# HIGHER LEVEL
# Chemistry
## for the IB Diploma
### 2nd Edition

**CATRIN BROWN • MIKE FORD**

76

Published by Pearson Education Limited, Edinburgh Gate, Harlow, Essex, CM20 2JE.

www.pearsonglobalschools.com

Text © Pearson Education Limited 2014
Edited by Tim Jackson
Proofread by Eilidh McGregor
Designed by Astwood Design
Typeset by Phoenix Photosetting, Chatham, Kent
Original illustrations © Pearson Education 2014
Illustrated by Tech-Set Ltd and Phoenix Photosetting
Cover design by Pearson Education Limited

The rights of Catrin Brown and Mike Ford to be identified as authors of this work have been asserted by them in accordance with the Copyright, Designs and Patents Act 1988.

First published 2014

25 24 23 22 21
IMP 15

**British Library Cataloguing in Publication Data**
A catalogue record for this book is available from the British Library

ISBN 978 1 447 95975 5
eBook only ISBN 978 1 447 95976 2

**Acknowledgements**
We would like to thank David Moore for his invaluable help with and feedback on this title.

The authors wish to thank Professor Colin Oloman, of the University of British Columbia, Canada for his valuable input and professional advice on the text.

We are grateful also to the following IB senior educators who provided useful feedback on the manuscript: Dr. Garth Irwin, Dr. Karen Mclean and Oksana Jajecznyk.

The authors and publisher would like to thank the R. Bruce Weisman laboratory at Rice University for permission to use their fullerene ozonide kinetics data and Dr. Julian Davies at University of British Columbia for permission to use his data on beta lactamase enzymes.

The author and publisher would like to thank the following individuals and organisations for permission to reproduce photographs:
(Key: b-bottom; c-centre; l-left; r-right; t-top)

**Alamy Images:** Clive Sawyer 254bl, Pictorial Press 59r, Shawn Hempel - Food 746bc; **Catrin Brown:** 27b, 127bc, 180tl, 311cr, 358bc, 383c, 420tl, 757cr; **Corbis:** David Lees 808br, Michael DeYoung / Design Pics 851bl, NASA 849b, Ted Levine 460c; **DK Images:** Clive Streeter 285t; **Eva Campbell:** 161b, 163tr, 171br, 420tl, 473bc, 476t, 477cr, 483t, 486tc, 503br, 757tr; **Fotolia.com:** Aaron Amat 42b, Africa Studio 140br, alessandrozocc 489tr, Andrej Kaprinay 942bc, bilderstoeckchen 214b, Can Balcioglu 216tl, cosma 446cr, goodluz 216tr, GoodMood Photo 11cr, jarerd 254br, joris484 837tr, Jürgen Fälchle 327cr, Kzenon 965bc, nikesidoroff 528c, Nikolai Sorokin 210c, photolife95 301tr, PixelThat 332cl, quayside 270c, sas 221bl, spotmatikphoto 255bl,

supakitmod 31br, Unclesam 935t; **Glow Images:** 769bc, Adam Gault 889tr; **Jupiterimages:** photos.com 255bl; **Pearson Education Ltd:** Trevor Clifford 961c, Sozaijiten 960c; **Phillipa Hudson:** 748t; **Rick Eppler estate:** 11br; **Science Photo Library Ltd:** A.dex,publiphoto Diffusion 884Bl, 59Bc, 100Cr, 130Bl, 211Cr, 215T, 249Cr, 326Bl, 478Br, 489Tl, 600Tl, 876Bl, 886Cl, 906Bl, 919Tr, 933Bc, 945Tr, Adam Hart-Davis 407Bc, 845C, Adrian Thomas 375Tr, Adrienne Hart-Davis 129T, 250Cl, 621Br, Aj Photo / Hop Americain 447Bl, Alexis Rosenfeld 817Cr, Andrew Lambert Photography 10Cl, 18B, 21Br, 23Br, 39Bc, 48B, 49Cr, 74Tl, 87Bc, 100Tc, 112Tr, 113C, 114Cl, 114Br, 115T, 117C, 121Cr, 125T, 132C, 132Bl, 142Tl, 142Tc, 187C, 248Bl, 248Br, 283C, 312Tl, 322Tl, 354Tl, 358Cl, 358Cr, 365Cr, 369Cr, 391Cl, 417Tr, 419Tr, 426Cl, 428Bc, 476Tc, 477Tl, 478Tl, 486Bl, 488Tl, 492Cl, 492Br, 493B, 502Tc, 504Cl, 509Tr, 531Cr, 637Cr, 708Tl, 873Tr, 917Br, 943Cr, Argonne National Laboratory 607Tr, 608C, Astier - Chru Lille 913Br, Astrid & Hanns-Frieder Michler 580C, 597Cr, 621C, Biophoto Associates 728Tc, 753Br, Bjorn Svensson 827Tr, Bob Edwards 930Bl, Brian Bell 683Bc, Bsip Vem 712Cl, Carlos Dominguez 455Bc, Carol And Mike Werner 799C, Charles Angelo 379B, Charles D. Winters 2C, 5Br, 16C, 39Tr, 96C, 112Cl, 114Tr, 123T, 313Tr, 324Tl, 338Cl, 347Br, 352Tl, 353Tr, 380Bl, 385Br, 407Tr, 418Tc, 448Bc, 451C, 491Tr, 655Cr, Chemical Design 742Tc, Chemical Design Ltd 645Bc, Chemical Design Ltd., Oxford 617Br, Chris Knapton 529C, Clive Freeman / Biosym Technologies 778Tl, Clive Freeman, The Royal Institution 203T, 479Bc, 606Tl, 691Cr, Cnri 911Cr, Cordelia Molloy 116Tl, 219Tl, 397Tr, 716Bl, 751Br, 946Br, Cristina Pedrazzini 532C, D. Phillips 310C, D. Phillips / The Population Council 711B, D. Vo Trung / Eurelios 697Br, David A. Hardy 70B, David Hay Jones 237Tr, David Mccarthy 606Br, David Nunuk 902Bl, David Parker 646Tc, David Scharf 172Tc, David Taylor 69Br, 629C, Dennis Flaherty 904Cl, Dept. Of Physics, Imperial College 71B, Digital Instruments / Veeco 628Tc, Dirk Wiersma 134Bl, 591Br, Dr David Wexler, Coloured By Dr Jeremy Burgess 944Tl, Dr Juerg Alean 794Tl, Dr Mark J. Winter 662T, 685Tc, Dr P. Marazzi 890Tl, 915Br, Dr Tim Evans 126Tl, 128Tl, 164Cl, 688Tl, 756C, Du Cane Medical Imaging Ltd 912Bc, Edward Kinsman 37Cr, 656Cl, Efda-Jet 796Cl, Emilio Segre Visual Archives 642Bc, Equinox Graphics 898Bl, 940Bl, Eye Of Science 172Bc, 411Tl, 461Br, Franz Himpsel / University Of Wisconsin 626Bc, Friedrich Saurer 943C, 943Cl, Geoff Kidd 740Bl, Geoff Tompkinson 560Tl, 860Tc, George Bernard 12R, Gustoimages 391Tr, Hank Morgan 62Tc, Hazen Group, Lawrence Berkley National Laboratory 760Bl, Heine Schneebeli 415Br, Hewlett-Packard Laboratories 629Tr, Hybrid Medical Animation 713T, 735Bc, J-L Charmet 431Bc, James Bell 610Tl, James King-Holmes 634Br, 654Bl, 931Br, James King-Holmes / Ocms 651Bc, James Prince 531C, Jean-Claude Revy, Ism 593Br, Jean-Loup Charmet 945Tl, Jeremy Walker 766C, 776B, Jerry Mason 69Tr, 69Cr, 133Br, 800C, Jim Dowdalls 870Bl, Jim Edds 8Bc, Jim Varney 925Br, John Bavosi 880Bl, 885Cr, John Mclean 484Tl, John Mead 770Tc, Juergen Berger 861C, Kenneth Eward / Biografx 75Tr, 166T, 188T, 231Tr, 631Cr, Kevin Curtis 944Br, Laguna Design 57Bl, 146Tc, 629Bc, 896Bc, 899Cr, Lawrence Berkeley National Laboratory 115B, 155Bc, 271C, Lawrence Lawry 168Br, Lawrence Livermore National Laboratory 586Cl, Leonard Lessin 521Bc, M.h. Sharp 611Cr, Manfred Kage 597Br, Mark Thomas 422Bl, Martin Bond 399C, Martin Shields 371Bc, Martyn F. Chillmaid 6Tl, 12L, 13Br, 48Tl, 112Tl, 112Tc, 184Bl, 245Tr, 278Tl, 284Cl, 301Br, 363Tr, 394Bc, 404C, 596Tl, 619C, 948Bl, Massimo Brega, The Lighthouse 713B, Mauro Fermariello 925Tr, 946Tr, Maximilian Stock Ltd 442C, Mehau Kulyk 529B, Mere Words 811Cl, Michael Donne 864Tl, Michael Szoenyi 353Cr, Mikkel Juul Jensen 840Bl, N K D Miller 879Br, Nasa 197C, 768Tl, Natural History Museum, London 670C, Nypl / Science Source 4Cl, Oulette & Theroux, Publiphoto Diffusion 914Tl, Pasieka 100Cl, 127Br, 139Br, 170Tr, 178Tl, 218Bl, 405Br, 582Tl, 586Tl, 672Tc, 732Bl, 872T, Patrick Landmann 587Bl, 756Tl, 797Cr, 803T, 811Tr, 813T, Paul J. Fusco 941Cr, Paul Rapson 466Bc, 677Br, 760Tc, 778Bl, Peggy Greb / Us Department Of Agriculture 657Bc, 948Br, Phantatomix 745Tr, Philippe Benoist / Look At Sciences 904Br, Philippe Plailly 56C, Philippe

Psaila 146Bc, 346Tl, Photostock-Israel 761Br, Physics Dept.,imperial College 58B, Physics Today Collection / American Institute Of Physics 626Cl, Pierre Philippon / Look At Sciences 431Cr, Power And Syred 695Bl, Prof. K Seddon & J. Van Den Berg / Queen's University, 371Tr, Prof. K.seddon & Dr. T.evans, Queen's University Belfast 517Tl, 517Tr, Laguna Design 903Tr, Ramon Andrade 3Dciencia 895Tr, 902C, Ray Ellis 775C, Ria Novosti 65Cr, 97Cr, 594Bc, 783Cr, 805C, Rich Treptow 182T, Robert Brook 634Tl, 635Bc, 738Tl, Russell Kightley 149Cr, 201Br, 202Tl, 630Cl, 861Br, 893Bc, 895C, Saturn Stills 705T, Scientifica, Visuals Unlimited 592C, Scott Camazine 887Br, Sheila Terry 4Br, 452Tc, 599Tr, 746Tl, Simon Fraser 329Tr, 344C, 397Br, 634Cl, 772Tl, Simon Fraser / Mauna Loa Observatory 824Br, Sinclair Stammers 687Br, St Mary's Hospital Medical School 876Tc, St. Bartholomew's Hospital 869Tr, Steve Gschmeissner 680Tr, Steve Horrell 614Bl, Susumu Nishinaga 138C, 143Tr, 168Bl, 877Br, Tek Image 549Br, Tom Mchugh 636Cl, Tony Craddock 637Br, Us Department Of Energy 294T, 797T, 804Tl, 933T, Us Dept. Of Energy 932Cl, Victor De Schwanberg 455Tc,Victor Habbick Visions 171tl, Vincent Moncorge / Look at Sciences 439tc, Volker Steger 92c, 842tc, Wladimir Bulgar 703b; **Shutterstock.com:** ggw1962 28bl, Susan Santa Maria 46b

**Cover images:** *Front:* **Alamy Images:** Olga Khoroshunova

All other images © Pearson Education

We are grateful to the following for permission to reproduce copyright material:

**Figures**

Figure on page 170 from p2 of http://www.nobelprize.org/nobel_prizes/physics/laureates/2010/popular-physicsprize2010.pdf © Airi Iliste/The Royal Swedish Academy of Sciences, © The Royal Swedish Academy of Sciences 2010; Figure on page 280 adapted from http://www.vernier.com/products/sensors/spectrometers/svis-pl/, with kind permission from Vernier Software & Technology; Figure on page 761 adapted from Fluorescent Guest Molecules Report Ordered Inner Phase of Host Capsules in Solution Author(s): Dalgarno, S. J. DOI: 10.1126/SCIENCE.1116579 Date: Sep 23, 2005 Volume: 309 Issue: 5743, reprinted with permission from AAAS; Figure on page 761 adapted from http://web.ornl.gov/sci/physical_sciences_directorate/highlight_improvedmethod_moyer.shtml; Figure on page 878 adapted from β-*lactamase enzymes identified during the age of antibiotics*, Professor Karen Bush with permission; Figure on page 548 adapted from University of California Museum of Paleontology's Understanding Science (http://www.understandingscience.org)., http://undsci.berkeley.edu/search/imagedetail.php?id=130&topic_id=&keywords=, Copyright 2006 by The University of California Museum of Paleontology, Berkeley, and the Regents of the University of California.

**Text**

Quote on page 973 from Richard Feynman The Physics Teacher Vol. 7, issue 6, 1969, pp. 313–320, reproduced with permission from American Association of Physics Teachers (c)1969; Extract on page 981 from *Physics and Philosophy: The Revolution in Modern Science ISBN-13: 978-0141182155* Penguin Modern Classics (Werner Heisenberg) p.25, with kind permission from Penguin Books Ltd.

Every effort has been made to contact copyright holders of material reproduced in this book. Any omissions will be rectified in subsequent printings if notice is given to the publishers.

# Contents

# Contents

# Introduction

## Authors' introduction to the second edition

Welcome to your study of IB Higher Level chemistry. This book is the second edition of the market-leading Pearson Baccalaureate HL chemistry book, first published in 2009. It has been completely rewritten to match the specifications of the new IB chemistry curriculum, and gives thorough coverage of the entire course content. While there is much new and updated material, we have kept and refined the features that made the first edition so successful. Our personal experience and intimate knowledge of the entire IB chemistry experience, through teaching and examining, curriculum review, moderating internal assessment and leading workshops for teachers in different continents, has given us a unique understanding of your needs in this course. We are delighted to share our enthusiasm for learning chemistry in the IB programme with you!

## Content

The book covers the three parts of the IB syllabus: the core, the AHL (additional higher level) material and the options, of which you will study one. Each chapter in the book corresponds to a topic or option in the IB guide, in the same sequence. The core and AHL material for a topic are combined in the same chapter, so that you can see the full development of each concept. The sequence of sub-topics within each chapter is given in the contents page.

Each chapter starts with a list of the Essential ideas from the IB chemistry guide, which summarize the focus of each sub-topic.

### Essential ideas

 **3.1**   The arrangement of elements in the Periodic Table helps to predict their electron configuration.

This is followed by an introduction, which gives the context of the topic and how it relates to your previous knowledge. The relevant sections from the IB chemistry guide for each sub-topic are then given as boxes showing Understanding, and Applications and skills, with notes for Guidance shown in italics where they help interpret the syllabus.

### Understandings:

- Atoms contain a positively charged dense nucleus composed of protons and neutrons (nucleons).

  **Guidance**
  *Relative masses and charges of the sub-atomic particles should be known, actual values are given in section 4 of the IB data booklet. The mass of the electron can be considered negligible.*

### Applications and skills:

- Use of the nuclear symbol notation $^{A}_{Z}X$ to deduce the number of protons, neutrons, and electrons in atoms and ions.

The text covers the course content using plain language, with all scientific terms explained and shown in bold as they are first introduced. It follows IUPAC nomenclature and definitions throughout.

We have been careful also to apply the same terminology you will see in IB examinations in all worked examples and questions.

## The nature of science

Throughout the course you are encouraged to think about the nature of scientific knowledge and the scientific process as it applies to chemistry. Examples are given of the evolution of chemical theories as new information is gained, the use of models to conceptualize our understanding, and the ways in which experimental work is enhanced by modern technologies. Ethical considerations, environmental impacts, the importance of objectivity, and the responsibilities regarding scientists' code of conduct are also considered here. The emphasis is not on learning any of these examples, but rather appreciating the broader conceptual themes in context. We have included at least one example in each sub-section, and hope you will come up with your own as you keep these ideas at the surface of your learning.

## Key to information boxes

A popular feature of the book is the different coloured boxes interspersed through each chapter. These are used to enhance your learning as explained using examples below.

**Nature of science**

This is an overarching theme in the course to promote concept-based learning. Through the book you should recognize some similar themes emerging across different topics. We hope they help you to develop your own skills in scientific literacy.

**NATURE OF SCIENCE**

The story of Fleming's discovery of penicillin is often described as serendipitous – a fortunate discovery made by chance or by accident. But it was more than that. Would not the majority of people who noticed the plates were contaminated simply have thrown them away, likely disappointed at the 'failed experiment'? The difference was that Fleming had the insight to observe the plates carefully and ask the right questions about why a clear ring appeared around the fungal growth. Scientists are trained to be observant and to seek explanations for what they see, and this must include the unexpected. As Louis Pasteur once famously said, 'Chance favours only the prepared mind'. Consider to what extent scientific discoveries are only possible to scientists who are trained in the principles of observation and interpretation.

The disposal of plastics is a major global problem. The very features that make plastics so useful, such as their impermeability to water and low reactivity, mean they are often non-biodegradable and so remain in landfill sites for indefinite periods of time. It is estimated that about 10% of plastics produced end up in the ocean, causing widespread hazards to marine life. Measures to try to address this problem include developments of more efficient recycling processes, biodegradable plastics, and plastic-feeding microorganisms. A reduction in the quantities of plastic produced and used is also urgently needed – which is something for which every individual can share responsibility.

**International-mindedness**

The impact of the study of chemistry is global, and includes environmental, political and socio-economic considerations. Examples of this are given to help you to see the importance of chemistry in an international context.

**Utilization**

Applications of the topic through everyday examples are described here, as well as brief descriptions of related chemical industries. This helps you to see the relevance and context of what you are learning.

Freeze-drying is an effective process for the preservation of food and some pharmaceuticals. It differs from standard methods of dehydration in that it does not use heat to evaporate water, but instead depends on the sublimation of ice. The substance to be preserved is first frozen, and then warmed gently at very low pressure which causes the ice to change directly to water vapour. The process is slow but has the significant advantage that the composition of the material, and so its flavour, are largely conserved. The freeze-dried product is stored in a moisture-free package that excludes oxygen, and can be reconstituted by the addition of water.

The person who researched and patented tetraethyl lead as a petroleum additive was the same person who later was responsible for the discovery and marketing of chlorofluorocarbons (CFCs) as refrigerants. Thomas Midgley of Ohio, USA, did not live to know the full extent that the long-term impact his findings would have on the Earth's atmosphere. He died in 1944, aged 55, from accidental strangulation after becoming entangled in ropes and pulleys he had devised to get himself in and out of bed following loss of use of his legs caused by polio. Perhaps his epitaph should have been 'The solution becomes the problem'.

  Interesting fact

These give background information that will add to your wider knowledge of the topic and make links with other topics and subjects. Aspects such as historic notes on the life of scientists and origins of names are included here.

 Laboratory work

These indicate links to ideas for lab work and experiments that will support your learning in the course, and help you prepare for the Internal Assessment. Some specific experimental work is compulsory, and further details of this are in the eBook.

 **Experiment to determine the empirical formula of MgO**

Full details of how to carry out this experiment with a worksheet are available online.

A sample of magnesium is heated and the change in mass recorded. From this, the ratio of moles of magnesium to oxygen can be determined.

Hess's law is a natural consequence of the law of conservation of energy. If you know the law of conservation of energy, do you automatically know Hess's law?

 TOK

These stimulate thought and consideration of knowledge issues as they arise in context. Each box contains open questions to help trigger critical thinking and discussion.

 Key fact

These key facts are drawn out of the main text and highlighted in bold. This will help you to identify the core learning points within each section. They also act as a quick summary for review.

 **The concentrations of $H^+$ and $OH^-$ are inversely proportional in an aqueous solution.**

In writing the ionization reactions of weak acids and bases, it is essential to use the equilibrium sign.

  Hints for success

These give hints on how to approach questions, and suggest approaches that examiners like to see. They also identify common pitfalls in understanding, and omissions made in answering questions.

Challenge yourself

These boxes contain open questions that encourage you to think about the topic in more depth, or to make detailed connections with other topics. They are designed to be challenging and to make you think.

**CHALLENGE YOURSELF**

6 Explain why oxygen behaves as a free radical despite having an even number of electrons.

## eBook

In the eBook you will find the following:

- Interactive glossary of scientific words used in the course
- Answers and worked solutions to all exercises in the book

- Fast facts and labs worksheets
- Interactive quizzes
- Animations
- Videos

For more details about your eBook, see the following section.

## Questions

There are three types of question in this book:

### 1. Worked example with Solution

These appear at intervals in the text and are used to illustrate the concepts covered.

They are followed by the solution, which shows the thinking and the steps used in solving the problem.

> **Worked example**
>
> Calomel is a compound once used in the treatment of syphilis. It has the empirical formula HgCl and a molar mass of 472.08 g mol$^{-1}$. What is its molecular formula?
>
> **Solution**
>
> First calculate the mass of the empirical formula:
> $$\text{mass(HgCl)} = 200.59 + 35.45 = 236.04 \text{ g mol}^{-1}$$
> $$(236.04) \times x = M = 472.08$$
> $$\therefore x = 2$$
> $$\text{molecular formula} = Hg_2Cl_2$$

### 2. Exercises

These questions are found throughout the text. They allow you to apply your knowledge and test your understanding of what you have just been reading.

The answers to these are given on the eBook at the end of each chapter.

> **Exercises**
>
> **64** Calculate the mass of potassium hydroxide, KOH, required to prepare 250 cm$^3$ of a 0.200 mol dm$^{-3}$ solution.

### 3. Practice questions

These questions are found at the end of each chapter. They are mostly taken from previous years' IB examination papers. The mark-schemes used by examiners when marking these questions are given in the eBook, at the end of each chapter.

---

**Practice questions**

**1** How many oxygen atoms are in 0.100 mol of $CuSO_4.5H_2O$?

**A** $5.42 \times 10^{22}$     **B** $6.02 \times 10^{22}$     **C** $2.41 \times 10^{23}$     **D** $5.42 \times 10^{23}$

---

## Answers and worked solutions

Full worked solutions to all exercises and practice questions can be found in the ebook, as well as regular answers.

 Hotlink boxes can be found at the end of each chapter, indicating that there are weblinks available for further study. To access these links go to www.pearsonhotlinks.com and enter the ISBN or title of this book. Here you can find links to animations, simulations, movie clips and related background material, which can help to deepen your interest and understanding of the topic.

We truly hope that this book and the accompanying online resources help you to enjoy this fascinating subject of IB Higher Level chemistry. We wish you success in your studies.

Catrin Brown and Mike Ford

# How to use your enhanced eBook

Jump to any page

Switch from single- to double-page view

Highlight parts of the text

Create notes

Search the whole book

Zoom

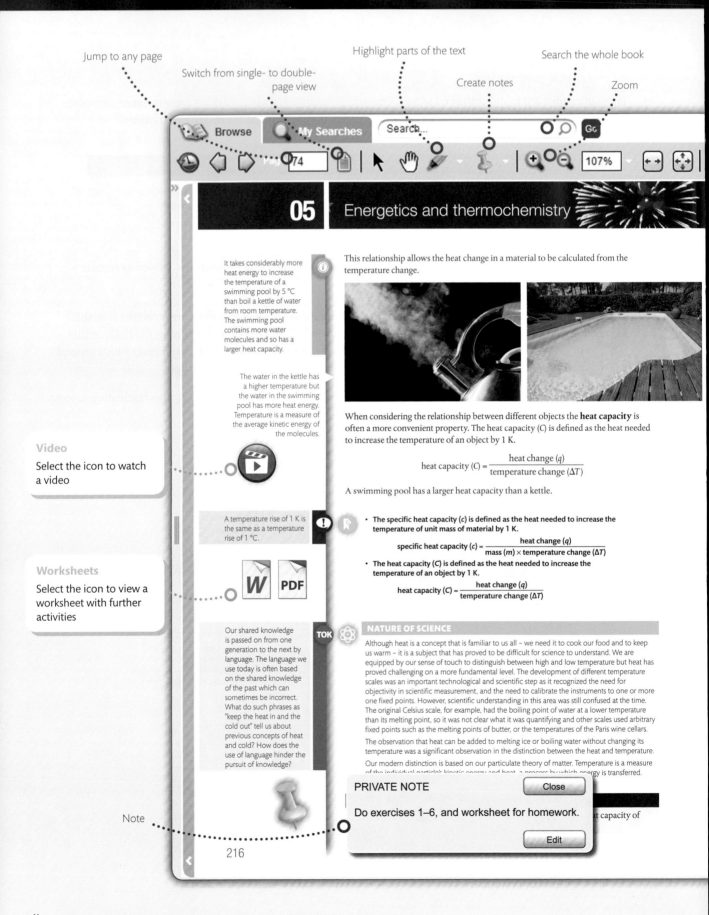

## Video
Select the icon to watch a video

## Worksheets
Select the icon to view a worksheet with further activities

Note

It takes considerably more heat energy to increase the temperature of a swimming pool by 5 °C than boil a kettle of water from room temperature. The swimming pool contains more water molecules and so has a larger heat capacity.

The water in the kettle has a higher temperature but the water in the swimming pool has more heat energy. Temperature is a measure of the average kinetic energy of the molecules.

A temperature rise of 1 K is the same as a temperature rise of 1 °C.

Our shared knowledge is passed on from one generation to the next by language. The language we use today is often based on the shared knowledge of the past which can sometimes be incorrect. What do such phrases as "keep the heat in and the cold out" tell us about previous concepts of heat and cold? How does the use of language hinder the pursuit of knowledge?

### 05 Energetics and thermochemistry

This relationship allows the heat change in a material to be calculated from the temperature change.

When considering the relationship between different objects the **heat capacity** is often a more convenient property. The heat capacity (C) is defined as the heat needed to increase the temperature of an object by 1 K.

$$\text{heat capacity } (C) = \frac{\text{heat change } (q)}{\text{temperature change } (\Delta T)}$$

A swimming pool has a larger heat capacity than a kettle.

- The specific heat capacity (c) is defined as the heat needed to increase the temperature of unit mass of material by 1 K.

$$\text{specific heat capacity } (c) = \frac{\text{heat change } (q)}{\text{mass } (m) \times \text{temperature change } (\Delta T)}$$

- The heat capacity (C) is defined as the heat needed to increase the temperature of an object by 1 K.

$$\text{heat capacity } (C) = \frac{\text{heat change } (q)}{\text{temperature change } (\Delta T)}$$

#### NATURE OF SCIENCE

Although heat is a concept that is familiar to us all – we need it to cook our food and to keep us warm – it is a subject that has proved to be difficult for science to understand. We are equipped by our sense of touch to distinguish between high and low temperature but heat has proved challenging on a more fundamental level. The development of different temperature scales was an important technological and scientific step as it recognized the need for objectivity in scientific measurement, and the need to calibrate the instruments to one or more one fixed points. However, scientific understanding in this area was still confused at the time. The original Celsius scale, for example, had the boiling point of water at a lower temperature than its melting point, so it was not clear what it was quantifying and other scales used arbitrary fixed points such as the melting points of butter, or the temperatures of the Paris wine cellars.

The observation that heat can be added to melting ice or boiling water without changing its temperature was a significant observation in the distinction between the heat and temperature.

Our modern distinction is based on our particulate theory of matter. Temperature is a measure of the individual particle's kinetic energy and heat, a process by which energy is transferred.

**PRIVATE NOTE**    Close

Do exercises 1–6, and worksheet for homework.

Edit

...t capacity of

216

See the definitions of key terms in the glossary

Create a bookmark

Switch to whiteboard view

**Animation**

Select the icon to see a related animation

## Solution

$$\text{heat change} = m \times c \times \Delta T$$
$$= 10.0 \text{ g} \times 0.385 \text{ J g}^{-1}\,^{\circ}\text{C}^{-1} \times -60.0\,^{\circ}\text{C (the value is negative as the Cu has lost heat)}$$
$$= -231 \text{ J}$$

### Exercises

1  When a sample of $NH_4SCN$ is mixed with solid $Ba(OH)_2.8H_2O$ in a glass beaker, the mixture changes to a liquid and the temperature drops sufficiently to freeze the beaker to the table. Which statement is true about the reaction?

  **A**   The process is endothermic and $\Delta H$ is –
  **B**   The process is endothermic and $\Delta H$ is +
  **C**   The process is exothermic and $\Delta H$ is –
  **D**   The process is exothermic and $\Delta H$ is +

2  Which one of the following statements is *true* of all exothermic reactions?

  **A**   They produce gases.
  **B**   They give out heat.
  **C**   They occur quickly.
  **D**   They involve combustion.

3  If 500 J of heat is added to 100.0 g samples of each of the substances below, which will have the largest temperature increase?

|   | Substance | Specific heat capacity / $J\,g^{-1}\,K^{-1}$ |
|---|---|---|
| **A** | gold | 0.129 |
| **B** | silver | 0.237 |
| **C** | copper | 0.385 |
| **D** | water | 4.18 |

4  The temperature of a 5.0 g sample of copper increases from 27 °C to 29 °C. Calculate how much heat has been added to the system. (Specific heat capacity of Cu = 0.385 $J\,g^{-1}\,K^{-1}$)

  **A**   0.770 J      **B**   1.50 J      **C**   3.00 J      **D**   3.85 J

5  Consider the specific heat capacity of the following metals.

| Metal | Specific heat capacity / $J\,g^{-1}\,K^{-1}$ |
|---|---|
| Al | 0.897 |
| Be | 1.82 |
| Cd | 0.231 |
| Cr | 0.449 |

1 kg samples of the metals at room temperature are heated by the same electrical heater for 10 min. Identify the metal which has the highest final temperature.

  **A**   Al      **B**   Be      **C**   Cd      **D**   Cr

6  The specific heat of metallic mercury is 0.138 $J\,g^{-1}\,^{\circ}\text{C}^{-1}$. If 100.0 J of heat is added to a 100.0 g sample of mercury at 25.0 °C, what is the final temperature of the mercury?

**Quiz**

Select the icon to take an interactive quiz to test your knowledge

**CHALLENGE YOURSELF**

2  Suggest an explanation for the pattern in specific heat capacities of the metals in Exercise 3.

**Worked solutions**

Select the icon at the end of the chapter to view worked solutions to exercises in this chapter

## Enthalpy changes and the direction of change

There is a natural direction for change. When we slip on a ladder, we go down, not up. The direction of change is in the direction of lower stored energy. In a similar way, we expect methane to burn when we strike a match and form carbon dioxide and water. The chemicals are changing in a way which reduces their enthalpy (Figure 5.5).

**Answers**

Select the icon at the end of the chapter to view answers to exercises in this chapter

217

# 01

## Stoichiometric relationships

## Essential ideas

**1.1** Physical and chemical properties depend on the ways in which different atoms combine.

**1.2** The mole makes it possible to correlate the number of particles with a mass that can be measured.

**1.3** Mole ratios in chemical equations can be used to calculate reacting ratios by mass and gas volume.

The reaction between ignited powdered aluminium and iron oxide, known as the thermite reaction:

$$2Al(s) + Fe_2O_3(s) \rightarrow Al_2O_3(s) + 2Fe(s)$$

Significant heat is released by the reaction, and it is used in welding processes including underwater welding. The stoichiometry of the reaction, as shown in the balanced equation, enables chemists to determine the reacting masses of reactants and products for optimum use.

The birth of chemistry as a physical science can be traced back to the first successful attempts to quantify chemical change. Carefully devised experiments led to data that revealed one simple truth. *Chemical change involves interactions between particles that have fixed mass.* Even before knowledge was gained of the atomic nature of these particles and of the factors that determine their interactions, this discovery became the guiding principle for modern chemistry. We begin our study with a brief introduction to this particulate nature of matter, and go on to investigate some of the ways in which it can be quantified.

The term **stoichiometry** is derived from two Greek words – *stoicheion* for element and *metron* for measure. Stoichiometry describes the relationships between the amounts of reactants and products during chemical reactions. As it is known that matter is conserved during chemical change, stoichiometry is a form of book-keeping at the atomic level. It enables chemists to determine what amounts of substances they should react together and enables them to predict how much product will be obtained. The application of stoichiometry closes the gap between what is happening on the atomic scale and what can be measured.

In many ways this chapter can be considered as a toolkit for the mathematical content in much of the course. It covers the universal language of chemistry, **chemical equations**, and introduces the **mole** as the unit of amount. Applications include measurements of mass, volume, and concentration.

You may choose not to work through all of this at the start of the course, but to come back to these concepts after you have gained knowledge of some of the fundamental properties of chemical matter in Chapters 2, 3, and 4.

## 1.1 Introduction to the particulate nature of matter and chemical change

### Understandings:

- Atoms of different elements combine in fixed ratios to form compounds, which have different properties from their component elements.

  **Guidance**
  *Names and symbols of the elements are in the IB data booklet in Section 5.*

- Mixtures contain more than one element and/or compound that are not chemically bonded together and so retain their individual properties.
- Mixtures are either homogeneous or heterogeneous.

## Applications and skills:

● Deduction of chemical equations when reactants and products are specified.

**Guidance**

*Balancing of equations should include a variety of types of reactions.*

● Application of the state symbols (s), (l), (g), and (aq) in equations.
● Explanation of observable changes in physical properties and temperature during changes of state.

**Guidance**

● *Names of the changes of state – melting, freezing, vaporization (evaporation and boiling), condensation, sublimation and deposition – should be covered.*
● *The term 'latent heat' is not required.*

 Antoine-Laurent Lavoisier (1743–1794) is often called the 'father of chemistry'. His many accomplishments include the naming of oxygen and hydrogen, the early development of the metric system, and a standardization of chemical nomenclature. Most importantly, he established an understanding of combustion as a process involving combination with oxygen from the air, and recognized that matter retains its mass through chemical change, leading to the law of conservation of mass. In addition, he compiled the first extensive list of elements in his book *Elements of Chemistry* (1789). In short, he changed chemistry from a qualitative to a quantitative science. But, as an unpopular tax collector in France during the French Revolution and Terror, he was tried for treason and guillotined in 1794. One and a half years after his death he was exonerated, and his early demise was recognized as a major loss to France.

## Chemical elements are the fundamental building blocks of chemistry

The English language is based on an alphabet of just 26 letters. But, as we know, combining these in different ways leads to an almost infinite number of words, and then sentences, paragraphs, books, and so on. It is similar to the situation in chemistry, where the 'letters' are the single substances known as **chemical elements**. There are

Antoine-Laurent Lavoisier, French chemist (1743–1794).

**A chemical element is a single pure substance, made of only one type of atom.**

Pictographic symbols used at the beginning of the 18th century to represent chemical elements and compounds. They are similar to those of the ancient alchemists. As more elements were discovered during the 18th century, attempts to devise a chemical nomenclature led to the modern alphabetic notational system. This system was devised by the Swedish chemist Berzelius and introduced in 1814.

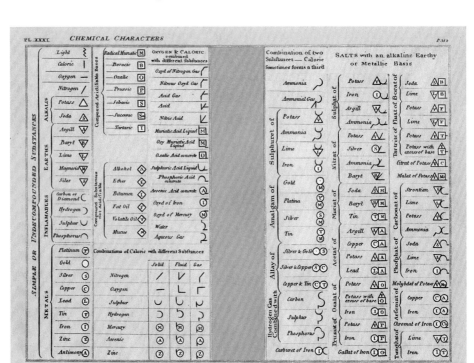

only about 100 of these, but because of the ways in which they combine with each other, they make up the almost countless number of different chemical substances in our world.

In Chapter 2 we will learn about atomic structure, and how each element is made up of a particular type of atom. The atoms of an element are all the same as each other (with the exception of isotopes, which we will also discuss in Chapter 2), and are different from those of other elements. It is this distinct nature of its atoms that gives each element its individual properties. A useful definition of an atom is that it is the smallest particle of an element to show the characteristic properties of that element.

To help communication in chemistry, each element is denoted by a **chemical symbol** of either one upper case letter, or one upper case letter followed by a lower case letter. A few examples are given below.

| Name of element | Symbol |
| --- | --- |
| carbon | C |
| fluorine | F |
| potassium | K |
| calcium | Ca |
| mercury | Hg |
| tungsten | W |

You will notice that often the letter or letters used are derived from the English name of the element, but in some cases they derive from other languages. For example, Hg for mercury comes from Latin, whereas W for tungsten has its origin in European dialects. Happily, these symbols are all accepted and used internationally, so they do not need to be translated. A complete list of the names of the elements and their symbols is given in Section 5 of the IB data booklet.

## Chemical compounds are formed from more than one element

Some elements, such as nitrogen and gold, are found in **native** form, that is uncombined with other elements in nature. But more commonly, elements exist in chemical combinations with other elements, in substances known as **chemical compounds**. Compounds contain a fixed proportion of elements, and are held together by chemical bonds (discussed in Chapter 4). The bonding between atoms in compounds changes their

Assorted minerals, including elements such as sulfur and silver, and compounds such as $Al_2O_3$ (sapphire) and $CaF_2$ (fluorite). Most minerals are impure and exist as mixtures of different elements and compounds.

The International Union of Pure and Applied Chemistry (IUPAC) was formed in 1919 by chemists from industry and academia. Since then it has developed into the world authority on chemical nomenclature and terminology. It has succeeded in fostering worldwide communications in the chemical sciences and in uniting academic, industrial, and public sector chemistry in a common language.

Chemistry is a very exact subject, and it is important to be careful in distinguishing between upper and lower case letters. For example, Co (cobalt, a metallic element) means something completely different from CO (carbon monoxide, a poisonous gas).

The number of elements that exist is open to change as new ones are discovered, although there is often a time-lag between a discovery and its confirmation by IUPAC. During this time a provisional systematic three-letter symbol is used, using Latin abbreviations to represent the atomic number. The letters u (un) = 1, b (bi) = 2, t (tri) = 3 and so on are used. So the provisional element of atomic number 118 will continue to be known as ununoctium or uuo until it is confirmed and a name formally agreed according to the process established by IUPAC.

**A compound is a chemical combination of different elements, containing a fixed ratio of atoms. The physical and chemical properties of a compound are different from those of its component elements.**

properties, so compounds have completely different properties from those of their component elements.

A classic example of this is that sodium, Na, is a dangerously reactive metal that reacts violently with water, while chlorine, $Cl_2$, is a toxic gas used as a chemical weapon. Yet when these two elements combine, they form the compound sodium chloride, NaCl, a white crystalline solid that we sprinkle all over our food.

Compounds are described using the chemical symbols for elements. A subscript is used to show the number of atoms of each element in a unit of the compound. Some examples are given below. (The reasons for the different ratios of elements in compounds will become clearer after we have studied atomic structure and bonding in Chapters 2 and 4.)

| Name of compound | Symbol | Name of compound | Symbol |
| --- | --- | --- | --- |
| sodium chloride | NaCl | water | $H_2O$ |
| potassium oxide | $K_2O$ | glucose | $C_6H_{12}O_6$ |
| calcium bromide | $CaBr_2$ | ammonium sulfate | $(NH_4)_2SO_4$ |

A combustion spoon holding sodium, Na, is lowered into a gas jar containing chlorine, $Cl_2$. The vigorous reaction produces white crystals of sodium chloride, NaCl.

$2Na(s) + Cl_2(g) \rightarrow 2NaCl(s)$

The properties of the compound are completely different from those of its component elements.

## Chemical equations summarize chemical change

The formation of compounds from elements is an example of **chemical change** and can be represented by a **chemical equation**. A chemical equation is a representation using chemical symbols of the simplest ratio of atoms, as elements or in compounds, undergoing chemical change. The left-hand side shows the **reactants** and the right-hand side the **products**.

For example:

$$\text{calcium} + \text{chlorine} \rightarrow \text{calcium chloride}$$
$$Ca + Cl_2 \rightarrow CaCl_2$$

As atoms are neither created nor destroyed during a chemical reaction, *the total number of atoms of each element must be the same on both sides of the equation.* This is known as **balancing the equation**, and uses numbers called **stoichiometric coefficients** to denote the number of units of each term in the equation.

For example:

$$\text{hydrogen} + \text{oxygen} \rightarrow \text{water}$$
$$2H_2 + O_2 \rightarrow 2H_2O$$

coefficients

| | total on left side | total on right side |
| --- | --- | --- |
| hydrogen atoms | 4 | 4 |
| oxygen atoms | 2 | 2 |

$$2H_2 + O_2 \longrightarrow 2H_2O$$

A chemical equation shows:

direction of change

reactants ⟶ products

Chemical equations are the universal language of chemistry. What other languages are universal, and to what extent do they help or hinder the pursuit of knowledge?

**TOK**

**Figure 1.1** When hydrogen and oxygen react to form water, the atoms are rearranged, but the number of atoms of each element remains the same.

Note that when the coefficient is 1, this does not need to be explicitly stated.

Chemical equations are used to show all types of reactions in chemistry, including reactions of decomposition, combustion, neutralization, and so on. Examples of these are given below and you will come across very many more during this course. Learning to write equations is an important skill in chemistry, which develops quickly with practice.

## Worked example

Write an equation for the reaction of thermal decomposition of sodium hydrogencarbonate ($NaHCO_3$) into sodium carbonate ($Na_2CO_3$), water ($H_2O$), and carbon dioxide ($CO_2$).

### Solution

First write the information from the question in the form of an equation, and then check the number of atoms of each element on both sides of the equation.

$$NaHCO_3 \rightarrow Na_2CO_3 + H_2O + CO_2$$

|                | total on left side | total on right side |
|----------------|:------------------:|:-------------------:|
| sodium atoms   | 1                  | 2                   |
| hydrogen atoms | 1                  | 2                   |
| carbon atoms   | 1                  | 2                   |
| oxygen atoms   | 3                  | 6                   |

In order to balance this we introduce coefficient 2 on the left.

$$2NaHCO_3 \rightarrow Na_2CO_3 + H_2O + CO_2$$

Finally check that it is balanced for each element.

> An equation by definition has to be *balanced*, so do not expect this to be specified in a question. After you have written an equation, *always* check the numbers of atoms of each element on both sides of the equation to ensure it is correctly balanced.

> When a question refers to 'heating' a reactant or to 'thermal decomposition', this does not mean the addition of oxygen, only that heat is the source of energy for the reaction. If the question refers to 'burning' or 'combustion', this indicates that oxygen is a reactant.

## NATURE OF SCIENCE

Early ideas to explain chemical change in combustion and rusting included the 'phlogiston' theory. This proposed the existence of a fire-like element that was released during these processes. The theory seemed to explain some of the observations of its time, although these were purely qualitative. It could not explain later quantitative data showing that substances actually gain rather than lose mass during burning. In 1783, Lavoisier's work on oxygen confirmed that combustion and rusting involve combination with oxygen from the air, so overturning the phlogiston theory. This is a good example of how the evolution of scientific ideas, such as how chemical change occurs, is based on the need for theories that can be tested by experiment. Where results are not compatible with the theory, a new theory must be put forward, which must then be subject to the same rigour of experimental test.

## Exercises

1   Write balanced chemical equations for the following reactions:

   **(a)** The decomposition of copper carbonate ($CuCO_3$) into copper(II) oxide ($CuO$) and carbon dioxide ($CO_2$).

   **(b)** The combustion of magnesium ($Mg$) in oxygen ($O_2$) to form magnesium oxide ($MgO$).

   **(c)** The neutralization of sulfuric acid ($H_2SO_4$) with sodium hydroxide ($NaOH$) to form sodium sulfate ($Na_2SO_4$) and water ($H_2O$).

   **(d)** The synthesis of ammonia ($NH_3$) from nitrogen ($N_2$) and hydrogen ($H_2$).

   **(e)** The combustion of methane ($CH_4$) to produce carbon dioxide ($CO_2$) and water ($H_2O$).

2   Write balanced chemical equations for the following reactions:

   **(a)** $K + H_2O \rightarrow KOH + H_2$      **(b)** $C_2H_5OH + O_2 \rightarrow CO_2 + H_2O$

   **(c)** $Cl_2 + KI \rightarrow KCl + I_2$      **(d)** $CrO_3 \rightarrow Cr_2O_3 + O_2$

   **(e)** $Fe_2O_3 + C \rightarrow CO + Fe$

>  Remember when you are balancing an equation, change the stoichiometric coefficient but never change the subscript in a chemical formula.

When balancing equations, start with the most complex species, and leave terms that involve a single element to last.

**3** Use the same processes to balance the following examples:

  **(a)** $C_4H_{10} + O_2 \rightarrow CO_2 + H_2O$
  **(b)** $NH_3 + O_2 \rightarrow NO + H_2O$
  **(c)** $Cu + HNO_3 \rightarrow Cu(NO_3)_2 + NO + H_2O$
  **(d)** $H_2O_2 + N_2H_4 \rightarrow N_2 + H_2O + O_2$
  **(e)** $C_2H_7N + O_2 \rightarrow CO_2 + H_2O + N_2$

A chemical equation can be used to assess the efficiency of a reaction in making a particular product. The **atom economy** is a concept used for this purpose and is defined as:

$$\% \text{ atom economy} = \frac{\text{mass of desired product}}{\text{total mass of products}} \times 100$$

Note that this is different from % yield discussed later in this chapter, which is calculated using only one product and one reactant. Atom economy is an indication of how much of the reactants ends up in the required products, rather than in waste products. A higher atom economy indicates a more efficient and less wasteful process. The concept is increasingly used in developments in green and sustainable chemistry. This is discussed further in Chapters 12 and 13.

## Mixtures form when substances combine without chemical interaction

A mixture is composed of two or more substances in which no chemical combination has occurred.

Air is described as a **mixture** of gases because the separate components – different elements and compounds – are interspersed with each other, but are not chemically combined. This means, for example, that the gases nitrogen and oxygen when mixed in air retain the same characteristic properties as when they are in the pure form. Substances burn in air because the oxygen present supports combustion, as does pure oxygen.

Another characteristic of mixtures is that their composition is not fixed. For example, air that we breathe in typically contains about 20% by volume oxygen, whereas the air that we breathe out usually contains only about 16% by volume oxygen. It is still correct to call both of these mixtures of air, because there is no fixed proportion in the definition.

Tide of oily water heading towards Pensacola Beach, Florida, USA, after the explosion of the offshore drilling unit in the Gulf of Mexico in 2010. The oil forms a separate layer as it does not mix with the water.

Air is an example of a **homogeneous mixture**, meaning that it has uniform composition and properties throughout. A solution of salt in water and a metal alloy such as bronze are also homogeneous. By contrast, a **heterogeneous mixture** such as water and oil has non-uniform composition, so its properties are not the same throughout. It is usually possible to see the separate components in a heterogeneous mixture but not in a homogeneous mixture.

Because the components retain their individual properties in a mixture, we can often separate them relatively easily. The technique we choose to achieve this will take advantage of a suitable difference in the physical properties of the components, as shown in the table below. Many of these are important processes in research and industry and are discussed in more detail in the following chapters.

| Mixture | Difference in property of components | Technique used |
|---|---|---|
| sand and salt | solubility in water | solution and filtration |
| hydrocarbons in crude oil | boiling point | fractional distillation |
| iron and sulfur | magnetism | response to a magnet |
| pigments in food colouring | adsorbtion to solid phase | paper chromatography |
| different amino acids | net charge at a fixed pH | gel electrophoresis |

## Matter exists in different states determined by the temperature and the pressure

From our everyday experience, we know that all matter (elements, compounds, and mixtures) can exist in different forms depending on the temperature and the pressure. Liquid water changes into a solid form, such as ice, hail, or snow, as the temperature drops and it becomes a gas, steam, at high temperatures. These different forms are known as the **states of matter** and are characterized by the different energies of the particles.

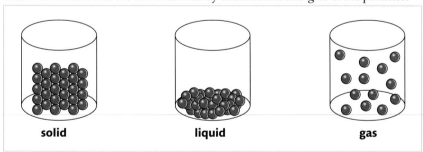

**solid**          **liquid**          **gas**

increasing temperature

increasing kinetic energy of particles

- particles close packed
- inter-particle forces strong, particles vibrate in position
- fixed shape
- fixed volume

- particles more spaced
- inter-particle forces weaker, particles can slide over each other
- no fixed shape
- fixed volume

- particles spread out
- inter-particle forces negligible, particles move freely
- no fixed shape
- no fixed volume

Ocean oil spills are usually the result of accidents in the industries of oil extraction or transport. The release of significant volumes of oil causes widespread damage to the environment, especially wildlife, and can have a major impact on local industries such as fishing and tourism. Efforts to reduce the impact of the spill include the use of dispersants, which act somewhat like soap in helping to break up the oil into smaller droplets so it can mix better with water. Concern is expressed, however, that these chemicals may increase the toxicity of the oil and they might persist in the environment. The effects of an oil spill often reach countries far from the source and are the subject of complex issues in international law. With the growth in demand for offshore drilling for oil and projected increases in oil pipelines, these issues are likely to become all the more pressing.

**Figure 1.2** Representation of the arrangement of the particles of the same substance in the solid, liquid, and gas states.

Depending on the chemical nature of the substance, matter may exist as atoms such as $Ar(g)$, or as molecules such as $H_2O(l)$, or as ions such as $Na^+$ and $Cl^-$ in $NaCl(aq)$. The term **particle** is therefore used as an inclusive term that is applied in this text to any or all of these entities of matter.

**Temperature is a measure of the average kinetic energy of the particles of a substance.**

This is known as the **kinetic theory** of matter. It recognizes that the average kinetic energy of the particles is directly related to the temperature of the system. The state of matter at a given temperature and pressure is determined by the strength of forces that may exist between the particles, known as **inter-particle forces**. The average kinetic energy is proportional to the temperature in kelvin, introduced on page 37.

### Worked example

Which of the following has the highest average kinetic energy?

A    He at 100 °C                              B    $H_2$ at 200 °C

C    $O_2$ at 300 °C                           D    $H_2O$ at 400 °C

### Solution

Answer = D. The substance at the highest temperature has the highest average kinetic energy.

Liquids and gases are referred to as **fluids**, which refers to their ability to flow. In the case of liquids it means that they take the shape of their container. Fluid properties are why **diffusion** occurs predominantly in these two states. Diffusion is the process by which the particles of a substance become evenly distributed, as a result of their random movements.

Kinetic energy (KE) refers to the energy associated with movement or motion. It is determined by the mass (*m*) and velocity or speed (*v*) of a substance, according to the relationship:

$$KE = \tfrac{1}{2}\,mv^2$$

As the kinetic energy of the particles of substances at the same temperature is equal, this means there is an inverse relationship between mass and velocity. This is why substances with lower mass diffuse more quickly than those with greater mass, when measured at the same temperature. This is discussed in more detail in Chapter 14.

**State symbols** are used to show the states of the reactants and products taking part in a reaction. These are abbreviations, which are given in brackets after each term in an equation, as shown below.

| State | Symbol | Example |
|---|---|---|
| solid | (s) | Mg(s) |
| liquid | (l) | $Br_2$(l) |
| gas | (g) | $N_2$(g) |
| aqueous (dissolved in water) | (aq) | HCl(aq) |

For example:

$$2Na(s) + 2H_2O(l) \rightarrow 2NaOH(aq) + H_2(g)$$

Bromine liquid, $Br_2$(l), had been placed in the lower gas jar only, and its vapour has diffused to fill both jars. Bromine vaporizes readily at room temperature and the gas colour allows the diffusion to be observed. Because gas molecules can move independently of each other and do so randomly, a gas spreads out from its source in this way.

### Exercises

**4**   Classify the following mixtures as homogeneous or heterogeneous:

(a) sand and water                    (b) smoke
(c) sugar and water                   (d) salt and iron filings
(e) ethanol and water in wine         (f) steel

## Exercises

**5** Write balanced equations for the following reactions and apply state symbols to all reactants and products, assuming room temperature and pressure unless stated otherwise. If you are not familiar with the aqueous solubilities of some of these substances, you may have to look them up.

**(a)** $KNO_3 \rightarrow KNO_2 + O_2$ (when heated, 500°C)
**(b)** $CaCO_3 + H_2SO_4 \rightarrow CaSO_4 + CO_2 + H_2O$
**(c)** $Li + H_2O \rightarrow LiOH + H_2$
**(d)** $Pb(NO_3)_2 + NaCl \rightarrow PbCl_2 + NaNO_3$ (all reactants are in aqueous solution)
**(e)** $C_3H_6 + O_2 \rightarrow CO_2 + H_2O$ (combustion reaction)

**6** A mixture of two gases, X and Y, which both have strong but distinct smells, is released. From across the room the smell of X is detected more quickly than the smell of Y. What can you deduce about X and Y?

**7** Ice floats on water. Comment on why this is not what you would expect from the kinetic theory of matter.

## Matter changes state reversibly

As the movement or kinetic energy of the particles increases with temperature, they will overcome the inter-particle forces and change state. These state changes occur at a fixed temperature and pressure for each substance, and are given specific names shown below.

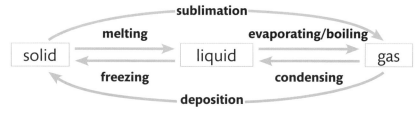

Sublimation, the direct inter-conversion of solid to gas without going through the liquid state, is characteristic at atmospheric pressure of some substances such as iodine, carbon dioxide, and ammonium chloride. Deposition, the reverse of sublimation that changes a gas directly to solid, is responsible for the formation of snow, frost, and hoar frost.

Note that evaporation involves the change of liquid to gas, but, unlike boiling, evaporation occurs only at the surface and takes place at temperatures below the boiling point.

Drying clothes. The heat of the Sun enables all the water to evaporate from the clothes.

Ice crystals, known as Hair Ice, formed by deposition on dead wood in a forest on Vancouver Island, Canada.

Boiling, on the other hand, is a volume phenomenon, characterized by particles leaving throughout the body of the liquid – which is why bubbles occur. Boiling occurs at a specific temperature, determined by when the vapour pressure reaches the external pressure. The influence of pressure on the temperature at which this occurs is demonstrated in Figure 1.3.

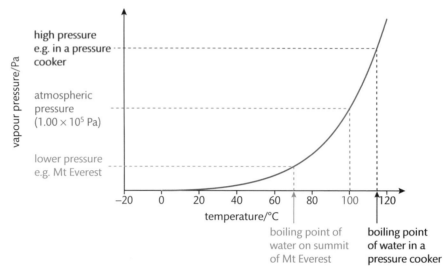

**Figure 1.3** Graph showing the increase in vapour pressure with temperature. This explains why boiling point changes with pressure. The boiling point of water at three different pressures is shown.

A pressure cooker is a sealed container in which a higher pressure can be generated. This raises the boiling point of water and so cooking time decreases. Conversely, at altitude, where the atmospheric pressure is lower, the boiling point of water is reduced so it takes much longer to cook food.

A butane gas camping stove. Butane, $C_4H_{10}$, is stored as a liquid because the high pressure in the canister raises its boiling point. When the valve is opened the release of pressure causes the butane to boil, releasing a gas that can be burned.

## CHALLENGE YOURSELF

1 Propane ($C_3H_8$) and butane ($C_4H_{10}$) are both commonly used in portable heating devices. Their boiling points are butane –1 °C and propane –42 °C. Suggest why butane is less suitable for use in very cold climates.

▲ Macrophotograph of freeze-dried instant coffee granules.

 Freeze-drying is an effective process for the preservation of food and some pharmaceuticals. It differs from standard methods of dehydration in that it does not use heat to evaporate water, but instead depends on the sublimation of ice. The substance to be preserved is first frozen, and then warmed gently at very low pressure which causes the ice to change directly to water vapour. The process is slow but has the significant advantage that the composition of the material, and so its flavour, are largely conserved. The freeze-dried product is stored in a moisture-free package that excludes oxygen, and can be reconstituted by the addition of water.

At night as the temperature is lowered, the rate of condensation increases. As the air temperature drops below its saturation point, known as the **dew point**, the familiar condensed water called **dew** forms. The temperature of the dew point depends on the atmospheric pressure and the water content of the air – that is, the relative humidity. A relative humidity of 100% indicates that the air is maximally saturated with water and the dew point is equal to the current temperature. Most people find this uncomfortable, as the condensation inhibits the evaporation of sweat, one of the body's main cooling mechanisms.

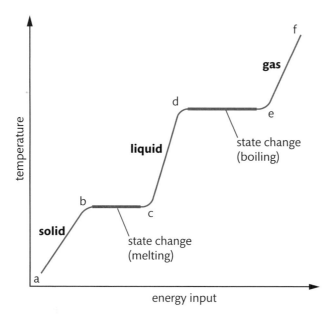

**Figure 1.4** Temperature change versus energy input at fixed pressure as a solid substance is heated. The flat regions shown in red are where the state change is occurring, as heat energy is used to overcome the inter-particle forces.

A fourth state of matter, plasma, exists only at conditions of very high temperatures and pressures, such as are commonly found in space. It is characterized by atoms that have been stripped of their electrons, and so exist as positively charged ions in loose association with their electrons. Plasma is a fluid, like liquid and gas, but also generates electromagnetic forces due to the charged particles present. All matter in the stars, including our Sun, exists in the plasma state.

Simple experiments can be done to monitor the temperature change while a substance is heated and changes state. Figure 1.4 shows a typical result. The graph can be interpreted as follows:

a–b   As the solid is heated, the vibrational energy of its particles increases and so the temperature increases.

b–c   This is the melting point. The vibrations are sufficiently energetic for the molecules to move away from their fixed positions and form liquid. Energy added during this stage is used to break the inter-particle forces, not to raise the kinetic energy, so the temperature remains constant.

c–d   As the liquid is heated, the particles gain kinetic energy and so the temperature increases.

d–e   This is the boiling point. There is now sufficient energy to break all of the inter-particle forces and form gas. Note that this state change needs more energy than melting, as all the inter-particle forces must be broken. The temperature remains constant as the kinetic energy does not increase during this stage. Bubbles of gas are visible throughout the volume of the liquid.

e–f   As the gas is heated under pressure, the kinetic energy of its particles continues to rise, and so does the temperature.

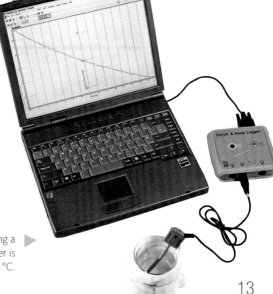

Experiment to measure the change in temperature of water using a temperature probe. In this example, the temperature of the water is decreasing as it cools from about 90 °C.

The global demand for refrigeration and air-conditioning systems is increasing sharply with increases in population and industrialization. It is estimated that world consumption of energy for cooling could increase tenfold by 2050, and that China will surpass the USA as the world's biggest user of energy for cooling by 2020. The increased energy demand has significant consequences for the environment, as both the energy use and the release of refrigerants such as HFCs contribute to greenhouse gas emissions, linked to climate change.

The process of refrigeration is usually based on energy changes during the evaporation and condensation cycle under changing pressure of a volatile liquid known as the **refrigerant**. At low pressure the liquid vaporizes and absorbs heat, causing cooling of the surroundings. Chlorofluorocarbons (CFCs) were commonly widely used as refrigerants, but these are now mostly phased out owing to their harmful role in causing ozone depletion. This is discussed further in Chapter 4. CFCs are largely replaced by hydrofluorocarbons (HFCs).

## Exercises

**8** A closed flask contains a pure substance, a brown liquid that is at its boiling point. Explain what you are likely to observe in the flask, and distinguish between the inter-particle distances and the average speeds of the particles in the two states present.

**9** During very cold weather, snow often gradually disappears without melting. Explain how this is possible.

**10** Explain why a burn to the skin caused by steam is more serious than a burn caused by the same amount of boiling water at the same temperature.

**11** Which of the following occurs at the melting point when solid sulfur is converted to its liquid form?

   I    movement of the particles increases
   II   distance between the particles increases

   **A**   I only
   **B**   II only
   **C**   Both I and II
   **D**   Neither I nor II

**12** You are given a liquid substance at 80 °C and told that it has a melting point of 35 °C. You are asked to take its temperature at regular time intervals while it cools to room temperature (25 °C). Sketch the cooling curve that you would expect to obtain.

The International Bureau of Weights and Measures (BIPM according to its French initials) is an international standards organization, which aims to ensure uniformity in the application of SI units around the world.

The SI (Systeme International d'Unites) refers to the metric system of measurement based on seven base units. These are metre (m) for length, kilogram for mass (kg), second (s) for time, ampere (A) for electric current, kelvin (K) for temperature, candela (cd) for luminous intensity, and mole (mol) for amount. All other units are derived from these. The SI system is the world's most widely used system of measurement.

# 1.2 The mole concept

## Understandings:

- The mole is a fixed number of particles and refers to the amount, $n$, of substance.

  *Guidance*
  *The value of the Avogadro's constant ($L$ or $N_A$) is given in the data booklet in section 2 and will be given for Paper 1 questions.*

- Masses of atoms are compared on a scale relative to $^{12}C$ and are expressed as relative atomic mass ($A_r$) and relative formula/molecular mass ($M_r$).

- Molar mass ($M$) has the units g mol$^{-1}$.

  *Guidance*
  *The generally used unit of molar mass (g mol$^{-1}$) is a derived SI unit.*

- The empirical and molecular formula of a compound give the simplest ratio and the actual number of atoms present in a molecule respectively.

## Applications and skills:

- Calculation of the molar masses of atoms, ions, molecules, formula units.
- Solution of problems involving the relationship between the number of particles, the amount of substance in moles, and the mass in grams.
- Interconversion of the percentage composition by mass and the empirical formula.
- Determination of the molecular formula of a compound from its empirical formula and molar mass.
- Obtaining and using experimental data for deriving empirical formulas from reactions involving mass changes.

## The Avogadro constant defines the mole as the unit of amount in chemistry

A problem in studying chemical change is that atoms are too small to measure individually. For example, even a relatively large atom like gold (Au) has a mass of $3.27 \times 10^{-25}$ kg – not a very useful figure when it comes to weighing it in a laboratory. But it's not really a problem, because all we need to do is to weigh an appropriately large number of atoms to give a mass that will be a useful quantity in grams. And in any case, atoms do not react individually but in very large numbers, so this approach makes sense. So how many atoms shall we lump together in our base unit of amount?

To answer this, let's first consider that atoms of different elements have different masses because they contain different numbers of particles, mostly **nucleons** in their nucleus, as we will discuss in Chapter 2. This means we can compare their masses with each other in relative terms. For example, an atom of oxygen has a mass approximately 16 times greater than an atom of hydrogen, and an atom of sulfur has a mass about twice that of an atom of oxygen. Now the good news is that these ratios will stay the same when we increase the number of atoms, *so long as we ensure we have the same number of each type.*

Amedeo Avogadro (1776–1856) was an Italian scientist who made several experimental discoveries. He clarified the distinction between atoms and molecules, and used this to propose the relationship between gas volume and number of molecules. His ideas were not, however, accepted in his time, largely due to a lack of consistent experimental evidence. After his death, when his theory was confirmed by fellow Italian Cannizzaro, his name was given in tribute to the famous constant that he helped to establish.

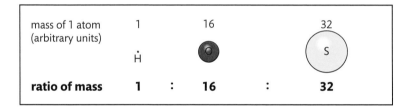

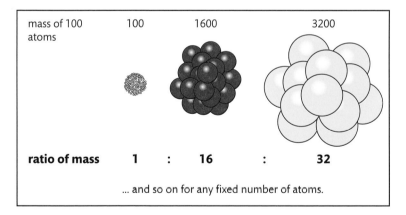

**Figure 1.5** 100 atoms of H, O, and S have the same mass ratio as one atom of each element, 1:16:32.

Now if we could take $6 \times 10^{23}$ atoms of hydrogen, it happens that this would have a mass of 1 g. It follows from the ratios above, that *the same number of atoms* of oxygen would have a mass of 16 g while *the same number of atoms* of sulfur has a mass of 32 g. So we now have a quantity of atoms that we can measure in grams.

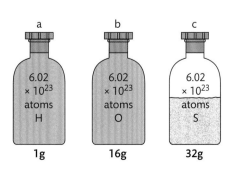

**Figure 1.6** $6.02 \times 10^{23}$ atoms of H, O, and S have the same mass ratio by mass as one atom of each element. This number of atoms gives an amount that we can see and measure in grams. (Note that this is illustrative only; in reality hydrogen and oxygen do not occur stably as single atoms, but as diatomic molecules – as explained in Chapter 4.)

This number, accurately stated as $6.02214129 \times 10^{23}$, is known as the **Avogadro number**, and it is the basis of the unit of **amount** used in chemistry known as the **mole**. In other words, a mole of a substance contains the Avogadro number of particles. Mole, the unit of amount, is one of the base units in the SI system and has the unit symbol **mol**.

So 'mole' is simply a word that represents a number, just as 'couple' is a word for 2, 'dozen' is a word for 12, and 'score' is a word that was commonly used for 20. A mole is a very large number, bigger than we can easily imagine or ever count, but it is nonetheless a fixed number. So a mole of any substance contains that Avogadro number, $6.02 \times 10^{23}$, of particles. You can refer to a mole of atoms, molecules, ions, electrons, and so on – it can be applied to any entity as it is just a number. And from this, we can easily calculate the number of particles in any portion or multiple of a mole of a substance.

Each beaker contains one mole, $6.02 \times 10^{23}$ particles, of a specific element. Each has a characteristic mass, known as its molar mass. From left to right the elements are tin (Sn), magnesium (Mg), iodine (I), and copper (Cu)

What ways of knowing can we use to grasp the magnitude of Avogadro's constant even though it is beyond the scale of our everyday experience?

Avogadro's number is so large that we cannot comprehend its scale. For example:

- $6.02 \times 10^{23}$ pennies distributed equally to everyone alive would make everyone on Earth a dollar trillionaire;
- $6.02 \times 10^{23}$ pencil erasers would cover the Earth to a depth of about 500 m;
- $6.02 \times 10^{23}$ drops of water would fill all the oceans of the Earth many times over.

When doing multiplication or division, the answer is given to the same number of significant figures as the data value with the least number of significant figures. When doing addition or subraction, the answer is given to the same number of decimal places as the data value with the least number of decimal places.

### Worked example

A tablespoon holds 0.500 moles of water. How many molecules of water are present?

**Solution**

1.00 mole of water has $6.02 \times 10^{23}$ molecules of water

$\therefore$ 0.500 moles of water has $\dfrac{0.500}{1.00} \times 6.02 \times 10^{23}$ molecules

$= 3.01 \times 10^{23}$ molecules of water

## Worked example

A solution of water and ammonia contains $2.10 \times 10^{23}$ molecules of $H_2O$ and $8.00 \times 10^{21}$ molecules of $NH_3$. How many moles of hydrogen atoms are present?

### Solution

First total the number of hydrogen atoms:

from water $H_2O$:     number of H atoms $= 2 \times (2.10 \times 10^{23})$

$= 4.20 \times 10^{23}$

from ammonia $NH_3$:    number of H atoms $= 3 \times (8.00 \times 10^{21})$

$= 0.240 \times 10^{23}$

$\therefore$ total H atoms $= (4.20 \times 10^{23}) + (0.240 \times 10^{23})$

$= 4.44 \times 10^{23}$

To convert atoms to moles, divide by the Avogadro constant:

$$\frac{4.44 \times 10^{23}}{6.02 \times 10^{23}} = 0.738 \text{ mol H atoms}$$

divide by Avogadro constant, $L$

number of particles ($N$)          number of moles ($n$)

multiply by Avogadro constant, $L$

## Exercises

**13** Calculate how many hydrogen atoms are present in :

(a) 0.020 moles of $C_2H_5OH$
(b) 2.50 moles of $H_2O$
(c) 0.10 moles of $Ca(HCO_3)_2$

**14** Propane has the formula $C_3H_8$. If a sample of propane contains 0.20 moles of C, how many moles of H are present?

**15** Calculate the amount of sulfuric acid, $H_2SO_4$, which contains $6.02 \times 10^{23}$ atoms of oxygen.

Dealing with Avogadro's constant to calculate the number of particles in a sample has its uses, but it still leaves us with numbers that are beyond our comprehension. What is much more useful, as you have probably realized, is the link between the Avogadro number and the mass of one mole of a substance, which is based on the relative atomic mass.

## Relative atomic mass is used to compare the masses of atoms

On page 15 the numbers used to compare the masses of the elements H, O and S are only approximate. A slight complexity is that most elements exist naturally with atoms that differ in their mass. These different atoms are known as **isotopes**, and we will look at them in Chapter 2. So a sample of an element containing billions of atoms will include a mix of these isotopes according to their relative abundance. The mass of an individual atom in the sample is therefore taken as a **weighted average** of these different masses.

Relative atomic mass, $A_r$, is the weighted average of one atom of an element relative to one-twelfth of an atom of carbon-12.

The nomenclature and the reference point used for describing atomic mass have been a subject for debate since John Dalton's work on atomic structure in the early 1800s. The original term 'atomic weight' is now considered largely obsolete. Chemists and physicists previously used two different reference points for mass based on isotopes of oxygen, but since the 1960s, the unified scale based on carbon-12 ($^{12}C$) has gained wide acceptance. The current IUPAC definition of the *unified atomic mass unit* is one-twelfth of the mass of a carbon-12 atom in its ground state with a mass of $1.66 \times 10^{-27}$ kg.

$A_r$ values are often rounded to whole numbers for quick calculations, but when using values from the IB data booklet for calculations, it is usually best to use the exact values given in Section 6.

**CHALLENGE YOURSELF**

**2** Three of the compounds in the photograph are hydrated, containing water of crystallization, as described on page 23. Use the formulas given in the caption and the masses marked on the photograph to deduce which compounds are hydrated, and the full formula of each.

The relative scale for comparing the mass of atoms needs a reference point. The international convention for this is to take the specific form of carbon known as the **isotope carbon-12** (see Chapter 2) as the standard, and assign this a value of 12 units. In other words, one-twelfth of an atom of carbon-12 has a value of exactly 1.

Putting all this together, we can define the **relative atomic mass** as follows:

$$\text{relative atomic mass } A_r = \frac{\text{weighted average of one atom of the element}}{\frac{1}{12}\text{mass of one atom of carbon-12}}$$

Values for $A_r$ do not have units as it is a relative term, which simply compares the mass of atoms against the same standard. As they are average values, they are not whole numbers; the IB data booklet in Section 6 gives $A_r$ values to two decimal places. Some examples are given below.

| Element | Relative atomic mass ($A_r$) |
| --- | --- |
| hydrogen, H | 1.01 |
| carbon, C | 12.01 |
| oxygen, O | 16.00 |
| sodium, Na | 22.99 |
| sulfur, S | 32.07 |
| chlorine, Cl | 35.45 |

You will notice that the $A_r$ of carbon is slightly greater than the mass of the isotope carbon-12 used as the standard, suggesting that carbon has isotopes with masses slightly greater than 12. In Chapter 2 we discuss how relative atomic mass is calculated from isotope abundances, using data from mass spectrometry.

## Relative formula mass is used to compare masses of compounds

We can extend the concept of relative atomic mass to compounds (and to elements occurring as molecules), to obtain the **relative formula mass**, $M_r$. This simply involves adding the relative atomic masses of all the atoms or ions present in its formula. Note that $M_r$, like $A_r$, is a relative term and so has no units.

One mole of different compounds, each showing the molar mass. The chemical formulas of these ionic compounds are, clockwise from lower left: $NaCl$, $FeCl_3$, $CuSO_4$, $KI$, $Co(NO_3)_2$, and $KMnO_4$.

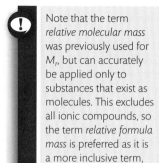

## Worked example

Use the values for $A_r$ in Section 6 of the IB data booklet to calculate the $M_r$ of the following:

(a) chlorine, $Cl_2$

$$M_r = 35.45 \times 2 = 70.90$$

(b) ammonium nitrate, $NH_4NO_3$

$$M_r = 14.01 + (1.01 \times 4) + 14.01 + (16.00 \times 3) = 80.06$$

(c) aluminium sulfate, $Al_2(SO_4)_3$

$$M_r = (26.98 \times 2) + [32.07 + (16.00 \times 4)] \times 3 = 342.17$$

## Molar mass is the mass of one mole of a substance

The Avogadro number is defined so that the mass of one mole of a substance is exactly equal to the substance's relative atomic mass expressed in grams. This is known as the **molar mass** and is given the symbol **M** with the unit $g\ mol^{-1}$, which is a derived SI unit. Using the examples discussed already in this chapter, we can now deduce the following:

| Element or compound | Molar mass ($M$) |
| --- | --- |
| hydrogen, H | $1.01\ g\ mol^{-1}$ |
| oxygen, O | $16.00\ g\ mol^{-1}$ |
| sulfur, S | $32.07\ g\ mol^{-1}$ |
| chlorine, $Cl_2$ | $70.90\ g\ mol^{-1}$ |
| ammonium nitrate, $NH_4NO_3$ | $80.06\ g\ mol^{-1}$ |
| aluminium sulfate, $Al_2(SO_4)_3$ | $342.17\ g\ mol^{-1}$ |

From our knowledge of molar mass we can state the definition of the mole as the mass of substance that contains as many particles as there are atoms in 12 g of carbon-12.

Now we are truly able to use the concept of the mole to make that all-important link between the number of particles and their mass in grams. The key to this is conversions of grams to moles and moles to grams. In the calculations that follow, we use the following notation:

- $n$ = number of moles (mol)
- $m$ = mass in grams (g)
- $M$ = molar mass ($g\ mol^{-1}$)

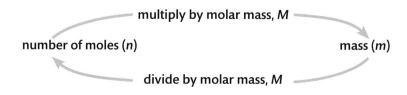

Dimensional analysis, or the factor-label method, is a widely used technique to determine conversion factors on the basis of cancelling the units. This method is not specifically used in the examples here, but the units *are* shown through the calculations. This method can be helpful to check that the units on both sides of the equation are balanced, and are appropriate for the answer, which is often a useful check on the steps taken. As in all cases, there is no one correct way to set out calculations, so long as the steps are clear.

Note the units cancel to give the correct units for mass. This is often a useful check that we are using the terms correctly in a calculation.

$$amount = \frac{mass}{molar\ mass}$$

$$n\ (mol) = \frac{m\ (g)}{M\ (g\ mol^{-1})}$$

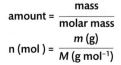

## Worked example

What is the mass of the following?

(a) 6.50 moles of NaCl

(b) 0.10 moles of OH⁻ ions

### Solution

In all these questions, we must first calculate the molar mass, M, to know the mass of 1 mole in g mol⁻¹. Multiplying M by the specified number of moles, n, will then give the mass, m, in grams.

(a) $M(NaCl) = 22.99 + 35.45 = 58.44\ g\ mol^{-1}$

$n(NaCl) = 6.50\ mol$

$\therefore m(NaCl) = 58.44\ g\ mol^{-1} \times 6.50\ mol = 380\ g$

(b) OH⁻ ions carry a charge because electrons have been transferred, but the change to the mass is negligible and so can be ignored in calculating M.

$M(OH^-) = 16.00 + 1.01 = 17.01\ g\ mol^{-1}$

$n(OH^-) = 0.10\ mol$

$\therefore m(OH^-) = 17.01\ g\ mol^{-1} \times 0.10\ mol = 1.7\ g$

## Worked example

What is the amount in moles of the following?

(a) 32.50 g $(NH_4)_2SO_4$

(b) 273.45 g $N_2O_5$

### Solution

Again we calculate the molar mass, M, to know the mass of one mole. Dividing the given mass, m, by the mass of one mole will then give the number of moles, n.

(a) $M((NH_4)_2SO_4) = [14.01 + (1.01 \times 4)] \times 2 + 32.07 + (16.00 \times 4) = 132.17\ g\ mol^{-1}$

$m((NH_4)_2SO_4) = 32.50\ g$

$\therefore n((NH_4)_2SO_4) = \frac{32.50\ g}{132.17\ g\ mol^{-1}} = 0.2459\ mol$

(b) $M(N_2O_5) = (14.01 \times 2) + (16.00 \times 5) = 108.02\ g\ mol^{-1}$

$m(N_2O_5) = 273.45\ g$

$\therefore n(N_2O_5) = \frac{273.45\ g}{108.02\ g\ mol^{-1}} = 2.532\ mol$

These simple conversions show that:

$$number\ of\ moles = \frac{mass}{molar\ mass} \qquad n\ (mol) = \frac{m\ (g)}{M\ (g\ mol^{-1})}$$

This is a very useful relationship, but it is hoped that you understand how it is derived, rather than rote learn it.

We can now put together the conversions shown on pages 17 and 19 to see the central role of the mole in converting from number of particles to mass in grams.

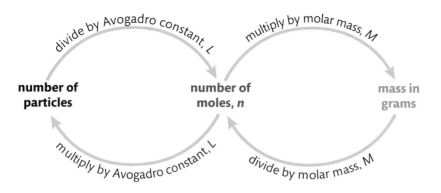

number of **particles** — divide by Avogadro constant, $L$ → **number of moles, $n$** — multiply by molar mass, $M$ → **mass in grams**

number of **particles** ← multiply by Avogadro constant, $L$ — **number of moles, $n$** ← divide by molar mass, $M$ — **mass in grams**

**Figure 1.7** Summary of the central role of the number of moles, $n$, in converting between the number of particles and the mass in grams.

 Calculations involving mass in chemistry always involve converting *grams to moles* and *moles to grams*. Think of these conversions as fundamental tools for chemists, and so make sure you are fully comfortable with carrying them out effectively.

## Exercises

\* indicates you should be able to do this question without a calculator.

Note that you should refer to section 6 of the IB data booklet for the values of $A_r$.

**16** Calculate the molar mass of the following compounds:

  **(a)** magnesium phosphate, $Mg_3(PO_4)_2$
  **(b)** ascorbic acid (vitamin C), $C_6H_8O_6$
  **(c)** calcium nitrate, $Ca(NO_3)_2$
  **(d)** hydrated sodium thiosulfate, $Na_2S_2O_3.5H_2O$

**17** Calcium arsenate, $Ca_3(AsO_4)_2$, is a poison which was widely used as an insecticide. What is the mass of 0.475 mol of calcium arsenate?

**18\*** How many moles of carbon dioxide are there in 66 g of carbon dioxide, $CO_2$?

**19** How many moles of chloride ions, $Cl^-$, are there in 0.50 g of copper(II) chloride, $CuCl_2$?

**20** How many carbon atoms are there in 36.55 g of diamond (which is pure carbon)?

**21\*** What is the mass in grams of a 0.500 mol sample of sucrose, $C_{12}H_{22}O_{11}$?

**22\*** Which contains the greater number of particles, 10.0 g of water ($H_2O$) or 10.0 g of mercury (Hg)?

**23\*** Put the following in descending order of mass?

  1.0 mol $N_2H_4$
  2.0 mol $N_2$
  3.0 mol $NH_3$
  25.0 mol $H_2$

## The empirical formula of a compound gives the simplest ratio of its atoms

Magnesium burns brightly in air to form a white solid product, and we might ask how many atoms of magnesium combine with how many atoms of oxygen in this reaction? Thanks to the mole, and its central role in relating the number of particles to a mass that can be measured, we can find the answer to this quite easily.

All we have to do is:

- burn a known mass of Mg, and from this calculate the moles of Mg;
- calculate the mass of oxygen that reacted from the increase in mass, and from this calculate the moles of O;
- express the ratio of moles Mg : moles O in its simplest form;
- the ratio of moles is the ratio of atoms, so we can deduce the simplest formula of magnesium oxide.

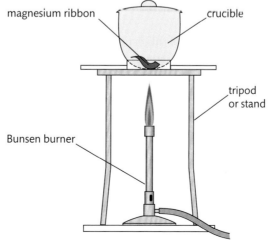

magnesium ribbon — crucible

tripod or stand

Bunsen burner

Magnesium burns with a bright white flame, combining with oxygen from the air to form the white solid magnesium oxide.

**Figure 1.8** Apparatus used to investigate mass changes on burning magnesium.

**Experiment to determine the empirical formula of MgO**

Full details of how to carry out this experiment with a worksheet are available online.

A sample of magnesium is heated and the change in mass recorded. From this, the ratio of moles of magnesium to oxygen can be determined.

### Sample results

| | Mass / g ± 0.001 | Observations |
|---|---|---|
| mass of crucible + lid | 19.777 | |
| mass of crucible + lid + Mg | 19.820 | magnesium metal has grey, shiny appearance |
| mass of crucible + lid + white solid product | 19.849 | metal burned with bright flame, leaving grey-white powder |

### Processed data

| | Magnesium, Mg | Oxygen, O |
|---|---|---|
| mass /g ± 0.002 | 0.043 | 0.029 |
| M / g mol$^{-1}$ | 24.31 | 16.00 |
| moles / mol | 0.00177 | 0.00181 |

ratio moles Mg : moles O = 1 : 1.02

So the ratio atoms Mg : atoms O approximates to 1 : 1

So the formula of magnesium oxide is MgO.

The fact that the experimental result is not exactly 1 : 1 indicates there are some errors in the experiment. We can consider possible systematic errors here, such as:

- the Mg weighed is not all pure;
- not all the Mg weighed reacted;
- the product was not magnesium oxide only;
- loss of Mg or of product occurred;
- change in the mass of the crucible occurred during handling and heating.

Modifications to the experimental design can be considered, which help to reduce the experimental error.

**The empirical formula is the simplest whole-number ratio of the elements in a compound.**

From the result of this experiment, we conclude that the formula of magnesium oxide is MgO. This is known as an **empirical formula**, which gives the simplest whole-number ratio of the elements in a compound.

## Worked example

Which of the following are empirical formulas?

I $C_6H_6$

II $C_3H_8$

III $N_2O_4$

IV $Pb(NO_3)_2$

## Solution

Only II and IV are empirical formulas, as their elements are in the simplest whole-number ratio.

I has the empirical formula CH; III has the empirical formula $NO_2$.

The formulas of all ionic compounds, made of a metal and a non-metal, such as magnesium oxide, are empirical formulas. This is explained when we look at ionic bonding in Chapter 4. But as we see in the worked example above, the formulas of covalently bonded compounds, usually made of different non-metal elements, are not always empirical formulas. This is explained in the next section on molecular formulas.

Empirical formulas can be deduced from experimental results, usually involving combustion, that give the masses of each of the elements present in a sample. It is a similar process to the one we used for magnesium oxide.

## Worked example

A sample of urea contains 1.120 g N, 0.161 g H, 0.480 g C, and 0.640 g O. What is the empirical formula of urea?

## Solution

- Convert the mass of each element to moles by dividing by its molar mass, $M$.
- Divide by the smallest number to give the ratio.
- Approximate to the nearest whole number.

|  | Nitrogen, N | Hydrogen, H | Carbon, C | Oxygen, O |
|---|---|---|---|---|
| mass / g | 1.120 | 0.161 | 0.480 | 0.640 |
| $M$ / g mol⁻¹ | 14.01 | 1.01 | 12.01 | 16.00 |
| number of moles / mol | 0.0799 | 0.159 | 0.0400 | 0.0400 |
| divide by smallest | 2.00 | 3.98 | 1.00 | 1.00 |
| nearest whole number ratio | 2 | 4 | 1 | 1 |

So the empirical formula of urea is $N_2H_4CO$, usually written as $CO(NH_2)_2$.

A modification of this type of question is to analyse the composition of a **hydrated salt**. These are compounds that contain a fixed ratio of water molecules, known as **water of crystallization**, within the crystalline structure of the compound. The water of crystallization can be driven off by heating, and the change in mass used to calculate the ratio of water molecules to the **anhydrous salt**. The formula of the hydrated salt is shown with a dot before the number of molecules of water, for example $CaCl_2.4H_2O$.

It is common for the composition data to be given in the form of percentages by mass, and we use these figures in the same way to deduce the ratio of atoms present. Percentage data effectively give us the mass present in a 100 g sample of the compound.

**Experiment to determine the formula of hydrated barium chloride, $BaCl_2.xH_2O$**

Full details of how to carry out this experiment with a worksheet are available online.

Hydrated copper (II) sulfate, $CuSO_4.5H_2O$, is blue due to the presence of water of crystallization within the structure of the crystals. The anhydrous form is white, as shown in the lower part of the tube. Heating removes the water molecules, leading to the colour being lost. The process is reversible, and the addition of water to the anhydrous crystals restores their blue colour.

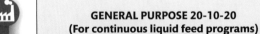

Fertilizers contain nutrients that are added to the soil, usually to replace those used by cultivated plants. The elements needed in the largest quantities, so-called **macronutrients**, include nitrogen, phosphorus, and potassium. Fertilizers are often labelled with an N-P-K rating, such as 30-15-30, to show the quantities of each of these three elements. The numbers indicate respectively the percentage by mass N, percentage by mass diphosphorus pentoxide, $P_2O_5$, and percentage by mass potassium oxide, $K_2O$. The percentage data for $P_2O_5$ and $K_2O$ represent the most oxidized forms of elemental phosphorus and potassium present in the fertilizer. Ammonium salts are the most common source of nitrogen used in fertilizers.

### GENERAL PURPOSE 20-10-20
**(For continuous liquid feed programs)**

| Guaranteed analysis | F1143 |
| --- | --- |
| Total nitrogen (N) | 20% |
| 7.77% ammoniacal nitrogen | |
| 12.23% nitrate nitrogen | |
| Available phosphate ($P_2O_5$) | 10% |
| Soluble potash ($K_2O$) | 20% |
| Magnesium (Mg)(Total) | 0.05% |
| 0.05% Water soluble magnesium (Mg) | |
| Boron (B) | 0.0068% |
| Copper (Cu) | 0.0036% |
| 0.0036% Chelated copper (Cu) | |
| Iron (Fe) | 0.05% |
| 0.05% Chelated iron (Fe) | |
| Manganese (Mn) | 0.025% |
| 0.025% Chelated manganese (Mn) | |
| Molybdenum (Mo) | 0.0009% |
| Zinc (Zn) | 0.0025% |
| 0.0025% Chelated zinc (Zn) | |

Derived from: ammonium nitrate, potassium phosphate, potassium nitrate, magnesium sulfate, boric acid, copper EDTA, manganese EDTA, iron EDTA, zinc EDTA, sodium molybdate. Potential acidity: 487 lbs. calcium carbonate equivalent per ton.

**Figure 1.9** The label on a fertilizer bag shows the percentage by mass of macro and micronutrients that it contains.

## CHALLENGE YOURSELF

**3** A fertilizer has an N-P-K rating of 18-51-20. Use the information in the box above to determine the percentage by mass of nitrogen, phosphorus, and potassium present.

When working with percentage figures, always check that they add up to 100. Sometimes an element is omitted from the data and you are expected to deduce its identity and percentage from information given.

### Worked example

The mineral celestine consists mostly of a compound of strontium, sulfur, and oxygen. It is found by combustion analysis to have the composition 47.70% by mass Sr, 17.46% S, and the remainder is O. What is its empirical formula?

### Solution

Here we need first to calculate the percentage of oxygen by subtraction of the total given masses from 100.

$$\% \text{ O} = 100 - (47.70 + 17.46) = 34.84$$

| | Strontium, Sr | Sulfur, S | Oxygen, O |
| --- | --- | --- | --- |
| % by mass | 47.70 | 17.46 | 34.84 |
| $M$ / g mol$^{-1}$ | 87.62 | 32.07 | 16.00 |
| number of moles/mol | 0.5443 | 0.5444 | 2.178 |
| divide by smallest | 1.000 | 1.000 | 4.001 |

So the empirical formula of the mineral is $SrSO_4$.

An understanding of percentage by mass data helps us to evaluate information that we commonly see on products such as foods, drinks, pharmaceuticals, household cleaners, as well as fertilizers. For example, a common plant fertilizer is labelled as pure sodium tetraborate pentahydrate, $Na_2B_4O_7.5H_2O$ and claims to be 15.2% boron. How accurate is this claim?

## Percentage composition by mass can be calculated from the empirical formula

We can see in the example above that, even though the mineral celestine has only one atom of strontium for every four atoms of oxygen, strontium nonetheless accounts for 47.70% of its mass. This, of course, is because an atom of strontium has significantly greater mass than an atom of oxygen, and the percentage by mass of an element in a compound depends on the total contribution of its atoms. We can calculate this as follows.

### Worked example

What is the percentage by mass of N, H, and O in the compound ammonium nitrate, $NH_4NO_3$?

### Solution

First calculate the molar mass $M$.

$$M(NH_4NO_3) = 14.01 + (1.01 \times 4) + 14.01 + (16.00 \times 3) = 80.06 \text{ g mol}^{-1}$$

Then for each element total the mass of its atoms, divide by $M$, and multiply by 100.

$$\% \text{ N} = \frac{14.01 \times 2}{80.06} \times 100 = 35.00\% \text{ by mass}$$

$$\% \text{ H} = \frac{1.01 \times 4}{80.06} \times 100 = 5.05\% \text{ by mass}$$

$$\% \text{ O} = \frac{16.00 \times 3}{80.06} \times 100 = 59.96\% \text{ by mass}$$

(alternatively, this last term can be calculated by subtraction from 100)

Finally check the numbers add up to 100%. Note that rounding here means that the total is 100.01%.

## The molecular formula of a compound gives the actual number of atoms in a molecule

The empirical formula gives us the simplest ratio of atoms present in a compound, but this often does not give the full information about the actual *number* of atoms in a molecule. For example, $CH_2$ is an empirical formula. There is no molecule that exists with just one atom of carbon and two atoms of hydrogen, but there are many molecules with multiples of this ratio, such as $C_2H_4$, $C_3H_6$, and so on. These formulas, which show all the atoms present in a molecule, are called **molecular formulas**.

The molecular formula shows all the atoms present in a molecule. It is a multiple of the empirical formula.

The molecular formula can be deduced from the empirical formula if the molar mass is known.

$$x \text{ (mass of empirical formula)} = M, \text{ where } x \text{ is an integer}$$

### Worked example

Calomel is a compound once used in the treatment of syphilis. It has the empirical formula HgCl and a molar mass of 472.08 g mol⁻¹. What is its molecular formula?

**TOK** Assigning numbers to the masses of elements has allowed chemistry to develop into a physical science. To what extent is mathematics effective in describing the natural world?

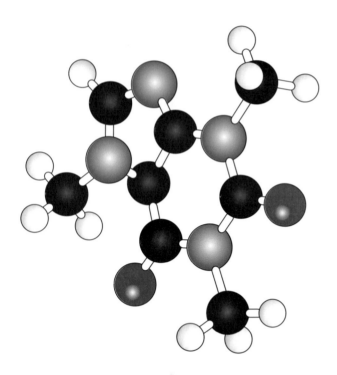

**Figure 1.10** A molecular model of the stimulant, caffeine. The atoms are colour coded as follows: black = carbon, grey = hydrogen, red = oxygen, blue = nitrogen. Can you deduce the molecular formula, the empirical formula, and the molar mass of caffeine?

### Solution

First calculate the mass of the empirical formula:

$$mass(HgCl) = 200.59 + 35.45 = 236.04 \text{ g mol}^{-1}$$

$$(236.04) \times x = M = 472.08$$

$$\therefore x = 2$$

$$\text{molecular formula} = Hg_2Cl_2$$

## Combustion analysis usually gives data on the mass of compounds formed

The data presented so far may suggest that combustion analysis directly gives information on the relative masses of individual elements in a compound. In fact this is rarely the case, but instead elements are converted into new compounds, typically their oxides, by reaction with oxygen. So the primary data obtained are the masses of carbon dioxide, water, sulfur dioxide, and so on, which are measured by infra-red absorption, as described in Chapter 11. Processing these data simply involves an extra step.

### Worked example

A 0.5438 g sample of a compound known to contain only carbon, hydrogen, and oxygen was burned completely in oxygen. The products were 1.0390 g $CO_2$ and 0.6369 g $H_2O$. Determine the empirical formula of the compound.

### Solution

First we must convert the mass of each compound to moles in the usual way. From the number of moles of $CO_2$ and $H_2O$ we can deduce the number of moles of C atoms and H atoms.

$$n(CO_2) = \frac{1.0390 \text{ g}}{12.01 + (16.00 \times 2) \text{ g mol}^{-1}} = 0.02361 \text{ mol } CO_2 \Rightarrow 0.02361 \text{ mol C atoms}$$

$$n(H_2O) = \frac{0.6369 \text{ g}}{(1.01 \times 2) + 16.00 \text{ g mol}^{-1}} = 0.03534 \text{ mol } H_2O \Rightarrow 0.03534 \times 2 = 0.07068 \text{ mol H atoms}$$

In order to know the mass of O in the original sample, we must convert the number of moles of C and H atoms to mass by multiplying by their molar mass, $M$.

$$\text{mass C} = 0.02361 \text{ mol} \times 12.01 \text{ g mol}^{-1} = 0.2836 \text{ g}$$

$$\text{mass H} = 0.07068 \text{ mol} \times 1.01 \text{ g mol}^{-1} = 0.07139 \text{ g}$$

$$\therefore \text{mass O} = 0.5438 - (0.2836 + 0.07139) = 0.1888 \text{ g}$$

$$\text{mol O atoms} = \frac{0.1888 \text{ g}}{16.00 \text{ g mol}^{-1}} = 0.01180 \text{ mol}$$

Now we can proceed as with the previous examples, converting mass of O to moles and then comparing the mole ratios.

|  | Carbon, C | Hydrogen, H | Oxygen, O |
|---|---|---|---|
| mass / g |  |  | 0.1888 |
| moles | 0.02361 | 0.07068 | 0.01180 |
| divide by smallest | 2.001 | 5.999 | 1.000 |
| nearest whole number ratio | 2 | 6 | 1 |

So the empirical formula is $C_2H_6O$.

## Exercises

**24** Give the empirical formulas of the following compounds:

  **(a)** ethyne, $C_2H_2$
  **(b)** glucose, $C_6H_{12}O_6$
  **(c)** sucrose, $C_{12}H_{22}O_{11}$
  **(d)** octane, $C_8H_{18}$
  **(e)** oct-1-yne, $C_8H_{14}$
  **(f)** ethanoic acid, $CH_3COOH$

**25** A sample of a compound contains only the elements sodium, sulfur, and oxygen. It is found by analysis to contain 0.979 g Na, 1.365 g S, and 1.021 g O. Determine its empirical formula.

**26** A sample of a hydrated compound was analysed and found to contain 2.10 g Co, 1.14 g S, 2.28 g O, and 4.50 g $H_2O$. Determine its empirical formula.

**27** A street drug has the following composition: 83.89% C, 10.35% H, 5.76% N. Determine its empirical formula.

**28** The following compounds are used in the production of fertilizers. Determine which has the highest percentage by mass of nitrogen: $NH_3$, $CO(NH_2)_2$, $(NH_4)_2SO_4$.

**29** A compound has a formula $M_3N$ where M is a metal element and N is nitrogen. It contains 0.673 g of N per gram of the metal M. Determine the relative atomic mass of M and so its identity.

**30** Compounds of cadmium are used in the construction of photocells. Deduce which of the following has the highest percentage by mass of cadmium: CdS, CdSe, CdTe.

**31** Benzene is a hydrocarbon, a compound of carbon and hydrogen only. It is found to contain 7.74% H by mass. Its molar mass is 78.10 g mol$^{-1}$. Determine its empirical and molecular formulas.

**32** A weak acid has a molar mass of 162 g mol$^{-1}$. Analysis of a 0.8821 g sample showed the composition by mass is 0.0220 g H, 0.3374 g P, and the remainder was O. Determine its empirical and molecular formulas.

**33** ATP is an important molecule in living cells. A sample with a mass of 0.8138 g was analysed and found to contain 0.1927 g C, 0.02590 g H, 0.1124 g N, and 0.1491 g P. The remainder was O. Determine the empirical formula of ATP. Its formula mass was found to be 507 g mol$^{-1}$. Determine its molecular formula.

**34** A 0.30 g sample of a compound that contains only carbon, hydrogen, and oxygen was burned in excess oxygen. The products were 0.66 g of carbon dioxide and 0.36 g of water. Determine the empirical formula of the compound.

**35** You are asked to write your name on a suitable surface, using a piece of chalk that is pure calcium carbonate, $CaCO_3$. How could you calculate the number of carbon atoms in your signature?

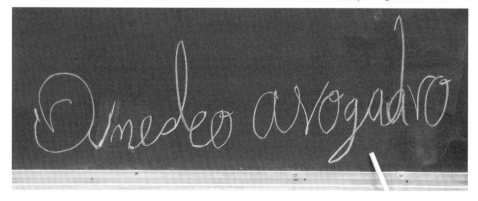

How many atoms of calcium are in Avogadro's name written in chalk?

## 1.3 Reacting masses and volumes

### Understandings:

- Reactants can be either limiting or excess.
- The experimental yield can be different from the theoretical yield.
- Avogadro's law enables the mole ratio of reacting gases to be determined from volumes of the gases.
- The molar volume of an ideal gas is a constant at specified temperature and pressure.

  **Guidance**
  *Values for the molar volume of an ideal gas are given in the IB data booklet in Section 2.*

- The molar concentration of a solution is determined by the amount of solute and the volume of solution.

  **Guidance**
  *The use of square brackets to denote molar concentration is required.*

- A standard solution is one of known concentration.

### Applications and skills:

- Solution of problems relating to reacting quantities, limiting and excess reactants, and theoretical, experimental, and percentage yields.
- Calculation of reacting volumes of gases using Avogadro's law.
- Solution of problems and analysis of graphs involving the relationship between temperature, pressure, and volume for a fixed mass of an ideal gas.
- Solution of problems relating to the ideal gas equation.

  **Guidance**
  *The ideal gas equation, PV = nRT, and the value of the gas constant (R), are given in the IB data booklet in Sections 1 and 2.*

- Explanation of the deviation of real gases from ideal behaviour at low temperature and high pressure.
- Obtaining and using experimental values to calculate the molar mass of a gas from the ideal gas equation.
- Solution of problems involving molar concentration, amount of solute, and volume of solution.

  **Guidance**
  *Units of concentration to include: g dm$^{-3}$, mol dm$^{-3}$, and parts per million (ppm).*

- Use of the experimental method of titration to calculate the concentration of a solution by reference to a standard solution.

### Chemical equations show reactants combining in a fixed molar ratio

Chemical change, as summarized in chemical equations, is simply an expression of reactants combining in fixed ratios to form products. The most convenient means to express this ratio is as moles, as that gives us a means of relating the number of particles that react to the mass that we can measure. So, for example, when methane, $CH_4$, burns in air, we can conclude the following, all from the balanced chemical equation:

|  | $CH_4(g)$ | + $2O_2(g)$ | $\rightarrow$ | $CO_2(g)$ | + $2H_2O(g)$ |
|---|---|---|---|---|---|
| Reacting ratio by mole: | 1 mole | 2 moles | | 1 mole | 2 moles |
| Reacting ratio by mass: | 16.05 g | 64.00 g | | 44.01 g | 36.04 g |

80.05 g reactant        80.05 g product

(The figures for total mass of reactant and product are just a check, as we know something would be wrong if they did not equate.)

The Bunsen burner controls the combustion of methane, $CH_4$, and is often used as a source of heat in the laboratory.

This simple interpretation of equations, going directly from coefficients to molar ratios, opens the door to a wide range of calculations involving reacting masses.

## Worked example

Calculate the mass of carbon dioxide produced from the complete combustion of 1.00 g of methane.

### Solution

Write the balanced equation and deduce the mole ratio as above. Then pick out from the question the terms that we need to analyse, here they are marked in red; these are the species where we need to convert moles to grams.

$$CH_4(g) + 2O_2(g) \rightarrow CO_2(g) + 2H_2O(g)$$

Reacting ratio by mole:     1 mole                    1 mole

Reacting ratio by mass / g:  16.05                     44.01

For 1.00 g methane:          1.00                        $x$

Now solve the ratio, shown here using cross-multiplication, to determine the value of $x$.

$$\frac{g\ CH_4}{g\ CO_2} = \frac{16.05}{44.01} = \frac{1.00}{x}$$

$$x = \frac{1.00 \times 44.01}{16.05} = 2.74\ g\ CO_2$$

All questions on reacting ratios involve a variation of this approach:
- write the balanced equation;
- work out the mole ratio for the species identified in the question;
- work out the reacting ratio by mass for these species, using $m = n\,M$;
- insert the data from the question and solve the ratio.

## Worked example

Iodine chloride, ICl, can be made by the following reaction:

$$2I_2 + KIO_3 + 6HCl \rightarrow 5ICl + KCl + 3H_2O$$

Calculate the mass of iodine, $I_2$, needed to prepare 28.60 g of ICl by this reaction.

### Solution

The relevant terms from the question are $I_2$ and ICl, so these are our focus.

$$2I_2 + KIO_3 + 6HCl \rightarrow 5ICl + KCl + 3H_2O$$

reacting ratio by mole:  2 moles                    5 moles

reacting ratio by mass:  $2 \times (126.90 \times 2)$     $5 \times (126.90 + 35.45)$
                         $= 507.60\ g$                   $= 811.75\ g$

For 28.60 g ICl:          $x$                        28.60 g

$$\frac{g\ I_2}{g\ ICl} = \frac{507.60}{811.75} = \frac{x}{28.60}$$

$$x = \frac{507.60 \times 28.60}{811.75}\ g\ I_2 = 17.88\ g\ I_2$$

The term **carbon footprint** refers to the mass of carbon dioxide and other greenhouse gases such as methane that an individual emits in a 1-year period. It is often expressed as the carbon dioxide equivalent, or $CO_2e$, to represent the total climate change impact of all the greenhouse gases caused by an item or activity. It includes emissions from fuels used in transport, services such as heating, production and consumption of food, and the direct and indirect emissions from manufactured goods and construction. It is extremely difficult to measure all sources accurately, but the fundamental concept uses the type of calculation shown here. The carbon footprint is a measure of an individual's consumption of resources, and suggests the link between this and the enhanced greenhouse effect. There is further discussion of carbon footprints in Chapter 12.

Remember to convert between mass and moles by using $n = \dfrac{m}{M}$ or

$m = n\,M$

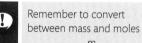

It is common for people to waste time solving questions like this by doing the mole to gram conversions for *all* the species represented in the equation. You can save yourself a lot of trouble by focusing *only* on the terms indicated in the question, as shown in this example.

### The theoretical yield is determined by the limiting reactant

Imagine that you are following a recipe to make 12 cookies. It calls for you to mix two eggs with four cups of flour. The problem is that you only have one egg. You will quickly realize that this means you can use only two cups of flour and end up with only six cookies. We could say that the number of eggs *limited* the amount of product.

In many chemical reactions the relative amounts of reactants available to react together will similarly affect the amount of product. The reactant that determines the quantity of product is known as the **limiting reactant**. Other reactants will therefore not be fully used, and are said to be in **excess**. Identifying the limiting reactant is therefore a crucial step before we can calculate the expected quantity of product. The **theoretical yield**, which is usually expressed in grams or moles, refers to the maximum amount of product obtainable, assuming 100% of the limiting reactant is converted to product.

Note that identification of the limiting reactant depends on the *mole ratios* in the balanced chemical equation for the reaction. This means that if reactant quantities are given in grams, they must first be converted to moles.

The concept of limiting reactant is often useful in the design of experiments and synthetic processes. By deliberately making one reactant available in an amount greater than that determined by its mole ratio in the balanced equation, it ensures that the other reactant is limiting and so will be fully used up. For example, in order to remove lead ions in lead nitrate from a contaminated water supply, sodium carbonate, $Na_2CO_3$, is added to precipitate lead carbonate, as shown in the equation:

$Pb(NO_3)_2(aq) + Na_2CO_3(aq)$
  limiting      excess
$\rightarrow PbCO_3(s) + 2NaNO_3(aq)$

By using excess $Na_2CO_3$, this ensures that *all* the lead ions react and so are removed from the water supply.

#### Worked example

Nitrogen gas ($N_2$) can be prepared from this reaction:

$$2NH_3(g) + 3CuO(s) \rightarrow N_2(g) + 3Cu(s) + 3H_2O(g)$$

If 18.1 g $NH_3$ are reacted with 90.40 g CuO, determine the mass of $N_2$ that can be formed.

#### Solution

First we must determine the limiting reactant. We convert the mass of reactants to moles, and then compare the mole ratio in the balanced equation with the mole ratio of reactants given.

$$n(NH_3) = \frac{18.1\,g}{14.01 + (3 \times 1.01)\,g\,mol^{-1}} = 1.06\,mol\,NH_3$$

$$n(CuO) = \frac{90.40\,g}{63.55 + 16.00\,g\,mol^{-1}} = 1.14\,mol\,CuO$$

mole ratio from equation: $\frac{NH_3}{CuO} = \frac{2}{3} = 0.667$

mole ratio from given masses: $\frac{NH_3}{CuO} = \frac{1.06}{1.14} = 0.930$

As the ratio $NH_3 : CuO$ of the given masses is *larger* than the required ratio in the equation, it means $NH_3$ is in excess and CuO is the limiting reactant.

This means that the amount of $N_2$ that can form will be determined by the amount of CuO. This is now similar to the earlier questions, where we write out the equation and focus on the terms identified in the question.

$$2NH_3(g) + 3CuO(s) \rightarrow N_2(g) + 3Cu(s) + 3H_2O(g)$$

reacting ratio by mole:  3 moles  1 mole
for 1.14 moles CuO:  1.14  $x$

mole ratio $\frac{CuO}{N_2} = \frac{3}{1} = \frac{1.14}{x}$   $\therefore x = \frac{1.14 \times 1}{3} = 0.380\,mol\,N_2$

$\therefore$ mass $N_2 = 0.380\,mol \times M(N_2)\,g\,mol^{-1} = 0.380\,mol \times 28.02\,g\,mol^{-1} = 10.7\,g\,N_2$

There are alternate approaches to determining the limiting reactant, such as calculating which given amount of reactant would yield the smallest amount of product. But in essence, all questions on limiting reactant and theoretical yield involve comparing the mole ratio of given masses of reactants with the coefficients in the equation. This is a summary of the steps:

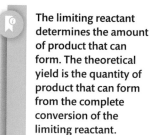

- write the balanced equation and focus on the mole ratio of reactants;
- convert the given mass of reactants to moles;
- compare the given mole ratios with the ratio of coefficients in the equation;
- identify the limiting reactant from the above ratios;
- calculate the moles of product from the given moles of limiting reactant.

Sometimes it is useful to measure how much excess reactant will remain when all the limiting reactant has been used up and the reaction stops. One example of this is a technique called **back-titration**, which analyses excess acid or alkali after a reaction is complete, and so indirectly measures the amount of a limiting reactant. This is explained on page 50.

A simple example of how to calculate the excess is shown below, using an example of burning $CH_4$ when 1 mole of $CH_4$ and 1 mole of $O_2$ are supplied.

$$CH_4(g) \ + \ 2O_2(g) \ \rightarrow \ CO_2(g) \ + \ 2H_2O(g)$$

| | | | | |
|---|---|---|---|---|
| reacting ratio by mole: | 1 | 2 | | |
| reactant ratio given: | 1 | 1 | | |

$\Rightarrow O_2$ is limiting reactant

mole ratio at the end of reaction:  0.5  0  0.5  1

So 0.5 moles $CH_4$ will be un-reacted at the end of the reaction.

We will study more examples of this type of question in the next section.

## The percentage yield can be calculated from the experimental and theoretical yields

The answer to the Worked example above, 10.7 g $N_2$ is known as the theoretical yield, because it assumes that *all* of the CuO was converted to $N_2$ with no loss, impurities present, wastage, or incomplete reaction. In reality, all of the above happen to different extents in most chemical reactions, and so the theoretical yield is usually different from the actual or **experimental yield**.

When we compare the experimental yield with the theoretical yield, we get a measure of the efficiency of the conversion of reactants to products. This is usually expressed as the **percentage yield**, defined as follows:

$$\text{percentage yield} = \frac{\text{experimental yield}}{\text{theoretical yield}} \times 100\%$$

In your own experiments, you may often be able to calculate the percentage yield of product in evaluating the results. In industry, this is a very important calculation to determine the efficiency of a process such as the synthesis of a drug in the pharmaceutical industry. Many aspects of green chemistry focus on ways to increase the yield of product by reducing wastage.

The limiting reactant determines the amount of product that can form. The theoretical yield is the quantity of product that can form from the complete conversion of the limiting reactant.

▲ Industrial plants such as this oil refinery need to be able to track the efficiency of the chemical reactions taking place. Measuring the yield of product is an essential part of this.

## CHALLENGE YOURSELF

4   Percentage yield and the atom economy are different concepts, but both can be used to assess aspects of the overall efficiency of a chemical process. See if you can find a reaction that has a high percentage yield under certain conditions, but a low atom economy.

## Worked example

The previous Worked example on the synthesis of $N_2$ from $NH_3$ and CuO had a theoretical yield of 10.7 g $N_2$ from the starting amounts of reactants. Under the same conditions, an experiment produced 8.35 g $N_2$. Determine the percentage yield.

### Solution

$$\text{percentage yield} = \frac{\text{experimental yield}}{\text{theoretical yield}} \times 100\%$$

$$\therefore \text{percentage yield} = \frac{8.35\text{ g}}{10.7\text{ g}} \times 100 = 78.0\%$$

## Exercises

**36**  Iron ore can be reduced to iron by the following reaction:

$$Fe_2O_3(s) + 3H_2(g) \rightarrow 2Fe + 3H_2O(l)$$

   **(a)**  How many moles of Fe can be made from 1.25 moles of $Fe_2O_3$?
   **(b)**  How many moles of $H_2$ are needed to make 3.75 moles of Fe?
   **(c)**  If the reaction yields 12.50 moles of $H_2O$, what mass of $Fe_2O_3$ was used up?

**37**  Lighters commonly use butane, $C_4H_{10}$, as the fuel.

   **(a)**  Formulate the equation for the combustion of butane.
   **(b)**  Determine the mass of butane that burned when 2.46 g water were produced.

**38**  Booster rockets for the space shuttle use the following reaction:

$$3Al(s) + 3NH_4ClO_4(s) \rightarrow Al_2O_3(s) + AlCl_3(s) + 3NO(g) + 6H_2O(g)$$

   Calculate the mass of $NH_4ClO_4$ that should be added to this fuel mixture to react completely with every kilogram of Al.

**39**  Limestone is mostly calcium carbonate, $CaCO_3$, but also contains other minerals. When heated, the $CaCO_3$ decomposes into CaO and $CO_2$. A 1.605 g sample of limestone was heated and gave off 0.657 g of $CO_2$.

   **(a)**  Formulate the equation for the thermal decomposition of calcium carbonate.
   **(b)**  Determine the percentage mass of $CaCO_3$ in the limestone.
   **(c)**  State the assumptions that you are making in this calculation.

**40**  Methanol, $CH_3OH$, is a useful fuel that can be made as follows:

$$CO(g) + 2H_2(g) \rightarrow CH_3OH(l)$$

   A reaction mixture used 12.0 g of $H_2$ and 74.5 g of CO.

   **(a)**  Determine the theoretical yield of $CH_3OH$.
   **(b)**  Calculate the amount of the excess reactant that remains unchanged at the end of the reaction.

**41**  The dry-cleaning solvent 1,2-dichloroethane, $C_2H_4Cl_2$, is prepared from the following reaction:

$$C_2H_4(g) + Cl_2(g) \rightarrow C_2H_4Cl_2(l)$$

   Determine the mass of product that can be formed from 15.40 g of $C_2H_4$ and 3.74 g of $Cl_2$.

**42**  Calcium carbonate, $CaCO_3$, is able to remove sulfur dioxide, $SO_2$, from waste gases by a reaction in which they react in a 1:1 stoichiometric ratio to form equimolar amounts of $CaSO_3$. When 255 g of $CaCO_3$ reacted with 135 g of $SO_2$, 198 g of $CaSO_3$ were formed. Determine the percentage yield of $CaSO_3$.

**43**  Pentyl ethanoate, $CH_3COOC_5H_{11}$, which smells like bananas, is produced from the esterification reaction:

$$CH_3COOH(aq) + C_5H_{11}OH(aq) \rightarrow CH_3COOC_5H_{11}(aq) + H_2O(l)$$

   A reaction uses 3.58 g of $CH_3COOH$ and 4.75 g of $C_5H_{11}OH$ and has a yield of 45.00%. Determine the mass of ester that forms.

**44**  A chemist has to make a 100 g sample of chlorobenzene, $C_6H_5Cl$, from the following reaction:

$$C_6H_6 + Cl_2 \rightarrow C_6H_5Cl + HCl$$

   Determine the minimum quantity of benzene, $C_6H_6$, that can be used to achieve this with a yield of 65%.

## Avogadro's law directly relates gas volumes to moles

All the examples above use mass as a way to measure amount, the number of moles. But in the laboratory we often work with liquids and gases, where *volume* is a more convenient measure. So what is the relationship between gas volume and number of moles?

Consider the following demonstration, where two gas jars are each filled with different gases – hydrogen ($H_2$) in flask A and bromine ($Br_2$) in flask B. The flasks are at the same temperature and pressure and have equal volumes.

It is known, from many experimental measurements on gas volumes, that the number of particles in the two flasks above is the same. At first this might seem surprising – after all bromine molecules are much larger and heavier than hydrogen molecules. But we need to consider the nature of the gaseous state, and as we learned on page 9, remember that the particles in a gas are widely spaced out with only negligible forces between them. In simple terms, most of a gas volume is empty space. And for this reason the chemical nature of the gas is irrelevant to its volume. Gas volume is determined only by the number of particles and by the temperature and pressure.

This understanding is known as Avogadro's law, which states that:

**Equal volumes of all gases, when measured at the same temperature and pressure, contain an equal number of particles.**

Alternatively, it can be stated that equal numbers of particles of all gases, when measured at the same temperature and pressure, occupy equal volumes.

Using V for volume and $n$ for number of moles:

$$V \propto n$$

This relationship enables us to relate gas volumes (of any gas) to the number of moles, and so to reacting ratios in equations.

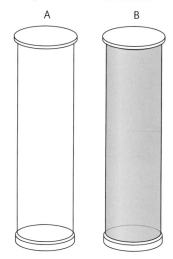

**Figure 1.11** Flask A contains hydrogen molecules, flask B contains bromine molecules. The two flasks are under the same conditions of temperature and pressure.

Airbags have become a standard safety fitting in many vehicles. They are designed to act as a cushion or shock absorber by inflating rapidly on sudden impact of the vehicle during a collision. Airbags work on the principle of a chemical reaction triggered by the impact producing a gaseous product that causes a sudden volume change. The key reaction used is the conversion of sodium azide, $NaN_3$, to nitrogen gas, $N_2$. To avoid the production of dangerously reactive sodium metal, potassium nitrate, $KNO_3$, and silicon dioxide, $SiO_2$, are also included so that harmless silicates are produced instead.

Illustration of an airbag and seatbelt in action during a car accident. On impact, the airbag inflates and the seatbelt slows the forward force of the body, protecting the driver's head and chest.

### Worked example

$40 \, cm^3$ of carbon monoxide are reacted with $40 \, cm^3$ of oxygen in the reaction:

$$2CO(g) + O_2(g) \rightarrow 2CO_2(g)$$

What volume of carbon dioxide is produced? (Assume all volumes are measured at the same temperature and pressure.)

## CHALLENGE YOURSELF

5 Use the explanation on page 33 to deduce the chemical equations for the reactions taking place in a deployed airbag.

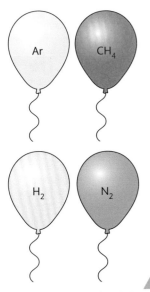

**Figure 1.12** These four balloons are all filled with 1 dm³ of gas. At 25 °C and 100 kPa, they each contain 0.044 mol or $2.65 \times 10^{22}$ atoms or molecules. Which balloon is the heaviest?

Note that STP (standard temperature and pressure) is not the same as the 'standard state', which is used in thermodynamic data and is explained in Chapter 5.

STP refers to a temperature of 273 K and a pressure of 100 kPa.

34

### Solution

First identify the mole ratios in the equation:

$$2CO(g) + O_2(g) \rightarrow 2CO_2(g)$$
2 moles    1 mole    2 moles

The mole ratio is equal to the ratio of reacting gas volumes, so:

$$2CO(g) + O_2(g) \rightarrow 2CO_2(g)$$
40 cm³    20 cm³    40 cm³

Therefore 40 cm³ of carbon dioxide are produced. (Oxygen is in excess by 20 cm³.)

### Worked example

When 10 cm³ of a gaseous hydrocarbon (a compound containing only carbon and hydrogen) is burned in excess oxygen, the products consist of 30 cm³ of carbon dioxide and 30 cm³ of water vapour, measured under the same conditions of temperature and pressure. Determine the molecular formula of the hydrocarbon.

### Solution

'Excess' oxygen indicates that the combustion reaction is complete.

$$C_xH_y + \text{excess } O_2 \rightarrow CO_2 + H_2O$$

volumes:                    10 cm³           30 cm³  30 cm³

ratio of volumes / mole ratio:    1           3      3

∴ 1 molecule hydrocarbon $\rightarrow$ 3 molecules $CO_2$ + 3 molecules $H_2O$
                                    3 C atoms          6 H atoms

The molecular formula is $C_3H_6$.

## All gases under the same conditions have the same molar volume

On the basis of Avogadro's law, the volume occupied by one mole of any gas, known as the **molar volume**, must be the same for *all* gases when measured under the same conditions of temperature and pressure.

At standard temperature and pressure (STP), one mole of a gas has a volume of $2.27 \times 10^{-2} \, m^3 \, mol^{-1}$ ($=22.7 \, dm^3 \, mol^{-1}$). The conditions at STP are:
• a temperature of 0 °C (273 K)
• pressure of 100 kPa.

The molar volume can be used to calculate the amount of gas in a similar way to the use of molar mass earlier in this chapter. Here though the calculations are easier, as all gases have the same molar volume under the same conditions.

$$\text{number of moles of gas } (n) = \frac{\text{volume } (V)}{\text{molar volume}}$$

## Worked example

What volume of oxygen at standard temperature and pressure would be needed to completely burn 1 mole of butane, $C_4H_{10}$?

**Solution**

As always, start with the balanced equation and pick out the terms from the question.

$$2C_4H_{10}(g) + 13O_2(g) \rightarrow 8CO_2(g) + 10H_2O(g)$$

mole / volume ratio:   1      6.5

6.5 moles of gas at STP have volume = 6.5 mol × 22.7 dm$^3$ mol$^{-1}$ = 147.6 dm$^3$

## Worked example

Calculate the volume occupied by 0.0200 g of He at standard temperature and pressure.

**Solution**

First convert the mass of He to moles.

$$n = \frac{m}{M} = \frac{0.0200 \text{ g}}{4.00 \text{ g mol}^{-1}} = 0.00500 \text{ mol}$$

volume = 0.00500 mol × 22.7 dm$^3$ mol$^{-1}$ = 0.114 dm$^3$

## A note about units of volume

The metric unit m$^3$ is widely used in industrial and engineering calculations, but is too large to be convenient for many volume measurements in the laboratory. Instead, dm$^3$ and cm$^3$ are commonly used, so it is important to be able to interconvert these.

| | |
|---|---|
| 1 dm$^3$ = 10$^{-3}$ m$^3$ | 1000 dm$^3$ = 1 m$^3$ |
| 1 cm$^3$ = 10$^{-3}$ dm$^3$ | 1000 cm$^3$ = 1 dm$^3$ |

divide by 1000          divide by 1000

**cm$^3$** ⇌ **dm$^3$** ⇌ **m$^3$**

multiply by 1000       multiply by 1000

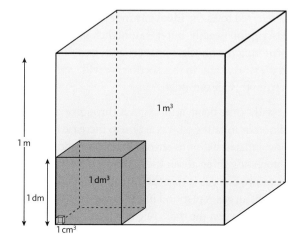

The litre (l or L) is widely used in place of dm$^3$, and millilitre (ml or mL) in place of cm$^3$. You will not be penalized for the use of these terms in an examination, but they will not be used in examination questions so it is essential that you know the correct use of m$^3$, dm$^3$, and cm$^3$.

The value of the molar volume and the conditions for STP are given in section 2 of the IB data booklet.

CODATA (Committee on Data for Science and Technology) is an interdisciplinary scientific committee of the International Council of Science. It was established in 1966 to promote the worldwide compilation and sharing of reliable numerical data, such as the molar volume of a gas.

**Figure 1.13** The three cubes are not to scale. 1 m$^3$ = 1000 dm$^3$ = 1 000 000 cm$^3$. In the laboratory, volumes are usually measured in cm$^3$ or dm$^3$ and often these measurements need to be converted to m$^3$ in calculations.

## Exercises

**45** How many moles are present in each of the following at STP?

    **(a)** 54.5 dm³ CH₄     **(b)** 250.0 cm³ CO     **(c)** 1.0 m³ O₂

**46** What is the volume of each of the following at STP?

    **(a)** 44.00 g N₂     **(b)** 0.25 mol NH₃

**47** Pure oxygen gas was first prepared by heating mercury(II) oxide, HgO.

$$2HgO(s) \rightarrow 2Hg(l) + O_2(g)$$

What volume of oxygen at STP is released by heating 12.45 g of HgO?

**48** Which sample contains more molecules, 3.14 dm³ of bromine, Br₂, or 11.07 g of chlorine, Cl₂ when measured at the same temperature and pressure?

**49** Calcium reacts with water to produce hydrogen.

$$Ca(s) + 2H_2O(l) \rightarrow Ca(OH)_2(aq) + H_2(g)$$

Calculate the volume of gas at STP produced when 0.200 g of calcium reacts completely with water.

**50** Dinitrogen oxide, N₂O, is a greenhouse gas produced from the decomposition of artificial nitrate fertilizers. Calculate the volume at STP of N₂O produced from 1.0 g of ammonium nitrate, when it reacts according to the equation:

$$NH_4NO_3(s) \rightarrow N_2O(g) + 2H_2O(l)$$

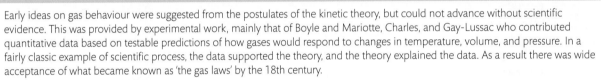

## NATURE OF SCIENCE

Early ideas on gas behaviour were suggested from the postulates of the kinetic theory, but could not advance without scientific evidence. This was provided by experimental work, mainly that of Boyle and Mariotte, Charles, and Gay-Lussac who contributed quantitative data based on testable predictions of how gases would respond to changes in temperature, volume, and pressure. In a fairly classic example of scientific process, the data supported the theory, and the theory explained the data. As a result there was wide acceptance of what became known as 'the gas laws' by the 18th century.

It is interesting to consider on the other hand why Avogadro's hypothesis was not widely accepted initially. Experiments led him to suggest that equal volumes of all gases at the same temperature and pressure contain the same number of molecules, but data to confirm this was somewhat lacking. In addition, his ideas conflicted with Dalton's atomic theory, which suggested that particles in gases could be only single atoms, not molecules as Avogadro proposed. It took the logical argument of Cannizzaro nearly 50 years later to show that Avogadro's hypothesis could be explained, and moreover used as a means to determine molecular mass. Following this, the relationship between gas volume and number of molecules became widely accepted and known as Avogadro's law. History has shown that the acceptance of scientific ideas by the scientific community is sometimes influenced by the time and manner of their presentation, as well as by their power to explain existing ideas.

## The gas laws describe pressure, volume, and temperature relationships for all gases

The kinetic theory of matter, summarized on page 9, describes gases as largely empty space containing free moving particles of negligible volume having no inter-particle forces. This is often referred to as the **ideal gas** model. In effect it is an approximation, as no gas fits this description exactly, but it is nonetheless a useful means for predicting and interpreting the physical properties of gases under typical conditions of temperature and pressure. Later in this section we will explore situations when gas behaviour deviates from this ideal model.

**An ideal gas is one that obeys the ideal gas laws.**

You will be familiar with some behaviour of gases through everyday experiences such as blowing up a balloon or inflating a bicycle tyre to increase the pressure. Perhaps you have noticed how inflated balloons shrivel in colder conditions and expand when it is warmer? The interesting thing about these simple observations of the volume, pressure, and temperature of a gas is that they are not dependent on the chemical nature of the gas. In fact, all gases respond in the same way to changes in volume, pressure, and temperature when the mass of gas is fixed. These relationships are summarized as the **gas laws** and are discussed below.

## A note about units of temperature

In all work on gases, it is essential to use values for temperature recorded in kelvin (K), not in Celsius (°C). Temperature in kelvin is known as the **absolute temperature**, and is based on a scale where absolute zero, 0 K, is the point of zero kinetic energy of particles. This coincides with −273.15 °C. As the interval on the Kelvin scale is the same as that on the Celsius scale, conversion between the two simply involves addition or subtraction of 273.15 (commonly approximated to 273).

$$\text{temperature (K)} = \text{temperature (°C)} + 273.15$$

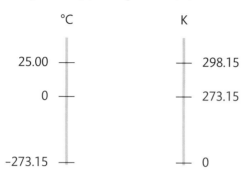

| °C | K |
|---|---|
| 25.00 | 298.15 |
| 0 | 273.15 |
| −273.15 | 0 |

William Thomson (1824–1907), who became known as Lord Kelvin later in life, completed most of his work at the University of Glasgow, Scotland. His concept of the absolute temperature scale followed from his recognition of the relationship between heat energy and the ability to do work. The existence of a minimum possible temperature at which no heat can be extracted from the system and so no work done, led him to the definition of absolute zero in 1848. This in turn led to the formulation of the laws of thermodynamics. Kelvin is considered one of the great scientists of the 19th century, and is buried next to Isaac Newton in London.

## A note about units of pressure

The SI unit of pressure is the Pascal (Pa), which is equal to $N\ m^{-2}$. Pressure is now commonly given in bars, where $10^5$ Pa = 1 bar, as this is conveniently close to 1 atmospheric pressure.

### NATURE OF SCIENCE

The definition of absolute zero (0 K) as the temperature where a substance has no kinetic energy, suggests it is the point at which all motion in particles ceases. It is the lowest possible temperature. Zero kelvin has not been achieved, although modern technologies, which improve cooling methods and use magnets to contain the gas, are helping scientists to reach values ever closer to this. Researchers in Finland have achieved temperatures as low as 100 pK ($1 \times 10^{-10}$ K) in a piece of rhodium metal. Ultra-low temperature research has led to observations of phenomena such as quantum fluid behaviour and superconductivity, and could lead to improvements in precision measurements such as those used in atomic clocks and sensors for gravity and rotation. Science progresses as improvements in technology give access to new information, and studies in one field open up possibilities in another. Superconductivity is discussed further in Chapter 12.

## 1 Relationship between volume and pressure

The volume of a gas is always the volume of its container as the particles spread out fully. Its pressure is the result of the particles colliding with the walls of the container, and will increase when the frequency or energy of these collisions increases.

If the temperature is held constant, it is found that increasing the pressure on a fixed mass of gas decreases its volume. In other words, the pressure of a gas is inversely proportional to its volume, and the product of pressure and volume is a constant.

**TOK** The ideal gas equation can be deduced from a small number of assumptions of ideal behaviour. What is the role of reason, perception, intuition, and imagination in the development of scientific models?

The so-called mentos-soda fountain reaction. Dissolved carbon dioxide in the soda changes quickly into gas in the presence of the candy mint mentos. The sudden pressure change causes the soda to be ejected in a fountain of foam.

Different countries continue to use a variety of units for pressure, including millimetres of mercury (mm Hg), torr, pounds per square inch (psi), and atmosphere (atm).

In all the examples here, use of the term 'pressure' assumes 'absolute pressure', which is referenced against a perfect vacuum. This is in contrast to the gauge pressure, which is measured relative to atmospheric pressure.

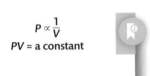

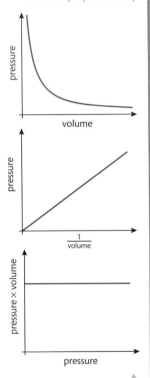

**Figure 1.14** As the pressure on a gas is increased, its volume decreases proportionately.

**Figure 1.15** Boyle's law. Gas pressure is inversely proportional to its volume.

**Figure 1.16** Charles' law. Gas volume is proportional to the absolute temperature. Note the dotted line represents an extrapolation, as data at temperatures down to 0 K are not obtainable.

$$V \propto T$$
$$\frac{V}{T} = \text{a constant}$$

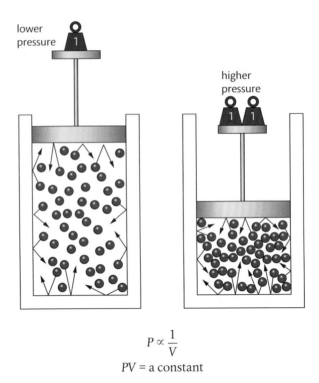

$$P \propto \frac{1}{V}$$
$$PV = \text{a constant}$$

This relationship is often known as **Boyle's law**, as it was first established by Robert Boyle in 1662. Application of this relationship is found in the compression of gases under pressure, often useful in transport and storage.

## 2 Relationship between volume and temperature

An increase in temperature represents an increase in the average kinetic energy of the particles. If the pressure is held constant, it is found that increasing the temperature of a fixed mass of gas increases its volume. In other words, the volume of a gas is directly proportional to its absolute temperature, and volume divided by absolute temperature is a constant.

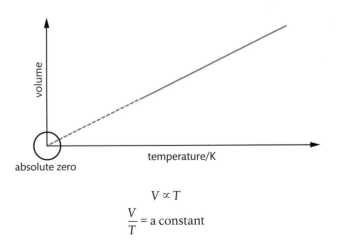

$$V \propto T$$
$$\frac{V}{T} = \text{a constant}$$

**TOK** The SI base unit of temperature is the kelvin, which has a natural basis for its definition of zero. By contrast, zero in the imperial scale of degree Celsius is arbitrarily defined. What are the implications of using a scale based on natural or arbitrary values?

This relationship is often known as **Charles' law**, as it was first established by Frenchman Jacques Charles in the late 18th century. You can demonstrate this relationship by immersing dented table tennis balls in warm water. As the air inside the ball equilibrates to the temperature of the water, it expands, pushing the dents out on the surface.

## 3 Relationship between pressure and temperature

An increase in temperature increases the average kinetic energy of the particles. The particles move faster and collide with the walls of the container with more energy and more frequency, raising the pressure. If the volume is held constant, it is found that increasing the temperature of a fixed mass of gas proportionately raises its pressure. In other words, the pressure of a gas is directly proportional to the absolute temperature, and pressure divided by temperature is a constant.

$$P \propto T$$

$$\frac{P}{T} = \text{a constant}$$

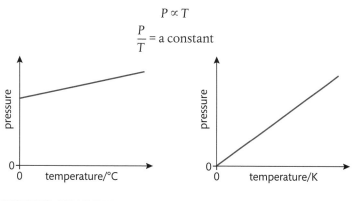

Balloons dipped in a mixture of dry ice (solid $CO_2$) and water rapidly deflate as the air inside contracts at low temperature.

**Figure 1.17** Gas pressure is proportional to the absolute temperature.

 Always be certain to use temperature in kelvin only when applying these relationships.

UN No. 1950
**Automotive Paint**

FLAMMABLE

Keep out of reach of children.
Keep away from sources of ignition –
No smoking.
Do not breathe spray.
Avoid contact with skin and eyes.
Use only in well ventilated areas.
Caution: Pressurised container. Protect from sunlight and do not expose to temperatures exceeding 50°C. Do not pierce or burn even after use. Do not spray on a naked flame or any incandescent material.

Automotive Chemicals Ltd.,
Bury, Lancashire, England. Tel. 061 764 5981    400 m

The label on the aerosol can warns of the dangers of exposing the pressurized contents to high temperature.

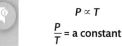

$$P \propto T$$

$$\frac{P}{T} = \text{a constant}$$

Pressurized cans, such as soda or beer, often carry a warning to be stored in a cool place. This is because at higher temperatures the pressure inside the can at fixed volume is able to rise to the point of causing the can to explode.

These three gas laws applied to a fixed mass of gas can be summarized as follows:

$$P \propto \frac{1}{V} \text{ at constant temperature}$$

$$V \propto T \text{ at constant pressure}$$

$$P \propto T \text{ at constant volume}$$

These can be combined to give one equation for a fixed mass of gas:

$$\frac{PV}{T} = \text{a constant} \text{ or}$$

$$\frac{P_1V_1}{T_1} = \frac{P_2V_2}{T_2} \text{ (where 1 and 2 refer to initial and final conditions respectively)}$$

Application of this enables gas volume, pressure, and temperature to be calculated as conditions change.

$$\frac{P_1V_1}{T_1} = \frac{P_2V_2}{T_2}$$

## Worked example

What happens to the volume of a fixed mass of gas when its pressure and its absolute temperature are both doubled?

### Solution

$$\frac{P_1V_1}{T_1} = \frac{P_2V_2}{T_2}$$

$P_2 = 2 \times P_1$ and $T_2 = 2 \times T_1$, so these can be substituted into the equation:

$$\frac{P_1V_1}{T_1} = \frac{2P_1V_2}{2T_1}$$

We can cancel $P_1$ and $T_1$ from both sides and 2s on the right side, leaving

$$V_1 = V_2$$

The volume does not change.

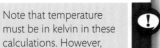

Note that temperature must be in kelvin in these calculations. However, the units of volume and pressure are not specified, so long as they are consistent on both sides of the equation.

## Worked example

The molar volume of a gas at STP is 22.7 dm³ mol⁻¹. Calculate the molar volume at 25 °C at the same pressure.

### Solution

As the pressure is not changing, we do not need to insert $P_1$ and $P_2$ into the combined gas equation. Temperature must be converted from °C to K.

$$T_1 = 273 \text{ K}, T_2 = 25 + 273 = 298 \text{ K}$$

$$\frac{V_1}{T_1} = \frac{V_2}{T_2}$$

$$\frac{22.7 \text{ dm}^3}{273 \text{ K}} = \frac{V_2}{298 \text{ K}}$$

$$V_2 = \frac{298 \times 22.7 \text{ dm}^3}{273} = 24.8 \text{ dm}^3$$

## The ideal gas equation is derived from the combined gas equation and Avogadro's law

The combined gas equation tells us that

$$\frac{PV}{T} = \text{a constant}$$

The value of the constant is directly proportional to the fixed mass of gas, or the number of moles, $n$.

So $\dfrac{PV}{T} \propto n$

This can be made into an equation by introducing a constant, **R**, known as the **universal gas constant**.

$\therefore \dfrac{PV}{T} = n\,R$, which is usually written as $\boldsymbol{PV = nRT}$

This equation is known as the **ideal gas equation**, and is given in Section 1 of the IB data booklet. The value of $R$ can be calculated by substituting known values into the equation, such as those for the molar volume of a gas at STP. In this case:

$$P = 10^5\,\text{Pa (N m}^{-2}),\ V = 2.27 \times 10^{-2}\,\text{m}^3,\ T = 273\,\text{K},\ n = 1$$

$$\therefore 10^5\,\text{N m}^{-2} \times 2.27 \times 10^{-2}\,\text{m}^3 = 1\,\text{mol} \times R \times 273\,\text{K}$$

$$R = 8.31\,\text{N m K}^{-1}\,\text{mol}^{-1} \text{ or } 8.31\,\text{J K}^{-1}\,\text{mol}^{-1}$$

This value for $R$, the gas constant, is given in Section 2 in the IB data booklet and should be used for all calculations involving the ideal gas equation.

Use of the ideal gas equation enables us to calculate how systems respond to changes in pressure, volume, and temperature, and to calculate molar mass. Gas density can also be derived by applying the relationship $\text{density} = \dfrac{\text{mass}}{\text{volume}}$.

These calculations usually involve simply substituting values into the equation, but the use of units needs special attention here. The guidelines below, based on the use of SI units only, should help you avoid some of the common mistakes that arise.

- Pressure, $P$: must be in Pa (N m$^{-2}$); if kPa are given, multiply by $10^3$.
- Volume, $V$: must be in m$^3$; if dm$^3$ are given, divide by $10^3$, if cm$^3$ are given divide by $10^6$.
- Number of moles, $n$: this is often derived by application of $n = \dfrac{m}{M}$.
- Temperature, $T$: must be in kelvin; if °C is given, add 273.15.

**The ideal gas equation is $PV = nRT$**

Many sources give data for ideal gas law questions in non-SI units such as atmosphere, which require a mathematical conversion. You will not be expected to be familiar with these conversions in IB examinations.

### Worked example

A helium party balloon has a volume of 18.0 dm$^3$. At 25 °C the internal pressure is 108 kPa. Calculate the mass of helium in the balloon.

#### Solution

First ensure all data are in SI units:

$$P = 108\,\text{kPa} = 108 \times 10^3\,\text{Pa}$$

$$V = 18.0\,\text{dm}^3 = 18.0 \times 10^{-3}\,\text{m}^3$$

$$T = 25\,°\text{C} = 298\,\text{K}$$

As this example shows, if pressure is given in kPa *and* volume is given in dm³, the same answer is obtained if these values are used directly in the ideal gas equation in place of Pa and m³.

$$PV = nRT$$

$$108 \times 10^3 \, Pa \times 18.0 \times 10^{-3} \, m^3 = n \times 8.31 \, J \, K^{-1} \, mol^{-1} \times 298 \, K$$

$$\therefore n(He) = 0.785 \, mol$$

$$\therefore mass \, (He) = n \, M = 0.785 \, mol \times 4.00 \, g \, mol^{-1} = 3.14 \, g$$

## Worked example

A sample of gas has a volume of 445 cm³ and a mass of 1.500 g at a pressure of 95 kPa and a temperature of 28 °C. Calculate its molar mass.

### Solution

Substitute $n = \dfrac{m}{M}$ into the ideal gas equation, and rearrange to solve for M.

$$M = \frac{mRT}{PV}$$

Ensure all data are in SI units:

$$P = 95 \, kPa = 95 \times 10^3 \, Pa$$

$$V = 445 \, cm^3 = 445 \times 10^{-6} \, m^3$$

$$T = 28 \, °C = 301 \, K$$

$$\therefore M = \frac{1.500 \, g \times 8.31 \, J \, K^{-1} \, mol^{-1} \times 301 \, K}{95 \times 10^3 \, Pa \times 445 \times 10^{-6} \, m^3} = 88.8 \, g \, mol^{-1}$$

## Worked example

A gas has a density of 1.65 g dm⁻³ at 27 °C and 92.0 kPa. Determine its molar mass.

### Solution

Blowing up a balloon increases its volume as the number of particles increases. What do you think would happen to this inflated balloon on the top of a very high mountain?

$$density \, data \Rightarrow 1.65 \, g \, occupies \, 1.00 \, dm^3$$

As in the example above, substitute data with correct units into $M = \dfrac{mRT}{PV}$

$$\therefore \frac{1.65 \, g \times 8.31 \, J \, K^{-1} \, mol^{-1} \times 300 \, K}{92.0 \times 10^3 \, Pa \times 1.00 \times 10^{-3} \, m^3} = 44.7 \, g \, mol^{-1}$$

**Experiment to calculate the molar mass of carbon dioxide by application of the ideal gas equation**

Full details with a worksheet are available online.

A known mass of $CuCO_3(s)$ is heated and the gas evolved collected by displacement of water. The volume of the gas, the room temperature, and pressure are recorded.

$$CuCO_3(s) \rightarrow CuO(s) + CO_2(g)$$

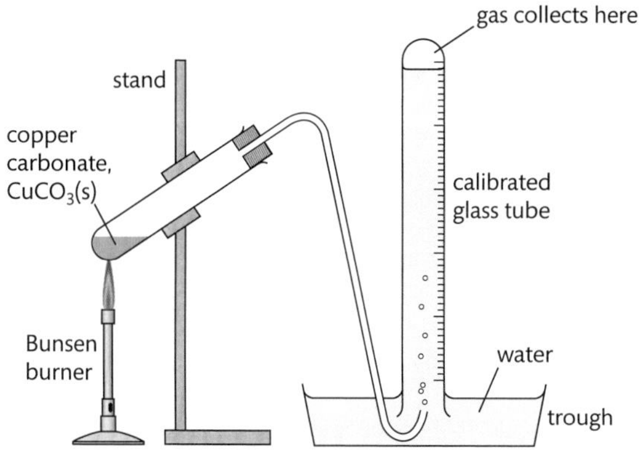

**Figure 1.18** Experiment to calculate the molar mass of carbon dioxide.

### Sample results

| | Trial 1 | Observations |
|---|---|---|
| mass of boiling tube + $CuCO_3$ before heating / g ± 0.001 | 33.910 | $CuCO_3$ is a green powder |
| mass of boiling tube + $CuCO_3$ after heating / g ± 0.001 | 33.822 | the contents of the tube are black after heating |
| mass change (mass $CO_2$) / g ± 0.002 | 0.088 | |
| volume of gas collected / $cm^3$ ± 0.1 | 38.1 | the gas collected is colourless |
| temperature / K ± 0.1 | 293.0 | |
| pressure / kPa ± 0.1 | 101.3 | |

### Processed data

$$M(CO_2) = \frac{mRT}{PV} = \frac{0.088\ g \times 8.31\ J\ mol^{-1}\ K^{-1} \times 293.0\ K}{101.3\ kPa \times 0.0381\ dm^3}$$

experimental value $M(CO_2) = 55.5\ g\ mol^{-1}$

theoretical value $M(CO_2) = 44.01\ g\ mol^{-1}$

$\therefore$ % error = 26.1%

The percentage error can be analysed in consideration of systematic errors such as:

- gas collected may not be pure $CO_2$;
- $CO_2$ may be soluble in water;
- air in the tube is collected with the gas;
- gas collected has not equilibrated to room temperature.

Modifications to the experimental design should suggest ways to reduce the impact of these errors. Note that repeat trials and error propagation are not shown here.

**NATURE OF SCIENCE**

Scientists often use models, which may be simple or complex, to explain concepts that are not observable. By their nature, models are thinking tools and so they all have limitations. Models are often tested against experimental results, and should be able to explain phenomena that are seemingly different from the ones used to develop the model. Sometimes, when a model does not seem consistent with data or observations, it may need to be modified or replaced. At other times it can be retained, with limitations to its usefulness agreed.

The ideal gas model has all of these characteristics. While it provides a useful conceptual image of gas behaviour, and is consistent with some testable predictions, there are limitations to this, as we will see below. These do not mean, however, that the model should be discarded – rather they alert us to the fact that the model is in some ways an over-simplification, and cannot apply accurately under all conditions.

### Exercises

**51** A 2.50 $dm^3$ container of helium at a pressure of 85 kPa was heated from 25 °C to 75 °C. The volume of the container expanded to 2.75 $dm^3$. What was the final pressure of the helium?

**52** After a sample of nitrogen with a volume of 675 $cm^3$ and a pressure of $1.00 \times 10^5$ Pa was compressed to a volume of 350 $cm^3$ and a pressure of $2.00 \times 10^5$ Pa, its temperature was 27.0 °C. Determine its initial temperature.

**53** The absolute temperature of 4.0 $dm^3$ of hydrogen gas is increased by a factor of three and the pressure is increased by a factor of four. Deduce the final volume of the gas.

**54** To find the volume of a flask, it was first evacuated so that it contained no gas at all. When 4.40 g of carbon dioxide was introduced, it exerted a pressure of 90 kPa at 27 °C. Determine the volume of the flask.

**55** An unknown noble gas has a density of 5.84 g $dm^{-3}$ at STP. Calculate its molar mass, and so identify the gas.

**56** A 12.1 mg sample of a gas has a volume of 255 $cm^3$ at a temperature of 25.0 °C and a pressure of 1300 Pa. Determine its molar mass.

**57** Which has the greater density at STP, hydrogen or helium?

**58** Calculate the volume of oxygen at STP required for the complete combustion of 125 g of octane, $C_8H_{18}$, to form carbon dioxide and water.

**59** A sample of an unknown gas with a mass of 3.620 g occupied a volume of 1120 $cm^3$ at a pressure of 99 kPa and a temperature of 25.0 °C. The sample contained 2.172 g O and 1.448 g S. Determine the empirical and molecular fomula of the gas.

**60** A road cyclist pumps his tyres up very hard before a trip over a high mountain pass at high altitude. Near the summit one of his tyres explodes. Suggest why this may have occurred.

## Real gases show deviation from ideal behaviour

An ideal gas is defined as one that obeys the ideal gas law $PV = nRT$ under all conditions. This means that for one mole of gas, the relationship $PV/RT$ should be equal to 1. So a graph of $PV/RT$ against $P$ for one mole of an ideal gas is a horizontal line of intercept 1 (Figure 1.19).

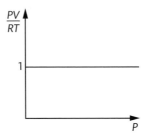

**Figure 1.19** For one mole of an ideal gas, the relationship $PV/RT$ is a constant at all pressures.

But, as we noted earlier, there is no such thing as an ideal gas. All gases, known as **real gases**, deviate to some extent from ideal behaviour. So, for real gases the value of $PV/RT$ for one mole will vary. An example of the extent of this variation from 1 at different conditions is shown in Figure 1.20.

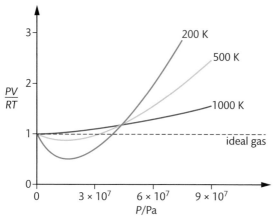

**Figure 1.20** The deviation from ideal behaviour of nitrogen at different temperatures and pressures.

We can draw the following conclusions from the graph:

- the gas behaves most like an ideal gas at low pressure and shows the greatest deviation at high pressure;
- the gas behaves most like an ideal gas at high temperature and shows the greatest deviation at low temperature.

To interpret these findings, it will be helpful to question the validity of two assumptions made in describing an ideal gas in the kinetic molecular theory:

1  the volume of the gas particles is negligible;
2  there are no attractive forces between the particles.

1. At relatively low pressure, such as $1 \times 10^5$ Pa (STP), the volume occupied by the particles of a typical gas is only about 0.05% of the total volume, so it is reasonably valid to describe this as negligible. But with increasing pressure as the space between the particles is reduced, this percentage increases and with a pressure of $5 \times 10^5$ Pa, the volume of the particles is about 20% of the total volume – certainly not negligible. As a result, the volume of a real gas at high pressure is larger than that predicted from the ideal gas law and $PV/nRT > 1$.

2. When a gas is at moderately low pressure, the particles are so widely spaced that interactive forces are highly unlikely, so this assumption is valid. But at pressures up to about $3 \times 10^7$ Pa, as the particles approach more closely, attractive forces strengthen between them. These have the effect of reducing the pressure of the gas, so $PV/nRT < 1$. Low temperatures increase this deviation because the lower kinetic energy of the particles increases the strength of inter-particle forces. At even higher pressures, the non-zero volume of the particles becomes more important and this effect dominates where the graph rises.

Overall, we can conclude that real gases deviate from ideal behaviour when either or both of the assumptions above are not valid. This occurs at high pressure and low temperature. It makes sense intuitively that a gas behaves in a less perfect way under these conditions, which are the closest to it changing into a liquid.

Attempts to modify the ideal gas equation to take these factors into account and make it apply accurately to real gases led to the **van der Waals' equation**, formulated in 1873. This has correction terms for both the volume of the particles and the inter-particle attractions, and these are specific to different gases. Happily, for a wide range of conditions under which gases are studied, the ideal gas equation is a sufficiently accurate expression, and has the big advantage that it is a single equation for all gases.

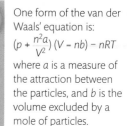

One form of the van der Waals' equation is:
$$\left(p + \frac{n^2a}{V^2}\right)(V - nb) = nRT$$
where $a$ is a measure of the attraction between the particles, and $b$ is the volume excluded by a mole of particles.

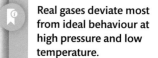

**Real gases deviate most from ideal behaviour at high pressure and low temperature.**

## Exercises

**61 (a)** List the main features of the kinetic theory for ideal gases.

**(b)** Explain the reason for the difference in behaviour between real and ideal gases at low temperature.

**62** Ammonia, $NH_3$, forms a relatively strong type of intermolecular attraction known as a hydrogen bond, whereas methane, $CH_4$, does not. Explain the relative deviation from ideal behaviour that each gas is likely to show.

**63** Gases deviate from ideal gas behaviour because their particles:

    **A** have negligible volume
    **B** have forces of attraction between them
    **C** are polyatomic
    **D** are not attracted to one another

## The concentration of a solution depends on moles of solute and volume of solution

Liquids, like gases, can conveniently be quantified by measuring their volume rather than their mass. Some liquids in common use are pure substances, such as water ($H_2O$), bromine ($Br_2$), and hexane ($C_6H_{14}$), but more commonly liquids are **solutions** containing two or more components.

A solution is a homogeneous mixture of two or more substances, which may be solids, liquids, or gases, or a combination of these. The **solvent** is the component present in the greatest quantity, in which the **solute** is dissolved. Some examples of solutions include:

- solid/solid: metal alloy such as brass (copper and zinc);
- solid/liquid: seawater (salts and water), copper sulfate(aq) (copper sulfate and water);
- liquid/liquid: wine (ethanol and water);
- gas/liquid: fizzy drinks (carbon dioxide and water).

In this section we will be considering solutions made by dissolving a solid solute in a liquid solvent.

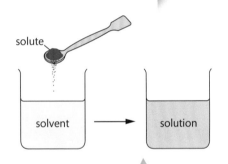

solute

solvent → solution

**Figure 1.21** A solution is made by dissolving a solute in a solvent

Unlike gases, the volume of a liquid is not directly related to its amount. Instead, for solutions, we express the amount through its **concentration**. The concentration of a solution ($c$) is determined by the amount of solute ($n$) and the volume of solution ($V$). It is usually expressed as $mol\,dm^{-3}$.

> The concentration of a solution refers to the amount of solute per volume of solution. It has the units $mol\,dm^{-3}$ or $g\,dm^{-3}$.

$$\text{concentration of solution } (mol\,dm^{-3}) = \frac{\text{amount of solute (mol)}}{\text{volume of solution } (dm^3)} \quad \text{or} \quad c = \frac{n}{V}$$

$\therefore$ amount of solute (mol) = conc. ($mol\,dm^{-3}$) × volume ($dm^3$)     or    $n = cV$

Square brackets are often used to represent 'concentration of' a particular substance; such as $[HCl] = 1.0\,mol\,dm^{-3}$.

Different types of laboratory glassware, which are identified in **Figure 1.22**. Note that beakers and conical flasks are generally not used for measuring volume.

Chemists routinely prepare solutions of known concentration, known as **standard solutions**. The mass of solute required is accurately measured and then transferred carefully to a volumetric flask, which is accurately calibrated for a specific volume. The solvent is added steadily with swirling to help the solute to dissolve, until the final level reaches the mark on the flask.

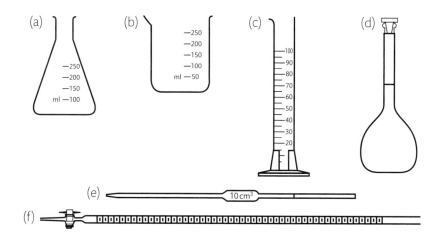

**Figure 1.22** Glassware commonly used in the laboratory: (a) conical or Erlenmeyer flask – its shape makes it easy to mix liquids as the flask can be easily swirled; (b) beaker; (c) measuring cylinder; (d) volumetric flask; (e) pipette; (f) burette. Standard solutions are prepared using volumetric flasks.

> Note that concentration is specified per volume of final *solution*, not per volume of *solvent* added. This is because volume changes occur on dissolving the solute.

> The term *molarity*, M, has been widely used to express amount concentration, but it is falling out of common usage. It will not be used in IB examination questions, so make sure you are fully familiar with the terms mol dm⁻³ and g dm⁻³. (Note that *M* is used specifically to refer to molar mass.)

## Worked example

Explain how you would prepare 100 cm³ of a 0.100 mol dm⁻³ solution of NaCl.

### Solution

Ensure that cm³ are converted to dm³ by dividing by 1000.

$$n = cV$$

$$n = 0.100 \text{ mol dm}^{-3} \times \frac{100}{1000} \text{ dm}^3 = 0.0100 \text{ mol}$$

$M(\text{NaCl}) = 22.99 + 35.45 = 58.44 \text{ g mol}^{-1}$

$\therefore$ mass required $= 0.0100 \text{ mol} \times 58.44 \text{ g mol}^{-1} = 0.584 \text{ g}$

Add 0.584 g NaCl(s) to a 100 cm³ volumetric flask, and make up to the mark with distilled water.

Concentration can also be expressed in mass (g dm⁻³).

## Worked example

Calculate the concentration of a 0.0400 mol dm⁻³ solution of sodium carbonate, $Na_2CO_3$, in g dm⁻³.

### Solution

$M(\text{Na}_2\text{CO}_3) = (22.99 \times 2) + 12.01 + (16.00 \times 3) = 105.99 \text{ g mol}^{-1}$

$m = nM \therefore m = 0.0400 \text{ mol} \times 105.99 \text{ g mol}^{-1} = 4.24 \text{ g}$

$\therefore [\text{Na}_2\text{CO}_3] = 4.24 \text{ g dm}^{-3}$

## CHALLENGE YOURSELF

**6** When sodium hydroxide pellets (NaOH) dissolve in water, there is a *decrease* in the total volume of the solution. Explain what might cause this.

> A standard solution is one of accurately known concentration.

> number of moles of solute (mol) = concentration of solute (mol dm⁻³) × volume of solution (dm³)
>
> $$n = cV$$

| Sodium | Na$^+$ | 13.2 |
| Calcium | Ca$^{2+}$ | 29.1 |
| Magnesium | Mg$^{2+}$ | 3.0 |
| Chloride | Cl$^-$ | 31.1 |
| Sulphate | SO$_4^{2-}$ | 42.7 |
| Nitrate | NO$_3^-$ | <0.5 |

PET

Label on sparkling water listing the mineral content in milligrams per dm$^3$.

The increased popularity in many countries of bottled water over tap water for drinking has raised several concerns, including the environmental costs of transport and packaging, and the source of the water and its solute (dissolved mineral) content. Significant differences exist in the regulation of the bottled water industry in different countries. In the USA, the FDA (Food and Drug Administration) requires that mineral waters contain between 500 and 1500 mg dm$^{-3}$ of total dissolved solids. In Europe, mineral water is defined by its origin rather than by content, and the EU (European Union) prohibits the treatment of any water bottled from a source. The global cost of bottled water exceeds billions of dollars annually. As the United Nations General Assembly has explicitly recognized that access to safe, clean, and affordable drinking water is a human right, there is an urgent need for money and technology to be diverted to improving tap water supplies globally to help make this a reality for all.

A different unit of concentration is known as **ppm**, parts per million. It denotes one part per $10^6$ by mass, and is useful in describing very low concentrations such as found in air and water pollution.

$$\text{parts per million (ppm)} = \frac{\text{mass of component}}{\text{total mass of solution}} \times 10^6$$

A concentration of 1 ppm for a substance means that each kilogram of solution contains 1 milligram of solute. Assuming a density of 1 g cm$^{-3}$, 1 ppm also means that each dm$^3$ of solution contains 1 mg of solute. An advantage of these values based on mass is that they are not temperature dependent.

## Dilutions of solutions reduce the concentration

A common practice in laboratory work is to make a **dilution** from a more concentrated starting solution, called the **stock solution**, by adding solvent. For all aqueous solutions, distilled water, rather than tap water, must be used.

Series of dilutions of cobalt(II) chloride solutions. In coloured solutions such as these, the effect of lowering the concentration of the solution can be observed.

As a solution is diluted, the number of moles of solute remains the same, but as they become spread through a larger volume, the concentration is decreased. In other words, the number of moles, $n$ = a constant, and as $n = cV \Rightarrow cV$ must be constant through dilution.

$$\therefore c_1V_1 = c_2V_2$$

where $c_1$ and $V_1$ refer to the initial concentration and volume and $c_2$ and $V_2$ refer to the diluted concentration and volume.

This equation provides an easy way to calculate concentration changes on dilution.

## Worked example

Determine the final concentration of a 75 cm³ solution of HCl of concentration 0.40 mol dm⁻³, which is diluted to a volume of 300 cm³.

### Solution

$$c_1V_1 = c_2V_2$$

$c_1 = 0.40$ mol dm⁻³    $V_1 = 75$ cm³    $V_2 = 300$ cm³

∴ $(0.40$ mol dm⁻³$)$ $(75$ cm³$)$ = $c_2$ $(300$ cm³$)$

$c_2$ diluted concentration = $0.10$ mol dm⁻³

A quick check shows that the volume has increased four times, so the concentration must have decreased four times.

In precise work, dilution should be carried out using volumetric flasks so the final volume of the solution is measured, taking account of volume changes that may occur on dilution.

## The concentration of a solution can be determined by volumetric analysis

Suppose we have an unlabelled bottle of hydrochloric acid, HCl, and want to know its concentration. We can find this out by reacting the acid with a standard solution of an alkali such as NaOH, and determining the exact volumes that react together. From the stoichiometry of the reaction, when we know the volumes of both solutions and the concentration of one of them, we can use the mole ratio to calculate the unknown concentration as follows.

▲ Redox titration experiment. The burette tap controls the flow of the orange potassium dichromate(VI) solution into the conical flask containing iron(II) ions. The equivalence point occurs when the exact volumes of the two solutions have reacted completely.

$$HCl(aq) + NaOH(aq) \rightarrow NaCl(aq) + H_2O(l)$$

mole ratio:    1    :    1
volume:    known        known(by titration)
conc.:    unknown = $x$        known (standard solution)

• moles NaOH can be calculated as follows:
  $n(NaOH) = c(NaOH) \times V(NaOH)$
• from the mole ratio in the equation:
  $n(NaOH) = n(HCl)$
• ∴ concentration of HCl, $x$, can be calculated from:
  $n(HCl) = x \times V(HCl)$

This is an example of a process called **volumetric analysis**. Most commonly, a technique called **titration** is used to determine the reacting volumes precisely. A **pipette** is used to measure a known volume of one of the solutions into a **conical flask**. The other solution is put into a **burette**, a calibrated glass tube that can deliver precise volumes into the conical flask through opening the tap at the bottom. The point at which the two solutions have reacted completely, the **equivalence point**, is usually determined by an **indicator** that is added to the solution in the conical

Burettes generally read to ± 0.05 cm³, so be sure to record your results to this precision. Readings such as 0, 12.0, or 3.5 are not acceptable but should be recorded as 0.00, 12.00, and 3.50 respectively.

flask and changes colour at its **end-point**. Different indicators are chosen for specific titrations, so that their end-point corresponds to the equivalence point of the titration. This is explained more fully in Chapter 8.

Titration usually involves multiple trials to obtain a more accurate result of the volume required to reach the equivalence point; this volume is known as the titre. A good titration result is one that gives consistent results within 0.05 cm³ of each other.

### Worked example

25.00 cm³ of 0.100 mol dm⁻³ sodium hydrogencarbonate, $NaHCO_3$, solution were titrated with dilute sulfuric acid, $H_2SO_4$.

$$2NaHCO_3(aq) + H_2SO_4(aq) \rightarrow Na_2SO_4(aq) + 2H_2O(l) + 2CO_2(g)$$

15.20 cm³ of the acid were needed to neutralize the solution. Calculate the concentration of the acid.

### Solution

We can calculate the amount of $NaHCO_3$ as we are given both the volume and the concentration.

$$n = cV$$

$$n(NaHCO_3) = 0.100 \text{ mol dm}^{-3} \times \frac{25.00}{1000} \text{ dm}^3 = 2.500 \times 10^{-3} \text{ mol}$$

Look at the mole ratio in the equation:

$$2n(NaHCO_3) = n(H_2SO_4)$$

$$\therefore n(H_2SO_4) = 0.5 \times 2.500 \times 10^{-3} \text{ mol} = 1.250 \times 10^{-3} \text{ mol}$$

$$c = \frac{n}{V} = \frac{1.250 \times 10^{-3} \text{ mol}}{15.20/1000 \text{ dm}^3} = 0.0822 \text{ mol dm}^{-3}$$

$$\therefore [H_2SO_4] = 0.0822 \text{ mol dm}^{-3}$$

Here is a summary of the steps in volumetric analysis calculations:

### Back titration

- first write the equation for the reaction;
- look for the reactant whose volume and concentration are given and calculate its number of moles from $n = cV$;
- use this answer and the mole ratio in the equation to determine the number of moles of the other reactant;
- use the number of moles and volume of the second reactant to calculate its concentration from $c = \frac{n}{V}$.

As the name implies, a back titration is done in reverse by returning to the end-point after it is passed. It is used when the end-point is hard to identify or when one of the reactants is impure. A known excess of one of the reagents is added to the reaction mixture, and the unreacted excess is then determined by titration against a standard solution. By subtracting the amount of unreacted reactant from the original amount used, the reacting amount can be determined.

An antacid tablet with a mass of 0.300 g and containing $NaHCO_3$ was added to 25.00 $cm^3$ of 0.125 mol $dm^{-3}$ hydrochloric acid. After the reaction was complete, the excess hydrochloric acid required 3.50 $cm^3$ of 0.200 mol $dm^{-3}$ NaOH to reach the equivalence point in a titration. Calculate the percentage of $NaHCO_3$ in the tablet.

## Solution

original reaction:    $NaHCO_3(s) + HCl(aq) \rightarrow NaCl(aq) + H_2O(l) + CO_2(g)$
mole ratio:              1      :     1

First calculate the total amount of HCl added, which is a known excess.

$$n(\text{HCl total}) = \frac{25.00}{1000} \text{ dm}^3 \times 0.125 \text{ mol dm}^{-3} = 0.00313 \text{ mol HCl total}$$

titration reaction:    $HCl(aq) + NaOH(aq) \rightarrow NaCl(aq) + H_2O(l)$
mole ratio:             1     :     1

$$n(\text{NaOH}) = 0.00350 \text{ dm}^3 \times 0.200 \text{ mol dm}^{-3} = 0.000700 \text{ mol}$$

$n(\text{NaOH}) = n(\text{HCl unreacted}) = 0.000700$ mol HCl unreacted

$\therefore n(\text{HCl reacted}) = 0.00313 - 0.000700 = 0.00243$ mol

$\therefore$ from the mole ratio in the first equation $n(\text{NaHCO}_3) = 0.00243$ mol

$M(\text{NaHCO}_3) = 22.99 + 1.01 + 12.01 + (16.00 \times 3) = 84.01 \text{ g mol}^{-1}$

$$m = nM = 0.00243 \text{ mol} \times 84.01 \text{ g mol}^{-1} = 0.204 \text{ g}$$

$$\text{percentage by mass in tablet} = \frac{0.204}{0.300} \times 100 = 68.0\%$$

Note that there are several assumptions made in this calculation. These include the fact that all the $NaHCO_3$ did react with the acid, and that the only component of the tablet that reacted with HCl is $NaHCO_3$. You may like to think how you could test the validity of these assumptions in the laboratory.

## Exercises

**64** Calculate the mass of potassium hydroxide, KOH, required to prepare 250 $cm^3$ of a 0.200 mol $dm^{-3}$ solution.

**65** Calculate the mass of magnesium sulfate heptahydrate, $MgSO_4.7H_2O$, required to prepare 0.100 $dm^3$ of a 0.200 mol $dm^{-3}$ solution.

**66** Calculate the number of moles of chloride ions in 0.250 $dm^3$ of 0.0200 mol $dm^{-3}$ zinc chloride, $ZnCl_2$, solution.

**67** 250 $cm^3$ of a solution contains 5.85 g of sodium chloride. Calculate the concentration of sodium chloride in mol $dm^{-3}$.

**68** Concentrated nitric acid, $HNO_3$, is 16.0 mol $dm^{-3}$. What volume would you need to prepare 100 $cm^3$ of 0.50 mol $dm^{-3}$ $HNO_3$?

**69** In a titration a 15.00 $cm^3$ sample of $H_2SO_4$ required 36.42 $cm^3$ of 0.147 mol $dm^{-3}$ NaOH solution for complete neutralization. What is the concentration of the $H_2SO_4$?

**70** Gastric juice contains hydrochloric acid, HCl. A 5.00 $cm^3$ sample of gastric juice required 11.00 $cm^3$ of 0.0100 mol $dm^{-3}$ KOH for neutralization in a titration. What was the concentration of HCl in this fluid? If we assume a density of 1.00 g $cm^{-3}$ for the fluid, what was the percentage by mass of HCl?

**71** Sodium sulfate, $Na_2SO_4$, reacts in aqueous solution with lead nitrate, $Pb(NO_3)_2$, as follows:

$$Na_2SO_4(aq) + Pb(NO_3)_2(aq) \rightarrow PbSO_4(s) + 2NaNO_3(aq)$$

In an experiment, 35.30 $cm^3$ of a solution of sodium sulfate reacted exactly with 32.50 $cm^3$ of a solution of lead nitrate. The precipitated lead sulfate was dried and found to have a mass of 1.13 g. Determine the concentrations of the original solutions of lead nitrate and sodium sulfate. State what assumptions are made.

## Challenge problems

**72** The fertilizer tri-ammonium phosphate is made from 'phosphate rock' by:

1   reacting the phosphate rock with sulfuric acid, $H_2SO_4$, to produce phosphoric acid, $H_3PO_4$;
2   reacting the phosphoric acid with ammonia, $NH_3$, to give tri-ammonium phosphate, $(NH_4)_3PO_4$.

If the phosphate rock contains 90% by mass $Ca_3(PO_4)_2$ from which the overall yield of tri-ammonium phosphate is 95%, calculate the mass of phosphate rock required to make 1000 tonnes of tri-ammonium phosphate.

**73** The combustion of both ammonia, $NH_3$, and hydrazine, $N_2H_4$, in oxygen gives nitrogen and water only. When a mixture of ammonia and hydrazine is burned in pure oxygen, the volumetric $N_2 : H_2O$ ratio in the product gas is 0.40. Calculate the % by mass of ammonia in the original mixture. What assumptions are being made here?

**74** Sulfuric acid, $H_2SO_4$, is produced from sulfur in a three-step process:

1   $S(s) + O_2(g) \rightarrow SO_2(g)$
2   $2SO_2(g) + O_2(g) \rightarrow 2SO_3(g)$
3   $SO_3(g) + H_2O(l) \rightarrow H_2SO_4(l)$

Assuming 100% conversion and yield for each step, what is the minimum mass of sulfur in kg needed to produce 980 tonnes of $H_2SO_4$?

**75** The concentration of hydrogen peroxide, $H_2O_2$, in excess aqueous sulfuric acid, $H_2SO_4$, can be determined by redox titration using potassium permanganate, $KMnO_4$ as follows:

$$2KMnO_4(aq) + 5H_2O_2(l) + 3H_2SO_4(aq) \rightarrow 2MnSO_4(aq) + K_2SO_4(aq) + 8H_2O(l) + 5O_2(g)$$

A 10.00 $cm^3$ sample of $H_2O_2$ solution requires 18.00 $cm^3$ of a 0.05 mol $dm^{-3}$ solution of $KMnO_4$ to reach the equivalence point in a titration. Calculate the concentration of $H_2O_2$ in the solution.

**76** Mixtures of sodium carbonate, $Na_2CO_3$, and sodium hydrogencarbonate, $NaHCO_3$, in aqueous solution are determined by titration with hydrochloric acid, HCl, in a two-step procedure.

1   Titrate to the phenolphthalein end-point:

$$Na_2CO_3(s) + HCl(aq) \rightarrow NaHCO_3(aq) + NaCl(aq)$$

2   Continue titration to the methyl orange end-point:

$$NaHCO_3 + HCl \rightarrow NaCl + H_2O + CO_2$$

For an X $cm^3$ sample of a sodium carbonate / sodium hydrogencarbonate mixture titrated with Y mol $dm^{-3}$ HCl, the respective end-points are Step 1 = P $cm^3$ HCl, Step 2 = Q $cm^3$ HCl. Derive relationships between X, Y, P, and Q to obtain the concentrations of sodium carbonate and sodium hydrogencarbonate in the original mixture.

**77** A sealed vessel with fixed total internal volume 2.00 $m^3$ contains 0.720 kg pentane, $C_5H_{12}$, and oxygen only. The pentane is ignited and undergoes 100% conversion to carbon dioxide and water. Subsequently the temperature and pressure in the vessel are respectively 740 K, 400 kPa. Calculate the initial amount and mass in kg of oxygen in the vessel.

## Practice questions

**1**   How many oxygen atoms are in 0.100 mol of $CuSO_4.5H_2O$?

**A**  $5.42 \times 10^{22}$     **B**  $6.02 \times 10^{22}$     **C**  $2.41 \times 10^{23}$     **D**  $5.42 \times 10^{23}$

**2**   What is the sum of the coefficients when the following equation is balanced using whole numbers?

$$\_\_\_ Fe_2O_3(s) + \_\_\_ CO(g) \rightarrow \_\_\_ Fe(s) + \_\_\_ CO_2(g)$$

**A**  5        **B**  6        **C**  8        **D**  9

**3** Four identical containers under the same conditions are filled with gases as shown below. Which container and contents will have the highest mass?

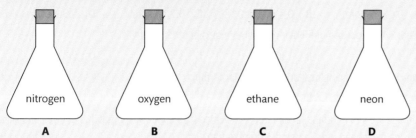

| nitrogen | oxygen | ethane | neon |
| A | B | C | D |

**4** 1.0 dm³ of an ideal gas at 100 kPa and 25 °C is heated to 50 °C at constant pressure. What is the new volume in dm³?

**A** 0.50      **B** 0.90      **C** 1.1      **D** 2.0

**5** What is the amount, in moles, of sulfate ions in 100 cm³ of 0.020 mol dm⁻³ $FeSO_4(aq)$?

**A** $2.0 \times 10^{-3}$      **B** $2.0 \times 10^{-2}$      **C** $2.0 \times 10^{-1}$      **D** 2.0

**6** 1.7 g of $NaNO_3$ ($M_r = 85$) is dissolved in water to prepare 0.20 dm³ of solution. What is the concentration of the resulting solution in mol dm⁻³?

**A** 0.01      **B** 0.1      **C** 0.2      **D** 1.0

**7** What mass, in g, of hydrogen is formed when 3 mol of aluminium react with excess hydrochloric acid according to the following equation?

$$2Al(s) + 6HCl(aq) \rightarrow 2AlCl_3(aq) + 3H_2(g)$$

**A** 3.0      **B** 4.5      **C** 6.0      **D** 9.0

**8** The relative molecular mass of a gas is 56 and its empirical formula is $CH_2$. What is the molecular formula of the gas?

**A** $CH_2$      **B** $C_2H_4$      **C** $C_3H_6$      **D** $C_4H_8$

**9** What is the sum of all coefficients when the following equation is balanced using the smallest possible whole numbers?

$$\underline{\quad} C_2H_2 + \underline{\quad} O_2 \rightarrow \underline{\quad} CO_2 + \underline{\quad} H_2O$$

**A** 5      **B** 7      **C** 11      **D** 13

**10** What is the total number of hydrogen atoms in 1.0 mol of benzamide, $C_6H_5CONH_2$?

**A** 7      **B** $6.0 \times 10^{23}$      **C** $3.0 \times 10^{24}$      **D** $4.2 \times 10^{24}$

**11** Chloroethene, $C_2H_3Cl$, reacts with oxygen according to the equation below:

$$2C_2H_3Cl(g) + 5O_2(g) \rightarrow 4CO_2(g) + 2H_2O(g) + 2HCl(g)$$

What is the amount, in mol, of $H_2O$ produced when 10.0 mol of $C_2H_3Cl$ and 10.0 mol of $O_2$ are mixed together, and the above reaction goes to completion?

**A** 4.00      **B** 8.00      **C** 10.0      **D** 20.0

**12** What is the concentration of NaCl, in mol dm⁻³, when 10.0 cm³ of 0.200 mol dm⁻³ NaCl solution is added to 30.0 cm³ of 0.600 mol dm⁻³ NaCl solution?

**A** 0.450      **B** 0.300      **C** 0.500      **D** 0.800

**13** On analysis, a compound with molar mass 60 g mol⁻¹ was found to contain 12 g of carbon, 2 g of hydrogen, and 16 g of oxygen. What is the molecular formula of the compound?

**A** $CH_2O$      **B** $CH_4O$      **C** $C_2H_4O$      **D** $C_2H_4O_2$

**14** 300 cm$^3$ of water is added to a solution of 200 cm$^3$ of 0.5 mol dm$^{-3}$ sodium chloride. What is the concentration of sodium chloride in the new solution?

    **A**  0.05 mol dm$^{-3}$    **B**  0.1 mol dm$^{-3}$    **C**  0.2 mol dm$^{-3}$    **D**  0.3 mol dm$^{-3}$

**15** What is the approximate molar mass, in g mol$^{-1}$, of $MgSO_4.7H_2O$?

    **A**  120          **B**  130          **C**  138          **D**  246

**16** Which is both an empirical and a molecular formula?

    **A**  $C_5H_{12}$         **B**  $C_5H_{10}$         **C**  $C_4H_8$         **D**  $C_4H_{10}$

**17** Airbags are an important safety feature in vehicles. Sodium azide, potassium nitrate, and silicon dioxide have been used in one design of airbag.

Two students looked at data in a simulated computer-based experiment to determine the volume of nitrogen generated in an airbag.

Sodium azide, a toxic compound, undergoes the following decomposition reaction under certain conditions.

$$2NaN_3(s) \rightarrow 2Na(s) + 3N_2(g)$$

Using the simulation program, the students entered the following data into the computer.

| Temperature (T) / °C | Mass of $NaN_3$(s) (m) / kg | Pressure (p) / atm |
| --- | --- | --- |
| 25.00 | 0.0650 | 1.08 |

    **(a)** Stage the number of significant figures for the temperature, mass, and pressure data.    (1)

    **(b)** Calculate the amount, in mol, of sodium azide present.    (1)

    **(c)** Determine the volume of nitrogen gas, in dm$^3$, produced under these conditions based on this reaction.    (4)

    *(Total 6 marks)*

**18** An important environmental consideration is the appropriate disposal of cleaning solvents. An environmental waste treatment company analysed a cleaning solvent, **J**, and found it to contain the elements carbon, hydrogen, and chlorine only. The chemical composition of **J** was determined using different analytical chemistry techniques.

Combustion reaction:

Combustion of 1.30 g of J gave 0.872 g $CO_2$ and 0.089 g $H_2O$.

Precipitation reaction with $AgNO_3$(aq):

0.535 g of J gave 1.75 g AgCl precipitate.

    **(a)** Determine the percentage by mass of carbon and hydrogen in **J**, using the combustion data.    (3)

    **(b)** Determine the percentage by mass of chlorine in **J**, using the precipitation data.    (1)

    **(c)** The molar mass was determined to be 131.38 g mol$^{-1}$. Deduce the molecular formula of **J**.    (3)

    *(Total 7 marks)*

**19** Nitrogen monoxide may be removed from industrial emissions via a reaction with ammonia as shown by the equation below:

$$4NH_3(g) + 6NO(g) \rightarrow 5N_2(g) + 6H_2O(l)$$

30.0 dm$^3$ of ammonia reacts with 30.0 dm$^3$ of nitrogen monoxide at 100 °C. Identify which gas is in excess and by how much and calculate the volume of nitrogen produced.    (2)

**20** The percentage by mass of calcium carbonate in eggshell was determined by adding excess hydrochloric acid to ensure that all the calcium carbonate had reacted. The excess acid left was then titrated with aqueous sodium hydroxide.

(a) A student added 27.20 cm$^3$ of 0.200 mol dm$^{-3}$ HCl to 0.188 g of eggshell. Calculate the amount, in mol, of HCl added. (1)

(b) The excess acid requires 23.80 cm$^3$ of 0.100 mol dm$^{-3}$ NaOH for neutralization. Calculate the amount, in mol, of acid that is in excess. (1)

(c) Determine the amount, in mol, of HCl that reacted with the calcium carbonate in the eggshell. (1)

(d) State the equation for the reaction of HCl with the calcium carbonate in the eggshell. (2)

(e) Determine the amount, in mol, of calcium carbonate in the sample of the eggshell. (2)

(f) Calculate the mass and the percentage by mass of calcium carbonate in the eggshell sample. (3)

(g) Deduce one assumption made in arriving at the percentage of calcium carbonate in the eggshell sample. (1)

*(Total 11 marks)*

**21** A 2.450 g sample of a mixture of sodium chloride and calcium chloride was dissolved in distilled water. The chloride solution was treated with excess silver nitrate solution, $AgNO_3$(aq). The precipitated silver chloride, $AgCl$(s), was collected, washed and dried. The mass of the dried silver chloride was 6.127 g. Calculate the percent by mass of the sodium chloride and calcium chloride in the original mixture. (2)

**22** A hydrate of potassium carbonate has the formula $K_2CO_3.xH_2O$. A 10.00 g sample of the hydrated solid is heated, and forms 7.93 g of anhydrous salt.

(a) Calculate the number of moles of water in the hydrated sample. (1)

(b) Calculate the number of moles of anhydrous salt that form. (1)

(c) Determine the formula of the hydrate. (1)

(d) How could you determine when all the hydrated salt has been converted into anhydrous form? (1)

*(Total 4 marks)*

**23** 625 cm$^3$ of ammonia, $NH_3$, at 42°C and 160 kPa is combined with 740 cm$^3$ of hydrogen chloride at 57°C and 113.3 kPa. The reaction produces ammonium chloride as follows:

$$NH_3(g) + HCl(g) \rightarrow NH_4Cl(s)$$

(a) Which reactant is in excess? (1)

(b) Which reactant is limiting? (1)

(c) What mass of ammonium chloride forms? (1)

*(Total 3 marks)*

 To access weblinks on the topics covered in this chapter, please go to www.pearsonhotlinks.com and enter the ISBN or title of this book.

# 02

## Atomic structure

# Essential ideas

**2.1** The mass of an atom is concentrated in its minute, positively charged nucleus.

**2.2** The electron configuration of an atom can be deduced from its atomic number.

**12.1** The quantized nature of energy transitions is related to the energy states of electrons in atoms and molecules.

'All things are made from atoms.' This is one of the most important ideas that the human race has learned about the universe. Atoms are everywhere and they make up everything. You are surrounded by atoms – they make up the foods you eat, the liquids you drink, and the fragrances you smell. Atoms make up you! To understand the world and how it changes you need to understand atoms.

The idea of atoms has its origins in Greek and Indian philosophy nearly 2500 years ago, but it was not until the 19th century that there was experimental evidence to support their existence. Although atoms are too small ever to be seen directly by a human eye, they are fundamental to chemistry. All the atoms in a piece of gold foil, for example, have the same chemical properties. The atoms of gold, however, have different properties from the atoms of aluminium. This chapter will explain how they differ. We will explore their structure and discover that different atoms are made from different combinations of the same sub-atomic particles.

This exploration will take us into some difficult areas because our everyday notion of particles following fixed trajectories does not apply to the microscopic world of the atom. To understand the block structure of the Periodic Table we need to use **quantum theory** and adopt a wave description of matter. These ideas are revolutionary. As Niels Bohr, one of the principal scientists involved in the development of quantum theory said, 'Anyone who is not shocked by quantum theory has not understood it.'

Picture of individual atoms. This is a scanning tunnelling micrograph of gold atoms on a graphite surface. The gold atoms are shown in yellow, red, and brown and the graphite (carbon) atoms are shown in green.

**TOK**

Richard Feynman: "… if all of scientific knowledge were to be destroyed, and only one sentence passed on to the next generation of creatures, what statement would contain the most information in the fewest words? I believe it is the atomic hypothesis … that *all things are made of atoms*." Are the models and theories which scientists create accurate descriptions of the natural world, or are they primarily useful interpretations for prediction, explanation, and control of the natural world?

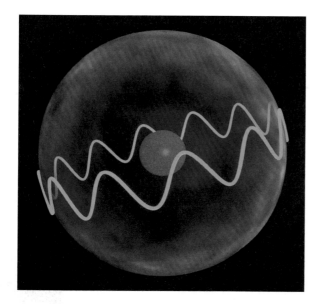

The hydrogen atom shown as a nucleus (a proton, pink), and an electron orbiting in a wavy path (light blue). It is necessary to consider the wave properties of the electron to understand atomic structure in detail.

A billion of your atoms once made up Shakespeare, another billion made up Beethoven, another billion St. Peter and another billion the Buddha. Atoms can rearrange in chemical reactions but they cannot be destroyed.

## 2.1 The nuclear atom

## Understandings:

- Atoms contain a positively charged dense nucleus composed of protons and neutrons (nucleons).

**Guidance**
*Relative masses and charges of the sub-atomic particles should be known, actual values are given in section 4 of the IB data booklet. The mass of the electron can be considered negligible.*

- Negatively charged electrons occupy the space outside the nucleus.
- The mass spectrometer is used to determine the relative atomic mass of an element from its isotopic composition.

**Guidance**
*The operation of the mass spectrometer is not required.*

## Applications and skills:

- Use of the nuclear symbol notation $^A_Z X$ to deduce the number of protons, neutrons, and electrons in atoms and ions.
- Calculations involving non-integer relative atomic masses and abundance of isotopes from given data, including mass spectra.

**Guidance**
*Specific examples of isotopes need not be learned.*

## Dalton's model of the atom

One of the first great achievements of chemistry was to show that all matter is built from about 100 **elements**. As mentioned in Chapter 1, the elements are substances which cannot be broken down into simpler components by chemical reactions. They are the simplest substances and their names are listed in your IB data booklet (section 5). Different elements have different chemical properties but gold foil, for example, reacts in essentially the same way as a single piece of gold dust. Indeed if the gold dust is cut into smaller and smaller pieces, the chemical properties would remain essentially the same until we reached an **atom**. This is the smallest unit of an element. There are only 92 elements which occur naturally on earth and they are made up from only 92 different types of atom. (This statement will be qualified when isotopes are discussed later in the chapter.)

**An element is a substance that cannot be broken down into simpler substances by a chemical reaction.**

The word 'atom' comes from the Greek words for 'not able to be cut'.

Scanning tunnelling microscope (STM) image of the surface of pure gold. STM provides a magnification of 250 000 times, which records the surface structure at the level of the individual atoms. Gold exists in many forms – gold foil, nuggets, blocks, etc., which all contain the same type of atoms. The 'rolling hills' structure seen here is the result of changes in the surface energy as the gold cooled from its molten state. STM is based on quantum mechanical effects, and is described on page 92.

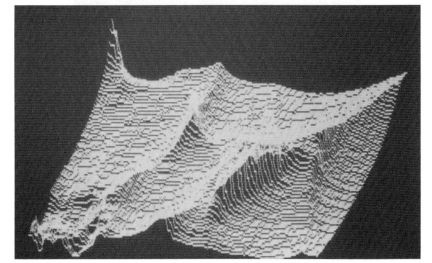

## NATURE OF SCIENCE

The idea that matter is made up from elements and atoms dates back to the Indian philosophy of the sixth century BCE and the Greek philosophy of Democritus (460 BCE to 370 BCE). These ideas were speculative as there was little evidence to support them. A significant development for chemistry came with the publication of Robert Boyle's *Skeptical Chemist* of 1661 which emphasized the need for scientific knowledge to be justified by evidence from practical investigations. Boyle was the first to propose the modern concept of an element as a substance which cannot be changed into anything simpler.

The modern idea of the atom dates from the beginning of the 19th century. John Dalton noticed that the elements hydrogen and oxygen always combined together in fixed proportions. To explain this observation he proposed that:

• all matter is composed of tiny indivisible particles called atoms;
• atoms cannot be created or destroyed;
• atoms of the same element are alike in every way;
• atoms of different elements are different;
• atoms can combine together in small numbers to form **molecules**.

Using this model we can understand how elements react together to make new substances called **compounds**. The compound water, for example, is formed when two hydrogen atoms combine with one oxygen atom to produce one water molecule. If we repeat the reaction on a larger scale with $2 \times 6.02 \times 10^{23}$ atoms of hydrogen and $6.02 \times 10^{23}$ atoms of oxygen, $6.02 \times 10^{23}$ molecules of water will be formed. This leads to the conclusion (see Chapter 1) that 2.02 g of hydrogen will react with 16.00 g of oxygen to form 18.02 g of water. This is one of the observations Dalton was trying to explain.

## NATURE OF SCIENCE

Dalton was a man of regular habits. 'For fifty-seven years... he measured the rainfall, the temperature... Of all that mass of data, nothing whatever came. But of the one searching, almost childlike question about the weights that enter the construction of simple molecules – out of that came modern atomic theory. That is the essence of science: ask an impertinent question: and you are on the way to the pertinent answer.' (J. Bronowski)

Dalton was the first person to assign chemical symbols to the different elements.

## CHALLENGE YOURSELF

**2** It is now known that some of these substances are not elements but compounds. Lime, for example, is a compound of calcium and oxygen. Can you find any other examples in this list and explain why the elements had not been extracted at this time?

John Dalton's symbols for the elements.

## CHALLENGE YOURSELF

**1** Can you think of any evidence based on simple observations that supports the idea that water is made up from discrete particles?

Although John Dalton (1766–1844) was a school teacher from Manchester in England, his name has passed into other languages. The internationally recognized term for colour-blindness, *Daltonisme* in French, for example, derives from the fact the he suffered from the condition.

 **TOK**

'What we observe is not nature itself but nature exposed to our mode of questioning.' (Werner Heisenberg). How does the knowledge we gain about the natural world depend on the questions we ask and the experiments we perform?

**A compound is a substance made by chemically combining two or more elements. It has different properties from its constituent elements.**

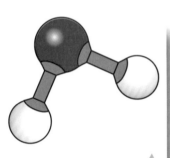

**Figure 2.1** A model of a water molecule made from two hydrogen atoms and one oxygen atom. Dalton's picture of the atom as a hard ball is the basis behind the molecular models we use today.

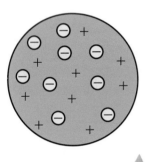

**Figure 2.2** Thomson's 'plum pudding' model of the atom. The electrons (yellow) are scattered in a positively charged sponge-like substance (pink).

When Geiger and Marsden reported to Rutherford that they had seen nothing unusual with most of the alpha particles passing straight through the gold and a small number being deflected by small angles, he asked them to look and see if any of the alpha particles had bounced back. This was a very unusual suggestion to make at the time, with little logical justification. What is the role of intuition in the pursuit of scientific knowledge?

**TOK**

Following his example, the formation of water (described above) can be written using modern notation:

$$2H + O \rightarrow H_2O$$

But what are atoms really like? It can be useful to think of them as hard spheres (Figure 2.1), but this tells us little about how the atoms of different elements differ. To understand this, it is necessary to probe deeper.

**NATURE OF SCIENCE**

Dalton's atomic theory was not accepted when it was first proposed. Many scientists, such as Kelvin for example, considered it as nothing more than a useful fiction which should not be taken too seriously. Over time, as the supporting evidence grew, there was a general shift in thinking which led to its widespread acceptance. These revolutions in understanding or **'paradigm shifts'** are characteristic of the evolutions of scientific thinking.

## Atoms contain electrons

The first indication that atoms were destructible came at the end of the 19th century when the British scientist J. J. Thomson discovered that different metals produce a stream of negatively charged particles when a high voltage is applied across two electrodes. As these particles, which we now know as **electrons**, were the same regardless of the metal, he suggested that they are part of the make-up of all atoms.

**NATURE OF SCIENCE**

The properties of electrons, or cathode rays as they were first called, could only be investigated once powerful vacuum pumps had been invented – and once advances had been made in the use and understanding of electricity and magnetism. Improved instrumentation and new technology have often been the drivers for new discoveries.

As it was known that the atom had no net charge, Thomson pictured the atom as a 'plum pudding', with the negatively charged electrons scattered in a positively charged sponge-like substance (Figure 2.2).

## Rutherford's model of the atom

Ernest Rutherford (1871–1937) and his research team working at Manchester University in England, tested Thomson's model by firing alpha particles at a piece of gold foil. We now know that alpha particles are helium nuclei, composed of two protons and two neutrons, with a positive charge. They are emitted by nuclei with too many protons to be stable. If Thomson's model was correct, the alpha particles should either pass straight through or get stuck in the positive 'sponge'. Most of the alpha particles did indeed pass straight through, but a very small number were repelled and bounced back. Ernest Rutherford recalled that 'It was quite the most incredible thing that has happened to me. It was as if you had fired a (artillery) shell at a piece of tissue paper and it came back and hit you.'

The large number of undeflected particles led to the conclusion that the atom is mainly empty space. Large deflections occur when the positively charged alpha particles collide with and are repelled by a dense, positively charged centre called the **nucleus** (Figure 2.3). The fact that only a small number of alpha particles bounce back suggests that the nucleus is very small.

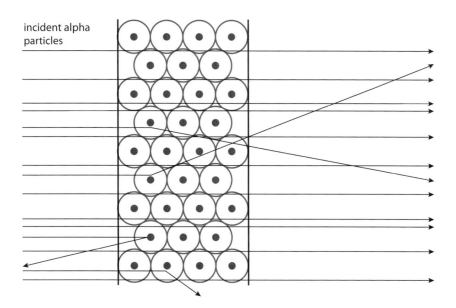

incident alpha particles

**Figure 2.3** Rutherford's model of the atom accounts for the experimental observations. Most of the alpha particles pass straight through but a small number collide with and are repelled by a positively charged nucleus.

**NATURE OF SCIENCE**

Our knowledge of the nuclear atom came from Rutherford's experiments with the relatively newly discovered alpha particles. Scientific knowledge grows as new evidence is gathered as a result of new technologies and instrumentation.

The European Organization for Nuclear Research (CERN) is run by twenty European Member States, with involvements from scientists from many other countries. It operates the world's largest particle physics research centre, including particle accelerators and detectors used to study the fundamental constituents of matter.

## Sub-atomic particles

A hundred or so years after Dalton first proposed his model, these experiments and many others showed that atoms are themselves made up from smaller or **sub-atomic** particles. The nucleus of an atom is made up of **protons** and **neutrons**, collectively called **nucleons**. Both the protons and neutrons have almost the same mass as a hydrogen nucleus and account for the most of the mass of the atom. **Electrons**, which have a charge equal and opposite to that of the proton, occupy the space in the atom outside of the nucleus.

These particles are described by their *relative* masses and charges which have no units. The absolute masses and charges of these fundamental particles are given in section 4 of the IB data booklet.

PET (positron-emission tomography) scanners give three-dimensional images of tracer concentration in the body, and can be used to detect cancers. The patient is injected with a tracer compound labelled with a positron-emitting isotope. The positrons collide with electrons after travelling a short distance ($\approx$1 mm) within the body. Both particles are destroyed with the production of two photons, which can be collected by the detectors surrounding the patient, and used to generate an image.

| Particle | Relative mass | Relative charge |
|----------|---------------|-----------------|
| proton   | 1             | +1              |
| electron | 0.0005        | −1              |
| neutron  | 1             | 0               |

**NATURE OF SCIENCE**

The description of sub-atomic particles offered here is sufficient to understand chemistry but incomplete. Although the electron is indeed a fundamental particle, we now know that the protons and neutrons are both themselves made up from more fundamental particles called quarks. We also know that all particles have anti-particles. The positron is the anti-particle of an electron; it has the same mass but has an equal and opposite positive charge. When particles and anti-particles collide they destroy each other and release energy in the form of high-energy photons called gamma rays. Our treatment of sub-atomic particles is in line with the principle of Occam's razor, which states that theories should be as simple as possible while maximizing explanatory power.

View of a patient undergoing a positron-emission tomography (PET) brain scan. A radioactive tracer is injected into the patient's bloodstream, which is then absorbed by active tissues of the brain. The PET scanner detects photons emitted by the tracer and produces 'slice' images.

As you are made from atoms, you are also mainly empty space. The particles which make up your mass would occupy the same volume as a flea if they were all squashed together, but a flea with your mass. This gives you an idea of the density of the nucleus.

**TOK**

None of these sub-atomic particles can be (or ever will be) directly observed. Which ways of knowing do we use to interpret indirect evidence gained through the use of technology.

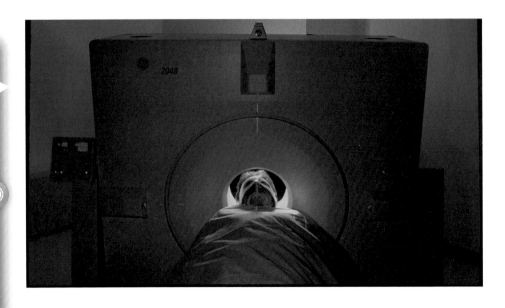

## Bohr model of the hydrogen atom

The Danish physicist Niels Bohr pictured the hydrogen atom as a small 'solar system', with an electron moving in an orbit or energy level around the positively charged nucleus of one proton (Figure 2.4). The electrostatic force of attraction between the oppositely charged sub-atomic particles prevents the electron from leaving the atom. The nuclear radius is $10^{-15}$ m and the atomic radius $10^{-10}$ m, so most of the volume of the atom is empty space.

The existence of neutrally charged neutrons is crucial for the stability of nuclei of later elements, which have more than one proton. Without the neutrons, the positively charged protons would mutually repel each other and the nucleus would fall apart.

**Figure 2.4** The simplest atom. Only one proton and one electron make up the hydrogen atom. The nuclear radius is $10^{-15}$ m and the atomic radius $10^{-10}$ m. Most of the volume of the atom is empty – the only occupant is the negatively charged electron. It is useful to think of the electron orbiting the nucleus in a similar way to the planets orbiting the sun. The absence of a neutron is significant – it would be essentially redundant as there is only one proton.

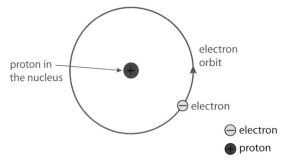

**Figure 2.5** A helium atom. The two neutrons allow the two protons, which repel each other, to stay in the nucleus.

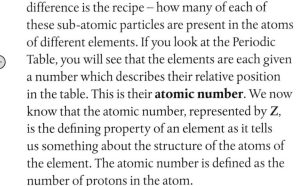

**The atomic number (Z) is defined as the number of protons in the nucleus.**

## Atomic number and mass number

We are now in a position to understand how the atoms of different elements differ. They are all made from the same basic ingredients, the sub-atomic particles. The only difference is the recipe – how many of each of these sub-atomic particles are present in the atoms of different elements. If you look at the Periodic Table, you will see that the elements are each given a number which describes their relative position in the table. This is their **atomic number**. We now know that the atomic number, represented by **Z**, is the defining property of an element as it tells us something about the structure of the atoms of the element. The atomic number is defined as the number of protons in the atom.

As an atom has no overall charge, the positive charge of the protons must be balanced by the negative charge of the electrons. The atomic number is also equal to the number of electrons.

The electron has such a very small mass that it is essentially ignored in mass calculations. The mass of an atom depends on the number of protons and neutrons only. The **mass number**, given the symbol **A**, is defined as the number of protons plus the number of neutrons in an atom. An atom is identified in the following way:

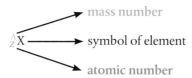

We can use these numbers to find the composition of any atom.

$$\text{number of protons (p)} = \text{number of electrons} = Z$$
$$\text{number of neutrons (n)} = A - \text{number of protons} = A - Z$$

Consider an atom of aluminium:

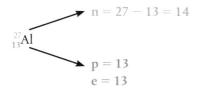

An aluminium atom is made from 13 protons and 13 electrons. An atom of gold on the other hand has 79 protons and 79 electrons. Can you find gold in the Periodic Table?

## Isotopes

Find chlorine in the Periodic Table. There are two numbers associated with the element, as shown below.

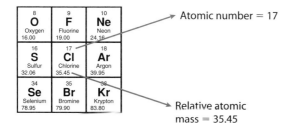

How can an element have a fractional relative atomic mass if both the proton and neutron have a relative mass of 1? One reason is that atoms of the same element with different mass numbers exist, so it is necessary to work within an average value – as discussed in Chapter 1.

To have different mass numbers, the atoms must have different numbers of neutrons – all the atoms have the same number of protons as they are all chlorine atoms. Atoms of the same element with different numbers of neutrons are called **isotopes**.

The isotopes show the same chemical properties, as a difference in the number of neutrons makes no difference to how they react and so they occupy the same place in the Periodic Table.

 Make sure you have a precise understanding of the terms identified in the subject guide. The atomic number, for example, is defined in terms of the number of protons, not electrons.

 **The mass number (A) is the number of protons plus the number of neutrons in an atom. As it gives the total number of nucleons in the nucleus, it is sometimes called the nucleon number.**

 **Isotopes are atoms of the same element with different mass numbers.**

The word 'isotope' derives from the Greek for 'same place'. As isotopes are atoms of the same element, they occupy the same place in the Periodic Table.

A common error is to misunderstand the meaning of 'physical property'. A difference in the number of neutrons is not a different physical property. A physical property of a substance can be measured without changing the chemical composition of the substance, e.g. melting point, density.

Radioisotopes are used in nuclear medicine for diagnostics, treatment, and research, as tracers in biochemical and pharmaceutical research, and as 'chemical clocks' in geological and archaeological dating.

Radioactive isotopes are extremely hazardous and their use is of international concern. The International Atomic Energy Agency (IAEA) promotes the peaceful use of nuclear energy. The organization was awarded the Nobel Peace Prize in 2005.

**When an atom loses electrons, a positive ion is formed and when it gains electrons, a negative ion is formed. Positive ions are called cations and negative ions are called anions.**

Chlorine exists as two isotopes, $^{35}$Cl and $^{37}$Cl. The average relative mass of the isotopes is, however, not 36, but 35.45. This value is closer to 35 as there are more $^{35}$Cl atoms in nature – it is the more abundant isotope. In a sample of 100 chlorine atoms, there are 77.5 atoms of $^{35}$Cl and 22.5 atoms of the heavier isotope, $^{37}$Cl.

To work out the average mass of one atom we first have to calculate the total mass of the hundred atoms:

$$\text{total mass} = (77.5 \times 35) + (22.5 \times 37) = 3545$$

$$\text{relative average mass} = \frac{\text{total mass}}{\text{number of atoms}} = \frac{3545}{100} = 35.45$$

The two isotopes are both atoms of chlorine with 17 protons and 17 electrons.

- $^{35}$Cl; number of neutrons = 35 − 17 = 18
- $^{37}$Cl; number of neutrons = 37 − 17 = 20

Although both isotopes essentially have the same chemical properties, the difference in mass does lead to different physical properties such as boiling and melting points. Heavier isotopes move more slowly at a given temperature and these differences can be used to separate isotopes.

### Exercises

**1** State two physical properties other than boiling and melting point that would differ for the two isotopes of chlorine.

**2** Explain why the relative atomic mass of tellurium is greater than the relative atomic mass of iodine, even though iodine has a greater atomic number.

Uranium exists in nature as two isotopes, uranium-235 and uranium-238. One key stage in the Manhattan Project (the development of the atomic bomb during World War II) was the enrichment of uranium with the lighter and less abundant isotope, as this is the atom which splits more easily. It is only 0.711% abundant in nature. First the uranium was converted to a gaseous compound (the hexafluoride $UF_6$). Gaseous molecules with the lighter uranium isotope move faster than those containing the heavier isotope at the same temperature and so the isotopes could be separated. Isotope enrichment is employed in many countries as part of nuclear energy and weaponry programmes. This is discussed in more detail in Chapter 14.

### NATURE OF SCIENCE

Science is a collaborative endeavour and it is common for scientists to work in teams between disciplines, laboratories, organizations, and countries. The Manhattan Project, which produced the first nuclear bomb, employed more than 130 000 people working in secret at different production and research sites. Today such collaboration is facilitated by virtual communication which allows scientists around the globe to work together.

## Ions

The atomic number is defined in terms of number of protons because it is a fixed characteristic of the element. The number of protons identifies the element in the same way your fingerprints identify you. The number of protons and neutrons never changes during a chemical reaction. It is the electrons which are responsible for chemical change. Chapter 4 will examine how atoms can lose or gain electrons to form **ions**. When the number of protons in a particle is no longer balanced by the number of electrons, the particles has a non-zero charge. When an atom loses electrons it forms a positive ion or **cation**, as the number of protons is now greater than the number of electrons. Negative ions or **anions** are formed when atoms gain electrons. The magnitude of the charge depends on the number of electrons lost or gained. The loss or gain of electrons makes a very big difference to the chemical properties. You swallow sodium ions, $Na^+$, every time you eat table salt, whereas (as you will discover in Chapter 3) sodium atoms, Na, are dangerously reactive.

An aluminium ion is formed when the atom loses three electrons. There is no change in the atomic or mass numbers of an ion because the number of protons and neutrons remains the same.

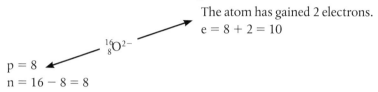

The atom has lost 3 electrons.
e = 13 − 3 = 10

$^{27}_{13}Al^{3+}$

p = 13
n = 27 − 13 = 14

Oxygen forms the oxide ion when the atom gains two electrons.

The atom has gained 2 electrons.
e = 8 + 2 = 10

$^{16}_{8}O^{2-}$

p = 8
n = 16 − 8 = 8

The element radium was first discovered by the Polish–French scientist Marie Curie. She is the only person to win Nobel Prizes in both Physics and Chemistry. The Curies were a remarkable family for scientific honours – Marie shared her first prize with husband Pierre, and her daughter Irène shared hers with her husband Frédéric. All the Curies' prizes were for work on radioactivity.

## Worked example

Identify the sub-atomic particles present in an atom of $^{226}$Ra.

### Solution

The number identifying the atom is the atomic number. We can find the atomic number from the IB data booklet (section 5).

We have Z = 88 and A = 226

In other words:

- number of protons (p) = 88
- number of electrons (e) = 88
- number of neutrons (n) = 226 − 88 = 138

## Worked example

Most nutrient elements in food are present in the form of ions. The calcium ion $^{40}Ca^{2+}$, for example, is essential for healthy teeth and bones. Identify the sub-atomic particles present in the ion.

### Solution

We can find the atomic number from the IB data booklet (section 5). We have Z = 20 and A = 40:

- number of protons (p) = 20
- number of neutrons (n) = 40 − 20 = 20

As the ion has a positive charge of 2+ there are two more protons than electrons:

- number of electrons = 20 − 2 = 18

## Worked example

Identify the species with 19 protons, 20 neutrons and 18 electrons.

**Solution**

- the number of protons tells us the atomic number; $Z = 19$ and so the element is potassium: K
- the mass number $= p + n = 19 + 20 = 39$: $^{39}_{19}K$
- the charge will be $= p - e = 19 - 18 = +1$ as there is one extra proton: $^{39}_{19}K^+$

## Exercises

**3** Use the Periodic Table to identify the sub-atomic particles present in the following species.

| | Species | No. of protons | No. of neutrons | No. of electrons |
|---|---|---|---|---|
| **(a)** | $^7Li$ | | | |
| **(b)** | $^1H$ | | | |
| **(c)** | $^{14}C$ | | | |
| **(d)** | $^{19}F^-$ | | | |
| **(e)** | $^{56}Fe^{3+}$ | | | |

**4** Isoelectronic species have the same number of electrons. Identify the following isoelectronic species by giving the correct symbol and charge. You will need a Periodic Table.

The first one has been done as an example.

| | Species | No. of protons | No. of neutrons | No. of electrons |
|---|---|---|---|---|
| | $^{40}Ca^{2+}$ | 20 | 20 | 18 |
| **(a)** | | 18 | 22 | 18 |
| **(b)** | | 19 | 20 | 18 |
| **(c)** | | 17 | 18 | 18 |

**5** Which of the following species contain more electrons than neutrons?

**A** $^2_1H$      **B** $^{11}_5B$      **C** $^{16}_8O^{2-}$      **D** $^{19}_9F^-$

**6** Which of the following gives the correct composition of the $^{71}Ga^+$ ion present in the mass spectrometer when gallium is analysed.

| | Protons | Neutrons | Electrons |
|---|---|---|---|
| **A** | 31 | 71 | 30 |
| **B** | 31 | 40 | 30 |
| **C** | 31 | 40 | 32 |
| **D** | 32 | 40 | 31 |

## Relative atomic masses of some elements

An instrument known as a **mass spectrometer** can be used to measure the mass of individual atoms. The mass of a hydrogen atom is $1.67 \times 10^{-24}$ g and that of a carbon atom is $1.99 \times 10^{-23}$ g. As the masses of all elements are in the range $10^{-24}$ to $10^{-22}$ g and these numbers are beyond our direct experience, it makes more sense to use relative values. The mass needs to be recorded relative to some agreed standard. As carbon is a very common element which is easy to transport and store because it is a solid, its isotope, $^{12}C$, was chosen as the standard in 1961. As discussed in Chapter 1 this is given a relative mass of exactly 12, as shown below.

| Element | Symbol | Relative atomic mass |
|---|---|---|
| carbon | C | 12.011 |
| chlorine | Cl | 35.453 |
| hydrogen | H | 1.008 |
| iron | Fe | 55.845 |
| **Standard isotope** | **Symbol** | **Relative atomic mass** |
| carbon-12 | $^{12}C$ | 12.000 |

Carbon-12 is the most abundant isotope of carbon but carbon-13 and carbon-14 also exist. This explains why the average value for the element is greater than 12.

## Mass spectra

The results of the analysis by the mass spectrometer are presented in the form of a **mass spectrum**. The horizontal axis shows the mass/charge ratio of the different ions on the carbon-12 scale, which in most cases can be considered equivalent to their mass. The percentage abundance of the ions is shown on the vertical scale.

The mass spectrum of gallium in Figure 2.6 shows that in a sample of 100 atoms, 60 have a mass of 69 and 40 have a mass of 71. We can use this information to calculate the relative atomic mass of the element.

total mass of 100 atoms = $(60 \times 69) + (40 \times 71) = 6980$

relative average mass = $\dfrac{\text{total mass}}{\text{number of atoms}} = \dfrac{6980}{100} = 69.80$

> The relative atomic mass of an element ($A_r$) is the average mass of an atom of the element, taking into account all its isotopes and their relative abundance, compared to one atom of carbon-12.

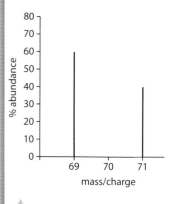

**Figure 2.6** Mass spectrum for gallium. The number of lines indicates the number of isotopes (two in this case), the value on the x-axis indicates their mass number (69 and 71) and the y-axis shows the percentage abundance.

### Worked example

Deduce the relative atomic mass of the element rubidium from the data given in Figure 2.7.

#### Solution

Consider a sample of 100 atoms.

total mass of 100 atoms = $(85 \times 77) + (87 \times 23) = 8546$

relative atomic mass = average mass of atom = $\dfrac{\text{total mass}}{\text{number of atoms}} = \dfrac{8546}{100} = 85.46$

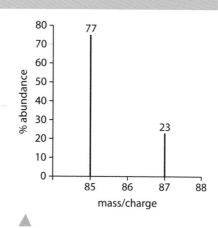

**Figure 2.7** Mass spectrum for rubidium.

## Worked example

Boron exists in two isotopic forms, $^{10}B$ and $^{11}B$. $^{10}B$ is used as a control for nuclear reactors. Use your Periodic Table to find the abundances of the two isotopes.

### Solution

Consider a sample of 100 atoms.

Let $x$ atoms be $^{10}B$ atoms. The remaining atoms are $^{11}B$.

number of $^{11}B$ atoms $= 100 - x$

total mass of 100 atoms $= x \times 10 + (100 - x) \times 11 = 10x + 1100 - 11x = 1100 - x$

$$\text{average mass} = \frac{\text{total mass}}{\text{number of atoms}} = \frac{1100 - x}{100}$$

From the Periodic Table, the relative atomic mass of boron = 10.81.

$$10.81 = \frac{1100 - x}{100}$$
$$1081 = 1100 - x$$

$$x = 1100 - 1081 = 19$$

The abundances are $^{10}B = 19\%$ and $^{11}B = 81\%$

## Exercises

**7** What is the same for an atom of phosphorus-26 and an atom of phosphorus-27?

   **A** atomic number and mass number
   **B** number of protons and electrons
   **C** number of neutrons and electrons
   **D** number of protons and neutrons

**8** Use the Periodic Table to find the percentage abundance of neon-20, assuming that neon has only one other isotope, neon-22.

**9** The relative abundances of the two isotopes of chlorine are shown in this table:

| Isotope | Relative abundance |
|---------|--------------------|
| $^{35}Cl$ | 75% |
| $^{37}Cl$ | 25% |

Use this information to deduce the mass spectrum of chlorine gas, $Cl_2$.

**10** Magnesium has three stable isotopes – $^{24}Mg$, $^{25}Mg$, and $^{26}Mg$. The lightest isotope has an abundance of 78.90%. Calculate the percentage abundance of the other isotopes.

**11** The Geiger–Marsden experiment, supervised by Ernest Rutherford, gave important evidence for the structure of the atom. Positively charged alpha particles were fired at a piece of gold foil. Most of the particles passed through with only minor deflections but a small number rebounded from the foil.

How did this experiment change our knowledge of the atom?

   **A** It provided evidence for the existence of discrete atomic energy levels.
   **B** It provided evidence for a positively charged dense nucleus.
   **C** It provided evidence that electrons move in unpredictable paths around the nucleus.
   **D** It provided evidence for the existence of an uncharged particle in the nucleus.

In 1911, a 40 kg meteorite fell in Egypt. Isotopic and chemical analysis of oxygen extracted from this meteorite show a different relative atomic mass to that of oxygen normally found on Earth. This value matched measurements made of the Martian atmosphere by the Viking landing in 1976, showing that the meteorite had originated from Mars.

## 2.2 Electron configuration

## Understandings:

- Emission spectra are produced when photons are emitted from atoms as excited electrons return to a lower energy level.
- The line emission spectrum of hydrogen provides evidence for the existence of electrons in discrete energy levels, which converge at higher energies.

### Guidance
*The names of the different series in the hydrogen line spectrum are not required.*

- The main energy level or shell is given an integer number, **n**, and can hold a maximum number of electrons, $2n^2$.
- A more detailed model of the atom describes the division of the main energy level into s, p, d, and f sub-levels of successively higher energies.
- Sub-levels contain a fixed number of orbitals, regions of space where there is a high probability of finding an electron.
- Each orbital has a defined energy state for a given electronic configuration and chemical environment and can hold two electrons of opposite spin.

## Applications and skills:

- Description of the relationship between colour, wavelength, frequency, and energy across the electromagnetic spectrum.

### Guidance
*Details of the electromagnetic spectrum are given in the IB data booklet in section 3.*

- Distinction between a continuous spectrum and a line spectrum.
- Description of the emission spectrum of the hydrogen atom, including the relationships between the lines and energy transitions to the first, second, and third energy levels.
- Recognition of the shape of an s orbital and the $p_x$, $p_y$, and $p_z$ atomic orbitals.
- Application of the Aufbau principle, Hund's rule, and the Pauli exclusion principle to write electron configurations for atoms and ions up to $Z = 36$.

### Guidance
- *Full electron configurations (e.g. $1s^2 2s^2 2p^6 3s^2 3p^4$) and condensed electron configurations (e.g. [Ne] $3s^2 3p^4$) should be covered.*
- *Orbital diagrams should be used to represent the character and relative energy of orbitals. Orbital diagrams refer to arrow-in-box diagrams, such as the one given below.*

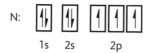

*The electron configurations of Cr and Cu as exceptions should be covered.*

Atoms of different elements give out light of a distinctive colour when an electric discharge is passed through a vapour of the element. Similarly, metals can be identified by the colour of the flame produced when their compounds are heated in a Bunsen burner. Analysis of the light emitted by different atoms has given us insights into the electron configurations within the atom.

To interpret these results we must consider the nature of electromagnetic radiation.

## The electromagnetic spectrum

Electromagnetic radiation comes in different forms of differing energy. The visible light we need to see the world is only a small part of the full spectrum, which ranges from low-energy radio waves to high-energy gamma rays. All electromagnetic waves

**(a)**

**(b)**

**(c)**

▲
Flame tests on the compounds of (a) sodium, (b) potassium, and (c) copper.

Flame colours can be used to identify unknown compounds.

69

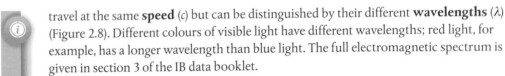

All electromagnetic waves travel at the same speed, $c = 3.00 \times 10^8$ m s$^{-1}$. This is the cosmic speed limit as, according to Einstein's Theory of Relativity, nothing in the universe can travel faster than this.

travel at the same **speed** ($c$) but can be distinguished by their different **wavelengths** ($\lambda$) (Figure 2.8). Different colours of visible light have different wavelengths; red light, for example, has a longer wavelength than blue light. The full electromagnetic spectrum is given in section 3 of the IB data booklet.

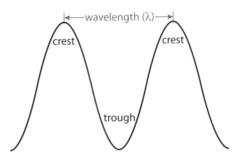

**Figure 2.8** Snapshot of a wave at a given instant. The distance between successive crests or peaks is called the wavelength ($\lambda$).

The number of waves which pass a particular point in 1 s is called the **frequency** ($\nu$); the shorter the wavelength, the higher the frequency. Blue light has a higher frequency than red light.

The wavelength and frequency are related by the equation:

$$c = \nu \lambda$$

The distance between two successive crests (or troughs) is called the wavelength ($\lambda$). The frequency ($\nu$) of the wave is the number of waves which pass a point in one second. The wavelength and frequency are related by the equation $c = \nu \lambda$ where $c$ is the speed of light.

where $c$ is the speed of light.

White light is a mixture of light waves of differing wavelengths or colours. We see this when sunlight passes through a prism to produce a **continuous spectrum** or as a rainbow when light is scattered through water droplets in the air.

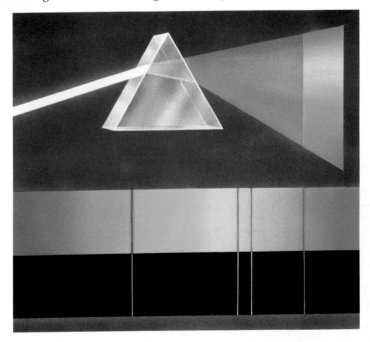

A continuous spectrum is produced when white light is passed through a prism. The different colours merge smoothly into one another. The two spectra below the illustration of the prism show, (top) a continuous spectrum with a series of discrete absorption lines and (bottom) a line emission spectrum.

As well as visible light, atoms emit infrared radiation, which has a longer wavelength than red light, and ultraviolet radiation, with a shorter wavelength than violet light. The complete electromagnetic spectrum is shown in Figure 2.9.

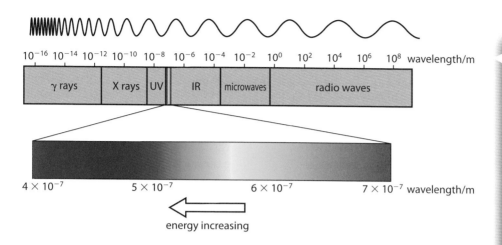

**Figure 2.9** The changing wavelength (in m) of electromagnetic radiation through the spectrum is shown by the trace across the top. At the short wavelength end (on the left) of the spectrum are γ rays, X rays, and ultraviolet light. In the centre of the spectrum are wavelengths that the human eye can see, known as visible light. Visible light comprises light of different wavelengths, energies, and colours. At the longer wavelength end of the spectrum (on the right) are infrared radiation, microwaves, and radio waves. The visible spectrum gives us only a small window to see the world.

## Atomic absorption and emission line spectra

When electromagnetic radiation is passed through a collection of atoms some of the radiation is absorbed and used to excite the atoms from a lower energy level to a higher energy level. The spectrometer analyses the transmitted radiation relative to the incident radiation and an **absorption spectrum** is produced.

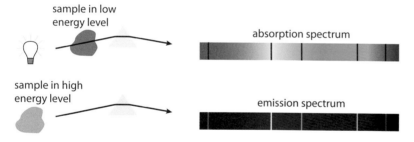

**Figure 2.10** The origin of absorption and emission spectra. An absorption spectrum shows the radiation absorbed as atoms move from a lower to a higher energy level. An emission spectrum is produced when an atom moves from a higher to a lower level.

When white light is passed through hydrogen gas, an absorption **line spectrum** is produced with some colours of the continuous spectrum missing. If a high voltage is applied to the gas, a corresponding **emission** line spectrum is produced.

**Investigating flame tests**

Full details of how to carry out this experiment with a worksheet are available online.

Visible emission spectrum of hydrogen. These lines form the Balmer series and you should note that they converge at higher energies. Similar series are found in the ultraviolet region – the Lyman Series – and in the infrared region – the Paschen series.

The colours present in the emission spectrum are the same as those that are missing from the absorption spectra. As different elements have different line spectra they can be used like barcodes to identify unknown elements. They give us valuable information about the electron configurations of different atoms.

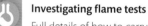 Emission spectra could be observed using discharge tubes of different gases and a spectroscope.

The elemental composition of stars can be determined by analysing their absorption spectra. This is discussed in more detail in Chapter 14.

The element helium was discovered in the Sun before it was found on Earth. Some unexpected spectral lines were observed when the absorption spectra of sunlight was analysed. These lines did not correspond to any known element. The new element was named after the Greek word *helios*, which means 'Sun'. Emission and absorption spectra can be used like barcodes to identify the different elements.

## Evidence for the Bohr model

How can a hydrogen atom absorb and emit energy? A simple picture of the atom was considered earlier with the electron orbiting the nucleus in a circular energy level. Niels Bohr proposed that an electron moves into an orbit or higher energy level further from the nucleus when an atom absorbs energy. The **excited state** produced is, however, unstable and the electron soon falls back to the lowest level or **ground state**. The energy the electron gives out when it falls into lower levels is in the form of electromagnetic radiation. One packet of energy (quantum) or **photon** is released for each electron transition (Figure 2.11). Photons of ultraviolet light have more energy than photons of infrared light. The energy of the photon is proportional to the frequency of the radiation.

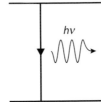

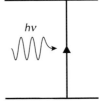

excited state

ground state

When an atom falls from excited state to the ground state, light of a specific frequency $v$ is emitted.

When an atom moves from the ground state to an excited state, light of a specific frequency $v$ is absorbed.

**Figure 2.11** Emission and absorption spectra are the result of an energy transition between the ground and excited states.

* A continuous spectrum shows an unbroken sequence of frequencies, such as the spectrum of visible light.

* A line emission spectrum has only certain frequencies of light as it is produced by excited atoms and ions as they fall back to a lower energy level.

* A line absorption spectrum is a continuous spectrum except for certain colours which are absorbed as the atoms are excited to higher energy levels.

The energy of the photon of light emitted is equal to the energy change in the atom:

$$\Delta E_{electron} = E_{photon}$$

It is also related to the frequency of the radiation by the Planck equation:

$$E_{photon} = h\,v$$

This equation and the value of $h$ (the Planck constant) are given in sections 1 and 2 of the IB data booklet.

This leads to:

$$\Delta E_{electron} = h\,v$$

This is a very significant equation as it shows that line spectra allow us to glimpse the inside of the atom. The atoms emit photons of certain energies which give lines of certain frequencies, because the electron can only occupy certain orbits. The energy levels can be thought of as a staircase. The electron cannot change its energy in a continuous way, in the same way that you cannot stand between steps; it can only change its energy by discrete amounts. This energy of the atom is **quantized**. The line spectrum is crucial evidence for quantization: if the energy were not quantized, the emission spectrum would be continuous.

The idea that electromagnetic waves can be thought of as a stream of photons or quanta is one aspect of quantum theory. The theory has implications for human knowledge and technology. The key idea is that energy can only be transferred in discrete amounts or quanta. Quantum theory shows us that our everyday experience cannot be transferred to the microscopic world of the atom and has led to great technological breakthroughs such as the modern computer. It has been estimated that 30% of the gross national product of the USA depends on the application of quantum theory. In the modern world our scientific understanding has led to many technological developments. These new technologies in their turn drive developments in science. The implications of the quantum theory for the electron are discussed in more detail later (page 74). Note that 'discrete' has a different meaning to 'discreet'.

When asked to distinguish between a line spectrum and a continuous spectrum, references should be made to discrete or continuous energy levels and all or specific colours, wavelengths, or frequencies.

The amount of light absorbed at particular frequency depends on the identity and concentration of atoms present. Atomic absorption spectroscopy is used to measure the concentration of metallic elements.

## The hydrogen spectrum

The hydrogen atom gives out energy when an electron falls from a higher to a lower energy level. Hydrogen produces visible light when the electron falls to the second energy level ($n = 2$). The transitions to the first energy level ($n = 1$) correspond to a higher energy change and are in the ultraviolet region of the spectrum. Infrared radiation is produced when an electron falls to the third or higher energy levels (Figure 2.12).

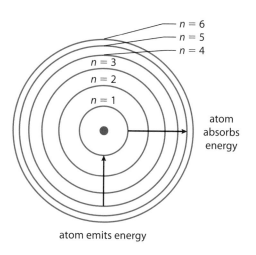

atom emits energy

**Figure 2.12** When an electron is excited from a lower to a higher energy level, energy is absorbed and a line in an absorption spectrum is produced. When an electron falls from a higher to a lower energy level, radiation is given out by the atom and a line in an emission spectrum is produced.

The pattern of the lines in Figure 2.12 gives us a picture of the energy levels in the atom. The lines **converge** at higher energies because the energy levels inside the atoms are closer together at higher energy. When an electron is at the highest energy $n = \infty$, it is no longer in the atom and the atom has been ionized. The energy needed to remove an electron from the ground state of an atom in a mole of gaseous atoms, ions, or molecules is called the **ionization energy**. Ionization energies can also be used to support this model of the atom (see page 85).

The energy of a photon of electromagnetic radiation is directly proportional to its frequency and inversely proportional to its wavelength. It can be calculated from the Planck equation ($E = h \nu$), which is given in section 1 of the IB data booklet.

The first ionization energy of an element is the minimum energy needed to remove one mole of electrons from one mole of gaseous atoms in their ground state.

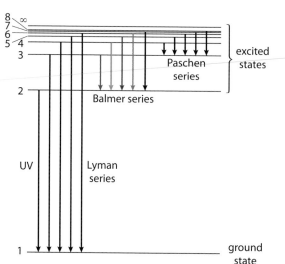

**Figure 2.13** Energy levels of the hydrogen atom showing the transitions which produce the Lyman, Balmer, and Paschen series. The transition $1 \rightarrow \infty$ corresponds to ionization:

$$H(g) \rightarrow H^+(g) + e^-$$

This is discussed in more detail later.

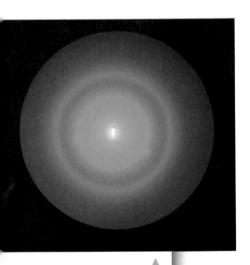

Demonstration of wave–particle duality. An electron gun has been fired at a thin sheet of graphite. The electrons passed through the graphite and hit a luminescent screen, producing the pattern of rings associated with diffraction. Diffraction occurs when a wave passes through an aperture similar in size to its wavelength. Quantum theory shows that electrons have wavelengths inversely proportional to their momentum (momentum is the product of their mass and velocity).

The Uncertainty Principle **TOK** can be thought of as an extreme example of the observer effect discussed on page 958. The significance of the Uncertainty Principle is that it shows the effect cannot be decreased indefinitely by improving the apparatus. There is an inherent uncertainty in our measurements. What are the implications of this for the limits of human knowledge?

## Wave and particle models

Although the Bohr model of the atom was able to explain the emission spectrum of hydrogen with great success, it failed to predict the spectral lines of atoms with more than one electron. The model is a simplification. To develop the model of the atom further, we need to reconsider the nature of light and matter.

We saw earlier that light could either be described by its frequency, $v$, which is a wave property, or by the energy of individual particles, $E$ (called photons or quanta of light), which make up a beam of light. The two properties are related by the Planck equation $E = h\,v$. Both wave and particle models have traditionally been used to explain scientific phenomena and you may be tempted to ask which model gives the 'true' description of light. We now realize that neither model gives a complete explanation of light's properties – both models are needed.

- The diffraction, or spreading out, of light that occurs when light passes through a small slit can only be explained by a wave model.
- The scattering of electrons that occurs when light is incident on a metal surface is best explained using a particle model of light.

In a similar way, quantum theory suggests that it is sometimes preferable to think of an electron (or indeed any particle) as having wave properties. The diffraction pattern produced when a beam of electrons is passed through a thin sheet of graphite demonstrates the wave properties of electrons. To understand the electron configurations of atoms it is useful to consider a wave description of the electron.

 **NATURE OF SCIENCE**

Models are used in science to explain processes that may not be observable. The models can be simple or complex in nature but must match the experimental evidence if they are to be accepted. The power of the wave and particle models is that they are based on our everyday experience, but this is also their limitation. We should not be too surprised if this way of looking at the world breaks down when applied to the atomic scale, as this is beyond our experience. The model we use depends on the phenomena we are trying to explain.

When differences occur between the theoretical predictions and experimental data, the models must be modified or replaced by new models. Bohr's model of the hydrogen atom was very successful in explaining the line spectra of the hydrogen atom but had some difficulties. It could not explain the spectra of more complex atoms, or the relative intensities of the lines in the hydrogen spectra. It also suffered from a fundamental weakness in that it was based on postulates which combined ideas from classical and quantum physics in an ad hoc manner, with little experimental justification: ideally models should be consistent with the assumptions and premises of other theories. A modification of Bohr's model could only be achieved at the expense of changing our model of the electron as a particle. Dalton's atomic model and quantum theory are both examples of such radical changes of understanding, often called **paradigm shifts**.

## The Uncertainty Principle

Another fundamental problem with the Bohr model is that it assumes the electron's trajectory can be precisely described. This is now known to be impossible, as any attempt to measure an electron's position will disturb its motion. The act of focusing radiation to locate the electron gives the electron a random 'kick' which sends it hurtling off in a random direction.

According to Heisenberg's **Uncertainty Principle** we cannot know where an electron is at any given moment in time – the best we can hope for is a probability picture of where the electron is *likely* to be. The possible positions of an electron are spread out in space in the same way as a wave is spread across a water surface.

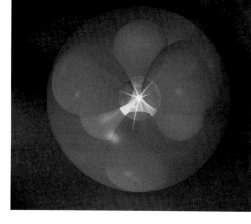

## Schrödinger model of the hydrogen atom

We have seen that the electron can be considered to have wave properties and that only a probability description of its location is possible at a given time. Both of these ideas are encapsulated in the Schrödinger model of the hydrogen atom. Erwin Schrödinger (1887–1961) proposed that a wave equation could be used to describe the behaviour of an electron in the same way that a wave equation could be used to described the behaviour of light. The equation can be applied to multi-electron systems and its solutions are known as **atomic orbitals**. An atomic orbital is a region around an atomic nucleus in which there is a 90% probability of finding the electron. The shape of the orbitals will depend on the energy of the electron. When an electron is in an orbital of higher energy it will have a higher probability of being found further from the nucleus.

### Exercises

**12** Emission and absorption spectra both provide evidence for:

**A** the existence of neutrons      **B** the existence of isotopes
**C** the existence of atomic energy levels      **D** the nuclear model of the atom

**13** The diagram shows the lowest five electron energy levels in the hydrogen atom.

$$n = 5$$
$$n = 4$$
$$n = 3$$
$$n = 2$$
$$n = 1$$

Deduce how many different frequencies in the visible emission spectrum of atomic hydrogen would arise as a result of electron transitions between these levels.

**A** 3      **B** 4      **C** 6      **D** 10

**14** Identify which of the following provide evidence to support the Bohr model of the hydrogen atom?

I    The energy of the lines in the emission spectra of atomic hydrogen.
II    The energy of the missing lines in the absorption spectra of helium as seen from the sun.
III   The relative intensity of the different spectral lines in the emission spectrum of atomic hydrogen.

**A** I only      **B** II only      **C** I and II      **D** I and III

Our model of the atom owes a great deal to the work of Niels Bohr and Werner Heisenberg, who worked together in the early years of quantum theory before World War II. But they found themselves on different sides when war broke out. The award-winning play and film *Copenhagen* is based on their meeting in the eponymous city in 1941 and explores their relationship, the uncertainty of the past, and the moral responsibilities of the scientist.

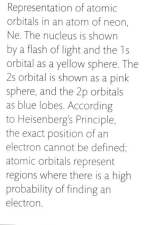

Representation of atomic orbitals in an atom of neon, Ne. The nucleus is shown by a flash of light and the 1s orbital as a yellow sphere. The 2s orbital is shown as a pink sphere, and the 2p orbitals as blue lobes. According to Heisenberg's Principle, the exact position of an electron cannot be defined; atomic orbitals represent regions where there is a high probability of finding an electron.

**TOK** In our efforts to learn as much as possible about the atom, we have found that certain things can never be known with certainty. Much of our knowledge must always remain uncertain. Some suggest that Heisenberg's Uncertainty Principle has major implications for *all* areas of knowledge. Does science have the power to inform thinking in other areas of knowledge such as philosophy and religion? To what extent should philosophy and religion take careful note of scientific developments?

The progressive nature of scientific knowledge is illustrated by the Nobel Prizes awarded between 1922 and 1933. The Physics prize was awarded to Bohr in 1922, Heisenberg in 1932, and Schrödinger in 1933.

## CHALLENGE YOURSELF

**3** State **two** ways in which the Schrödinger model of the hydrogen atom differs from that of the Bohr model.

# Atomic orbitals

## The first energy level has one 1s orbital

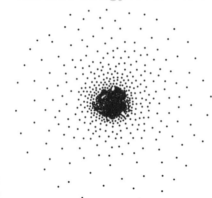

We saw that the electron in hydrogen occupies the first energy level in the ground state, which can hold a maximum of two electrons. To highlight the distinction between this wave description of the electron provided by the Schrödinger model and the circular orbits of the Bohr atom, we say the electron occupies a 1s orbital.

The dots in Figure 2.14 represent locations where the electron is most likely to be found. The denser the arrangement of dots, the higher the probability that the electron occupies this region of space. The electron can be found anywhere within a spherical space surrounding the nucleus.

**Figure 2.14** An electron in a 1s atomic orbital. The density of the dots gives a measure of the probability of finding the electron in this region.

The first energy level consists of a 1s atomic orbital which is spherical in shape.

**The electrons in the Bohr model occupy orbits, which are circular paths. An orbital, which is a wave description of the electron, shows the volume of space in which the electron is likely to be found.**

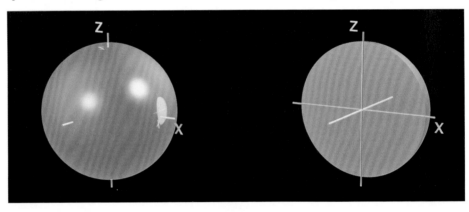

## The second energy level has a 2s and 2p level

The second energy level of the Bohr model is split into two **sub-levels** in the Schrödinger model. Further evidence of sub-shells comes from a consideration of patterns in first ionization energies, which will be discussed on page 90. The 2s sub-level is made up from one 2s orbital and can hold a maximum of two electrons, and the 2p sub-level is made up from three 2p orbitals and can hold six electrons.

The 2s orbital has the same symmetry as a 1s orbital but extends over a larger volume. So electrons in a 2s orbital are, on average, further from the nucleus than electrons in 1s orbitals and are at higher energy.

The 2s electron orbital. Just as a water wave can have crests and troughs, an orbital can have positive and negative areas. The blue area shows positive values, and the gold area negative. As it is the magnitude of the wave, not the sign, which determines the probability of finding an electron at particular positions, the sign is often not shown.

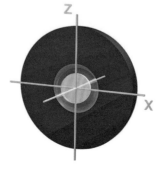

The 2p sub-level contains three 2p atomic orbitals of equal energy which are said to be **degenerate**. They all have the same dumbbell shape; the only difference is their orientation in space. They are arranged at right angles to each other with the nucleus at the centre.

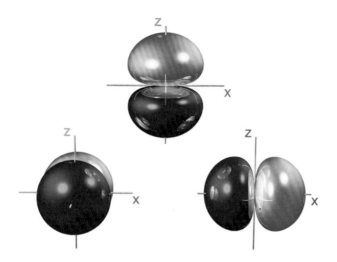

From left to right, the $p_y$, $p_z$, and $p_x$ atomic orbitals, localized along the $y$, $z$, and $x$-axes respectively (the $y$-axis comes out of the page). As they have the same energy, they are said to be degenerate. They form the 2p sub-level.

*(i)* If you wanted to be absolutely 100% sure of where the electron is you would have to draw an orbital the size of the universe.

## d and f orbitals

We have seen that the first energy level is made up from one sub-level and the second energy level is made up from two sub-levels. This pattern can be generalized; the $n$th energy level of the Bohr atom is divided into $n$ sub-levels. The third energy level is made up from three sub-levels: the 3s, 3p, and 3d. The d sub-level is made up from five d atomic orbitals.

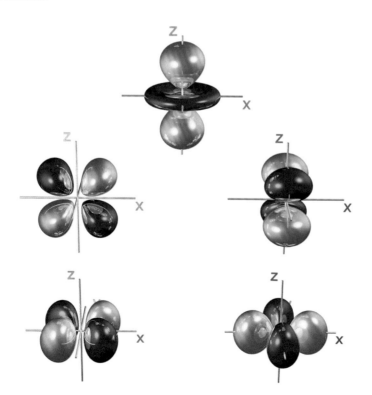

The five electron orbitals found in the 3d sub-level. Four of the orbitals are made up of four lobes, centred on the nucleus.

*(!)* You are expected to know the shapes and names of the s and p atomic orbitals, but not of the d atomic orbitals.

The labels s, p, d, and f relate to the nature of the spectral lines the model was attempting to explain. The corresponding spectroscopic terms are *sharp*, *principal*, *diffuse*, and *fine*.

The letters **s**, **p**, **d**, and **f** are used to identify different sub-levels and the atomic orbitals which comprise them. The fourth level ($n = 4$) is similarly made up from four sub-levels. The 4f sub-levels are made up from seven f atomic orbitals, but you are not required to know the shapes of these orbitals.

## Worked example

Draw the shapes of a 1s orbital and a $2p_x$ orbital.

### Solution

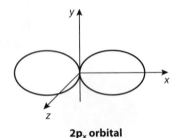

**1s orbital**                    **$2p_x$ orbital**

**Figure 2.15** A simple two-dimensional drawing is sufficient.

## Electron spin and the Pauli Exclusion Principle

The atomic orbitals associated with the different energy levels are shown in Figure 2.16. This diagram is a simplification, as the relative energy of the orbitals depends on the atomic number. This is discussed in more detail later. The relative energies of the 4s and 3d atomic orbitals is chemically significant.

**Figure 2.16** The relative energies of the atomic orbitals up to the 4p sub-level. The 3d sub-level falls below the 4s level for elements $Z > 20$.

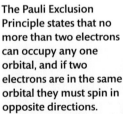

the 3d sub-level falls below the 4s level for elements $Z > 20$.

**The Pauli Exclusion Principle** states that no more than two electrons can occupy any one orbital, and if two electrons are in the same orbital they must spin in opposite directions.

An electron is uniquely characterized by its atomic orbital and spin. If two electrons occupied the same orbital spinning in the same direction, they would be the same electron.

Each atomic orbital can hold a maximum of two electrons. These electrons can occupy the same region of space despite their mutual repulsion as they spin in opposite directions.

## Exercises

**15** List the 4d, 4f, 4p, and 4s atomic orbitals in order of increasing energy.

**16** State the number of 4d, 4f, 4p, and 4s atomic orbitals.

## Sub-levels of electrons

The number of electrons in the sub-levels of the first four energy levels are shown in the table below.

| Level | Sub-level | Maximum number of electrons in sub-level | Maximum number of electrons in level |
|---|---|---|---|
| $n = 1$ | 1s | 2 | 2 |
| $n = 2$ | 2s | 2 | 8 |
| | 2p | 6 | |
| $n = 3$ | 3s | 2 | 18 |
| | 3p | 6 | |
| | 3d | 10 | |
| $n = 4$ | 4s | 2 | 32 |
| | 4p | 6 | |
| | 4d | 10 | |
| | 4f | 14 | |

We can see the following from the table.

- The $n$th energy level of the Bohr atom is divided into $n$ sub-levels. For example, the fourth level ($n = 4$) is made up from four sub-levels. The letters s, p, d, and f are used to identify different sub-levels.
- Each main level can hold a maximum of $2n^2$ electrons. The 3rd energy level, for example, can hold a maximum of 18 electrons ($2 \times 3^2 = 18$).
- s sub-levels can hold a maximum of 2 electrons.
- p sub-levels can hold a maximum of 6 electrons.
- d sub-levels can hold a maximum of 10 electrons.
- f sub-levels can hold a maximum of 14 electrons.

## Aufbau Principle: orbital diagrams

The electron configuration of the ground state of an atom of an element can be determined using the **Aufbau Principle**, which states that electrons are placed into orbitals of lowest energy first. Boxes can be used to represent the atomic orbitals, with single-headed arrows to represent the spinning electrons. The **electron configurations** of the first five elements are shown in Figure 2.17. The number of electrons in each sub-level is given as a superscript.

*Aufbau* means 'building up' in German.

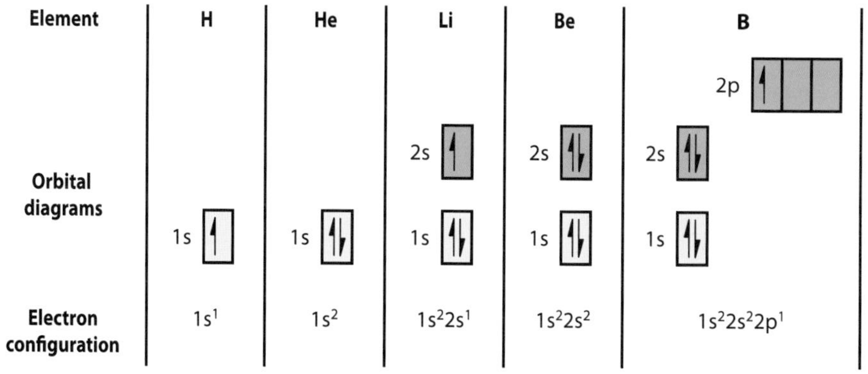

| Element | H | He | Li | Be | B |
|---|---|---|---|---|---|
| Orbital diagrams | 1s ↑ | 1s ↑↓ | 2s ↑ / 1s ↑↓ | 2s ↑↓ / 1s ↑↓ | 2p ↑ / 2s ↑↓ / 1s ↑↓ |
| Electron configuration | $1s^1$ | $1s^2$ | $1s^2 2s^1$ | $1s^2 2s^2$ | $1s^2 2s^2 2p^1$ |

**Figure 2.17** The electron configuration of the first five elements.

The next element in the Periodic Table is carbon. It has two electrons in the 2p sub-level. These could either pair up, and occupy the same p orbital, or occupy separate p orbitals. Following **Hund's third rule**, we can place the two electrons in separate orbitals because this configuration minimizes the mutual repulsion between them. As the 2p orbitals are perpendicular to each other and do not overlap, the two 2p electrons are unlikely to approach each other too closely. The electrons in the different 2p orbitals have parallel spins, as this leads to lower energy. The electron configurations of carbon and nitrogen are shown in Figure 2.18.

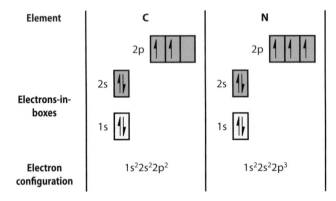

**Figure 2.18** Electron configurations of carbon and nitrogen.

> **Hund's rule:** If more than one orbital in a sub-level is available, electrons occupy different orbitals with parallel spins.

> **Do you need a useful mnemonic to the order of filling orbitals?** Figure 2.19 shows orbitals filled to sub-level 7s. Follow the arrows to see the order in which the sub-levels are filled.

The 2p electrons begin to pair up for oxygen ($1s^2 2s^2 2p_x^2 2p_y^1 2p_z^1$) and fluorine ($1s^2 2s^2 2p_x^2 2p_y^2 2p_z^1$). The 2p sub-shell is completed for neon ($1s^2 2s^2 2p_x^2 2p_y^2 2p_z^2$).

## Exercises

**17** Apply the *orbital diagram* method to determine the electron configuration of calcium.

**18** Deduce the number of unpaired electrons present in a phosphorus atom.

| 7s | 7p | 7d | 7f | 7g | 7h | 7h |
|----|----|----|----|----|----|----|
| 6s | 6p | 6d | 6f | 6g | 6h | |
| 5s | 5p | 5d | 5f | 5g | | |
| 4s | 4p | 4d | 4f | | | |
| 3s | 3p | 3d | | | | |
| 2s | 2p | | | | | |
| 1s | | | | | | |

**Figure 2.19** Order of filling sub-levels: 1s, 2s, 2p, 3s, 3p, 4s, 3d, 4p, 5s, 4d, 5p, 6s, 4f, 5d, 6p, 7s, 5f, 6d, 7s.

> The mathematical nature of the orbital description is illustrated by some simple relationships:
> - number of sub-levels at *n*th main energy level = $n$
> - number of orbitals at *n*th energy level = $n^2$
> - number of electrons at *n*th energy level = $2n^2$
> - number of orbitals at *l*th sub-level = $(2l + 1)$ where $n$ and $l$ are sometimes known as quantum numbers.

| Sub-level | s | p | d | f |
|-----------|---|---|---|---|
| *l* | 0 | 1 | 2 | 3 |

# The relative energy of the orbitals depends on the atomic number

The energy of an orbital depends on the attractions between the electrons and the nucleus and inter-electron repulsions. As these interactions change with the nuclear charge and the number of the electrons, that is the atomic number, so does the relative energy of the orbitals. All the sub-levels in the third energy level (3s, 3p, and 3d), for example, have the same energy for the hydrogen atom and only become separated as extra protons and electrons are added. The situation is particularly complicated when we reach the d block elements. The 3d and 4s levels are very close in energy and their relative separation is very sensitive to inter-electron repulsion. For the elements potassium and calcium, the 4s orbitals are filled before the 3d sub-level. Electrons are, however, first lost from the 4s sub-level when transitional metals form their ions, as once the 3d sub-level is occupied the 3d electrons push the 4s electrons to higher energy.

When the transition metal atoms form ions they lose electrons from the 4s sub-level before the 3d sub-level.

## Worked example

State the full electron configuration of vanadium and deduce the number of unpaired electrons.

### Solution

The atomic number of vanadium gives the number of electrons: Z = 23.

So the electronic configuration is: $1s^2 2s^2 2p^6 3s^2 3p^6 4s^2 3d^3$. Note: the 3d sub-level is filled after the 4s sub-level.

It is useful, however, to write the electronic configuration with the 3d sub-shell before the 4s: $1s^2 2s^2 2p^6 3s^2 3p^6 3d^3 4s^2$ as the 3d sub-level falls below the 4s orbital once the 4s orbital is occupied (i.e. for elements after Ca).

Three 3d orbitals each have an unpaired electron. Number of unpaired electrons = 3.

The worked example asked for the full electron configuration. Sometimes it is convenient to use an abbreviated form, where only the outer electrons are explicitly shown. The inner electrons are represented as a noble gas core. Using this notation, the electron configuration of vanadium is written [Ar] $3d^3 4s^2$, where [Ar] represents the electron configuration of Ar, which is $1s^2 2s^2 2p^6 3s^2 3p^6$.

The electron configurations of the first 30 elements are tabulated below.

**TOK** The abstract language of mathematics provides a powerful tool for describing the behaviour of electrons in the atom. The shapes and equations it generates have elegance and symmetry. What do such results tell us about the relationship between the natural sciences, mathematics, and the natural world?

| Element | Electron configuration | Element | Electron configuration | Element | Electron configuration |
|---|---|---|---|---|---|
| $_1$H | $1s^1$ | $_{11}$Na | $1s^2 2s^2 2p^6 3s^1$ | $_{21}$Sc | [Ar] $3d^1 4s^2$ |
| $_2$He | $1s^2$ | $_{12}$Mg | $1s^2 2s^2 2p^6 3s^2$ | $_{22}$Ti | [Ar] $3d^2 4s^2$ |
| $_3$Li | $1s^2 2s^1$ | $_{13}$Al | $1s^2 2s^2 2p^6 3s^2 3p^1$ | $_{23}$V | [Ar] $3d^3 4s^2$ |
| $_4$Be | $1s^2 2s^2$ | $_{14}$Si | $1s^2 2s^2 2p^6 3s^2 3p^2$ | $_{24}$Cr | [Ar] $3d^5 4s^1$ |
| $_5$B | $1s^2 2s^2 2p^1$ | $_{15}$P | $1s^2 2s^2 2p^6 3s^2 3p^3$ | $_{25}$Mn | [Ar] $3d^5 4s^2$ |
| $_6$C | $1s^2 2s^2 2p^2$ | $_{16}$S | $1s^2 2s^2 2p^6 3s^2 3p^4$ | $_{26}$Fe | [Ar] $3d^6 4s^2$ |
| $_7$N | $1s^2 2s^2 2p^3$ | $_{17}$Cl | $1s^2 2s^2 2p^6 3s^2 3p^5$ | $_{27}$Co | [Ar] $3d^7 4s^2$ |
| $_8$O | $1s^2 2s^2 2p^4$ | $_{18}$Ar | $1s^2 2s^2 2p^6 3s^2 3p^6$ | $_{28}$Ni | [Ar] $3d^8 4s^2$ |
| $_9$F | $1s^2 2s^2 2p^5$ | $_{19}$K | $1s^2 2s^2 2p^6 3s^2 3p^6 4s^1$ | $_{29}$Cu | [Ar] $3d^{10} 4s^1$ |
| $_{10}$Ne | $1s^2 2s^2 2p^6$ | $_{20}$Ca | $1s^2 2s^2 2p^6 3s^2 3p^6 4s^2$ | $_{30}$Zn | [Ar] $3d^{10} 4s^2$ |

The term 'valence' is derived from the Latin word for 'strength'.

The electrons in the outer energy level are mainly responsible for compound formation and are called **valence electrons**. Lithium has one valence electron in the outer second energy level ($2s^1$), beryllium has two ($2s^2$), boron has three ($2s^2p^1$), etc. The number of valence electrons follows a periodic pattern, which is discussed fully in Chapter 3. Atoms can have many other electron arrangements when in an excited state. Unless otherwise instructed, assume that you are being asked about ground-state arrangements.

For the d block elements three points should be noted:

- the 3d sub-level is written with the other $n = 3$ sub-levels as it falls below the 4s orbital once the 4s orbital is occupied (i.e. for elements after Ca), as discussed earlier;
- chromium has the electron configuration [Ar] $3d^5 4s^1$;
- copper has the electron configuration [Ar] $3d^{10}4s^1$.

To understand the electron configurations of copper and chromium it is helpful to consider the orbital diagram arrangements in Figure 2.20. As the 4s and 3d orbitals are close in energy, the electron configuration for chromium with a half-full d sub-level is relatively stable as it minimizes electrostatic repulsion, with six singly occupied atomic orbitals. This would be the expected configuration using Hund's rule if the 4s and 3d orbitals had exactly the same energy. Half-filled and filled sub-levels seem to be particularly stable: the configuration for copper is similarly due to the stability of the full d sub-level.

**Figure 2.20** The electron configuration of the 3rd and 4th energy levels for chromium and copper.

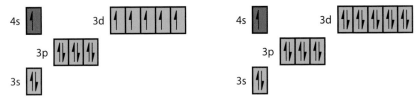

chromium: [Ar]$3d^5 4s^1$          copper: [Ar]$3d^{10}4s^1$

## Exercises

**19** Identify the sub-level which does not exist.

   **A** 5d      **B** 4d      **C** 3f      **D** 2p

**20** Which is the correct order of orbital filling according to the Aufbau Principle?

   **A** 4s 4p 4d 4f      **B** 4p 4d 5s 4f      **C** 4s 3d 4p 5s      **D** 4d 4f 5s 5p

**21** State the full ground-state electron configuration of the following elements.

   **(a)** V      **(b)** K      **(c)** Se      **(d)** Sr

**22** Determine the total number of electrons in d orbitals in a single iodine atom.

   **A** 5      **B** 10      **C** 15      **D** 20

**23** Identify the excited state (i.e. not a ground state) in the following electron configurations.

   **A** [Ne] $3s^2 3p^3$      **B** [Ne] $3s^2 3p^3 4s^1$      **C** [Ne] $3s^2 3p^6 4s^1$      **D** [Ne] $3s^2 3p^6 3d^1 4s^2$

**24** Deduce the number of unpaired electrons present in the ground state of a titanium atom.

   **A** 1      **B** 2      **C** 3      **D** 4

## Electron configuration of ions

As discussed earlier, positive ions are formed by the loss of electrons. These electrons are lost from the outer sub-levels. The electron configurations of the different aluminium ions formed when electrons are successively removed are for example:

- $Al^+$ is $1s^22s^22p^63s^2$
- $Al^{2+}$ is $1s^22s^22p^63s^1$
- $Al^{3+}$ is $1s^22s^22p^6$, etc.

When positive ions are formed for transition metals, the outer 4s electrons are removed before the 3d electrons, as discussed earlier.

For example, Cr is [Ar] $3d^54s^1$ and $Cr^{3+}$ is [Ar] $3d^3$

The electron configuration of negative ions is determined by adding the electrons into the next available electron orbital:

S is $1s^22s^22p^63s^23p^4$ and $S^{2-}$ is $1s^22s^22p^63s^23p^6$

## Worked example

State the ground-state electron configuration of the $Fe^{3+}$ ion.

### Solution

First find the electron configuration of the atom. Fe has 26 electrons: $1s^22s^22p^63s^23p^64s^23d^6$

As the 3d sub-level is below the 4s level for elements after calcium we write this as $1s^22s^22p^63s^23p^63d^64s^2$

Now remove the two electrons from the 4s sub-level and one electron from the 3d sub-level.

Electron configuration of $Fe^{3+}$ is $1s^22s^22p^63s^23p^63d^5$

Note the abbreviated electron configuration using the noble gas core is not acceptable when asked for the *full* electron configuration.

## Exercises

**25** State the full ground-state electron configuration of the following ions.

    **(a)** $O^{2-}$     **(b)** $Cl^-$     **(c)** $Ti^{3+}$     **(d)** $Cu^{2+}$

**26** State the electron configuration of the following transition metal ions by filling in the boxes below. Use arrows to represent the electron spin.

| | Ion | 3d | | | | | 4s |
|---|---|---|---|---|---|---|---|
| **(a)** | $Ti^{2+}$ | | | | | | |
| **(b)** | $Fe^{2+}$ | | | | | | |
| **(c)** | $Ni^{2+}$ | | | | | | |
| **(d)** | $Zn^{2+}$ | | | | | | |

**27 (a)** State the full electron configuration for neon.

    **(b)** State the formulas of two oppositely charged ions which have the same electron configuration as neon.

## Electronic configuration and the Periodic Table

We are now in a position to understand the structure of the Periodic Table (Figure 2.21):

- elements whose valence electrons occupy an s sub-level make up the **s block**;
- elements with valence electrons in p orbitals make up the **p block**;
- the **d block** and the **f block** are similarly made up of elements with outer electrons in d and f orbitals.

**Figure 2.21** The block structure of the Periodic Table is based on the sub-levels of the atom. H and He are difficult elements to classify. Although they have electron configurations that place them in the s block, their chemistry is not typical of Group 1 or Group 2 elements.

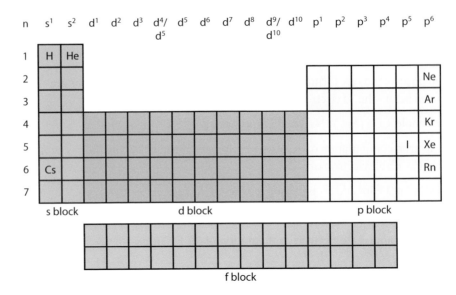

**The *ns* and *np* sub-levels are filled for elements in Period *n*. However the (*n* – 1)d sub-level is filled for elements in Period *n*.**

Some versions of the Periodic Table use the numbering 3–7 for Groups 13–17. In this version Group 3 elements have 3 valence electrons and Group 7 elements have 7 valence electrons. Although this is simpler in some respects it can lead to problems. How do you refer to the d-block elements? After extensive discussions, the IUPAC concluded that the 1 to 18 numbering provides the most clear and unambiguous labelling system. The Periodic Table has to meet the needs of young students and Nobel Prize winners alike.

Do atomic orbitals exist or are they primarily useful inventions to aid our understanding? What consequences might questions about the reality of scientific entities have for the public perception and understanding of the subject? If they are only fictions, how is it that they can yield such accurate predictions?

The position of an element in the Periodic Table is based on the occupied sub-level of highest energy in the ground-state atom. Conversely, the electron configuration of an element can be deduced directly from its position in the Periodic Table.

Here are some examples.

- Caesium is in Group 1 and Period 6 and has the electronic configuration: $[Xe]\ 6s^1$.
- Iodine is in Group 17 and in Period 5 and has the configuration: $[Kr]\ 5s^2 4d^{10} 5p^5$. Placing the 4d sub-level before the 5s gives $[Kr]\ 4d^{10} 5s^2 5p^5$. Iodine has 7 valence electrons in agreement with the pattern discussed on page 82.

## Exercises

**28** Use the Periodic Table to find the full ground-state electron configuration of the following elements.
   **(a)** Cl        **(b)** Nb        **(c)** Ge        **(d)** Sb

**29** Identify the elements which have the following ground-state electron configurations.
   **(a)** $[Ne]\ 3s^2 3p^2$        **(b)** $[Ar]\ 3d^5 4s^2$        **(c)** $[Kr]\ 5s^2$
   **(d)** $1s^2 2s^2 2p^6 3s^2 3p^6 3d^1 4s^2$

**30** State the total number of p orbitals containing one or more electrons in tin.

**31** How many electrons are there in all the d orbitals in an atom of barium?

**32** State the electron configuration of the ion $Cd^{2+}$.

## CHALLENGE YOURSELF

**4** Only a few atoms of element 109, meitnerium, have ever been made. Isolation of an observable quantity of the element has never been achieved, and may well never be. This is because meitnerium decays very rapidly.
   **(a)** Suggest the electron configuration of the ground-state atom of the element.
   **(b)** There is no g block in the Periodic Table as no elements with outer electrons in g orbitals exist in nature or have been made artificially. Suggest a minimum atomic number for such an element.

**5** State the full electron configuration of $U^{2+}$.

**6** Consider how the shape of the Periodic Table is related to the three-dimensional world we live in.
   **(a)** How many 3p and 3d orbitals would there be if there were only the *x* and *y* dimensions?
   **(b)** How many groups in the p and d block would there be in such a two-dimensional world?

We have seen how the model of the atom has changed over time. All these theories are still used today. Dalton's model adequately explains many properties of the states of matter, the Bohr model is used to explain chemical bonding, and the structure of the Periodic Table is explained by the wave description of the electron. In science we often follow Occam's razor and use the simplest explanation which can account for the phenomena. As Einstein said 'Explanations should be made as simple as possible, but not simpler.'

# 12.1 Electrons in atoms

## Understandings:

- In an emission spectrum, the limit of convergence at higher frequency corresponds to the first ionization energy.
- Trends in first ionization energy across periods account for the existence of main energy levels and sub-levels in atoms.
- Successive ionization energy data for an element give information that shows relations to electron configurations.

## Applications and skills:

- Solving problems using $E = h\nu$.

  **Guidance**
  *The value of Planck's constant and $E = h\nu$ are given in the IB data booklet in sections 1 and 2.*

- Calculation of the value of the first ionization energy from spectral data which gives the wavelength or frequency of the convergence limit.

  **Guidance**
  *Use of the Rydberg formula is not expected in calculations of ionization energy.*

- Deduction of the group of an element from its successive ionization energy data.
- Explanation of the trends and discontinuities in data on first ionization energy across a period.

## Ionization energy

The first ionization energy is the energy needed to remove one mole of electrons from the ground state of one mole of the gaseous atom. For hydrogen it corresponds to the following change with the electron being removed from the 1s orbital:

$$H(g) \rightarrow H^+(g) + e^-$$

Once removed from the atom, the electron is an infinite distance away from the nucleus and can considered to be in the $n = \infty$ energy level.

We saw earlier that the energy levels in the hydrogen converge at higher energy. This allows us to calculate the ionization energy from the convergence limit at higher frequency.

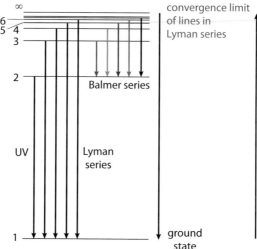

**Figure 2.22** The transition from $n = 1$ to $n = \infty$ corresponds to ionization.

**NATURE OF SCIENCE**

The best data for making accurate and precise descriptions is often quantitative as it is then amenable to mathematical analysis. The data can often be presented in a variety of formats that can be analysed. Scientists look for patterns in an attempt to discover relationships. The frequencies of the lines in the Lyman series, for example, can be analysed in different ways.

### Method 1

The frequencies of the lines in the Lyman series are shown below. All the transitions involve the electron falling from the excited levels with $n \geq 1$ to the $n = 1$ energy level. The difference between the frequencies in successive lines is given in the third column.

| Excited energy level | Frequency, $\nu$ / $\times 10^{14}$ s$^{-1}$ | $\Delta\nu$ / $\times 10^{14}$ s$^{-1}$ |
|:---:|:---:|:---:|
| 2 | 24.66 | 4.57 |
| 3 | 29.23 | 1.60 |
| 4 | 30.83 | 0.74 |
| 5 | 31.57 | 0.40 |
| 6 | 31.97 | 0.24 |
| 7 | 32.21 | 0.16 |
| 8 | 32.37 | |

As we are interested in the frequency of the line at which convergence occurs ($\Delta\nu = 0$), we have plotted a graph of $\nu$ against $\Delta\nu$ (Figure 2.23).

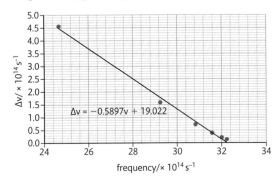

**Figure 2.23** A graph showing the frequency of the line emitted against the difference in frequency between successive lines in the Lyman series of the hydrogen atom.

As we can see, the points fit an approximate straight line with the equation:
$$\Delta\nu = -0.5897\nu + 19.022$$

This allows us to find the frequency at which convergence occurs ($\Delta\nu = 0$):
$$-0.5897\nu + 19.022 = 0$$

$$\nu = \frac{19.022}{0.5897} \times 10^{14}\ \text{s}^{-1} = 32.26 \times 10^{14}\ \text{s}^{-1}$$

### Method 2

Alternatively, a graph of the frequencies of the lines plotted against $1/n^2$ produces a straight line (Figure 2.24).

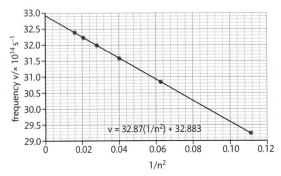

**Figure 2.24**

continued

*continued ....*

The frequency corresponding to $n = \infty$ can be read as the intercept on the y-axis and equals $32.883 \times 10^{14}$ s$^{-1}$.

The second method produced the best-fit straight line. We can use the frequency obtained to calculate the ionization energy.

Using the equation $E = h\nu$ we have the ionization energy for one atom:

$$E = 32.883 \times 10^{14} \text{ s}^{-1} \times 6.63 \times 10^{-34} \text{ J s}$$

So for one mole the ionization energy is given by:

$$\text{I.E.} = 32.883 \times 10^{14} \text{ s}^{-1} \times 6.63 \times 10^{-34} \text{ J s} \times 6.02 \times 10^{23} \text{ mol}^{-1}$$
$$= 1312 \text{ kJ mol}^{-1}$$

This agrees with the value given in section 8 of the IB data booklet.

The Bohr model of the atom (1913) was able to explain the relationship between the frequency of the lines and the *n* values for the energy levels, but Bohr was unable to provide experimental evidence to support his postulates. They were inconsistent as they came from an unjustified mixture of classical and quantum physics. In general scientists strive to develop hypotheses and theories that are compatible with accepted principles and that simplify and unify existing ideas. A deeper understanding needed the wave description of the electron suggested by de Broglie (1926).

Many scientific discoveries have involved flashes of intuition and many have come from speculation or simple curiosity about particular phenomena. Broglie speculated on the wave properties of particles by combining results from Einstein's theory of relativity with Planck's quantum theory.

Given that $E = h\nu$ from the Planck equation and $E = mc^2$ from Einstein's theory of special relativity, we have: $h\nu = mc^2$

This can be simplified to $h\nu/c = mc$ (for a photon $mc$ is the momentum $p$) to give

$$\frac{h\nu}{c} = \frac{h}{\lambda} = p$$

de Broglie suggested this result could be generalized for all particles; particles with greater momentum will have an associated shorter wavelength. Using this idea the energy levels of the hydrogen atom can be associated with standing waves of specific wavelength. The circumference of the orbit of the $n = 1$ energy level, for example, is equal to the wavelength of the de Broglie wave. The wave properties of the electrons, first suggested by de Broglie, were confirmed later by the **Davisson–Germer experiment** in which electrons were diffracted. To be scientific, an idea (e.g. a theory or hypothesis) must be testable.

Ionization energies can also be used to support this model of the atom.

## CHALLENGE YOURSELF

7  Use the graph produced by method 1 to calculate the ionization energy of hydrogen.
8  The convergence limit in the Balmer series corresponds to a frequency of $8.223 \times 10^{14}$ s$^{-1}$. Use this value along with other data given above to calculate the ionization energy.

An electron diffraction tube. The electrons fired at a thin sheet of graphite produce the patterns of rings associated with diffraction. de Broglie (1892–1987) correctly deduced that the electrons would have wavelengths inversely proportional to their momentum.

**TOK**

The de Broglie equation shows that macroscopic particles have too short a wavelength for their wave properties to be observed. Is it meaningful to talk of properties which can never be observed from sense perception?

## Patterns in successive ionization energies give evidence for the energy levels in the atom

Additional evidence for electron configuration in atoms comes from looking at patterns of successive ionization energies. For aluminium, the first ionization energy corresponds to the following process:

$$Al(g) \rightarrow Al^+(g) + e^-$$

The second ionization energy corresponds to the change:

$$Al^+(g) \rightarrow Al^{2+}(g) + e^-$$

and so on …

The ionization energies for aluminium are shown in Figure 2.25 and follow a similar pattern to the electron configuration.

**Figure 2.25** Successive ionization energies for aluminium. Note the jumps between the 3rd and 4th and between the 11th and 12th ionization energies as electrons are removed from lower energy levels. The wide range in values is best presented on a log scale.

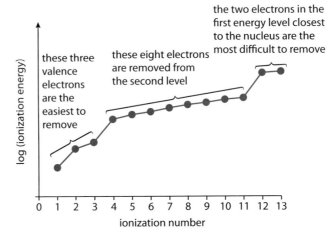

**TOK**

How does the method of data presentation influence how the data are interpreted? The use of scale can clarify important relationships but can also be used to manipulate data. How can you as a knower distinguish between the use and abuse of data presentation?

The electron configurations of aluminium ions as electrons are successively removed are shown in the table below.

| Ion | Electron configuration | Ion | Electron configuration |
|---|---|---|---|
| Al | $1s^2 2s^2 2p^6 3s^2 3p^1$ | $Al^{6+}$ | $1s^2 2s^2 2p^3$ |
| $Al^+$ | $1s^2 2s^2 2p^6 3s^2$ | $Al^{7+}$ | $1s^2 2s^2 2p^2$ |
| $Al^{2+}$ | $1s^2 2s^2 2p^6 3s^1$ | $Al^{8+}$ | $1s^2 2s^2 2p^1$ |
| $Al^{3+}$ | $1s^2 2s^2 2p^6$ | $Al^{9+}$ | $1s^2 2s^2$ |
| $Al^{4+}$ | $1s^2 2s^2 2p^5$ | $Al^{10+}$ | $1s^2 2s^1$ |
| $Al^{5+}$ | $1s^2 2s^2 2p^4$ | $Al^{11+}$ | $1s^2$ |

The graph in Figure 2.25 shows two key points.

1 There is an increase in successive ionization energies. The first ionization energy involves the separation of an electron from a singly charged ion and the second the separation of an electron from a doubly charged ion. The process becomes more difficult as there is increasing attraction between the higher charged positive ions and the oppositely charged electron.

2 There are jumps when electrons are removed from levels closer to the nucleus. The first three ionization energies involve the removal of electrons from the third level.

The 3p electron is removed first, followed by the electrons from the 3s orbital. An electron is removed from the second level for the fourth ionization energy. This electron is closer to the nucleus and is more exposed to the positive charge of the nucleus and so needs significantly more energy to be removed. There is similarly a large jump for the 12th ionization energy as it corresponds to an electron being removed from the 1s orbital.

## A closer look at successive ionization energies gives evidence for the sub-levels

A closer look at the successive ionization energies shows evidence of the sub-levels present with each level. The log graph of all 13 ionization energies showed a 2, 8, 3 pattern in successive ionization energies, which reflects the electron arrangement of the atom, with two electrons in the first level, eight electrons at the second energy level, and three valence electrons in the outer shell. Now we will consider the fourth to eleventh ionization energies in more detail. These correspond to the removal of the eight electrons in the second energy level (Figure 2.26).

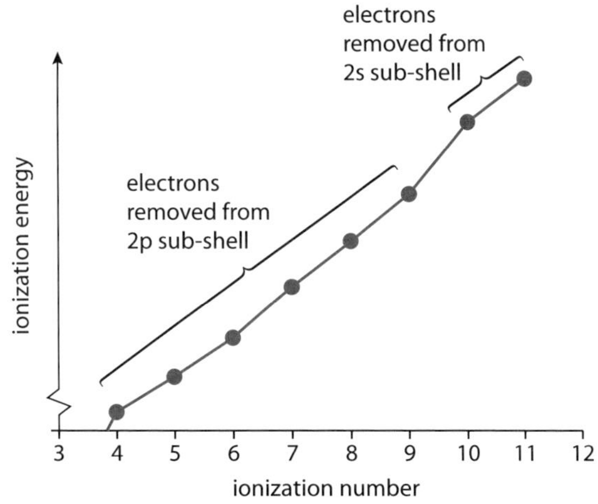

The jump between the ninth and tenth ionization energies shows that the eleventh electron is more difficult to remove than we would expect from the pattern of the six previous electrons. This suggests that the second energy level is divided into two **sub-levels**.

This evidence confirms that the **2s sub-level** can hold a maximum of two electrons, and the **2p sub-level** can hold six electrons.

TOK Which of Dalton's five proposals (page 59) do we now hold to be 'true'? How does scientific knowledge change with time? Are the models and theories of science accurate descriptions of the natural world, or just useful interpretations to help predict and explain the natural world?

**Figure 2.26** Successive ionization energies for aluminium. The jump between the ninth and tenth ionization energies indicates that the second energy level is divided into sub-levels. The smaller jump between the sixth and seventh ionization energies should also be noted and is discussed more fully in the text.

### Worked example

A graph of some successive ionization energies of aluminium is shown in Figure 2.26.

(a) Explain why there is a large increase between the ninth and tenth ionization energies.

(b) Explain why the increase between the sixth and seventh values is greater than the increase between the fifth and sixth values.

### Solution

(a) The ninth ionization energy corresponds to the change:

$$Al^{8+}(g) \rightarrow Al^{9+}(g) + e^-$$

$Al^{8+}$ has the configuration $1s^2 2s^2 2p^1$. The electron is removed from a 2p orbital.

The tenth ionization energy corresponds to the change:

$$Al^{9+}(g) \rightarrow Al^{10+}(g) + e^-$$

$Al^{9+}$ has the configuration $1s^2 2s^2$. The electron is removed from a 2s orbital.

Electrons in a 2s orbital are of lower energy. They are closer to the nucleus and experience a stronger force of electrostatic attraction and so are more difficult to remove.

(b) The sixth ionization energy corresponds to the change:

$$Al^{5+}(g) \rightarrow Al^{6+}(g) + e^-$$

$Al^{5+}$ has the configuration $1s^2 2s^2 2p^4$ ($1s^2 2s^2 2p_x^2 2p_y^1 2p_z^1$). The electron is removed from a doubly occupied 2p orbital.

The seventh ionization energy corresponds to the change:

$$Al^{6+}(g) \rightarrow Al^{7+}(g) + e^-$$

The electron is removed from singly occupied 2p orbital.

An electron in a doubly occupied orbital is repelled by its partner, as it has the same negative charge, and so is easier to remove than electrons in half-filled orbitals, which do not experience this force of repulsion (Figure 2.27).

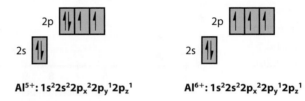

**$Al^{5+}$: $1s^2 2s^2 2p_x^2 2p_y^1 2p_z^1$**      **$Al^{6+}$: $1s^2 2s^2 2p_x^2 2p_y^1 2p_z^1$**

**Figure 2.27** The electron removed from the $Al^{5+}$ ion is removed from a doubly occupied 2p orbital. This is easier to remove as it is repelled by its partner.

Further evidence of sub-shells comes from a consideration of patterns in first ionization energies.

**Figure 2.28** The first ionization energies of the first 20 elements.

## Trends in first ionization energy across periods accounts or the existence of main energy levels and sub-levels in atoms

The periodic arrangement of the elements in the Periodic Table is also reflected by patterns in first ionization energies.

1 Ionization energy generally increases from left to right across a period, as the nuclear charge increases. As the electrons are removed from the same main energy level, there is an increase in the force of electrostatic attraction between the nucleus and outer electrons.

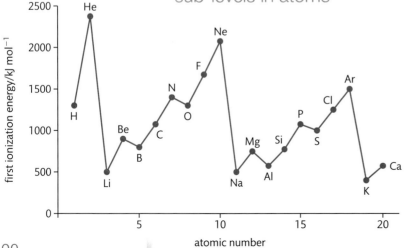

2 Ionization energy decreases down a group as a new energy level, which is further from the nucleus, is occupied. Less energy is required to remove outer electrons that are further from the attractive pull of the nucleus.

3 There are regular discontinuities in the trend across a period, which are explored below. These provide further evidence for the existence of sub-shells.

## Worked example

Further evidence for the existence of sub-shells comes from a study of first ionization energies.

(a) In Period 2 there is a decrease in first ionization energies between Be and B, and in Period 3 there is a decrease between Mg and Al. Explain this decrease in ionization energies between Group 2 and Group 13 elements.

(b) In Period 2 there is a decrease in first ionization energies between N and O, and in Period 3 a decrease between P and S. Explain the decrease in ionization energies between Group 15 and Group 16 elements.

## Solution

(a) The Group 2 elements have the electron configuration $ns^2$. The Group 13 elements have the electron configuration $ns^2np^1$.

The electron removed when the Group 13 elements are ionized is a p electron. The electron removed when the Group 2 elements are ionized is an s electron. Electrons in p orbitals are of higher energy and further away from the nucleus than s electrons and so are easier to remove than electrons in an s orbital.

(b) Group 15 elements have the configuration $ns^2np_x^1np_y^1np_z^1$. Group 16 elements have the configuration $ns^2np_x^2np_y^1np_z^1$. For Group 16 elements, the electron is removed from a doubly occupied 2p orbital. An electron in a doubly occupied orbital is repelled by its partner and so is easier to remove than an electron in a half-filled orbital.

**TOK**

Patterns in successive ionization energies of a given element and in first ionization energies of different elements both provide evidence to support the orbital model of electron configuration. Which source do you find most compelling? What constitutes good evidence within the natural sciences?

Databases could be used for compiling graphs of trends in ionization energies.

## Exercises

33 The first four ionization energies for a particular element are 738, 1450, 7730, and 10 550 kJ mol⁻¹ respectively. Deduce the group number of the element.

**A** 1 **B** 2 **C** 3 **D** 4

34 Successive ionization energies for an unknown element are given in the table below.

| First ionization energy / kJ mol⁻¹ | Second ionization energy / kJ mol⁻¹ | Third ionization energy / kJ mol⁻¹ | Fourth ionization energy / kJ mol⁻¹ |
|---|---|---|---|
| 590 | 1145 | 4912 | 6491 |

Identify the element.

**A** K **B** Ca **C** S **D** Cl

35 The successive ionization energies (in kJ mol⁻¹) for carbon are tabulated below.

| 1st | 2nd | 3rd | 4th | 5th | 6th |
|---|---|---|---|---|---|
| 1086 | 2352 | 4619 | 6220 | 37820 | 47280 |

**(a)** Explain why there is a large increase between the fourth and fifth values.
**(b)** Explain why there is an increase between the second and third values.

36 Sketch a graph to show the expected pattern for the first seven ionization energies of fluorine.

## Exercises

**37** The first ionization energies of the Period 3 elements Na to Ar are given in Section 8 of the IB data booklet.

   **(a)** Explain the general increase in ionization energy across the period.
   **(b)** Explain why the first ionization energy of magnesium is greater than that of aluminium.
   **(c)** Explain why the first ionization energy of sulfur is less than that of phosphorus.

One of the first advances in nanotechnology was the invention of the **scanning tunnelling microscope** (STM). The STM does not 'see' atoms, but 'feels' them. An ultra-fine tip scans a surface and records a signal as the tip moves up and down depending on the atoms present. The STM also provides a physical technique for manipulating individual atoms. They can be positioned accurately in just the same way as using a pair of tweezers.

The head of a variable temperature scanning tunnelling microscope.

The use of the scanning tunnelling microscope has allowed us to 'see' individual atoms. Does technology blur the distinction between simulation and reality?

 **TOK**  Waves can be thought of as a carrier of information. The precision of the information they provide is based on their wavelength or the momentum of the associated particles. Electrons can be accelerated to high momenta which allows electron microscopy to be used to show more precise detail than that provided by light microscopy. This has led to many advances in biology, such as the ultrastructure of cells and viruses. The scanning tunnelling microscope (STM) uses a stylus of a single atom to scan a surface and provide a three-dimensional image at the atomic level.

CERN, the European Organization for Nuclear Research, an international organization set up in 1954, is the world's largest particle physics laboratory. The laboratory, situated near Geneva, shares data with scientists of over 100 nationalities from 600 or more universities and research facilities.

### NATURE OF SCIENCE

This chapter has highlighted the need for experimental evidence to support our scientific theories:

- the hydrogen emission spectra provides evidence for the existence of energy levels;
- patterns in ionization energies provided evidence for the sub-levels in other elements;
- the Davisson–Germer experiment supports de Broglie's hypothesis.

Scientific ideas often start as speculations which are only later confirmed experimentally. The existence of the Higgs' boson was, for example, first suggested by the physicist Peter Higgs after he had spent a weekend walking in the Scottish mountains in 1964 thinking about the missing pieces in the jig-saw of the standard model of particle physics and why the fundamental particles have mass. It was, however, only detected in 2012 when two separate international teams working at the Large Hadron Collider at CERN independently announced that they had collected evidence to support the existence of the Higgs' boson. This discovery was greatly facilitated by the growth in computing power and sensor technology. Experiments in CERN's Large Hadron Collider regularly produce 23 petabytes of data per second, which is equivalent to 13.3 years of high definition TV content per second.

## Practice questions

**1** What is the electron configuration of the Cr²⁺ ion?

  **A** [Ar] $3d^54s^1$      **B** [Ar] $3d^34s^1$      **C** [Ar] $3d^64s^1$      **D** [Ar] $3d^44s^0$

**2** What is the relative atomic mass of an element with the following mass spectrum?

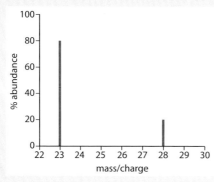

  **A** 24            **B** 25            **C** 26            **D** 27

**3** Which is correct for the following regions of the electromagnetic spectrum?

| | Ultraviolet (UV) | | Infrared (IR) | |
|---|---|---|---|---|
| **A** | high energy | short wavelength | low energy | low frequency |
| **B** | high energy | low frequency | low energy | long wavelength |
| **C** | high frequency | short wavelength | high energy | long wavelength |
| **D** | high frequency | long wavelength | low frequency | low energy |

**4** An ion has the electron configuration $1s^22s^22p^63s^23p^63d^{10}$. Which ion could it be?

  **A** Ni²⁺          **B** Cu⁺          **C** Cu²⁺          **D** Co³⁺

**5** Which describes the visible emission spectrum of hydrogen?

  **A** a series of lines converging at longer wavelength

  **B** a series of regularly spaced lines

  **C** a series of lines converging at lower energy

  **D** a series of lines converging at higher frequency

**6** Which statements about the isotopes of chlorine, $^{35}_{17}Cl$ and $^{37}_{17}Cl$, are correct?

  I    They have the same chemical properties.

  II   They have the same atomic number.

  III  They have the same physical properties.

  **A** I and II only      **B** I and III only      **C** II and III only      **D** I, II, and III

**7** Which statement about the numbers of protons, electrons, and neutrons in an atom is always correct?

  **A** The number of neutrons minus the number of electrons is zero.

  **B** The number of protons plus the number of neutrons equals the number of electrons.

  **C** The number of protons equals the number of electrons.

  **D** The number of neutrons equals the number of protons.

**8** Which quantities are the same for all atoms of chlorine?

  I    number of protons

  II   number of neutrons

  III  number of electrons

  **A** I and II only      **B** I and III only      **C** II and III only      **D** I, II, and III

**9** In the emission spectrum of hydrogen, which electronic transition would produce a line in the visible region of the electromagnetic spectrum?

**A** $n = 2 \rightarrow n = 1$    **B** $n = 3 \rightarrow n = 2$    **C** $n = 2 \rightarrow n = 3$    **D** $n = \infty \rightarrow n = 1$

**10** How many electrons does the ion $^{31}_{15}P^{3-}$ contain?

**A** 12          **B** 15          **C** 16          **D** 18

**11** A sample of iron has the following isotopic composition by mass.

| Isotope | $^{54}Fe$ | $^{56}Fe$ | $^{57}Fe$ |
|---|---|---|---|
| Relative abundance / % | 5.95 | 91.88 | 2.17 |

Calculate the relative atomic mass of iron based on this data, giving your answer to two decimal places.       (2)

*(Total 2 marks)*

**12** The electron configuration of chromium can be expressed as $[Ar]4s^x3d^y$.

**(a)** Explain what the square brackets around argon, [Ar], represent.   (1)

**(b)** State the values of $x$ and $y$.   (1)

**(c)** Annotate the diagram below showing the 4s and 3d orbitals for a chromium atom using an arrow, ↑ and ↓, to represent a spinning electron.

4s                                3d                 (1)

*(Total 3 marks)*

**13 (a)** Explain why the relative atomic mass of cobalt is greater than the relative atomic mass of nickel, even though the atomic number of nickel is greater than the atomic number of cobalt.(1)

**(b)** Deduce the numbers of protons and electrons in the ion $Co^{2+}$.   (1)

**(c)** Deduce the electron configuration for the ion $Co^{2+}$.   (1)

*(Total 3 marks)*

**14** The graph represents the energy needed to remove nine electrons, one at a time, from an atom of an element. Not all of the electrons have been removed.

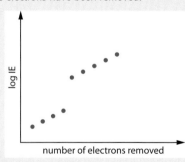

Which element could this be?

**A** C            **B** Si            **C** P            **D** S

**15** The graph below represents the successive ionization energies of sodium. The vertical axis plots log (ionization energy) instead of ionization energy to allow the data to be represented without using an unreasonably long vertical axis.

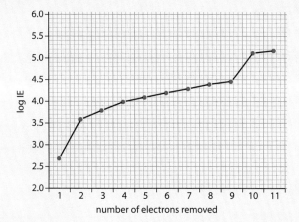

State the full electron configuration of sodium and explain how the successive ionization energy data for sodium are related to its electron configuration.

*(Total 4 marks)*

To access weblinks on the topics covered in this chapter, please go to www.pearsonhotlinks.com and enter the ISBN or title of this book.

# 03 Periodicity

# Essential ideas

**3.1** The arrangement of elements in the Periodic Table helps to predict their electron configuration.

**3.2** Elements show trends in their physical and chemical properties across periods and down groups.

**13.1** The transition elements have characteristic properties; these properties are related to their all having incomplete d sub-levels.

**13.2** d orbitals have the same energy in an isolated atom, but split into two sub-levels in a complex ion. The electric field of ligands cause the d orbitals in complex ions to split so that the energy of an electron transition between them corresponds to a photon of visible light.

The Periodic Table is the 'map' of chemistry; it suggests new avenues of research for the professional chemist and is a guide for students – as it disentangles a mass of observations and reveals hidden order. Chemistry is not the study of a random collection of elements, but of the trends and patterns in their chemical and physical properties.

The Periodic Table is a remarkable demonstration of the order of the subject. It was first proposed in 1869 by the Russian chemist Dmitri Mendeleyev. Previous attempts had been made to impose order on the then known 62 elements, but Mendeleyev had the insight to realize that each element has its allotted place, so he left gaps where no known elements fitted into certain positions. As a scientific idea it was extremely powerful as it made predictions about the unknown elements that fitted these gaps, predictions which could be tested. When these elements were later discovered, the agreement between the predicted properties and the actual properties was remarkable.

Water being dripped into a dish containing potassium metal. Potassium reacts violently and exothermically with water, producing potassium hydroxide and hydrogen gas. The reaction is explosive because the generated heat causes the hydrogen to ignite.

Mendeleyev grouped the known elements into families, leaving gaps corresponding to elements that should exist but which had not yet been discovered.

 **TOK** What is the role of imagination and creativity in the sciences? To what extent might the formulation of a hypothesis be comparable to imagining and creating a work of art?

**TOK** Which attributes of the IB Learner Profile are demonstrated by Mendeleyev's work on the Periodic Table?

Mendeleyev's Periodic Table of 1869. The noble gas elements had not been discovered. Reading from top to bottom and left to right, the first four gaps were waiting for scandium (1879), gallium (1875), germanium (1886) and technetium (1937).

| | | | | | | |
|---|---|---|---|---|---|---|
| | | K = 39 | Rb = 85 | Cs = 133 | — | — |
| | | Ca = 40 | Sr = 87 | Ba = 137 | — | — |
| | | — | ?Yt = 88? | ?Di = 138? | Er = 178? | — |
| | | Ti = 48? | Zr = 90 | Ce = 140? | ?La = 180? | Tb = 231 |
| | | V = 51 | Nb = 94 | — | Ta = 182 | — |
| | | Cr = 52 | Mo = 96 | — | W = 184 | U = 240 |
| | | Mn = 55 | — | — | — | — |
| | | Fe = 56 | Ru = 104 | — | Os = 195? | — |
| | | Co = 59 | Rh = 104 | — | Ir = 197 | — |
| **Typische Elemente** | | Ni = 59 | Pd = 106 | — | Pt = 198? | — |
| H = 1 | Li = 7 · Na = 23 | Cu = 63 | Ag = 108 | — | Au = 199? | — |
| | Be = 9,4 · Mg = 24 | Zn = 65 | Cd = 112 | — | Hg = 200 | — |
| | B = 11 · Al = 27,3 | — | In = 113 | — | Tl = 204 | — |
| | C = 12 · Si = 28 | — | Sn = 118 | — | Pb = 207 | — |
| | N = 14 · P = 31 | As = 75 | Sb = 122 | — | Bi = 208 | — |
| | O = 16 · S = 32 | Se = 78 | Te = 125? | — | — | — |
| | F = 19 · Cl = 35,5 | Br = 80 | J = 127 | — | — | — |

Mendeleyev had no knowledge of the structure of the atom, which we discussed in Chapter 2. With the benefit of hindsight it is clear that the periodicity of the elements is a direct consequence of the periodicity of the electron configurations within the atom.

The position of an element in the Periodic Table is based on the sub-level of the highest-energy electron in the ground-state atom.

## 3.1 The Periodic Table

### Understandings:
- The Periodic Table is arranged into four blocks associated with the four sub-levels: s, p, d, and f.
- The Periodic Table consists of groups (vertical columns) and periods (horizontal rows).

  *Guidance*
  *The group numbering scheme from group 1 to group 18, as recommended by IUPAC, should be used.*
- The period number (*n*) is the outer energy level that is occupied by electrons.
- The number of the principal energy level and the number of the valence electrons in an atom can be deduced from its position on the Periodic Table.
- The Periodic Table shows the positions of metals, non-metals and metalloids.

  *Guidance*
  *The terms alkali metals, halogens, noble gases, transition metals, lanthanoides and actinoides should be known.*

### Applications and skills:
- Deduction of the electron configuration of an atom from the element's position on the Periodic Table, and vice versa.

### Periods and groups

If you have visited a large supermarket you will appreciate the importance of a classification system. Similar products are grouped together to help you find what you want. In the same way, a chemist knows what type of element to find in different parts of the Periodic Table. The elements are placed in order of increasing atomic number (Z), which we now know is a fundamental property of the element – the number of protons in the nucleus of its atoms. As there are no gaps in the sequence of atomic numbers we can be confident that the search for new elements in nature is over.

The only way to extend the Periodic Table is by making elements artificially. Today there are over 110 elements recognized by the International Union of Pure and Applied Chemistry (IUPAC). The columns of the table are called **groups** and the rows **periods**.

In the IB data booklet Periodic Table the main groups are numbered from 1 to 18.

As discussed in Chapter 2, the position of an element is related to the electron configuration of its atoms.

Elements whose valence electrons occupy an s sub-level make up the **s block**, elements with valence electrons in p orbitals make up the **p block**, and the **d block** and **f block** are similarly made up of elements with outer electrons in d and f orbitals. The element sodium, for example, is in Period 3 as it has three occupied principal energy levels, and is in Group 1 of the s block as there is one electron in the valence energy level [Ne] $3s^1$. Bromine is in Period 4 and in Group 17 of the p block as it has seven electrons in the fourth principal energy level, and seventeen more electrons than the previous noble gas, argon: [Ar] $3d^{10}4s^24p^5$ (Figure 3.1).

Mendeleyev is said to have made his discovery after a dream. When he awoke he set out his chart in virtually its final form. He enjoyed playing a form of patience (solitaire) and wrote the properties of each element on cards which he arranged into rows and columns.

IUPAC is an international, non-governmental body with a membership made up of chemists which has the aim of fostering worldwide communication in chemistry.

| | s¹ | s² | d¹ | d² | d³ | d⁵s¹ | d⁵ | d⁶ | d⁷ | d⁸ | d¹⁰s¹ | d¹⁰ | p¹ | p² | p³ | p⁴ | p⁵ | p⁶ |
|---|----|----|----|----|----|------|----|----|----|----|-------|-----|----|----|----|----|----|----|
| | 1 | 2 | 3 | 4 | 5 | 6 | 7 | 8 | 9 | 10 | 11 | 12 | 13 | 14 | 15 | 16 | 17 | 18 |

| Period | | | | | | | | | | | | | | | | | | |
|---|---|---|---|---|---|---|---|---|---|---|---|---|---|---|---|---|---|---|
| 1 | H hydrogen 1 | | | | | | | | | | | | | | | | | He helium 2 |
| 2 | Li lithium 3 | Be beryllium 4 | | | | | | | | | | | B boron 5 | C carbon 6 | N nitrogen 7 | O oxygen 8 | F fluorine 9 | Ne neon 10 |
| 3 | Na sodium 11 | Mg magnesium 12 | | | | | | | | | | | Al aluminium 13 | Si silicon 14 | P phosphorus 15 | S sulfur 16 | Cl chlorine 17 | Ar argon 18 |
| 4 | K potassium 19 | Ca calcium 20 | Sc scandium 21 | Ti titanium 22 | V vanadium 23 | Cr chromium 24 | Mn manganese 25 | Fe iron 26 | Co cobalt 27 | Ni nickel 28 | Cu copper 29 | Zn zinc 30 | Ga gallium 31 | Ge germanium 32 | As arsenic 33 | Se selenium 34 | Br bromine 35 | Kr krypton 36 |
| 5 | Rb rubidium 37 | Sr strontium 38 | Y yttrium 39 | Zr zirconium 40 | Nb niobium 41 | Mo molybdenum 42 | Tc technetium 43 | Ru ruthenium 44 | Rh rhodium 45 | Pd palladium 46 | Ag silver 47 | Cd 48 | In indium 49 | Sn tin 50 | Sb antimony 51 | Te tellurium 52 | I iodine 53 | Xe xenon 54 |
| 6 | Cs caesium 55 | Ba barium 56 | 57–71 see below | Hf hafnium 72 | Ta tantalum 73 | W tungsten 74 | Re rhenium 75 | Os osmium 76 | Ir iridium 77 | Pt platinum 78 | Au gold 79 | Hg mercury 80 | Tl thallium 81 | Pb lead 82 | Bi bismuth 83 | Po polonium 84 | At astatine 85 | Rn radon 86 |
| 7 | Fr francium 87 | Ra radium 88 | 89–103 see below | Rf rutherfordium 104 | Db dubnium 105 | Sg seaborgium 106 | Bh bohrium 107 | Hs hassium 108 | Mt meitnerium 109 | Ds darmstadtium 110 | Rg roentgenium 111 | Cp copernicium 112 | Uut ununtrium 113 | Fl flerovium 114 | Uup ununpentium 115 | Lv Livermorium 116 | Uus Ununseptium 117 | Uuo Ununoctium 118 |

| La lanthanum 57 | Ce cerium 58 | Pr praseodymium 59 | Nd neodymium 60 | Pm promethium 61 | Sm samarium 62 | Eu europium 63 | Gd gadolinium 64 | Tb terbium 65 | Dy dysprosium 66 | Ho holmium 67 | Er erbium 68 | Tm thulium 69 | Yb ytterbium 70 | Lu Lutetium 71 |
|---|---|---|---|---|---|---|---|---|---|---|---|---|---|---|
| Ac actinium 89 | Th thorium 90 | Pa protactinium 91 | U uranium 92 | Np neptunium 93 | Pu plutonium 94 | Am americium 95 | Cm curium 96 | Bk berkellium 97 | Cf californium 98 | Es einsteinium 99 | Fm fermium 100 | Md mendelevium 101 | No nobelium 102 | Lr Lawrencium 103 |

**Figure 3.1** The Periodic Table. The rows are called periods. The period number gives the number of occupied electron principal energy levels. The columns in the Periodic Table are called groups. The colours show the blocks formed by the elements with their outer electrons in the same electron sub-level: s block (blue), d block (yellow), p block (red), f block (green). It is these outer electrons that determine an element's chemical properties.

The discovery of the elements was an international endeavour. This is illustrated by some of their names. Some derive from the place where they were made, some derive from the origins of their discoverers, and some derive from the geographical origins of the minerals from which they were first isolated. The Periodic Table of chemical elements hangs in front of chemistry classrooms and in science laboratories throughout the world.

The rows in the Periodic Table are called periods. The period number gives the number of occupied electron principal energy levels. The columns in the Periodic Table are called groups.

## Worked example

How many electrons are in the outer shell of iodine?

### Solution

Find the element in the Periodic Table. It is Period 5, so has the noble gas core of Kr, with electrons added to 5s, then 4d, and then 5p.

As it is Group 17 it has the configuration: [Kr] $5s^2 4d^{10} 5p^5$ or [Kr] $4d^{10} 5s^2 5p^5$ and so has seven electrons in its valence energy level.

## CHALLENGE YOURSELF

1 Four elements derive their name from a small town called Ytterby, just outside Stockholm, Sweden. Try to find their names.

## Exercises

1 Use the IB Periodic Table to identify the position of the following elements:

| | Element | Period | Group |
|---|---|---|---|
| **(a)** | helium | | |
| **(b)** | chlorine | | |
| **(c)** | barium | | |
| **(d)** | francium | | |

2 Phosphorus is in Period 3 and Group 15 of the Periodic Table.

(a) Distinguish between the terms 'period' and 'group'.

(b) State the electron configuration of phosphorus and relate it to its position in the Periodic Table.

3 How many valence (outer shell) electrons are present in the atoms of the element with atomic number 51?

The lanthanides with scandium and yttrium are sometimes called rare earth metals. They are not, however, that rare. Cerium for example is the 26th most abundant element in the earth's crust.

## Metals and non-metals

Non-metallic elements. Clockwise from top left, they are sulfur (S), bromine (Br), phosphorus (P), iodine (I) and carbon (C). Non-metals are generally poor conductors of both heat and electricity. Graphite, an allotrope of carbon, is unusual in that it is a non-metal that does conduct electricity.

One of the key features of the Periodic Table is that the metals, metalloids, and non-metals occupy different regions. The non-metals are found on the upper right-hand side of the p block. The **halogens**, for example, are a reactive group of non-metals in Group 17 and the **noble gases** are a very unreactive family of non-metals found at the extreme right-hand side in Group 18. Metallic elements are found on the left-hand side of the table in the s block, in the central d block, and the island of the f block. The alkali metals, for example, are a reactive group of metals in Group 1 of the s block. The lanthanoides and actinoides are metals which make up the first and second row of the f block.

The metalloid elements have the characteristics of both metals and non-metals. Their physical properties and appearance most resemble the metals, although chemically they have more in common with the non-metals. In the Periodic Table the metalloid elements silicon, germanium, arsenic, antimony, tellurium, and polonium form a diagonal staircase between the metals and non-metals.

### CHALLENGE YOURSELF

**2** How many elements in the IB Periodic Table are liquids and how many are gases?

Silicon is a metalloid. There is enough silicon in this piece to make many hundreds of computers.

Europium (Eu), is one of the lanthanoides. It is a hard silvery-white metallic element and is used in television screens and fluorescent light bulbs.

### CHALLENGE YOURSELF

**3** Distinguish between the terms 'metalloid' and 'semiconductor'.

 The element europium is used in the security marking of euro notes and other banknotes. When placed in UV radiation europium compounds fluoresce, making the security markers visible.

 **The lanthanoides and actinoides both make up the f block of the Periodic Table.**

### CHALLENGE YOURSELF

**4** State the electron configuration of europium.

## Exercises

**4** Which of the following elements is a metalloid?

   **A** calcium         **B** manganese        **C** germanium       **D** magnesium

**5** Which of the following materials is the best conductor of electricity in the solid state?

   **A** silicon           **B** graphite            **C** phosphorus      **D** antimony

**6** Which of the following properties is used to arrange the elements in the modern Periodic Table?

   **A** relative atomic mass      **B** number of valence electrons

   **C** atomic number            **D** effective nuclear charge

## NATURE OF SCIENCE

Scientists attempt to discover relationships by looking for patterns, trends, and discrepancies. Classification is an important aspect of scientific work. In the 18th century, Antoine Lavoisier tried to bring order to the confusing number of elements by classifying the elements into groups such as gases, non-metals, and metals. Some classification systems are, however, more useful than others and classifications based on quantitative data are more useful than those on qualitative data. The publication of 1858 by Stanislao Cannizzaro of a list of atomic masses allowed the elements to be placed in some sort of order.

One of the first attempts to classify the elements was made by Johann Döbereiner (1780–1849) who organized the elements into groups of three or 'triads' with similar properties (such as lithium, sodium, and potassium), where the average mass of the first and third element equalled the mass of the second. This pattern is approximately true for several triads of elements. The average relative mass of lithium and potassium, the first and third elements in a triad, for example = (6.94 + 39.10)/2 = 23.02 which is very close to the relative atomic mass of sodium (22.99), the second element in the triad.

In 1862 Alexandre de Chancourtois wrote a list of the elements on a tape and wound it in a spiral and noticed that chemically similar elements formed vertical groups.

John Newlands developed this idea and noted that many similar elements occur in intervals, rather like the seven notes in a musical scale. His law of octaves stated that any given element will be similar in its properties to the eighth element following it in the table.

Mendeleyev recognized that the breakdown in the periodicity of Newlands' octaves was due to the table's incomplete nature as some elements were yet to be discovered. Mendeleyev left gaps for these elements to ensure that periodicity was maintained, and predicted the physical and chemical properties of these missing elements. This was a key step in the scientific process as his precise predictions could be confirmed or falsified with the discovery of the new elements.

The discovery of elements such as gallium and germanium confirmed Mendeleyev's ideas. One advantage of Mendeleyev's table over previous attempts was that it exhibited similarities not only in small units such as the triads, but showed similarities in an entire network of vertical, horizontal, and diagonal relationships.

Mendeleyev did not propose an explanation for his periodic law. This had to await the discovery of the electron by Thomson in 1897 and the work of Rutherford and Bohr at the beginning of the 20th century.

'Theories' and 'laws' are terms which have a special meaning in science and it is important to distinguish these from their everyday use. Scientific laws are descriptive, normative statements derived from observations of regular patterns of behaviour. They do not necessarily explain a phenomenon. Newlands' law of octaves and Mendeleyev's periodic law, for example, tell us that there is pattern in the properties of the elements but they do not attempt to explain these patterns.

 **TOK** The patterns observed in the evolution of the Periodic Table were as a result of inductive reasoning. What do these patterns illustrate about the problems of induction? Is induction ever a reliable source for knowledge?

 The development of the Periodic Table took many years and involved scientists from different countries building upon the foundations of each other's work and ideas.

## 3.2 Periodic trends

### Understandings:

- Vertical and horizontal trends in the Periodic Table exist for atomic radius, ionic radius, ionization energy, electron affinity, and electronegativity.

  **Guidance**
  *Only examples of general trends across periods and down groups are required. For ionization energy the discontinuities in the increase across a period should be covered.*

- Trends in metallic and non-metallic behaviour are due to the trends above.
- Oxides change from basic through amphoteric to acidic across a period.

### Applications and skills:

- Prediction and explanation of the metallic and non-metallic behaviour of an element based on its position in the Periodic Table.
- Discussion of the similarities and differences in the properties of elements in the same group, with reference to alkali metals (Group 1) and halogens (Group 17).

  **Guidance**
  *Group trends should include the treatment of the reactions of alkali metals with water, alkali metals with halogens and halogens with halide ions.*

- Construction of equations to explain the pH changes for reactions of $Na_2O$, $MgO$, $P_4O_{10}$, and the oxides of nitrogen and sulfur with water.

## Physical properties

The elements in the Periodic Table are arranged to show how the properties of the elements repeat periodically. This **periodicity** of the elements is reflected in their physical properties. The atomic and ionic radii, electronegativity, and ionization energy are of particular interest as they explain the periodicity of the chemical properties.

The concept of effective nuclear charge is helpful in explaining trends in both physical and chemical properties.

### Effective nuclear charge

The **nuclear charge** of the atom is given by the atomic number and so increases by one between successive elements in the table, as a proton is added to the nucleus. The outer electrons which determine many of the physical and chemical properties of the atom do not, however, experience the full attraction of this charge as they are **shielded** from the nucleus and repelled by the inner electrons. The presence of the inner electrons reduces the attraction of the nucleus for the outer electrons (Figure 3.2). The **effective charge** 'experienced' by the outer electrons is less than the full nuclear charge.

Consider, for example, a sodium atom. The nuclear charge is given by the atomic number of element (Z = 11). The outer electron in the 3s orbital is, however, shielded from these 11 protons by the 10 electrons in the first and second principal energy levels ($1s^2 2s^2 2p^6$).

Consider the first four elements in Period 3, as shown in the table on page 103.

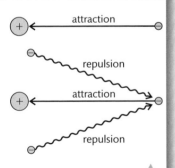

**Figure 3.2** An electron in the hydrogen atom experiences the full attraction of the nuclear charge, but in a many-electron atom the attraction for the nucleus is reduced as the outer electron is repelled by inner electrons.

| Element | Na | Mg | Al | Si |
|---|---|---|---|---|
| Nuclear charge | 11 | 12 | 13 | 14 |
| Electron configuration | [Ne] $3s^1$ | [Ne] $3s^2$ | [Ne] $3s^23p^1$ | [Ne] $3s^23p^2$ |
| Effective nuclear charge | $\approx 11 - 10$ $\approx +1$ | $\approx 12 - 10$ $\approx +2$ | $\approx 13 - 10$ $\approx +3$ | $\approx 14 - 10$ $\approx +4$ |

As the period is crossed from left to right, one proton is added to the nucleus and one electron is added to the valence electron energy level. The effective charge increases with the nuclear charge as there is no change in the number of inner electrons, as all the atoms have a noble gas structure of 10 electrons ([Ne] = $1s^22s^22p^6$).

If we assume that the noble gas core is completely shielding, then the 10 inner electrons of the neon core make the effective nuclear charge 10 less than the nuclear charge.

The changes down a group can be illustrated by considering the elements in Group 1, as shown in the table below:

| Element | Nuclear charge | Electron configuration |
|---|---|---|
| Li | 3 | $1s^22s^1$ |
| Na | 11 | $1s^22s^22p^63s^1$ |
| K | 19 | $1s^22s^22p^63s^23p^64s^1$ |

As we descend the group, the increase in the nuclear charge is largely offset by the increase in the number of inner electrons; both increase by eight between successive elements in the group. The effective nuclear charge experienced by the outer electrons remains approximately +1 down the group.

## Atomic radius

The concept of atomic radius is not as straightforward as you may think. We saw in the last chapter that electrons occupy atomic orbitals, which give a probability description of the electrons' locations, but do not have sharp boundaries. The atomic radius r is measured as half the distance between neighbouring nuclei (Figure 3.3). For many purposes, however, it can be considered as the distance from the nucleus to the outermost electrons of the Bohr atom.

Table 8 in the IB data booklet shows that atomic radii increase down a group and decrease across a period. To explain the trend down a group consider, for example, the Group 1 elements – as shown in the table below.

| Element | Period | No. of occupied principal energy levels | Atomic radius/$10^{-12}$ m |
|---|---|---|---|
| Li | 2 | 2 | 152 |
| Na | 3 | 3 | 186 |
| K | 4 | 4 | 231 |
| Rb | 5 | 5 | 244 |
| Cs | 6 | 6 | 262 |

The effective nuclear charge experienced by an atom's outer electrons increases with the group number of the element. It increases across a period but remains approximately the same down a group.

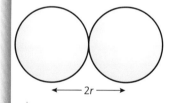

Figure 3.3 The atomic radius r is measured as half the distance between neighbouring nuclei.

The atomic radii increase down a group, as the number of occupied electron shells (given by the period number) increases.

The trend across a period is illustrated by the Period 3 elements, as shown below.

| Element | Na | Mg | Al | Si | P | S | Cl | Ar |
|---|---|---|---|---|---|---|---|---|
| Atomic radius/$10^{-12}$ m | 186 | 160 | 143 | 117 | 110 | 104 | 99 | – |

All these elements have three occupied principal energy levels. The attraction between the nucleus and the outer electrons increases as the nuclear charge increases so there is a general decrease in atomic radii across the period.

The decrease in radii across a period is quite significant; a chlorine atom, for example, has a radius that is about half that of a sodium atom.

## Ionic radius

The atomic and ionic radii of the Period 3 elements are shown in the table below.

| Element | Na | Mg | Al | Si | P | S | Cl |
|---|---|---|---|---|---|---|---|
| Atomic radius/$10^{-12}$ m | 186 | 160 | 143 | 117 | 110 | 104 | 99 |
| Ionic radius/$10^{-12}$ m | 98 ($Na^+$) | 65 ($Mg^{2+}$) | 45 ($Al^{3+}$) | 42 ($Si^{4+}$); 271 ($Si^{4-}$) | 212 ($P^{3-}$) | 190 ($S^{2-}$) | 181 ($Cl^-$) |

Five trends can be identified.

- Positive ions are smaller than their parent atoms. The formation of positive ions involves the loss of the outer shell. The $Na^+$ ion, for example, is formed by the removal of the 3s electron from the Na atom.
- Negative ions are larger than their parent atoms. The formation of negative ions involves the addition of electrons into the outer shell. $Cl^-$ is formed by the addition of an electron into the 3p sub-shell. The increased electron repulsion between the electrons in the outer principal energy level causes the electrons to move further apart and so increases the radius of the outer shell.
- The ionic radii decrease from Groups 1 to 14 for the positive ions. The ions $Na^+$, $Mg^{2+}$, $Al^{3+}$, and $Si^{4+}$ all have the same electron configuration ($1s^22s^22p^6$). The decrease in ionic radius is due to the increase in nuclear charge with atomic number across the period. The increased attraction between the nucleus and the electrons pulls the outer shell closer to the nucleus.
- The ionic radii decrease from Groups 14 to 17 for the negative ions. The ions $Si^{4-}$, $P^{3-}$, $S^{2-}$ and $Cl^-$ have the same electron configuration ($1s^22s^22p^63s^23p^6$). The decrease in ionic radius is due to the increase in nuclear charge across the period, as explained above. The positive ions are smaller than the negative ions, as the former have only two occupied electron principal energy levels and the latter have three. This explains the big difference between the ionic radii of the $Si^{4+}$ and $Si^{4-}$ ions and the discontinuity in the middle of the table.
- The ionic radii increase down a group as the number of electron energy levels increases.

### Worked example

Describe and explain the trend in radii of the following atoms and ions:

$O^{2-}$, $F^-$, Ne, $Na^+$, and $Mg^{2+}$.

## Solution

The ions and the Ne atom have 10 electrons and the electron configuration $1s^2 2s^2 2p^6$.

The nuclear charges increase with atomic number:

O: Z = +8

F: Z = +9

Ne: Z = +10

Na: Z = +11

Mg: Z = +12

The increase in nuclear charge results in increased attraction between the nucleus and the outer electrons. The ionic radii decrease as the atomic number increases.

### Exercises

**7**  **(a)**  Explain what is meant by the atomic radius of an element.
   **(b)**  The atomic radii of the elements are found in Table 9 of the IB data booklet.
     **(i)**  Explain why no values for ionic radii are given for the noble gases.
     **(ii)**  Describe and explain the trend in atomic radii across the Period 3 elements.
**8**  $Si^{4+}$ has an ionic radius of $4.2 \times 10^{-11}$ m and $Si^{4-}$ has an ionic radius of $2.71 \times 10^{-10}$ m. Explain the large difference in size between the $Si^{4+}$ and $Si^{4-}$ ions.

## Ionization energies

First ionization energies are a measure of the attraction between the nucleus and the outer electrons. They were defined in Chapter 2 (page 73), where they provided evidence for the electron configuration of the atoms of different elements (Figure 3.4).

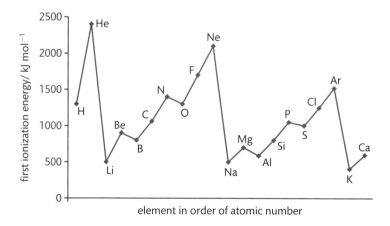

Two general trends can be identified from Figure 3.4.

- Ionization energies increase across a period. The increase in effective nuclear charge causes an increase in the attraction between the outer electrons and the nucleus and makes the electrons more difficult to remove.
- Ionization energies decrease down a group. The electron removed is from the energy level furthest from the nucleus. Although the nuclear charges increase, the effective nuclear charge is about the same, owing to shielding of the inner electrons, and so the increased distance between the electron and the nucleus reduces the attraction between them.

> The first ionization energy of an element is the energy required to remove one mole of electrons from one mole of gaseous atoms in their ground state.

**Figure 3.4**  First ionization energies of the first 20 elements.

The small departures from these trends provide evidence for division of energy levels into sub-levels, as discussed in Chapter 2 (page 90). Thus, the Group 13 elements, with the electron configuration $ns^2np^1$, have lower first ionization energies than Group 2 elements, with the configuration $ns^2$, as p orbitals have higher energy than s orbitals. The drop between Groups 15 and 16 occurs as the electron removed from a Group 16 element, unlike a Group 15 element, is taken from a doubly occupied p orbital. This electron is easier to remove as it is repelled by its partner.

The trend in ionization energy is the reverse of the trend in atomic radii. Both trends are an indication of the attraction between the nucleus and the outer electrons.

### Electron affinity

The first **electron affinity** of an element ($\Delta H_{ea}^{\ominus}$) is the energy change when one mole of electrons is added to one mole of gaseous atoms to form one mole of gaseous ions:

$$X(g) + e^- \rightarrow X^-(g)$$

Values are tabulated in Table 8 of the IB data booklet. The noble gases do not generally form negatively charged ions so electron affinity values are not available for these elements. As the added electron is attracted to the positively charged nucleus the process is generally exothermic. The second and third electron affinities are defined similarly. The second electron affinity for oxygen, for example, corresponds to the change:

$$O^-(g) + e^- \rightarrow O^{2-}(g)$$

This process is endothermic as the added electron is repelled by the negatively charged oxide ($O^-$) ion, and energy needs to be available for this to occur.

The electron affinities of the first 18 elements are shown below. The pattern in electron affinities is related to that observed with first ionization energy but generally displaced to the right by one and inverted. The minimum values for electron affinities occur for the Group 17 elements whereas the values for ionization energy reach a maximum for Group 18.

Electron affinities can be thought of as the negative of first ionization energy of the anion.

- The Group 17 elements have incomplete outer energy levels and a high effective nuclear charge of approximately +7 and so attract electrons the most.
- The Group 1 metals have the lowest effective nuclear charge of approximately +1 and so attract the extra electron the least.

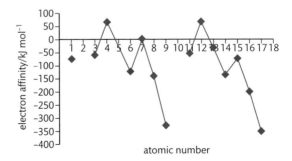

**Figure 3.5** The electron affinities of the first 18 elements. Note there are no values assigned to the noble gases.

The electron affinities reach a maximum for Group 2 and Group 5 elements. Group 2 elements have an electron configuration $ns^2$, so the added electron must be placed into a 2p orbital which is further from the nucleus and so experiences reduced electrostatic attraction due to shielding from electrons in the ns orbital. The value for beryllium is actually endothermic as there is electrostatic repulsion between the electrons of the Be atom and the added electron. The electrons in the 1s and 2s orbitals of Be also shield the added electron from the positively charged nucleus.

Group 15 elements have the configuration $ns^2np_x^1p_y^1p_z^1$ so the added electron must occupy a p orbital that is already singly occupied: the attraction between the electron and atom is less than expected as there is increased inter-electron repulsion. The value is only just exothermic for nitrogen.

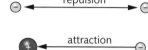

## Electronegativity

The **electronegativity** of an element is a measure of the ability of its atoms to attract electrons in a covalent bond (see Chapter 4). It is related to ionization energy as it is also a measure of the attraction between the nucleus and its outer electrons – in this case *bonding electrons*.

An element with a high electronegativity has strong electron pulling power and an element with a low electronegativity has weak pulling power. The concept was originally devised by the American chemist Linus Pauling and his values are given in the IB data booklet (Section 8). The general trends are the same as those for ionization energy.

• Electronegativity increases from left to right across a period owing to the increase in nuclear charge, resulting in an increased attraction between the nucleus and the bond electrons.
• Electronegativity decreases down a group. The bonding electrons are furthest from the nucleus and so there is reduced attraction.

The most electronegative element is on the top right of the Periodic Table and the least electronegative element on the bottom left. As the concept does not apply to the Group 18 elements, which do not form covalent bonds, Pauling assigned the highest value of 4.0 to fluorine and the lowest value of 0.7 to caesium.

Although the general trends in ionization energy and electronegativity are the same, they are distinct properties. Ionization energies can be measured directly and are a property of gaseous atoms. Elements with high electronegativities have the most exothermic electron affinities, but again care should be taken to avoid confusion between the terms. Electron affinities are properties of isolated gaseous atoms whereas electronegativity is a property of an atom in a molecule. Electronegativity values are derived indirectly from experimental bond energy data.

## Metals have lower ionization energies and electronegativities than non-metals

The ability of metals to conduct electricity is due to the availability of their valence electrons to move away from the atomic nucleus. This can be related to their low ionization energies and electronegativities. There is a transition from metal to metalloid and non-metal from left to right as these properties increase. The diagonal band of metalloids which divides the metals from the non-metals can also be related to the similar electronegativities of these elements.

**The electron affinity of an atom is the energy change that occurs when one mole of electrons is added to one mole of gaseous atoms.**

**Figure 3.6** Energy is needed to bring two particles of the same charge closer together as they repel reach other: this is an endothermic process. Particles of the opposite charge attract each other. They will spontaneously move closer together: it is an exothermic process.

**Electronegativity is the ability of an atom to attract electrons in a covalent bond.**

Linus Pauling has the unique distinction of winning two *unshared* Nobel Prizes – one for Chemistry in 1954 and one for Peace in 1962. His Chemistry Prize was for improving our understanding of the chemical bond and his Peace Prize was for his campaign against nuclear weapons testing.

## Exercises

**9** Which of the following is a property of gaseous atoms?

   I    ionization energy
   II   electron affinity
   III  electronegativity

   **A**  I and II      **B**  I and III      **C**  II and III      **D**  I, II, and III

**10** Which of the following changes is endothermic?

   I    $Ca(g) \rightarrow Ca^+(g) + e^-$
   II   $I(g) + e^- \rightarrow I^-(g)$
   III  $O^- + e^- \rightarrow O^{2-}(g)$

   **A**  I and II      **B**  I and III      **C**  II and III      **D**  I, II, and III

**11** Identify the element which is likely to have an electronegativity value most similar to that of lithium?

   **A**  beryllium      **B**  sodium      **C**  magnesium      **D**  hydrogen

**12** The graph represents the variation of a property of the Group 2 elements.

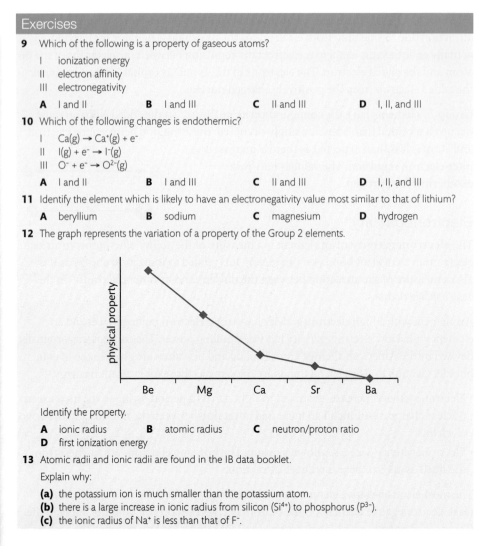

   Identify the property.

   **A**  ionic radius      **B**  atomic radius      **C**  neutron/proton ratio
   **D**  first ionization energy

**13** Atomic radii and ionic radii are found in the IB data booklet.

   Explain why:

   **(a)** the potassium ion is much smaller than the potassium atom.
   **(b)** there is a large increase in ionic radius from silicon ($Si^{4+}$) to phosphorus ($P^{3-}$).
   **(c)** the ionic radius of $Na^+$ is less than that of $F^-$.

## Melting points

Comparisons between melting points of different elements are more complex as they depend on both the type of bonding and the structure (Chapter 4). Trends down Groups 1 and 17 can, however, be explained simply, as the elements within each group bond in similar ways. Trends in melting points down Group 1 and Group 17 are shown in the table below.

| Element | Melting point / K | Element | Melting point / K |
|---------|-------------------|---------|-------------------|
| Li | 454 | $F_2$ | 54 |
| Na | 371 | $Cl_2$ | 172 |
| K | 337 | $Br_2$ | 266 |
| Rb | 312 | $I_2$ | 387 |
| Cs | 302 | $At_2$ | 575 |

Melting points decrease down Group 1. The elements have metallic structures which are held together by attractive forces between **delocalized** outer electrons and the positively charged ions. This attraction decreases with distance.

Melting points increase down Group 17. The elements have molecular structures which are held together by London (dispersion) forces. These increase with the number of electrons in the molecule. This is explained more fully in Chapter 4.

Melting points generally rise across a period and reach a maximum at Group 14. They then fall to reach a minimum at Group 18. In Period 3, for example, the bonding changes from metallic (Na, Mg, and Al) to giant covalent (Si) to weak van der Waals' attraction between simple molecules ($P_4$, $S_8$, $Cl_2$) and single atoms (Ar) (Figure 3.7). All the Period 3 elements are solids at room temperature except chlorine and argon.

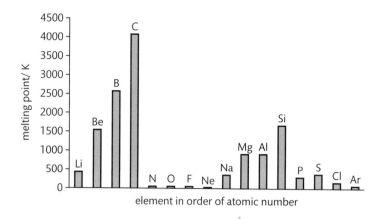

**Figure 3.7** The melting points show a periodic pattern as the bonding changes from metallic, to giant covalent, to simple molecular.

**TOK**
No one knows how high the atomic number of the elements will go, but it is expected that all new elements will fit into the current scheme. Could there ever be an 'end' to science? Could we reach a point where everything important in a scientific sense is known?

## Exercises

**14** Explain why sulfur has a higher melting point than phosphorus.

**15** Which physical property generally increases down a group but decreases from left to right across a period?

   **A** melting point    **B** electronegativity    **C** ionization energy    **D** atomic radius

**16** The elements in the Periodic Table are arranged in order of increasing:

   **A** relative atomic mass
   **B** ionic radii
   **C** nuclear charge
   **D** ionization energy

**17** What is the order of decreasing radii for the species $Cl$, $Cl^+$, and $Cl^-$?

**18** Which one of the following elements has the highest electronegativity?

   **A** Be       **B** Cl       **C** Ca       **D** Br

**19** Which properties of the Period 3 elements increase from sodium to argon:

   **A** nuclear charge and atomic radius
   **B** atomic radius and electronegativity
   **C** nuclear charge and electronegativity
   **D** nuclear charge, atomic radius, and electronegativity

**20** The following graph shows the variation of a physical property, X, of the first 20 elements in the Periodic Table with the atomic number.

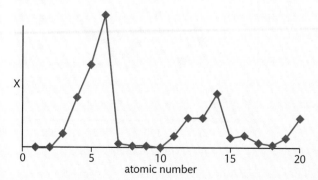

Identify the property X.

   **A** atomic radius    **B** first ionization energy
   **C** ionic radius    **D** melting point

## Exercises

**21** Identify the graph which shows the correct ionic radii for the isoelectronic ions Cl⁻, K⁺, and Ca²⁺?

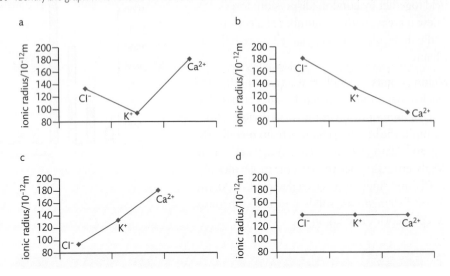

### NATURE OF SCIENCE

Although Mendeleyev is given most of the credit for arranging the elements into a Periodic Table in 1869, the periodicity in the physical properties was independently demonstrated the same year by the German chemist Lothar Meyer. Meyer plotted a range of physical properties against relative atomic mass. The graph of density against relative atomic mass is shown in Figure 3.8. Elements in the same group occur at similar points on the curve. The noble gases, for example, are all near the minimum points in the curve.

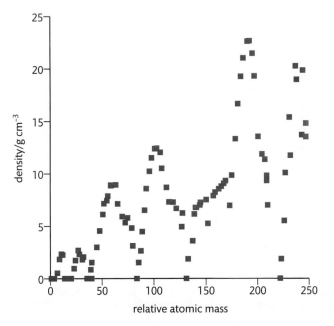

**Figure 3.8** The relationship between relative atomic mass and density.

Many scientific laws and theories have often been developed independently by different scientists working in different countries. This illustrates the objective nature of science.

# Chemical properties

The chemical properties of an element are determined by the electron configuration of its atoms. Elements of the same group have similar chemical properties as they have the same number of valence electrons in their outer energy level. The alkali metals in Group 1, for example, all have one electron in their outer shell and the halogens in Group 17 have seven outer electrons. The trends in their chemical properties can be accounted for by the trends in their properties discussed earlier.

## Group 18: the noble gases

To understand the reactivity of the elements it is instructive to consider Group 18, which contains the least reactive elements – the noble gases. This chemically aloof family of elements was only discovered at the end of the 19th century after Mendeleyev first published his table.

- They are colourless gases.
- They are monatomic: they exist as single atoms.
- They are very unreactive.

Their lack of reactivity can be explained by the inability of their atoms to lose or gain electrons. They do not generally form positive ions as they have the highest ionization energies. They do not form negative ions as extra electrons would have to be added to an empty outer energy level shell where they would experience a negligible effective nuclear force, with the protons shielded by an equal number of inner electrons. With the exception of helium, they have complete valence energy levels with eight electrons; a **stable octet**. Helium has a complete principal first energy level with two electrons.

The reactivity of elements in other groups can be explained by their unstable incomplete electron energy levels. They lose or gain electrons so as to achieve the electron configuration of their nearest noble gas.

- Elements in Groups 1, 2, and 13 lose electrons to adopt the arrangement of the nearest noble gas with a lower atomic number. They are generally metals.
- Elements in Groups 15 to 17 gain electrons to adopt the electron configuration of the nearest noble gas on their right in the Periodic Table. They are generally non-metals.
- The metalloids in the middle of the table show intermediate properties.

## Group 1: the alkali metals

All the elements are silvery metals and are too reactive to be found in nature. They are usually stored in oil to prevent contact with air and water. The properties of the first three elements are summarized in the table below.

| Physical properties | Chemical properties |
|---|---|
| <ul><li>They are good conductors of electricity and heat.</li><li>They have low densities.</li><li>They have grey shiny surfaces when freshly cut with a knife.</li></ul> | <ul><li>They are very reactive metals.</li><li>They form ionic compounds with non-metals.</li></ul> |

Chemical properties of an element are largely determined by the number of valence electrons in their outer energy level.

NATURE OF SCIENCE

The electron arrangement description of the atom is sufficient to explain the chemical properties of elements in the s and p blocks. We will follow Occam's razor and use this simple but incomplete model. The principle of Occam's razor is often used as a guide to developing a scientific theory. The theory should be as simple as possible while maximizing explanatory power.

TOK

What characteristics must an explanation possess to be considered 'good' within the natural sciences? What is the difference between explanations in the different areas of knowledge?

Group 18 used to be called the 'inert gases' as it was thought that they were completely unreactive. No compounds of helium or neon have ever been found. The first compound of xenon was made in 1962 and compounds of krypton and argon have now been prepared. The most reactive element in the group has the lowest ionization energy as reactions involve the withdrawal of electrons from the parent atom.

▲ Lithium is a soft reactive metal. When freshly cut, it has a metallic lustre. However, it rapidly reacts with oxygen in the air, giving it a dark oxide coat.

It has been estimated that at any one time there are only 17 francium atoms on the Earth.

▲ Sodium is softer and more reactive than lithium.

▲ Potassium is softer and more reactive than sodium.

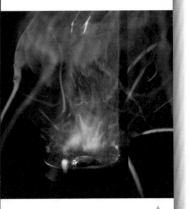

▲ Potassium reacting with water. The heat generated causes the hydrogen to ignite.

Note that the metal hydroxide is produced when Group 1 elements are added to water. A common mistake is to give the oxide as the product.

Observations must be something that can be observed. You cannot usually identify chemicals by simple observations. If you are asked to describe what you would see, saying 'a gas was produced' would gain more marks than 'hydrogen was produced'.

They form single charged ions, $M^+$, with the stable octet of the noble gases when they react. Their low ionization energies give an indication of the ease with which the outer electron is lost. Reactivity increases down the group as the elements with higher atomic number have the lowest ionization energies. Their ability to conduct electricity and heat is also due to the mobility of their outer electron.

## Reaction with water

The alkali metals react with water to produce hydrogen and the metal hydroxide. When you drop a piece of one of the first three elements into a small beaker containing distilled water, the following happens.

- Lithium floats and reacts slowly. It releases hydrogen but keeps its shape.
- Sodium reacts with a vigorous release of hydrogen. The heat produced is sufficient to melt the unreacted metal, which forms a small ball that moves around on the water surface.
- Potassium reacts even more vigorously to produce sufficient heat to ignite the hydrogen produced. It produces a lilac coloured flame and moves excitedly on the water surface.

The metals are called alkali metals because the resulting solution is alkaline owing to the presence of the hydroxide ion formed.

For example, with potassium:

$$2K(s) + 2H_2O(l) \rightarrow 2KOH(aq) + H_2(g)$$

As KOH is an ionic compound (Chapter 4) which dissociates in water, it is more appropriate to write the equation as:

$$2K(s) + 2H_2O(l) \rightarrow 2K^+(aq) + 2OH^-(aq) + H_2(g)$$

The reaction becomes more vigorous as the group is descended. The most reactive element, caesium, has the lowest ionization energy and so forms positive ions most readily.

### Exercises

**22** State two observations you could make during the reaction between sodium and water. Give an equation for the reaction.

**23** Which property increases down Group 1 from lithium to caesium?

    **A**  electronegativity    **B**  first ionization energy    **C**  melting point
    **D**  chemical reactivity

## Group 17: the halogens

The Group 17 elements exist as diatomic molecules, $X_2$. Their physical and chemical properties are summarized in the table below.

| Physical properties | Chemical properties |
|---|---|
| • They are coloured.<br>• They show a gradual change from gases ($F_2$ and $Cl_2$), to liquid ($Br_2$), and solids ($I_2$ and $At_2$). | • They are very reactive non-metals. Reactivity decreases down the group.<br>• They form ionic compounds with metals and covalent compounds with other non-metals. |

The trend in reactivity can be explained by their readiness to accept electrons, as illustrated by their very exothermic electron affinities discussed earlier. The nuclei have a high effective charge, of approximately +7, and so exert a strong pull on any electron from other atoms. This electron can then occupy the outer energy level of the halogen atom and complete a stable octet. The attraction is greatest for the smallest atom fluorine, which is the most reactive non-metal in the Periodic Table. Reactivity decreases down the group as the atomic radius increases and the attraction for outer electrons decreases.

### Reaction with Group 1 metals

The halogens react with the Group 1 metals to form ionic **halides**. The halogen atom gains one electron from the Group 1 element to form a halide ion $X^-$. The resulting ions both have the stable octet of the noble gases. For example:

$$2Na(s) + Cl_2(g) \rightarrow 2NaCl(s)$$

The electrostatic force of attraction between the oppositely charged $Na^+$ and $Cl^-$ ions bonds the ions together. The outer electron moves like a harpoon from the sodium to the chlorine. Once the transfer is complete the ions are pulled together by the mutual attraction of their opposite charges (Figure 3.9).

The names of diatomic elements all end in *-ine* or *-gen*.

**Group 1 and Group 17 are on opposite sides of the Periodic Table and show opposite trends in their reactivities and melting points.**

From left to right: chlorine ($Cl_2$), bromine ($Br_2$), and iodine ($I_2$). These are toxic and reactive non-metals. Chlorine is a green gas at room temperature. Bromine is a dark liquid, although it readily produces a brown vapour. Iodine is a crystalline solid.

Two halogens are named by their colours: *chloros* means 'yellowish green' and *ioeides* is 'violet' in Greek. One is named by its smell: *'bromos'* is the Greek word for 'stench'.

**TOK** Chlorine was used as a chemical weapon during World War I. Should scientists be held morally responsible for the applications of their discoveries?

**TOK** The electron involved in the bonding of sodium is described as a harpoon. How useful are similes and metaphors in the sciences? Does the language we use in the sciences have a descriptive or interpretive function?

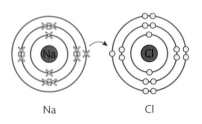
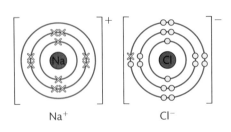

**Figure 3.9** The high effective charge of the chlorine nucleus pulls the outer electron from the sodium atom. Once the transfer is complete the ions are pulled together by electrostatic attraction.

Sodium reacting with chlorine to form sodium chloride (NaCl, table salt). The violent reaction is exothermic and releases much heat.

When chlorine water is added to the colourless potassium bromide solution, bromine (yellow/orange) is formed. Bromine is displaced from solution by the more reactive chlorine.

**The more reactive halogen displaces the ions of the less reactive halogen from its compounds.**

The most vigorous reaction occurs between the elements which are furthest apart in the Periodic Table: the most reactive alkali metal, francium, at the bottom of Group 1, with the most reactive halogen, fluorine, at the top of Group 17.

## Displacement reactions

The relative reactivity of the elements can also be seen by placing them in direct competition for an extra electron. When chlorine is bubbled through a solution of potassium bromide the solution changes from colourless to orange owing to the production of bromine:

$$2KBr(aq) + Cl_2(aq) \rightarrow 2KCl(aq) + Br_2(aq)$$

$$2Br^-(aq) + Cl_2(aq) \rightarrow 2Cl^-(aq) + Br_2(aq)$$

A chlorine nucleus has a stronger attraction for an electron than a bromine nucleus because of its smaller atomic radius and so takes the electron from the bromide ion. The chlorine has gained an electron and so forms the chloride ion, $Cl^-$. The bromide ion loses an electron to form bromine.

Other reactions are:

$$2I^-(aq) + Cl_2(aq) \rightarrow 2Cl^-(aq) + I_2(aq)$$

The colour changes from colourless to dark orange/brown owing to the formation of iodine.

$$2I^-(aq) + Br_2(aq) \rightarrow 2Br^-(aq) + I_2(aq)$$

The colour darkens owing to the formation of iodine. To distinguish between bromine and iodine more effectively, the final solution can be shaken with a hydrocarbon solvent. Iodine forms a violet solution and bromine a dark orange solution as shown in the photo.

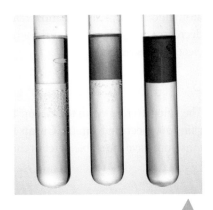

Solutions of chlorine (left), bromine (middle), and iodine (right) in water (lower part) and cyclohexane (upper part). Chlorine dissolves in water, but the halogens are generally more soluble in non-polar solvents like cyclohexane.

## The halides

The halogens form insoluble salts with silver. Adding a solution containing the halide to a solution containing silver ions produces a **precipitate** that is useful in identifying the halide ion.

$$Ag^+(aq) + X^-(aq) \rightarrow AgX(s)$$

This is shown in this photo.

Silver halide precipitates formed by reacting silver nitrate ($AgNO_3$) with solutions of the halides. From left to right, these are silver chloride (AgCl), silver bromide (AgBr), and silver iodide (AgI).

## Exercises

**24** How do the reactivities of the alkali metals and the halogens vary down the group?

**25** Which property of the halogens increases from fluorine to iodine?

   **A** ionic charge         **C** melting point of the element

   **B** electronegativity     **D** chemical reactivity with metals

**26** Which pair of elements reacts most readily?

   **A** $Li + Br_2$      **B** $Li + Cl_2$      **C** $K + Br_2$      **D** $K + Cl_2$

**27** Chlorine is a greenish-yellow gas, bromine is a dark red liquid, and iodine is a dark grey solid. Identify the property which most directly causes these differences in volatility.

   **A** the halogen–halogen bond energy

   **B** the number of neutrons in the nucleus of the halogen atom

   **C** the number of outer electrons in the halogen atom

   **D** the number of electrons in the halogen molecule

**28** A paper published in April 2010 by Yu. Ts. Oganessian and others claims the synthesis of isotopes of a new element with atomic number 117. One of the isotopes is $^{293}_{117}Uus$. Which of the following statements is correct?

   **A** the nucleus of the atom has a relative charge of +117

   **B** $^{293}_{117}Uus$ has a mass number of 117

   **C** there are 262 neutrons in $^{293}_{117}Uus$

   **D** the atomic number is 293 – 117

## NATURE OF SCIENCE

Element 117 would be a new halogen. Whereas the discovery of the early elements involved the practical steps of extraction and isolation often performed by one individual, later elements are made by teams of scientists working together. New elements are as much invented as discovered, but their existence provides further knowledge about the natural world. The first synthetic elements were the transuranics. They are radioactive elements which are heavier than uranium, the heaviest natural element.

Claims that a new halogen, element 117, had been made were first made in April 2010 but these findings have yet to be confirmed. Scientists publish their own results in scientific journals after their work has been reviewed by several experts working in the same field. This process is called peer review. If the element turns out to have the properties predicted of a halogen below astatine, it will provide more evidence to support our model of the atom and the Periodic Table.

Glenn Seaborg (1912–1999) pointing to the element seaborgium (Sg). Seaborg discovered the transuranic element plutonium (Pu) in 1940. Seaborg also discovered americium (Am) and seven other transuranics. He won the 1951 Nobel Prize in Chemistry.

**TOK** How can the production of artificial elements give us more knowledge of the natural world?

## Bonding of the Period 3 oxides

The transition from metallic to non-metallic character is illustrated by the bonding of the Period 3 oxides. Ionic compounds are generally formed between metal and non-metal elements and so the oxides of elements Na to Al have **giant ionic** structures. Covalent compounds are formed between non-metals, so the oxides of phosphorus, sulfur, and chlorine are **molecular covalent**. The oxide of silicon, which is a metalloid, has a **giant covalent** structure.

The ionic character of a compound depends on the *difference* in electronegativity between its elements. Oxygen has an electronegativity of 3.4, so the ionic character of the oxides decreases from left to right, as the electronegativity values of the Period 3 elements approach this value (Figure 3.10).

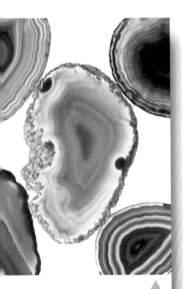

Cut and polished slices of agate. Agate is a variety of quartz (silicon dioxide). The colours are formed by impurities and the concentric bands are formed as successive layers of the oxide precipitate out of solution during formation of the agate.

**Figure 3.10** Electronegativities increase across the period and approach 3.4, the value for oxygen.

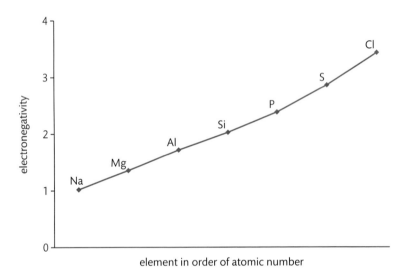

The oxides become more ionic down a group as the electronegativity decreases.

The conductivity of the molten oxides gives an experimental measure of their ionic character, as is shown in the table below. They only conduct electricity in the liquid state, when the ions are free to move.

Note that the maximum oxidation number of a Period 3 element is related to the group number. It is +1 for elements in Group 1, +2 for elements in Group 2, +3 for elements in Group 13, +4 for elements in Group 14, and so on. Oxidation numbers are discussed in Chapter 9.

| Formula of oxide | $Na_2O(s)$ | $MgO(s)$ | $Al_2O_3(s)$ | $SiO_2(s)$ | $P_4O_{10}(s)/$ $P_4O_6(s)$ | $SO_3(l)/$ $SO_2(g)$ | $Cl_2O_7(l)/$ $Cl_2O(g)$ |
|---|---|---|---|---|---|---|---|
| Oxidation number | +1 | +2 | +3 | +4 | +5/+3 | +6/+4 | +7/+1 |
| Electrical conductivity in molten state | high | high | high | very low | none | none | none |
| Structure | giant ionic | | | giant covalent | molecular covalent | | |

## Acid–base character of the Period 3 oxides

The acid–base properties of the oxides are closely linked to their bonding and structure. Metallic elements, which form ionic oxides, are basic; non-metal oxides, which are covalent, are acidic. Aluminium oxide, which can be considered as an ionic oxide with some covalent character, shows amphoteric properties – reacting with both acids and bases. The acid–base properties of Period 3 oxides are shown in the table below.

| Formula of oxide | $Na_2O(s)$ | $MgO(s)$ | $Al_2O_3(s)$ | $SiO_2(s)$ | $P_4O_{10}(s)$/ $P_4O_6(s)$ | $SO_3(l)$/ $SO_2(g)$ | $Cl_2O_7(l)$/ $Cl_2O(g)$ |
|---|---|---|---|---|---|---|---|
| Acid–base character | basic | | amphoteric | acidic | | | |

Oxides of metals are ionic and basic. Oxides of the non-metals are covalent and acidic. Aluminium oxide is amphoteric.

Amphoteric oxides show both acidic and basic properties.

Non-metal oxides are responsible for acid rain. This is discussed in more detail in Chapter 8.

Aqueous solutions of the oxides of some elements with universal indicator. Sulfur trioxide forms sulfuric acid in water, which is highly acidic. Sodium oxide forms sodium hydroxide, which is a strong alkali. Non-metal oxides have low pH and metal oxides have high pH. The acidity of the iron compounds is discussed later in the chapter.

Alkalis are bases which are soluble in water. They form hydroxide ions in aqueous solution.

## Basic oxides

Sodium oxide and magnesium oxide dissolve in water to form alkaline solutions owing to the presence of hydroxide ions:

$$Na_2O(s) + H_2O(l) \rightarrow 2NaOH(aq)$$

$$MgO(s) + H_2O(l) \rightarrow Mg(OH)_2(aq)$$

A basic oxide reacts with an acid to form a salt and water. The oxide ion combines with two $H^+$ ions to form water:

$$O^{2-}(s) + 2H^+(aq) \rightarrow H_2O(l)$$

$$Li_2O(s) + 2HCl(aq) \rightarrow 2LiCl(aq) + H_2O(l)$$

$$MgO(s) + 2HCl(aq) \rightarrow MgCl_2(aq) + H_2O(l)$$

## Acidic oxides

The non-metallic oxides react readily with water to produce acidic solutions. Phosphorus(V) oxide reacts with water to produce phosphoric(V) acid:

$$P_4O_{10}(s) + 6H_2O(l) \rightarrow 4H_3PO_4(aq)$$

Phosphorus(III) oxide reacts with water to produce phosphoric(III) acid:

$$P_4O_6(s) + 6H_2O(l) \rightarrow 4H_3PO_3(aq)$$

When an element forms a number of different oxides it is useful to use the oxidation number of the element to distinguish between them. The oxidation number is shown by a Roman numeral. Oxidation numbers are discussed in more detail in Chapter 9. It is worth noting here that the oxidation numbers of sulfur, phosphorus, and chlorine remain unchanged as their oxides are added to water, in the examples shown. This is not always the case. For example, the oxidation number of one of the chlorine atoms increases, and the other decreases, when the gas is added to water.

$$Cl_2(g) + H_2O(l) \rightleftharpoons HOCl(aq) + HCl(aq)$$

**0**      **+1**      **−1** oxidation number of Cl

Sulfur trioxide reacts with water to produce sulfuric(VI) acid:

$$SO_3(l) + H_2O(l) \rightarrow H_2SO_4(aq)$$

Sulfur dioxide reacts with water to produce sulfuric(IV) acid:

$$SO_2(g) + H_2O(l) \rightarrow H_2SO_3(aq)$$

Dichlorine heptoxide ($Cl_2O_7$) reacts with water to produce chloric(VII) acid ($HClO_4$):

$$Cl_2O_7(l) + H_2O(l) \rightarrow 2HClO_4(aq)$$

Dichlorine monoxide ($Cl_2O$) reacts with water to produce chloric(I) acid (HClO):

$$Cl_2O(l) + H_2O(l) \rightarrow 2HClO(aq)$$

Silicon dioxide does not react with water, but reacts with concentrated alkalis to form silicates:

$$SiO_2(s) + 2OH^-(aq) \rightarrow SiO_3{}^{2-}(aq) + H_2O(l)$$

**TOK**

The Periodic Table has been called the most elegant classification chart ever devised. Is it a description or an explanation of periodic trends? Do other unifying systems exist in other areas of knowledge? To what extent do the classification systems we use affect the knowledge we obtain?

## Amphoteric oxides

Aluminium oxide does not affect the pH when it is added to water as it is essentially insoluble. It has amphoteric properties, however, as it shows both acid and base behaviour. For example, it behaves as a base as it reacts with sulfuric acid:

$$Al_2O_3(s) + 6H^+ \rightarrow 2Al^{3+}(aq) + 3H_2O(l)$$

$$Al_2O_3(s) + 3H_2SO_4(aq) \rightarrow Al_2(SO_4)_3(aq) + 3H_2O(l)$$

and behaves as an acid when it reacts with alkalis such as sodium hydroxide:

$$Al_2O_3(s) + 3H_2O(l) + 2OH^-(aq) \rightarrow 2Al(OH)_4{}^-(aq)$$

### Exercises

**29** An oxide of a Period 3 element is a solid at room temperature and forms a basic oxide. Identify the element.

   **A** Mg       **B** Al       **C** P       **D** S

**30** Which pair of elements has the most similar chemical properties?

   **A** N and S       **B** N and P       **C** P and Cl       **D** N and Cl

**31** Identify the oxide which forms an acidic solution when added to water.

   **A** $Na_2O(s)$       **B** MgO(s)       **C** $SiO_2(s)$       **D** $SO_3(g)$

**32 (a)** Use the data below to identify the state of the four oxides listed under standard conditions.

High melting points are associated with ionic or covalent giant structures, low melting points with molecular covalent structures.

| Oxides | Melting point / K | Boiling point / K |
| --- | --- | --- |
| MgO | 3125 | 3873 |
| $SiO_2$(quartz) | 1883 | 2503 |
| $P_4O_{10}$ | 297 | 448 |
| $SO_2$ | 200 | 263 |

**(b)** Explain the difference in melting points by referring to the bonding and structure in each case.

**(c)** The oxides are added to separate samples of pure water. State whether the resulting liquid is acidic, neutral, or alkaline. Describe all chemical reactions by giving chemical equations.

**(d)** Use chemical equations to describe the reactions of aluminium oxide with:

   **(i)** hydrochloric acid

   **(ii)** sodium hydroxide

Make sure that you understand all the chemical equations presented in this topic. You could be expected to reproduce them under exam conditions.

**33** Describe the acid–base character of the oxides of the Period 3 elements Na to Ar. For sodium oxide and sulfur trioxide, write balanced equations to illustrate their acid–base character.

# 13.1 First-row d-block elements

## Understandings:

- Transition elements have variable oxidation numbers, form complex ions with ligands, have coloured compounds, and display catalytic and magnetic properties.

  ### Guidance
  *Common oxidation numbers of the transition metal ions are listed in the IB Data booklet in sections 9 and 14.*

- Zn is not considered to be a transition element as it does not form ions with incomplete d orbitals.
- Transition elements show an oxidation number of +2 when the s electrons are removed.

## Applications and skills:

- Explanation of the ability of transition metals to form variable oxidation states from successive ionization energies.
- Explanation of the nature of the coordinate bond within a complex ion.
- Deduction of the total charge given the formula of the ion and ligands present.
- Explanation of the magnetic properties in transition metals in terms of unpaired electrons.

The elements of the d block have properties which have allowed us to advance technologically throughout the ages. To many people, a typical metal is a transition metal of the d block. We use the strength of iron and its alloy steel to construct buildings and machines, the electrical conductivity and low reactivity of copper to direct the flow of electricity and water, and we treasure gold and silver because of their appearance and rarity.

The ten elements of the first row of the d-block elements from Sc to Zn show a 'lull' in the periodic patterns we have seen in elements of the s and p blocks. The 10 d-block elements have similar physical and chemical properties.

**TOK** The medical symbols for female and male originate from the alchemical symbols for copper and iron. What role has the pseudoscience of alchemy played in the development of modern science?

## Transition elements have characteristic properties

### Electron configuration

The similarity in the properties of first row d-block elements is illustrated by the relatively small range in atomic radii (Figure 3.11).

To understand the trend in atomic radii it is instructive to consider the electron configuration of the elements, summarized in the table on page 120. The unusual electron configurations of chromium (Cr) and copper (Cu) are due to the stability of the half-filled and filled 3d sub-level respectively. This is discussed on page 82.

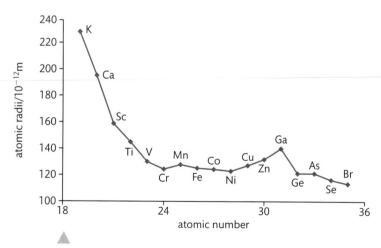

**Figure 3.11** Atomic radii across Period 4.

| Element | Core | 3d | | | | | 4s |
|---|---|---|---|---|---|---|---|
| Sc | [Ar] | ↑ | | | | | ↑↓ |
| Ti | [Ar] | ↑ | ↑ | | | | ↑↓ |
| V | [Ar] | ↑ | ↑ | ↑ | | | ↑↓ |
| Cr | [Ar] | ↑ | ↑ | ↑ | ↑ | ↑ | ↑ |
| Mn | [Ar] | ↑ | ↑ | ↑ | ↑ | ↑ | ↑↓ |
| Fe | [Ar] | ↑↓ | ↑ | ↑ | ↑ | ↑ | ↑↓ |
| Co | [Ar] | ↑↓ | ↑↓ | ↑ | ↑ | ↑ | ↑↓ |
| Ni | [Ar] | ↑↓ | ↑↓ | ↑↓ | ↑ | ↑ | ↑↓ |
| Cu | [Ar] | ↑↓ | ↑↓ | ↑↓ | ↑↓ | ↑↓ | ↑ |
| Zn | [Ar] | ↑↓ | ↑↓ | ↑↓ | ↑↓ | ↑↓ | ↑↓ |

The relatively small decrease in atomic radii across the d block is due to the correspondingly small increase in effective nuclear charge experienced by the outer 4s electrons. The increase in nuclear charge due to the added proton is largely offset by the addition of an electron in an *inner* 3d sub-level. This similarity in atomic radii explains the ability of the transition metals to form alloys: the atoms of one d-block metal can be replaced by atoms of another without too much disruption of the solid structure. The small increase in effective nuclear charge also accounts for the small range in first ionization energies across the first transition series. As discussed in Chapter 2 (page 83), it is the 4s electrons which are removed first when the atom is ionized.

## Exercises

**34** State the electron configuration of the following metal ions by filling in the boxes below. Use arrows to represent the electron spin.

| Ion | 3d | | | | | 4s |
|---|---|---|---|---|---|---|
| Sc$^{3+}$ | | | | | | |
| Ti$^{3+}$ | | | | | | |
| Ni$^{2+}$ | | | | | | |
| Zn$^{2+}$ | | | | | | |

## Physical properties

The transition elements are all metals with the following general physical properties:

- high electrical and thermal conductivity
- high melting point
- malleable – they are easily beaten into shape
- high tensile strength – they can hold large loads without breaking
- ductile – they can be easily drawn into wires
- iron, cobalt, and nickel are ferromagnetic.

These properties can be explained in terms of the strong metallic bonding found in the elements. As the 3d electrons and 4s electrons are close in energy, they are all involved in bonding, and form part of the delocalized sea of electrons which holds the metal lattice together (Chapter 4). This large number of delocalized electrons accounts for the strength of the metallic bond and the high electrical conductivity. The smaller atomic radii of the d-block metals compared to their s-block neighbours also account, in part, for their higher densities.

The magnetic properties of the transition metal elements and compounds are discussed in more detail later.

## Chemical properties

The chemical properties of the transition metals are very different from those of the s-block metals. Transition metals:

- form compounds with more than one oxidation number
- form a variety of complex ions
- form coloured compounds
- act as catalysts when either elements or compounds.

These properties are discussed in more detail later in the chapter.

## Zinc is not a transition metal

The absence of zinc (Zn) from the collection of coloured ions in the photo above is significant. Zinc compounds do not generally form coloured solutions. Zinc is a d-block element but not a transition metal as it does not display the characteristic properties listed earlier; it shows only the +2 oxidation state in its compounds. The reason for its exceptional behaviour can be traced to the electronic configuration of its atom and the $Zn^{2+}$ ion – the d sub-level is complete in both species (see the table on page 122). The electron configuration of the transition metal ions $Ti^{2+}$ and $Cu^{2+}$ are included for comparison. $Sc^{3+}$(aq) is also colourless in aqueous solution as it has no d electrons, but it is a transition metal as its atom has an incomplete d sub-shell, and the $Sc^{2+}$ ion, although not common, does exist with a single d electron.

The properties and uses of the transition metals make them important commodities on the international stock exchange. The mining and extraction of these elements is an important industrial process in the economic development of some countries.

Transition element ions are coloured in aqueous solutions. From left to right the transition metal ions are: $Ti^{2+}$(aq), $V^{3+}$(aq), $VO^{2+}$(aq), $Cr^{3+}$(aq), $Cr_2O_7^{2-}$(aq), $Mn^{2+}$(aq), $MnO_4^-$(aq), $Fe^{3+}$(aq), $Co^{2+}$(aq), $Ni^{2+}$(aq), and $Cu^{2+}$(aq).

**Transition metals are element whose atoms have an incomplete d sub-shell, or which can give rise to cations with an incomplete d sub-shell.**

| Ion | Core | 3d | | | | | 4s |
|-----|------|----|----|----|----|----|----|
| Sc³⁺ | [Ar] | | | | | | |
| Ti²⁺ | [Ar] | ↑ | ↑ | | | | |
| Cu²⁺ | [Ar] | ↑↓ | ↑↓ | ↑↓ | ↑↓ | ↑ | |
| Zn²⁺ | [Ar] | ↑↓ | ↑↓ | ↑↓ | ↑↓ | ↑↓ | |

## Explanation of variable oxidation number of transition elements

One of the key features of transition metal chemistry is the wide range of oxidation numbers that the metals display in their compounds. This should be contrasted with the s-block metals, which show only the oxidation state corresponding to their group number in their compounds. Calcium, for example, only shows the +2 state whereas titanium shows the +4 , +3, and +2 states (Figure 3.12). The difference in behaviour can be related to patterns in successive ionization energies.

| Element | Electron configuration |
|---------|------------------------|
| Ca | $1s^22s^22p^63s^23p^64s^2$ |
| Ti | $1s^22s^22p^63s^23p^63d^24s^2$ |

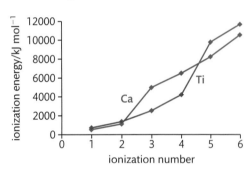

**Figure 3.12** Successive ionization energies for Ca and Ti.

The Ca³⁺ ion is energetically unstable because there is a large jump in ionization energy as the third electron is removed from the inner 3p orbital. The increase in successive energies for titanium is more gradual as the 3d and 4s orbitals are close in energy. Titanium shows the +2, +3, and +4 oxidation states. A large jump occurs between the fourth and fifth ionization energies, as the inner 3p electron is removed, so titanium does not form the +5 state.

The oxidation states of the d block elements are summarized below. The more common oxidation states are highlighted in blue.

The oxidation states of vanadium and manganese can be investigated experimentally.

| Sc | Ti | V | Cr | Mn | Fe | Co | Ni | Cu | Zn |
|----|----|----|----|----|----|----|----|----|----|
| | | | | | | | | +1 | |
| +2 | +2 | +2 | +2 | +2 | +2 | +2 | +2 | +2 | +2 |
| +3 | +3 | +3 | +3 | +3 | +3 | +3 | +3 | +3 | |
| | +4 | +4 | +4 | +4 | +4 | +4 | +4 | | |
| | | +5 | +5 | +5 | +5 | +5 | | | |
| | | | +6 | +6 | +6 | | | | |
| | | | | +7 | | | | | |

The following points are important and should be noted.

Chromium chloride $CrCl_3$ (violet) and chromium nitrate $Cr(NO_3)_3$ (green) illustrate chromium in the oxidation state +3. In potassium chromate $K_2CrO_4$ (yellow) and potassium dichromate $K_2Cr_2O_7$ (orange) chromium has an oxidation state of +6.

- All the transition metals show both the +2 and +3 oxidation states. The $M^{3+}$ ion is the stable state for the elements from scandium to chromium, but the $M^{2+}$ state is more common for the later elements. The increased nuclear charge of the later elements makes it more difficult to remove a third electron.
- The maximum oxidation state of the elements increases in steps of +1 and reaches a maximum at manganese. These states correspond to the use of both the 4s and 3d electrons in bonding. Thereafter, the maximum oxidation state decreases in steps of −1.
- Oxidation states above +3 generally show covalent character. Ions of higher charge have such a large charge density that they polarize negative ions and increase the covalent character of the compound (see Figure 3.13).
- Compounds with higher oxidation states tend to be oxidizing agents. The use of potassium dichromate(VI) ($K_2Cr_2O_7$), for example, in the oxidation of alcohols is discussed in Chapter 10.

▲

**Figure 3.13** The high charge density of the transition metal ions $M^{n+}$ pulls the weakly held outer electrons of the $X^-$ ion. This polarization of negative ions increases the covalent character of the compounds of the transition metal ions with oxidation number greater than +3.

## Exercises

**35** Identify the property/properties which are characteristic of an element found in the d block of the Periodic Table.

   **A**   all the compounds of the element are ionic
   **B**   the element exhibits a variety of oxidation states and colours in its compounds
   **C**   the element has a low melting point
   **D**   the element is a good conductor of heat and electricity

**36** Identify the oxidation number which is the most common among the first-row transition elements.

   **A**   +1          **B**   +2          **C**   +4          **D**   +6

**37** An element has the electronic configuration $1s^2 2s^2 2p^6 3s^2 3p^6 3d^3 4s^2$. Which oxidation state(s) would this element show?

   **A**   +2 and +3 only     **B**   +2 and +5 only     **C**   +3 and +5 only     **D**   +2, +3, +4, and +5

**38 (a)** State the full electron configuration of zinc (Zn).
   **(b)** State the full electron configuration of $Zn^{2+}$.
   **(c)** Explain why zinc is not classed as a transition metal.

**39** State the oxidation states shown by calcium and chromium, and explain the difference in their behaviour.

**NATURE OF SCIENCE**

Science involves the investigation of patterns and trends. The d block elements follow certain patterns of behaviour, but scandium, zinc, chromium, and copper show significant discrepancies. Scientific knowledge is provisional and continues to evolve; scandium is sometimes classed as a transition element due to the rarity of the +2 oxidation state, but this is now considered to be incorrect.

## Complex ions

**Complex ions**

Full details of how to carry out this experiment with a worksheet are available online.

Transition metal ions in solution have a high charge density and attract water molecules which form coordinate bonds with the positive ions to form a **complex ion**.

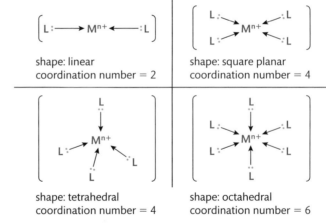

**Figure 3.14** The complex ion $[Fe(H_2O)_6]^{3+}$. The water molecules are ligands as they form coordinate bonds to the central ion.

More generally a complex is formed when a central ion is surrounded by molecules or ions which possess a lone pair of electrons. These surrounding species (**ligands**), are attached via a coordinate bond. All ligands have at least one atom with a lone pair of electrons which is used to form a coordinate bond with the central metal ion.

A coordinate bond uses a lone pair of electrons to form a covalent bond.

A ligand is a species that uses a lone pair of electrons to form a coordinate bond with a metal ion.

The word 'ligand' is derived from *ligandus*, the Latin word for 'bound'.

The number of coordinate bonds from the ligands to the central ion is called the **coordination number**. The shapes of some complex ions and their coordination numbers are shown in Figure 3.15.

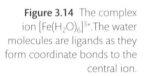

shape: linear
coordination number = 2

shape: square planar
coordination number = 4

shape: tetrahedral
coordination number = 4

shape: octahedral
coordination number = 6

**Figure 3.15** Shapes and coordination numbers of some complex ions.

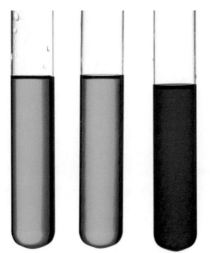

In aqueous solution, water molecules generally act as ligands but these can be replaced in a process known as ligand exchange. As complexes often have distinctive colours they can be used in qualitative analysis.

A solution of pale blue copper(II) sulfate contains $[Cu(H_2O)_6]^{2+}$(left). The yellow $[CuCl_4]^{2-}$ complex, formed when concentrated hydrochloric acid is added (centre) gives a vivid green colour in the presence of $[Cu(H_2O)_6]^{2+}$. The dark blue $[Cu(H_2O)_2(NH_3)_4]^{2+}$ complex is formed when ammonia is added.

Some examples of complex ions are shown in the table below.

| Complex | Ligand | Coordination number | Oxidation number of central ion | Shape |
|---|---|---|---|---|
| $[Fe(H_2O)_6]^{3+}$ | $H_2O$ | 6 | +3 | octahedral |
| $[Co(NH_3)_6]^{3+}$ | $NH_3$ | 6 | +3 | octahedral |
| $[CuCl_4]^{2-}$ | $Cl^-$ | 4 | +2 | tetrahedral |
| $[Fe(CN)_6]^{3-}$ | $CN^-$ | 6 | +3 | octahedral |
| $[Ag(NH_3)_2]^+$ | $NH_3$ | 2 | +1 | linear |
| $MnO_4^-$ | $O^{2-}$ | 4 | +7 | tetrahedral |
| $Ni(CO)_4$ | $CO$ | 4 | 0 | tetrahedral |
| $PtCl_2(NH_3)_2$ | $Cl^-$ and $NH_3$ | 4 | +2 | square planar |

## Polydentate ligands act as chelating agents

Some species have more than one lone pair available to form a coordinate bond with the central transition ion. $EDTA^{4-}$ (old name ethylenediaminetetraacetic acid) is an example of a polydentate ligand as it has six atoms (two nitrogen atoms and four oxygen atoms) with lone pairs available to form coordinate bonds.

**Figure 3.16** The polydentate ligand $EDTA^{4-}$ can take the place of six monodentate ligands as it has six lone pairs available.

EDTA$^{4-}$ is thus equivalent to six monodentate ligands and is described as a hexadentate (six-toothed) ligand. It can occupy all the octahedral sites and grip the central ion in a six-pronged claw called a **chelate**.

> A chelate is a complex containing at least one polydentate ligand. The name is derived from the Greek word for *claw*.

Chelates are very important in foods and all biological systems. EDTA$^{4-}$ forms chelates with many metal ions and is widely used as a food additive as it removes transition ions from solution and so inhibits enzyme-catalysed oxidation reactions.

## Exercises

**40** Identify the species which cannot act as a ligand:

| | | | |
|---|---|---|---|
| **A** $H_2O$ | **B** CO | **C** $CH_4$ | **D** $Cl^-$ |

**41** Consider the reaction below:

$$[Cu(H_2O)_6]^{2+}(aq) + 4HCl(aq) \rightarrow [CuCl_4]^{2-}(aq) + 6H_2O(aq) + 4H^+(aq)$$

Which of the following is acting as a ligand?

| | | | |
|---|---|---|---|
| **A** $H^+$ only | **B** $H^+$ and $Cl^-$ only | **C** $H_2O$ and $Cl^-$ only | **D** $H^+$, $H_2O$, and $Cl^-$ |

**42** The colour and formulas of some coordination compounds of hydrated forms of chromium(III) chloride are listed in this table.

| | I | II | III |
|---|---|---|---|
| Formula | $[Cr(H_2O)_6]Cl_3$ | $[CrCl(H_2O)_5]Cl_2.H_2O$ | $[CrCl_2(H_2O)_4]Cl.2H_2O$ |
| Colour | purple | blue-green | green |

What are the charges on each of the complex ions?

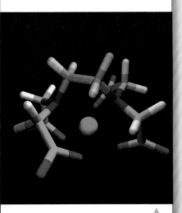

Computer graphic of a molecule of the chelating agent ethyldiaminetetraacetic acid surrounding a magnesium ion (Mg, green sphere). The atoms (tubes) of the molecule are colour-coded: carbon (light blue), nitrogen (dark blue), hydrogen (white) and oxygen (red). EDTA is used to preserve DNA (deoxyribonucleic acid) samples by removing the magnesium ions that aid the degradation of DNA. It is also used to detoxify patients suffering from heavy metal poisoning (chelation therapy).

| | I | II | III |
|---|---|---|---|
| **A** | 0 | 0 | 0 |
| **B** | + | 2+ | 3+ |
| **C** | 2+ | 3+ | + |
| **D** | 3+ | 2+ | + |

**43** Identify the feature which is an essential characteristic of all ligands.

    **A** a negative charge
    **B** an electronegative atom
    **C** the presence of a non-bonding pair of electrons
    **D** the presence of two or more atoms

**44** Elements with atomic number 21 to 30 are Sc, Ti, V, Cr, Mn, Fe, Co, Ni, Cu, and Zn.

    **(a)** Identify which of the d-block elements is not considered to be a transition metal.
    **(b)** Deduce the oxidation state of the transition metal in the following species.
        **(i)** $Fe_3O_4$
        **(ii)** $MnO_4^-$
        **(iii)** $CrO_4^{2-}$
        **(iv)** $[Fe(CN)_6]^{4-}$

## CHALLENGE YOURSELF

**5** Assuming the transition metal ion, $M^{n+}$, is originally surrounded by water molecules, the ligand replacement reaction can be represented as:

$$[M(H_2O)_6]^{n+} + EDTA^{4-} \rightarrow$$
$$[M(EDTA)]^{n-4} + 6H_2O$$

Predict the entropy change for this reaction and explain the stability of the chelate formed.

## Transition metals and their ions are important catalysts

The use of the transition elements in construction was discussed earlier. The use of the metals and their compounds as catalysts is also of economic importance. A catalyst is a substance which alters the rate of reaction, by providing an alternative reaction pathway with a lower activation energy (see Chapter 6).

Catalysts play an essential role in the chemical industry as they allow chemical processes to proceed at an economical rate.

## Transition metals and their ions as heterogeneous catalysts

In **heterogeneous** catalysis, the catalyst is in a different state from the reactants. The ability of transition metals to use their 3d and 4s electrons to form weak bonds to reactant molecules makes them effective heterogeneous catalysts as they provide a surface for the reactant molecules to come together with the correct orientation.

Examples of transition metals as heterogeneous catalysts include the following.

More details of heterogeneous and homogeneous catalysis are discussed in Chapter 12.

• Iron (Fe) in the Haber process:

$$N_2(g) + 3H_2(g) \rightleftharpoons 2NH_3(g)$$

Ammonia ($NH_3$) is the raw material for a large number of other useful chemical products such as fertilizers, plastics, drugs, and explosives.

• Nickel (Ni) in the conversion of alkenes to alkanes:

The action of transition metal catalysis such as manganese (IV) oxide in the decomposition of hydrogen peroxide, and cobalt chloride in the decomposition of potassium sodium tartrate.

This reaction allows unsaturated vegetable oils with a carbon–carbon double bond to be converted to margarine.

• Palladium (Pd) and platinum (Pt) in catalytic converters:

$$2CO(g) + 2NO(g) \rightarrow 2CO_2(g) + N_2(g)$$

This reaction removes harmful primary pollutants from a car's exhaust gases.

• $MnO_2$ in the decomposition of hydrogen peroxide:

$$2H_2O_2(aq) \rightarrow 2H_2O(l) + O_2(g)$$

• $V_2O_5$ in the Contact process:

$$2SO_2(g) + O_2(g) \rightleftharpoons 2SO_3(g)$$

Sulfur trioxide ($SO_3$) is used in the production of sulfuric acid, the manufacturing world's most important chemical.

Heterogeneous catalysis is generally preferred in industrial processes as the catalyst can be easily removed by filtration from the reaction mixture after use.

## Ions of transition metals as homogeneous catalysts

**Homogeneous** catalysts are in the same state of matter as the reactants. The ability of transition metals to show variable oxidation states allows them to be particularly effective homogeneous catalysts in redox reactions. As many of the enzyme-catalysed cell reactions in the body involve transition metals as homogeneous catalysis, they are of fundamental biological importance. Examples include the following.

The molecular structure of a heme group of the blood protein hemoglobin, which carries oxygen and carbon dioxide around the body. The $Fe^{2+}$ (red) ion is bonded to four nitrogen atoms (yellow). The flat group of four rings around the $Fe^{2+}$ ion gives oxygen easy access to the iron from above, allowing binding and release without any chemical change.

• $Fe^{2+}$ in heme: oxygen is transported through the bloodstream by forming a weak bond with the heme group of hemoglobin. This group contains a central $Fe^{2+}$ ion surrounded by four nitrogen atoms. The $O_2$–$Fe^{2+}$ bond is easily broken when the oxygen needs to be released.

• $Co^{3+}$ in vitamin $B_{12}$. Part of the vitamin $B_{12}$ molecule consists of an octahedral $Co^{3+}$ complex. Five of the sites are occupied by

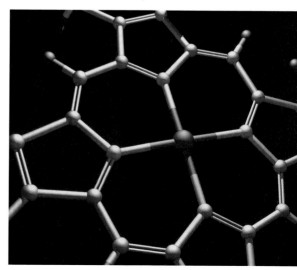

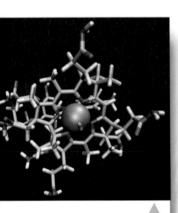

Vitamin $B_{12}$. The central $Co^{3+}$(purple) is coordinated to five nitrogen atoms (blue).

nitrogen atoms, leaving the sixth site available for biological activity. Vitamin $B_{12}$ is needed for the production of red blood cells and for a healthy nervous system.

As homogeneous catalysts mix effectively with the reactants, they work under the mild conditions of the human body.

### Exercises

**45** Study the structure of heme shown in the picture on page 127.

   **(a)** What is the oxidation state of the central iron ion?
   **(b)** What is the geometry of the nitrogen atoms around the central iron ion?
   **(c)** Explain why the complex is ideally suited to carry oxygen around the body

**46** Name the catalyst in each of the following processes:

   **(a)** The hydrogenation of vegetable oils to form margarine:

$$R^1\text{–}CH=CH\text{–}R^2 + H_2 \rightarrow R^1\text{–}CH_2\text{–}CH_2\text{–}R^2$$

   **(b)** The manufacture of sulfuric acid in the Contact process.
   **(c)** The removal of carbon monoxide and nitrogen monoxide from exhaust emissions.

**47 (a)** Distinguish between homogeneous catalysis and heterogeneous catalysis.
   **(b)** Explain why the transition metals make effective heterogeneous catalysts.
   **(c)** Explain why heterogeneous catalysts are generally used in industrial processes.

## The magnetic properties of the transition metals and their compounds

Every spinning electron in an atom or molecule can behave as a tiny magnet. Electrons with opposite spins behave like minute bar magnets with opposing orientation and so have no net magnetic effect. Most substances have paired electrons that pair up and so are non-magnetic. Some transition metals and their compounds are unusual in having some electrons that remain unpaired, which when aligned lead to magnetic properties.

### Substances can be distinguished by their response to externally applied magnetic fields

Materials are classified as diamagnetic, paramagnetic, or ferromagnetic based on their behaviour when placed in an external magnetic field.

- **Diamagnetism** is a property of all materials and produces a very weak opposition to an applied magnetic field.
- **Paramagnetism**, which only occurs with substances which have unpaired electrons, is stronger than diamagnetism. It produces magnetization proportional to the applied field and in the same direction.
- **Ferromagnetism** is the largest effect, producing magnetizations sometimes orders of magnitude greater than the applied field.

Most materials are diamagnetic as the orbital motion of their electrons produces magnetic fields which oppose any external field. Paramagnetism is a property of single atoms or ions with unpaired spinning electrons, whereas ferromagnetism only occurs if there is long range ordering of the unpaired electrons.

### Iron, cobalt, and nickel are ferromagnetic

Iron, nickel, and cobalt are ferromagnetic; the unpaired d electrons in large numbers of atoms line up with parallel spins in regions called **domains**. Although these domains are generally randomly oriented with respect to each another, they can become more ordered if exposed to an external magnetic field. The magnetism remains after the external magnetic field is removed, as the domains remain aligned due to the long range interaction between the unpaired electrons in the different atoms.

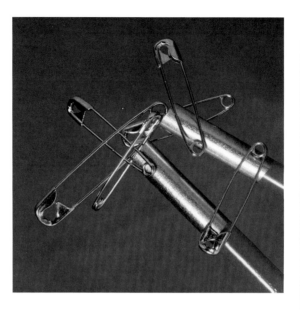

## Transition metals and their complexes show paramagnetic properties

Transition metal complexes with unpaired electrons show paramagnetic properties as they are pulled into a magnetic field. Paramagnetic and diamagnetic complexes can be distinguished using the experimental arrangement in Figure 3.17. The sample to be tested, shown in green, is placed in an electromagnet. When the field is turned on paramagnetic materials are attracted into the magnetic field of the electromagnet and so will move downwards causing the blue counterweight to move up; the sample appears to have increased in mass. Diamagnetic materials will move out of the field in the opposite direction and so will appear to have reduced in mass.

Paramagnetism increases with the number of unpaired electrons so generally increases from left to right across the Periodic Table, reaches a maximum at chromium, and decreases. Zinc has no unpaired electrons and so is diamagnetic.

The presence of electron spin was first demonstrated in the Stern–Gerlach experiment. A beam of silver atoms divided into two as it travelled through an electromagnetic field. Atoms with the unpaired electron spinning ↑ moved in the opposite direction to those atoms with electrons spinning ↓.

The action at a distance of invisible magnetic forces mystified early thinkers, who drew parallels between magnetism and other areas of human experiences – such as infection and love. Remnants of this confusion are reflected in our language; the French word for 'magnet' is *aimant*. Language allows knowledge to be passed on to others and to be accumulated over time for future generations. This is how knowledge is 'shared', but outdated ideas and theories can be communicated in the same way. How does the vocabulary we use help and hinder the pursuit of knowledge?

**TOK**

A horseshoe magnet holding some safety-pins. Magnetic objects have the capability to retain a certain amount of magnetization once exposed to an external magnetic field. Domains in the crystalline structure of these metals are small regions, 0.1–1 mm across, in which the magnetic moment of each atom has the same direction. When an external field is applied all the domains are lined up with the field, providing the high magnetization.

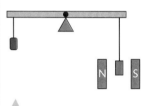

**Figure 3.17** Diamagnetic and paramagnetic materials will move in different directions in the field produced by an electromagnet. The sample, shown in green, will appear to increase in mass when the field is turned on if it is paramagnetic, and will appear to decrease in mass if it is diamagnetic.

**NATURE OF SCIENCE**

Magnetism was used in navigation by the Chinese long before it was explained scientifically. Historically, technology emerged before science. Materials were often used practically long before there was an understanding of why they possessed their properties.

In today's world the reverse is often the case, with scientific understanding leading to technological developments, which in turn drive further developments in scientific ideas.

## Exercises

**48** Which of the following elements would be expected to be paramagnetic?

   **A**   Ca         **B**   Zn         **C**   He         **D**   Mn

**49** Which of the elements is the most paramagnetic?

   **A**   Sc         **B**   Ti         **C**   V         **D**   Cr

**50** Explain why chromium is the most paramagnetic element in the first transition series and why zinc is diamagnetic.

# 13.2 Coloured complexes

## Understandings:

- The d sub-level splits into two sets of orbitals of different energy in a complex ion.
- Complexes of d-block elements are coloured, as light is absorbed when an electron is excited between the d orbitals.
- The colour absorbed is complementary to the colour observed.

### Guidance

*The relation between the colour observed and absorbed is illustrated by the colour wheel in the IB Data booklet in section 17.*

## Applications and skills:

- Explanation of the effect of the identity of the metal ion, the oxidation number of the metal, and the identity of the ligand on the colour of transition metal ion complexes.

### Guidance

*Students are not expected to recall the colour of specific complex ions.*

- Explanation of the effect of different ligands on the splitting of the d orbitals in transition metal complexes and colour observed using the spectrochemical series.

### Guidance

*The spectrochemical series is given in the IB data booklet in section 15. A list of polydentate ligands is given in the data booklet in section 16. Students are not expected to know the different splitting patterns and their relation to the coordination number. Only the splitting of the 3-d orbitals in an octahedral crystal field is required.*

The colours of complex ions can be experimentally investigated.

The colour of transition metal ions (shown in the table below) can be related to the presence of partially filled d orbitals. The ion $Sc^{3+}$ is colourless because the 3d sub-level is empty; $Zn^{2+}$ is colourless because the 3d sub-level is full.

| Ion | Electron configuration | Colour |
|---|---|---|
| $Sc^{3+}$ | [Ar] | colourless |
| $Ti^{3+}$ | [Ar] $3d^1$ | violet |
| $V^{3+}$ | [Ar] $3d^2$ | green |
| $Cr^{3+}$ | [Ar] $3d^3$ | violet |
| $Mn^{2+}$ | [Ar] $3d^5$ | pink |
| $Fe^{3+}$ | [Ar] $3d^5$ | yellow |
| $Fe^{2+}$ | [Ar] $3d^6$ | green |
| $Co^{2+}$ | [Ar] $3d^7$ | pink |
| $Ni^{2+}$ | [Ar] $3d^8$ | green |
| $Cu^{2+}$ | [Ar] $3d^9$ | blue |
| $Zn^{2+}$ | [Ar] $3d^{10}$ | colourless |

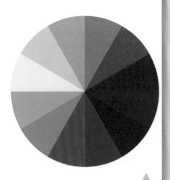

**Figure 3.18** The colour wheel. There is a colour wheel in section 17 of the IB Data booklet.

## The visible spectrum

The visible spectrum ranges from 400 nm to about 700 nm. The colour we see depends on wavelength.

| Colour | Wavelength range / nm |
|--------|----------------------|
| Red | 630–700 |
| Orange | 590–630 |
| Yellow | 560–590 |
| Green | 490–560 |
| Blue | 450–490 |
| Violet | 400–450 |

The colour of a substance is determined by which colour(s) of light it absorbs and which colour(s) it transmits or reflects (the complementary colour(s)). Copper sulfate, for example, appears turquoise because it absorbs orange light. Orange and turquoise are complementary colours; they are opposite each other in the colour wheel (Figure 3.18).

## Transition metals appear coloured because they absorb visible light

As discussed in Chapter 2, white light is composed of all the colours of the visible spectrum. Transition metal compounds appear coloured because their ions absorb some of these colours. $[Fe(H_2O)_6]^{3+}$, for example, appears yellow because it absorbs light in the blue region of the spectrum (Figures 3.19 and 3.20).

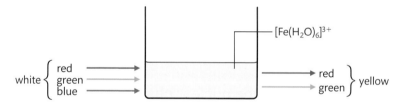

## Transition metals absorb light because the d orbitals split into two sub-levels

The d orbitals in an isolated transition metal atom are said to be degenerate as they all have the same energy. However, in the electric field produced by the ligand's lone pair of electrons, they split into two sub-levels. Consider, for example, the octahedral complex $[Ti(H_2O)_6]^{3+}$ with the water molecules placed along the x-, y-, and z-axes (Figure 3.21).

When light passes through a solution of $[Ti(H_2O)_6]^{3+}$, one 3d electron is excited from the lower to the higher energy sub-level (Figure 3.22). A photon of green light is absorbed and light of the complementary colour (purple) is transmitted, which accounts for the purple colour of a solution of $[Ti(H_2O)_6]^{3+}$.

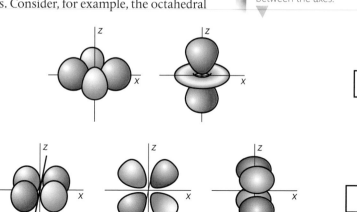

**Figure 3.19** Complementary colours. Yellow light (a mixture of red and green light) added to blue light makes white light. White light changes to yellow when the blue is removed.

**Figure 3.20** The ion $Fe^{3+}$ appears yellow because it absorbs blue light. Yellow is the complementary colour to blue.

**Figure 3.21** An electron in a d orbital orientated along the bond axis has a higher energy than an electron in one of the three orbitals which point between the axes.

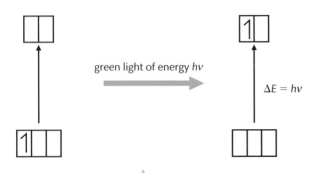

green light of energy $h\nu$

$\Delta E = h\nu$

**Figure 3.22** Green light of energy $h\nu$ excites an electron from a d orbital of lower energy to a d orbital of higher energy. The transmitted light is purple.

Cobalt chloride paper is used to indicate the presence of water. The colour changes from blue to pink as the ligands change from $Cl^-$ ions to $H_2O$ molecules.

$[Mn(H_2O)_6]^{2+}$ (on the left) is pale pink and $[Fe(H_2O)_6]^{3+}$ (on the right) is yellow/brown. Both have the same electron configuration. The manganate ion, $MnO_4^-$ (in the centre) shows manganese in a +7 oxidation state. It has a distinctive intense purple colour.

The energy separation between the orbitals is $\Delta E$ and hence the colour of the complex depends on the following factors:

- the nuclear charge and the identity of the central metal ion;
- the charge density of the ligand;
- the geometry of the complex ion (the electric field created by the ligand's lone pair of electrons depends on the geometry of the complex ion);
- the number of d electrons present and hence the oxidation number of the central ion.

Each of these factors is discussed in turn below.

 Don't confuse the colour of transition metal ions, produced as a result of light being absorbed as electrons jump between the split d sub-levels, with the emission of colour produced when excited electrons return to the ground state.

## The colour depends on the nuclear charge and identity of the central metal ion

The strength of the coordinate bond between the ligand and the central metal ion depends on the electrostatic attraction between the lone pair of electrons and the nuclear charge of the central ion. Ligands interact more effectively with the d orbitals of ions with a higher nuclear charge. For example, $[Mn(H_2O)_6]^{2+}$ and $[Fe(H_2O)_6]^{3+}$ both have the same electron configuration but the iron nucleus has a higher nuclear charge and so has a stronger interaction with the water ligands. Manganese(II) compounds are pale pink in aqueous solution as the ions absorb in the green region of the visible spectrum of light, whereas iron(III) compounds are yellow/brown as they absorb higher energy light in the blue region of the spectrum.

## Charge density of the ligand

The spectrum of the copper complex formed when four of the water molecule ligands are replaced by four ammonia molecules is shown in Figure 3.23. The $[Cu(NH_3)_4(H_2O)_2]^{2+}$ complex absorbs the shorter wavelength yellow light, therefore the complex has a deep blue colour. Ammonia has a greater charge density than water and so produces a larger split in the d orbitals. The higher charge density of the ammonia compared to water also explains their relative base strengths.

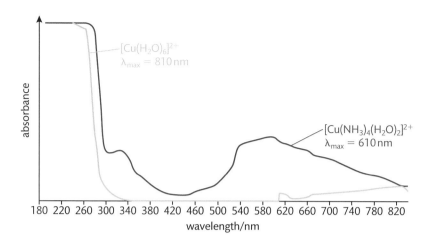

**Figure 3.23** The electronic UV–vis absorption spectrum of some copper complexes. $[Cu(H_2O)_6]^{2+}$ absorbs light in the orange region of the spectrum and so appears turquoise. $[Cu(NH_3)_4(H_2O)_2]^{2+}$ absorbs light in the yellow region of the spectrum and so appears dark blue.

The **spectrochemical series** arranges the ligands according to the energy separation, $\Delta E$, between the two sets of d orbitals. The wavelength at which maximum absorbance occurs, $\lambda_{max}$, decreases with the charge density of the ligand, as shown in the table below. The large iodide ion, which has the lowest charge density, repels the d electrons the least and so produces a small splitting. The smaller chloride ion, with a relatively high charge density, has a larger splitting. The large splitting of the $CN^-$ ion and carbon monoxide is more complex and is partly due to the presence of $\pi$ bonding in the ligand; electrons in the p orbitals on the carbon atoms can interact with the d orbitals of the transition metal. The spectrochemical series is given in section 15 of the IB Data booklet.

| Ligand | $I^-$ | $Br^-$ | $S^{2-}$ | $Cl^-$ | $H_2O$ | $OH^-$ | $NH_3$ | $CN^-$ | CO |
|---|---|---|---|---|---|---|---|---|---|
| $\lambda_{max}$ | longest wavelength | wavelength increasing ← | | | | | | | shortest wavelength |
| $\Delta E$ | weakest field | $\Delta E$ increasing → | | | | | | | strongest field |

## Geometry of the complex

The change of the colour in the cobalt complex in the photo on the right is also in part due to the change in coordination number and geometry of the complex ion. The splitting in energy of the d orbitals depends on the relative orientation of the ligand and the d orbitals.

## Number of d electrons and oxidation state of the central metal ion

The strength of the interaction between the ligand and the central metal ion and the amount of electron repulsion between the ligand and the d electrons depends on the number of d electrons and hence the oxidation state of the metal. For example, $[Fe(H_2O)_6]^{2+}$ absorbs violet light and so appears green/yellow, whereas $[Fe(H_2O)_6]^{3+}$ absorbs blue light and appears orange/brown.

The pink solution (left) contains the complex ion $[Co(H_2O)_6]^{2+}$. If concentrated hydrochloric acid is added (centre), a blue colour is seen. The chloride ions of the acid displace the water in the cobalt complex, forming a new complex ion, $[CoCl_4]^{2-}$, with a characteristic blue colour. Adding water (right) reverses the reaction.

### NATURE OF SCIENCE

The colour of transition metal complexes can be explained through the use of models and theories based on how electrons are distributed in d orbitals. A detailed understanding needs a consideration of the three-dimensional symmetry of the complex ions. The ability to visualize the three-dimensional arrangement of atoms and ions is a key skill of the chemist.

Emeralds are green due to trace amounts of chromium.

## Worked example

State the formula and the shape of the complex ion formed in the following reactions.

(a) Some iron metal is dissolved in sulfuric acid and then left exposed to air until a yellow solution is formed.

(b) Concentrated hydrochloric acid is added to aqueous copper sulfate solution to form a yellow solution.

(c) A small volume of sodium chloride is added to aqueous silver nitrate solution. The white precipitate dissolves to form a colourless solution when ammonia solution is added.

### Solution

(a) $[Fe(H_2O)_6]^{3+}$

The oxidation state is +3 as the complex is left exposed to air.

The shape is octahedral as the coordination number = 6 (see left).

(b) The complex $[CuCl_4]^{2-}$ is yellow.

The shape is tetrahedral as the coordination number = 4 (see left).

(c) $NaCl(aq) + AgNO_3(aq) \rightarrow AgCl(s) + NaNO_3(aq)$

The complex $[Ag(NH_3)_2]^+$ is linear as the coordination number is 2.

$[H_3N—Ag—NH_3]^+$

## Exercises

**52** The colour of transition metal complexes depends on several factors.

    **(a)** Suggest why the colour of $[Cr(H_2O)_6]^{3+}$ is different from the colour of $[Fe(H_2O)_6]^{3+}$.

    **(b)** Suggest why the colour of $[Fe(H_2O)_6]^{2+}$ is different from the colour of $[Fe(H_2O)_6]^{3+}$.

    **(c)** Suggest why the colour of $[Fe(NH_3)_6]^{2+}$ is different from the colour of $[Fe(H_2O)_6]^{3+}$.

**53** Explain why $Fe^{2+}(aq)$ is coloured and can behave as a reducing agent, whereas $Zn^{2+}(aq)$ is not coloured and does not behave as a reducing agent.

**54** The absorption spectrum of $[Ti(H_2O)_6]^{3+}$ is shown below. Use the colour wheel to suggest a colour for the complex.

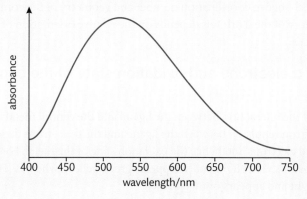

**55 (a)** Draw a diagram to show how the electrons are arranged in $Fe^{2+}$ when it is present in the $[Fe(H_2O)_6]^{2+}$ ion.

    **(b)** Predict whether the splitting of the d orbitals in $[Fe(CN)_6]^{4-}$ would be less than or greater than the splitting in $[Fe(H_2O)_6]^{2+}$.

**56 (a)** Explain why $[Fe(H_2O)_6]^{3+}$ and $[Cr(H_2O)_6]^{3+}$ have different colours.

    **(b)** Explain why $[Fe(H_2O)_6]^{3+}$ and $[Fe(H_2O)_6]^{2+}$ have different colours.

## NATURE OF SCIENCE

Colour is a trans-disciplinary subject that is of interest to the artist and the scientist alike. Science looks for the hidden structures and processes at smaller dimensions to explain observable phenomena. The poet John Keats criticised Newton for destroying the poetry of the rainbow by reducing it to the colours of a prism, but an explanation of colour in terms of electron transitions and molecular symmetries adds to our appreciation and understanding of the natural word.

## Practice questions

1   Which property generally decreases across Period 3?

   **A**  atomic number      **B**  electronegativity      **C**  atomic radius
   **D**  first ionization energy

2   Which statements about Period 3 are correct?
   I    The electronegativity of the elements increases across Period 3.
   II   The atomic radii of the elements decreases across Period 3.
   III  The oxides of the elements change from acidic to basic across Period 3.

   **A**  I and II only      **B**  I and III only      **C**  II and III only      **D**  I, II, and III

3   Which property decreases down Group 17 in the Periodic Table?

   **A**  melting point      **B**  electronegativity      **C**  atomic radius      **D**  ionic radius

4   Which oxides produce an acidic solution when added to water?
   I    $P_4O_{10}$
   II   MgO
   III  $SO_3$

   **A**  I and II only      **B**  I and III only      **C**  II and III only      **D**  I, II, and III

5   The $x$-axis of the graph on the right represents the atomic number of the elements in Period 3. Which variable could represent the $y$-axis?

   **A**  melting point      **B**  electronegativity      **C**  ionic radius      **D**  atomic radius

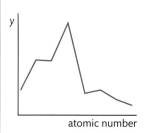

6   Which is the best definition of *electronegativity*?

   **A**  Electronegativity is the energy required for a gaseous atom to gain an electron.
   **B**  Electronegativity is the attraction of an atom for a bonding pair of electrons.
   **C**  Electronegativity is the attraction between the nucleus and the valence electrons of an atom.
   **D**  Electronegativity is the ability of an atom to attract electrons from another atom.

7   What happens when sodium is added to water?
   I    a gas is evolved
   II   the temperature of the water increases
   III  a clear, colourless solution is formed

   **A**  I and II only      **B**  I and III only      **C**  II and III only      **D**  I, II, and III

8   What are the products of the reaction between chlorine and water?

   **A**  $O_2$, $H_2$, and HCl      **B**  $H_2$ and $OCl_2$      **C**  HCl and HOCl      **D**  HOCl, $H_2$, and $Cl_2$

9   Which statements are correct for the complex ion $[CuCl_4]^{2-}$?
   I    The oxidation number of Cu in the complex ion is +2.
   II   The coordination number of the copper ion is 4.
   III  Chloride ions are behaving as ligands.

   **A**  I and II only      **B**  I and III only      **C**  II and III only      **D**  I, II, and III

**10** In which complexes does iron have an oxidation number of +3?

   I   $[Fe(H_2O)_6]^{3+}$

   II  $[Fe(H_2O)_5(CN)]^{2+}$

   III $[Fe(CN)_6]^{3-}$

   **A** I and II only      **B** I and III only      **C** II and III only      **D** I, II, and III

**11** Which transition element, or compound of a transition element, is used as a catalyst in the Contact process?

   **A** Fe             **B** $MnO_2$         **C** $V_2O_5$         **D** Ni

**12** Which process is responsible for the colour of a transition metal complex?

   **A** the absorption of light when electrons move between s orbitals and d orbitals

   **B** the emission of light when electrons move between s orbitals and d orbitals

   **C** the absorption of light when electrons move between different d orbitals

   **D** the emission of light when electrons move between different d orbitals

**13 (a)** Define the term *first ionization energy*. (2)

   **(b)** Explain why the first ionization energy of magnesium is higher than that of sodium. (2)

                                                        *(Total 4 marks)*

**14** Samples of sodium oxide and sulfur trioxide are added to separate beakers of water. Deduce the equation for each reaction and identify each oxide as acidic, basic, or neutral.

                                                        *(Total 3 marks)*

**15** Describe and explain what you will see if chlorine gas is bubbled through a solution of

   **(a)** potassium iodide (2)

   **(b)** potassium fluoride (1)

                                                        *(Total 3 marks)*

**16** The Periodic Table shows the relationship between electron configuration and the properties of elements and is a valuable tool for making predictions in chemistry.

   **(a)** Identify the property used to arrange the elements in the Periodic Table. (1)

   **(b)** Outline two reasons why electronegativity increases across Period 3 in the Periodic Table and one reason why noble gases are not assigned electronegativity values. (3)

                                                        *(Total 4 marks)*

**17 (a)** Outline two reasons why a sodium ion has a smaller radius than a sodium atom. (2)

   **(b)** Explain why the ionic radius of $P^{3-}$ is greater than the ionic radius of $Si^{4+}$. (2)

                                                        *(Total 4 marks)*

**18** Sodium oxide, $Na_2O$, is a white solid with a high melting point.

   **(a)** Explain why solid sodium oxide is a non-conductor of electricity. (1)

   **(b)** Molten sodium oxide is a good conductor of electricity. State the half-equation for the reaction occurring at the positive electrode during the electrolysis of molten sodium oxide. (1)

   **(c) (i)** State the acid/base nature of sodium oxide. (1)

       **(ii)** State the equation for the reaction of sodium oxide with water. (1)

                                                        *(Total 4 marks)*

**19** The graph below of the first ionization energy plotted against atomic number for the first 20 elements shows periodicity.

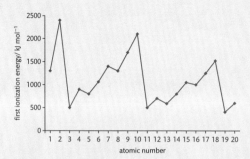

(a) Define the term *first ionization energy* and state what is meant by the term *periodicity*. (2)

(b) State the electron configuration of argon and explain why the noble gases, helium, neon, and argon, show the highest first ionization energies for their respective periods. (3)

(c) A graph of atomic radius plotted against atomic number shows that the atomic radius decreases across a period. Explain why chlorine has a smaller atomic radius than sodium. (1)

(d) Explain why a sulfide ion, $S^{2-}$, is larger than a chloride ion, $Cl^-$. (1)

(e) Explain why the melting points of the Group 1 metals (Li to Cs) decrease down the group whereas the melting points of the Group 17 elements (F to I) increase down the group. (3)

*(Total 10 marks)*

**20** When concentrated hydrochloric acid is added to a solution containing hydrated copper(II) ions, the colour of the solution changes from light blue to green. The equation for the reaction is:

$$[Cu(H_2O)_6]^{2+}(aq) + 4Cl^-(aq) \rightarrow [CuCl_4]^{2-}(aq) + 6H_2O(l)$$

(a) Explain what the square brackets around the copper containing species represent. (1)

(b) Explain why the $[Cu(H_2O)_6]^{2+}$ ion is coloured and why the $[CuCl_4]^{2-}$ ion has a different colour. (2)

*(Total 3 marks)*

To access weblinks on the topics covered in this chapter, please go to www.pearsonhotlinks.com and enter the ISBN or title of this book.

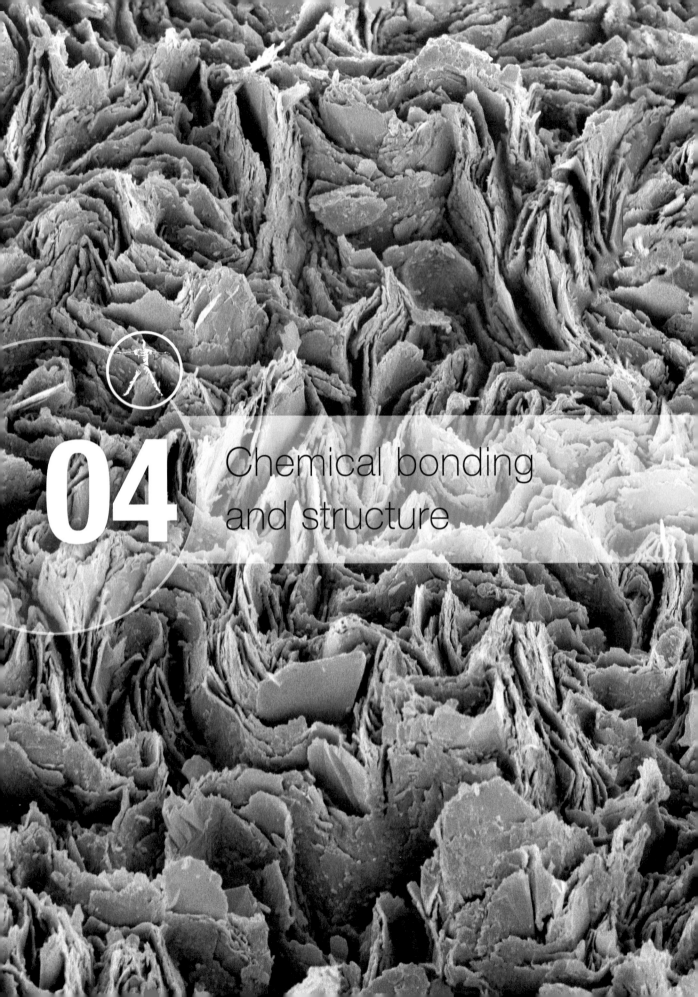

**04** Chemical bonding
and structure

# Essential ideas

**4.1**  Ionic compounds consist of ions held together in lattice structures by ionic bonds.

**4.2**  Covalent compounds form by the sharing of electrons.

**4.3**  Lewis (electron dot) structures show the electron domains in the valence shell and are used to predict molecular shape.

**4.4**  The physical properties of molecular substances result from different types of forces between their molecules.

**4.5**  Metallic bonds involve a lattice of cations with delocalized electrons.

**14.1**  Larger structures and more in-depth explanations of bonding systems often require more sophisticated concepts and theories of bonding.

**14.2**  Hybridization results from the mixing of atomic orbitals to form the same number of new equivalent hybrid orbitals that can have the same mean energy as the contributing atomic orbitals.

Scanning electron micrograph of graphite shows its layered structure. Graphite is a form of pure carbon, in which the bonding of atoms within a layer is much stronger than the forces between the layers. An understanding of bonding enables scientists to explain and predict many of the properties of materials.

We learned in Chapter 2 that all elements are made of atoms but that there are only about 100 chemically different types of atom. Yet we know that we live in a world made up of literally millions of different substances: somehow these must all be formed from just these 100 atomic building blocks. The extraordinary variety arises from the fact that atoms readily combine with each other and they do so in a myriad of different ways. They come together in small numbers or large, with similar atoms or very different atoms, but always the result of the combination is a stable association known as a **chemical bond**. Atoms linked together by bonds therefore have very different properties from their parent atoms.

In this chapter we will study the main types of chemical bonds – the ionic bond, the covalent bond, and the metallic bond – and also consider other forces that help to hold substances together. Our study of the covalent bond at this level will use some of the concepts from quantum mechanical theory developed in Chapter 2 to explain the shapes and properties of molecules in more detail. As electrons are the key to the formation of all these bonds, a solid understanding of electron configurations will help you.

Chemical reactions take place when some bonds break and others re-form. Being able to predict and understand the nature of the bonds within a substance is therefore central to explaining its chemical reactivity.

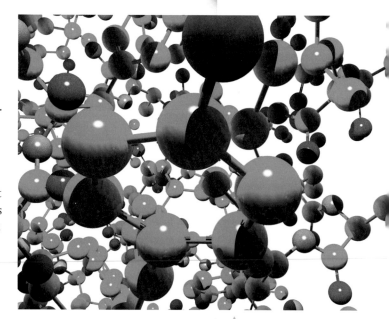

A molecule of insulin, the hormone essential for the regulation of glucose in the body. The ball-and-stick model shows all the atoms and bonds within the protein molecule. Insulin was the first protein to have its entire structure elucidated.

# 4.1 Ionic bonding and structure

## Understandings:

- Positive ions (cations) form by metals losing valence electrons.
- Negative ions (anions) form by non-metals gaining electrons.
- The number of electrons lost or gained is determined by the electron configuration of the atom.
- The ionic bond is due to electrostatic attraction between oppositely charged ions.
- Under normal conditions, ionic compounds are usually solids with lattice structures.

## Applications and skills:

- Deduction of the formula and name of an ionic compound from its component ions, including polyatomic ions.

  ### Guidance
  *Students should be familiar with the names of these polyatomic ions: $NH_4^+$, $OH^-$, $NO_3^-$, $HCO_3^-$, $CO_3^{2-}$, $SO_4^{2-}$, and $PO_4^{3-}$*

- Explanation of the physical properties of ionic compounds (volatility, electrical conductivity, and solubility) in terms of their structure.

## Ions form when electrons are transferred

**An ion is a charged particle. Ions form from atoms or from groups of atoms by loss or gain of one or more electrons.**

All atoms are electrically neutral, even though they contain charged particles known as protons and electrons. This is because the number of protons (+) is equal to the number of electrons (−), and so their charges cancel each other out. The positively charged protons, located within the nucleus of the atom, are not transferred during chemical reactions. Electrons, however, positioned outside the nucleus, are less tightly held and outer electrons, known as **valence electrons**, can be transferred when atoms react together. When this happens the atom is no longer neutral, but instead carries an electric charge and is called an **ion**. The charge on the ion which forms is therefore determined by how many electrons are lost or gained.

We learned in Chapter 3 that the group number in the Periodic Table relates to the number of electrons in the outer shell of the atoms of all the elements in that group. We also learned that Group 18 elements, known as the **noble gases**, where the atoms all have full outer shells of electrons, are especially stable and have almost no tendency to react at all. This full outer shell behaves in a sense like the 'ultimate goal' for other atoms: they react to gain the stability associated with this by losing or gaining the appropriate number of electrons, whichever is the easiest (in energetic terms).

It may help you to remember: CATion is PUSSYtive and aNion is Negative.

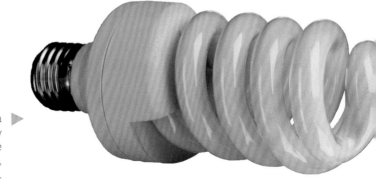

An energy-efficient light bulb. A compact fluorescent lamp has a gas-filled glass tube which contains a small amount of mercury vapour mixed with argon under low pressure. As argon is a noble gas, it is very unreactive owing to its stable electron arrangement, so it helps to provide an inert environment.

- Elements that have a small number of electrons in their outer shells (Groups 1, 2, and 13) will lose those electrons and form positive ions called **cations**. These elements are the **metals**.
- Elements that have higher numbers of electrons in their outer shells (Groups 15, 16, and 17) will gain electrons and form negative ions called **anions**. These elements are the **non-metals**.

We are now able to summarize how the position of an element in the Periodic Table enables us to predict the type of ion that it will form.

| Group number | Example | Number of valence electrons | Electrons lost or gained | Number of electrons transferred | Charge on ion formed | Type of element |
|---|---|---|---|---|---|---|
| 1 | sodium | 1 | lost | 1 | 1+ | metal |
| 2 | calcium | 2 | lost | 2 | 2+ | metal |
| 13 | aluminium | 3 | lost | 3 | 3+ | metal |
| 14 | carbon | 4 | – | – | – | non-metal |
| 15 | phosphorus | 5 | gained | 3 | 3– | non-metal |
| 16 | oxygen | 6 | gained | 2 | 2– | non-metal |
| 17 | bromine | 7 | gained | 1 | 1– | non-metal |

Note that elements in Group 14, having four electrons in their outer shell, do not have a tendency to gain or to lose electrons, and so they generally do not form ions. This is because the energy involved in transferring four electrons would simply be too large to be favourable. These elements therefore react to form a different type of bond, which we will discuss later in this chapter.

When an atom loses electrons it forms a positive ion, called a cation. When an atom gains electrons it forms a negative ion, called an anion. The number of charges on the ion formed is equal to the number of electrons lost or gained.

Metals form cations by losing valence electrons. Non-metals form anions by gaining electrons.

**TOK** Do we have direct or indirect evidence for the existence of ions? Is there an important difference between the two types of evidence?

## Worked example

Refer to the Periodic Table to deduce the charge on the ion formed when the following elements react:

**(i)** lithium
**(ii)** sulfur
**(iii)** argon

### Solution

**(i)** lithium is in Group 1 so forms $Li^+$
**(ii)** sulfur is in Group 16 so forms $S^{2-}$
**(iii)** argon is in Group 18 so does not form ions

For some elements though, it is difficult to predict the ion that will form from its position in the Periodic Table. For example, as we learned in Chapter 3, the metals occurring in the middle of the Periodic Table, known as the **transition elements**, have an electron configuration that allows them to lose different numbers of electrons from their d sub-shell and so form stable ions with different charges. The transition element iron, Fe, for example, can form $Fe^{2+}$ by losing two electrons or $Fe^{3+}$ by losing three electrons, depending on the reacting conditions. The two ions have distinct properties, such as forming compounds with different colours.

Compounds containing different ions of iron can be distinguished by colour: the left beaker contains $Fe^{2+}(aq)$ and the right beaker $Fe^{3+}(aq)$. Similar colour changes occur when iron rusts as it reacts with oxygen to form these different ions.

Fehling's reagent uses the different colours of the copper ions to test for simple sugars. The left tube containing the blue $Cu^{2+}$ ion changes to the red $Cu^+$ ion seen on the right when warmed with glucose or other 'reducing sugars'.

Likewise, the element copper can exist as $Cu^{2+}$ and $Cu^+$ and again these ions can be distinguished by colour.

Other examples of elements that form ions that are not obvious from their group number are:

• lead, Pb, despite being in Group 14, forms a stable ion $Pb^{2+}$
• tin, Sn, also in Group 14, can form $Sn^{4+}$ and $Sn^{2+}$
• silver, Ag, forms the ion $Ag^+$
• hydrogen, H, can form $H^-$ (hydride) as well as the more common $H^+$.

When the charge on an ion needs to be specified, the oxidation number is given in Roman numerals in brackets after the name of the element. For example, the red $Cu^+$ ion shown above can be written as copper(I) oxide. Oxidation numbers are explained fully in Chapter 9.

Finally, there are some ions that are made up of more than one atom which together have experienced a loss or gain of electrons and so carry a charge. These species are called **polyatomic ions**, and many of them are found in commonly occurring compounds. It will help you to become familiar with the examples in the table below, as you will often use them when writing formulas and equations. (Note that this information is not supplied in the IB data booklet.)

> **!** When writing the symbol for ions, note the charge is written as a superscript with the number first and the charge next, e.g. $N^{3-}$. When an ion X carries a charge of 1+ or 1– it is written just as $X^+$ or $X^-$.

> **!** Note the common names of some compounds give a clue to their composition. Here you can see that the ending '-ate' refers to ions that contain oxygen bonded to another element.

| Polyatomic ion name | Charge on ion | Symbol | Example of compound containing this ion |
|---|---|---|---|
| nitrate | 1– | $NO_3^-$ | lead nitrate |
| hydroxide | 1– | $OH^-$ | barium hydroxide |
| hydrogencarbonate | 1– | $HCO_3^-$ | potassium hydrogencarbonate |
| carbonate | 2– | $CO_3^{2-}$ | magnesium carbonate |
| sulfate | 2– | $SO_4^{2-}$ | copper sulfate |
| phosphate | 3– | $PO_4^{3-}$ | calcium phosphate |
| ammonium | 1+ | $NH_4^+$ | ammonium chloride |

We will learn how to write the formulas for these compounds in the next section.

# Ionic compounds form when oppositely charged ions attract

Ions do not form in isolation. Rather the process of **ionization** – where electrons are transferred between atoms – occurs when an atom that loses electrons passes them directly to an atom that gains them. Typically, this means electrons are transferred from a metal element to a non-metal element. For example, sodium (metal) passes an electron to chlorine (non-metal) when they react together.

$$\text{Na} \cdot \quad + \quad \overset{\times\times}{\underset{\times\times}{\times}\text{Cl}\times} \quad \longrightarrow \quad [\text{Na}]^+ \quad [\overset{\times\times}{\underset{\times\times}{\cdot}\text{Cl}\times}]^-$$

| $1s^22s^22p^63s^1$ | $1s^22s^22p^63s^23p^5$ | $1s^22s^22p^6$ | $1s^22s^22p^63s^23p^6$ |
|---|---|---|---|
| sodium atom | chlorine atom | sodium ion | chloride ion |

Note that both ion products, $Na^+$ and $Cl^-$, have the electron configuration of a noble gas.

Now the oppositely charged ions resulting from this electron transfer are attracted to each other and are held together by electrostatic forces. These forces are known as an **ionic bond**, and ions held together in this way are known as **ionic compounds**.

Remember that in forming the ionic compound there is no net loss or gain of electrons, and so the ionic compound, like the atoms that formed it, must be electrically neutral. Writing the formula for the ionic compound therefore involves *balancing the total number of positive and negative charges*, taking into account the different charges on each ion.

For example, magnesium oxide is made up of magnesium ions $Mg^{2+}$ and oxide ions $O^{2-}$. Here each magnesium atom has transferred *two* electrons to each oxygen atom and so the compound contains equal numbers of each ion. Its formula, $Mg^{2+}O^{2-}$, is usually written as MgO. But when magnesium reacts with fluorine, each Mg loses *two* electrons, whereas each F gains only *one* electron. So it will take two fluorine atoms to combine with each magnesium atom, and the compound that results will therefore have the ratio Mg : F = 1 : 2. This is written as $Mg^{2+}F^-_2$ or $MgF_2$.

## Worked example

Write the formula for the compound that forms between aluminium and oxygen.

### Solution

1   Check the Periodic Table for the ions that each element will form.
    aluminium in Group 13 will form $Al^{3+}$; oxygen in Group 16 will form $O^{2-}$

2   Write the number of the charge above the ion:    **3**    **2**
                                                      Al     O

Cross-multiply these numbers

Or you can directly balance the charges: here you need 6 of each charge:
$$2 \times Al^{3+} = 6+ \text{ and } 3 \times O^{2-} = 6-$$

3   Write the final formula using subscripts to show the number of ions: $Al_2O_3$

Coloured scanning electron micrograph of crystals of table salt, sodium chloride, NaCl. The very reactive elements sodium and chlorine have combined together to form this stable compound containing $Na^+$ and $Cl^-$ ions.

> The ionic bond is due to electrostatic attraction between oppositely charged ions.

> Note that in many non-metal elements the ending of the name changes to '-ide' when ions are present. For example, *chlorine* (the element) becomes *chloride* (the ion), *oxygen* becomes *oxide*, *nitrogen* becomes *nitride*, etc.

> Note the convention in naming ionic compounds that the positive ion is written first and the negative ion second.

> Note that the formula of the compound shows the *simplest ratio* of the ions it contains. So, for example, magnesium oxide is not $Mg_2O_2$ but MgO.

It is common practice to leave the charges out when showing the final formula. If the formula contains more than one polyatomic ion, brackets are used around the ion before the subscript.

### Worked example

Write the formula for ammonium phosphate.

### Solution

The compound contains two polyatomic ions, and you need to know these:

$$NH_4^+ \text{ and } PO_4^{3-}$$

Balancing the charges: $3 \times NH_4^+ = 3+$ and $1 \times PO_4^{3-} = 3-$ or:

Following the steps above:

$$\begin{matrix} 1 & \diagdown\!\!\!\!\diagup & 3 \\ NH_4^+ & & PO_4^{3-} \end{matrix}$$

So the formula is $(NH_4)_3PO_4$.

### Exercises

1. Write the formula for each of the compounds in the table on page 142.
2. Write the formula for each of the following compounds:

    **(a)** potassium bromide
    **(b)** zinc oxide
    **(c)** sodium sulfate
    **(d)** copper(II) bromide
    **(e)** chromium(III) sulfate
    **(f)** aluminium hydride

3. Name the following compounds:

    **(a)** $Sn_3(PO_4)_2$
    **(b)** $Ti(SO_4)_2$
    **(c)** $Mn(HCO_3)_2$
    **(d)** $BaSO_4$
    **(e)** $Hg_2S$

4. What are the charges on the positive ions in each of the compounds in Q3 above?
5. What is the formula of the compound that forms from element A in Group 2 and element B in Group 15?
6. Explain what happens to the electron configurations of Mg and Br when they react to form the compound magnesium bromide.

## Ionic compounds have a lattice structure

The forces of electrostatic attraction between ions in a compound cause the ions to surround themselves with ions of opposite charge. As a result, the ionic compound takes on a predictable three-dimensional crystalline structure known as an **ionic lattice**. The details of the lattice's geometry vary in different compounds, depending mainly on the sizes of the ions, but it always involves this fixed arrangement of ions based on a repeating unit. The term **coordination number** is used to express the number of ions that surround a given ion in the lattice. For example, in the sodium chloride lattice, the coordination number is six because each $Na^+$ ion is surrounded by six $Cl^-$ ions and each $Cl^-$ ion is surrounded by six $Na^+$ ions.

Note that the lattice consists of a very large number of ions and it can grow indefinitely. As ionic compounds do not therefore exist as units with a fixed number of ions, their formulas are simply an expression of the *ratio* of ions present. The simplest ratio is known as the **formula unit**, which is an empirical formula, as described in Chapter 1.

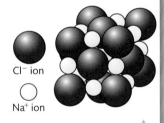

$Cl^-$ ion

$Na^+$ ion

**Figure 4.1** The NaCl lattice is built up from oppositely charged sodium and chloride ions.

Make sure that you avoid the term 'molecular formula' when describing ionic compounds, but instead use the term formula unit.

We will learn in Chapter 5 that **lattice energy** is a measure of the strength of attraction between the ions within the lattice. This is greater for ions that are small and highly charged, as they have a larger charge density.

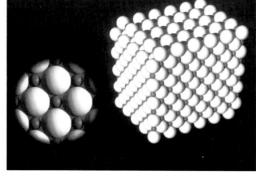

## The physical properties of ionic compounds reflect their lattice structure

Physical properties are those that can be examined without chemically altering the substance. Our knowledge of ionic bonds and lattice structure helps us to interpret and explain some of these properties for ionic compounds.

### Melting points and boiling points

Ionic compounds tend to have high melting and boiling points as the forces of electrostatic attraction between the ions in the lattice are strong and so require large amounts of heat energy to break. These compounds are therefore solids at room temperature, and will only melt at very high temperatures. Sodium chloride, for example, remains solid until about 800 °C.

The melting and boiling points are generally higher when the charge on the ions is greater, due to the increased attraction between the ions. For example, the table below compares the melting points of sodium oxide and magnesium oxide.

| Ionic compound | Charge on metal ion | Melting point |
|---|---|---|
| $Na_2O$ | 1+ | 1132 °C |
| MgO | 2+ | 2800 °C |

The high melting points of ionic compounds become an economic consideration in many industrial processes, such as the electrolysis of molten ionic compounds discussed in Chapter 9. It can be very expensive to maintain such high temperatures, and this is an important factor in considering suitable methods to extract a reactive metal such as aluminium from its ore.

**Volatility** is a term used to describe the tendency of a substance to vaporize. In summary, ionic compounds can be described as having a low volatility or being non-volatile. Our everyday encounter with them as crystalline solids with low odour is consistent with this.

### Solubility

Solubility refers to the ease with which a solid (the solute) becomes dispersed through a liquid (the solvent) to form a solution. You probably know from common observations that common salt, sodium chloride, readily dissolves in water but does not dissolve in oil. Why is this? There are several factors involved, but in general, solubility is determined by the degree to which the separated particles of solute are able to form bonds or attractive forces with the solvent.

Ionic liquids are efficient solvents with low volatility and are being used increasingly as solvents in Green Chemistry for energy applications and industrial processes. They are usually made of organic salts.

## CHALLENGE YOURSELF

1 The melting point of aluminium oxide, $Al_2O_3$, is slightly lower than that of magnesium oxide, despite the 3+ charge on the aluminium ion. What factors might help to explain this?

 **Ionic compounds have low volatility.**

**Ionic compounds are generally soluble in ionic or polar solvents but not soluble in non-polar solvents.**

**Figure 4.2** Dissolving of NaCl in water involves the attraction of the polar water molecules to the opposite charged ions in the NaCl lattice, and the hydration of the separated ions.

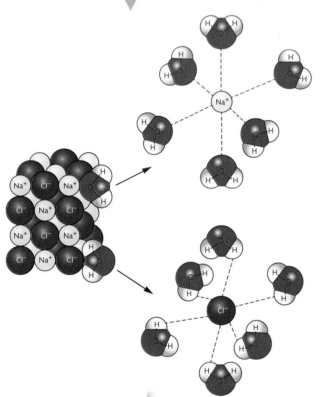

Consider an ionic compound being placed in water. As we will learn in the next section, water molecules are polar, which means they have some separation of charge in their structure. At the contact surface, the partial charges in the water molecules are attracted to ions of opposite charge in the lattice, which may cause the ions to dislodge from their position. As these ions separate from the lattice, they become surrounded by water molecules and are said to be **hydrated**. When this happens the solid is dissolved. State symbols are used to show this change as follows:

$$NaCl(s) \xrightarrow{+H_2O} NaCl(aq)$$

$$NaCl(s) \xrightarrow{+H_2O} Na^+(aq) + Cl^-(aq)$$

If a liquid other than water is able to dissolve the solid, the ions are said to be **solvated** and an appropriate state symbol to denote the solvent is used.

In the case of solvents like oil or hexane, $C_6H_{14}$, which are non-polar and so have no charge separation, there is no attraction between the liquid and the ions. So here the ions remain tightly bound to each other in the lattice, and the solid is insoluble.

This suggests that solubility trends are based on the similar chemical nature of the solute and solvent, as this is most likely to lead to successful interactions between them. The expression '*like dissolves like*' is often used to capture this notion. Note though that this is a generalized statement and somewhat over-simplified as there are some important exceptions.

## Electrical conductivity

Condom conductivity test. Condoms are tested for holes by being filled with water and placed in a solution of NaCl, and then attached to electrodes. The current will not be conducted across the insulating material of the condom, but if there is a hole the current will be conducted into the salty water, triggering an alarm. All condoms are conductivity tested in this way.

**Ionic compounds do not conduct electricity in the solid state, but conduct when molten or in aqueous solution.**

The ability of a compound to conduct electricity depends on whether it contains ions that are able to move and carry a charge. Ionic compounds are not able to conduct electricity in the solid state as the ions are firmly held within the lattice and so cannot move. However, when the ionic compound is either present in the liquid state (molten), or dissolved in water (aqueous solution), the ions *will* be able to move. Therefore ionic compounds as liquids or aqueous solutions do show electrical conductivity.

## Brittleness

Ionic compounds are usually brittle, which means the crystal tends to shatter when force is applied. This is because movement of the ions within the lattice places ions of the same charge alongside each other, so the repulsive forces cause it to split.

## Different ionic compounds have a different extent of ionic character

A **binary** compound is one that contains only two elements. We have seen that in order for any two elements to react to form an ionic compound, they must have *very different tendencies to lose or gain electrons*. A relatively simple assessment of this can be made by looking at their positions on the Periodic Table. Metals on the left lose electrons most easily, while non-metals on the right gain electrons most easily. Also, we learned in Chapter 3 that the tendency to lose electrons and form positive ions increases *down* a group, whereas the tendency to gain electrons and form negative ions increases *up* a group. So the highest tendency to react together and form ionic compounds will be between metals on the *bottom left* and non-metals on the *top right* of the Periodic Table.

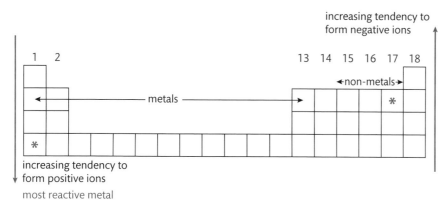

Another way to judge the tendency of two elements to form an ionic compound is by looking at **electronegativity values**. As explained in Chapter 3 on page 107, electronegativity is a measure of the ability of an atom to attract electrons in a covalent bond, and is described using the Pauling scale of values. These are given in section 8 of the IB data booklet and are summarized here.

**Figure 4.3** The pairs of elements that react most easily to form ionic compounds are metals on the bottom left of the Periodic Table and non-metals on the top right, indicated here by asterisks.

**Figure 4.4** Periodic trends in electronegativity values show an increase along a period and up a group.

| | | | | | | | | | | | | | | | | | |
|---|---|---|---|---|---|---|---|---|---|---|---|---|---|---|---|---|---|
| 1<br>H<br>2.2 | | | | | | | | | | | | | | | | | |
| 3<br>Li<br>1.0 | 4<br>Be<br>1.6 | | | | | | | | | | | 5<br>B<br>2.0 | 6<br>C<br>2.6 | 7<br>N<br>3.0 | 8<br>O<br>3.4 | 9<br>F<br>4.0 | |
| 11<br>Na<br>0.9 | 12<br>Mg<br>1.3 | | | | | | | | | | | 13<br>Al<br>1.6 | 14<br>Si<br>1.9 | 15<br>P<br>2.2 | 16<br>S<br>2.6 | 17<br>Cl<br>3.2 | |
| 19<br>K<br>0.8 | 20<br>Ca<br>1.0 | 21<br>Sc<br>1.4 | 22<br>Ti<br>1.5 | 23<br>V<br>1.6 | 24<br>Cr<br>1.7 | 25<br>Mn<br>1.6 | 26<br>Fe<br>1.8 | 27<br>Co<br>1.9 | 28<br>Ni<br>1.9 | 29<br>Cu<br>1.9 | 30<br>Zn<br>1.7 | 31<br>Ga<br>1.8 | 32<br>Ge<br>2.0 | 33<br>As<br>2.2 | 34<br>Se<br>2.6 | 35<br>Br<br>3.0 | |
| 37<br>Rb<br>0.8 | 38<br>Sr<br>1.0 | 39<br>Y<br>1.2 | 40<br>Zr<br>1.3 | 41<br>Nb<br>1.6 | 42<br>Mo<br>2.2 | 43<br>Tc<br>2.1 | 44<br>Ru<br>2.2 | 45<br>Rh<br>2.3 | 46<br>Pd<br>2.2 | 47<br>Ag<br>1.9 | 48<br>Cd<br>1.7 | 49<br>In<br>1.8 | 50<br>Sn<br>2.0 | 51<br>Sb<br>2.1 | 52<br>Te<br>2.1 | 53<br>I<br>2.7 | |
| 55<br>Cs<br>0.8 | 56<br>Ba<br>0.9 | 57<br>La*<br>1.1 | 72<br>Hf<br>1.3 | 73<br>Ta<br>1.5 | 74<br>W<br>1.7 | 75<br>Re<br>1.9 | 76<br>Os<br>2.2 | 77<br>Ir<br>2.2 | 78<br>Pt<br>2.2 | 79<br>Au<br>2.4 | 80<br>Hg<br>1.9 | 81<br>Tl<br>1.8 | 82<br>Pb<br>1.8 | 83<br>Bi<br>1.9 | 84<br>Po<br>2.0 | 85<br>At<br>2.2 | |
| 87<br>Fr<br>0.7 | 88<br>Ra<br>0.9 | 89<br>Ac*<br>1.1 | | | | | | | | | | | | | | | |

Pauling electronegativity values

<1.0 | 1.0 – 1.4 | 1.5 – 1.9 | 2.0 – 2.4 | 2.5 – 2.9 | 3.0 – 4.0

The determining factor in ionic bond formation is the *difference* in electronegativity values. It is generally recognized that a difference of 1.8 units or more on the Pauling scale will give a compound that is predominantly ionic.

> **The extent of ionic character is determined by the *difference* in electronegativity of the bonded elements.**

### Worked example

Explain which of the following pairs will be most likely to form an ionic bond.

**A**  Be and F          **B**  Si and O          **C**  N and Cl          **D**  K and S

### Solution

Consider the difference in electronegativity of each pair:

**A**  1.6 and 4.0          **B**  1.9 and 3.4          **C**  3.0 and 3.2          **D**  0.8 and 2.6

A has the greatest difference, so $BeF_2$ is the most ionic.

### Exercises

7  Which fluoride is the most ionic?

    **A**  NaF        **B**  CsF        **C**  $MgF_2$        **D**  $BaF_2$

8  Which pair of elements reacts most readily?

    **A**  $Li + Br_2$      **B**  $Li + Cl_2$      **C**  $K + Br_2$      **D**  $K + Cl_2$

9  You are given two white solids and told that only one of them is an ionic compound. Describe three tests you could carry out to determine which it is.

The fact that compounds differ in their extent of ionic character suggests that other types of bonding are involved, and we will consider these in the next section. We will see that the distinction between ionic and covalent bonds is not black and white, but is best described as a **bonding continuum** with all intermediate types possible.

| **ionic compounds** | **covalent compounds** |
| --- | --- |
| reactive metal + reactive non-metal | two non-metals |
| electronegativity difference > 1.8 | electronegativity difference << 1.8 |

**polar covalent compounds**
0 < electronegativity difference < 1.8

## 4.2  Covalent bonding

## Understandings:

- A covalent bond is formed by the electrostatic attraction between a shared pair of electrons and the positively charged nuclei.
- Single, double, and triple covalent bonds involve one, two, and three shared pairs of electrons respectively.
- Bond length decreases and bond strength increases as the number of shared electrons increases.
- Bond polarity results from the difference in electronegativities of the bonded atoms.

### Guidance
*Bond polarity can be shown either with partial charges, dipoles, or vectors.*

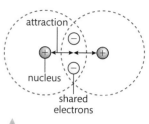

▲ **Figure 4.5** In a covalent bond the shared electrons are attracted to the nuclei of both atoms.

## Applications and skills:

● Deduction of the polar nature of a covalent bond from electronegativity values.

### Guidance

*Electronegativity values are given in section 8 of the data booklet.*

## A covalent bond forms by atoms sharing electrons

When atoms of two non-metals react together, each is seeking to gain electrons in order to achieve the stable electron structure of a noble gas. By sharing an electron pair they are effectively each able to achieve this. The shared pair of electrons is concentrated in the region between the two nuclei and is attracted to them both. It therefore holds the atoms together by electrostatic attraction and is known as a **covalent bond**. A group of atoms held together by covalent bonds forms a **molecule**.

For example, two hydrogen atoms form a covalent bond as follows.

$$H^{\times} + \cdot H \longrightarrow \quad \substack{\times \\ \bullet}$$

two hydrogen     a molecule of
atoms (2H)      hydrogen ($H_2$)

Note that in the molecule $H_2$ each hydrogen atom has a share of two electrons so it has gained the stability of the electron arrangement of the noble gas helium, He.

The formation of the covalent bond stabilizes the atoms so energy is released as the bond forms. The forces of attraction between the nuclei and shared electrons are balanced by the forces of repulsion between the two nuclei, and this holds the atoms at a fixed distance apart. Figure 4.6 shows how the bond forms at this point of lowest energy as two hydrogen atoms approach each other and their electron density shifts.

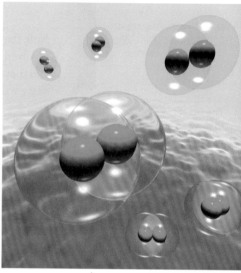

Computer artwork of hydrogen molecules. Each molecule consists of two hydrogen atoms bonded covalently.

**Figure 4.6** When two hydrogen atoms form a covalent bond, the distance between them corresponds to the lowest energy. The letters A, B, and C show the correspondence between shifts in electron density and the distance apart of the atoms.

> A covalent bond is the electrostatic attraction between a pair of electrons and positively charged nuclei. A molecule is a group of atoms held together by covalent bonds.

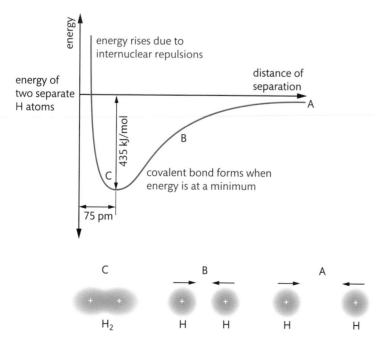

Similarly, two chlorine atoms react together to form a chlorine molecule in which both atoms have gained a share of eight electrons in their outer shells (the electron arrangement of argon, Ar). This tendency of atoms to form a stable arrangement of eight electrons in their outer shell is referred to as the **octet rule**. The diagrams below only show the outer electrons, not the inner full shells, as the outer electrons are the only electrons that take part in bonding.

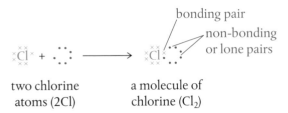

two chlorine atoms (2Cl)       a molecule of chlorine ($Cl_2$)

Note that in the chlorine molecule, each atom has three pairs of electrons that are not involved in forming the bond. These are known as **non-bonding pairs**, or **lone pairs**, and they play an important role in determining the shape of more complex molecules, as we will see later.

Hydrogen and chlorine also react together to form a molecule of hydrogen chloride, HCl, which has the structure shown below. Note that the formation of the covalent bond enables both H and Cl to gain a stable outer shell.

$$\cdot + \times^{\times}_{\times}Cl^{\times}_{\times} \longrightarrow H\times^{\times}_{\times}Cl^{\times}_{\times}$$

## Atoms can share more than one pair of electrons to form multiple bonds

Sometimes it seems there are not enough electrons to achieve octets on all the atoms in the molecule. In these cases, the atoms will have to share more than one electron pair, in other words form a multiple bond. A **double bond** forms when two electron pairs, a total of four electrons, are shared; a **triple bond** forms when three electron pairs, a total of six electrons, are shared.

For example, the two most abundant gases in the air, oxygen and nitrogen, both exist as diatomic molecules containing multiple bonds:

$$O\times^{\times}_{\times}O \quad \text{or} \quad O{=}O \quad \text{double bond}$$

$$\times N^{\times} \quad \text{or} \quad \times N{\equiv}N\colon \quad \text{triple bond}$$

As shown above, it is often convenient to use a line to represent a shared pair of electrons, two lines to represent a double bond, and three lines a triple bond. Despite this notation, we will learn in Section 14.1 (page 185) that multiple bonds contain unequal bonds. Double bonds contain one sigma bond and one pi bond, triple bonds contain one sigma bond and two pi bonds.

## Short bonds are strong bonds

Every covalent bond is characterized by two values.

Data on both these values are given in sections 10 and 11 of the IB data booklet.

---

Molecules contain a fixed number of atoms. Those containing two atoms are described as *diatomic*, those containing three atoms are *triatomic*.

It is sometimes useful to use different symbols or colours to distinguish between the electrons of different atoms, as you see here, but in reality all electrons are the same so it is not always necessary to do this. What *is* crucial is to have the correct number of valence electrons in the atoms.

The octet rule states that when atoms react, they tend to achieve an outer shell with eight electrons.

Note the octet rule would better be considered as a guideline only, as there are exceptions – notably hydrogen, the transition elements, radicals, and atoms that form an incomplete or expanded octet.

Note that the terms *valence electrons* and *outer shell electrons* are used interchangeably. They both refer to the electrons that take part in bonding.

The triple bond in nitrogen ($N_2$) is difficult to break, making the molecule very stable. This is why, although nitrogen makes up about 78% of the atmosphere, it does not readily take part in chemical reactions. For example, although the element is essential for all life forms, $N_2$ from the atmosphere is only rarely used directly by organisms as their source of nitrogen for synthesis reactions.

- **Bond length**: a measure of the distance between the two bonded nuclei.
- **Bond strength**: usually described in terms of **bond enthalpy**, which will be discussed in Chapter 5, and is effectively a measure of the energy required to break the bond.

As atomic radius increases as we go down a group, we would expect the atoms to form molecules with longer bonds. For example:

Cl₂ bond length 199 pm

Br₂ bond length 228 pm

As a result, the shared electron pair is further from the pull of the nuclei in the larger molecules, and so the bond would be expected to be weaker. Data on Group 17 elements, which exist as diatomic molecules, mostly confirm these trends.

$(F_2 \quad F–F)$
$Cl_2 \quad Cl–Cl$
$Br_2 \quad Br–Br$
$I_2 \quad I–I$

bond length increases
bond enthalpy decreases

## CHALLENGE YOURSELF

2  Fluorine, $F_2$, is shown in brackets opposite, as a close look at its bond enthalpy data shows that it is an outlier in the trends described here. What explanation might account for this?

Multiple bonds have a greater number of shared electrons and so have a stronger force of electrostatic attraction between the bonded nuclei. This means there is a greater pulling power on the nuclei, bringing them closer together, resulting in bonds that are shorter and stronger than single bonds. We can see this by comparing different bonds involving the same atoms, such as in the hydrocarbons.

| Hydrocarbon | $C_2H_6$ | $C_2H_4$ | $C_2H_2$ |
|---|---|---|---|
| Structural formula | 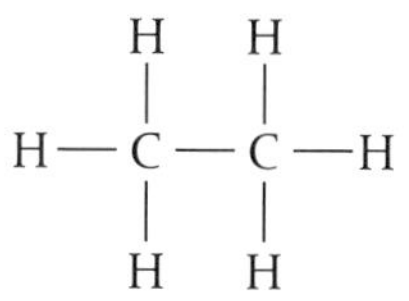 H–C–C–H (with H atoms) | 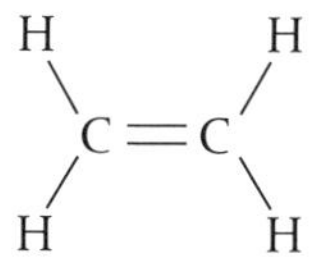 C=C (with H atoms) | $H—C\equiv C—H$ |
| Bond between carbon atoms | single | double | triple |
| Bond length / pm | 154 | 134 | 120 |
| Bond enthalpy / kJ mol⁻¹ | 346 | 614 | 839 |

These data confirm that triple bonds are stronger and shorter than double bonds, which are shorter and stronger than single bonds. Note though that the double bond is not twice as strong as the single bond, due to the fact that it is made up of two different bonds – one sigma bond and one pi bond that is weaker. These bonds will be described more fully in Section 14.1.

Also, we can compare two different carbon–oxygen bonds within the molecule ethanoic acid, $CH_3COOH$.

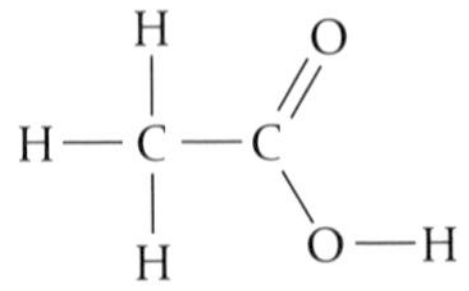

$$H - C - C \bigg\langle{O \atop O-H}$$

|  | C — O | C = O |
|---|---|---|
| Bond length / pm | 143 | 122 |
| Bond enthalpy / kJ mol$^{-1}$ | 358 | 804 |

single bonds       double bonds       triple bonds

→ decreasing length, increasing strength

## Polar bonds result from unequal sharing of electrons

Not all sharing is equal. It may be the case that you share this textbook with a class mate, but if you have it for more than half the time, it clearly belongs more to you than to your friend. So it is with electron pairs. In simple terms, if they spend more time with one atom than the other, they are not equally shared. This occurs when there is a difference in the electronegativities of the bonded atoms as the more electronegative atom exerts a greater pulling power on the shared electrons and so gains more 'possession' of the electron pair. The bond is now unsymmetrical with respect to electron distribution and is said to be **polar**.

The term **dipole** is often used to indicate the fact that this type of bond has two separated opposite electric charges. The more electronegative atom with the greater share of the electrons, has become partially negative or **δ–**, and the less electronegative atom has become partially positive or **δ+**.

For example, in HCl the shared electron pair is pulled more strongly by the Cl atom than the H atom, resulting in a polar molecule.

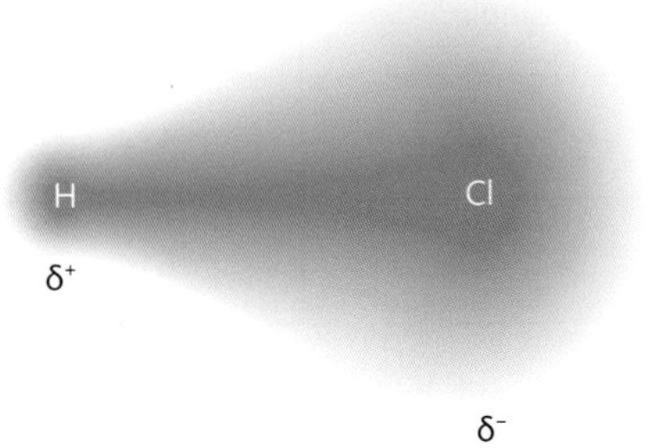

**Figure 4.7** The distribution of electrons in the H–Cl bond is unsymmetrical, with a greater electron density over the Cl atom.

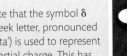

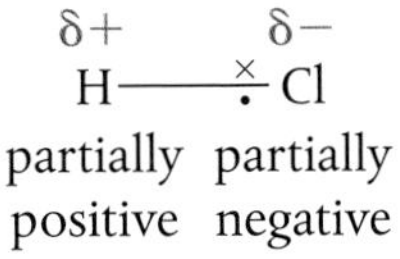

Note that the symbol δ (Greek letter, pronounced 'delta') is used to represent a partial charge. This has no fixed value, but is always less than the unit charge associated with an ion such as X$^+$ or X$^-$.

δ+     δ–
H —— × Cl
partially   partially
positive   negative

In water, the electronegativity difference results in polar O–H bonds with the electron density greater on the oxygen.

The extent of polarity in a covalent bond varies, depending on how big a difference exists in the electronegativity values of the two bonded atoms. We can estimate this from knowledge of the periodic trends in electronegativity, discussed in Chapter 3 and summarized here.

electronegativity increases across a period

electronegativity increases up a group

As fluorine is in the top right of the Periodic Table, it is clearly the most electronegative atom, so we can predict it will have the greater electron density whenever it is bonded to another element. Fluorine has a value of 4.0 on the Pauling scale of electronegativity given on page 147, and all other elements have lower values. This scale can be used to assess the relative polarity of a bond. For example, the table below compares the polarities of the hydrogen halides.

| | Electronegativity values of atoms | | Difference in electronegativity |
|---|---|---|---|
| H–F | 2.2 | 4.0 | 1.8 |
| H–Cl | 2.2 | 3.2 | 1.0 |
| H–Br | 2.2 | 3.0 | 0.8 |
| H–I | 2.2 | 2.7 | 0.5 |

increasing bond polarity

There are several ways to denote the polar nature of a bond in a structure. One is to write the partial charges $\delta+$ and $\delta-$ over the less electronegative and more electronegative atom respectively. Another is to represent the direction of electron pull as a vector with an arrow on the bond indicating the pull on the electrons by the more electronegative atoms. The dipole notation is also useful. As you can see in the diagram of water here, it is quite acceptable to show more than one way together.

## CHALLENGE YOURSELF

3 Oxygen is a very electronegative element with a value of 3.4 on the Pauling scale. Can you determine the formula of a compound in which oxygen would have a partial positive charge?

### Worked example

Use the electronegativity values on page 147 to put the following bonds in order of decreasing polarity.

N–O in $NO_2$      N–F in $NF_3$      H–O in $H_2O$      N–H in $NH_3$

**Solution**

bond polarity:                    H–O > N–F > N–H > N–O

difference in electronegativity values:    1.2    1.0    0.8    0.4

A microwave oven generates microwaves that have lower frequencies and longer wavelengths than visible light. Microwaves are used for cooking because certain wavelengths are absorbed by polar molecules, notably water, and also by sugar and fat. The absorption causes the water to heat up and cook the food, leaving the oven surface and containers of glass, plastic, or ceramic unaffected.

In a covalent bond, the greater the difference in the electronegativity values of the atoms, the more polar the bond.

The only bonds that are truly non-polar are bonds between the same atoms such the bonds in $F_2$, $H_2$, and $O_2$, because clearly here the *difference* in electronegativity is zero. These are sometimes referred to as **pure covalent** to express this. All other bonds have some degree of polarity, although it may be very slight. The C–H bond, ubiquitous in organic chemistry, is often considered to be largely non-polar, although in fact carbon is slightly more electronegative than hydrogen. As we will see in Chapter 10, the low polarity of the C–H bond is an important factor in determining the properties of organic compounds.

The presence of polar bonds in a molecule has a significant effect on its properties. Effectively, the partial separation of charges introduces some ionic nature into covalent bonds, so the more polar the bond, the more like an ionic compound the molecule behaves. Polar bonds are therefore considered to be intermediates in relation to pure covalent bonds and ionic bonds, part of the bonding continuum that was mentioned on page 148. We now see why the boundaries between ionic and covalent bonds are somewhat 'fuzzy', and why it is often appropriate to describe substances using terms such as 'predominantly' covalent or ionic, or of being 'strongly' polar.

The idea of the bonding continuum is summarized below.

| Ionic | Polar covalent | Pure covalent |
|---|---|---|
| complete transfer of electrons | partial transfer of electrons<br>unequal sharing of electrons | equal sharing of electrons |
| $Na^+Cl^-$ | HF, HCl, HBr, HI | $Cl_2$ |
| ionic lattice | | discrete molecules |
| + – | δ+ δ– | ● ● |

### NATURE OF SCIENCE

Scientists observe the natural world where variations in structure or properties are often continuous rather than discontinuous. In other words, a spectrum of intermediates exists and this can make classification difficult. At the same time, the properties of such intermediates can strengthen our understanding. For example, we have seen here that the existence of polar covalent molecules in the bonding continuum adds to our interpretation of electron behaviour in bond formation.

## Exercises

**10** Which substance contains only ionic bonds?

    **A** $NaNO_3$     **B** $H_3PO_4$     **C** $NH_4Cl$     **D** $CaCl_2$

**11** Which of the following molecules contains the shortest bond between carbon and oxygen?

    **A** $CO_2$     **B** $H_3COCH_3$     **C** CO     **D** $CH_3COOH$

**12** For each of these molecules, identify any polar bonds and label them using δ+ and δ– appropriately:

    **(a)** HBr     **(b)** $CO_2$     **(c)** ClF
    **(d)** $O_2$     **(e)** $NH_3$

**13** Use the electronegativity values in Section 8 of the IB data booklet to predict which bond in each of the following pairs is more polar.

    **(a)** C–H or C–Cl     **(b)** Si–Li or Si–Cl     **(c)** N–Cl or N–Mg

# 4.3 Covalent structures

## Understandings:

- Lewis (electron dot) structures show all the valence electrons in a covalently bonded species.
    - **Guidance**
        - *The term 'electron domain' should be used in place of 'negative charge centre'.*
        - *Electron pairs in a Lewis (electron dot) structure can be shown as dots, crosses, a dash, or any combination.*
        - *Coordinate covalent bonds should be covered.*
- The 'octet rule' refers to the tendency of atoms to gain a valence shell with a total of 8 electrons.
- Some atoms, like Be and B, might form stable compounds with incomplete octets of electrons.
- Resonance structures occur when there is more than one possible position for a double bond in a molecule.
- Shapes of species are determined by the repulsion of electron pairs according to VSEPR theory.
- Carbon and silicon form giant covalent/network covalent/macromolecular structures.
    - **Guidance**
    - *Allotropes of carbon (diamond, graphite, graphene, $C_{60}$ buckminsterfullerene) and $SiO_2$ should be covered.*

## Applications and skills:

- Deduction of Lewis (electron dot) structure of molecules and ions showing all valence electrons for up to four electron pairs on each atom.
- The use of VSEPR theory to predict the electron domain geometry and the molecular geometry for species with two, three, and four electron domains.
- Prediction of bond angles from molecular geometry and presence of non-bonding pairs of electrons.
- Prediction of molecular polarity from bond polarity and molecular geometry.
- Deduction of resonance structures, including $C_6H_6$, $CO_3^{2-}$, and $O_3$.
- Explanation of the properties of giant covalent compounds in terms of their structures.

## Lewis diagrams are used to show the arrangement of electrons in covalent molecules

When describing the structure of covalent molecules, the most convenient method is known as a **Lewis structure**. This uses a simple notation of dots and crosses to represent the outer energy level, or valence shell, electrons of all the atoms in the molecule. It can be derived as follows.

Gilbert Newton Lewis (1875–1946) was one of the greatest and most influential American chemists of the last century. He formulated the idea that the covalent bond consists of a shared pair of electrons, proposed the electron pair theory of acid/base reactions, and was the first person to produce a pure sample of deuterium oxide (heavy water). He also published important theories on chemical thermodynamics and first coined the term 'photon' for the smallest unit of radiant energy. Since 1916 his dot diagrams for covalent structures have been used almost universally.

Steps to follow in drawing a Lewis structure.

**1** Calculate the total number of valence electrons in the molecule by multiplying the number of valence electrons of each element by the number of atoms of the element in the formula and totalling these.

**2** Draw the skeletal structure of the molecule to show how the atoms are linked to each other.

**4** Add more electron pairs to complete the octets (8 electrons) around the atoms (other than hydrogen which must have 2 electrons and the exceptions noted below).

**3** Use a pair of crosses, a pair of dots, or a single line to show one electron pair and put a pair in each bond between atoms.

**5** If there are not enough electrons to complete the octets, form double bonds and if necessary triple bonds.

**6** Check that the total number of electrons in your finished structure is equal to your calculation in the first step.

Electron pairs can be represented by dots, crosses, a combination of dots and crosses, or by a line. Use whichever notation you prefer, but be prepared to recognize all versions. The important thing is to be clear and consistent, and to avoid vague and scattered dots.

## Worked example

Draw the Lewis structure for the molecule $CCl_4$.

### Solution

Note that in Lewis structures, as in the examples on page 157, only the valence electrons are shown, as these are the only ones that take part in bonding.

**1** Total number of valence electrons = $4 + (7 \times 4) = 32$

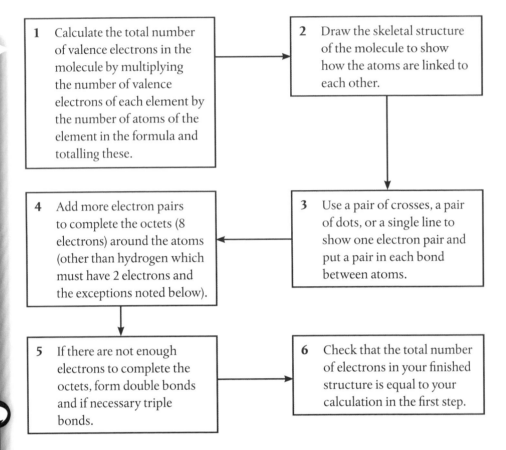

**2** Skeletal structure  **3** Bonded pairs  **4** Completed Lewis structure

(32 electrons)

There are several different ways of drawing Lewis structures, and some alternative acceptable forms are shown below.

The table on page 157 shows some examples of molecules with their Lewis structures.

| Molecule | Total number of valence electrons | Lewis structure | |
|---|---|---|---|
| $CH_4$ | $4 + (1 \times 4) = 8$ | H⋮C⋮H with H above and H below (dot representation) | H—C—H with H above and H below (line representation) |
| $NH_3$ | $5 + (1 \times 3) = 8$ | H⋮N⋮H with H below (dot representation) | H—N—H with H below (line representation) |
| $H_2O$ | $(1 \times 2) + 6 = 8$ | H⋮O⋮H (dot representation) | H—O—H (line representation) |
| $CO_2$ | $4 + (6 \times 2) = 16$ | O⋮⋮C⋮⋮O (dot representation) | O=C=O (line representation) |
| $HCN$ | $1 + 4 + 5 = 10$ | H⋮C⋮⋮N⋮ (dot representation) | H—C≡N (line representation) |

When drawing the Lewis structure of ions, note that you must:

• calculate valence electrons as above and then add one electron for each negative charge and subtract one electron for each positive charge;
• put the Lewis structure in a square bracket with the charge shown outside.

## Worked example

Draw the Lewis structures for:

(i) $OH^-$

(ii) $SO_4^{2-}$

### Solution

(i) valence electrons = $6 + 1 + 1 = 8$

$$\left[ \ddot{O} \, H \right]^{-}$$

(ii) valence electrons = $6 + (6 \times 4) + 2 = 32$

$$\left[ \begin{array}{c} O \\ O\ S\ O \\ O \end{array} \right]^{2-}$$

When drawing the Lewis structure of an ion, make sure you remember to put a square bracket around the structure with the charge shown clearly outside the bracket.

## In coordinate bonds both shared electrons come from one atom

The examples so far involve covalent bonds where each bonded atom contributes one electron to the shared pair. However, sometimes the bond forms by *both* the electrons in the pair originating from the same atom. This means that the other atom accepts and gains a share in a donated electron pair. Such bonds are called **coordinate bonds**, also known as **dative bonds**. An arrow on the head of the bond is sometimes used to show a coordinate bond, with the direction indicating the origin of the electrons.

For example:

$$H_3O^+ \quad \left[H \overset{\times\times}{\underset{H}{:O:}} H\right]^+ \qquad \left[H - \overset{\times\times}{\underset{H}{O}} \to H\right]^+$$

$$NH_4^+ \quad \left[H \overset{H}{\underset{H}{:N:}} H\right]^+ \qquad \left[\overset{H}{\underset{H}{H - N \to H}}\right]^+$$

$$CO \qquad :C \overset{\times\times}{\underset{\times\times}{::}} O \times \qquad :C \equiv O \times$$

Note that in CO the triple bond consists of two bonds that involve sharing an electron from each atom, and the third bond is a coordinate bond where both electrons come from the oxygen. The three bonds are nonetheless identical to each other. This illustrates an important point about coordinate bonds: once they are formed, they are no different from other covalent bonds. Understanding the origin of bonding electrons can be important, however, in interpreting some reaction mechanisms, such as Lewis acid/base behaviour, as we will learn in Chapter 8.

> **A coordinate bond is a covalent bond in which both the shared electrons are provided by one of the atoms.**

## The octet rule is not always followed

There are a few molecules that are exceptions to the octet rule. Small atoms such as beryllium (Be) and boron (B) form stable molecules in which the central atom has fewer than eight electrons in its valence shell. This is known as an **incomplete octet**. For example, the structures of $BeCl_2$ and $BF_3$ are shown below.

$BeCl_2$  valence electrons $= 2 + (7 \times 2) = 16$

$$\overset{\times\times}{\underset{\times\times}{\times Cl}} \overset{\bullet}{:} Be \overset{\times\times}{:} \underset{\times\times}{Cl \times}$$

$BF_3$  valence electrons $= 3 + (7 \times 3) = 24$

$$\overset{\times\times}{\underset{\times\times}{\times F}} \overset{\bullet}{:} B \overset{\times\times}{:} \underset{\times\times}{F \times}$$
$$\overset{\bullet}{\underset{\times\times}{\times F \times}}$$

Molecules with incomplete octets are said to be **electron deficient**, and have a tendency to accept an electron pair from a molecule with a lone pair, such as $NH_3$ or $H_2O$. This leads to the formation of a coordinate compound in which the central atom has now gained an octet.

$$\underset{\underset{H}{|}}{\overset{\overset{H}{|}}{H - N}} \to \underset{\underset{F}{|}}{\overset{\overset{F}{|}}{B}} - F$$

> Remember to include *all lone pairs* in your Lewis structures. Structures which show only bonded pairs, e.g. H–Cl, are structural formulas, not Lewis structures.

$BF_3$ is an important catalyst in several synthetic reactions as a result of this tendency to accept electrons.

## Exercises

**14** Draw the Lewis structures of:
   (a) HF      (b) $CF_3Cl$      (c) $C_2H_6$      (d) $PCl_3$
   (e) $C_2H_4$   (f) $C_2H_2$

**15** How many valence electrons are in the following molecules?
   (a) $BeCl_2$   (b) $BCl_3$      (c) $CCl_4$      (d) $PH_3$
   (e) $SCl_2$   (f) $NCl_3$

**16** Use Lewis structures to show the formation of a coordinate bond between $H_2O$ and $H^+$.

**17** Draw the Lewis structures of:

    **(a)** $NO_3^-$            **(b)** $NO^+$            **(c)** $NO_2^-$            **(d)** $O_3$

    **(e)** $N_2H_4$

! Note that hydrogen, H, which forms only one bond, must always be in a terminal position and can never be a central atom in a molecule.

Molecules that have an expanded octet have central atoms that are larger and are found in Period 3 (and beyond), where the valence shell can hold 18 electrons. Their structures, involving five and six electron pairs, are discussed in Section 14.1.

# VSEPR theory: The shape of a molecule is determined by repulsion between electron domains

Once we know the Lewis structure of a molecule, we can predict exactly how the bonds will be orientated with respect to each other in space – in other words, the three-dimensional shape of the molecule. This is often a crucial feature of a substance in determining its reactivity. For example, biochemical reactions depend on a precise 'fit' between the enzyme, which controls the rate of the reaction, and the reacting molecule, known as the substrate. Anything that changes the shape of either of these may therefore alter the reaction dramatically; many drugs work in this way.

Predictions of molecular shape are based on the **Valence Shell Electron Pair Repulsion (VSEPR) theory**. As its name suggests, this theory is based on the simple notion that *because electron pairs in the same valence shell carry the same charge, they repel each other and so spread themselves as far apart as possible.*

Before applying this theory, it is useful to clarify some of the language involved because the term VS**EP**R, evidently referring to Electron Pairs, is actually an over-simplification. As we have seen, molecules frequently contain multiple pairs of shared electrons, and these behave as a single unit in terms of repulsion because they are orientated together. So a better, more inclusive, term than electron pair is **electron domain**. This includes all electron locations in the valence shell, be they occupied by lone pairs, single, double, or triple bonded pairs. What matters in determining shape is the *total number of electron domains*, and this can be determined from the Lewis structure.

**TOK** People often find this topic easier to understand when they can build and study models of the molecules in three dimensions. Does this suggest different qualities to the knowledge we acquire in different ways?

## Worked example

How many electron domains exist in the central atom of the following molecules whose Lewis structures are shown?

         (i)                (ii)               (iii)

### Solution

Each electron domain is ringed in red.

         (i)                (ii)               (iii)

**(i)** 4 electron domains: 3 bonding and 1 non-bonding

**(ii)** 2 electron domains: 2 bonding and 0 non-bonding

**(iii)** 3 electron domains: 2 bonding and 1 non-bonding

Technically then, VSEPR theory should be called Valence Shell Electron Domain Repulsion. It can be summarized as follows:

• The repulsion applies to electron domains, which can be single, double, or triple bonding electron pairs, or non-bonding pairs of electrons.
• The total number of electron domains around the central atom determines the geometrical arrangement of the electron domains.
• The shape of the molecule is determined by the angles between the bonded atoms.
• Non-bonding pairs (lone pairs) have a higher concentration of charge than a bonding pair because they are not shared between two atoms, and so cause slightly more repulsion than bonding pairs. The repulsion decreases in the following order:

lone pair–lone pair > lone pair–bonding pair > bonding pair–bonding pair

As a result, molecules with lone pairs on the central atom have some distortions in their structure that reduce the angle between the bonded atoms.

Note that in the diagrams in this section, non-bonding electrons on the surrounding atoms have been omitted for clarity – these are therefore *not* Lewis structures.

## Species with two electron domains

Molecules with two electron domains will position them at **180°** to each other, giving a **linear** shape to the molecule.

**The repulsion between electron pairs varies as follows:**

strongest repulsion ↑ lone pair–lone pair
                   lone pair–bonding pair
weakest repulsion  | bonding pair–bonding pair

$$BeCl_2 \quad Cl-Be-Cl$$
$$CO_2 \quad O=C=O \quad \Big\} \quad \textbf{linear } \mathbf{180°}$$
$$C_2H_2 \quad H-C\equiv C-H$$

## Species with three electron domains

Molecules with three electron domains will position them at **120°** to each other, giving a **triangular planar** shape to the electron domain geometry. If all three electron domains are bonding, the shape of the molecule will also be triangular planar.

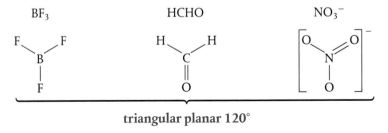

triangular planar 120°

> **Note that when you are asked to draw a Lewis structure, you must show all the non-bonding pairs on all the atoms.**

> **The electron domain geometry is determined by the positions of *all* the electron domains, but the molecular geometry depends only on the positions of the *bonded* atoms.**

However, if one of the electron domains is a lone pair, this will not be 'seen' in the overall shape of the molecule, as it is part of the central atom. The molecular shape is determined by the positions of the atoms fixed by the bonding pairs only. A further consideration is that, as described above, lone pairs cause slightly more repulsion than bonding pairs, so in their presence the angles are slightly altered.

For example, as shown on page 159, the Lewis structure of ozone, $O_3$, has three electron domains. Therefore the electron domain geometry of the molecule is triangular planar. But, as only two of the three electron domains are bonding electrons, the molecular geometry will not be triangular planar. The red outline below shows the positions of the bonding electrons that determine the shape. The molecule is described as **bent** or **V-shaped**. The lone pair of electrons distorts the shape slightly, so the angle is slightly less than 120°; it is approximately 117°.

bond angle 117°

**bent or V-shaped**

! If there are lone pairs on the central atom, the electron domain geometry and the molecular geometry will not be the same as each other.

## Species with four electron domains

Molecules with four electron domains will position them at **109.5°** to each other, giving a **tetrahedral** shape to the electron domains. If all four electron domains are bonding, the shape of the molecule will also be tetrahedral.

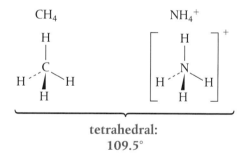

tetrahedral:
**109.5°**

However, if one or more of the electron domains is a lone pair, we must again focus on the number of bonded pairs to determine the shape of the molecule. The table on page 162 compares molecules with 0, 1, and 2 lone pairs respectively.

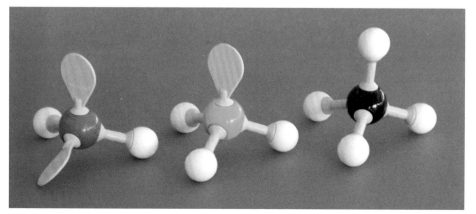

Models of $H_2O$, $NH_3$, and $CH_4$ showing the different molecular geometry due to the different numbers of lone pairs on the central atom.

| | $CH_4$ | $NH_3$ | $H_2O$ |
|---|---|---|---|
| Lewis structure | H—C—H (with H above and below) | H—N—H (with lone pair above, H below) | H—O—H (with two lone pairs) |
| Number of electron domains | 4 | 4 | 4 |
| Electron domain geometry | tetrahedral | tetrahedral | tetrahedral |
| Number of lone pairs | 0 | 1 | 2 |
| Number of bonded electron domains | 4 | 3 | 2 |
| Molecular geometry | tetrahedral | trigonal pyramidal | bent or V-shaped |
| Bond angles | 109.5° | approximately 107° | approximately 105° |

Note that the presence of two lone pairs in $H_2O$ causes more repulsion than the single lone pair in $NH_3$. This is why the bond angle is reduced further in $H_2O$ from the 109.5° of the symmetrical tetrahedron.

Here is a summary of the steps used in determining the shape of a molecule.

1   Draw the Lewis structure, following the steps on page 156.
2   Count the total number of electron domains on the central atom.
3   Determine the electron domain geometry as follows:
    2 electron domains → linear
    3 electron domains → triangular planar
    4 electron domains → tetrahedral
4   Determine the molecular geometry from the number of bonding electron domains.
5   Consider the extra repulsion caused by the lone pairs and adjust the bond angles accordingly.

> Always draw the Lewis structure before attempting to predict the shape of a molecule, as you have to know the total number of bonding pairs and lone pairs around the central atom.

> **With 4 electron domains on the central atom:** 0 lone pairs → tetrahedral, 1 lone pair → trigonal pyramid, 2 lone pairs → V-shaped.

## Exercises

**18** Predict the shape and bond angles of the following molecules:
   **(a)** $H_2S$     **(b)** $CF_4$     **(c)** HCN     **(d)** $NF_3$
   **(e)** $BCl_3$     **(f)** $NH_2Cl$     **(g)** $OF_2$

**19** Predict the shape and bond angles of the following ions:
   **(a)** $CO_3^{2-}$     **(b)** $NO_3^-$     **(c)** $NO_2^+$     **(d)** $NO_2^-$
   **(e)** $ClF_2^+$     **(f)** $SnCl_3^-$

**20** How many electron domains are there around the central atom in molecules that have the following shapes?
   **(a)** tetrahedral     **(b)** bent     **(c)** linear
   **(d)** trigonal pyramidal     **(e)** triangular planar

# Molecules with polar bonds are not always polar

We have learned that the polarity of a *bond* depends on the charge separation between its two bonded atoms, which is a result of differences in their electronegativities. The polarity of a *molecule*, however, depends on:

• the polar bonds that it contains;
• the way in which such polar bonds are orientated with respect to each other, in other words, on the shape of the molecule.

If the bonds are of equal polarity (i.e. involving the same elements) *and* are arranged symmetrically with respect to each other, their charge separations will oppose each other and so will effectively cancel each other out. In these cases the molecule will be non-polar, despite the fact that it contains polar bonds. It is a bit like a game of tug-of-war between players who are equally strong and symmetrically arranged.

The molecules below are all non-polar because the dipoles cancel out. The arrows, shown here in blue, are the notation for a dipole that results from the pull of electrons in the bond towards the more electronegative atom.

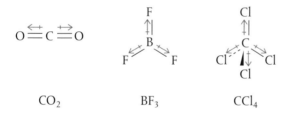

CO$_2$            BF$_3$            CCl$_4$

However, if *either* the molecule contains bonds of different polarity, *or* its bonds are not symmetrically arranged, then the dipoles will not cancel out, and the molecule will be polar. Another way of describing this is to say that it has a net **dipole moment**, which refers to its turning force in an electric field. This is what would happen in a game of tug-of-war if the players were not equally strong or were not pulling in exactly opposite directions.

The molecules below are all polar because the dipoles do not cancel out.

CH$_3$Cl            NH$_3$            H$_2$O

VSEPR theory in nature. Different numbers of snowberries growing together spontaneously adopt the geometry of maximum repulsion. Clockwise from the top: four berries form a tetrahedral shape bond angle 109.5°, three berries form a triangular planar shape bond angle 120°, and two berries are linear bond angle 180°. What other examples of VSEPR shapes can you find in nature?

**Figure 4.8** Equal and opposite pulls cancel each other out.

**Figure 4.9** When the pulls are not equal and opposite there is a net pull.

 Bond dipoles can be thought of as vectors, so the polarity of a molecule is the resultant force. This approach may help you to predict the overall polarity from considering the sum of the bond dipoles.

## Exercises

**21** Predict whether the following will be polar or non-polar molecules:

    **(a)** PH$_3$     **(b)** CF$_4$     **(c)** HCN     **(d)** BeCl$_2$
    **(e)** C$_2$H$_4$     **(f)** ClF     **(g)** F$_2$     **(h)** BF$_3$

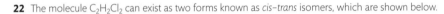

**22** The molecule $C_2H_2Cl_2$ can exist as two forms known as *cis–trans* isomers, which are shown below.

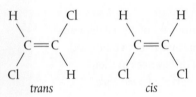

*trans*         *cis*

Determine whether either of these has a net dipole moment.

## CHALLENGE YOURSELF

**4** If you were given two solutions and told one contained a polar substance and the other a non-polar substance, suggest experiments that might enable you to identify which is which.

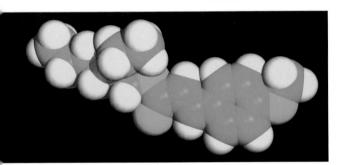

Computer graphic of a molecule of the sunscreen $C_{18}H_{26}O_3$. Carbon atoms are shown in green, hydrogen atoms in yellow, and oxygen atoms in blue. Note the benzene ring and carbon–carbon double bonds in the molecule. Sunscreens help to protect the skin from sun damage by absorbing UV radiation and releasing it as heat. They are able to do this due to the many double bonds and delocalized electrons in their structure.

# Electrons in multiple bonds can sometimes spread themselves between more than one bonding position

Our account of covalent bonding so far describes a bond as a pair of electrons held in a specific position within a molecule. However, in some molecules bonding electrons are less restricted than this. Instead of being confined to one location they show a tendency to be shared between more than one bonding position, and are said to be **delocalized**. Free from the constraints of a single bonding position, delocalized electrons spread themselves out, giving greater stability to the molecule or ion.

Delocalization is a characteristic of electrons in multiple bonds when there is more than one possible position for a double bond within a molecule. For example, let us look again at the Lewis structure of ozone, $O_3$, from page 159,

$$\overset{\times\times}{\underset{\times\times}{O}}=\overset{\times\times}{O}-\overset{\times\times}{\underset{\times\times}{O}}{\times}$$

We can see that a different Lewis structure would be equally valid:

$$\times\overset{\times\times}{\underset{\times\times}{O}}-\overset{\times\times}{O}=\overset{\times\times}{\underset{\times\times}{O}}$$

These structures suggest that the molecule should contain one oxygen–oxygen double bond and one oxygen–oxygen single bond, which we would expect to be different in bond length and bond strength. However, experimental data reveal that ozone actually contains two *equal* oxygen–oxygen bonds, intermediate in length and strength between single and double bonds.

| | O–O single bond | O=O double bond | Oxygen–oxygen bonds in $O_3$ |
|---|---|---|---|
| Bond length / pm | 148 | 121 | 127 |
| Bond enthalpy / kJ mol$^{-1}$ | 144 | 498 | 364 |

We can explain this by considering that the electrons from the double bond have delocalized and spread themselves equally between both possible bonding positions. The true structure for ozone is a blend or hybrid of the Lewis structures shown above.

$$O \text{---} O \text{---} O$$

This cannot be accurately represented by a single Lewis structure, so a concept known as **resonance** is introduced. The Lewis structures that can be drawn are known as

**resonance structures**, depicted as shown below, while it is recognized that neither of these is the correct structure. The true structure is an intermediate form, known as the **resonance hybrid**.

$$O=O-O \longleftrightarrow O-O=O$$

It is as if you were trying to explain to someone what a mule (a cross between a horse and a donkey) looks like: you might draw a horse and a donkey and a double-headed arrow between them implying the mule is an intermediate. You wouldn't mean that the animal is a horse one minute and a donkey the next! Likewise, resonance structures do not represent forms that flip from one to the other. Resonance structures can be drawn for any molecule in which there is more than one possible position for a double bond; the number of structures will equal the number of different possible positions.

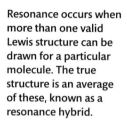

Resonance occurs when more than one valid Lewis structure can be drawn for a particular molecule. The true structure is an average of these, known as a resonance hybrid.

## Worked example

Draw the resonance structures for the carbonate ion $CO_3^{2-}$.

### Solution

Count the number of valence electrons: $4 + (6 \times 3) + 2 = 24$

Draw the Lewis structure, noting that there are three possible positions for the double bond. This means there will be three resonance structures, as follows:

$$\left[ \begin{array}{c} O \\ C \\ O \end{array} O \right]^{2-} \longleftrightarrow \left[ \begin{array}{c} O \\ C \\ O \end{array} O \right]^{2-} \longleftrightarrow \left[ \begin{array}{c} O \\ C \\ O \end{array} O \right]^{2-}$$

Some other ions and molecules that have delocalized electrons and so can be represented by resonance structures are shown in the table below.

You can deduce how many resonance structures exist for a molecule or ion by looking at the number of possible positions for its double bond.

| Species name and formula | Number of valence electrons | Resonance structures |
|---|---|---|
| nitrate(V), $NO_3^-$ | 24 | $\left[ \begin{array}{c} O \\ N \\ O \end{array} O \right]^- \longleftrightarrow \left[ \begin{array}{c} O \\ N \\ O \end{array} O \right]^- \longleftrightarrow \left[ \begin{array}{c} O \\ N \\ O \end{array} O \right]^-$ |
| nitrate(III), $NO_2^-$ | 18 | $\left[ O-N=O \right]^- \longleftrightarrow \left[ O=N-O \right]^-$ |
| methanoate, $HCOO^-$ | 18 | $\left[ H-C{\overset{O}{\underset{O}{}}} \right]^- \longleftrightarrow \left[ H-C{\overset{O}{\underset{O}{}}} \right]^-$ |

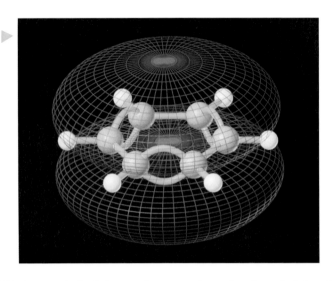

**NATURE OF SCIENCE**

Models and
representations such
as Lewis structures
and molecular models
are useful tools in
science. They can help
understanding and
the communication of
complex information
effectively. But there are
also often limits to the
usefulness of a model. The
difficulty of representing
a resonance hybrid
through a Lewis structure
is an example of this. It
demands that we extend
our interpretation of the
Lewis structure to include
the existence of molecules
with delocalized electrons.

Benzene, $C_6H_6$, is a particularly interesting case of a molecule with delocalized
electrons. The six carbon atoms are arranged in a hexagonal ring, each also bonded to
a hydrogen atom in a triangular planar arrangement with 120° bond angles. A possible
Lewis structure is:

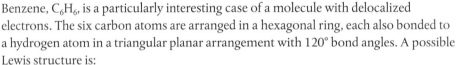

But we can see there are other possible positions for the double bonds, indicating the
existence of resonance structures.

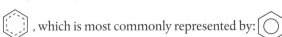

In Chapter 10 we will discuss evidence that indicates that benzene's properties cannot
be explained by either of these Lewis structures. The true form is the resonance hybrid:

⬡ , which is most commonly represented by: ⬡

The circle inside the hexagon represents delocalized pi electrons, which are spread
equally through the ring, rather than being in confined double bonds. As we would
expect, this results in carbon–carbon bonds that are equal in length and strength, and
intermediate between those of single and double bonds.

**Bond order** is a measure of the number of electrons involved in bonds between two atoms. Values for bond order are: single bonds = 1, double bonds = 2, triple bonds = 3. Resonance hybrids have fractional values of bond order. The carbon-carbon bonds in benzene have a bond order of 1.5.

|  | C–C single bond | C=C double bond | Carbon–carbon bonds in benzene |
|---|---|---|---|
| Bond length / pm | 154 | 134 | 140 |
| Bond enthalpy / kJ mol$^{-1}$ | 346 | 614 | 507 |

Resonance gives great stability to the benzene molecule, making it chemically quite unreactive. In our study of organic chemistry we will learn that this is unusual given its high ratio of carbon to hydrogen (unsaturation). The explanation in Chapter 10 will use concepts of hybridization and pi bonding, introduced later in this chapter.

## Worked example

Compare the structures of $CH_3COOH$ and $CH_3COO^-$ with reference to their possible resonance structures.

### Solution

Draw the Lewis structure of each, and note if there is more than one possible position for a double bond to be placed.

$$CH_3COOH \qquad H - \overset{\overset{\textstyle H}{|}}{\underset{\underset{\textstyle H}{|}}{C}} - \overset{\overset{\textstyle O}{/\!/}}{\underset{\underset{\textstyle O-H}{\diagdown}}{C}}$$

There is only one possible Lewis structure, so the molecule has one carbon–oxygen double bond and one carbon–oxygen single bond.

$$CH_3COO^- \qquad \left[ H - \overset{\overset{\textstyle H}{|}}{\underset{\underset{\textstyle H}{|}}{C}} - \overset{\overset{\textstyle O}{/\!/}}{\underset{\underset{\textstyle O}{\diagdown}}{C}} \right]^- \longleftrightarrow \left[ H - \overset{\overset{\textstyle H}{|}}{\underset{\underset{\textstyle H}{|}}{C}} - \overset{\overset{\textstyle O}{\diagup}}{\underset{\underset{\textstyle O}{/\!/}}{C}} \right]^-$$

Two resonance structures exist, so the ion exists as a hybrid with two equal carbon–oxygen bonds, intermediate in length and strength between the two carbon–oxygen bonds in $CH_3COOH$.

$$\left[ H - \overset{\overset{\textstyle H}{|}}{\underset{\underset{\textstyle H}{|}}{C}} - \overset{\overset{\textstyle O}{/\!/}}{\underset{\underset{\textstyle O}{\diagup\!\!\!\cdot}}{C}} \right]^-$$

Resonance is an important concept that gives special properties to the structures where it occurs. We have seen its influence on bond lengths and strengths, which in turn can influence reactivity. The different strengths of organic acids and bases, for example, can often be explained by resonance.

The current model of benzene with a symmetrical ring of delocalized electrons developed when predictions based on the so-called Kekulé model with alternating double bonds failed to match observations. Differences between the calculated and measured values of bond energy and bond length, and the ability to undergo addition reactions all indicated that the Kekulé model was not correct. Progress in science sometimes depends on the need to abandon a model or an interpretation if it cannot explain valid experimental results.

Exercises

**23** Put the following species in order of increasing carbon–oxygen bond length:

$$CO \qquad CO_2 \qquad CO_3^{2-} \qquad CH_3OH$$

**24** By reference to their resonance structures, compare the nitrogen–oxygen bond lengths in nitrate(V) ($NO_3^-$) and nitric(V) acid ($HNO_3$).

## Some covalent substances form giant molecular crystalline solids

Most covalent substances exist as discrete molecules with a finite number of atoms. However, there are some that have a very different structure, a crystalline lattice in which the atoms are linked together by covalent bonds. Effectively, the crystal is a single molecule with a regular repeating pattern of covalent bonds, so has no finite size. It is referred to as a **giant molecular** or **network covalent** structure or **macromolecular structure**. As we might expect, such crystalline structures have very different properties from other smaller covalent molecules. A few examples are considered here.

### Allotropes of carbon

**Allotropes** are different forms of an element in the same physical state, such as oxygen ($O_2$) and ozone ($O_3$) which both exist as gases. Different bonding within these structures gives rise to distinct forms with different properties.

Carbon has several allotropes and these are described and compared in the table on page 169.

References to hybridization are explained in Section 14.2 of this chapter.

**CHALLENGE YOURSELF**

**5** For the most part, good electrical conductors are also good thermal conductors, but this is not the case with diamond. Can you think why this might be, and whether there are other substances that are not electrical conductors but good thermal conductors?

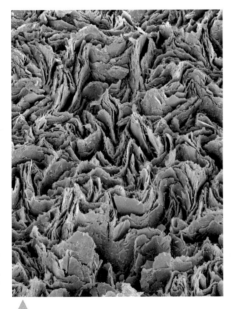

▲ Coloured scanning electron micrograph of layers making up the core of a graphite pencil. Because graphite is a soft form of carbon, the tip of the pencil disintegrates under pressure to leave marks on the paper.

▲ Cut and polished diamond. Diamond is a naturally occurring form of carbon that has crystallized under great pressure. It is the hardest known mineral. Beautiful crystals are found in South Africa, Russia, Brazil, and Sierra Leone.

| | Graphite | Diamond | Fullerene $C_{60}$ | Graphene |
|---|---|---|---|---|
| **Structure** | Each C atom is $sp^2$ hybridized and covalently bonded to 3 others, forming hexagons in parallel layers with bond angles of 120°. The layers are held only by weak London dispersion forces so they can slide over each other. | Each C atom is $sp^3$ hybridized and covalently bonded to 4 others tetrahedrally arranged in a regular repetitive pattern with bond angles of 109.5°. | Each C atom is $sp^2$ hybridized and bonded in a sphere of 60 carbon atoms, consisting of 12 pentagons and 20 hexagons. Structure is a closed spherical cage in which each carbon is bonded to 3 others. (Note it is not a giant molecule as it has a fixed formula.) | Each C atom is covalently bonded to 3 others, as in graphite, forming hexagons with bond angles of 120°. But it is a single layer, so exists as a two-dimensional material only. It is often described as a honeycomb or chicken wire structure. |
| **Electrical conductivity** | Good electrical conductor; contains one non-bonded, delocalized electron per atom that gives electron mobility. | Non-conductor of electricity; all electrons are bonded and so non-mobile. | A semiconductor at normal temperature and pressure due to some electron mobility; easily accepts electrons to form negative ions. | Very good electrical conductor; one delocalized electron per atom gives electron mobility across the layers. |
| **Thermal conductivity** | Not a good conductor, unless the heat can be forced to conduct in a direction parallel to the crystal layers. | Very efficient thermal conductor, better than metals. | Very low thermal conductivity. | Best thermal conductivity known, even better than diamond. |
| **Appearance** | Non-lustrous, grey crystalline solid. | Highly transparent, lustrous crystal. | Yellow crystalline solid, soluble in benzene. | Almost completely transparent. |
| **Special properties** | Soft and slippery due to slippage of layers over each other; brittle; very high melting point; the most stable allotrope of carbon. | The hardest known natural substance; it cannot be scratched by anything; brittle; very high melting point. | Very light and strong; reacts with K to make superconducting crystalline material; low melting point. | The thickness of just one atom so the thinnest material ever to exist; but also the strongest – 100 times stronger than steel; very flexible; very high melting point. |
| **Uses** | A dry lubricant; in pencils; electrode rods in electrolysis. | Polished for jewellery and ornamentation; tools and machinery for grinding and cutting glass. | Lubricants, medical, and industrial devices for binding specific target molecules; related forms are used to make nanotubes and nanobuds used as capacitors in electronics industry, and catalysts. | TEM (transmission electron microscopy) grids, photo-voltaic cells, touch screens, high performance electronic devices; many applications are still being developed. |

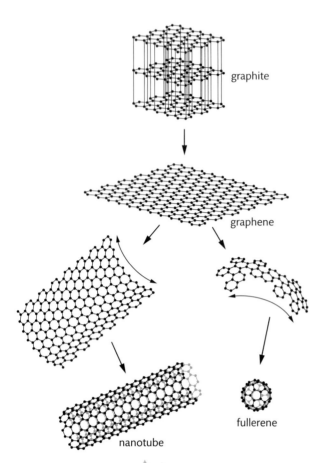

graphite

graphene

nanotube

fullerene

**Figure 4.10** Graphite occurs naturally, and a single separated layer is graphene. A rolled up layer of graphene is a nanotube, and a closed cage is fullerene.

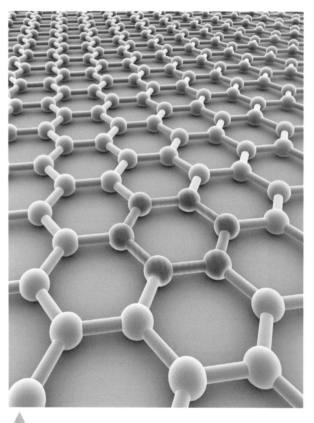

Graphene is a planar sheet of carbon atoms arranged in a hexagonal pattern.

Graphene is a relatively new form of carbon, isolated for the first time in 2004. Given its hardness, strength, lightness, flexibility, conductivity, and chemical inertness, it has enormous potential applications. Currently though, many of these are only in the development stage as they are dependent on the production of large sheets of pure graphene, which is difficult to achieve economically. But this is an intense field of research and breakthroughs are common. Some of the potential applications and advantages of graphene are as follows:

• new conductive materials could be made by mixing graphene with plastics;
• transistors of graphene are predicted to be faster and smaller than silicon transistors in electronics;
• touch screens of graphene printed on thin plastic instead of coatings layered onto glass would be light, flexible, and almost unbreakable;
• supercapacitors for storing charge could replace batteries and more efficiently power mobile devices and electric cars;
• solar panels in which photovoltaic cells (that generate electricity from sunlight) contain graphene would be light and flexible, and so could be wrapped around any surface such as clothing, furniture, or vehicles.

**TOK** Whether graphene will realize its potential and lead to innovative materials and applications remains an open question. What is the role of imagination in helping to direct the research focus of scientists?

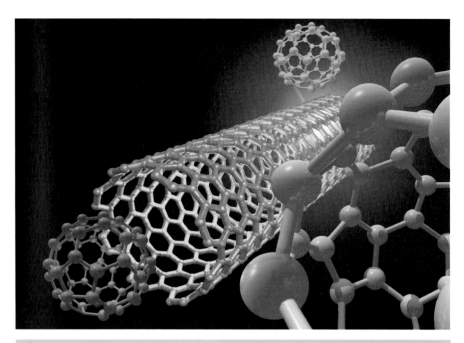

The name 'fullerene' was given to the newly discovered spheres $C_{60}$ in honour of the American architect R. Buckminster Fuller. He had designed the World Exhibition building in Montreal, Canada, on the same concept of hexagons and a small number of pentagons to create a curved surface known as a geodesic dome. The dome of the Epcot Centre in Disney World, Florida, is similarly designed. Perhaps more familiarly it is also the structure of a European soccer ball. The term 'buckyballs' has slipped into common usage, derived from the full name of the structure 'buckminsterfullerene'.

## NATURE OF SCIENCE

The discoveries of the allotropes of carbon – buckminsterfullerene and graphene – illustrate the importance of collaboration between scientists.

The discovery of fullerenes in 1985 was the result of teamwork between scientists with different experience and research objectives. Harold Kroto from the UK was interested in red giant stars and how carbon might polymerize near them. Robert Curl and Richard Smalley working in Texas, USA, had developed a technique using a laser beam for evaporating and analysing different substances. When they worked together and applied this technique to graphite, clusters of stable $C_{60}$ and $C_{70}$ spheres were formed. The three scientists shared the Nobel Prize in Chemistry for 1996.

The isolation of graphene was announced by Kostya Novoselov and Andre Geim in 2004, both working at the University of Manchester, UK. It led to their shared award of the Nobel Prize in Physics in 2010. Novoselov and Geim were research collaborators over many years in different countries, originally as research student and supervisor respectively. Their work involved the use of adhesive tape to rip successively thinner flakes off graphite and analyse them by attachment to a layer of silicon oxide. Many scientists over many years had attempted to isolate graphene, and through their successes and failures indirectly contributed to the later discovery.

The development of structures such as nanotubes, nanobuds, and graphene is part of the growing science of **nanotechnology** (Chapter 12), which deals with the atomic scale manipulation of matter. An interesting development is a new material called **graphone**, which is made by adding hydrogen to graphene. Controlling the amount of hydrogen coverage gives variable magnetic properties, which may in turn lead to wider graphene applications. A further development is fluorographene, which has one fluorine atom attached to each carbon atom giving a rippled rather than a flat structure. As all the electrons are held in bonds, it is an insulator.

## CHALLENGE YOURSELF

6   Graphite is thermodynamically more stable than diamond. The reaction

$$C(diamond) \rightarrow C(graphite)$$

is accompanied by a loss of energy, $\Delta H = -2$ kJ mol$^{-1}$.

But we commonly hear that 'diamonds are forever'. Are they?

The structure of fullerene has the same arrangements of hexagons and pentagons as a soccer ball.

## Silicon and silicon dioxide

Silicon is the most abundant element in the Earth's crust after oxygen, occurring as silica ($SiO_2$) in sand and in the silicate minerals. Since silicon is just below carbon in Group 14, the possibility of silicon-based life has been proposed. But unlike carbon, silicon is not able to form long chains, multiple bonds, or rings so cannot compete with the diversity possible in organic chemistry, based on carbon. However, there is some evidence that the first forms of life were forms of clay minerals that were probably based on the silicon atom.

Coloured scanning electron micrograph of the surface of a microprocessor computer chip. Silicon chips are tiny pieces of silicon as small as 1 $mm^2$ made to carry minute electrical circuits used in computers and transistors. Silicon is the most widely used semiconductor.

Like carbon, silicon is a Group 14 element and so its atoms have four valence shell electrons. In the elemental state, each silicon atom is covalently bonded to four others in a tetrahedral arrangement. This results in a giant lattice structure much like diamond.

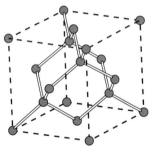

The silicon crystal structure and the arrangement of bonds around a central silicon atom.

Silicon dioxide, $SiO_2$, commonly known as silica or quartz, also forms a giant covalent structure based on a tetrahedral arrangement. But here the bonds are between silicon and oxygen atoms, where each Si atom is covalently bonded to four O atoms, and each O to two Si atoms. You can think of the oxygen atoms as forming bridges between the tetrahedrally bonded silicon atoms.

Quartz crystals shown in a coloured scanning electron micrograph. Quartz is a form of silica ($SiO_2$) and the most abundant mineral in the Earth's crust. Quartz is used in optical and scientific instruments and in electronics such as quartz watches.

Note here the formula $SiO_2$ refers to the *ratio* of atoms within the giant molecule – it is an empirical formula and the actual number of atoms present will be a very large multiple of this. As the atoms are strongly held in tetrahedral positions that involve all four silicon valence electrons, the structure has the following properties:

- strong;
- insoluble in water;
- high melting point;
- non-conductor of electricity.

These are all properties we associate with glass and sand – different forms of silica.

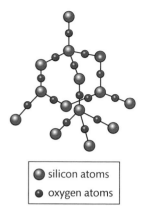

**Figure 4.11** The structure of quartz $SiO_2$.

- silicon atoms
- oxygen atoms

## Exercises

**25** Describe the similarities and differences you would expect in the properties of silicon and diamond.

**26** Explain why graphite and graphene are good conductors of electricity whereas diamond is not.

# 4.4 Intermolecular forces

## Understandings:

- Intermolecular forces include London (dispersion) forces, dipole–dipole forces, and hydrogen bonding.

### Guidance

*The term 'London (dispersion) forces' refers to instantaneous dipole–induced dipole forces that exist between any atoms or groups of atoms and should be used for non-polar entities. The term 'van der Waals' is an inclusive term, which includes dipole–dipole, dipole–induced dipole, and London (dispersion) forces.*

- The relative strengths of these interactions are London (dispersion) forces < dipole–dipole forces < hydrogen bonds.

## Applications and skills:

- Deduction of the types of intermolecular force present in substances, based on their structure and chemical formula.
- Explanation of the physical properties of covalent compounds (volatility, electrical conductivity, and solubility) in terms of their structure and intermolecular forces.

Covalent bonds hold atoms together *within* molecules, but of course molecules do not exist in isolation. A gas jar full of chlorine, $Cl_2$, for example, will contain millions of molecules of chlorine. So what are the forces that exist *between* these molecules, the so-called **intermolecular forces**? The answer depends on the polarity and size of the molecules involved, and so the intermolecular forces will vary for different molecules. We will consider three types of intermolecular force here, and see how they differ from each other in origin and in strength.

The strength of intermolecular forces determines the physical properties of a substance. Volatility, solubility, and conductivity can all be predicted and explained from knowledge of the nature of the forces between molecules.

Note that the prefix *intra-* refers to *within*, whereas the prefix *inter-* refers to *between*. For example, the Internet gives communication between many different places, while an intranet works within an organization.

intramolecular
(covalent bond)

intermolecular

Fritz London (1900–1954) was a German physicist who pioneered the interpretation of covalent bond formation and intermolecular forces in the emerging field of quantum mechanics. As he was of Jewish descent, he had to leave his university post in Germany during the Nazi regime before World War II, and completed most of his research in Duke University, USA.

# London (dispersion) forces

Non-polar molecules such as chlorine, $Cl_2$, have no permanent separation of charge within their bonds because the shared electrons are pulled equally by the two chlorine atoms. In other words, they do not have a permanent dipole. Likewise, atoms of a noble gas such as argon exist as non-polar particles.

However, because electrons behave somewhat like mobile clouds of negative charge, the density of this cloud may at any one moment be greater over one region of a molecule or atom than over another region. When this occurs, a weak dipole known as a **temporary** or **instantaneous dipole** is formed. This will not last for more than an instant as the electron density is constantly changing, but it may influence the electron distribution in a neighbouring atom or molecule, causing an **induced dipole**.

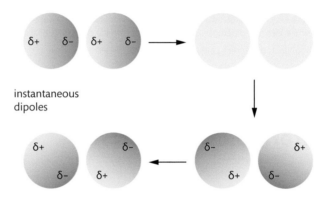

**Figure 4.12** A series of instantaneous views of electron density in an atom. Each image is like a snap-shot of a possible electron distribution at a moment in time. Although the instantaneous dipole varies, it always leads to an attractive force with its neighbour.

As a result, weak forces of attraction, known as **London (dispersion) forces**, will occur between opposite ends of these two temporary dipoles in the molecules. These are the weakest form of intermolecular force. Their strength increases with increasing molecular size; this is because the greater number of electrons within a molecule increases the probability of temporary dipoles developing.

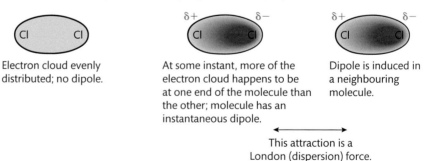

**Figure 4.13** Instantaneous dipole–induced dipole cause London (dispersion) forces between molecules of $Cl_2$.

London (dispersion) forces are the *only* forces that exist between non-polar molecules. Such molecules generally have low melting and boiling points, because relatively little energy is required to break the weak London (dispersion) forces and separate the molecules from each other. This is why many non-polar elements and compounds are gases at room temperature, for example $O_2$, $Cl_2$, and $CH_4$. Boiling point data also indicate how the strength of London (dispersion) forces increases with increasing molecular size. This is shown in the tables on page 175 that compare the boiling points of the halogens (Group 17 elements) and of the family of hydrocarbons known as the alkanes.

| Element | $M_r$ | Boiling point / °C | State at room temperature |
|---------|-------|--------------------|---------------------------|
| $F_2$ | 38 | −188 | gas |
| $Cl_2$ | 71 | −34 | gas |
| $Br_2$ | 160 | 59 | liquid |
| $I_2$ | 254 | 185 | solid |

boiling point increases with increasing number of electrons

| Alkane | $M_r$ | Boiling point / °C |
|--------|-------|--------------------|
| $CH_4$ | 16 | −164 |
| $C_2H_6$ | 30 | −89 |
| $C_3H_8$ | 44 | −42 |
| $C_4H_{10}$ | 58 | −0.5 |

boiling point increases with increasing number of electrons

Although London (dispersion) forces are weak, they are responsible for the fact that non-polar substances can be condensed to form liquids and sometimes solids at low temperatures. For example, nitrogen gas, $N_2$, liquefies below −196 °C, and even helium gas has been liquefied at the extremely low temperature of −269 °C.

London (dispersion) forces are also components of the forces between polar molecules, but often get somewhat overlooked because of the presence of stronger forces.

When asked to name forces between molecules, London dispersion forces should be given in all cases, regardless of what additional forces may be present.

## Dipole–dipole attraction

Polar molecules such as hydrogen chloride, HCl, have a permanent separation of charge within their bonds as a result of the difference in electronegativity between the bonded atoms. One end of the molecule is electron deficient with a partial positive charge (δ+), while the other end is electron rich with a partial negative charge (δ−). This is known as a **permanent dipole**. It results in opposite charges on neighbouring molecules attracting each other, generating a force known as a **dipole–dipole attraction**.

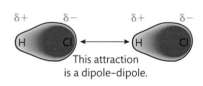

This attraction is a dipole–dipole.

Figure 4.14 Permanent dipoles cause forces of dipole–dipole attraction between molecules of HCl.

The strength of this intermolecular force will vary depending on the distance and relative orientation of the dipoles. But dipole–dipole forces are generally stronger than London dispersion forces, as we might expect from their origin in permanent rather than instantaneous dipoles. These forces cause the melting and boiling points of polar compounds to be higher than those of non-polar substances of comparable molecular mass.

When examining the boiling points of different substances to see the effect of different intermolecular forces, it is important to compare substances with similar molecular mass. Otherwise the difference could be attributed solely to stronger London dispersion forces in the molecules with more electrons.

| | $C_3H_8$ | $CH_3OCH_3$ |
|--|----------|-------------|
| Molar mass / g mol$^{-1}$ | 44 | 46 |
| Intermolecular attraction | London dispersion forces | London dispersion forces and dipole–dipole attraction |
| Boiling point / K | 229 | 249 |

175

Johannes van der Waals (1837–1923) from the Netherlands established himself as an eminent physicist on the publication of his very first paper, his PhD thesis. His study of the continuity of the gas and liquid state from which he put forward his 'equation of state' led James Clerk Maxwell to comment, 'there can be no doubt that the name of van der Waals will soon be among the foremost in molecular science'. Van der Waals did indeed fulfil this early promise, being awarded the Nobel Prize in Physics in 1910.

Note that dipole–dipole attractions can occur between any combinations of polar molecules, such as between $PCl_3$ and $CHCl_3$, and generally lead to the solubility of polar solutes in polar solvents.

The umbrella term **van der Waals' forces** is used to include both London dispersion forces and dipole–dipole attractions. It also covers a less common type of attraction known as dipole–induced dipole. In other words, van der Waals' forces refers to all forces between molecules that do not involve electrostatic attractions between ions or bond formation. We can summarize this as follows:

London dispersion force, e.g.    $Cl_2$----$Cl_2$

dipole–dipole attraction       $HCl$----$HCl$   } van der Waals forces

dipole–induced dipole        $HCl$----$Cl_2$

In some cases, van der Waals' forces may occur within a molecule (intramolecularly) if the different groups can position themselves appropriately. This is an important feature of proteins, for example, which is discussed in detail in Chapter 13.

## Hydrogen bonding

When a molecule contains hydrogen covalently bonded to a very electronegative atom (fluorine, nitrogen, or oxygen), these molecules are attracted to each other by a particularly strong type of intermolecular force called a **hydrogen bond**. The

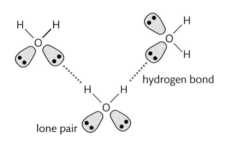

**Figure 4.15** Hydrogen bonding between water molecules.

hydrogen bond is in essence a particular case of dipole–dipole attraction. The large electronegativity difference between hydrogen and the bonded fluorine, oxygen, or nitrogen results in the electron pair being pulled away from the hydrogen. Given its small size and the fact that it has no other electrons to shield the nucleus, the hydrogen now exerts a strong attractive force on a lone pair in the electronegative atom of a neighbouring molecule. This is the hydrogen bond.

Hydrogen bonds are the strongest form of intermolecular attraction. Consequently, they cause the boiling points of substances that contain them to be significantly higher than would be predicted from their molar mass. We can see this in Figure 4.16, in which boiling points of the hydrides from Groups 14 to 17 are compared down the Periodic Table.

**TOK**

There is ongoing debate about the nature of the hydrogen bond and IUPAC define six criteria that should be used as evidence for its occurrence. To what extent does a specialized vocabulary help or hinder the growth of knowledge?

**Figure 4.16** Periodic trends in the boiling points of the hydrides of Groups 14–17.

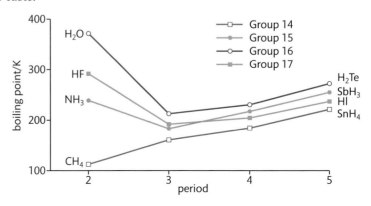

In all four groups there is a general trend that boiling point increases down the group as molar mass increases. The anomalies are $NH_3$, HF, and $H_2O$, which all have significantly higher boiling points than would be expected from their molar mass. This can only be explained by the presence of hydrogen bonding in these molecules. If it wasn't for the fact that it is hydrogen bonded, $H_2O$ would be a gas not a liquid at room temperature.

Likewise, when we compare the boiling points of some organic molecules that have similar or equal values of molar mass, we find a higher value where hydrogen bonding occurs between the molecules. For example, the following table compares two different forms of $C_2H_6O$, known as isomers, both with a molar mass of 46.

| $CH_3–O–CH_3$ | $CH_3CH_2–O–H$ |
|---|---|
| methoxymethane | ethanol |
| $M = 46$ g mol$^{-1}$ | $M = 46$ g mol$^{-1}$ |
| does not form hydrogen bonds | forms hydrogen bonds |
| boiling point = −23 °C | boiling point = +79 °C |

Water makes a particularly interesting case for the study of hydrogen bonding. Here, because of the two hydrogen atoms in each molecule and the two lone pairs on the oxygen atom, each $H_2O$ can form up to *four* hydrogen bonds with neighbouring molecules. Liquid water contains fewer than this number, but in the solid form, ice, each $H_2O$ is maximally hydrogen bonded in this way. The result is a tetrahedral arrangement that holds the molecules a fixed distance apart, forming a fairly open structure, which is actually *less* dense than the liquid. This is a remarkable fact – in nearly all other substances the solid form with closer packed particles is *more* dense than its liquid. The fact that ice floats on water is evidence of the power of hydrogen bonds in holding the molecules together in ice. This density change means that water expands on freezing, which can lead to all kinds of problems in cold climates such as burst pipes and cracked machinery. The same force of expansion is at work in the Earth's crust, fragmenting and splitting rocks, ultimately forming sand and soil particles. The humble hydrogen bond is truly responsible for massive geological changes!

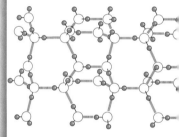

**Figure 4.17** The arrangement of water molecules in ice. Each molecule is held by hydrogen bonds to four other molecules in a tetrahedral arrangement.

Icebergs float on water. Hydrogen bonds create a very open structure in ice which is less dense than liquid water.

 Make sure you realize that although hydrogen bonds are strong in relation to other types of intermolecular force, they are very much weaker (about 15–20 times) than covalent bonds and ionic bonds.

177

In these examples we have looked at hydrogen bonds as an intermolecular force, that is, *between* molecules, but like van der Waals' forces, they can occur *within* large molecules where they play a key role in determining properties. Proteins, for example, are fundamentally influenced by hydrogen bonding – you can read about this in Chapter 13, Option B Biochemistry. Another fascinating example is DNA (deoxyribonucleic acid) which, as the chemical responsible for storing the genetic information in cells, is able to replicate itself exactly, a feat only possible because of its use of hydrogen bonding.

We can now summarize the intermolecular forces we have discussed in this section.

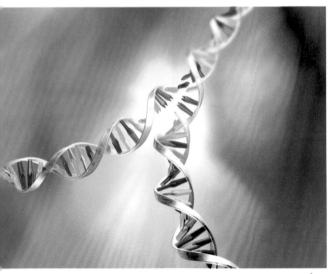

Computer artwork of a DNA molecule replicating. DNA is composed of two strands, held together by hydrogen bonds and twisted into a double helix. Before replication the strands separate from each other by breaking the hydrogen bonds and each strand then acts as a template for the synthesis of a new molecule of DNA.

Make sure you realize that when a covalent substance melts or boils, it is the bonds *between* the molecules that break, not the covalent bonds *within* the molecules. When you boil a kettle of water, you do not fill the kitchen with separated oxygen and hydrogen atoms.

|  |  | Non-polar molecules | Polar molecules | Molecules which contain H–O, H–N, or H–F |
|---|---|---|---|---|
| **London dispersion forces** | } van der Waals' forces | ✓ | ✓ | ✓ |
| **Dipole–dipole attractions** |  |  | ✓ | ✓ |
| **Hydrogen bonding** |  |  |  | ✓ |

increasing strength of intermolecular force

## The physical properties of covalent compounds are largely a result of their intermolecular forces

If we know the type of intermolecular force in a substance, we are in a good position to predict its physical properties.

### Melting and boiling points

Changing state by melting or boiling both involve separating particles by overcoming the forces between them. So the stronger the intermolecular forces, the more energy will be required to do this, and the higher will be the substance's melting and boiling points.

Covalent substances generally have lower melting and boiling points than ionic compounds. The forces to be overcome to separate the molecules are the relatively weak intermolecular forces, which are significantly easier to break than the electrostatic attractions in the ionic lattice. This is why many covalent substances are liquids or gases at room temperature.

As discussed on page 174, the strength of the intermolecular forces increases with increasing molecular size and with an increase in the extent of polarity within the molecule, and so these features help us to predict relative melting and boiling points.

## Worked example

Put the following molecules in order of increasing boiling point and explain your choice:

$$CH_3CHO \qquad CH_3CH_2OH \qquad CH_3CH_2CH_3$$

### Solution

First check the value of $M$ for each molecule:

$CH_3CHO = 44$

$CH_3CH_2OH = 46$

$CH_3CH_2CH_3 = 44$, so they are all very similar.

Now consider the type of bonding and intermolecular attractions:

| CH₃CHO | CH₃CH₂OH | CH₃CH₂CH₃ |

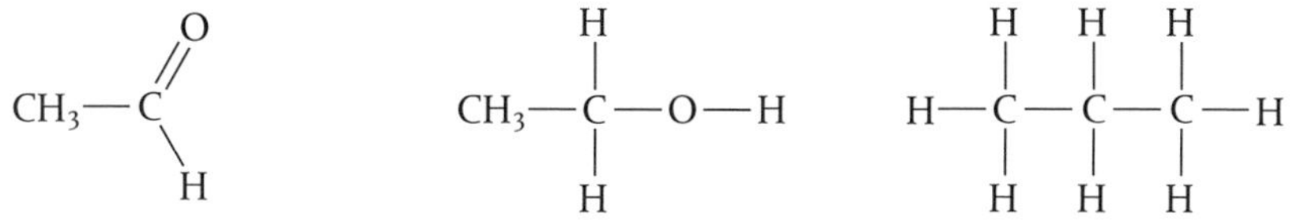

polar bonds ⇒
dipole–dipole

O–H bond ⇒ H bonding

non-polar bonds ⇒
London (dispersion) forces

So the order, starting with the lowest boiling point, will be:

$$CH_3CH_2CH_3 < CH_3CHO < CH_3CH_2OH$$

By contrast, macromolecular or giant covalent structures have high melting and boiling points, often at least as high as those of ionic compounds. This is because covalent bonds must be broken in these compounds for the change of state to occur. Diamond, for example, remains solid until about 4000 °C.

## Solubility

Non-polar substances are generally able to dissolve in non-polar solvents by the formation of London dispersion forces between solute and solvent. For example, the halogens, all of which are non-polar molecules (e.g. $Br_2$), are readily soluble in the non-polar solvent paraffin oil. It is another example of *like dissolves like*, which is a useful guiding principle here.

Likewise, polar covalent compounds are generally soluble in water, a highly polar solvent. Here the solute and solvent interact through dipole interactions and hydrogen bonding. Common examples include the aqueous solubility of HCl, glucose ($C_6H_{12}O_6$), and ethanol ($C_2H_5OH$). Biological systems are mostly based on polar covalent molecules in aqueous solution.

The solubility of polar compounds is, however, reduced in larger molecules where the polar bond is only a small part of the total structure. The non-polar parts of the molecule, unable to associate with water, reduce its solubility. For example, while ethanol ($C_2H_5OH$) is readily soluble in water, the larger alcohol heptanol ($C_7H_{15}OH$) is

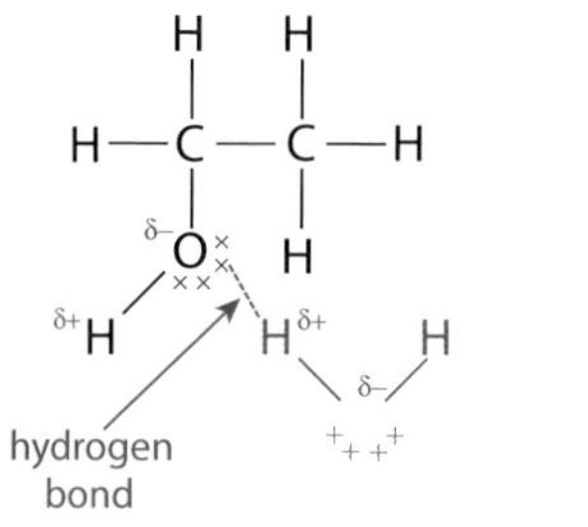

**Figure 4.18** Water and ethanol form hydrogen bonds and mix readily, as we know from the homogeneous nature of alcoholic drinks.

The moss plant *Philonotis fontana* has a waxy substance on its surface which repels water. The wax is a large non-polar covalent molecule that is unable to form hydrogen bonds with water.

Dry-cleaning is a process where clothes are washed without water. Instead, a less polar organic liquid is used which may be a better solvent for stains caused by large non-polar molecules such as grass and grease.

**Non-polar covalent substances dissolve best in non-polar solvents, polar substances dissolve best in polar solvents.**

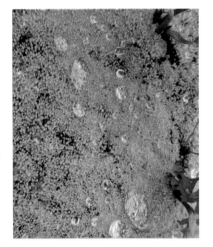

not. The difference is the size of the non-polar hydrocarbon group.

It follows from this that non-polar covalent substances do not dissolve well in water. Nitrogen, $N_2$, for example, has very low solubility in water at normal pressure, as do hydrocarbons such as candle wax and large covalent molecules such as chlorophyll. If you think about the substances that mark clothes and are not easily removed with water – grease, red wine, grass stains, and gravy are good examples – they are all relatively large insoluble non-polar molecules.

Likewise, polar substances have low solubility in non-polar solvents as they will remain held to each other by their dipole–dipole attractions and cannot interact well with the solvent. You can observe this by putting some sugar into cooking oil, and noticing that it does not dissolve.

Giant molecular substances are generally insoluble in all solvents, as too much energy would be required to break the strong covalent bonds in their structure. Beaches made primarily of sand, $SiO_2$, do not dissolve when the tide comes in and a diamond ring can safely be immersed in water.

### Electrical conductivity

Covalent compounds do not contain ions, and so are not able to conduct electricity in the solid or liquid state. Some polar covalent molecules, however, in conditions where they can ionize will conduct electricity. For example, HCl dissolved in water (hydrochloric acid) is an electrical conductor as it dissociates into $H^+(aq) + Cl^-(aq)$.

As discussed on page 169, the giant covalent molecules graphite and graphene are electrical conductors due to mobile electrons. In addition, fullerene and silicon have semiconductivity properties. Diamond is a non-conductor of electricity.

### Summary of physical properties

We can now summarize the physical properties of ionic and covalent compounds, though it should be recognized that the table below gives only general trends and does not apply universally.

| | Ionic compounds | Polar covalent compounds | Non-polar covalent compounds | Giant covalent |
|---|---|---|---|---|
| Volatility | low | higher | highest | low |
| Solubility in polar solvent, e.g. water | soluble | solubility increases as polarity increases | non-soluble | non-soluble |
| Solubility in non-polar solvent, e.g. hexane | non-soluble | solubility increases as polarity decreases | soluble | non-soluble |
| Electrical conductivity | conduct when molten (l) or dissolved in water (aq) | non-conductors | non-conductors | non-conductors except graphite, graphene and semi-conductivity of Si and fullerene |

**Investigation of the physical properties of a variety of substances**

Full detais of how to carry out this experiment with a worksheet are available online.

## Exercises

**27** The physical properties of five solids labelled A, B, C, D, and E are summarized below. The substances are: an ionic compound, a non-polar molecular solid, a metal, a polar molecular solid, and a giant molecular substance. Classify each correctly.

| Sample | Solubility in water | Conductivity of solution | Conductivity of solid | Relative melting point |
|--------|--------------------|-----------------------|---------------------|----------------------|
| A | insoluble | – | yes | third to melt |
| B | insoluble | – | no | highest |
| C | soluble | no | no | second to melt |
| D | insoluble | – | no | lowest |
| E | soluble | yes | no | fourth to melt |

**28** Which substance is the most soluble in water?

**A** $CH_3OH$      **B** $CH_4$      **C** $C_2H_6$      **D** $C_2H_5OH$

**29** State the intermolecular forces that exist between molecules of each of the following:

  **(a)** dry ice, $CO_2(s)$      **(b)** $NH_3(l)$      **(c)** $N_2(l)$      **(d)** $CH_3OCH_3$

**30** Which of each pair has the lower boiling point?

  **(a)** $C_2H_6$ and $C_3H_8$      **(b)** $H_2O$ and $H_2S$      **(c)** $Cl_2$ and $Br_2$      **(d)** HF and HCl

# 4.5 Metallic bonding

## Understandings:

- A metallic bond is the electrostatic attraction between a lattice of positive ions and delocalized electrons.
- The strength of a metallic bond depends on the charge of the ions and the radius of the metal ion.
- Alloys usually contain more than one metal and have enhanced properties.

  *Guidance*
  *Examples of various alloys should be covered.*

## Applications and skills:

- Explanation of electrical conductivity and malleability in metals.
- Explanation of trends in melting points of metals.

  *Guidance*
  *Trends should be limited to s- and p-block elements.*

- Explanation of the properties of alloys in terms of non-directional bonding.

Metals are found on the left of the Periodic Table and have a small number of electrons in their outer shell. These are atoms with low ionization energies, and typically react with other elements by losing their valence electrons and forming positive ions. So these elements are characterized by having a loose control over their outer shell electrons.

In the elemental state, when there is no other element present to accept the electrons and form an ionic compound, the outer electrons are held only loosely by the metal atom's nucleus and so tend to 'wander off' or, more correctly, become **delocalized**. As we saw in Section 4.3, delocalized electrons are not fixed in one position. This means that in metals they are no longer associated closely with any one metal nucleus but instead can spread themselves through the metal structure. The metal atoms without

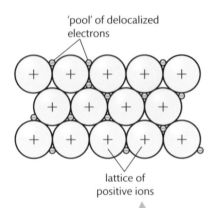

'pool' of delocalized electrons

lattice of positive ions

**Figure 4.19** A model of metallic bonding. It is often described as a lattice of cations surrounded by a sea of electrons.

Copper is one of the oldest metals ever used. It is malleable, ductile, and a good conductor of heat and electricity. Brass and bronze are copper alloys.

**Metallic bonds are the strong forces of attraction between delocalized electrons and positive ions.**

The extraction of metals from their ores is a major part of industry and development in many countries, but is associated with some complex environmental issues. These include the destruction of landscapes by strip mining, the 'tailings' or waste material that accumulate in spoil tips, and the release of toxic materials that leach out of waste and pollute the environment. An important step to reduce the impact of these effects is to maximize the reuse and recycling of all metal objects, and avoid metal dumping. Despite their apparent abundance, metals are a precious resource, available only at considerable cost.

these electrons have become positively charged ions and form a regular lattice structure through which these electrons can move freely.

You can think of it like a close neighbourhood of families where the children do not belong specifically to any one set of parents but are free to wander between the homes. This arrangement causes a close association between the families. Likewise in metals there is a force of electrostatic attraction between the lattice of cations and the delocalized electrons, and this is known as **metallic bonding**.

The strength of the metallic bond is determined by:

• the number of delocalized electrons;
• the charge on the cation;
• the radius of the cation.

The greater the number of delocalized electrons and the smaller the cation, the greater the binding force between them. For example, if we compare:

• sodium, Na, Group 1, electron configuration $1s^22s^22p^63s^1$ and
• magnesium, Mg, Group 2, electron configuration $1s^22s^22p^63s^2$

we can deduce that Na will have one delocalized electron per atom and the $Na^+$ ion, whereas Mg will have two delocalized electrons per atom and the $Mg^{2+}$ ion. In addition, the radius of $Mg^{2+}$ is slightly smaller than that of $Na^+$. These factors all indicate that Mg has stronger metallic bonding than Na, which can be confirmed by a comparison of their melting points.

|  | **Na** | **Mg** |
|---|---|---|
| Melting point / °C | 98 | 650 |

The strength of metallic bonding tends to decrease down a group as the size of the cation increases, reducing the attraction between the delocalized electrons and the positive charges. Again melting points confirm this.

|  | **Na** | **K** | **Rb** |
|---|---|---|---|
| Melting point / °C | 98 | 63 | 39 |

The transition elements tend to have very strong metallic bonds due to the large number of electrons that can become delocalized, from both 3d and 4s sub-shells.

Metals share characteristic physical properties, which can be explained through this model of metallic bonding. They are summarized below.

| Metallic property | Explanation | Application |
|---|---|---|
| good electrical conductivity | delocalized electrons are highly mobile, and so can move through the metal structure in response to an applied voltage | electrical circuits use copper |
| good thermal conductivity | delocalized electrons and close packed ions enable efficient transfer of heat energy | cooking utensils |
| malleable, can be shaped under pressure | movement of delocalized electrons is non-directional and essentially random through the cation lattice, so the metallic bond remains intact while the conformation changes under applied pressure | moulded into many forms including machinery and structural components of buildings and vehicles |
| ductile, can be drawn out into threads | | electric wires and cables |
| high melting points | a lot of energy is required to break the strong metallic bonds and separate the atoms | high speed tools and turbine engines; tungsten has the highest melting point |
| shiny, lustrous appearance | delocalized electrons in metal crystal structure reflect light | ornamental structures |

## Alloys are solutions of metals with enhanced properties

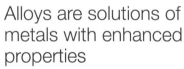

Alloys are produced by adding one metal element to another metal (or carbon) in the molten state, so that the different atoms can mix. As the mixture solidifies, ions of the different metals are scattered through the lattice and bound by the delocalized electrons, so they contain metallic bonds. The production of alloys is possible because of the non-directional nature of the delocalized electrons, and the fact that the lattice can accommodate ions of different size.

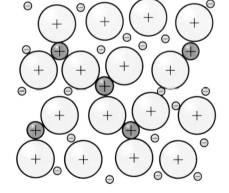

**Figure 4.20** Alloys consist of different metal ions and a sea of delocalized electrons. The smaller ions are able to fit in the spaces between the larger ions in the lattice structure.

**Alloys are solid solutions usually containing more than one metal, and held together by metallic bonding.**

Alloys have properties that are distinct from their component elements due to the different packing of the cations in the lattice. The alloy is often more chemically stable, and also often stronger and more resistant to corrosion.

| Name of alloy | Component metals | Properties and uses |
|---|---|---|
| steel | iron with carbon and other elements | high tensile strength but corrodes, used as structural material |
| stainless steel | iron with other elements such as nickel and chromium | widely used in domestic and industrial appliances due to strength and corrosion resistance |
| brass | copper and zinc | variety of plumbing fittings |
| bronze | copper and tin | coins, medals, tools, heavy gears |
| pewter | tin and antimony and copper | decorative objects |
| duralumin | aluminium, copper, and manganese | aircraft, boats, and machinery due to high strength and resistance to corrosion |
| Nichrome | nickel and copper | heating elements in toasters, electric heaters |
| solder | lead and tin | low melting point, used in joining two metals together, especially in electric circuitry |
| sterling silver | silver and copper | jewellery, art objects |

 You do not need to learn all these examples, but you should be able to use the examples you choose to explain why the structure of alloys gives them enhanced properties compared with their component metals.

 Steel manufacture is one of the world's largest industries and is sometimes used as a measure of a country's development and economic progress. Many countries are investing in technologies to become self sufficient in steel making. Production has increased steadily in Asia, which in 2013 accounted for about 65% of global steel production, with China and India the major contributors. Steel is the most recycled material in the world and, in developed countries, recycling accounts for almost half of the steel produced.

 Naturally occurring alloys have been used by humans since ancient times, and civilizations learned to make alloys by smelting, largely influenced by the availability of native metals. The Bronze Age in Europe dates from about 2500 BCE, while in the Middle East, brass was produced from about 400 BCE. The availability of these alloys played a major part in establishing cultures and trading relationships.

## Exercises

**31** Which is the best definition of metallic bonding?

   **A** the attraction between cations and anions
   **B** the attraction between cations and delocalized electrons
   **C** the attraction between nuclei and electron pairs
   **D** the attraction between nuclei and anions

**32** Aluminium is a widely used metal. What properties make it suitable for the following applications?

   **(a)** baking foil
   **(b)** aircraft bodywork
   **(c)** cooking pans
   **(d)** tent frames

**33** Suggest two ways in which some of the properties of aluminium can be enhanced.

Nichrome wire is used in carrying out flame tests in the laboratory. It is a convenient material because it is resistant to oxidation at high temperatures.

# 14.1 Further aspects of covalent bonding and structure

## Understandings:

- Covalent bonds result from the overlap of atomic orbitals. A sigma bond ($\sigma$) is formed by the direct head-on/end-to-end overlap of atomic orbitals, resulting in electron density concentrated between the nuclei of the bonding atoms. A pi bond ($\pi$) is formed by the sideways overlap of atomic orbitals, resulting in electron density above and below the plane of the nuclei of the bonding atoms.

### Guidance
*The linear combination of atomic orbitals to form molecular orbitals should be covered in the context of the formation of sigma ($\sigma$) and pi ($\pi$) bonds.*

- Formal charge (FC) can be used to decide which Lewis (electron dot) structure is preferred from several. The FC is the charge an atom would have if all atoms in the molecule had the same electronegativity. FC = (number of valence electrons) − ½(number of bonding electrons) − (number of non-bonding electrons). The Lewis (electron dot) structure with the atoms having FC values closest to zero is preferred.
- Exceptions to the octet rule include some species having incomplete octets and expanded octets.

### Guidance
*Molecular polarities of geometries corresponding to five and six electron domains should also be covered.*

- Delocalization involves electrons that are shared by/between all atoms in a molecule or ion as opposed to being localized between a pair of atoms.
- Resonance involves using two or more Lewis (electron dot) structures to represent a particular molecule or ion. A resonance structure is one of two or more alternative Lewis (electron dot) structures for a molecule or ion that cannot be described fully with one Lewis (electron dot) structure alone.

## Applications and skills:

- Prediction whether sigma ($\sigma$) or pi ($\pi$) bonds are formed from the linear combination of atomic orbitals.
- Deduction of the Lewis (electron dot) structures of molecules and ions showing all valence electrons for up to six electron pairs on each atom.
- Application of FC to ascertain which Lewis (electron dot) structure is preferred from different Lewis (electron dot) structures.
- Deduction using VSEPR theory of the electron domain geometry and molecular geometry with five and six electron domains and associated bond angles.
- Explanation of the wavelength of light required to dissociate oxygen and ozone.
- Description of the mechanism of the catalysis of ozone depletion when catalysed by CFCs and $NO_x$.

## Some molecules contain a central atom with an expanded octet

In Section 4.3 we explored the shapes of molecules having two, three, and four electron domains – that is those with up to eight electrons, an octet, around the central atom. The octet, being associated with a special stability for most atoms, is the most common electron arrangement.

However, when the central atom is an element from the Period 3 or below, we sometimes find compounds in which there are more than eight electrons around the central atom. This is known as an **expanded octet**. This arrangement is possible because the d orbitals available in the valence shell of these atoms have energy values relatively close to those of the p orbitals. So promotion of electrons, for example

**Exceptions to the octet rule:**

- small atoms like Be and B form stable molecules with fewer than an octet of electrons

- atoms of elements in Period 3 and below may expand their octet by using d orbitals in their valence shell.

from 3p to empty 3d orbitals, will allow additional electron pairs to form. This is how elements such as phosphorus and sulfur expand their octets, forming species with five or six electron domains. These will have characteristic shapes, as discussed below. In the following diagrams, as before, non-bonding electron pairs on the surrounding atoms are not shown, to aid clarity, so these are *not* Lewis (electron dot) structures.

## Species with five electron domains

Molecules with five electron domains will position them in a **triangular bipyramidal** shape, which has angles of 90°, 120°, and 180°. If all five electron domains are bonding electrons, the shape of the molecule is also triangular bipyramidal.

$$PCl_5$$

However, as we saw in the examples with three and four electron domains on pages 160–1, if one or more of the electron domains are non-bonding electrons, then the shape of the *molecule* will be different as it is determined by the positions only of the *bonded atoms*.

In determining the position of the non-bonding pairs of electrons, remember that they cause greater repulsion than bonding pairs so will arrange themselves in the position offering the greatest distance from a neighbouring pair. In the triangular bipyramidal structure this will mean in the equatorial plane, as shown in the examples below.

• One non-bonding pair gives an **unsymmetrical tetrahedron** or **see-saw** shape.

$$SF_4$$

There will be some distortion of the shape due to the greater repulsion of the non-bonding pair of electrons, so bond angles will be 90°, 117°, and 180°.

• Two non-bonding pairs gives a **T-shaped** structure.

$$ClF_3$$

The bond angles are 90° and 180°.

With 5 electron domains on the central atom:
0 lone pairs → triangular bipyramidal,
1 lone pair → see-saw,
2 lone pairs → T-shaped,
3 lone pairs → linear.

Compounds containing two different halogen atoms bonded together are called interhalogen compounds. They are interesting because they contain halogen atoms in unusual oxidation states: the more electronegative halogen has its typical negative oxidation number whereas the less electronegative halogen has a positive oxidation number. For example in $ClF_3$ described here, the oxidation number of each F is −1 and the oxidation number of Cl is +3. You can read more about oxidation numbers in Chapter 9.

- Three non-bonding pairs gives a **linear** shape.

  For example $I_3^-$

The bond angle is 180°.

Iodine starch test. The bottle should more accurately be labelled 'Iodine solution' as it contains $I_2(s)$ dissolved in $KI(aq)$. The $I_3^-$ species present in this solution turns from orange to blue-black when mixed with starch – confirming the presence of starch in the potato.

The species $I_3^-$ described here as having a linear structure is the form of iodine used in the widely used starch test. The iodine reagent is made by dissolving iodine in water in the presence of potassium iodide, forming the soluble tri-iodide ion.

$$I_2(s) + I^-(aq) \rightarrow I_3^-(aq)$$

When this species is added to starch it slides into coils in the starch structure causing an intense blue-black colour.

## Species with six electron domains

Molecules with six electron domains will position them in an **octahedral** shape with angles of 90°. So a molecule having all six of its electron domains as bonding pairs of electrons will have this symmetrical octahedral shape.

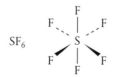

$SF_6$

The bond angles are 90°.

The shape of a molecule in which there are one or more non-bonding pairs of electrons is based on considering where the non-bonding pairs will be placed for maximum repulsion.

- One non-bonding pair gives a **square pyramidal** shape.

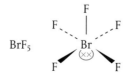

$BrF_5$

The eight-sided octahedral shape is determined by the six electron domains directed to each corner.

This is a shape commonly found in the complexes of metal ions with ligands, described more fully in Section 13.2.

With 6 electron domains on the central atom:
0 lone pairs → octahedral,
1 lone pair → square pyramidal,
2 lone pairs → square planar.

Molecular model of iodine pentafluoride, $IF_5$. The iodine atom is shown in orange, fluorine atoms in red, and the lone pair on the iodine atom in blue. Like $BrF_5$ described in the text, this molecule has a square pyramidal shape that maximizes the distance between the valence shell electron pairs.

Due to their stable electron configuration, Group 18 compounds are very unreactive. Compounds exist only between the elements with larger atoms having lower ionization energies, and the most electronegative elements fluorine and oxygen. Xenon tetrafluoride ($XeF_4$), described here, is stable at normal temperatures and occurs as colourless crystals. Its square planar structure was determined by NMR spectroscopy and X-ray crystallography in 1963.

• Two non-bonding pairs will maximize their distance apart by arranging those pairs at 180° to each other. This gives a **square planar** shape.

$XeF_4$

## Worked example

Predict the shape and bond angles found in $PF_6^-$.

**Solution**

First work out its Lewis (electron dot) structure following the steps on page 156.

$$\text{total number of valence electrons} = 5 + (7 \times 6) + 1 = 48$$

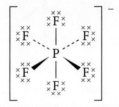

So there are six charge centres around the central atom P, which will be arranged in an octahedral shape. All angles are 90°.

## Summary of shapes of molecules predicted from VSEPR theory

The shapes of molecules for two, three, four, five, and six electron domains are summarized in the table on page 189.

| Number of electron domains | Electron domain geometry | Number of bonding electron domains | Number of non-bonding pairs of electrons | Molecular geometry | Example | |
|---|---|---|---|---|---|---|
| 2 | linear | 2 | 0 | linear | $CO_2$ | $O=C=O$ |
| 3 | planar triangular | 3 | 0 | planar triangular | $BF_3$ | |
| 3 | planar triangular | 2 | 1 | V-shaped | $SO_2$ | |
| 4 | tetrahedral | 4 | 0 | tetrahedral | $CH_4$ | |
| 4 | tetrahedral | 3 | 1 | pyramidal | $NH_3$ | |
| 4 | tetrahedral | 2 | 2 | V-shaped | $H_2O$ | |
| 5 | triangular bipyramidal | 5 | 0 | triangular bipyramidal | $PCl_5$ | |
| 5 | triangular bipyramidal | 4 | 1 | unsymmetrical tetrahedron/see-saw | $SF_4$ | |
| 5 | triangular bipyramidal | 3 | 2 | T-shaped | $ClF_3$ | |
| 5 | triangular bipyramidal | 2 | 3 | linear | $I_3^-$ | |
| 6 | octahedral | 6 | 0 | octahedral | $SF_6$ | |
| 6 | octahedral | 5 | 1 | square pyramidal | $BrF_5$ | |
| 6 | octahedral | 4 | 2 | square planar | $XeF_4$ | |

## Molecular geometry determines molecular polarity

We saw in Section 4.3 that the polarity of a molecule can be determined from the orientation of its polar bonds, and whether the bond dipoles cancel or not. We can apply this same principle to molecules in which the central atom has an expanded octet.

If there are no lone pairs and all the atoms attached to the central atom are the same, the molecules are non-polar as there is no net dipole. For example, $PCl_5$ and $SF_6$ are both non-polar.

Non-polar molecules:

PCl₅          SF₆

If the atoms attached to the central atom are not all the same, there may or may not be a net dipole depending on the symmetry. For example, $SBrF_5$ has a net dipole and is polar; $PCl_3F_2$ has no net dipole due to cancellation, so it is non-polar.

net dipole          no net dipole

The presence of lone pairs often, but not always, results in a polar molecule. It again depends on symmetry and whether dipoles cancel. For example, $ClF_3$ is polar, whereas $XeF_4$ is not.

net dipole          no net dipole

## Exercises

**34** Predict the shapes and bond angles of the following molecules and ions:

    **(a)** $XeF_2$     **(b)** $ClO_3^-$     **(c)** $OF_2$     **(d)** $XeO_4$
    **(e)** $PCl_6^-$     **(f)** $IF_4^+$

**35** How many electron domains are there around the central atom in molecules that have the following geometry?

    **(a)** square planar     **(b)** octahedral     **(c)** square pyramidal
    **(d)** trigonal bipyramidal     **(e)** linear

**36** What bond angles do you expect for each of the following?

    **(a)** the F–Kr–F angle in $KrF_4$
    **(b)** the Cl–P–Cl angle in $PCl_3$
    **(c)** the F–S–F angle in $SF_6$

**37** Determine whether the species in Q14 (a)–(f) (page 158) are polar or non-polar.

**38** Which of the following molecules would be expected to be polar?

    **(a)** $ClBr_3$     **(b)** $IO_4^-$     **(c)** $TeF_6$     **(d)** $BrF_4^-$
    **(e)** $PCl_4^+$     **(f)** $FCl_2^+$

# Formal charge is a useful tool for comparing Lewis (electron dot) structures

It is sometimes possible to follow the rules for drawing Lewis (electron dot) structures, and come up with more than one possible structure that seems to be acceptable. This happens especially with molecules that are able to form an expanded octet, where we can broaden our study of resonance structures. A classic example is sulfur dioxide, $SO_2$,

which in different sources is represented as: (i)

(ii) as a structure with an expanded octet on S

These three are all resonance structures as they differ only in the distribution of electrons, not in the position of the atoms in the skeletal structure. They all have the same shape with a bond angle of approximately 117°.

Can we determine which of these represents the most stable structure? A useful tool to use for this is the concept of **formal charge**. This treats covalent bonds as if they were purely covalent with equal electron distribution – so for this, forget about electronegativity differences between the atoms. The idea is to count how many electrons 'belong' to (are assigned to) each atom in the Lewis (electron dot) structure, and compare this with the number of valence electrons in the non-bonded atom. The difference between these two is the formal charge. It can be expressed as:

**formal charge (FC)** = number of valence electrons in unbonded atom (V) − **number of electrons assigned to atom in Lewis (electron dot) structure**

- The number of valence electrons (V) is determined from the element's group in the Periodic Table.
- The number of electrons assigned to an atom in the Lewis (electron dot) structure is calculated by assuming that:
  (a) each atom has an equal share of a bonding electron pair (one electron per atom), even if it is a coordinate bond (½B);
  (b) an atom owns its lone pairs completely (L).

This means that:

**number of electrons assigned = ½ number of electrons in bonded pairs (½B) + number of electrons in lone pairs (L)**

So overall:

$$FC = V - (\tfrac{1}{2}B + L)$$

Low formal charges mean that less charge transfer has taken place in forming a structure from its atoms, and in general this represents the most stable or preferred structure.

We can now apply the formula for formal charge to the different Lewis (electron dot) structures for $SO_2$ shown above, and consider the formal charge of each atom in turn for both structures.

Formal charge (FC) is determined for each atom in a structure from:

$$FC = V - (\tfrac{1}{2}B + L)$$

where V = valence electrons, B = number of bonding electrons, L = number of lone pair electrons.

191

**(i)**  $\longleftrightarrow$     **(ii)**

| | |
|---|---|
| S: 3 bonding pairs | S: 4 bonding pairs |
| 1 lone pair | 1 lone pair |
| FC = 6 − (3 + 2) = +1 | FC = 6 − (4 + 2) = 0 |
| left O: 2 bonding pairs | left O: 2 bonding pairs |
| 2 lone pairs | 2 lone pairs |
| FC = 6 − (2 + 4) = 0 | FC = 6 − (2 + 4) = 0 |
| right O: 1 bonding pair | right O: 2 bonding pairs |
| 3 lone pairs | 2 lone pairs |
| FC = 6 − (1 + 6) = −1 | FC = 6 − (2 + 4) = 0 |

The formal charges in each resonance structure can be summarized as follows:

(i)

(ii)

We can conclude that structure (ii) where all atoms have a formal charge of zero is the most stable structure for $SO_2$.

This example shows the use of formal charge in determining which of several possible Lewis (electron dot) structures is the more stable or preferred structure. In fact, all resonance structures contribute to the electronic structure of the molecule, and the real or observed structure is a combination of them. The more stable structure, the one with the lowest formal charge, contributes more than the less stable structures.

> Equivalent Lewis structures are those that contain the same numbers of single and multiple bonds, such as the resonance structures of ozone. Non-equivalent Lewis structures contain different numbers of single and multiple bonds, such as the two structures of $SO_2$ discussed here. Note that the concept of formal charges is used to compare the stabilities of non-equivalent structures, but not for equivalent structures, as they are the same.

## Worked example

Use the concept of formal charge to determine which of the following Lewis (electron dot) structures for $XeO_3$ is preferred?

### Solution

| | | |
|---|---|---|
| Xe | FC = 8 − (4 + 2)= +2 | FC = 8 − (6 + 2) = 0 |
| left O | FC = 6 − (1 + 6) = −1 | FC = 6 − (2 + 4) = 0 |
| central O | FC = 6 − (2 + 4) = 0 | FC = 6 − (2 + 4) = 0 |
| right O | FC = 6 − (1 + 6) = −1 | FC = 6 − (2 + 4) = 0 |

> In general, the Lewis (electron dot) structure with the atoms having values for formal charge closest to zero is preferred.

The structure on the right with the lowest formal charge is preferred.

Note that the sum of the formal charges for a species must be zero for a neutral molecule or equal to the charge on the ion.

Formal charge is a useful tool but, because it ignores differences in electronegativity values, it does not give the full picture. So, a useful guideline to follow is that the most stable of several Lewis (electron dot) structures is the structure that has:

• the lowest formal charges *and*
• negative values for formal charge on the more electronegative atoms.

For example, two Lewis (electron dot) structures with formal charges are shown for $N_2O$.

(i)                    (ii)

$$\overset{\,}{\underset{0}{\text{N}}}\equiv\overset{+}{\underset{+1}{\text{N}}}-\overset{-}{\underset{-1}{\text{O}}} \qquad \overset{-}{\underset{-1}{\text{N}}}=\overset{+}{\underset{+1}{\text{N}}}=\overset{\,}{\underset{0}{\text{O}}}$$

We can see that both structures have the same difference for formal charge, which suggests equal stability. But (i) has the negative charge over the more electronegative atom, O, and so it is preferred.

Formal charge can help explain the allocation of charges on transition states in reaction mechanisms.

Formal charge is described here as a tool that helps us to consider the relative stability of molecular structures. In Chapter 9 we will introduce the concept of oxidation number, which similarly considers electron distributions within structures. While formal charge treats covalent bonds as if they were pure covalent bonds with electrons shared equally between atoms, oxidation number treats covalent bonds as if they were ionic with transfer of electrons between atoms. So these two models can be viewed as opposite approaches, and in reality neither accurately describes the real charge on atoms. But they both can be useful models, depending on the circumstances.

By using formal charge in some situations, and oxidation numbers in another, scientists are applying the principle of Occam's razor. This recognizes that the simplest explanation is often the most appropriate, as it can maximize the explanatory power of a theory.

## Ozone: a case study in resonance, molecular polarity, and formal charge

Our introduction to resonance on pages 164–5 used ozone, $O_3$, as an example. We can now develop this study further, using some of our later work on molecular polarity and formal charge. The explanations here include sigma and pi bond formation and hybridization, which will make more sense after you have read Section 14.2. Ozone is a particularly interesting molecule because of its role in the stratosphere, in air pollution, and in water purification, and understanding its structure is key to these properties.

The Lewis (electron dot) structures of ozone $\overset{\times\times}{\text{O}}=\overset{\times\times}{\text{O}}-\overset{\times\times}{\underset{\times\times}{\text{O}}}\times \longleftrightarrow \times\overset{\times\times}{\underset{\times\times}{\text{O}}}-\overset{\times\times}{\text{O}}=\overset{\times\times}{\text{O}}$ indicate that the central atom has three electron domains with a triangular planar geometry. As only two of the domains are bonding, the molecular geometry is bent or V shaped. The greater repulsion of the lone pair gives a bond angle of about 117°.

## CHALLENGE YOURSELF

7  There are several covalently bonded molecules and ions that contain transition metals, such as $FeBr_3$ and $MnO_4^-$. What problems arise in determining the formal charge of species like these?

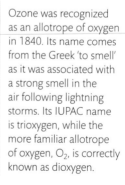

Ozone was recognized as an allotrope of oxygen in 1840. Its name comes from the Greek 'to smell' as it was associated with a strong smell in the air following lightning storms. Its IUPAC name is trioxygen, while the more familiar allotrope of oxygen, $O_2$, is correctly known as dioxygen.

The double bond is composed of a sigma (σ) bond from the overlap of hybrid orbitals, and a pi (π) bond from the overlap of unhybridized p orbitals. The electrons in the pi bond are less tightly held so become delocalized through the structure, giving rise to the resonance forms. The true structure is a resonance hybrid. As there are three pairs of electrons in two bonding positions, the bond order is 1.5. This means that the bonds are intermediate in length and strength between single and double oxygen-oxygen bonds.

The bonds in ozone are between oxygen atoms only, so they are clearly non-polar. So the fact that it is a polar molecule may seem surprising. It can be explained, however, by checking the formal charges on each atom, which show the uneven distribution of electrons through the structure.

This gives a net dipole across the molecule, making it polar. This can be shown as follows.

## Ozone is an essential component of the stratosphere

The layer of gas tens of kilometres above us, known as the **atmosphere**, is essential for life on Earth. It traps heat, creating a temperature appropriate for life, while at the same time blocks some of the dangerous radiation from the Sun and prevents it from reaching Earth. It also contains oxygen, essential to life. The different regions of the atmosphere are shown in Figure 4.21. The region from approximately 12–50 kilometres above the Earth is known as the **stratosphere**.

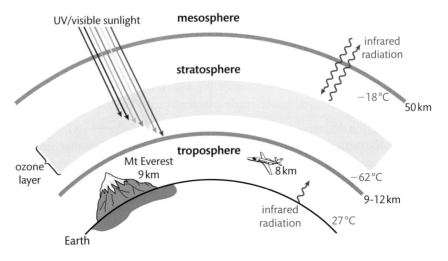

**Figure 4.21** Regions of the atmosphere. The ozone layer is in the lower part of the stratosphere, approximately 20–30 kilometres above Earth.

**Regions of the atmosphere**

UV/visible sunlight — mesosphere — infrared radiation — stratosphere — −18 °C — 50 km — ozone layer — Mt Everest 9 km — troposphere — 8 km — −62 °C — 9-12 km — infrared radiation — 27 °C — Earth

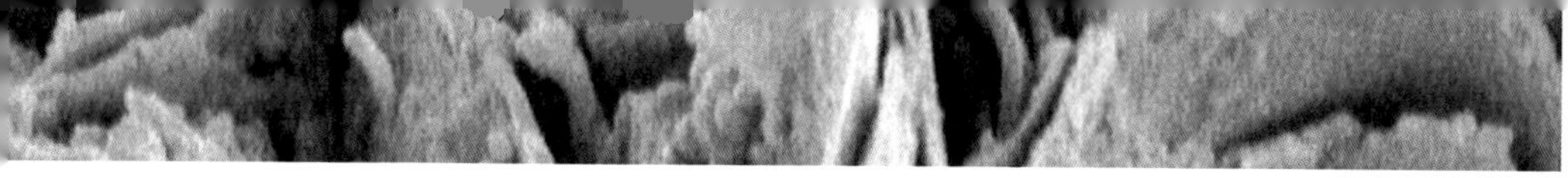

The lower part of the stratosphere, known as the **ozone layer**, contains 90% of the atmospheric ozone, although the concentration is less than 10 parts per million. Ozone levels are maintained through a cycle of reactions involving the formation and breakdown of oxygen and ozone as described in Chapter 5, pages 236–237.

Two key steps in the ozone cycle are shown below. The symbol O· represents a species known as a **free radical** that has an unpaired electron and so is highly reactive.

A free radical is a reactive species that contains an unpaired electron.

## Oxygen dissociation

$$O_2(g) \xrightarrow{\lambda < 242\,nm} O\cdot(g) + O\cdot(g)$$

## Ozone dissociation

1  $O_3(g) \xrightarrow[\text{fast}]{\lambda < 330\,nm} O\cdot(g) + 2O_2(g)$

2  $O_3(g) + O\cdot(g) \xrightarrow[\text{slow}]{} 2O_2(g)$  $\Delta H$ = negative (exothermic reaction)

We can see that the breakdown of $O_2$ involves shorter wavelength light ($\lambda$ <242 nm) than the breakdown of $O_3$ ($\lambda$ < 330 nm). The difference is due to the relative strengths of the O–O bonds in the two molecules as we saw on page 164. The stronger bonds in $O_2$ require the higher energy radiation of the shorter wavelength to break.

| | **Oxygen $O_2$** | **Ozone $O_3$** |
|---|---|---|
| | 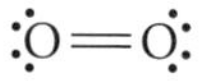 :O=O: | 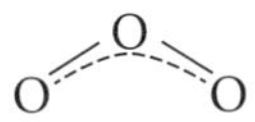 O—O—O |
| **bond order** | 2 | 1.5 |
| **bond enthalpy** | 498 kJ mol$^{-1}$ | 364 kJ mol$^{-1}$ |
| **dissociated by UV light** | <242 nm | <330 nm |

Oxygen contains stronger bonds than ozone, and so is dissociated by light of shorter wavelength.

The fact that ozone absorbs radiation of wavelengths in the range 200 nm to 315 nm is very significant. This corresponds to the higher range of ultraviolet light, known as UV-B and UV-C, which can cause damage to living tissue. So the ozone layer plays a vital role in protecting life on Earth from this radiation. This is a direct consequence of the specific nature of the bonding in ozone molecules.

The absorption of UV radiation by ozone is also a major source of heat in the stratosphere, and is the reason why the temperature in the stratosphere rises with height. This is explained further in Chapter 5, page 237. Ozone therefore also plays an additional role in determining the temperature structure of the Earth's atmosphere.

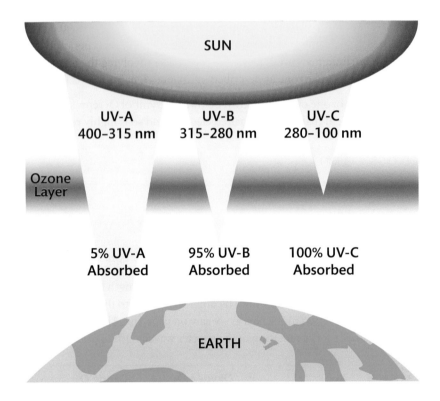

**Figure 4.22** The ozone layer is responsible for absorbing much of the harmful UV radiation.

## Catalytic destruction of ozone

Ozone's ability to absorb UV radiation also means that it is unstable, and it reacts easily with compounds found in the stratosphere that have been released through human activities. Chief amongst these are nitrogen oxides, known as $NO_x$, and chlorofluorocarbons, known as **CFCs**. These compounds produce highly reactive free radicals that catalyse the decomposition of ozone to oxygen.

Nitrogen monoxide, NO, is produced in vehicle engines by direct combination of nitrogen and oxygen from the air at high temperatures. It is a free radical as it has an odd number of electrons. Nitrogen dioxide, $NO_2$, forms from the oxidation of nitrogen oxide and is also a free radical. The reactions of nitrogen oxides with ozone are as follows:

$$NO \cdot (g) + O_3(g) \rightarrow NO_2 \cdot (g) + O_2(g)$$

$$NO_2 \cdot (g) + O \cdot (g) \rightarrow NO \cdot (g) + O_2(g)$$

$NO \cdot (g)$ has acted as a catalyst because it is regenerated during the reaction and the net change is the breakdown of ozone:

$$O_3(g) + O \cdot (g) \rightarrow 2O_2(g)$$

Chlorofluorocarbons were widely used in aerosols, refrigerants, solvents, and plastics due to their low reactivity and low toxicity in the troposphere. But when they get into the stratosphere, the higher energy UV radiation breaks them down, releasing free chlorine atoms, which are also reactive free radicals. For example, the CFC known as Freon undergoes photochemical decomposition as follows:

$$CCl_2F_2(g) \rightarrow CClF_2 \cdot (g) + Cl \cdot (g)$$

The weaker C–Cl bond breaks in preference to the C–F bond, and the chlorine radicals catalyse the decomposition of ozone.

$$Cl\cdot(g) + O_3(g) \rightarrow O_2(g) + ClO\cdot(g)$$

$$ClO\cdot(g) + O\cdot(g) \rightarrow O_2(g) + Cl\cdot(g)$$

Here $Cl\cdot(g)$ has acted as a catalyst and the net reaction is again:

$$O_3(g) + O\cdot(g) \rightarrow 2O_2(g)$$

These reactions, and others like them, have upset the balance of the ozone cycle described on pages 236–237 and led to thinning of the ozone layer, which was first noted in the 1970s. The increased UV radiation reaching the Earth has been most pronounced in the polar regions, and has been a source of global concern ever since.

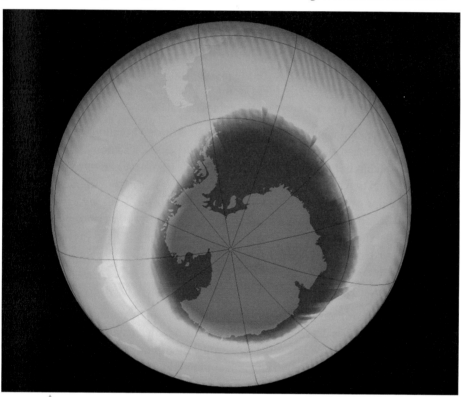

Satellite image of the ozone hole over Antarctica in 2010. Ozone layer thicknesses are colour coded from purple (lowest) through blue, cyan, and green to yellow (highest). The ozone hole was at its annual maximum, covering an area of over 22 million square kilometres. Although CFCs responsible for much of the damage were phased out from the 1980s, damage to the ozone did not peak until 2006. Ozone-depleting chemicals in the stratosphere persist at high concentrations.

Chemicals that have the effect of breaking down ozone in the stratosphere are collectively known as ozone-depleting chemicals (ODCs). Once their destructive effects became known, many countries started banning their use. An international response was developed through the Montreal Protocol, which was originally signed in 1987 but subsequently has passed many revisions. In total, the treaties have been ratified by 197 countries and the European Union, and it has been described as 'perhaps the single most successful international agreement to date.' Opinions vary on the extent to which the ozone layer can recover over time. It has been suggested that full compliance with the terms of the Montreal Protocol by all nations could lead to its restoration by 2050, but other estimates are less optimistic. A major problem is the persistence of ODCs in the stratosphere, despite the fact that they are no longer released in large quantities.

**TOK** In relation to environmental concerns of global significance, what is the balance between the responsibility of the individual, scientists, and governments?

## NATURE OF SCIENCE

The global reduction in the production of ozone-depleting chemicals has to a certain extent been possible because of research into substitute chemicals and technologies that can replace the compounds being phased out. While scientific innovation is held largely responsible for ozone depletion, the response to the problem also relies heavily on the work of scientists. Risk assessment and application of the precautionary principle are essential approaches to help ameliorate some negative unintended consequences of scientific advances. In addition, continuous monitoring of environmental and health outcomes through data collection and sharing is essential.

## CHALLENGE YOURSELF

8 Consider why the depletion of the ozone layer is greater in the winter months over polar regions.

### Exercises

39 Use the concept of formal charge to explain why $BF_3$ is an exception to the octet rule.

40 Draw two different Lewis (electron dot) structures for $SO_4^{2-}$, one of which obeys the octet rule for all its atoms, the other which has an octet for S expanded to 12 electrons. Use formal charges to determine which is the preferred structure.

41 Explain why ozone can be dissociated by light with a longer wavelength than that required to decompose oxygen.

42 Outline ways in which ozone levels are decreased by human activities, using equations to support your answer.

## Atomic orbitals overlap to form two types of covalent bond: sigma and pi

The VSEPR theory discussed in Sections 4.3 and 14.1 gives us a model for predicting the shapes of molecules and ions. But if we stop and think for a moment, it also raises a big question. How can we explain angles such as 109.5°, when the shapes of orbitals described in Chapter 2 are spherical (s orbitals) or dumb-bell shaped orientated at 90° to each other (p orbitals)? Clearly, these atomic orbitals must undergo some changes during the bonding process to explain the angles that arise.

A full explanation of the interaction between orbitals during bonding, and the resulting electron distributions in covalent bonds, depends on a knowledge of wave mechanics which is not discussed here. But, in simple terms, we can think of a bond as forming when two atomic orbitals, each containing one electron, overlap to form a new **molecular orbital** that is at a lower energy. The shape of this molecular orbital can be predicted from the shapes of the two atomic orbitals, as described below. We will see that there are two main types of molecular orbital, each representing a particular type of covalent bond.

### The sigma (σ) bond

When two atomic orbitals overlap along the bond axis – an imaginary line between the two nuclei – the bond is described as a **sigma bond**, denoted using the Greek letter σ. This type of bond forms by the overlap of s orbitals, p orbitals, and hybrid orbitals (to be described in the next section) in different combinations. It is always the bond that forms in a single covalent bond.

All single covalent bonds are sigma bonds. Sigma bonds form by overlap of orbitals along the bond axis.

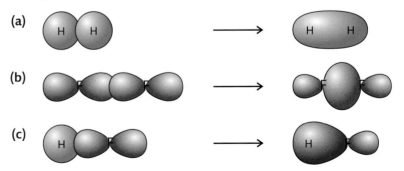

**Figure 4.23** Formation of sigma bond by overlap of (a) s orbitals, e.g. H + H → $H_2$, (b) p orbitals end-on, e.g. F + F → $F_2$. and (c) s and p orbitals, e.g. H + F → HF. The symbol for the element denotes the position of the nucleus. In all cases, the electron density is greatest along the bond axis.

In a sigma bond the electron density is concentrated between the nuclei of the bonded atoms.

## The pi (π) bond

When two p orbitals overlap *sideways*, the electron density of the molecular orbital is concentrated in two regions, above and below the plane of the bond axis. This is known as a **pi bond**, denoted using the Greek letter π. This type of bond only forms by the overlap of p orbitals alongside the formation of a sigma bond. In other words, pi bonds only form within a double bond or a triple bond.

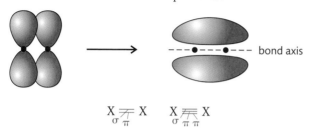

**Figure 4.24** Formation of pi bond by sideways overlap of p orbitals. The electron density is greatest in two regions above and below the bond axis.

The formation of pi bonds within multiple bonds is described more fully in the next section. Pi bonds are weaker than sigma bonds as their electron density is further from the positive charge of the nucleus, and so they break more easily during chemical reactions. We will see in Chapter 10 how this causes molecules with carbon–carbon double bonds to be more reactive than those with only single bonds.

Note that even though the pi bond has two distinct areas of electron density, it is only *one* bond containing a pair of electrons. Both of the electrons can be found anywhere in the two lobes.

**Double covalent bonds contain one sigma bond and one pi bond.**

**Triple covalent bonds contain one sigma bond and two pi bonds.**

The combinations of atomic orbitals giving rise to each type of bond are summarized in the table below.

| Atomic orbitals which overlap | Type of bond | Example of bond and molecule |
|---|---|---|
| s and s | sigma | H−H in $H_2$ |
| s and p | sigma | H−Cl in HCl |
| p and p end-on | sigma | Cl−Cl in $Cl_2$ |
| hybrid orbitals and s | sigma | C−H in $CH_4$ |
| hybrid orbitals with hybrid orbitals | sigma | C−C in $CH_4$<br>one of the C=C in $C_2H_4$<br>one of the C≡C in $C_2H_2$ |
| p and p sideways | pi | one of the C=C in $C_2H_4$<br>two of the C≡C in $C_2H_2$ |

# 14.2 Hybridization

## Understandings:

- A hybrid orbital results from the mixing of different types of atomic orbitals on the same atom.

## Applications and skills:

- Explanation of the formation of $sp^3$, $sp^2$, and sp hybrid orbitals in methane, ethene, and ethyne.
- Identification and explanation of the relationships between Lewis (electron dot) structures, electron domains, molecular geometries, and types of hybridization.

### Guidance
*Students need only consider species with $sp^3$, $sp^2$, and sp hybridization.*

## The formation of covalent bonds often starts with the excitation of the atoms

Carbon is of great interest in this study as it forms such a vast number of covalently bonded compounds (see Chapter 10). In all of these, carbon forms *four* covalent bonds. Yet if we consider the electron configuration in the carbon atom, we would not predict this as it has only *two* singly occupied orbitals available for bonding.

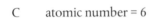

C        atomic number = 6        electron configuration $1s^2 2s^2 2p_x^1 2p_y^1$

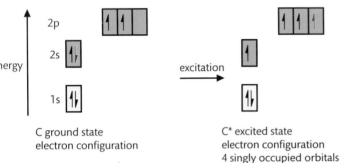

energy

2p

2s

1s

C ground state
electron configuration

excitation

C* excited state
electron configuration
4 singly occupied orbitals
are available for bonding

**Figure 4.25** Excitation of carbon showing promotion of the paired s orbital electron (shown in red) to the empty 2p orbital, making four singly occupied orbitals available for bonding.

The fact that carbon can – and does – form four covalent bonds indicates that this lowest energy or **ground-state** electron configuration changes during bonding. A process known as **excitation** occurs in which an electron is promoted within the atom from the 2s orbital to the vacant 2p orbital. The atom now has four singly occupied orbitals available for bonding. Remember from Hund's rule in Chapter 2 that all the electrons in singly occupied orbitals in the same sub-shell have parallel spin.

The amount of energy put in to achieve this is more than compensated by the extra energy released on forming four bonds.

## Hybridization involves mixing atomic orbitals to form new hybrid atomic orbitals

So the process of excitation explains how carbon is able to form four covalent bonds. But look again at the atomic orbitals now available for bonding – they are not all the same: there is one s orbital, and three p orbitals at a slightly higher energy. So if these were used in forming the covalent bonds, we would expect unequal bonds. The fact that methane, $CH_4$, has four *identical* carbon–hydrogen bonds suggests that these orbitals have been changed and somehow made equal during the bonding process. Again the details of this are complex and depend on an understanding of quantum mechanics, but in essence unequal atomic orbitals within an atom mix to form new **hybrid atomic orbitals** which are the same as each other, but different from the original orbitals. This mixing of orbitals is known as **hybridization**. Hybrid orbitals have different energies, shapes, and orientation in space from their parent orbitals and are able to form stronger bonds by allowing for greater overlap.

**Hybridization is the process where atomic orbitals within an atom mix to produce hybrid orbitals of intermediate energy. The atom is able to form stronger covalent bonds using these hybrid orbitals.**

The explanations given here to explain the formation of covalent bonds, including hybridization, are based primarily on the so-called **valence bond** theory. An alternate theory, known as **molecular orbital** theory, sometimes gives a more accurate picture, especially for describing delocalized pi electrons. This theory, focusing on the wave nature of electrons, considers them combining either constructively to form a lower energy **bonding molecular orbital**, or destructively to form a higher energy **anti-bonding molecular orbital**. The details are not discussed here but form an important part of more advanced work on covalent bonding.

Hybridization can involve different numbers and types of orbital, leading to the formation of distinct hybrid orbitals. We will discuss those involving s and p orbitals here.

A simple analogy may help you to picture this somewhat abstract topic.

- If you were to mix one bucket of white paint with three buckets of red paint, you would make *four* buckets of equal dark pink paint. Similarly, hybridization of one s orbital with three p orbitals produces *four* so-called **sp³ hybrid orbitals** that are equal to each other. Their shape and energy have properties of both s and p, but are more like p than s.
- Mixing one bucket of white paint with two buckets of red paint would produce *three* buckets of equal lighter pink paint; likewise hybridization of one s orbital with two p orbitals will produce *three* equal **sp² hybrid orbitals**.
- Finally, hybridization of one s orbital with one p orbital will produce *two* equal **sp hybrid orbitals**.

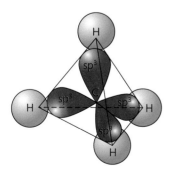

The different types of hybrid orbital have different orientations, defining the shapes of the molecules, as we will see in the examples described below using carbon compounds.

## sp³ hybridization

When carbon forms four single bonds, it undergoes sp³ hybridization, producing four equal orbitals.

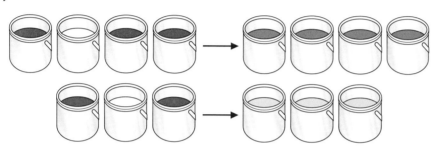

These orbitals orientate themselves at 109.5°, forming a tetrahedron. Each hybrid orbital overlaps with the atomic orbital of another atom forming four sigma bonds.

For example, methane, $CH_4$.

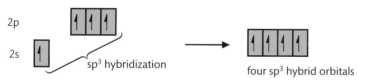

◀ **Figure 4.28** Structure of methane. The tetrahedral shape is formed by the four sp³ hybrid orbitals, which each overlap with the s orbital of an H atom. All bonds are sigma bonds.

Computer artwork of methane molecule, $CH_4$, clearly showing the tetrahedral shape with angles of 109.5° between the atoms. The carbon atom is sp³ hybridized, forming four sigma bonds with hydrogen atoms. ▶

**Figure 4.26** Mixing red and white paint makes the hybrid colour pink. The number of buckets and the shade of pink depend on the original number of buckets of red and white. Similarly, hybridizing one s orbital with three p orbitals makes four equal sp³ hybrid orbitals, whereas one s orbital hybridized with two p orbitals produces three equal sp² orbitals.

> The overlap of a hybrid orbital with *any* other atomic orbital (s, p, or another hybrid orbital) always forms a sigma bond.

**Figure 4.27** sp³ hybridization.

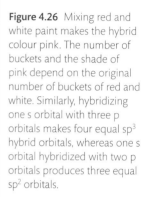

## sp² hybridization

When carbon forms a double bond, it undergoes sp² hybridization, producing three equal orbitals.

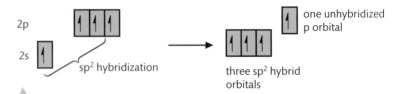

2p

2s

sp² hybridization

three sp² hybrid orbitals

one unhybridized p orbital

▲ **Figure 4.29** sp² hybridization.

These orbitals orientate themselves at 120°, forming a triangular planar shape. Each hybrid orbital overlaps with a neighbouring atomic orbital, forming three sigma bonds.

For example, ethene, $C_2H_4$.

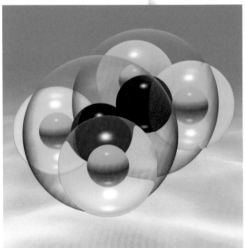

▲ Computer model of a molecule of ethene, $C_2H_4$. Carbon atoms are shown in black and hydrogen atoms in green. The double bond between the two sp² hybridized carbon atoms consists of one sigma bond and one pi bond.

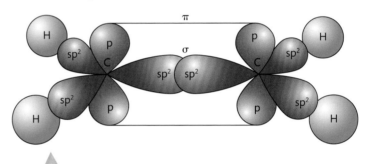

▲ **Figure 4.30** Structure of ethene. The three sp² hybrid orbitals on each carbon atom form a triangular planar shape, overlapping to form one C–C and two C–H sigma bonds. The unhybridized p orbitals on each carbon atom overlap to form a pi bond.

As the two carbon atoms approach each other, the p orbitals in each atom that did not take part in hybridization and have so retained their dumb-bell shape, overlap sideways. They form a pi bond with its characteristic lobes of electron density above and below the bond axis. So the double bond between the carbon atoms consists of one sigma bond and one pi bond.

## sp hybridization

When carbon forms a triple bond, it undergoes sp hybridization, producing two equal orbitals.

**Figure 4.31** sp hybridization.

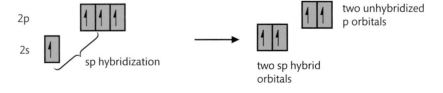

2p

2s

sp hybridization

two sp hybrid orbitals

two unhybridized p orbitals

These orbitals orientate themselves at 180°, giving a linear shape. Overlap of the two hybrid orbitals with other atomic orbitals forms two sigma bonds.

For example, ethyne, $C_2H_2$.

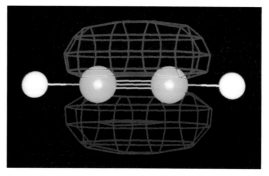

Computer graphics representation of an ethyne, $C_2H_2$, molecule. This linear molecule's two sp hybridized carbon atoms are shown as green spheres with hydrogen atoms in white. The red and blue regions represent the electron distribution in the two pi bonds.

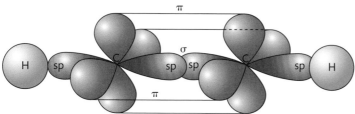

**Figure 4.32** Structure of ethyne. The two sp hybrid orbitals on each carbon atom form a linear shape, overlapping to form one C–C and one C–H sigma bonds. The unhybridized p orbitals on each carbon atom overlap to form two pi bonds.

Each carbon has two unhybridized p orbitals that are orientated at 90° to each other. As these overlap each other sideways, two pi bonds form representing four lobes of electron density around the atoms. These coalesce into a cylinder of negative charge around the atom, making the molecule susceptible to attack by **electrophilic reagents** (those that are attracted to electron-dense regions). This is discussed in Chapter 10.

## Hybridization in molecules with expanded octets

Molecules which have electrons in d orbitals can undergo hybridization involving these too. For example, $PCl_5$, described earlier, has $sp^3d$ hybridization which produces five equivalent orbitals orientated to the corners of a triangular bipyramid. Knowledge of this is not required at this level.

## Lone pairs can be involved in hybridization too

The examples above all use orbitals with bonding electrons in the hybridization process. But non-bonding pairs of electrons can also take part in hybridization. For example, in ammonia, $NH_3$, the non-bonding pair on the N atom resides in a $sp^3$ hybrid orbital.

# Hybridization can also be used to predict molecular shape

Although we have focused mostly here on examples from organic chemistry (those involving carbon), this concept of hybridization can be used to explain the shape of any molecule. And conversely the shape of a molecule can be used to determine the type of hybridization that has occurred. The relationship is as follows:

- tetrahedral arrangement ↔ $sp^3$ hybridized
- triangular planar arrangement ↔ $sp^2$ hybridized
- linear arrangement ↔ sp hybridized

So now we can look again at the geometric arrangement of the electron domains predicted by VSEPR theory on page 159, and deduce the hybridization involved.

**TOK**

Electron orbitals do not exist as physical entities, but their description as a volume of space provides a convenient basis to explain electron properties and bonding. Their true definition depends on a mathematical equation describing the electron's wave function. Hybridization, for the purposes of explanations of bonding, is termed a mixing process, but in reality is likewise based on complex mathematical manipulation. In the world of electronic communication we similarly use familiar terms to describe entities which do not really exist as such – cyberspace, viruses, firewalls, and so on. To what extent do you think this use of language and imagery enhances or masks our understanding of what is represented?

| Number of electron domains | Electron domain geometry | Molecular geometry | Example | | Hybridization |
|---|---|---|---|---|---|
| 2 | linear | linear | $CO_2$ | $O = C = O$ | sp |
| 3 | planar triangular | planar triangular | $BCl_3$ |  | $sp^2$ |
| 3 | planar triangular | V-shaped | $SO_2$ | | $sp^2$ |
| 4 | tetrahedral | tetrahedral | $CH_4$ | | $sp^3$ |
| 4 | tetrahedral | pyramidal | $NH_3$ | | $sp^3$ |
| 4 | tetrahedral | V-shaped | $H_2O$ | | $sp^3$ |

VSEPR theory, applied to hybridized orbitals in the same way as to electron domains, explains the geometry of the hybrid atomic orbitals. It therefore relates the shape of the molecule to the hybridization and to the number of electron domains.

number of electron domains ↔ **shape of molecule** ↔ hybridization

## Worked example

Urea $H_2N - C - NH_2$ (with O double-bonded to C) is present in solution in animal urine. What is the hybridization of C and N in the molecule, and what are the approximate bond angles?

### Solution

Start with the Lewis (electron dot) structure.

Because there are three electron domains around the C atom, they are arranged in a triangular planar shape with angles of 120°. The C atom must be $sp^2$ hybridized to give this shape. There are four electron domains around each N atom, so they are arranged tetrahedrally. The N atoms must be $sp^3$ hybridized to give this shape.

## Exercises

**43** What is the difference in spatial distribution between electrons in a pi bond and electrons in a sigma bond?

**44** Give examples of sigma bonds in molecules that form from overlap of the following orbitals. The first one is completed for you as an example.

(a) s–s: <u>answer</u> H–H in $H_2$

| | | | |
|---|---|---|---|
| (b) s–p | (c) p–p end-on | (d) $sp^3$–s | (e) $sp^2$–s |
| (f) sp–s | (g) $sp^2$–p | | |

**45** What hybridization would you expect for the coloured atom in each of the following?

(a) $H_2C=O$  (b) $BH_4^-$  (c) $SO_3$
(d) $BeCl_2$  (e) $CH_3COOH$

**46** Cyclohexane $C_6H_{12}$ 

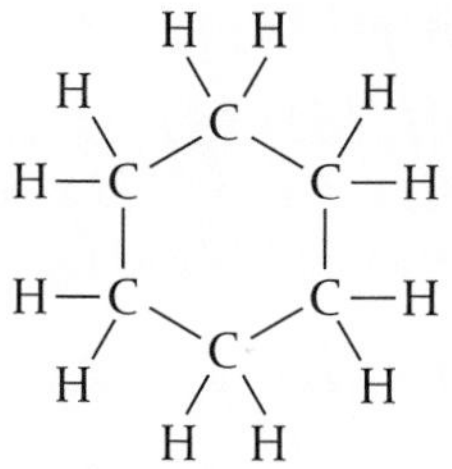

has a puckered, non-planar shape whereas benzene

$C_6H_6$ 

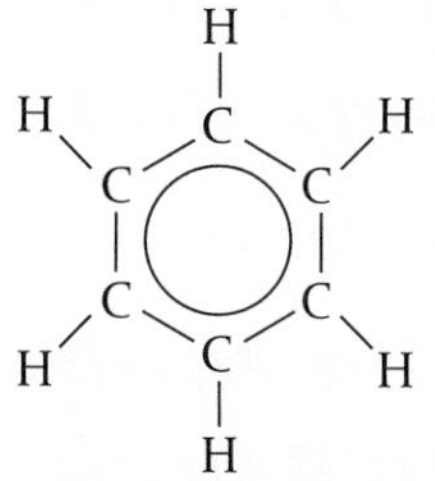

is planar.

Explain this difference by making reference to the C–C–C bond angles and the type of hybridization of carbon in each molecule.

## Practice questions

**1** Which bonds are arranged in order of increasing polarity?

**A** H–F < H–Cl < H–Br < H–I

**B** H–I < H–Br < H–F < H–Cl

**C** H–I < H–Br < H–Cl < H–F

**D** H–Br < H–I < H–Cl < H–F

**2** Which row correctly describes the bonding type and melting point of carbon and carbon dioxide?

| | Carbon | | Carbon dioxide | |
|---|---|---|---|---|
| A | covalent bonding | high melting point | covalent bonding | low melting point |
| B | ionic bonding | low melting point | ionic bonding | high melting point |
| C | ionic bonding | high melting point | ionic bonding | low melting point |
| D | covalent bonding | low melting point | covalent bonding | high melting point |

**3** What is the correct order of increasing boiling points?

**A** $CH_3CH_3 < CH_3CH_2Cl < CH_3CH_2Br < CH_3CH_2I$

**B** $CH_3CH_2Cl < CH_3CH_2Br < CH_3CH_3 < CH_3CH_2I$

**C** $CH_3CH_2I < CH_3CH_2Br < CH_3CH_2Cl < CH_3CH_3$

**D** $CH_3CH_2Br < CH_3CH_2Cl < CH_3CH_2I < CH_3CH_3$

**4** Which statements about hybridization are correct?

I   The hybridization of carbon in diamond is $sp^3$.

II   The hybridization of carbon in graphite is $sp^2$.

III   The hybridization of carbon in $C_{60}$ fullerene is $sp^3$.

**A** I and II only     **B** I and III only     **C** II and III only     **D** I, II. and III

**5** How many $\sigma$ and $\pi$ bonds are present in a molecule of propyne, $CH_3CCH$?

|   | $\sigma$ | $\pi$ |
|---|---|---|
| **A** | 5 | 3 |
| **B** | 6 | 2 |
| **C** | 7 | 1 |
| **D** | 8 | 0 |

**6** Which compound forms hydrogen bonds in the liquid state?

**A** $C_2H_5OH$     **B** $CHCl_3$     **C** $CH_3CHO$     **D** $(CH_3CH_2)_3N$

**7** Which molecule has a non-bonding (lone) pair of electrons around the central atom?

**A** $BF_3$     **B** $SO_2$     **C** $PCl_5$     **D** $SiF_4$

**8** Which species does not have delocalized electrons?

**A** $NO_3^-$     **B** $NO_2^-$     **C** $O_3$     **D** $C_3H_6$

**9** Which species contain a coordinate covalent bond?

I   HCHO

II   CO

III   $H_3O^+$

**A** I and II only     **B** I and III only     **C** II and III only     **D** I, II, and III

**10** Which molecule has an octahedral shape?

**A** $SF_6$     **B** $PCl_5$     **C** $XeF_4$     **D** $BF_3$

**11** Which statements about $\sigma$ and $\pi$ bonds are correct?

I   $\sigma$ bonds result from the axial overlap of orbitals.

II   $\sigma$ bonds only form from s orbitals.

III   $\pi$ bonds result from the sideways overlap of parallel p orbitals.

**A** I and II only     **B** I and III only     **C** II and III only     **D** I, II, and III

**12** In which substance does a carbon atom have $sp^2$ hybridization?

**A** 2-methylbutan-1-ol **B** propyne, $CH_3CCH$ **C** $C_{60}$, fullerene     **D** diamond

**13** The Lewis structure of $XeF_2$ contains two bonding pairs of electrons and three non-bonding pairs of electrons (lone pairs) around the central xenon atom. What is the shape of the $XeF_2$ molecule?

**A** bent     **B** trigonal bipyramidal

**C** square planar     **D** linear

**14** Which substance can form intermolecular hydrogen bonds in the liquid state?

    **A** $CH_3OCH_3$         **B** $CH_3CH_2OH$         **C** $CH_3CHO$         **D** $CH_3CH_2CH_3$

**15** What is the type of hybridization of the silicon and oxygen atoms in silicon dioxide?

| | Silicon | Oxygen |
|---|---|---|
| **A** | $sp^3$ | $sp^3$ |
| **B** | $sp^3$ | $sp^2$ |
| **C** | $sp^2$ | $sp^3$ |
| **D** | $sp^2$ | $sp^2$ |

**16** Based on the types of intermolecular force present, explain why butan-1-ol has a higher boiling point than butanal. (2)

**17 (a)** For each of the species $PBr_3$ and $SF_6$:

    **(i)** deduce the Lewis (electron dot) structure

    **(ii)** predict the shape and bond angle.

    **(iii)** predict and explain the molecular polarity. (8)

  **(b) (i)** Compare the formation of sigma ($\sigma$) and pi ($\pi$) bonds between the carbon atoms in a molecule of ethyne. (2)

    **(ii)** Identify the number of sigma and pi bonds present in *trans*-but-2-ene-1,4-dioic acid. (1)

    **(iii)** Explain why the melting point of *trans*-but-2-ene-1,4-dioic acid is higher than that of *cis*-but-2-ene-1,4-dioic acid. (1)

    **(iv)** Explain why *cis*-but-2-ene-1,4-dioic acid forms *cis*-but-2-ene-1,4-dioic anhydride when heated, whereas no cyclic anhydride forms when *trans*-but-2-ene-1,4-dioic acid is heated. (1)

*cis*-but-2-ene-1,4-dioic anhydride

  **(c)** Deduce the hybridization of each oxygen atom in *cis*-but-2-ene-1,4-dioic acid. (1)

*(Total 14 marks)*

**18** Carbon and silicon belong to the same group of the periodic table.

  **(a)** Describe and compare three features of the structure and bonding in the three allotropes of carbon: diamond, graphite, and $C_{60}$ fullerene. (6)

  **(b)** Both silicon and carbon form oxides.

    **(i)** Describe the structure and bonding in $SiO_2$. (2)

    **(ii)** Explain why silicon dioxide is a solid and carbon dioxide is a gas at room temperature. (2)

  **(c)** Describe the bonding within the carbon monoxide molecule. (2)

  **(d)** Describe the delocalization of pi ($\pi$) electrons and explain how this can account for the structure and stability of the carbonate ion, $CO_3^{2-}$. (3)

  **(e)** Explain the meaning of the term *hybridization*. State the type of hybridization shown by the carbon atoms in carbon dioxide, diamond, graphite, and the carbonate ion. (5)

*(Total 20 marks)*

19 Methoxymethane, $CH_3OCH_3$, and ethanol, $C_2H_5OH$, have the same relative molecular mass. Explain why methoxymethane has a much lower boiling point than ethanol. (3)

20 But-2-ene is a straight-chain alkene with formula $C_4H_8$.
The molecule contains both sigma and pi bonds.
(a) Explain the formation of the pi bond. (2)
(b) For each of the carbon atoms, C1 and C2, identify the type of hybridization shown. (1)
*(Total 3 marks)*

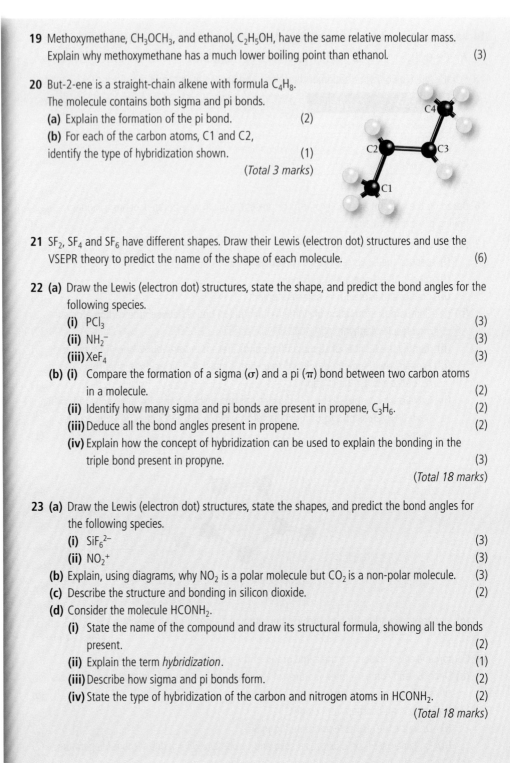

21 $SF_2$, $SF_4$ and $SF_6$ have different shapes. Draw their Lewis (electron dot) structures and use the VSEPR theory to predict the name of the shape of each molecule. (6)

22 (a) Draw the Lewis (electron dot) structures, state the shape, and predict the bond angles for the following species.
   (i) $PCl_3$ (3)
   (ii) $NH_2^-$ (3)
   (iii) $XeF_4$ (3)
   (b) (i) Compare the formation of a sigma ($\sigma$) and a pi ($\pi$) bond between two carbon atoms in a molecule. (2)
   (ii) Identify how many sigma and pi bonds are present in propene, $C_3H_6$. (2)
   (iii) Deduce all the bond angles present in propene. (2)
   (iv) Explain how the concept of hybridization can be used to explain the bonding in the triple bond present in propyne. (3)
*(Total 18 marks)*

23 (a) Draw the Lewis (electron dot) structures, state the shapes, and predict the bond angles for the following species.
   (i) $SiF_6^{2-}$ (3)
   (ii) $NO_2^+$ (3)
   (b) Explain, using diagrams, why $NO_2$ is a polar molecule but $CO_2$ is a non-polar molecule. (3)
   (c) Describe the structure and bonding in silicon dioxide. (2)
   (d) Consider the molecule $HCONH_2$.
   (i) State the name of the compound and draw its structural formula, showing all the bonds present. (2)
   (ii) Explain the term *hybridization*. (1)
   (iii) Describe how sigma and pi bonds form. (2)
   (iv) State the type of hybridization of the carbon and nitrogen atoms in $HCONH_2$. (2)
*(Total 18 marks)*

**24** Assign formal charges to the atoms in the following structures. In each case, which of the two do you think is the more important contributor to the resonance hybrid and why? (6)

(a) (i)

$$\underset{H}{\overset{H}{{\diagup}}}\hspace{-2pt}C{=}N{=}\overset{\times\times}{\underset{\times\times}{N}}$$

(ii)

$$\underset{H}{\overset{H}{{\diagup}}}\hspace{-2pt}C{-}\overset{\times\times}{\underset{\times\times}{N}}{=}\overset{\times\times}{\underset{\times\times}{N}}$$

(b) (i)

$$\left[\overset{\times\times}{\underset{\times\times}{O}}{-}\overset{}{\underset{}{Cl}}{-}\overset{\times\times}{\underset{\times\times}{O}}\right]^{-}$$

(ii)

$$\left[\overset{\times\times}{\underset{\times\times}{O}}{-}\overset{}{\underset{}{Cl}}{=}\overset{\times\times}{\underset{\times\times}{O}}\right]^{-}$$

## NATURE OF SCIENCE

A model of the lattice structure of NaCl, with sodium ions shown in green and chloride ions shown in black. Can you suggest in what ways this model may not be an accurate representation of the real structure of sodium chloride? Compare it with the models pictured on page 145, and consider which you think may be the better model.

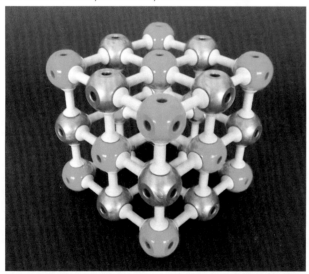

To access weblinks on the topics covered in this chapter, please go to www.pearsonhotlinks.com and enter the ISBN or title of this book.

# 05 Energetics and thermochemistry

# Essential ideas

**5.1** The enthalpy changes from chemical reactions can be calculated from their effect on the temperature of their surroundings.

**5.2** In chemical transformations energy can neither be created nor destroyed (the first law of thermodynamics).

**5.3** Energy is absorbed when bonds are broken and is released when bonds are formed.

**15.1** The concept of the energy change in a single step reaction being equivalent to the summation of smaller steps can be applied to changes involving ionic compounds.

**15.2** A reaction is spontaneous if the overall transformation leads to an increase in total entropy (system plus surroundings). The direction of spontaneous change always increases the total entropy of the universe at the expense of energy available to do useful work. This is known as the second law of thermodynamics.

All chemical reactions are accompanied by energy changes. Energy changes are vital. Our body's processes are dependent on the energy changes which occur during respiration, when glucose reacts with oxygen. Modern lifestyles are dependent on the transfer of energy that occurs when fuels burn. As we explore the source of these energy changes, we will deepen our understanding of why bonds are broken and formed during a chemical reaction, and why electron transfer can lead to the formation of stable ionic compounds. The questions of why things change will lead to the development of the concept of entropy. We will see that this concept allows us to give the same explanation for a variety of physical and chemical changes: the universe is becoming more disordered. This provides us with a signpost for the direction of all change. The distinction between the quantity and quality of energy will lead to the development of the concept of free energy, a useful accounting tool for chemists to predict the feasibility of any hypothetical reaction.

We will see how creative thinking, accurate calculations, and careful observations and measurement can work together to lead to a deeper understanding of the relationship between heat and chemical change.

The burning of a firework increases the disorder in the universe, as both energy and matter become dispersed. This is the natural direction of change.

James Prescott Joule (1818–89) was devoted to making accurate measurements of heat. The SI unit of energy is named after him.

# 5.1 Measuring energy changes

## Understandings:
- Heat is a form of energy.
- Temperature is a measure of the average kinetic energy of the particles.
- Total energy is conserved in chemical reactions.
- Chemical reactions that involve transfer of heat between the system and the surroundings are described as endothermic or exothermic.
- The enthalpy change ($\Delta H$) for chemical reactions is indicated in kJ mol$^{-1}$.
- $\Delta H$ values are usually expressed under standard conditions, known as $\Delta H^{\ominus}$, including standard states.

*Guidance*
*Enthalpy changes of combustion ($\Delta H_c^{\ominus}$) and formation ($\Delta H_f^{\ominus}$) should be covered.*

## Applications and skills:

- Calculation of the heat change when the temperature of a pure substance is changed using $q = mc\Delta T$.

**Guidance**
*The specific heat capacity of water is provided in the IB Data booklet in section 2.*

- A calorimetry experiment for an enthalpy of reaction should be covered and the results evaluated.

**Guidance**
- *Consider reactions in aqueous solution and combustion reactions.*
- *Standard state refers to the normal, most pure stable state of a substance measured at 100 kPa.*
- *Temperature is not a part of the definition of standard state, but 298 K is commonly given as the temperature of interest.*
- *Students can assume the density and specific heat capacities of aqueous solutions are equal to those of water, but should be aware of this limitation.*
- *Heat losses to the environment and the heat capacity of the calorimeter in experiments should be considered, but the use of a bomb calorimeter is not required.*

The joule is the unit of energy and work. You do 1 J of work when you exert a force of 1 N over a distance of 1 m. 1 J of energy is expended every time the human heart beats.

**Energy is conserved in chemical reactions.**

surroundings

system

**Figure 5.1** The system is the sample or reaction vessel of interest. The surroundings are the rest of the universe.

**Enthalpy (*H*) is a measure of the amount of heat energy contained in a substance. It is stored in the chemical bonds and intermolecular forces as potential energy. When substances react, the difference in the enthalpy between the reactants and products (at constant pressure) results in a heat change which can be observed.**

## Energy and heat transfer energy

**Energy** is a measure of the ability to do **work**, that is to move an object against an opposing force. It comes in many forms and includes heat, light, sound, electricity, and chemical energy – the energy released or absorbed during chemical reactions. This chapter will focus on reactions which involve heat changes. Heat is a mode of energy transfer which occurs as a result of a temperature difference and produces an increase in disorder in how the particles behave. Heat increases the average kinetic energy of the molecules in a disordered fashion. This is to be contrasted with work, which is a more ordered process of transferring energy. When you do work on a beaker of water, by lifting it from a table, for example, you raise all the molecules above the table in the same way.

## System and surroundings

Chemical and physical changes take place in many different environments such as test tubes, polystyrene cups, industrial plants and living cells. It is useful in these cases to distinguish between the **system** – the area of interest and the **surroundings** – in theory everything else in the universe (Figure 5.1). Most chemical reactions take place in an **open system** which can exchange energy and matter with the surroundings. A **closed system** can exchange energy but not matter with the surroundings. Although energy can be exchanged between a system and the surroundings, the total energy cannot change during the process; any energy lost by the system is gained by the surroundings and vice versa.

## The heat content of a system is its enthalpy

Although, according to the conservation of energy, the total energy of the system and surroundings cannot change during a process, heat can be transferred between a system and its surroundings energy. The heat content of a system is called its **enthalpy**, a name which comes from the Greek word for 'heat inside'. A system acts like a reservoir of heat. When heat is added to a system from the surroundings its enthalpy increases. Changes in enthalpy are denoted by $\Delta H$. $\Delta H$ is positive when heat is added to the system.

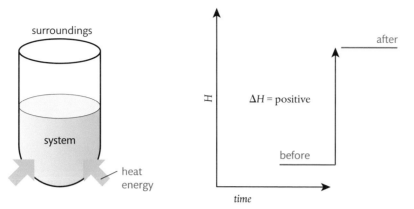

**Figure 5.2** When heat is gained by the system from the surroundings, the enthalpy of the system increases and $\Delta H$ is positive.

When heat is released from the system to the surroundings the enthalpy of the system decreases and $\Delta H$ is negative.

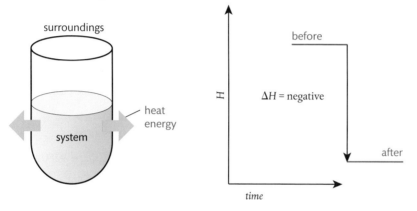

**Figure 5.3** When heat is lost from the system to the surroundings the enthalpy of the system decreases and $\Delta H$ is negative.

**TOK** How important are technical terms such as *enthalpy* in different areas of knowledge? Is their correct use a necessary or sufficient indicator of understanding?

## Exothermic and endothermic reactions

The enthalpy ($H$) of the system is stored in the chemical bonds and intermolecular forces as potential energy. When substances react, the difference in the enthalpy between the reactants and products produces an enthalpy change which can be observed. Most chemical reactions, including most combustion and all neutralization reactions, are exothermic. They give out heat and result in a transfer of enthalpy from the chemicals to the surroundings and $\Delta H_{\text{reaction}}$ is negative.

A few reactions are **endothermic** as they result in an energy transfer from the surroundings to the system. In this case the products have more enthalpy than the reactants and $\Delta H$ is positive.

**For exothermic reactions heat is given out by the system and $\Delta H$ is negative.**

**For endothermic reactions heat is absorbed by the system and $\Delta H$ is positive.**

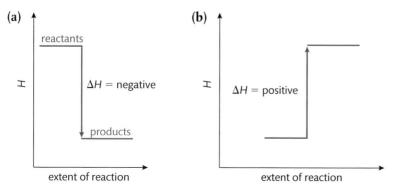

**Figure 5.4** (a) An exothermic reaction. The enthalpy of the products is less than the enthalpy of the reactants. (b) An endothermic reaction. The enthalpy of the products is greater than the enthalpy of the reactants.

## Standard enthalpy changes

As the enthalpy of a system also depends on the intermolecular forces of the reactants and products, the enthalpy change for a reaction depends on the conditions under which the reaction occurs. The **standard enthalpy changes**, $\Delta H^{\ominus}$, given in the literature are measured under the following conditions:

- a pressure of 100 kPa
- concentration of 1 mol dm$^{-3}$ for all solutions
- all substances in their standard states.

Temperature is not part of the definition of standard state, but 298K is usually given as the specified temperature.

## Thermochemical equations

The combustion of methane can be described by the thermochemical equation:

$$CH_4(g) + 2O_2(g) \rightarrow CO_2(g) + 2H_2O(l) \qquad \Delta H^{\ominus} = -890 \text{ kJ mol}^{-1}$$

This is a shorthand way of expressing information that *one mole* of methane gas reacts with *two moles* of oxygen gas to give *one mole* of gaseous carbon dioxide and *two moles* of liquid water and *releases* 890 kJ of heat energy.

The thermochemical equation for photosynthesis can be represented as:

$$6CO_2(g) + 6H_2O(l) \rightarrow C_6H_{12}O_6(aq) + 6O_2(g) \qquad \Delta H^{\ominus}_{\text{reaction}} = +2802.5 \text{ kJ mol}^{-1}$$

which means that 2802.5 kJ of energy is absorbed when one mole of glucose is formed under standard conditions from gaseous carbon dioxide and liquid water.

Photosynthesis is an endothermic reaction which occurs in green leaves.

Scientists share their knowledge using a precise language. In everyday language heat and work are both nouns and verbs, whereas in science they are nouns which describe energy transfer processes. Heat is often said to flow from high temperature to low temperature. This image originates from the incorrect outdated view that heat was a liquid, *calorique*, which was included in Lavoisier's list of chemical elements. Heat is now more correctly characterized as a process of energy transfer.

Enthalpy is a word rarely used in non-scientific discourse; it is an abstract entity with a precise mathematical definition. At this level we need not concern ourselves with absolute enthalpy values but only enthalpy changes which can be determined from temperature changes at constant pressure which can be measured.

The use of appropriate terminology is a key issue with scientific literacy and the public understanding of science and scientists need to take this into account when communicating with the public.

| | Noms nouveaux. | Noms anciens correspondans. |
|---|---|---|
| | Lumière......... | Lumière. |
| Substances simples qui appartiennent aux trois règnes & qu'on peut regarder comme les élémens des corps. | Calorique........ | Chaleur. Principe de la chaleur. Fluide igné. Feu. Matière du feu & de la chaleur. |
| | Oxygène......... | Air déphlogistiqué. Air empiréal. Air vital. Base de l'air vital. |
| | Azote........... | Gaz phlogistique. Mofete. Base de la mofete. |
| | Hydrogène...... | Gaz inflammable. Base du gaz inflammable. |
| Substances simples non métalliques oxidables & acidifiables. | Soufre........... Phosphore....... Carbone........ Radical muriatique. Radical fluorique . Radical boracique. | Soufre. Phosphore. Charbon pur. Inconnu. Inconnu. Inconnu. |
| Substances simples métalliques oxidables & acidifiables. | Antimoine....... Argent........... Arsenic.......... Bismuth......... Cobolt.......... Cuivre.......... Etain........... Fer............. Manganèse...... Mercure......... Molybdène...... Nickel.......... Or............. Platine.......... Plomb.......... Tungstène...... Zinc........... | Antimoine. Argent. Arsenic. Bismuth. Cobolt. Cuivre. Etain. Fer. Manganèse. Mercure. Molybdène. Nickel. Or. Platine. Plomb. Tungstene. Zinc. |
| Substances simples salifiables terreuses. | Chaux.......... Magnésie........ Baryte......... Alumine........ Silice.......... | Terre calcaire, chaux. Magnésie, base du sel d'Epsom. Barote, terre pesante. Argile, terre de l'alun, base de l'alun. Terre siliceuse, terre vitrifiable. |

Lavoisier's list of chemical elements includes heat (*calorique*) which was thought to be a liquid.

The SI unit of temperature is the kelvin (K), but the Celsius scale (°C), which has the same incremental scaling, is commonly used in most countries. The USA, however, continues to use the Fahrenheit (°F) scale for all non-scientific communication.

## Temperature is a measure of average kinetic energy

The movement or kinetic energy of the particles of a substance depends on the temperature. If the temperature of a substance is decreased, the average kinetic energy of the particles also decreases. **Absolute zero** (−273 °C) is the lowest possible temperature attainable as this is the temperature at which all movement has stopped. The **Kelvin scale** emphasizes this relationship between average kinetic energy and temperature. The absolute temperature, measured in kelvin, is directly proportional to the average kinetic energy of its particles.

## Heat changes can be calculated from temperature changes

If the same amount of heat is added to two different objects, the temperature change will not be the same, as the average kinetic energy of the particles will not increase by the same amount. The object with the smaller number of particles will experience the larger temperature increase, as the same energy is shared amongst a smaller collection of particles.

In general, the increase in temperature when an object is heated depends on:

• the mass of the object
• the heat added
• the nature of the substance.

The specific heat capacity is the property of a substance which gives the heat needed to increase the temperature of unit mass by 1 K. The specific heat capacity depends on the number of particles present in a unit mass sample, which in turn will depend on the mass of the individual particles.

heat change ($q$) = mass ($m$) × specific heat capacity ($c$) × temperature change ($\Delta T$)

**heat change = $m \times c \times \Delta T$**

**heat change (J) = $m$ (g) × $c$ (J g$^{-1}$ K$^{-1}$) × $\Delta T$ (K)**

**When the heat is absorbed by water, $c$ = 4.18 J g$^{-1}$ K$^{-1}$**

**This value is given in the IB data booklet.**

It takes considerably more heat energy to increase the temperature of a swimming pool by 5 °C than boil a kettle of water from room temperature. The swimming pool contains more water molecules and so has a larger heat capacity.

The water in the kettle has a higher temperature but the water in the swimming pool has more heat energy. Temperature is a measure of the average kinetic energy of the molecules.

This relationship allows the heat change in a material to be calculated from the temperature change.

When considering the relationship between different objects the **heat capacity** is often a more convenient property. The heat capacity (C) is defined as the heat needed to increase the temperature of an object by 1 K.

$$\text{heat capacity } (C) = \frac{\text{heat change } (q)}{\text{temperature change } (\Delta T)}$$

A swimming pool has a larger heat capacity than a kettle.

A temperature rise of 1 K is the same as a temperature rise of 1 °C.

- **The specific heat capacity (c) is defined as the heat needed to increase the temperature of unit mass of material by 1 K.**

$$\text{specific heat capacity } (c) = \frac{\text{heat change } (q)}{\text{mass } (m) \times \text{temperature change } (\Delta T)}$$

- **The heat capacity (C) is defined as the heat needed to increase the temperature of an object by 1 K.**

$$\text{heat capacity } (C) = \frac{\text{heat change } (q)}{\text{temperature change } (\Delta T)}$$

**TOK**

Our shared knowledge is passed on from one generation to the next by language. The language we use today is often based on the shared knowledge of the past which can sometimes be incorrect. What do such phrases as "keep the heat in and the cold out" tell us about previous concepts of heat and cold? How does the use of language hinder the pursuit of knowledge?

### NATURE OF SCIENCE

Although heat is a concept that is familiar to us all – we need it to cook our food and to keep us warm – it is a subject that has proved to be difficult for science to understand. We are equipped by our sense of touch to distinguish between high and low temperature but heat has proved challenging on a more fundamental level. The development of different temperature scales was an important technological and scientific step as it recognized the need for objectivity in scientific measurement, and the need to calibrate the instruments to one or more one fixed points. However, scientific understanding in this area was still confused at the time. The original Celsius scale, for example, had the boiling point of water at a lower temperature than its melting point, so it was not clear what it was quantifying and other scales used arbitrary fixed points such as the melting points of butter, or the temperatures of the Paris wine cellars.

The observation that heat can be added to melting ice or boiling water without changing its temperature was a significant observation in the distinction between the heat and temperature.

Our modern distinction is based on our particulate theory of matter. Temperature is a measure of the individual particle's kinetic energy and heat, a process by which energy is transferred.

### Worked example

How much heat is released when 10.0 g of copper with a specific heat capacity of $0.385 \, \text{J g}^{-1}\,^{\circ}\text{C}^{-1}$ is cooled from 85.0 °C to 25.0 °C?

## Solution

$$\text{heat change} = m \times c \times \Delta T$$

$$= 10.0\,\text{g} \times 0.385\,\text{J}\,\text{g}^{-1}\,°\text{C}^{-1} \times -60.0\,°\text{C} \text{ (the value is negative as the Cu has lost heat)}$$

$$= -231\,\text{J}$$

## Exercises

**1** When a sample of $NH_4SCN$ is mixed with solid $Ba(OH)_2.8H_2O$ in a glass beaker, the mixture changes to a liquid and the temperature drops sufficiently to freeze the beaker to the table. Which statement is true about the reaction?

**A** The process is endothermic and $\Delta H$ is –
**B** The process is endothermic and $\Delta H$ is +
**C** The process is exothermic and $\Delta H$ is –
**D** The process is exothermic and $\Delta H$ is +

**2** Which one of the following statements is *true* of all exothermic reactions?

**A** They produce gases.
**B** They give out heat.
**C** They occur quickly.
**D** They involve combustion.

**3** If 500 J of heat is added to 100.0 g samples of each of the substances below, which will have the largest temperature increase?

|   | Substance | Specific heat capacity / $J\,g^{-1}\,K^{-1}$ |
|---|---|---|
| **A** | gold | 0.129 |
| **B** | silver | 0.237 |
| **C** | copper | 0.385 |
| **D** | water | 4.18 |

**4** The temperature of a 5.0 g sample of copper increases from 27 °C to 29 °C. Calculate how much heat has been added to the system. (Specific heat capacity of Cu = $0.385\,J\,g^{-1}\,K^{-1}$)

**A** 0.770 J    **B** 1.50 J    **C** 3.00 J    **D** 3.85 J

**5** Consider the specific heat capacity of the following metals.

| Metal | Specific heat capacity / $J\,g^{-1}\,K^{-1}$ |
|---|---|
| Al | 0.897 |
| Be | 1.82 |
| Cd | 0.231 |
| Cr | 0.449 |

1 kg samples of the metals at room temperature are heated by the same electrical heater for 10 min. Identify the metal which has the highest final temperature.

**A** Al    **B** Be    **C** Cd    **D** Cr

**6** The specific heat of metallic mercury is $0.138\,J\,g^{-1}\,°C^{-1}$. If 100.0 J of heat is added to a 100.0 g sample of mercury at 25.0 °C, what is the final temperature of the mercury?

## CHALLENGE YOURSELF

**2** Suggest an explanation for the pattern in specific heat capacities of the metals in Exercise 3.

# Enthalpy changes and the direction of change

There is a natural direction for change. When we slip on a ladder, we go down, not up. The direction of change is in the direction of lower stored energy. In a similar way, we expect methane to burn when we strike a match and form carbon dioxide and water. The chemicals are changing in a way which reduces their enthalpy (Figure 5.5).

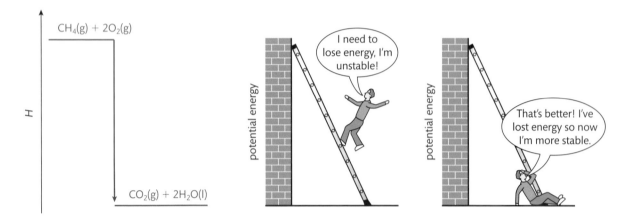

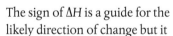

**Figure 5.5** An exothermic reaction can be compared to a person falling off a ladder. Both changes lead to a decrease in stored energy. The state of lower energy is more stable. The mixture of carbon dioxide and water is more stable than a mixture of methane and oxygen.

Diamonds are not forever as they are unstable relative to graphite.

$$C(\text{diamond}) \rightarrow C(\text{graphite})$$
$$\Delta H = -1.9 \text{ kJ mol}^{-1}$$

However, the change is very slow.

Diamond is a naturally occurring form of carbon that has crystallized under great pressure. It is unstable relative to graphite.

There are many examples of exothermic reactions and we generally expect a reaction to occur if it leads to a reduction in enthalpy. In the same way that a ball is more stable on the ground than in mid-air, we can say that the products in an exothermic reaction are more stable than the reactants. It is important to realize that stability is a relative term. Hydrogen peroxide, for example, is stable with respect to its elements but unstable relative to its decomposition to water and oxygen (Figure 5.6).

The sign of $\Delta H$ is a guide for the likely direction of change but it is not completely reliable. We do not expect a person to fall up a ladder but some endothermic reactions can occur. For example, the reaction:

$$6SOCl_2(l) + FeCl_3.6H_2O(s) \rightarrow FeCl_3(s) + 6SO_2(g) + 12HCl(g) \qquad \Delta H = +11271 \text{ kJ mol}^{-1}$$

is extremely endothermic. Endothermic reactions are less common and occur when there is an increase in disorder of the system, for example owing to the production of gas. This is discussed in more detail later in the chapter.

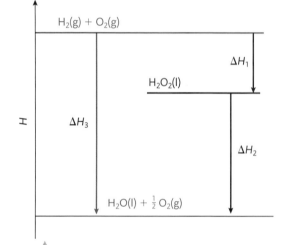

**Figure 5.6** Hydrogen peroxide is stable relative to the hydrogen and oxygen but unstable relative to water.

## Measuring enthalpy changes of combustion

For liquids such as ethanol, the enthalpy change of combustion can be determined using the simple apparatus shown in Figure 5.7.

The standard enthalpy change of combustion ($\Delta H_c^{\ominus}$) is the enthalpy change for the complete combustion of one mole of a substance in its standard state in excess oxygen under standard conditions.

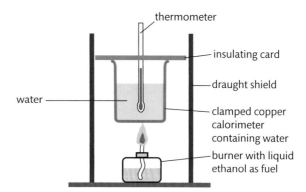

thermometer

insulating card

draught shield

water

clamped copper calorimeter containing water

burner with liquid ethanol as fuel

Sherbet contains sodium hydrogencarbonate and tartaric acid. When sherbet comes into contact with water on the tongue an endothermic reaction takes place. The sherbet absorbs heat energy from the water on the tongue creating a cold sensation.

▲ **Figure 5.7** The heat produced by the combustion of the fuel is calculated from the temperature change of the water in the metal calorimeter. Copper is a good conductor of heat, so heat from the flame can be transferred to the water.

The temperature of the water increases as it has increased its heat content, owing to the heat released by the combustion reaction. There is a decrease of enthalpy during the reaction.

## Calculating enthalpies of reaction from temperature changes

When the heat released by an exothermic reaction is absorbed by water, the temperature of the water increases. The heat produced by the reaction can be calculated if it is assumed that all the heat is absorbed by the water.

$$\Delta H_{reaction} = -\Delta H(water) = -m(H_2O) \times c(H_2O) \times \Delta T(H_2O)$$

As the water has gained the heat produced by the reaction, the enthalpy change of reaction is negative when the temperature of the water increases.

When an endothermic reaction is carried out in solution, the heat absorbed by the reaction is taken from the water so the temperature of the water decreases. As the reaction has taken in the heat lost by the water, the enthalpy change of reaction is positive.

As the heat change observed depends on the amount of reaction, for example the number of moles of fuel burned, enthalpy changes are usually expressed in kJ mol$^{-1}$.

**!** It is important to state all assumptions when processing data. Simple treatments of heat of combustion reactions assume that all the heat is absorbed by the water, but the heat absorbed by the copper calorimeter can also be calculated.

The energy content of different foods and fuels could also be investigated.

### Worked example

Calculate the enthalpy of combustion of ethanol from the following data. Assume all the heat from the reaction is absorbed by the water. Compare your value with the IB data booklet value and suggest reasons for any differences.

| | |
|---|---|
| Mass of water in copper calorimeter / g | 200.00 |
| Temperature increase in water / °C | 13.00 |
| Mass of ethanol burned / g | 0.45 |

## Solution

$$\text{number of moles of ethanol} = \frac{m(C_2H_5OH)}{M(C_2H_5OH)} \text{ mol}$$

$$M(C_2H_5OH) = (12.01 \times 2) + (6 \times 1.01) + 16.00 = 46.08 \text{ g mol}^{-1}$$

$$\Delta H_{reaction} = -m(H_2O) \times c(H_2O) \times \Delta T(H_2O)$$

$$\Delta H_c = \Delta H_{reaction} \text{ (for one mole of ethanol)}$$

$$= \frac{-m(H_2O) \times c(H_2O) \times \Delta T(H_2O)}{m(C_2H_5OH) / M(C_2H_5OH)} \text{ J mol}^{-1}$$

$$= \frac{-200 \text{ g} \times 4.18 \text{ J g}^{-1}°C^{-1} \times 13.00°C}{0.45g / 46.08 \text{ g mol}^{-1}} \text{ J mol}^{-1}$$

$$= -1112\,883 \text{ J mol}^{-1}$$

$$= -1112.883 \text{ kJ mol}^{-1}$$

$$= -1100 \text{ kJ mol}^{-1}$$

The precision of the final answer is limited by the precision of the mass of the ethanol (see Chapter 11).

The IB data booklet value is $-1367$ kJ mol$^{-1}$. The difference between the values can be accounted for by any of the following factors:

- Not all the heat produced by the combustion reaction is transferred to the water. Some is needed to heat the copper calorimeter and some has passed to the surroundings.
- The combustion of the ethanol is unlikely to be complete owing to the limited oxygen available, as assumed by the literature value.
- The experiment was not performed under standard conditions.

> It is important that you record qualitative as well as quantitative data when measuring enthalpy changes – for example, evidence of incomplete combustion in an enthalpy of combustion determination. When asked to evaluate experiments and suggest improvements, avoid giving trivial answers such as incorrect measurement. Incomplete combustion, for example, can be reduced by burning the fuel in oxygen. Heat loss can be reduced by insulating the apparatus.

> **Combustion reactions are generally exothermic, so $\Delta H_c$ values are generally negative.**

## Exercises

**7**  The mass of the burner and its content is measured before and after the experiment. The thermometer is read before and after the experiment. What are the expected results?

| | Mass of burner and contents | Reading on thermometer |
|---|---|---|
| **A** | decreases | increases |
| **B** | decreases | stays the same |
| **C** | increases | increases |
| **D** | increases | stays the same |

**8**  The experimental arrangement in Figure 5.7 is used to determine the enthalpy of combustion of an alcohol. Which of the following would lead to an experimental result which is **less** exothermic than the literature value?

I   Heat loss from the sides of the copper calorimeter.
II  Evaporation of alcohol during the experiment.
III The thermometer touches the bottom of the calorimeter.

**A**  I and II only   **B**  I and III only   **C**  II and III only   **D**  I, II, and III

**9** A copper calorimeter was used to determine the enthalpy of combustion of butan-1-ol. The experimental value obtained was −2100 ± 200 kJ mol⁻¹ and the data booklet value is −2676 kJ mol⁻¹. Which of the following accounts for the difference between the two values?

I   random measurement errors
II  incomplete combustion
III heat loss to the surroundings

**A** I and II only     **B** I and III only     **C** II and III only     **D** I, II, and III

**10** 1.10 g of glucose was completely burnt in a copper calorimeter. The temperature of the water increased from 25.85 °C to 36.50 °C.

**(a)** Calculate the enthalpy of combustion of glucose from the data below.

| Mass of water / g | 200.00 |
|---|---|
| Specific heat capacity of water / g⁻¹ K⁻¹ | 4.18 |
| Mass of copper / g | 120.00 |
| Specific heat capacity of copper / g⁻¹ K⁻¹ | 0.385 |

**(b)** Draw an enthalpy level diagram to represent this reaction.

**11** The heat released from the combustion of 0.0500 g of white phosphorus increases the temperature of 150.00 g of water from 25.0 °C to 31.5 °C. Calculate a value for the enthalpy change of combustion of phosphorus. Discuss possible sources of error in the experiment.

## NATURE OF SCIENCE

Qualitative and quantitative experimental data are the lifeblood of science. The best data for making accurate and precise descriptions and predictions are often quantitative data that are amenable to mathematical analysis but qualitative observations always have a role in chemistry: the lower than expected exothermic value for a heat of combustion of a hydrocarbon for example is often as a result of incomplete combustion. The evidence for this comes from any black soot and residue observed during the experiment.

The combustion of fossil fuel, which meets many of our energy needs, produces carbon dioxide which is a greenhouse gas. It is important we are aware of how our lifestyle contributes to global warming. It is a global problem but we need to act locally to solve it. Global warming is discussed in more detail in Chapter 12.

**Calorimetry – comparing pentane and hexane**

Full details of how to carry out this experiment with a worksheet are available online.

A common error when calculating heat changes is using the incorrect mass of substance heated.

**Figure 5.8** A simple calorimeter. The polystyrene is a very good thermal insulator with a low heat capacity.

## Enthalpy changes of reaction in solution

The enthalpy changes of reaction in solution can be calculated by carrying out the reaction in an insulated system, for example, a polystyrene cup (Figure 5.8). The heat released or absorbed by the reaction can be measured from the temperature change of the water.

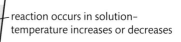

reaction occurs in solution– temperature increases or decreases

insulating polystyrene cup traps heat or keeps out heat from the surroundings

221

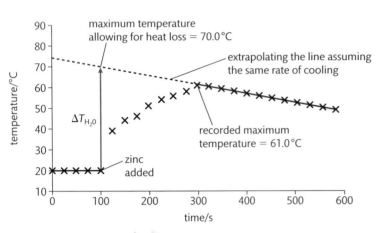

**Figure 5.9** A known volume of copper sulfate solution is added to the calorimeter and its temperature measured every 25 s. Excess zinc powder is added after 100 s and the temperature starts to rise until a maximum after which it falls in an approximately linear fashion.

In the previous calculation, we assumed that all the heat produced in the reaction is absorbed by water. One of the largest sources of error in experiments conducted in a polystyrene cup is heat loss to the environment. Consider, for example, the exothermic reaction between zinc and aqueous copper sulfate (Figure 5.9):

$$Cu^{2+}(aq) + Zn(s) \rightarrow Cu(s) + Zn^{2+}(aq)$$

Heat is lost from the system as soon as the temperature rises above the temperature of the surroundings, in this case 20 °C, and so the maximum recorded temperature is lower than the true value obtained in a perfectly insulated system. We can make some allowance for heat loss by extrapolating the cooling section of the graph to the time when the reaction started (100 s).

To proceed we can make the following assumptions:

1 no heat loss from the system
2 all the heat goes from the reaction to the water
3 the solution is dilute: $V(CuSO_4) = V(H_2O)$
4 water has a density of $1.00$ g cm$^{-3}$.

$$\Delta H(\text{system}) = 0 \text{ (assumption 1)}$$

$$\Delta H(\text{system}) = \Delta H(\text{water}) + \Delta H_{\text{reaction}} \text{ (assumption 2)}$$

$$\Delta H_{\text{reaction}} = -\Delta H(\text{water})$$

For an exothermic reaction, $\Delta H_{\text{reaction}}$ is negative as heat has passed from the reaction into the water.

$$\Delta H(\text{water}) = m(H_2O) \times c(H_2O) \times \Delta T(H_2O)$$

The limiting reactant must be identified in order to determine the molar enthalpy change of reaction.

$$\Delta H_{\text{reaction}} = \frac{-m(H_2O) \times c(H_2O) \times \Delta T(H_2O)}{\text{moles of limiting reactant}}$$

As the zinc was added in excess, the copper sulfate is the limiting reactant. From Chapter 1 (page 30):

$$\text{number of moles } (n) = \text{concentration (mol dm}^{-3}) \times \text{volume } (V \text{ cm}^3)$$

There are 1000 cm$^3$ in 1 dm$^3$
$$\text{volume } (V \text{ dm}^3) = \text{volume } (V \text{ cm}^3) / 1000 \text{ (cm}^3 \text{ dm}^{-3})$$

$$\text{number of moles of } CuSO_4 \ (n(CuSO_4)) = [CuSO_4] \times \frac{V(CuSO_4)}{1000} \text{ mol}$$

$$\Delta H_{\text{reaction}} = \frac{-m(H_2O) \times c(H_2O) \times \Delta T(H_2O)}{n(CuSO_4)} \text{ J mol}^{-1}$$

$$= \frac{-m(H_2O) \times c(H_2O) \times \Delta T(H_2O)}{[CuSO_4] \times V(CuSO_4)/1000} \text{ J mol}^{-1}$$

$$\Delta H_{\text{reaction}} = \frac{-m(H_2O) \times c(H_2O) \times \Delta T(H_2O)}{[CuSO_4] \times V(CuSO_4)/1000} \text{ J (assumption 3)}$$

$$\Delta H_{\text{reaction}} = \frac{c(H_2O) \times \Delta T(H_2O)}{[CuSO_4]/1000} \text{ (assumption 4)}$$

$$\Delta H_{\text{reaction}} = \frac{c(H_2O) \times \Delta T(H_2O)}{[CuSO_4]} \text{ kJ mol}^{-1}$$

## Worked example

The neutralization reaction between solutions of sodium hydroxide and sulfuric acid was studied by measuring the temperature changes when different volumes of the two solutions were mixed. The total volume was kept constant at 120.0 cm³ and the concentrations of the two solutions were both 1.00 mol dm⁻³ (Figure 5.10).

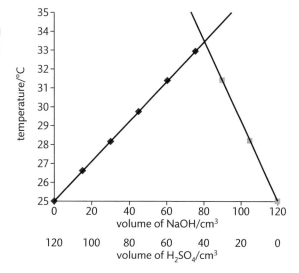

Key
- ■ Volume of NaOH added
- ▨ Volume of $H_2SO_4$ added

**Figure 5.10** Temperature changes produced when different volumes of sodium hydroxide and sulfuric acid are mixed.

(a) Determine the volumes of the solutions which produce the largest increase in temperature.

(b) Calculate the heat produced by the reaction when the maximum temperature was produced.

(c) Calculate the heat produced for one mole of sodium hydroxide.

(d) The literature value for the enthalpy of neutralization is = −57.5 kJ mol⁻¹.

Calculate the percentage error value and suggest a reason for the discrepancy between the experimental and literature values.

### Solution

(a) From the graph: $V(NaOH) = 80.0 \text{ cm}^3$
$$V(H_2SO_4) = 40.0 \text{ cm}^3$$

(b) Assuming 120.0 cm³ of the solution contains 120.0 g of water and all the heat produced by the neutralization reaction passes into the water.

$$\Delta H_{\text{reaction}} = -m(H_2O) \times c(H_2O) \times \Delta T(H_2O) \text{ J}$$

$$= -120.0 \text{ g} \times 4.18 \text{ J g}^{-1} \text{ K}^{-1} \times (33.5 - 25.0) \text{ K}$$

$$= -4264 \text{ J}$$

**(c)** $\Delta H_{\text{reaction}} = \dfrac{-4264}{n(\text{NaOH})}$ J mol$^{-1}$

$= \dfrac{-4264}{1.00 \times 80.0/1000}$ J mol$^{-1}$

$= \dfrac{-4264}{80.0}$ kJ mol$^{-1}$

$= -53.3$ kJ mol$^{-1}$

**(d)** % error $= \dfrac{-57.5--53.3}{-57.5} \times 100\% = 7\%$

The calculated value assumes:

- no heat loss from the system
- all heat is transferred to the water
- the solutions contain 120 g of water.
- There are also uncertainties in the temperature, volume, and concentration measurements.

The literature value assumes standard conditions.

A common error is to miss out or incorrectly state the units and to miss out the negative sign for $\Delta H$.

### NATURE OF SCIENCE

The accurate determination of enthalpy changes involves making careful observations and measurements, which inevitably have experimental uncertainties. The calculated enthalpy values are also dependent on the assumptions made. All these elements should be considered when reporting and evaluating experimental enthalpy values.

Mathematics is a powerful tool in the sciences, but scientific systems are often too complex to treat rigorously. These underlying assumptions, made to make a problem solvable, should not be ignored when evaluating quantitative data generated by a mathematical model.

## CHALLENGE YOURSELF

**3** A piece of brass is held in the flame of a Bunsen burner for several minutes. The brass is then quickly transferred into an aluminium calorimeter which contains 200.00 g of water. Determine the temperature of the Bunsen flame from the following data.

| | |
|---|---|
| $m$(brass) / g | 21.20 |
| $m$(aluminium calorimeter) / g | 80.00 |
| $c$(brass) / J g$^{-1}$ K$^{-1}$ | 0.400 |
| $c$(Al) / J g$^{-1}$ K$^{-1}$ | 0.900 |
| Initial temperature of water / °C | 24.50 |
| Final temperature of water / °C | 77.50 |

### Exercises

**12** Calculate the molar enthalpy change from the data in Figure 5.9. The copper sulfate has a concentration of 1.00 mol dm$^{-3}$ and a volume of 1.00 dm$^3$.

**13** Calculate the enthalpy of neutralization based on the following data.

| | |
|---|---|
| Initial temperature of solutions / °C | 24.5 |
| Concentration of KOH(aq) / mol dm$^{-3}$ | 0.950 |
| Concentration of HNO$_3$(aq) / mol dm$^{-3}$ | 1.050 |
| Volume of HCl(aq) / cm$^3$ | 50.00 |
| Volume of NaOH(aq) / cm$^3$ | 50.00 |
| Final temperature of mixture / °C | 32.3 |

State the assumptions you have made in your calculation.

**14** A student added 5.350 g of ammonium chloride to 100.00 cm$^3$ of water. The initial temperature of the water was 25.55 °C but it decreased to 21.79 °C. Calculate the enthalpy change that would occur when 1 mol of the solute is added to 1.000 dm$^3$ of water.

**15** Explain the meaning of the term $\Delta H$ and describe how it is measured.

The temperature of the Bunsen flame and the enthalpy of fusion can be investigated.

# 5.2 Hess's law

## Understandings:

- The enthalpy change for a reaction that is carried out in a series of steps is equal to the sum of the enthalpy changes for the individual steps.

## Applications and skills:

- Application of Hess's law to calculate enthalpy changes.
- Calculation of $\Delta H$ reactions using $\Delta H_f^{\ominus}$ data.

### Guidance

- Enthalpy of formation data can be found in the data booklet in section 12.
- An application of Hess's law is

$$\Delta H_{reactions} = \sum(\Delta H_f^{\ominus}(products)) - \sum(\Delta H_f^{\ominus}(reactants))$$

- Determination of the enthalpy change of a reaction that is the sum of multiple reactions with known enthalpy changes.

## Enthalpy cycles

As it is sometimes difficult to measure the enthalpy change of a reaction directly, chemists have developed a method which uses an indirect route. The enthalpy change for a particular reaction is calculated from the known enthalpy change of other reactions. Consider the **energy cycle** in Figure 5.11: in the clockwise route, the carbon and hydrogen are first combined to form ethanol and then ethanol is burned. In the anticlockwise route, the elements are burned separately. The experimentally determined enthalpy changes are included in the figure.

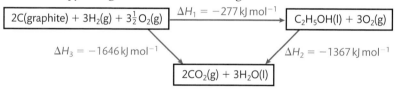

**Figure 5.11** In the clockwise route, the elements are first combined to form ethanol and then ethanol is burned. In the anticlockwise route, the elements are burned separately.

Consider the clockwise route:

$$\Delta H_1 + \Delta H_2 = -277 + -1367 = -1644 \text{ kJ mol}^{-1}$$

Consider the anticlockwise route:

$$\Delta H_3 = -1646 \text{ kJ mol}^{-1}$$

Given the uncertainty of the experimental values, we can conclude that:

$$\Delta H_3 = \Delta H_1 + \Delta H_2$$

The values are the same as both changes correspond to the combustion of two moles of carbon and three moles of hydrogen. The result is a consequence of the law of conservation of energy, otherwise it would be possible to devise cycles in which energy was created or destroyed (Figure 5.12). Consider a clockwise cycle in which carbon and hydrogen and oxygen are converted to ethanol and then carbon dioxide and water, which are then converted to the original elements.

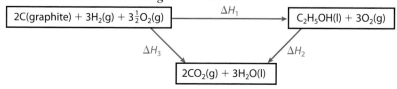

**Figure 5.12** There is no net chemical change in a complete cycle as the starting reactants and final products are the same.

From the law of conservation of energy:

in Figure 5.12, the enthalpy change in a complete cycle = 0

$$= \Delta H_1 + \Delta H_2 - \Delta H_3$$

therefore $\Delta H_1 + \Delta H_2 = \Delta H_3$

This result can be generalized and is known as **Hess's law**.

## Using Hess's law

Hess's law states that the enthalpy change for any chemical reaction is independent of the route provided the starting conditions and final conditions, and reactants and products, are the same.

**Hess's law states that the enthalpy change for any chemical reaction is independent of the route, provided the starting conditions and final conditions, and reactants and products, are the same.**

The importance of Hess's law is that it allows us to calculate the enthalpy changes of reactions that we cannot measure directly in the laboratory. For example, although the elements carbon and hydrogen do not combine directly to form propane, $C_3H_8$, the enthalpy change for the reaction:

$$3C(\text{graphite}) + 4H_2(g) \rightarrow C_3H_8(g)$$

can be calculated from the enthalpy of combustion data of the elements and the compound (Figure 5.13).

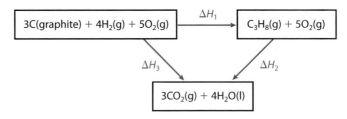

**Figure 5.13** $\Delta H_1 + \Delta H_2 = \Delta H_3$, therefore $\Delta H_1 = \Delta H_3 - \Delta H_2$. Although $\Delta H_1$ cannot be measured directly it can be calculated from the enthalpy of combustion of carbon, hydrogen, and propane.

The steps in an enthalpy cycle may be hypothetical and may refer to reactions that do not actually take place. The only requirement is that the individual chemical reactions in the sequence must balance. The relationship between the different reactions is clearly shown in an energy level diagram (Figure 5.14).

**Figure 5.14** Energy level diagram used to obtain the enthalpy of formation of propane indirectly.

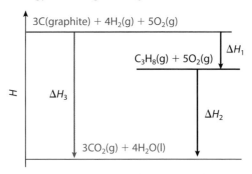

**Reversing the direction of a reaction reverses the sign of ΔH.**

### Worked example

$$S(s) + 1\tfrac{1}{2}O_2(g) \rightarrow SO_3(g) \qquad \Delta H^\ominus = -395 \text{ kJ} \quad (1)$$

$$SO_2(g) + \tfrac{1}{2}O_2(g) \rightarrow SO_3(g) \qquad \Delta H^\ominus = -98 \text{ kJ} \quad (2)$$

Calculate the standard enthalpy change, $\Delta H^\ominus$, for the reaction:

$$S(s) + O_2(g) \rightarrow SO_2(g)$$

## Solution

We can think of the reaction as a journey from $S(s)$ to $SO_2(g)$. As the standard enthalpy change cannot be measured directly, we must go by an alternative route suggested by the equations given.

Reaction 1 starts from the required starting point:

$$S(s) + 1\tfrac{1}{2}O_2(g) \rightarrow SO_3(g) \qquad \Delta H^\ominus = -395 \text{ kJ} \qquad (1)$$

Reaction 2 relates $SO_3(g)$ to $SO_2(g)$. To finish with the required product, we reverse the chemical change and the sign of enthalpy change:

$$SO_3(g) \rightarrow SO_2(g) + \tfrac{1}{2}O_2(g) \qquad \Delta H^\ominus = +98 \text{ kJ} \qquad (2)$$

We can now combine these equations:

$$S(s) + \tfrac{3}{2}O_2(g) + SO_3(g) \rightarrow SO_3(g) + SO_2(g) + \tfrac{1}{2}O_2(g) \qquad \Delta H^\ominus = -395 + 98 \text{ kJ}$$

Simplifying:

$$S(s) + \tfrac{2}{2}\cancel{\tfrac{3}{2}}O_2(g) + \cancel{SO_3(g)} \rightarrow \cancel{SO_3(g)} + SO_2(g) + \cancel{\tfrac{1}{2}O_2(g)} \qquad \Delta H^\ominus = -297 \text{ kJ}$$

$$S(s) + O_2(g) \rightarrow SO_2(g) \qquad \Delta H^\ominus = -297 \text{ kJ}$$

The enthalpy change for the decomposition of metal carbonates can be determined by adding the metal carbonate and metal oxide to dilute acids using Hess's Law.

## Exercises

**16** The diagram illustrates the enthalpy changes of a set of reactions.

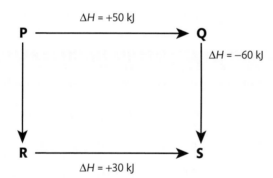

Which of the following statements are correct?

| | | |
|---|---|---|
| I | $P \rightarrow S$ | $\Delta H = -10$ kJ |
| II | $R \rightarrow Q$ | $\Delta H = +90$ kJ |
| III | $P \rightarrow R$ | $\Delta H = +20$ kJ |

**A** I and II only     **B** I and III only     **C** II and III only     **D** I, II, and III

**17** Calculate the enthalpy change, $\Delta H^\ominus$, for the reaction:

$$C(graphite) + \tfrac{1}{2}O_2(g) \rightarrow CO(g)$$

from the information below:

$$C(graphite) + O_2(g) \rightarrow CO_2(g) \qquad \Delta H^\ominus = -394 \text{ kJ}$$
$$CO(g) + \tfrac{1}{2}O_2(g) \rightarrow CO_2(g) \qquad \Delta H^\ominus = -283 \text{ kJ}$$

**18** Calculate the enthalpy change, $\Delta H^\ominus$, for the reaction:

$$2NO(g) + O_2(g) \rightarrow 2NO_2(g)$$

from the information below:

$$N_2(g) + O_2(g) \rightarrow 2NO(g) \qquad \Delta H^\ominus = +180.5 \text{ kJ}$$
$$N_2(g) + 2O_2(g) \rightarrow 2NO_2(g) \qquad \Delta H^\ominus = +66.4 \text{ kJ}$$

**19** Calculate the enthalpy change for the dimerization of nitrogen dioxide:

$$2NO_2(g) \rightarrow N_2O_4(g)$$

It is good practice to give the enthalpy changes for endothermic reactions have an explicitly + value.

from the following data:

$$\tfrac{1}{2}N_2(g) + O_2(g) \rightarrow NO_2(g) \qquad \Delta H^{\ominus} = +33.2 \text{ kJ mol}^{-1}$$
$$N_2(g) + 2O_2(g) \rightarrow N_2O_4(g) \qquad \Delta H^{\ominus} = +9.16 \text{ kJ mol}^{-1}$$

**20** The thermochemical equations for three related reactions are shown.

$$CO(g) + \tfrac{1}{2}O_2(g) \rightarrow CO_2(g) \qquad \Delta H_1 = -283 \text{ kJ mol}^{-1}$$
$$2H_2(g) + O_2(g) \rightarrow 2H_2O(l) \qquad \Delta H_2 = -572 \text{ kJ mol}^{-1}$$
$$CO_2(g) + H_2(g) \rightarrow CO(g) + H_2O(l) \qquad \Delta H_3 = ???$$

Determine $\Delta H_3$

**A** $+289$ kJ mol$^{-1}$    **B** $-3$ kJ mol$^{-1}$    **C** $-289$ kJ mol$^{-1}$    **D** $-855$ kJ mol$^{-1}$

## Standard enthalpy changes of reaction

As discussed earlier, the enthalpy change of a reaction depends on the physical state of the reactants and the products and the conditions under which the reaction occurs. For this reason, **standard enthalpy changes**, $\Delta H^{\ominus}$, which are measured under standard conditions of 298 K (25 °C) and $1.00 \times 10^5$ Pa, are generally tabulated.

The **standard enthalpy change of formation**, $\Delta H_f^{\ominus}$, of a substance is the enthalpy change that occurs when one mole of the substance is formed from its elements in their standard states. These standard measurements are taken at a temperature of 298 K (25 °C) and a pressure of $1.00 \times 10^5$ Pa. They are important as they:

- give a measure of the stability of a substance relative to its elements
- can be used to calculate the enthalpy changes of all reactions, either hypothetical or real.

> The standard enthalpy of formation of a substance is the enthalpy change that occurs when one mole of the substance is formed from its elements in their standard states under standard conditions of 298 K (25 °C) and 1.00 × 10⁵ Pa.

> Be careful with definitions of all key terms. Many students have difficulty defining standard enthalpy of formation – they refer to the energy required rather than enthalpy change and do not refer to the formation of one mole of substance in its standard state.

> The standard enthalpy change of formation of an element in its most stable form is zero. There is no chemical change and so no enthalpy change when an element is formed from itself.

### Worked example

The enthalpy of formation of ethanol is given in section 12 of the IB data booklet. Give the thermochemical equation which represents the standard enthalpy of formation of ethanol.

**Solution**

The value from the IB data booklet = $-278$ kJ mol$^{-1}$

Ethanol ($C_2H_5OH$) is made from the elements (C(graphite)) and hydrogen ($H_2(g)$) and oxygen ($O_2(g)$).

$$\_C(graphite) + \_H_2(g) + \_O_2(g) \rightarrow C_2H_5OH(l)$$

Balance the equation:

$$2C(graphite) + 3H_2(g) + \tfrac{1}{2}O_2(g) \rightarrow C_2H_5OH(l) \qquad \Delta H = -278 \text{ kJ mol}^{-1}$$

Note that as the enthalpy change of formation refers to one mole of product, there are fractional coefficients in the balanced equation.

### Exercises

**21** Which of the following does **not** have a standard heat of formation value of **zero** at 25 °C and 1.00 × 10⁵ Pa?

   **A** $Cl_2(g)$      **B** $I_2(s)$      **C** $Br_2(g)$      **D** Na(s)

**22** Which of the following does **not** have a standard heat of formation value of **zero** at 25 °C and 1.00 × 10⁵ Pa?

   **A** H(g)      **B** Hg(s)      **C** C(diamond)      **D** Si(s)

**23** For which equation is the enthalpy change described as an enthalpy change of formation?

  **A**  $CuSO_4(aq) + Zn(s) \rightarrow ZnSO_4(aq) + Cu(s)$

  **B**  $Cu(s) + S(s) + 2O_2(g) \rightarrow CuSO_4(aq)$

  **C**  $5H_2O(l) + CuSO_4(s) \rightarrow CuSO_4.5H_2O(s)$

  **D**  $Cu(s) + S(s) + 2O_2(g) \rightarrow CuSO_4(s)$

**24 (a)** Write the thermochemical equation for the standard enthalpy of formation of propanone ($CH_3COCH_3$).

  **(b)** State the conditions under which standard enthalpy changes are measured.

## Using standard enthalpy changes of formation

Standard enthalpy changes of formation can be used to calculate the standard enthalpy change of any reaction. Consider the general energy cycle in Figure 5.15.

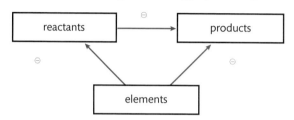

We have from the diagram:

$$\Sigma\Delta H_f^{\ominus}(\text{reactants}) + \Delta H_{\text{reaction}} = \Sigma\Delta H_f^{\ominus}(\text{products})$$

This gives the general expression for $\Delta H_{\text{reaction}}$ of any reaction

$$\Delta H_{\text{reaction}} = \Sigma\Delta H_f^{\ominus}(\text{products}) - \Sigma\Delta H_f^{\ominus}(\text{reactants})$$

**Figure 5.15** The chemical change elements → products can either occur directly or indirectly. The total enthalpy change must be the same for both routes. $\Sigma$ means 'the sum of '.

## Worked example

Calculate the enthalpy change for the reaction

$$C_3H_8(g) + 5O_2(g) \rightarrow 3CO_2(g) + 4H_2O(g)$$

from the following standard enthalpy changes of formation.

| Substance | $\Delta H_f^-$ / kJ mol$^{-1}$ |
|-----------|--------------------------------|
| $C_3H_8(g)$ | −105 |
| $CO_2(g)$ | −394 |
| $H_2O(l)$ | −286 |

$\Delta H_{\text{reaction}} =$
$\Sigma\Delta H_f^{\ominus}(\text{products}) -$
$\Sigma\Delta H_f^{\ominus}(\text{reactants})$

### Solution

First, write down the equation with the corresponding enthalpies of formation underneath:

$$C_3H_8(g) \quad + \quad 5O_2(g) \quad \rightarrow \quad 3CO_2(g) \quad + \quad 4H_2O(g)$$

$$\quad -105 \qquad\qquad >0 \qquad\qquad 3(-394) \qquad 4(-286) \qquad \Delta H_f^{\ominus} / \text{kJ mol}^{-1}$$

As the standard enthalpies of formation are given per mole they must be multiplied by the number of moles in the balanced equation, shown in red above.

Write down the general expression for the $\Delta H_{\text{reaction}}$

$$\Delta H_{\text{reaction}} = \Sigma\Delta H_f^{\ominus}(\text{products}) - \Sigma\Delta H_f^{\ominus}(\text{reactants})$$

**NATURE OF SCIENCE**

Heat is a tool that drives a country's industrial development and an individual's life, and a concept that has enlightened our understanding of why things change in the natural world.

The scientific understanding and harnessing of the energy has helped make the modern world what it is. The conservation of energy, on which Hess's law is based, developed as a result of practical considerations about the use and effect of heat and work. Hess's law is now important on both a practical and theoretical level as it allows us to predict the energy changes of possible and impossible reactions. The study of energetics shows how scientific theories evolve and generally accommodate the assumptions and premises of other theories, creating a consistent understanding across a range of phenomena and disciplines.

and express $\Delta H_{reaction}$ in terms of the data given:

$$\Delta H^{\ominus}_{reaction} = 3(-394) + 4(-286) - (-105)$$
$$= -2221 \text{ kJ mol}^{-1}$$

## Exercises

**25** Calculate $\Delta H^{\ominus}$ (in kJ mol$^{-1}$) for the reaction

$$Fe_3O_4(s) + 2C(graphite) \rightarrow 3Fe(s) + 2CO_2(g)$$

from the data below:

|  | $\Delta H_f^{\ominus}$ / kJ mol$^{-1}$ |
| --- | --- |
| $Fe_3O_4(s)$ | −1118 |
| $CO_2(g)$ | −394 |

**26** Calculate $\Delta H^{\ominus}$ (in kJ mol$^{-1}$) for the reaction

$$2NO_2(g) \rightarrow N_2O_4(g)$$

from the data below:

|  | $\Delta H_f^{\ominus}$ / kJ mol$^{-1}$ |
| --- | --- |
| $NO_2(g)$ | +33.2 |
| $N_2O_4(g)$ | +9.2 |

**27** Hydrogen peroxide slowly decomposes into water and oxygen:

$$2H_2O_2(l) \rightarrow 2H_2O(l) + O_2(g)$$

Calculate the enthalpy change of this reaction from the data table.

|  | $\Delta H_f^{\ominus}$ / kJ mol$^{-1}$ |
| --- | --- |
| $H_2O_2(l)$ | −188 |
| $H_2O(l)$ | −286 |

   **A** +98 kJ mol$^{-1}$    **B** −98 kJ mol$^{-1}$    **C** +196 kJ mol$^{-1}$    **D** −196 kJ mol$^{-1}$

**28** Calculate the enthalpy change for the hypothetical reduction of magnesium oxide by carbon, according to the equation below from the data given. Comment on its feasibility.

$$2MgO(s) + C(s) \rightarrow CO_2(g) + 2Mg(s)$$

|  | $\Delta H_f^{\ominus}$ / kJ mol$^{-1}$ |
| --- | --- |
| $CO_2(g)$ | −394 |
| $MgO(l)$ | −602 |

# 5.3 Bond enthalpies

## Understandings:
- Bond forming releases energy and bond breaking requires energy.
- Average bond enthalpy is the energy needed to break one mole of a bond in a gaseous molecule averaged over similar compounds.

## Applications and skills:
- Calculation of the enthalpy changes from known bond enthalpy values and comparison of these to experimentally measured values.

Chemical reactions involve the breaking and making of bonds. To understand the energy changes in a chemical reaction, we need to look at the energies needed to break the bonds that hold the atoms together in the reactants and the energy released when new bonds are formed in the products.

## Breaking bonds is an endothermic process

A covalent bond is due to the electrostatic attraction between the shared pair of electrons and the positive nuclei of the bonded atoms. Energy is needed to separate the atoms in a bond.

The bond enthalpy is the energy needed to break one mole of bonds in gaseous molecules under standard conditions.

The energy change, for example, during the formation of two moles of chlorine atoms from one mole of chlorine molecules can be represented as:

$$Cl_2(g) \rightarrow 2Cl(g) \qquad \Delta H^\ominus = +242 \text{ kJ mol}^{-1}$$

A chemical reaction involves the breaking and making of bonds. 500 to 1000 kJ of heat are typically needed to break one mole of chemical bonds. This image shows a change in the bond between the atoms represented by the yellow and the dark blue.

The situation is complicated in molecules which contain more than two atoms. Breaking the first O–H bond in a water molecule requires more heat energy than breaking the second bond:

$$H_2O(g) \rightarrow H(g) + OH(g) \qquad \Delta H^\ominus = +502 \text{ kJ mol}^{-1}$$

$$OH(g) \rightarrow H(g) + O(g) \qquad \Delta H^\ominus = +427 \text{ kJ mol}^{-1}$$

Similarly the energy needed to break the O–H in other molecules such as ethanol, $C_2H_5OH$, is different. In order to compare bond enthalpies which exist in different environments, **average bond enthalpies** are tabulated.

Using Hess's law:

$$H_2O(g) \rightarrow H(g) + OH(g) \qquad \Delta H = +502 \text{ kJ mol}^{-1}$$

$$OH(g) \rightarrow H(g) + O(g) \qquad \Delta H = +427 \text{ kJ mol}^{-1}$$

Average bond enthalpy over numbers on right

$$H_2O(g) \rightarrow H(g) + H(g) + OH(g) \qquad \Delta H = +502 + 427 \text{ kJ mol}^{-1}$$

$$\text{Average bond enthalpy } E(\text{O–H}) = \frac{+502 + 427}{2} \text{ kJ mol}^{-1}$$

$$= \frac{929}{2}$$

$$= 464.5 \text{ kJ mol}^{-1}$$

This value should be compared with the bond enthalpies given in the table on page 232 which are calculated from a wide range of molecules. Multiple bonds generally have higher bond enthalpies and shorter bond lengths than single bonds.

| Bond | E(X–Y) / kJ mol⁻¹ | Bond length / 10⁻⁹ m |
|------|------|------|
| H–H | +436 | 0.074 |
| C–C | +347 | 0.154 |
| C=C | +614 | 0.134 |
| C–H | +414 | 0.108 |
| O=O | +498 | 0.121 |
| O–H | +463 | 0.097 |
| C=O | +804 | 0.122 |
| Cl–Cl | +242 | 0.199 |

All bond enthalpies refer to reactions in the gaseous state so that the enthalpy changes caused by the formation and breaking of intermolecular forces can be ignored.

**The average bond enthalpy is the energy needed to break one mole of bonds in gaseous molecules under standard conditions averaged over similar compounds.**

**Note carefully the definition of bond enthalpy. A common error is to fail to indicate that all the species have to be in the gaseous state.**

## Making bonds is an exothermic process

The same amount of energy is absorbed when a bond is broken as is given out when a bond is made (Figure 5.16). For example:

$$H(g) + H(g) \rightarrow H_2(g)$$

$$\Delta H^\ominus = -436 \text{ kJ mol}^{-1}$$

**Endothermic processes involve the separation of particles which are held together by a force of attraction.**

**Exothermic processes involve the bringing together of particles which have an attractive force between them.**

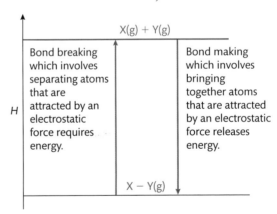

**Figure 5.16** The energy changes that occur when bonds are broken and bonds are formed.

### Worked example

Which of the following processes are endothermic?

A  $2Cl(g) \rightarrow Cl_2(g)$
B  $Na(g) \rightarrow Na^+(g) + e^-$
C  $Na^+(g) + Cl^-(g) \rightarrow NaCl(s)$
D  $Na(g) \rightarrow Na(s)$

### Solution

Only one of the processes involves the separation of particles:

$$Na(g) \rightarrow Na^+(g) + e^-$$

In this case, a negatively charged electron is separated from a positive ion Na⁺(g).

Answer = B

**29** Which of the following processes are endothermic?

I $H_2O(s) \rightarrow H_2O(g)$
II $CO_2(g) \rightarrow CO_2(s)$
III $O_2(g) \rightarrow 2O(g)$

**A** I and II only  **B** I and III only  **C** II and III only  **D** I, II, and III

**30** Identify the equation which represents the bond enthalpy for the H–Cl bond.

**A** $HCl(g) \rightarrow H(g) + Cl(g)$
**B** $HCl(g) \rightarrow \frac{1}{2}H_2(g) + \frac{1}{2}Cl_2(g)$
**C** $HCl(g) \rightarrow H^+(g) + Cl^-(g)$
**D** $HCl(aq) \rightarrow H^+(aq) + Cl^-(aq)$

**31** Which of the following processes are endothermic?

I $CO_2(g) \rightarrow CO_2(s)$
II $H_2O(s) \rightarrow H_2O(g)$
III $O_2(g) \rightarrow 2O(g)$

**A** I and II only  **B** I and III only  **C** II and III only  **D** I, II, and III

**32** Identify the bonds which are broken in the following process.

$$C_2H_6(g) \rightarrow 2C(g) + 6H(g)$$

# Using bond enthalpies to calculate the enthalpy changes of reaction

We are now in a position to understand how energy changes occur in chemical reactions. Consider, for example, the complete combustion of methane when we use a Bunsen burner:

$$\begin{array}{c} H \\ | \\ H-C-H + 2O{=}O \rightarrow O{=}C{=}O + 2H-O-H \\ | \\ H \end{array}$$

Energy is needed to break the C—H and O=O bonds in the reactants, but energy is given out when the C=O and O—H bonds are formed. The reaction is exothermic overall as the bonds which are formed are stronger than the bonds which are broken. A reaction is endothermic when the bonds broken are stronger than the bonds which are formed.

## Worked example

Use bond enthalpies to calculate the heat of combustion of methane, the principal component of natural gas.

### Solution

1  Write down the equation for the reaction showing all the bonds. This has already been done above.

2  Draw a table which shows the bonds which are broken and those that are formed during the reaction with the corresponding energy changes.

## CHALLENGE YOURSELF

4 Compare the value of the enthalpy of combustion of methane obtained in the worked example to that in section 13 of the IB data booklet and use Hess's law to estimate the strength of a hydrogen bond.

| Bonds broken | $\Delta H$ / kJ mol$^{-1}$ (endothermic) | Bonds formed | $\Delta H$ / kJ mol$^{-1}$ (exothermic) |
|---|---|---|---|
| 4 C–H | 4 (+414) | 2 C=O | 2 (–804) |
| 2 O=O | 2 (+498) | 4 O–H | 4 (–463) |
| Total | = +2652 | | = +3460 |

$$\Delta H = \Sigma E(\text{bonds broken}) - \Sigma E(\text{bonds formed})$$

$$\Delta H^{\ominus} = +2652 + (-3460) \text{ kJ mol}^{-1} = -808 \text{ kJ mol}^{-1}$$

The value calculated from the bond enthalpies should be compared with the experimental value of $-891$ kJ mol$^{-1}$ measured under standard conditions given in section 13 of the IB data booklet. The values are different because the standard state of water is liquid and the bond enthalpy calculation assumes that the reaction occurs in the gaseous state. The use of average bond enthalpies is an additional approximation.

> Make sure that you select the correct values for the bond enthalpies. For example don't confuse C=C with C—C, and use the correct coefficients for the number of bonds broken and formed.

## Exercises

33 Which of the following is equivalent to the bond enthalpy of the carbon–oxygen bond in carbon monoxide?

**A** $CO(g) \rightarrow C(s) + O(g)$      **C** $CO(g) \rightarrow C(s) + \frac{1}{2}O_2(g)$
**B** $CO(g) \rightarrow C(g) + O(g)$      **D** $CO(g) \rightarrow C(g) + \frac{1}{2}O_2(g)$

34 Use the bond enthalpies below to calculate $\Delta H^{\ominus}$ for the reaction:

$$H_2C{=}CH_2 + H_2 \rightarrow H_3C{-}CH_3$$

| Bond | Bond enthalpy / kJ mol$^{-1}$ |
|---|---|
| C—C | +347 |
| C=C | +612 |
| H—H | +436 |
| C—H | +413 |

35 Use the bond enthalpies below to calculate $\Delta H^{\ominus}$ for the reaction:

$$2H_2(g) + O_2(g) \rightarrow 2H_2O(g)$$

| Bond | Bond enthalpy / kJ mol$^{-1}$ |
|---|---|
| O=O | +498 |
| H—H | +436 |
| O—H | +464 |

36 The hydrogenation of the alkene double bond in unsaturated oils is an important reaction in margarine production. Calculate the enthalpy change when one mole of C=C bonds is hydrogenated from the bond energy data shown.

| Bond | Bond enthalpy / kJ mol$^{-1}$ |
|---|---|
| H—H | 436 |
| C—C | 347 |
| C—H | 412 |
| C=C | 612 |

**A** $-224$ kJ mol$^{-1}$    **B** $-123$ kJ mol$^{-1}$    **C** $+123$ kJ mol$^{-1}$    **D** $+224$ kJ mol$^{-1}$

37 Use the bond enthalpy data given to calculate the enthalpy change of reaction between methane and fluorine:

$$C_2H_4(g) + F_2(g) \rightarrow CH_2FCH_2F(g)$$

| Bond | Bond enthalpy / kJ mol$^{-1}$ |
|------|------|
| C—C | 347 |
| C=C | 612 |
| F—F | 158 |
| H—F | 568 |
| C—F | 467 |

**A** +776          **B** +164          **C** –511          **D** –776

**38** Use the bond enthalpies given in section 11 of the IB data booklet to estimate the enthalpy of combustion of ethanol and comment on the reliability of your result.

## Ozone depletion

The Earth is unique among the planets in having an atmosphere that is chemically active and rich in oxygen. Oxygen is present in two forms, normal oxygen ($O_2$) and ozone ($O_3$), and both forms play a key role in protecting life on the Earth's surface from harmful ultraviolet (UV) radiation. They form a protective screen which ensures that radiation that reaches the surface of the Earth is different from that emitted by the Sun. As discussed in Chapter 4, $O_2$ and $O_3$ differ in their bonding as follows:

| :O=O: | :Ö:  ⟷  :Ö: |
|-------|-------------|
| $O_2$; double bonds | $O_3$; the oxygen to oxygen bond is between a single bond and a double bond |

### The bonds in oxygen and ozone are broken by UV of different wavelengths

The bonds in oxygen and ozone are both broken when they absorb UV radiation of sufficient energy. The double bond in $O_2$ is stronger than the 1.5 bond in ozone and so is broken by radiation of higher energy and shorter wavelengths.

The energy $E_{photon}$ of a photon of light is related to its frequency $\nu$ by Planck's equation (see Chapter 2):

$$E_{photon} = h\nu$$

The wavelength $\lambda$ is related to the frequency: $\nu = c/\lambda$ where $c$ is the speed of light. Substituting for $\nu$ in Planck's equation:

$$E_{photon} = \frac{h \times c}{\lambda}$$

As oxygen has the strongest bond, shorter wavelength radiation is needed to break its bonds. The wavelengths of light needed to break the bonds in ozone are calculated in the following example.

## CHALLENGE YOURSELF

**5** Suggest, based on the discussion of bonding and structure in Chapter 4, why graphite is more stable than diamond.

Don't confuse the different methods of calculating enthalpy changes. A common error when using bond enthalpies is the reversal of the sign.

The correct expression is:

$\Delta H = \sum E(\text{bonds broken}) - \sum E(\text{bonds formed})$

This should be contrasted with the expression using standard enthalpies of formation:

$\Delta H_{reaction} = \sum \Delta H_f^{\ominus}(\text{products}) - \sum \Delta H_f^{\ominus}(\text{reactants})$

The depletion of the ozone layer is an important transdisciplinary topic. It is also discussed in Chapter 4.

### Worked example

The bond energy in ozone is 363 kJ mol$^{-1}$. Calculate the wavelength of UV radiation needed to break the bond.

**Solution**

One mole of photons are needed to break one mole of bonds. The energy of a mole of photons is the energy of one photon multiplied by Avogadro's number (L) (page 15).

$$L \times E_{photon} = 363 \text{ kJ} = 363\,000 \text{ J}$$

$$E_{photon} = \frac{363\,000}{6.02 \times 10^{23}} \text{ J}$$

$$\lambda = \frac{hc}{E_{photon}}$$

$$= 6.63 \times 10^{-34} \text{ Js} \times 3.00 \times 10^{8} \text{ ms}^{-1} \times \frac{6.02 \times 10^{23}}{363000} \text{ J}^{-1}$$

$$= 3.30 \times 10^{-7} \text{ m}$$

$$= 330 \text{ nm}$$

Any radiation in the UV region with a wavelength smaller than 330 nm breaks the bond in ozone.

## The natural formation and depletion of ozone

The temperature of the atmosphere generally decreases with height but at 12 km above the Earth's surface the temperature starts to rise because ultraviolet radiation is absorbed in a number of photochemical reactions.

In the stratosphere, the strong covalent double bond in normal oxygen $O_2$ is broken by high-energy UV radiation with a wavelength shorter than 242 nm to form two oxygen atoms:

$$O_2(g) \xrightarrow{\text{UV light, } \lambda < 242 \text{ nm}} O\bullet(g) + O\bullet(g)(\text{atomic oxygen})$$

The oxygen atoms have unpaired electrons. They are reactive **free radicals** and so react with another oxygen molecule to form ozone.

$$O\bullet(g) + O_2(g) \rightarrow O_3(g)$$

This second step is *exothermic*; bonds are formed and the energy given out raises the temperature of the stratosphere.

As the bonds in ozone are weaker than the double bond in oxygen, ultraviolet light of lower energy is needed to break them:

$$O_3(g) \xrightarrow{\text{UV light, } \lambda < 330 \text{ nm}} O\bullet(g) + O_2(g)$$

The oxygen atoms then react with another ozone molecule to form two oxygen molecules.

$$O_3(g) + O\bullet(g) \rightarrow 2O_2(g)$$

As bonds are formed this is another exothermic reaction which produces heat that maintains the relatively high temperature of the stratosphere. The level of ozone in the

A free radical is a species with an unpaired electron.

## CHALLENGE YOURSELF

**6** Explain why oxygen behaves as a free radical despite having an even number of electrons.

stratosphere – less than 10 ppm – stays at a constant level if the rate of formation of ozone is balanced by its rate of removal. This is known as a **steady state**. The whole process is described by the Chapman Cycle.

Step 1
$$O_2 \xrightarrow[\substack{\text{high} \\ \text{energy} \\ \text{UV } \lambda < 242nm}]{} 2O^\bullet$$

Step 2
$$O^\bullet + O_2 \underset{\substack{\text{Step 3} \\ \text{lower} \\ \text{energy}}}{\overset{\text{Step 2}}{\rightleftharpoons}} O_3$$

Step 4
$$O_3 + O^\bullet \xrightarrow[\text{(slow)}]{} 2O_2$$

This cycle of reactions is significant because dangerous ultraviolet light has been absorbed and the stratosphere has become warmer. Both these processes are essential for the survival of life on Earth.

▲ Technician releasing a balloon to measure stratospheric ozone over the Arctic. This research was part of a joint project by NASA and the European Union to look at the amount and rate of stratospheric ozone depletion.

## Exercises

**39** The concentration of ozone in the upper atmosphere is maintained by the following reactions.

I    $O_2 \rightarrow 2O\bullet$
II   $O_2 + O\bullet \rightarrow O_3$
III  $O_3 \rightarrow O_2 + O\bullet$

The presence of chlorofluorocarbons (CFCs) in the upper atmosphere has led to a reduction in ozone concentration.

**(a)** Identify the step which is exothermic.
**(b)** Identify with reference to the bonding in $O_2$ and $O_3$, the most endothermic step.

**40** Use section 11 of the IB data booklet to calculate the minimum wavelength of radiation needed to break the O=O double bond in $O_2$.

**41** Explain why ozone can be decomposed by light with a longer wavelength than that required to decompose oxygen.

Ozone depletion is a global political issue. Consider the following quote from Maneka Gandhi, former Indian Minister of the Environment and delegate to the *Montreal Protocol*. 'India recognizes the threat to the environment and the necessity for a global burden sharing to control it. But is it fair that the industrialized countries who are responsible for the ozone depletion should arm-twist the poorer nations into bearing the cost of their mistakes?'

Stratospheric ozone depletion is a particular concern in the polar regions of the planet, although the pollution that causes it comes from a variety of regions and sources. International action and cooperation have helped to ameliorate the ozone depletion problem.

# 15.1 Energy cycles

## Understandings:
- Representative equations (e.g. $M^+(g) \rightarrow M^+(aq)$) can be used for enthalpy/energy of hydration, ionization, atomization, electron affinity, lattice, covalent bond, and solution.
- Enthalpy of solution, hydration enthalpy, and lattice enthalpy are related in an energy cycle.

## Applications and skills:

- Construction of Born–Haber cycles for Group 1 and 2 oxides and chlorides.
- Construction of energy cycles from hydration, lattice, and solution enthalpy. For example, dissolution of solid NaOH or $NH_4Cl$ in water.
- Calculation of enthalpy changes from Born–Haber or dissolution energy cycles.

  **Guidance**
  - The following enthalpy/energy terms should be covered: ionization, atomization, electron affinity, lattice, covalent bond, hydration, and solution.
  - Values for lattice enthalpies (section 18), enthalpies of aqueous solutions (section 19), and enthalpies of hydration (section 20) are given in the data booklet.
- Relate size and charge of ions to lattice and hydration enthalpies.

  **Guidance**
  Polarizing effect of some ions producing covalent character in some largely ionic substances will not be assessed.
- Perform lab experiments which could include single replacement reactions in aqueous solutions.

## First ionization energies and electron affinities

In Chapter 4 we discussed the formation of ionic compounds such as sodium chloride. Metal atoms lose electrons and non-metal atoms gain electrons.

The first ionization energy ($\Delta H_i^\ominus$) corresponds to the energy needed to form the positive ion.

$$Na(g) \rightarrow Na^+(g) + e^-(g) \qquad \Delta H_i^\ominus = +496 \text{ kJ mol}^{-1}$$

This process was discussed in Chapters 2 and 3, where we saw that sodium, which is on the left of the Periodic Table, has a relatively low ionization energy. The first **electron affinity** ($\Delta H_e^\ominus$) is the enthalpy change when one mole of gaseous atoms attracts one mole of electrons. Values are tabulated in section 7 of the IB data booklet. For chlorine:

$$Cl(g) + e^-(g) \rightarrow Cl^-(g) \qquad \Delta H_e^\ominus = -349 \text{ kJ mol}^{-1}$$

As the electron is attracted to the positively charged nucleus of the Cl atom, the process is exothermic.

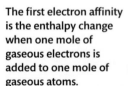

**The first ionization energy is the minimum energy required to remove one mole of electrons from one mole of gaseous atoms.**

**The first electron affinity is the enthalpy change when one mole of gaseous electrons is added to one mole of gaseous atoms.**

## Lattice enthalpies

Add the equations for first ionization energy and first electron affinity:

$$Na(g) + Cl(g) \rightarrow Na^+(g) + Cl^-(g) \qquad \Delta H^\ominus = -349 + 496 = +147 \text{ kJ mol}^{-1}$$

We can now see that the electron transfer process is endothermic overall and so energetically unfavourable, despite the fact that it leads to the formation of ions with stable noble gas electron configurations. To understand the formation of ionic compounds, we need to look deeper. The oppositely charged gaseous ions come together to form an **ionic lattice**; this is a very exothermic process as there is strong attraction between the oppositely charged ions:

$$Na^+(g) + Cl^-(g) \rightarrow NaCl(s) \qquad \Delta H^\ominus = -790 \text{ kJ mol}^{-1}$$

It is this step of the process which explains the readiness of sodium and chlorine to form an ionic compound.

The **lattice enthalpy** ($\Delta H_{lat}^\ominus$) expresses this enthalpy change in terms of the reverse endothermic process. The lattice enthalpy relates to the formation of gaseous ions

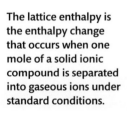

**The lattice enthalpy is the enthalpy change that occurs when one mole of a solid ionic compound is separated into gaseous ions under standard conditions.**

Although some texts use an exothermic definition of lattice energy, it is the endothermic definition which is given in section 18 of the IB data booklet.

from one mole of a solid crystal breaking into gaseous ions. For example, sodium chloride:

$$NaCl(s) \rightarrow Na^+(g) + Cl^-(g) \qquad \Delta H^{\ominus}_{lat} = +790 \text{ kJ mol}^{-1}$$

## Experimental lattice enthalpies and the Born–Haber cycle

Experimental lattice energies cannot be determined directly. An energy cycle based on Hess's law, known as the **Born–Haber cycle** is used. The formation of an ionic compound from its elements is supposed to take place in a number of steps including the formation of the solid lattice from its constituent gaseous ions. From Hess's law, the enthalpy change for the overall formation of the solid must be equal to the sum of the enthalpy changes accompanying the individual steps.

Consider, for example, the formation of sodium chloride:

$$Na(s) + \tfrac{1}{2}Cl_2(g) \rightarrow NaCl(s) \qquad \Delta H^{\ominus}_f(NaCl) = -411 \text{ kJ mol}^{-1}$$

This can be considered to take place in several steps as shown in the table below.

| Step | $\Delta H^{\ominus}$ / kJ mol$^{-1}$ |
|---|---|
| Sodium is atomized to form one mole of gaseous ions:<br>$$Na(s) \rightarrow Na(g)$$<br>The corresponding enthalpy change is known as the enthalpy change of atomization. | $\Delta H^{\ominus}_{atom}(Na) = +107$ |
| One mole of chlorine atoms is formed as ½ mole of Cl—Cl bonds break:<br>$$\tfrac{1}{2}Cl_2(g) \rightarrow Cl(g)$$<br>$E$ = bond enthalpy, page 233<br>Enthalpy of atomization of chlorine | $\tfrac{1}{2}E(Cl—Cl) = \tfrac{1}{2}(+242)$ |
| One electron is removed from the outer shell of the gaseous sodium atom:<br>$$Na(g) \rightarrow Na^+(g) + e^-$$<br>Ionization energy of sodium | $\Delta H^{\ominus}_i(Na) = +496$ |
| One electron is added to the outer shell of the gaseous chlorine atom:<br>$$Cl(g) + e^- \rightarrow Cl^-(g)$$<br>Electron affinity of chlorine | $\Delta H^{\ominus}_e(Cl) = -349$ |
| The gaseous ions come together to form one mole of solid sodium chloride:<br>$$Na^+(g) + Cl^-(g) \rightarrow NaCl(s)$$<br>– Lattice enthalpy of sodium chloride | $-\Delta H^{\ominus}_{lat} = ???$ |

These changes are best illustrated using an energy level diagram (Figure 5.17).

The enthalpy change of atomization $\Delta H^{\ominus}_{atom}$ is the enthalpy change that occurs when one mole of gaseous atoms is formed from the element in its standard state.

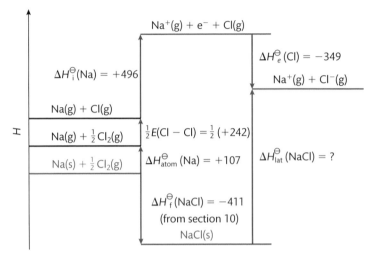

**Figure 5.17** Born–Haber cycle for sodium chloride. The enthalpy change of formation of sodium chloride, shown in blue, can be equated to a combination of the enthalpy changes associated with the changes shown in red.

Note changes from original bond energy for $Cl_2$ = 242 and the arrow for lattice energy has been inverted.

$$\Delta H_f^\ominus(NaCl) = \Delta H_{atom}^\ominus(Na) + \Delta H_i^\ominus(Na) + \tfrac{1}{2}E(Cl-Cl) + \Delta H_e^\ominus(Cl) - \Delta H_{lat}^\ominus(NaCl)$$

This allows an equation for the lattice enthalpy to be expressed in terms of experimentally verifiable quantities:

$$\Delta H_{lat}^\ominus(NaCl) = \Delta H_{atom}^\ominus(Na) + \Delta H_i^\ominus(Na) + \tfrac{1}{2}E(Cl-Cl) + \Delta H_e^\ominus(Cl) - \Delta H_f^\ominus(NaCl)$$

$$\Delta H_{lat}^\ominus(NaCl) = +107 + 496 + \tfrac{1}{2}(+242) - 349 - (-411)\ \text{kJ mol}^{-1}$$

$$= +786\ \text{kJ mol}^{-1}$$

## Worked example

(a) Write an equation to represent the lattice energy of magnesium oxide, MgO.

(b) Write an equation to represent the second electron affinity of oxygen and comment on the relative values of the first and second values given in section 8 of the IB data booklet.

(c) Use the following data, and further information from sections 8 and 11 of the IB data booklet to construct a Born–Haber cycle for magnesium oxide.

(d) Calculate the lattice energy of magnesium oxide.

Additional data:

• enthalpy change of atomization for Mg(s) = +148 kJ mol$^{-1}$
• second ionization energy of magnesium = +1451 kJ mol$^{-1}$
• enthalpy change of formation of MgO(s) = −602 kJ mol$^{-1}$

### Solution

(a) $MgO(s) \rightarrow Mg^{2+}(g) + O^{2-}(g)$

(b) $O^-(g) + e^-(g) \rightarrow O^{2-}(g)$

The first electron affinity corresponds to the attraction of an outer electron into the outer energy level of an oxygen atom. This is an exothermic process.

The second electron affinity corresponds to a negatively charged oxide ion accepting an additional outer electron into an outer energy level despite the mutual repulsion between the negatively charged species. This is an endothermic process.

(c) Note the enthalpy change of atomization for oxygen = half the bond energy for $O_2$ (Figure 5.18).

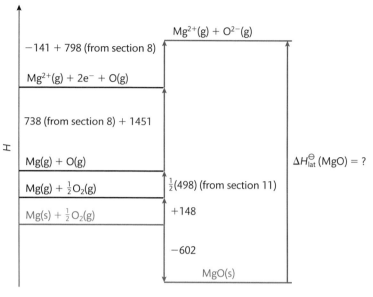

**Figure 5.18** Born–Haber cycle for magnesium oxide.

(d) From the diagram we have

$$\Delta H^{\ominus}_{lat}(MgO) = +602 + 148 + \tfrac{1}{2}(498) + (738 + 1451) + (753 - 142) \text{ kJ mol}^{-1}$$

$$\Delta H^{\ominus}_{lat}(MgO) = +3799 \text{ kJ mol}^{-1}$$

## Exercises

**42** Identify the process which has the sign of its associated enthalpy change different from the rest.
   **A** $Cl(g) + e^- \rightarrow Cl^-(g)$    **C** $KCl(g) \rightarrow K^+(g) + Cl^-(g)$
   **B** $K(g) \rightarrow K^+(g) + e^-$    **D** $Cl_2(g) \rightarrow 2Cl(g)$

**43** Which equation represents the electron affinity of potassium?
   **A** $K(g) \rightarrow K^+(g) + e^-$    **B** $K(g) \rightarrow K^-(g) + e^-$    **C** $K(g) + e^- \rightarrow K^-(g)$    **D** $K^+(g) + e^- \rightarrow K(g)$

**44** Identify the process which corresponds to the standard enthalpy change of atomization of bromine.
   **A** $Br_2(g) \rightarrow 2Br(g)$    **B** $Br_2(l) \rightarrow 2Br(g)$    **C** $\tfrac{1}{2}Br_2(g) \rightarrow Br(g)$    **D** $\tfrac{1}{2}Br_2(l) \rightarrow Br(g)$

**45 (a)** Write an equation to represent the lattice energy of potassium oxide, $K_2O$.
   **(b)** The Born–Haber cycle shown may be used to calculate the lattice energy of potassium oxide (Figure 5.19).

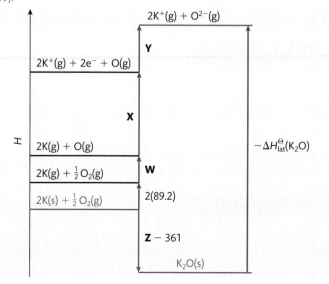

**Figure 5.19** Born–Haber cycle for potassium oxide.

Identify the enthalpy changes labelled by the letters **W**, **X**, **Y** and **Z**.

**(c)** Use the energy cycle, and further information from sections 8 and 11 of the IB data booklet to calculate an experimental value for the lattice energy of potassium oxide.

## Theoretical lattice enthalpies can be calculated from the ionic model

Theoretical lattice enthalpies can be calculated by assuming the crystal is made up from perfectly spherical ions. This **ionic model** assumes that the only interaction is due to electrostatic forces between the ions. Consider, for example, the formation of the ion pair in Figure 5.20.

The energy needed to separate the ions depends on the product of the ionic charges and the sum of the ionic radii.

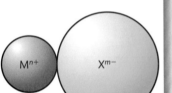

**Figure 5.20** An ion pair of cation and anion. Note that both ions are spherical. This is one of the assumptions of the ionic model.

- An increase in the ionic radius of one of the ions decreases the attraction between the ions.
- An increase in the ionic charge increases the ionic attraction between the ions.

To calculate the lattice energy for one mole, more ion interactions need to be considered as a solid crystal forms (Figure 5.21). The overall attraction between the positive and negative ions predominates over the repulsion of ions with the same charge as ions are generally surrounded by neighbouring ions of opposite charge.

This leads to the general expression:

$$\Delta H^{\ominus}_{lat} = \frac{Knm}{R_{M^{n+}} + R_{X^{m-}}}$$

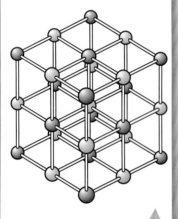

**Figure 5.21** The cubic crystal consists of an ionic lattice of sodium ($Na^+$) and chloride ($Cl^-$) ions. Sodium ions are represented by red spheres, chloride ions as green spheres. Ionic crystals tend to be hard and brittle, due to the strong electrostatic forces between the constituent ions.

where K is a constant that depends on geometry of the lattice and $n$ and $m$ are the magnitude of charges on the ions. As the ionic radii ($R_{M^{n+}} + R_{X^{m-}}$) can be determined from X-ray diffraction measurements of the crystal, theoretical values can be calculated once the geometry of the solid lattice is known.

## Exercises

**46** Which one of the following compounds would be expected to have the highest lattice enthalpy?

   **A** $Na_2O$        **B** $MgO$        **C** $CaO$        **D** $KCl$

**47** Theoretical lattice enthalpies can be calculated on the ionic model. The values for the sodium halides are tabulated below.

| Halide | $\Delta H^{\ominus}_{lat}$/ kJ mol$^{-1}$ |
|--------|------|
| NaF | +910 |
| NaCl | +769 |
| NaBr | +732 |
| NaI | +682 |

Explain the trend in lattice enthalpies of sodium halides.

**48** The theoretical lattice enthalpies, based on the ionic model, of sodium chloride and magnesium oxide are shown below.

| Compound | $\Delta H^{\ominus}_{lat}$ / kJ mol$^{-1}$ |
|----------|------|
| NaCl | +769 |
| MgO | +3795 |

Explain why magnesium oxide has the higher lattice enthalpy compared to sodium chloride.

# Lattice enthalpies depend on the size and charge of the ions.

The lattice enthalpies of the group 1 halides are given below. Remember from Chapter 3 that ion radius increases going down a group of the Periodic Table.

|  | $F^-$ | $Cl^-$ | $Br^-$ | $I^-$ |
|---|---|---|---|---|
| $Li^+$ | 1049 | 864 | 820 | 764 |
| $Na^+$ | 930 | 790 | 754 | 705 |
| $K^+$ | 829 | 720 | 691 | 650 |
| $Rb^+$ | 795 | 695 | 668 | 632 |
| $Cs^+$ | 759 | 670 | 647 | 613 |

The lattice enthalpies of the Group 1 halides

We can see that the lattice enthalpies decrease as the size of the cation or anion increases. LiF contains the ions with the smallest ionic radii and has the highest lattice enthalpy, and CsI contains the largest ions and the smallest lattice enthalpy.

The effect of charge is seen in the following comparisons.

|  | $\Delta H^\ominus_{lattice}$ (kJ mol$^{-1}$) |  | $\Delta H^\ominus_{lattice}$ (kJ mol$^{-1}$) | Explanation of difference |
|---|---|---|---|---|
| NaCl | 1049 | $MgCl_2$ | 2540 | $MgCl_2$ has more than double the lattice enthalpy of NaCl as $Mg^{2+}$ has double the charge of $Na^+$ and a smaller ionic radius. |
| $CaF_2$ | 2651 | CaO | 3401 | CaO has higher lattice enthalpy than $CaF_2$ as $O^{2-}$ has double the charge of $F^-$. The value is less than double as $O^{2-}$ has a larger ionic radius than $F^-$ |

So overall, we can see that lattice enthalpies are greater when ionic compounds form between smaller, more highly charged ions, that is those with the greatest charge density.

Lattice enthalpy decreases with increasing ion radius and increases with increasing ion charge.

The enthalpy change of solution is the enthalpy change when one mole of a solute is dissolved in a solvent to infinite dilution under standard conditions of temperature (298 K) and pressure ($1.0 \times 10^5$ Pa).

**Figure 5.22** Ionic compounds generally dissolve in the polar solvent water. (a) Ionic lattice are often broken up by polar water molecules. At the contact surface, partial charges in the water molecules are attracted to ions of opposite charge in the lattice, which may cause them to dislodge from their positions. (b) The partially negatively oxygen atoms in the polar water molecules are attracted to the positive ions. (c) The partially positively hydrogen atoms in the polar water molecules are attracted to the negative ions.

## Exercises

**49** Identify the compound which has the greatest lattice energy.

  **A**  sodium chloride

  **B**  potassium chloride

  **C**  magnesium bromide

  **D**  calcium bromide

**50** The lattice enthalpy values for sodium fluoride and magnesium chloride are shown below.

$$NaF(s) \quad \Delta H^{\ominus} = +930 \text{ kJ mol}^{-1}$$
$$MgCl_2(s) \quad \Delta H^{\ominus} = +2540 \text{ kJ mol}^{-1}$$

Identify which of the following statements help(s) to explain the relative value of the lattice enthalpies.

  I  The ionic charge of sodium is less than that of magnesium.

  II  The ionic radius of the chloride is larger than that of flouride.

  **A**  I only  **B**  II only  **C**  I and II  **D**  Neither I nor II

**51** The lattice enthalpies of silver bromide and sodium bromide are given below.

| | $\Delta H^{\ominus}$/ kJ mol$^{-1}$ | | $\Delta H^{\ominus}$/ kJ mol$^{-1}$ |
|---|---|---|---|
| AgBr | 905 | KBr | 691 |

Explain the relative values of the lattice enthalpies with reference to the bonding.

## Enthalpies of solution

In exercise 14 you were asked to calculate the enthalpy change that occurs when ammonium chloride is added to 1 dm$^3$ of water:

$$NH_4Cl(s) \xrightarrow{H_2O} NH_4^+(aq) + Cl^-(aq) \qquad \Delta H^{\ominus}_{sol} = +14.78 \text{ kJ mol}^{-1}$$

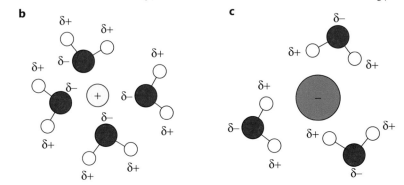

As the exercise demonstrates, these enthalpies of solutions can calculated by measuring the temperature change in solution. As the interaction between the solute and the solvent water molecules depends on the concentration of the solution; the enthalpy of solution strictly refers to the ideal situation of infinite dilution. The enthalpy of solution is obtained practically by measuring enthalpy changes for solutions with increasing volumes of water until a limit is reached.

Ionic compounds like NaCl and NH$_4$Cl dissolve very readily in water as the ions are strongly attracted to the polar solvent water. The partial positive charge on the hydrogen atoms in the water molecules are attracted to the negative ions and the partial negative change of the oxygen is attracted to the positive ions.

Ions separated from the lattice in this way become surrounded by water molecules and are said to be **hydrated**. The strength of interaction between the polar water molecules and the separated ions is given by their **hydration enthalpies**.

# The hydration enthalpy of an ion depends on the attraction between the ions and the polar water molecules

The enthalpy of hydration of a compound is the enthalpy change that occurs when one mole of its constituent gaseous ions is dissolved to form an infinitely dilute solution. The enthalpy of hydration of individual ions, although more useful, cannot generally be measured directly; as positive ions and negative ions are both present in a compound and it is difficult to disentangle the contribution of each ion.

This problem is resolved by measuring the enthalpy of hydration of the $H^+$ ion separately using an indirect spectral technique:

$$H^+(g) \rightarrow H^+(aq) \qquad \Delta H_{hyd}^\ominus = -1130 \text{ kJ mol}^{-1}$$

and then combining this value with the hydration enthalpy of different compounds to obtain values for individual ions.

The enthalpy change of hydration of an ion is the enthalpy change that occurs when one mole of gaseous ions is dissolved to form an infinitely dilute solution of one mole of aqueous ions.

$$M^{n+}(g) \rightarrow M^{n+}(aq) \qquad \Delta H_{hyd}^\ominus(M^{n+})$$

$$X^{m-}(g) \rightarrow X^{m-}(aq) \qquad \Delta H_{hyd}^\ominus(X^{m-})$$

As there is a force of attraction between the ions and the polar water molecules, it is an exothermic process and the enthalpy changes are negative.

Consider the following hydration energies of the Group 1 cations and Group 17 anions.

| Cations | $\Delta H_{hyd}^\ominus$ / kJ mol$^{-1}$ | Anions | $\Delta H_{hyd}^\ominus$ / kJ mol$^{-1}$ |
|---|---|---|---|
| Li$^+$ | −538 | F$^-$ | −504 |
| Na$^+$ | −424 | Cl$^-$ | −359 |
| K$^+$ | −340 | Br$^-$ | −328 |
| Rb$^+$ | −315 | I$^-$ | −287 |

The values become less exothermic as the groups are descended and the ionic radius increases. The electrostatic attraction between the ions and the water molecule decreases with increasing distance.

The hydration enthalpies of the ions are approximately inversely proportional to the ionic radii:

$$\Delta H_{hyd}^\ominus \approx \frac{-A}{R_{ionic}}$$

where A is a constant. So the smallest ion, Li$^+$, has the most exothermic hydration ion and the largest ion, I$^-$, has the least exothermic value.

Similarly across periods 3: the hydration enthalpies of the metal become more exothermic as the ionic charge increases and the ionic radius decreases. Both changes lead to increased attraction between the positive ion and the partially negatively charged oxygen atoms in the water molecules.

This suggests a relationship of the form:

$$\Delta H_{hyd}^\ominus \approx -Bn / R_{ionic}$$

where n is the charge of the ion and B is a constant. Al$^{3+}$ has the most exothermic hydration enthalpy because it has the highest charge and the smallest radius.

The heat produced when water is added to anhydrous copper(II) sulfate (white) is enough to produce steam and disturb the powder. The hydrated ions can remain in the solid lattice as blue crystals or form a solution if more water is added.

The enthalpy change of hydration of an ion is the enthalpy change that occurs when one mole of gaseous ions is dissolved to form an infinitely dilute solution of one mole of aqueous ions under standard conditions of temperature and pressure.

## CHALLENGE YOURSELF

7 Ag$^+$ has a more exothermic enthalpy of hydration than Na$^+$ but has a larger ionic radius. Suggest an explanation for this.

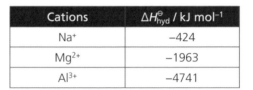

| Cations | $\Delta H^{\ominus}_{hyd}$ / kJ mol$^{-1}$ |
|---------|------------|
| Na$^+$ | −424 |
| Mg$^{2+}$ | −1963 |
| Al$^{3+}$ | −4741 |

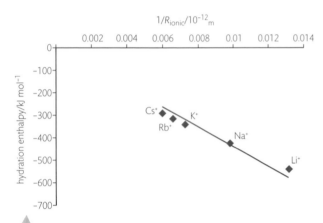

**Figure 5.23** The hydration enthalpies of the Group 1 metal ions plotted against $1/R_{ionic}$. The hydration enthalpies of the ions are approximately inversely proportional to the ionic radii: $\Delta H^{\ominus}_{hyd} \approx -A/R_{ionic}$.

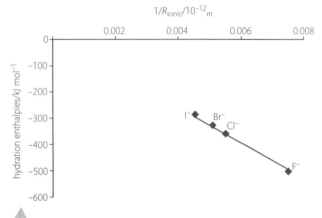

**Figure 5.24** The hydration enthalpies of the halides (Group 17) ions plotted against $1/R_{ionic}$. The hydration enthalpies of the ions are approximately inversely proportional to the ionic radii: $\Delta H^{\ominus}_{hyd} \approx -A/R_{ionic}$.

**Calculation of enthalpy changes in aqueous solution**

Full details of how to carry out this experiment with a worksheet are available online.

# The enthalpy change of solution is related to the lattice enthalpy and the hydration enthalpies of the constituent ions

The solution of a substance can be understood by imagining that the solid is first sublimed into gaseous ions, which are then plunged into water.

$$\Delta H^{\ominus}_{sol}(NaCl) = \Delta H^{\ominus}_{lattice}(NaCl) + \Delta H^{\ominus}_{hyd}(Na^+) + \Delta H^{\ominus}_{hyd}(Cl^-)$$
$$= +790 - 424 - 359 \text{ kJ mol}^{-1}$$
$$= +7 \text{ kJ mol}^{-1}$$

**Figure 5.25** An energy cycle which relates the enthalpy of solution of an ionic compound to its lattice enthalpy and the hydration enthalpies of its constituent ions.

Na$^+$(g) + Cl$^-$(g)

H

$\Delta H^{\ominus}_{lattice}(NaCl) = +790$ kJ mol$^{-1}$

$\Delta H^{\ominus}_{hyd}(Na^+) + \Delta H^{\ominus}_{hyd}$ (Cl$^-$) = −424 − 359 kJ mol$^{-1}$

Na$^+$(aq) + Cl$^-$(aq)

$\Delta H^{\ominus}_{sol}(NaCl) = +7$ kJ mol$^{-1}$

NaCl(s)

The value obtained by the energy cycle should be compared with the value in the data booklet in section 19, which is $\Delta H^{\ominus}_{sol}(NaCl) = +3.88$ kJ mol$^{-1}$. The disagreement between the two values illustrates a general problem when a small numerical value is calculated from the difference of two large numerical values.

## Exercises

**52** Discuss the relative enthalpies of hydration of the $K^+$ and $F^-$ ions in relation to their ionic radii.

**53 (a)** Use an energy cycle to calculate the enthalpy of solution of potassium chloride from data in sections 18 and 20 of the IB data booklet.

**(b)** Calculate the % inaccuracy of your value by comparing with the value in section 19 and comment on the disagreement between the two values.

A UK newspaper, in an attempt to gauge scientific literacy amongst some prominent public figures asked the question: Why does salt dissolve in water?

Here are some of their answers:

**Geologist/ TV presenter**: The chlorine joins with the water and the sodium ions float free.

**Writer/Critic broadcaster**: It must be because it absorbs water to the point at which it disintegrates.

**TV Presenter/Poet**: It forms another compound.

**Cultural historian**: The sodium molecules join up with the hydrogen and oxygen molecules.

**Brain scientist**: Because sodium and chloride disassociate and $H_2O$ is hydrogen and oxygen.

**Political journalist**: Because it's less dense.

**Human fertility expert and science TV presenter**: It's to do with ions isn't it? Do you know, I'm not sure I can really explain it.

**Author, broadcaster**: No idea.

The article argued that despite the importance of science to people's lives most adults have very little understanding of how the world works. An understanding of the nature of science is vital when society needs to make decisions involving scientific findings and issues. Scientists are well placed to explain to the public their issues and findings, but outside their specializations, as some of these responses show, they may be no more qualified than ordinary citizens to advise others on scientific issues.

**CHALLENGE YOURSELF**

**8** So why does salt dissolve in water?

# 15.2 Entropy and spontaneity

## Understandings:

• Entropy ($S$) refers to the distribution of available energy among the particles. The more ways the energy can be distributed the higher the entropy.

• Gibbs free energy ($G$) relates the energy that can be obtained from a chemical reaction to the change in enthalpy ($\Delta H$), change in entropy ($\Delta S$), and absolute temperature.

### Guidance

*$\Delta G$ is a convenient way to take into account both the direct entropy change resulting from the transformation of the chemicals, and the indirect entropy change of the surroundings as a result of the gain/loss of heat energy. Examine various reaction conditions that affect $\Delta G$.*

• Entropy of gas > liquid > solid under same conditions.

## Applications and skills:

• Prediction of whether a change will result in an increase or decrease in entropy by considering the states of the reactants and products.

• Calculation of entropy changes ($\Delta S$) from given values ($S^\ominus$).

• Application of $\Delta G^\ominus = \Delta H^\ominus - T\Delta S^\ominus$ in predicting spontaneity and calculation of various conditions of enthalpy and temperature that will affect this.

### Guidance

*Thermodynamic data are given in section 12 of the data booklet.*

• Relation of $\Delta G$ to position of equilibrium.

## Entropy is a more complete direction of change

If a bottle of a carbonated drink is left open, we expect it to find it 'flat' after a couple of days. The carbon dioxide escapes from solution and diffuses or spreads out into the wider surroundings. We do not expect all the carbon dioxide to return at a later date. In a similar way, a hot cup of coffee will cool down and lose some heat to the surroundings. The heat will not return. Both these examples illustrate a general principle: energy and matter tend to disperse and the universe becomes more disordered. These are both examples of **spontaneous change**; they occur naturally without the need to do work. We can reverse the natural tendency of change but only at the expense of doing work. Similarly, sodium and chlorine have a natural tendency to react together to form sodium chloride. We can reverse this process and split sodium chloride into its constituents, but only at the expense of using valuable electrical energy, as discussed in Chapter 9.

Bubbles rise and escape from a carbonated drink. This illustrates a general principle: matter and energy tend to disperse and become more disordered. Such everyday experiences can be expressed more precisely when the degree of disorder of a system is quantified by its **entropy** (S). Entropy (S) refers to the distribution of available energy among the particles. The more ways the energy can be distributed the higher the entropy. Ordered states, with a small energy distribution are said to have low entropy; disordered states, with a high energy distribution, have high entropy. As time moves forward, matter and energy become more disordered, and the total entropy of the universe increases.

This is an expression of the Second Law of Thermodynamics, which is one of the most important laws in science (Figure 5.26).

> Spontaneous changes occur without the need to do work. A spontaneous reaction occurs without adding energy (beyond that required to overcome the activation energy barrier – see Chapter 6).

> Entropy (*S*) refers to the distribution of available energy among the particles.

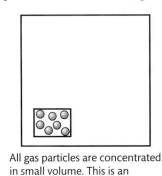

All gas particles are concentrated in small volume. This is an ordered state with low entropy.

Time

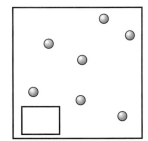

The gas particles are dispersed throughout the room. This is a disordered state with high entropy.

**Figure 5.26** Particles naturally adopt a more disordered state with higher entropy. A mixed up system allows the energy to be distributed in more ways than one in which different particles are separated. This illustrates the Second Law of Thermodynamics: spontaneous processes always occur with an increase of entropy in the universe.

A piece of potassium manganate(VII) was placed at the bottom of the beaker at 12 o'clock. Two hours later it has diffused throughout the water:

$$KMnO_4(s) \rightarrow K^+(aq) + MnO_4^-(aq)$$

The aqueous ions have higher entropy than the solid crystal. Entropy increases with time.

The Second Law of Thermodynamics has been called the most fundamental law in all of science and some, including Albert Einstein, have argued that it is one of the few laws which will never be overthrown. It is important, however, to understand that it is a statement of experience which cannot be proved. It has been shown to apply to all known spontaneous changes. It is not impossible for the disordered arrangement in Figure 5.26 to spontaneously change into the more ordered arrangement, but it is statistically unlikely that the motion of all the particles would be spontaneously coordinated to find them all back in the box at the same instant. This is particularly true given that even a small volume of gas contains a very large number of molecules. The Second Law of Thermodynamics was first formulated to explain how steam engines work, but is now used to explain the big bang, and the expansion of the universe. It is one of the most fundamental scientific laws, and it has been said that 'not knowing the Second Law of Thermodynamics is like never having read a work of Shakespeare'.

To get a better understanding of the statistical nature of the Second Law developed by Ludwig Boltzmann, we need to adopt a statistical approach based on the number of different microscopic arrangements of the same macroscopic state.

Consider the example of an idealized hot cup of coffee with all the stored heat $4Q$ localized in the four cells of the cup. Each cell can only hold a maximum of one unit $Q$ of energy. There is only one microscopic state consistent with this macroscopic state.

TOK Which ways of knowing have been used to construct the Second Law of Thermodynamics? To what extent is certainty attainable within each of the ways of knowing or within each of the areas of knowledge?

**Coffee cup (4 cells)    Surroundings (12 cells)**

| Q | Q | | |
|---|---|---|---|
| Q | Q | | |
| | | | |
| | | | |

◀ **Figure 5.27** The hot cup of coffee is a low entropy state: $W = 1$.

We now allow one unit of heat $Q$ to flow from the cup to the surroundings. We have the possibilities of four different microscopic states with $3Q$ in the cup, as we can have one of any four boxes empty and twelve different microscopic states with unit $Q$ spread around the room, in any of twelve possible cells. The mixed-up state has more possible distributions and so a higher entropy.

**Coffee cup (4 cells)    Surroundings (12 cells)**

| Q | | | |
|---|---|---|---|
| | | | Q |
| Q | Q | | |
| | | | |
| | | | |

◀ **Figure 5.28** A cooler cup of coffee. There are 4 × 12 different states with $3Q$ in the cup $1Q$ in the surroundings. $W = 48$. The entropy has increased.

In this approach:

$$W(\text{total}) = W(\text{surroundings}) \times W(\text{coffee cup})$$

*continued ...*

▲ Ludwig Boltzmann (1844–1906). Boltzmann extended the kinetic theory of gases and used the mechanics and statistics of large numbers of particles to give definitions of heat and entropy. Boltzmann suffered life-long depression and he committed suicide at age 62. Boltzmann's formula is engraved on his tombstone.

**NATURE OF SCIENCE**

*continued ...*

A more convenient approach, adopted by Ludwig Boltzmann, is to use a function ($S$) based on the natural logarithms of W:

$$S = k \ln W \text{ with } k \text{ being a constant}$$

This gives the property:

$$S(\text{total}) = k \ln W(\text{total}) = k \ln W(\text{coffee cup}) \times W(\text{surroundings})$$
$$= k \ln W(\text{coffee cup}) + k \ln W \, W(\text{surroundings})$$
$$S(\text{total}) = S(\text{coffee cup}) + S(\text{surroundings})$$

The function $S$ is consistent with our previous interpretation of entropy, with the Boltzmann constant $k$.

The same diagrams and mathematics can essentially be used to explain why perfume molecules spread around a room. The use of abstract mathematics may make the subject more challenging but it does broaden the scope of scientific understanding.

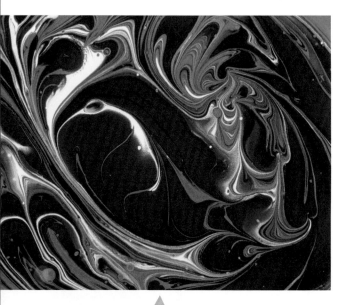

The entropy of the universe increases as the red and blue paints are mixed.

The power of the Second Law of Thermodynamics is that it offers an explanation for all change. For example, a hot cup of coffee naturally cools when left, for essentially the same reason that a gas disperses – the energy disperses so as to lead to the situation with the widest energy distribution. This change results in an increase in entropy of the universe. Another example is seen in the mixing of different colours of paint.

## Predicting entropy changes

As the solid state is the most ordered state and the gaseous state the most disordered, we can predict that the entropy of a system increases as a solid changes to a liquid and as a liquid changes to a gas.

Similarly, doubling the number of particles present in a sample also increases the opportunity for a system to become disordered and for its entropy to increase. More precisely, it can be shown that doubling the amount of a substance doubles the entropy. Similar considerations allow us to predict the entropy changes of the system ($\Delta S$) during any physical or chemical change. Some examples are tabulated below.

| Change | $\Delta S$ |
|---|---|
| solid → liquid | increase (+) |
| solid → gas | increase (+) |
| liquid → gas | increase (+) |
| liquid → solid | decrease (−) |
| gas → solid | decrease (−) |
| gas → liquid | decrease (−) |

When predicting entropy changes, the change due to a change in the number of particles in the gaseous state is usually greater than any other possible factor.

## Worked example

Predict the entropy change $\Delta S$ for the following changes.

(a) $Br_2(l) \rightarrow Br_2(g)$

(b) $2Cu(s) + O_2(g) \rightarrow 2CuO(s)$

(c) $Ag^+(aq) + Br^-(aq) \rightarrow AgBr(s)$

(d) $H_2(g) + Cl_2(g) \rightarrow 2HCl(g)$

(e) $CH_4(g) + 2O_2(g) \rightarrow CO_2(g) + 2H_2O(l)$

(f) $Cu^{2+}(aq) + Zn(s) \rightarrow Cu(s) + Zn^{2+}(aq)$

### Solution

(a) One mole of liquid is changing into one mole of gas. There is an increase in disorder and an increase in entropy. $\Delta S$ is positive.

(b) There is decrease in the number of moles of gas during the reaction. This leads to a reduction in disorder in the products. $\Delta S$ is negative.

(c) There are two moles of aqueous ions on the left-hand side and one mole of solid on the right-hand side. There is a decrease in disorder and there will be a decrease in entropy. $\Delta S$ is negative.

(d) There are two moles of gas in the reactants and in the products. There is no significant change in disorder. The entropy change will be close to zero. $\Delta S \approx 0$.

(e) There are three moles of gas in the reactants and one mole of gas in the products. There is a decrease in disorder and so there will be a decrease in entropy. $\Delta S$ is negative.

(f) One mole of solid and one mole of aqueous ions are changed into one mole of solid and one mole of aqueous ions. The entropy change will be close to zero. $\Delta S \approx 0$.

> **TOK** Entropy is a technical term which has a precise meaning. How important are such technical terms in different areas of knowledge?

## Exercises

**54** Identify the process expected to have a value of $\Delta S$ closest to zero?

    **A** $C_2H_4(g) + H_2(g) \rightarrow C_2H_6(g)$     **C** $CaCO_3(s) \rightarrow CaO(s) + CO_2(g)$

    **B** $H_2(g) + Cl_2(g) \rightarrow 2HCl(g)$     **D** $H_2O(l) \rightarrow H_2O(g)$

**55** Identify the processes which have an associated increase in entropy.

    I   $Br_2(g) \rightarrow Br_2(l)$

    II  $Br_2(g) \rightarrow 2Br(g)$

    III $KBr(s) \rightarrow K^+(aq) + Br^-(aq)$

    **A** I and II     **B** I and III     **C** II and III     **D** I, II, and III

**56** Which is the best description of the entropy and enthalpy changes accompanying the sublimation of iodine: $I_2(s) \rightarrow I_2(g)$?

    **A** $\Delta S$ +, $\Delta H$ +, reaction is endothermic

    **B** $\Delta S$ +, $\Delta H$ –, reaction is exothermic

    **C** $\Delta S$ –, $\Delta H$ +, reaction is endothermic

    **D** $\Delta S$ –, $\Delta H$ –, reaction is exothermic

**57** Identify the reaction which has the largest increase in entropy?

    **A** $AgNO_3(aq) + NaCl(aq) \rightarrow AgCl(s) + NaNO_3(aq)$

    **B** $H_2(g) + Cl_2(g) \rightarrow 2HCl(g)$

    **C** $C_2H_4(g) + H_2(g) \rightarrow C_2H_6(g)$

    **D** $Mg(s) + H_2SO_4(aq) \rightarrow MgSO_4(aq) + H_2(g)$

**58** Predict the entropy change $\Delta S$ for the following reactions.

    (a) $N_2(g) + 3H_2(g) \rightarrow 2NH_3(g)$

    (b) $3Fe(s) + 4H_2O(g) \rightarrow Fe_3O_4(s) + 4H_2(g)$

    (c) $Ba(OH)_2 \cdot 8H_2O(s) + 2NH_4SCN(s) \rightarrow Ba(SCN)_2(aq) + 2NH_3(aq) + 10H_2O(l)$

> **!** Explanations to changes in entropy must refer to changes in state and the number of moles. Change in number of moles of gas is often the key factor.

251

## Absolute entropy

The absolute entropy of different substances can be calculated. As entropy depends on the temperature and pressure, tabulated entropy values refer to standard conditions and are represented as $S^{\ominus}$. Some values are shown in the table below.

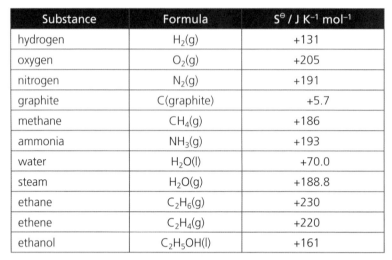

| Substance | Formula | $S^{\ominus}$ / J K$^{-1}$ mol$^{-1}$ |
|---|---|---|
| hydrogen | $H_2(g)$ | +131 |
| oxygen | $O_2(g)$ | +205 |
| nitrogen | $N_2(g)$ | +191 |
| graphite | C(graphite) | +5.7 |
| methane | $CH_4(g)$ | +186 |
| ammonia | $NH_3(g)$ | +193 |
| water | $H_2O(l)$ | +70.0 |
| steam | $H_2O(g)$ | +188.8 |
| ethane | $C_2H_6(g)$ | +230 |
| ethene | $C_2H_4(g)$ | +220 |
| ethanol | $C_2H_5OH(l)$ | +161 |

Section 12 of the IB data booklet has a list of values for organic compounds. The units will be explained later.

As expected, the entropy values increase in the order: solid, liquid, gas. It should be noted that all entropy values are positive. A perfectly ordered solid at absolute zero has an entropy of zero. All other states, which are more disordered, have positive entropy values.

## Calculating entropy changes

The entropy change of the system during a reaction can be calculated from the differences between the total entropy of the products and the total entropy of the reactants.

$$\sum S^{\ominus}(\text{reactants}) \xrightarrow{\Delta S^{\ominus}_{\text{reaction}}} \sum S^{\ominus}(\text{products})$$

$$\Delta S^{\ominus}_{\text{reaction}} = \sum S^{\ominus}(\text{products}) - \sum S^{\ominus}(\text{reactants})$$

The strategy and potential pitfalls of solving problems related to entropy change are similar to those discussed when calculating enthalpy changes.

### Worked example

Calculate the entropy change for the hydrogenation of ethene

$$C_2H_4(g) + H_2(g) \rightarrow C_2H_6(g)$$

using the entropy values given in section 12 in the IB data booklet and the table above.

**Solution**

When asked to calculate an entropy change it is always a good idea to start by predicting the sign of $\Delta S^{\ominus}_{\text{reaction}}$.

$$C_2H_4(g) + H_2(g) \rightarrow C_2H_6(g)$$

Two moles of gas are converted to one mole of gas: there will be a decrease in disorder and a decrease in entropy. So $\Delta S^{\ominus}_{\text{reaction}}$ will be negative.

Write down the equation with the corresponding entropy values below:

$$C_2H_4(g) \quad + \quad H_2(g) \quad \rightarrow \quad C_2H_6(g)$$
$$\quad\ 220 \qquad\qquad 131 \qquad\qquad 230 \qquad\qquad\qquad S^{\ominus}/J\,K^{-1}\,mol^{-1}$$

$$\Delta S^{\ominus}_{\text{reaction}} = \Sigma S^{\ominus}(\text{products}) - \Sigma S^{\ominus}(\text{reactants})$$

$$= 230 - (220 + 131) = -121\ J\,K^{-1}\,mol^{-1}$$

## Exercises

**59** Sketch a graph to show how the entropy of a solid changes as the temperature increases.

**60** Calculate the entropy change $\Delta S$ for the Haber process, shown below, using tabulated standard molar entropies at 25 °C.

$$N_2(g) + 3H_2(g) \rightarrow 2NH_3(g)$$

**61** Calculate the standard entropy change associated with the formation of methane from its elements.

## Spontaneity

This discussion of the direction of change based on entropy changes is incomplete. Earlier in the chapter, we suggested that enthalpy changes could be used as an indicator of the direction of change; but this left endothermic reactions unexplained. Similarly, we have also discussed the need for the entropy to increase during spontaneous changes, but we have seen that many reactions occur with a decrease of entropy. This section resolves these issues.

## Entropy changes of the surroundings

So far, our discussion of entropy has focussed on the entropy of the substances present in the system. To consider the total entropy change of a reaction, we must also consider the accompanying entropy change in the surroundings.

Consider again the reaction between zinc and copper sulfate, discussed earlier.

$$Cu^{2+}(aq) + Zn(s) \rightarrow Cu(s) + Zn^{2+}(aq) \qquad \Delta H^{\ominus}_{\text{reaction}} = -217\ kJ\,mol^{-1},\ \Delta S^{\ominus}_{\text{reaction}} \approx 0$$

How does this reaction increase the total entropy of the universe?

The key to answering this question is an appreciation that adding heat to the surroundings results in a general dispersal of heat into the surrounding universe. The reaction can be compared to the cooling of a hot cup of coffee discussed earlier. Both result in an increase in total entropy as heat is dispersed.

The change of the entropy of the surroundings, $\Delta S$(surroundings), can be calculated from the enthalpy change in the system, $\Delta H$(system), and the absolute temperature, $T$.

**Figure 5.29** Both an exothermic reaction and a cooling coffee cup increase the entropy of the universe.
▼

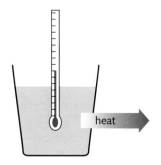

The entropy of the surroundings increases as the heat given out by the reaction increases the disorder of the surroundings.

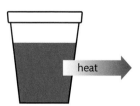

The entropy of the surroundings increases as the heat given out by the hot coffee increases the disorder of the surroundings.

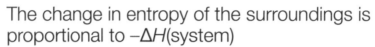

## The change in entropy of the surroundings is proportional to −Δ*H*(system)

We have seen that exothermic reactions, with a negative value for Δ*H*(system) result in an increase in the entropy of the surroundings. This explains the inclusion of the negative sign when relating Δ*H*(system) to Δ*S*(surroundings).

$$\Delta S(\text{surroundings}) \propto -\Delta H(\text{system})$$

We are now in a position to understand why exothermic reactions are generally more common than endothermic reactions. The key is not the decrease in energy of the system but the associated increase in entropy of the surroundings.

## The change in entropy is inversely proportional to the absolute temperature

To understand the relationship between the enthalpy change of reaction and the entropy change of the surroundings, it is helpful to recognize that the impact of a transfer of heat to the surroundings depends on the current state of disorder in the surroundings. If the surroundings are hot, the addition of a little extra heat makes little difference to the disorder. But if the surroundings are cold, the same amount of heat could cause a dramatic change in entropy. This explains the inclusion of absolute temperature, *T*, in the denominator in the expression:

$$\Delta S(\text{surroundings}) \propto 1/T$$

The impact of an addition of heat depends on the present state of disorder, as indicated by the absolute temperature.

A busy street is a 'hot' and disordered environment; a quiet library is a 'cold' and ordered environment. Which do you think would cause more disruption: sneezing in a busy street or in a quiet library?

## Δ*S*(surroundings) and an explanation of the units of entropy

An expression consistent with the above discussion is

$$\Delta S(\text{surroundings}) = \frac{-\Delta H(\text{system})}{T} \quad (T \text{ must be measured in K})$$

For the displacement reaction discussed, at *T* = 25 °C = 298 K

$$\Delta S(\text{surroundings}) = -\frac{-217 \text{ kJ mol}^{-1}}{298 \text{ K}} = +0.729 \text{ kJ K}^{-1} \text{ mol}^{-1} = 729 \text{ J K}^{-1} \text{ mol}^{-1}$$

We can now see the origins of the units used for entropy in the values tabulated earlier.

Entropies are generally expressed in the units $J K^{-1} mol^{-1}$.

These are consistent with its characterization as a distribution of available energy.

## Calculating total entropy changes and understanding endothermic reactions

The Second Law of Thermodynamics tells us that for a spontaneous change:

$$\Delta S(\text{total}) = \Delta S(\text{system}) + \Delta S(\text{surroundings}) > 0$$

Substitute for $\Delta S(\text{surroundings})$ from the expression developed earlier:

$$\Delta S(\text{total}) = \Delta S(\text{system}) - \frac{\Delta H(\text{system})}{T} > 0$$

This equation allows us to understand how endothermic reactions can occur. Endothermic reactions occur if the change of entropy of the system can compensate for the negative entropy change of the surroundings produced as the heat flows from the surroundings to the system. For example, the strongly endothermic reaction

$$Ba(OH)_2 \cdot 8H_2O(s) + 2NH_4SCN(s) \rightarrow Ba(SCN)_2(aq) + 2NH_3(aq) + 10H_2O(l)$$

is possible as there is a very large increase in disorder and entropy of the system. Three moles of solid are converted to ten moles of liquid and three moles of compounds in aqueous solution.

This emphasizes a general point. We must consider the universe (i.e. both the system and the surroundings) when applying the Second Law of Thermodynamics. Order may increase in local areas but only at the expense of greater disorder elsewhere in the universe. For chemical reactions, neither $\Delta H(\text{system})$ nor $\Delta S(\text{system})$ alone can reliably be used to predict the feasibility of a reaction.

> If a system were at absolute zero, an additional small amount of heat energy would lead to an infinite increase in entropy. Such a state is impossible. Absolute zero can never be achieved.

> Such local manifestations of order as the development of life, and the construction of beautiful buildings, are only possible at the expense of greater disorder generated elsewhere in the universe.

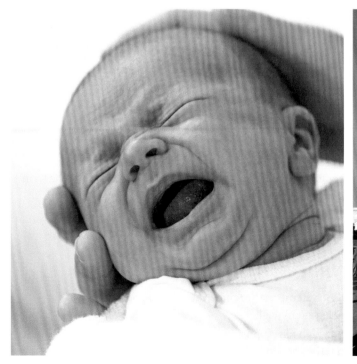

Photosynthesis is a remarkable reaction. There is a decrease in entropy of the system as the particles adopt more ordered structures and the reaction is endothermic as the system absorbs energy:

$$6CO_2(g) + 6H_2O(l) \rightarrow C_6H_{12}O_6(g) + 6H_2O(l)$$

This does not break the Second Law of Thermodynamics as the increase in entropy of the Sun more than compensates for the local decrease in entropy in a green leaf.

## Gibbs free energy is a useful accounting tool

We have seen that for chemical reactions neither $\Delta H$(system) nor $\Delta S$(system) alone can reliably be used to predict the feasibility of a reaction. The ultimate criterion for the feasibility of a reaction is:

$$\Delta S(\text{total}) = \Delta S(\text{system}) - \frac{\Delta H(\text{system})}{T} > 0$$

This expression can be tidied up. Multiplying by $T$ (as they are always positive)

$$T\Delta S(\text{total}) = T\Delta S(\text{system}) - \Delta H(\text{system}) > 0$$

Multiplying by $-1$ and reversing the inequality:

$$-T\Delta S(\text{total}) = -T\Delta S(\text{system}) + \Delta H(\text{system}) < 0$$

**$\Delta G$(system) must be negative for a spontaneous process.**

This combination of entropy and enthalpy of a system gives a new function known as the **Gibbs free energy** ($\Delta G$(system)):

$$\Delta G(\text{system}) = \Delta H(\text{system}) - T\Delta S(\text{system}) < 0$$

That is, $\Delta G$(system) must be negative for a spontaneous process.

Whereas $\Delta H$(system) is a measure of the *quantity* of heat change during a chemical reaction, $\Delta G$(system) gives a measure of the *quality* of the energy available. It is a measure of the energy which is free to do useful work rather than just leave a system as heat. Spontaneous reactions have negative free energy changes because they can do useful work. Josiah Willard Gibbs (1839–1903) was the first to develop this concept.

## Using $\Delta G$(system) to predict the feasibility of a change

We can use the expression $\Delta G$(system) to predict how a system changes as the temperature is changed. We generally assume that both the enthalpy and entropy changes of the system do not change with temperature.

Using the expression:

$$\Delta G(\text{system}) = \Delta H(\text{system}) - T\Delta S(\text{system}) < 0$$

we can think of the temperature, $T$, as a tap which adjusts the significance of the term $\Delta S$(system) in determining the value of $\Delta G$(system).

• At low temperature:
    $\Delta G$(system) $\approx \Delta H$(system), as $T\Delta S$(system) $\approx 0$
  That is, all exothermic reactions can occur at low temperatures.
• At high temperature:
    $\Delta G$(system) $\approx -T\Delta S$(system), as the temperature is sufficiently high to make the term $\Delta H$(system) negligible.
This means all reactions which have a positive value of $\Delta S$(system) can be feasible at high temperatures even if they are endothermic.

## Worked example

(a) Give an equation for the boiling of water.

(b) Predict a sign for the enthalpy change and entropy change for this process.

(c) Predict a value for the sign of $\Delta G$ at low and high temperatures.

(d) Suggest why water boils at 100 °C.

(e) Use the entropy values in the table on page 252 to calculate the entropy change for this process.

(f) Use the data below to calculate the enthalpy change for the process.

|  | $\Delta H_f^{\ominus}$/ kJ mol$^{-1}$ |
| --- | --- |
| $H_2O(l)$ | −286 |
| $H_2O(g)$ | −242 |

(g) Deduce the boiling point of water from your calculations. Describe any assumptions you have made.

## Solution

(a)
$$H_2O(l) \rightarrow H_2O(g)$$

(b) As there is an increase in moles of gas, $\Delta S$(system) is positive. The process involves the breaking of intermolecular (hydrogen) bonds so $\Delta H$(system) is positive.

(c) At low temperature: $\Delta G$(system) $\approx \Delta H$(system) and so is positive.
At high temperature: $\Delta G$(system) $\approx -T\Delta S$(system) and so is negative.

(d) The change only occurs at higher temperatures where $\Delta G$ is negative.
$$\Delta G = 0 \text{ at } 100 \text{ °C}$$

(e)
$$H_2O(l) \quad \rightarrow \quad H_2O(g)$$
$$+70.0 \qquad\qquad +188.8$$

$$\Delta S^{\ominus}/ \text{J K}^{-1} \text{mol}^{-1}$$

$$\Delta S^{\ominus}_{reaction} = \Sigma S^{\ominus}(\text{products}) - \Sigma S^{\ominus}(\text{reactants})$$

$$= +188.8 - (70) = +118.8 \text{ J K}^{-1} \text{mol}^{-1}$$

(f)
$$\Delta H^{\ominus}_{reaction} = \Sigma \Delta H^{\ominus}(\text{products}) - \Sigma \Delta H^{\ominus}(\text{reactants})$$
$$= -242 - (-286) = +44 \text{ kJ mol}^{-1}$$

(g) At the boiling point: $\Delta G$(system) = $\Delta H$(system) $-T\Delta S$(system) = 0

$$T = \frac{\Delta H(\text{system})}{\Delta S(\text{system})}$$

$$T = \frac{44 \text{ kJ mol}^{-1}}{118.8 \times 10^{-3} \text{ kJ K}^{-1} \text{mol}^{-1}} = 370 \text{ K}$$

It is assumed that $\Delta H$(system) and $\Delta S$(system) do not change with temperature.

## Exercises

**62** Ammonium chloride dissolves in water spontaneously in an endothermic process. Identify the best explanation for these observations.

   **A**   Endothermic processes are energetically favourable.

   **B**   The bonds in solid $NH_4Cl$ are very weak.

   **C**   The entropy change of the system drives the process.

   **D**   The entropy change of the surroundings drives the process

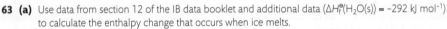

**63 (a)** Use data from section 12 of the IB data booklet and additional data $(\Delta H_f^\ominus(H_2O(s)) = -292 \text{ kJ mol}^{-1})$ to calculate the enthalpy change that occurs when ice melts.

**(b)** The entropy change when ice melts is 22.0 J K$^{-1}$ mol$^{-1}$. Deduce a value for the melting point of ice.

**64** Identify the combination of $\Delta H$ and $\Delta S$ which results in a reaction being spontaneous at low temperatures but non-spontaneous at higher temperatures?

**A** $\Delta S$ – and $\Delta H$ –     **B** $\Delta S$ + and $\Delta H$ –     **C** $\Delta S$ – and $\Delta H$ +     **D** $\Delta S$ + and $\Delta H$ +

**65** Identify the combination of $\Delta H$ and $\Delta S$ which leads to a reaction that is **not** spontaneous at low temperatures but becomes spontaneous at higher temperatures?

**A** $\Delta H$ – and $\Delta S$ –     **B** $\Delta H$ – and $\Delta S$ +     **C** $\Delta H$ + and $\Delta S$ –     **D** $\Delta H$ + and $\Delta S$ +

**66** The $\Delta H$ and $\Delta S$ values for the combustion of hydrogen are both negative. Which is the correct description of this reaction at different temperatures?

|   | Low temperature | High temperature |
|---|---|---|
| **A** | not spontaneous | not spontaneous |
| **B** | spontaneous | not spontaneous |
| **C** | spontaneous | spontaneous |
| **D** | not spontaneous | spontaneous |

**67** The decomposition of limestone can be represented by the equation:

$$CaCO_3(s) \rightarrow CaO(s) + CO_2(g)$$

**(a)** Predict a sign for the enthalpy change of the reaction.
**(b)** Predict a sign for the entropy change of the reaction.
**(c)** Deduce how the stability of limestone changes with temperature.

## The effect of $\Delta H^\ominus$, $\Delta S^\ominus$, and $T$ on the spontaneity of reaction

The effect of temperature on the spontaneous reactions for different reactions is summarized in the table below.

| $\Delta H^\ominus$ | $\Delta S^\ominus$ | $T$ | $\Delta G$ | Spontaneity |
|---|---|---|---|---|
| positive (endothermic) | positive (more disordered products) | low | positive $\approx \Delta H^\ominus$ | not spontaneous |
| positive (endothermic) | positive (more disordered products) | high | negative $\approx -T\Delta S^\ominus$ | spontaneous |
| positive (endothermic) | negative (more ordered products) | low | positive $\approx \Delta H^\ominus$ | not spontaneous |
| positive (endothermic) | negative (more ordered products) | high | positive $\approx -T\Delta S^\ominus$ | not spontaneous |
| negative (exothermic) | positive (more disordered products) | low | negative $\approx \Delta H^\ominus$ | spontaneous |
| negative (exothermic) | positive (more disordered products) | high | negative $\approx -T\Delta S^\ominus$ | spontaneous |
| negative (exothermic) | negative (more ordered products) | low | negative $\approx -T\Delta S^\ominus$ | spontaneous |
| negative (exothermic) | negative (more ordered products) | high | positive $\approx -T\Delta S^\ominus$ | not spontaneous |

Work through all the different set of conditions to make sure that you agree with the results of this table. Do not memorize it!

## Calculating $\Delta G$ values

There are two routes to calculating changes in Gibbs free energy during a reaction. $\Delta G$ (at 298 K) can be calculated from tabulated values of $\Delta G_f^\ominus$ in the same way enthalpy changes are calculated. $\Delta G$ values are, however, very sensitive to changes to temperature, and $\Delta G$ values calculated using this method are not applicable when the temperature is changed. Changes in free energy at other temperatures can be obtained by applying the equation:

$$\Delta G(\text{system}) = \Delta H(\text{system}) - T\Delta S(\text{system})$$

## Calculating $\Delta G_{\text{reaction}}$ from $\Delta G_f^{\ominus}$

$\Delta G_{\text{reaction}}$ for reactions at 298 K can be calculated from $\Delta G_f^{\ominus}$ values in the same way $\Delta H_{\text{reaction}}$ can be calculated from $\Delta H_f^{\ominus}$ values (Figure 5.30).

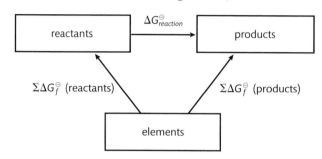

$$\Delta G_{\text{reaction}} = \Sigma\Delta G_f^{\ominus}(\text{products}) - \Sigma\Delta G_f^{\ominus}(\text{reactants})$$

Values of $\Delta G$ can only give information about the feasibility of a reaction. They give no information about the reaction's rate. Some spontaneous reactions need to be heated to occur. The reactants need energy to overcome the activation energy barrier. This is discussed further in Chapter 6.

**Figure 5.30** A Gibbs free energy cycle.

### Worked example

Calculate $\Delta G_{\text{reaction}}$ for the reaction

$$2Al(s) + Fe_2O_3(s) \rightarrow 2Fe(s) + Al_2O_3(s)$$

from the following data.

| Compound | $\Delta G_f^{\ominus}$/kJ mol$^{-1}$ |
|----------|------------------|
| $Fe_2O_3(s)$ | −742 |
| $Al_2O_3(s)$ | −1582 |

Comment on the significance of the value obtained.

### Solution

First, write the chemical equation with the values below:

$$2Al(s) \quad + \quad Fe_2O_3(s) \quad \rightarrow \quad 2Fe(s) \quad + \quad Al_2O_3(s)$$
$$2 \times 0 \qquad\quad -742 \qquad\qquad\quad 2 \times 0 \qquad\quad -1582 \qquad\qquad \Delta G_f^{\ominus}/ \text{ kJ mol}^{-1}$$

Note: $\Delta G_f^{\ominus}(\text{element})$ is zero by definition just as it is for $\Delta H_f^{\ominus}(\text{element})$.

$$\Delta G_{\text{reaction}} = \Sigma\Delta G_f^{\ominus}(\text{products}) - \Sigma\Delta G_f^{\ominus}(\text{reactants})$$
$$= -1582 - -742 \text{ kJ mol}^{-1}$$
$$= -840 \text{ kJ mol}^{-1}$$

The reaction is spontaneous under standard conditions.

### Exercises

**68** The enthalpy and entropy changes for the reaction

$$A(s) + B(aq) \rightarrow C(aq) + D(g)$$

are $\Delta H^{\ominus} = 100$ kJ mol$^{-1}$ and $\Delta S^{\ominus} = 100$ J K$^{-1}$ mol$^{-1}$

  **A**  The reaction is not spontaneous at any temperature.
  **B**  The reaction is spontaneous at all temperatures.
  **C**  The reaction is spontaneous at all temperatures below 1000 °C.
  **D**  The reaction is spontaneous at all temperatures above 1000 K.

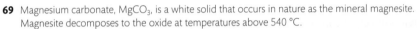

**69** Magnesium carbonate, $MgCO_3$, is a white solid that occurs in nature as the mineral magnesite. Magnesite decomposes to the oxide at temperatures above 540 °C.

$$MgCO_3(s) \rightarrow MgO(s) + CO_2(g)$$

Identify the correct description of this reaction at 800 °C.

|   | $\Delta G$ | $\Delta H$ | $\Delta S$ |
|---|---|---|---|
| **A** | + | + | + |
| **B** | + | − | − |
| **C** | − | + | + |
| **D** | − | + | − |

**70** Calculate $\Delta G_{reaction}$ for the thermal decomposition of calcium carbonate

$$CaCO_3(s) \rightarrow CaO(s) + CO_2(g)$$

from the following data, and comment on the significance of the value obtained.

| Compound | $\Delta G_f^{\ominus}$ / kJ mol$^{-1}$ |
|---|---|
| $CaCO_3(s)$ | −1129 |
| $CaO(s)$ | −604 |
| $CO_2(g)$ | −394 |

## Using $\Delta S_{reaction}^{\ominus}$ and $\Delta H_{reaction}^{\ominus}$ values to calculate $\Delta G_{reaction}^{\ominus}$ at all temperatures

As the standard values of $\Delta G_f^{\ominus}$ refer to standard conditions, they can only be used to calculate $\Delta G_{reaction}^{\ominus}$ at 298 K.

When the system is the reaction we have:

$$\Delta G_{reaction} = \Delta H_{reaction} - T\Delta S_{reaction}$$

Here $\Delta G_{reaction}$ can now be calculated at any temperature with $\Delta H_{reaction} = \Delta H_{reaction}^{\ominus}$ and $\Delta S_{reaction} = \Delta S_{reaction}^{\ominus}$ effectively constant.

$$\Delta G_{reaction} = \Delta H_{reaction}^{\ominus} - T\Delta S_{reaction}^{\ominus}$$

### Worked example

Calculate $\Delta G_{reaction}$ at 298 K for the thermal decomposition of calcium carbonate from the following data.

| Compound | $\Delta H_f^{\ominus}$/ kJ mol$^{-1}$ | $S^{\ominus}$/ J K$^{-1}$ mol$^{-1}$ |
|---|---|---|
| $CaCO_3(s)$ | −1207 | +92.9 |
| $CaO(s)$ | −635 | +39.7 |
| $CO_2(g)$ | −394 | +214 |

### Solution

First calculate $\Delta H_{reaction}$. Write the chemical equation with the $\Delta H_f^{\ominus}$ values in the appropriate places.

$$CaCO_3(s) \quad \rightarrow \quad CaO(s) \quad + \quad CO_2(g)$$
$$-1207 \qquad\qquad -635 \qquad\quad -394 \qquad\qquad\qquad \Delta H_f^{\ominus}/ \text{kJ mol}^{-1}$$

Using the equation

$$\Delta H^{\ominus}_{reaction} = \Sigma \Delta H^{\ominus}_f(products) - \Sigma \Delta H^{\ominus}_f(reactants)$$

$$= (-635 + -394) - (-1207) \text{ kJ mol}^{-1}$$

$$= +178 \text{ kJ mol}^{-1}$$

Now calculate the standard entropy change of reaction. As always predict whether the value is positive or negative.

One mole of solid is converted to one mole of solid and one mole of gas. There is an increase in disorder and an increase in entropy. $\Delta S^{\ominus}_{reaction}$ is positive.

And now do the calculation:

$$CaCO_3(s) \rightarrow CaO(s) + CO_2(g) \qquad \Delta S^{\ominus} / \text{J K}^{-1} \text{ mol}^{-1}$$
$$+92.9 \qquad\quad +39.7 \qquad +214$$

Using the equation:

$$\Delta S^{\ominus}_{reaction} = \Sigma S^{\ominus}(products) - \Sigma S^{\ominus}(reactants)$$

$$= (39.7 + 214) - (+92.9) \text{ J K}^{-1} \text{ mol}^{-1}$$

$$= +160.8 \text{ J K}^{-1} \text{ mol}^{-1}$$

Now calculate the change in Gibbs free energy of the reaction.

$$\Delta G_{reaction} = \Delta H^{\ominus}_{reaction} - T\Delta H^{\ominus}_{reaction}$$

$$= +178 - (298 \times 160.8 \times 10^{-3}) \text{ kJ mol}^{-1}$$

$$= +130 \text{ kJ mol}^{-1}$$

Note as the temperature is 298 K this value agrees with that calculated in the previous exercise using free energy of formation data.

> ⚠ Don't forget to convert so as to use consistent units for $\Delta H^{\ominus}_{reaction}$ and $\Delta S^{\ominus}_{reaction}$ when calculating $\Delta G_{reaction}$. Temperatures in all free energy calculations must be in kelvin. Note also the use of J and kJ.

## Exercises

**71** Calculate $\Delta G_{reaction}$ at 2000 K for the thermal decomposition of calcium carbonate from the data given in the worked example.

**72** Which property of an element has a value of zero in its standard state?

   I     $\Delta H^{\ominus}_f$
   II   $S^{\ominus}$
   III  $\Delta G^{\ominus}_f$

  **A**  I and II       **B**  I and III       **C**  II and III       **D**  I, II, and III

**73** The standard enthalpy change for the formation of ethanol, $C_2H_5OH(l)$, and its molar entropy are given in section 12 of the IB data booklet.

  **(a)** Write an equation for the formation of ethanol.
  **(b)** Calculate the entropy change for this process. The entropies of its constituent elements are:
     $C(graphite) = 5.7 \text{ J K}^{-1} \text{ mol}^{-1}$
     $H_2(g) = 65.3 \text{ J K}^{-1} \text{ mol}^{-1}$
     $O_2(g) = 102.5 \text{ J K}^{-1} \text{ mol}^{-1}$
  **(c)** Calculate the standard free energy change of formation of ethanol at 500 K.
  **(d)** Deduce whether the reaction is spontaneous at 500 K, and give a reason.
  **(e)** Predict the effect, if any, of an increase in temperature on the spontaneity of this reaction.

## Gibbs free energy and equilibrium

So far we have considered reactions in which it is assumed that all the reactants are converted into products. Many reactions do not go to completion but instead reach equilibrium, as will be discussed in Chapter 7. The extent of reaction can be quantified by the ratio of the concentrations: [products]/[reactants]. The boundary between partial and complete reaction is of course not clearly defined, but as $\Delta G°_{reaction}$ becomes more negative, the reaction favours products. When $\Delta G°_{reaction}$ is below $-30$ kJ mol$^{-1}$ the reaction can considered as complete.

For values of $\Delta G°_{reaction}$ between $-30$ and $0$ kJ mol$^{-1}$ there will be an equilibrium mixture with products predominating.

The table below summarizes the relationship between $\Delta G°_{reaction}$ and the extent of reaction.

| $\Delta G^{\ominus}_{reaction}$ | Extent of reaction |
|---|---|
| $\Delta G^{\ominus}_{reaction} > +30$ kJ mol$^{-1}$ | spontaneous change impossible : no reaction $\dfrac{[products]}{[reactants]} \ll 1$ |
| $0$ kJ mol$^{-1} < \Delta G^{\ominus}_{reaction} < +30$ kJ mol$^{-1}$ | partial reaction producing equilibrium mixture $\dfrac{[products]}{[reactants]} < 1$ |
| $\Delta G^{\ominus}_{reaction} = 0$ kJ mol$^{-1}$ | partial reaction producing equilibrium mixture $\dfrac{[products]}{[reactants]} = 1$ |
| $0$ kJ mol$^{-1} > \Delta G^{\ominus}_{reaction} > -30$ kJ mol$^{-1}$ | partial reaction producing equilibrium mixture $\dfrac{[products]}{[reactants]} > 1$ |
| $\Delta G^{\ominus}_{reaction} < -30$ kJ mol$^{-1}$ | complete reaction $\dfrac{[products]}{[reactants]} \gg 1$ |

The relationships between free energy, entropy and equilibrium are discussed more fullly in Chapter 7, page 335.

### CHALLENGE YOURSELF

9 For the reaction A → B, $K_c = \dfrac{[products]}{[reactants]} = \dfrac{[B]}{[A]}$

Find a mathematical function of $K_c$ which gives values of $\Delta G^{\ominus}_{reaction}$ consistent with the table.

**74** What signs of $\Delta H^{\ominus}_{reaction}$ and $\Delta S^{\ominus}_{reaction}$ for a reaction result in a complete reaction at all temperatures?

| | $\Delta H^{\ominus}_{reaction}$ | $\Delta S^{\ominus}_{reaction}$ |
|---|---|---|
| **A** | − | − |
| **B** | + | − |
| **C** | − | + |
| **D** | + | + |

**75** Which conditions correspond to a system of equilibrium?

I   The entropy of the system is at a maximum.
II  The free energy of a system is at a minimum.
III $\Delta G^{\ominus}_{reaction} = 0$

**A** I and II only      **B** I and III only      **C** II and III only      **D** I, II, and III

**76** Which values correspond to a reaction that can be reversed by changing the temperature.

| | $\Delta H^{\ominus}_{reaction}$ | $\Delta S^{\ominus}_{reaction}$ |
|---|---|---|
| I | − | − |
| II | + | − |
| III | + | + |

**A** I and II only      **B** I and III only      **C** II and III only      **D** I, II, and III

**77** Propene reacts with hydrogen in the presence of a nickel catalyst to form propane.

$$C_3H_6(g) + H_2(g) \rightarrow C_3H_8(g)$$

$\Delta H^{\ominus}_{reaction} = -123 \text{ kJ mol}^{-1}$; $\Delta S^{\ominus}_{reaction} = -128 \text{ J K mol}^{-1}$

Estimate the temperature range in which a mixture of all three gases will be present.

**78** The Haber process is an important process in which ammonia is formed from nitrogen and hydrogen:

$$N_2(g) + 3H_2(g) \rightarrow 2NH_3(g)$$

$\Delta S^{\ominus}_{reaction} = -198 \text{ J K}^{-1} \text{ mol}^{-1}$; $\Delta H^{\ominus}_{reaction} = -93 \text{ J K}^{-1} \text{ mol}^{-1}$

Estimate the temperature range in which a mixture of all three gases will be present.

## Practice questions

**1** A pure aluminium block with a mass of 10 g is heated so that its temperature increases from 20 °C to 50 °C. The specific heat capacity of aluminium is $8.99 \times 10^{-1} \text{ J g}^{-1} \text{ K}^{-1}$. Which expression gives the heat energy change in kJ?

**A** $10 \times 8.99 \times 10^{-1} \times 303$

**B** $10 \times 8.99 \times 10^{-1} \times 30$

**C** $\dfrac{10 \times 8.99 \times 10^{-1} \times 303}{1000}$

**D** $\dfrac{10 \times 8.99 \times 10^{-1} \times 30}{1000}$

**2** Which processes have a negative enthalpy change?

I   $2CH_3OH(l) + 3O_2(g) \rightarrow 2CO_2(g) + 4H_2O(l)$

II  $HCl(aq) + NaOH(aq) \rightarrow NaCl(aq) + H_2O(l)$

III $H_2O(g) \rightarrow H_2O(l)$

**A** I and II only      **B** I and III only      **C** II and III only      **D** I, II, and III

**3** Identical pieces of magnesium are added to two beakers, A and B, containing hydrochloric acid. Both acids have the same initial temperature but their volumes and concentrations differ.

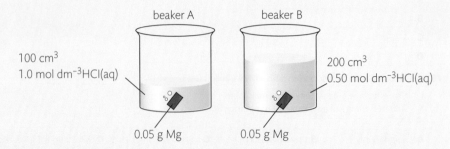

beaker A

beaker B

100 cm³
1.0 mol dm⁻³HCl(aq)

200 cm³
0.50 mol dm⁻³HCl(aq)

0.05 g Mg

0.05 g Mg

Which statement is correct?

**A** The maximum temperature in A will be higher than in B.

**B** The maximum temperature in A and B will be equal.

**C** It is not possible to predict whether A or B will have the higher maximum temperature.

**D** The temperature in A and B will increase at the same rate.

**4** Consider the following reactions.

$$Cu_2O(s) + \tfrac{1}{2}O_2(g) \rightarrow 2CuO(s) \qquad\qquad \Delta H^{\ominus} = -144 \text{ kJ}$$

$$Cu_2O(s) \rightarrow Cu(s) + CuO(s) \qquad\qquad \Delta H^{\ominus} = +11 \text{ kJ}$$

What is the value of $\Delta H^{\ominus}$, in kJ, for this reaction?

$$Cu(s) + \tfrac{1}{2}O_2(g) \rightarrow CuO(s)$$

**A** $-144 + 11$   **B** $+144 - 11$   **C** $-144 - 11$   **D** $+144 + 11$

**5** Which equation best represents the bond enthalpy of HCl?

**A** $HCl(g) \rightarrow H^+(g) + Cl^-(g)$

**B** $HCl(g) \rightarrow H(g) + Cl(g)$

**C** $HCl(g) \rightarrow \tfrac{1}{2}H_2(g) + \tfrac{1}{2}Cl_2(g)$

**D** $2HCl(g) \rightarrow H_2(g) + Cl_2(g)$

**6** Consider the equations below.

$$CH_4(g) + O_2(g) \rightarrow HCHO(l) + H_2O(l) \qquad\qquad \Delta H^{\ominus} = x$$

$$HCHO(l) + \tfrac{1}{2}O_2(g) \rightarrow HCOOH(l) \qquad\qquad \Delta H^{\ominus} = y$$

$$2HCOOH(l) + \tfrac{1}{2}O_2(g) \rightarrow (COOH)_2(s) + H_2O(l) \qquad\qquad \Delta H^{\ominus} = z$$

What is the enthalpy change of the reaction below?

$$2CH_4(g) + 3\tfrac{1}{2}O_2(g) \rightarrow (COOH)_2(s) + 3H_2O(l)$$

**A** $x + y + z$   **B** $2x + y + z$   **C** $2x + 2y + z$   **D** $2x + 2y + 2z$

**7** Which process represents the C–Cl bond enthalpy in tetrachloromethane?

**A** $CCl_4(g) \rightarrow C(g) + 4Cl(g)$

**B** $CCl_4(g) \rightarrow CCl_3(g) + Cl(g)$

**C** $CCl_4(l) \rightarrow C(g) + 4Cl(g)$

**D** $CCl_4(l) \rightarrow C(s) + 2Cl_2(g)$

**8** What is the energy, in kJ, released when 1.00 mol of carbon monoxide is burned according to the following equation?

$$2CO(g) + O_2(g) \rightarrow 2CO_2(g) \qquad\qquad \Delta H^{\ominus} = -564 \text{ kJ}$$

**A** 141   **B** 282   **C** 564   **D** 1128

**9** Methanol is made in large quantities as it is used in the production of polymers and in fuels. The enthalpy of combustion of methanol can be determined theoretically or experimentally.

$$CH_3OH(l) + 1\frac{1}{2}O_2(g) \rightarrow CO_2(g) + 2H_2O(g)$$

**(a)** Using the information from section 11 of the IB data booklet, determine the theoretical enthalpy of combustion of methanol. (3)

**(b)** The enthalpy of combustion of methanol can also be determined experimentally in a school laboratory. A burner containing methanol was weighed and used to heat water in a test tube, as illustrated below.

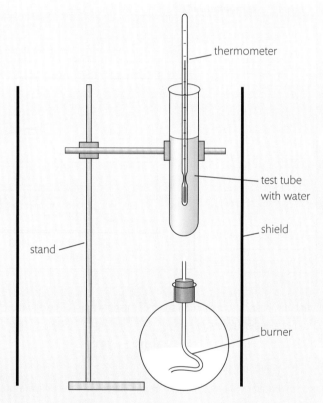

The following data were collected.

| Initial mass of burner and methanol / g | 80.557 |
|---|---|
| Final mass of burner and methanol / g | 80.034 |
| Mass of water in test tube / g | 20.000 |
| Initial temperature of water / °C | 21.5 |
| Final temperature of water / °C | 26.4 |

**(i)** Calculate the amount, in mol, of methanol burned. (2)

**(ii)** Calculate the heat absorbed, in kJ, by the water. (3)

**(iii)** Determine the enthalpy change, in kJ mol$^{-1}$, for the combustion of 1 mole of methanol. (2)

**(c)** The data booklet value for the enthalpy of combustion of methanol is −726 kJ mol$^{-1}$. Suggest why this value differs from the values calculated in parts (a) and (b).

**(i)** Part (a) (1)

**(ii)** Part (b) (1)

*(Total 12 marks)*

**10** The data below are from an experiment to measure the enthalpy change for the reaction of aqueous copper(II) sulfate, $CuSO_4(aq)$, and zinc, $Zn(s)$.

$$Cu^{2+}(aq) + Zn(s) \rightarrow Cu(s) + Zn^{2+}(aq)$$

$50.0$ cm$^3$ of $1.00$ mol dm$^{-3}$ copper(II) sulfate solution was placed in a polystyrene cup and zinc powder was added after 100 seconds. The temperature–time data were taken from a data-logging software program. The table shows the initial 23 readings.

| | A | B | C | D | E | F | G | H |
|---|---|---|---|---|---|---|---|---|
| 1 | time/s | temperature/°C | | | | | | |
| 2 | 0.0 | 24.8 | | | | | | |
| 3 | 1.0 | 24.8 | | | | | | |
| 4 | 2.0 | 24.8 | | | | | | |
| 5 | 3.0 | 24.8 | | | | | | |
| 6 | 4.0 | 24.8 | | | | | | |
| 7 | 5.0 | 24.8 | | | | | | |
| 8 | 6.0 | 24.8 | | | | | | |
| 9 | 7.0 | 24.8 | | | | | | |
| 10 | 8.0 | 24.8 | | | | | | |
| 11 | 9.0 | 24.8 | | | | | | |
| 12 | 10.0 | 24.8 | | | | | | |
| 13 | 11.0 | 24.8 | | | | | | |
| 14 | 12.0 | 24.8 | | | | | | |
| 15 | 13.0 | 24.8 | | | | | | |
| 16 | 14.0 | 24.8 | | | | | | |
| 17 | 15.0 | 24.8 | | | | | | |
| 18 | 16.0 | 24.8 | | | | | | |
| 19 | 17.0 | 24.8 | | | | | | |
| 20 | 18.0 | 24.8 | | | | | | |
| 21 | | | | | | | | |
| 22 | | | | | | | | |
| 23 | | | | | | | | |
| 24 | | | | | | | | |

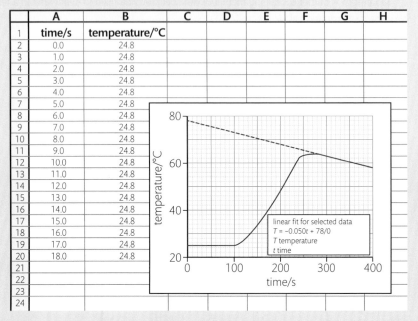

A straight line has been drawn through some of the data points. The equation for this line is given by the data-logging software as

$$T = -0.050t + 78.0$$

where $T$ is the temperature at time $t$.

**(a)** The heat produced by the reaction can be calculated from the temperature change, $\Delta T$, using the expression below.

heat change = volume of $CuSO_4(aq)$ × specific heat capacity of $H_2O$ × $\Delta T$

Describe **two** assumptions made in using this expression to calculate heat changes. (2)

**(b) (i)** Use the data presented by the data-logging software to deduce the temperature change, $\Delta T$, which would have occurred if the reaction had taken place instantaneously with no heat loss. (2)

**(ii)** State the assumption made in part (b)(i). (1)

**(iii)** Calculate the heat, in kJ, produced during the reaction using the expression given in part (a). (1)

**(c)** The colour of the solution changed from blue to colourless. Deduce the amount, in moles, of zinc which reacted in the polystyrene cup. (1)

**(d)** Calculate the enthalpy change, in kJ mol$^{-1}$, for this reaction. (1)

*(Total 8 marks)*

11 Two students were asked to use information from the data booklet to calculate a value for the enthalpy of hydrogenation of ethene to form ethane.

$$C_2H_4(g) + H_2(g) \rightarrow C_2H_6(g)$$

John used the average bond enthalpies from section 10. Marit used the values of enthalpies of combustion from section 13.

**(a)** Calculate the value for the enthalpy of hydrogenation of ethene obtained using the average bond enthalpies given in section 11. (2)

**(b)** Marit arranged the values she found in section 12 into an energy cycle.

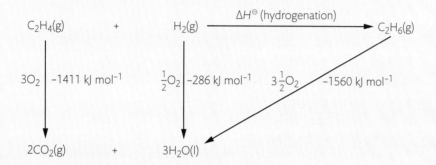

Calculate the value for the enthalpy of hydrogenation of ethene from the energy cycle. (1)

**(c)** Suggest **one** reason why John's answer is slightly less accurate than Marit's answer. (1)

**(d)** John then decided to determine the enthalpy of hydrogenation of cyclohexene to produce cyclohexane.

$$C_6H_{10}(l) + H_2(g) \rightarrow C_6H_{12}(l)$$

**(i)** Use the average bond enthalpies to deduce a value for the enthalpy of hydrogenation of cyclohexene. (1)

**(ii)** The percentage difference between these two methods (average bond enthalpies and enthalpies of combustion) is greater for cyclohexene than it was for ethene. John's hypothesis was that it would be the same. Determine why the use of average bond enthalpies is less accurate for the cyclohexene equation shown above, than it was for ethene. Deduce what extra information is needed to provide a more accurate answer. (2)

*(Total 7 marks)*

12 Hydrazine is a valuable rocket fuel. The equation for the reaction between hydrazine and oxygen is given below.

$$N_2H_4(l) + O_2(g) \rightarrow N_2(g) + 2H_2O(l)$$

Use the bond enthalpy values from section 10 of the data booklet to determine the enthalpy change for this reaction. (3)

13 The following reactions take place in the ozone layer by the absorption of ultraviolet light.

I   $O_3 \rightarrow O_2 + O\bullet$

II   $O_2 \rightarrow O\bullet + O\bullet$

State and explain, by reference to the bonding, which of the reactions, I or II, requires a shorter wavelength. (2)

**14** Which ionic compound has the greatest lattice enthalpy?

    **A** MgO           **B** CaO           **C** NaF           **D** KF

**15** Which step(s) is/are endothermic in the Born–Haber cycle for the formation of LiCl?

    **A** $\frac{1}{2}Cl_2(g) \rightarrow Cl(g)$ and $Li(s) \rightarrow Li(g)$

    **B** $Cl(g) + e^- \rightarrow Cl^-(g)$ and $Li(g) \rightarrow Li^+(g) + e^-$

    **C** $Li^+(g) + Cl^-(g) \rightarrow LiCl(s)$

    **D** $\frac{1}{2}Cl_2(g) \rightarrow Cl(g)$ and $Cl(g) + e^- \rightarrow Cl^-(g)$

**16** Which reaction has the greatest increase in entropy?

    **A** $SO_2(g) + 2H_2S(g) \rightarrow 2H_2O(l) + 3S(s)$

    **B** $CaO(s) + CO_2(g) \rightarrow CaCO_3(s)$

    **C** $CaC_2(s) + 2H_2O(l) \rightarrow Ca(OH)_2(s) + C_2H_2(g)$

    **D** $N_2(g) + O_2(g) \rightarrow 2NO(g)$

**17** Which change will **not** increase the entropy of a system?

    **A** increasing the temperature

    **B** changing the state from liquid to gas

    **C** mixing different types of particles

    **D** a reaction where four moles of gaseous reactants changes to two moles of gaseous products

**18** What is the standard free energy change, $\Delta G^\ominus$, in kJ, for the following reaction?

$$C_2H_5OH(l) + 3O_2(g) \rightarrow 2CO_2(g) + 3H_2O(g)$$

| Compound | $\Delta G_f^\ominus$ / kJ mol$^{-1}$ |
|---|---|
| $C_2H_5OH(l)$ | −175 |
| $CO_2(g)$ | −394 |
| $H_2O(g)$ | −229 |
| $O_2(g)$ | 0 |

    **A** −1650       **B** −1300       **C** −448       **D** +1300

**19** What is the standard entropy change, $\Delta S^\ominus$, for the following reaction?

$$2CO(g) + O_2(g) \rightarrow 2CO_2(g)$$

| | CO(g) | $O_2(g)$ | $CO_2(g)$ |
|---|---|---|---|
| $S^\ominus$ / J K$^{-1}$ mol$^{-1}$ | 198 | 205 | 214 |

    **A** −189       **B** −173       **C** +173       **D** +189

**20** A reaction has a standard enthalpy change, $\Delta H^\ominus$, of +10.00 kJ mol$^{-1}$ at 298 K. The standard entropy change, $\Delta S^\ominus$, for the same reaction is +10.00 J K$^{-1}$ mol$^{-1}$. What is the value of $\Delta G^\ominus$ for the reaction in kJ mol$^{-1}$?

    **A** +9.75       **B** +7.02       **C** −240       **D** −2970

**21** The lattice enthalpy of magnesium chloride can be calculated from the Born–Haber cycle shown below.

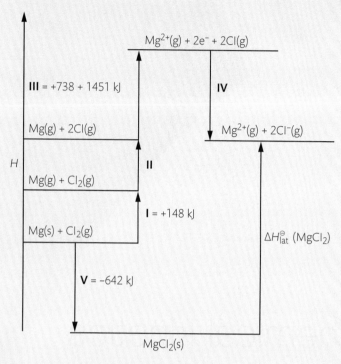

$Mg^{2+}(g) + 2e^- + 2Cl(g)$

**III** = +738 + 1451 kJ

**IV**

$Mg(g) + 2Cl(g)$

$Mg^{2+}(g) + 2Cl^-(g)$

$H$

**II**

$Mg(g) + Cl_2(g)$

**I** = +148 kJ

$Mg(s) + Cl_2(g)$

$\Delta H^{\ominus}_{lat} (MgCl_2)$

**V** = −642 kJ

$MgCl_2(s)$

**(a)** Identify the enthalpy changes labelled **I** and **V** in the cycle. (2)

**(b)** Use the ionization energies given in the cycle above and further data from the data booklet to calculate a value for the lattice enthalpy of magnesium chloride. (4)

**(c)** The theoretically calculated value for the lattice enthalpy of magnesium chloride is +2326 kJ. Explain the difference between the theoretically calculated value and the experimental value. (2)

**(d)** The experimental lattice enthalpy of magnesium oxide is given in section 18 of the data booklet. Explain why magnesium oxide has a higher lattice enthalpy than magnesium chloride. (2)

*(Total 10 marks)*

To access weblinks on the topics covered in this chapter, please go to www.pearsonhotlinks.com and enter the ISBN or title of this book.

# 06

# Chemical kinetics

## Essential ideas

**6.1** The greater the probability that molecules will collide with sufficient energy and proper orientation, the higher the rate of reaction.

**16.1** Rate expressions can only be determined empirically and these limit possible reaction mechanisms. In particular cases, such as a linear chain of elementary reactions, no equilibria, and only one significant activation barrier, the rate equation is equivalent to the slowest step of the reaction.

**16.2** The activation energy of a reaction can be determined from the effect of temperature on reaction rate.

Copper is commonly used in roofing due to its durability; however, over time it reacts with oxygen and turns green. Scientists have found ways to both accelerate and slow down this reaction in order to get the desired appearance of the metal.

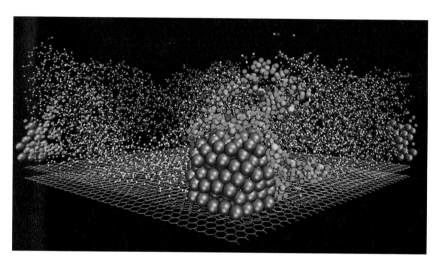

Computer simulation of fuel cell nanocatalysts. Platinum nanoparticles, shown in yellow, on a carbon substrate, shown as the green grid, are being investigated for their catalytic activity in fuel cell reactions. The red and white molecules are water, and the coloured chains are fragments of a polymer used in the proton exchange membranes. Research and development in fuel cell technology rely on an understanding of the factors that control reaction rates, including the action of catalysts.

The word **kinetics**, derived from the Greek word *kinesis*, refers to movement. The word 'cinema' (kine-ma) has the same origin and is used to describe 'the movies'. Movement in chemistry refers to the progress of a reaction, so kinetics is the study of how fast a reaction goes.

Imagine you are cooking in the kitchen. As you drop an egg into hot fat in the pan it immediately changes to a white solid; meanwhile a container of milk that was left out of the refrigerator is slowly turning sour. We observe a similar wide variation in the rate of reactions that we study in the laboratory, and these data can be very useful. Kinetic studies are of prime importance in industry because they give information on how quickly products form and on the conditions that give the most efficient and economic yield. They can also be useful in situations where we want to slow reactions down – for example, those that cause the destruction of ozone in the stratosphere, or the reactions where pollutants in the air combine to produce smog. At other times, it is important to know for how long a certain reaction will continue – for example, the radioactive effect from radioactive waste. Knowledge of reaction kinetics also gives insights into how reactions happen at the molecular level by suggesting a sequence of bond breaking and bond making, known as the **reaction mechanism**.

This chapter begins with a study of reaction rates and a consideration of how these are measured in different cases. Through the postulates of the **collision theory**, we will come to understand why different factors affect the rate of reactions, and then go on to develop mathematical equations to explore these relationships.

**Collision theory and rates of reaction**

## Understandings:

- Species react as a result of collisions of sufficient energy and proper orientation.
- The rate of reaction is expressed as the change in concentration of a particular reactant/product per unit time.
- Concentration changes in a reaction can be followed indirectly by monitoring changes in mass, volume, and colour.
- Activation energy ($E_a$) is the minimum energy that colliding molecules need in order to have successful collisions leading to a reaction.
- By decreasing $E_a$, a catalyst increases the rate of a chemical reaction, without itself being permanently chemically changed.

## Applications and skills:

- Description of the kinetic theory in terms of the movement of particles whose average kinetic energy is proportional to temperature in kelvin.
- Analysis of graphical and numerical data from rate experiments.

    ### Guidance
    - *Calculation of reaction rates from tangents of graphs of concentration, volume, or mass vs time should be covered.*
    - *Students should be familiar with the interpretation of graphs of changes in concentration, volume, or mass against time.*

- Explanation of the effects of temperature, pressure/concentration, and particle size on rate of reaction.
- Construction of Maxwell–Boltzmann energy distribution curves to account for the probability of successful collisions and factors affecting these, including the effect of a catalyst.
- Investigation of rates of reaction experimentally and evaluation of the results.
- Sketching and explanation of energy profiles with and without catalysts.

## Rate of reaction is defined as the rate of change in concentration

When we are interested in how quickly something happens, the factor that we usually measure is **time**. For example, in a sports race the competitors are judged by the time it takes them to reach the finishing line. However, if we want to compare their performance in different races over different distances, we would need to express this as a **rate** – in other words how they performed *per unit time*.

Rate takes the reciprocal value of time, so is expressed *per unit time* or in SI units *per second* (symbol = $s^{-1}$).

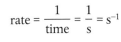

$$\text{rate} = \frac{1}{\text{time}} = \frac{1}{s} = s^{-1}$$

In the study of chemical reactions we use the concept of **rate of reaction** to describe how quickly a reaction happens. As the reaction proceeds, reactants are converted into products, and so the concentration of reactants decreases as the concentration of products increases. The graphs in Figures 6.1 and 6.2 show sketches of typical data from reactions.

Note that because time and rate are reciprocal values, as one increases, the other decreases. So in the example of a race, the racer with the *shortest time* wins the race, because they had the *highest rate*.

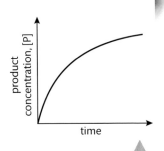

**Figure 6.1** Concentration of product against time.

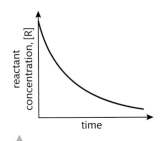

**Figure 6.2** Concentration of reactant against time.

The rate of a reaction depends on how quickly the concentration of either reactant or product changes with respect to time. It can be defined as follows:

$$\text{rate of reaction} = \frac{\text{increase in product conc.}}{\text{time taken}} \quad \text{or} \quad \frac{\text{decrease in reactant conc.}}{\text{time taken}}$$

Using $\Delta$ to represent 'change in', [R] for concentration of reactant, and [P] for concentration of product, we can express this as

$$\text{rate of reaction} = \frac{\Delta[P]}{\Delta t} \quad \text{or} \quad -\frac{\Delta[R]}{\Delta t}$$

The negative sign in the reactant expression indicates that reaction concentration is decreasing, but, by convention, rate is expressed as a positive value.

As rate = change in concentration per time, its units are **mol dm$^{-3}$ s$^{-1}$**.

Figure 6.3 represents graphs of two different reactions showing the change in concentration of reactant against time. We can see that the concentration of reactants is decreasing more quickly in reaction A than in reaction B – the curve is steeper. The steepness, or gradient, of the curve is a measure of the change in concentration per unit time, in other words, the rate of the reaction.

Because the graphs are curves and not straight lines, the gradient is not constant and so can only be given for a particular value of time. We can measure this by drawing a tangent to the curve at the specified time point and measuring its gradient. This is shown in Figure 6.4 for the time point 120 seconds. Note that the gradient of this graph is negative as the reactant concentration is decreasing, but rate is expressed as a positive value.

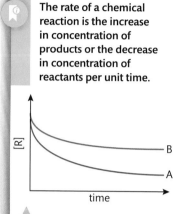

The rate of a chemical reaction is the increase in concentration of products or the decrease in concentration of reactants per unit time.

**Figure 6.3** Reactant concentration against time for two different reactions A and B.

**Figure 6.4** Measuring the gradient of the tangent to the curve at time $t$ = 120 seconds. The measured rate of the reaction is 8.48 × 10$^{-3}$ mol dm$^{-3}$ s$^{-1}$ at this time.

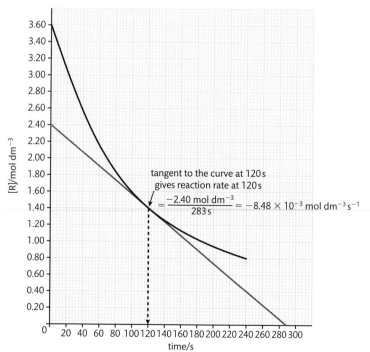

Note the difference between the two instructions 'draw a graph' and 'sketch a graph'. *Drawing* is based on actual data so scales must be chosen appropriately and data points and units clearly marked; *sketching* is a way of showing a trend in the variables, without reference to specific data. Note that in both cases the axes must be clearly labelled with the dependent variable on the *y*-axis and the independent variable on the *x*-axis.

273

The shape of the curve indicates that the rate of the reaction is not constant during the reaction, but is greatest at the start and slows down as the reaction proceeds. This is illustrated in Figure 6.5, which shows the calculation of reaction rate at two different times during a reaction.

- $t = 0$ s rate $= 2.9 \times 10^{-2}$ mol dm$^{-3}$ s$^{-1}$
- $t = 90$ s rate $= 7.2 \times 10^{-3}$ mol dm$^{-3}$ s$^{-1}$

**Figure 6.5** Measuring the gradient of the tangent to the curve at two different times during a reaction. The rate decreases as the reaction proceeds.

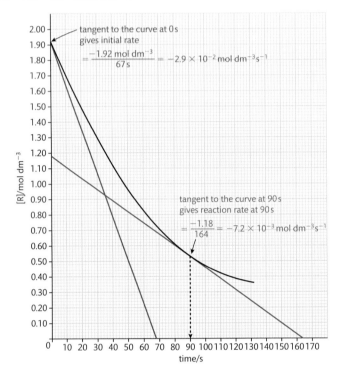

You will get a more accurate value for the slope of the tangent if you draw it as long as you reasonably can so that the 'y' value (concentration) and the 'x' value (time) are as large as possible.

**The rate of a reaction is not constant during a reaction, but is greatest at the start and decreases as the reaction proceeds.**

The rate is greatest at the start because this is when the reactant concentration is highest. The effect of concentration on reaction rate is discussed later in this chapter. Because of this variation in rate as a reaction proceeds, in order to compare the rates of reactions under different conditions it is common to compare the **initial rate** of each reaction by taking the tangent to the curve at $t = 0$. As we will see later in this chapter, initial rates data are very useful in analysing the effect of concentration on rate.

## Measuring rates of reaction uses different techniques depending on the reaction

**TOK**

Note that the balanced equation of a reaction gives us no information about its rate. We can obtain this information only from experimental (empirical) data. Is there a fundamental difference between knowledge claims based on conclusions from theoretical data and those based on experimental data?

Choosing whether to measure the change in concentration of reactants or products, and the technique with which to measure that change really depends on what is the most convenient for a particular reaction. This is different for different reactions. In most cases the concentration is not measured directly, but is measured by means of a signal which is related to the changing concentration. If, for example, a reaction produces a coloured precipitate as product, the change in colour could be measured; if a reaction gives off a gas, then the change in volume or change in mass could be measured. The raw data collected using these 'signals' will be in a variety of units, rather than as concentrations measured in mol dm$^{-3}$ directly. This is generally not a problem, as it still enables us to determine the rate of the reaction. Many of the experiments used here can be carried out using data-logging devices. Some examples of common techniques in relation to specific reactions are discussed below.

# 1 Change in volume of gas produced

This is a convenient method if one of the products is a gas. Collecting the gas and measuring the change in volume at regular time intervals enables a graph to be plotted of volume against time. A **gas syringe** can be used for this purpose. It consists of a ground glass barrel and plunger, which moves outwards as the gas collects and is calibrated to record the volume directly. Alternatively, the gas can be collected by displacement of water from an inverted burette. Note though that the displacement method can only be used if the gas collected has low solubility in water. Data loggers are also available for continuous monitoring of volume change against time. The rate of reaction of a metal with dilute acid to release hydrogen gas can be followed in this way.

$$Mg(s) + 2HCl(aq) \rightarrow MgCl_2(aq) + H_2(g)$$

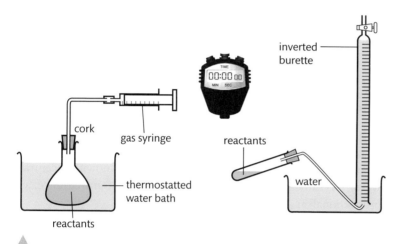

▲ **Figure 6.6** Experiments to measure rate of reaction by following change in volume against time.

# 2 Change in mass

Many reactions involve a change in mass, and it may be convenient to measure this directly. If the reaction is giving off a gas, the corresponding decrease in mass can be measured by standing the reaction mixture directly on a balance. This method is unlikely to work well where the evolved gas is hydrogen, as it is too light to give significant changes in mass. The method allows for continuous readings, so a graph can be plotted directly of mass against time. For example, the release of carbon dioxide from the reaction between a carbonate and dilute acid can be followed in this way.

$$CaCO_3(s) + 2HCl(aq) \rightarrow CaCl_2(aq) + CO_2(g) + H_2O(l)$$

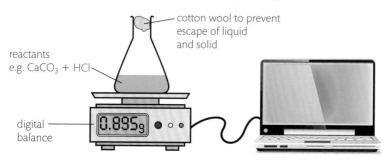

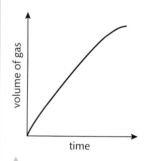

▲ **Figure 6.7** Volume of gas against time.

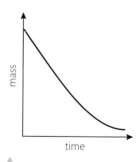

▲ **Figure 6.9** Mass against time.

**Figure 6.8** Experiment to measure rate of reaction by following change in mass against time.

## 3 Change in transmission of light: colorimetry/spectrophotometry

This technique can be used if one of the reactants or products is coloured and so gives characteristic absorption in the visible region (wavelengths about 320–800 nm). Sometimes an indicator can be added to generate a coloured compound that can then be followed in the reaction. A colorimeter or spectrophotometer works by passing light of a selected wavelength through the solution being studied and measures the intensity of the light transmitted by the reaction components. As the concentration of the coloured compound increases, it absorbs proportionally more light, so less is transmitted. A photocell generates an electric current according to the amount of light transmitted and this is recorded on a meter or connected to a computer.

**Figure 6.10** A spectrophotometer measures absorbance, which directly relates to concentration. Light of a specific wavelength is selected from an internal source and passes through the solution placed in the cuvette. The transmitted light passes through a diffraction grating, then the diffracted light is collected and changed into a digital signal by the CCD detector.

The method allows for continuous readings to be made, so a graph of absorbance against time can be plotted directly. It is possible to convert the absorbance values into concentrations using a standard curve based on readings of known concentration. Often, however, it is sufficient to record absorbance itself (or transmittance, which is inversely proportional) as a function against time.

For example, the reaction between the dye crystal violet and sodium hydroxide solution can be written in an abbreviated form as follows:

$$CV^+ + OH^- \rightarrow CVOH$$

The initial crystal violet solution ($CV^+$) is coloured but this slowly changes to a colourless solution as the product (CVOH) is formed. So we can determine the rate of product formation by measuring the *decrease in absorbance* that occurs as the coloured reactant is depleted. The screen shot shows data from this reaction, with absorbance at 591 nm measured against time.

Results of an experiment to determine the rate of reaction by following change in absorbance against time using a digital spectrophotometer.

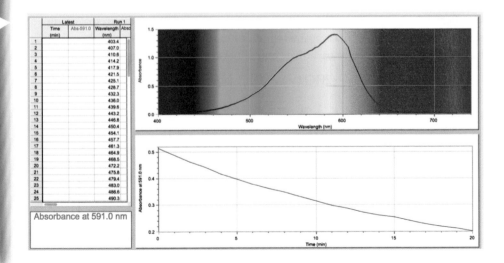

An example of the use of absorbance data to follow concentration changes is given in section 16.1 of this chapter. In Chapter 13, Biochemistry, we discuss the use of a calibration curve to determine concentration from absorbance data using the Beer–Lambert law.

## 4 Change in concentration measured using titration

In some reactions it may be possible to measure the concentration of one of the reactants or products by titrating it against a known 'standard' (see Chapter 1). However, because this technique involves chemically changing the reaction mixture, it cannot be done continuously as the reaction proceeds. Instead, samples must be withdrawn from the reaction mixture at regular time intervals and then analysed by titration. A problem here is that the process of titration takes time, during which the reaction mixture in the sample will continue to react. To overcome this, a technique known as **quenching** can be used, where a substance is introduced which effectively stops the reaction in the sample at the moment it is withdrawn. It is rather like obtaining a 'freeze frame' shot of the reaction at a particular interval of time. In order to see how concentration changes as the reaction proceeds, it is necessary to repeat this process at several intervals of time.

For example, the reaction between $H_2O_2$ and acidified KI yields $I_2$, which can be titrated against sodium thiosulfate, $Na_2S_2O_3$ to determine its concentration. Sodium carbonate, $Na_2CO_3$, is used to quench the reaction by neutralising the added acid.

$$H_2O_2(aq) + 2H^+(aq) + 2I^-(aq) \rightarrow I_2(aq) + 2H_2O(l)$$

## 5 Change in concentration measured using conductivity

The total electrical conductivity of a solution depends on the total concentration of its ions and on their charges. If this changes when reactants are converted to products, it can provide a convenient method to follow the progress of the reaction. Conductivity can be measured directly using a conductivity meter which involves immersing inert electrodes in the solution. As with colorimetry, the apparatus can be calibrated using solutions of known concentration so that readings can be converted into the concentrations of the ions present.

For example, in the reaction:

$$BrO_3^-(aq) + 5Br^-(aq) + 6H^+(aq) \rightarrow 3Br_2(aq) + 3H_2O(l)$$

the sharp decrease in the concentration of ions (12 on the reactants side and 0 on the products side) will give a corresponding decrease in the electrical conductivity of the solution as the reaction proceeds.

## 6 Non-continuous methods of detecting change during a reaction: 'clock reactions'

Sometimes it is difficult to record the continuous change in the rate of a reaction. In these cases, it may be more convenient to measure the time it takes for a reaction to reach a certain chosen fixed point – that is, something observable which can be used as an arbitrary 'end point' by which to stop the clock. The time taken to reach this point for the same reaction under different conditions can then be compared and used as a means of judging the different rates of the reaction. Note though the limitation of this method is that the data obtained give only an average rate over the time interval.

In all these reactions the goal is to measure change in concentration against time. This allows a comparison of reaction rates under different conditions. But because the rate is dependent on temperature, it is essential to control the temperature throughout these experiments. It is sometimes suitable to carry out the reactions in a thermostatically controlled water bath.

Experiments can be done to investigate the rate of reaction with changing reactant concentration, termperature, particle size, and catalyst. Full details of how to carry out an experiment on the effect of concentration, with a worksheet are available online.

For example, the following can be measured:

- the time taken for a certain size piece of magnesium ribbon to react completely with dilute acid, until it is no longer visible

$$Mg(s) + 2HCl\,(aq) \rightarrow MgCl_2(aq) + H_2(g)$$

- the time taken for a solution of sodium thiosulfate with dilute acid to become opaque by the precipitation of sulfur, so that a cross viewed through the solution is no longer visible

$$Na_2S_2O_3(aq) + 2HCl(aq) \rightarrow 2NaCl(aq) + SO_2(aq) + H_2O(l) + S(s)$$

Recording the increase in opaqueness during a reaction. Sodium thiosulfate (left) is a clear liquid, which reacts with hydrochloric acid (upper centre) to form an opaque solution (right). A cross (left) drawn onto paper is placed under the reaction beaker to allow the end point to be confirmed. The experiment is timed from when the reactants are mixed until the cross disappears from sight.

## Exercises

1   Consider the following reaction:

$$2MnO_4^-(aq) + 5C_2O_4^{2-}(aq) + 16H^+(aq) \rightarrow 2Mn^{2+}(aq) + 10CO_2(g) + 8H_2O(l)$$

Describe three different ways in which you could measure the rate of this reaction.

2   Which units are used to express the rate of a reaction?

   **A**  mol dm$^{-3}$ time      **B**  mol$^{-1}$ dm$^3$ time$^{-1}$      **C**  mol dm$^{-3}$ time$^{-1}$      **D**  mol time$^{-1}$

3   The reaction between calcium carbonate and hydrochloric acid is carried out in an open flask. Measurements are made to determine the rate of the reaction.

$$CaCO_3(s) + 2HCl(aq) \rightarrow CaCl_2(aq) + H_2O(l) + CO_2(g)$$

   **(a)**  Suggest three different types of data that could be collected to measure the rate of this reaction.
   **(b)**  Explain how you would expect the rate of the reaction to change with time and why.

4   The following data were collected for the reaction

$$2H_2O_2(aq) \rightarrow 2H_2O(l) + O_2(g) \text{ at } 390\,°C$$

| [H$_2$O$_2$] / mol dm$^{-3}$ | Time / s | [H$_2$O$_2$] / mol dm$^{-3}$ | Time / s |
|---|---|---|---|
| 0.200 | 0 | 0.070 | 120 |
| 0.153 | 20 | 0.063 | 140 |
| 0.124 | 40 | 0.058 | 160 |
| 0.104 | 60 | 0.053 | 180 |
| 0.090 | 80 | 0.049 | 200 |
| 0.079 | 100 | | |

Draw a graph of concentration against time and determine the reaction rate after 60 s and after 120 s.

The Kelvin scale of temperature gives a natural measure of the kinetic energy of gas, whereas the Celsius scale is based on the properties of water. Are physical properties such as temperature invented or discovered?

**TOK**

## Collision theory

### Kinetic energy and temperature

Since the early 18th century, theories have been developed to explain the fact that gases exert a pressure. These theories developed alongside a growing understanding of the atomic and molecular nature of matter, and were extended to include the behaviour of particles in all states of matter. Today they are summarized as the **kinetic-molecular theory of matter** (see Chapter 1).

The essence of kinetic molecular theory is that particles in a substance move randomly as a result of the **kinetic energy** that they possess. Because of the random nature of these movements and collisions, not all particles in a substance at any one time have the same values of kinetic energy, but will have instead a range of values. A convenient way to describe the kinetic energy of a substance is therefore to take the *average* of these values, and this is directly related to its **absolute temperature** – that is, its temperature measured in kelvin.

Increasing temperature therefore means an increase in the average kinetic energy of the particles of a substance. As we supply a substance with extra energy through heating it, we raise the average kinetic energy of the particles and so also raise its temperature. When we compare the behaviour of the particles in the three states of matter from solid, through liquid, to gas, the differences are a result of this increase in the average kinetic energy of the particles, as described on page 9.

For a given substance this can be summarized as follows:

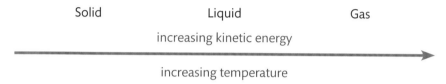

| Solid | Liquid | Gas |

increasing kinetic energy

increasing temperature

## The Maxwell–Boltzmann distribution curve

The fact that particles in a gas at a particular temperature show a range in their values of kinetic energy is expressed by the **Maxwell–Boltzmann distribution curve**.

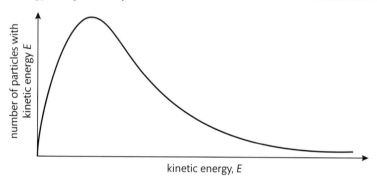

Like other distribution curves, this shows the number having a particular value, in this case of particles with a particular value of kinetic energy (or the probability of that value occurring) plotted against the values for kinetic energy. The area under the curve represents the total number of particles in the sample.

Although their names are linked in the famous energy distribution curve discussed here, James Clerk Maxwell and Ludwig Boltzmann were two people with very different outlooks on life. Maxwell was a Scottish physicist, known for his insatiable curiosity and overflowing humour. His wife worked alongside him in many of his experiments. Boltzmann, an Austrian, was prone to depression and eventually took his own life while on a family holiday, seemingly believing that his work was not valued. Nonetheless as peers during the 19th century, both seeking to explain the observed properties of gases, they refined and developed each other's ideas, culminating in the distribution curve that bears their two names.

## How reactions happen

When reactants are placed together, the kinetic energy that their particles possess causes them to collide with each other. The energy of these collisions may result in some bonds between the reactants being broken, and some new bonds forming. As a result, products form and the reaction 'happens'.

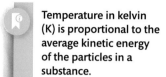

Temperature in kelvin (K) is proportional to the average kinetic energy of the particles in a substance.

There is more heat in an iceberg than in a cup of boiling coffee.

As heat is a form of energy, the total heat in the iceberg will be the sum of all the energy of all its particles. The iceberg's *temperature* is of course much lower than that of the cup of coffee, which means its particles have, on average, much lower kinetic energy. But because there are vastly more particles in the iceberg than the cup of coffee, its *total* energy is greater.

**Figure 6.11** The Maxwell–Boltzmann distribution curve.

**Figure 6.12** Particles react by colliding.

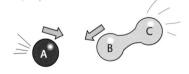

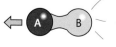

279

It follows that the rate of the reaction will depend on the number of collisions between particles which are 'successful', that is, which lead to the formation of products. But a very important point is that *not all collisions will be successful*. There are two main factors that influence this:

- energy of collision and
- geometry of collision.

### i Energy of collision

In order for a collision to lead to reaction, the particles must have a certain minimum value for their kinetic energy, known as the **activation energy**, $E_a$. This energy is necessary for overcoming repulsion between molecules, and often for breaking some bonds in the reactants before they can react. When this energy is supplied, the reactants achieve the **transition state** from which products can form. The activation energy therefore represents an energy barrier for the reaction, and it has a different value in different reactions.

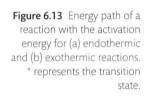

Activation energy ($E_a$) is defined as the minimum value of kinetic energy which particles must have before they are able to react.

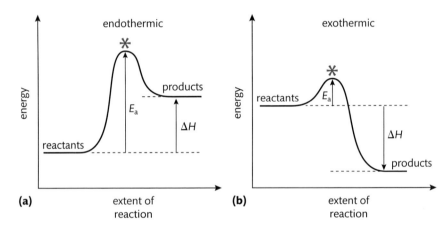

**Figure 6.13** Energy path of a reaction with the activation energy for (a) endothermic and (b) exothermic reactions. * represents the transition state.

We can think of the activation energy as a 'threshold value' – a bit like a pass mark in an examination: values greater than this mark achieve a pass, lower values do not achieve a pass. The activation energy threshold similarly determines which particles react and which do not. So only particles that have a kinetic energy value greater than the activation energy will have successful collisions. Note that particles with lower values of kinetic energy may still collide, but these collisions will not be 'successful' in the sense of causing a reaction.

It therefore follows that the rate of the reaction depends on the proportion of particles that have values for kinetic energy greater than the activation energy.

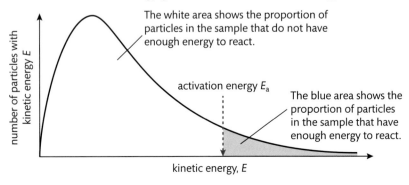

**Figure 6.14** Maxwell–Boltzmann distribution showing how the activation energy, $E_a$, distinguishes between particles which have greater or lesser values of kinetic energy.

The magnitude of the activation energy varies greatly from one reaction to another, and it is an important factor in determining the overall rate of the reaction. In general, reactions with high activation energy proceed more slowly than those with low activation energy. In section 16.2 of this chapter, we will learn how activation energy can be calculated.

## ii  Geometry of collision

Because collisions between particles are random, they are likely to occur with the particles in many different orientations. In some reactions this can be crucial in determining whether or not the collisions will be successful, and therefore what proportion of collisions will lead to a reaction.

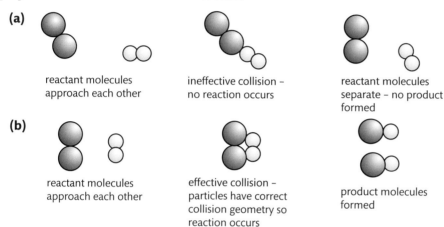

**(a)**

reactant molecules approach each other

ineffective collision – no reaction occurs

reactant molecules separate – no product formed

**(b)**

reactant molecules approach each other

effective collision – particles have correct collision geometry so reaction occurs

product molecules formed

**Figure 6.15** The effect of collision geometry. In (a) the particles do not have the correct collision geometry and no reaction occurs. In (b) the particles collide with the correct geometry, enabling products to form.

## Summary

The rate of a reaction depends on the frequency of collisions which occur between particles possessing both:

• values of kinetic energy greater than the activation energy and
• appropriate collision geometry.

Understanding this theory will help us to investigate and explain the factors that influence the rate of reaction.

**In order to react, particles must collide with kinetic energy greater than the activation energy and have the correct collision geometry.**

### Exercises

**5**  Which statement is correct for a collision between reactant particles that leads to reaction?

  **A**  Colliding particles must have different energy.
  **B**  Colliding particles must have the same energy.
  **C**  Colliding particles must have kinetic energy greater than the average kinetic energy.
  **D**  Colliding particles must have kinetic energy greater than the activation energy.

**6**  Which of the following determine whether a reaction will occur?

  I    the orientation of the molecules
  II   the energy of the molecules
  III  the volume of the container

  **A**  I and II          **B**  I and III          **C**  II only          **D**  I, II, and III

**7**  If we compare two reactions, one which requires the simultaneous collision of three molecules and the other which requires a collision between two molecules, which reaction would you expect to be faster? Explain why.

Be careful not to confuse the question of 'how fast?' a reaction goes with the question of 'how far?' it goes. We are discussing only the first question here. The question of how far a reaction goes, which influences the *yield* of the reaction, will be discussed in Chapter 7, Equilibrium.

## Factors affecting rate of reaction

From the collision theory we know that any factor which increases the number of successful collisions will increase the rate of the reaction. We will investigate five such factors here.

### 1 Temperature

Increasing the temperature causes an increase in the average kinetic energy of the particles. We can see this by comparing Maxwell–Boltzmann distribution curves of the same sample of particles at two different temperatures.

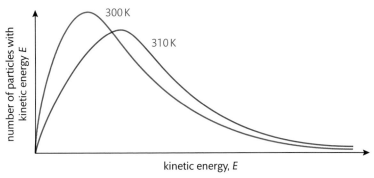

**Figure 6.16** Maxwell–Boltzmann distribution curves for a sample of gas at 300 K and 310 K. At the higher temperature the curve has shifted to the right and become broader, showing a larger number of particles with higher values for kinetic energy.

The area under the two curves is equal as this represents the total number of particles in the sample. But at the higher temperature, more of the particles have higher values for kinetic energy and the peak of the curve shifts to the right. In Figure 6.17, we can see how this shift increases the proportion of particles that have values for kinetic energy greater than that of the activation energy.

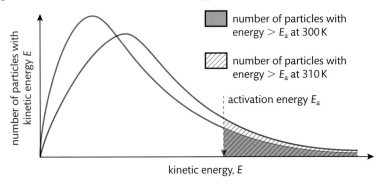

**Figure 6.17** Maxwell–Boltzmann distribution curves for a sample of gas at two different temperatures, showing the higher proportion of particles with kinetic energy greater than the activation energy at the higher temperature.

So, as temperature increases, there is an increase in collision frequency due to the higher kinetic energy, but more importantly there is an increase in the frequency of collisions involving particles with the necessary activation energy to overcome the activation energy barrier. Consequently, there is an increase in the frequency of *successful* collisions and so an increase in the rate of reaction. Many reactions double their reaction rate for every 10 °C increase in temperature. In section 16.2 of this chapter, we will explore this further through a study of the mathematical relationship between temperature and rate of reaction.

## 2 Concentration

Increasing the concentration of reactants increases the rate of reaction. This is because as concentration increases, the frequency of collisions between reactant particles increases, as shown in Figure 6.18. The frequency of successful collisions therefore increases too.

We can see the effect of concentration by following the rate of a reaction as it progresses. As reactants are used up, their concentration falls and the rate of the reaction decreases, giving the typical rate curve we saw in Figure 6.2.

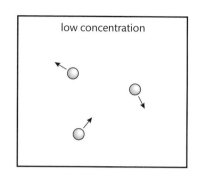

low concentration

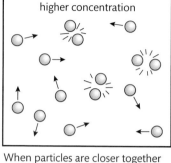

higher concentration

When particles are closer together they have a greater chance of reacting.

**Figure 6.18** Effect of concentration on collision frequency.

## 3 Particle size

Decreasing the particle size increases the rate of reaction. This is important in heterogeneous reactions where the reactants are in different phases, such as a solid reacting with a solution. Subdividing a large particle into smaller parts increases the total surface area and therefore allows more contact and a higher probability of collisions between the reactants. You know, for example, how much easier it is to start a fire using small pieces of wood, rather than a large log – it's because with the small pieces there is more contact between the wood and the oxygen with which it is reacting. In reactions involving dispersions, stirring may help to decrease particle size and so increase the rate.

The effect of concentration on the rate of reaction between zinc and sulfuric acid. The tube on the left has a more concentrated solution of the acid, the one on the right a more dilute solution. The product, hydrogen gas, is seen collecting much more quickly in the presence of the more concentrated acid.

The effect of particle size can be demonstrated in the reaction between marble ($CaCO_3$) and hydrochloric acid. When marble chips are replaced with powder, the effervescence caused by carbon dioxide release is much more vigorous.

This effect of particle size on reaction rate can be quite dramatic. It has been responsible for many industrial accidents involving explosions of flammable dust powders – for example coal dust in mines and flour in mills.

Specimens of the extinct mammal the mammoth, dated as 10 000 years old, have been found perfectly preserved in the Arctic ice, whereas individual specimens of a similar age found in California, have only bones that remain. This is an illustration of the effect of the low temperature in the Arctic decreasing the rate of the reactions of decay. The same concept is used in the process of refrigerating or freezing food to preserve it.

## 4 Pressure

For reactions involving gases, increasing pressure increases the rate of reaction. This is because the higher pressure compresses the gas, effectively increasing its concentration. This will increase the frequency of collisions.

## 5 Catalyst

A catalyst is a substance that increases the rate of a chemical reaction without itself undergoing permanent chemical change. Most catalysts work by providing an alternate route for the reaction that has a lower activation energy.

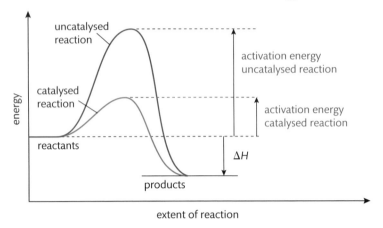

**Figure 6.19** Effect of a catalyst on lowering the activation energy of a reaction.

Milk powder dropped on a flame. As milk powder is dropped onto a flame the fine particles expose a huge surface area to the flame, leading to very fast burning.

This means that without increasing the temperature, a larger number of particles will now have values of kinetic energy greater than the activation energy, and so will be able to undergo successful collisions. Think again of activation energy as being like the pass mark in an examination: the effect of the catalyst is like lowering the pass mark. This means that with the same work in the tests, a higher number of people would be able to achieve a pass!

Figure 6.20 uses the Maxwell–Boltzmann distribution to show how a catalyst increases the proportion of particles having values of kinetic energy greater than the activation energy.

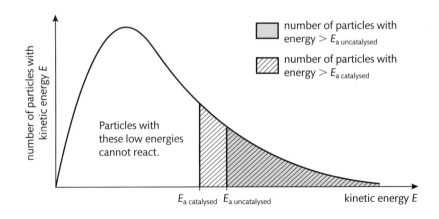

**Figure 6.20** Effect of catalyst on increasing the proportion of particles able to react.

Catalysts bring about an equal reduction in the activation energy of both the forward and the reverse reactions, so they do not change the position of equilibrium or the yield (Chapter 7). However, because of their ability to increase the rate of reactions, they influence the rate of formation of product and so play an essential role in the efficiency of many industrial processes. Without catalysts, many reactions would proceed too slowly, or would have to be conducted at such high temperatures that they would simply not be worthwhile. This is why the discovery of the 'best' catalyst for a particular reaction is a very active area of research, and often the exact specification of a catalyst used in an industrial process is a matter of secrecy.

**A catalyst is a substance that increases the rate of a chemical reaction without itself undergoing permanent chemical change.**

A catalytic converter. This device catalyses reactions which convert the toxic emissions from an internal combustion engine into less harmful ones. It is estimated that catalytic converters can reduce pollution emission by 90% without loss of engine performance or fuel economy.

The development of the process of *catalytic reforming*, by which linear hydrocarbons are converted into branched or cyclic molecules which burn more smoothly, is often credited with having played a major role in World War II. Aircraft fuel using such hydrocarbons increased the performance of the European allies' planes to the point where they were able to gain victory in the skies.

Every biological reaction is controlled by a catalyst, known as an **enzyme**. Thousands of different enzymes exist as they are each specific for a particular biochemical reaction. Enzymes are finding increasingly widespread uses in many domestic and industrial processes, from biological detergents to acting as 'biosensors' in medical studies. Some of these applications, like cheese making, are centuries old, but others are developing rapidly, constituting the field known as **biotechnology**. Enzyme kinetics is discussed further in Chapter 13, Biochemistry.

Catalysis is also an important aspect of Green Chemistry, which seeks to reduce the negative impact of chemical processes on the environment. Catalysts can replace stoichiometric reagents, and can greatly enhance the selectivity of processes. As they are effective in very small quantities and can frequently be reused, catalysts do not contribute to the chemical waste, and so they increase the atom economy. Some examples of Green Chemistry catalysts in organic synthesis reactions are discussed in Chapter 10.

Depletion of the protective ozone layer in the stratosphere has been caused largely by the catalytic effects of CFCs and nitrogen oxides, as discussed in Chapter 4. These chemicals are produced from a variety of sources and often have their most destructive effect far from the country of their origin. International action and cooperation have played an important part in ameliorating the effects of ozone depletion, and continuing adherence by all countries to international treaties is essential.

## Exercises

**8** Which of the following statements is correct?

  **A**  A catalyst increases the rate of the forward reaction only.
  **B**  A catalyst increases the rate of the forward and backward reactions.
  **C**  A catalyst increases the yield of product formed.
  **D**  A catalyst increases the activation energy of a reaction.

**9** Which statements are correct for the effects of catalyst and temperature on the rate of reaction?

| | Adding a catalyst | Increasing the temperature |
|---|---|---|
| **A** | collision frequency increases | collision frequency increases |
| **B** | activation energy decreases | collision frequency increases |
| **C** | collision frequency increases | activation energy increases |
| **D** | activation energy increases | activation energy decreases |

**10** In the reaction between marble (calcium carbonate) and hydrochloric acid, which set of conditions would give the highest rate of reaction?

$$CaCO_3(s) + 2HCl \rightarrow CaCl_2(aq) + CO_2(g) + H_2O(l)$$

  **A**  marble chips and 1.0 mol dm$^{-3}$ HCl
  **B**  marble powder and 1.0 mol dm$^{-3}$ HCl
  **C**  marble chips and 0.1 mol dm$^{-3}$ HCl
  **D**  marble powder and 0.1 mol dm$^{-3}$ HCl

**11** A sugar cube cannot be ignited with a match, but a sugar cube coated in ashes will ignite. Suggest a reason for this observation.

12 Catalytic converters are now used in most cars to convert some components of exhaust gases into less environmentally damaging molecules. One of these reactions converts carbon monoxide and nitrogen monoxide into carbon dioxide and nitrogen. The catalyst usually consists of metals such as platinum or rhodium.

(a) Write an equation for this reaction.

(b) Explain why it is important to reduce the concentrations of carbon monoxide and nitrogen monoxide released into the atmosphere.

(c) Why do you think the converter sometimes consists of small ceramic beads coated with the catalyst?

(d) Suggest why the converter usually does not work effectively until the car engine has warmed up.

(e) Discuss whether the use of catalytic converters in cars solves the problem of car pollution.

# 16.1 Rate expression and reaction mechanism

## Understandings:

- Reactions may occur by more than one step and the slowest step determines the rate of reaction (rate-determining step/RDS).

   **Guidance**
   *Use potential energy level profiles to illustrate multi-step reactions; showing the higher $E_a$ in the rate-determining step in the diagram.*

- The molecularity of an elementary step is the number of reactant particles taking part in that step.

   **Guidance**
   *Catalysts are involved in the rate-determining step.*

- The order of a reaction can be either integer or fractional in nature. The order of a reaction can describe, with respect to a reactant, the number of particles taking part in the rate-determining step.

- Rate equations can only be determined experimentally.

   **Guidance**
   *Any experiment which allows students to vary concentrations to see the effect upon the rate and hence determine a rate equation is appropriate.*

- The value of the rate constant ($k$) is affected by temperature and its units are determined from the overall order of the reaction.

- Catalysts alter a reaction mechanism, introducing a step with lower activation energy.

## Applications and skills:

- Deduction of the rate expression for an equation from experimental data and solving problems involving the rate expression.

- Sketching, identifying, and analysing graphical representations for zero, first, and second-order reactions.

   **Guidance**
   *Consider concentration–time and rate–concentration graphs.*

- Evaluation of proposed reaction mechanisms to be consistent with kinetic and stoichiometric data.

   **Guidance**
   *Reactions where the rate-determining step is not the first step should be considered.*

## The rate law for a reaction is derived from experimental data

Let us look in more detail at some typical data from a study of the change in concentration of a reactant during a reaction. We will investigate an unusual but simple reaction in which an oxidized form of buckminsterfullerene, $C_{60}O_3$, decomposes into $C_{60}O$ by releasing $O_2$ when its solution in methylbenzene is warmed to room temperature.

$$C_{60}O_3 \rightarrow C_{60}O + O_2$$

The reaction can be followed by recording the change in absorbance of light of a certain wavelength (as described on page 276) as this is directly proportional to the concentration of $C_{60}O_3$. In other words, observing absorbance as a function of time gives a measure of concentration as a function of time. The table and graph below show some experimental results.

| Time / minutes | $C_{60}O_3$ absorbance at 23 °C | Time / minutes | $C_{60}O_3$ absorbance at 23 °C |
|---|---|---|---|
| 3 | 0.04241 | 57 | 0.01106 |
| 9 | 0.03634 | 63 | 0.00955 |
| 15 | 0.03121 | 69 | 0.00827 |
| 21 | 0.02680 | 75 | 0.00710 |
| 27 | 0.02311 | 81 | 0.00616 |
| 33 | 0.01992 | 87 | 0.00534 |
| 39 | 0.01721 | 93 | 0.00461 |
| 45 | 0.01484 | 99 | 0.00395 |
| 51 | 0.01286 | | |

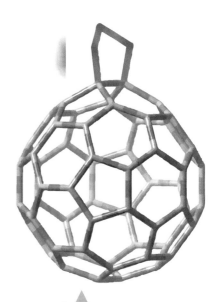

**Figure 6.21** The structure of oxidized buckminsterfullerene, $C_{60}O_3$, showing its three-oxygen bridge. Fullerenes are allotropes of carbon, made of a closed cage of hexagons and pentagons. Their structure is discussed in Chapter 4.

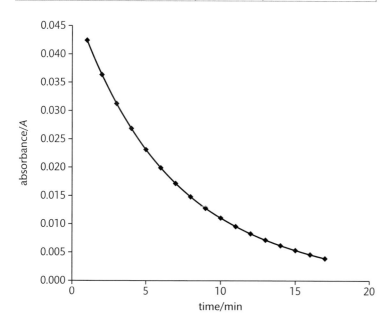

**Figure 6.22** Absorbance–time graph for decomposition of $C_{60}O_3$.

We established in section 6.1 that the rate of the reaction is equal to the rate of change in the concentration of reactant, $C_{60}O_3$.

$$\text{rate} = -\frac{\Delta[C_{60}O_3]}{\Delta t}$$

Note that the value for the change in concentration here is negative as concentration is decreasing, but by convention rate is expressed as a positive value. The rate can be evaluated at each time interval by measuring the gradient of the tangent to the curve at that particular value of time, or from the data table by calculating the change in absorbance divided by the change in time at each step. When the rate calculated in this way is plotted as a function of time, we obtain the graph shown in Figure 6.23.

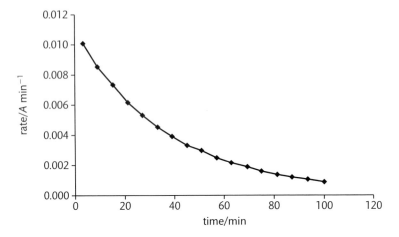

**Figure 6.23** Rate–time graph for decomposition of $C_{60}O_3$.

This shows that the rate changes over the course of time, slowing as the concentration of $C_{60}O_3$ decreases. This graph mirrors the one in Figure 6.22 where absorbance also decreases with time. The similarity of the graph of concentration of $C_{60}O_3$ (shown by absorbance) against time with that of rate against time, suggests that the rate must be related to the concentration at each time.

We can confirm this by plotting the rate of the reaction against the absorbance of $C_{60}O_3$, as shown in Figure 6.24.

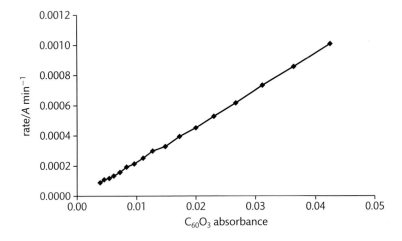

**Figure 6.24** Rate–absorbance graph for $C_{60}O_3$ decomposition.

The straight-line graph obtained in Figure 6.24 confirms that the rate of the reaction is directly proportional to the concentration of the reactant $C_{60}O_3$.

$$\text{reaction rate} \propto [C_{60}O_3]$$

This proportional relationship is converted into an equation by introducing a constant. So:

$$\text{reaction rate} = k\,[C_{60}O_3]$$

where $k$ is the **rate constant**.

This equation is known as the **rate expression** or the **rate law** for this reaction. In this case it is called a **first-order** rate expression because the concentration of the reactant is raised to the power one. It has been shown by experiment that the rate of all reactions can similarly be shown to depend on the concentration of one or more of the reactants, and that the exact relationship depends on the particular reaction.

In general, the rate is proportional to the product of the concentrations of the reactants, each raised to a power. For the reaction:

$$A + B \rightarrow products$$

$$rate \propto [A]^m [B]^n \text{ or } rate = k [A]^m [B]^n$$

The powers to which the concentrations of reactants are raised in the rate expression, $m$ and $n$, are known as the **orders** of the reaction with respect to reactants A and B respectively. The **overall order** for the reaction is the sum of the individual orders, $m + n$. The rate constant, $k$, has a fixed value for a particular reaction at a specified temperature. Once the value of $k$ and the orders of the reaction are known, the rate expression enables us to calculate the rate of reaction at any concentration of reactants.

## Worked example

The reaction:

$$2H_2(g) + 2NO(g) \rightarrow 2H_2O(g) + N_2(g)$$

is shown to be second order with respect to NO and first order with respect to $H_2$.

Give the rate equation for this reaction and its overall order.

### Solution

Second order with respect to NO means that the concentration of NO must be raised to the power 2 in the rate equation; first order for $H_2$ means that the concentration of $H_2$ must be raised to the power 1, and this exponent is not usually shown. Therefore

$$rate = k [NO]^2 [H_2]$$

The overall order of the reaction = 2 + 1 = 3; it is a third-order reaction.

The example above of the reaction between $H_2$ and NO illustrates the point that the orders of reaction with respect to reactants do not necessarily correspond to their coefficients in the reaction equation. The orders can in fact *only* be determined by experiment (empirically). The table below gives examples of some reaction equations and the empirically derived orders of the reactions with respect to individual reactants, and so the overall order. As you can see, there is no predictable relationship between the coefficients in the equation and the values for the order of reaction with respect to the reactants.

| | Equation for the reaction | Order with respect to reactant 1 | Order with respect to reactant 2 | Overall order of the reaction |
|---|---|---|---|---|
| 1 | $H_2(g) + I_2(g) \rightarrow 2HI(g)$ | $H_2$: 1st | $I_2$, 1st | 2nd |
| 2 | $2H_2O_2(aq) \rightarrow 2H_2O(l) + O_2(g)$ | $H_2O_2$: 1st | – | 1st |
| 3 | $S_2O_8^{2-}(aq) + 2I^-(aq) \rightarrow 2SO_4^{2-}(aq) + I_2(aq)$ | $S_2O_8^{2-}$: 1st | $I^-$, 1st | 2nd |
| 4 | $2N_2O_5(g) \rightarrow 4NO_2(g) + O_2(g)$ | $N_2O_5$: 1st | – | 1st |

Note that the rate constant is written with a lower case $k$. Do not confuse this with equilibrium constants which are written with an upper case $K$.

This apparent disconnect between the reaction equation and the rate expression begs the question: what *does* determine the order of the reaction? The quick answer to this is the **reaction mechanism**, and we will explore this relationship fully on pages 296.

## Exercises

**13** Write the rate expression for each of the reactions in the table on page 289.

**14** The rate expression for the reaction

$$NO(g) + O_3(g) \rightarrow NO_2(g) + O_2(g)$$

is rate = $k$ [NO] [$O_3$]. What is the order with respect to each reactant and what is the overall order?

**15** The reaction

$$CH_3Cl(aq) + OH^-(aq) \rightarrow CH_3OH(aq) + Cl^-(aq)$$

is found to be second order overall. Give three possible rate expressions consistent with this finding.

Make sure that you include the correct units for $k$ in all calculations. You should check that the units are consistent with the data, so that the rate will always have the units of concentration time$^{-1}$.

## Units of $k$ vary depending on the overall order of the reaction

The table below shows how the rate constant $k$ has different units, depending on the overall order of the reaction. Note that these examples measure rate per second, so this would have to be changed if the rate given were, for example, per minute.

| Zero order | First order | Second order | Third order |
|---|---|---|---|
| rate = $k$ | rate = $k$ [A] | e.g. rate = $k$ [A]$^2$ | e.g. rate = $k$ [A]$^3$ |
| $k$ = units of rate<br>= **mol dm$^{-3}$ s$^{-1}$** | $k = \dfrac{\text{units of rate}}{\text{units of concentration}}$<br><br>$= \dfrac{\text{mol dm}^{-3}\text{ s}^{-1}}{\text{mol dm}^{-3}}$<br><br>$= \textbf{s}^{-1}$ | $k = \dfrac{\text{units of rate}}{(\text{units of concentration})^2}$<br><br>$= \dfrac{\text{mol dm}^{-3}\text{ s}^{-1}}{(\text{mol dm}^{-3})^2}$<br><br>$= \textbf{mol}^{-1}\textbf{ dm}^3\textbf{ s}^{-1}$ | $k = \dfrac{\text{units of rate}}{(\text{units of concentration})^3}$<br><br>$= \dfrac{\text{mol dm}^{-3}\text{ s}^{-1}}{(\text{mol dm}^{-3})^3}$<br><br>$= \textbf{mol}^{-2}\textbf{ dm}^6\textbf{ s}^{-1}$ |

The value of $k$ can be calculated from the rate expression when the concentrations of reactants and the corresponding rate are known. Its value increases with increasing temperature, a relationship that we will explore further in section 16.2.

## Worked example

A reaction has the rate expression rate = $k$ [A]$^2$ [B].

Calculate the value of $k$, including units, for the reaction when the concentrations of both A and B are $2.50 \times 10^{-2}$ mol dm$^{-3}$ and the reaction rate is $7.75 \times 10^{-5}$ mol dm$^{-3}$ min$^{-1}$.

### Solution

Substituting the values into the rate expression gives

$$7.75 \times 10^{-5} \text{ mol dm}^{-3}\text{ min}^{-1} = k \, (2.50 \times 10^{-2} \text{ mol dm}^{-3})^2 \times (2.50 \times 10^{-2} \text{ mol dm}^{-3})$$

Therefore $k = \dfrac{7.75 \times 10^{-5} \text{ mol dm}^{-3}\text{ min}^{-1}}{(2.50 \times 10^{-2})^3 \, (\text{mol dm}^{-3})^3}$

$= 4.96$ mol$^{-2}$ dm$^6$ min$^{-1}$

Reactions which are zero order overall are relatively uncommon. They occur when the rate of the reaction is independent of the concentration of the reactants. An example would be the decomposition of gaseous ammonia using a catalyst of heated platinum.

$$2NH_3(g) \xrightarrow{\text{Pt(s)}} N_2(g) + 3H_2(g)$$

The rate depends on the number of $NH_3$ molecules attached to the surface of the catalyst, which is very small relative to the total number of $NH_3$ molecules. So increasing the concentration of the reactant will not affect the rate.

## Exercises

**16** Give the units of $k$ in each of the rate expressions below:

(a) rate = $k [NO_2]^2$      (c) rate = $k [NH_3]^0$      (e) rate = $k [H_2] [I_2]$
(b) rate = $k [CH_3CH_2Br]$      (d) rate = $k [NO]^2 [Br_2]$

**17** The reaction $2N_2O_5(g) \rightarrow 4NO_2(g) + O_2(g)$ has a value of $k = 6.9 \times 10^{-4}$ s$^{-1}$ at a certain temperature. Deduce the rate expression for this reaction.

**18** A reaction involving A and B is found to be zero order with respect to A and second order with respect to B. When the initial concentrations of A and B are $1.0 \times 10^{-3}$ mol dm$^{-3}$ and $2.0 \times 10^{-3}$ mol dm$^{-3}$ respectively, the initial rate of the reaction is $4.5 \times 10^{-4}$ mol dm$^{-3}$ min$^{-1}$. Calculate the value of the rate constant for the reaction.

# Graphical representations of reaction kinetics

In our study here we will investigate reactions where the order with respect to a particular reactant is zero, first, or second. In more complex reactions, other values for order are possible, including fractional and negative values. As we saw at the beginning of this section it is possible to establish the order of a reaction with respect to a reactant from graphical representations of experimental data. However, as you will see below, concentration–time graphs do not lead to a clear distinction between first and second order. Rate–concentration graphs, on the other hand, clearly reveal the difference. Both are shown below for each case, with reference to a single reactant, A.

## Zero-order reaction

Here the concentration of reactant A does not affect the rate of the reaction.

$$\text{rate} = k [A]^0 \text{ or rate} = k$$

So the concentration–time graph is a straight line, showing a constant rate (Figure 6.25). The gradient of the line = $k$. The rate–concentration graph is a horizontal line (Figure 6.26).

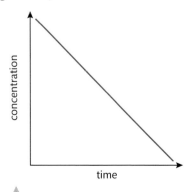

▲ **Figure 6.25** Concentration–time graph for a zero-order reaction.

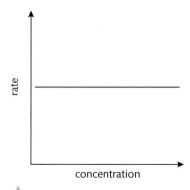

▲ **Figure 6.26** Rate–concentration graph for a zero-order reaction.

## First-order reaction

Here the rate is directly proportional to the concentration of A.

$$\text{rate} = k\,[\text{A}]$$

So the concentration–time graph is a curve showing rate decreasing with concentration (Figure 6.27); the rate–concentration graph is a straight line passing through the origin with gradient $k$ (Figure 6.28).

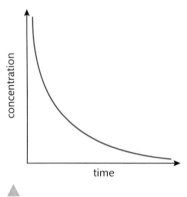

▲ **Figure 6.27** Concentration–time graph for a first-order reaction.

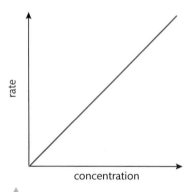

▲ **Figure 6.28** Rate–concentration graph for a first-order reaction.

## Second-order reaction

Here the rate is proportional to the square of the concentration of A.

$$\text{rate} = k\,[\text{A}]^2$$

So the concentration–time graph is also a curve, steeper at the start than the first-order graph and levelling off more (Figure 6.29). The rate–concentration graph is a parabola, characteristic of the square function (Figure 6.30). The gradient here is proportional to the concentration and is initially zero.

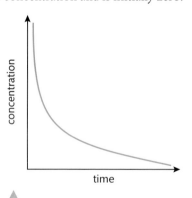

▲ **Figure 6.29** Concentration–time graph for a second-order reaction.

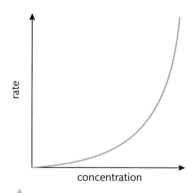

▲ **Figure 6.30** Rate–concentration graph for a second-order reaction.

## Summary

The relationships of concentration–time and rate–concentration graphs for zero-, first-, and second-order reactions are shown in Figures 6.31 and 6.32 for comparison.

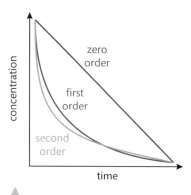

**Figure 6.31** Concentration–time graphs for zero-, first-, and second-order reactions.

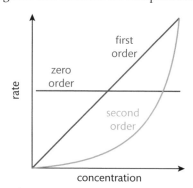

**Figure 6.32** Rate–concentration graphs for zero-, first-, and second-order reactions.

## First-order reactions have a constant half-life

There is one additional feature of the concentration–time graph for the first-order reaction worth mentioning. On these graphs, if we measure the time it takes for a concentration of reactant to decrease to half its original value, we find that this interval is independent of the starting concentration. This value, known as the **half-life**, $t_{1/2}$, for the reactant, is therefore a constant, as shown in Figure 6.33.

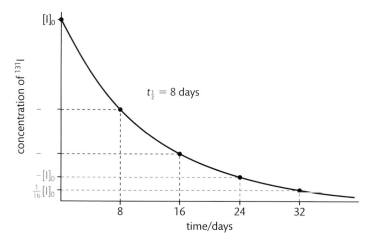

**Figure 6.33** First-order radioactive decay of iodine-131 showing constant half-life.

Constant half-life is a feature only of first-order reaction kinetics, so it can be used to establish that a reaction is first order with respect to that reactant. The shorter the value of the half-life, the faster the reaction.

Radioactive decay reactions follow first-order kinetics and are often described in terms of the half-life of the isotopes involved. For example, iodine-131, as shown in Figure 6.33, has a half-life of 8 days. This radioisotope is used in the diagnosis and treatment of thyroid cancer. In Chapter 15, Medicinal chemistry, we discuss the uses of this and other radiosotopes in the treatment of disease.

> **If a reactant has a constant half-life, then the reaction must be first order with respect to that reactant.**

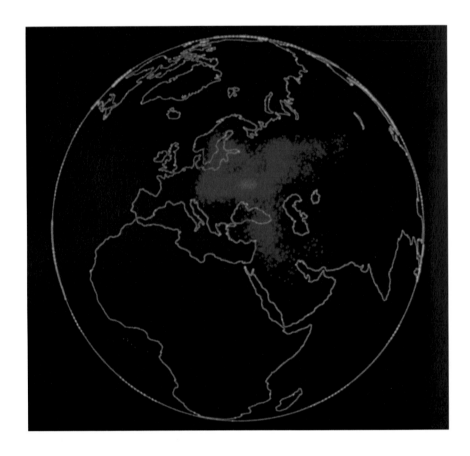

Computer simulation of the distribution of radioactivity in the northern hemisphere 6 days after the accident at the Chernobyl nuclear power station. High-altitude winds carried radioactivity over the Middle East, whilst lower level winds carried radioactivity north over Scandinavia and west over Poland.

The range of values for half-lives of different isotopes varies enormously from 4.5 billion years for uranium-238 to milliseconds for carbon-17. The duration of the half-life is of prime relevance in assessing the health dangers associated with radioactivity. When the nuclear facility in Chernobyl, Ukraine, exploded in April 1986, many different isotopes were released. Of these, iodine-131 had decayed almost completely after about 6 weeks, but caesium-137 with a half-life of 30 years and strontium-90 with a half-life of 29 years will remain in the soil and concentrate in food chains for over 300 years. These are considered to be the most devastating consequence of the accident.

## Determination of the order of a reaction

Methods for determining the overall order of a reaction depend on determining the order with respect to each reactant in turn. There are two main methods for doing this, although only one of these, the initial rates method, is covered at this level. It is discussed here with respect to two reactants, denoted 'A' and 'B' in these examples.

### Initial rates method

This involves carrying out a number of separate experiments with different starting concentrations of reactant A, and measuring the initial rate of each reaction. The concentrations of other reactants are held constant, so that the effect of [A] on reaction rate can be seen. The process can then be repeated for reactant B.

By analysing the data, the order of the reaction can be deduced as follows.

- If changing the concentration of A has no effect on the rate, the reaction must be zero order with respect to A.
- If changes in the concentration of A produce directly proportional changes in the rate of the reaction, the reaction must be first order with respect to A. In other words, in a first-order reaction, doubling the concentration of A leads to doubling of the rate, tripling [A] leads to a tripling of the rate, etc.
- If changes in the concentration of A lead to the square of that change in the rate of the reaction, then the reaction must be second order with respect to A. For example, doubling [A] would lead to a four-fold increase in the rate of reaction, and tripling [A] would lead to a nine-fold increase in the rate.

Use the data in the table below to work out the order of reaction with respect to reactants A and B, and so write the rate expression for this reaction.

| Experiment number | Initial concentrations / mol dm$^{-3}$ | | Initial rate of reaction / mol dm$^{-3}$ s$^{-1}$ |
|---|---|---|---|
| | [A] | [B] | |
| 1 | 0.10 | 0.10 | $2.0 \times 10^{-4}$ |
| 2 | 0.20 | 0.10 | $4.0 \times 10^{-4}$ |
| 3 | 0.30 | 0.10 | $6.0 \times 10^{-4}$ |
| 4 | 0.30 | 0.20 | $2.4 \times 10^{-3}$ |
| 5 | 0.30 | 0.30 | $5.4 \times 10^{-3}$ |

**Solution**

The concentration of B is constant in the first three experiments, so we can use these to deduce the effect of A on the rate of the reaction. We can find the change in rate by dividing one value by the other. Comparing experiments 1 and 2, doubling [A] leads to a doubling of the rate; from experiments 1 and 3, tripling [A] leads to a tripling of the rate. So the reaction must be first order with respect to A.

The concentration of A is held constant in the last three experiments, so these are used to deduce the effect of B on the rate. Comparing experiments 3 and 4, doubling [B] leads to a quadruple ($2^2$) change in the rate; comparing experiments 3 and 5, tripling [B] leads to a nine-fold ($3^2$) change in the rate. So the reaction must be second order with respect to B.

Therefore the rate expression for this reaction is rate = $k$ [A] [B]$^2$.

The table below summarizes the deductions used in analysing data of this type.

| | Change in rate of zero-order reaction | Change in rate of first-order reaction | Change in rate of second-order reaction |
|---|---|---|---|
| **[A] doubles** | no change | rate doubles (×2) | rate ×4 |
| **[A] triples** | no change | rate triples (×3) | rate ×9 |
| **[A] increases four-fold** | no change | rate increases four-fold (×4) | rate ×16 |

## Use of the integrated form of the rate expression

In more advanced studies of kinetics, mathematical analysis involving the calculus is used. By taking the integrated form of the rate expression, direct graphical analysis of functions of concentration against time leads to identification of the order. This mathematical analysis is not covered in this course.

Experiments can be done to determine the order of reaction by altering reactant concentrations.

### Exercises

**19** The reaction between $NO_2$ and $F_2$ gives the following rate data at a certain temperature. What is the order of reaction with respect to $NO_2$ and $F_2$?

| $[NO_2]$ / mol dm$^{-3}$ | $[F_2]$ / mol dm$^{-3}$ | Rate / mol dm$^{-3}$ min$^{-1}$ |
|---|---|---|
| 0.1 | 0.2 | 0.1 |
| 0.2 | 0.2 | 0.4 |
| 0.1 | 0.4 | 0.2 |

|   | **NO$_2$ order** | **F$_2$ order** |
|---|---|---|
| **A** | first | first |
| **B** | first | second |
| **C** | second | first |
| **D** | second | second |

**20** The following data were obtained for the reaction of NO(g) with $O_2$(g) to form $NO_2$(g) at 25 °C.

| Experiment | [NO] / mol dm$^{-3}$ | $[O_2]$ / mol dm$^{-3}$ | Initial rate / mol dm$^{-3}$ s$^{-1}$ |
|---|---|---|---|
| 1 | 0.30 | 0.20 | $2.0 \times 10^{-3}$ |
| 2 | 0.30 | 0.40 | $4.0 \times 10^{-3}$ |
| 3 | 0.60 | 0.80 | $3.2 \times 10^{-2}$ |

Calculate the order with respect to the two reactants and write the rate expression for the reaction.

**21** If a reaction A + 2B → products has the rate expression rate = $k\,[A]^2$, deduce the rates in experiments 2 and 3 in the table below.

| Experiment | [A] / mol dm$^{-3}$ | [B] / mol dm$^{-3}$ | Rate / mol dm$^{-3}$ s$^{-1}$ |
|---|---|---|---|
| 1 | 0.01 | 0.01 | $3.8 \times 10^{-3}$ |
| 2 | 0.02 | 0.01 |  |
| 3 | 0.02 | 0.02 |  |

### NATURE OF SCIENCE

Chemical kinetic data are derived entirely from experiment, and cannot be deduced from knowledge of the reaction's stoichiometry. This requires objectivity on the part of the researcher, as results can sometimes be different from what might be expected. Kinetic data, when interpreted alongside stoichiometric data, can provide valuable insights into the nature of chemical change.

**TOK**

The study of kinetics enables us to accumulate evidence in support of a particular reaction mechanism. This is an example of inductive reasoning, discussed in the TOK chapter on page 951. But there may be alternate reaction pathways that are also consistent with the data. In the examples given here, can you suggest alternate possible reaction mechanisms and what further evidence might support them?

## Reaction mechanism

### Most reactions involve a series of small steps

Most reactions that occur at a measurable rate occur as a series of simple steps, each involving a small number of particles, as described in the collision theory discussed in section 6.1. This sequence of steps is known as the **reaction mechanism**. The individual steps, called **elementary steps**, usually cannot be observed directly, so the mechanism is in effect a *theory* about the sequence of events in progressing from reactants to products. Chemists derive evidence to support such reaction mechanisms from many sources, and the study of kinetics often gives very important clues. It is worth noting though, that while kinetic evidence can help to support a particular mechanism, it cannot *prove* it to be correct – only that it is consistent with the observed data.

Often the products of a single step in the mechanism are used in a subsequent step. They exist only as reaction **intermediates**, not as final products. The sum of the individual steps in the mechanism must equal the overall equation for the reaction and intermediates on both sides cancel out.

For example, in the reaction

$$NO_2(g) + CO(g) \rightarrow NO(g) + CO_2(g)$$

it has been shown that the mechanism involves the following elementary steps:

step 1:  $NO_2(g) + \cancel{NO_2(g)} \rightarrow NO(g) + \cancel{NO_3(g)}$

step 2:  $\underline{\cancel{NO_3(g)} + CO(g) \rightarrow \cancel{NO_2(g)} + CO_2(g)}$

overall reaction:  $NO_2(g) + CO(g) \rightarrow NO(g) + CO_2(g)$

The overall reaction is obtained by cancelling molecules that appear on both sides.

$NO_3$ is an intermediate in this reaction, being produced and consumed in different steps, so it does not appear in the overall equation.

The term **molecularity** is used in reference to an elementary step to indicate the number of reactant species involved. So **unimolecular** refers to an elementary step that involves a single reactant particle, **bimolecular** refers to an elementary step with two reactant particles. In the $NO_2 + CO$ reaction above, both the elementary steps are bimolecular. Because of collision theory, and the extremely low probability of more than two particles colliding at the same time with sufficient energy and in the correct orientation, **termolecular** reactions (those that involve three reactant particles) are rare.

## The rate-determining step is the slowest step in the reaction mechanism

When city planners are trying to improve traffic flow through a particular area, they always look at the place where traffic is moving the most slowly – perhaps a crowded junction or a merge lane. They know that this is the place that is limiting the overall flow. Similarly, in chemical reactions that involve several steps, the overall rate of reaction is determined by the slowest step in the sequence. This is therefore called the **rate-determining step**. Products of the reaction can only appear as fast as the products of this elementary step. So the rate-determining step determines the overall rate of the reaction.

Potential energy level profiles can be used to illustrate the progress of a multi-step reaction. An example is shown in Figure 6.34.

The two maxima represent the transition states (as

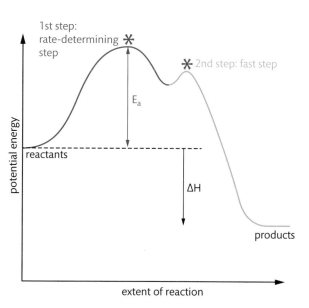

Figure 6.34 Potential energy level profile showing a two-step reaction.

**NATURE OF SCIENCE**

The simultaneous collision of three particles with sufficient energy and the correct orientation is so unlikely statistically that reaction mechanisms usually exclude termolecular reactions and propose instead a stepwise mechanism. In this way, scientists are applying the principle of Occam's razor – that theories need to be as simple as possible while maximizing explanatory power.

**The slowest step in a reaction mechanism is called the rate-determining step. This step determines the overall rate of the reaction.**

explained in Figure 6.13 on page 280), and the minimum between them represents the intermediate species present after the first step. In this example, the energy of the transition state of the first step is higher than that of the second step, so the first step will be the slowest step and will determine the rate of the reaction. The activation energy for the overall reaction is equal to the activation energy of this rate-determining step. Catalysts usually alter the reaction mechanism by providing an alternate pathway for the rate-determining step that has a lower activation energy.

## The rate expression for an overall reaction is determined by the reaction mechanism

As the rate of reaction depends on the rate of the rate-determining step, it follows that the rate expression for the overall reaction must depend on the rate law for the rate-determining step. So how can this be determined?

Because the rate-determining step is an elementary step, a single molecular event, its rate law comes directly from its molecularity. Collision theory informs us that the concentration of each reactant in the rate-determining step must appear in the rate law for that step, raised to the power of its stoichiometric coefficient in the equation. The table below shows the relationship between equations for elementary steps and their rate laws. (Remember these relationships exist *only for elementary steps* and not for deriving the rate expression for the overall reaction from the stoichiometric coefficients.)

| Equation for rate-determining step | Molecularity | Rate law |
|---|---|---|
| A → products | unimolecular | rate = $k$ [A] |
| 2A → products | bimolecular | rate = $k$ [A]$^2$ |
| A + B → products | bimolecular | rate = $k$ [A] [B] |

The rate law for the rate-determining step, predictable from its equation, leads us to the rate expression for the overall reaction. If the rate-determining step is the first step in the mechanism, or the only step in a single-step mechanism, then its rate law is the same as the rate expression for the overall reaction.

### Worked example

The reaction

$$2NO_2Cl(g) \rightarrow 2NO_2(g) + Cl_2(g)$$

is believed to have the following mechanism:

| | | |
|---|---|---|
| step 1: | $NO_2Cl(g) \rightarrow NO_2(g) + Cl(g)$ | slow: the rate-determining step |
| step 2: | $NO_2Cl(g) + Cl(g) \rightarrow NO_2(g) + Cl_2(g)$ | fast |

overall:   $2NO_2Cl(g) \rightarrow 2NO_2(g) + Cl_2(g)$

Deduce the rate expression and the overall order of the reaction.

### Solution

The rate expression for the overall reaction is that of step 1, the rate-determining step.

rate = $k$ [NO$_2$Cl]

This is a first-order reaction.

When the rate-determining step is not the first step in the mechanism, it is a bit more complicated as in this case its reactant concentrations will depend on an earlier step, so this must also be taken into account.

## Worked example

For the reaction:

$$2NO(g) + O_2(g) \rightarrow 2NO_2(g)$$

the following reaction mechanism has been proposed.

| step 1: | $NO(g) + NO(g) \rightarrow N_2O_2(g)$ | fast |
| step 2: | $N_2O_2(g) + O_2(g) \rightarrow 2NO_2(g)$ | slow: the rate-determining step |
| overall: | $2NO(g) + O_2(g) \rightarrow 2NO_2(g)$ | |

Deduce the rate expression and the order for this reaction.

### Solution

So the rate depends on step 2 for which the rate law is:

$$\text{rate} = k\,[N_2O_2]\,[O_2]$$

But $N_2O_2$ is a product of step 1, so the concentration of this intermediate depends on $[NO]^2$. Therefore we substitute this into the equation above.

The rate expression for the overall reaction is:

$$\text{rate} = k\,[NO]^2\,[O_2]$$

It is a third-order reaction.

These examples explain why the order of the reaction with respect to each reactant is not linked to their coefficients in the overall equation for the reaction, but is instead determined by their coefficients in the equation for the rate-determining step.

Perhaps you can now understand what it means for a reaction to be zero order with respect to a particular reactant? We know that the concentration of this reactant does not affect the rate of the reaction – and this is because it does not take part in the rate-determining step. If a reactant does appear in the rate expression, then that reactant or something derived from it must take part in the rate-determining step.

The mechanisms given above are described as 'possible mechanisms' because they fit the empirical findings – that is both the kinetic data and the overall stoichiometry of the reaction. Mechanisms that do not satisfy one of these criteria must be rejected. Remember though that we can go no further in accepting a mechanism than to state that it is consistent with the data; it cannot be proven to be correct.

In summary, we can see that kinetic data give us information about reaction mechanisms, and so insights into the detailed processes of bond making and bond breaking. Good examples of this are covered in Chapter 10 – in the hydrolysis of halogenoalkanes, the different mechanisms of the reactions for primary and tertiary molecules are interpreted in terms of differences in their bonding.

Evaluation of a proposed mechanism for a reaction involves checking that it is consistent with kinetic data and the overall stoichiometry of the reaction.

Reaction mechanisms can be supported by indirect evidence but cannot be observed. What evidence would be needed to accept a proposed reaction mechanism as certain?

TOK

## Exercises

**22** If the reaction $NO_2(g) + CO(g) \rightarrow CO_2(g) + NO(g)$ occurs by a one-step collision process, what would be the expected rate expression for the reaction?

**23** $2NO_2(g) \rightarrow 2NO(g) + O_2(g)$ is shown experimentally to be second order with respect to $NO_2$. Is this consistent with the following mechanism?

$$NO_2 + NO_2 \rightarrow NO_3 + NO \quad \text{slow: the rate-determining step}$$

$$NO_3 + NO \rightarrow 2NO + O_2 \quad \text{fast}$$

**24** Which statement or statements about the following reaction at 450 °C is/are correct?

$$2SO_2(g) + O_2(g) \rightarrow 2SO_3(g)$$

I    The reaction must involve a collision between one $O_2$ and two $SO_2$ molecules.
II   Every collision between $SO_2$ and $O_2$ will produce $SO_3$.
III  The rate-determining step is the slowest step of the reaction.

**A**  I and III         **C**  III only
**B**  II only           **D**  None of the statements is correct

**25** If the mechanism of a reaction is:

$$AB_2 + AB_2 \rightarrow A_2B_4 \quad \text{slow}$$

$$A_2B_4 \rightarrow A_2 + 2B_2 \quad \text{fast}$$

**(a)** What is the overall equation for the reaction?
**(b)** What is the rate expression for this reaction?
**(c)** What units will the rate constant have in this expression?

# 16.2 Activation energy

## Understandings:

- The Arrhenius equation uses the temperature dependence of the rate constant to determine the activation energy.

### Guidance
*Use energy level diagrams to illustrate multi-step reactions showing the RDS in the diagram.*

- A graph of $1/T$ against $\ln k$ is a linear plot with gradient $-E_a/R$ and intercept $\ln A$.
- The frequency factor (or pre-exponential factor) $(A)$ takes into account the frequency of collisions with proper orientations.

## Applications and skills:

- Analysing graphical representation of the Arrhenius equation in its linear form $\ln k = \dfrac{-E_a}{RT} + \ln A$.
- Using the Arrhenius equation $k = Ae^{\frac{-E_a}{RT}}$.

### Guidance
- *Consider various data sources in using the linear expression $\ln k = \dfrac{-E_a}{RT} + \ln A$.*
- *The expression $\ln \dfrac{k_1}{k_2} = \dfrac{E_a}{R}\left(\dfrac{1}{T_2} - \dfrac{1}{T_1}\right)$ is given in the data booklet.*
- Describing the relationships between temperature and rate constant; frequency factor and complexity of molecules colliding.
- Determining and evaluating values of activation energy and frequency factors from data.

## The rate constant $k$ is temperature dependent

We learned in section 6.2 that the rate of reactions increases with increasing temperature, and that the common relationship is that a 10 °C increase in temperature leads to a doubling of the rate. This is often referred to as a rule of thumb, not a law

The term 'rule of thumb', used to describe a guideline or rough measure, is of unknown origin. The phrase exists in other languages including Scandinavian languages, Dutch, Turkish, and Persian, and it is likely that it refers to one of the numerous ways that thumbs have been used to estimate things. You may like to consider a rule of thumb as something which 'thumb times it works and thumb times it doesn't'.

of nature, as there are many reactions that respond very differently to temperature changes. In this section we will find out more about why this is so.

From the rate expressions developed in section 16.1 we know that the rate of reaction depends on two things: the rate constant, $k$, and the concentrations of reactants, raised to a power. Since increasing temperature does not change the values of reactant concentrations, its effect must therefore be on the value of $k$. So $k$ is a general measure of the rate of a reaction at a particular temperature.

In section 6.1 we used collision theory to explain the effect of increasing temperature on reaction rate: principally by increasing the number of collisions that involve particles having the necessary activation energy, $E_a$, a greater proportion of collisions leads to reaction. Maxwell–Boltzmann distribution curves can be used to show the changing distribution of kinetic energies with increasing temperature, as we saw on page 282. From this, we can predict that the value of the activation energy will determine the extent of the change in the number of particles that can react at higher temperature. When the activation energy is large, a temperature rise will cause a significant increase in the number of particles that can react. On the other hand, a low value for activation energy will mean that the same temperature rise will have a proportionately smaller effect on the reaction rate. Thus the temperature dependence of $k$ depends on the value of the activation energy.

Clearly, a mathematical relationship must exist between temperature, the rate constant, and the activation energy, and we will explore this below.

## The temperature dependence of the rate constant is expressed in the Arrhenius equation

Svante Arrhenius (page 347) showed that the fraction of molecules with energy greater than activation energy, $E_a$, at temperature $T$ is proportional to the expression $e^{-E_a/RT}$ where $R$ is the gas constant (= 8.31 J K$^{-1}$ mol$^{-1}$) and $T$ is the absolute temperature (in K). This must mean that the reaction rate, and therefore also the rate constant, are also proportional to this value. So we can write

$$k \propto e^{\frac{-E_a}{RT}} \text{ or } k = Ae^{\frac{-E_a}{RT}}$$

where $A$ is the **Arrhenius constant**, often called the **frequency factor** or **pre-exponential factor**. It takes into account the frequency with which successful collisions will occur, based on collision geometry and energy requirements. It is a constant for a reaction and has units the same as $k$, which therefore vary depending on the order of the reaction.

The equation $k = Ae^{\frac{-E_a}{RT}}$ is known as the **Arrhenius equation** and is given in section 1 of the IB data booklet.

## Using the Arrhenius equation to calculate activation energy

Simple manipulations of the Arrhenius equation give equations which can be used to calculate activation energy from experimental data.

The flight of insects like this common wasp depends on the release of energy from chemical reactions in their cells. The rate of these reactions is affected significantly by changes in the external temperature, slowing down when it is cooler. This is why wasps are only active during the warmer months, and why it is so much easier to swat a fly, for example, on a cold day.

Laboratory temperature sensor. The sensor is at the end of the metal rod and has been placed in a beaker of ice. Data-logging devices like this allow continuous temperature measurements to be made and analysed on a computer.

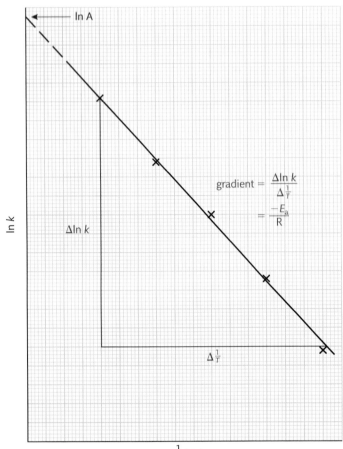

**Figure 6.35** An Arrhenius plot showing that ln $k$ versus $1/T$ gives a straight line with intercept ln $A$ on the $y$-axis and gradient = $-E_a/R$.

The value of $A$, the Arrhenius constant, indicates the frequency of collisions and the probability that collisions have proper orientations.

## The equation of a straight line

If we take the natural logarithm (logarithm to base e) of both sides of the equation above, we find that

$$\ln k = -\frac{E_a}{RT} + \ln A$$

This is a form of the equation for a straight line $y = mx + c$. So a graph of ln $k$ ($y$-axis) against $1/T$ ($x$-axis) will give a straight line with gradient ($m$) $= -E_a/R$. This is known as an **Arrhenius plot** and an example is shown in Figure 6.35.

This form of the Arrhenius equation is also given in Table 1 of the IB data booklet.

As R is a constant (8.31 J K$^{-1}$ mol$^{-1}$), it is therefore a simple operation to derive $E_a$ from the measured gradient of this graph.

$$\text{gradient} = -\frac{E_a}{R}$$

Therefore, $E_a$ (J mol$^{-1}$) = measured gradient (K) × 8.31 (J K$^{-1}$ mol$^{-1}$).

### Worked example

The following data were collected for a reaction.

| Rate constant / s$^{-1}$ | Temperature / °C | Rate constant / s$^{-1}$ | Temperature / °C |
|---|---|---|---|
| $2.88 \times 10^{-4}$ | 320 | $1.26 \times 10^{-3}$ | 380 |
| $4.87 \times 10^{-4}$ | 340 | $1.94 \times 10^{-3}$ | 400 |
| $7.96 \times 10^{-4}$ | 360 | | |

Determine the activation energy for the reaction in kJ mol$^{-1}$ by a graphical method.

**Solution**

Convert the values of $k$ to ln $k$ and the values for temperature to $1/T$ (remember to convert °C to K by adding 273). Draw an Arrhenius plot of ln k against $1/T$ and measure its gradient.

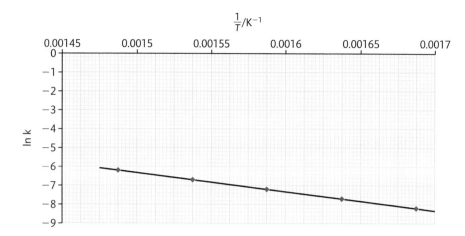

measured gradient $= -9518.65$ K

$$\text{gradient} = -\frac{E_a}{R}$$

$E_a \text{ (J mol}^{-1}) = 9518.65 \text{ (K)} \times 8.31 \text{ (J K}^{-1} \text{ mol}^{-1})$

Therefore $E_a = 79.1 \text{ kJ mol}^{-1}$

## Solving simultaneous equations

Activation energy can also be calculated from values of the rate constant, $k$, at only two temperatures. The formula is derived as follows:

At temperature $T_1$ where the rate constant is $k_1$:

$$\ln k_1 = -\frac{E_a}{RT_1} + \ln A$$

At temperature $T_2$ where the rate constant is $k_2$:

$$\ln k_2 = -\frac{E_a}{RT_2} + \ln A$$

By subtracting the second equation from the first, we can derive the following equation:

$$\ln\frac{k_1}{k_2} = \frac{E_a}{R}\left(\frac{1}{T_2} - \frac{1}{T_1}\right)$$

This equation is also given in section 1 of the IB data booklet.

### Worked example

The table below shows data of rate constants for the gas-phase decomposition of hydrogen iodide at two different temperatures.

$$2HI(g) \rightarrow H_2(g) + I_2(g)$$

| Temperature / °C | Rate constant / mol dm$^{-3}$ s$^{-1}$ |
|---|---|
| 283 | $3.52 \times 10^{-7}$ |
| 508 | $3.95 \times 10^{-2}$ |

Calculate the activation energy for the reaction.

**Calculation of the activation energy of a reaction**
Full details of how to carry out this experiment with a worksheet are available online.

## Solution

Convert temperatures in °C to K: $T_1 = 556$ K and $T_2 = 781$ K.

Substituting the values into the equation:

$$\ln\left(\frac{k_1}{k_2}\right) = \frac{E_a}{R}\left(\frac{1}{T_2} - \frac{1}{T_1}\right)$$

$$\ln\left(\frac{3.52\times10^{-7} \text{ mol dm}^{-3}\text{ s}^{-1}}{3.95\times10^{-2} \text{ mol dm}^{-3}\text{ s}^{-1}}\right) = \frac{E_a}{8.31 \text{ J K}^{-1}\text{ mol}^{-1}}\left(\frac{1}{781 \text{ K}} - \frac{1}{556 \text{ K}}\right)$$

$$E_a = 1.87 \times 10^5 \text{ J mol}^{-1}$$

So the Arrhenius equation enables us to calculate the activation energy of a reaction. The relationship also supports the observation that increasing the temperature by 10 K (which is of course the same as 10 °C) doubles the value of the rate constant and hence the rate of reaction when the activation energy is in a fairly narrow range around 50 kJ mol$^{-1}$. This is the situation for a large number of common reactions, hence the rule of thumb is justified. But for reactions that have particularly large or particularly small values for activation energy, then we find that the rise in temperature has a very different effect on the rate constant. This is applied in materials research, where the temperature sensitivity of reactions is crucial. For example, research into the temperature dependence of memory devices such as flash drives is based on the Arrhenius equation, and helps manufacturers predict the memory retention under different conditions.

### NATURE OF SCIENCE

The effect of increasing temperature on increasing the rate of reactions is widely observed in everyday examples such as puddles of water drying up more quickly when the weather is warmer. This temperature effect on rate can be broadly understood and explained in terms of the kinetic molecular theory and collision theory. But this approach is only qualitative. The significance of the Arrhenius equation is that it proposes a quantitative model to explain the effect of temperature change on reaction rate. Because this leads to testable predictions, it means that data can be generated which lend support to the theory.

### Exercises

**26** Consider the following statements:

I     The rate constant of a reaction increases with increase in temperature.
II    Increase in temperature decreases the activation energy of the reaction.
III   The term $A$ in the Arrhenius equation ($k = Ae^{-E_a/RT}$) relates to the energy requirements of the collisions.

Which statement(s) is/are correct?

   **A**   I only           **B**   II only           **C**   I and III only       **D**   II and III only

**27** To what does $A$ refer in the Arrhenius equation $k = Ae^{-E_a/RT}$?

   **A**   activation energy     **B**   kinetic energy     **C**   rate constant     **D**   collision geometry

**28** The rate of a chemical reaction increases with increasing temperature. This increase in rate is due to:

I     an increase in the collision rate
II    an increase in the activation energy
III   an increase in the rate constant

   **A**   I and II only       **B**   I and III only       **C**   II and III only       **D**   I, II, and III

**29** Rate constants for the reaction

$$NO_2(g) + CO(g) \rightarrow NO(g) + CO_2(g) \text{ are given below.}$$

At 700 K, $k = 1.3$ mol dm$^{-3}$ s$^{-1}$

At 800 K, $k = 23.0$ mol dm$^{-3}$ s$^{-1}$

Calculate the value of the activation energy in kJ mol$^{-1}$.

1 Which graph represents a reaction that is first order with respect to reactant A?

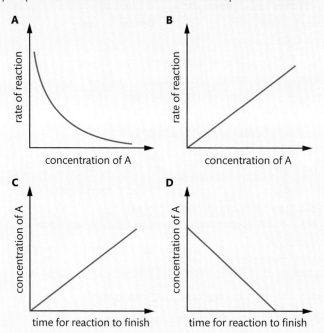

2 Curve X on the graph below shows the volume of oxygen formed during the catalytic decomposition of a 1.0 mol dm$^{-3}$ solution of hydrogen peroxide:

$$2H_2O_2(aq) \rightarrow O_2(g) + 2H_2O(l)$$

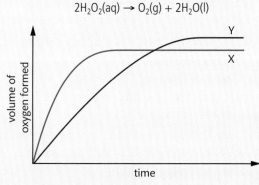

Which change would produce the curve Y?

A adding water

B adding some 0.1 mol dm$^{-3}$ hydrogen peroxide solution

C using a different catalyst

D lowering the temperature

3 Bromine and nitrogen(II) oxide react according to the following equation.

$$Br_2(g) + 2NO(g) \rightarrow 2NOBr(g)$$

Which rate equation is consistent with the experimental data?

| [Br$_2$] / mol dm$^{-3}$ | [NO] / mol dm$^{-3}$ | Rate / mol dm$^{-3}$ s$^{-1}$ |
|---|---|---|
| 0.10 | 0.10 | $1.0 \times 10^{-6}$ |
| 0.20 | 0.10 | $4.0 \times 10^{-6}$ |
| 0.20 | 0.40 | $4.0 \times 10^{-6}$ |

A rate $= k$ [Br$_2$]$^2$ [NO]          C rate $= k$ [Br$_2$]$^2$

B rate $= k$ [Br$_2$] [NO]$^2$          D rate $= k$ [NO]$^2$

**4** Which step is the rate-determining step of a reaction?

**A** the step with the lowest activation energy    **C** the step with the highest activation energy

**B** the final step                                      **D** the first step

**5** Consider the following reaction.

$$2NO(g) + 2H_2(g) \rightarrow N_2(g) + 2H_2O(g)$$

A proposed reaction mechanism is:

| | |
|---|---|
| $NO(g) + NO(g) \rightleftharpoons N_2O_2(g)$ | fast |
| $N_2O_2(g) + H_2(g) \rightarrow N_2O(g) + H_2O(g)$ | slow |
| $N_2O(g) + H_2(g) \rightarrow N_2(g) + H_2O(g)$ | fast |

What is the rate expression?

**A** rate $= k [H_2] [NO]^2$                       **C** rate $= k [NO]^2 [H_2]^2$

**B** rate $= k [N_2O_2] [H_2]$                 **D** rate $= k [NO]^2 [N_2O_2]^2 [H_2]$

**6** Which changes increase the rate of the reaction below?

$$C_4H_{10}(g) + Cl_2(g) \rightarrow C_4H_9Cl(l) + HCl(g)$$

I    increase of pressure

II   increase of temperature

III  removal of HCl(g)

**A** I and II only       **B** I and III only       **C** II and III only       **D** I, II, and III

**7** What happens when the temperature of a reaction increases?

**A** the activation energy increases             **C** the enthalpy change increases

**B** the rate constant increases                   **D** the order of the reaction increases

**8** Which experimental procedure could be used to determine the rate of reaction for the reaction between a solution of cobalt chloride, $CoCl_2(aq)$, and concentrated hydrochloric acid, $HCl(aq)$?

$$Co(H_2O)_6^{2+}(aq) + 4Cl^-(aq) \rightleftharpoons CoCl_4^{2-}(aq) + 6H_2O(l)$$

**A** measure the change in pH in a given time

**B** measure the change in mass in a given time

**C** use a colorimeter to measure the change in colour in a given time

**D** measure the change in volume of the solution in a given time

**9** Powdered manganese(IV) oxide, $MnO_2(s)$, increases the rate of the decomposition reaction of hydrogen peroxide, $H_2O_2(aq)$. Which statements about $MnO_2$ are correct?

I    The rate is independent of the particle size of $MnO_2$.

II   $MnO_2$ provides an alternative reaction pathway for the decomposition with a lower activation energy.

III  All the $MnO_2$ is present after the decomposition of the hydrogen peroxide is complete.

**A** I and II only       **B** I and III only       **C** II and III only       **D** I, II, and III

**10** Consider the following reaction.

$$NO_2(g) + CO(g) \rightarrow NO(g) + CO_2(g)$$

At $T < 227\ °C$ the rate expression is rate $= k [NO_2]^2$. Which of the following mechanisms is consistent with this rate expression?

| | | | | |
|---|---|---|---|---|
| **A** | $NO_2 + NO_2 \rightleftharpoons N_2O_4$ | fast | **C** $NO_2 \rightarrow NO + O$ | slow |
| | $N_2O_4 + 2CO \rightarrow 2NO + 2CO_2$ | slow | $CO + O \rightarrow CO_2$ | fast |
| **B** | $NO_2 + CO \rightarrow NO + CO_2$ | slow | **D** $NO_2 + NO_2 \rightarrow NO_3 + NO$ | slow |
| | | | $NO_3 + CO \rightarrow NO_2 + CO_2$ | fast |

**11 (a)** Nitrogen monoxide, NO, is involved in the decomposition of ozone according to the following mechanism.

$$O_3 \rightarrow O_2 + O\bullet$$
$$O_3 + NO \rightarrow NO_2 + O_2$$
$$NO_2 + O\bullet \rightarrow NO + O_2$$

Overall: $2O_3 \rightarrow 3O_2$

State and explain whether or not NO is acting as a catalyst. (2)

**(b)** The following is a proposed mechanism for the reaction of $NO(g)$ with $H_2(g)$.

Step 1:  $2NO(g) \rightarrow N_2O_2(g)$
Step 2:  $N_2O_2(g) + H_2(g) \rightarrow N_2O(g) + H_2O(g)$

**(i)** Identify the intermediate in the reaction. (1)
**(ii)** The observed rate expression is rate $= k\,[NO]^2\,[H_2]$. Assuming that the proposed mechanism is correct, comment on the relative speeds of the two steps. (1)

**(c)** The following two-step mechanism has been suggested for the reaction of $NO_2(g)$ with CO (g), where $k_2 \gg k_1$.

Step 1:  $NO_2(g) + NO_2(g) \rightarrow NO(g) + NO_3(g)$
Step 2:  $NO_3(g) + CO(g) \rightarrow NO_2(g) + CO_2(g)$
Overall:  $NO_2(g) + CO(g) \rightarrow NO(g) + CO_2(g)$

The experimental rate expression is rate $= k_1\,[NO_2]^2$. Explain why this mechanism produces a rate expression consistent with the experimentally observed one. (2)

**(d)** HI(g) decomposes into $H_2(g)$ and $I_2(g)$ according to the reaction below.

$$2HI(g) \rightarrow H_2(g) + I_2(g)$$

The reaction was carried out at different temperatures and a value of the rate constant, $k$, was obtained for each temperature. A graph of $\ln k$ against $\dfrac{1}{T}$ is shown below.

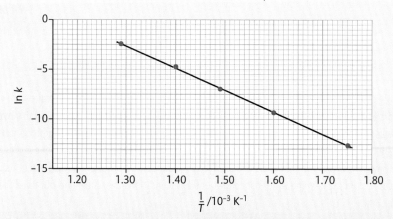

Calculate the activation energy, $E_a$, for the reaction using these data and Section 1 of the IB Data booklet, showing your working. (4)

*(Total 10 marks)*

**12** Hydrogen and nitrogen(II) oxide react according to the following equation.

$$2H_2(g) + 2NO(g) \rightleftharpoons N_2(g) + 2H_2O(g)$$

At time $= t$ seconds, the rate of the reaction is
rate $= k\,[H_2(g)]\,[NO(g)]^2$

(a) Explain precisely what the square brackets around nitrogen(II) oxide, [NO(g)], represent in this context. (1)

(b) Deduce the units for the rate constant $k$. (1)

*(Total 2 marks)*

**13** Consider the following graph of ln $k$ against $\frac{1}{T}$ (temperature in kelvin) for the second-order decomposition of $N_2O$ into $N_2$ and O:

$$N_2O \rightarrow N_2 + O$$

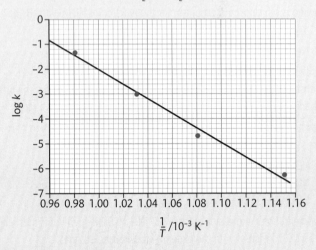

(a) State how the rate constant, $k$, varies with temperature, $T$. (1)

(b) Determine the activation energy, $E_a$, for this reaction. (3)

(c) The rate expression for this reaction is rate $= k\,[N_2O]^2$ and the rate constant is 0.244 $dm^3\ mol^{-1}\ s^{-1}$ at 750 °C. A sample of $N_2O$ of concentration 0.200 mol $dm^{-3}$ is allowed to decompose. Calculate the rate when 10% of the $N_2O$ has reacted. (2)

*(Total 6 marks)*

**14** Alex and Hannah were asked to investigate the kinetics involved in the iodination of propanone. They were given the following equation by their teacher:

$$CH_3COCH_3(aq) + I_2(aq) \xrightarrow{H^+(aq)} CH_2ICOCH_3(aq) + HI(aq)$$

Alex's hypothesis was that the rate will be affected by changing the concentrations of the propanone and the iodine, as the reaction can happen without a catalyst. Hannah's hypothesis was that as the catalyst is involved in the reaction, the concentrations of the propanone, iodine, and the hydrogen ions will all affect the rate.

They carried out several experiments varying the concentration of one of the reactants or the catalyst whilst keeping other concentrations and conditions the same, and obtained the results below.

| Experiment | Composition by volume of mixture / $cm^3$ | | | | Initial rate / mol $dm^{-3}\ s^{-1}$ |
|---|---|---|---|---|---|
| | 1.00 mol $dm^{-3}$ $CH_3COCH_3(aq)$ | water | 1.00 mol $dm^{-3}$ $H^+(aq)$ | $5.00 \times 10^{-3}$ mol $dm^{-3}$ $I_2$ in KI | |
| 1 | 10.0 | 60.0 | 10.0 | 20.0 | $4.96 \times 10^{-6}$ |
| 2 | 10.0 | 50.0 | 10.0 | 30.0 | $5.04 \times 10^{-6}$ |
| 3 | 5.0 | 65.0 | 10.0 | 20.0 | $2.47 \times 10^{-6}$ |
| 4 | 10.0 | 65.0 | 5.0 | 20.0 | $2.51 \times 10^{-6}$ |

**(a)** Explain why they added water to the mixtures. (1)

**(b) (i)** Deduce the order of reaction for each substance and the rate expression from the results. (2)

**(ii)** Comment on whether Alex's or Hannah's hypothesis is correct. (1)

**(c)** Using the data from Experiment 1, determine the concentration of the substances used and the rate constant for the reaction including its units. (3)

**(d) (i)** This reaction uses a catalyst. Sketch and annotate the Maxwell–Boltzmann energy distribution curve for a reaction with and without a catalyst on labelled axes. (3)

**(ii)** Describe how a catalyst works. (1)

*(Total 11 marks)*

**15** The diagram below shows a potential energy level profile for a reaction. It occurs by the following mechanism:

$$W + XY \rightarrow WY + X$$
$$WY + Z \rightarrow W + YZ$$

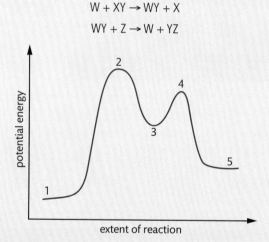

**(a)** Deduce the equation for the overall reaction. (1)

**(b)** Label each step 1–5 as reactant, product, transition state, or intermediate. (3)

**(c)** Identify the species present at each step. (3)

**(d)** Determine which step is the rate-determining step and deduce the rate expression for the overall reaction. (2)

**(e)** Consider whether the reaction is catalysed, and if so identify the catalyst. (1)

**(f)** Add labelled arrows to the diagram to show the activation energy, $E_a$, and the enthalpy change, $\Delta H$. (2)

*(Total 12 marks)*

To access weblinks on the topics covered in this chapter, please go to www.pearsonhotlinks.com and enter the ISBN or title of this book.

**07**

Equilibrium

## Essential ideas

**7.1** Many reactions are reversible. These reactions will reach a state of equilibrium when the rates of the forward reaction and reverse reaction are equal. The position of equilibrium can be controlled by changing the conditions.

**17.1** The position of equilibrium can be quantified by the equilibrium law. The equilibrium constant for a particular reaction only depends on the temperature.

Electron micrograph of a section through human lung tissue, showing air spaces called alveoli. Equilibrium considerations help us to understand how oxygen and carbon dioxide are exchanged between the blood and the air in these spaces.

Imagine that you are part way along an escalator (a moving staircase) that is moving up and you decide to run down. If you can run down at exactly the same speed as the escalator is moving up, you will have no *net* movement. So, if someone were to take a picture of you at regular time intervals, it would seem as if you were not moving at all. Of course, in reality both you and the escalator *are* moving, but because there is no net change neither movement is observable. In chemical reactions a similar phenomenon occurs when a reaction takes place at the same rate as its reverse reaction, so no net change is observed. This is known as the **equilibrium state**.

In this chapter, we explore some of the features of the equilibrium state and learn how to derive and use the equilibrium constant expression. Application of the **equilibrium law** enables us to quantify reaction components and to predict how far reactions will proceed under different conditions. Industrial processes rely significantly on this type of study to determine the conditions that will maximize the yield of product. Equilibrium studies are also important in many biochemical and environmental processes, such as predicting the solubility of gases in the blood and knowing how certain chemicals in the atmosphere may react together to form pollutants that contribute to climate change. By the end of this chapter, you will be ready to tackle some of these applications in subsequent chapters.

Snow and ice-covered peak in the Cordillera Huayhuash, Peru. Equilibrium considerations help explain the relationship between water vapour in the clouds and precipitations in the form of liquid (rain) and solid (snow) at different temperatures and pressures.

# 7.1 Equilibrium

## Understandings:

- A state of equilibrium is reached in a closed system when the rates of the forward and reverse reactions are equal.

### Guidance
*Physical and chemical systems should be covered.*

- The equilibrium law describes how the equilibrium constant ($K_c$) can be determined for a particular chemical equation.
- The magnitude of the equilibrium constant indicates the extent of a reaction at equilibrium and is temperature dependent.
- The reaction quotient ($Q$) measures the relative amount of products and reactants present during a reaction at a particular point in time. $Q$ is the equilibrium expression with non-equilibrium concentrations. The position of the equilibrium changes with changes in concentration, pressure, and temperature.
- A catalyst has no effect on the position of equilibrium or the equilibrium constant.

## Applications and skills:

- The characteristics of chemical and physical systems in a state of equilibrium.
- Deduction of the equilibrium constant expression ($K_c$) from an equation for a homogeneous reaction.
- Determination of the relationship between different equilibrium constants ($K_c$) for the same reaction at the same temperature.

  **Guidance**
  *Relationship between $K_c$ values for reactions that are multiples or inverses of one another should be covered.*

- Application of Le Chatelier's principle to predict the qualitative effects of changes of temperature, pressure, and concentration on the position of equilibrium and on the value of the equilibrium constant.

  **Guidance**
  *Specific details of any industrial process are not required.*

## Physical systems

Consider what happens when some bromine, $Br_2$, is placed in a sealed container at room temperature.

As bromine is a **volatile** liquid, with a boiling point close to room temperature, a significant number of particles (molecules of $Br_2$) will have enough energy to escape from the liquid state and form vapour in the process known as **evaporation**. As the container is sealed, the bromine vapour cannot escape and so its concentration will increase. Some of these vapour molecules will collide with the surface of the liquid, lose energy, and become liquid in the process known as **condensation**.

$$Br_2(l) \underset{\text{condensation}}{\overset{\text{evaporation}}{\rightleftharpoons}} Br_2(g)$$

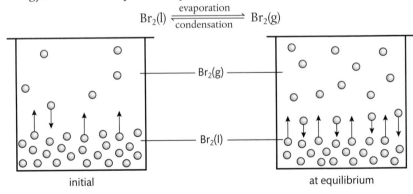

initial      at equilibrium

The rate of condensation increases with the increase in concentration of vapour, as more vapour particles collide with the surface of the liquid. Eventually, the rate of condensation is *equal* to the rate of evaporation, and at this point there will be no net change in the amounts of liquid and gas present (Figure 7.2). We say that the system has reached **equilibrium**. This will only occur in a closed system, where the $Br_2(g)$ cannot escape as vapour but may condense back into the liquid.

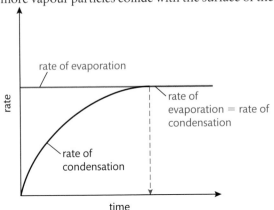

Bromine stored in a sealed jar. The system is in dynamic equilibrium, so the concentrations of liquid and vapour do not change at constant temperature.

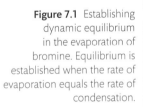

Bromine is the only non-metallic element that is liquid at room temperature. It is extremely toxic and takes its name from a Greek word meaning stench.

**Figure 7.1** Establishing dynamic equilibrium in the evaporation of bromine. Equilibrium is established when the rate of evaporation equals the rate of condensation.

**Figure 7.2** The rates of evaporation and condensation as liquid–vapour equilibrium is established in a closed system. The rate of evaporation is constant, while the rate of condensation increases with increasing concentration of vapour. Equilibrium is established when the two rates are equal.

# Chemical systems

Consider the reaction of dissociation between hydrogen iodide (HI) and its elements hydrogen ($H_2$) and iodine ($I_2$). Hydrogen and hydrogen iodide are both colourless, whereas iodine is released as a purple gas, so this helps us to see what is happening.

$$2HI(g) \rightleftharpoons H_2(g) + I_2(g)$$
colourless gas    colourless gas    purple gas

If we carry out this reaction starting with hydrogen iodide in a sealed container, there will at first be an increase in the purple colour owing to the production of iodine gas. But after a while this increase in colour will stop, and it may appear that the reaction too has stopped. In fact, what has happened is that the rate of the dissociation of HI is fastest at the start when the concentration of HI is greatest and falls as the reaction proceeds. Meanwhile, the reverse reaction, which initially has a zero rate because there is no $H_2$ and $I_2$ present, starts slowly and increases in rate as the concentrations of $H_2$ and $I_2$ increase. Eventually, the rate of dissociation of HI has become equal to the rate of the reverse reaction of association between $H_2$ and $I_2$, so the concentrations remain constant. This is why the colour in the flask remains the same. At this point, equilibrium has been reached. It is described as **dynamic** because both forward and backward reactions are still occurring.

If we were to analyse the contents of the flask at this point, we would find that HI, $H_2$, and $I_2$ would all be present and that if there were no change in conditions, their concentrations would remain constant over time. We refer to this as the **equilibrium mixture**.

If we reversed the experiment and started with $H_2$ and $I_2$ instead of HI, we would find that eventually an equilibrium mixture would again be achieved in which the concentrations of $H_2$, $I_2$, and HI would remain constant. These relationships are shown in Figure 7.3.

Iodine gas in a stoppered flask. Iodine is a crystalline solid at room temperature, but sublimes on heating to form a purple gas.

TOK The study of chemical change often involves both the macroscopic and microscopic scales. Which ways of knowing do we use in moving from the macroscopic to the microscopic?

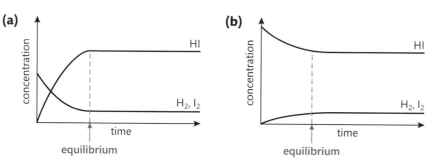

**Figure 7.3** Equilibrium is reached when the concentrations of reactants and products become constant. Note the same equilibrium mixture is reached starting from (a) a mixture of $H_2$ and $I_2$ or (b) from pure HI.

# The equilibrium state has specific characteristics

In studies of equilibria we are dealing with reversible reactions – those that occur in both directions. The convention is to describe the reaction from left to right (reactants to products) as the **forward reaction**, and the reaction from right to left (products to reactants) as the **backward** or **reverse reaction**. The symbol $\rightleftharpoons$ is used to show that the reaction is an equilibrium reaction.

forward
reaction
reactants $\rightleftharpoons$ products
backward
reaction

The examples of physical and chemical systems discussed have shown that:

     " At equilibrium the rate of the forward reaction is equal to the rate of the backward reaction. "

Strictly speaking, all reactions can be considered as equilibrium reactions. However, in many cases the equilibrium mixture consists almost entirely of products – that is, it is considered to have gone virtually to completion. By convention we use the symbol $\rightarrow$ rather than the equilibrium symbol in these cases. In other reactions there may be so little product formed that it is undetectable and the reaction is considered to have effectively not happened.

Make sure that you use the equilibrium symbol $\rightleftharpoons$ when writing equations for reactions where the reverse reactions are significant. For example, it must be used when explaining the behaviour of weak acids and bases (Chapter 8).

These reactions have also shown some of the main features of the equilibrium state, and these can now be summarized as they apply to *all* reactions at equilibrium.

| | Feature of equilibrium state | Explanation |
|---|---|---|
| 1 | Equilibrium is dynamic | The reaction has not stopped but both forward and backward reactions are still occurring at the same rate. |
| 2 | Equilibrium is achieved in a closed system | A closed system has no exchange of matter with the surroundings, so equilibrium is achieved where both reactants and products can react and recombine with each other. |
| 3 | The concentrations of reactants and products remain constant at equilibrium | They are being produced and destroyed at an equal rate. |
| 4 | At equilibrium there is no change in macroscopic properties | Macroscopic properties are observable properties such as colour and density. These do not change as they depend on the concentrations of the components of the mixture. |
| 5 | Equilibrium can be reached from either direction | The same equilibrium mixture will result under the same conditions, no matter whether the reaction is started with all reactants, all products, or a mixture of both. |

It is important to understand that even though the concentrations of reactant and product are *constant* at equilibrium, this in no way implies that they are *equal*. In fact, most commonly there will be a much higher concentration of either reactant or product in the equilibrium mixture, depending both on the reaction and on the conditions. We can see, for example, in Figure 7.3 that when the dissociation of HI reaches equilibrium, there is a higher concentration of HI than of $H_2$ and $I_2$.

Thinking back to the analogy in the introduction to this chapter, of you running in the opposite direction on a moving staircase where the top and bottom represent reactants and products respectively, it would be possible for you to be 'at equilibrium' near the top of the staircase, near the bottom, or anywhere in between. As long as you were moving at the same speed as the staircase you would still have no net change in position.

At equilibrium the rate of the forward reaction is equal to the rate of the backward reaction.

The proportion of reactant and product in the equilibrium mixture is referred to as its **equilibrium position**. Reactions where the mixture contains predominantly products are said to 'lie to the right' and reactions with predominantly reactants are said to 'lie to the left'. It is, however, often useful to be able to capture this information mathematically to compare the equilibrium mixtures of different reactions and the effect of different conditions. In the next section we will look at how this is done.

What are the differences between theories and analogies as forms of explanation?

TOK

**NATURE OF SCIENCE**

At equilibrium no change is observed on the macroscopic level, although particles are reacting at the microscopic level. These changes can be deduced using techniques such as isotopic labelling, which allow the progress of a specific reactant to be followed. Our power of understanding is enhanced by contributions from instrumentation and sensors that may gather information beyond human sense perception.

**1** Which statements are correct for a reaction at equilibrium?

I The forward and reverse reactions both continue.
II The rates of the forward and reverse reactions are equal.
III The concentrations of reactants and products are equal.

**A** I and II only      **B** I and III only      **C** II and III only      **D** I, II, and III

**2** Which statement is always true for a chemical reaction that has reached equilibrium at constant temperature?

**A** The yield of product(s) is greater than 50%.
**B** The rate of the reverse reaction is lower than that of the forward reaction.
**C** The amounts of reactants and products do not change.
**D** Both forward and reverse reactions have stopped.

**3** Which statement is *not* true for a mixture of ice and water at equilibrium at constant temperature?

**A** The rates of melting and freezing are equal.
**B** The amounts of ice and water are equal.
**C** The same position of equilibrium can be reached by cooling water and by heating ice.
**D** There is no observable change in the system.

## The equilibrium constant $K_c$ can be predicted from a reaction's stoichiometry

Consider now the reaction

$$H_2(g) + I_2(g) \rightleftharpoons 2HI(g)$$

If we were to carry out a series of experiments on this reaction with different starting concentrations of $H_2$, $I_2$, and HI, we could wait until each reaction reached equilibrium and then measure the composition of each equilibrium mixture. Here are some typical results obtained at 440 °C.

| | Initial concentration / mol dm⁻³ | Equilibrium concentration / mol dm⁻³ |
|---|---|---|
| $H_2$ | 0.100 | 0.0222 |
| $I_2$ | 0.100 | 0.0222 |
| HI | 0.000 | 0.156 |

Experiment I

| | Initial concentration / mol dm⁻³ | Equilibrium concentration / mol dm⁻³ |
|---|---|---|
| $H_2$ | 0.000 | 0.0350 |
| $I_2$ | 0.0100 | 0.0450 |
| HI | 0.350 | 0.280 |

Experiment II

| | Initial concentration / mol dm⁻³ | Equilibrium concentration / mol dm⁻³ |
|---|---|---|
| $H_2$ | 0.0150 | 0.0150 |
| $I_2$ | 0.000 | 0.0135 |
| HI | 0.127 | 0.100 |

Experiment III

At a glance these data may not appear to show any pattern. However, there is a predictable relationship among the different compositions of these equilibrium mixtures, and the key to discovering it is in the stoichiometry of the reaction equation.

Sometimes you may see the equilibrium sign written with unequal arrows such as ⇌. This is used to represent the reaction that lies in favour of products. Likewise, ⇌ is used to represent a reaction that lies in favour of reactants.

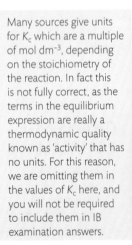

Remember square brackets [ ] are commonly used to show concentration in mol dm⁻³.

Many sources give units for $K_c$ which are a multiple of mol dm⁻³, depending on the stoichiometry of the reaction. In fact this is not fully correct, as the terms in the equilibrium expression are really a thermodynamic quality known as 'activity' that has no units. For this reason, we are omitting them in the values of $K_c$ here, and you will not be required to include them in IB examination answers.

**The equilibrium constant $K_c$ has a fixed value for a particular reaction at a specified temperature. The only thing that changes the value of $K_c$ for a reaction is the temperature.**

The equilibrium constant expression will only give the value $K_c$ when the concentrations used in the equation are the *equilibrium* concentrations for all reactants and products. Strictly speaking, the subscript 'eqm' should always be used in the equation, but by convention this is generally left out. However, make completely sure that the only values you substitute into an equation to calculate $K_c$ are the equilibrium concentrations.

$$H_2(g) + I_2(g) \rightleftharpoons 2HI(g)$$

If we take the *equilibrium* concentrations and process them in the following way:

$$\frac{[HI]^2_{eqm}}{[H_2]^1_{eqm}[I_2]^1_{eqm}}$$

2 = coefficient of HI in the reaction equation

1 = coefficient of $H_2$ in the reaction equation

1 = coefficient of $I_2$ in the reaction equation

we find the following results:

**Experiment I**

$$\frac{(0.156)^2}{0.0222 \times 0.0222} = 49.4$$

**Experiment II**

$$\frac{(0.280)^2}{0.035 \times 0.0450} = 49.8$$

**Experiment III**

$$\frac{(0.100)^2}{0.0150 \times 0.0135} = 49.4$$

Clearly this way of processing the equilibrium data produces a constant value within the limits of experimental accuracy. This constant is known as the **equilibrium constant, $K_c$**. It has a fixed value for this reaction *at a specified temperature*.

In fact, every reaction has its own particular value of $K_c$ which can be derived in a similar way. First we use the balanced reaction equation to write the **equilibrium constant expression**.

For the reaction:

$$aA + bB \rightleftharpoons cC + dD$$

the equilibrium constant expression is

$$\frac{[C]^c_{eqm}[D]^d_{eqm}}{[A]^a_{eqm}[B]^b_{eqm}} = K_c$$

The value for $K_c$ can then be determined by substituting the equilibrium concentrations of all reactants and products into this equation.

Note:

- The equilibrium constant expression has the concentrations of products in the numerator and the concentrations of reactants in the denominator.
- Each concentration is raised to the power of its coefficient in the balanced equation. (Where it is equal to one it does not have to be given.)
- Where there is more than one reactant or product the terms are multiplied together.

### Worked example

Write the equilibrium expression for the following reactions.

(i)  $2H_2(g) + O_2(g) \rightleftharpoons 2H_2O(g)$

(ii)  $Cu^{2+}(aq) + 4NH_3(aq) \rightleftharpoons [Cu(NH_3)_4]^{2+}$

**Solution**

(i)  $K_c = \dfrac{[H_2O]^2}{[H_2]^2[O_2]}$

(ii)  $K_c = \dfrac{[[Cu(NH_3)_4]^{2+}]}{[Cu^{2+}][NH_3]^4}$

## Exercises

4  Write the equilibrium constant expression for the following reactions:

(a)  $2NO(g) + O_2(g) \rightleftharpoons 2NO_2(g)$
(b)  $4NH_3(g) + 7O_2(g) \rightleftharpoons 4NO_2(g) + 6H_2O(g)$
(c)  $CH_3Cl(aq) + OH^-(aq) \rightleftharpoons CH_3OH(aq) + Cl^-(aq)$

5  Write the equations for the reactions represented by the following equilibrium constant expressions

(a)  $K_c = \dfrac{[NO_2]^2}{[N_2O_4]}$

(b)  $K_c = \dfrac{[CO][H_2]^3}{[CH_4][H_2O]}$

6  Write the equilibrium constant expressions for the following chemical reactions:

(a)  fluorine gas and chlorine gas combine to form $ClF_3(g)$
(b)  NO dissociates into its elements
(c)  methane, $CH_4$, and steam react to form carbon monoxide and hydrogen

## The magnitude of $K_C$ gives information on the extent of reaction

Different reactions have different values of $K_c$. What does this value tell us about a particular reaction?

As the equilibrium constant expression puts products on the numerator and reactants on the denominator, a high value of $K_c$ will mean that at equilibrium there are proportionately more products than reactants. In other words, such an equilibrium mixture lies to the right and the reaction goes almost to completion. By contrast, a low value of $K_c$ must mean that there are proportionately less products with respect to reactants, so the equilibrium mixture lies to the left and the reaction has barely taken place.

Consider the following three reactions and their $K_c$ values measured at 550 K.

$H_2(g) + I_2(g) \rightleftharpoons 2HI(g)$        $K_c = 2$
$H_2(g) + Br_2(g) \rightleftharpoons 2HBr(g)$      $K_c = 10^{10}$
$H_2(g) + Cl_2(g) \rightleftharpoons 2HCl(g)$      $K_c = 10^{18}$

The large range in their $K_c$ values tells us about the differing extents of these reactions. We can deduce that the reaction between $H_2$ and $Cl_2$ has taken place the most fully at this temperature, while $H_2$ and $I_2$ have reacted the least.

A good rule of thumb to apply to these situations is that if $K_c \gg 1$, the reaction is considered to go almost to completion (very high conversion of reactants into products), and if $K_c \ll 1$, the reaction hardly proceeds.

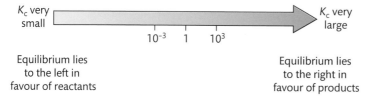

Equilibrium lies to the left in favour of reactants       Equilibrium lies to the right in favour of products

Note that the magnitude of $K_c$ does not give us any information on the *rate* of the reaction. It informs us of the nature of the equilibrium mixture, but not on how quickly the equilibrium state will be achieved.

The equilibrium constant expressions described here apply to homogeneous reactions, that is reactions where reactants and products are in the same phase, as gases, liquids, or in solution. It is good practice always to include state symbols in your equations to ensure this is being applied correctly.

## CHALLENGE YOURSELF

2  Why do you think the reactions of the three halogens $Cl_2$, $Br_2$, and $I_2$, with $H_2$ have such different values for their equilibrium constant at the same temperature? What can you conclude about the strength of bonding in the three hydrogen halides?

**Figure 7.4**  The larger the value of $K_c$, the further the equilibrium mixture lies to the right.

**The magnitude of the equilibrium constant $K_c$ gives information about how far a reaction goes at a particular temperature, but not about how fast it will achieve the equilibrium state.**

317

## The reaction quotient, $Q$, enables us to predict the direction of reaction

Remember that the value of $K_c$ is calculated from substituting the *equilibrium* concentrations of all reactants and products into the equilibrium constant expression. Any other values used will not give the equilibrium value $K_c$ for that reaction at that temperature.

This in itself can be useful. If we take the concentrations of the reactants and products at one moment in time when the reaction is not at equilibrium, and substitute these into the equilibrium constant expression, we obtain a value known as the **reaction quotient, Q**. As time passes and the reaction continues, the concentrations of all reaction components change and eventually reach the equilibrium concentrations. In other words, the value of Q changes in the direction of $K_c$. This enables us to predict the direction in which the reaction will proceed.

For example, if we again consider the reaction:

$$H_2(g) + I_2(g) \rightleftharpoons 2HI(g)$$

for which $K_c = 49.5$ at 440 °C, as we saw on page 316.

The table below shows experimental data for the concentrations of the reaction components from experiments I and II at a time when the reaction mixture was not at equilibrium.

|  | Experiment I: concentration at time $t$ / mol dm$^{-3}$ | Experiment II: concentration at time $t$ / mol dm$^{-3}$ |
|---|---|---|
| $H_2$ | 0.0500 | 0.0250 |
| $I_2$ | 0.0500 | 0.0350 |
| HI | 0.100 | 0.300 |

The reaction quotient, $Q$, is a measure of the relative amounts of reactants and products present in a reaction at a particular time. Its value is determined from substituting concentrations of reaction components, all measured at the same time, into the equilibrium expression.

The equilibrium constant expression $= \dfrac{[HI]^2}{[H_2][I_2]}$

Experiment I, time $t$ $\quad Q = \dfrac{(0.100)^2}{(0.0500)(0.0500)} = 4.00$

Experiment II, time $t$ $\quad Q = \dfrac{(0.300)^2}{(0.0250)(0.0350)} = 103$

In experiment I, $Q < K_c$ and so Q must increase as the reaction moves towards equilibrium. This means that the net reaction must be to the right, in favour of products.

In experiment II, $Q > K_c$ and so Q must decrease as the reaction moves towards equilibrium. This means that the net reaction must be to the left, in favour of reactants.

We can summarize the use of the reaction quotient, $Q$, in determining the direction of reaction as follows:

- if $Q = K_c$, reaction is at equilibrium, no net reaction occurs;
- if $Q < K_c$, reaction proceeds to the right in favour of products;
- if $Q > K_c$, reaction proceeds to the left in favour of reactants.

Note that the value of $Q$ for a reaction does not have a fixed value as it can be measured at any point in time, whereas the value of $K_c$ for a reaction is a constant at a specified temperature.

Comparison of the value of the reaction quotient, $Q$, at a specific time in a reaction with the value of $K_c$ for the reaction, enables us to predict the direction of change.

## Worked example

The equilibrium constant $K_c$ for the reaction

$$N_2(g) + 3H_2(g) \rightleftharpoons 2NH_3(g)$$

is $1.7 \times 10^2$ at 500 K.

Determine whether the reaction mixture is at equilibrium when the concentrations of the components at this temperature are as follows:

$[N_2] = 1.50$

$[H_2] = 1.00$

$[NH_3] = 8.00$.

If it is not at equilibrium, state and explain in which direction the reaction will proceed.

### Solution

First write the equilibrium constant expression.

$$\frac{[NH_3]^2}{[N_2][H_2]^3}$$

Calculate the value of $Q$ at these conditions by substituting the given concentration values into the equilibrium expression.

$$Q = \frac{(8.00)^2}{(1.50)(1.00)^3} = 42.7$$

Compare the value of $Q$ at the given conditions with $K_c$.

$$42.7 < 1.7 \times 10^2$$

Therefore the reaction is not at equilibrium. It will proceed to the right in favour of products, as the value of $Q$ must increase to be equal to $K_c$ at equilibrium.

The reaction quotient $Q$ is used in the calculation of the electrode potential of a half-cell operating under non-standard conditions in the Nernst equation. This is discussed in topic C.6 in Chapter 14, Energy.

## Relationships between $K_c$ for different equations of a reaction

As $K_c$ is defined with products on the numerator and reactants on the denominator, each raised to the power of their stoichiometric coefficients in the balanced equation, we can manipulate its value according to changes made to these terms. For this discussion we will consider the generic reaction:

$$aA + bB \rightleftharpoons cC + dD$$

for which the equilibrium constant is:

$$K_c = \frac{[C]^c[D]^d}{[A]^a[B]^b}$$

### 1 $K_c$ for the inverse reaction

The inverse reaction

$$cC + dD \rightleftharpoons aA + bB$$

defines the products as reactants and vice versa. We will denote its equilibrium constant as $K_c'$.

$$K_c' = \frac{[A]^a [B]^b}{[C]^c [D]^d}$$

We can see that $K_c' = \dfrac{1}{K_c}$ or $K_c' = K_c^{-1}$.

In other words the equilibrium constant for a reaction is the reciprocal of the equilibrium constant for its inverse reaction.

### 2 $K_c$ for a multiple of a reaction

Consider now the reaction

$$2aA + 2bB \rightleftharpoons 2cC + 2dD$$

We will denote its equilibrium constant as $K_c^x$.

$$K_c^x = \frac{[C]^{2c} [D]^{2d}}{[A]^{2a} [B]^{2b}}$$

We can see that each term has been squared in $K_c^x$ relative to its value in $K_c$.

So $K_c^x = K_c^2$.

By similar thinking, we can conclude that tripling of the stoichiometric coefficients would lead to a cubing of the value of $K_c$, halving of the stoichiometric coefficients would lead to a square rooting of the value of $K_c$, and so on.

These manipulations of the value of $K_c$ are summarized below.

| | Effect on equilibrium expression | Effect on $K_c$ |
|---|---|---|
| inversing the reaction | inverts the expression | $\dfrac{1}{K_c}$ or $K_c^{-1}$ |
| doubling the reaction coefficients | squares the expression | $K_c^2$ |
| tripling the reaction coefficients | cubes the expression | $K_c^3$ |
| halving the reaction coefficients | square roots the expression | $\sqrt{K_c}$ |
| adding together two reactions | multiplies the two expressions | $K_c^i \times K_c^{ii}$ |

## Worked example

The equilibrium constant for the reaction

$$2HI(g) \rightleftharpoons H_2(g) + I_2(g)$$

is 0.04 at a certain temperature. What would be the value of the equilibrium constant, $K_c'$, for the following reaction at the same temperature?

$$\tfrac{1}{2}H_2(g) + \tfrac{1}{2}I_2(g) \rightleftharpoons HI(g)$$

**Solution**

$$K_c = \frac{\left[H_2\right]\left[I_2\right]}{\left[HI\right]^2}$$

$$K_c' = \frac{\left[HI\right]}{\left[H_2\right]^{1/2}\left[I_2\right]^{1/2}}$$

Note that the reaction is reversed and the coefficients in the equation are halved. Overall, the value of $K_c'$ is the square root of the value of the reciprocal of $K_c$.

So $K_c' = \dfrac{1}{\sqrt{K_c}}$ or $\sqrt{(K_c)^{-1}}$.

$$\therefore K_c' = \sqrt{\frac{1}{0.04}} = 5.0$$

## Exercises

**7** When the following reactions reach equilibrium, does the equilibrium mixture contain mostly reactants or mostly products at the specified temperature? Assume that the value for $K_c$ given corresponds to the temperature of the reaction mixture.

(a) $N_2(g) + 2H_2(g) \rightleftharpoons N_2H_4(g)$  $K_c = 7.4 \times 10^{-26}$
(b) $N_2(g) + O_2(g) \rightleftharpoons 2NO(g)$  $K_c = 2.7 \times 10^{-18}$
(c) $2NO(g) + O_2(g) \rightleftharpoons 2NO_2(g)$  $K_c = 6.0 \times 10^{13}$

**8** The equilibrium constant for the reaction:

$$H_2O(g) + Cl_2O(g) \rightleftharpoons 2HOCl(g)$$

is 0.0900 at 298 K.

Determine whether the following sets of conditions represent an equilibrium mixture for the reaction at this temperature. For those not at equilibrium, determine in which direction the reaction will proceed.

|     | $[H_2O]$ | $[Cl_2O]$ | $[HOCl]$ |
|-----|----------|-----------|----------|
| (a) | 0.100    | 0.100     | 1.00     |
| (b) | 0.49     | 0.040     | 0.042    |
| (c) | 0.19     | 0.00033   | 0.083    |

**9** At a given temperature, the reaction

$$2SO_2(g) + O_2(g) \rightleftharpoons 2SO_3(g)$$

has a value of $K_c = 278$. Determine values of $K_c$ for the following reactions at this temperature.

(a) $4SO_2(g) + 2O_2(g) \rightleftharpoons 4SO_3(g)$
(b) $2SO_3(g) \rightleftharpoons 2SO_2(g) + O_2(g)$
(c) $SO_3(g) \rightleftharpoons SO_2(g) + \tfrac{1}{2}O_2(g)$

# When equilibrium is disrupted

A system remains at equilibrium so long as the rate of the forward reaction equals the rate of the backward reaction. But as soon as this balance is disrupted by any change

Henri-Louis Le Chatelier was a French chemist who published his equilibria principle in 1884. Amongst other research, he also investigated the possibility of ammonia synthesis, but abandoned his efforts after suffering a devastating explosion in his laboratory. After Haber's later elucidation of the conditions required in the reaction, Le Chatelier realized that he had been very close to the discovery himself. Late in his life he wrote 'I let the discovery of the ammonia synthesis slip through my hands. It was the greatest blunder of my career.' We can only speculate on how history might have been re-written if this discovery had in fact been made in France rather than in Germany before World War I.

Experiment to show the effect of changing the concentration of chloride ions on the cobalt chloride equilibrium reaction:

$$[Co(H_2O)_6]^{2+}(aq) + 4Cl^-(aq) \rightleftharpoons CoCl_4^{2-}(aq) + 6H_2O(l)$$

The flask on the left has a low concentration of chloride ions, giving the pink colour of the complex ion with water. As the concentration of chloride ions is increased, the equilibrium shifts to the right, changing the colour from pink to blue. Adding water would shift the equilibrium in the opposite direction. Cobalt chloride is often used to test for the presence of water because of this colour change.

**Figure 7.5** Effects of the addition of reactant and removal of product on the equilibrium $N_2(g) + 3H_2(g) \rightleftharpoons 2NH_3(g)$. When $H_2$ is added some $N_2$ reacts and more $NH_3$ is formed as the equilibrium shifts to the right. When $NH_3$ is removed, more $N_2$ reacts with $H_2$ as the equilibrium again shifts to the right. After each change a new equilibrium mixture is achieved.

in conditions that unequally affects the rates of these reactions, the equilibrium condition will no longer be met. It has been shown, however, that equilibria respond in a predictable way to such a situation, based on a principle known as **Le Chatelier's principle**. This states that *a system at equilibrium when subjected to a change will respond in such a way as to minimize the effect of the change.* Simply put, this means that whatever we do to a system at equilibrium, the system will respond in the opposite way. Add something and the system will react to remove it, remove something and the system will react to replace it. After a while, a new equilibrium will be established and this will have a different composition from the earlier equilibrium mixture. Applying the principle therefore enables us to predict the qualitative effect of typical changes that occur to systems at equilibrium.

## Changes in concentration

Suppose an equilibrium is disrupted by an increase in the concentration of one of the reactants. This will cause the rate of the forward reaction to increase while the backward reaction will not be affected, so the reaction rates will no longer be equal. When equilibrium re-establishes itself, the mixture will have new concentrations of all reactants and products, and the equilibrium will have shifted in favour of products. The value of $K_c$ will be unchanged. This is in keeping with the prediction from Le Chatelier's principle: addition of reactant causes the system to respond by removing reactant – this favours the forward reaction and so shifts the equilibrium to the right.

Similarly, the equilibrium could be disrupted by a decrease in the concentration of product by removing it from the equilibrium mixture. As the rate of the backward reaction is now decreased, there will be a shift in the equilibrium in favour of the products. A different equilibrium position will be achieved, but the value of $K_c$ will be unchanged. Again this confirms the prediction from Le Chatelier's principle: removal of product causes the system to respond by making more product – this favours the forward reaction and so shifts the equilibrium to the right.

The graph in Figure 7.5 illustrates these disruptions to equilibrium for the reaction

$$N_2(g) + 3H_2(g) \rightleftharpoons 2NH_3(g)$$

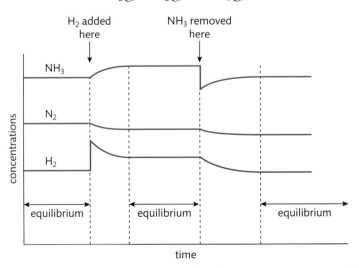

After $H_2$ is added, the concentrations of $N_2$ and $H_2$ decrease (in a $1:3$ ratio in keeping with their reaction stoichiometry), while the concentration of $NH_3$ rises (in a $2:1$ ratio relative to $N_2$) as the rate of the forward reaction increases and the equilibrium shifts to the right. The new equilibrium mixture has a higher proportion of products. In the second part of the graph, removal of $NH_3$ from the equilibrium mixture causes a decrease in the concentrations of $N_2$ and $H_2$ as they react to form more $NH_3$.

Often in an industrial process the product will be removed as it forms. This ensures that the equilibrium is continuously pulled to the right, so increasing the yield of product.

Applying Le Chatelier's principle, can you think what concentration changes would cause an equilibrium to shift to the left? The answer is either an increase in concentration of product or a decrease in concentration of reactant.

## Changes in pressure

Equilibria involving gases will be affected by a change in pressure if the reaction involves a change in the number of molecules. This is because there is a direct relationship between the number of gas molecules and the pressure exerted by a gas in a fixed volume. So if such a reaction at equilibrium is subject to an increase in pressure, the system responds to decrease this pressure by favouring the side with the smaller number of molecules. Conversely, a decrease in pressure will cause a shift in the equilibrium position to the side with the larger number of molecules of gas. A different equilibrium position will be achieved but the value of $K_c$ will be unchanged, so long as the temperature remains the same.

For example, consider the reaction used in the production of methanol:

$$CO(g) + 2H_2(g) \rightleftharpoons CH_3OH(g)$$

In total there are three molecules of gas on the left side and one molecule of gas on the right side. So here high pressure will shift the equilibrium to the right, in favour of the smaller number of gas molecules, which increases the yield of $CH_3OH$.

Note that many common equilibrium reactions do not involve a change in the number of gas molecules and so are not affected by changes in pressure. For example, the reaction

$$H_2(g) + I_2(g) \rightleftharpoons 2HI(g)$$

has two molecules of gas on both sides of the equation. Changing pressure for this reaction will affect the rate of the reaction but not the position of equilibrium or the value of $K_c$.

## Changes in temperature

We have noted that $K_c$ is temperature dependent, so changing the temperature will change $K_c$. However, in order to predict *how* it will change we must examine the enthalpy changes (see Chapter 5) of the forward and backward reactions. Remember that an exothermic reaction releases energy ($\Delta H$ negative), whereas an endothermic reaction absorbs energy ($\Delta H$ positive). The enthalpy changes of the forward and backward reactions are equal and opposite to each other.

So if we apply Le Chatelier's principle, including the energy change in the chemical reaction, we can predict how the reaction will respond to a change in temperature.

Consider the reaction:

$$\begin{array}{ccc} 2NO_2(g) & \rightleftharpoons & N_2O_4(g) \\ \text{brown} & & \text{colourless} \end{array} \qquad \Delta H = -57 \text{ kJ mol}^{-1}$$

Changes in the concentration of reactants or products alter the equilibrium position and so change the composition of the equilibrium mixture. But the value of $K_c$ stays the same.

Changes in pressure or volume will affect the position of equilibrium of a reaction if it involves a change in the number of gas molecules. The value of $K_c$ remains unchanged.

When describing the effects of volume or pressure on equilibrium reactions, you must state it depends on the relative number of *gas* molecules on both sides of the equation. Solids and liquids are hardly affected by changes in pressure.

An increase in pressure favours the side of an equilibrium reaction that has the smaller number of gas molecules.

When $\Delta H$ is given for an equilibrium reaction, by convention its sign refers to the forward reaction. So a negative sign for $\Delta H$ means that the forward reaction is exothermic, and the backward reaction is endothermic.

## CHALLENGE YOURSELF

4 Use information from this section to explain why there is very little NO in the atmosphere under ordinary conditions, and why severe air pollution is often characterized by a brownish haze.

The negative sign of $\Delta H$ tells us that the forward reaction is exothermic and so releases heat. If this reaction at equilibrium is subjected to a decrease in temperature, the system will respond by producing heat and it does this by favouring the forward exothermic reaction. This means that the equilibrium will shift to the right, in favour of the product $N_2O_4$. A new equilibrium mixture will be achieved and the value of $K_c$ will increase. So here we can see that the reaction will give a higher yield of products at a *lower temperature*.

Conversely, increasing the temperature favours the backward endothermic reaction, and so shifts the equilibrium to the left, decreasing the value of $K_c$. The reaction mixture becomes a darker colour as the concentration of $NO_2$ increases.

The table below illustrates the effect of temperature on the value of $K_c$ for this reaction.

| Temperature / $K$ | $K_c$ for $2NO_2(g) \rightleftharpoons N_2O_4(g)$ |
|---|---|
| 273 | 1300 |
| 298 | 170 |

Even though in this case a lower temperature will produce an equilibrium mixture with a higher proportion of products, remember from Chapter 6 that low temperature also causes a lower rate of reaction. And so, although a higher yield will be produced eventually, it may simply take too long to achieve this from practical and economic considerations if this was an industrial-scale reaction. We will come back to this point later in this chapter.

Now consider the following reaction:

$$N_2(g) + O_2(g) \rightleftharpoons 2NO(g) \qquad \Delta H = +181 \text{ kJ mol}^{-1}$$

In this case we can see that the forward reaction is endothermic and so absorbs heat. So here the effect of a decreased temperature will be to favour the backward exothermic reaction. Therefore the equilibrium will shift to the left, in favour of reactants, and $K_c$ will decrease. At higher temperatures, the forward endothermic reaction is favoured, so the equilibrium shifts to the right and $K_c$ will increase.

The table below illustrates the effect of temperature on the value of $K_c$ for this reaction.

| Temperature / $K$ | $K_c$ for $N_2(g) + O_2(g) \rightleftharpoons 2NO(g)$ |
|---|---|
| 298 | $4.5 \times 10^{-31}$ |
| 900 | $6.7 \times 10^{-10}$ |
| 2300 | $1.7 \times 10^{-3}$ |

The reaction

$$N_2(g) + O_2(g) \rightleftharpoons 2NO(g)$$

takes place in motor vehicles where the heat released by the combustion of the fuel is sufficient to cause the nitrogen and oxygen gases from the air to combine together in this way. Unfortunately, the product NO is toxic, and, worse still, quickly becomes converted into other toxins that form the components of acid rain and smog. It is therefore of great interest to vehicle manufacturers to find ways of lowering the temperature during combustion in order to reduce the production of NO in the reaction above.

These examples illustrate that, unlike changes in concentration and pressure, changes in temperature *do* cause the value of $K_c$ to change. An increase in temperature increases the value of $K_c$ for an endothermic reaction and decreases the value of $K_c$ for an exothermic reaction. This is because changes in temperature have a different effect

Experiment to show the effect of temperature on the reaction that converts $NO_2$ (brown) to $N_2O_4$ (colourless). As the temperature is increased, more $NO_2$ is produced and the gas becomes darker, as seen in the tube on the left.

**TOK**

Combustion reactions are generally described as exothermic, but the reaction

$N_2(g) + O_2(g) \rightleftharpoons 2NO(g)$

is endothermic. When is it appropriate to refer to an 'exception to a rule', and when does the rule need to be reconsidered?

**Increasing the temperature causes an increase in the value of $K_c$ for an endothermic reaction and a decrease in the value of $K_c$ for an exothermic reaction.**

on the rates of the forward and backward reactions, due to their different activation energies, as discussed in Chapter 6. In the next chapter, we will use this fact to explain why the pH of pure water is temperature dependent.

## Addition of a catalyst

As we learned in Chapter 6, a catalyst speeds up the rate of a reaction by providing an alternate reaction pathway that has a transition state with a lower activation energy, $E_a$. This increases the number of particles that have sufficient energy to react without raising the temperature.

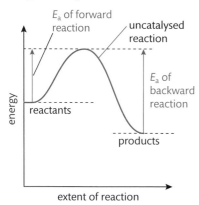
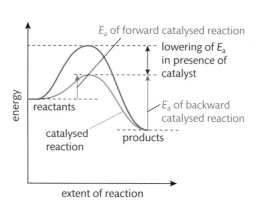

Because the forward and backward reactions pass through the same transition state, a catalyst lowers the activation energy by the same amount for the forward and backward reactions. So the rate of both these reactions will be increased by the same factor, as shown in Figure 7.6. The catalyst will therefore have no effect on the position of equilibrium, or on the value of $K_c$. In other words the catalyst will not increase the equilibrium yield of product in a reaction. It will, however, speed up the attainment of the equilibrium state and so cause products to form more quickly. Catalysts are generally not shown in the reaction equation or in the equilibrium constant expression as they are not chemically changed at the end of the reaction, and have no effect on the equilibrium concentrations.

Catalysts are widely used in industrial processes to increase the rate of product formation, and are involved in every single biochemical reaction. One of the key principles of Green Chemistry is that catalytic reagents, chosen to be as selective as possible, are superior to stoichiometric reagents as they are not consumed in the reaction. Catalysts, including the differences between homogeneous and heterogeneous catalysts, are discussed in more detail in Option A Materials, topic A.3.

## Summary

We can now summarize the effects of concentration, pressure, temperature, and catalyst on the position of equilibrium and on the value of $K_c$.

| | Effect of ... | Change in position of equilibrium | Change in value of $K_c$ |
|---|---|---|---|
| 1 | concentration | changes | no change |
| 2 | pressure | changes if reaction involves a change in the number of gas molecules | no change |
| 3 | temperature | changes | changes |
| 4 | catalyst | no change | no change |

**Observations of shifts in the position of chemical equilibria**
Full details of how to carry out this experiment with a worksheet are available online.

Catalysts do not change the position of equilibrium or the yield of a single reaction, but they enable the equilibrium mixture to be achieved more quickly. Catalysts do not change the value of $K_c$.

A particular reaction at a specified temperature can have many different possible equilibrium positions, but only one value for the equilibrium constant $K_c$.

**NATURE OF SCIENCE**

Knowledge of how systems at equilibrium respond to change has many applications, as we will see in the next section. Le Chatelier's principle is a useful predictive tool for this purpose, and has the advantage of being relatively simple to apply and effective. But it has some disadvantages too. Firstly, it leads only to qualitative predictions of the system's response. In some cases, such as investigations of when a precipitate will form in aqueous solution, this is insufficient. Secondly, Le Chatelier's principle offers no *explanation* for the response – it predicts what will happen, but not why. It can even be misleading in that it can suggest a false sense of purpose to systems' responses if the language used is such as 'the system tries to…'.

On the other hand, use of the reaction quotient, $Q$, to predict the consequence of change can often provide an effective explanation. As disturbances in concentration or pressure change the value of $Q$, the system responds as $Q$ progresses towards $K_c$. But changes in temperature are different because they change the value of $K_c$ – in this case the system responds as $Q$ progresses towards the new value of $K_c$. The response of $K_c$ to temperature can be explained through thermodynamics and the fact that the forward and backward reactions respond differently to temperature changes due to their different activation energies. Increased temperature favours the endothermic reaction as it has the higher activation energy. Scientific explanations often draw on different approaches and theories in this way. So long as the approaches do not contradict each other, together they can clarify and strengthen the understanding.

---

**Note that you are not expected to learn specific conditions for any reaction, so there is no need to focus on the names of catalysts, specific temperature used, etc. But you should be able to apply an understanding of equilibria to any given example, and predict the conditions likely to be effective.**

Fritz Haber 1868–1934

## Exercises

**10** The manufacture of sulfur trioxide can be represented by the equation below:

$$2SO_2(g) + O_2(g) \rightleftharpoons 2SO_3(g) \qquad \Delta H^{\ominus} = -197 \text{ kJ mol}^{-1}$$

What happens when a catalyst is added to an equilibrium mixture from this reaction?

**A** The rate of the forward reaction increases and that of the reverse reaction decreases.
**B** The rates of both forward and reverse reactions increase.
**C** The value of $\Delta H^{\ominus}$ increases.
**D** The yield of sulfur trioxide increases.

**11** What will happen to the position of equilibrium and the value of the equilibrium constant when the temperature is increased in the following reaction?

$$Br_2(g) + Cl_2(g) \rightleftharpoons 2BrCl(g) \qquad \Delta H^{\ominus} = +14 \text{ kJ}$$

| | Position of equilibrium | Value of equilibrium constant |
|---|---|---|
| **A** | shifts towards the reactants | decreases |
| **B** | shifts towards the reactants | increases |
| **C** | shifts towards the products | decreases |
| **D** | shifts towards the products | increases |

**12** Which changes will shift the position of equilibrium to the right in the following reaction?

$$2CO_2(g) \rightleftharpoons 2CO(g) + O_2(g)$$

I   adding a catalyst
II  decreasing the oxygen concentration
III increasing the volume of the container

**A** I and II only    **B** I and III only    **C** II and III only    **D** I, II, and III

**13** For each of the following reactions, predict in which direction the equilibrium will shift in response to an increase in pressure:

**(a)** $2CO_2(g) \rightleftharpoons 2CO(g) + O_2(g)$
**(b)** $CO(g) + 2H_2 \rightleftharpoons CH_3OH(g)$
**(c)** $H_2(g) + Cl_2(g) \rightleftharpoons 2HCl(g)$

**14** How will the equilibrium:

$$CH_4(g) + 2H_2S(g) \rightleftharpoons CS_2(g) + 4H_2(g) \qquad \Delta H = +ve$$

respond to the following changes?

**(a)** addition of $H_2(g)$
**(b)** addition of $CH_4(g)$
**(c)** a decrease in the volume of the container
**(d)** removal of $CS_2(g)$
**(e)** increase in temperature

**15** The reaction

$$2CO(g) + O_2(g) \rightleftharpoons 2CO_2(g) \qquad \Delta H = -566 \text{ kJ mol}^{-1}$$

takes place in catalytic converters in cars. If this reaction is at equilibrium, will the amount of CO increase, decrease, or stay the same when:

**(a)** the pressure is increased by decreasing the volume?
**(b)** the pressure is increased by adding $O_2(g)$?
**(c)** the temperature is increased?
**(d)** a platinum catalyst is added?

## Equilibrium theory is applied in many industrial processes

In reactions involving the manufacture of a chemical it is obviously a goal to obtain as high a conversion of reactant to product as possible. Application of Le Chatelier's principle enables chemists to choose conditions that will cause the equilibrium to lie to the right, and so help to achieve this. But the *yield* of a reaction is only part of the consideration. The *rate* is also clearly of great significance as it would be of limited value if a process were able to claim a high equilibrium yield of product, but took several years to achieve this. The economics of the process will depend on considerations of both the equilibrium and the kinetics of the reaction – in other words on how far and how fast the reaction will proceed. Sometimes these two criteria work against each other, and so the best compromise must be reached. A few case studies of industrial processes are discussed here.

### The Haber process: the production of ammonia, NH₃

Fritz Haber was born in what is now Poland but moved to Germany early in his career. Together with Carl Bosch, also of Germany, he developed the process for the industrial synthesis of ammonia from its elements, and the first factory for ammonia production opened in Germany in 1913, just before World War I. This development had enormous significance for the country at war: it enabled the continued production of explosives despite the fact that imports of nitrate from Chile, used for producing nitric acid and explosives such as TNT, were barred through the blockaded ports. This effectively enabled Germany to continue its war efforts for another 4 years. Haber was awarded the Nobel Prize in Chemistry in 1918. In many ways history has recorded this as a controversial choice – not only had Haber's work helped to prolong the war, he had also been responsible for the development and use of chlorine as the first poison gas. Ironically, despite his evident patriotism towards Germany, he was expelled from the country in 1933 when the rising tide of anti-Semitism conflicted with his Jewish ancestry.

The book *The alchemy of air: a Jewish genius, a doomed tycoon, and the scientific discovery that fed the world but fueled the rise of Hitler* is written by Thomas Hager. It is a fascinating account of the historic discovery of the process to synthesize ammonia, and its continuing mixed consequences – these include the revolution in global food production, the death of millions through wars, and growing concerns of nitrate pollution and obesity.

The Haber process is based on the reaction

$$N_2(g) + 3H_2(g) \rightleftharpoons 2NH_3(g) \qquad \Delta H = -93 \text{ kJ mol}^{-1}$$

The following information can be derived from this equation:

• all reactants and products are gases;
• there is a change in the number of gas molecules as the reaction proceeds: four gas molecules on the left and two on the right;

It is estimated that as much as 130 million tonnes of ammonia, $NH_3$, are produced worldwide every year. China is responsible for nearly one-third of this, and India, Russia, and the USA also produce significant amounts. Approximately 80% of the ammonia is used to make fertilizers, notably ammonium nitrate, $NH_4NO_3$. Other uses include synthesis of textiles such as nylon and powerful explosives. In April 2013, a major explosion occurred in a fertilizer factory in Texas, USA, killing and injuring hundreds of people. It was caused by a fire in a stock of 250 000 kilograms of ammonium nitrate. Accidents such as this in industrial plants raise many questions regarding health and safety, storage, and handling of chemicals and the balance of responsibility between companies, governments, and individuals.

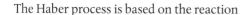

▲ Tractor applying a chemical solution of fertilizer to the soil. Ammonium salts such as ammonium nitrate and sulfate are particularly effective fertilizers as they supply nitrogen needed by plants and are readily soluble. It is estimated that without the use of ammonium fertilizers, two billion people would starve.

- the forward reaction is exothermic so releases heat; the backward reaction is endothermic so absorbs heat.

Application of Le Chatelier's principle to this reaction enables us to consider the optimum conditions.

- Concentration: the reactants nitrogen and hydrogen are supplied in the molar ratio 1:3 in accordance with their stoichiometry in the equation. The product ammonia is removed as it forms, thus helping to pull the equilibrium to the right and increasing the yield.
- Pressure: as the forward reaction involves a decrease in the number of gas molecules, it will be favoured by a *high pressure*. The usual pressure used in the Haber process is about $2 \times 10^7$ Pa.
- Temperature: as the forward reaction is exothermic, it will be favoured by a lower temperature. However, too low a temperature would cause the reaction to be uneconomically slow, and so a *moderate temperature* of about 450 °C is used.
- Catalyst: a catalyst will speed up the rate of production and so help to compensate for the moderate temperature used. A catalyst of finely divided iron is used, with small amounts of aluminium and magnesium oxides added to improve its activity. More recently, ruthenium has become the catalyst of choice, and this has helped reduce the energy requirement.

In fact, the Haber process achieves a conversion of $H_2$ and $N_2$ into $NH_3$ of only about 10–20% per pass through the reactor. After separation of the $NH_3$ product, the unconverted reactants are recycled to the reactor to obtain an overall yield of about 95%. This recycling of unconverted reactants is commonly used in industrial processes, and allows processes with low equilibrium yield to be made commercially viable.

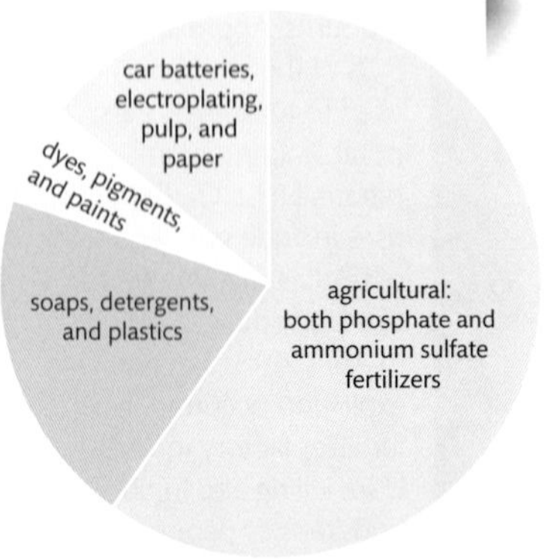

## The Contact process: the production of sulfuric acid $H_2SO_4$

The Contact process involves a series of three simple reactions:

(i) the combustion of sulfur to form sulfur dioxide;

(ii) the oxidation of sulfur dioxide to sulfur trioxide:

$$2SO_2(g) + O_2(g) \rightleftharpoons 2SO_3(g) \qquad \Delta H = -196 \text{ kJ mol}^{-1}$$

(iii) The combination of sulfur trioxide with water to produce sulfuric acid.

It has been shown that the overall rate of the process depends on step (ii), the oxidation of sulfur dioxide. So applying Le Chatelier's principle to this step, we can predict the conditions that will most favour the formation of product. These are summarized in the table below.

| | Influence on reaction | Condition used |
|---|---|---|
| pressure | forward reaction involves reduction in the number of molecules of gas from three molecules reactant to two molecules product: high pressure will favour product | $2 \times 10^5$ Pa (this gives a very high equilibrium yield, so still higher pressure is not needed) |
| temperature | forward reaction is exothermic: low temperature will increase the equilibrium yield, but decrease the rate | 450 °C |
| catalyst | increases the rate of reaction | vanadium(V) oxide |

**Figure 7.7** The uses of sulfuric acid.

More sulfuric acid by mass is produced worldwide than any other chemical. It has been found that the production of sulfuric acid closely mirrors historical events such as major wars that affect a country's economy. For this reason some economists use sulfuric acid production as a measure of a country's industrial strength. Sulfuric acid is used directly or indirectly in nearly all industrial processes, including the production of fertilizers, detergents, and paints and in ore processing, steel production, and water treatment. Approximately 250 million tonnes are produced annually across all continents.

The process gets its name the *Contact process* from the fact that molecules of the gases $O_2$ and $SO_2$ react in *contact* with the surface of the solid catalyst $V_2O_5$.

## The production of methanol

$$CO(g) + 2H_2(g) \rightleftharpoons CH_3OH(g) \qquad \Delta H = -90 \text{ kJ mol}^{-1}$$

Again, Le Chatelier's principle can be used to consider the conditions that will optimize the production.

| | Influence on reaction | Condition used |
|---|---|---|
| pressure | forward reaction involves reduction in the number of molecules of gas from three molecules reactant to one molecule product: high pressure will favour product | $5$–$10 \times 10^6$ Pa |
| temperature | forward reaction is exothermic: low temperature will increase the equilibrium yield, but decrease the rate | 250 °C |
| catalyst | increases the rate of reaction | $Cu$-$ZnO$-$Al_2O_3$ |

▲ Land contaminated by waste impurities from an old sulfuric acid plant close to a residential area in Bilbao, Spain. The waste largely derives from smelting and combustion processes. The full consideration of any industrial process must include an assessment of its impact on the environment, both locally and globally.

### NATURE OF SCIENCE

Scientific research is largely influenced by the social context, which helps to determine funding and set priorities. A good example is Haber's work on ammonia synthesis, which became pressing in Germany in the early years of the 20th century. Scientific discoveries often have significant economic, ethical, and political implications. Some of these may be unintended consequences of the discovery, such as the environmental degradation caused by the excess use of nitrate fertilizers as an outcome of the Haber process. This raises the question of who must take moral responsibility for the applications of scientific discoveries. The process of science includes risk benefit analyses, risk assessment, and ethical considerations, but sometimes the full consequences cannot be predicted and do not become known until much later.

### Exercises

**16** In the Haber process for the synthesis of ammonia, what effects does the catalyst have?

| | Rate of formation of $NH_3(g)$ | Amount of $NH_3(g)$ formed |
|---|---|---|
| **A** | increases | increases |
| **B** | increases | decreases |
| **C** | increases | no change |
| **D** | no change | increases |

**17** $2SO_2(g) + O_2(g) \rightleftharpoons 2SO_3(g)$ $\quad \Delta H^\ominus = -200$ kJ

According to the above information, what temperature and pressure conditions produce the greatest amount of $SO_3$?

| | Temperature | Pressure |
|---|---|---|
| **A** | low | low |
| **B** | low | high |
| **C** | high | high |
| **D** | high | low |

**18** Predict how you would expect the value for $K_c$ for the Haber process to change as the temperature is increased. Explain the significance of this in terms of the reaction yield.

## CHALLENGE YOURSELF

**5** Consider the atom economy of the reactions described here using the formula

$$\text{atom economy} = \frac{\text{mass of desired product}}{\text{total mass of reactants}} \times 100$$

Explain how this is different from the reaction yield.

Methanol is used as a **chemical feedstock**, that is used to make other chemicals. A high proportion is converted into methanal, HCHO, which is then converted into plastics, paints, explosives, and plywood. Methanol is used as a laboratory solvent, as an antifreeze agent, and in the process of producing biodiesel fuel from fats. Interest has also focused on the potential of methanol as an energy storage molecule in the so-called 'methanol economy'. In on-going efforts to reduce dependence on imported fossil fuels, China has greatly increased production capacity and consumption of methanol for its transportation sector, and plans to produce five million alternative-energy vehicles a year by 2020.

## Understandings:

- Le Chatelier's principle for changes in concentration can be explained by the equilibrium law.
- The position of equilibrium corresponds to a maximum value of entropy and a minimum in the value of the Gibb's free energy.
- The Gibbs free energy change of a reaction and the equilibrium constant can both be used to measure the position of an equilibrium reaction and are related by the equation, $\Delta G = -RT \ln K$.

### Guidance
- The expression $\Delta G = -RT \ln K$ is given in the data booklet in section 1.
- Students will not be expected to derive the expression $\Delta G = -RT \ln K$.

## Applications and skills:

- Solution of homogeneous equilibrium problems using the expression for $K_c$.

### Guidance
The use of quadratic equations will not be assessed.

- Relationship between $\Delta G$ and the equilibrium constant.
- Calculations using the equation $\Delta G^\circ = RT \ln K$.

So far we have learned how to derive the equilibrium constant $K_c$ from the equation for a reaction, and have considered in qualitative terms what its value tells us about the composition of an equilibrium mixture. We now want to take this further by quantifying these values.

There are two processes involved here, which we will consider in turn:

- calculation of the equilibrium constant, $K_c$
- calculation of the concentrations of reactants and products present at equilibrium.

As we will see, the equilibrium constant expression is the key to all these calculations.

In the examples here we will consider only **homogeneous equilibria**, that is those where reactants and products are all in the same phase, as gases or solutions.

**TOK**

The study of systems at equilibrium uses mathematics. Does this indicate that the systems are inherently mathematical, or have we constructed the mathematics to fit the system?

## Calculating the equilibrium constant from initial and equilibrium concentrations

If we know the equilibrium concentrations of all reactants and products in a reaction, we can simply substitute these into the equilibrium expression to calculate $K_c$ – as we did on page 316. The first step in such a calculation is always to write the equilibrium expression from the chemical equation.

### Worked example

Hydrogen can be prepared by the combination of carbon monoxide and water at 500 °C. At equilibrium the concentrations in the reaction mixture were found to be:

| | | | |
|---|---|---|---|
| CO | 0.150 mol dm$^{-3}$ | H$_2$O | 0.0145 mol dm$^{-3}$ |
| H$_2$ | 0.200 mol dm$^{-3}$ | CO$_2$ | 0.0200 mol dm$^{-3}$ |

Calculate the equilibrium constant for the reaction at this temperature.

## Solution

First write the equation for the reaction, making sure it is correctly balanced:

$$CO(g) + H_2O(g) \rightleftharpoons H_2(g) + CO_2(g)$$

Next write the equilibrium expression:

$$K_c = \frac{[H_2][CO_2]}{[CO][H_2O]}$$

Now substitute the given values for each component:

$$K_c = \frac{(0.200)(0.0200)}{(0.150)(0.0145)} = 1.84$$

 Remember to check that the precision of your answer is consistent with the data given in the question – the answer here must be given to three significant figures.

More commonly, we may first have to work out the value for the equilibrium concentration for one or more reactants or products from data on initial concentrations and equilibrium concentrations of other components. The important thing here is to be sure that only *equilibrium* concentrations are substituted into the equilibrium expression. The steps given below will help you to do this. These steps will be a useful guide through many calculations in this chapter and the work on acids and bases that follows.

1   Write the balanced equation.
2   Under the equation, write in the values of the concentrations of each component using three rows: *initial, change,* and *equilibrium*.
   * *Initial* represents the concentration originally placed in the flask; unless stated otherwise, we assume the initial product concentration is zero.
   * *Change* represents the amount that reacts to reach equilibrium. A minus sign for reactants represents a decrease in concentration as they are used up, and a plus sign for products represents an increase in concentration as they form. The changes that occur must be in the same ratio as the coefficients in the balanced equation, so if we know one of the change values we can deduce the others.
   * *Equilibrium* is the concentration present in the equilibrium mixture. This can be calculated by applying the amount of change to the initial concentration for each component.

      equilibrium concentration = initial concentration ± change in concentration
3   Write the expression for $K_c$ from the balanced equation. Substitute the values for equilibrium concentration and calculate $K_c$.

### Worked example

A student placed 0.20 mol of $PCl_3(g)$ and 0.10 mol of $Cl_2(g)$ into a 1.0 dm³ flask at 350 °C. The reaction, which produced $PCl_5$, was allowed to come to equilibrium, at which time it was found that the flask contained 0.12 mol of $PCl_3$. What is the value of $K_c$ for this reaction?

#### Solution

1   Write the equation for the reaction.

$$PCl_3(g) + Cl_2(g) \rightleftharpoons PCl_5(g)$$

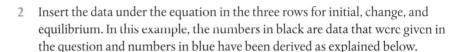

The example above involved a 1 dm³ reaction volume, so we could use the given amounts in mol directly as concentration in mol dm⁻³. Sometimes though we will need to calculate concentrations from given amounts and volumes. For example, if the data were given for a 3 dm³ volume, we would need to divide the amounts in mol by 3 to express this as mol dm⁻³. The volume must also be taken into account in this way when the reaction involves a change in the number of molecules of gas.

2　Insert the data under the equation in the three rows for initial, change, and equilibrium. In this example, the numbers in black are data that were given in the question and numbers in blue have been derived as explained below.

|  | $PCl_3(g)$ | + | $Cl_2(g)$ | $\rightleftharpoons$ | $PCl_5(g)$ |
|---|---|---|---|---|---|
| initial (mol dm⁻³) | 0.20 | | 0.10 | | 0.00 |
| change (mol dm⁻³) | −0.08 | | −0.08 | | +0.08 |
| equilibrium (mol dm⁻³) | 0.12 | | 0.02 | | 0.08 |

The change in concentration of $PCl_3$, the amount that reacted to reach equilibrium, is $0.20 - 0.12 = 0.08$. It is given a minus sign to show that the concentration decreases by this amount. As $PCl_3$ and $Cl_2$ react in a 1:1 ratio and form a 1:1 ratio of $PCl_5$, the same change in concentration must apply to $Cl_2$ and $PCl_5$. The equilibrium concentrations are calculated by applying the change amount to the initial values.

3　$K_c = \dfrac{[PCl_5]}{[PCl_3][Cl_2]} = \dfrac{0.08}{0.12 \times 0.02} = 33$

## Worked example

The oxidation of NO to form $NO_2$ occurs during the formation of smog. When 0.60 mol of NO was reacted with 0.60 mol of $O_2$ in a 2.0 dm³ container at 500 °C, the equilibrium mixture was found to contain 0.20 mol of $NO_2$. Calculate the equilibrium constant for the reaction at this temperature.

### Solution

1　$2NO + O_2 \rightleftharpoons 2NO_2$

2　Insert the data from the question under the equation. Note that because the volume is 2 dm³ the amounts must be divided by two to give concentration as mol dm⁻³. As before, derived data are shown in blue, with explanations for these below.

|  | $2NO$ | + | $O_2$ | $\rightleftharpoons$ | $2NO_2$ |
|---|---|---|---|---|---|
| initial (mol dm⁻³) | 0.30 | | 0.30 | | 0.00 |
| change (mol dm⁻³) | −0.10 | | −0.05 | | +0.10 |
| equilibrium (mol dm⁻³) | 0.20 | | 0.25 | | 0.10 |

The change in concentration of $NO_2$, the amount that had formed at equilibrium, is +0.10. From the stoichiometry of the reaction, for every two moles of $NO_2$ that form, two moles of NO and one mole of $O_2$ are used. Therefore we can deduce the corresponding changes in concentration for NO and $O_2$ and use these values to calculate the equilibrium concentrations of all components.

3　$K_c = \dfrac{[NO_2]^2}{[NO]^2[O_2]} = \dfrac{(0.10)^2}{(0.20)^2 \times 0.25} = 1.0$

Aerial view over Los Angeles showing a thick smog. The formation of smog involves several chemical equilibria including those involving nitrogen and sulfur oxides.

Don't miss out the step showing the equilibrium constant expression. It will help to ensure you substitute the values correctly, and even if you make a mistake with the numbers, you can still get credit for this part of your answer.

## Calculating equilibrium concentrations from the equilibrium constant

If we know the value of $K_c$ and the equilibrium concentrations of all but one of the components, we can calculate the remaining equilibrium concentration simply by substituting the values into the equilibrium expression.

The reaction:

$$CO(g) + 2H_2(g) \rightleftharpoons CH_3OH(g)$$

has $K_c = 0.500$ at 350 K. If the concentrations at equilibrium are:

CO    0.200 mol dm$^{-3}$

H$_2$    0.155 mol dm$^{-3}$

what is the equilibrium concentration of CH$_3$OH?

**Solution**

Write the equilibrium expression:

$$K_c = \frac{[CH_3OH]}{[CO][H_2]^2}$$

Substitute the data from the question and solve the equation to give the unknown concentration.

$$0.500 = \frac{[CH_3OH]}{(0.200)(0.155)^2}$$

Therefore $[CH_3OH] = 0.00240$ mol dm$^{-3}$ or $2.40 \times 10^{-3}$ mol dm$^{-3}$

A more complex situation arises when we need to calculate equilibrium concentrations given $K_c$ and initial concentrations. Here we use algebra to deduce the concentrations that have reacted to reach equilibrium and so calculate the equilibrium concentrations. The process developed in the previous section will also help to set the data out clearly here.

## Worked example

The equilibrium constant $K_c$ for the reaction

$$SO_3(g) + NO(g) \rightleftharpoons NO_2(g) + SO_2(g)$$

was found to be 6.78 at a specified temperature. If the initial concentrations of NO and SO$_3$ were both 0.0300 mol dm$^{-3}$, what would be the equilibrium concentration of each component?

**Solution**

To calculate the equilibrium concentrations of the reactants and products, we need to know how much has reacted, in other words the change in concentration:

let the change in concentration of NO = $-x$

therefore change in concentration of SO$_3$ = $-x$

and change in concentration of both NO$_2$ and SO$_2$ = $+x$ (due to the 1 : 1 stoichiometry)

Insert the relevant data from the question under the equation:

|  | SO$_3$(g) + | NO(g) $\rightleftharpoons$ | NO$_2$(g) + | SO$_2$(g) |
|---|---|---|---|---|
| initial (mol dm$^{-3}$) | 0.0300 | 0.0300 | 0.00 | 0.00 |
| change (mol dm$^{-3}$) | $-x$ | $-x$ | $+x$ | $+x$ |
| equilibrium (mol dm$^{-3}$) | $0.0300 - x$ | $0.0300 - x$ | $x$ | $x$ |

Always look for a way to simplify calculations of this type, for example, by taking the square root of both sides of the equation. If you think you need to use the quadratic equation to solve equilibria calculations at this level, you have almost certainly made a mistake or have missed a simplifying step – so go back and look again.

Write the equilibrium expression and substitute the equilibrium concentrations.

$$K_c = \frac{[NO_2][SO_2]}{[SO_3][NO]} = \frac{x^2}{(0.0300 - x)^2} = 6.78$$

This can be solved by taking the square root of both sides of the equation and collecting the terms in $x$.

$$\frac{x}{0.0300 - x} = \sqrt{6.78} = 2.60$$

$$x(1 + 2.60) = 2.60 \times 0.0300 = 0.0780$$

$$x = \frac{0.0780}{3.60} = 0.0217$$

The equilibrium concentration of each component can now be calculated.

$[SO_3]$ = $0.0300 - 0.0217 = 0.00830$ mol dm$^{-3}$

$[NO]$ = $0.0300 - 0.0217 = 0.00830$ mol dm$^{-3}$

$[NO_2]$ = $0.0217$ mol dm$^{-3}$

$[SO_2]$ = $0.0217$ mol dm$^{-3}$

> Do not make the mistake of stopping when you have calculated $x$. The question asks for the equilibrium concentrations so you must substitute the value for $x$ in the expressions you derived for the equilibrium concentrations to give the answer.

## Calculating equilibrium concentrations when $K_c$ is very small

> **TOK** What ways of knowing do we use when we make an assumption in a calculation to simplify the mathematics? What is the difference between intuition and reason in this context?

In some reactions the value of $K_c$ is very small, less than $10^{-3}$. As we learned in section 7.1, this represents a reaction in which the forward reaction has hardly proceeded and the equilibrium mixture consists almost entirely of reactants. In other words, the change in reactant concentrations is close to zero, as the equilibrium concentrations of reactants are approximately equal to their initial concentrations:

$$[\text{reactant}]_{\text{initial}} \approx [\text{reactant}]_{\text{equilibrium}}$$

This situation is common in the study of weak acids and bases as they dissociate only slightly, and so this approximation will help you in these calculations in Chapter 8.

> The approximation made in this calculation that $[\text{reactant}]_{\text{initial}} \approx [\text{reactant}]_{\text{equilibrium}}$ assumes that the value of $x$ is extremely small, so that subtracting $x$ (or in this case $2x$) from the initial concentration will not make a difference to the result within the precision used. You can check this assumption against your answer: subtracting $5.3 \times 10^{-7}$ from $0.10$ will still give $0.10$ when rounded to this precision. Note though that multiplying or dividing by $x$, however small its value, will make a significant difference to the answer, so the values of $x$ on the numerator in the $K_c$ expression must be retained through the calculation.

### Worked example

The thermal decomposition of water has a very small value of $K_c$. At 1000 °C, $K_c = 7.3 \times 10^{-18}$ for the reaction

$$2H_2O(g) \rightleftharpoons 2H_2(g) + O_2(g)$$

A reaction is set up at this temperature with an initial $H_2O$ concentration of 0.10 mol dm$^{-3}$. Calculate the $H_2$ concentration at equilibrium.

### Solution

We need to know the change in concentration of $H_2$, so we could assign this as $x$. But from the stoichiometry of the reaction, this would make change in $[O_2] = \frac{1}{2}x$. So it will make the calculation easier if we proceed as follows:

    let change in concentration of $H_2 = 2x$

    therefore change in concentration of $O_2 = x$

    so change in concentration of $H_2O = -2x$ (due to the 2:2:1 stoichiometry)

Insert the relevant data from the question under the equation.

|  | $2H_2O(g)$ | $\rightleftharpoons$ | $2H_2(g)$ | + | $O_2(g)$ |
|---|---|---|---|---|---|
| initial (mol dm$^{-3}$) | 0.10 | | 0.00 | | 0.00 |
| change (mol dm$^{-3}$) | $-2x$ | | $+2x$ | | $+x$ |
| equilibrium (mol dm$^{-3}$) | $0.10 - 2x$ | | $2x$ | | $x$ |
| | $\approx 0.10$ | | | | |

The approximation $[H_2O]_{initial} \approx [H_2O]_{equilibrium}$ follows from the very small value of $K_c$.

Write the equilibrium expression and substitute the equilibrium concentrations.

$$K_c = \frac{[H_2]^2[O_2]}{[H_2O]^2} = \frac{(2x)^2 x}{(0.10)^2} = 7.3 \times 10^{-18}$$

This can now be solved for $x$.

$4x^3 = (7.3 \times 10^{-18})(0.010) = 7.3 \times 10^{-20}$

$x = 2.632 \times 10^{-7}$

The equilibrium concentration of $H_2$ can now be calculated.

$[H_2]_{equilibrium} = 2x = 5.3 \times 10^{-7}$ mol dm$^{-3}$

When using approximations of this type given a very small value of $K_c$, be sure to note in your answer where you are making the approximation and why it is justified.

As a rule of thumb, when $K_c < 10^{-3}$, approximations of this type are justified.

## Exercises

**19** The dissociation of hydrogen iodide into its elements takes place in a 1.0 dm$^3$ container at 440 °C. When 1.0 mole of hydrogen iodide is used, it is found to have decreased to 0.78 moles at equilibrium.

   **(a)** Calculate the equilibrium constant for this reaction at this temperature.
   **(b)** Deduce whether the dissociation reaction is endothermic or exothermic, given that at 600 °C the value of $K_c$ is 0.04.

**20** The reaction $N_2(g) + O_2(g) \rightleftharpoons 2NO(g)$ is carried out in a closed container with initial concentrations of both reactants of 1.6 mol dm$^{-3}$. $K_c$ for the reaction is $1.7 \times 10^{-3}$.

   Calculate the concentration of $NO(g)$ at equilibrium.

**21 (a)** The reaction $CO(g) + H_2O(g) \rightleftharpoons H_2(g) + CO_2(g)$ was studied at 550 °C. When 4.0 moles of CO and 6.4 moles of $H_2O$ were introduced into a 1 dm$^3$ vessel, the equilibrium mixture was found to contain 3.2 moles of both $H_2$ and $CO_2$.

   Calculate the concentrations of CO and $H_2O$ at equilibrium and the value of $K_c$.

   **(b)** At the same temperature and pressure a different experiment was found to have 4.0 moles of both CO and $H_2O$, and 3.0 moles of both $H_2$ and $CO_2$ present in the mixture after a period of reaction. Show mathematically that this mixture had not reached equilibrium, and in which direction it will react.

## Free energy and equilibrium

Different reactions have widely differing values of their equilibrium constant $K_c$, reflecting the range in the direction and extent of the chemical reaction. In some cases, such as the ionization of water, the reaction barely takes place, while other reactions, such as the combustion of methane, go almost to completion. What determines this fundamental difference between reactions?

To answer this, we will visit again some of the thermodynamic concepts we learned in Chapter 5. Remember that the Gibbs free energy change, $\Delta G$, is a measure of the work that is available from a system. Its sign is used to predict the spontaneity of a reaction.

$\Delta G^{\ominus}$ = **negative** $\Rightarrow$ **reaction proceeds in the forward direction**

$\Delta G^{\ominus}$ = **positive** $\Rightarrow$ **reaction proceeds in the backward direction**

$\Delta G^{\ominus}$ = **0** $\Rightarrow$ **reaction is at equilibrium**

**Equilibrium occurs when a reaction mixture is at the minimum value of Gibbs free energy.**

**Figure 7.8** The total free energy of a reaction mixture as the reaction progresses. Starting with either pure reactants or pure products, the free energy decreases as the reaction moves towards equilibrium. In (a) $G^{\ominus}_{reactants} > G^{\ominus}_{products}$ so $\Delta G^{\ominus}$ is negative for the reaction and it progresses forward towards equilibrium. The equilibrium mixture consists largely of products. In (b) $G^{\ominus}_{reactants} < G^{\ominus}_{products}$ so $\Delta G^{\ominus}$ is positive for the reaction and very little reaction occurs before equilibrium. The equilibrium mixture consists largely of reactants.

The free energy change $\Delta G^{\ominus}$ can be calculated for a reaction from the equation:

$$\Delta G^{\ominus} = G^{\ominus}_{products} - G^{\ominus}_{reactants}$$

so at equilibrium:

$$G^{\ominus}_{products} = G^{\ominus}_{reactants}$$

Consider what happens to the total free energy during a reaction, such as when a fully charged battery is used until it is fully discharged (dead).

• At the start of the reaction, the total free energy of the reactants is greater than that of the products so a lot of work is available. $\Delta G^{\ominus}$ is negative and the reaction proceeds in the forward direction.

• As the battery discharges, the reaction continues converting reactants to products. So the total free energy of the reactants decreases while the free energy of the products increases. $\Delta G^{\ominus}$ becomes less negative and less work is available.

• The system reaches equilibrium when the total free energies of the reactants and products are equal and no work can be extracted from the system. The battery is dead.

As the reaction progresses, there is a decrease in the total free energy as work is done by the system. Figure 7.8 shows that this occurs whether the reaction starts with pure reactants or with pure products. Because the free energy decreases in both directions, the reaction must go through a composition which corresponds to the minimum value of free energy. This is the equilibrium state where the net reaction stops. The relative amounts of reactants and products at equilibrium, the composition of this equilibrium mixture, is determined by the difference in free energy between the reactants and products.

The decrease in free energy during the reaction appears as work done by the system or as an increase in the entropy. Therefore the system has the highest possible value of entropy when free energy is at a minimum – in other words at equilibrium.

So $\Delta G^{\ominus}$ can be used to predict the spontaneity of a reaction and the position of equilibrium as follows.

• A reaction with a value of $\Delta G^{\ominus}$ that is both large and negative, appears to occur spontaneously and has an equilibrium mixture with a high proportion of products.

• A reaction with a value of $\Delta G^{\ominus}$ that is large and positive, appears to be non-spontaneous as only minute amounts of product form. It has an equilibrium mixture that is predominantly reactants.

(a)

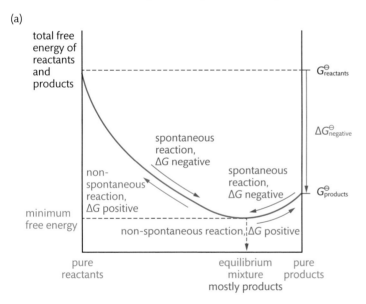

(b)

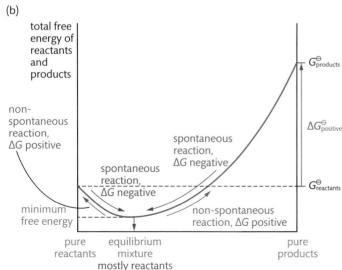

# $K_c$ can be calculated from thermodynamic data

We have now identified two terms which relate to the position of equilibrium:

- $K_c$, the equilibrium constant;
- $\Delta G^{\ominus}$, the change in free energy.

Clearly these terms must be related to each other. The equation which shows this relationship is derived from the principles of thermodynamics.

$$\Delta G^{\ominus} = -RT \ln K$$

This equation is given in section 1 of the IB data booklet. In this equation:

$\Delta G^{\ominus}$ = standard free energy change of the reaction

$R$ = the gas constant 8.31 J K$^{-1}$ mol$^{-1}$

$T$ = the absolute temperature, in kelvin

$\ln K$ = the natural logarithm of the equilibrium constant, $K_c$.

From this equation we can deduce relationships between $\Delta G^{\ominus}$ and $K_c$ for a reaction. These are summarized below.

| $\Delta G^{\ominus}$ | $\ln K$ | $K$ | Equilibrium mixture |
|---|---|---|---|
| $\Delta G^{\ominus}$ negative | $\ln K$ positive | $K > 1$ | mainly products |
| $\Delta G^{\ominus}$ positive | $\ln K$ negative | $K < 1$ | mainly reactants |
| $\Delta G^{\ominus} = 0$ | $\ln K = 0$ | $K = 1$ | appreciable amounts of both reactants and products |

The equation can also be used to calculate the equilibrium constant from the standard free energy change of a reaction and vice versa. This can be useful in situations where the equilibrium constant is difficult to measure directly, for example because a reaction may be too slow to reach equilibrium, or where the amounts of some of the components are too small to measure.

## Worked example

The esterification reaction that produces ethyl ethanoate has a free energy change $\Delta G^{\ominus} = -4.38$ kJ mol$^{-1}$.

$$CH_3COOH(aq) + C_2H_5OH(aq) \rightleftharpoons CH_3COOC_2H_5(aq) + H_2O(aq)$$

Calculate the value of the equilibrium constant of this reaction at 298 K.

### Solution

$$\Delta G^{\ominus} = -RT \ln K_c$$

$\therefore -4.38 \times 1000$ J mol$^{-1} = -(8.31$ J K$^{-1}$ mol$^{-1}) \times (298$ K$) \times \ln K_c$

$\ln K_c = \dfrac{-4380 \text{ J mol}^{-1}}{2478 \text{ J mol}^{-1}} = 1.77$

$\therefore K_c = e^{1.77} = 5.9$

We have now answered the question about what determines the fact that different reactions have such different values of equilibrium constant. The answer is the value of $\Delta G^{\ominus}$. Remember from Chapter 5 that this in turn depends on the values of enthalpy change ($\Delta H$) and entropy change ($\Delta S$) for the reaction.

**The position of equilibrium corresponds to a maximum value of entropy for the system.**

**The equilibrium constant for a reaction is determined by the sign and value of its free energy change, $\Delta G^{\ominus}$, through the equation $\Delta G^{\ominus} = -RT \ln K_c$.**

In essence, Le Chatelier's principle can be summarized as a system which is stressed when it is disturbed from its position of lowest free energy, responding by spontaneously relaxing back to this lowest energy state, the equilibrium position. The principle is sometimes used to describe negative feedback cycles, and links are made to other disciplines such as politics and economics. Although these applications may be useful in a general sense to enhance understanding, they must be subject to the checks and balances of the scientific process if they are to be claimed as scientifically valid. Without evidence which is testable and therefore falsifiable, these extensions of the principle have no scientific basis, and might be considered as pseudoscience.

## Kinetics and equilibrium

Rusting of iron is a complex process, but it can be represented by the equation:

$$4Fe(s) + 3O_2(g) \rightleftharpoons 2Fe_2O_3(s)$$

This is a heterogeneous equilibrium as its reaction components are in different phases, so we will not derive the equilibrium expression here. We can, however, calculate the value of the equilibrium constant from $\Delta G^{\ominus} = 1490 \times 10^6$ J, using the equation $\Delta G^{\ominus} = -RT \ln K_c$. This gives a value of $K_c = 10^{261}$. This very large value indicates that this is a thermodynamically favourable reaction, which will proceed towards completion. Clearly $\Delta G^{\ominus}$ is large and negative. But we know that rusting is a slow process, which can take years to complete.

This is an example of what has been mentioned earlier in this chapter – the magnitude of the equilibrium constant gives no information on the rate of reaction. Nonetheless, a study of the relative values of the rate constants for the forward and backward steps can help to explain some aspects of equilibria and Le Chatelier's principle.

We will consider a reaction which we will assume occurs in a single step. In other words, the overall reaction is an elementary bimolecular reaction (see Chapter 6).

$$A + B \rightleftharpoons C + D$$

In this case (and only in this case), we can write the rate laws for the forward and backward reactions from the stoichiometry of the reaction.

$$\text{rate of forward reaction} = k \, [A] \, [B]$$

$$\text{rate of backward reaction} = k' \, [C] \, [D]$$

where $k$ = rate constant for the forward reaction and $k'$ = rate constant for the backward reaction.

The equilibrium constant expression for this reaction is:

$$K_c = \frac{[C][D]}{[A][B]}$$

At equilibrium, the rate of the forward reaction = rate of backward reaction, so

$$k \, [A] \, [B] = k' \, [C] \, [D]$$

Rearranging this gives

$$\frac{k}{k'} = \frac{[C][D]}{[A][B]} \quad \text{or} \quad K_c = \frac{k}{k'}$$

In other words, the equilibrium constant is the ratio of the rate constants of the forward and backward reactions. This equation provides a fundamental link between chemical equilibrium and chemical kinetics.

Rusting of iron is a slow reaction which proceeds in the forward direction. In other words, it has a high equilibrium constant but a small rate constant.

The position of equilibrium is determined by the relative values of the rate constants of the forward and backward reactions.

- If $k \gg k' \Rightarrow K_c$ is large and the reaction progresses towards completion.
- If $k \ll k' \Rightarrow K_c$ is small and the reaction barely takes place.

We can finish this study by using the relationship between equilibrium constant and rate constants for a reaction to add to our interpretation of how equilibrium responds to changing conditions.

- Concentration: Increasing the concentration of reactant increases the rate of the forward reaction and so shifts the equilibrium to the right. Increasing the concentration of product increases the rate of the backward reaction and so shifts the equilibrium to the left. The value of the equilibrium constant stays constant because concentration changes do not affect the values of the rate constants.
- Catalyst: Adding a catalyst increases the values of $k$ and $k'$ by the same factor so the ratio of their values, the equilibrium constant, is not affected.
- Temperature dependence of $K_c$: From the Arrhenius equation, $k = Ae^{\frac{-E_a}{RT}}$, we know that the rate constant increases with increasing temperature. But because the activation energies of the forward and backward reactions are different, their rate constants $k$ and $k'$ are differently affected by temperature. So the ratio $k/k'$, the equilibrium constant, is temperature dependent. For an endothermic reaction, in which $E_a$(forward reaction) $> E_a$(backward reaction), the increase in temperature has a greater effect on increasing $k$ than $k'$, so $K_c$ increases as temperature increases.

## NATURE OF SCIENCE

Le Chatelier's principle enables qualitative predictions about changes to systems at equilibrium to be made, but we rely on thermodynamics for an explanation of these changes. Several seemingly different approaches can be used, but because they are applications of the same thermodynamic and kinetic concepts they support the same conclusions. Quantitative measurements provide evidence for equilibrium theory and enable us to make calculations of related variables.

## Exercises

**22** Which of the following correctly describes the entropy and free energy of a system at equilibrium?

|   | Entropy $S$ | Free energy $G$ |
|---|---|---|
| **A** | maximum value | maximum value |
| **B** | minimum value | maximum value |
| **C** | maximum value | minimum value |
| **D** | minimum value | minimum value |

**23** What is the sign of $\Delta G^{\ominus}$ for a reaction when:

(a) $K_c = 1$
(b) $K > 1$
(c) $K < 1$

**24 (a)** The ionization of water has an equilibrium constant $1.00 \times 10^{-14}$ at 298 K.

$$H_2O(l) \rightleftharpoons H^+(aq) + OH^-(aq)$$

Calculate $\Delta G^{\ominus}$ for this reaction at this temperature.

**(b)** At 313 K the equilibrium constant has a value of $2.92 \times 10^{-14}$. What can you conclude about the enthalpy change $\Delta H$ of the reaction?

## Practice questions

1 Which statement about chemical equilibria implies they are dynamic?

   A The position of equilibrium constantly changes.

   B The rates of forward and backward reactions change.

   C The reactants and products continue to react.

   D The concentrations of the reactants and products continue to change.

2 The reaction below represents the Haber process for the industrial production of ammonia.

$$N_2(g) + 3H_2(g) \rightleftharpoons 2NH_3(g) \qquad \Delta H^\ominus = -92 \text{ kJ}$$

The optimum conditions of temperature and pressure are chosen as a compromise between those that favour a high yield of ammonia and those that favour a fast rate of production. Economic considerations are also important. Which statement is correct?

   A A higher temperature would ensure a higher yield and a faster rate.

   B A lower pressure would ensure a higher yield at a lower cost.

   C A lower temperature would ensure a higher yield and a faster rate.

   D A higher pressure would ensure a higher yield at a higher cost.

3 What is the effect of an increase of temperature on the yield and the equilibrium constant for the following reaction?

$$2H_2(g) + CO(g) \rightleftharpoons CH_3OH(l) \qquad \Delta H^\ominus = -128 \text{ kJ}$$

|   | Yield | Equilibrium constant |
|---|-------|---------------------|
| A | increases | increases |
| B | increases | decreases |
| C | decreases | increases |
| D | decreases | decreases |

4 Consider the equilibrium between methanol, $CH_3OH(l)$, and methanol vapour, $CH_3OH(g)$.

$$CH_3OH(l) \rightleftharpoons CH_3OH(g)$$

What happens to the position of equilibrium and the value of $K_c$ as the temperature decreases?

|   | Position of equilibrium | Value of $K_c$ |
|---|------------------------|----------------|
| A | shifts to the left | decreases |
| B | shifts to the left | increases |
| C | shifts to the right | decreases |
| D | shifts to the right | increases |

5 0.50 mol of $I_2(g)$ and 0.50 mol of $Br_2(g)$ are placed in a closed flask. The following equilibrium is established.

$$I_2(g) + Br_2(g) \rightleftharpoons 2IBr(g)$$

The equilibrium mixture contains 0.80 mol of $IBr(g)$. What is the value of $K_c$?

   A 0.64       B 1.3       C 2.6       D 64

6 An increase in temperature increases the amount of chlorine present in the following equilibrium.

$$PCl_5(s) \rightleftharpoons PCl_3(l) + Cl_2(g)$$

What is the best explanation for this?

   A The higher temperature increases the rate of the forward reaction only.

   B The higher temperature increases the rate of the reverse reaction only.

**C** The higher temperature increases the rate of both reactions but the forward reaction is affected more than the reverse.

**D** The higher temperature increases the rate of both reactions but the reverse reaction is affected more than the forward.

**7** Consider the following reversible reaction.

$$Cr_2O_7^{2-}(aq) + H_2O(l) \rightleftharpoons 2CrO_4^{2-}(aq) + 2H^+(aq)$$

What will happen to the position of equilibrium and the value of $K_c$ when more $H^+$ ions are added at constant temperature?

| | Position of equilibrium | Value of $K_c$ |
|---|---|---|
| **A** | shifts to the left | decreases |
| **B** | shifts to the right | increases |
| **C** | shifts to the right | does not change |
| **D** | shifts to the left | does not change |

**8** Consider this equilibrium reaction in a sealed container:

$$H_2O(g) \rightleftharpoons H_2O(l)$$

What will be the effect on the equilibrium of increasing the temperature from 20 °C to 30 °C?

**A** More of the water will be in the gaseous state at equilibrium.

**B** More of the water will be in the liquid state at equilibrium.

**C** At equilibrium the rate of condensation will be greater than the rate of evaporation.

**D** At equilibrium the rate of evaporation will be greater than the rate of condensation.

**9** Which statement is correct for the equilibrium:

$$H_2O(l) \rightleftharpoons H_2O(g)$$

in a closed system at 100 °C?

**A** All the $H_2O(l)$ molecules have been converted to $H_2O(g)$.

**B** The rate of the forward reaction is greater than the rate of the reverse reaction.

**C** The rate of the forward reaction is less than the rate of the reverse reaction.

**D** The pressure remains constant.

**10 (a)** Consider the following equilibrium:

$$2SO_2(g) + O_2(g) \rightleftharpoons 2SO_3(g) \qquad \Delta H^\ominus = -198 \text{ kJ mol}^{-1}$$

   **(i)** Deduce the equilibrium constant expression, $K_c$, for the reaction. (1)

   **(ii)** State and explain the effect of increasing the pressure on the yield of sulfur trioxide. (2)

   **(iii)** State and explain the effect of increasing the temperature on the yield of sulfur trioxide. (2)

   **(iv)** State the effects of a catalyst on the forward and reverse reactions, on the position of equilibrium, and on the value of $K_c$. (3)

**(b)** When a mixture of 0.100 mol NO, 0.051 mol $H_2$, and 0.100 mol $H_2O$ were placed in a 1.0 dm³ flask at 300 K, the following equilibrium was established.

$$2NO(g) + 2H_2(g) \rightleftharpoons N_2(g) + 2H_2O(g)$$

At equilibrium, the concentration of NO was found to be 0.062 mol dm⁻³. Determine the equilibrium constant, $K_c$, of the reaction at this temperature. (4)

*(Total 12 marks)*

**11** Consider the following equilibrium reaction.

$$Cl_2(g) + SO_2(g) \rightleftharpoons SO_2Cl_2(g) \qquad\qquad \Delta H^{\ominus} = -84.5 \text{ kJ}$$

In a 1.00 dm$^3$ closed container, at 375 °C, $8.60 \times 10^{-3}$ mol of $SO_2$ and $8.60 \times 10^{-3}$ mol of $Cl_2$ were introduced. At equilibrium, $7.65 \times 10^{-4}$ mol of $SO_2Cl_2$ was formed.

**(a)** Deduce the equilibrium constant expression, $K_c$, for the reaction. (1)

**(b)** Determine the value of the equilibrium constant, $K_c$. (3)

**(c)** If the temperature of the reaction is changed to 300 °C, predict, stating a reason in each case, whether the equilibrium concentration of $SO_2Cl_2$ and the value of $K_c$ will increase or decrease. (3)

**(d)** If the volume of the container is changed to 1.50 dm$^3$, predict, stating a reason in each case, how this will affect the equilibrium concentration of $SO_2Cl_2$ and the value of $K_c$. (3)

**(e)** Suggest, stating a reason, how the addition of a catalyst at constant pressure and temperature will affect the equilibrium concentration of $SO_2Cl_2$. (2)

*(Total 12 marks)*

**12** The Haber process enables the large-scale production of ammonia needed to make fertilizers. The equation for the Haber process is given below.

$$N_2(g) + 3H_2(g) \rightleftharpoons 2NH_3(g)$$

The percentage of ammonia in the equilibrium mixture varies with temperature.

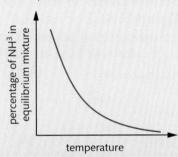

**(a)** Use the graph to deduce whether the forward reaction is exothermic or endothermic and explain your choice. (2)

**(b)** State and explain the effect of increasing the pressure on the yield of ammonia. (2)

**(c)** Deduce the equilibrium constant expression, $K_c$, for the reaction. (1)

**(d)** A mixture of 1.00 mol $N_2$ and 3.00 mol $H_2$ was placed in a 1.0 dm$^3$ flask at 400 °C. When the system was allowed to reach equilibrium, the concentration of $NH_3$ was found to be 0.062 mol dm$^{-3}$. Determine the equilibrium constant, $K_c$, of the reaction at this temperature. (3)

**(e)** Iron is used as a catalyst in the Haber process. State the effect of a catalyst on the value of $K_c$. (1)

*(Total 9 marks)*

**13** An example of a homogeneous reversible reaction is the reaction between hydrogen and iodine.

$$H_2(g) + I_2(g) \rightleftharpoons 2HI(g)$$

**(a)** Outline the characteristics of a homogeneous chemical system that is in a state of equilibrium. (2)

**(b)** Deduce the expression for the equilibrium constant, $K_c$. (1)

(c) Predict what would happen to the position of equilibrium if the pressure is increased from 1 atm to 2 atm. (1)

(d) The value of $K_c$ at 500 K is 160 and the value of $K_c$ at 700 K is 54. Deduce what this information tells us about the enthalpy change of the forward reaction. (1)

(e) At a temperature just above 700 K it is found that when 1.60 mol of hydrogen and 1.00 mol of iodine are allowed to reach equilibrium in a 4.00 dm³ flask, the amount of hydrogen iodide formed in the equilibrium mixture is 1.80 mol. Determine the value of the equilibrium constant at this temperature. (4)

(f) The reaction can be catalysed by adding platinum metal. State and explain what effect the addition of platinum would have on the value of the equilibrium constant. (2)

*(Total 11 marks)*

14 (a) What is the value of $\Delta G^\ominus$ for a reaction in which $K = 1$? (1)

(b) Nitrogen oxide, NO, is oxidized in the air to $NO_2$.

$$2NO(g) + O_2(g) \rightleftharpoons 2NO_2(g)$$

At 298 K, the value of $K_c$ for this reaction is $1.7 \times 10^{12}$. Calculate the value of $\Delta G^\ominus$ for the reaction. (3)

*(Total 4 marks)*

15 Hydrogen and iodine react together as follows:

$H_2(g) + I_2(g) \rightleftharpoons 2HI(g)$

(a) 6.0 moles of $H_2(g)$ and 3.0 moles of $I_2(g)$ are placed in a 1.0 dm³ flask. At the temperature of the reaction, $K_c = 4.00$. Calculate the equilibrium concentrations of $H_2(g)$, $I_2(g)$ and HI. (3)

(b) At a different temperature, the value of $K_c$ for the reaction is 51.50. A sample of HI was placed into a 1.0 dm³ flask at this temperature. At equilibrium, 0.218 mol $H_2(g)$ was present.

(i) How much HI was originally placed into the flask? (1)

(ii) How much $I_2$ and HI were present at equilibrium? (2)

*(Total 6 marks)*

To access weblinks on the topics covered in this chapter, please go to www.pearsonhotlinks.com and enter the ISBN or title of this book.

# 08

# Acids and bases

# Essential ideas

Acid–base theory informs much of our research into rainwater pollution and other aspects of environmental change.

The burning feeling of acid indigestion, the sour taste of grapefruit, and the vinegary smell of wine that has been exposed to the air are just some of the everyday encounters we have with acids. Likewise alkalis, or bases, are familiar substances – for example in baking soda, in household cleaners that contain ammonia, and in medication against indigestion. So what are the defining properties of these two groups of substances?

This question has intrigued chemists for centuries. The word 'acid' is derived from the Latin word *acetum* meaning sour – early tests to determine whether a substance was acidic were based on tasting! But it was learned that acids had other properties in common too: for example they changed the colour of the dye litmus from blue to red and they corroded metals. Similarly, alkalis were known to have distinctive properties such as being slippery to the touch, being able to remove fats and oils from fabrics, and turning litmus from red to blue. The name alkali comes from the Arabic word for plant ash, *alkalja*, where they were first identified. Early theories about acids and alkalis focused only on how they reacted together – it was actually suggested that the sourness of acids came from their possession of sharp angular spikes which became embedded in soft, rounded particles of alkali!

Over the last 120 years, our interpretation of acid–base behaviour has evolved alongside an increasing knowledge of atomic structure and bonding. In this chapter, we explore the modern definitions of acids and bases and learn how these help us to interpret and predict their interactions. Acid–base theory is central to topics such as air and water pollution, how global warming may affect the chemistry of the oceans, the action of drugs in the body, and many other aspects of cutting-edge research. As most acid–base reactions involve equilibria, much of the approach and mathematical content is based on work covered in Chapter 7. It is strongly recommended that you are familiar with this work before starting this chapter.

◄ A food scientist testing a sample of a batch of orange juice in a factory in France. pH measurements are an important part of the quality control of the product.

# 8.1 Theories of acids and bases

## Understandings:
- A Brønsted–Lowry acid is a proton/H⁺ donor and a Brønsted–Lowry base is a proton/H⁺ acceptor.
  - **Guidance**
    *Students should know the representation of a proton in aqueous solution as both $H^+(aq)$ and $H_3O^+(aq)$.*
- Amphiprotic species can act as both Brønsted–Lowry acids and bases.
- A pair of species differing by a single proton is called a conjugate acid–base pair.

## Applications and skills:
- Deduction of the Brønsted–Lowry acid and base in a chemical reaction.
  - **Guidance**
    *The location of the proton transferred should be clearly indicated. For example, $CH_3COOH/CH_3COO-$ rather than $C_2H_4O_2/C_2H_3O_2^-$.*
- Deduction of the conjugate acid or conjugate base in a chemical reaction.
  - **Guidance**
    *Lewis theory is not required here.*

## Early theories

The famous French chemist Lavoisier proposed in 1777 that oxygen was the 'universal acidifying principle'. He believed that an acid could be defined as a compound of oxygen and a non-metal. In fact, the name he gave to the newly discovered gas *oxygen* means 'acid-former'. This theory, however, had to be dismissed when the acid HCl was proven to be made of hydrogen and chlorine only – no oxygen. To hold true, of course, any definition of an acid has to be valid for *all* acids.

A big step forward came in 1887 when the Swedish chemist Arrhenius suggested that an acid could be defined as a substance that dissociates in water to form hydrogen ions ($H^+$) and anions, while a base dissociates into hydroxide ($OH^-$) ions and cations. He also recognized that the hydrogen and hydroxide ions could form water, and the cations and anions form a salt. In a sense, Arrhenius was very close to the theory that is widely used to explain acid and base properties today, but his focus was only on aqueous systems. A broader theory was needed to account for reactions occurring without water, and especially for the fact that some insoluble substances show base properties.

Svante August Arrhenius (1859–1927) wrote up his ideas on acids dissociating into ions in water as part of his doctoral thesis while a student at Stockholm University. But his theory was not well received and he was awarded the lowest possible class of degree. Later, his work gradually gained recognition and he received one of the earliest Nobel Prizes in Chemistry in 1903.

Arrhenius may be less well known as the first person documented to predict the possibility of global warming as a result of human activity. In 1896, aware of the rising levels of $CO_2$ caused by increased industrialization, he calculated the likely effect of this on the temperature of the Earth. Today, over 100 years later, the significance of this relationship between increasing $CO_2$ and global temperatures has become a subject of major international concern.

## Brønsted–Lowry: a theory of proton transfer

In 1923 two chemists, Martin Lowry of Cambridge, England, and Johannes Brønsted of Copenhagen, Denmark, working independently, published similar conclusions regarding the definitions of acids and bases. Their findings overcame the limitations of Arrhenius' work and have become established as the **Brønsted–Lowry theory**.

This theory focuses on the transfer of $H^+$ ions during an acid–base reaction: acids donate $H^+$ while bases accept $H^+$. For example, in the reaction between HCl and $NH_3$:

$$HCl + NH_3 \rightleftharpoons NH_4^+ + Cl^-$$

HCl transfers $H^+$ to $NH_3$ and so acts as an acid; $NH_3$ accepts the $H^+$ and so acts as a base.

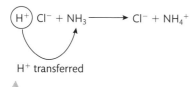

**Figure 8.1** HCl transfers $H^+$ to $NH_3$.

Hydrogen atoms contain just one proton and one electron, so when they ionize by losing the electron, all that is left is the proton. Therefore *$H^+$ is equivalent to a proton*, and we will use the two terms interchangeably here.

The Brønsted–Lowry theory can therefore be stated as:

• a Brønsted–Lowry acid is a proton ($H^+$) donor;
• a Brønsted–Lowry base is a proton ($H^+$) acceptor.

**NATURE OF SCIENCE**

The evolution of theories to explain acid–base chemistry and develop general principles is a fascinating tale of the scientific process in action. Some theories have arisen and been disproved, such as Lavoisier's early definition of an acid as a compound containing oxygen. Falsification of an idea when it cannot be applied in all cases is an essential aspect of the scientific process. Other theories have proved to be too limited in application, such as Arrhenius' theory which could not be generalized beyond aqueous solutions.

On the other hand, Brønsted–Lowry theory (as well as an alternate broader theory known as Lewis theory that is described later), has stood the test of time and experimentation. This indicates that it has led to testable predictions which have supported the theory, and enabled wide ranging applications to be made.

Reaction between vapours of HCl and $NH_3$ forming the white smoke of ammonium chloride $NH_4Cl$.

$$HCl(aq) + NH_3(aq) \rightarrow NH_4Cl(s)$$

**NATURE OF SCIENCE**

Brønsted and Lowry's work on acid–base theory may be a good example of what is sometimes referred to as 'multiple independent discovery'. This refers to cases where similar discoveries are made by scientists at almost the same time, even though they have worked independently from each other. Examples include the independent discovery of the calculus by Newton and Leibniz, the formulation of the mechanism for biological evolution by Darwin and Wallace, and derivation of the pressure–volume relationships of gases by Boyle and Mariotte. Nobel Prizes in Chemistry are commonly awarded to more than one person working in the same field, who may have made the same discovery independently. Multiple independent discoveries are likely increasing as a result of communication technology, which enables scientists who may be widely separated geographically to have access to a common body of knowledge as the basis for their research.

When a discovery is made by more than one scientist at about the same time, ethical questions can arise, such as whether the credit belongs to one individual or should be shared, and whether there are issues regarding intellectual property and patent rights. Historically, these issues have been settled in very different ways in different cases. Nonetheless, the peer review process in science aims to ensure that credit is correctly awarded to the scientist or scientists responsible for a discovery, and that published work represents a new contribution to work in that field.

**A Brønsted–Lowry acid is a proton (H⁺) donor.**

**A Brønsted–Lowry base is a proton (H⁺) acceptor.**

## Conjugate pairs

The act of donating cannot happen in isolation – there must always be something present to play the role of acceptor. In Brønsted–Lowry theory, an acid can therefore only behave as a proton donor if there is also a base present to accept the proton.

Let's consider the acid–base reaction between a generic acid HA and base B:

$$HA + B \rightleftharpoons A^- + BH^+$$

We can see that HA acts as an acid, donating a proton to B while B acts as a base, accepting the proton from HA. But if we look also at the reverse reaction, we can pick out another acid–base reaction: here $BH^+$ is acting as an acid, donating its proton to $A^-$ while $A^-$ acts as a base accepting the proton from $BH^+$. In other words acid HA has reacted to form the base $A^-$, while base B has reacted to form acid $BH^+$.

conjugate acid–base pair

$$HA + B \rightleftharpoons A^- + BH^+$$

conjugate acid–base pair

Acids react to form bases and vice versa. The acid–base pairs related to each other in this way are called **conjugate acid–base pairs**, and you can see that they *differ by just one proton*. It is important to be able to recognize these pairs in a Brønsted–Lowry acid–base reaction.

One example of a conjugate pair is $H_2O$ and $H_3O^+$, which is found in all acid–base reactions in aqueous solution. The reaction

$$H_2O(l) + H^+(aq) \rightleftharpoons H_3O^+(aq)$$

occurs when a proton released from an acid readily associates with $H_2O$ molecules forming $H_3O^+$. In other words, protons become hydrated. $H_3O^+$ is variously called the hydroxonium ion, the oxonium ion, or the hydronium ion and is always the form of hydrogen ions in aqueous solution. However, for most reactions it is convenient simply to write it as $H^+(aq)$. Note that in this pair $H_3O^+$ is the conjugate acid and $H_2O$ its conjugate base.

Note that $H_3O^+(aq)$ and $H^+(aq)$ are both used to represent a proton in aqueous solution.

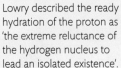

Lowry described the ready hydration of the proton as 'the extreme reluctance of the hydrogen nucleus to lead an isolated existence'.

## Worked example

Label the conjugate acid–base pairs in the following reaction:

$$CH_3COOH(aq) + H_2O(l) \rightleftharpoons CH_3COO^-(aq) + H_3O^+(aq)$$

**Solution**

$$CH_3COOH \,/\, CH_3COO^-$$
$$\quad\text{acid}\qquad\quad\text{base}$$
$$\underbrace{\qquad\qquad\qquad}_{\text{conjugate pair}}$$

$$H_2O \,/\, H_3O^+$$
$$\text{base}\quad\text{acid}$$
$$\underbrace{\qquad\qquad}_{\text{conjugate pair}}$$

The fact that in a conjugate pair the acid always has one proton more than its conjugate base, makes it easy to predict the formula of the corresponding conjugate for any given acid or base.

## Worked example

1 Write the conjugate base for each of the following.

   (a) $H_3O^+$      (b) $NH_3$      (c) $H_2CO_3$

2 Write the conjugate acid for each of the following.

   (a) $NO_2^-$      (b) $OH^-$      (c) $CO_3^{2-}$

**Solution**

1 To form the base from these species, remove one $H^+$

   (a) $H_2O$      (b) $NH_2^-$      (c) $HCO_3^-$

2 To form the acid from these species, add one $H^+$

   (a) $HNO_2$      (b) $H_2O$      (c) $HCO_3^-$

## Some species can act as acids and as bases

You may be surprised to see water described in the answers to the Worked examples above as a base (Q1, part a), and as an acid (Q2, part b), as you are probably not used to thinking of water as an acid, or as a base, but rather as a neutral substance. The point is that Brønsted–Lowry theory describes acids and bases in terms of how they react together, so it all depends on what water is reacting with. Consider the following:

$$CH_3COOH + H_2O \rightleftharpoons CH_3COO^- + H_3O^+$$
$$\quad\text{acid}\qquad\text{base}\qquad\quad\text{base}\qquad\text{acid}$$

$$NH_3 + H_2O \rightleftharpoons NH_4^+ + OH^-$$
$$\text{base}\quad\text{acid}\qquad\text{acid}\quad\text{base}$$

So with $CH_3COOH$, water acts as a Brønsted–Lowry base, but with $NH_3$ it acts as a Brønsted–Lowry acid.

Notice that water is not the only species that can act as both an acid and a base – for example, we see in the Worked example below that $HCO_3^-$ behaves similarly. Substances which can act as Brønsted–Lowry acids and bases in this way are said to be **amphiprotic**. What are the features that enable these species to have this 'double identity'?

When writing the conjugate acid of a base, add one $H^+$; when writing the conjugate base of an acid, remove one $H^+$. Remember to adjust the charge by the 1+ removed or added.

**The acid and base in a conjugate acid-base pair differ by just one proton.**

*Amphoteros* is a Greek word meaning 'both'. For example amphibians are adapted both to water and to land.

**An amphiprotic substance is one which can act as both a proton donor and a proton acceptor.**

Terminology in science has to be used appropriately according to the context. *Amphiprotic* specifically relates to Brønsted–Lowry acid–base theory, where the emphasis is on the transfer of a proton. The term *amphoteric*, on the other hand, has a broader meaning as it is used to decribe a substance which can act as an acid and as a base, including reactions that do not involve the transfer of a proton. For example, as described in Chapter 3, aluminium oxide is an amphoteric oxide as it reacts with both dilute acids and alkalis. We will see in section 18.1 that this acid–base behaviour is best described by a different theory, the Lewis theory. Note that all amphiprotic substances are also amphoteric, but the converse is not true. The fact that the two terms exist reflects the fact that different theories are used to describe acid–base reactions.

To act as a Brønsted–Lowry acid, they must be able to dissociate and release $H^+$.

To act as a Brønsted–Lowry base, they must be able to accept $H^+$, which means they must have a lone pair of electrons.

So substances that are amphiprotic according to Brønsted–Lowry theory must possess both a lone pair of electrons and hydrogen that can be released as $H^+$.

### Worked example

Write equations to show $HCO_3^-$ acting (a) as a Brønsted–Lowry acid and (b) as a Brønsted–Lowry base.

### Solution

(a) to act as an acid, it donates $H^+$
$$HCO_3^-(aq) + H_2O(l) \rightleftharpoons CO_3^{2-}(aq) + H_3O^+(l)$$

(b) to act as a base, it accepts $H^+$
$$HCO_3^-(aq) + H_2O(l) \rightleftharpoons H_2CO_3(aq) + OH^-(aq)$$

### Exercises

1 Deduce the formula of the conjugate acid of the following:
  (a) $SO_3^{2-}$  (c) $C_2H_5COO^-$  (e) $F^-$
  (b) $CH_3NH_2$  (d) $NO_3^-$  (f) $HSO_4^-$

2 Deduce the formula of the conjugate base of the following:
  (a) $H_3PO_4$  (c) $H_2SO_3$  (e) $OH^-$
  (b) $CH_3COOH$  (d) $HSO_4^-$  (f) $HBr$

3 For each of the following reactions, identify the Brønsted–Lowry acids and bases and the conjugate acid–base pairs:
  (a) $CH_3COOH + NH_3 \rightleftharpoons NH_4^+ + CH_3COO^-$
  (b) $CO_3^{2-} + H_3O^+ \rightleftharpoons H_2O + HCO_3^-$
  (c) $NH_4^+ + NO_2^- \rightleftharpoons HNO_2 + NH_3$

4 Show by means of equations how the anion in $K_2HPO_4$ is amphiprotic.

## 8.2 Properties of acids and bases

## Understandings:

- Most acids have observable characteristic chemical reactions with reactive metals, metal oxides, metal hydroxides, hydrogen carbonates, and carbonates.

  *Guidance*
  *Bases which are not hydroxides, such as ammonia, soluble carbonates, and hydrogen carbonates should be covered.*

- Salt and water are produced in exothermic neutralization reactions.

## Applications and skills:

- Balancing chemical equations for the reaction of acids.
- Identification of the acid and base needed to make different salts.
- Candidates should have experience of acid–base titrations with different indicators.

  *Guidance*
  *The colour changes of different indicators are given in the data booklet in section 22.*

While we have commented that ideas regarding the defining nature of acids and bases have been long debated, the recognition of what these substances *do* has been known for centuries.

We will look here at some typical reactions of acids and bases in aqueous solutions where $H^+$ is the ion common to all acids. The bases considered here are those that neutralize acids to produce water, which include:

- metal oxides and hydroxides;
- ammonia;
- soluble carbonates ($Na_2CO_3$ and $K_2CO_3$) and hydrogencarbonates ($NaHCO_3$ and $KHCO_3$).

The soluble bases are known as **alkalis**. When dissolved in water they all release the hydroxide ion $OH^-$. For example:

$$K_2O(s) + H_2O(l) \rightarrow 2K^+(aq) + 2OH^-(aq)$$

$$NH_3(aq) + H_2O(l) \rightleftharpoons NH_4^+(aq) + OH^-(aq)$$

$$CO_3^{2-}(aq) + H_2O(l) \rightleftharpoons HCO_3^-(aq) + OH^-(aq)$$

$$HCO_3^-(aq) \rightleftharpoons CO_2(g) + OH^-(aq)$$

## Acids react with metals, bases, and carbonates to form salts

The term **salt** refers to the ionic compound formed when the hydrogen of an acid is replaced by a metal or another positive ion. Salts form by reaction of acids with metals or bases. The familiar example, sodium chloride, NaCl, known as common salt, is derived from the acid HCl by reaction with a base that contains Na, such as NaOH. The terms **parent acid** and **parent base** are sometimes used to describe this relationship between an acid, a base, and their salt.

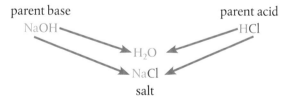

There are three main types of reaction by which acids react to form salts.

## 1 Acid + metal → salt + hydrogen

$$2HCl(aq) + Zn(s) \rightarrow ZnCl_2(aq) + H_2(g)$$

$$H_2SO_4(aq) + Fe(s) \rightarrow FeSO_4(aq) + H_2(g)$$

$$2CH_3COOH(aq) + Mg(s) \rightarrow Mg(CH_3COO)_2(aq) + H_2(g)$$

We can also write these as ionic equations. For example:

$$2H^+(aq) + 2Cl^-(aq) + Zn(s) \rightarrow Zn^{2+}(aq) + 2Cl^-(aq) + H_2(g)$$

**Figure 8.2** The relationship between alkalis and bases.

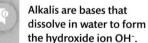

Alkalis are bases that dissolve in water to form the hydroxide ion $OH^-$.

In acid–base theory the words ionization and dissociation are often used interchangeably as acid dissociation always leads to ion formation.

Species which do not change during a reaction, like $Cl^-$ here, are called **spectator ions** and can be cancelled out. So the net reaction is:

$$2H^+(aq) + Zn(s) \rightarrow Zn^{2+}(aq) + H_2(g)$$

These reactions of metals with acids are the reason why acids have corrosive properties on most metals, and why, for example, it is important to keep car battery acid well away from the metal bodywork of the car.

You can demonstrate the release of hydrogen from acids in simple experiments by adding a small piece of metal to a dilute solution of the acid. There is a big range, however, in the reactivity of metals in these reactions. More reactive metals such as sodium and potassium in Group 1 would react much too violently, while copper and other less reactive metals such as silver and gold will usually not react at all. This is partly why these less reactive metals are so valuable – they are much more resistant to corrosion. We will consider this differing reactivity in Chapter 9. Another point to note is that although the common acid nitric acid, $HNO_3$, does react with metals, it usually does not release hydrogen owing to its oxidizing properties (Chapter 9).

## 2 Acid + base → salt + water

$$HCl(aq) + NaOH(aq) \rightarrow NaCl(aq) + H_2O(l)$$

$$HNO_3(aq) + NH_4OH(aq) \rightarrow NH_4NO_3(aq) + H_2O(l)$$

$$2CH_3COOH(aq) + CuO(s) \rightarrow Cu(CH_3COO)_2(aq) + H_2O(l)$$

These reactions between acids and bases are known as **neutralization** reactions. They can all be represented by one common ionic equation that shows the net reaction clearly:

$$H^+(aq) + OH^-(aq) \rightarrow H_2O(l)$$

Neutralization reactions of acids with bases are exothermic – heat is released. The **enthalpy of neutralization** is defined as the enthalpy change that occurs when an acid and a base react together to form one mole of water. For reactions between all strong acids and strong bases, the enthalpy change is very similar with $\Delta H = -57$ kJ mol$^{-1}$ approximately. This is because the net reaction is the same, involving the formation of water from its ions.

There are times when neutralization reactions are useful to help reduce the effect of an acid or a base. For example, treatment for acid indigestion often involves using 'antacids' which contain a mixture of weak alkalis such as magnesium hydroxide and aluminium hydroxide. As we will learn in section 8.5, in places where the soil has become too acidic, the growth of many plants will be restricted. Adding a weak alkali such as lime, CaO, can help to reduce the acidity and so increase the fertility of the soil.

## 3 Acid + carbonate → salt + water + carbon dioxide

$$2HCl(aq) + CaCO_3(s) \rightarrow CaCl_2(aq) + H_2O(l) + CO_2(g)$$

$$H_2SO_4(aq) + Na_2CO_3(aq) \rightarrow Na_2SO_4(aq) + H_2O(l) + CO_2(g)$$

$$CH_3COOH(aq) + KHCO_3(aq) \rightarrow KCH_3COO(aq) + H_2O(l) + CO_2(g)$$

These reactions can also be represented as an ionic equation:

$$2H^+(aq) + CO_3^{2-}(aq) \rightarrow H_2O(l) + CO_2(g)$$

Magnesium reacting with HCl.

$Mg(s) + 2HCl(aq) \rightarrow$ $MgCl_2(aq) + H_2(g)$

The tiny bubbles are hydrogen gas being liberated.

**Acid + reactive metal → salt + hydrogen**

Bee stings are slightly acidic, and so have traditionally been treated by using a mild alkali such as baking soda ($NaHCO_3$). Wasp stings, on the other hand, are claimed to be alkali, and so are often treated with the weak acid, ethanoic acid ($CH_3COOH$) found in vinegar. Whether these claims are valid is, however, open to dispute as the pH of wasp stings is actually very close to neutral. Nonetheless the healing powers of vinegar are well documented and vigorously defended.

**Acid + carbonate → salt + water + carbon dioxide**

**Neutralization reactions occur when an acid and base react together to form a salt and water. They are exothermic reactions.**

The reactions, like the reaction of acids with metals, involve a gas being given off so they visibly produce bubbles, known as **effervescence**.

Rain water dissolves some carbon dioxide from the air to form a weak solution of carbonic acid, $H_2CO_3$.

$$H_2O(l) + CO_2(g) \rightleftharpoons H_2CO_3(aq)$$

Greater pressure, such as that found in capillary beds of limestone ($CaCO_3$) rocks, increases the tendency of $CO_2$ to dissolve, giving rise to a more acidified solution. This then reacts on the limestone as follows:

$$H_2CO_3(aq) + CaCO_3(s) \rightleftharpoons Ca(HCO_3)_2(aq)$$

$CaCO_3$, limestone, is virtually insoluble whereas the product calcium hydrogencarbonate, $Ca(HCO_3)_2$, is soluble and washes away, leading to erosion of the rocks. This is why caves commonly form in limestone regions. Inside the cave where the pressure is lower, the reaction above may be reversed, as less $CO_2$ dissolves. In this case $CaCO_3$ comes out of solution and precipitates, giving rise to the formations known as stalagtites and stalagmites.

Similar reactions of rain water dissolving $CaCO_3$ rocks can give rise to water supplies with elevated levels of $Ca^{2+}$ ions, known as 'hard water'.

In section 8.5, these reactions between acids and metals and metal carbonates are discussed in the context of the environmental problem known as acid deposition.

## Acids and bases can be distinguished using indicators

Indicators act as chemical detectors, giving information about a change in the environment. The indicators most widely used in chemistry are **acid–base indicators** that change colour reversibly according to the concentration of $H^+$ ions in the solution. This happens because they are weak acids and bases whose conjugates have different colours. The colour change means that they can be used to identify the pH of a substance. Indicators are generally used either as aqueous solutions or absorbed onto 'test paper'.

Probably the best known acid–base indicator is **litmus**, which is a dye derived from lichens, and which turns pink in the presence of acid and blue in the presence of alkalis. It is widely used to test for acids or alkalis, but is not so useful in distinguishing between different strengths of acid or alkali.

Other indicators give different colours in different solutions of acid and alkali. Some common examples are given in the table here, and there are more in section 22 of your IB data booklet.

| Indicator | Colour in acid | Colour in alkali |
|---|---|---|
| litmus | pink | blue |
| methyl orange | red | yellow |
| phenolphthalein | colourless | pink |

Many of these indicators are derived from natural substances such as extracts from flower petals and berries. A common indicator in the laboratory is **universal indicator**, which is formed by mixing together several indicators. It changes colour

Kitchen chemistry. Baking soda ($NaHCO_3$) and vinegar ($CH_3COOH$) react together in a powerful acid–base reaction, releasing carbon dioxide gas.

$$NaHCO_3(s) + CH_3COOH(aq) \rightarrow NaCH_3COO(aq) + H_2O(l) + CO_2 (g)$$

Limestone rock shaped by natural chemical erosion in Switzerland. Rainwater, a weak solution of $H_2CO_3$, reacts with the calcium carbonate, slowly dissolving it.

Litmus indicator compared in acidic and alkaline solutions.

> **!** Be careful not to assume that indicator tests always show acids as pink and alkalis as blue. This is true with litmus, but other indicators give many different colours including pink in alkali.

many times across a range of different acids and alkalis and so can be used to measure the concentration of $H^+$ on the pH scale. We will discuss this later in the chapter.

In section 18.3 (page 378), we will learn in more detail how indicators work and how they are used in quantitative experimental work.

## Acid–base titrations are based on neutralization reactions

Neutralization reactions are often used in the laboratory to calculate the exact concentration of an acid or an alkali when the other concentration is known. As we learned in Chapter 1, the solution of known concentration is known as the standard solution. The technique known as **acid–base titration** involves reacting together a carefully measured volume of one of the solutions, and adding the other solution gradually until the so-called **equivalence point** is reached where they exactly neutralize each other. A convenient way to determine when the equivalence point has been reached is to use an indicator, chosen to change colour as the acid and base exactly neutralize each other.

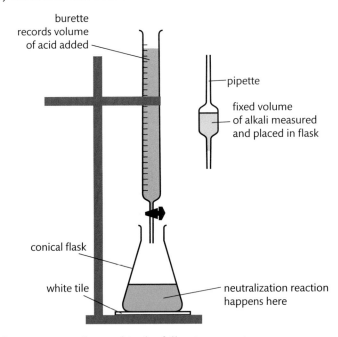

**Figure 8.3** Simple titration apparatus.

For example, titration can be used in the following experiments:

- to calculate the concentration of ethanoic acid in vinegar by titration with a standard solution of aqueous sodium hydroxide, using phenolphthalein indicator;
- to calculate the concentration of sodium hydroxide by titration with a standard solution of hydrochloric acid, using methyl orange indicator.

A good indicator is one that gives a distinct or sharp colour change at the equivalence point.

In section 18.3 we will study additional examples of titrations and learn how to choose an indicator that is appropriate for specific combinations of acid and base.

**Acid–base titration to calculate the concentration of ethanoic acid in vinegar**

Full details of how to carry out this experiment with a worksheet are available online.

## Exercises

**5** Write equations for the following reactions:

**(a)** sulfuric acid and copper oxide
**(b)** nitric acid and sodium hydrogencarbonate
**(c)** phosphoric acid and potassium hydroxide
**(d)** ethanoic acid and aluminium

**6** An aqueous solution of which of the following reacts with calcium metal?

**A** ammonia          **C** potassium hydroxide
**B** hydrogen chloride      **D** sodium hydrogencarbonate

**7** Which of the following is / are formed when a metal oxide reacts with a dilute acid?

I    a metal salt
II   water
III   carbon dioxide gas

**A** I only      **B** I and II only      **C** II and III only      **D** I, II, and III

**8** Suggest by name a parent acid and parent base that could be used to make the following salts. Write equations for each reaction.

**(a)** sodium nitrate         **(c)** copper(II) sulfate
**(b)** ammonium chloride    **(d)** potassium methanoate

When you need to choose a base in solution to make a specific salt, it is useful to know some simple solubility rules.

- The only soluble carbonates and hydrogencarbonates are $(NH_4)_2CO_3$, $Na_2CO_3$, $K_2CO_3$, $NaHCO_3$, $KHCO_3$, and $Ca(HCO_3)_2$.

- The only soluble hydroxides are $NH_4OH$, $LiOH$, $NaOH$, and $KOH$.

# 8.3   The pH scale

## Understandings:

- $pH = -\log [H^+(aq)]$ and $[H^+] = 10^{-pH}$.
- A change of one pH unit represents a 10-fold change in the hydrogen ion concentration $[H^+]$.

### Guidance
*Knowing the temperature dependence of $K_w$ is not required.*

- pH values distinguish between acidic, neutral, and alkaline solutions.
- The ionic product constant, $K_w = [H^+] [OH^-] = 10^{-14}$ at 298 K.

## Applications and skills:

- Solving problems involving pH, $[H^+]$, and $[OH^-]$.

### Guidance
- *Students should be concerned only with strong acids and bases in this sub-topic.*
- *Students will not be assessed on pOH values.*

- Students should be familiar with the use of a pH meter and universal indicator.

The Danish chemist Søren Peder Lauritz Sorensen (1868–1939) developed the pH concept in 1909, originally proposing that it be formulated as $p_H$. He did not account for his choice of the letter 'p' though it has been suggested to originate from the German word *potenz* for power. It could equally well derive from the Latin, Danish, or French terms for the same word.

## pH is a logarithmic expression of $[H^+]$

Chemists realized a long time ago that it would be useful to have a quantitative scale of acid strength based on the concentration of hydrogen ions. As the majority of acids encountered are weak, the hydrogen ion concentration expressed directly as mol dm$^{-3}$ produces numbers with large negative exponents; for example the $H^+$ concentration in our blood is $4.6 \times 10^{-8}$ mol dm$^{-3}$. Such numbers are not very user-friendly when it comes to describing and comparing acids. The introduction of the pH scale in 1909 by Sorensen led to wide acceptance owing to its ease of use. It is defined as follows:

$$pH = -\log_{10} [H^+]$$

In other words, pH is the negative number to which the base 10 is raised to give the $[H^+]$. This can also be expressed as:

$$[H^+] = 10^{-pH}$$

- A solution that has $[H^+] = 0.1$ mol dm$^{-3}$ $\Rightarrow [H^+] = 10^{-1}$ mol dm$^{-3}$ $\Rightarrow$ pH = 1.
- A solution that has $[H^+] = 0.01$ mol dm$^{-3}$ $\Rightarrow [H^+] = 10^{-2}$ mol dm$^{-3}$ $\Rightarrow$ pH = 2.

Now we can explore some of the features of the pH scale that help to make it so convenient.

## pH numbers are usually positive and have no units

Although the pH scale is theoretically an infinite scale (and can even extend into negative numbers), most acids and bases encountered will have positive pH values and fall within the range 0–14, corresponding to $[H^+]$ from 1.0 mol dm$^{-3}$ to $10^{-14}$ mol dm$^{-3}$.

## The pH number is inversely related to the $[H^+]$

Solutions with a higher $[H^+]$ have a lower pH and vice versa. So stronger and more concentrated acids have a lower pH, weaker and more dilute acids have a higher pH.

## A change of one pH unit represents a 10-fold change in $[H^+]$

This means increasing the pH by one unit represents a decrease in $[H^+]$ by 10 times; decreasing by one pH unit represents an increase in $[H^+]$ by 10 times.

$$pH = -\log_{10}[H^+];$$
$$[H^+] = 10^{-pH}$$

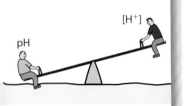

**Figure 8.4** The inverse relationship between pH and H$^+$.

**Figure 8.5** The pH scale at 298 K and pH values of some common substances.

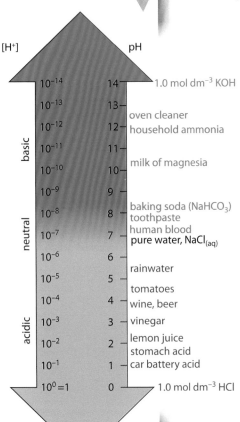

### NATURE OF SCIENCE

The use of a logarithmic scale to represent data enables a wide range of values to be presented as a smaller range of simpler numbers. We see here that the pH scale takes a range of hydrogen ion concentrations from $10^0$ to $10^{-14}$ and effectively compresses it to a much smaller scale of numbers, 0–14. On page 88, we saw that the use of a logarithmic scale to represent the ionization energies of aluminium similarly makes a wide range of data easier to interpret. In cases of exponential change, a log base scale shows the data as a straight line, so outliers where the change is greater or less than exponential can be easily identified.

But use of a logarithmic scale can also be misleading, as it can obscure the scale of change if not interpreted correctly. For example, a small change in pH represents a dramatic difference in the hydrogen ion concentration of a solution. Keep this in mind when you read reports of changes in pH, for example of rainfall as a result of pollution. A reported change from pH 5.5 to pH 4.5 may not sound much, but in fact it represents a *ten-fold increase* in the hydrogen ion concentration – hugely significant to the acidic properties. As we will learn in section 18.3 (page 378), the pH of our blood is carefully controlled by chemicals called buffers to remain at 7.4; a change of only half a pH unit on either side of this is known to be fatal. Communication of data in science takes different forms and uses different scales, and must always be interpreted in the context used.

Logarithmic scales are used in other disciplines where they can help in the presentation of data. In medicine, the logarithmic decay of levels of drugs in the blood against time is used. In seismic studies, the Richter scale is a logarithmic expression of the relative energy released during earthquakes. In sense perception the decibel scale of sound intensity and the scale for measuring the visible brightness of stars (their magnitude) are also logarithmic scales.

## Worked example

If the pH of a solution is changed from 3 to 5, deduce how the hydrogen ion concentration changes.

### Solution

$pH = 3 \Rightarrow [H^+] = 10^{-3}$ mol dm$^{-3}$; $pH = 5 \Rightarrow [H^+] = 10^{-5}$ mol dm$^{-3}$

So $[H^+]$ has changed by $10^{-2}$ or decreased by 100.

The pH scale is a measure of $[H^+]$ and so at first glance may appear to be more suited for the measurement of acids than of bases. But we can in fact use the same scale to describe the alkalinity of a solution. As will be explained on page 359, this is because the relationship between $[H^+]$ and $[OH^-]$ is inverse in aqueous solutions, and so lower $[H^+]$ (higher pH) means higher $[OH^-]$ and vice versa. Therefore the scale of pH numbers represents a range of values from strongly acidic through to strongly alkaline.

| pH 0 | pH 7 | pH 14 |
|---|---|---|
| increasing [H$^+$] increasing acidity | neutral | increasing [OH$^-$] increasing alkalinity |

## pH calculations

From the definition of pH we can:

(i)   calculate the value of pH from a known concentration of $H^+$;
(ii)  calculate the concentration of $H^+$ from a given pH.

## Worked example

A sample of lake water was analysed at 298 K and found to have $[H^+] = 3.2 \times 10^{-5}$ mol dm$^{-3}$. Calculate the pH of this water and comment on its value.

### Solution

$$pH = -\log_{10} [H^+]$$
$$= -\log_{10} (3.2 \times 10^{-5}) = -(-4.49485)$$
$$pH = 4.49$$

At 298 K this pH < 7, and the lake water is therefore acidic.

## Worked example

Human blood has a pH of 7.40. Calculate the concentration of hydrogen ions present.

### Solution

$$[H^+] = 10^{-pH}$$
$$= 10^{-7.40} = 4.0 \times 10^{-8}$$
$$[H^+] = 4.0 \times 10^{-8} \text{ mol dm}^{-3}$$

In the last 40 years, researchers have developed so-called 'super acids' by mixing together various substances. These are several orders of magnitude more acidic than conventional acids, and one example known as 'magic acid' is even able to dissolve candle wax.

In pH calculations you will need to be able to work out logarithms to base 10 and anti-logarithms. Make sure that you are familiar with these operations on your calculator.

Note that the logarithms used in all the work on acids and bases are logarithms to base 10 (log). Do not confuse these with natural logarithms, to base e, (ln).

The rule to follow for significant figures in logarithms is that *the number of decimal places in the logarithm should equal the number of significant figures in the number*. In other words, the number to the left of the decimal place in the logarithm is not counted as a significant figure (this is because it is derived from the exponential part of the number). In the first example here, the number given has two significant figures (3.2) and so the answer is given to two decimal places (.49).

**Use of a pH meter and universal indicator in measuring pH**

Full details of how to carry out this experiment with a worksheet are available online.

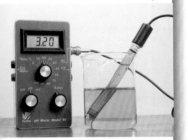

A digital probe showing a pH of 3.20 for the solution in the beaker. The temperature dial is adjusted to the room temperature, allowing the pH meter to compensate for the temperature.

The pH scale and universal indicator. The tubes contain universal indicator added to solutions of pH 0–14 from left to right

Victoria Falls on the Zimbabwe–Zambia border. It is estimated that $6.25 \times 10^8$ dm³ of water flow over the falls every minute. According to the ionization constant discussed here, for every billion of these molecules only two are ionized, and that proportion gets even smaller at lower temperatures.

We are using $H^+(aq)$ throughout this chapter as a simplified form of $H_3O^+(aq)$. This is acceptable in most situations, but don't forget that $H^+$ in aqueous solution always exists as $H_3O^+(aq)$.

## Measuring pH

An easy way to measure pH is with universal indicator paper or solution. The substance tested will give a characteristic colour, which can then be compared with a colour chart supplied with the indicator. Narrower range indicators give a more accurate reading than broad range, but they always depend on the ability of the user's eyes to interpret the colour.

A more objective and usually more accurate means is by using a **pH meter** or probe that directly reads the $[H^+]$ concentration through a special electrode. pH meters can record to an accuracy of several decimal points. They must, however, be calibrated before each use with a buffer solution, and standardized for the temperature, as pH is a temperature-dependent measurement.

## The ionization of water

As the majority of acid–base reactions involve ionization in aqueous solution, it is useful to consider the role of water in more detail. Water itself does ionize, albeit only very slightly at normal temperatures and pressures, so we can write an equilibrium expression for this reaction.

$$H_2O(l) \rightleftharpoons H^+(aq) + OH^-(aq)$$

Therefore $K_c = \dfrac{[H^+][OH^-]}{[H_2O]}$

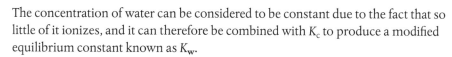

The concentration of water can be considered to be constant due to the fact that so little of it ionizes, and it can therefore be combined with $K_c$ to produce a modified equilibrium constant known as $K_w$.

$$K_c[H_2O] = [H^+][OH^-]$$

Therefore $K_w = [H^+][OH^-]$

$K_w$ is known as the **ionic product constant of water** and has a fixed value at a specified temperature. At 298 K, $K_w = 1.00 \times 10^{-14}$.

In pure water because $[H^+] = [OH^-]$, it follows that $[H^+] = \sqrt{K_w}$

So, at 298 K, $[H^+] = 1.00 \times 10^{-7}$ which gives pH = 7.00

This is consistent with the widely known value for the pH of water at room temperature.

## The relationship between H⁺ and OH⁻ is inverse

Because the product $[H^+] \times [OH^-]$ gives a constant value, it follows that the concentrations of these ions must have an inverse relationship. In other words, in aqueous solutions the higher the concentration of $H^+$ the lower the concentration of $OH^-$. Solutions are defined as acidic, neutral, or basic according to their relative concentrations of these ions as shown below.

|  |  | at 298 K |
|---|---|---|
| Acidic solutions are defined as those in which | $[H^+] > [OH^-]$ | pH < 7 |
| Neutral solutions are defined as those in which | $[H^+] = [OH^-]$ | pH = 7 |
| Alkaline solutions are defined as those in which | $[H^+] < [OH^-]$ | pH > 7 |

So if we know the concentration of either $H^+$ or $OH^-$, we can calculate the other from the value of $K_w$.

$$[H]^+ = \frac{K_w}{[OH]^-} \quad \text{and} \quad [OH]^- = \frac{K_w}{[H]^+}$$

### Worked example

A sample of blood at 298 K has $[H^+] = 4.60 \times 10^{-8}$ mol dm⁻³.

Calculate the concentration of $OH^-$ and state whether the blood is acidic, neutral, or basic.

### Solution

At 298 K, $K_w = 1.00 \times 10^{-14} = [H^+][OH^-]$

$$[OH]^- = \frac{1.00 \times 10^{-14}}{4.60 \times 10^{-8}} = 2.17 \times 10^{-7} \text{ mol dm}^{-3}$$

As $[OH^-] > [H^+]$ the solution is basic.

Calculations involving $[H^+]$, $[OH^-]$, and pH, as well as the pOH scale, are considered in more detail in section 18.2, page 366.

Water is a pure liquid so its concentration is just a function of its density, which is 1.00 g cm⁻³.

From $n = \frac{m}{M}$, this gives

$n(H_2O) = \frac{1000}{18}$ in 1 dm³

so concentration $(H_2O) = 55$ mol dm⁻³.

The value $K_w = 1.00 \times 10^{-14}$ at 298 K is given in section 2 of the IB data booklet so does not have to be learned.

$K_w = [H^+][OH^-]$

**The concentrations of H⁺ and OH⁻ are inversely proportional in an aqueous solution.**

**9** What happens to the pH of an acid when 10 cm³ of it is added to 90 cm³ of water?

**10** Beer has a hydrogen ion concentration of $1.9 \times 10^{-5}$ mol dm⁻³. What is its pH?

**11** An aqueous solution has a pH of 9 at 25 °C. What are its concentrations for H⁺ and OH⁻?

**12** For each of the following aqueous solutions, calculate [OH⁻] from [H⁺] or [H⁺] from [OH⁻]. Classify each solution as acidic, basic, or neutral at 298 K.

**(a)** $[H^+] = 3.4 \times 10^{-9}$ mol dm⁻³
**(b)** $[OH^-] = 0.010$ mol dm⁻³
**(c)** $[OH^-] = 1.0 \times 10^{-10}$ mol dm⁻³
**(d)** $[H^+] = 8.6 \times 10^{-5}$ mol dm⁻³

**13** What is the pH of 0.01 mol dm⁻³ solution of HCl which dissociates fully?

$$HCl(aq) \rightarrow H^+(aq) + Cl^-(aq)$$

**14** For each of the following biological fluids, calculate the pH from the given concentration of H⁺ or OH⁻ ions.

**(a)** bile: $[OH^-] = 8 \times 10^{-8}$ mol dm⁻³
**(b)** gastric juice: $[H^+] = 10^{-2}$ mol dm⁻³
**(c)** urine: $[OH^-] = 6 \times 10^{-10}$ mol dm⁻³

**15** A solution of sodium hydroxide is prepared by adding distilled water to 6.0 g NaOH to make 1.0 dm³ of solution. What is the pH of this solution? Assume that NaOH dissociates completely in solution:

$$NaOH(aq) \rightarrow Na^+(aq) + OH^-(aq)$$

# 8.4 Strong and weak acids and bases

## Understandings:

- Strong and weak acids and bases differ in the extent of ionization.

### Guidance
*The terms ionization and dissociation can be used interchangeably.*

- Strong acids and bases of equal concentrations have higher conductivities than weak acids and bases.

### Guidance
*See section 21 in the data booklet for a list of weak acids and bases.*

- A strong acid is a good proton donor and has a weak conjugate base.
- A strong base is a good proton acceptor and has a weak conjugate acid.

## Applications and skills:

- Distinction between strong and weak acids and bases in terms of the rates of their reactions with metals, metal oxides, metal hydroxides, metal hydrogen carbonates, and metal carbonates and their electrical conductivities for solutions of equal concentrations.

## The strength of an acid or base depends on its extent of ionization

We have seen that the reactions of acids and bases are dependent on the fact that they dissociate in solution, acids to produce H⁺ ions and bases to produce OH⁻ ions. As we will see here, the extent of this dissociation is what defines the strength of an acid or a base.

Consider the acid dissociation reaction:

$$HA(aq) + H_2O(l) \rightleftharpoons A^-(aq) + H_3O^+(aq)$$

If this acid dissociates fully, it will exist entirely as ions in solution. It is said to be a **strong acid**. For example, hydrochloric acid, HCl, is a strong acid.

The reaction is written without the equilibrium sign.

$$HCl(aq) + H_2O(l) \rightarrow H_3O^+(aq) + Cl^-(aq)$$

If, on the other hand, the acid dissociates only partially, it produces an equilibrium mixture in which the undissociated form dominates. It is said to be a **weak acid**. For example, ethanoic acid, $CH_3COOH$, is a weak acid.

$$CH_3COOH(aq) + H_2O(l) \rightleftharpoons H_3O^+(aq) + CH_3COO^-(aq)$$

Here it is essential to use the equilibrium sign for its dissociation reaction.

Strong acids are good proton donors. As their dissociation reactions go to completion, their conjugate bases are not readily able to accept a proton. For example, HCl reacts to form the conjugate base $Cl^-$, which shows virtually no basic properties.

| $HCl(aq)$ | + | $H_2O(l)$ | $\rightarrow$ | $H_3O^+(aq)$ | + | $Cl^-(aq)$ |
|---|---|---|---|---|---|---|
| strong acid | | base | | conjugate acid | | conjugate base |

Weak acids are poor proton donors. As their dissociation reactions are equilibria which lie to the left, in favour of reactants, their conjugate bases are readily able to accept a proton. For example, $CH_3COOH$ reacts to form the conjugate base $CH_3COO^-$, which is a stronger base than $Cl^-$.

| $CH_3COOH(aq)$ | + | $H_2O(l)$ | $\rightleftharpoons$ | $H_3O^+(aq)$ | + | $CH_3COO^-(aq)$ |
|---|---|---|---|---|---|---|
| weak acid | | base | | conjugate acid | | conjugate base |

So acid dissociation reactions favour the production of the weaker conjugate.

In a similar way, bases can be described as strong or weak on the basis of the extent of their ionization. For example, NaOH is a **strong base** because it ionizes fully.

$$NaOH(aq) \rightarrow Na^+(aq) + OH^-(aq)$$

Its dissociation is written without equilibrium signs.

(Note that it is the $OH^-$ ions that show Brønsted–Lowry base behaviour by accepting protons.)

On the other hand, $NH_3$ is a **weak base** as it ionizes only partially, so its equilibrium lies to the left and the concentration of ions is low.

$$NH_3(aq) + H_2O(l) \rightleftharpoons NH_4^+(aq) + OH^-(aq)$$

Strong bases are good proton acceptors; they react to form conjugates that do not show acidic properties. Weak bases are poor proton acceptors; they react to form conjugates with stronger acidic properties than the conjugates of strong bases. Base ionization reactions favour the production of the weaker conjugate.

In section 18.2 (page 366), we will learn how we can quantify the strength of an acid or base in terms of the equilibrium constant for its dissociation reaction, and look in more detail at the relationship between the strength of acid–base conjugate pairs.

The strength of an acid or base is therefore a measure of how readily it dissociates in aqueous solution. This is an inherent property of a particular acid or base, dependent on its bonding. Do not confuse acid or basic *strength* with its *concentration*, which is a variable depending on the number of moles per unit volume, according to how much solute has been added to the water. Note, for example, it is possible for an acid or base

Strong acids and strong bases ionize almost completely in solution; weak acids and weak bases ionize only partially in solution.

In writing the ionization reactions of weak acids and bases, it is essential to use the equilibrium sign.

361

to be strong but present in a dilute solution, or weak and present in a concentrated solution.

**NATURE OF SCIENCE**

The use of advanced analytical techniques has allowed the strengths of different acids and bases to be quantified and compared. Experimental evidence has been obtained from accurate pH and concentration measurements. Sometimes the results may seem surprising, and this has led to a fuller exploration of the factors involved at the molecular level. For example, the relative acidic strengths of the hydrogen halides (HF, HCl, HBr, and HI) are found to increase down the group, despite the decreasing polarity of the molecules. This is explained by the decreasing bond strength of H–halogen as the halogen atom increases in size. In other cases, such as the organic acids, factors such as electronegativity, ion stability, and inductive effects are used to explain the patterns in acid strength. Theories must explain experimental evidence and be subject to testable predictions.

## Weak acids and bases are much more common than strong acids and bases

It is often useful to know which of the acids and bases we come across are strong and which are weak. Fortunately this is quite easy as there are very few common examples of strong acids and bases, so this short list can be committed to memory. You will then know that any other acids and bases you come across are likely to be weak.

| | Acid | | Base | |
|---|---|---|---|---|
| common examples of **strong** forms | HCl | hydrochloric acid | LiOH | lithium hydroxide |
| | $HNO_3$ | nitric acid | NaOH | sodium hydroxide |
| | $H_2SO_4$ | sulfuric acid | KOH | potassium hydroxide |
| | | | $Ba(OH)_2$ | barium hydroxide |
| some examples of **weak** forms | $CH_3COOH$ and other organic acids | ethanoic acid | $NH_3$ | ammonia |
| | $H_2CO_3$ | carbonic acid | $C_2H_5NH_2$ and other amines | ethylamine |
| | $H_3PO_4$ | phosphoric acid | | |

Note that amines such as ethylamine, $C_2H_5NH_2$, can be considered as organic derivatives of $NH_3$ in which one of the hydrogen atoms has been replaced by an alkyl (hydrocarbon) group. There are literally hundreds of acids and bases in organic chemistry (Chapter 10), nearly all of which are weak in comparison with the strong inorganic acids listed here. Many of these are listed in section 21 of the IB data booklet. Amino acids, the building blocks of proteins, as their name implies contain both the basic –$NH_2$ amino group and the –COOH acid group. The 'A' in DNA, the store of genetic material, stands for 'acid', in this case the acid present is phosphoric acid.

## Distinguishing between strong and weak acids and bases

Due to their greater ionization in solution, strong acids and strong bases will contain a *higher concentration of ions* than weak acids and weak bases. This then can be used as a means of distinguishing between them. Note though that such comparisons will only be valid when solutions of the same concentration (mol dm⁻³) are compared at the same temperature. We will consider here three properties that depend on the concentration of ions and so can be used for this purpose.

## 1  Electrical conductivity

Electrical conductivity of a solution depends on the concentration of mobile ions. Strong acids and strong bases will therefore show higher conductivity than weak acids and bases – so long as solutions of the same concentration are compared. This can be measured using a conductivity meter or probe, or by using the conductivity setting on a pH meter.

## 2  Rate of reaction

The reactions of acids described in section 8.2 depend on the concentration of $H^+$ ions. They will therefore happen at a greater rate with stronger acids.

These different rates of reactions may be an important consideration, for example, regarding safety in the laboratory, but they usually do not provide an easy means of quantifying data to distinguish between weak and strong acids.

## 3  pH

Because it is a measure of the $H^+$ concentration, the pH scale can be used directly to compare the strengths of acids (providing they are of equal molar concentration). Remember the higher the $H^+$ concentration, the lower the pH value. Universal indicator or a pH meter can be used to measure pH.

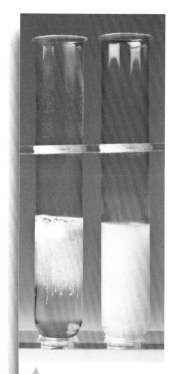

The different rates of reaction between magnesium metal and hydrochloric acid and ethanoic acid. The mass and surface area of the magnesium added and the concentrations and volumes of the acids are equal in both tubes. The higher rate with the strong acid HCl is shown on the left, where large bubbles of hydrogen form. The slower reaction with $CH_3COOH$, shown on the right, causes smaller bubbles of hydrogen gas, which gives the milky appearance.

### Exercises

**16** Which of the following 1 mol dm⁻³ solutions will be the poorest conductor of electricity?

   **A**  HCl       **B**  $CH_3COOH$     **C**  NaOH       **D**  NaCl

**17** Which methods will distinguish between equimolar solutions of a strong base and a strong acid?

   I    Add magnesium to each solution and look for the formation of gas bubbles.
   II   Add aqueous sodium hydroxide to each solution and measure the temperature change.
   III  Use each solution in a circuit with a battery and lamp and see how brightly the lamp glows.

   **A**  I and II only    **B**  I and III only    **C**  II and III only    **D**  I, II, and III

**18** Which acid in each of the following pairs has the stronger conjugate base?

   **(a)**  $H_2CO_3$ or $H_2SO_4$
   **(b)**  HCl or HCOOH

# 18.1  Lewis acids and bases

## Understandings:

- A Lewis acid is a lone pair acceptor and a Lewis base is a lone pair donor.
  ### Guidance
  - Relations between Brønsted–Lowry and Lewis acids and bases should be discussed.
  - Both organic and inorganic examples should be studied.
- When a Lewis base reacts with a Lewis acid a coordinate bond is formed.
- A nucleophile is a Lewis base and an electrophile is a Lewis acid.

## Applications and skills:

- Application of Lewis acid–base theory to inorganic and organic chemistry to identify the role of the reacting species.

## Lewis theory focuses on electron pairs

Gilbert Lewis, whose name famously belongs to electron dot structures for representing covalent bonding (Chapter 4), used such structures in interpreting Brønsted–Lowry theory. Realizing that the base must have a lone pair of electrons, he reasoned that the entire reaction could be viewed in terms of the electron pair rather than in terms of proton transfer. For example, the reaction previously described in which ammonia acts as a base can be represented as follows:

The curly arrow (shown in blue) is a convention used to show donation of a pair of electrons. $H^+$ is acting as an electron pair acceptor and the nitrogen atom in ammonia is acting as an electron pair donor. From such thinking Lewis developed a new, broader definition of acids and bases.

- A Lewis acid is a lone pair acceptor.
- A Lewis base is a lone pair donor.

Lewis bases and Brønsted–Lowry bases are therefore the same group of compounds: by either definition they are species that must have a lone pair of electrons.

In the case of acids, however, the Lewis definition is broader than the Brønsted–Lowry theory: no longer restricted just to $H^+$, an acid by Lewis definition is any species capable of accepting a lone pair of electrons. Of course this *includes* $H^+$ with its vacant orbital (so all Brønsted–Lowry acids *are* Lewis acids) – but it will also include molecules that have an incomplete valence shell. Lewis acid–base reactions result in the formation of a covalent bond, which will always be a **coordinate bond** because both the electrons come from the base.

Here is another example:

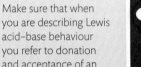

$BF_3$ has an incomplete octet so is able to act as a Lewis acid and accept a pair of electrons; $NH_3$ acts as a Lewis base, donating its lone pair of electrons. The arrow on the covalent bond denotes the fact that it is a coordinate bond with both electrons donated from the nitrogen.

Other good examples of Lewis acid–base reactions are found in the chemistry of the transition elements. As we learned in Chapter 3, these metals in the middle of the Periodic Table often form ions with vacant orbitals in their d subshell. So they are able to act as Lewis acids and accept lone pairs of electrons when they bond with ligands to form complex ions.

**A Lewis acid is lone pair acceptor. A Lewis base is a lone pair donor.**

Make sure that when you are describing Lewis acid–base behaviour you refer to donation and acceptance of an electron *pair*. If you omit the word pair, you would be describing a redox reaction which is entirely different.

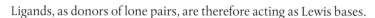

Ligands, as donors of lone pairs, are therefore acting as Lewis bases.

For example, $Cu^{2+}$ in aqueous solution reacts as follows:

$$Cu^{2+}(aq) + 6H_2O(l) \rightarrow [Cu(H_2O)_6]^{2+}(aq)$$

$Cu^{2+}$ is a Lewis acid and $H_2O$ is a Lewis base.

Typical ligands found in complex ions include $H_2O$, $CN^-$, and $NH_3$. Note that these all possess lone pairs of electrons, the defining feature of their Lewis base properties.

## Nucleophiles and electrophiles

At about the same time as Lewis developed his acid–base theory, alternate language was being introduced to describe the behaviour of reactants with respect to electron pairs.

A **nucleophile** ('likes nucleus') is an electron-rich species that donates a lone pair to form a new covalent bond in a reaction.

An **electrophile** ('likes electrons') is an electron-deficient species that accepts a lone pair from another reactant to form a new covalent bond.

These terms are often used to describe reactions in terms of electron-rich nucleophiles attacking electron-deficient electrophiles, and are depicted using curly arrows to show electron movements. Several examples from organic chemistry are discussed in Chapter 10.

Clearly these terms are the same as those derived by Lewis. In other words, a nucleophile is a Lewis base and an electrophile is a Lewis acid.

• Examples of nucleophiles / Lewis bases:

• Examples of electrophiles / Lewis acids:

The reaction below shows the hydroxide ion, $OH^-$, acting as a nucleophile on an organic molecule known as a halogenoalkane. This reaction is discussed in detail on page 498. We can see that $OH^-$ is a Lewis base as it is donating a lone pair of electrons.

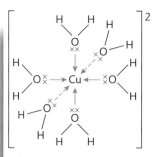

**Figure 8.6** In the complex ion $[Cu(H_2O)_6]^{2+}$, $Cu^{2+}$ has acted as a Lewis acid and the $H_2O$ ligands as Lewis bases. The bonds within the complex ion are coordinate bonds, as indicated by the arrows. For clarity only one lone pair (out of two) is shown on each O atom in $H_2O$.

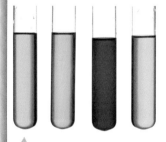

Copper ions ($Cu^{2+}$) forming different complex ions with distinct colours. From left to right the ligands are $H_2O$, $Cl^-$, $NH_3$, and the organic group EDTA. The $Cu^{2+}$ ion has acted as the Lewis acid, the ligands as Lewis bases.

A nucleophile is a Lewis base and an electrophile is a Lewis acid.

**TOK** Different approaches and vocabulary can sometimes be used to explain the same phenomenon. Does the use of language as a way of knowing help us to judge these competing approaches?

## Comparison of Brønsted–Lowry and Lewis theories of acids and bases

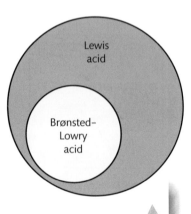

**Figure 8.7** Relationship between Brønsted–Lowry acids and Lewis acids.

| Theory | Definition of acid | Definition of base |
|---|---|---|
| Brønsted–Lowry | proton donor | proton acceptor |
| Lewis | electron pair acceptor | electron pair donor |

• Although all Brønsted–Lowry acids are Lewis acids, not all Lewis acids are Brønsted–Lowry acids. The term Lewis acid is usually reserved for those species which can *only* be described by Lewis theory, that is those that do not release $H^+$.

• Many reactions cannot be described as Brønsted–Lowry acid–base reactions, but do qualify as Lewis acid–base reactions. These are reactions where no transfer of $H^+$ occurs.

**NATURE OF SCIENCE**

Lewis acid–base theory is compatible with Brønsted–Lowry theory, it does not falsify it. By changing the perspective of acid–base reactions from the proton to the lone pair of electrons, it opens up a wider field of application. The proton no longer has a central role, it is just one example of a lone pair acceptor. Lewis acids include a wide range of both organic and inorganic species that are not recognized as acids in Brønsted–Lowry theory. Yet, in many cases, as we will see in the following sections, Brønsted–Lowry theory is sufficient and could be considered a more useful theory for the description of acid–base reactions, especially those occurring in aqueous solution.

### Exercises

**19** For each of the following reactions identify the Lewis acid and the Lewis base.

    **(a)** $4NH_3(aq) + Zn^{2+}(aq) \rightarrow [Zn(NH_3)_4]^{2+}(aq)$

    **(b)** $2Cl^-(aq) + BeCl_2(aq) \rightarrow [BeCl_4]^{2-}(aq)$

    **(c)** $Mg^{2+}(aq) + 6H_2O(l) \rightarrow [Mg(H_2O)_6]^{2+}(aq)$

**20** Which of the following could not act as a ligand in a complex ion with a transition metal?

    **A** $Cl^-$     **B** $NCl_3$     **C** $PCl_3$     **D** $CH_4$

**21** Which of the following reactions represents an acid–base reaction according to Lewis theory but not according to Brønsted-Lowry theory?

    **A** $NH_3(aq) + HCl(aq) \rightleftharpoons NH_4Cl(aq)$

    **B** $2H_2O(l) \rightleftharpoons H_3O^+(aq) + OH^-(aq)$

    **C** $Cu^{2+}(aq) + 4NH_3(aq) \rightleftharpoons [Cu(NH_3)_4]^{2+}(aq)$

    **D** $BaO(s) + H_2O(l) \rightleftharpoons Ba^{2+}(aq) + 2OH^-(aq)$

## 18.2 Calculations involving acids and bases

### Understandings:

• The expression for the dissociation constant of a weak acid ($K_a$) and a weak base ($K_b$).

• For a conjugate acid–base pair, $K_a \times K_b = K_w$.

    ***Guidance***

    • *The value $K_w$ depends on the temperature.*

    • *Only examples involving the transfer of one proton will be assessed.*

    • *Calculations of pH at temperatures other than 298 K can be assessed.*

• The relationship between $K_a$ and $pK_a$ is $pK_a = -\log K_a$ and between $K_b$ and $pK_b$ is $pK_b = -\log K_b$.

## Applications and skills:

- Solution of problems involving [$H^+$(aq)], [$OH^-$(aq)], pH, pOH, $K_a$, $pK_a$, $K_b$, and $pK_b$.

  **Guidance**
  - *Students should state when approximations are used in equilibrium calculations.*
  - *The use of quadratic equations will not be assessed.*

- Discussion of the relative strengths of acids and bases using values of $K_a$, $pK_a$, $K_b$, and $pK_b$.

  **Guidance**
  *The calculation of pH in buffer solutions will only be assessed in options B.7 and D.4.*

We have learned that acids and bases differ in their strength according to the equilibrium position of their ionization reactions. They can also be prepared in different concentrations of aqueous solution according to the ratio of acid or base to water used. Both these factors, strength and concentration, influence the pH of a solution. In this section we will learn how to quantify these relationships.

## $K_w$ is temperature dependent

The ionic product constant of water, $K_w$, was derived on pages 358–359.

$$K_w = [H^+][OH^-] = 1.00 \times 10^{-14} \text{ at } 298 \text{ K}$$

As $K_w$ is an equilibrium constant, its value must be temperature dependent. The reaction for the dissociation of water is endothermic (it involves bond breaking) and so, as we learned in Chapter 7, an increase in temperature will shift the equilibrium to the right and increase the value of $K_w$. This represents an increase in the concentrations of $H^+$(aq) and $OH^-$(aq), and so a decrease in pH. Conversely, a reduction in temperature, through its effect on shifting the equilibrium to the left, decreases the value of $K_w$, representing lower ion concentrations and so higher pH values. Some data to illustrate these trends are given in the table below.

| Temperature / °C | $K_w$ | [$H^+$] in pure water ($\sqrt{K_w}$) | pH of pure water ($-\log_{10}[H^+]$) |
|---|---|---|---|
| 0 | $1.5 \times 10^{-15}$ | $0.39 \times 10^{-7}$ | 7.47 |
| 10 | $3.0 \times 10^{-15}$ | $0.55 \times 10^{-7}$ | 7.27 |
| 20 | $6.8 \times 10^{-15}$ | $0.82 \times 10^{-7}$ | 7.08 |
| 25 | $1.0 \times 10^{-14}$ | $1.00 \times 10^{-7}$ | 7.00 |
| 30 | $1.5 \times 10^{-14}$ | $1.22 \times 10^{-7}$ | 6.92 |
| 40 | $3.0 \times 10^{-14}$ | $1.73 \times 10^{-7}$ | 6.77 |
| 50 | $5.5 \times 10^{-14}$ | $2.35 \times 10^{-7}$ | 6.63 |

In other words, the pH of pure water is 7.00 only when the temperature is 298 K. Note that at temperatures above and below this, despite changes in the pH value, water is still a neutral substance as its $H^+$(aq) concentration is equal to its $OH^-$(aq) concentration. It does not become acidic or basic as we heat it and cool it respectively!

The temperature dependence of $K_w$ means that the temperature should always be stated alongside pH measurements.

**TOK** Because many people are so familiar with the value 7.00 as the pH of water, it is often more difficult to convince them that water with a pH of greater or less than this is still neutral. Can you think of other examples where entrenched prior knowledge might hinder a fuller understanding of new knowledge? Are we likely to misinterpret experimental data when it does not fit with our expectations based on prior knowledge?

## pH and pOH scales are inter-related

In section 8.3 we learned that the pH scale was introduced in order to simplify the expression of the $H^+$ concentration in a solution, and in particular it helps us to compare different solutions in terms of their $H^+$ content. The same rationale can be applied to the $OH^-$ ions. Like $H^+$ ions, $OH^-$ ions are often present in low concentrations in solutions and so have negative exponents when expressed as mol dm$^{-3}$ that can be awkward to work with. The parallel scale, known as the **pOH scale**, is therefore used to describe the $OH^-$ content of solutions.

- $pOH = -\log_{10}[OH^-]$;
- $[OH^-] = 10^{-pOH}$

- $pH = -\log_{10}[H^+]$;
- $[H^+] = 10^{-pH}$

As explained on page 356, the logarithmic nature of these scales means that a change of one unit in pH or pOH represents a 10× change in $[H^+]$ or $[OH^-]$ respectively. The scales are inverse, so the higher the $H^+$ or $OH^-$ concentration, the smaller the pH or pOH value. These values are usually positive and have no units.

**In all aqueous solutions at 298 K: pH + pOH = 14**

From the relationship $[H^+][OH^-] = K_w = 1.00 \times 10^{-14}$ at 298 K, it follows that

$$10^{-pH} \times 10^{-pOH} = 1.00 \times 10^{-14} \text{ at } 298 \text{ K}$$

By taking the negative logarithm to base 10 of both sides, we get

$$pH + pOH = 14.00 \text{ at } 298 \text{ K}$$

**Figure 8.8** Relationship between $[H^+]$, $[OH^-]$, pH, and pOH at 298 K.

The relationships between pH, $[H^+]$, pOH, and $[OH^-]$ are shown in Figure 8.8.

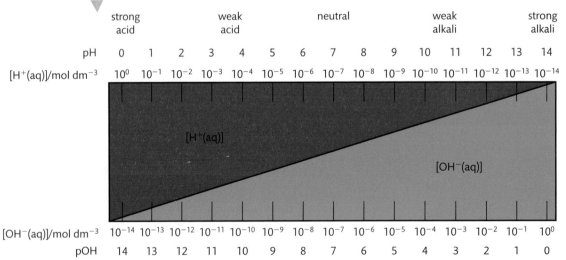

In the same way as the negative logarithms to base 10 of $H^+$ and $OH^-$ are known as pH and pOH respectively, the same terminology can be applied to $K_w$ to derive **p$K_w$**.

- $pK_w = -\log_{10}(K_w)$
- $K_w = 10^{-pK_w}$

**pH + pOH = p$K_w$**

So we can rewrite the expression above in a form that will apply to all temperatures:

$$pH + pOH = pK_w$$

# Summary of the relationships between [H⁺], [OH⁻], pH, and pOH

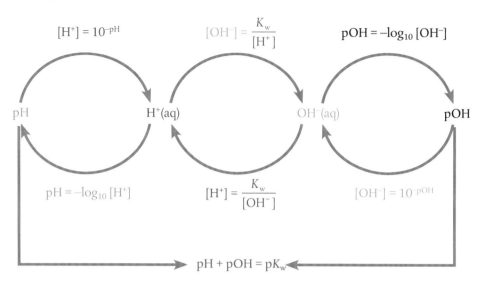

$$[H^+] = 10^{-pH}$$

$$[OH^-] = \frac{K_w}{[H^+]}$$

$$pOH = -\log_{10}[OH^-]$$

pH      H⁺(aq)      OH⁻(aq)      pOH

$$pH = -\log_{10}[H^+]$$

$$[H^+] = \frac{K_w}{[OH^-]}$$

$$[OH^-] = 10^{-pOH}$$

$$pH + pOH = pK_w$$

## Converting H⁺ and OH⁻ into pH and pOH

Many calculations on acids and bases involve inter-conversions of [H⁺] and pH, as we saw in section 8.3, and we can extend these now to include [OH⁻] and pOH.

### Worked example

Lemon juice has a pH of 2.90 at 25 °C. Calculate its [H⁺], [OH⁻], and pOH.

**Solution**

$$[H^+] = 10^{-pH} = 10^{-2.90} = 1.3 \times 10^{-3}\ \text{mol dm}^{-3}$$

$pH + pOH = 14.00$ at 298 K, so $pOH = 14.00 - 2.90 = 11.10$

$$[OH^-] = 10^{-pOH} = 10^{-11.10} = 7.7 \times 10^{-12}\ \text{mol dm}^{-3}$$

or $K_w = [H^+][OH^-]$ so $1.00 \times 10^{-14} = (1.3 \times 10^{-3}) \times [OH^-]$

$$[OH^-] = 7.7 \times 10^{-12}\ \text{mol dm}^{-3}$$

## Strong acids and bases: pH and pOH can be deduced from their concentrations

We assume full dissociation for strong acids and bases. Because of this we can deduce the ion concentrations and so calculate the pH or pOH directly from the initial concentration of the solution. Note that the pH and pOH are derived from the *equilibrium* concentrations of H⁺ and OH⁻. In these examples we will use the same notation as in Chapter 7, black for data that are given in the questions and blue for derived data.

## Worked example

Calculate the pH of the following at 298 K:

(a) 0.10 mol dm$^{-3}$ NaOH(aq)

(b) 0.15 mol dm$^{-3}$ H$_2$SO$_4$(aq)

### Solution

(a) $\qquad\qquad\qquad\qquad$ NaOH(aq) → Na$^+$(aq) + OH$^-$(aq)

initial (mol dm$^{-3}$) $\qquad\qquad$ 0.10

equilibrium (mol dm$^{-3}$) $\qquad\qquad\qquad\qquad\qquad\qquad$ 0.10

pOH = $-\log_{10}$ (0.10) = 1.0, therefore pH = 13.0

(b) $\qquad\qquad\qquad\qquad$ H$_2$SO$_4$(aq) → 2H$^+$(aq) + SO$_4{}^{2-}$(aq)

initial (mol dm$^{-3}$) $\qquad\qquad$ 0.15

equilibrium (mol dm$^{-3}$) $\qquad\qquad\qquad\qquad$ 0.30

pH = $-\log_{10}$ (0.30) = 0.52

## Exercises

**22** At the temperature of the human body, 37 °C, the value of $K_w$ = 2.4 × 10$^{-14}$.

Calculate [H$^+$], [OH$^-$], pH, pOH, and p$K_w$ of water at this temperature. Is it acidic, basic, or neutral?

**23** The pH of a sample of milk is 6.77 at 298 K. Calculate its pOH, [H$^+$], and [OH$^-$]. Deduce whether it is acidic, basic, or neutral.

**24** Calculate the pH of the following solutions:

(a) 0.40 mol dm$^{-3}$ HCl

(b) 3.7 × 10$^{-4}$ mol dm$^{-3}$ KOH

(c) 5.0 × 10$^{-5}$ mol dm$^{-3}$ Ba(OH)$_2$

**25** Which values are correct for a solution of NaOH of concentration 0.010 mol dm$^{-3}$ at 298 K?

A $\quad$ [H$^+$] = 1.0 × 10$^{-2}$ mol dm$^{-3}$ and pH = 2.00

B $\quad$ [OH$^-$] = 1.0 × 10$^{-2}$ mol dm$^{-3}$ and pH = 12.00

C $\quad$ [H$^+$] = 1.0 × 10$^{-12}$ mol dm$^{-3}$ and pOH = 12.00

D $\quad$ [OH$^-$] = 1.0 × 10$^{-12}$ mol dm$^{-3}$ and pOH = 2.00

# Dissociation constants express the strength of weak acids and bases

Weak acids and bases, unlike strong acids and bases, do not dissociate fully. This means we *cannot* deduce the concentrations of ions in their solutions from the initial concentrations, as the ion concentrations will depend on the extent of dissociation that has occurred. So we need some means of quantifying the extent of dissociation – and the process takes us back to equilibrium considerations.

The dissociation reactions of weak acids and weak bases can be represented as equilibrium expressions, each with their own equilibrium constant. The value of this constant will convey information about the position of equilibrium, and therefore on the extent of dissociation of the acid or base.

Consider the generic weak acid HA dissociating in water:

$$HA(aq) + H_2O(l) \rightleftharpoons H_3O^+(aq) + A^-(aq)$$

$$K_c = \frac{[H_3O^+][A^-]}{[HA][H_2O]}$$

Given that the concentration of water is considered to be a constant, we can combine this with $K_c$ to produce a modified equilibrium constant known as $\textbf{K}_\textbf{a}$.

$$K_c[H_2O] = \frac{[H_3O^+][A^-]}{[HA]}$$

Therefore $K_a = \dfrac{[H_3O^+][A^-]}{[HA]}$

$K_a$ is known as the **acid dissociation constant**. It will have a fixed value for a particular acid at a specified temperature.

As the value of $K_a$ depends on the position of the equilibrium of acid dissociation, it gives a direct measure of the strength of an acid. *The higher the value of $K_a$ at a particular temperature, the greater the dissociation, and so the stronger the acid.* Note that because $K_a$ is an equilibrium constant, its value does not depend on the concentration of the acid or on the presence of other ions. We will return to this point in our study of buffer solutions in section 18.3 (page 378).

Similarly, we can consider the ionization of a base using the generic weak base B.

$$B(aq) + H_2O(l) \rightleftharpoons BH^+(aq) + OH^-(aq)$$

$$K_c = \frac{[BH^+][OH^-]}{[B][H_2O]}$$

Again we can combine the constants to give a modified equilibrium constant $\textbf{K}_\textbf{b}$.

$$K_c[H_2O] = \frac{[BH^+][OH^-]}{[B]}$$

Therefore $K_b = \dfrac{[BH^+][OH^-]}{[B]}$

$K_b$ is known as the **base dissociation constant**. It will have a fixed value for a particular base at a specified temperature.

As with $K_a$, the value of $K_b$ relates to the position of the equilibrium and so in this case to the strength of the base. *The higher the value of $K_b$ at a particular temperature, the greater the ionization and so the stronger the base.*

Note that the term **acid dissociation constant** is sometimes used interchangeably with the term **acid ionization constant**. You should be comfortable to recognize either terminology in textbooks and questions.

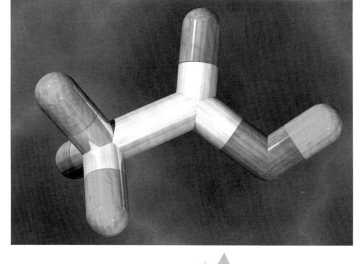

Computer model of a molecule of ethanoic acid, $CH_3COOH$. The atoms (tubes) are colour coded: carbon is white, hydrogen is green, and oxygen is purple. Ethanoic acid is a weak acid, and is used in many of the examples in this chapter. It is used in the production of plastics and also as a preservative.

$$K_a = \frac{[H_3O^+][A^-]}{[HA]}$$

$$K_b = \frac{[BH^+][OH^-]}{[B]}$$

The values of $K_a$ and $K_b$ are constant for a specific acid and base respectively, at a specified temperature. Their values give a measure of the strength of the acid or base.

A pH probe interfaced to a computer showing ammonia solution to have a pH of 11.2. It is a weak base, used in many of the examples in this chapter.

371

### Worked example

Write the expressions for $K_a$ and $K_b$ for the following acid and base.

(a) $CH_3COOH(aq)$

(b) $NH_3(aq)$

**Solution**

First write the equation for the equilibrium reactions – remembering that acids donate $H^+$ and bases accept $H^+$.

(a) $CH_3COOH(aq) \rightleftharpoons CH_3COO^-(aq) + H^+(aq)$

$$K_a = \frac{[CH_3COO^-][H^+]}{[CH_3COOH]}$$

(b) $NH_3(aq) + H_2O(l) \rightleftharpoons NH_4^+(aq) + OH^-(aq)$

$$K_b = \frac{[NH_4^+][OH^-]}{[NH_3]}$$

### Exercises

**26** Write the expressions for $K_b$ for the following:

(a) $C_2H_5NH_2(aq)$

(b) $HSO_4^-(aq)$

(c) $CO_3^{2-}(aq)$

**27** Place the following acids in order of increasing strength.

$H_3PO_4 \quad K_a = 7.1 \times 10^{-3}$

$HNO_2 \quad K_a = 7.1 \times 10^{-4}$

$H_2SO_3 \quad K_a = 1.2 \times 10^{-2}$

**28** Why do you think we do not usually use the concept of $K_a$ and $K_b$ to describe the strength of strong acids and bases?

## Calculations involving $K_a$ and $K_b$

The values of $K_a$ and $K_b$ enable us to compare the strengths of weak acids and bases, and to calculate ion concentrations present at equilibrium and so the pH and pOH values. Examples of these calculations are given below. Note that many of these questions are approached in a similar manner to those given in Chapter 7. It is assumed here that you are familiar with that work, so it may be useful for you to refresh your memory of section 17.1 before continuing.

The following points are to remind you of some key points and guide you in all the calculations that follow:

• The given concentration of an acid or base is its *initial* concentration – before dissociation occurs.

• The pH (or pOH) of a solution refers to the concentration of $H^+$ ions (or $OH^-$ ions) at *equilibrium*.

• The concentration values substituted into the expressions for $K_a$ and $K_b$ must be the *equilibrium* values for all reactants and products.

• When the extent of dissociation is very small (very low value for $K_a$ or $K_b$) it is appropriate to use the approximations:

$$[acid]_{initial} \approx [acid]_{equilibrium}$$

$$[base]_{initial} \approx [base]_{equilibrium}$$

Make sure you clearly state when an approximation is made in a calculation, and justify it in terms of the small value of $K$.

# 1 Calculation of $K_a$ and $K_b$ from pH and initial concentration

## Worked example

Calculate $K_a$ at 298 K for a 0.01 mol dm$^{-3}$ solution of ethanoic acid (CH$_3$COOH). It has a pH of 3.4 at this temperature.

### Solution

Write the equation for the dissociation of the acid. Insert the data in three rows: initial, change, and equilibrium. As in Chapter 7, numbers in black are data that were given in the question, numbers in blue have been derived.

From the pH we get the [H$^+$] at equilibrium:

pH $3.4 \Rightarrow$ [H$^+$] $= 10^{-3.4} = 4.0 \times 10^{-4}$ mol dm$^{-3}$

From the stoichiometry of the reaction we know that [H$^+$] = [CH$_3$COO$^-$]

|  | CH$_3$COOH(aq) | $\rightleftharpoons$ CH$_3$COO$^-$(aq) + | H$^+$(aq) |
|---|---|---|---|
| initial (mol dm$^{-3}$) | 0.01 | 0.00 | 0.00 |
| change (mol dm$^{-3}$) | $-4 \times 10^{-4}$ | $+4 \times 10^{-4}$ | $+4 \times 10^{-4}$ |
| equilibrium (mol dm$^{-3}$) | $0.01 - (4 \times 10^{-4})$ | $4 \times 10^{-4}$ | $4 \times 10^{-4}$ |
|  | $\sim 0.01$ | | |

The approximation $0.01 \approx 0.01 - (4 \times 10^{-4})$ is valid within the precision of this data.

Write the expression for $K_a$ and substitute the equilibrium values.

$$K_a = \frac{[CH_3COO^-][H^+]}{[CH_3COOH]} = \frac{(4 \times 10^{-4})^2}{0.01} = 1.6 \times 10^{-5}$$

## Worked example

Calculate the $K_b$ for a 0.100 mol dm$^{-3}$ solution of methylamine, CH$_3$NH$_2$ at 25 °C. Its pH is 11.80 at this temperature.

### Solution

At 25 °C (298 K), pH + pOH = 14.00. Therefore pH $11.80 \Rightarrow$ pOH = 2.20

[OH$^-$] $= 10^{-pOH} = 10^{-2.20} = 6.3 \times 10^{-3}$

From the stoichiometry of the reaction [OH$^-$] = [CH$_3$NH$_3^+$]

|  | CH$_3$NH$_2$(aq) + | H$_2$O(l) $\rightleftharpoons$ | CH$_3$NH$_3^+$(aq) + | OH$^-$(aq) |
|---|---|---|---|---|
| initial (mol dm$^{-3}$) | 0.100 | | 0.000 | 0.000 |
| change (mol dm$^{-3}$) | $-0.00630$ | | $+0.00630$ | $+0.00630$ |
| equilibrium (mol dm$^{-3}$) | 0.0937 | | 0.00630 | 0.00630 |

$$K_b = \frac{[CH_3NH_3^+][OH^-]}{[CH_3NH_2]} = \frac{(0.00630)^2}{0.0937} = 4.22 \times 10^{-4}$$

## 2 Calculation of $[H^+]$ and pH, $[OH^-]$ and pOH from $K_a$ and $K_b$

### Worked example

A $0.75$ mol dm$^{-3}$ solution of ethanoic acid has a value for $K_a = 1.8 \times 10^{-5}$ at a specified temperature. What is its pH at this temperature?

#### Solution

To calculate pH we need to know $[H^+]$ at equilibrium, and therefore the amount of dissociation of the acid that has occurred: this is the 'change' amount in the reaction.

So let the change in concentration of $CH_3COOH = -x$

Therefore change in concentration of $CH_3COO^-$ and $H^+ = +x$

| | $CH_3COOH(aq)$ | $\rightleftharpoons$ $CH_3COO^-(aq)$ | + $H^+(aq)$ |
|---|---|---|---|
| initial (mol dm$^{-3}$) | 0.75 | 0.00 | 0.00 |
| change (mol dm$^{-3}$) | $-x$ | $+x$ | $+x$ |
| equilibrium (mol dm$^{-3}$) | $0.75 - x$ | $x$ | $x$ |
| | $\sim 0.75$ | | |

As $K_a$ is very small, $x$, the amount of dissociation, is also extremely small and it is valid to approximate $[CH_3COOH]_{initial} \approx [CH_3COOH]_{equilibrium}$.

$$K_a = \frac{[CH_3COO^-][H^+]}{[CH_3COOH]} = \frac{x^2}{0.75} = 1.8 \times 10^{-5}$$

Therefore $x = \sqrt{1.8 \times 10^{-5} \times 0.75} = 3.7 \times 10^{-3}$

$[H^+] = 3.7 \times 10^{-3} \Rightarrow pH = 2.4$

### Worked example

A $0.20$ mol dm$^{-3}$ aqueous solution of ammonia has $K_b$ of $1.8 \times 10^{-5}$ at 298 K. What is its pH?

#### Solution

Let the change in concentration of $NH_3 = -x$

Therefore change in concentration of $NH_4^+$ and $OH^- = +x$

| | $NH_3(aq)$ | + $H_2O(l)$ | $\rightleftharpoons$ $NH_4^+(aq)$ | + $OH^-(aq)$ |
|---|---|---|---|---|
| initial (mol dm$^{-3}$) | 0.20 | | 0.00 | 0.00 |
| change (mol dm$^{-3}$) | $-x$ | | $+x$ | $+x$ |
| equilibrium (mol dm$^{-3}$) | $0.20 - x$ | | $x$ | $x$ |
| | $\approx 0.20$ | | | |

As $K_b$ is very small, $x$ the amount of dissociation is also extremely small, and so it is valid to approximate $[NH_3]_{initial} \approx [NH_3]_{equilibrium}$

$$K_b = \frac{[NH_4^+][OH^-]}{[NH_3]} = \frac{x^2}{0.20} = 1.8 \times 10^{-5}$$

Therefore $x = \sqrt{1.8 \times 10^{-5} \times 0.20} = 1.9 \times 10^{-3}$

$[OH^-] = 1.9 \times 10^{-3}$

$pOH = -\log_{10}(1.9 \times 10^{-3}) = 2.72$

Therefore at 298 K, $pH = 14.00 - 2.72 = 11.28$

**29** The acid dissociation constant of a weak acid has a value of $1.0 \times 10^{-5}$ mol dm$^{-3}$. What is the pH of a 0.1 mol dm$^{-3}$ aqueous solution of HA?

    **A** 2            **B** 3            **C** 5            **D** 6

**30** Calculate the $K_b$ of ethylamine, $C_2H_5NH_2$, given that a 0.10 mol dm$^{-3}$ solution has a pH of 11.86.

**31** What are the [H$^+$] and [OH$^-$] in a 0.10 mol dm$^{-3}$ solution of an acid that has $K_a = 1.0 \times 10^{-7}$?

# p$K_a$ and p$K_b$

We have seen that $K_a$ and $K_b$ values give us a direct measure of the relative strengths of weak acids and bases. But as these values are characteristically very small, they usually involve dealing with numbers with negative exponents, which we have acknowledged before are clumsy to use as the basis for comparisons. They also span a wide range of values. So, in the same way as with the concentrations of H$^+$ and OH$^-$ ions and $K_w$, and for the same reason, we can convert $K_a$ and $K_b$ values into their negative logarithms to the base 10, known as **p$K_a$** and **p$K_b$**.

- $pK_a = -\log_{10} K_a$;
- $K_a = 10^{-pK_a}$

- $pK_b = -\log_{10} K_b$;
- $K_b = 10^{-pK_b}$

Some examples of $K_a$ and p$K_a$, $K_b$ and p$K_b$ values are given below, all at 298 K.

| Acid | Formula | $K_a$ | p$K_a$ |
|---|---|---|---|
| methanoic | HCOOH | $1.8 \times 10^{-4}$ | 3.75 |
| ethanoic | $CH_3COOH$ | $1.8 \times 10^{-5}$ | 4.76 |
| propanoic | $C_2H_5COOH$ | $1.4 \times 10^{-5}$ | 4.87 |

| Base | Formula | $K_b$ | p$K_b$ |
|---|---|---|---|
| ammonia | $NH_3$ | $1.8 \times 10^{-5}$ | 4.75 |
| methylamine | $CH_3NH_2$ | $4.6 \times 10^{-4}$ | 3.34 |
| ethylamine | $C_2H_5NH_2$ | $4.5 \times 10^{-4}$ | 3.35 |

The following points follow from the table.

**1  p$K_a$ and p$K_b$ numbers are usually positive and have no units.**

Although the derivation of $K_a$ and $K_b$ can be applied to any acid or base, it is really useful mostly for weak acids and bases where the extent of dissociation is small. The fact that these have negative powers means that their p$K_a$ and p$K_b$ values will be positive, as we can see in the examples in the table above.

**2  The relationship between $K_a$ and p$K_a$ and between $K_b$ and p$K_b$ is inverse.**

Stronger acids or bases with higher values for $K_a$ or $K_b$ have lower values for p$K_a$ or p$K_b$.

▲ Stinging nettle plants. The leaves are covered in sharp hairs which when touched inject a painful mixture of chemicals including the weak acid methanoic acid HCOOH into the skin. The stinging sensation can be relieved by rubbing the skin with leaves of a plant such as dock, which has a mildly basic sap and so helps to neutralize the acid.

## CHALLENGE YOURSELF

**1** In organic acids and bases, increasing the length of the carbon chain *decreases* the acid strength of the –COOH group but *increases* the basic strength of $C_2H_5NH_2$ relative to $CH_3NH_2$. Can you suggest why this is so? Hint: think about the electron density distributions in the molecules.

3    A change of one unit in $pK_a$ or $pK_b$ represents a 10 fold change in the value of $K_a$ or $K_b$.

This is because the scale is logarithmic to base 10.

4    $pK_a$ and $pK_b$ must be quoted at a specified temperature.

This is because the values are derived from the temperature-dependent constants, $K_a$ and $K_b$.

Table 21 in the IB data booklet gives $pK_a$ and $pK_b$ values for a range of common weak acids and bases. These are the data commonly quoted to describe acid and base strengths, so in calculation questions you may first need to convert $pK_a$ and $pK_b$ into $K_a$ or $K_b$ values. This is done by taking anti-logarithms, as we did with pH, pOH, and $pK_w$.

## Relationship between $K_a$ and $K_b$, $pK_a$ and $pK_b$ for a conjugate pair

Consider the $K_a$ and $K_b$ expressions for a conjugate acid–base pair HA and $A^-$.

$$HA(aq) \rightleftharpoons H^+(aq) + A^-(aq) \qquad K_a = \frac{[H^+][A^-]}{[HA]}$$

$$A^-(aq) + H_2O(l) \rightleftharpoons HA(aq) + OH^-(aq) \qquad K_b = \frac{[HA][OH^-]}{[A^-]}$$

$$K_a \times K_b = \frac{[H^+][\cancel{A^-}]}{[\cancel{HA}]} \times \frac{[\cancel{HA}][OH^-]}{[\cancel{A^-}]}$$

Therefore $K_a \times K_b = [H^+] \times [OH^-] = K_w$

By taking negative logarithms of both sides:

$pK_a + pK_b = pK_w$

At 298 K, $K_w = 1.00 \times 10^{-14}$ so $pK_w = 14.00$

Therefore $pK_a + pK_b = 14.00$ at 298 K

This relationship holds for any conjugate acid–base pair in aqueous solution, so from the value of $K_a$ of the acid we can calculate $K_b$ for its conjugate base. It shows that the higher the value of $K_a$ for the acid, the lower the value of $K_b$ for its conjugate base. In other words, stronger acids have weaker conjugate bases, and vice versa. This gives a quantitative basis for the relative strengths of conjugate acid–base pairs, discussed qualitatively on page 361. It makes sense in the context of equilibrium positions. For a conjugate pair such as

$$HA(aq) \rightleftharpoons H^+(aq) + A^-(aq)$$

the weaker the acid HA, the further this equilibrium lies to the left; this means the stronger the base $A^-$, the greater its tendency to accept the proton. So acids and bases react to form the weaker conjugate, as illustrated in Figure 8.9.

---

$pK_a = -\log_{10} K_a$; $K_a = 10^{-pK_a}$
$pK_b = -\log_{10} K_b$; $K_b = 10^{-pK_b}$

- the larger the $pK_a$, the weaker the acid
- the larger the $pK_b$, the weaker the base

---

For any conjugate acid–base pair:

- $K_a \times K_b = K_w$
- $pK_a + pK_b = pK_w$
- $pK_a + pK_b = 14$ at 298 K

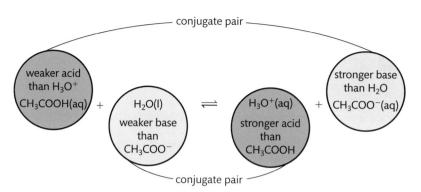

Figure 8.9 The reaction between $CH_3COOH$ and $H_2O$. At equilibrium the mixture lies in favour of the weaker conjugates, the acid $CH_3COOH$ and the base $H_2O$.

The inverse relationship between the strengths of acids and their conjugate bases is shown in Figure 8.10.

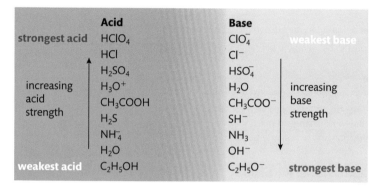

Figure 8.10 The relative strengths of some acids and their conjugate bases in aqueous solution.

## NATURE OF SCIENCE

The application of the equilibrium law to acid–base equilibria leads to a number of different derived equilibrium constants. These can be used to solve a wide range of numerical problems, which allow the strength of acids and bases to be determined. Explanation of patterns and trends in the relative strengths of acids and bases is based on interpretations of their molecular structures. This flow of understanding and knowledge across a range of phenomena is central to the study of chemistry.

## Exercises

**32** A weak acid HA has a $pK_a$ of 4.92. What will be the $[H^+]$ and pH of a 0.030 mol dm$^{-3}$ solution of this acid?

**33** What is the relationship between $K_a$ and $pK_a$?

   **A**    $pK_a = -\log K_a$

   **B**    $pK_a = \dfrac{1.0 \times 10^{-14}}{K_a}$

   **C**    $pK_a = \log K_a$

   **D**    $pK_a = \dfrac{1.0}{K_a}$

**34** The $pK_a$ of HCN is 9.21 and that of HF is 3.17. Which is the stronger acid?

**35** Look at the data in Q34. What are the $pK_b$ values of CN$^-$ and F$^-$? Which is the stronger base?

**36 (a)** The $pK_a$ of ethanoic acid, $CH_3COOH$, at 298 K is 4.76. What is the $pK_b$ of its conjugate base $CH_3COO^-$?

   **(b)** The $pK_a$ of methanoic acid, HCOOH, at 298 K is 3.75. Is its conjugate base weaker or stronger than that of ethanoic acid?

# 18.3 pH curves

## Understandings:

- The characteristics of the pH curves produced by the different combinations of strong and weak acid and bases.
- An acid–base indicator is a weak acid or a weak base where the components of the conjugate acid–base pair have different colours.

### Guidance
- For an indicator which is a weak acid:

$$HIn(aq) \rightleftharpoons H^+(aq) + In^-(aq)$$
$$\text{colour A} \qquad\qquad \text{colour B}$$

- For an indicator which is a weak base:

$$BOH(aq) \rightleftharpoons B^+(aq) + OH^-(aq)$$
$$\text{colour A} \quad\ \text{colour B}$$

- Examples of indicators are listed in the data booklet in section 22.

- The relationship between the pH range of an acid–base indicator, which is a weak acid, and its $pK_a$ value.

### Guidance
The colour change can be considered to take place over a range of $pK_a \pm 1$.

- The buffer region on the pH curve represents the region where small additions of acid or base result in little or no change in pH.
- The composition and action of a buffer solution.

## Applications and skills:

- The general shapes of graphs of pH against volume for titrations involving strong and weak acids and bases with an explanation of their important features.

### Guidance
- Only examples involving the transfer of one proton will be assessed. Important features are:
  - intercept with pH axis
  - equivalence point
  - buffer region
  - points where $pK_a = pH$ or $pK_b = pOH$

- Selection of an appropriate indicator for a titration, given the equivalence point of the titration and the end-point of the indicator.
- While the nature of the acid–base buffer always remains the same, buffer solutions can be prepared by either mixing a weak acid/base with a solution of a salt containing its conjugate, or by partial neutralization of a weak acid/base with a strong acid/base.
- Prediction of the relative pH of aqueous salt solutions formed by the different combinations of strong and weak acid and base.

### Guidance
- Salts formed from the four possible combinations of strong and weak acids and bases should be considered. Calculations are not required.
- The acidity of hydrated transition metal ions is covered in topic 13. The treatment of other hydrated metal ions is not required.

## Buffer solutions

A buffer refers to something that acts to reduce the impact of one thing on another – a little bit like a shock absorber. For example, buffers in the computer world are areas shared by hardware devices that operate at different speeds. In acid–base chemistry, a buffer acts to reduce the pH impact of added acid or base on a chemical system. It is defined as follows:

pH buffers are not the only type of buffer in physical science. Other examples include thermal buffers that help to maintain a constant temperature, and mineral redox buffers which help to stabilize oxidation states in natural rock systems. But buffering pH is by far the most common application, and so the term 'buffer' in chemistry is generally used synonymously with 'pH buffer'.

It is defined as follows:

**A buffer solution is resistant to changes in pH on the addition of small amounts of acid or alkali.**

To understand the importance of buffers, it is useful to see how added acid or alkali changes the pH of a non-buffered solution. This is shown below.

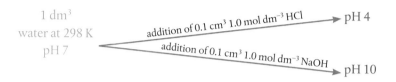

$$1 \text{ dm}^3 \text{ water at 298 K} \quad \text{pH 7}$$

addition of 0.1 cm³ 1.0 mol dm⁻³ HCl → pH 4

addition of 0.1 cm³ 1.0 mol dm⁻³ NaOH → pH 10

Note the volume added here is merely 0.1 cm³ – just a few drops. Evidently, water is very vulnerable to significant fluctuations in its pH and this can have major impacts on chemical reactions in aqueous solutions. However, biological systems are able to operate efficiently only within a narrow range of pH, principally because of the effect that pH change has on enzyme activity and so on all biochemical reactions. These systems are therefore dependent on buffers, and mammalian blood is an excellent example of a complex natural buffer. Ocean chemistry also includes effective buffer systems, which help to maintain the conditions suitable for life. Many chemical processes such as electrophoresis and fermentation, the dyes industry, and calibration of instruments depend on effective buffering.

> When giving the definition of a buffer, be sure to include the 'small amount' for the added acid or alkali. Otherwise you imply that buffers have infinite ability to maintain the pH, which is not the case.

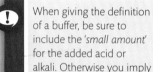

Ocean water has a pH around 8–9, controlled by several buffer systems. The carbonate and hydrogencarbonate ions, existing in equilibrium: $CO_3^{2-} + H^+ \rightleftharpoons HCO_3^-$, are crucial to the buffering action. The ocean has the capacity to absorb huge amounts of $CO_2$ from the atmosphere, so acts as a $CO_2$ 'sink', which is very important in helping to alleviate the effects of increasing atmospheric $CO_2$. But as $CO_2$ dissolves in the ocean, it makes the water more acidic, releasing $H^+$ that shifts the equilibrium and reduces the concentration of $CO_3^{2-}$. Coral reefs are directly affected by this, as they depend on the carbonate ion to build their structures, and have shown serious decline with decreasing carbonate levels. Of potentially greater impact still is the fact that the decrease in pH of the water may set up a feedback loop, reducing the ocean's buffering capacity and so diminish its ability to take up additional $CO_2$ from the atmosphere. Many research scientists believe that ocean acidification is potentially the most serious of all predicted outcomes of increase in atmospheric $CO_2$.

> Note that although buffers maintain the pH close to a set value, they do not all work at pH 7. Different buffer solutions can be made to buffer at almost any pH.

Turret coral on the Great Barrier Reef, Australia. Corals depend on carbonate ions in the ocean to build their hard structures made from calcium carbonate. In many parts of the world coral reefs are threatened by changes in the ocean chemistry, especially the loss of buffering capacity and decreasing pH that is a result of increasing atmospheric carbon dioxide.

### How buffers work

There are two main types of buffer solution – acidic buffers that maintain the pH at a value less than 7 and basic buffers that maintain the pH at a value greater than 7. We will see that both are a *mixture* of two solutions, composed in such a way that they each contain the *two* species of a conjugate acid–base pair. The key to understanding their buffering action is to focus on the equilibria in the solutions and to pick out the species that respond to added $H^+$ and $OH^-$. These are shown in red below.

### 1   Acidic buffers

#### Composition of the buffer solution

Made by mixing an aqueous solution of a weak acid with a solution of its salt of a strong alkali. For example:

$$CH_3COOH(aq) \quad and \quad NaCH_3COO(aq)$$
weak acid $\qquad\qquad$ salt of weak acid
with strong alkali

The following equilibria exist in a solution of this mixture:

$$(i) \quad CH_3COOH(aq) \rightleftharpoons CH_3COO^-(aq) + H^+(aq)$$

$CH_3COOH(aq)$ is a weak acid, so equilibrium lies to the left.

$$(ii) \quad NaCH_3COO(aq) \rightarrow Na^+(aq) + CH_3COO^-(aq)$$

$CH_3COO^-(aq)$ is a soluble salt, so is fully dissociated in solution.

So the mixture contains relatively high concentrations of both $CH_3COOH$ and $CH_3COO^-$, that is an acid and its conjugate base. These can be considered as 'reservoirs', ready to react with added $OH^-$ and $H^+$ respectively in neutralization reactions.

#### Response to added acid and base

• Addition of acid ($H^+$):

$\quad$ $H^+$ will combine with the base $CH_3COO^-$ to form $CH_3COOH$, therefore removing most of the added $H^+$.

$$CH_3COO^-(aq) + H^+(aq) \rightleftharpoons CH_3COOH(aq)$$

• Addition of base ($OH^-$):

$\quad$ $OH^-$ will combine with the acid $CH_3COOH$ to form $CH_3COO^-$ and $H_2O$, so removing most of the $OH^-$.

$$CH_3COOH(aq) + OH^-(aq) \rightleftharpoons CH_3COO^-(aq) + H_2O(l)$$

Consequently, as the added $H^+$ and $OH^-$ are used in these reactions, they do not persist in the solution and so the pH is largely unchanged.

### 2   Basic buffers

#### Composition of the buffer solution

Made by mixing an aqueous solution of a weak base with its salt of a strong acid. For example:

$$NH_3(aq) \quad and \quad NH_4Cl(aq)$$
weak base $\qquad$ salt of weak base
with strong acid

Bottle containing a buffer solution for maintaining pH at 10.00. Note the fact that this is temperature dependent. Buffers are often supplied as concentrate or as tablets and can be diluted to give a larger volume. Dilution does not change the ratio of acid to salt or base to salt so the pH remains constant whatever the volume.

Certified
**Buffer Solution Concentrate**
**For pH 10.00**
± .02 @ 25°C.

The following equilibria exist in solution:

$$\text{(i)} \quad NH_3(aq) + H_2O(l) \rightleftharpoons NH_4^+(aq) + OH^-(aq)$$

$NH_3(aq)$ is a weak base, so equilibrium lies to the left.

$$\text{(ii)} \quad NH_4Cl(aq) \rightarrow NH_4^+(aq) + Cl^-(aq)$$

$NH_4^+(aq)$ is a soluble salt, so is fully dissociated in solution.

So here the mixture contains relatively high concentrations of both $NH_3(aq)$ and $NH_4^+(aq)$ – that is a base and its conjugate acid. These species will again act as reservoirs, ready to react with added $H^+$ and $OH^-$ respectively in neutralization reactions.

### Response of buffer to added acid or alkali

• Addition of acid ($H^+$):

   $H^+$ will combine with the base $NH_3$ to form $NH_4^+$, therefore removing most of the added $H^+$.

$$NH_3(aq) + H^+ \rightleftharpoons NH_4^+(aq)$$

• Addition of base ($OH^-$):

   $OH^-$ will combine with the acid $NH_4^+$ and form $NH_3$ and $H_2O$, so removing most of the $OH^-$.

$$NH_4^+(aq) + OH^-(aq) \rightleftharpoons NH_3(aq) + H_2O(l)$$

So, as with the acidic buffer, the removal of the added $H^+$ and $OH^-$ by reactions with the components of the buffer solution means that they do not persist in the solution and so do not alter the pH.

### In summary:

Buffer solutions are a mixture containing both an acid and a base of a weak conjugate pair. The buffer's acid neutralizes added alkali, and the buffer's base neutralizes added acid, and so pH change is resisted.

### Making buffer solutions

The pH of a buffer is determined by the interactions of its components. Specifically it depends on:

1  the $pK_a$ or $pK_b$ of its acid or base;
2  the *ratio* of the initial concentrations of acid and salt, or base and salt, used in its preparation.

The calculation of the pH of a buffer is covered in more detail in the Biochemistry (B.7) and Medicinal chemistry (D.4) option topics in Chapters 13 and 15.

Buffer solutions can be prepared by starting with an acid or base that has a $pK_a$ or $pK_b$ value as close as possible to the required pH or pOH of the buffer. This is then either:

• mixed with a solution of a salt containing its conjugate or
• partially neutralized by a strong base or acid

The neutralization reaction should ensure that approximately one half of the starting acid or base is converted into salt. After reaction, the mixture will contain

A buffer solution is resistant to changes in pH on the addition of small amounts of acid or alkali.

The pH of a buffer is determined by the $pK_a/pK_b$ of its acid/base and the ratio of its concentration of acid and salt/base and salt.

the unreacted acid or base and its salt in equimolar amounts. An example of this is illustrated below using simple mole ratios.

$$CH_3COOH(aq) + NaOH(aq) \rightarrow NaCH_3COO(aq) + H_2O(l)$$

|  | $CH_3COOH$ | $NaOH$ | $NaCH_3COO$ | $H_2O$ |
|---|---|---|---|---|
| initial amounts in moles | 2 | 1 | 0 | 0 |
| change during reaction | −1 | −1 | +1 | +1 |
| final amounts in moles | 1 | 0 | 1 | 1 |

The final mixture, containing equal amounts of the weak acid $CH_3COOH$ and its salt $NaCH_3COO$, is a buffer solution.

### Worked example

State whether each of the following mixtures will form a buffer solution when dissolved in 1.00 dm$^3$ of water.

(a) 0.20 mol $NaHCO_3$ and 0.20 mol $Na_2CO_3$

(b) 0.20 mol $CH_3COOH$ and 0.10 mol $HCl$

(c) 0.20 mol $NH_3$ and 0.10 mol $HCl$

(d) 0.10 mol $H_3PO_4$ and 0.20 mol $NaOH$

### Solution

(a) Solution contains $HCO_3^-$ and $CO_3^{2-}$, a conjugate pair, so it is a buffer.

(b) Solution contains two acids – it is not a buffer.

(c) $NH_3$ and $HCl$ react together forming 0.10 mol $NH_4Cl$ and 0.10 mol $NH_3$ unreacted; it is a buffer.

(d) $H_3PO_4$ and $NaOH$ react together forming 0.20 mol $Na_2HPO_4$

$$H_3PO_4(aq) + 2NaOH(aq) \rightarrow Na_2HPO_4 + 2H_2O(l)$$

it is not a buffer.

## Factors that can influence buffers

Now that we know what determines the pH of a buffer, we can predict how it will respond in certain situations.

### 1 Dilution

$K_a$ and $K_b$ are equilibrium constants and so are not changed by dilution. Dilution also does not change the *ratio* of acid or base to salt concentration, as both components will be decreased by the same amount. Therefore diluting a buffer does not change its pH.

Nonetheless, diluting a buffer does alter the amount of acid or base it can absorb without significant changes in pH – the so-called **buffering capacity**. This depends on the molar concentrations of its components, so decreases as they are lowered by dilution.

### 2 Temperature

As temperature affects the values of $K_a$ and $K_b$, it does affect the pH of the buffer. This is why a constant temperature should be maintained in all work involving buffers, such as calibration of pH meters. Temperature fluctuations must also be minimized in many medical procedures such as blood transfusions, due to the effect on the buffers in the blood.

---

**Dilution does not change the pH of a buffer, but it lowers its buffering capacity.**

## CHALLENGE YOURSELF

**2** Contrast and explain how the pH of each of the following types of solution responds to dilution:
  **(a)** strong acid
  **(b)** weak acid
  **(c)** buffer

At high altitudes, where the air pressure and therefore the concentration of $O_2$ is significantly less than at sea level, some people suffer from altitude sickness. This is a potentially fatal condition that involves an increase in the pH of the blood (alkalosis). The causes are complex but stem from a decrease in $CO_2$ in the blood, resulting from hyperventilation. Drugs that can alleviate the symptoms lower the concentration of $HCO_3^-$ through stimulating its excretion by the kidneys. This shifts the equilibrium:

$$CO_2(aq) + H_2O(l) \rightleftharpoons H^+(aq) + HCO_3^-(aq)$$

to the right and so acidifies the blood. Indigenous cultures in the Andes have used coca leaves for centuries to alleviate mild symptoms of altitude sickness, although the way in which this may be achieved is not fully understood.

Climbers in the Andes, Peru. At high altitudes like this, the lower concentration of oxygen in the air makes it more difficult to do vigorous exercise. Climbers need to acclimatize to the level of oxygen available in order to avoid problems caused by alkalosis of the blood.

## Exercises

**37** Which mixture would produce a buffer solution when dissolved in 1.0 dm³ of water?

**A** 0.50 mol of $CH_3COOH$ and 0.50 mol of NaOH
**B** 0.50 mol of $CH_3COOH$ and 0.25 mol of NaOH
**C** 0.50 mol of $CH_3COOH$ and 1.00 mol of NaOH
**D** 0.50 mol of $CH_3COOH$ and 0.25 mol of $Ba(OH)_2$

**38** A buffer solution can be prepared by adding which of the following to 50 cm³ of 0.10 mol dm⁻³ $CH_3COOH(aq)$?

I   50 cm³ of 0.10 mol dm⁻³ $NaCH_3COO(aq)$
II  25 cm³ of 0.10 mol dm⁻³ NaOH(aq)
III 50 cm³ of 0.10 mol dm⁻³ NaOH(aq)

**A** I only          **B** I and II only          **C** II and III only          **D** I, II, and III

**39** State and explain which of the following has the greater buffering capacity:

**(i)** 100 cm³ 0.30 mol dm⁻³ $HNO_2$ and 0.30 mol dm⁻³ $NaNO_2$ or
**(ii)** 100 cm³ 0.10 mol dm⁻³ $HNO_2$ and 0.10 mol dm⁻³ $NaNO_2$.

## Salt hydrolysis

We saw on page 351 that a neutralization reaction between an acid and a base produces a salt – an ionic compound containing a cation from the parent base and an anion from the parent acid. The cation is the conjugate acid of the parent base and the anion is the conjugate base of the parent acid.

$$\text{parent base} + \text{parent acid} \rightarrow \text{salt} + \text{water}$$
$$\text{MOH} \qquad\qquad \text{HA} \qquad \text{M}^+\text{A}^- \quad \text{H}_2\text{O}$$

But although salts are the products of a neutralization reaction, they do not all form neutral aqueous solutions. Their pH in solution depends on whether and to what extent their ions, which are conjugate acids and bases, react with water and hydrolyse it, releasing $H^+$ or $OH^-$ ions. Remember in section 18.2 we showed through $pK_a$ and $pK_b$ values that the weaker the acid or base the stronger its conjugates, and vice versa. The relative strengths of the conjugate acids and bases in the salt determines the extent of hydrolysis reactions and so the pH of the salt solution.

### Salt of strong acid and strong base – no hydrolysis

The reaction between a strong acid and a strong base forms a salt in which both the conjugate acid and the conjugate base are weak. As a result there is virtually no hydrolysis of ions, and the pH is close to neutral. For example:

$$HCl(aq) \quad + \quad NaOH(aq) \quad \rightarrow \quad NaCl(aq) \quad + \quad H_2O(l)$$
$$\text{pH approximately 7}$$

Solutions of salts of strong acids with strong bases have a pH ≈ 7 at 298 K.

### Salt of weak acid and strong base – anion hydrolysis

The anion ($A^-$) is a conjugate base of the parent acid. When the acid is weak this conjugate base is strong enough to cause hydrolysis:

$$A^-(aq) + H_2O(l) \rightleftharpoons HA(aq) + OH^-(aq)$$

The release of $OH^-$ causes the pH of the solution to *increase*.

For example, the salt $NaCH_3COO$, containing the conjugate base $CH_3COO^-$, causes hydrolysis:

$$CH_3COO^-(aq) + H_2O(l) \rightleftharpoons CH_3COOH(aq) + OH^-(aq)$$

Solutions of salts of weak acids with strong bases have a pH > 7 at 298 K.

### Salt of strong acid and weak base – cation hydrolysis

The cation ($M^+$) is a conjugate of the parent base. When the base is weak and this conjugate is a non-metal (e.g. $NH_4^+$), it is able to hydrolyse water:

$$M^+(aq) + H_2O(l) \rightleftharpoons MOH(aq) + H^+(aq)$$

The release of $H^+$ causes the pH of the solution to *decrease*.

For example:

$$NH_4^+(aq) + H_2O(l) \rightleftharpoons NH_4OH(aq) + H^+(aq)$$

Solutions of salts of strong acids with weak bases have a pH < 7 at 298 K.

When the cation is a metal ion, the situation is a little more complex as it depends on the metal's charge density. Metal ions that have a high charge density, such as $Al^{3+}$ and $Fe^{3+}$, carry out hydrolysis, releasing $H^+$ from water. As a result they form acidic solutions.

### Salt of weak acid and weak base

When a weak acid reacts with a weak base, they form a salt in which both the conjugates are relatively strong and carry out hydrolysis. The pH of the solution therefore depends on the relative $K_a$ and $K_b$ values of the acids and bases involved.

**Salts of strong acids and strong bases are neutral.**

**Salts of weak acids and strong bases are basic.**

**Salts of strong acids and weak bases are acidic.**

## Summary

The pH of a salt solution depends on the relative hydrolysis of its anions and cations, which can be deduced from the relative strengths of the parent acids and bases. The table below summarizes this.

| Neutralization reaction | Example of parent acid and base | Salt formed | Hydrolysis of ions | Type of salt solution | pH of salt solution |
|---|---|---|---|---|---|
| strong acid and strong base | $HCl(aq) + NaOH(aq)$ | $NaCl(aq)$ | neither ion hydrolyses | neutral | 7 |
| weak acid and strong base | $CH_3COOH(aq) + NaOH(aq)$ | $NaCH_3COO(aq)$ | anion hydrolyses | basic | >7 |
| strong acid and weak base | $HCl(aq) + NH_3(aq)$ | $NH_4Cl(aq)$ | cation hydrolyses | acidic | <7 |
| weak acid and weak base | $CH_3COOH(aq) + NH_3(aq)$ | $NH_4CH_3COO(aq)$ | anion and cation hydrolyse | depends on relative strengths of conjugates | cannot generalize |

### Exercises

**40** Predict for each salt in aqueous solution whether the pH will be greater than, less than, or equal to 7.

(a) $NaCl$  
(b) $FeCl_3$  
(c) $NH_4NO_3$  
(d) $Na_2CO_3$

**41** Which compound will dissolve in water to give a solution with a pH greater than 7?

**A** sodium chloride  
**B** potassium carbonate  
**C** ammonium nitrate  
**D** lithium sulfate

**42** Deduce whether the pH of the resulting salt solution will be greater than, less than, or equal to 7 when the following solutions exactly neutralize each other.

(a) $H_2SO_4(aq) + NH_3(aq)$  
(b) $H_3PO_4(aq) + KOH(aq)$  
(c) $HNO_3(aq) + Ba(OH)_2(aq)$

## Acid–base titrations

The neutralization reactions between acids and bases described above can be investigated quantitatively using titration, as introduced in section 8.2. Titration is one of the most widely used procedures in chemistry. Quality control of food and drink production, health and safety checks in the cosmetic industry, and clinical analysis in medical services are just some examples of its use.

Controlled volumes of one reactant are added from a **burette** to a fixed volume of the other reactant that has been carefully measured using a **pipette** and placed in a conical flask. The reaction between acid and base takes place in the flask until the **equivalence point** or **stoichiometric point** is reached, where they exactly neutralize each other. An indicator or a pH meter are used to detect the exact volume needed to reach equivalence.

Addition of base from the burette to an acid in the conical flask containing phenolphthalein indicator. As the neutralization reaction happens, the change in the pH of the reaction mixture causes a change in the colour of the indicator. Drop-wise addition of the base ensures that an accurate measure of the equivalence point can be made.

385

When a base is added to an acid in the neutralization reaction, there is a change in pH as we would expect. But this change does not show a linear relationship with the volume of base added, partly due to the logarithmic nature of the pH scale. The easiest way to follow the reaction is to record pH using a pH meter or data-logging device as a function of volume of base added, and plot these values as **pH curves**.

pH curves can also be derived from theory – by calculating the pH at different volumes of base added. The process is a lot more laborious but produces the same results. Some sample calculations for the first titration discussed (strong acid–strong base) are given here to illustrate how this is done. Similar calculations based on the processes used earlier in this chapter can be done for the other three reactions.

It is found that in most titrations a big jump in pH occurs at equivalence, and this is known as the **point of inflection**. The equivalence point is determined as being half-way up this jump.

We will consider all four combinations of strong and weak acid and base here, and will see that the pH curves have specific features that relate to the strengths of the acid and base. To make comparisons of the curves easier, these examples all use:

- $0.10$ mol dm$^{-3}$ solutions of all acids and bases;
- an initial volume of $50.0$ cm$^3$ of acid in the conical flask with base added from the burette;
- acids and bases which all react in a $1:1$ ratio, so that equivalence is achieved at equal volumes for these equimolar solutions (i.e. when $50$ cm$^3$ of base has been added to the $50$ cm$^3$ of acid).

At the equivalence point, the acid and base have exactly neutralized each other, so the solution contains salt and water only. Remember that the pH of this solution depends on hydrolysis by ions in the salt, determined by the relative strengths of the parent acid and base – as explained on pages 384–385.

> The equivalence point occurs when stoichiometrically equivalent amounts of acid and base have reacted together. At this point the solution contains salt and water only.

## 1 Strong acid and strong base

For example:

$$HCl(aq) + NaOH(aq) \rightarrow NaCl(aq) + H_2O(l)$$

- pH at equivalence $= 7$ as neither ion hydrolyses appreciably.

The calculations in the section below are a sample to show the reasons for the shape of the pH curve. In this example we assume full dissociation because these are strong acids and bases. Note also that as the base is added to the acid, neutralization of some of the acid occurs, while excess acid remains – until equivalence where the amounts of acid and base have fully reacted. After equivalence the mixture contains excess base. As the volume changes during the addition, this must be taken into account in determining the concentrations.

As the volume of base added increases, we can see how the resulting pH changes.

| Volume of base added | | | | |
|---|---|---|---|---|
| 0.00 cm³ (flask contains acid only) | 25.00 cm³ | 49.00 cm³ | 50.00 cm³ (contents of flask at equivalence) | 51.00 cm³ (flask contains excess base) |
| | (flask contains excess acid) | | | |
| $[acid]_{initial} =$ 0.10 mol dm⁻³ $[H^+] = 1 \times 10^{-1}$ **pH = 1.0** | $n(acid\ initial) = cV =$ $0.10 \times 0.050 =$ 0.0050 mol <br><br> $n(base\ added) = cV$ $= 0.10 \times 0.0250 =$ 0.00250 mol <br><br> $n(acid\ remaining) =$ $0.0050 - 0.00250 =$ 0.00250 <br><br> $n(H^+) = 0.00250$ mol <br><br> new volume = 0.0750 dm³ <br><br> so $[H^+] = 0.0333$ <br><br> **pH = 1.5** | $n(acid\ initial)$ $= 0.0050$ mol <br><br> $n(base\ added)$ $= cV\ = 0.10 \times 0.0490$ $= 0.00490$ <br><br> $n(acid\ remaining)$ $= 0.0050 - 0.00490$ $= 0.00010$ mol <br><br> $n(H^+) = 0.00010$ mol <br><br> new volume = 0.0990 dm³ <br><br> so $[H^+] = 0.00101$ <br><br> **pH = 3.0** | All of the acid has been neutralized by the base; the solution contains $NaCl + H_2O$ only <br><br><br> **pH = 7.0** | $n(base\ added) = cV =$ $0.10 \times 0.0510 =$ 0.00510 <br><br> $n(base\ remaining) =$ $0.00510 - 0.0050 =$ 0.00010 <br><br><br> $n(OH^-) = 0.00010$ mol <br><br> new volume = 0.101 dm³ <br><br> so $[OH^-] = 0.00099$ <br><br> so pOH = 3 <br><br> **pH = 11.0** |

These calculations show that the initial pH is low as this is a strong acid. As base is added, the increase in pH is at first very gradual, so that even when the mixture is only 1.0 cm³ away from equivalence it is still a long way below pH 7. A small addition of base around the equivalence point causes a dramatic rise in pH, with an increase of about eight units from pH 3 to 11.

The pH curve showing these pH changes over the full range of addition of base is shown in Figure 8.11.

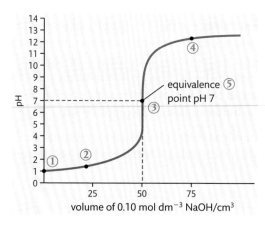

**Figure 8.11** Titration curve for strong acid–strong base.

The following points can be deduced from the graph:

1  initial pH = 1 (pH of strong acid);
2  pH changes only gradually until equivalence;
3  very sharp jump in pH at equivalence: from pH 3 to pH 11;

4  after equivalence the curve flattens out at a high value (pH of strong base).

5  **pH at equivalence = 7.**

## 2  Weak acid and strong base

For example:

$$CH_3COOH(aq) + NaOH(aq) \rightleftharpoons NaCH_3COO(aq) + H_2O(l)$$

• pH at equivalence > 7 as the anion hydrolysis releases OH⁻.

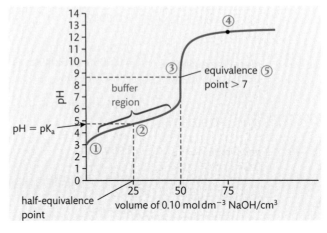

**Figure 8.12**  Titration curve for weak acid–strong base.

The following points can be deduced from the graph:

1  initial pH fairly high (pH of weak acid);

2  pH stays relatively constant until equivalence – labelled as buffer region;

3  jump in pH at equivalence from about pH 7.0–11.0, which is not as much of a jump as for a strong acid–strong base titration;

4  after equivalence the curve flattens out at a high value (pH of strong base);

5  **pH at equivalence is > 7.**

The reaction mixture after addition of 25cm³ of base is of particular interest. It is labelled as the **half-equivalence** point in the graph as it represents where exactly half of the acid has been neutralized by base and converted into salt, while the other half of the acid in the flask remains unreacted. This mixture, having equal quantities of a weak acid and its salt, is therefore a buffer. This explains why the pH in this region is shown to be relatively resistant to change in pH on the addition of small amounts of base and why it is labelled as the **buffer region** in the graph above.

The pH at the half-equivalence point gives us an easy way to calculate $pK_a$. Because at this point [acid] = [salt], we can substitute these values into the equilibrium expression of the acid:

$$K_a = \frac{[H^+][A^-]}{[HA]}$$

so if we assume that [acid] = [HA] and [salt] = [A⁻], then [HA] = [A⁻] and so we can cancel these terms in the equilibrium expression:

∴ $K_a = [H^+]$ and $pK_a = pH$

We can read the pH at the half-equivalence point directly from the graph, and so deduce the $pK_a$ of the acid as shown. Note that a parallel calculation of $pK_b$ can be done when a titration is carried out with acid added to base.

One drop of solution delivered from a burette has a volume of about 0.05 cm³.

Most burettes have 0.1 cm³ as the smallest division, so on this analogue scale you should record all readings to one half of this, that is ±0.05 cm³. This is explained further in Chapter 11.

Note that acids and bases react in stoichiometric ratios, irrespective of whether they are weak or strong. In other words equivalence is achieved with the same volume of alkali added to the strong acid, HCl, as to the weak acid, CH₃COOH, given that they are equimolar solutions.

## CHALLENGE YOURSELF

**3**  How can we justify the assumption that [acid] = [HA] and [salt] = [A⁻]? When might this not be a valid approximation to make?

## 3 Strong acid and weak base

For example:

$$HCl(aq) + NH_3(aq) \rightleftharpoons NH_4Cl(aq)$$

• pH at equivalence < 7 as cation hydrolysis releases $H^+$.

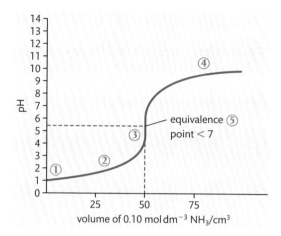

The following points can be deduced from the graph:

1 initial pH =1 (strong acid);

2 pH stays relatively constant through the buffer region to equivalence;

3 jump in pH at equivalence from about pH 3.0–7.0;

4 after equivalence the curve flattens out at a fairly low pH (pH of weak base);

5 **pH at equivalence is < 7.**

## 4 Weak acid and weak base

For example:

$$CH_3COOH(aq) + NH_3(aq) \rightleftharpoons NH_4CH_3COO(aq)$$

• pH at equivalence is difficult to define.

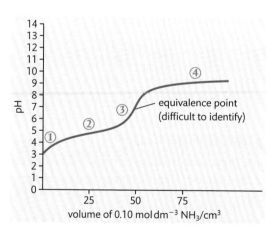

### CHALLENGE YOURSELF

4 Explain how you would modify the titration shown here for a strong acid and weak base to enable you to calculate the $K_b$ of $NH_3$. Show the steps you would use, and justify with equations

**Figure 8.13** Titration curve for strong acid–weak base.

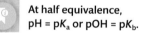 **At half equivalence, pH = p$K_a$ or pOH = p$K_b$.**

**Figure 8.14** Titration curve for weak acid–weak base.

The following points can be deduced from the graph:

1 initial pH is fairly high (pH of weak acid);
2 addition of base causes the pH to rise steadily;
3 change in pH at the equivalence point is much less sharp than in the other titrations;
4 after equivalence the curve flattens out at a fairly low pH (pH of weak base).

This titration does not give a clearly defined equivalence point as there is no significant jump in pH to identify, due to several equilibria being involved. For this combination of acid and base, it is better to use other techniques, such as conductimetric measurements, to determine the equivalence point.

pH curves can equally well be described in terms of the addition of acid to a base, in which case the curves will be the inverse of those described here.

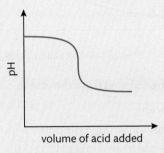

Be sure to check which way round the data are given when answering questions on this topic. Note that this is the way a titration must be performed to calculate $K_b$ of a weak base.

## Exercises

**43** Separate 20.0 cm³ solutions of a weak acid and a strong acid of the same concentration are titrated with NaOH solution. Which will be the same for these two titrations?

I initial pH
II pH at equivalence point
III volume of NaOH required to reach the equivalence point

**A** I only      **B** II only      **C** I and II only      **D** III only

**44** Sketch a graph for the pH change as 0.1 mol dm⁻³ HCl(aq) is added to 25 cm³ of 0.1 mol dm⁻³ NH₃(aq). Mark on your graph the pH at equivalence and the buffer region.

**45** Titration experiments can be used to deduce the $pK_a$ of a weak acid. Taking the neutralization reaction between CH₃COOH and NaOH as an example, show how the $pK_a$ for the acid can be deduced from *two* different points on the titration curve.

## Indicators signal change in pH

We learned in section 8.2 that acid–base indicators are substances whose colour depends on the pH of the solution. They therefore signal a change in pH by undergoing a distinct colour change.

These indicators are themselves weak acids or weak bases in which the undissociated and dissociated forms have different colours. If we consider an indicator HIn that is a weak acid, it exists in equilibrium in solution as follows:

$$HIn(aq) \rightleftharpoons H^+(aq) + In^-(aq)$$

colour A                  colour B

By applying Le Chatelier's principle, we can predict how this equilibrium will respond to a change in the pH of the medium.

- Increasing [H⁺]: the equilibrium will shift to the left in favour of HIn.
- Decreasing [H⁺]: the equilibrium will shift to the right in favour of In⁻.

In other words, at low pH colour A will dominate and at higher pH colour B will dominate.

For example, methyl orange is an indicator that is red when placed in a solution of acid such as HCl. As an alkali is added and the pH increases, the indicator changes to yellow. We can show this in an equation using HMet to represent the weak acid and Met⁻ to represent its conjugate base.

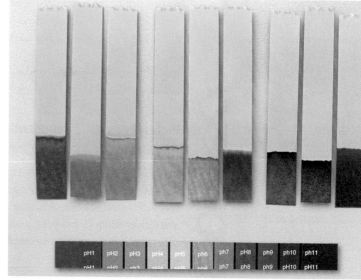

$$HMet(aq) \rightleftharpoons H^+(aq) + Met^-(aq)$$

Methyl orange indicator changes colour when added to an acid or alkali. It turns red in acid (left) and yellow in alkali (right).

Universal indicator paper showing a range of colours in response to being dipped in solutions of different pH. The light green is neutral, the orange and red are increasingly acidic, whereas the dark green and purple are increasingly alkaline. Universal indicator is made of a mix of indicators so that it changes colour across the pH range. Other indicators change colour at a fixed end-point, as described in this section.

## Indicators change colour when the pH is equal to their pKₐ

The change in colour of methyl orange, known as its **change point** or **end-point**, happens in the range pH 3.1–4.4. What determines the pH at which this occurs for an indicator?

We can answer this by considering the equilibrium expression for the above reaction.

The acid dissociation constant is defined as follows:

$$K_a = \frac{[H^+][In^-]}{[HIn]}$$

At the point where the equilibrium is balanced between the acid and its conjugate base, that is where [In⁻] = [HIn], the indicator is exactly in the middle of its colour change. As these values cancel in the equation

$$K_a = \frac{[H^+][\cancel{In^-}]}{[\cancel{HIn}]}$$

the expression becomes simplified as $K_a = [H^+]$ or $pK_a = pH$.

## CHALLENGE YOURSELF

5 What structural features might indicators possess that could explain the fact that they change colour on gain or loss of H⁺?

**Indicators are substances that change colour reversibly according to the pH of the solution.**

The end-point of an indicator is the pH at which it changes colour. This occurs at the pH equal to its $pK_a$.

Remember that not all indicators change colour at pH 7. Different indicators change colour at a wide range of pH values, from acidic to basic.

Make sure that you do not confuse the terms 'equivalence point' and 'end-point'.

• The equivalence point is where stoichiometrically equal amounts of acid and base have neutralized each other.

• The end-point is the pH at which the indicator changes colour.

A titration is set up so that the pH of these two points coincides.

At this point, the addition of a very small volume of acid or base will shift the equilibrium as described above, and so cause the indicator to change colour – this is its end-point. We can see from the equation above that this occurs at the pH equal to the $pK_a$ of the indicator. It follows that different indicators, having different $pK$ values, will have different end-points and so will change colour at different pH values. A selection of indicator end-points is given in section 22 of the IB data booklet.

## Indicators can be used to signal the equivalence point in titrations

Because indicators give us a visible cue when pH changes, they can be used to identify the equivalence points in titrations, given that this is the place where the pH changes most dramatically. An indicator will be effective in signalling the equivalence point of a titration when *its end-point coincides with the pH at the equivalence point.* This means that different indicators must be used for different titrations, depending on the pH at the equivalence point.

The following steps will help you to choose an appropriate indicator for a particular titration.

1 Determine what combination of weak and strong acid and base are reacting together.

2 Deduce the pH of the salt solution at equivalence from the nature of the parent acid and base (page 384).

3 Choose an indicator with an end-point in the range of the equivalence point by consulting data tables.

For example, in the titration of a weak acid with a strong base the equivalence point occurs in the range pH 7–11. An appropriate indicator would therefore be one whose end-point lies in this range, such as phenolphthalein (end-point range 8.2–10.0) as shown in Figure 8.15.

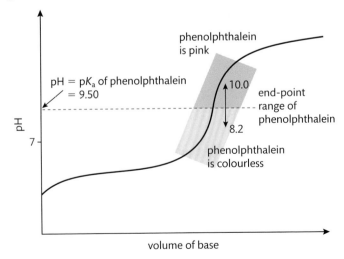

**Figure 8.15** A weak acid–strong base titration showing how phenolphthalein will change colour and so effectively signal when equivalence is reached.

The table on page 393 gives examples of suitable indicators for the different titrations.

| Reactants in titration | pH range at equivalence | Example of suitable indicators | $pK_a$ | End-point range of indicator and colour change |
|---|---|---|---|---|
| strong acid + strong base | 3–11 | phenolphthalein | 9.50 | 8.2–10.0; colourless to pink |
| | | methyl orange | 3.46 | 3.2–4.4; red to yellow |
| weak acid + strong base | 7–11 | phenolphthalein | 9.50 | 8.2–10.0; colourless to pink |
| | | phenol red | 8.00 | 6.6–8.0; yellow to red |
| strong acid + weak base | 3–7 | methyl orange | 3.46 | 3.2–4.4; red to yellow |
| | | bromophenol blue | 4.10 | 3.0–4.6; yellow to blue |
| weak acid + weak base | this combination of acid and base does not give a significant change in pH at equivalence, so there is no suitable indicator to use here | | | |

Our eyes are able to identify the distinct colour of one form of an indicator (e.g. HIn) when the ratio of its concentration to that of the other form (In⁻) is about 10:1. So for a transition to be observed from the colour of HIn to the colour of In⁻ at the end-point, the ratio of these concentrations must change from 10:1 to 1:10. This represents a range of two pH units. This is why there is a range of ±1 pH units on either side of the value of $pK_a$ at which the eye can definitely notice the colour change occurring. This is given as the **end-point range** in the table.

When an indicator is used to detect the equivalence point in a titration, a few drops of it are added to the solution in the conical flask at the start of the procedure. As the other solution is added from the burette and the neutralization reaction occurs, the exact volume at which the indicator changes colour can be recorded as the equivalence point. A difference of just one drop of added solution from the burette should produce the dramatic change in colour at this point.

## Exercises

**46** Which statement about indicators is always correct?

   **A** The mid-point of an indicator's colour change is at pH = 7.
   **B** The pH range is greater for indicators with higher $pK_a$ values.
   **C** The colour red indicates an acidic solution.
   **D** The $pK_a$ value of an indicator is within its pH range.

**47** Bromocresol green has a pH range of 3.8–5.4 and changes colour from yellow to blue as the pH increases.

   **(a)** Of the four types of titration shown in the table above, state in which two of these this indicator could be used.
   **(b)** Suggest a value for the $pK_a$ of this indicator.
   **(c)** What colour will the indicator be at pH 3.6?

# 8.5 Acid deposition

## Understandings:

- Rain is naturally acidic because of dissolved $CO_2$ and has a pH of 5.6. Acid deposition has a pH below 5.6.
- Acid deposition is formed when nitrogen or sulfur oxides dissolve in water to form $HNO_3$, $HNO_2$, $H_2SO_4$, and $H_2SO_3$.
- Sources of the oxides of sulfur and nitrogen and the effects of acid deposition should be covered.

## Applications and skills:

- Balancing the equations that describe the combustion of sulfur and nitrogen to their oxides and the subsequent formation of $H_2SO_3$, $H_2SO_4$, $HNO_2$, and $HNO_3$.
- Distinction between the pre-combustion and post-combustion methods of reducing sulfur oxide emissions.
- Deduction of acid deposition equations for acid deposition with reactive metals and carbonates.

## Causes of acid deposition

All rain water is naturally acidic owing to the presence of dissolved carbon dioxide, which dissolves in water to form the weak acid carbonic acid, $H_2CO_3$.

$$H_2O(l) + CO_2(g) \rightleftharpoons H_2CO_3(aq)$$

Carbonic acid ionizes to form the following equilibrium:

$$H_2CO_3(aq) \rightleftharpoons H^+(aq) + HCO_3^-(aq)$$

This gives a solution with a minimum pH of 5.6. **Acid rain** refers to solutions with a pH below 5.6, and which therefore contain additional acids. The main contributors to acid rain are the oxides of sulfur and nitrogen, which are primary pollutants. Acid rain is a secondary pollutant produced when these acidic gases dissolve in water.

**Acid deposition** is a broader term than acid rain and includes all processes by which acidic components as precipitates or gases leave the atmosphere. There are two main types of acid deposition:

- wet acid deposition: rain, snow, sleet, hail, fog, mist, dew fall to ground as aqueous precipitates;
- dry acid deposition: acidifying particles, gases fall to ground as dust and smoke, later dissolve in water to form acids.

Test tubes containing normal rain water (left) and acid rain (right) with universal indicator solution added to show acidity. The normal rain water has a pH of above 5.6, while the acid rain has a lower pH. In this example the pH = 4.0.

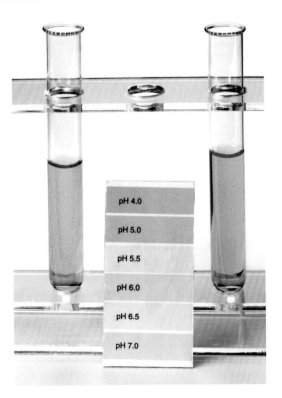

**Rain water is naturally acidic due to dissolved $CO_2$. Rain water with a pH < 5.6 is known as acid rain.**

## Sulfur oxides

Sulfur dioxide, $SO_2$, is produced from the burning of fossil fuels, particularly coal and heavy oil in power plants used to generate electricity. It is also released in industrial processes of smelting where metals are extracted from their ores. It is estimated that about 50% of annual global emissions of sulfur dioxide come from coal.

$$S(s) + O_2(g) \rightarrow SO_2(g)$$

Sulfur dioxide is a colourless gas with a sharp smell. It dissolves in water to form sulfurous acid, $H_2SO_3(aq)$.

$$H_2O(l) + SO_2(g) \rightarrow H_2SO_3(aq)$$

Sulfur dioxide can also be oxidized to sulfur trioxide, $SO_3$, which then dissolves in water to form sulfuric acid, $H_2SO_4$.

$$2SO_2(g) + O_2(g) \rightarrow 2SO_3(g)$$

$$H_2O(l) + SO_3(g) \rightarrow H_2SO_4(aq)$$

There are several mechanisms that might occur in these reactions, and the chemistry is complex given the wide range of conditions and other chemicals found in the atmosphere. During sunlight hours photo-oxidation may occur, and oxidation may also be catalysed by tiny particles of metal present in the clouds, such as iron or manganese. Ozone ($O_3$) or hydrogen peroxide ($H_2O_2$) present as pollutants in the atmosphere, can be involved. A more detailed study involves hydroxyl free radicals, •HO, which form by reactions between water and atomic oxygen or ozone. A free radical possesses an unpaired electron and so is a short-lived and reactive species. It is shown with the symbol •.

$$\bullet HO + SO_2 \rightarrow \bullet HOSO_2$$

$$\bullet HOSO_2 + O_2 \rightarrow \bullet HO_2 + SO_3$$

## Nitrogen oxides

Nitrogen monoxide, NO, is produced mainly from internal combustion engines, where the burning of the fuel releases heat energy that causes nitrogen and oxygen from the air to combine.

$$N_2(g) + O_2(g) \rightarrow 2NO(g) \qquad\qquad \Delta H = +181 \text{ kJ mol}^{-1}$$

A similar reaction gives rise directly to the brown gas, nitrogen dioxide, $NO_2$.

$$N_2(g) + 2O_2(g) \rightarrow 2NO_2(g)$$

Nitrogen dioxide also forms from the oxidation of nitrogen monoxide:

$$2NO(g) + O_2(g) \rightarrow 2NO_2(g)$$

Nitrogen dioxide dissolves in water to form a mixture of nitrous acid ($HNO_2$) and nitric acid ($HNO_3$).

$$H_2O(l) + 2NO_2(g) \rightarrow HNO_2(aq) + HNO_3(aq)$$

Alternatively, nitrogen dioxide can be oxidized to form nitric acid.

$$2H_2O(l) + 4NO_2(g) + O_2(g) \rightarrow 4HNO_3(aq)$$

## CHALLENGE YOURSELF

6 What is the source of sulfur in fossil fuels? Consider why some fuels such as coal contain higher amounts of sulfur.

 Free radicals are discussed in more detail in Chapters 4 and 10.

## CHALLENGE YOURSELF

7 How can you explain the fact that the reaction of nitrogen and oxygen is endothermic, whereas other combustion reactions are exothermic?

## CHALLENGE YOURSELF

8 By reference to Chapter 9, deduce the oxidation states of S and N in each of the species given here, and suggest names using oxidation numbers for $HNO_2$, $HNO_3$, $H_2SO_3$, and $H_2SO_4$.

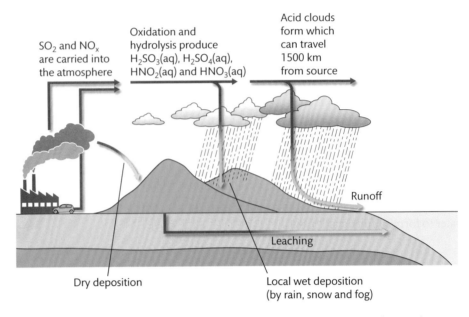

SO$_2$ and NO$_x$ are carried into the atmosphere

Oxidation and hydrolysis produce H$_2$SO$_3$(aq), H$_2$SO$_4$(aq), HNO$_2$(aq) and HNO$_3$(aq)

Acid clouds form which can travel 1500 km from source

Runoff

Leaching

Dry deposition

Local wet deposition (by rain, snow and fog)

Several other oxides of nitrogen exist, and the term NO$_x$ is used somewhat variably. But in atmospheric chemistry it refers specifically to the total of the two oxides of nitrogen NO and NO$_2$ present.

One of the most controversial aspects of acid deposition is that its effects often occur far from the source of the pollutants, due to atmospheric weather patterns. In many cases, this means countries are suffering the impact of other countries' industrial processes. Legislation to reduce the impact of acid deposition has therefore been the subject of intense political debate, and several international protocols have developed. These have led to significant reductions in sulfur emissions in many countries, but reduction in nitrogen oxide emissions has been less effective.

These reactions also proceed via different mechanisms, depending on the conditions and chemical cocktail in the atmosphere. Photo-oxidation, the presence of ozone, and hydroxyl free radicals (•HO) all contribute to the production of nitrous acid and nitric acid.

$$\bullet HO + NO \rightarrow HNO_2$$
$$\bullet HO + NO_2 \rightarrow HNO_3$$

In summary, a complex set of reactions in the atmosphere converts the primary pollutants SO$_2$ and NO into acid rain. The main active components of acid rain are H$_2$SO$_3$(aq), H$_2$SO$_4$(aq), HNO$_2$(aq), and HNO$_3$(aq).

## Effects of acid deposition

### Impact on materials

The building materials marble and limestone are both forms of calcium carbonate, CaCO$_3$. Both sulfur dioxide (in dry deposition) and sulfuric acid (in acid rain) react with this, forming the calcium salt, CaSO$_4$:

$$2CaCO_3(s) + 2SO_2(g) + O_2(g) \rightarrow 2CaSO_4(aq) + 2CO_2(g)$$

$$CaCO_3(s) + H_2SO_4(aq) \rightarrow CaSO_4(aq) + H_2O(l) + CO_2(g)$$

As calcium sulfate is somewhat more soluble than calcium carbonate, it washes out of the limestone or flakes off. Calcium sulfate has a greater molar volume than calcium carbonate, so its formation causes expansion and stress in the stonework. A similar reaction occurs with nitric acid, forming the soluble nitrate salt:

$$CaCO_3(s) + 2HNO_3(aq) \rightarrow Ca(NO_3)_2(aq) + H_2O(l) + CO_2(g)$$

These reactions all lead to erosion of structures, and many historic buildings and statues have suffered in this way.

Acid deposition also affects metals, causing corrosion. Again components of both dry deposition and acid rain react with metals such as iron, forming the salt. This enables ionic conductivity to occur, which leads to an increase in the rate of electrochemical corrosion reactions such as rusting:

$$Fe(s) + SO_2(g) + O_2(g) \rightarrow FeSO_4(s)$$

$$Fe(s) + H_2SO_4(aq) \rightarrow FeSO_4(aq) + H_2(g)$$

In addition, acid rain is able to react with and so remove the protective oxide layer on the surface of metals such as aluminium:

$$Al_2O_3(s) + 6HNO_3(aq) \rightarrow 2Al(NO_3)_3(aq) + 3H_2O(l)$$

As a result, acid rain causes significant damage to metallic structures such as bridges, rail road tracks, and vehicles.

You should be able to write equations for the reactions between the different components of acid rain and reactive metals and metal carbonates, similar to those developed in section 8.2. Note though that nitric acid, $HNO_3$, does not react as a typical acid releasing hydrogen from metals, as it is an oxidizing agent and releases NO instead. (So in fact this reaction releases more pollutant into the air to form more acid rain.)

Marble statue damaged by acid rain.

## Impact on plant life

Acid rain has been shown to be a direct cause of slower growth, injury, or death of plants. One of its effects is to cause important minerals such as $Mg^{2+}$, $Ca^{2+}$, and $K^+$ held in the soil to become soluble and so wash away in a process called **leaching**, before they can be absorbed by plants. Without sufficient $Mg^{2+}$ ions, for example, a plant cannot synthesize chlorophyll and so cannot make its food through photosynthesis. At the same time, acid rain causes the release of substances that are toxic to plants, such as $Al^{3+}$, which damage plant roots. In addition, dry deposition can directly affect plants by blocking the pores for gas exchange, known as stomata. Forests in hilly regions seem to be particularly vulnerable because they tend to be surrounded by acidic clouds and mists. Some of the worst effects on forests have been in Europe, though the impact is seen worldwide.

## Impact on water

Acid rain has caused a number of lakes to become 'dead' – unable to support life. Many fish including trout and perch cannot survive at pH values below 5. Below pH 4, rivers are effectively dead as toxic $Al^{3+}$ ions normally trapped in the rock as insoluble aluminium hydroxide leach out under acid conditions:

$$Al(OH)_3(s) + 3H^+(aq) \rightarrow Al^{3+}(aq) + 3H_2O(l)$$

Aluminium ions interfere with the operation of the fish's gills and reduce their ability to take in oxygen.

Acid rain also contributes to an additional problem known as **eutrophication**. This is over-fertilization of bodies of water, and can be caused by nitrates present in acid rain. It results in algal blooms leading to oxygen depletion, and sometimes the death of the lake or stream.

Woodland devastated by the effects of acid rain in the Czech Republic, near the border with Germany. This is one of the most affected areas in Europe.

## Impact on human health

Acid rain does not directly affect human health but its components can react to form fine sulfate and nitrate particles that can travel long distances and be present in inhaled air. These particles irritate the respiratory tract and increase the risk of illnesses such as asthma, bronchitis, and emphysema. They can also cause irritation to the eyes. The release of toxic metal ions such as $Al^{3+}$, $Pb^{2+}$, and $Cu^{2+}$ by the reaction of acid rain on metal structures such as pipes is also a potential health risk.

## Responses to acid deposition

The link between increasing industrialization causing atmospheric pollution and acid rain was first described in Manchester, England, in 1852. However, the phenomenon did not gain widespread attention until the 1970s when some of the impacts described above became evident in several countries. As a result, many governments responded with measures aimed to reduce the emissions of nitrogen and sulfur oxides. Some of these are summarized below.

## Reduction of SO$_2$ emissions

### i) Pre-combustion methods

These are processes that reduce or remove the sulfur present in coal or oil before combustion. Where the sulfur is present as a metal sulfide, it can be removed by crushing the coal and washing with water. The high density metal sulfide sinks to the bottom and so separates from the clean coal. **Hydrodesulfurization** (HDS) is a catalytic process that removes sulfur from refined petroleum products by reacting it with hydrogen to form hydrogen sulfide, $H_2S$. This is a highly toxic gas, so it is captured and later converted into elemental sulfur for use in the manufacture of sulfuric acid, $H_2SO_4$.

### ii) Post-combustion methods

**Flue-gas desulfurization** can remove up to 90% of $SO_2$ from flue gas in the smoke stacks of coal-fired power stations before it is released into the atmosphere. The process uses a wet slurry of $CaO$ and $CaCO_3$ which reacts with $SO_2$ to form the neutral product calcium sulfate, $CaSO_4$.

$$CaO(s) + SO_2(g) \rightarrow CaSO_3(s)$$

$$CaCO_3(s) + SO_2(g) \rightarrow CaSO_3(s) + CO_2(g)$$

$$2CaSO_3(s) + O_2(g) \rightarrow 2CaSO_4(s)$$

The calcium sulfate has industrial uses such as making plasterboard.

## Reduction of NOx emissions

### i) Catalytic converters in vehicles

Exhaust gases can be controlled by the use of catalytic converters in which the hot gases are mixed with air and passed over a platinum- or palladium-based catalyst. The reaction converts toxic emissions into relatively harmless products. For example:

$$2CO(g) + 2NO(g) \rightarrow 2CO_2(g) + N_2(g)$$

### ii) Lower temperature combustion

As mentioned in Chapter 7, the formation of nitrogen monoxide is reduced at lower temperature. Recirculating the exhaust gases back into the engine lowers the temperature to reduce the nitrogen oxide in the emissions.

## Other options

In addition to finding ways to reduce the emission of the primary pollutants when fossil fuels are burned, other solutions to the problems of acid deposition include lowering the demand for fossil fuels. More efficient energy transfer systems, greater use of public transport, and switching to renewable energy sources are all part of this.

The restoration of ecosystems damaged by acid rain is a long-term process. One method is to use calcium oxide (CaO), known as lime, or calcium hydroxide ($Ca(OH)_2$) to neutralize the acid.

$$CaO(s) + H_2SO_4(aq) \rightarrow CaSO_4(s) + H_2O(l)$$

$$Ca(OH)_2(s) + H_2SO_4(aq) \rightarrow CaSO_4(s) + 2H_2O(l)$$

Response to acid rain in Sweden. The dosing column is adding $Ca(OH)_2$ to the stream, to help neutralize the acidity of the water.

## Exercises

**48 (a)** Explain why natural rain has a pH of around 5.6. Give a chemical equation to support your answer.

**(b)** Acid rain may be 50 times more acidic than natural rain. One of the major acids present in acid rain originates mainly from burning coal. State the name of the acid and give equations to show how it is formed.

**(c)** The second major acid responsible for acid rain originates mainly from internal combustion engines. State the name of this acid and state two different ways in which its production can be reduced.

**(d)** Acid rain has caused considerable damage to buildings and statues made of marble ($CaCO_3$). Write an equation to represent the reaction of acid rain with marble.

**(e)** State three consequences of acid rain.

**(f)** Suggest a method of controlling acid rain, not involving a chemical reaction, for reducing sulfur dioxide emissions from power stations.

**49** The table gives some substances found in air.

| Name | Formula |
|------|---------|
| sulfur dioxide | $SO_2$ |
| nitrogen monoxide | $NO$ |
| particulates | – |

**(a)** Identify the pollutant(s) which contribute(s) to acid rain.

**(b)** Identify the pollutant(s) which come(s) mainly from power stations.

**(c)** The presence of one of these pollutants makes the ill effects of the others worse. Identify the pollutant and explain why it has this effect.

**(d)** Emissions of one of these pollutants have been controlled by reaction with calcium oxide. Identify this pollutant and write an equation for the reaction with calcium oxide.

**(e)** Identify the pollutants that come primarily from motor vehicles and describe the basis for their production.

**50 (a)** Describe the difference in dispersion between dry acid deposition and wet acid deposition.

**(b)** Explain the physical and chemical processes involved in the development of wet acid deposition.

**51** Identify the free radical involved in the formation of sulfuric acid and nitric acid in acid rain and explain how it is formed.

## Practice questions

**1** The $K_b$ value for a base is $5.0 \times 10^{-2}$ mol dm$^{-3}$ at 298 K. What is the $K_a$ value for its conjugate acid at this temperature?

**A** $5.0 \times 10^{-2}$     **B** $2.0 \times 10^{-6}$     **C** $2.0 \times 10^{-12}$     **D** $2.0 \times 10^{-13}$

**2** Which combination will form a buffer solution?

**A** 100 cm$^3$ of 0.10 mol dm$^{-3}$ hydrochloric acid with 50 cm$^3$ of 0.10 mol dm$^{-3}$ sodium hydroxide

**B** 100 cm$^3$ of 0.10 mol dm$^{-3}$ ethanoic acid with 50 cm$^3$ of 0.10 mol dm$^{-3}$ sodium hydroxide

**C** 50 cm$^3$ of 0.10 mol dm$^{-3}$ hydrochloric acid with 100 cm$^3$ of 0.10 mol dm$^{-3}$ sodium hydroxide

**D** 50 cm$^3$ of 0.10 mol dm$^{-3}$ ethanoic acid with 100 cm$^3$ of 0.10 mol dm$^{-3}$ sodium hydroxide

**3** Equal volumes and concentrations of hydrochloric acid and ethanoic acid are titrated with sodium hydroxide solutions of the same concentration. Which statement is correct?

**A** The initial pH values of both acids are equal.

**B** At the equivalence points, the solutions of both titrations have pH values of 7.

**C** The same volume of sodium hydroxide is needed to reach the equivalence point.

**D** The pH values of both acids increase equally until the equivalence points are reached.

**4** Bromophenol blue changes from yellow to blue over the pH range of 3.0 to 4.6. Which statement is correct?

**A** Molecules of bromophenol blue, HIn, are blue.

**B** At pH < 3.0, a solution of bromophenol blue contains more ions, In$^-$, than molecules, HIn.

**C** The p$K_a$ of bromophenol blue is between 3.0 and 4.6.

**D** Bromophenol blue is a suitable indicator to titrate ethanoic acid with potassium hydroxide solution.

**5** What is the $K_b$ expression for the reaction of ethylamine with water?

**A** $K_b = [CH_3CH_2NH_3^+] [OH^-]$

**B** $K_b = \dfrac{[CH_3CH_2NH_3^+][OH^-]}{[CH_3CH_2NH_2]}$

**C** $K_b = \dfrac{[CH_3CH_2NH_3^+][H_2O]}{[CH_3CH_2NH_2]}$

**D** $K_b = [CH_3CH_2NH_2] [H_2O]$

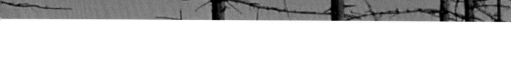

**6** $pK_w$ for water at 10 °C = 14.54. What is the pH of the pure water at this temperature?

    **A** 6.73         **B** 7.00         **C** 7.27         **D** 7.54

**7** What is $K_b$ for the aqueous fluoride ion given that $K_w$ is $1.0 \times 10^{-14}$ and $K_a$ for HF is $6.8 \times 10^{-4}$ at 298 K?

    **A** $\dfrac{1}{6.8 \times 10^{-4}}$

    **B** $(6.8 \times 10^{-4})\,(1.0 \times 10^{-14})$

    **C** $\dfrac{1.0 \times 10^{-14}}{6.8 \times 10^{-4}}$

    **D** $6.8 \times 10^{-4}$

**8** If 20 cm³ samples of 0.1 mol dm⁻³ solutions of the acids below are taken, which acid would require a different volume of 0.1 mol dm⁻³ sodium hydroxide for complete neutralization?

    **A** nitric acid     **B** sulfuric acid     **C** ethanoic acid     **D** hydrochloric acid

**9** Which mixture of acid and alkali would produce a buffer solution?

| | Acid | Alkali |
|---|---|---|
| **A** | 40 cm³ 0.1 mol dm⁻³ HCl | 60 cm³ 0.1 mol dm⁻³ NaOH |
| **B** | 60 cm³ 0.1 mol dm⁻³ HCl | 40 cm³ 0.1 mol dm⁻³ NaOH |
| **C** | 40 cm³ 0.1 mol dm⁻³ HCl | 60 cm³ 0.1 mol dm⁻³ NH₃ |
| **D** | 60 cm³ 0.1 mol dm⁻³ HCl | 40 cm³ 0.1 mol dm⁻³ NH₃ |

**10** Ammonia acts as a weak base when it reacts with water. What is the $K_b$ expression for this reaction?

    **A** $\dfrac{[NH_4^+][OH^-]}{[NH_3][H_2O]}$     **B** $\dfrac{[NH_3][H_2O]}{[NH_4^+][OH^-]}$     **C** $\dfrac{[NH_3]}{[NH_4^+][OH^-]}$     **D** $\dfrac{[NH_4^+][OH^-]}{[NH_3]}$

**11** The indicator HIn is used in a titration between an acid and base. Which statement about the dissociation of the indicator, HIn, is correct?

$$HIn(aq) \rightleftharpoons H^+(aq) + In^-(aq)$$
$$\text{colour A} \qquad\qquad\qquad \text{colour B}$$

    **A** In a strongly alkaline solution, colour B would be observed.

    **B** In a strongly acidic solution, colour B would be observed.

    **C** $[In^-]$ is greater than $[HIn]$ at the equivalence point.

    **D** In a weakly acidic solution colour B would be observed.

**12** Which salt dissolves in water to form an acidic solution?

    **A** ammonium nitrate         **C** potassium chloride

    **B** sodium ethanoate         **D** sodium hydrogencarbonate

**13** Which of the following mixtures of equimolar solutions produces a buffer with pH < 7 at 298 K?

    **A** 50 cm³ HCl(aq) and 150 cm³ NH₃(aq)

    **B** 50 cm³ CH₃COOH(aq) and 50 cm³ HCl(aq)

    **C** 100 cm³ CH₃COOH(aq) and 50 cm³ NaOH(aq)

    **D** 50 cm³ CH₃COOH(aq) and 50 cm³ NH₃(aq)

**14** Hypochlorous acid, HOCl(aq), is an example of a weak acid.

**(a)** State the expression for the ionic product constant of water, $K_w$. (1)

**(b)** A household bleach contains sodium hypochlorite, NaOCl(aq), at a concentration of 0.705 mol dm$^{-3}$. The hypochlorite ion, OCl$^-$(aq), is a weak base.

$$OCl^-(aq) + H_2O(l) \rightleftharpoons HOCl(aq) + OH^-(aq)$$

**(i)** The p$K_a$ value of HOCl(aq) is 7.52. Determine the $K_b$ value of OCl$^-$(aq) assuming a temperature of 298 K. (1)

**(ii)** Determine the concentration of OH$^-$(aq), in mol dm$^{-3}$, at equilibrium and state **one** assumption made in arriving at your answer other than a temperature of 298 K. (3)

**(iii)** Calculate the pH of the bleach. (2)

*(Total = 7 marks)*

**15 (a) (i)** Define the terms *acid* and *base* according to the Brønsted–Lowry theory. Distinguish between a weak base and a strong base. State **one** example of a weak base. (3)

**(ii)** Weak acids in the environment may cause damage. Identify a weak acid in the environment **and** outline **one** of its effects. (2)

**(iii)** The graph below indicates the pH change during the titration of 20.0 cm$^3$ of 0.100 mol dm$^{-3}$ of CH$_3$COOH(aq) with 0.100 mol dm$^{-3}$ KOH(aq). From the graph, identify the volume of KOH(aq) and the pH at the equivalence point. (2)

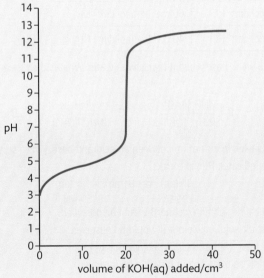

**(iv)** Explain how the graph could be used to determine the p$K_a$ of ethanoic acid **and** determine the p$K_a$ value for these data. (2)

**(v)** Sketch a graph, similar to the previous graph, to indicate the change in pH during a titration of 25.0 cm$^3$ of 0.100 mol dm$^{-3}$ HNO$_3$(aq) with 0.100 mol dm$^{-3}$ OH$^-$(aq). On your graph, clearly indicate the starting pH value, the equivalence point, the pH at the equivalence point, and the final pH reached. (4)

**(b) (i)** Describe how an indicator works. (3)

**(ii)** Using Table 16 of the Data Booklet, identify the most appropriate indicator for the titration of ethanoic acid with potassium hydroxide. Explain your choice. (2)

*(Total = 18 marks)*

**16** Ammonia can be converted into nitric acid ($HNO_3(aq)$) and hydrocyanic acid ($HCN(aq)$). The $pK_a$ of hydrocyanic acid is 9.21.

  **(a)** Distinguish between the terms *strong acid* and *weak acid* and state the equations used to show the dissociation of each acid in aqueous solution. (3)

  **(b)** Deduce the expression for the ionization constant, $K_a$, of hydrocyanic acid and calculate its value from the $pK_a$ value given. (2)

  **(c)** Use your answer from part (b) to calculate the $[H^+]$ and the pH of an aqueous solution of hydrocyanic acid of concentration 0.108 mol dm$^{-3}$. State **one** assumption made in arriving at your answer. (4)

  *(Total = 9 marks)*

To access weblinks on the topics covered in this chapter, please go to www.pearsonhotlinks.com and enter the ISBN or title of this book.

09 Redox processes

# Essential ideas

**9.1** Redox (reduction–oxidation) reactions play a key role in many chemical and biochemical processes.

**9.2 and 19.1** Voltaic cells convert chemical energy to electrical energy and electrolytic cells convert electrical energy to chemical energy. Energy conversions between electrical and chemical energy lie at the core of electrochemical cells.

The vigorous reaction here shows the redox change that occurs when magnesium metal and copper oxide are heated together, forming magnesium oxide and copper.
$Mg(s) + CuO(s) Æ MgO(s) + Cu(s)$.
Redox reactions occur when electrons are transferred between species, and are the basis of electrochemistry.

Oxygen makes up only about 20% by volume of the air, yet it is the essential component for so many reactions. Without it fuels would not burn, iron would not rust, and we would be unable to obtain energy from our food molecules through respiration. Indeed, animal life on the planet did not evolve until a certain concentration of oxygen had built up in the atmosphere over 600 million years ago. The term **oxidation** has been in use for a long time to describe these and other reactions where oxygen is involved in chemical change. Oxidation, though, is only half of the story, as it is always accompanied by the opposite process **reduction**, which was originally thought of in terms of loss of oxygen.

Later, however, the terms widened to include a much broader range of reactions. We now define these two processes, oxidation and reduction, as occurring whenever electrons are transferred from one reactant to another – and many of these reactions do not use oxygen. For example, photosynthesis, the process by which plants store chemical energy from light energy, involves oxidation and reduction reactions, although oxygen itself is not a reactant.

Transferring electrons from one substance to another leads to a flow of electrons, in other words an electric current. So, chemical reactions can be used to generate electricity – a simple **voltaic cell** or **battery** works in this way. By reversing the process and using an electric current to drive reactions of oxidation and reduction, stable compounds can be broken down into their elements. This is the process known as **electrolysis**. These applications of oxidation and reduction, collectively known as **electrochemical cells**, have truly revolutionized our world. For example, it would be hard to imagine life without the many battery-powered mobile devices we use every day, or without metals such as aluminium that are only available from electrolysis. An understanding of oxidation and reduction is therefore at the heart of the study of a large branch of chemistry both in the laboratory and beyond.

Coloured X-ray of a smart phone, showing its rechargeable battery. Mobile devices such as this are powered by electrical energy generated from the reactions of oxidation and reduction occurring within the battery.

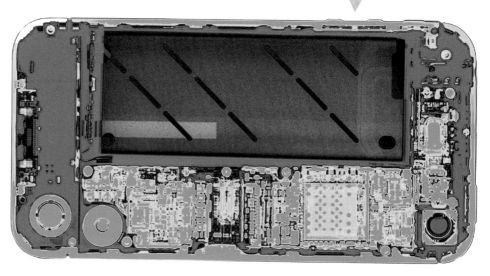

## Understandings:

- Oxidation and reduction can be considered in terms of oxygen gain/hydrogen loss, electron transfer, or change in oxidation number.
- An oxidizing agent is reduced and a reducing agent is oxidized.

**Guidance**

*Oxidation states should be represented with the sign given before the number, e.g. +2 not 2+.*

- Variable oxidation numbers exist for transition metals and for most main-group non-metals.

**Guidance**

*The oxidation state of hydrogen in metal hydrides (–1) and oxygen in peroxides (–1) should be covered.*

- The activity series ranks metals according to the ease with which they undergo oxidation.

**Guidance**

*A simple activity series is given in the IB data booklet in section 25.*

- The Winkler method can be used to measure biochemical oxygen demand (BOD), used as a measure of the degree of pollution in a water sample.

## Applications and skills:

- Deduction of the oxidation state of an atom in an ion or a compound.
- Deduction of the name of a transition metal compound from a given formula, applying oxidation numbers represented by Roman numerals.

**Guidance**

*Oxidation number and oxidation state are often used interchangeably, though IUPAC does formally distinguish between the two terms. Oxidation numbers are represented by Roman numerals according to IUPAC.*

- Identification of the species oxidized and reduced and the oxidizing and reducing agents, in redox reactions.
- Deduction of redox reactions using half-equations in acidic or neutral solutions.
- Deduction of the feasibility of a redox reaction from the activity series or reaction data.
- Solution of a range of redox titration problems.
- Application of the Winkler method to calculate BOD.

## Introduction to oxidation and reduction

Early attempts to define oxidation and reduction were based on observations of the gain and loss of oxygen and hydrogen during chemical change. They can be summarized as follows.

| Oxidation | Reduction |
|-----------|-----------|
| gain of oxygen | loss of oxygen |
| loss of hydrogen | gain of hydrogen |

These definitions are still useful in some cases, particularly in organic chemistry, but they have largely been replaced by a more inclusive approach. It is now recognized that oxidation and reduction occur during chemical change whenever there is a shift in electron density from one atom to another. In other words, the focus has become the transfer of electrons, whether complete or partial, whether oxygen and hydrogen are involved or not. Some examples will help to explain this.

When magnesium is burned in air, it gives a bright white flame with the production of a white powder, magnesium oxide:

$$2Mg(s) + O_2(g) \rightarrow 2MgO(s)$$

The fact that magnesium gains oxygen in this reaction makes it easy to see why we say it is an **oxidation** reaction and that magnesium has been oxidized. However, during the same reaction a small amount of the magnesium combines with the nitrogen of the air too, forming magnesium nitride. It may be less obvious that this is also an oxidation reaction and that again magnesium is oxidized.

$$3Mg(s) + N_2(g) \rightarrow Mg_3N_2(s)$$

What do these two reactions have in common which means they can both be defined in this way? If we divide them into so-called **half-equations**, each showing what happens to one reactant, we can examine what is happening in terms of electrons.

$$2Mg(s) \rightarrow 2Mg^{2+}(s) + 4e^-$$
$$O_2(g) + 4e^- \rightarrow 2O^{2-}(s)$$
$$\overline{2Mg(s) + O_2(g) \rightarrow 2MgO(s)}$$

$$3Mg(s) \rightarrow 3Mg^{2+}(s) + 6e^-$$
$$N_2(g) + 6e^- \rightarrow 2N^{3-}(s)$$
$$\overline{3Mg(s) + N_2(g) \rightarrow Mg_3N_2(s)}$$

In both reactions Mg is forming $Mg^{2+}$ by losing electrons, while O and N are forming $O^{2-}$ and $N^{3-}$ respectively by gaining electrons. It is this transfer of electrons that now defines oxidation, and its opposite reaction, reduction.

Magnesium ribbon burning in air. It forms mostly magnesium oxide with small amounts of magnesium nitride.

" Oxidation is the loss of electrons, reduction is the gain of electrons. "

So in the reactions above, magnesium is oxidized while oxygen and nitrogen are reduced. Clearly each process is dependent on the other, so oxidation and reduction will always occur together and reactions of this type are known as **redox reactions**.

It may help you to remember OILRIG: Oxidation Is Loss (of electrons), Reduction Is Gain (of electrons).

The free-radical theory of ageing suggests that the physiological changes associated with ageing are the result of oxidative reactions in cells causing damage to membranes and large molecules such as DNA. These changes accumulate with time and may explain the increase in degenerative diseases, such as cancer, with age. The theory suggests that supplying cells with anti-oxidants will help to slow down the damaging oxidative reactions. Anti-oxidants are particularly abundant in fresh fruit and vegetables, as well as in red wine, tea, and cocoa. Although there is strong evidence that anti-oxidant supplementation may help protect against certain diseases, it has not yet been shown to produce a demonstrated increase in the human life span.

Fresh fruits and vegetables are good sources of anti-oxidants, which may help prevent damaging oxidative reactions in cells.

**Oxidation is the loss of electrons, reduction is the gain of electrons.**

## Oxidation numbers enable us to track redox change

In reactions involving ions, such as the examples above, it is easy to identify the electron transfers occurring. But what about reactions where electrons are not transferred but instead are shared in a covalent bond, such as the combination of hydrogen and oxygen to produce water? Can oxidation and reduction be identified here too?

$$2H_2(g) + O_2(g) \rightarrow 2H_2O(l)$$

Note that the charge on an ion X is written with the number first then the charge: e.g. $X^{2+}$. The oxidation state is written with the charge first then the number: e.g. +2.

The answer is 'yes', through the introduction of the concept of **oxidation state**. This is a value we assign to each atom in a compound that is a measure of the electron control or possession it has relative to the atom in the pure element. Oxidation state can be defined as the apparent charge that an atom has in a molecule or ion. It is as if we exaggerate the unequal sharing in a covalent bond, based on electronegativity differences, to the point where each atom has complete gain or loss of the electrons shared – in other words, has formed ions. This enables us to keep track of the relative electron density in a compound and how it changes during a reaction. There are two parts to the oxidation state:

- the sign: '+' means the atom has lost electron control, '–' means it has gained electron control;
- its value: this refers to the number of electrons over which control has changed.

The oxidation state is written with the sign first, followed by the number, e.g. +2 or −3.

## Strategy for assigning oxidation states

There are a few simple rules to follow which help in determining the oxidation state of an atom in any species. We will use blue to show oxidation states throughout this text.

1  Atoms in the free (uncombined) element have an oxidation state of zero: for example,

2  In simple ions, the oxidation state is the same as the charge on the ion: for example,

**TOK**
What ways of knowing can we use to distinguish between the charge on an ion and the oxidation state?

3  The oxidation states of all the atoms in a neutral (uncharged) compound must add up to zero:

for example, in $H_2SO_4$ the sum of oxidation states = 0.

4  The oxidation states of all the atoms in a polyatomic ion must add up to the charge on the ion:

for example, in $SO_4^{2-}$ the sum of oxidation states = −2.

5  The usual oxidation state for an element is the same as the charge on its most common ion:

for example, Group 1 elements have oxidation state = +1, H is usually +1, O is usually −2.

6  Most main group non-metals, the elements at the bottom of Group 14, and transition elements have oxidation states that vary in different compounds – depending on the conditions and other elements present. So for N, P, S, Sn, Pb, and all transition elements, the oxidation state of the element in a particular species needs to be determined on a case-by-case basis.

The table on page 409 summarizes some useful information about oxidation states.

| Element | Usual oxidation state | Exceptions | Explanation |
|---------|----------------------|-----------|-------------|
| Li, Na, K | +1 | | |
| Mg, Ca | +2 | | |
| F | −1 | | there are no exceptions because F is the most electronegative element |
| O | −2 | peroxides such as $H_2O_2$, where it is −1; $OF_2$, where it is +2 | |
| H | +1 | metal hydrides such as NaH, where it is −1 | H is more electronegative than Na and so gains electron control |
| Cl | −1 | when it is combined with O or F | Cl is less electronegative than O and F, and so loses electron control |

When working out the oxidation states of atoms in compounds, it is usually best to assign the oxidation state to the atoms that are easy to predict first, then use Rules 3 and 4 above to find the more unpredictable elements by subtraction.

## Worked example

Assign oxidation states to all the elements in (a) $H_2SO_4$ and (b) $SO_3^{2-}$.

### Solution

(a) We can assign H and O as follows:

Note that the oxidation states apply to each atom and that here the sum of all the oxidation states must be zero as $H_2SO_4$ is electrically neutral.

Therefore, $2(+1) + S + 4(-2) = 0 \Rightarrow S = +6$

(b) Here we start by assigning O:

Note that here the oxidation states must add up to −2, the charge on the ion.

Therefore, $S + 3(-2) = -2 \Rightarrow S = +4$

The oxidation state of a transition metal in a complex ion can be worked out from the charges on the ligands and the overall charge. Remember from Chapter 3 that ligands are either neutral or negatively charged.

## Worked example

Assign oxidation states to the metal ion in (a) $[Co(NH_3)_6]^{3+}$ and (b) $[CuCl_4]^{2-}$.

### Solution

(a) $NH_3$ is a neutral ligand, so the charge on the complex is the same as the charge on the metal ion: $\therefore$ Co = +3

(b) Cl has a 1− charge $\therefore$ (charge on Cu) + (4 × 1−) = 2−

$\therefore$ Cu = +2

## Interpreting oxidation states

We can see that an element such as sulfur can have a wide range of oxidation states in different compounds.

| $H_2S$ | S | $SCl_2$ | $SO_2$, $SO_3^{2-}$ | $SO_3$, $H_2SO_4$ |
| -2 | 0 | +2 | +4 | +6 |

increasing oxidation state

What is the significance of these different values? Because the oxidation state is a measure of the electron control that an atom has, it follows that the higher the positive number, the more the atom has lost control over electrons, in other words the more oxidized it is. Likewise, the greater the negative number, the more it has gained electron control, so the more reduced it is. Therefore $H_2S$ represents sulfur in its most reduced form (lowest oxidation number), and $SO_3$ and $H_2SO_4$ represent sulfur in its most oxidized form (highest oxidation number).

**A redox reaction is a chemical reaction in which changes in the oxidation states occur.**

It follows that any change in oxidation states during a reaction is an indication that redox processes are occurring: an increase in oxidation number represents oxidation, and a decrease in oxidation number represents reduction.

So, going back to the reaction between hydrogen and oxygen discussed earlier, we can now clearly follow the redox process:

**Oxidation occurs when there is an increase in oxidation state of an element, reduction occurs when there is a decrease in oxidation state of an element.**

$$2H_2(g) + O_2(g) \rightarrow 2H_2O(l)$$
$$0 \qquad 0 \qquad +1 \ -2$$

Hydrogen has been oxidized (oxidation state increased from 0 to +1) and oxygen has been reduced (oxidation state decreased from 0 to −2).

Use oxidation states to deduce which species is oxidized and which is reduced in the following reactions:

(a) $Ca(s) + Sn^{2+}(aq) \rightarrow Ca^{2+}(aq) + Sn(s)$

(b) $4NH_3(g) + 5O_2(g) \rightarrow 4NO(g) + 6H_2O(l)$

**Solution**

(a) $Ca(s) + Sn^{2+}(aq) \rightarrow Ca^{2+}(aq) + Sn(s)$
$\quad\ 0 \qquad +2 \qquad\ +2 \qquad\ 0$

Ca is oxidized because its oxidation state increases from 0 to + 2; $Sn^{2+}$ is reduced because its oxidation state decreases from +2 to 0.

(b) $4NH_3(g) + 5O_2(g) \rightarrow 4NO(g) + 6H_2O(l)$
$\quad\ -3\ +1 \qquad\ 0 \qquad\ +2\ -2 \quad\ +1\ -2$

$NH_3$ is oxidized because the oxidation state of N increases from −3 to +2; $O_2$ is reduced because its oxidation state decreases from 0 to −2.

Coloured scanning electron micrograph (SEM) of rust on painted sheet metal. Rust is hydrated iron oxide resulting from electrochemical reactions between iron and atmospheric water vapour and oxygen. Rusting spontaneously causes iron to revert to its more stable oxidized state, unless this is prevented by protecting the iron. Rust flakes off the surface of the iron, causing it to be degraded and weakened.

## Systematic names of compounds use oxidation numbers

We have seen that elements such as sulfur exhibit different oxidation states in different compounds. In these cases it is useful to include information about the oxidation state in the name. Traditional names used descriptive language that became associated with a particular oxidation state. For example, ferrous and ferric iron oxides referred to FeO and $Fe_2O_3$, in which Fe has oxidation states $+2$ and $+3$ respectively.

The IUPAC system, founded in 1919, introduced a nomenclature using **oxidation numbers** to make the names more recognizable and unambiguous. This system uses a Roman numeral corresponding to the oxidation state which is inserted in brackets after the name of the element. For example copper(I) oxide contains copper in the oxidation state $+1$. Different compounds in which the same elements have different oxidation states are then shown with different oxidation numbers, such as copper(I) oxide and copper(II) oxide.

The table shows some common examples.

Oxidation state is shown with a '+' or '–' sign and an Arabic numeral, e.g $+2$.

Oxidation number is shown by inserting a Roman numeral in brackets after the name or symbol of the element.

| Formula of compound | Oxidation state | Name using oxidation number | Formula of compound | Oxidation state | Name using oxidation number |
|---|---|---|---|---|---|
| FeO | Fe $+2$ | iron(II) oxide | $MnO_4^-$ | Mn $+7$ | manganate(VII) ion |
| $Fe_2O_3$ | Fe $+3$ | iron(III) oxide | $K_2Cr_2O_7$ | Cr $+6$ | potassium dichromate(VI) |
| $Cu_2O$ | Cu $+1$ | copper(I) oxide | $Cr_2O_3$ | Cr $+3$ | chromium(III) oxide |
| CuO | Cu $+2$ | copper(II) oxide | NO | N $+2$ | nitrogen(II) oxide |
| $MnO_2$ | Mn $+4$ | manganese(IV) oxide | $NO_2$ | N $+4$ | nitrogen(IV) oxide |

Although we have made the distinction here between oxidation number and oxidation state according to IUPAC guidelines, in reality this is not the main point of this discussion. In fact many sources use oxidation number and oxidation state interchangeably, so it is not too important. What does matter though, is the information represented in these values in terms of the electron density associated with an atom in a compound.

The IUPAC system aims to help chemists communicate more easily in all languages by introducing systematic names into compounds. However, its success in achieving this will be determined by how readily it is adopted. What do you think might prevent chemists using exclusively the 'new names'?

## Worked example

Deduce the name of the following compounds using oxidation numbers.

(a) $V_2O_5$  (b) $Ni(OH)_2$  (c) $TiCl_4$

### Solution

1. First deduce the oxidation state:
   (a) $V_2O_5$      V is $+5$
   (b) $Ni(OH)_2$    Ni is $+2$
   (c) $TiCl_4$      Ti is $+4$

2. Then the corresponding Roman numeral is inserted after the name of the element. There is no space between the name and the number, and the number is placed in brackets.
   (a) vanadium(V) oxide
   (b) nickel(II) hydroxide
   (c) titanium(IV) chloride

Although this nomenclature can theoretically be used in the naming of all compounds, it is really only worthwhile when an element has more than one common oxidation state. For example $Na_2O$ could be called sodium(I) oxide, but as we know Na always has oxidation state $+1$, it is perfectly adequate to call it simply sodium oxide.

### NATURE OF SCIENCE

Oxidation state and formal charge (introduced in Chapter 4) are both useful tools for electron book-keeping, but they are based on very different premises. Oxidation state is derived by assuming bonds are ionic unless they are between the same element; formal charge is assigned by assuming bonds are pure covalent. Each model has its usefulness and its limitations, as discussed on pages 193 and 415.

## Redox equations

### Writing half-equations

Although we have seen that oxidation cannot take place without reduction and vice versa, it is sometimes useful to separate out the two processes from a redox equation and write separate equations for the oxidation and reduction processes. These are therefore called **half-equations**. Electrons are added on one side of each equation to balance the charges.

## Worked example

Deduce the two half-equations for the following reaction

$$Zn(s) + Cu^{2+}(aq) \rightarrow Zn^{2+}(aq) + Cu(s)$$

### Solution

Assign oxidation states so we can see what is being oxidized and what is reduced.

$$Zn(s) + Cu^{2+}(aq) \rightarrow Zn^{2+}(aq) + Cu(s)$$
$$\quad 0 \qquad +2 \qquad\qquad +2 \qquad\quad 0$$

Here we can see that Zn is being oxidized and $Cu^{2+}$ is being reduced.

oxidation: $\quad\quad\quad$ $Zn(s) \rightarrow Zn^{2+}(aq) + 2e^-$ $\quad\quad$ electrons are lost

reduction: $\quad\quad\quad$ $Cu^{2+}(aq) + 2e^- \rightarrow Cu(s)$ $\quad\quad$ electrons are gained

Note there must be equal numbers of electrons in the two half-equations, so that when they are added together the electrons cancel out.

## Writing redox equations using half-equations

Sometimes we may know the species involved in a redox reaction, but not the overall equation so we need to work this out, making sure it is balanced for both atoms and charge. A good way to do this is to write half-equations for the oxidation and reduction processes separately, and then add these two together to give the overall reaction. Many of these reactions take place in acidified solutions and we therefore use $H_2O$ and/ or $H^+$ ions to balance the half-equations. The process is best broken down into a series of steps, as shown in the example below.

### Worked example

Write an equation for the reaction in which $NO_3^-$ and Cu react together in acidic solution to produce NO and $Cu^{2+}$.

#### Solution

1. Assign oxidation states to determine which atoms are being oxidized and which are being reduced:

$$NO_3^-(aq + Cu(s) \rightarrow NO(g) + Cu^{2+}(aq) \quad\quad \text{equation is unbalanced}$$
$$\phantom{NO_3^-}{+5}\;{-2}\phantom{aq +}{0}\phantom{Cu(s) \rightarrow}{+2}{-2}\phantom{NO(g) +}{+2}$$

Therefore Cu is being oxidized ($0 \rightarrow +2$) and N is being reduced ($+5 \rightarrow +2$).

2. Write half-equations for oxidation and reduction.
   (a) Balance the atoms other than H and O:

   oxidation: $\quad$ $Cu(s) \rightarrow Cu^{2+}(aq)$
   reduction: $\quad$ $NO_3^-(aq) \rightarrow NO(g)$

   In this example the Cu and N are already balanced.
   (b) Balance each half-equation for O by adding $H_2O$ as needed.
   Here the reduction equation needs two more O atoms on the right-hand side:

   reduction: $\quad$ $NO_3^-(aq) \rightarrow NO(g) + 2H_2O(l)$

   (c) Balance each half-equation for H by adding $H^+$ as needed.
   Here the reduction equation needs four H atoms on the left-hand side:

   reduction: $\quad$ $NO_3^-(aq) + 4H^+(aq) \rightarrow NO(g) + 2H_2O(l)$

   (d) Balance each half-equation for charge by adding electrons to the side with the more positive charge. (Electrons will be products in the oxidation equation and reactants in the reduction equation.)

   oxidation: $\quad$ $Cu(s) \rightarrow Cu^{2+}(aq) + 2e^-$
   reduction: $\quad$ $NO_3^-(aq) + 4H^+(aq) + 3e^- \rightarrow NO(g) + 2H_2O(l)$

   (e) Now check that each half-equation is balanced for atoms and for charge.

Photochromic lenses darken in response to increasing light intensity and become lighter in dim light. The change is brought about by a redox reaction between silver chloride and copper(I) chloride, which are both embedded in the lens. In bright light $Ag^+$ ions oxidize $Cu^+$ forming Ag and $Cu^{2+}$:

$$Ag^+(s) + Cu^+(s) \rightarrow$$
$$Ag(s) + Cu^{2+}(s)$$

The silver metal produced creates a film over the lens, cutting out glare. In dim light the reaction reverses as $Cu^{2+}$ oxidizes Ag, and the lens clears.

413

3 Equalize the number of electrons in the two half-equations by multiplying each appropriately.

Here the equation of oxidation must be multiplied by 3, and the equation of reduction by 2, to give six electrons in both equations:

oxidation: $3Cu(s) \rightarrow 3Cu^{2+}(aq) + 6e^-$

reduction: $2NO_3^-(aq) + 8H^+(aq) + 6e^- \rightarrow 2NO(g) + 4H_2O(l)$

4 Add the two half-equations together, cancelling out anything that is the same on both sides, which includes the electrons.

$$3Cu(s) + 2NO_3^-(aq) + 8H^+(aq) \rightarrow 3Cu^{2+}(aq) + 2NO(g) + 4H_2O(l)$$

The final equation should be balanced for atoms and charge and have no electrons.

**Summary of steps in writing redox equations.**

1 Assign oxidation states to determine which atoms are being oxidized and which are being reduced.

2 Write half-equations for oxidation and reduction as follows:

(a) balance the atoms other than H and O;

(b) balance each half-equation for O by adding $H_2O$ as needed;

(c) balance each half-equation for H by adding $H^+$ as needed;

(d) balance each half-equation for charge by adding electrons to the sides with the more positive charge.

(e) check that each half-equation is balanced for atoms and for charge.

3 Equalize the number of electrons in the two half-equations by multiplying each appropriately.

4 Add the two half-equations together, cancelling out anything that is the same on both sides.

## Exercises

1 Assign oxidation states to all elements in the following compounds:

(a) $NH_4^+$     (d) $SO_2$     (g) $MnO_2$     (i) $K_2Cr_2O_7$

(b) $CuCl_2$     (e) $Fe_2O_3$     (h) $PO_4^{3-}$     (j) $MnO_4^-$

(c) $H_2O$     (f) $NO_3^-$

2 Use oxidation states to deduce which species is oxidized and which is reduced in the following reactions:

(a) $Sn^{2+}(aq) + 2Fe^{3+}(aq) \rightarrow Sn^{4+}(aq) + 2Fe^{2+}(aq)$

(b) $Cl_2(aq) + 2NaBr(aq) \rightarrow Br_2(aq) + 2NaCl(aq)$

(c) $2FeCl_2(aq) + Cl_2(aq) \rightarrow 2FeCl_3(aq)$

(d) $2H_2O(l) + 2F_2(g) \rightarrow 4HF(aq) + O_2(g)$

(e) $I_2(aq) + SO_3^{2-}(aq) + H_2O(l) \rightarrow 2I^-(aq) + SO_4^{2-}(aq) + 2H^+(aq)$

3 Deduce the half-equations of oxidation and reduction for the following reactions:

(a) $Ca(s) + 2H^+(aq) \rightarrow Ca^{2+}(aq) + H_2(g)$

(b) $2Fe^{2+}(aq) + Cl_2(aq) \rightarrow 2Fe^{3+}(aq) + 2Cl^-(aq)$

(c) $Sn^{2+}(aq) + 2Fe^{3+}(aq) \rightarrow Sn^{4+}(aq) + 2Fe^{2+}(aq)$

(d) $Cl_2(aq) + 2Br^-(aq) \rightarrow 2Cl^-(aq) + Br_2(aq)$

4 Write balanced equations for the following reactions that occur in acidic solutions:

(a) $Zn(s) + SO_4^{2-}(aq) \rightarrow Zn^{2+}(aq) + SO_2(g)$

(b) $I^-(aq) + HSO_4^-(aq) \rightarrow I_2(aq) + SO_2(g)$

(c) $NO_3^-(aq) + Zn(s) \rightarrow NH_4^+(aq) + Zn^{2+}(aq)$

(d) $I_2(aq) + OCl^-(aq) \rightarrow IO_3^-(aq) + Cl^-(aq)$

(e) $MnO_4^-(aq) + H_2SO_3(aq) \rightarrow SO_4^{2-}(aq) + Mn^{2+}(aq)$

**5** Which equation represents a redox reaction?

   **A**  $NaOH(aq) + HNO_3(aq) \rightarrow NaNO_3(aq) + H_2O(l)$

   **B**  $Zn(s) + 2HCl(aq) \rightarrow ZnCl_2(aq) + H_2(g)$

   **C**  $CuO(s) + 2HCl(aq) \rightarrow CuCl_2(aq) + H_2O(l)$

   **D**  $MgCO_3(s) + 2HNO_3(aq) \rightarrow Mg(NO_3)_2(aq) + H_2O(l) + CO_2(g)$

**6** The oxidation state of chromium is the same in all the following compounds except:

   **A**  $CrCl_3$       **B**  $Cr_2O_3$       **C**  $Cr_2(CO_3)_3$       **D**  $CrO_3$

**7** Deduce the names of the following compounds, using their oxidation numbers:

   **(a)** $Cr_2O_3$       **(c)** $HNO_3$       **(d)** $HNO_2$       **(e)** $PbO_2$

   **(b)** $CuCl$

We have seen that oxidation states have several important uses as they enable us to:

- track redox changes in reactions;
- apply systematic names to compounds;
- determine reacting ratios in redox reactions.

At the same time, because they do not have a structural basis, oxidation states can raise some potential misunderstandings or ambiguities.

- Oxidation states do not distinguish between partial and complete transfer of electrons: +4 for C in $CO_2$ or +7 for Mn in $KMnO_4$ do not represent losses of 4 and 7 electrons respectively.
- In some cases, especially in organic chemistry, oxidation states have fractional values: in propane, $C_3H_8$, the oxidation state of C is $-2\frac{2}{3}$.
- Oxidation states and Lewis (electron dot) structures sometimes suggest conflicting information: $CH_4$, $C_2H_6$, and $C_3H_8$ are all similarly bonded molecules, but their C atoms have different oxidation states, $-4$, $-3$, and $-2\frac{2}{3}$ respectively.

In $S_2O_3{}^{2-}$, the rules would suggest oxidation states of +2 on each S atom, but from the Lewis

structure,  , values of +2 and +6 seem more appropriate.

Overall, oxidation states are best considered as a very useful tool that chemists use widely, while also keeping an eye on their limitations.

# Oxidizing and reducing agents

We have seen that redox reactions *always* involve the simultaneous oxidation of one reactant with the reduction of another as electrons are transferred between them. The reactant that accepts electrons is called the **oxidizing agent** as it brings about oxidation of the other reactant. In the process it becomes reduced. Likewise the reactant that supplies the electrons is known as the **reducing agent**, because it brings about reduction and itself becomes oxidized. Sometimes the terms **reductant** and **oxidant** are used in place of reducing agent and oxidizing agent respectively.

Molten iron being tapped from a blast furnace for transfer to the steel-making furnace. Iron is extracted from its ore $Fe_2O_3$ by reducing it with carbon in the form of coke. Although blast furnaces existed in China from about the 5th century BCE and were widespread across Europe, a major development occurred in England in 1709. Substitution of the reducing agent charcoal for coke produced a less brittle form of iron. This accelerated the iron trade and was a key factor in the British Industrial Revolution.

For example, in the reaction where iron (Fe) is extracted from its ore ($Fe_2O_3$):

$$\underset{\substack{\text{oxidizing} \\ \text{agent}}}{Fe_2O_3(s)} + \underset{\substack{\text{reducing} \\ \text{agent}}}{3C(s)} \rightarrow 2Fe(s) + 3CO(g)$$
$$+3 \qquad\qquad 0 \qquad\qquad 0 \qquad\quad +2$$

(The oxidation state of O is not shown as it does not change during the reaction.)

The reducing agent C brings about the reduction of Fe ($+2 \rightarrow 0$), while it is oxidized to CO ($0 \rightarrow +2$). The oxidizing agent $Fe_2O_3$ brings about the oxidation of C, while itself is reduced to Fe.

Some examples of useful oxidizing and reducing agents are given below:

- oxidizing agent: $O_2$, $O_3$, $H^+/MnO_4^-$, $H^+/Cr_2O_7^{2-}$, $F_2$, $Cl_2$, conc. $HNO_3$, $H_2O_2$
- reducing agent: $H_2$, C, CO, $SO_2$, reactive metals

Note that whether a species acts as an oxidizing or as a reducing agent actually depends on what it is reacting with. For example, water can act as an oxidizing agent and be reduced to hydrogen, for example by sodium, or act as a reducing agent and be oxidized to oxygen, for example by fluorine.

- $H_2O$ acting as an oxidizing agent:

$$2H_2O(l) + 2Na(s) \rightarrow 2NaOH(aq) + H_2(g)$$
$$+1 \qquad\qquad\qquad\qquad\qquad\qquad 0$$

- $H_2O$ acting as a reducing agent:

$$2H_2O(l) + 2F_2(g) \rightarrow 4HF(aq) + O_2(g)$$
$$-2 \qquad\qquad\qquad\qquad\qquad\qquad 0$$

In fact, water is weak both as an oxidizing agent and as a reducing agent, which is why it is such a useful solvent for many redox reactions.

Treatment of drinking water to kill pathogens commonly uses oxidizing agents such as chlorine and ozone. The process is effective and relatively cheap, yet millions of people worldwide lack access to clean drinking water. 'Access to safe water is a fundamental human need and therefore a human right.' Kofi Annan, United Nations Secretary General. In 2010 this human right was passed into international law, but this does not yet make it a reality for millions of people in developing countries.

## More reactive metals are stronger reducing agents

Of course not all oxidizing and reducing agents are of equal strength. Some will be stronger than others, depending on their relative tendencies to lose or gain electrons. We learned in Chapter 4 that metals have a tendency to lose electrons and form positive ions, so they will act as reducing agents, pushing their electrons on to another substance. More reactive metals lose their electrons more readily and so we might expect that they will be stronger reducing agents than less reactive metals.

We can check this out by seeing if one metal is able to reduce the ions of another metal in solution. If we immerse zinc in a solution of copper sulfate, a reaction occurs. The blue colour of the solution fades, the pinkish-brown colour of copper metal appears and there is a rise in temperature. What is happening is that the $Cu^{2+}$ ions are being displaced from solution as they are reduced by Zn. At the same time Zn dissolves as it is oxidized to $Zn^{2+}$.

$$Zn(s) + CuSO_4(aq) \rightarrow ZnSO_4(aq) + Cu(s)$$

In a redox equation the substance that is reduced is the oxidizing agent, the substance that is oxidized is the reducing agent.

## CHALLENGE YOURSELF

1 Hydrogen peroxide, $H_2O_2$, can also act as an oxidizing agent and as a reducing agent. With reference to the oxidation states of its atoms, suggest why this is so and which behaviour is more likely.

**Single replacement reactions involving metals with metal ions**

Full details of how to carry out this experiment with a worksheet are available online.

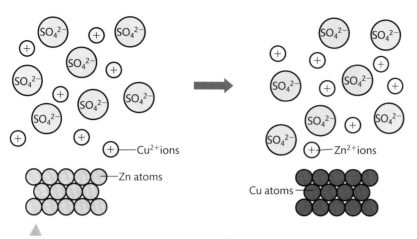

Figure 9.1 The reaction of zinc with copper(II) sulfate solution.

We can write this as an ionic equation without showing the sulfate ions as these act as spectator ions and are not changed during the reaction.

$$Zn(s) + Cu^{2+}(aq) \rightarrow Zn^{2+}(aq) + Cu(s)$$

So zinc has acted as the reducing agent – it is therefore the more reactive metal. We can think of it as having the reducing strength to 'force' copper ions to accept the electrons.

We could confirm this by trying the reaction the other way round, with copper metal immersed in a solution of zinc ions. Can you predict what will happen? The answer is there will be no reaction, because Cu is not a strong enough reducing agent to reduce $Zn^{2+}$. This is another way of saying that it is a less reactive metal, less able to push the electrons onto $Zn^{2+}$.

More reactive metals are stronger reducing agents than less reactive metals.

By comparing **displacement** reactions like these between different combinations of metals and their ions, we can build up a list of relative strengths of the metals as reducing agents. This is called the **activity series** and it enables us to predict whether a particular redox reaction between a metal and the ions of another metal will be feasible. Later in this chapter we will learn how to quantify these differences in metal reactivity, which is of great importance in many industrial processes. For example, the extraction of a metal from its ore often involves choosing a suitable reducing agent by reference to these data.

A more reactive metal is able to reduce the ions of a less reactive metal.

Here is a small part of the activity series of metals:

Mg    strongest reducing agent, most readily becomes oxidized

Al

Zn

Fe

Pb

Cu

Ag    weakest reducing agent, least readily becomes oxidized

A simple activity series is given in section 25 of the IB data booklet and is not something that needs to be learned. The important thing is that you are able to interpret it and to deduce it from given data.

417

Redox reactions between a metal and the oxide of a less reactive metal can also confirm the activity series. Here powdered aluminium reduces iron oxide, forming aluminium oxide and iron. $2Al(s) + Fe_2O_3(s) \rightarrow Al_2O_3(s) + 2Fe(s)$. This shows that aluminium is a stronger reducing agent than iron. The reaction is exothermic, creating short bursts of extremely high temperatures.

## Worked example

Refer to the activity series given on page 417 to predict whether the following reactions will occur:

(a) $ZnCl_2(aq) + 2Ag(s) \rightarrow 2AgCl(s) + Zn(s)$
(b) $2FeCl_3(aq) + 3Mg(s) \rightarrow 3MgCl_2(aq) + 2Fe(s)$

**Solution**

(a) This reaction would involve Ag reducing $Zn^{2+}$ in $ZnCl_2$. But Ag is a weaker reducing agent than Zn, so this will not occur.
(b) This reaction involves Mg reducing $Fe^{3+}$ in $FeCl_3$. Mg is a stronger reducing agent than Fe, so this will occur.

We can investigate how some non-metals such as carbon and hydrogen would fit into this activity series of metals by similar types of displacement reactions. Carbon is able to reduce the oxides of iron and metals below it in the series, which provides one of the most effective means for the extraction of these metals. The position of hydrogen relative to the metals is discussed in section 19.1 on pages 432–435.

## More reactive non-metals are stronger oxidizing agents

In a similar way, the different strengths of non-metals as oxidizing agents can be compared. For example, the halogens (Group 17 elements) react by gaining electrons and forming negative ions, and so act as oxidizing agents by removing electrons from other substances. We learned in Chapter 3 that their tendency to do this decreases down the group, so we would expect the following trend.

**More reactive non-metals are stronger oxidizing agents than less reactive non-metals.**

F strongest oxidizing agent, most readily becomes reduced

Cl

Br

I weakest oxidizing agent, least readily becomes reduced

Again this can be verified by reacting one halogen with solutions containing the ions of another halogen (known as halide ions). For example:

$$Cl_2(aq) + 2KI(aq) \rightarrow 2KCl(aq) + I_2(aq)$$

Here the $Na^+$ ions are spectator ions so we can write the ionic equation without showing them:

$$Cl_2(aq) + 2I^-(aq) \rightarrow 2Cl^-(aq) + I_2(aq)$$

The reaction occurs because Cl is a stronger oxidizing agent than I and so is able to remove electrons from it. In simple terms, you can think of it as a competition for electrons where the stronger oxidizing agent, in this case chlorine, will always 'win'.

Chlorine gas bubbling through a clear solution of potassium iodide KI. The solution is turning brown due to the formation of iodine in solution, as chlorine oxidizes the iodide ions and forms chloride ions.

## Exercises

8 Identify the oxidizing agents and the reducing agents in the following reactions:
   (a) $H_2(g) + Cl_2(g) \rightarrow 2HCl(g)$
   (b) $2Al(s) + 3PbCl_2(s) \rightarrow 2AlCl_3(s) + 3Pb(s)$
   (c) $Cl_2(aq) + 2KI(aq) \rightarrow 2KCl(aq) + I_2(aq)$
   (d) $CH_4(g) + 2O_2(g) \rightarrow CO_2(g) + 2H_2O(l)$

9 Use the two reactivity series given to predict whether reactions will occur between the following reactants, and write equations where relevant.
   (a) $CuCl_2 + Ag$    (b) $Fe(NO_3)_2 + Al$    (c) $NaI + Br_2$    (d) $KCl + I_2$

10 (a) Use the following reactions to deduce the order of reactivity of the elements W, X, Y, Z, putting the most reactive first.

   $W + X^+ \rightarrow W^+ + X$        $X + Z^+ \rightarrow X^+ + Z$
   $Y^+ + Z \rightarrow$ no reaction        $X + Y^+ \rightarrow X^+ + Y$

   (b) Which of the following reactions would you expect to occur according to the reactivity series you established in part (a)?
   (i) $W^+ + Y \rightarrow W + Y^+$
   (ii) $W^+ + Z \rightarrow W + Z^+$

**A more reactive non-metal is able to oxidize the ions of a less reactive non-metal.**

## Redox titrations

As with acid–base titrations (discussed in Chapter 8), redox titrations are used to determine the unknown concentration of a substance in solution. But in this case, the technique is based on a redox reaction between the two reactants, and finds the equivalence point where they have reacted stoichiometrically by transferring electrons. The two types of titration are compared below.

| Acid–base titration | Redox titration |
|---|---|
| neutralization reaction between acid and base | redox reaction between oxidizing agent and reducing agent |
| protons are transferred from acid to base | electrons are transferred from reducing agent to oxidizing agent |

Redox titrations are carried out in much the same way as acid–base titrations, using a burette and pipette to measure volumes accurately, and a standard solution of

## CHALLENGE YOURSELF

2 Reactions in which the same element is simultaneously oxidized and reduced is known as **disproportionation**. Show how this happens in the reaction when $Cl_2$ and NaOH react to produce NaCl, NaClO, and $H_2O$.

one reactant. An indicator is usually used to signal the equivalence point, although some redox changes are accompanied by a colour change and may not need an external indicator. From the volume of the solution added from the burette to reach equivalence, which is known as the **titre**, the concentration of the other reactant can be determined. The calculations are based on the redox equation, which is typically developed from the half-equations.

Redox titrations are commonly used in the food and beverages industry, in the pharmaceutical industry, and in water and environmental analysis. For example, wines can be analysed for the presence of sulfur dioxide, and the vitamin C content of foods can be determined in this way. Some examples of common redox titrations that can be carried out in the laboratory are given below, and more details on how to carry out these experiments can be found online.

## 1 Analysis of iron with manganate(VII)

This redox titration uses $KMnO_4$ in an acidic solution as the oxidizing agent, which oxidizes $Fe^{2+}$ ions to $Fe^{3+}$. During the reaction $MnO_4^-$ is reduced to $Mn^{2+}$, so the overall equation is:

$$5Fe^{2+} + MnO_4^- + 8H^+ \rightarrow 5Fe^{3+} + Mn^{2+} + 4H_2O$$
$$\text{purple} \qquad\qquad\qquad \text{colourless}$$

The reaction is accompanied by a colour change from deep purple to colourless, so the reaction acts as its own indicator, signalling the equivalence point.

### Worked example

All the iron in a 2.000 g tablet was dissolved in an acidic solution and converted to $Fe^{2+}$. This was then titrated with $KMnO_4$. The titration required 27.50 cm$^3$ of 0.100 mol dm$^{-3}$ $KMnO_4$. Calculate the total mass of iron in the tablet and its percentage by mass. Describe what would be observed during the reaction, and how the equivalence point can be detected.

#### Solution

First we need the balanced equation for the reaction, which is solved by the half-equation method described earlier.

oxidation: $Fe^{2+} \rightarrow Fe^{3+} + e^-$

reduction: $MnO_4^- + 8H^+ + 5e^- \rightarrow Mn^{2+} + 4H_2O$

overall: $5Fe^{2+} + MnO_4^- + 8H^+ \rightarrow 5Fe^{3+} + Mn^{2+} + 4H_2O$

Next we need to know the amounts of reactants used to reach equivalence. We start with $KMnO_4$ as we know both its concentration and its volume.

$$n = cV$$

$$n(MnO_4^-) = 0.100 \text{ mol dm}^{-3} \times \frac{27.50}{1000} \text{ dm}^3 = 0.00275 \text{ mol MnO}_4^-$$

From the equation for the reaction we know the reacting ratio:

$MnO_4^- : Fe^{2+} = 1 : 5$

$\therefore$ mol $Fe^{2+} = 0.00275$ mol $MnO_4^- \times 5 = 0.01375$ mol

The browning of fruit when it is exposed to the air is an oxidation reaction. It occurs when phenols released in damaged cells are oxidized with molecular oxygen at alkaline pH. The brown products are tannins. Food chemists are often interested in slowing down these reactions using reducing agents such as $SO_2$ or vitamin C, for example in lemon juice.

**Redox titration**
Full details of how to carry out this experiment with a worksheet are available online.

$M(\text{Fe}) = 55.85 \text{ g mol}^{-1}$

$$n = \frac{m}{M}$$

$\therefore m(\text{Fe}) = 0.01375 \text{ mol} \times 55.85 \text{ g mol}^{-1} = 0.7679 \text{ g}$

$\% \text{ Fe in tablet} = \dfrac{0.768 \text{ g}}{2.000 \text{ g}} \times 100 = 38.39\%$

$\therefore$ Fe in tablet = 0.768 g, 38.4%

$MnO_4^-$ in the burette is purple, but forms a nearly colourless solution in the flask as it reacts to form $Mn^{2+}$. But when the reducing agent $Fe^{2+}$ in the flask has been used up at equivalence, $MnO_4^-$ ions will not react and the purple colour will persist.

## 2 Iodine–thiosulfate reaction

Several different redox titrations use an oxidizing agent to react with excess iodide ions to form iodine.

$$2I^-(\text{aq}) + \text{oxidizing agent} \rightarrow I_2(\text{aq}) + \text{reduced product}$$

Examples of oxidizing agents used in this way include $KMnO_4$, $KIO_3$, $K_2Cr_2O_7$, and $NaOCl$.

The liberated iodine, $I_2$, is then titrated with sodium thiosulfate, $Na_2S_2O_3$, using starch as an indicator.

Redox equations:

oxidation: $2S_2O_3^{2-} \rightarrow S_4O_6^{2-} + 2e^-$

reduction: $I_2 + 2e^- \rightarrow 2I^-$

The overall equation is:

$$2S_2O_3^{2-}(\text{aq}) + I_2(\text{aq}) \rightarrow 2I^-(\text{aq}) + S_4O_6^{2-}(\text{aq})$$
deep blue in<br>presence of starch

The starch indicator is added during the titration (not at the start) and forms a deep blue colour by forming a complex with free $I_2$. As the $I_2$ is reduced to $I^-$ during the reaction, the blue colour disappears, marking the equivalence point.

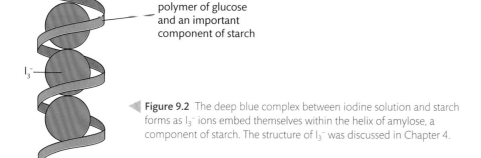

amylose helix, a polymer of glucose and an important component of starch

$I_3^-$

**Figure 9.2** The deep blue complex between iodine solution and starch forms as $I_3^-$ ions embed themselves within the helix of amylose, a component of starch. The structure of $I_3^-$ was discussed in Chapter 4.

Because iodine, $I_2$, has a very low solubility in water, it is used instead in the form of 'iodine solution', which is made by dissolving $I_2$ in iodide ions, forming the complex ion $I_3^-$(aq). It is the $I_3^-$ ion that gives the deep blue complex with starch. Even though $I_3^-$ is the reactant, it is still valid to use $I_2$ in the equations, as this is the 'active ingredient'. Technically, starch is not a redox indicator as such, as it responds to the disappearance of $I_2$, rather than to a change in the redox potential of the solution.

## CHALLENGE YOURSELF

3 From your knowledge of the structure of $I_3^-$, consider why it forms a stable complex in the hydrophobic interior of the amylose helix.

Household bleach is an oxidizing agent that contains sodium hypochlorite, NaOCl, as the active ingredient. It reacts with iodide ions in acidic solution as follows:

$$OCl^-(aq) + 2I^-(aq) + 2H^+(aq) \rightarrow I_2(aq) + Cl^-(aq) + H_2O(l)$$

A 10.00 cm³ sample of bleach was reacted with a solution of excess iodide ions, and the liberated iodine was then titrated with $Na_2S_2O_3$. The titration required 38.65 cm³ of 0.0200 mol dm⁻³ $Na_2S_2O_3$. Determine the concentration of $OCl^-$ in the bleach.

### Solution

First we need the balanced equation for the titration, which is solved by the half-equation method on page 413.

$$2Na_2S_2O_3(aq) + I_2(aq) \rightarrow 2NaI(aq) + Na_2S_4O_6(aq)$$

Next we calculate the number of moles of $Na_2S_2O_3$ as we know both its concentration and its volume.

$$n = cV$$

$$n(S_2O_3{}^{2-}) = 0.0200 \text{ mol dm}^{-3} \times \frac{38.65}{1000} \text{ dm}^3 = 7.73 \times 10^{-4} \text{ mol } S_2O_3{}^{2-}$$

From the equation for the reaction we know the reacting ratio

$$S_2O_3{}^{2-} : I_2 = 2:1$$

$$\therefore \text{ mol } I_2 = 7.73 \times 10^{-4} \times 0.5 = 3.865 \times 10^{-4}$$

This is a back-titration as the $I_2$ was liberated by the reaction of $I^-$ with $OCl^-$, as given in the question. The reacting ratio is

$$OCl^-(aq) : I_2(aq) = 1:1$$

$$\therefore \text{ mol } OCl^- = \text{mol } I_2 = 3.865 \times 10^{-4}$$

The concentration of the $OCl^-$ in the bleach can now be calculated.

$$n(OCl^-) = cV$$

$$\therefore 3.865 \times 10^{-4} \text{ mol} = c \times \frac{10.00}{1000} \text{ dm}^3$$

$$[OCl^-] = 0.0387 \text{ mol dm}^{-3}$$

---

In titration calculations, always look first for the reactant where you know both its reacting volume *and* its concentration. Start by using these data to calculate the number of moles. Then use the reacting ratio in the equation to deduce the moles of the other reactant.

---

A canal in England covered in a bloom of duckweed. This is an aquatic weed that thrives in water that contains pollutants such as phosphates. This is known as eutrophication. The bloom blocks out sunlight to deeper layers of the water ecosystem, and so lowers the level of dissolved oxygen.

## 3 Winkler method for calculating dissolved oxygen

The **dissolved oxygen** content of water is one of the most important indicators of its quality, as oxygen is essential to the survival of aquatic life. As the level of pollution in water increases, the dissolved oxygen content generally decreases, as the oxygen is used by bacteria in decomposition reactions. The **biological oxygen demand** (BOD) is therefore used as a means of measuring the degree of pollution. BOD is defined as the amount of oxygen used to decompose the organic matter in a sample of water over a specified time period, usually five days at a specified temperature. A high BOD indicates a greater quantity of degradable organic waste in the water, which means a lower level of dissolved oxygen.

The BOD of a body of water increases with the addition of nitrates and phosphates in the run-off from soil, resulting from the excess use of inorganic fertilizers and detergents. These ions promote the growth of plants resulting in **blooms** of algae and aquatic weeds, which lead to a decrease in the dissolved oxygen content of the water. This is known as **eutrophication**, and significantly impacts the ability of lakes to support biodiversity. According to a United Nations report, eutrophication has increased significantly in most major lakes worldwide since the 1970s, and is a particular problem in Europe, Japan, China, and the Great Lakes of North America. Remedial action involves better treatment of waste-water and diversions of agricultural run-offs, but nitrates and phosphates continue to be released from the high concentrations stored in soil sediments. As is the case with some other environmental problems, the impact of damaging practices often persists long after corrective actions have been taken.

Redox titrations can be used to measure the dissolved oxygen in water, and from this calculate the BOD in a process known as the **Winkler method**. The principle is based on a sequence of redox reactions as follows.

1   The dissolved oxygen, $O_2(g)$, in the water is 'fixed' by the addition of a manganese(II) salt such as $MnSO_4$. Reaction of this salt with $O_2$ in basic solution causes oxidation of Mn(II) to higher oxidation states, such as Mn(IV):

$$2Mn^{2+}(aq) + O_2(g) + 4OH^-(aq) \rightarrow 2MnO_2(s) + 2H_2O(l)$$
$$+2 \qquad\qquad\qquad\qquad +4$$

2   Acidified iodide ions, $I^-$, are added to the solution, and are oxidized by the Mn(IV) to $I_2$:

$$MnO_2(s) + 2I^-(aq) + 4H^+(aq) \rightarrow Mn^{2+}(aq) + I_2(aq) + 2H_2O(l)$$
$$+4 \qquad\qquad\qquad\qquad +2$$

3   The iodine produced is then titrated with sodium thiosulfate, as described earlier:

$$2S_2O_3^{2-}(aq) + I_2(aq) \rightarrow 2I^-(aq) + S_4O_6^{2-}(aq)$$

So we can see that in the overall sequence, for every 1 mole of $O_2$ in the water, 4 mol of $S_2O_3^{2-}$ are used.

### Worked example

A 500 cm³ sample of water was collected and tested for dissolved oxygen by the addition of $MnSO_4$ in basic solution, followed by the addition of acidified KI. It was found that 12.50 cm³ of 0.0500 mol dm⁻³ $Na_2S_2O_3(aq)$ was required to react with the iodine produced. Calculate the dissolved oxygen content of the water in g dm⁻³, using the equations given above.

### Solution

Start with calculating the amount of $S_2O_3^{2-}$, as we are given both its volume and its concentration.

$$n = cV$$

$$n(S_2O_3^{2-}) = 0.0500 \text{ mol dm}^{-3} \times \frac{12.50}{1000} \text{ dm}^3 = 6.25 \times 10^{-4} \text{ mol}$$

From the reacting ratio in step 3, $S_2O_3^{2-} : I_2 = 2 : 1$

$\therefore n(I_2) = 0.5 \times 6.25 \times 10^{-4} = 3.175 \times 10^{-4} \text{ mol}$

From the reacting ratio in step 2, $I_2 : MnO_2 = 1 : 1$

$\therefore n(MnO_2) = 3.175 \times 10^{-4}$ mol

From the reacting ratio in step 1, $MnO_2 : O_2(g) = 2 : 1$

$\therefore n(O_2) = 0.5 \times 3.175 \times 10^{-4}$ mol $= 1.5875 \times 10^{-4}$ mol

(We could also go directly from a ratio of $O_2 : S_2O_3^{2-} = 1 : 4$)

Finally express the amount of $O_2(g)$ as g dm$^{-3}$

$$m(O_2) = n \times M = 1.5875 \times 10^{-4} \text{ mol} \times 32.00 \text{ g mol}^{-1} = 5.080 \times 10^{-3} \text{ g in } 500 \text{ cm}^3$$

$\therefore$ dissolved oxygen = 0.0102 g dm$^{-3}$

### NATURE OF SCIENCE

We have seen that oxidation and reduction can be defined in different ways, and that these different definitions do not contradict but are consistent with each other. Which definition we choose to apply will be determined by the particular example, and by which approach gives the simplest, most useful interpretation of the type of reaction occurring.

| Oxidation | Reduction |
|---|---|
| gain of oxygen | loss of oxygen |
| loss of hydrogen | gain of hydrogen |
| loss of electrons | gain of electrons |
| increase in oxidation state | decrease in oxidation state |
| brought about by an oxidizing agent that becomes reduced | brought about by a reducing agent that becomes oxidized |

We have seen similar situations earlier in this text where different theories used to describe the same phenomenon persist. Sometimes the theories are distinct, such as the particle–wave theories of electron behaviour, at other times, one represents a broader generalization of the other, such as the distinction between Brønsted–Lowry and Lewis acid–base behaviour. As long as a theory leads to testable predictions and can be supported by experimental data, it has validity and contributes to the understanding of the phenomenon.

### Exercises

**11** A bag of 'road salt', used to melt ice and snow from roads, contains a mixture of calcium chloride, $CaCl_2$, and sodium chloride, NaCl. A 2.765 g sample of the mixture was analysed by first converting all the calcium into calcium oxalate, $CaC_2O_4$. This was then dissolved in $H_2SO_4$, and titrated with 0.100 mol dm$^{-3}$ KMnO$_4$ solution. The titration required 24.65 cm$^3$ of KMnO$_4$(aq) and produced Mn$^{2+}$(aq), $CO_2$(g), and $H_2O$(l).

(a) What would be observed at the equivalence point of the titration?
(b) Write the half-equation for the oxidation reaction, starting with $C_2O_4^{2-}$.
(c) Write the half-equation for the reduction reaction, starting with MnO$_4^-$.
(d) Write the overall equation for the redox reaction.
(e) Determine the number of moles of $C_2O_4^{2-}$.
(f) Deduce the number of moles of Ca$^{2+}$ in the original sample.
(g) What was the percentage by mass of $CaCl_2$ in the road salt?

**12** Alcohol levels in blood can be determined by a redox titration with potassium dichromate, $K_2Cr_2O_7$, according to the following equation.

$$C_2H_5OH(aq) + 2Cr_2O_7^{2-}(aq) + 16H^+(aq) \rightarrow 2CO_2(g) + 4Cr^{3+}(aq) + 11H_2O(l)$$

(a) Determine the alcohol percentage in the blood by mass if a 10.000 g sample of blood requires 9.25 cm$^3$ of 0.0550 mol dm$^{-3}$ K$_2$Cr$_2$O$_7$ solution to reach equivalence.
(b) Describe the change in colour that would be observed during the titration.

# 9.2 & 19.1 Electrochemical cells

## Understandings:

### Voltaic (Galvanic) cells

- Voltaic cells convert energy from spontaneous, exothermic chemical processes to electrical energy.
- Oxidation occurs at the anode (negative electrode) and reduction occurs at the cathode (positive electrode) in a voltaic cell.
- A voltaic cell generates an electromotive force (EMF) resulting in the movement of electrons from the anode (negative electrode) to the cathode (positive electrode) via the external circuit. The EMF is termed the cell potential ($E^{\ominus}$).
- The standard hydrogen electrode (SHE) consists of an inert platinum electrode in contact with 1 mol dm$^{-3}$ hydrogen ion and hydrogen gas at 100 kPa and 298 K. The standard electrode potential ($E^{\ominus}$) is the potential (voltage) of the reduction half-equation under standard conditions measured relative to the SHE. Solute concentration is 1 mol dm$^{-3}$ or 100 kPa for gases. $E^{\ominus}$ of the SHE is 0 V.
- $G^{\ominus} = -nFE^{\ominus}$. When $E^{\ominus}$ is positive, $\Delta G^{\ominus}$ is negative indicative of a spontaneous process. When $E^{\ominus}$ is negative, $\Delta G^{\ominus}$ is positive indicative of a non-spontaneous process. When $E^{\ominus}$ is 0, then $\Delta G^{\ominus}$ 0.

#### Guidance
- $\Delta G^{\ominus} = -nFE^{\ominus}$ is given in the data booklet in section 1.
- Faraday's constant = 96 500 C mol$^{-1}$ is given in the data booklet in section 2.

### Electrolytic cells

- Electrolytic cells convert electrical energy to chemical energy, by bringing about non-spontaneous processes.
- Oxidation occurs at the anode (positive electrode) and reduction occurs at the cathode (negative electrode) in an electrolytic cell.
- When aqueous solutions are electrolysed, water can be oxidized to oxygen at the anode and reduced to hydrogen at the cathode.
- Current, duration of electrolysis, and charge on the ion affect the amount of product formed at the electrodes during electrolysis.

#### Guidance
Electrolytic processes to be covered in theory should include the electrolysis of aqueous solutions (e.g. sodium chloride, copper(II) sulfate, etc.) and water using both inert platinum or graphite electrodes and copper electrodes.

- Electroplating involves the electrolytic coating of an object with a metallic thin layer.

#### Guidance
The term cells in series should be understood.

## Applications and skills:

- Construction and annotation of both types of electrochemical cells.

#### Guidance
For voltaic cells, a cell diagram convention should be covered.

- Explanation of how a redox reaction is used to produce electricity in a voltaic cell and how current is conducted in an electrolytic cell.
- Distinction between electron and ion flow in both electrochemical cells.
- Performance of laboratory experiments involving a typical voltaic cell using two metal/metal-ion half-cells.
- Deduction of the products of the electrolysis of a molten salt.

#### Guidance
Explanations should refer to $E^{\ominus}$ values, nature of the electrode, and concentration of the electrolyte.

- Calculation of cell potentials using standard electrode potentials.
- Prediction of whether a reaction is spontaneous or not using $E^{\ominus}$ values.
- Determination of standard free-energy changes ($\Delta G^{\ominus}$) using standard electrode potentials.
- Explanation of the products formed during the electrolysis of aqueous solutions.
- Perform lab experiments that could include single replacement reactions in aqueous solutions.
- Determination of the relative amounts of products formed during electrolytic processes.
- Explanation of the process of electroplating.

The fact that redox reactions involve transfers of electrons immediately suggests a link between this type of chemical reactivity and electricity. The main applications of this are collectively known as **electrochemical cells**, of which there are two main types.

electrochemical cells

**voltaic (galvanic) cells**
generate electricity from chemical reactions

**electrolytic cells**
drive chemical reactions using electrical energy

We will consider each of these types of cell in turn.

Building voltaic cells with different combinations of metals/metal ion electrodes will help in the understanding of this topic. Full details with a worksheet are available online.

# Voltaic cells

## Voltaic cells generate electricity from spontaneous redox reactions

Let us consider again the reaction we discussed on pages 416–417 in which zinc reduced copper ions. Remember that here zinc was the reducing agent and became oxidized while copper ions were reduced. When the reaction is carried out in a single test tube, as shown in the photo on page 417, the electrons flow spontaneously from the zinc to the copper ions in the solution, and as we noted, energy is released in the form of heat as it is an exothermic reaction. There is, however, a different way of organizing this reaction so that the energy released in the redox reaction, instead of being lost as heat, is available as electrical energy. It is really just a case of separating the two half-reactions

oxidation $\quad$ $Zn(s) \rightarrow Zn^{2+}(aq) + 2e^-$ and
reduction $\quad$ $Cu^{2+}(aq) + 2e^- \rightarrow Cu(s)$

into so-called **half-cells**, and allowing the electrons to flow between them only through an external circuit. This is known as a **voltaic** or a **galvanic cell**, and we will see how it is constructed in the next section.

## Half-cells generate electrode potentials

There are many types of half-cell but probably the simplest is made by putting a strip of metal into a solution of its ions.

A copper half-cell consisting of a piece of copper metal dipping into a solution of a copper salt. An equilibrium is set up between the Cu metal and its ions:

$Cu^{2+}(aq) + 2e^- \rightleftharpoons Cu(s)$

**Figure 9.3** Copper and zinc half-cells.

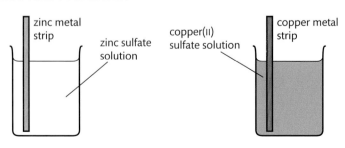

In the zinc half-cell, zinc atoms will form ions by releasing electrons that will make the surface of the metal negatively charged with respect to the solution.

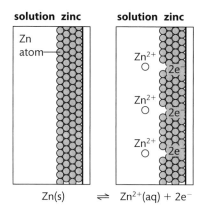

$$Zn(s) \rightleftharpoons Zn^{2+}(aq) + 2e^-$$

**Figure 9.4** Zinc atoms form zinc ions by releasing electrons. An equilibrium is set up between the metal and its solution of ions.

There will therefore be a charge separation, known as an **electrode potential**, between the metal and its ions in solution. At the same time, ions in the solution gain electrons to form Zn atoms, so an equilibrium exists as follows:

$$Zn^{2+}(aq) + 2e^- \rightleftharpoons Zn(s)$$

The position of this equilibrium determines the size of the electrode potential in the half-cell, and depends on the reactivity of the metal.

Because copper is the less reactive metal, in its half-cell the equilibrium position for the equivalent reaction:

$$Cu^{2+}(aq) + 2e^- \rightleftharpoons Cu(s)$$

lies further to the right. In other words, copper has less of a tendency to lose electrons than zinc. Consequently, there are fewer electrons on the copper metal strip, so it will develop a higher (or less negative) electrode potential than the zinc half-cell.

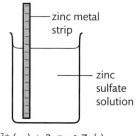

$$Zn^{2+}(aq) + 2e^- \rightleftharpoons Zn(s)$$

Some zinc atoms from the metal strip release electrons, giving it a negative charge.

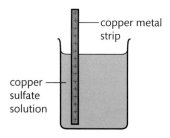

$$Cu^{2+}(aq) + 2e^- \rightleftharpoons Cu(s)$$

Some copper ions in the solution accept electrons from the copper rod giving it a positive charge.

The equilibrium as written for the copper half-cell lies further to the right than the equilibrium in the zinc half-cell.

**Figure 9.5** The zinc half-cell develops a negative potential with respect to the copper half-cell.

In general the more reactive a metal, the more negative its electrode potential in its half-cell.

## Two connected half-cells make a voltaic cell

If we now connect these two half-cells by an external wire, electrons will have a tendency to flow spontaneously from the zinc half-cell to the copper half-cell because of their different electrode potentials. The half-cells connected in this way are often called **electrodes**, and their name gives us information about the type of reaction that occurs there. The electrode where oxidation occurs is called the **anode**, in this case it is the zinc electrode and it has a negative charge:

$$Zn(s) \rightarrow Zn^{2+}(aq) + 2e^-$$

The electrode where reduction occurs is called the **cathode**, in this case it is the copper electrode and it has a positive charge:

$$Cu^{2+}(aq) + 2e^- \rightarrow Cu(s)$$

A potential difference will, however, only be generated between the electrodes when the circuit is complete.

Oxidation always occurs at the anode; reduction always occurs at the cathode. In the voltaic cell, the anode has a negative charge and the cathode has a positive charge.

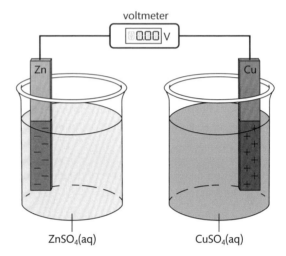

Figure 9.6 This cell has an incomplete circuit – no voltage is generated. A salt bridge must be added to allow ions to flow between the two electrodes.

The voltaic cell therefore must have the following connections between the half-cells.

• An external electronic circuit, connected to the metal electrode in each half-cell. A voltmeter can also be attached to this external circuit to record the voltage generated. Electrons will flow from the anode to the cathode through the wire.

• A salt bridge completes the circuit. The salt bridge is a glass tube or strip of absorptive paper that contains an aqueous solution of ions. Movement of these ions neutralizes any build-up of charge and maintains the potential difference. Anions move in the salt bridge from the cathode to the anode, which opposes the flow of electrons in the external circuit. Cations move in the salt bridge from the anode to the cathode. The

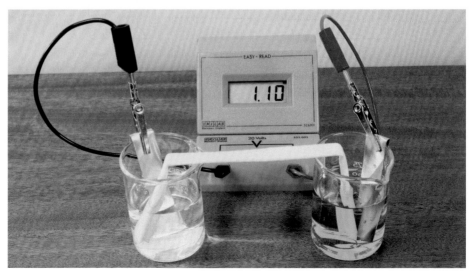

Zinc–copper voltaic cell showing a copper half-cell and a zinc half-cell connected by a salt bridge that appears white. Electrons flow from the zinc electrode to the copper electrode through the electrical wires, while ions flow through the salt bridge to complete the circuit. The voltmeter is showing 1.10 V, the potential difference of this cell.

solution chosen is often aqueous $NaNO_3$ or $KNO_3$ as these ions will not interfere with the reactions at the electrodes. Without a salt bridge, no voltage is generated.

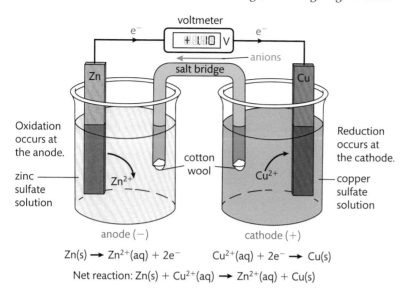

Figure 9.7 A copper–zinc voltaic cell.

Zn(s) → Zn²⁺(aq) + 2e⁻     Cu²⁺(aq) + 2e⁻ → Cu(s)

Net reaction: Zn(s) + Cu²⁺(aq) → Zn²⁺(aq) + Cu(s)

You may be familiar with the sensation of a mild electric shock when you happen to bite some aluminium foil on a tooth that has a filling. The filling is made of an amalgam of mercury and either tin or silver, and creates a voltaic cell when it touches the foil. Aluminium is the anode, the filling is the cathode, and the saliva is the electrolyte 'salt bridge'. A weak current flows between the electrodes and is detected by the sensitive nerves in the teeth.

A voltaic cell converts the energy released from a spontaneous, exothermic reaction into electrical energy.

## Cell diagram convention

Rather than always drawing out all the components of a voltaic cell, a shorthand version known as a **cell diagram convention** can be used. This has the following features:

- a single vertical line represents a phase boundary such as that between a solid electrode and an aqueous solution within a half-cell;
- a double vertical line represents the salt bridge;
- the aqueous solutions of each electrode are placed next to the salt bridge;
- the anode is generally put on the left and the cathode on the right, so electrons flow from left to right;
- spectator ions are usually omitted from the diagram;
- if a half-cell includes two ions, they are separated by a comma because they are in the same phase (see page 434).

The cell diagram convention is shown below for the copper–zinc cell.

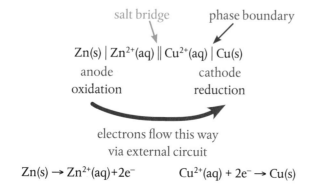

The placing of the anode and cathode on the left and right is not universally used. The important thing is that the diagram is clearly labelled and leads to the correct interpretation of the direction of electron flow and the interpretation of $E^\ominus$ data as described in the next section.

429

## Different half-cells make voltaic cells with different voltages

Any two half-cells can be connected together similarly to make a voltaic cell. For any such cell the direction of electron flow and the voltage generated will be determined by the *difference* in reducing strength of the two metals. In most cases this can be judged by the relative position of the metals in the reactivity series. For example if we changed the copper half-cell in the example above to a silver half-cell, a larger voltage would be produced because the difference in electrode potentials of zinc and silver is greater than between that of zinc and copper. Electrons would flow from zinc (anode) to silver (cathode), as shown in Figure 9.8.

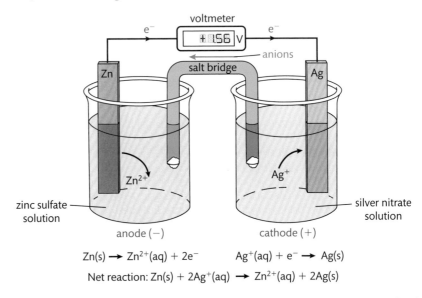

$$Zn(s) \rightarrow Zn^{2+}(aq) + 2e^-  \qquad Ag^+(aq) + e^- \rightarrow Ag(s)$$
$$\text{Net reaction: } Zn(s) + 2Ag^+(aq) \rightarrow Zn^{2+}(aq) + 2Ag(s)$$

**Figure 9.8** A silver–zinc voltaic cell.

**Electrons always flow in the external circuit from anode to cathode.**

If we now make a voltaic cell with one copper electrode and one silver electrode, the direction of electron flow would be *away* from copper towards silver. In other words, copper will be the anode and silver the cathode. This is due to the greater reducing power of copper – it has the lower electrode potential.

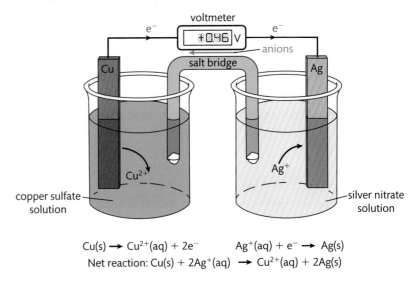

$$Cu(s) \rightarrow Cu^{2+}(aq) + 2e^-  \qquad Ag^+(aq) + e^- \rightarrow Ag(s)$$
$$\text{Net reaction: } Cu(s) + 2Ag^+(aq) \rightarrow Cu^{2+}(aq) + 2Ag(s)$$

**Figure 9.9** A silver–copper voltaic cell.

We can now summarize the parts of a voltaic cell and the direction of movement of electrons and ions:

- electrons flow from anode to cathode through the external circuit;
- anions migrate from cathode to anode through the salt bridge;
- cations migrate from anode to cathode through the salt bridge.

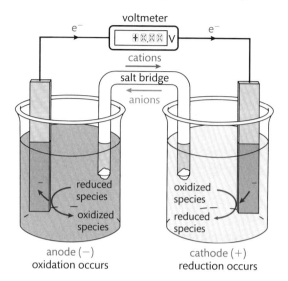

USB batteries. These rechargeable batteries are charged by plugging them into the USB port of a computer.

Batteries are an application of a voltaic cell, making electrical energy available as a source of power. Our reliance on batteries increases as global demand for mobile electronic devices such as smart phones, laptops, and tablets continues to grow. China is the largest market, while India and South Korea are growing the fastest. The largest growth is in the area of rechargeable batteries, with estimates placing the global market up to 100 billion US dollars. While demand for batteries looks set to continue, concern over toxicity and environmental damage from battery disposal has meant that mercury and cadmium batteries are being phased out in many places. The different types of batteries and their relative advantages are explained more fully in Option C, Energy.

## Exercises

**13** Use the metal reactivity series in section 25 of the IB data booklet to predict which electrode will be the anode and which will be the cathode when the following half-cells are connected. Write half-equations for the reactions occurring at each electrode.

   **(a)** $Zn/Zn^{2+}$ and $Fe/Fe^{2+}$
   **(b)** $Fe/Fe^{2+}$ and $Mg/Mg^{2+}$
   **(c)** $Mg/Mg^{2+}$ and $Cu/Cu^{2+}$

**14 (a)** Draw a voltaic cell with one half-cell consisting of Mg and a solution of $Mg^{2+}$ ions and the other consisting of Zn and a solution of $Zn^{2+}$ ions. Label the electrodes with name and charge, the direction of electron and ion movement, and write equations for the reactions occurring at each electrode.

   **(b)** Draw a cell diagram to represent the above voltaic cell.

**15** Predict what would happen if an iron spatula was left in a solution of copper sulfate overnight.

INVENTIONS ILLUSTRES
La pile de Volta

Italian physicist Count Alessandro Volta (1745–1827) demonstrates his newly-invented battery or 'voltaic pile' to Napoleon Bonaparte in 1801. Constructed from alternating discs of zinc and copper with pieces of cardboard soaked in brine between the metals, his voltaic pile was the first battery that produced a reliable, steady current of electricity.

The first observations of the link between electricity and chemical change are usually credited to the Italian scientist Luigi Galvani in 1791. He discovered what he called 'animal electricity' by accident, when he noticed twitching in the leg muscles of a dead frog when it was in contact with two different metals. After many experiments, he concluded that the contractions were caused by an electrical fluid that was carried to the muscles in the nerves. His contemporary and fellow countryman Alessandro Volta, however, had an intuition that the source of the electricity was not biological, but originated instead from the interaction between two metals. He set out to prove it by building a 'voltaic pile' from pairs of metals separated by a conducting solution, and demonstrated that this generated an electric current. The fact that the terms galvanic cell and voltaic cell are still both used reflects the recognition given to both men in the discovery.

The invention of the battery shows how a chance observation, followed by experimentation, debate, and the testing of hypotheses led to the development of theory with testable predictions which is then supported by evidence.

## Standard electrode potentials

**Quick reference of units and terms used in electrochemistry**

Here are some definitions of terms used in electrochemistry and an introduction to the units used.

- The SI unit of electric current ($I$) is the **ampere**, usually known as **amp (A)**. It is an SI base unit, from which other units are derived.

- The SI unit of electric charge ($Q$) is the **coulomb (C)**. It is the amount of charge transported in 1 second by a current of 1 ampere. The charge on a single electron is $1.602 \times 10^{-19}$ C, so one mole of electrons carries a charge of 96485.34 C mol$^{-1}$, known as a **faraday (F)**.

  So the familiar equation $Q = I \times t$ can also be written as $C = A \times s$

  The charge on a single electron is $1.602 \times 10^{-19}$ C, so 1 mol of electrons carries a charge of 96485.34 C mol$^{-1}$.

- The SI unit of potential difference is the **volt (V)**. It is equal to the difference in electric potential between two points on a conducting wire, and defined as the amount of energy (J) that can be delivered by a coulomb of electric charge (C). $V = J \times C^{-1}$

- The **electromotive force (EMF)** of a cell is the greatest potential difference that it can generate. It is measured in volts. In practice, because of its internal resistance, it is measurable only when the cell is not supplying current. We will use the term **cell potential** $E_{cell}$ to describe the potential difference when generating electrical energy.

- Cells in series are connected along the same path, so the same current flows through all components.

## Comparisons of half-cell electrode potentials need a reference point

A voltaic cell generates a potential difference known as the **electromotive force (EMF)**. As electrons tend to flow from the half-cell with the more negative potential to the half-cell with the more positive potential, the potential generated is called the **cell potential** or **electrode potential** and is given the symbol **E**. The magnitude of this voltage depends on the *difference* in the tendencies of these two half-cells to undergo reduction. Clearly, the electrode potential of a single half-cell cannot be measured in isolation, but only when electrons flow as it is linked in this way to another half-cell. Therefore, in order to draw up a list of the relative reducing power of different half-cells, it is necessary to compare them all with some fixed reference point that acts as a standard for measurement. It is similar to the way in which heights of mountains can be compared with each other because each is given a height relative to an agreed zero point, in this case sea level.

In electrochemistry, the reference standard is the **standard hydrogen electrode**, sometimes known as **SHE**. As we will see, this gives us a baseline for measuring and comparing the electrode potentials of other half-cells.

## The standard hydrogen electrode

The standard hydrogen electrode (sometimes called the standard hydrogen half-cell) is a modified form of the pH electrode encountered in Chapter 8.

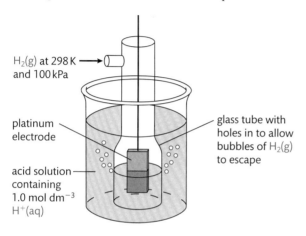

$H_2(g)$ at 298 K and 100 kPa

platinum electrode

glass tube with holes in to allow bubbles of $H_2(g)$ to escape

acid solution containing 1.0 mol dm$^{-3}$ H$^+$(aq)

**Figure 9.11** The standard hydrogen electrode (SHE).

Do not confuse *absorption* with *adsorption*. Absorption occurs when something is taken up through the *volume* of another substance, such as a sponge taking up water; adsorption occurs only at the *surface*, and so depends on the surface area.

Platinum is used as the conducting metal in the electrode because it is fairly inert and will not ionize, and it also acts as a catalyst for the reaction of proton reduction. It is used in the form of 'platinized platinum', which means the surface of the metal is coated with very finely divided platinum (sometime known as platinum black). This causes the electrode reaction to happen rapidly as the large surface area helps in the adsorption of hydrogen gas. Note that the concentration of H$^+$(aq) is 1.0 mol dm$^{-3}$ (pH = 0) and the pressure of H$_2$(g) is 100 kPa at 298 K.

As the electrode is immersed in the acidic solution, it is alternately bathed in H$^+$(aq) and H$_2$(g), setting up an equilibrium between the adsorbed layer of H$_2$(g) and aqueous H$^+$ ions.

$$2H^+(aq) + 2e^- \rightleftharpoons H_2(g)$$

The reaction is reversible, occurring as reduction of H$^+$ (forward reaction) or as oxidation of H$_2$ (backward reaction), depending on the electrode potential of the half-cell to which it is linked, as we will see below.

**The standard hydrogen electrode is assigned an electrode potential value of 0 V.**

The hydrogen half-cell is arbitrarily assigned an electrode potential of zero volts, 0 V. This gives us a means to measure and compare electrode potentials of any other half-cell to which it is connected.

### NATURE OF SCIENCE

The standard electrode potential concept brings a quantitative approach to the study of electrochemistry. As there is no absolute reference point, a convenient reference standard is chosen, in much the same way as we saw with entropy in Chapter 5. This lends itself to mathematical analysis and enables scientists to recognize patterns, trends, and discrepancies.

## Measuring standard electrode potentials

As electrode potentials depend on the concentrations of ions, gas pressures, purity of substance, and temperature, these must all be controlled in order to make valid comparisons between different half-cells. So **standard conditions** are used in these measurements, defined as follows:

- all solutions must have a concentration of $1.0\ mol\ dm^{-3}$;
- all gases must be at a pressure of 100 kPa;
- all substances used must be pure;
- temperature is 298 K;
- if the half-cell does not include a solid metal, platinum is used as the electrode.

Half-cells under these conditions are known as **standard half-cells**.

**Figure 9.12** $Fe^{2+}(aq)/Fe^{3+}(aq)$ half-cell. As it does not include a metal electrode, platinum is used as a point for the entry and exit of electrons into the half-cell. The platinum does not take part in the redox reaction. The standard hydrogen electrode uses platinum for the same purpose.

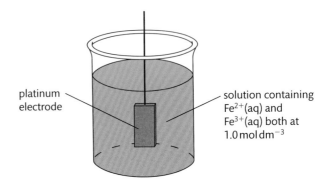

platinum electrode

solution containing $Fe^{2+}(aq)$ and $Fe^{3+}(aq)$ both at $1.0\ mol\ dm^{-3}$

When the standard hydrogen electrode is connected to another standard half-cell by an external circuit with a high-resistance voltmeter and a salt bridge, the EMF generated is known as the **standard electrode potential** of that half-cell. It is given the symbol $E^{\ominus}$. ($E$ refers to electrode potential and the superscript $\ominus$ refers to standard conditions, as introduced in Chapter 5.)

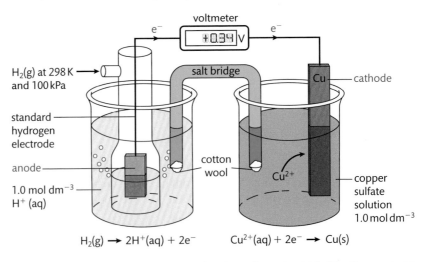

voltmeter
$+0.34$ V

$H_2(g)$ at 298 K and 100 kPa

salt bridge

Cu — cathode

standard hydrogen electrode

anode

cotton wool

$Cu^{2+}$

$1.0\ mol\ dm^{-3}$ $H^+(aq)$

copper sulfate solution $1.0\ mol\ dm^{-3}$

$H_2(g) \rightarrow 2H^+(aq) + 2e^-$     $Cu^{2+}(aq) + 2e^- \rightarrow Cu(s)$

**Figure 9.13** Measuring the standard electrode potential for $Cu^{2+}(aq)/Cu(s)$.

For example, as shown in Figure 9.12, $E^{\ominus}$ for the $Cu^{2+}(aq)/Cu(s)$ half-cell is +0.34 V.

The positive value for $E^{\ominus}$ indicates that this half-cell has a greater tendency to be reduced than $H^+$. So electrons tend to flow from the hydrogen half-cell, which is therefore oxidized, to the copper half-cell, which is reduced.

$$H_2(g) \rightarrow 2H^+(aq) + 2e^-$$

$$Cu^{2+}(aq) + 2e^- \rightarrow Cu(s)$$

The hydrogen half-cell is the anode and the copper half-cell is the cathode, defined by the processes that occur there. The overall reaction is therefore:

$$Cu^{2+}(aq) + H_2(g) \rightarrow 2H^+(aq) + Cu(s) \qquad E^\ominus_{cell} = +0.34 \text{ V}$$

Copper is somewhat of an unusual metal in this respect, having a higher tendency to be reduced than $H^+$. More reactive metals lose their electrons very readily and so bring about the reduction of $H^+$. In these cases, the electron flow will be towards hydrogen and the $E^\ominus$ of the metal half-cell will be negative.

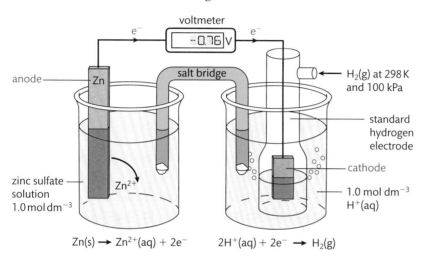

$$Zn(s) \rightarrow Zn^{2+}(aq) + 2e^- \qquad 2H^+(aq) + 2e^- \rightarrow H_2(g)$$

For example, as shown in Figure 9.14, $E^\ominus$ for the $Zn^{2+}(aq)/Zn(s)$ half-cell is −0.76 V.

The negative value for $E^\ominus$ indicates that this half-cell has less of a tendency to be reduced than $H^+$. So electrons flow from the zinc half-cell, which is therefore oxidized, to the hydrogen half-cell, which is reduced.

$$Zn(s) \rightarrow Zn^{2+}(aq) + 2e^-$$

$$2H^+(aq) + 2e^- \rightarrow H_2(g)$$

So the zinc half-cell is the anode and the hydrogen half-cell is the cathode. The overall reaction is therefore:

$$Zn(s) + 2H^+(aq) \rightarrow Zn^{2+}(aq) + H_2(g) \qquad E^\ominus_{cell} = -0.76 \text{ V}$$

These two examples also explain something we observed in Chapter 8. Most metals react with dilute acids, forming a salt with the liberation of hydrogen, but copper is unable to react in this way. We now see that this is because copper has a higher $E^\ominus$ than hydrogen, and so cannot reduce $H^+$. This is true for any metal that has a positive value for $E^\ominus$.

We can represent the zinc–hydrogen cell using the cell diagram convention we introduced earlier.

$$Zn(s) \mid Zn^{2+}(aq) \parallel H^+(aq) \mid H_2(g) \mid Pt(s)$$

anode half-cell          cathode half-cell
oxidation                reduction

Figure 9.14 Measuring the standard electrode potential for $Zn^{2+}(aq)/Zn(s)$.

## Standard electrode potentials are given for the reduction reaction

Given that half-cell reactions exist as equilibria and can occur as oxidation or as reduction, for purposes of standardizing the data there has to be an agreed convention. The standard electrode potential is always given for the *reduction* reaction, in other words for the reaction with the oxidized species on the left and the reduced species on the right. For this reason, standard electrode potential values, $E^{\ominus}$, are sometimes known as **standard reduction potentials**.

A selection of standard electrode potential values is given in section 24 in the IB data booklet. Data from this table corresponding to half-cells discussed so far in this chapter are given here.

| | Oxidized species | | Reduced species | $E^{\ominus}$ / V, at 298 K |
|---|---|---|---|---|
| increasing tendency to occur as reduction | $Zn^{2+}(aq) + 2e^-$ | $\rightleftharpoons$ | $Zn(s)$ | −0.76 |
| | $H^+(aq) + e^-$ | $\rightleftharpoons$ | $\frac{1}{2}H_2(g)$ | 0.00 |
| | $Cu^{2+}(aq) + 2e^-$ | $\rightleftharpoons$ | $Cu(s)$ | +0.34 |
| | $Ag^+(aq) + e^-$ | $\rightleftharpoons$ | $Ag(s)$ | +0.80 |

The following points should be noted:

• all $E^{\ominus}$ values refer to the reduction reaction;
• the $E^{\ominus}$ values do not depend on the total number of electrons, so do not have to be scaled up or down according to the stoichiometry of the equation;
• the more positive the $E^{\ominus}$ value for a half-cell, the more readily it is reduced.

It follows that electrons always flow through the external circuit in a voltaic cell from the half-cell with the more negative standard electrode potential to the half-cell with the more positive electrode potential. So the half-cell with the more negative electrode potential (−) is the anode as oxidation occurs there, and the half-cell with the more positive electrode potential (+) is the cathode as reduction occurs there.

**In a voltaic cell the half-cell with the higher (more positive) electrode potential is the cathode (+), and the half-cell with the lower (more negative) electrode potential is the anode (−).**

**Electrons always flow towards the half-cell with the highest $E^{\ominus}$ value.**

## Using standard electrode potential data

Because the heights of mountains are all measured relative to sea level, we can deduce the difference in height between any two mountains and in which direction we would be going – uphill or downhill. In a similar way, the fact that standard electrode potential data are all referenced to the same point provides a relative scale for us to make predictions about redox reactions and the direction of electron flow. We will look at three specific applications of using $E^{\ominus}$ data here.

### 1 Calculating the cell potential, $E^{\ominus}_{cell}$

From the $E^{\ominus}$ values for any two half-cells, we can calculate the EMF for a voltaic cell in which they are connected. By deducing the direction of electron flow, we can also predict the outcome of a redox reaction.

The half-cell with the higher $E^{\ominus}$ value will be reduced, and the half-cell with the lower $E^{\ominus}$ value will be oxidized. As the cell potential is the difference in the tendencies of these two half-cells to be reduced, we can calculate it by substituting the appropriate values into the following expression:

$$E^{\ominus}_{cell} = E^{\ominus}_{\text{half-cell where reduction occurs}} - E^{\ominus}_{\text{half-cell where oxidation occurs}}$$

Note the following:

- The $E^{\ominus}$ values used in this expression must be the *reduction* potentials as supplied in data tables. Do not invert them before substituting into the equation!
- The $E^{\ominus}$ values do not have to be multiplied according to the stoichiometry of the redox equation. This is because they are intensive quantities and do not depend on the total number of electrons shown in the equation.

## Worked example

Calculate the EMF for a voltaic cell constructed from a zinc half-cell and a copper half-cell, and identify the anode and cathode. Write the equation for the overall cell reaction.

### Solution

Standard electrode potential data for these half-cells at 298 K are:

$$Zn^{2+}(aq) + 2e^- \rightleftharpoons Zn(s) \qquad E^{\ominus} = -0.76 \text{ V}$$

$$Cu^{2+}(aq) + 2e^- \rightleftharpoons Cu(s) \qquad E^{\ominus} = +0.34 \text{ V}$$

So the copper half-cell will be reduced (higher value for $E^{\ominus}$), and the zinc half-cell will be oxidized. Electrons flow from zinc to copper.

$$E^{\ominus}_{cell} = E^{\ominus}_{\text{half-cell where reduction occurs}} - E^{\ominus}_{\text{half-cell where oxidation occurs}}$$

$$E^{\ominus}_{cell} = E^{\ominus}_{Cu^{2+}} - E^{\ominus}_{Zn^{2+}} = +0.34 - (-0.76) \text{ V} = +1.10 \text{ V}$$

The zinc half-cell is the anode and the copper half-cell is the cathode.

$$Zn(s) + Cu^{2+}(aq) \rightarrow Zn^{2+}(aq) + Cu(s)$$

This confirms the value shown on the photograph on page 428.

$$E^{\ominus}_{cell} = E^{\ominus}_{\text{half-cell where reduction occurs}} - E^{\ominus}_{\text{half-cell where oxidation occurs}}$$

$E^{\ominus}$ / V

$-0.76$  $Zn^{2+}(aq) + 2e^- \rightarrow Zn(s)$

$0.00$  $+1.10 \text{ V}$

$+0.34$  $Cu^{2+}(aq) + 2e^- \rightarrow Cu(s)$

Cathodic protection. Blocks of zinc are bolted on to the iron posts to help protect the iron from corrosion. As zinc is preferentially oxidized, it acts as the anode where **sacrificial corrosion** occurs, $Zn(s) \rightarrow Zn^{2+}(aq) + 2e^-$. This leaves the iron unaffected at the cathode. Photographed in Haida Gwaii, Canada.

## Worked example

Determine $E^{\ominus}_{cell}$ for the voltaic cell based on the following two half-cells, for which $E^{\ominus}$ values are given. Write the equation for the overall reaction, and represent the cell with a cell diagram.

(i)  $MnO_4^-(aq) + 8H^+(aq) + 5e^- \rightleftharpoons Mn^{2+}(aq) + 4H_2O(l)$ $\qquad E^{\ominus} = +1.51 \text{ V}$

(ii) $IO_4^-(aq) + 2H^+(aq) + 2e^- \rightleftharpoons IO_3^-(aq) + H_2O(l)$ $\qquad E^{\ominus} = +1.60 \text{ V}$

**Solution**

$IO_4^-$(aq) will be reduced, as it has the higher $E^\ominus$ value, and $Mn^{2+}$(aq) will be oxidized.

$$E^\ominus_{cell} = E^\ominus_{\text{half-cell where reduction occurs}} - E^\ominus_{\text{half-cell where oxidation occurs}}$$

$$= +1.60\,V - (+1.51\,V)$$

$$= +0.09\,V$$

To balance the equations for electrons, multiply (i) by 2 and (ii) by 5. Then add the two half-equations together, cancelling out terms on both sides.

$$5IO_4^-(aq) + 2Mn^{2+}(aq) + 3H_2O(l) \rightarrow 5IO_3^-(aq) + 2MnO_4^-(aq) + 6H^+(aq)$$

$$Pt(s) \mid Mn^{2+}(aq), 2MnO_4^-(aq) \parallel IO_4^-(aq), IO_3^-(aq) \mid Pt(s)$$

anode half-cell      cathode half-cell

oxidation           reduction

Note that Pt is used in both half-cells since it is stable in these conditions and they do not contain a metal to conduct.

## 2 Determining spontaneity of a reaction

As $E^\ominus$ values can be used to predict the redox change that will occur among a mixture of reactants, it follows we can use them to determine whether a particular reaction will occur spontaneously. This is based on the fact that *a voltaic cell will always run in the direction that gives a positive value for the $E^\ominus_{cell}$.*

- If $E^\ominus_{cell}$ is positive, the reaction is spontaneous as written.
- If $E^\ominus_{cell}$ is negative, the reaction is non-spontaneous, and the reverse reaction is spontaneous.

**Worked example**

Use $E^\ominus$ values to determine whether the reaction

$$Ni(s) + Mn^{2+}(aq) \rightarrow Ni^{2+}(aq) + Mn(s)$$

will occur spontaneously under standard conditions.

**Solution**

The data values are as follows:

$$Ni^{2+}(aq) + 2e^- \rightarrow Ni(s) \qquad\qquad E^\ominus = -0.26\,V$$

$$Mn^{2+}(aq) + 2e^- \rightarrow Mn(s) \qquad\qquad E^\ominus = -1.18\,V$$

In the reaction given, Ni is being oxidized and $Mn^{2+}$ is being reduced.

Substituting in the equation:

$$E^\ominus_{cell} = E^\ominus_{\text{half-cell where reduction occurs}} - E^\ominus_{\text{half-cell where oxidation occurs}}$$

$$E^\ominus_{cell} = E^\ominus_{Mn^{2+}} - E^\ominus_{Ni^{2+}} = -1.19 - (-0.26) = -0.93\,V$$

The negative sign for $E^\ominus_{cell}$ tells us that this reaction will not happen spontaneously. In this mixture the reaction that occurs will be the reverse reaction,

$$Ni^{2+}(aq) + Mn(s) \rightarrow Ni(s) + Mn^{2+}(aq)$$

---

When substituting $E^\ominus$ values into the equation for $E^\ominus_{cell}$ used here, make sure you use the values with the sign given for the *reduction* reaction, i.e. exactly as in the data table. The subtraction in the equation for the half-cell undergoing oxidation reverses its sign, so you must not do this first.

$E^\ominus_{cell}$ **is positive for all spontaneous reactions.**

Microbial fuel cell (MFC) technology generates electricity directly from the degradation of organic material, such as that found in sewage. These fuel cells consist of a chamber filled with organic sewage and small electrodes. Sewage bacteria oxidize the organic compounds, transferring electrons directly to the anode, which then flow via an external circuit to the cathode generating electricity. MFCs are actively researched in several countries, with the hope that they may enable sewage treatment plants to become energy self-sufficient.

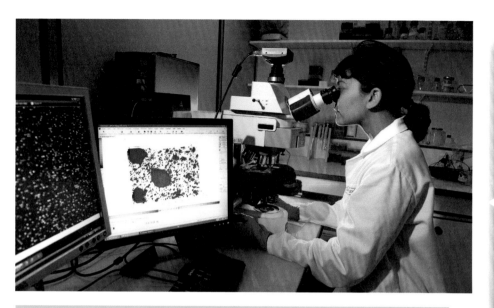

Researcher using a microscope to study bacteria used in microbial fuel cells in France. Microbial fuel cells are an exciting area of research, with the potential of turning waste to energy.

## NATURE OF SCIENCE

Research into microbial fuel cells (MFCs) is a good example of the interdisciplinary nature of much scientific research. In this case, the combination of expertise in engineering and design technology with microbiology, molecular biology, and chemistry helps scientists understand how microbial ecosystems work and can be used to generate electricity. Teamwork and collaboration can create a synergy, in which the combined product of understanding is greater than the individual contributions. In research this can help to achieve a common goal that is beyond one scientific field.

## Electrode potential and free energy change ($E_{cell}$ and $\Delta G$)

We have now come across two quantitative measures of the spontaneity of a reaction, $E^{\ominus}_{cell}$ and the free energy, $\Delta G^{\ominus}$, introduced in Chapter 5. These two values are directly related through the equation:

$$\Delta G^{\ominus} = -nFE^{\ominus}$$

where

- $n$ = number of moles of electrons transferred in the reaction;
- $F$ = the charge carried by 1 mole of electrons, known as the Faraday constant (it has a value of approximately 96 500 C mol$^{-1}$).

The units of the terms in this equation confirm the relationship:

$$\Delta G^{\ominus} \text{ (J)} = -n \text{ (mol) } F \text{ (C mol}^{-1}) E^{\ominus} \text{ (V) as J = C} \times \text{V}$$

The negative sign in the equation indicates that $E$ and $\Delta G$ have opposite signs:

- when $E^{\ominus}_{cell}$ is positive, $\Delta G^{\ominus}$ is negative $\Rightarrow$ reaction is spontaneous;
- when $E^{\ominus}_{cell}$ is negative, $\Delta G^{\ominus}$ is positive $\Rightarrow$ reaction is non-spontaneous;
- when $E^{\ominus}_{cell}$ is 0, $\Delta G^{\ominus}$ is 0 $\Rightarrow$ reaction is at equilibrium.

Because of the direct relationship between $E^{\ominus}_{cell}$ and $\Delta G^{\ominus}$, the more positive the value of $E^{\ominus}_{cell}$, the more energetically favourable is the reaction. It also follows that a voltmeter can be considered as an indirect measure of free-energy change as well as of electrode potential.

This equation enables us to calculate the free-energy change of a reaction from standard electrode potential data.

The equation $\Delta G^{\ominus} = -nFE^{\ominus}$ and the value of $F$ are given in sections 1 and 2 of the IB data booklet.

## CHALLENGE YOURSELF

5 Derive a more precise value of the Faraday constant using information in the IB data booklet.

### Worked example

Calculate the standard free-energy change at 298 K for the zinc–copper voltaic cell, which has a standard cell potential of +1.10 V.

**Solution**

First write the equation for the overall cell reaction, as we need to know the number of electrons transferred. We deduced this on page 437.

$$Zn(s) + Cu^{2+}(aq) \rightarrow Zn^{2+}(aq) + Cu(s)$$

$$\Delta G^{\ominus} = -nFE^{\ominus}$$

$$= -2 \text{ (mol e}^-) \times 96\,500 \text{ (C mol}^{-1}) \times 1.10 \text{ (V)}$$

$$= 212{,}000 \text{ J}$$

$$\therefore \Delta G^{\ominus} = -212 \text{ kJ}$$

In practice, voltaic cells rarely run under standard conditions, and in any case the concentrations change as the reaction proceeds. A modification of the equation above, known as the **Nernst equation**, is used to calculate cell potentials under non-standard conditions. This is discussed in Option C, Energy.

## 3   Comparing relative oxidizing and reducing power of half-cells

The calculations using $E^{\ominus}$ values for half-reactions confirm the order of the activity series discussed earlier in this chapter. In quantitative terms, we can now say that a metal is able to reduce the ions of another metal that has a higher $E^{\ominus}$ value. Metals with low $E^{\ominus}$ values (most negative) are therefore the strongest reducing agents. Likewise, a non-metal is able to oxidize the ions of another non-metal that has a lower $E^{\ominus}$ value. Non-metals with high $E^{\ominus}$ values are therefore the strongest oxidizing agents.

These trends are summarized below.

|  | Oxidized species |  | Reduced species | $E^{\ominus}$ / V |  |
|---|---|---|---|---|---|
| increasing strength as oxidizing agent | $Zn^{2+}(aq) + 2e^-$ | $\rightleftharpoons$ | $Zn(s)$ | −0.76 | increasing strength as reducing agent |
| | $H^+(aq) + e^-$ | $\rightleftharpoons$ | $\frac{1}{2}H_2(g)$ | 0.00 | |
| | $Cu^{2+}(aq) + 2e^-$ | $\rightleftharpoons$ | $Cu(s)$ | +0.34 | |
| | $\frac{1}{2}I_2(s) + e^-$ | $\rightleftharpoons$ | $I^-(aq)$ | +0.54 | |
| | $\frac{1}{2}Cl_2(g) + e^-$ | $\rightleftharpoons$ | $Cl^-(aq)$ | +1.36 | |

### Worked example

A solution containing potassium manganate(VII) and concentrated hydrochloric acid reacts to form chlorine gas. Identify the strongest oxidizing agent in the solution and calculate the standard cell potential.

**Solution**

First consider the ions present in solution and extract the relevant half-equations from section 24 in the IB data booklet.

$$MnO_4^-(aq) + 8H^+ + 5e^- \rightarrow Mn^{2+}(aq) + 4H_2O(l) \qquad E^\ominus = +1.51 \text{ V}$$

$$\tfrac{1}{2}Cl_2(g) + e^- \rightarrow Cl^-(aq) \qquad E^\ominus = +1.36 \text{ V}$$

$MnO_4^-(aq)$ is the stronger oxidizing agent as it has the higher value for $E^\ominus$ so it will be reduced.

$$E^\ominus_{cell} = E^\ominus_{\text{half-cell where reduction occurs}} - E^\ominus_{\text{half-cell where oxidation occurs}}$$

$$E^\ominus_{cell} = E^\ominus_{MnO_4^-} - E^\ominus_{Cl_2} = +1.51 - (+1.36) = +0.15 \text{ V}$$

## A little caution about interpreting $E^\ominus$ data

Note that although $E^\ominus$ data give information on the energetic feasibility of a reaction and the products of a redox reaction, they do not give any information on the rate. So a reaction that is predicted to be spontaneous may give no observable sign of reaction because the activation energy may be too high for the reaction to occur at an appreciable rate. As we saw in Chapters 6 and 7, feasibility and rate are two different considerations.

In addition, the $E^\ominus$ values that we have used throughout these examples relate only to standard conditions, and any changes in temperature, concentration, or pressure will alter the values, possibly even changing whether a reaction is spontaneous or not.

In summary, the interpretation of electrode potential data involves recognizing one fundamental fact: *electrons always tend to flow towards the half-cell with the highest $E^\ominus$ value.* All other deductions and interpretations follow from this.

**The higher the value of $E^\ominus$ of a half-cell, the stronger the oxidizing agent; the lower the value of $E^\ominus$, the stronger the reducing agent.**

## Exercises

**16** Given the standard electrode potentials of the following reactions:

$$Cr^{3+}(aq) + 3e^- \rightarrow Cr(s) \qquad E^\ominus = -0.75 \text{ V}$$
$$Cd^{2+}(aq) + 2e^- \rightarrow Cd(s) \qquad E^\ominus = -0.40 \text{ V}$$

calculate the cell potential for

$$2Cr(s) + 3Cd^{2+}(aq) \rightarrow 2Cr^{3+}(aq) + 3Cd(s)$$

**17** From the half-equations below, determine the cell reaction and standard cell potential.

$$BrO_3^-(aq) + 6H^+(aq) + 6e^- \rightarrow Br^-(aq) + 3H_2O \qquad E^\ominus = +1.44 \text{ V}$$
$$I_2(s) + 2e^- \rightarrow 2I^-(aq) \qquad E^\ominus = +0.54 \text{ V}$$

**18** From the following data

$$Cu^{2+}(aq) + 2e^- \rightarrow Cu(s) \qquad E^\ominus = +0.34 \text{ V}$$
$$Mg^{2+}(aq) + 2e^- \rightarrow Mg(s) \qquad E^\ominus = -2.37 \text{ V}$$
$$Zn^{2+}(aq) + 2e^- \rightarrow Zn(s) \qquad E^\ominus = -0.76 \text{ V}$$

identify the strongest oxidizing agent and the strongest reducing agent.

**19** Using the data for $E^\ominus$ values in questions 16–18, predict whether a reaction will be spontaneous between the following pairs.

**(a)** $Cu^{2+}(aq) + I_2(s)$
**(b)** $Cd(s)$ and $BrO_3^-(aq)$ in acidic solution
**(c)** $Cr(s)$ and $Mg^{2+}(aq)$

Write equations and calculate the cell potentials for the reactions that will occur as written.

**20** The standard electrode potential for the reaction

$$Al(s) + Cr^{3+}(aq) \rightarrow Al^{3+}(aq) + Cr(s)$$

is 0.92 V at 298 K. What is the standard free-energy change for this reaction?

# Electrolytic cells

## An external source of electricity drives non-spontaneous redox reactions

Worker siphoning off molten aluminium in an aluminium processing plant. Electrolysis of a solution of alumina ($Al_2O_3$) dissolved in cryolite is used to reduce the $Al^{3+}$ ions at the cathode. The molten aluminium is siphoned off and cooled before any further processing.

As we have seen, a voltaic cell takes the energy of a spontaneous redox reaction and harnesses it to generate electrical energy. An **electrolytic cell** does the reverse: it uses an external source of electrical energy to bring about a redox reaction that would otherwise be non-spontaneous. You can think of it in terms of an external power supply pumping electrons into the electrolytic cell, driving reactions of oxidation and reduction. As the word *electro-lysis* suggests, it is the process where electricity is used to bring about reactions of chemical breakdown.

The reactant in the process of electrolysis is present in the **electrolyte**. This is a liquid, usually a molten ionic compound or a solution of an ionic compound. As the electric current passes through the electrolyte, redox reactions occur at the **electrodes**, removing the charges on the ions and forming products that are electrically neutral. The ions are therefore said to be **discharged** during this process.

Reactive metals, including aluminium, lithium, magnesium, sodium, and potassium, are found naturally in compounds such as $Al_2O_3$ and NaCl where they exist as positive ions. Extraction of the metal therefore involves reduction of these ions. But this is a problem because, as we saw earlier, the $E^{\ominus}$ values of these reactive metal ions are so low that there are no good reducing agents available to do this.

In these cases, the only effective source of reduction is directly with electrons, using electrolysis. This means that electrolysis is the *only* means of extracting these metals from their ores. As we will see, it is also the process used in the production of many non-metal elements of industrial importance, and in the related procedures of electroplating and anodization.

The components of an electrolytic cell are shown in Figure 9.15 and described below.

 **Electrodes are electronically conducting, electrolytes are ionically conducting.**

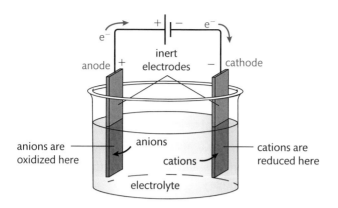

**Figure 9.15** Components of an electrolytic cell.

- The source of electric power is a battery or a DC power source. This is shown in diagrams as $\mid\mid$ where the longer line represents the positive terminal and the shorter line the negative terminal.
- The electrodes are immersed in the electrolyte and connected to the power supply. They must not touch each other! Electrodes are made from a conducting substance – generally a metal or graphite. They are described as **inert** when they do not take part in the redox reactions.
- Electric wires connect the electrodes to the power supply.

The power source pushes electrons towards the negative electrode where they enter the electrolyte. This is the cathode. Electrons are released at the positive terminal, the anode, and returned to the source. The current is passed through the electrolyte, not by electrons but by the ions as they are mobile and migrate to the electrodes. The chemical reactions occurring at each electrode remove the ions from the solution and so enable the process to continue.

## Redox reactions occur at the electrodes

The ions in the electrolyte migrate to the electrodes by attraction of opposite charges. So positive ions (cations) are attracted to the negative electrode, the cathode, while negative ions (anions) are attracted to the positive electrode, the anode. At the electrodes, redox reactions occur, oxidation at the anode and reduction at the cathode, which result in the ions being discharged. In aqueous solutions, water can be oxidized to oxygen at the anode and reduced to hydrogen at the cathode.

- At the negative electrode (cathode): $M^+ + e^- \rightarrow M$
  cations gain electrons so are reduced.
- At the positive electrode (anode): $A^- \rightarrow A + e^-$
  anions lose electrons so are oxidized.

### Terminology of electrodes – a reminder

You will notice that the charges on the electrodes are inverted in an electrolytic cell compared with a voltaic cell. This is because it is the nature of the redox reaction, not the electrical charge, which defines the electrode: oxidation *always* occurs at the anode and reduction at the cathode, so electrons flow from anode to cathode. This never changes.

Michael Faraday, the English physicist and chemist (1791–1867), first defined and introduced the names electrolyte, electrode, anode, cathode, ion, anion, and cation, all of which are derived from Greek, into scientific language in 1834. He recognized the need to clarify the terminology, seeing the electrodes as surfaces where the current enters (anode) and leaves (cathode) the 'decomposing body' (electrolyte). He was referring to the established convention that current direction is always stated in reverse direction to electron flow. Faraday rather modestly suggested his names would be used only when necessary to avoid confusion, saying '*I am fully aware that names are one thing and science another*'.

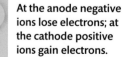

**At the anode negative ions lose electrons; at the cathode positive ions gain electrons.**

| | Voltaic cell | | Electrolytic cell | |
|---|---|---|---|---|
| Anode | oxidation occurs here | negative | oxidation occurs here | positive |
| Cathode | reduction occurs here | positive | reduction occurs here | negative |

The anode is the electrode where oxidation occurs, the cathode is the electrode where reduction occurs. In an electrolytic cell, the anode is positive and the cathode is negative.

## Determining the products in electrolytic cells

We can apply our knowledge of redox chemistry to electrolytic cells, determining the reactions that occur at the electrodes, and so predicting the products released. The following steps are a useful summary.

> **1** Identify all the ions present in the electrolyte and determine which will migrate to which electrode: anions to anode, and cations to cathode.

> **2** Where there is more than one possible reaction at each electrode, determine which will occur, as will be discussed on page 447. Write the half-equation for the reaction at each electrode, showing electrons released at the anode in oxidation and taken up at the cathode in reduction.

> **3** Balance the electrons lost and gained at the anode and the cathode, then add the two half-equations to write the equation for the net reaction.

> **4** Consider what changes would be observed in the cell as a result of the redox processes occurring. These may include colour changes in the electrolyte, precipitation of solid, gas discharge, or pH changes.

To help with this topic, you might find it useful to review the structure of ionic compounds, and particularly why they conduct when molten or in aqueous solution, but not when solid. See pages 145–146.

## The electrolysis of molten salts

When the electrolyte is a molten salt, the only ions present are those from the compound itself as there is no solvent. So, usually, only one ion migrates to each electrode, and it is straightforward to predict the reactions that will occur.

### Worked example

Describe the reactions that occur at the two electrodes during the electrolysis of molten lead(II) bromide. Write an equation for the overall reaction and comment on any likely changes that would be observed.

**Solution**

1 Deduce the ions present in the electrolyte and to which electrode they will be attracted:

$$PbBr_2(l) \rightarrow Pb^{2+}(l) + 2Br^-(l)$$

to cathode   to anode

2   Half-equations at the electrodes are:
    anode, $Br^-$ is oxidized:

$$2Br^-(l) \rightarrow Br_2(l) + 2e^-$$

cathode, $Pb^{2+}$ is reduced:

$$Pb^{2+}(l) + 2e^- \rightarrow Pb(l)$$

3   Overall reaction: $Pb^{2+}(l) + 2Br^-(l) \rightarrow Pb(l) + Br_2(l)$
4   The observable changes will be a brown liquid with a strong smell ($Br_2$) at the anode and the appearance of a grey metal (Pb) at the cathode.

Lead(II) bromide has a relatively low melting point of 373 °C, so this electrolysis experiment can be carried out in a school laboratory. Unfortunately though, as the two products lead and bromine are both toxic, it may not be practical to do this.

Most other ionic compounds have very high melting points, so electrolysis of their molten salts involves working at high temperatures, which can only be generated and maintained under industrial conditions. Sometimes in industrial processes another compound is added to lower the melting point to make it more economical. For example, the electrolysis of molten sodium chloride used in the extraction of sodium uses an electrolyte of molten sodium chloride to which some molten calcium chloride has been added. This has a melting point of about 580 °C, considerably lower than the 801 °C for pure NaCl. It is obviously important though that the presence of the added $CaCl_2$ does not interfere with the discharge of sodium at the cathode. We can check that this is the case by looking at the $E^\ominus$ values for the two metal ions.

$$Ca^{2+}(aq) + 2e^- \rightarrow Ca(s) \qquad E^\ominus = -2.87 \text{ V}$$

$$Na^+(aq) + e^- \rightarrow Na(s) \qquad E^\ominus = -2.71 \text{ V}$$

From its higher $E^\ominus$ value, we can deduce that $Na^+$ will be reduced in preference to $Ca^{2+}$, so the addition of $CaCl_2$ will not interfere with the production of Na at the cathode.

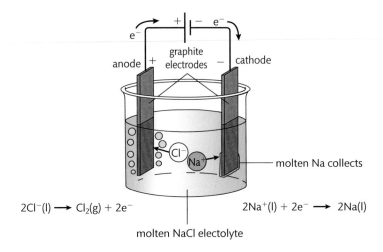

$$2Cl^-(l) \rightarrow Cl_2(g) + 2e^-$$
molten NaCl electolyte
$$2Na^+(l) + 2e^- \rightarrow 2Na(l)$$
molten Na collects

**NATURE OF SCIENCE**

The applications of electrochemical cells are so widespread in society that it is not surprising they have also raised some difficult questions. The global demand for energy and metals drives research and development in this field, and leads to significant economic and environmental impacts. Some of these have been discussed here, such as the problems of disposal of batteries and the significant release of greenhouse gases in many electrolytic processes. Others include the release of toxic by-products such as mercury and the continuing use of asbestos in some electrolytic cells despite the fact that it is banned from many other applications. In addition, there are high energy costs of maintaining the required conditions in electrolytic cells. Innovations in science often involve both benefit and burden, and so place responsibilities on scientists, industries, and governments to monitor.

**Figure 9.16** Electrolysis of molten sodium chloride. Chloride ions are oxidized at the anode and sodium ions are reduced at the cathode. The overall equation is $2NaCl(l) \rightarrow 2Na(l) + Cl_2(g)$.

## Worked example

Describe what you would expect to observe during the electrolysis of molten copper(II) chloride. Explain your answer in terms of the redox reactions occurring at the electrodes, including equations in your answer.

### Solution

1

$$CuCl_2(l) \rightarrow Cu^{2+}(l) + 2Cl^-(l)$$

to cathode    to anode

2   Half-equations at the electrodes are:
anode, $Cl^-$ is oxidized:

$$2Cl^-(l) \rightarrow Cl_2(l) + 2e^-$$

cathode, $Cu^{2+}$ is reduced:

$$Cu^{2+}(l) + 2e^- \rightarrow Cu(l)$$

3   Overall reaction: $Cu^{2+}(l) + 2Cl^-(l) \rightarrow Cu(l) + Cl_2(g)$

4   The observable changes will be a pale green gas with a pungent smell ($Cl_2$) around the anode, and a pinkish metallic solid (Cu) at the cathode. The bright blue colour of the solution will fade.

In the next section we will see how $E^\ominus$ data are used in similar ways to determine which ion is discharged when there is more than one anion or cation attracted to the same electrode.

Aluminium is a unique metal: strong, flexible, lightweight, corrosion-resistant, and 100% recyclable. Its commercial manufacture began in the 1880s when electrolysis made it possible to extract it from its ore bauxite, $Al_2O_3$. It is therefore a young metal in contrast to tin, lead, and iron, which have been in use for thousands of years, but in this short time it has become the world's second most used metal after steel. Aluminium production is, however, very energy intensive and also is associated with the production of perfluorocarbons (PFCs), strong greenhouse gases. A major emphasis must therefore be placed on recycling the metal as this uses only 5% of the energy and has only 5% of the greenhouse gas emissions compared with new production. Countries vary in the success of their recycling programmes; in the recycling of aluminium beverage cans Japan and Brazil are world leaders with rates over 95% cans recycled.

The aluminium drink can is the world's most recycled container, with approximately 70% of all cans being recycled worldwide.

**21** Write half-equations for the electrode reactions occurring during the electrolysis of the following molten salts using graphite electrodes.

   **(a)** KBr                    **(b)** $MgF_2$              **(c)** ZnS

**22** Magnesium metal is produced by the electrolysis of molten magnesium chloride using inert electrodes.

   **(a)** Make a fully labelled drawing of the electrolytic cell, including the charges on the electrodes and the direction of electron and ion migration.

   **(b)** Write equations for the reactions occurring at each electrode and the overall cell reaction.

**23** Which statement is *not* correct for the electrolysis of molten copper(II) chloride?

   **A**   Copper ions and chloride ions move through the electrolyte.

   **B**   Oxidation of chloride takes place at the anode.

   **C**   Electrons move through the external circuit.

   **D**   Oxidation of chlorine takes place at the cathode.

# Electrolysis of aqueous solutions

When electrolysis is carried out on an aqueous solution, predicting the products at the electrodes is more difficult because water itself can be oxidized or reduced.

- At the cathode, $H_2O$ can be reduced to $H_2$:

$$2H_2O(l) + 2e^- \rightarrow H_2(g) + 2OH^-(aq)$$

- At the anode, $H_2O$ can be oxidized to $O_2$:

$$2H_2O(l) \rightarrow 4H^+(aq) + O_2(g) + 4e^-$$

So when a solute $M^+A^-$ is in an aqueous solution, there is more than one redox reaction possible at each electrode. Specifically:

- at the anode: either $A^-$ or $H_2O$ can be oxidized;
- at the cathode: either $M^+$ or $H_2O$ can be reduced.

The discharge of an ion at the electrode in these cases is known as **selective discharge**. The outcome is determined by the following factors:

- **the relative $E^\ominus$ values of the ions;**
- **the relative concentrations of the ions in the electrolyte;**
- **the nature of the electrode.**

These are discussed below with reference to specific examples, using the steps given earlier.

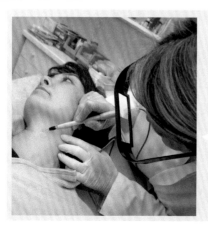

Electrolysis is used to remove unwanted hairs permanently. The needle is inserted into the hair shaft and passes an electric current through the follicle. Electrolytic reactions result in the production of NaOH, which destroys the hair follicle.

## Electrolysis of water

As we learned in Chapter 8, the ionization of pure water is extremely low, so it is not a good conductor of electricity. However, the addition of ions increases its conductivity, so usually some ionic compound such as NaOH (which as we will see will not interfere with the discharge of the ions from water) is added when this electrolysis is performed.

1   Ions present:

$$NaOH(aq) \rightarrow Na^+(aq) + OH^-(aq)$$

                      ↓            ↓
                     to          to
               cathode   anode

2   At the cathode, possible reactions are:

$$Na^+(aq) + e^- \rightarrow Na(s) \qquad E^\ominus = -2.71 \text{ V}$$
$$2H_2O(l) + 2e^- \rightarrow H_2(g) + 2OH^-(aq) \qquad E^\ominus = -0.83 \text{ V}$$

So $H_2O$ is preferentially reduced and $H_2(g)$ will be discharged.

At the anode, possible reactions are:

$$4OH^-(aq) \rightarrow 2H_2O(l) + O_2(g) + 4e^- \qquad -E^\ominus = -0.40 \text{ V}$$
$$2H_2O(l) \rightarrow 4H^+(aq) + O_2(g) + 4e^- \qquad -E^\ominus = -1.23 \text{ V}$$

Note because these reactions are written as oxidations, the sign of the electrode potential has been reversed. Based on these values, $OH^-(aq)$ is preferentially oxidized and $O_2(g)$ is discharged.

3   The overall balanced equation is:

$$2H_2O(l) \rightarrow 2H_2(g) + O_2(g)$$

4   The observed changes at the electrodes will be:
   - colourless gas evolved at both anode ($O_2$) and cathode ($H_2$)
   - ratio by volumes of the gases is 2 $H_2$ : 1 $O_2$ (by application of Avogadro's law on gas volumes)
   - the pH at the anode will decrease as $H^+$ is released, while the pH at the cathode will increase as $OH^-$ is released.

## Electrolysis of NaCl(aq)

NaCl(aq) is sometimes known as **brine**. Electrolysis of this solution leads to the production of $H_2(g)$ , $Cl_2(g)$, and NaOH(aq), all of which are of commercial importance.

1  Ions present:

$$NaCl(aq) \rightarrow Na^+(aq) + Cl^-(aq)$$

to cathode    to anode

2  At the cathode the possible reactions are the same as above in the electrolysis of water. So $H_2O$ is preferentially reduced and $H_2(g)$ will be discharged.

$$2H_2O(l) + 2e^- \rightarrow H_2(g) + 2OH^-(aq)$$

At the anode, possible reactions are:

$$2H_2O(l) \rightarrow 4H^+(aq) + O_2(g) + 4e^- \qquad -E^\ominus = -1.23\ V$$

$$2Cl^-(aq) \rightarrow Cl_2(g) + 2e^- \qquad -E^\ominus = -1.36\ V$$

Although the $E^\ominus$ value favours the oxidation of $H_2O$ leading to the discharge of $O_2$, the situation here is a bit more complicated.

- When the concentration of $Cl^-$ is low, $H_2O$ is oxidized, leading to the release of $O_2$ as given in the electrolysis of water.
- But when, more typically, the concentration of NaCl is greater than about 25% by mass of the solution, the $Cl^-$ is preferentially oxidized, leading to the release of $Cl_2(g)$. The industrial electrolysis of brine uses a saturated solution of aqueous NaCl to ensure the discharge of $Cl_2(g)$.

3  The overall balanced equation when $Cl^-$ is discharged is:

$$2NaCl(aq) + 2H_2O(l) \rightarrow H_2(g) + Cl_2(g) + 2Na^+(aq) + 2OH^-(aq)$$

4  The observed changes at the electrodes (assuming $Cl^-$ discharged) will be:
- gas evolved at both anode ($Cl_2$) and cathode ($H_2$);
- $Cl_2(g)$ identified at the anode through strong smell and bleaching effect on damp blue litmus paper;
- an increase in pH of the electrolyte will occur due to release of $OH^-$.

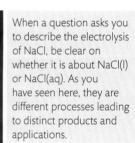

When a question asks you to describe the electrolysis of NaCl, be clear on whether it is about NaCl(l) or NaCl(aq). As you have seen here, they are different processes leading to distinct products and applications.

The commercial electrolysis of aqueous sodium chloride, known as the **chlor-alkali** industry, has been in operation since 1892. It is of major significance economically because of the simultaneous yield of $Cl_2$ and NaOH. One process, the mercury cell, produces chlorine-free NaOH, but is associated with serious health and environmental concerns because of the use of mercury, a known toxin. In 2013 the United Nations Environment Programme agreed to a deadline for the phase-out of mercury cells by 2025, and this was accepted by more than 140 countries.

The explanation given here about the preferential discharge of $Cl^-$ when its concentration is high is valid, but somewhat of a simplification. A fuller interpretation includes the fact that $E^\ominus$ values reflect equilibrium conditions, but as ion distributions change while the current flows these potentials also change. In effect a higher voltage, known as **overvoltage**, must be applied to discharge an ion in an operating cell. In the electrolysis of NaCl(aq) where the pH increases during the reaction, there is a significant increase in the overvoltage for the oxidation of water, thus favouring the discharge of $Cl^-$ at the anode. Electrode kinetics is also a factor; modern chlor-alkali anodes are titanium metal coated with a few microns of Ir and Ru oxides that catalyse the preferential oxidation of $Cl^-$ to $Cl_2$.

The electrolytic processes involving copper are respectively called 'electro-winning' (C anode) and 'electro-refining' (Cu anode). In industry the electro-winning anode is usually a lead/antimony alloy.

**Selective discharge of an ion during electrolysis depends on relative $E^\ominus$ values, the ion concentration, and the nature of the electrode.**

## Electrolysis of $CuSO_4(aq)$

$CuSO_4(aq)$ is a bright blue colour, due to the presence of the hydrated $Cu^{2+}$ ion. Electrolysis of this solution yields different products depending on the nature of the electrodes. We will describe the reactions with (a) C electrodes and (b) Cu electrodes here, following the same steps according to the numbered sequence on page 444.

1   Ions present:

$$CuSO_4(aq) \rightarrow Cu^{2+}(aq) + SO_4^{2-}(aq)$$
$$\downarrow \qquad \qquad \downarrow$$
$$\text{to} \qquad \quad \text{to}$$
$$\text{cathode} \qquad \text{anode}$$

### (a) Carbon (graphite) or other 'inert' electrodes

2   At the cathode, possible reactions are:

$$Cu^{2+}(aq) + 2e^- \rightarrow Cu(s) \qquad\qquad E^\ominus = +0.34\ \text{V}$$
$$2H_2O(l) + 2e^- \rightarrow H_2(g) + 2OH^-(aq) \qquad E^\ominus = -0.83\ \text{V}$$

So $Cu^{2+}$ is preferentially reduced and Cu(s) is discharged.

At the anode, $H_2O$ is preferentially oxidized:

$$2H_2O(l) \rightarrow 4H^+(aq) + O_2(g) + 4e^- \qquad -E^\ominus = -1.23\ \text{V}$$

3   The overall balanced equation is:
$$2CuSO_4(aq) + 2H_2O(l) \rightarrow 2Cu(s) + O_2(g) + 4H^+(aq) + 2SO_4^{2-}(aq)$$

4   The observed changes at the electrodes are as follows:
   • pinky brown colour of copper deposited on cathode;
   • colourless gas ($O_2$) evolved at the anode;
   • decrease in pH of the solution due to release of $H^+$ ions;
   • loss of intensity of blue colour due to discharge of $Cu^{2+}(aq)$.

### (b) Copper electrodes

2   At the cathode: the reaction will be as above with discharge of $Cu^{2+}$:
$$Cu^{2+}(aq) + 2e^- \rightarrow Cu(s)$$

At the anode: the reaction is different from above. The Cu electrode itself is oxidized, supplying electrons for the reaction and dissolving as $Cu^{2+}(aq)$:

$$Cu(s) \rightarrow Cu^{2+}(aq) + 2e^-$$

3   So the net reaction is the movement of $Cu^{2+}(aq)$ from where it is produced at the anode to the cathode where it is discharged as Cu(s).

4   The observed changes at the electrodes are as follows:
   • pinky brown colour of Cu deposited on cathode;
   • disintegration of Cu anode;
   • no change in the pH of the solution;
   • no change in the intensity of the blue colour of the solution as $Cu^{2+}$ ions are both formed and removed from the solution so their concentration remains constant.

An application of this is used in the purification of copper. The process uses electrolysis of a solution containing $Cu^{2+}(aq)$ with an impure copper anode and a small pure copper cathode. As the cell runs, the anode erodes as copper is transferred to the cathode, which therefore increases in mass. Impurities collect as sludge in the bottom of the cell.

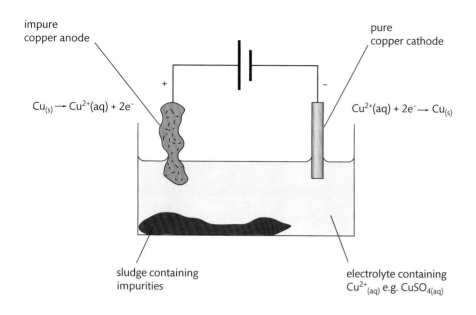

impure
copper anode

pure
copper cathode

$Cu_{(s)} \rightarrow Cu^{2+}(aq) + 2e^-$

$Cu^{2+}(aq) + 2e^- \rightarrow Cu_{(s)}$

+ −

sludge containing
impurities

electrolyte containing
$Cu^{2+}_{(aq)}$ e.g. $CuSO_{4(aq)}$

**Figure 9.17** The purification of copper using electrolysis. Reactions at the electrodes result in a net transfer of copper from the anode to the cathode.

A close-up photograph of the coil-shape electrodes used in electrolysis of aqueous tin(II) chloride, $SnCl_2$(aq). Deduce which electrode is which and write electrode reactions for the changes shown. What can you deduce about the electrode potential of $Sn^{2+}$?

## Exercises

**24** Deduce the products formed during the electrolysis of an aqueous solution of potassium fluoride. Write an equation for the reaction at the anode and explain your reasoning.

**25 (a)** Describe fully all the changes you would expect to see during the electrolysis of $CuCl_2$(aq) using carbon electrodes. Write equations to support your predicted observations.
  **(b)** How would your answer to (a) change if Cu electrodes were used instead?

**26** Write an equation for a reaction that occurs during the electrolysis of NaCl(aq) that does not occur during the electrolysis of NaCl(l).

## Factors affecting the amount of product in electrolysis

Michael Faraday, who, as noted earlier, coined the terminology used in much of this work, also showed that the amounts of products at the electrodes depend on the quantity of electric charge passed through the cell.

Historical artwork of Michael Faraday's experiments on electrolysis in 1833. By passing electricity through molten tin chloride he was able to show that the amounts of tin produced at the cathode and chlorine gas produced at the anode were proportional to the amount of electricity.

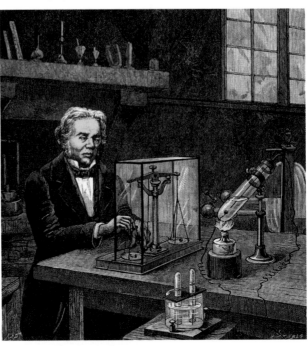

We can quantify electric charge as follows:

- charge = current × time

  So: Charge, $Q$ measured in coulomb (C), depends on the current, $I$ measured in amperes (A) and the time, $t$ measured in seconds (s).

- The charge carried by one mole of electrons, known as a Faraday ($F$) introduced on page 432, is 96 500 C.

We can now relate laboratory measurements to the amounts of product as follows.

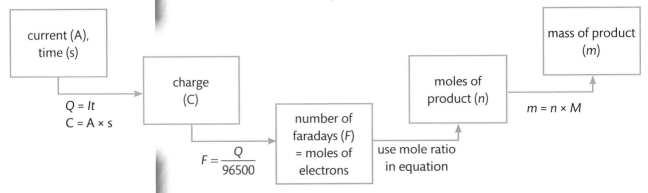

current (A), time (s)

$Q = It$
$C = A \times s$

charge (C)

$F = \dfrac{Q}{96500}$

number of faradays ($F$) = moles of electrons

use mole ratio in equation

moles of product ($n$)

$m = n \times M$

mass of product ($m$)

### Worked example

(a) How many grams of copper are deposited on the cathode of an electrolytic cell containing $CuCl_2$(aq) if a current of 2.00 A is run for 15.0 minutes?

(b) How would the amount differ if the same conditions were applied using CuCl(aq) instead?

## Solution

(a) We first calculate the charge then the moles of electrons:

$$\text{charge} = \text{current} \times \text{time}$$
$$= 2.00 \text{ A} \times (15.0 \times 60 \text{ s})$$
$$= 1800 \text{ C}$$

$$F = \frac{1800 \text{ C}}{96500 \text{ C mol}^{-1}} = 0.01865 \text{ mol of e}^-$$

Then use the mole ratio in the electrode half-equation to determine the moles of product:

$$Cu^{2+}(aq) + 2e^- \rightarrow Cu(s)$$

$\Rightarrow$ 2 mol e$^-$ : 1 mol Cu

$$\therefore 0.01865 \text{ mol e}^- \rightarrow \frac{0.01865 \text{ mol e}^-}{2 \text{ mol e}^-} \times 1 \text{ mol Cu} = 0.00933 \text{ mol Cu}$$

$$m = n \times M$$
$$= 0.00933 \text{ mol} \times 63.55 \text{ g mol}^{-1}$$
$$= 0.593 \text{ g Cu}$$

(b) The equation for discharge from CuCl(aq) is

$$Cu^+(aq) + e^- \rightarrow Cu(s)$$

$\Rightarrow$ 1 mol e$^-$ : 1 mol Cu

$\therefore$ 0.01865 mol e$^- \rightarrow$ 0.01865 mol Cu

$$m = n \times M$$

$\therefore$ 0.01865 mol e$^- \times$ 63.55 g mol$^{-1}$ = 1.19 g Cu

We see that the same quantity of electric charge produces twice as much copper from Cu$^+$ as from Cu$^{2+}$. This shows that the charge on the ion also influences the amount of product and enables us to determine relative amounts. For example, in the electrolysis of NaCl(l) and PbBr$_2$(l) discussed earlier we can deduce:

NaCl(l) electrolyte

at cathode:     Na$^+$(l)   +   e$^-$   $\rightarrow$   Na(l)

                1 mole of    1 mole
                electrons    of Na

PbBr$_2$(l) electrolyte

at cathode:     Pb$^{2+}$(l)   +   2e$^-$   $\rightarrow$   Pb(s)

                2 moles of    1 mole
                electrons    of Pb

So to produce 1 mole of Pb requires twice the quantity of electricity required to produce 1 mole of Na.

**The amount of product formed in electrolysis is determined by the current, duration, and the charge on the ion.**

## Worked example

If a current of 2.00 A is passed through a solution of $AgNO_3$ for 10 minutes it is found that 0.0124 moles of Ag are formed.

(a) How much would form if a current of 1.00 A is passed through the same solution for 30 minutes?

(b) What amount of Cu would form if the quantity of electricity in (a) was passed through a solution of $CuSO_4$?

### Solution

(a) charge = current × time

$$\text{amount of product} = 0.0124 \text{ mol} \times \frac{1.00 \text{ A}}{2.00 \text{ A}} \times \frac{30 \text{ min}}{10 \text{ min}} = 0.0186 \text{ mol Ag}$$

(b) $Ag^+(aq) + e^- \rightarrow Ag(s)$
$Cu^{2+}(aq) + 2e^- \rightarrow Cu(s)$

So the same quantity of electricity will produce 2 Ag : 1 Cu

$$\text{therefore yield Cu} = \frac{0.0186 \text{ mol}}{2} = 0.0093 \text{ mol Cu}$$

In summary, we can conclude that the amount of products formed in electrolysis are determined by:

1 the current;
2 the duration of the electrolysis;
3 the charge on the ion.

## Electroplating: a widely used application of electrolysis

During the electrolysis of $CuSO_4(aq)$, we saw that Cu(s) is deposited on the cathode when either graphite or copper electrodes are used. This is one example of **electroplating**, the process of using electrolysis to deposit a layer of a metal on top of another metal or other conductive object. An electrolytic cell used for electroplating has the following features:

• an electrolyte containing the metal ions which are to be deposited;
• the cathode made of the object to be plated;
• sometimes the anode is made of the same metal which is to be coated because it may be oxidized to replenish the supply of ions in the electrolyte.

Techniques for electroplating plastics have developed over the last 50 years or so, and P–O–P (plated on plastic) components are now commonplace. These products have the appearance of a high quality metal with the advantage of significant weight reduction. This is particularly important in the automobile industry, and used for example in chromium-plated car trim. But as plastics are not conductors, they must first be treated in an aggressive chromic/sulfuric acid bath to make small pits on their surface. They are then placed in a palladium chloride bath to deposit metal particles in the pits, after which the plastics can be electroplated with chromium or other metals.

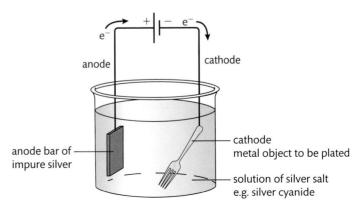

**Figure 9.18** Apparatus for electroplating silver.

Reduction of the metal ions at the cathode leads to their deposition on its surface. The process can be controlled by altering the current and the time according to how thick a layer of metal is desired.

Electroplating serves many different purposes, some of which are outlined here.

- Decorative purposes. For example, covering a metal with a layer of a more expensive or decorative metal, such as silver- and nickel-plating of cutlery.
- Corrosion control. For example, iron with a layer of zinc deposited on its surface, known as **galvanized iron**, is protected from corrosion as the zinc will be preferentially oxidized. This is sometimes called **sacrificial protection**.
- Improvement of function. For example electroplating with chromium improves the wear on steel parts such as crankshafts and hand tools.

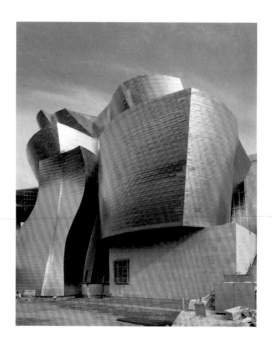

Metal-coated beetles. The metal has been added by electroplating.

Anodizing is an electrolytic process in which a metal anode is oxidized to deposit a metal oxide coat on the surface of the metal. This surface coat protects the underlying metal from corrosion. It is commonly applied to aluminium and chromium, and enables these metals to be used much more extensively than would be possible with the uncoated metal. For example, anodized aluminium is commonly used in cooking utensils and does not react even when heated despite its relatively high position in the reactivity series.

## Summary of voltaic and electrolytic cells

We have seen that voltaic and electrolytic cells are the reverse of each other. A voltaic cell converts chemical energy to electrical energy when a reaction with a positive value for $E$ proceeds towards equilibrium; an electrolytic cell converts electrical energy to chemical energy when an electric current drives a reaction with a negative value for $E$ away from equilibrium. These relationships, together with the free-energy change $\Delta G$, for the different cells are summarized below.

The Guggenheim museum, Bilbao, Spain, which opened in 1997, is sheathed in panels of titanium. Although the metal is very resistant to corrosion, when it is anodized using electrolysis, the layer of titanium oxide deposited on its surface changes its optical properties, causing it to have different colours in different lights.

| Type of cell | $E_{cell}$ | $\Delta G$ | Type of reaction |
|---|---|---|---|
| voltaic | > 0 | < 0 | spontaneous |
| electrolytic | < 0 | > 0 | non-spontaneous |
| equilibrium | 0 | 0 | dead battery |

## Exercises

**27** If a quantity of electricity is passed through a molten sample of aluminium chloride, it is found that 0.2 moles of chlorine are formed. What is the mass of aluminium formed at the other electrode?

**28** Which of the following will cause the largest amount of copper to be deposited during electrolysis?

   **A**  $Cu(I)Cl(aq)$, 5.00 A, 10 min         **C**  $Cu(I)Cl(aq)$, 2.00 A, 30 min
   **B**  $Cu(II)Cl_2$, 5.00 A, 10 min         **D**  $Cu(II)Cl_2$, 2.00 A, 30 min

**29** A metal spoon is plated with silver using an aqueous solution of $AgNO_3$ and an impure silver anode. Predict how the masses of the two electrodes will change with time and what other changes might be visible.

## Practice questions

**1** Four electrolytic cells are constructed. Which cell would produce the greatest mass of metal at the negative electrode (cathode)?

| | Electrolyte | Current / A | Time / s |
|---|---|---|---|
| **A** | 1.0 mol dm$^{-3}$ CuSO$_4$(aq) | 1.0 | 500 |
| **B** | 1.0 mol dm$^{-3}$ AgNO$_3$(aq) | 2.0 | 250 |
| **C** | 1.0 mol dm$^{-3}$ CuSO$_4$(aq) | 1.0 | 750 |
| **D** | 1.0 mol dm$^{-3}$ AgNO$_3$(aq) | 1.5 | 250 |

**2** Which species could be reduced to form $NO_2$?

   **A**  $N_2O$         **B**  $NO_3^-$         **C**  $HNO_2$         **D**  $NO$

**3** The standard electrode potentials for two metals are given below.

$Al^{3+}(aq) + 3e^- \rightleftharpoons Al(s)$                        $E^{\ominus} = -1.66$ V
$Ni^{2+}(aq) + 2e^- \rightleftharpoons Ni(s)$                        $E^{\ominus} = -0.23$ V

What is the equation and cell potential for the spontaneous reaction that occurs?

   **A**  $2Al^{3+}(aq) + 3Ni(s) \rightarrow 2Al(s) + 3Ni^{2+}(aq)$         $E^{\ominus} = +1.89$ V
   **B**  $2Al(s) + 3Ni^{2+}(aq) \rightarrow 2Al^{3+}(aq) + 3Ni(s)$         $E^{\ominus} = +1.89$ V
   **C**  $2Al^{3+}(aq) + 3Ni(s) \rightarrow 2Al(s) + 3Ni^{2+}(aq)$         $E^{\ominus} = +1.43$ V
   **D**  $2Al(s) + 3Ni^{2+}(aq) \rightarrow 2Al^{3+}(aq) + 3Ni(s)$         $E^{\ominus} = +1.43$ V

**4** For the electrolysis of aqueous copper(II) sulfate, which of the following statements is correct?

   **A**  Cu and $O_2$ are produced in a mol ratio of $1:1$
   **B**  $H_2$ and $O_2$ are produced in a mol ratio of $1:1$
   **C**  Cu and $O_2$ are produced in a mol ratio of $2:1$
   **D**  $H_2$ and $O_2$ are produced in a mol ratio of $2:1$

**5** Consider the following reaction.

$$MnO_4^-(aq) + 8H^+(aq) + 5Fe^{2+}(aq) \rightarrow Mn^{2+}(aq) + 5Fe^{3+}(aq) + 4H_2O(l)$$

Which statement is correct?

   **A**  $MnO_4^-$ is the oxidizing agent and it loses electrons.
   **B**  $MnO_4^-$ is the reducing agent and it loses electrons.
   **C**  $MnO_4^-$ is the oxidizing agent and it gains electrons.
   **D**  $MnO_4^-$ is the reducing agent and it gains electrons.

**6** What condition is necessary for the electroplating of silver, Ag, onto a steel spoon?

**A** The spoon must be the positive electrode.

**B** The silver electrode must be the negative electrode.

**C** The spoon must be the negative electrode.

**D** The electrolyte must be acidified.

**7** What is the reducing agent in the reaction below?

$$2MnO_4^-(aq) + Br^-(aq) + H_2O(l) \rightarrow 2MnO_2(s) + BrO_3^-(aq) + 2OH^-(aq)$$

**A** $Br^-$      **B** $BrO_3^-$      **C** $MnO_4^-$      **D** $MnO_2$

**8** Which changes could take place at the positive electrode (cathode) in the voltaic cell?

I    $Zn^{2+}(aq)$ to $Zn(s)$

II   $Cl_2(g)$ to $Cl^-(aq)$

III $Mg(s)$ to $Mg^{2+}(aq)$

**A** I and II only      **B** I and III only      **C** II and III only      **D** I, II, and III

**9** How do the products compare at each electrode when aqueous 1 mol dm$^{-3}$ magnesium bromide and molten magnesium bromide are electrolysed?

$$E^\ominus \text{ / V}$$

$Mg^{2+}(aq) + 2e^- \rightleftharpoons Mg(s)$      $-2.37$

$\frac{1}{2}Br_2(l) + e^- \rightleftharpoons Br^-(aq)$      $+1.07$

$\frac{1}{2}O_2(g) + 2H^+(aq) + 2e^- \rightleftharpoons H_2O(l)$      $+1.23$

| | Positive electrode (anode) | Negative electrode (cathode) |
|---|---|---|
| **A** | same | same |
| **B** | same | different |
| **C** | different | same |
| **D** | different | different |

**10** What happens at the negative electrode in a voltaic cell and in an electrolytic cell?

| | Voltaic cell | Electrolytic cell |
|---|---|---|
| **A** | oxidation | reduction |
| **B** | reduction | oxidation |
| **C** | oxidation | oxidation |
| **D** | reduction | reduction |

**11** What is the cell potential, in V, for the reaction that occurs when the following two half-cells are connected?

$$E^\ominus \text{ / V}$$

$Fe^{2+}(aq) + 2e^- \rightleftharpoons Fe(s)$      $-0.44$

$Cr_2O_7^{2-}(aq) + 14H^+(aq) + 6e^- \rightleftharpoons 2Cr^{3+}(aq) + 7H_2O(l)$      $+1.33$

**A** $+0.01$      **B** $+0.89$      **C** $+1.77$      **D** $+2.65$

**12 (a)** An electrochemical cell is made from an iron half-cell connected to a cobalt half-cell:
The standard electrode potential for $Fe^{2+}(aq) + 2e^- \rightleftharpoons Fe(s)$ is −0.45 V. The total cell potential obtained when the cell is operating under standard conditions is 0.17 V. Cobalt is produced during the spontaneous reaction.

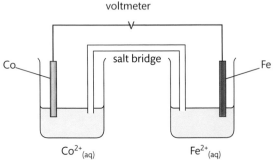

voltmeter
V
salt bridge
Co
Fe
$Co^{2+}{}_{(aq)}$
$Fe^{2+}{}_{(aq)}$

**(i)** Define the term *standard electrode potential* and state the meaning of the minus sign in the value of −0.45 V. (3)

**(ii)** Calculate the value for the standard electrode potential for the cobalt half-cell. (1)

**(iii)** Deduce which species acts as the oxidizing agent when the cell is operating. (1)

**(iv)** Deduce the equation for the spontaneous reaction taking place when the iron half-cell is connected instead to an aluminium half-cell. (2)

**(v)** Explain the function of the salt bridge in the electrochemical cell. (2)

**(b)** Deduce the oxidation number of cobalt in the following species.

**(i)** $[Co(H_2O)_6]^{2+}$ (1)

**(ii)** $Co_2(SO_4)_3$ (1)

**(iii)** $[CoCl_4]^{2-}$ (1)

**(c)** An electrolytic cell is made using a very dilute solution of sodium chloride.

**(i)** Draw a labelled diagram of the cell. Use an arrow to show the direction of the electron flow and identify the positive and negative electrodes. (3)

**(ii)** Give all the formulas of all the ions present in the solution. (2)

**(iii)** Predict the products obtained at each electrode and state the half-equation for the formation of each product. (3)

**(iv)** Deduce the molar ratios of the products obtained at the two electrodes. (1)

**(d)** Predict the products by giving the relevant half-equation for the reaction occurring at each electrode if the electrolyte of the cell described in part (c) was changed to:

**(i)** concentrated sodium chloride (2)

**(ii)** molten sodium bromide (2)

*(Total 25 marks)*

**13 (a)** Outline two differences between an electrolytic cell and a voltaic cell. (2)

**(b)** Explain why solid sodium chloride does not conduct electricity but molten sodium chloride does. (2)

**(c)** Molten sodium chloride undergoes electrolysis in an electrolytic cell. For each electrode deduce the half-equation and state whether oxidation or reduction takes place. Deduce the equation of the overall cell reaction including state symbols. (5)

**(d)** Electrolysis has made it possible to obtain reactive metals such as aluminium from their ores, which has resulted in significant developments in engineering and technology. State one reason why aluminium is preferred to iron in many uses. (1)

**(e)** Electroplating is an important application of electrolysis. State the composition of the electrodes and the electrolyte used in the silver electroplating process. (3)

*(Total 13 marks)*

**14** Consider the following half-cell reactions and their standard electrode potentials.

$$E^\ominus \,/\, V$$

$$Ni^{2+}(aq) + 2e^- \rightleftharpoons Ni(s) \qquad -0.26$$
$$Al^{3+}(aq) + 3e^- \rightleftharpoons Al(s) \qquad -1.66$$

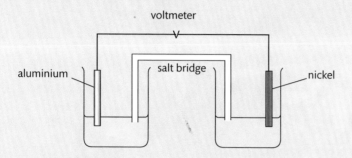

**(a)** Deduce a balanced equation for the overall reaction which will occur spontaneously when these two half-cells are connected. (2)

**(b)** Determine the cell potential when the two half-cells are connected. (1)

**(c)** On the cell diagram below, label the negative electrode (anode), the positive electrode (cathode), and the directions of the movement of electrons and ion flow. (4)

*(Total 7 marks)*

To access weblinks on the topics covered in this chapter, please go to www.pearsonhotlinks.com and enter the ISBN or title of this book.

# 10

# Organic chemistry

## Essential ideas

**10.1** Organic chemistry focuses on the chemistry of compounds containing carbon.

**10.2** Structure, bonding and chemical reactions involving functional group interconversions are key strands in organic chemistry.

**20.1** Key organic reaction types include nucleophilic substitution, electrophilic addition, electrophilic substitution, and redox reactions. Reaction mechanisms vary and help in understanding the different types of reaction taking place.

**20.2** Organic synthesis is the systematic preparation of a compound from a widely available starting material or the synthesis of a compound via a synthetic route that often can involve a series of different steps.

**20.3** Stereoisomerism involves isomers which have different arrangements of atoms in space but do not differ in connectivity or bond multiplicity (i.e. whether single, double, or triple) between the isomers themselves.

The skier's clothing and equipment such as backpack and goggles, are made almost entirely of organic compounds which have been artificially synthesized. Organic chemists use knowledge of the functional groups in molecules to design compounds with the required properties such as weatherproofing, breathability, strength, flexibility, and insulation.

Organic chemistry is one of the major branches of chemistry. It includes the study of:

- all biological molecules – from simple sugars to complex nucleic acids
- all fossil fuels – including oil, coal, and natural gas
- nearly all synthetic materials – such as nylon, Lycra®, and Gore-Tex®
- many domestic and industrial products – such as paints, detergents, and refrigerants.

So what defines an organic compound? Simply, it is a compound that contains carbon and, in nearly all cases, also contains hydrogen in a covalently bonded structure. Other elements such as oxygen, nitrogen, chlorine, and sulfur are often also present, but it is carbon that is the key. Amazingly, this single element is able to form a larger number of compounds than all the other elements put together. This is because carbon forms four strong covalent bonds with other carbon atoms or with other elements, especially hydrogen. Carbon's ability to link to itself to form chains and rings, known as **catenation**, is one of the main reasons for the vast number of organic compounds that exist.

In this chapter, we will start with a study of the classification of organic compounds and learn how each compound can be described specifically by name and formula. The presence of specific **functional groups** in organic molecules brings order to the almost overwhelming diversity of structures, and enables organic chemists to predict and explain characteristic reactions and mechanisms. Examples of reactions and synthetic pathways discussed here give insights into the applications of organic chemistry in medicine, agriculture, and the food and petro-chemicals industries, which are developed further in the chapters on the Option topics.

False-colour scanning electron micrograph (SEM) of a Velcro® hook. Velcro® is a nylon material manufactured in two separate pieces – one with a hooked surface and the other with a smooth surface made up of loops. When the two surfaces are brought together they form a strong bond, allowing for quick closure on clothing, etc. Velcro® is an example of a product of research and development in organic chemistry.

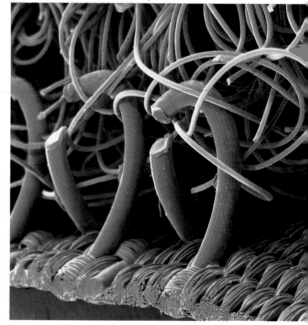

# 10 Organic chemistry

## Definitions and conventions used in organic chemistry

The study of organic chemistry involves recognizing several different types of reactant and reaction. You should find the following summary a useful reference as you work through the chapter.

### Types of reactant

| Saturated | Unsaturated |
| --- | --- |
| • compounds which contain only single bonds <br> • for example: alkanes | • compounds which contain double or triple bonds <br> • for example: alkenes, arenes |

| Aliphatics | Arenes |
| --- | --- |
| • compounds which do not contain a benzene ring; may be saturated or unsaturated <br> • for example: alkanes, alkenes | • compounds which contain a benzene ring; they are all unsaturated compounds <br> • for example: benzene, phenol |

| Electrophile (electron-seeking) | Nucleophile (nucleus-seeking) |
| --- | --- |
| • an electron-deficient species which is therefore attracted to parts of molecules which are electron rich <br> • electrophiles are positive ions or have a partial positive charge <br> • for example: $NO_2^+$, $H^+$, $Br^{\delta+}$ | • an electron-rich species which is therefore attracted to parts of molecules which are electron deficient <br> • nucleophiles have a lone pair of electrons and may also have a negative charge <br> • for example: $Cl^-$, $OH^-$, $NH_3$ |

### Types of reaction

| Addition | • occurs when two reactants combine to form a single product <br> • characteristic of unsaturated compounds <br> • for example <br><br> $$C_2H_4 + Br_2 \rightarrow C_2H_4Br_2$$ |
| --- | --- |
| Substitution | • occurs when one atom or group of atoms in a compound is replaced by a different atom or group <br> • characteristic of saturated compounds and aromatic compounds <br> • for example <br><br> $$CH_4 + Cl_2 \rightarrow CH_3Cl + HCl$$ |

| **Addition–elimination** | <ul><li>occurs when two reactants join together (addition) and in the process a small molecule such as $H_2O$, HCl, or $NH_3$ is lost (elimination)</li><li>reaction occurs between a functional group in each reactant</li><li>also called **condensation** reaction</li><li>for example</li></ul> |
|---|---|

$$ROH + R'COOH \rightarrow R'COOR + H_2O$$

R — OH + (O=)C—R' (with HO below C) → R—O—C(=O)—R' + **H₂O**

alcohol  acid    ester

## Types of bond breaking (bond fission)

| **Homolytic fission** | **Heterolytic fission** |
|---|---|
| <ul><li>is when a covalent bond breaks by splitting the shared pair of electrons between the two products</li><li>produces two free radicals, each with an unpaired electron</li></ul> $$X\!:\!X \rightarrow X^{\bullet} + X^{\bullet}$$ | <ul><li>is when a covalent bond breaks with both the shared electrons going to one of the products</li><li>produces two oppositely charged ions</li></ul> $$X\!:\!X \rightarrow X\!:^{-} + X^{+}$$ |

## Convention for depicting organic reaction mechanisms

Describing organic reaction mechanisms often involves showing the movement of electrons within bonds and between reactants. The convention adopted for this is a **curly arrow**, drawn from the site of electron availability, such as a pair of non-bonding electrons, to the site of electron deficiency, such as an atom with a partial positive charge.

For example:

| X⌒Y | represents the electron pair being pulled towards Y so Y becomes $\delta-$ and X becomes $\delta+$ |
|---|---|
| X: (arrow to) C $\delta+$ | the nucleophile X: is attracted to the electron-deficient C ($\delta+$) |

A 'normal' double-barbed arrow (⌒➤) represents the motion of an electron pair (as above). Often the mechanism involves several steps. The electrons are transferred ultimately to an atom or group of atoms that then detaches itself and is known as the **leaving group**. We will use blue throughout this chapter to show curly arrows and the pull of electrons.

Note that a single-barbed arrow (⌒➢), known as a **fish-hook**, represents the movement of a single electron. These single arrows are often used in reactions involving radicals.

# 10.1 Fundamentals of organic chemistry

## Understandings:

- A homologous series is a series of compounds of the same family, with the same general formula, which differ from each other by a common structural unit.
- Structural formulas can be represented in full and condensed format.
- Structural isomers are compounds with the same molecular formula but different arrangements of atoms.
- Functional groups are the reactive parts of molecules.
- Saturated compounds contain single bonds only and unsaturated compounds contain double or triple bonds.
- Benzene is an aromatic, unsaturated hydrocarbon.

### Guidance
*The general formulas (e.g. $C_nH_{2n+2}$) of alkanes, alkenes, alkynes, ketones, alcohols, aldehydes, and carboxylic acids should be known.*

## Applications and skills:

- Explanation of the trends in boiling points of members of a homologous series.
- Distinction between empirical, molecular, and structural formulas.
- Identification of different classes: alkenes, alkynes, halogenoalkanes, alcohols, ethers, aldehydes, ketones, esters, carboxylic acids, amines, amides, nitriles, and arenes.
- Identification of typical functional groups in molecules, e.g. phenyl, hydroxyl, carbonyl, carboxyl, carboxamide, aldehyde, ester, ether, amine, nitrile, alkyl, alkenyl, and alkynyl.
- Construction of 3D models (real or virtual) of organic molecules.
- Application of IUPAC rules in the nomenclature of straight-chain and branched-chain isomers.
- Identification of primary, secondary, and tertiary carbon atoms in halogenoalkanes and alcohols and primary, secondary, and tertiary nitrogen atoms in amines.
- Discussion of the structure of benzene using physical and chemical evidence.

### Guidance
- *Skeletal formulas should be discussed in the course.*
- *The distinction between class names and functional group names needs to be made, e.g. for OH, hydroxy is the functional group whereas alcohol is the class name.*
- *The following nomenclature should be covered:*
  - *non-cyclic alkanes and halogenoalkanes up to halohexanes*
  - *alkenes up to hexene and alkynes up to hexyne*
  - *compounds up to six carbon atoms (in the basic chain for nomenclature purposes) containing only one of the classes of functional groups: alcohols, ethers, aldehydes, halogenoalkanes, ketones, esters, and carboxylic acids.*

The total number of organic compounds that exists on Earth is so large that it is impossible to estimate with any accuracy. In any case, it is increasing all the time as new materials are synthesized. But we do know that there are at least ten million different organic molecules currently on the planet and every one of them is unique in its chemical structure and specific properties. Of course it is not possible or necessary to study the features of all of the compounds in this large branch of chemistry, but it is useful instead to introduce some system of classification.

## Homologous series

Organic compounds are classified into 'families' of compounds known as **homologous series**. The members of each such series possess certain common features, as described in the following text.

For a long time it was believed that organic molecules were unique to living things, and could not therefore be synthesized outside a living organism. However, in 1828, the German chemist Friedrich Wöhler synthesized urea from inorganic reactants, commenting in a letter to Berzelius: 'I must tell you that I can make urea without the use of kidneys, either man or dog. Ammonium cyanate is urea'. This discovery, which like many great scientific discoveries was actually made by accident, destroyed the former belief in 'vitalism', and opened the door to the exploration of organic synthesis reactions. The development of new organic compounds is responsible for many of the innovations in our world today.

## Successive members of a homologous series differ by a —CH₂— group

Consider the following compounds of carbon and hydrogen where the carbons are all bonded by single covalent bonds.

$CH_4$

$$H-\underset{\underset{H}{|}}{\overset{\overset{H}{|}}{C}}-H$$

methane

$C_2H_6$

$$H-\underset{\underset{H}{|}}{\overset{\overset{H}{|}}{C}}-\underset{\underset{H}{|}}{\overset{\overset{H}{|}}{C}}-H$$

ethane

$C_3H_8$

$$H-\underset{\underset{H}{|}}{\overset{\overset{H}{|}}{C}}-\underset{\underset{H}{|}}{\overset{\overset{H}{|}}{C}}-\underset{\underset{H}{|}}{\overset{\overset{H}{|}}{C}}-H$$

propane

$C_4H_{10}$

$$H-\underset{\underset{H}{|}}{\overset{\overset{H}{|}}{C}}-\underset{\underset{H}{|}}{\overset{\overset{H}{|}}{C}}-\underset{\underset{H}{|}}{\overset{\overset{H}{|}}{C}}-\underset{\underset{H}{|}}{\overset{\overset{H}{|}}{C}}-H$$

butane

These are members of a homologous series known as the **alkanes**. It can be seen that neighbouring members differ from each other by —CH₂—. This same increment applies to successive members of each homologous series, and means that the molecular mass increases by a fixed amount as we go up a series.

## Members of a homologous series can be represented by the same general formula

The four alkanes shown above can all be represented by the general formula $C_nH_{2n+2}$.

Other homologous series are characterized by the presence of a particular **functional group**, and this will be shown in the general formula for the series. For example, the homologous series known as the **alcohols** possess the functional group —OH as shown below.

$CH_3OH$

$$H-\underset{\underset{H}{|}}{\overset{\overset{H}{|}}{C}}-O-H$$

methanol

$C_2H_5OH$

$$H-\underset{\underset{H}{|}}{\overset{\overset{H}{|}}{C}}-\underset{\underset{H}{|}}{\overset{\overset{H}{|}}{C}}-O-H$$

ethanol

$C_3H_7OH$

$$H-\underset{\underset{H}{|}}{\overset{\overset{H}{|}}{C}}-\underset{\underset{H}{|}}{\overset{\overset{H}{|}}{C}}-\underset{\underset{H}{|}}{\overset{\overset{H}{|}}{C}}-O-H$$

propanol

$C_4H_9OH$

$$H-\underset{\underset{H}{|}}{\overset{\overset{H}{|}}{C}}-\underset{\underset{H}{|}}{\overset{\overset{H}{|}}{C}}-\underset{\underset{H}{|}}{\overset{\overset{H}{|}}{C}}-\underset{\underset{H}{|}}{\overset{\overset{H}{|}}{C}}-O-H$$

butanol

These compounds can be represented by the general formula $C_nH_{2n+1}OH$.

The functional group is usually a small group of atoms attached to a carbon atom in a molecule, and it gives the characteristic properties to the compound.

## Members of a homologous series show a gradation in physical properties

As successive members of a homologous series differ by a —CH₂— group, they have successively longer carbon chains. This is reflected in a gradual trend in the physical properties of the members of the series. For example, the effect of the length of the carbon chain on the boiling point of the alkanes is shown in the table on page 466.

The word 'organic' is now used in several different contexts beyond the chemistry of carbon compounds. Examples include organic food, organic growth, and organic degeneration. To what extent does this common vocabulary represent a common origin in meaning? Does it confuse or enhance communication?

The trend in boiling points of the alkanes is of great significance in the oil industry, as it makes it possible to separate the many components of crude oil into **fractions** that contain molecules of similar molecular mass on the basis of their boiling points. As the crude oil is heated, the smaller hydrocarbons boil off first while larger molecules distil at progressively higher temperatures in the fractionating column. The different fractions are used as fuels, industrial lubricants, and as starting molecules in the manufacture of synthetic compounds.

| Alkane | | Boiling point / °C | |
|---|---|---|---|
| methane | $CH_4$ | −164 | gases at room temperature |
| ethane | $C_2H_6$ | −89 | |
| propane | $C_3H_8$ | −42 | |
| butane | $C_4H_{10}$ | −0.5 | |
| pentane | $C_5H_{12}$ | 36 | liquids at room temperature |
| hexane | $C_6H_{14}$ | 69 | |
| heptane | $C_7H_{16}$ | 98 | |
| octane | $C_8H_{18}$ | 125 | |

increasing boiling point

The data show that the boiling point increases with increasing carbon number. This is because of the increased instantaneous induced dipoles causing stronger London (dispersion) forces between the molecules as their molecular size increases. Note, though, that the increase is not linear, but steeper near the beginning as the influence of the increased chain length is proportionally greater for small molecules.

Other physical properties that show this predictable trend with increasing carbon number are density and viscosity.

Oil products. Containers of crude oil and various fractions obtained from it, on a background of a silhouetted oil refinery. The fractions are arranged here in order of increasing boiling point from left to right.

It is estimated that the top ten oil-producing countries of the world produce about two-thirds of the world's oil. This geo-political leverage of the major oil-exporting nations is an on-going challenge to countries that are dependent on imported oil.

### Members of a homologous series show similar chemical properties

As they have the same functional group, members of the same homologous series show similar chemical reactivity. For example:

- the alcohols have the —OH functional group, which can be oxidized to form organic acids
- the —COOH functional group, present in the homologous series of the **carboxylic acids**, is responsible for the acidic properties of these compounds.

It follows that if we know the characteristic reactions of a functional group, we will be able to predict the properties of all members of a series.

**The main features of a homologous series are as follows:**
- **Successive members of a homologous series differ by a —CH$_2$— group.**
- **Members of a homologous series can be represented by the same general formula.**
- **The members of a homologous series show a gradation in their physical properties.**
- **The members of a series have similar chemical properties.**

The study of organic chemistry is in some ways like the study of a language where rules have developed to enable communication to be clear and consistent. In order to describe an organic molecule in this way, there are two aspects to consider:

- the formula used to represent the molecule
- the specific name given to the molecule, known as its **nomenclature**.

We will discuss each of these in turn and learn the rules that will enable us to communicate effectively in this study.

**TOK** To what extent is chemistry a separate language? What are the main differences between the language of chemistry and your mother tongue?

## Formulas for organic compounds: empirical, molecular, and structural

The **empirical formula** of a compound is the simplest whole number ratio of the atoms it contains (see Chapter 1). For example, the empirical formula of ethane, $C_2H_6$, is $CH_3$. This formula can be derived from percentage composition data obtained from combustion analysis. It is, however, of rather limited use on its own, as it does not tell us the actual number of atoms in the molecule.

The **molecular formula** of a compound is the actual number of atoms of each element present in a molecule. For example, the molecular formula of ethane is $C_2H_6$. It is therefore a multiple of the empirical formula, and so can be deduced if we know both the empirical formula and the molar mass $M$. The relationship can be expressed as:

$$M = (\text{molar mass of empirical formula})_n$$

where $n$ is an integer.

So, for example, if we know that the empirical formula of ethane is $CH_3$, and its molar mass $M = 30 \text{ g mol}^{-1}$, using the formula above:

$$30 \text{ g mol}^{-1} = (\text{mass of } CH_3)_n \text{ so } 30 = (12 + (3 \times 1))_n, \text{ which gives } n = 2$$

Therefore the molecular formula of ethane is $(CH_3)_2$ or $C_2H_6$.

However, the molecular formula is also of quite limited value as the properties of a compound are determined not only by the atoms it contains, but also by how those atoms are arranged in relation to each other and in space.

The **structural formula** is a representation of the molecule showing how the atoms are bonded to each other. There are variations in the amount of detail this shows.

Be careful to mark all the hydrogen atoms with —H when drawing structural formulas. Leaving these out gives what is called a **skeletal structure** and is not acceptable as a structural formula.

- A **full structural formula** (graphic formula or displayed formula) shows every bond and atom. Usually 90° and 180° (and 120°) angles are used to show the bonds because this is the clearest representation on a two-dimensional page, although in most cases this is not the true geometry of the molecule.
- A **condensed structural formula** often omits bonds where they can be assumed, and groups atoms together. It contains the minimum information needed to describe the molecule non-ambiguously – in other words there is only one possible structure that could be described by this formula.
- A **stereochemical formula** attempts to show the relative positions of atoms and groups around carbon in three dimensions. The convention is that a bond sticking forwards from the page is shown as a solid, enlarging wedge, whereas a bond sticking behind the page is shown as a hashed line. A bond in the plane of the paper is a solid line. When carbon forms four single bonds, the arrangement is tetrahedral with bond angles of 109.5°; when it forms a double bond, the arrangement is triangular planar with bonds at 120°.

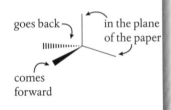

For example: methanol, $CH_3OH$ ethene, $C_2H_4$

The table below shows these different formulas applied to three compounds.

| Compound | Ethane | Ethanoic acid | Glucose |
|---|---|---|---|
| **Empirical formula** | $CH_3$ | $CH_2O$ | $CH_2O$ |
| **Molecular formula** | $C_2H_6$ | $C_2H_4O_2$ | $C_6H_{12}O_6$ |
| **Full structural formula** | | | |
| **Condensed structural formula** | $CH_3CH_3$ | $CH_3COOH$ | $CHO(HCOH)_4CH_2OH$ |

Sometimes we do not need to show the exact details of the hydrocarbon, or **alkyl**, part of the molecule, so we can abbreviate this to **R**. For molecules which contain a benzene ring, $C_6H_6$, known as **aromatic compounds**, we use ⬡ to show the ring.

## Nomenclature for organic compounds: the IUPAC system

For over a hundred years, chemists have recognized the need for a specific set of rules for the naming of organic compounds. IUPAC names are logically based on the chemistry of the compounds, and so give information about the functional groups present and the size of the molecules. Some guidelines for applying the IUPAC nomenclature are discussed below.

### Rule 1: Identify the longest straight chain of carbon atoms

The longest chain of carbon atoms gives the **stem** of the name as follows.

| Number of carbon atoms in longest chain | Stem in IUPAC name | Example of compound |
|---|---|---|
| 1 | meth- | $CH_4$, methane |
| 2 | eth- | $C_2H_6$, ethane |
| 3 | prop- | $C_3H_8$, propane |
| 4 | but- | $C_4H_{10}$, butane |
| 5 | pent- | $C_5H_{12}$, pentane |
| 6 | hex- | $C_6H_{14}$, hexane |

Note that 'straight chain' refers to continuous or unbranched chains of carbon atoms – it does not mean angles of 180°. Be careful when identifying the longest straight chain not to be confused by the way the molecule may appear on paper, because of the free rotation around carbon–carbon single bonds. For example, in Figure 10.1, all three structures are the same molecule pentane, $C_5H_{12}$, even though they may look different.

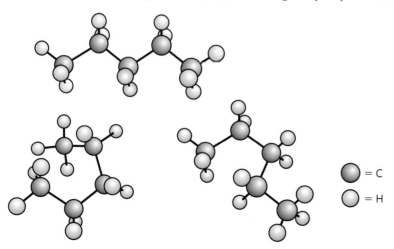

○ = C
○ = H

The international, non-governmental organization IUPAC (International Union of Pure and Applied Chemistry), first mentioned in Chapter 1, is best known for its system of nomenclature, now recognized as the world authority in this field. IUPAC terminology enables precise communication between scientists across international boundaries.

IUPAC nomenclature is seen commonly on labels of everyday substances such as foods, pharmaceuticals, toothpaste, and glue sticks.

**Figure 10.1** Different representations of the same molecule $C_5H_{12}$, pentane. These can all be interconverted by rotating the carbon–carbon bonds.

## Rule 2: Identify the functional group

The functional group usually determines the specific ending or **suffix** to the name, which replaces the '-ane' ending in the parent alk*ane*. The suffixes used for some common functional groups are shown in the table below. Note the distinction between *class*, which refers to the type of compound, and *functional group*, which refers to the site of reactivity in the molecule.

| Class | Functional group | Name of functional group | Suffix in IUPAC name | Example of compound | General formula |
|---|---|---|---|---|---|
| alkane | | | -ane | $C_2H_6$, ethane | $C_nH_{2n+2}$ |
| alkene | $\diagdown C = C \diagup$ | alkenyl | -ene | $H_2C = CH_2$, ethene | $C_nH_{2n}$ |
| alkyne | $-C \equiv C-$ | alkynyl | -yne | $HC \equiv CH$, ethyne | $C_nH_{2n-2}$ |
| alcohol | $-OH$ | hydroxyl | -anol | $C_2H_5OH$, ethanol | $C_nH_{2n+1}OH$ |
| ether | $R-O-R'$ | ether | -oxyalkane | $H_3C-O-C_2H_5$, methoxyethane | $R-O-R'$ |
| aldehyde | $-C \overset{O}{\underset{H}{\diagup}}$ | aldehyde (carbonyl) | -anal | $C_2H_5CHO$, propanal | $R-CHO$ |
| ketone | $\overset{R}{\underset{R'}{>}} C = O$ | carbonyl | -anone | $CH_3COCH_3$, propanone | $R-CO-R'$ |
| carboxylic acid | $-C \overset{O}{\underset{O-H}{\diagup}}$ | carboxyl | -anoic acid | $C_2H_5COOH$, propanoic acid | $C_nH_{2n+1}COOH$ |
| ester* | $-C \overset{O}{\underset{O-R}{\diagup}}$ | ester | -anoate | $C_2H_5COOCH_3$, methyl propanoate | $R-COO-R'$ |
| amide | $-C \overset{O}{\underset{N \diagdown H}{\diagdown}} H$ | carboxyamide | -anamide | $C_2H_5CONH_2$, propanamide | |
| amine | $-NH_2$ | amine | -anamine | $C_2H_5NH_2$, ethanamine | |
| nitrile | $-C \equiv N$ | nitrile | -anenitrile | $C_2H_5CN$, propanenitrile | |
| arene | $C_6H_5-$ | phenyl | -benzene | $C_6H_5CH_3$, methyl benzene | |

*Esters form when the alkyl group of an alcohol replaces the hydrogen of a carboxylic acid in a condensation reaction:

$$R-COOH + R'OH \rightarrow R-COO-R' + H_2O$$

They are named in a similar way to salts, which form when a metal has replaced the hydrogen of a carboxylic acid. Salts take the stem of the name from the parent acid. For example, $C_2H_5COONa$ is sodium propanoate. In esters, the alkyl group of the alcohol is the prefix, so $C_2H_5COOCH_3$ is methyl propanoate.

The position of a functional group is shown by a number between dashes inserted before the functional group ending. The number refers to the carbon atom to which the functional group is attached. The chain is numbered starting at the end that will give the smallest number to the group.

For example:

propan-2-ol

but-1-ene

here we number the carbon chain starting from the right-hand side so that the number of the group will be 1 and not 3

Sometimes a functional group can only be in one place, and in these cases we do not need to give a number to show its position.

For example:

butanoic acid

propanone

## Rule 3: Identify the side chains or substituent groups

Side chains, or functional groups in addition to the one used as the suffix, are known as **substituents** and are given as the first part or **prefix** of the name. Some common examples are shown in the table.

| Class | Functional group | Name of functional group | Prefix in IUPAC name | Example of compound |
| --- | --- | --- | --- | --- |
| alkane | | | methyl, ethyl, propyl, etc. | $CH_3CH(CH_3)C_2H_5$, 2-methylbutane $CH(C_2H_5)_3$, 3-ethylpentane $CH(C_3H_7)_3$, 4-propylheptane |
| halogenoalkane | —F, —Cl, —Br, —I | halogeno | fluoro, chloro, bromo, iodo | $C_2H_5Cl$, chloroethane $CH_3CH_2BrCH_3$, 2-bromopropane |
| amine | —$NH_2$ | amine | amino | $CH_2(NH_2)COOH$, 2-aminoethanoic acid |

You will notice that —$NH_2$ appears as both a possible suffix and a prefix. Usually when it is the only functional group it will take the suffix, but if there are two or more functional groups in the molecule it will be a prefix, as for example in *amino* acids.

As shown above, the position of the substituent groups is given by a number followed by a dash in front of its name showing the carbon atom to which it is attached, again numbering the chain to give the smallest number to the group.

For example:

H H H H
| | | |
H—C¹—C²—C—C—H
| | | |
H | H H
H—C—H
|
H

2-methylbutane

H H H H H
| | | | |
H—C—C—C—C²—C¹—H
| | | | |
H H H | H
H—C—H
|
H

2-methylpentane

If there is more than one substituent group of the same type, we use commas between the numbers and the prefixes di-, tri-, or tetra- before the name. Substituents are given in order of the number of the carbon atom to which they are attached; if there is more than one group on the same atom they are put in alphabetical order.

For example:

H H H
| | |
H—C—C—C—H
| | |
Cl Cl H

1,2-dichloropropane

H H H
| | |
H—C—C—C—H
| | |
Cl | H
H—C—H
|
H

1-chloro-2-methylpropane

H Br H
| | |
H—C—C—C—H
| | |
H Cl H

2-bromo-2-chloropropane

For example:

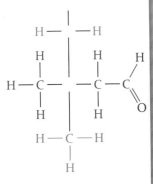

3,3-dimethylbutanal

## Summary

IUPAC nomenclature has three possible parts, which are usually written together as a single word.

**Prefix** ·········· **Stem** ·········· **Suffix**

position, number and name of substituents

number of carbon atoms in longest chain

class of compound determined by functional group

> There is an H in aldeHyde but not in ketone.

> When you are asked to name a compound from a condensed structural formula, it is a good idea to draw out the full structural formula first.

### Exercises

1  For each of the following molecules give its class and its IUPAC name:
   (a) $CH_3CH_2CH_2COOH$
   (b) $CHCl_2CH_2CH_3$
   (c) $CH_3CH_2COCH_3$
   (d) $CH_3COOCH_3$
   (e) $CH_3CH_2OCH_3$
   (f) $CH_3CH_2CH_2CH_2COOCH_2CH_3$

2  Give the structural formulas of the following molecules (condensed form is acceptable):
   (a) hexanoic acid
   (b) butanal
   (c) pent-1-ene
   (d) 1-bromo-2-methylbutane
   (e) ethyl methanoate
   (f) methoxypropane
   (g) but-2-yne

3  Which of the following is an amine?
   A  $CH_3CH_2NH_2$
   B  $CH_3CONH_2$
   C  $CH_3CH_2CN$
   D  $C_2H_5CONH(CH_3)$

4  Which compound is a member of the same homologous series as 1-bromopropane?
   A  1-iodopropane
   B  1,2-dibromopropane
   C  1-bromopropene
   D  1-bromopentane

Classification is an important aspect of many disciplines as it brings some order to large amounts of data, and helps in the recognition of patterns and trends. In organic chemistry it is particularly helpful, given the almost infinite number of compounds. The IUPAC nomenclature system described here is broadly accepted by scientists because it provides effective communication. Yet, in common with most systems of classification, there are limits to its usefulness. One of these is in biochemistry, where IUPAC nomenclature can result in seemingly complex and extended names for relatively simple molecules. For example, sucrose, $C_{12}H_{22}O_{11}$, becomes *(2R,3R,4S,5S,6R)-2-[(2S,3S,4S,5R)-3,4-dihydroxy-2,5-bis(hydroxymethyl)oxolan-2-yl] oxy-6-(hydroxymethyl)oxane-3,4,5-triol*. Although there is a place for such terminology, it is not widely used. Classification and nomenclature are artificial constructs, and when not helpful need not be used. In Chapters 13 and 15 we will commonly use non-IUPAC names for biological molecules for this reason.

## Structural isomers: different arrangements of the same atoms

The molecular formula of a compound shows the atoms that are present in the molecule, but gives no information on how they are arranged. Consider for example the formula $C_4H_{10}$. There are two possible arrangements for these atoms that correspond to different molecules with different properties.

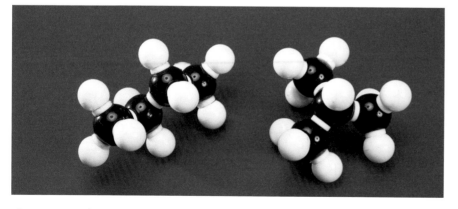

butane,
boiling point −0.5 °C

2-methylpropane,
boiling point −11.7 °C

Such molecules, having the same molecular formula but different arrangements of the atoms, are known as **structural isomers**.

Construction of 3D models and working with virtual models online is important experience that helps in gaining an understanding of the structural concepts described here. Full details with worksheets are available online.

**Structural isomers are molecules that have the same molecular formula but different arrangements of the atoms.**

Molecular models of the two isomers of $C_4H_{10}$. On the left is butane (sometimes called n-butane to denote a straight chain), and on the right is 2-methylpropane.

Each isomer is a distinct compound, having unique physical and chemical properties. As we will see, the number of isomers that exist for a molecular formula increases with the size of the molecule. This is one of the reasons for the vast number of compounds that can be formed from carbon.

Deducing the structural formulas and names for all possible isomers from a given molecular formula gives us a good opportunity to practise the earlier work on IUPAC nomenclature. We will apply this to isomers in the first six members of the alkanes, the alkenes, and the alkynes.

## Structural isomers in alkanes

- $C_4H_{10}$ has two isomers, as shown on page 473.
- $C_5H_{12}$ has the following isomers:

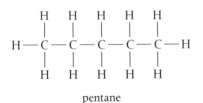

pentane

2-methylbutane

2,2-dimethylpropane

- $C_6H_{14}$ has the following five isomers

hexane

2-methylpentane

3-methylpentane

As we can see here the number of isomers that exist for a molecular formula increases as the molecular size increases. In fact the increase is exponential; there are 75 possible isomers of $C_{10}H_{22}$ and 366 319 of $C_{20}H_{42}$!

When drawing structural formulas, double check that you haven't drawn the same thing twice by drawing it the other way round.

2,2-dimethylbutane

2,3-dimethylbutane

Starting in 1923 a compound called tetraethyl lead – marketed as 'ethyl' from America – was added to petroleum in most parts of the world. It proved to be a very successful 'anti-knocking agent', allowing lower grades of fuel to be used in internal combustion engines without causing premature burning known as 'knocking'. Many decades and thousands of tonnes of lead emissions later, mounting concern about the effect of rising lead levels in the atmosphere led to the additive being banned in most countries from about 1986 onwards. Lead is a neurotoxin that is linked to many health effects, particularly brain damage. Since its phase-out from petroleum, blood levels of lead have fallen dramatically but still remain about 600 times higher than they were a century ago.

The person who researched and patented tetraethyl lead as a petroleum additive was the same person who later was responsible for the discovery and marketing of chlorofluorocarbons (CFCs) as refrigerants. Thomas Midgley of Ohio, USA, did not live to know the full extent that the long-term impact his findings would have on the Earth's atmosphere. He died in 1944, aged 55, from accidental strangulation after becoming entangled in ropes and pulleys he had devised to get himself in and out of bed following loss of use of his legs caused by polio. Perhaps his epitaph should have been 'The solution becomes the problem'.

## Structural isomers in alkenes

A different type of structural isomer occurs when the carbon–carbon double bond is found in different positions.

• $C_4H_8$ has the following straight-chain isomers:

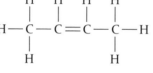

but-1-ene                           but-2-ene

Note that the molecules are named using the smallest numbered carbon that is part of the double bond.

• $C_5H_{10}$ has the following two straight-chain isomers.

pent-1-ene                          pent-2-ene

• $C_6H_{12}$ has the following three straight-chain isomers.

hex-1-ene                 hex-2-ene                 hex-3-ene

Similarly, the structures and names of the isomers of the alkynes can be deduced from considering different possible positions for the triple bond.

The existence of these different straight-chain and branched-chain isomers of the alkanes is of great significance in the petroleum industry. It has been found that branched-chain isomers generally burn more smoothly in internal combustion engines than straight-chain isomers, and so oil fractions with a higher proportion of these branched-chain isomers are considered to be of 'better grade'. This is often referred to as a higher 'octane number' and means that it fetches a higher price at the pump.

A good exercise when practising this work is to give the names that you give to isomers to one of your classmates, and see if they can correctly draw the structures. There should be only one possible structure for each name.

There are many different types of isomers, including those in which the molecules have different functional groups and so are members of different classes of compounds with very different reactivities. For example, the molecular formula $C_2H_6O$ describes both an alcohol and an ether.

Methoxymethane and ethanol are functional group isomers, both with the molecular formula $C_2H_6O$. Ethanol is widely used in alcoholic drinks while methoxymethane is a gas used in aerosol propellants.

Isomers are of great significance in biochemistry and the drugs industry, as discussed in more detail in Chapters 13 and 15. Later in this chapter, in section 20.3 page 514, we will study a type of isomerism known as stereoisomerism, where the molecules have the same structural formula but different spatial arrangements.

## Primary, secondary, and tertiary compounds

The activity of a functional group is often influenced by its position in the carbon chain, identified as follows.

A **primary carbon atom** is attached to the functional group and also to at least two hydrogen atoms. Molecules with this arrangement are known as primary molecules.

For example, ethanol, $C_2H_5OH$, is a primary alcohol and chloroethane, $C_2H_5Cl$, is a primary halogenoalkane.

A **secondary carbon atom** is attached to the functional group and also to one hydrogen atom and two alkyl groups. These molecules are known as secondary molecules. For example, propan-2-ol, $CH_3CH(OH)CH_3$, is a secondary alcohol, and 2-chloroethane, $CH_3CHClCH_3$, is a secondary halogenoalkane.

Butan-2-ol, a secondary alcohol. Carbon atoms are black, hydrogen atoms are white, and oxygen atoms are red. Note there is only one hydrogen atom on the carbon attached to the —OH group.

A **tertiary carbon atom** is attached to the functional group and is also bonded to three alkyl groups and so has no hydrogen atoms. These molecules are known as tertiary molecules. For example, 2-methylpropan-2-ol, $C(CH_3)_3OH$, is a tertiary alcohol, and 2-chloro-2-methylpropane, $C(CH_3)_3Cl$, is a tertiary halogenoalkane.

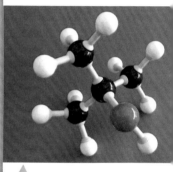

2-Methylpropan-2-ol, a tertiary alcohol. Carbon atoms are black, hydrogen atoms are white, and oxygen atoms are red. Note there are no hydrogen atoms on the carbon attached to the —OH group.

In amines, a similar classification can be applied according to the number of alkyl groups and hydrogen atoms bonded to the nitrogen atom.

## CHALLENGE YOURSELF

1  What is the hybridization of each carbon atom and each nitrogen atom in the tertiary amine drawn here?

## Arenes

**Arenes** are a class of compounds that are derived from **benzene**, $C_6H_6$. They form a special branch of organic compounds known as the **aromatics**, which have properties somewhat distinct from other organic compounds, which are known as **aliphatics**. Arenes contain the phenyl functional group:

$C_6H_5-$

The key to understanding the properties of arenes comes from a study of the parent arene molecule – benzene itself.

 Amines and amides, including the substituted derivatives, are widely found in many medicinal compounds. The hormone adrenaline, well known as the 'emergency' hormone as well as a transmitter in the nervous system, is a secondary amine.

Non-polar liquids like benzene can be separated from aqueous solutions using a separating funnel because they form a separate layer and the lower liquid can be drained. Here, the lower aqueous layer has been coloured purple to make the separation more visible.

## Benzene does not behave like other unsaturated molecules

The 1 : 1 ratio of carbon to hydrogen in benzene, $C_6H_6$, indicates a high degree of unsaturation, greater than that of alkenes or alkynes. Yet early observations on benzene indicated that it does not show the characteristic properties of possible structures such as:

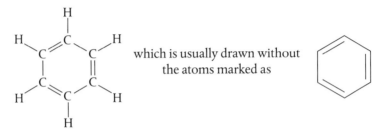

For example, benzene has no isomers, and is reluctant to undergo addition reactions – both features that would be expected from these molecules.

In 1865 Kekulé suggested a cyclic arrangement of the carbon atoms with alternating single and double bonds. This is 1,3,5-cyclohexatriene:

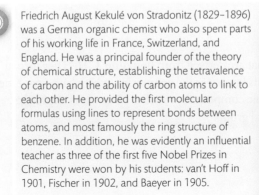

which is usually drawn without the atoms marked as

The symmetry of this model explained some of the known properties of benzene, such as the fact that it has no isomers, but again fell short of explaining benzene's atypical reactivity for such an unsaturated molecule. Clearly, modifications to the Kekulé structure were needed. Advances in technology, such as X-ray diffraction, provided data that helped to develop the current model of benzene structure.

Benzene is an important industrial solvent and is used in the synthesis of drugs, dyes, and plastics such as polystyrene. Because of its frequent use, benzene has become widespread in the environment of developed countries. In the USA, petroleum contains up to 2% benzene by volume and it may be as high as 5% in other countries. But benzene is a toxic compound and a known carcinogen. Chronic exposure at low levels can lead to aplastic anaemia and leukaemia. Regulating bodies in many countries have set permissible exposure limits for benzene levels in drinking water, foods, and air in the workplace.

Friedrich August Kekulé von Stradonitz (1829–1896) was a German organic chemist who also spent parts of his working life in France, Switzerland, and England. He was a principal founder of the theory of chemical structure, establishing the tetravalence of carbon and the ability of carbon atoms to link to each other. He provided the first molecular formulas using lines to represent bonds between atoms, and most famously the ring structure of benzene. In addition, he was evidently an influential teacher as three of the first five Nobel Prizes in Chemistry were won by his students: van't Hoff in 1901, Fischer in 1902, and Baeyer in 1905.

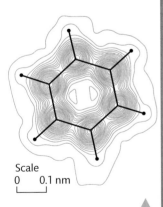

Scale
0    0.1 nm

**Figure 10.2** Electron density map for benzene at –3° C. The blue lines join parts of the molecule with equal electron density, showing that all bonds between carbon atoms are equal and of length 0.139 nm.

# The special stability of the benzene ring is the result of delocalized electrons

Benzene is a cyclic structure, in which a framework of single bonds attaches each carbon to the one on either side and to a hydrogen atom. Each of the six carbon atoms is $sp^2$ hybridized, and forms three sigma $\sigma$ bonds with angles of 120°, making a planar shape.

This leaves one unhybridized p electron on each carbon atom with its dumb-bell shape perpendicular to the plane of the ring. But instead of pairing up to form discrete alternating $\pi$ bonds, the p orbitals effectively overlap in both directions, spreading themselves out evenly to be shared by all six carbon atoms. This forms a **delocalized $\pi$ electron cloud** in which electron density is concentrated in two donut-shaped rings above and below the plane of the ring. This is a very stable arrangement and lowers the internal energy of the molecule.

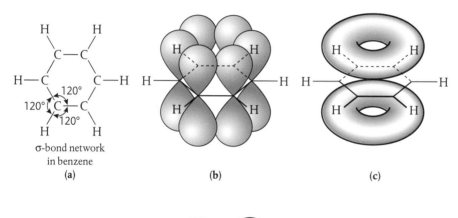

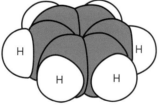

**Figure 10.3** The bonding in benzene. This is a symmetrical arrangement where all the p electrons are shared equally by all of the bonded carbon atoms. It is a very stable structure and lowers the internal energy of the molecule. **(a)** The $\sigma$-bond framework. **(b)** The unhybridized p orbitals before overlapping sideways. **(c)** The delocalized $\pi$ electrons form regions of high electron density above and below the planar benzene ring.

**Figure 10.4** A space-filling model of benzene, showing its planar shape.

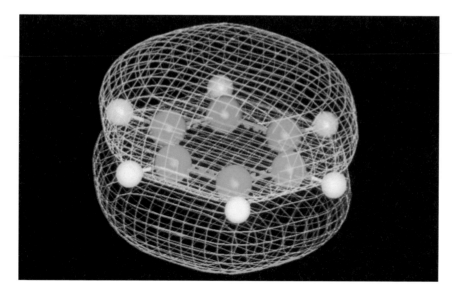

Computer graphics representation of the structure of benzene showing the delocalized electron clouds which confer great stability on the molecule. They appear as the blue and yellow cages above the flat plane of the molecule. Carbon atoms are shown in green and hydrogen atoms in white.

Make sure that when you are writing the structure of benzene you do not forget to include the ring inside the hexagon. If you do forget, and draw instead

, this denotes an entirely different structure, cyclohexane $C_6H_{12}$.

The usual convention for depicting this structure of benzene uses a ring inside the hexagon to denote the delocalized electrons.

This model is supported by evidence, and provides explanations for most observed properties of benzene, as described below.

| Property | Observation / evidence | Explanation |
|---|---|---|
| 1 Bond lengths | All carbon–carbon bond lengths in benzene are equal and intermediate in length between single and double bonds. | Each bond contains a share of three electrons between the bonded atoms.<br><br>X-ray bond length data / nm:<br><br>alkane single bond C—C 0.154 nm<br><br>alkene double bond C==C 0.134 nm<br><br>benzene 0.139 nm |
| 2 $\Delta H_{hydrogenation}$ for the reaction $C_6H_6 + 3H_2 \rightarrow C_6H_{12}$ | Theoretical value based on adding $H_2$ across three C==C double bonds = $-362$ kJ mol$^{-1}$<br><br>Experimental value for benzene = $-210$ kJ mol$^{-1}$<br><br>Benzene is more stable than predicted from the Kekulé structure by approx. 152 kJ mol$^{-1}$ | Delocalization minimizes the repulsion between electrons and so gives benzene a more stable structure, lowering its internal energy by 152 kJ mol$^{-1}$. This is the amount of energy that would have to be supplied in order to overcome the special stability of the delocalized ring. It is called the **resonance energy** or the **stabilization energy** of benzene. See Figure 10.5. |
| 3 Type of reactivity | Benzene is reluctant to undergo addition reactions and is more likely to undergo substitution reactions. | Addition reactions are energetically not favoured as they would involve disrupting the entire cloud of delocalized electrons. The resonance energy would have to be supplied and the product, without the delocalized ring of electrons, would be *less* stable. Benzene can instead undergo substitution reactions that preserve the stable ring structure. |
| 4 Isomers | Only one isomer exists of compounds such as 1,2-dibromobenzene. | As benzene is a symmetrical molecule with no alternating single and double bonds, all adjacent positions in the ring are equal.<br><br>For example 1,2-dibromobenzene, $C_6H_4Br_2$<br><br>Br<br>Br |

The reactivity of benzene is discussed further on page 508.

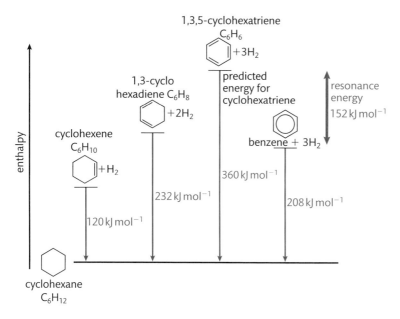

1,3,5-cyclohexatriene
$C_6H_6$
$+3H_2$

predicted energy for cyclohexatriene

1,3-cyclohexadiene $C_6H_8$
$+2H_2$

resonance energy
152 kJ mol$^{-1}$

cyclohexene
$C_6H_{10}$
$+H_2$

benzene + $3H_2$

enthalpy

360 kJ mol$^{-1}$

232 kJ mol$^{-1}$

208 kJ mol$^{-1}$

120 kJ mol$^{-1}$

cyclohexane
$C_6H_{12}$

**Figure 10.5** Enthalpy changes for the hydrogenation of benzene and related molecules. Note that the molecule 1,3,5-cyclohexatriene does not exist, so the value for its hydrogenation is theoretical only.

**NATURE OF SCIENCE**

The changing model of the structure of benzene has largely been a result of advances in technology and instrumentation. The Kekulé model seemed to explain many of the known properties of benzene at the time, but had to be reconsidered when quantitative data obtained through X-ray diffraction experimentation provided counter evidence, for example on bond lengths. The progress of science sometimes demands a refinement or abandonment of a model as new data is obtained, and the acceptance of this is dependent on the objectivity and openness of scientists.

## Trends in physical properties

We have seen that the structure of organic compounds can be thought of in two parts.

1   A framework consisting of carbon and hydrogen only, known as the **hydrocarbon skeleton**. This differs in size in different members of the same homologous series.

2   A functional group. This differs in identity in different homologous series.

Both of these components influence the physical properties of a compound. Most of these properties were discussed in relation to intermolecular forces in Chapter 4, page 178, and a few additional points are made here.

The increase in boiling point with carbon number that we saw in the alkanes applies to other homologous series. In general, the lower members of a series are likely to be gases or liquids at room temperature, while the higher members are more likely to be solids. Branching of the hydrocarbon chain also has an effect on volatility as it influences the strength of the intermolecular forces. Think, for example, how tree logs with lots of branches sticking out cannot stack together as closely as a pile of logs which have no branches. In a similar way branched-chain isomers have less contact with each other than their straight-chain isomers, and so have weaker intermolecular forces and so lower boiling points. We saw earlier that the straight-chain molecule butane has a higher boiling point (−0.5 °C) than its branched-chain isomer, 2-methylpropane (boiling point −11.7 °C).

Owing to their different polarities and resulting differences in intermolecular forces, functional groups have a significant effect on volatility. This can be summarized as follows.

| most volatile | least volatile |
|---|---|
| **alkane > halogenoalkane > aldehyde > ketone > alcohol > carboxylic acid** | |
| London (dispersion) force → dipole–dipole interaction → hydrogen bonding | |
| increasing strength of intermolecular attraction ⟶ | |
| increasing boiling point ⟶ | |

## Exercises

5   Draw and name all the structural isomers of $C_3H_3Cl_5$.

6   Which formula is that of a secondary halogenoalkane?

    **A** $CH_3CH_2CH_2CH_2Br$   **B** $CH_3CHBrCH_2CH_3$   **C** $(CH_3)_2CHCH_2Br$   **D** $(CH_3)_3CBr$

7   Describe the bonding in a benzene molecule and use it to explain benzene's energetic stability.

8   **(a)** When comparing the boiling points of different classes of compound, why is it important to choose molecules that have similar molar mass?

    **(b)** Explain how you would expect the solubility of alcohols in hexane to change with increasing chain length.

# 10.2 Functional group chemistry

## Understandings:

- **Alkanes:** have low reactivity and undergo free radical substitution reactions.
- **Alkenes:** are more reactive than alkanes and undergo addition reactions. Bromine water can be used to distinguish between alkenes and alkanes.
- **Alcohols:** undergo nucleophilic substitution reactions with acids (also called esterification or condensation) and some undergo oxidation reactions.
- **Halogenoalkanes:** are more reactive than alkanes. They can undergo (nucleophilic) substitution reactions. A nucleophile is an electron-rich species containing a lone pair that it donates to an electron-deficient carbon.
- **Polymers:** addition polymers consist of a wide range of monomers and form the basis of the plastics industry.
- **Benzene:** does not readily undergo addition reactions but does undergo electrophilic substitution reactions.

## Applications and skills:

- **Alkanes:**
  - Writing equations for the complete and incomplete combustion of hydrocarbons.
  - Explanation of the reaction of methane and ethane with halogens in terms of a free radical substitution mechanism involving photochemical homolytic fission.
- **Alkenes:**
  - Writing equations for the reactions of alkenes with hydrogen and halogens and of symmetrical alkenes with hydrogen halides and water.
  - Outline of the addition polymerization of alkenes.
  - Relationship between the structure of the monomer to the polymer and repeating unit.
- **Alcohols:**
  - Writing equations for the complete combustion of alcohols.
  - Writing equations for the oxidation reactions of primary and secondary alcohols (using acidified potassium dichromate(VI) or potassium manganate(VII) as oxidizing agents). Explanation of distillation and reflux in the isolation of the aldehyde and carboxylic acid products.
  - Writing the equation for the condensation reaction of an alcohol with a carboxylic acid, in the presence of a catalyst (e.g. concentrated sulfuric acid) to form an ester.
- **Halogenoalkanes:**
  - Writing the equation for the substitution reactions of halogenoalkanes with aqueous sodium hydroxide.

  ### Guidance
  - *Reference should be made to initiation, propagation, and termination steps in free radical substitution reactions. Free radicals should be represented by a single dot.*
  - *The mechanisms of $S_N1$ and $S_N2$ and electrophilic substitution reactions are not required.*

When asked to define a hydrocarbon, make sure you include the word *only* after the fact that they contain carbon and hydrogen – as otherwise your description would apply to *all* organic compounds!

# Alkanes

- General formula is $C_nH_{2n+2}$
- Alkanes are **saturated hydrocarbons**.

The term hydrocarbons refers to compounds which contain carbon and hydrogen *only*. Alkanes are said to be saturated because they contain all single carbon–carbon bonds.

Alkanes contain only C—C and C—H bonds, which are both strong bonds: C—C = 348 kJ mol$^{-1}$ and C—H = 412 kJ mol$^{-1}$. So these molecules will only react in the presence of a strong source of energy, strong enough to break these bonds. As a result, alkanes are stable under most conditions and can be stored, transported, and even compressed safely – which is one of the reasons why they are such useful compounds.

The C—C and C—H bonds are also characteristically non-polar, so these molecules are not susceptible to attack by most common reactants. These two factors taken together mean that alkanes are generally of very low reactivity.

There are, however, two reactions involving alkanes that we will consider here – combustion and substitution reactions.

## Combustion: alkanes as fuels

Alkanes are widely used as fuels, in internal combustion engines and household heating for example, because they release significant amounts of energy when they burn. In other words, the reactions of combustion are highly exothermic. This is mainly because of the large amount of energy released in forming the double bonds in $CO_2$ and the bonds in $H_2O$.

Alkanes burn in the presence of excess oxygen to produce carbon dioxide and water. This is known as complete combustion because the products are fully oxidized.

Molecular models of the first three members of the alkane homologous series: methane ($CH_4$), ethane ($C_2H_6$), and propane ($C_3H_8$). Carbon atoms are shown in black and hydrogen atoms in white. There is free rotation around the carbon–carbon bonds in these saturated molecules.

Methane, $CH_4$, is both a fuel and an atmospheric pollutant. As a greenhouse gas, it has a much higher potential for trapping infrared radiation than carbon dioxide. It is emitted from natural sources such as wetlands, but about 60% of $CH_4$ released is from human activities. The three main sources are the petroleum industry, domestic livestock, and landfill sites. Strategies to reduce $CH_4$ emission include its capture and use as a source of energy.

Aeroplane landing with exhaust behind. The burning of hydrocarbon fuels releases large amounts of carbon dioxide, as well as carbon monoxide and other pollutants, into the atmosphere.

Given all the negative environmental effects associated with the burning of fossil fuels, how can we make changes in our lifestyles to lessen these impacts?

## CHALLENGE YOURSELF

2 Use oxidation numbers to show the differences in the extent of oxidation in reactions of complete and incomplete combustion of hydrocarbons.

For example:

$$C_3H_8(g) + \tfrac{7}{2}O_2(g) \rightarrow 3CO(g) + 4H_2O(g)$$

However, when the oxygen supply is limited, incomplete combustion occurs giving rise to carbon monoxide and water. For example, per mole of propane:

This final equation for this reaction is:

$$2C_3H_8(g) + 7O_2(g) \rightarrow 6CO(g) + 8H_2O(g)$$

In conditions of extreme oxygen limitation, carbon will also be produced. For example:

$$C_3H_8(g) + 2O_2(g) \rightarrow 3C(g) + 4H_2O(g)$$

Other hydrocarbons, the alkenes, alkynes, and arenes, similarly undergo complete or incomplete combustion depending on the availability of oxygen, with the release of large amounts of energy. As the $C:H$ ratio increases with unsaturation, there is an increase in the smokiness of the flame, due to unburned carbon.

The products of all these reactions have serious impact on the environment, which is why the burning of these and other **fossil fuels** on a very large scale is widely recognized as a global problem.

- Carbon dioxide and water are both so-called **greenhouse gases**, which means that they absorb infrared radiation and so contribute to **global warming** and **climate change**. Rising levels of carbon dioxide are largely implicated in the increase in average world temperatures over the last century.
- Carbon monoxide is a toxin because it combines irreversibly with the hemoglobin in the blood and prevents it from carrying oxygen. Slow idling vehicle engines in regions of high traffic densities produce higher concentrations of carbon monoxide. It is essential to provide adequate ventilation when these fuels are being burned in a confined space, to avoid carbon monoxide poisoning which can be fatal.
- Unburned carbon is released into the air as particulates, which have a direct effect on human health, especially the respiratory system. In addition, these particulates act as catalysts in forming smog in polluted air, and have also been targeted as the source of another serious environmental problem known as **global dimming**.

## Substitution reactions of alkanes: halogenation

As alkanes are saturated molecules, the main type of reaction that they can undergo is **substitution**. This occurs when another reactant, such as a halogen, takes the place of a hydrogen atom in the alkane. For example, methane, $CH_4$, reacts with chlorine producing chloromethane and hydrogen chloride.

$$CH_4(g) + Cl_2(g) \xrightarrow{\text{UV light}} CH_3Cl(g) + HCl(g)$$

The reaction does not take place in the dark as the energy of UV light is necessary to break the covalent bond in the chlorine molecule. This splits it into chlorine atoms, which each have an unpaired electron and are known as **free radicals**. Once formed, these radicals will start a chain reaction in which a mixture of products including the halogenoalkane is formed. We can describe the reaction as a sequence of steps, known as the **reaction mechanism**.

## Initiation

$$Cl_2 \xrightarrow{\text{UV light}} 2\ Cl\bullet \text{ radicals}$$

$$\overset{\times\times}{\underset{\times\times}{\times}} Cl \overset{\times}{\underset{\times}{}} \overset{\times\times}{\underset{\times\times}{}} Cl \overset{\times}{\underset{\times}{\times}} \xrightarrow{\text{UV light}} \overset{\times\times}{\underset{\times\times}{\times}} \overset{\times}{Cl} {\times} \quad \overset{\times\times}{\underset{\times\times}{\times}} \overset{}{Cl} \overset{\times}{\underset{}{}}$$

2 chlorine radicals

This process occurs in the presence of ultra-violet light. It is known as **photochemical homolytic fission** because the bond between the chlorine atoms is broken, splitting the shared pair of electrons between the two atoms. *Homo-* means 'the same' and refers to the fact that the two products have an equal assignment of electrons from the bond.

This process can be shown using single-sided curly arrows, sometimes known as 'fish-hooks', to show the movement of a single electron.

$$\overset{\times\times}{\underset{\times\times}{\times}} Cl - \overset{\times\times}{\underset{\times\times}{}} Cl \overset{\times}{\underset{}{\times}} \longrightarrow \overset{\times\times}{\underset{\times\times}{\times}} \overset{\times}{Cl} {\times} \quad \overset{\times\times}{\underset{\times\times}{\times}} \overset{}{Cl} \overset{\times}{\underset{}{}}$$

## Propagation

Propagation reactions both use and produce free radicals. For example:

$$Cl\bullet + CH_4 \rightarrow CH_3\bullet + HCl$$

$$CH_3\bullet + Cl_2 \rightarrow CH_3Cl + Cl\bullet$$

$$CH_3Cl + Cl\bullet \rightarrow CH_2Cl\bullet + HCl$$

$$CH_2Cl\bullet + Cl_2 \rightarrow CH_2Cl_2 + Cl\bullet$$

There are many possible propagation steps, which all allow the reaction to continue. This is why this type of reaction is often called a **chain reaction**.

## Termination

Termination reactions remove free radicals from the mixture by causing them to react together and pair up their electrons. For example:

$$Cl\bullet + Cl\bullet \rightarrow Cl_2$$

$$CH_3\bullet + Cl\bullet \rightarrow CH_3Cl$$

$$CH_3\bullet + CH_3\bullet \rightarrow C_2H_6$$

Again there are many possible termination steps.

So the reaction mixture may contain mono- and di-substituted halogenoalkanes, as well as HCl and larger alkanes. A similar reaction occurs with other alkanes and with bromine. The change in colour from brown to colourless of bromine water when it reacts with an alkane occurs only in the presence of UV light, as shown in Figure 10.6. This reaction is sometimes used to distinguish between alkanes and alkenes.

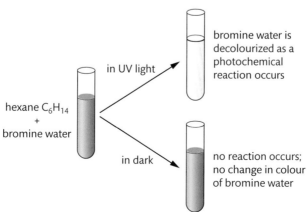

bromine water is decolourized as a photochemical reaction occurs

hexane $C_6H_{14}$ + bromine water

in UV light

in dark

no reaction occurs; no change in colour of bromine water

A free radical contains an unpaired electron and so is very reactive.

Homolytic fission occurs when a bond breaks by splitting the shared pair of electrons between the two products. It produces two free radicals, each with an unpaired electron:

$$X : X \rightarrow X\cdot + X\cdot$$

Make sure that you understand the difference between a free radical and an ion. A free radical has an unpaired electron but no net charge; an ion carries a charge.

**Figure 10.6** The reaction between hexane, $C_6H_{14}$, and bromine water takes place only in the presence of UV light.

Alkanes are saturated hydrocarbons and undergo substitution reactions.

## Alkenes

### CHALLENGE YOURSELF

3  The mechanism for the addition reactions of alkenes is completely different from the substitution reactions we discussed for alkanes; addition reactions involve **heterolytic fission**. Think about what this term suggests about the type of bond breaking involved. What might the mechanism for the addition reaction be, based on this? This is discussed later in this chapter.

• General formula $C_nH_{2n}$.
• Alkenes are **unsaturated hydrocarbons** containing a carbon–carbon double bond.

$$\underset{H}{\overset{H}{\diagdown}}C\underset{\pi}{\overset{\sigma}{=\!=\!=}}C\underset{H}{\overset{H}{\diagup}}$$

As we learned in Chapter 4, the double bond is made of two different bonds, one sigma, σ, and one pi, π. The carbon atoms are $sp^2$ hybridized, forming a trigonal planar shape with angles of 120°.

Alkenes are more reactive than alkanes as the double bond is the site of reactivity of the molecule. The π bond is relatively easily broken, which creates two new bonding positions on the carbon atoms. This enables alkenes to undergo **addition reactions** and so form a range of different saturated products. These are described in the following text.

### Addition of hydrogen

Hydrogen reacts with alkenes to form alkanes in the presence of a nickel catalyst at about 150 °C.

$$H{-}\underset{\overset{|}{H}}{\overset{\overset{H}{|}}{C}}{-}\underset{}{\overset{\overset{H}{|}}{C}}{=}\underset{}{\overset{\overset{H}{|}}{C}}{-}H + H_2 \longrightarrow H{-}\underset{\overset{|}{H}}{\overset{\overset{H}{|}}{C}}{-}\underset{\overset{|}{H}}{\overset{\overset{H}{|}}{C}}{-}\underset{\overset{|}{H}}{\overset{\overset{H}{|}}{C}}{-}H$$

$$\underset{\text{propene}}{CH_3CHCH_2} + H_2 \xrightarrow[150\,°C]{\text{Ni catalyst}} \underset{\text{propane}}{CH_3CH_2CH_3}$$

This process, known as **hydrogenation**, is used in the margarine industry to convert oils containing many unsaturated hydrocarbon chains into more saturated compounds which have higher melting points. This is done so that margarine will be a solid at room temperature. However, there are now widespread concerns about the health effects of so-called *trans* fats, produced by partial hydrogenation. This is discussed further in Chapter 13, Biochemistry.

Oct-1-ene, $C_8H_{16}$, an alkene, burning in a crucible. The flame is smoky due to unburned carbon, an indication of unsaturation.

## Addition of halogens

Halogens react with alkenes to produce dihalogeno compounds. These reactions happen quickly at room temperature, and are accompanied by the loss of colour of the reacting halogen. Note that the name and structure of the product indicates that a halogen atom attaches to each of the two carbon atoms of the double bond.

$$H-\underset{\underset{H}{|}}{\overset{\overset{H}{|}}{C}}-\overset{\overset{H}{|}}{C}=\overset{\overset{H}{|}}{C}-H + Br_2 \longrightarrow H-\overset{\overset{H}{|}}{\underset{\underset{H}{|}}{C}}-\overset{\overset{H}{|}}{\underset{\underset{Br}{|}}{C}}-\overset{\overset{H}{|}}{\underset{\underset{Br}{|}}{C}}-H$$

$$CH_3CHCH_2 + Br_2 \longrightarrow CH_3CHBrCH_2Br$$

propene           1,2-dibromopropane

## Addition of hydrogen halides

Hydrogen halides, such as HCl and HBr, react with alkenes to produce halogenoalkanes. These reactions take place rapidly in solution at room temperature.

$$H-\overset{\overset{H}{|}}{C}=\overset{\overset{H}{|}}{C}-H + HCl \longrightarrow H-\overset{\overset{H}{|}}{\underset{\underset{H}{|}}{C}}-\overset{\overset{H}{|}}{\underset{\underset{Cl}{|}}{C}}-H$$

$$CH_2CH_2 + HCl \longrightarrow CH_3CH_2Cl$$

ethene           chloroethane

All the hydrogen halides are able to react in this way, but the reactivity is in the order HI > HBr > HCl due to the decreasing strength of the hydrogen halide bond down Group 17. So HI, with the weakest bond, reacts the most readily.

The mechanism of these reactions is discussed in Section 20.1.

**Alkenes are unsaturated hydrocarbons and undergo addition reactions.**

## Addition of water

The reaction with water is known as **hydration**, and converts the alkene into an alcohol. In the laboratory, it can be achieved using concentrated sulfuric acid as a catalyst. The reaction involves an intermediate in which both $H^+$ and $HSO_4^-$ ions are added across the double bond, but this is quickly followed by hydrolysis with replacement of the $HSO_4^-$ by $OH^-$ and reformation of the $H_2SO_4$.

Be careful not to confuse the terms *hydrogenation* (addition of hydrogen) with *hydration* (addition of water).

$$\overset{\overset{H}{|}}{\underset{\underset{H}{|}}{C}}=\overset{\overset{H}{|}}{\underset{\underset{H}{|}}{C}} + H_2SO_4 \longrightarrow H-\overset{\overset{H}{|}}{\underset{\underset{H}{|}}{C}}-\overset{\overset{H}{|}}{\underset{\underset{OSO_3H}{|}}{C}}-H + H_2O \longrightarrow H-\overset{\overset{H}{|}}{\underset{\underset{H}{|}}{C}}-\overset{\overset{H}{|}}{\underset{\underset{H}{|}}{C}}-OH$$

$$CH_2CH_2 \xrightarrow{H_2SO_4(conc.)} CH_3CH_2(HSO_4) \xrightarrow{H_2O} CH_3CH_2OH + H_2SO_4$$

ethene      ethyl hydrogensulfate      ethanol

Conditions: heat with steam and catalyst of concentrated $H_2SO_4$

This reaction is of industrial significance because ethanol is a very important solvent, and so is manufactured on a large scale.

The modern process for ethanol synthesis is by direct catalytic hydration of ethene over a phosphoric acid catalyst absorbed on silica.

487

Two observable differences in the reactions of alkanes and alkenes have been mentioned in this section.

- Alkenes decolorize bromine water rapidly at room temperature, whereas alkanes will only do this in the presence of UV light.
- Alkenes burn with a dirtier, smokier flame than alkanes.

Either of these tests might be considered as a way to distinguish between the two classes of compound, but both rely on qualitative data and are subjective, based on the eye of the observer. Wherever possible, experiments are designed to produce quantitative data that is more objective and able to be analysed. Consider what instrumentation and sensors could be used to develop these observations into more rigorous tests to distinguish between saturated and unsaturated hydrocarbons.

 Use of bromine water to distinguish between an alkane (hexane) and an alkene (hex-1-ene). Without UV light, the brown colour is decolorized by the alkene but not by the alkane. This is due to the addition reaction that occurs with the unsaturated alkene that does not occur with the alkane.

## Polymerization of alkenes

Because alkenes readily undergo addition reactions by breaking their double bond, they can be joined together to produce long chains known as **addition polymers**. The alkene used in this reaction is known as the **monomer**, and its chemical nature determines the properties of the polymer. Polymers, typically containing thousands of molecules of the monomer, are a major product of the organic chemical industry and many of our most familiar and useful plastics are polymers of alkenes.

**Figure 10.7** People cannot form a chain until they unfold their arms to release their hands. Similarly, alkenes must break their double bonds in order to join together to form the polymer.

As polymers are such large molecules, their structures are shown using a **repeating unit**, which has open bonds at each end. It is put in a bracket with $n$ as subscript to denote the number of repeating units. For example, ethene polymerizes to form poly(ethene), commonly known as **polythene**.

$$n\begin{pmatrix} H & H \\ | & | \\ C = C \\ | & | \\ H & H \end{pmatrix} \longrightarrow \begin{pmatrix} H & H \\ | & | \\ -C - C- \\ | & | \\ H & H \end{pmatrix}_n$$

ethene                    the repeating unit

The disposal of plastics is a major global problem. The very features that make plastics so useful, such as their impermeability to water and low reactivity, mean they are often non-biodegradable and so remain in landfill sites for indefinite periods of time. It is estimated that about 10% of plastics produced end up in the ocean, causing widespread hazards to marine life. Measures to try to address this problem include developments of more efficient recycling processes, biodegradable plastics, and plastic-feeding microorganisms. A reduction in the quantities of plastic produced and used is also urgently needed – which is something for which every individual can share responsibility.

Waste plastic on a beach in Italy. Plastic waste from oceans is washed up on shores creating problems for wildlife and unsightly scenes such as this.

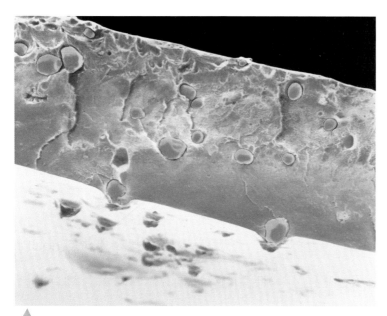

Coloured scanning electron micrograph of a section through a sheet of a biodegradable plastic. The orange spheres are granules of starch embedded in the plastic. When the plastic is buried in soil, the starch grains take up water and expand. This breaks the plastic into many small fragments, increasing the contact area with bacteria in the soil which digest the plastic. Such plastics help to address the major problem of waste plastic disposal.

Similarly, propene polymerizes to form poly(propene), often called polypropylene.

$$n\left(\begin{matrix} H & H \\ | & | \\ C=C \\ | & | \\ H & CH_3 \end{matrix}\right) \longrightarrow \left(\begin{matrix} H & H \\ | & | \\ C-C \\ | & | \\ H & CH_3 \end{matrix}\right)_n$$

propene          the repeating unit

Other common addition polymers include poly(chloroethene), also known as PVC, and PTFE, poly(tetrafluoroethene), often marketed as Teflon®. Their repeating units are given below.

$$\left(\begin{matrix} H & H \\ | & | \\ C-C \\ | & | \\ H & Cl \end{matrix}\right)_n \qquad \left(\begin{matrix} F & F \\ | & | \\ C-C \\ | & | \\ F & F \end{matrix}\right)_n$$

PVC                    PTFE

Polymers are discussed further in Chapter 12, Option Materials.

The example with propene shows that it is helpful to draw the structure of the monomer with the double bond in the *middle* and the other groups off at 90°. Then it is easy to see how the monomers link together when the double bond breaks.

## CHALLENGE YOURSELF

4  Draw the repeating unit in polystyrene, given that the formula of the monomer is $C_6H_5CHCH_2$.

Polythene has excellent insulating properties and is commonly used in household containers, carrier bags, water tanks, and piping. Polypropylene is used in the manufacture of clothing, especially thermal wear for outdoor activities. PVC is used in all forms of construction materials, packaging, electrical cable sheathing, etc. There is some controversy regarding its use, linked to health and environmental concerns, and some organizations are advocating its phase-out. PTFE has a very low surface friction so is widely used in non-stick pans. It also makes up one of the layers in waterproof, breathable fabrics such as GoreTex®. Its resistance to van der Waals' forces means that it is the only known surface to which a gecko cannot stick.

In summary, alkenes:

- readily undergo addition reactions
- are used as starting materials in the manufacture of many industrially important chemicals.

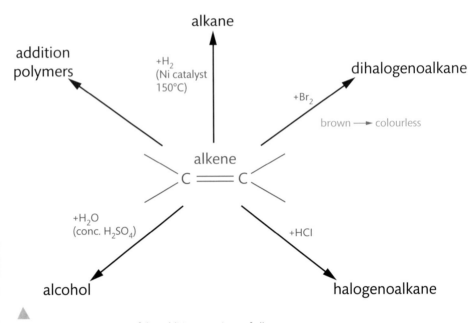

▲ **Figure 10.8** A summary of the addition reactions of alkenes.

**NATURE OF SCIENCE**

It is hard to assess the vastness of the scale of the impact that alkanes and alkenes have had on society. As fuels, alkanes have made energy widely available, and as chemical feedstock, alkenes have led to the synthesis of diverse plastics. Yet these innovations have come at significant cost to the environment, and the long-term consequences are still being determined. While scientific progress is responsible for both the intended and unintended consequences, it is scientists who must respond to the problems. The issues of climate change, air pollution, and plastic disposal are currently pressing areas of research and development.

## Exercises

9  Write equations for the following reactions:

   (a) incomplete combustion of pentane, forming $CO(g)$
   (b) complete combustion of butane
   (c) incomplete combustion of propyne, forming $C(s)$.

10 Write equations showing possible steps leading to a mixture of products in the reaction between bromine and ethane reacting together in UV light.

11 Give the name and structure of the products of the following reactions:

   (a) $CH_3CH_2CH=CH_2 + H_2$ over Ni catalyst
   (b) $CH_3CH=CHCH_3$ + conc. $H_2SO_4$
   (c) $CH_3CH=CHCH_3$ + HBr

12 What would you observe during the following experiments carried out in test tubes at room temperature?

   (a) some bromine water is added to cyclohexane in a test tube covered in aluminium foil
   (b) a few drops of methylbenzene are burned on a watch glass
   (c) some bromine water is added to propane in a test tube in UV light.

# Alcohols

- General formula $C_nH_{2n+1}OH$
- Alcohols have —OH functional group

The —OH group is polar, and so increases the solubility in water of the molecules, relative to alkanes of comparable molar mass. The most common alcohol, ethanol ($C_2H_5OH$), is soluble in water in all proportions, as we know from its presence in alcoholic drinks.

## Combustion: alcohols as fuels

Like the hydrocarbons, alcohols burn in oxygen to form carbon dioxide and water, along with the release of significant amounts of energy. Alcohols are an important fuel, used in alcohol burners, etc. The amount of energy released per mole of alcohol increases as we go up the homologous series, chiefly due to the increasing number of carbon dioxide molecules produced.

For example, the burning of methanol:

$$2CH_3OH(l) + 3O_2(g) \rightarrow 2CO_2(g) + 4H_2O(g) \qquad \Delta H_c^{\ominus} = -726.1 \text{ kJ mol}^{-1}$$

$\Rightarrow 1:1$ ratio of alcohol : $CO_2$

By comparison, the burning of pentanol:

$$2C_5H_{11}OH(g) + 15O_2(g) \rightarrow 10CO_2(g) + 12H_2O(g) \qquad \Delta H_c^{\ominus} = -3330.9 \text{ kJ mol}^{-1}$$

$\Rightarrow 1:5$ ratio of alcohol : $CO_2$ and a corresponding increase in the molar enthalpy of combustion.

As is the case with the hydrocarbons, in the presence of a limited supply of oxygen, alcohols will produce carbon monoxide instead of carbon dioxide.

## Oxidation of alcohols

Combustion involves the *complete* oxidation of the alcohol molecules, but it is also possible for them to react with oxidizing agents which selectively oxidize the carbon atom attached to the —OH group, keeping the carbon skeleton of the molecule intact. In this way, alcohols can be oxidized into other important organic compounds. The products of these reactions are determined by whether the alcohol is primary, secondary, or tertiary, as described on page 477.

Various oxidizing agents can be used for these reactions, but commonly the laboratory process uses acidified potassium dichromate(VI). This is a bright orange solution owing to the presence of Cr(VI), which is reduced to green Cr(III) as the alcohol is oxidized on heating. When writing these reactions it is often easier to show the oxidizing agent simply as '+ [O]'. The oxidation reactions of the different alcohols are as follows.

**Primary alcohols** are oxidized in a two-step reaction, first forming the **aldehyde**, which under prolonged conditions is oxidized further to the **carboxylic acid**. For example:

Alcohol burning in a beaker.

Methanol is considered to be a potential candidate to replace fuels based on crude oil. It can be burned directly as a fuel, or used in the production of hydrogen for fuel cells. It is synthesized on a large scale by the reduction of carbon dioxide and carbon monoxide.

Alcoholic drinks are widely consumed globally. However, as individuals' blood alcohol levels rise, they become impaired with loss of balance and judgment, and so most countries have set legal limits for consumption for activities such as driving. Analysis of ethanol concentration is based on samples of breath, blood, or urine. Common techniques use the oxidation reactions of ethanol in fuel cells or photocells (in which orange Cr(VI) is reduced to green Cr(III)) or infrared spectroscopy. Alcohol abuse is a major contributor to social and economic problems in some societies.

Distillation apparatus is used to separate liquids with different boiling points. In the oxidation of primary alcohols, the aldehyde has a lower boiling point than the alcohol or the acid, and so is collected as a gas and passes into the condensing tube, which is surrounded by cold flowing water. The gas condenses back into a liquid, which is collected in the beaker at the bottom. This prevents further oxidation of the aldehyde to the carboxylic acid.

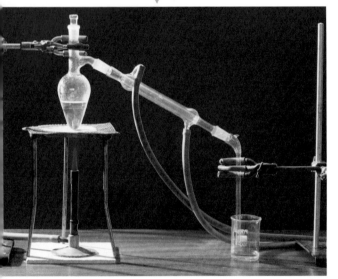

ethanol
primary alcohol

$\xrightarrow{\text{+[O], heat}}$

ethanal
aldehyde

$\xrightarrow[\text{reflux}]{\text{+[O], heat}}$

ethanoic acid
carboxylic acid

ethanol
primary alcohol

$\xrightarrow{\text{+ [O], heat}}$

ethanal
aldehyde

$\xrightarrow[\text{reflux}]{\text{+ [O], heat}}$

ethanoic acid
carboxylic acid

$H^+/Cr(VI) \xrightarrow{\hspace{5cm}} Cr(III)$

This is why when we leave a bottle of wine exposed to the air, bacteria slowly oxidize the ethanol to ethanoic acid, giving the smell of vinegar.

It is possible to stop the reaction after the first step and obtain the aldehyde product by using **distillation** to remove it from the reaction mixture. This is possible because aldehydes have lower boiling points than either alcohols or carboxylic acids, because they do not have hydrogen bonding between their molecules.

If, on the other hand, we want to obtain the carboxylic acid as the product, then we must leave the aldehyde in contact with the oxidizing agent for a prolonged period of time. This will be achieved most efficiently using apparatus for **reflux**.

When you are asked for the conditions for the oxidation reactions, make sure that you specify acidified oxidizing agent and heat, as well as distillation or reflux.

Student heating a pear-shaped flask with a Bunsen burner and using a reflux condenser. This collects and condenses vapours that would otherwise escape from the reaction mixture, and so enables the volatile components to remain in the reaction for long enough to complete their reaction. In this case it is used to oxidize a primary alcohol to completion, to the carboxylic acid.

**Secondary alcohols** are oxidized to the **ketone** by a similar process of oxidation.

$$\text{propan-2-ol} \xrightarrow[\text{reflux}]{+ [O],\ \text{heat}} \text{propanone} + H_2O$$
$$\text{CH}_3\text{CHOHCH}_3 \qquad\qquad (\text{CH}_3)_2\text{CO}$$
$$H^+/\text{Cr(VI)} \xrightarrow{\hspace{2cm}} \text{Cr(III)}$$

**Tertiary alcohols** are not readily oxidized under comparable conditions. This would involve breaking the carbon skeleton of the molecule, which requires significantly more energy. Therefore we will not see a colour change in the potassium dichromate(VI) oxidizing agent when it is reacted with a tertiary alcohol.

2-methylpropan-2-ol → no reaction

$$\text{2-methylpropan-2-ol} \xrightarrow{+ [O],\ \text{heat}} \text{no reaction}$$
$$H^+/\text{Cr(VI)} \xrightarrow{\hspace{2cm}} \text{no change in colour}$$

The colour of the solutions after oxidation with potassium dichromate(VI) solution, $K_2Cr_2O_7$, which is orange. Primary and secondary alcohols are oxidized, to carboxylic acids and ketones respectively, and the Cr(VI) is reduced to green Cr(III). Tertiary alcohols are not oxidized and do not react.

## Summary of oxidation of alcohols

|  | Oxidation product | Colour change with acidified $K_2Cr_2O_7$(aq) |
| --- | --- | --- |
| **primary alcohol** | aldehyde → carboxylic acid | orange → green |
| **secondary alcohol** | ketone | orange → green |
| **tertiary alcohol** | not oxidized | no colour change |

**Reactions of alcohols**
Full details of how to carry out this experiment with a worksheet are available online.

## Esterification reaction

Alcohols react with carboxylic acids to form esters in a **condensation** reaction in which water is also produced.

$$\text{carboxylic acid} + \text{alcohol} \rightleftharpoons \text{ester} + \text{water}$$

For example, the reaction between ethanoic acid and ethanol is as follows.

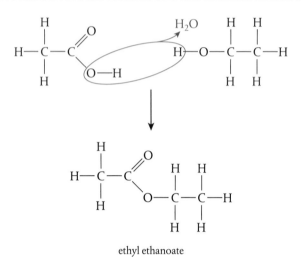

ethyl ethanoate

$$CH_3COOH + C_2H_5OH \xrightleftharpoons{\text{conc. } H_2SO_4} CH_3COOC_2H_5 + H\text{-}O\text{-}H$$

The reaction is an equilibrium reaction, and is catalysed by concentrated sulfuric acid, $H_2SO_4$. The ester has the lowest boiling point of the components of the reaction mixture and so can be separated by distillation. Esters have distinct smells that can often be detected if the reaction mixture is poured into a beaker of water. Unlike their parent acid and alcohol, esters have no free —OH groups so they cannot form hydrogen bonds and so are mostly quite insoluble and form a layer on the surface.

Some other esterification reactions are given below.

$$HCOOH + C_2H_5OH \rightleftharpoons HCOOC_2H_5 + H_2O$$
methanoic    ethanol      ethyl
acid                  methanoate

$$C_3H_7COOH + CH_3OH \rightleftharpoons C_3H_7COOCH_3 + H_2O$$
butanoic    methanol      methyl
acid                  butanoate

## Halogenoalkanes

- General formula is $C_nH_{2n+1}X$ (where X = halogen)
- Halogenoalkanes contain an atom of fluorine, chlorine, bromine, or iodine bonded to the carbon skeleton of the molecule.

Halogenoalkanes are saturated molecules so, like alkanes, their reactions involve substitution – that is the replacement of one atom by another atom or group. But, unlike the alkanes, the halogenoalkanes possess a polar bond and this makes them more reactive.

The preparation of aspirin involves an esterification reaction, converting the —OH group of the natural ingredient salicylic acid into an ester group. This improves the taste and tolerance of the drug in the body. The conversion of morphine into heroin similarly involves conversion of two —OH groups into ester groups. This change makes heroin a much more potent drug as it can be taken up by the non-polar environment of the brain more readily than morphine.

Esters are widely used in perfumes, artificial food flavourings, painkillers, and solvents for paints, varnishes, and so on. They are also used as plasticizers in the petro-chemicals industry, helping to soften plastics. Fats and oils are esters of glycerol and fatty acids, and the nucleic acids DNA and RNA contain phosphodiester links. These biological molecules are described in more detail in Chapter 13.

## Nucleophilic substitution reactions of halogenoalkanes

The polarity in halogenoalkanes is due to the fact that the halogen atom is more electronegative than carbon and so exerts a stronger pull on the shared electrons in the carbon–halogen bond. As a result the halogen gains a partial negative charge ($\delta-$), and the carbon gains a partial positive charge ($\delta+$) and is said to be **electron deficient**. It is this electron-deficient carbon that defines much of the reactivity of the halogenoalkanes.

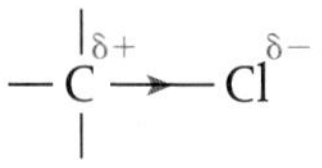

$$-\overset{|}{\underset{|}{C}}\overset{\delta+}{\longrightarrow} \overset{\delta-}{Cl}$$

**Nucleophiles** are reactants that are themselves electron rich, as they have a lone pair of electrons and may also carry a negative charge. These species are therefore attracted to the electron-deficient carbon atom in the halogenoalkane. This leads to reactions in which substitution of the halogen occurs, known as **nucleophilic substitution** reactions.

The hydroxide ion, $OH^-$, is a good nucleophile. For example, halogenoalkanes react with alkalis such as NaOH to form alcohols.

$$CH_3Cl \; + \; NaOH \; \rightarrow \; CH_3OH \; + \; NaCl$$
chloromethane — methanol

$$C_3H_7Br \; + \; NaOH \; \rightarrow \; C_3H_7OH \; + \; NaBr$$
1-bromopropane — propan-1-ol

The mechanism for these reactions is discussed in Section 20.1, page 498. These reactions, and others like them in which the halogen is substituted by another group, mean that halogenoalkanes can be converted into many other classes of compound and so are very useful intermediates in organic synthetic pathways. This is discussed further in Section 20.2, page 512.

Halogenoalkanes include CFCs, whose destructive effects on the ozone layer were discussed in Chapter 4, page 196.

A nucleophile is an electron-rich species that is attracted to parts of molecules that are electron deficient.

## Benzene

We saw on page 479 that the delocalized electrons in benzene give it a special stability. This means that addition reactions, which would lead to loss of the stable arene ring, are generally not favoured as the products would be of higher energy than the reactants. Instead, substitution reactions, in which one or more of the hydrogen atoms is replaced by an incoming group, occur more readily as these lead to products in which the arene ring is conserved. The delocalized ring of electrons, which represents an area of electron density, is the site of reactivity.

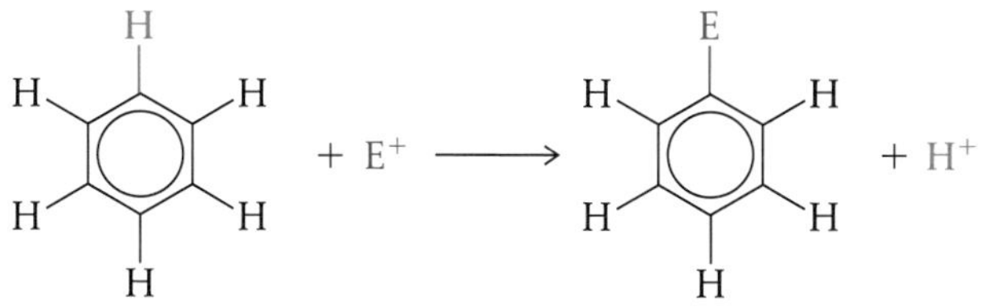

$$\text{benzene} \; + \; E^+ \; \longrightarrow \; \text{product} \; + \; H^+$$

**Figure 10.9** Electrophilic substitution reaction of benzene with a generic electrophile $E^+$. Note that the product has the arene ring conserved.

# Organic chemistry

## Electrophilic substitution reactions of benzene

**Electrophiles** are reactants that are themselves electron deficient, as they have a positive charge or a partial positive charge. These species are therefore attracted to the electron-rich benzene ring, leading to **electrophilic substitution** reactions.

For example, benzene reacts with the nitronium ion, $NO_2^+$ (derived from nitric acid, $HNO_3$), as follows:

$$C_6H_6 + HNO_3 \xrightarrow[50\,°C]{conc.\ H_2SO_4} C_6H_5NO_2 + H_2O$$

The reaction of benzene with halogens is as follows:

$$C_6H_6 + Cl_2 \xrightarrow{AlCl_3\ in\ dry\ ether} C_6H_5Cl + HCl$$

The mechanism for these reactions is discussed in Section 20.1, page 508.

### Exercises

**13** Write equations for
**(a)** the complete combustion of ethanol and propanol
**(b)** the esterification reaction between propanoic acid and butanol.

**14** Predict the products of heating the following alcohols with acidified potassium dichromate(VI) solution, and the colour changes that would be observed in the reaction mixture.
**(a)** butan-2-ol
**(b)** methanol (product collected by distillation immediately)
**(c)** 2-methylbutan-2-ol

**15** Explain what is meant by nucleophilic substitution, using the reaction between NaOH and chloroethane to illustrate your answer.

**16** Discuss why benzene, which is highly unsaturated, tends to undergo substitution reactions rather than addition reactions.

# 20.1 Types of organic reactions

## Understandings:

- **Nucleophilic substitution reactions:**
  - $S_N1$ represents a nucleophilic unimolecular substitution reaction and $S_N2$ represents a nucleophilic bimolecular substitution reaction. $S_N1$ involves a carbocation intermediate. $S_N2$ involves a concerted reaction with a transition state.
  - For tertiary halogenoalkanes the predominant mechanism is $S_N1$ and for primary halogenoalkanes it is $S_N2$. Both mechanisms occur for secondary halogenoalkanes.

- The rate-determining step (slow step) in an $S_N1$ reaction depends only on the concentration of the halogenoalkane, rate = k[halogenoalkane]. For $S_N2$, rate = k[halogenoalkane][nucleophile]. $S_N2$ is stereospecific with an inversion of configuration at the carbon.
- $S_N2$ reactions are best conducted using aprotic, polar solvents and $S_N1$ reactions are best conducted using protic, polar solvents.
- **Electrophilic addition reactions:**
  - An electrophile is an electron-deficient species that can accept electron pairs from a nucleophile. Electrophiles are Lewis acids.
  - Markovnikov's rule can be applied to predict the major product in electrophilic addition reactions of unsymmetrical alkenes with hydrogen halides and interhalogens. The formation of the major product can be explained in terms of the relative stability of possible carbocations in the reaction mechanism.
- **Electrophilic substitution reactions:**
  - Benzene is the simplest aromatic hydrocarbon compound (or arene) and has a delocalized structure of $\pi$ bonds around its ring. Each carbon to carbon bond has a bond order of 1.5. Benzene is susceptible to attack by electrophiles.
- **Reduction reactions:**
  - Carboxylic acids can be reduced to primary alcohols (via the aldehyde). Ketones can be reduced to secondary alcohols. Typical reducing agents are lithium aluminium hydride and sodium borohydride.

  ### Guidance
  - *Reference should be made to heterolytic fission for $S_N1$ reactions.*
  - *The difference between homolytic and heterolytic fission should be understood.*
  - *The difference between curly arrows and fish-hooks in reaction mechanisms should be emphasized.*
  - *Use of partial charges ($\delta+$ and $\delta-$) and wedge/dash three-dimensional representations using tapered bonds should be encouraged where appropriate in explaining reaction mechanisms.*
  - *Typical conditions and reagents of all reactions should be known (e.g. catalysts, reducing agents, reflux, etc.). However, more precise details such as specific temperatures need not be included.*

## Applications and skills:

- **Nucleophilic substitution reactions:**
  - Explanation of why hydroxide is a better nucleophile than water.
  - Deduction of the mechanism of the nucleophilic substitution reactions of halogenoalkanes with aqueous sodium hydroxide in terms of $S_N1$ and $S_N2$ mechanisms. Explanation of how the rate depends on the identity of the halogen (i.e. the leaving group), whether the halogenoalkane is primary, secondary, or tertiary and the choice of solvent.
  - Outline of the difference between protic and aprotic solvents.
- **Electrophilic addition reactions:**
  - Deduction of the mechanism of the electrophilic addition reactions of alkenes with halogens/interhalogens and hydrogen halides.
- **Electrophilic substitution reactions:**
  - Deduction of the mechanism of the nitration (electrophilic substitution) reaction of benzene (using a mixture of concentrated nitric acid and sulfuric acid).
- **Reduction reactions:**
  - Writing reduction reactions of carbonyl-containing compounds: aldehydes and ketones to primary and secondary alcohols and carboxylic acids to aldehydes, using suitable reducing agents.
  - Conversion of nitrobenzene to aniline via a two-stage reaction.

Organic reactions are broadly organized according to *what* happens (the type of reaction) and *how* it happens (the mechanism of the reaction). Again this system of classification helps us to focus on patterns and unifying themes, which is useful given the seemingly endless number of possible organic reactions. Different combinations of mechanism and reaction type are described below, with specific examples.

Many organic mechanisms describe the reactants according to electrophilic and nucleophilic behaviour, terms we introduced in Chapter 8, page 365, and again in this chapter on page 495.

- Nucleophiles are electron rich and attack areas of electron deficiency. They act as Lewis bases and donate a pair of electrons in forming a new covalent bond. Typical examples include $OH^-$, $H_2O$, $NH_3$, and $CN^-$.
- Electrophiles are electron deficient and accept electron pairs from a nucleophile. They act as Lewis acids. Typical examples include $H^+$, $Br^+$, and $NO_2^+$.

A convention used in depicting reaction mechanisms is the use of a **curly arrow**. The double-headed arrow ( ⌒→ ) represents the motion of an electron pair, with the tail showing where the pair comes from and the head of the arrow showing where it is going. We will show curly arrows in blue in this text.

Note the double-headed arrow for movement of an *electron pair* is distinct from the single-sided arrow or fish-hook which shows the movement of a *single electron*. The single-sided arrow was introduced in Section 10.1 to show electron movements in radical formation.

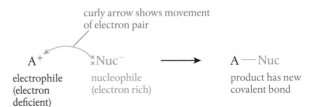

curly arrow shows movement of electron pair

$A^+$ — electrophile (electron deficient)

$Nuc^-$ — nucleophile (electron rich)

$A—Nuc$ — product has new covalent bond

## Nucleophilic substitution reactions: halogenoalkanes

The shorthand notation $S_N$ – substitution nucleophilic – is used for this type of reaction.

The polar carbon–halogen bond in halogenoalkanes means that the carbon atom is electron deficient, and it is attacked by nucleophiles such as $OH^-$. During these reactions, the carbon–halogen bond breaks and the halogen atom is released as a negative ion (the halide). This type of bond breakage, where both the shared electrons go to one of the products, is known as **heterolytic fission**. The halogen, because it becomes detached in the reaction, is known as the **leaving group**.

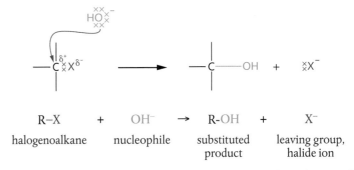

**Figure 10.10** Heterolytic fission of the carbon–halogen bond occurs during the substitution reaction. Note that X represents any halogen atom.

$R–X$ + $OH^-$ → $R–OH$ + $X^-$

halogenoalkane + nucleophile → substituted product + leaving group, halide ion

A nucleophile is an electron-rich species that is attracted to parts of molecules that are electron deficient.

The exact mechanism of these reactions depends on whether the halogenoalkane is primary, secondary, or tertiary – as described on page 476. We will discuss examples of two different mechanisms here when halogenoalkanes react with aqueous sodium hydroxide, NaOH, to produce alcohols. Similar reactions take place with water as the nucleophile, but they occur more slowly. Because $H_2O$ lacks a negative charge it is a weaker nucleophile than $OH^-$.

Heterolytic fission is when a bond breaks with both the shared electrons going to one of the products. It produces two oppositely charged ions.

$X : X \rightarrow X^+ + X:^-$

## Primary halogenoalkanes: $S_N2$ mechanism

Primary halogenoalkanes have at least two hydrogen atoms attached to the carbon of the carbon–halogen bond. For example chloroethane:

H—C—C—Cl (structure with H H on top, H H on bottom)

The overall reaction that occurs with NaOH is:

$$C_2H_5Cl + OH^- \rightarrow C_2H_5OH + Cl^-$$

As the hydrogen atoms are so small, the carbon atom is relatively open to attack by the nucleophile. An unstable **transition state** is formed in which the carbon is weakly bonded to both the halogen and the nucleophile. The carbon–halogen bond then breaks heterolytically, releasing $Cl^-$ and forming the alcohol product.

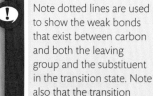

Effectively this is a one-step concerted reaction with an unstable transition state. Because the mechanism is dependent on the concentration of *both* the halogenoalkane and the hydroxide ion, it is known as a **bimolecular** reaction.

$$rate = k \text{ [halogenoalkane] [nucleophile]}$$

Therefore this mechanism is fully described as $S_N2$: substitution nucleophilic bimolecular.

Note that the nucleophile attacks the electrophilic carbon atom on the *opposite side* from the leaving group, which causes an **inversion** of the arrangement of the atoms around the carbon atom. The process can be likened to an umbrella blowing inside out, as shown in Figure 10.11.

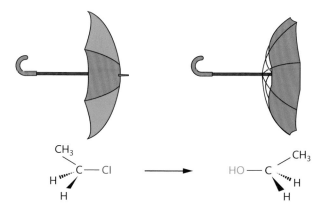

**Figure 10.11** An umbrella blowing inside out is somewhat similar to the inversion of the configuration at the electrophilic carbon atom in the $S_N2$ mechanism.

These configurations are a result of different spatial arrangements around tetrahedrally bonded carbon atoms. This topic is discussed more fully in Section 20.3, page 514. The $S_N2$ mechanism is described as **stereospecific** because the three-dimensional arrangement of the reactants determines the three-dimensional configuration of the products. This happens because bond formation comes before bond cleavage in the transition state, so the stereochemistry of the carbon attacked is not lost. Stereospecific reactions are important in the synthesis of biological molecules such as amino acids, and in many drug syntheses.

The $S_N2$ mechanism is favoured by polar, **aprotic solvents**. Aprotic solvents are those which are not able to form hydrogen bonds as they do not contain −OH or −NH bonds, although they may have strong dipoles. This means they solvate the metal cation (e.g. $Na^+$) rather than the nucleophile ($OH^-$). The unsolvated, bare nucleophile has a higher energy state and this increases the reaction rate. Suitable solvents include propanone, $(CH_3)_2CO$, and ethanenitrile, $CH_3CN$.

## Tertiary halogenoalkane: $S_N1$ mechanism

Tertiary halogenoalkanes have three alkyl groups attached to the carbon of the carbon–halogen bond. 2-chloro-2-methylpropane is an example:

$$H_3C - \underset{\underset{CH_3}{|}}{\overset{\overset{CH_3}{|}}{C}} - Cl$$

The overall reaction that occurs with NaOH is:

$$(CH_3)_3CCl \quad + \quad OH^- \quad \rightarrow \quad (CH_3)_3COH \quad + \quad Cl^-$$

2-chloro-2-methylpropane            2-methyl-propan-2-ol

Here the presence of the three alkyl groups around the carbon of the carbon–halogen bond causes what is called **steric hindrance**, meaning that these bulky groups make it difficult for an incoming group to attack this carbon atom. Instead, the first step of the reaction involves the halogenoalkane ionizing by breaking its carbon–halogen bond heterolytically. As the halide ion is detached, this leaves the carbon atom with a temporary positive charge, which is known as a **carbocation intermediate**. This is then attacked by the nucleophile in the second step of the reaction, leading to the formation of a new bond.

carbocation intermediate

A carbocation is a positive ion with the charge centred on a carbon atom.

Another reason which favours this mechanism in tertiary halogenoalkanes is that the carbocation is stabilized by the presence of the three alkyl groups, as each of these has an electron-donating or **positive inductive** effect, shown by the blue arrows in the diagram. This stabilizing effect helps the carbocation to persist for long enough for the second step to occur.

Because the slow step of this reaction, the rate-determining step, is determined by the concentration only of the halogenoalkane, it is described as a **unimolecular** reaction.

$$\text{rate} = k\,[\text{halogenoalkane}]$$

Therefore this reaction mechanism is fully described as $S_N1$: substitution nucleophilic unimolecular.

The carbocation intermediate has a planar shape, which means the nucleophile can attack from any position in the second step. This means that the $S_N1$ reaction is not stereospecific. It can in fact give rise to a mixture of optical isomers, known as a racemic mixture. This is explained further in Section 20.3.

The influence of solvents on the $S_N1$ reaction is mostly a result of their ability to stabilize the carbocation intermediate. Anything that stabilizes the intermediate will favour the reaction. Polar, **protic solvents** contain $-OH$ or $-NH$ and so are able to form hydrogen bonds. They are effective in stabilizing the positively charged intermediate by solvation involving ion–dipole interactions. Suitable solvents include water, alcohols, and carboxylic acids.

## Secondary halogenoalkanes

It is not possible to be precise about the mechanism of nucleophilic substitution in secondary halogenoalkanes, as data show that they usually undergo a mixture of both $S_N1$ and $S_N2$ mechanisms.

## Comparison of the rates of nucleophilic substitution reactions

### 1 The effect of the mechanism

Experimental data have shown that the $S_N1$ mechanism proceeds more quickly than the $S_N2$ mechanism. So substitution reactions occur more quickly with tertiary halogenoalkanes than with primary halogenoalkanes. Secondary halogenolkanes using a mixture of both mechanisms show an intermediate rate of reaction.

The relative rate of reactivity of the three classes of halogenoalkane when all other variables are kept constant is:

$$\text{tertiary} > \text{secondary} > \text{primary}$$
$$S_N1 \qquad S_N1 \text{ and } S_N2 \qquad S_N2$$

### 2 The influence of the leaving group (halogen)

There are two opposing factors to consider here.

#### (a) The polarity of the carbon–halogen bond

As the electronegativity of the halogens decreases in going down the group from fluorine to iodine, the carbon of the carbon–halogen bond becomes progressively less electron deficient and so less vulnerable to nucleophilic attack. So from this we would expect:

$$\text{fluoroalkane} > \text{chloroalkane} > \text{bromoalkane} > \text{iodoalkane}$$

Protic solvents contain $-OH$ or $-NH$ and are able to form hydrogen bonds. Aprotic solvents are those that are not able to form hydrogen bonds.

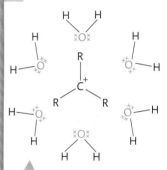

**Figure 10.12** Solvation of a carbocation by water. The ion is stabilized by ion–dipole interactions with the electron-rich oxygen atoms.

The rate of nucleophilic substitution reactions in halogenoalkanes is fastest with tertiary halogenoalkanes and slowest with primary halogenoalkanes.

## CHALLENGE YOURSELF

6 Think about the design of an experiment that would give the data needed to confirm the kinetics of these reactions. You might find it helpful to look back at Chapter 6.

The halogenoalkanes chlorobutane, bromobutane, and iodobutane after reaction with an alcoholic solution of aqueous silver nitrate. The colour of the precipitate of the silver halide – AgCl, AgBr, and AgI from left to right – appears as the halide ion is released during the substitution reaction.

(b) *The strength of the carbon–halogen bond*

Bond energy data show that the carbon–halogen bond decreases in strength from fluorine to iodine. As the substitution reaction involves breaking this bond, we would expect the ease of breaking bonds to be:

$$C—I > C—Br > C—Cl > C—F$$

Reaction rate data indicate that (b) above, the strength of the carbon–halogen bond, dominates the outcome here. The relative rate of reaction of the different halogens in halogenoalkanes when all other variables are kept constant is therefore:

$$\text{iodoalkanes} > \text{bromoalkanes} > \text{chloroalkanes} > \text{fluoroalkanes}$$

## 3 Choice of solvent

As explained above, the $S_N1$ mechanism is favoured by polar, protic solvents while the $S_N2$ mechanism is favoured by polar, aprotic solvents.

So, overall, the fastest reactions will occur with tertiary iodoalkanes in polar, protic solvents. Nucleophilic substitution reactions of halogenoalkanes can be followed by the appearance of the halide ion. Silver nitrate solution, $AgNO_3(aq)$, added to the reaction mixture reacts with the halide ion, forming a precipitate of the silver halide, each with a distinct colour.

The table below summarizes the differences in the two mechanisms of nucleophilic substitution reactions in halogenoalkanes.

## Summary

| | $S_N2$ | $S_N1$ |
|---|---|---|
| Favoured by | primary halogenoalkanes | tertiary halogenoalkanes |
| Nature of mechanism | concerted one-step mechanism with unstable transition state | two-step reaction via carbocation intermediate |
| Relative rate | lower | higher |
| Favoured solvent | polar, aprotic | polar, protic |
| Reaction profile | | |

Note that in these reactions, primary alcohols are produced from primary halogenoalkanes, secondary alcohols from secondary halogenoalkanes, and so on. This will be useful in the consideration of synthetic pathways in Section 20.2.

## Exercises

**17 (a)** Give the structural formulas of three isomers of $C_4H_9Br$ which can be classified as primary, secondary, or tertiary.

**(b)** Identify which of these isomers will react with aqueous sodium hydroxide almost exclusively by an $S_N1$ mechanism. Explain the symbols in the term $S_N1$.

**(c)** Using the formula RBr to represent a bromoalkane, write an equation for the rate-determining step of the reaction.

**18** Which compound reacts most readily by a $S_N1$ mechanism?

| | |
|---|---|
| **A** $(CH_3)_3CCl$ | **B** $CH_3CH_2CH_2CH_2Cl$ |
| **C** $(CH_3)_3CI$ | **D** $CH_3CH_2CH_2CH_2I$ |

**19** Suggest explanations for the following:

**(a)** Iodo- and bromo- compounds are more useful than chloro-compounds as intermediates in synthesis pathways.

**(b)** Two compounds X and Y have the same molecular formula, $C_4H_9Cl$. When each compound is reacted with dilute alkali and $AgNO_3(aq)$ is added, a white precipitate that darkens on exposure to air forms rapidly with X, but only slowly with Y.

Freshly picked ripe peaches. Ethene is produced in low levels by most parts of plants, regulating the ripening of fruit and the opening of flowers. Commercial suppliers take advantage of this by applying ethene to fruit to ensure that it is ripened at just the right time for sale.

## Electrophilic addition reactions: alkenes

Alkenes are unsaturated molecules, and as we saw on page 486, are important compounds in many synthesis pathways because of their readiness to undergo addition reactions.

To understand the mechanism of these reactions, it is useful to focus first on some key features of the carbon–carbon double bond.

The nature of the double bond in alkenes is:

**An addition reaction occurs when two reactants combine to form a single product. It is characteristic of unsaturated compounds containing double or triple bonds.**

- The carbon atoms of the double bond are $sp^2$ hybridized, forming a planar triangular shape, with bond angle 120°. This is a fairly open structure that makes it relatively easy for incoming groups to attack.

- The pi ($\pi$) bond represents an area of electron density above and below the plane of the bond axis. Because electrons in the $\pi$ bond are less closely associated with the nuclei, it is a weaker bond than the $\sigma$ bond and so breaks more easily during the addition reactions.

- Because it is an area of electron density, the $\pi$ bond is attractive to **electrophiles**, species that either are electron deficient or that become electron deficient in the presence of the $\pi$ bond.

When this bond breaks, reactants attach at each carbon atom:

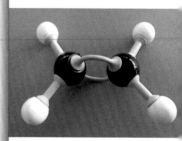

A molecular model of ethene, $C_2H_4$, showing the double bond between the two carbon atoms. This bond is the site of reactivity of alkenes and enables them to undergo addition reactions, producing a wide range of products.

503

An electrophile is an electron-deficient species that forms a bond by accepting an electron pair. Electrophiles are positive ions or have a partial positive charge.

Reactions between these reagents and alkenes are therefore known as **electrophilic addition reactions**. Good examples include the addition of halogens and hydrogen halides to alkenes, which happen readily under mild conditions. In these reactions the electrophile is produced through **heterolytic fission**, as described in detail in the following examples.

### Ethene + bromine

When ethene gas is bubbled through bromine at room temperature, the brown colour of the bromine fades as it reacts to form the saturated product 1,2-dibromoethane.

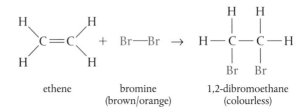

ethene                bromine                1,2-dibromoethane
                   (brown/orange)              (colourless)

We saw on page 488 that colour changes of this type are often used to show the presence of unsaturation.

The mechanism of the reaction is as follows:

• Bromine is a non-polar molecule, but as it approaches the electron rich region of the alkene, it becomes polarized by electron repulsion.

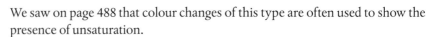

a bromine molecule is polarized by an alkene

The bromine test for an alkene. The tube on the right contains cyclohexene that has reacted with bromine water and decolorized it. This is because it contains a reactive double bond. The tube on the left contains benzene, which has not decolorized the bromine water. Although it is unsaturated, benzene does not readily undergo addition reactions due to its stable aromatic ring structure.

• The bromine atom nearest the alkene's double bond (shown in here red) gains a δ+ charge and acts as the electrophile. Note the curly arrow is always drawn in the direction in which the electron pair moves. The bromine molecule splits **heterolytically**, forming $Br^+$ and $Br^-$, and the initial attack on the ethene in which the π bond breaks is carried out by the positive ion, $Br^+$.

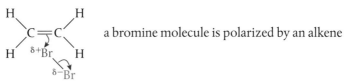

This step is slow, resulting in an unstable **carbocation** intermediate in which the carbon atom has a share in only six outer electrons and carries an overall positive charge.

• This unstable species then reacts rapidly with the negative bromide ion, $Br^-$, forming the product 1,2-dibromoethane.

1,2-dibromoethane

Overall the equation for the reaction is:

$$C_2H_4 + Br_2 \rightarrow CH_2BrCH_2Br$$

Similar reactions take place with other alkenes such as propene. For example:

$$C_3H_6 + Br_2 \rightarrow CH_3CH_2BrCH_2Br$$
1,2-dibromopropane

Evidence for this reaction mechanism can be gained by carrying out the same reaction, $C_2H_4$ and $Br_2$, with the additional presence of chloride ions, $Cl^-$. It is found that the products are $BrH_2CCH_2Br$ and $BrH_2CCH_2Cl$. This is consistent with the mechanism described, as the carbocation formed in the first step is equally ready to combine with $Br^-$ or $Cl^-$. The fact that no dichloro compound is ever formed in this reaction confirms that the initial attack was by the electrophile $Br^+$ formed from $Br_2$.

## Ethene + hydrogen bromide

When ethene gas is bubbled through a concentrated aqueous solution of hydrogen bromide, HBr, an addition reaction occurs fairly readily at room temperature, forming bromoethane.

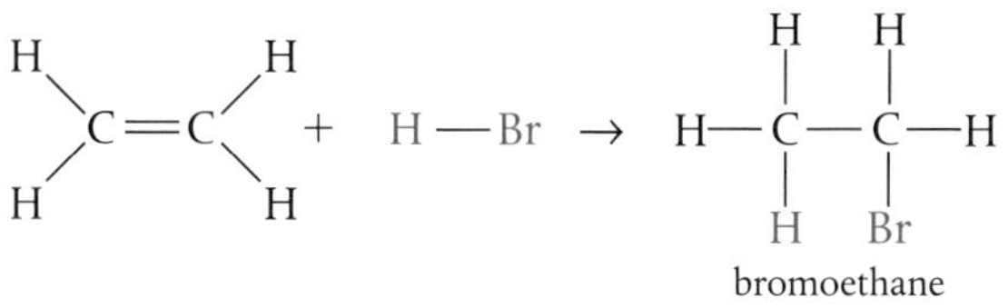

bromoethane

The reaction occurs by a similar mechanism to that described above. HBr as a polar molecule undergoes heterolytic fission to form $H^+$ and $Br^-$, and the electrophile, $H^+$, makes the initial attack on the alkene's double bond. The unstable carbocation intermediate that forms from this step then reacts quickly with $Br^-$ to form the addition product.

The mechanism is as follows:

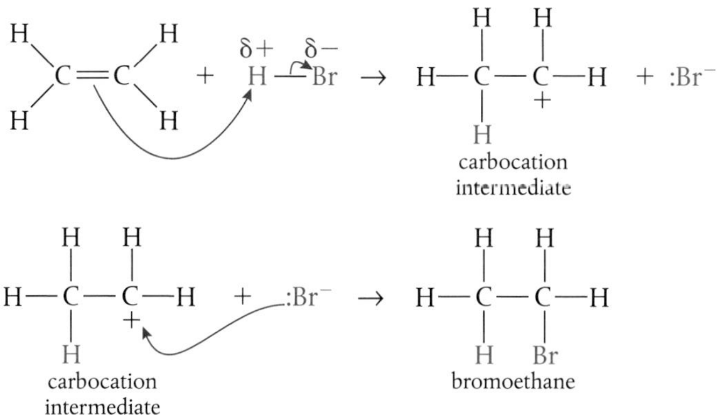

carbocation intermediate

carbocation intermediate     bromoethane

One piece of evidence that supports this mechanism is that the reaction is favoured by a polar solvent that facilitates the production of ions from heterolytic fission.

The other hydrogen halides react similarly with alkenes. HI reacts more readily than HBr due to its weaker bond and HCl less readily due to its stronger bond.

**CHALLENGE YOURSELF**

7 If this reaction is carried out with bromine water in place of pure bromine, predict how the product formed may be different and what colour change may be observed.

The compound 1,2-dichloroethane is synthesized by the addition of chlorine to ethene. It is one of the most widely used chemicals in the world, mostly as a starting material for the manufacture of the plastic PVC, poly(vinyl chloride).

## Propene + hydrogen bromide (unsymmetric addition)

When an unsymmetric alkene such as propene is reacted with a hydrogen halide such as HBr, there are theoretically two different products that can form. These are isomers of each other and they result from two possible pathways through the electrophilic addition mechanism described above.

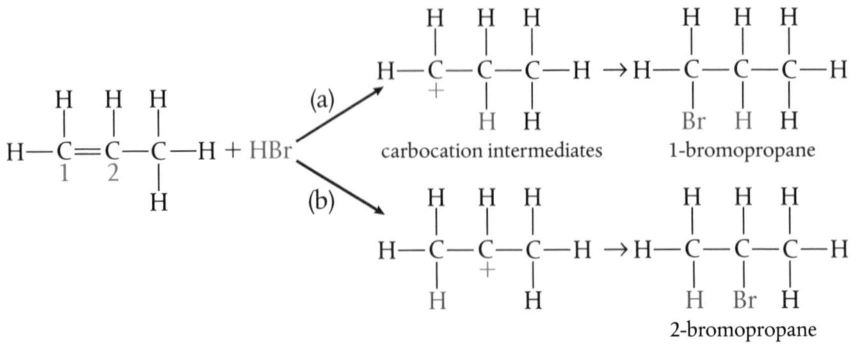

carbocation intermediates

1-bromopropane

2-bromopropane

The difference between these two depends on whether the attacking electrophile ($H^+$ formed from heterolytic fission of HBr) is more likely to bond to the carbon labelled 2, as in mechanism (a) above, or to carbon labelled 1, as in mechanism (b). So which is the more likely? The answer comes from considering which pathway will give the most stable carbocation during the addition process.

We saw on page 500 that alkyl groups around a carbocation stabilize it somewhat due to their **positive inductive effects**, meaning that they push electron density away from themselves and so lessen the density of the positive charge. In (a) above the carbocation is a **primary carbocation** and is stabilized by *only one* such positive inductive effect, whereas in (b), a **secondary carbocation** forms in which there are *two* such effects and the stabilization is greater. Consequently, the more stable carbocation in (b) will be more likely to persist and react with $Br^-$, leading to 2-bromopropane as the main product of the reaction.

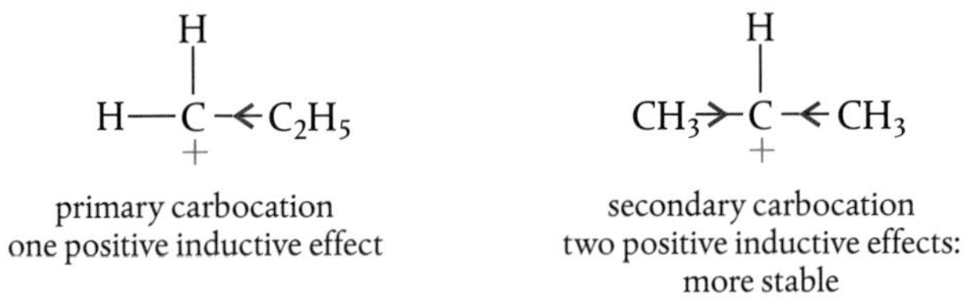

primary carbocation
one positive inductive effect

secondary carbocation
two positive inductive effects:
more stable

Therefore the correct mechanism for the reaction is:

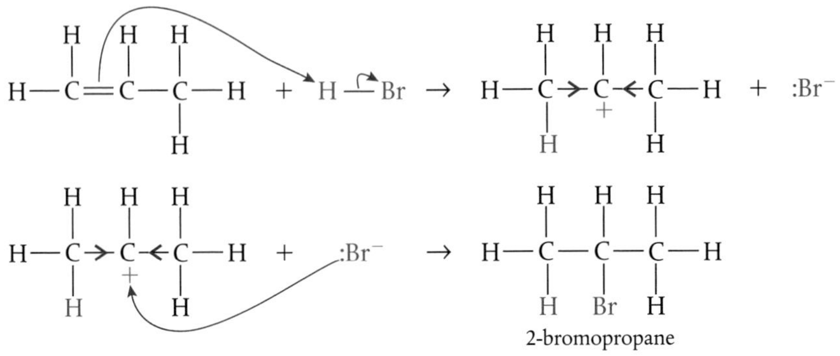

2-bromopropane

We can predict such an outcome for any reaction involving addition of a hydrogen halide to asymmetric alkenes by using what is known as **Markovnikov's rule**. This states: *the hydrogen will attach to the carbon that is already bonded to the greater number of hydrogens*. As we have seen, this is based on the fact that the mechanism that proceeds via the most stable carbocation will be favoured.

In more general terms Markovnikov's rule can be stated as *the more electropositive part of the reacting species bonds to the least highly substituted carbon atom in the alkene* (the one with the smaller number of carbons attached). Applying this rule enables us to predict the outcomes from any reactions involving unsymmetric reagents undergoing addition reactions with unsymmetric alkenes.

## Worked example

Write names and structures for the two possible products of the addition of the interhalogen compound BrCl to propene. Consider which is likely to be the major product and explain why.

### Solution

The two possible reactions are:

(i)

1-chloro-2-bromopropane

(ii)

1-bromo-2-chloropropane

Chlorine is more electronegative than bromine, so Br—Cl is polarized with Br δ+ and Cl δ−. Considering the carbocation that would be produced en route to each of these products by addition of the electrophile Br⁺:

(i)

primary carbocation

(ii)

secondary carbocation

We can see that the secondary carbocation in (ii) is more stable than the primary carbocation in (i) owing to the greater number of positive inductive effects to spread the density of the positive charge. So this mechanism is favoured, leading to the synthesis of 1-bromo-2-chloropropane as the major product.

Markovnikov's rule can be remembered as 'they that have are given more'. The carbon with the most hydrogens gets the incoming hydrogen; the carbon with the most substituents gets another substituent.

When asked to predict and explain the major product of an addition reaction with unsymmetric alkenes and reagents, it is not enough to state Markovnikov's rule, as this is not an explanation. Your answer must refer to the relative stabilities of the carbocations due to inductive effects.

**When an unsymmetrical reagent adds to an unsymmetrical alkene, the electrophilic portion of the reagent adds to the carbon that is bonded to the greater number of hydrogen atoms.**

Vladimir Markovnikov (1838–1904) was a Russian chemist who also studied in Germany under Erlenmeyer and Kolbe. He developed his famous rule in 1869 but as he refused to publish in a foreign language, these findings were unknown outside of Russia until 1899. It has been observed that his published work was not based on much of his own experimental work, and may have been more of an inspired guess. 1869 was also the year that Mendeleev, another Russian chemist, published his Periodic Table.

**20** Explain carefully why alkenes undergo electrophilic addition reactions. Outline the mechanism of the reaction between but-2-ene and bromine and name the product.

**21** Predict the major product of the reaction between but-1-ene and hydrogen bromide. Explain the basis of your prediction.

**22** By considering the polarity within the molecule ICl, determine how it would react with propene. Draw the structure and name the main product.

## Electrophilic substitution reactions: benzene

Despite its high unsaturation, benzene does not behave like alkenes in its characteristic reactions. Its unusual and highly stable aromatic ring determines that substitution, not addition, is its favoured reaction. Nonetheless, like alkenes, benzene is attractive to electrophiles because its ring is a region of electron density. The delocalized cloud of $\pi$ electrons seeks electron-deficient species and forms a new bond as a hydrogen atom is lost. The reactions are therefore **electrophilic substitution**.

The mechanism of the electrophilic substitution reactions of benzene follows a similar path with different electrophiles. The reaction has high activation energy and so proceeds rather slowly. This is because the first step in the mechanism, in which an electron pair from benzene is attracted to the electrophile, leads to a disruption of the symmetry of the delocalized $\pi$ system. The unstable carbocation intermediate that forms has both the entering atom or group and the leaving hydrogen temporarily bonded to the ring.

Using $E^+$ to represent an electrophile, we can show the reaction as follows.

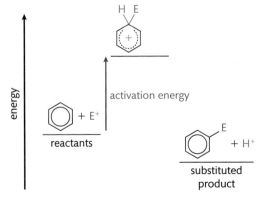

The incomplete circle inside the ring shows its loss of symmetry, with the positive charge distributed over the bulk of the molecule. Loss of a hydrogen ion, $H^+$, from this intermediate leads to the electrically neutral substitution product as two electrons from the C–H bond move to regenerate the aromatic ring. This product is more stable, as shown in Figure 10.13.

**Figure 10.13** The energy profile of an electrophilic substitution reaction in benzene.

These reactions can be used with different electrophiles to introduce different functional groups into the ring. We will illustrate the process with nitration.

## Nitration of benzene

The nitration of benzene is the substitution of —H by —NO$_2$ to form nitrobenzene, C$_6$H$_5$NO$_2$.

The electrophile for the reaction is NO$_2^+$, the nitronium ion. This is generated by using a **nitrating mixture**, a mixture of concentrated nitric and concentrated sulfuric acids at 50 °C. As the stronger of the two acids, sulfuric acid protonates the nitric acid, which then loses a molecule of water to produce NO$_2^+$.

$$\text{HNO}_3 + \text{H}_2\text{SO}_4 \rightleftharpoons \quad + \text{HSO}_4^- \rightleftharpoons \text{H}_2\text{O} + \text{NO}_2^+$$

nitric acid           nitronium ion

NO$_2^+$ is a strong electrophile and reacts with the π electrons of the benzene ring to form the carbocation intermediate. Loss of a proton from this leads to reformation of the arene ring in the product nitrobenzene, which appears as a yellow oil. The hydrogen ion released reacts with the base HSO$_4^-$ to reform sulfuric acid, H$_2$SO$_4$.

The overall reaction is:

$$\text{C}_6\text{H}_6 + \text{HNO}_3 \xrightarrow[50\,°\text{C}]{\text{conc. H}_2\text{SO}_4} \text{C}_6\text{H}_5\text{NO}_2 + \text{H}_2\text{O}$$

The analysis of reaction mechanisms gives a molecular level understanding to organic reactions. This has helped research and industrial chemists to devise the most efficient conditions for synthesis reactions, leading to developments of new materials with novel properties. Innovative products such as breathable fabrics, strong and biodegradable plastics, and new superconducting materials are all the results of such research. But organic chemistry involves working with some toxic reactants, and can be associated with products and by-products that have significant impact on the environment. This makes it all the more urgent to incorporate aspects of Green chemistry into modern organic synthesis. Examples of this include the use of more selective catalysts and safer solvents, in addition to maximizing the atom economy of a process to limit waste.

## Reduction reactions

It is often convenient in organic chemistry to analyse redox reactions in terms of gain and loss of oxygen or hydrogen, rather than in terms of electrons. In the following reactions, reduction can be identified where hydrogen is gained by a reactant.

Apparatus used to make nitrobenzene from benzene in the laboratory. The round-bottomed reaction flask is held in a beaker of cold water by a clamp. The dropping funnel above this contains benzene, which is added slowly to the nitrating mixture in the flask. The mixture of concentrated nitric and sulfuric acids reacts and gives out heat, which is why the cold water and controlled addition of benzene are necessary.

Most of the nitrobenzene produced by this reaction is converted to phenylamine, C$_6$H$_5$NH$_2$, by reduction, as described below. Smaller quantities of nitrobenzene are used in flavourings or perfume additives, but its use is limited due to its high toxicity.

### CHALLENGE YOURSELF

8 Relative to benzene, phenylamine is more reactive towards electrophilic substitution, whereas nitrobenzene is less reactive. Consider what this might suggest about the electron density in the ring in all three compounds, and why this might be the case.

## Reduction of carbonyl compounds

We saw that the oxidation of alcohols to carbonyl compounds (those that contain the $C=O$ group) takes place in the presence of a suitable oxidizing agent and yields different products depending on the alcohol and the conditions.

• primary alcohol → aldehyde → carboxylic acid
• secondary alcohol → ketone

We can reverse these reactions using a suitable reducing agent:

1  sodium borohydride, $NaBH_4$, in aqueous or alcoholic solution, or
2  lithium aluminium hydride, $LiAlH_4$, in anhydrous conditions, such as dry ether followed by aqueous acid.

Both reagents produce the hydride ion, $H^-$, which acts as a nucleophile on the electron-deficient carbonyl carbon. $NaBH_4$ tends to be the safer reagent, but it is not reactive enough to reduce carboxylic acids, so $LiAlH_4$ must be used for this. We can show these reactions using [+H] to represent reduction, in the same way as we used [+O] to represent oxidation of alcohols. Some examples are given below.

$$CH_3COOH \xrightarrow{[+H]} CH_3CHO \xrightarrow{[+H]} CH_3CH_2OH$$

| ethanoic acid | ethanal | ethanol |
|---|---|---|
| carboxylic acid | aldehyde | primary alcohol |

Conditions: heat with $LiAlH_4$ in dry ether. The reaction cannot be stopped at the aldehyde as it reacts too readily with $LiAlH_4$.

$$(CH_3)_2CO \xrightarrow{[+H]} (CH_3)_2CHOH$$

| propanone | propan-2-ol |
|---|---|
| ketone | secondary alcohol |

Conditions: heat with $NaBH_4$(aq).

## Reduction of nitrobenzene

Nitrobenzene, $C_6H_5NO_2$, can be converted into phenylamine, $C_6H_5NH_2$, in a two-stage reduction process.

1  $C_6H_5NO_2$ is reacted with a mixture of tin, Sn, and concentrated hydrochloric acid, HCl. The reaction mixture is heated under reflux in a boiling water bath. The product $C_6H_5NH_3^+$, phenylammonium ions, is protonated because of the acidic conditions.

nitrobenzene → (Sn/conc. HCl) → phenylammonium ions

2  $C_6H_5NH_3^+$ is reacted with sodium hydroxide, NaOH, to remove the $H^+$ and form the product phenylamine, $C_6H_5NH_2$.

+ OH⁻ → + $H_2O$

phenylamine

An example of Green Chemistry is the synthesis of phenylamine by electroreduction of nitrobenzene.

$$C_6H_5NO_2 + 6H^+ + 6e^- \rightarrow C_6H_5NH_2 + 2H_2O$$

The process avoids the use of Sn, HCl, and NaOH and their toxic by-products. Organic electro-synthesis offers many Green Chemistry alternatives, but the costs are currently higher than traditional methods.

Phenylamine is an important compound used in the manufacture of anti-oxidants, in the vulcanization of rubber, and in the synthesis of many pharmaceuticals. In addition, it can be converted into so-called **azo compounds**, which are of great importance in the production of dyes.

# Summary of reaction mechanisms

| Reaction mechanism | Reactants | | | Product |
|---|---|---|---|---|
| | Attacking species | Reactive site in molecule | | |
| Electrophilic addition | electrophile<br>• halogens<br>  X—X<br><br><br><br>• hydrogen halides<br>  H—X | pi bond in alkene<br><br>$\searrow C \overset{\pi}{=\!\!=} C \swarrow$ | | • dihalogenoalkane<br>    X   X<br>    \|   \|<br> —C—C—<br>    \|   \|<br><br>• halogenoalkane<br>    H   X<br>    \|   \|<br> —C—C—<br>    \|   \| |
| Electrophilic substitution | electrophile<br>• nitronium $NO_2{}^+$ | delocalized pi ring in benzene | | • nitrobenzene<br>    $NO_2$ |
| Nucleophilic substitution | nucleophile<br>• hydroxide $OH^-$ | $\delta+$ in C—X of halogenoalkanes<br><br>$-\overset{\delta+}{C}-X$ | | • alcohol<br>  \|<br>—C—OH<br>  \| |
| Free-radical mechanism | free radical from halogen X• | C—H bond in alkane | | • halogenoalkane<br>  \|<br>—C—X<br>  \| |
| Reduction | $H^-$ (hydride ion) | $\delta+$ in C=O<br><br>$R-\overset{\delta+}{C}\overset{\diagup O}{\diagdown}$ | • carboxylic acid<br><br><br><br><br>• aldehyde<br><br><br><br>• ketone | • primary alcohol<br>     H<br>     \|<br>R—C—OH<br>     \|<br>     H<br>• primary alcohol<br>     H<br>     \|<br>R—C—OH<br>     \|<br>     H<br>• secondary alcohol<br>     R<br>     \|<br>R—C—OH<br>     \|<br>     H |

**23** State the reactants used in converting benzene to nitrobenzene. Explain how they enable the nitration reaction to occur.

**24** Explain how the following reduction reactions are carried out in the laboratory:

(a) propanoic acid to propanol
(b) nitrobenzene to phenylamine
(c) ethanal to ethanol

# 20.2 Synthetic routes

## Understandings:

- The synthesis of an organic compound stems from a readily available starting material via a series of discrete steps. Functional group interconversions are the basis of such synthetic routes.
- Retro-synthesis of organic compounds.

**Guidance**
*Conversions with more than four stages will not be assessed in synthetic routes.*

## Applications and skills:

- Deduction of multi-step synthetic routes given starting reagents and the product(s).

**Guidance**
*Reaction types can cover any of the reactions covered in Topic 10 and Section 20.1.*

We can now summarize some of the reactions we have studied in this chapter, and see how they are inter-related. Separate summaries are given for aliphatic and aromatic compounds.

Organic synthesis is a major part of drug design. Often the process starts with a product isolated from a natural source, which acts as the 'lead' for analysis of its desirable properties, and for synthesis of related molecules. Examples include aspirin, Taxol, and mescaline. Some of these are discussed further in Option D, Medicinal Chemistry.

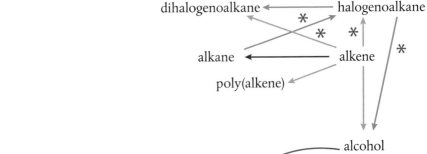

* = mechanism required

→ = oxidation

→ = reduction/addition of $H_2$

→ = substitution

→ = addition

→ = condensation

**Figure 10.14** Some pathways of conversion of organic compounds.

The development of new organic compounds – from drugs to dyes, clothing to construction materials – represents a major part of modern industrial chemistry. The oil industry is the main source of organic compounds for these processes, but it does not yield the required proportion of desired compounds. Therefore organic chemists typically have to convert compounds from one form into another, usually working with a readily available starting material and organizing several reactions in sequence, so that the product of one reaction is the reactant of the next. The series of discrete steps involved is known as a **synthetic route**. Functional group interconversions are the basis of a synthetic route, and we will look at examples from the reactions we have studied.

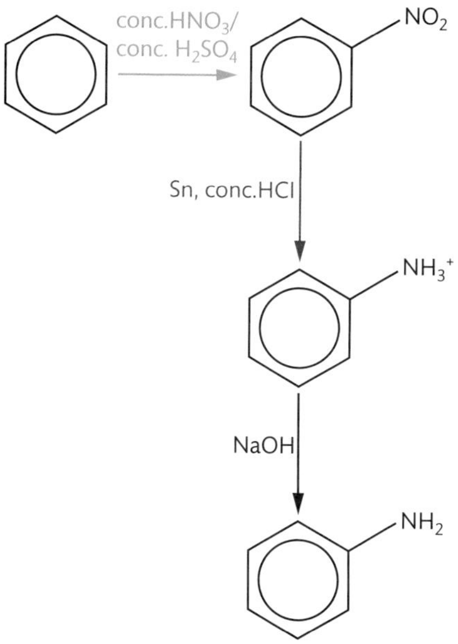

conc.HNO₃/ conc. H₂SO₄

NO₂

Sn, conc.HCl

NH₃⁺

NaOH

NH₂

**Figure 10.15** Some pathways of conversion of organic compounds.

## Retro-synthesis: working backwards

This branch of organic chemistry became established as a systematic discipline largely on the basis of the work of the American chemist E.J. Corey, for which he was awarded the Nobel Prize for Chemistry in 1990. He recognized that the desired product, known as the **target molecule**, itself could serve as the starting point for our thinking. By studying its functional groups, it can be strategically broken down into progressively smaller fragments known as **precursors**. Each precursor then becomes the target for further analysis, eventually yielding a familiar molecule from which the synthetic sequence can start.

> target molecule ⇒ precursor 1 ⇒ precursor 2 ⇒ starting material
>
> the symbol '⇒' means 'can be made from'

Corey introduced the term **retrosynthetic analysis** to describe this systematic backwards approach. It has led to the efficient syntheses of thousands of molecules, and now, enhanced by computer programming to select the best route, is a major aspect of the pharmaceutical and other industries.

One of the early developments from Corey's work on retro-synthesis was the development of synthetic versions of chemicals called prostaglandins. These are involved in many aspects of physiology, especially the control of blood pressure and high pressure in the eye, known as glaucoma. The first synthetic pathway for prostaglandin F2a involved 17 steps, but this has now been refined to a 7-step pathway.

### Worked example

Explain how propyl propanoate can be synthesized from a single carboxylic acid. Give equations and conditions for all reactions, and state the type of reaction occurring at the functional group at each step.

### Solution

Start by analysing the target molecule: the ester is the result of condensation between propanoic acid, $C_2H_5COOH$, and propanol, $C_3H_7OH$.

• Starting with $C_2H_5COOH$, a portion of it is reduced to $C_3H_7OH$ by heating with $LiAlH_4$ in dry ether followed by aqueous acid. The conditions must be applied for long enough to complete the reduction reaction via the aldehyde.

• Another portion of $C_2H_5COOH$ is reacted with the alcohol produced above. The mixture is heated with a catalyst of concentrated $H_2SO_4$.

$$C_2H_5COOH \xrightarrow[\text{2 aqueous } H^+]{\text{1 LiAlH}_4 \text{ in dry ether}} C_3H_7OH \qquad \text{reduction}$$

$$C_2H_5COOH + C_3H_7OH \underset{\text{conc. } H_2SO_4}{\rightleftharpoons} C_2H_5COOC_3H_7 + H_2O \qquad \text{condensation}$$

### Worked example

You are required to make butanone starting from any alkene of your choice. Show the steps involved in retro-synthesis to determine the identity of the alkene.

### Solution

Butanone, $CH_3COC_2H_5$, is a ketone. It can be made by oxidizing a secondary alcohol.

$$CH_3COC_2H_5 \Rightarrow CH_3CH(OH)C_2H_5 \qquad \text{oxidation using } H^+/K_2Cr_2O_7$$

The secondary alcohol is made by substitution of a secondary halogenoalkane.

$$CH_3CH(OH)C_2H_5 \Rightarrow CH_3CH(Br)C_2H_5 \qquad \text{substitution using NaOH}$$

The secondary halogenoalkane is made by addition to an alkene according to Markovnikov rules.

$$CH_3CH(Br)C_2H_5 \Rightarrow CH_2=CHCH_2CH_3 \qquad \text{addition using HBr}$$

Therefore but-1-ene is the starting material.

(The secondary alcohol could be made directly by hydration of the alkene, but is likely to give a better yield via the halogenoalkane.)

### Exercises

**25** Describe how ethyl ethanoate can be made from a single alcohol.

**26** You are required to convert the compound 1-chlorobutane into butanoic acid. Describe the steps you would use, giving reagents, conditions, and equations for each stage.

## 20.3 Stereoisomerism

## Understandings:

• Stereoisomers are sub-divided into two classes: conformational isomers, which interconvert by rotation about an $\sigma$ bond, and configurational isomers, which interconvert only by breaking and reforming a bond.
• Configurational isomers are further sub-divided into *cis–trans* and *E/Z* isomers and optical isomers.
• *Cis–trans* isomers can occur in alkenes or cycloalkanes (or hetero-analogues) and differ in the positions of atoms (or groups) relative to a reference plane. According to IUPAC, *E/Z* isomers refer to alkenes of the form R1R2C=CR3R4 (R1 ≠ R2, R3 ≠ R4) where neither R1 nor R2 need be different from R3 or R4.
• A chiral carbon is a carbon joined to four different atoms or groups.
• An optically active compound can rotate the plane of polarized light as it passes through a solution of the compound. Optical isomers are enantiomers.
• Enantiomers are non-superimposeable mirror images of each other. Diastereomers are not mirror images of each other.

- A racemic mixture (or racemate) is a mixture of two enantiomers in equal amounts and is optically inactive.

### Guidance
- *The term geometric isomers as recommended by IUPAC is now obsolete and cis–trans isomers and E/Z isomers should be encouraged in the teaching programme.*
- *In the E/Z system, the group of highest Cahn–Ingold–Prelog priority attached to one of the terminal doubly bonded atoms of the alkene (i.e. R1 or R2) is compared with the group of highest precedence attached to the other (i.e. R3 or R4). The stereoisomer is Z if the groups lie on the same side of a reference plane passing through the double bond and perpendicular to the plane containing the bonds linking the groups to the double-bonded atoms; the other stereoisomer is designated as E.*

## Applications and skills:
- Construction of 3-D models (real or virtual) of a wide range of stereoisomers.
- Explanation of stereoisomerism in non-cyclic alkenes and C3 and C4 cycloalkanes.
- Comparison between the physical and chemical properties of enantiomers.
- Description and explanation of optical isomers in simple organic molecules.
- Distinction between optical isomers using a polarimeter.

### Guidance
*Wedge-dash type representations involving tapered bonds should be used for representations of optical isomers.*

In Section 10.1 we introduced the concept of isomerism, and explored examples of structural isomers. We saw that these have atoms attached in different orders and so are fundamentally different compounds from each other. Structural isomers may have differences in the amounts of branching in their chains, or in the positions or the nature of functional groups.

Another type of isomerism, known as **stereoisomerism**, has molecules with atoms attached in the same order, but which differ from each other in their spatial or three-dimensional arrangement. Whereas structural isomers can be represented relatively easily in two dimensions on paper, the study of stereoisomerism requires three-dimensional representation.

Stereoisomerism can be further broken down into different types, as shown below.

Conformational isomers usually spontaneously interconvert by rotation, and so in most cases cannot be isolated separately. Some conformers of a compound, though, may be more stable than others, and so are favoured.

> You will probably find that your understanding of this topic will be greatly helped by looking at and building three-dimensional models of the different molecules, or working with simulations of virtual molecules.

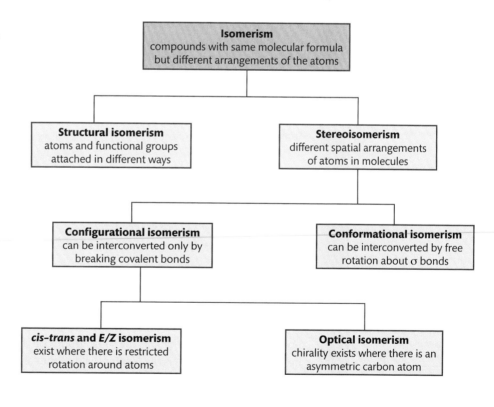

**Isomerism**
compounds with same molecular formula but different arrangements of the atoms

**Structural isomerism**
atoms and functional groups attached in different ways

**Stereoisomerism**
different spatial arrangements of atoms in molecules

**Configurational isomerism**
can be interconverted only by breaking covalent bonds

**Conformational isomerism**
can be interconverted by free rotation about σ bonds

**cis–trans and E/Z isomerism**
exist where there is restricted rotation around atoms

**Optical isomerism**
chirality exists where there is an asymmetric carbon atom

Configurational isomers have a permanent difference in their geometry. These isomers cannot be interconverted and they exist as separate compounds, with some distinct properties. We will study in turn the two main groups of configurational isomerism here.

## *cis–trans* and *E/Z* isomers

**Stereoisomers differ from each other in the spatial arrangement of their atoms.**

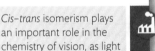

When there is some constraint in a molecule that restricts the free rotation of substituted groups, they become fixed in space relative to each other. In these cases, the position of the groups must be described with respect to a reference plane.

There are two circumstances where these isomers arise.

### 1 Double bonded molecules

The double bond consists of one sigma ($\sigma$) bond and one pi ($\pi$) bond, with the $\pi$ bond forming by sideways overlap of two p orbitals. Free rotation around this is not possible as it would push the p orbitals out of position, and the $\pi$ bond would break. The reference plane is perpendicular to the sigma bonds and passes through the double bond.

### 2 Cyclic molecules

Cycloalkanes contain a ring of carbon atoms that restricts rotation. The bond angles are strained from the tetrahedral angles in the parent alkane. For example, in cyclopropane the carbon atoms form a triangle with bond angles of 60°, and in cyclobutane the atoms form a puckered square with approximate angles of 90°. The reference plane is the plane of the ring.

When the molecule contains two or more different groups attached to the double bond or to the ring, these can be arranged to give two different isomers. The simplest examples, involving only two different substituents, form what are known as **cis** and **trans isomers**.

*Cis–trans* isomerism plays an important role in the chemistry of vision, as light causes a photochemical transformation between the isomers of the pigment rhodopsin. *Cis–trans* isomerism is a concern in the margarine industry, where partial hydrogenation of fats leads to the production of *trans* fats, associated with some negative health effects. A widely used chemotherapy drug used in the treatment of cancer is *cis*-platin, the activity of which is dependent on its stereochemistry.

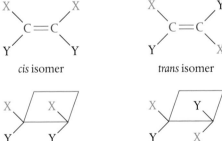

*cis* isomer      *trans* isomer

*cis* isomer      *trans* isomer

*Cis* refers to the isomer that has the same groups on the same side of the double bond or ring, while *trans* is the isomer that has the same groups on opposite sides, or across the reference plane. These prefixes are given in italics before the name of the compound.

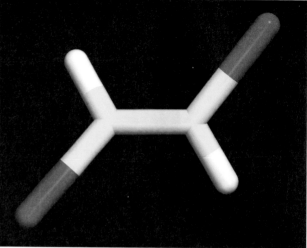

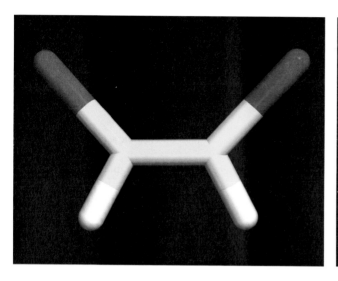

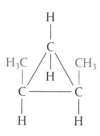

$$\underset{\text{cis-but-2-ene}}{\overset{H_3C}{\underset{H}{\Large C}}=\overset{CH_3}{\underset{H}{\Large C}}}$$

$$\underset{\text{trans-but-2-ene}}{\overset{H}{\underset{H_3C}{\Large C}}=\overset{CH_3}{\underset{H}{\Large C}}}$$

cis-1,2-dimethylcyclopropane

trans-1,2-dimethylcyclopropane

cis-1,3-dichlorocyclobutane

trans-1,3-dichlorocyclobutane

Molecular graphics of the geometric isomers of 1,2-dibromoethene. The atoms are shown as colour-coded cylinders, with carbon in yellow, hydrogen in white, and bromine in red. The *cis* form is on the left and the *trans* form on the right. The molecule cannot alternate between the two forms as there is restricted rotation about the carbon–carbon double bond.

Note from the example of 1,3-dichlorocyclobutane above, the substituted groups do not have to be on adjacent carbon atoms; it is their position relative to the plane of the ring that defines the isomer.

## Worked example

Draw and name the *cis–trans* isomers of butenedioic acid.

### Solution

As the carboxylic acid groups must be in the terminal positions and cannot be attached to a double bond, the condensed structural formula must be

## CHALLENGE YOURSELF

**9** *Cis–trans* isomerism can occur in inorganic as well as in organic compounds. Think about why it can occur in square planar or octahedral complexes, but not in tetrahedral molecules.

HOOC–CH=CH–COOH. To identify the geometric isomers, we need to represent the geometry of the molecule.

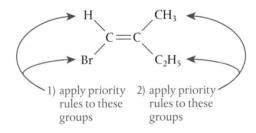

*cis*-butenedioic acid       *trans*-butenedioic acid

There are, however, many cases in alkenes where the *cis–trans* designation breaks down. This happens when the carbon atoms of the double bond are bonded to more than two different substituents. Consider, for example, 1-bromo-2-methylbut-1-ene.

As all the groups attached to the double bond are different, there are no 'same groups' to position relative to the reference plane. For these cases, a more comprehensive naming system has been developed, known as **E/Z isomers**.

*E/Z* isomerism is based on the so-called Cahn–Ingold–Prelog **rules of priority**, which are applied in turn to the groups on each end of the double bond.

1) apply priority rules to these groups     2) apply priority rules to these groups

The priority rules get complicated in many cases, but for our purposes can be summarized as follows:

- Rule 1: Look at the atom bonded to the carbon of the double bond. The atom with the higher atomic number has the higher priority.
- Rule 2: If the atoms are the same, for example if they are both carbon atoms, apply the same rule to the next bonded atom. This means that longer hydrocarbon chains have higher priority.

$$C_3H_7 > C_2H_5 > CH_3 > H \text{ and } Br > Cl > F$$

Next we compare the positions of the highest priority groups on the two carbons of the double bond.

- If the two highest priority groups are on the *same* side of the double bond then the isomer is 'Z'.
- If the two highest priority groups are on the *opposite* side of the double bond, they are labelled as 'E'.

When we apply these rules to the example above, we find:

**1**   Br has the higher priority of the two groups attached to the left-hand carbon and
**2**   $C_2H_5$ has the higher priority of the two groups attached to the right-hand carbon.

As the two highest priority groups are on the same side, this is the Z isomer. If they were on opposite sides it would be the E isomer.

(Z)-1-bromo-2-methylbut-1-ene          (E)-1-bromo-2-methylbut-1-ene

This process may sound more complicated than it really is, but becomes clearer with examples.

## Worked example

Draw and name, using the E/Z convention, the two stereoisomers of 3-methylpent-2-ene.

### Solution

Draw out the full structural formula, identifying the two groups attached to each carbon of the double bond.

Apply the priority rules in turn to the groups on each carbon of the double bond.

Draw the isomers with the highest priority groups on the same side (Z) and opposite sides (E) of the double bond.

(Z)-3-methylpent-2-ene          (E)-3-methylpent-2-ene

We can see that the E/Z convention has wider application than *cis–trans*, and is therefore being used increasingly in both organic and inorganic nomenclature.

*Cis* and *trans* and E/Z isomers may have some different physical properties depending on the influence of the substituted groups on polarity and the shape or symmetry of the molecules. Boiling points, melting points, and solubility data are therefore reported separately for each isomer.

Differences in the properties of the *cis* and *trans* isomers of butenedioic acid become very evident when examples of their roles in biology are compared. They are given distinct non-IUPAC names. Fumaric acid (*trans*) is an intermediate in the Krebs cycle, an essential part of the reactions of aerobic respiration for energy release in cells. By contrast, maleic acid (*cis*) is an inhibitor of reactions that interconvert amino acids, for example in the human liver. Their different biological activities are a consequence of their different shapes affecting their binding to enzymes, the biological catalysts that control all these reactions. More details on enzyme activity are given in Chapter 13, Option B – Biochemistry.

To remember which way round the E/Z classification is applied, it may help to think 'Z' is on the 'zame' side.

Often the E designation is *trans* and the Z designation is *cis*. But this is not always the case, as we can see in this example, where the E isomer is the *cis* form. So when asked for E/Z nomenclature, make sure you work it out from the priority rules, not from a possible *cis–trans* approach.

The E/Z notation is derived from German words. Z derives from *zusammen* meaning 'together' and E derives from *entgegen* meaning 'opposite'.

## CHALLENGE YOURSELF

10 *Cis*-butenedioic acid forms intramolecular hydrogen bonds at the expense of intermolecular hydrogen bonds. Consider what impact this may have on the physical properties and acid strength of the two isomers.

# Optical isomers

A carbon atom attached to four *different* atoms or groups is known as **chiral**. It is alternatively known as **asymmetric** or as a **stereocentre**. The four groups, arranged tetrahedrally around the carbon atom with bond angles of 109.5°, can be arranged in two different three-dimensional configurations which are mirror images of each other. This is known as **optical isomerism**. The term refers to the ways in which the isomers interact with plane-polarized light, which will be discussed below. They are said to be **chiral molecules** and have no plane of symmetry.

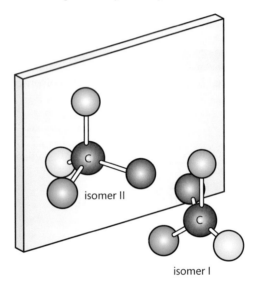

The word 'chiral' is derived from the Greek word for 'hand'. Lord Kelvin first introduced the term into science in 1904 with the now celebrated definition: 'I call any geometrical figure, or group of points, chiral, and say it has chirality if its image in a plane mirror, ideally realized, cannot be brought to coincide with itself.' His definition can therefore be applied much more generally to structures outside chemistry, such as knots.

**Figure 10.16** An asymmetric, or chiral, carbon atom, shown in black, is bonded to four different atoms or groups – shown here in different colours. This gives rise to two configurations which are mirror images of each other.

If you look at your two hands you will see that they also are mirror images. When you put them on top of each other, the fingers and thumbs do not line up – we say they are **non-superimposable**.

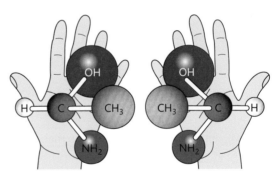

**Figure 10.17** Your two hands are non-superimposable mirror images.

Computer simulations and technologies such as 3D printing may facilitate our understanding of stereochemistry. To what extent do these approaches involve a different way of knowing than studies based on two-dimensional representations?

**TOK**

The same is true for optical isomers, and the two non-superimposable forms are known as **enantiomers**. A mixture containing equal amounts of the two enantiomers is known as a **racemic mixture** or a **racemate**. As we will see, such a mixture is said to be optically inactive.

Many molecules have more than one chiral centre, and so can give rise to different configurations at each position. Enantiomers have opposite configurations at *each* chiral centre, which is why the molecules are mirror images of each other. But when molecules have different configurations at one or more, *but not all*, chiral centres, they are known as **diastereomers** and are not mirror images of each other. Common sugars are often diastereomers of each other, such as glucose and galactose.

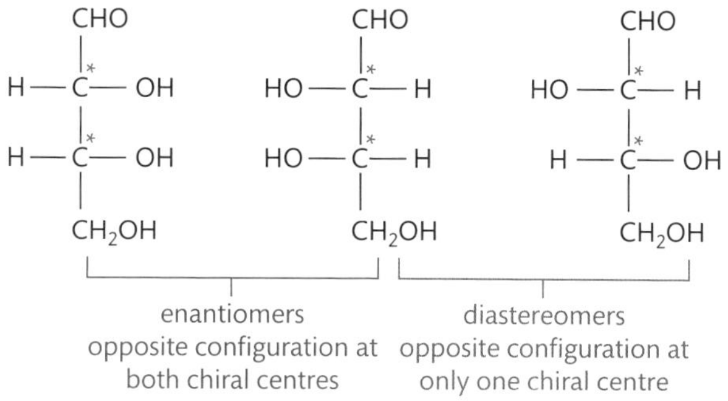

$$
\begin{array}{ccc}
\text{CHO} & \text{CHO} & \text{CHO} \\
\text{H---C*---OH} & \text{HO---C*---H} & \text{HO---C*---H} \\
\text{H---C*---OH} & \text{HO---C*---H} & \text{H---C*---OH} \\
\text{CH}_2\text{OH} & \text{CH}_2\text{OH} & \text{CH}_2\text{OH}
\end{array}
$$

enantiomers — opposite configuration at both chiral centres

diastereomers — opposite configuration at only one chiral centre

**Figure 10.18** Examples of four-carbon sugars showing the difference between enantiomers and diastereomers. Red asterisks mark the position of chiral carbon atoms. Note the diagram is simplified to two-dimensional representation for this purpose.

We can find optical activity in many of the molecules we have already encountered in this chapter. The clue is to look for any carbon atom that is bonded to four different groups. It is often useful to mark that carbon with a red asterisk.

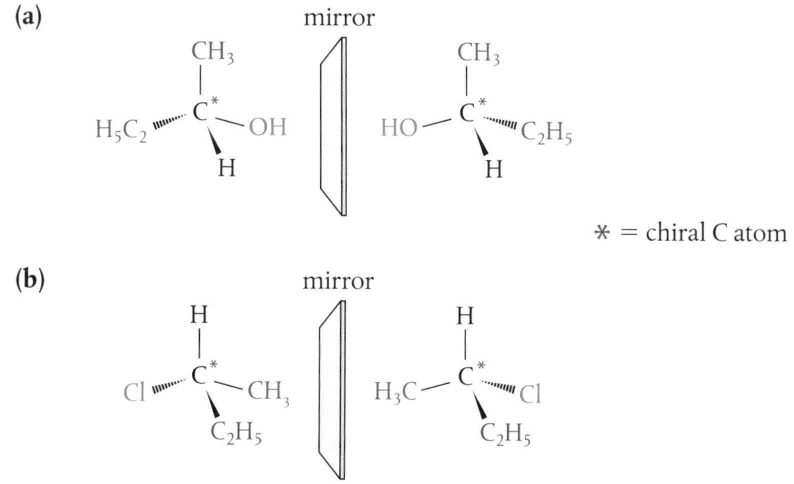

**(a)**

mirror

$$
\underset{H}{\overset{CH_3}{H_5C_2\text{---}\overset{\displaystyle |}{\underset{\displaystyle |}{C^*}}\text{---}OH}}
\qquad
\underset{H}{\overset{CH_3}{HO\text{---}\overset{\displaystyle |}{\underset{\displaystyle |}{C^*}}\text{---}C_2H_5}}
$$

∗ = chiral C atom

**(b)**

mirror

$$
\underset{C_2H_5}{\overset{H}{Cl\text{---}\overset{\displaystyle |}{\underset{\displaystyle |}{C^*}}\text{---}CH_3}}
\qquad
\underset{C_2H_5}{\overset{H}{H_3C\text{---}\overset{\displaystyle |}{\underset{\displaystyle |}{C^*}}\text{---}Cl}}
$$

A single chiral centre in a molecule gives rise to two stereoisomers. In general a molecule with $n$ chiral centres has a maximum of $2^n$ stereoisomers, although some may be too strained to exist. For example, cholesterol has eight chiral centres and so a possible $2^8 = 256$ stereoisomers. Only one is produced in biological systems.

Enantiomers have opposite configurations at all chiral centres and are mirror images of each other. Diastereomers have opposite configuration at some but not all chiral centres, and are not mirror images of each other.

**Figure 10.19** Enantiomers of (a) butan-2-ol and (b) 2-chlorobutane.

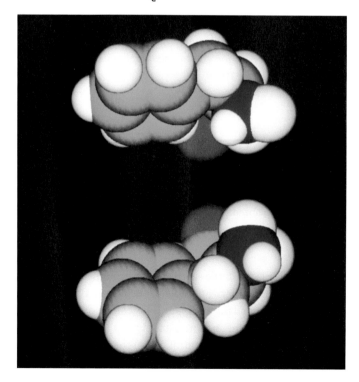

Molecular graphic of the two enantiomers of the amino acid phenylalanine, showing that they are mirror images of each other. Nearly all amino acids are chiral, but only one form, the l-form, occurs in biological systems.

# 10 Organic chemistry

When drawing enantiomers make sure that you use the wedge-dash type representation. It is best to write in the plane of the mirror first and then ensure that the same groups in the two molecules are an equal distance from this plane.

Note that when you are looking for a chiral carbon atom in a molecule you must look at the whole group bonded to the carbon, not just the immediately bonded atom. For example, $-CH_3$ is a different group from $-C_2H_5$.

## Worked example

Draw the enantiomers of 2-hydroxypropanoic acid (lactic acid). Mark the chiral carbon atom and show the plane of the mirror.

### Solution

First draw out the full structure and then identify the chiral carbon atom.

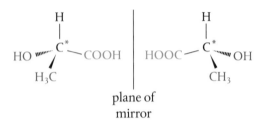

## Properties of enantiomers

Diastereomers usually differ from each other in their physical and chemical properties. Enantiomers, on the other hand, have identical physical and chemical properties – with two important exceptions.

## 1 Optical activity

As we know from their name, optical isomers show a difference in a specific interaction with light. A beam of ordinary light consists of electromagnetic waves that oscillate in an infinite number of planes at right angles to the direction of travel. If, however, this light is passed through a device called a **polarizer**, only the light waves oscillating in a single plane pass through, while light waves in all other planes are blocked out. This is known as **plane-polarized light**. A similar effect is achieved in polarized sunglasses or windshields to reduce glare.

In the early 1800s it was discovered that when a beam of plane-polarized light passes through a solution of optical isomers, they rotate the plane of polarization. The amount and direction of rotation can be measured with an instrument called a **polarimeter**, as shown in Figure 10.20.

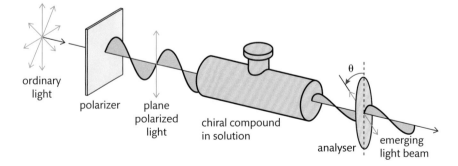

**Figure 10.20** Schematic representation of a polarimeter.

The solution of isomers is placed in the sample tube through which plane-polarized light is passed. Rotation of the polarization plane occurs and the light then passes through a second polarizer called the **analyser**. This can be rotated until the light passes through it and so the extent and direction of rotation can be deduced. In order to compare different solutions, the concentrations of the solutions, the wavelength of light used, and the sample path length must all be kept the same.

Separate solutions of enantiomers, at the same concentration, rotate plane-polarized light in equal amounts but opposite directions. This is what is meant by being optically active. A racemic mixture does not rotate the light and so is said to be optically inactive. Naturally occurring chiral molecules are optically active, in other words they exist as only one enantiomer. For example, morphine rotates plane-polarized light to the left so is said to be (–), whereas sucrose rotates it to the right and is said to be (+).

**The two enantiomers of a chiral compound rotate plane-polarized light in equal and opposite directions.**

## NATURE OF SCIENCE

The pioneer of polarimetry was Jean Baptiste Biot (1774–1862) who was a French physicist and older friend of the famous French bacteriologist Louis Pasteur (1822–1895). Biot showed that some crystals of quartz rotated the plane of polarized light while other crystals rotated it to the same extent in the opposite direction. Later, by showing the same effect in liquids such as turpentine, and in solutions of naturally occurring substance such as sugar he realized it must be a molecular property and coined the term 'optical activity'. In 1848 Pasteur, working on crystalline salts derived from wine, discovered that while tartaric acid showed optical activity, racemic acid with the same chemical composition does not, and deduced that this is because it contains an equal mixture of two isomers. Pasteur saw the huge significance of this. He reasoned that reactions outside the cell always produce an optically inactive mixture whereas biological activity is specific to one isomer. In his later work on the origin of life this became his guiding distinction between living and inanimate material.

Different notations are used to distinguish between the two enantiomers of a pair. (+) and (–) refer to the direction in which the plane polarized light is rotated, (+) for a clockwise direction and (–) for anticlockwise rotation. The lower case d- (dextrorotatory) and l- (laevorotatory) respectively are used as alternates for this but are becoming obsolete. Confusingly, small upper case d- and l- are a different, unrelated notation based on spatial configurations in comparison with the reference molecule glyceraldehyde. This latter system is widely used in naming many biological molecules such as amino acids and sugars. Other molecules are described by their absolute configuration, using *R* (rectus) for right or clockwise and *S* (sinister) for left or counterclockwise. The rules for determining the absolute configuration are based on atomic number and mass. Happily, we will not adopt any particular system here and you will not be expected to identify the specific enantiomer in any of these examples.

## 2 Reactivity with other chiral molecules

When a racemic mixture is reacted with a single enantiomer of another chiral compound, the two components of the mixture, the (+) and (–) enantiomers, react to produce different products. These products have distinct chemical and physical properties and so can be separated from each other relatively easily. This is therefore a means by which the two enantiomers can be separated from a racemic mixture, a process known as **resolution**.

The different reactivity of a pair of enantiomers with another chiral molecule is of particular significance in biological systems because these *are* chiral environments. An infamous example of this occurred in the 1960s when the drug thalidomide was prescribed to pregnant women for morning sickness. One enantiomer is therapeutic but the other produces severe malformations in the fetus. This tragedy largely spearheaded research into processes for the manufacture of a single enantiomer using a chiral catalyst. The process, known as **asymmetric synthesis**, led to the Nobel Prize in Chemistry in 2001. It is discussed in Chapter 15.

The human senses of smell and taste are responsive to chiral influences. For example, d-amino acids all taste sweet, whereas l-amino acids are often tasteless or bitter. We can distinguish between the smells of oranges and lemons due to the presence of different enantiomers of the compound limonene. This is because taste buds on the tongue and sense receptors in the nose contain chiral molecules and so interact differently with the different enantiomers. As a result, stereochemistry is a major aspect of the food and perfume industries, as well as being a key factor in the pharmaceutical industry.

## Exercises

**27** Which compound can exist as optical isomers?

  **A**  $CH_3CHBrCH_3$            **C**  $CH_3CHBrCOOH$

  **B**  $CH_2ClCH(OH)CH_2Cl$   **D**  $CH_3CCl_2CH_2OH$

**28** Write the structure of the first alkane to show optical isomerism.

**29** Draw and name the isomers of the following using the *E/Z* convention.

  **(a)** pent-2-ene

  **(b)** 2,3-dichlorobut-2-ene

## Practice questions

**1** Which reaction type is typical for halogenoalkanes?

  **A**  electrophilic substitution        **C**  nucleophilic substitution

  **B**  electrophilic addition            **D**  nucleophilic addition

**2** Which statement about the reactions of halogenoalkanes with potassium hydroxide is correct?

  **A**  Primary halogenoalkanes react mainly by an $S_N1$ mechanism.

  **B**  Bromoalkanes react faster than iodoalkanes.

  **C**  Tertiary halogenoalkanes react faster than primary halogenoalkanes.

  **D**  The primary product of the reaction is an aldehyde.

**3** Which molecule exhibits optical isomerism?

  **A**  3-iodopentane            **C**  1,3-diiodopropane

  **B**  2-iodo-2-methylpropane   **D**  2-iodobutane

**4** From which monomer is this polymer made?

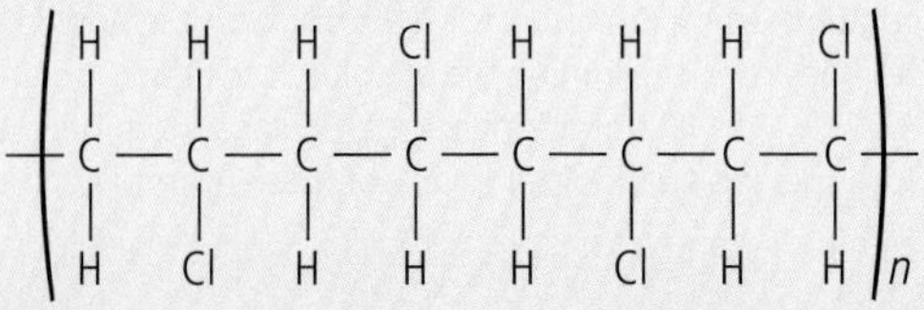

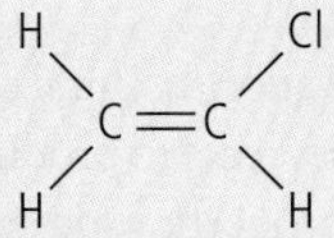

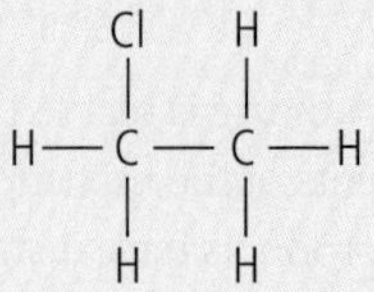

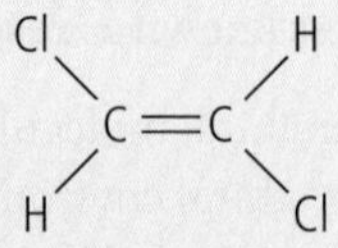

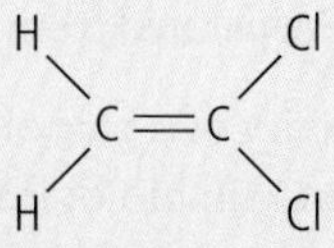

**5** What is the correct order of reaction types in the following sequence?

$$C_3H_7Br \xrightarrow{I} C_3H_7OH \xrightarrow{II} C_2H_5COOH \xrightarrow{III} C_2H_5COOC_2H_5$$

| | I | II | III |
|---|---|---|---|
| **A** | substitution | oxidation | condensation |
| **B** | addition | substitution | condensation |
| **C** | oxidation | substitution | condensation |
| **D** | substitution | oxidation | substitution |

**6** Which reactants could be used to form the compound below?

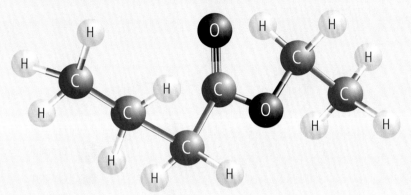

    **A**  butanoic acid and ethanol        **C**  ethanoic acid and propan-1-ol
    **B**  propanoic acid and ethanol       **D**  ethanoic acid and butan-1-ol

**7** Halogenoalkanes can undergo $S_N1$ and $S_N2$ reactions with aqueous sodium hydroxide. Which halogenoalkane will react fastest with a 0.1 mol dm$^{-3}$ solution of aqueous sodium hydroxide?

    **A**  2-chloro-2-methylpropane       **C**  1-chlorobutane
    **B**  2-iodo-2-methylpropane          **D**  1-iodobutane

**8** How many isomers can exist for a compound with the molecular formula $C_2H_2Cl_2$?

    **A**  1             **B**  2            **C**  3           **D**  4

**9** Which substances are possible products of the incomplete combustion of octane?

    **A**  carbon dioxide and hydrogen gas      **C**  carbon monoxide and hydrogen gas
    **B**  carbon monoxide and water vapour    **D**  methane and hydrogen gas

**10** How many chiral carbon atoms are present in a molecule of 2,3-dibromobutane?

    **A**  1             **B**  2            **C**  3           **D**  4

**11** Which reaction occurs via a free-radical mechanism?

    **A**  $C_2H_6 + Br_2 \rightarrow C_2H_5Br + HBr$       **C**  $C_4H_9I + OH^- \rightarrow C_4H_9OH + I^-$
    **B**  $C_2H_4 + Br_2 \rightarrow C_2H_4Br_2$           **D**  $(CH_3)_3Cl + H_2O \rightarrow (CH_3)_3COH + HI$

**12** Which compound could rotate the plane of polarization of polarized light?

    **A**  $(CH_3)_2CHCH_2Cl$    **B**  $CH_3CH_2CH_2CH_2Cl$  **C**  $CH_3CH_2CHClCH_3$  **D**  $(CH_3)_3CCl$

**13** Which conditions are required to obtain a good yield of a carboxylic acid when ethanol is oxidized using potassium dichromate(VI), $K_2Cr_2O_7$(aq)?

    I    add sulfuric acid
    II   heat the reaction mixture under reflux
    III  distil the product as the oxidizing agent is added

    **A**  I and II only      **B**  I and III only      **C**  II and III only      **D**  I, II, and III

**14** Which statement is correct about the enantiomers of a chiral compound?

    **A**  Their physical properties are different.
    **B**  All their chemical reactions are identical.
    **C**  A racemic mixture will rotate the plane of polarized light.
    **D**  They will rotate the plane of polarized light in opposite directions.

**15 (a)** Below are four structural isomers with molecular formula $C_4H_9Br$. State the name of each of the isomers A, B, C, and D.

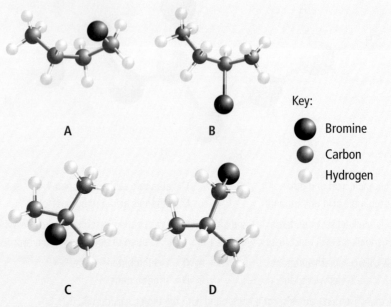

Key:
- Bromine
- Carbon
- Hydrogen

A

B

C

D

(4)

**(b) (i)** Identify the isomer(s) which will react with aqueous sodium hydroxide almost exclusively by an $S_N1$ mechanism. State the meaning of the symbols in the term $S_N1$ mechanism. (2)

**(ii)** Using the formula RBr to represent a bromoalkane, state an equation for the rate-determining step of this $S_N1$ reaction. (1)

**(iii)** Identify one isomer that will react with aqueous sodium hydroxide almost exclusively by an $S_N2$ mechanism. Draw the mechanism for this reaction using curly arrows to represent the movement of electron pairs. Include the structural formulas of the transition state and the organic product. (4)

**(c)** State and explain how the rates of the reactions in parts (b) (i) and (b) (iii) are affected when the concentration of the sodium hydroxide is doubled. (2)

**(d)** State and explain how the rate of reaction of 1-bromobutane with sodium hydroxide compares with that of 1-chlorobutane with sodium hydroxide. (2)

**(e)** Identify the isomer of $C_4H_9Br$ that can exist as stereoisomers. Outline how a polarimeter will distinguish between the isomers, and how their physical and chemical properties compare. (5)

*(Total 20 marks)*

**16** Alkenes are an economically and chemically important family of organic compounds.

**(a)** The reaction of alkenes with bromine water provides a test for unsaturation in the laboratory. Describe the colour change when bromine water is added to chloroethene. (1)

**(b)** Deduce the Lewis structure of chloroethene and identify the formula of the repeating unit of the polymer poly(chloroethene). (2)

**(c)** Besides polymerization, state **two** commercial uses of the reactions of alkenes. (2)

*(Total 5 marks)*

**17 (a)** Two compounds, **A** and **D**, each have the formula $C_4H_9Cl$.

Compound **A** is reacted with dilute aqueous sodium hydroxide to produce compound **B** with a formula of $C_4H_{10}O$. Compound **B** is then oxidized with acidified potassium manganate(VII) to produce compound **C** with a formula of $C_4H_8O$. Compound **C** resists further oxidation by acidified potassium manganate(VII).

Compound **D** is reacted with dilute aqueous sodium hydroxide to produce compound **E** with a formula of $C_4H_{10}O$. Compound **E** does not react with acidified potassium manganate(VII).

Deduce the structural formulas for compounds **A**, **B**, **C**, **D**, and **E**. (5)

**(b)** Deduce an equation for the reaction between propanoic acid and methanol. Identify the catalyst and state the name of the organic compound, **X**, formed. (4)

*(Total 9 marks)*

To access weblinks on the topics covered in this chapter, please go to www.pearsonhotlinks.com and enter the ISBN or title of this book.

**11** Measurement and data processing and analysis

## Essential ideas

**11.1** All measurement has a limit of precision and accuracy, and this must be taken into account when evaluating experimental results.

**11.2** Graphs are a visual representation of trends in data.

**11.3** Analytical techniques can be used to determine the structure of a compound, analyse the composition of a substance, or determine the purity of a compound. Spectroscopic techniques are used in the structural identification of organic and inorganic compounds.

**21.1** Although spectroscopic characterization techniques form the backbone of structural identification of compounds, typically no one technique results in a full structural identification of a molecule.

Sample preparation for research. Experimental conclusions must take into account any systematic errors and random uncertainties that could have occurred, for example, when measuring.

Science is a communal activity and it is important that information is shared openly and honestly. An essential part of this process is the way the international scientific community subjects the findings of scientists to intense critical scrutiny through the repetition of experiments and the peer review of results in journals and at conferences. All measurements have uncertainties and it is important these are reported when data are exchanged, as these limit the conclusions that can be legitimately drawn. Science has progressed and is one of the most successful enterprises in our culture because these inherent uncertainties are recognized. Chemistry provides us with a deep understanding of the material world but it does not offer absolute certainty.

Analytical chemistry plays a significant role in today's society. It is used in forensic, medical, and industrial laboratories and helps us monitor our environment and check the quality of the food we eat and the materials we use. Early analysts relied on their senses to discover the identity of unknown substances, but we now have the ability to probe the structure of substances using electromagnetic radiation beyond

The scales on two pieces of measuring glassware. The white numbers (left) belong to a measuring cylinder, while the black numbers (centre) mark out much smaller volumes on the side of a graduated pipette. A greater degree of measuring precision can be obtained by using the pipette rather than the cylinder.

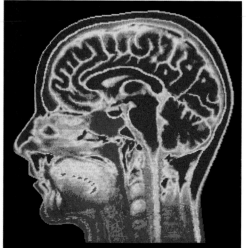

NMR is the basis of the diagnostic medical tool known as **magnetic resonance imaging** (MRI). This is a MRI scan of a normal brain. MRI is ideal for detecting brain tumours, infections in the brain, spine, and joints, and in diagnosing strokes and multiple sclerosis.

**TOK**

**TOK**

Scientists need to be principled and act with integrity and honesty.

'One aim of the physical sciences has been to give an exact picture of the material world. One achievement ... has been to prove that this aim is unattainable.' (J. Bronowski)

What are the implications of this claim for the aspirations of science?

the visible region. This has allowed us to discover how atoms are bonded in different molecules, and to detect minute quantities of substances in mixtures down to levels of parts per billion. No one method supplies us with all the information we need, so a battery of tools and range of skills have been developed.

Data collected from investigations are often presented in graphical form. This provides a pictorial representation of how one quantity is related to another. A graph is also a useful tool to assess errors as it identifies data points which do not fit the general trend and so gives another measure of the reliability of the data.

# 11.1 Uncertainties and errors in measurement and results

## Understandings:

- Qualitative data include all non-numerical information obtained from observations not from measurement.
- Quantitative data are obtained from measurements, and are always associated with random errors/ uncertainties, determined by the apparatus, and by human limitations such as reaction times.
- Propagation of random errors in data processing shows the impact of the uncertainties on the final result.
- Experimental design and procedure usually lead to systematic errors in measurement, which cause a deviation in a particular direction.
- Repeat trials and measurements will reduce random errors but not systematic errors.

  **Guidance**
  *SI units should be used throughout the programme.*

## Applications and skills:

- Distinction between random errors and systematic errors.
- Record uncertainties in all measurements as a range (±) to an appropriate precision.
- Discussion of ways to reduce uncertainties in an experiment.
- Propagation of uncertainties in processed data, including the use of percentage uncertainties.
- Discussion of systematic errors in all experimental work, their impact on the results, and how they can be reduced.
- Estimation of whether a particular source of error is likely to have a major or minor effect on the final result.
- Calculation of percentage error when the experimental result can be compared with a theoretical or accepted result.
- Distinction between accuracy and precision in evaluating results.

  **Guidance**
  - *Note that the data value must be recorded to the same precision as the random error.*
  - *The number of significant figures in a result is based on the figures given in the data. When adding or subtracting, the answer should be given to the least number of decimal places. When multiplying or dividing the final answer is given to the least number of significant figures.*

## Uncertainty in measurement

Measurement is an important part of chemistry. In the laboratory, you will use different measuring apparatus and there will be times when you have to select the instrument that is most appropriate for your task from a range of possibilities. Suppose, for example, you wanted 25 cm³ of water. You could choose from measuring cylinders, pipettes, burettes, volumetric flasks of different sizes, or even an analytical balance if you know the density. All of these could be used to measure a volume of 25 cm³, but with different levels of uncertainty.

## Uncertainty in analogue instruments

An uncertainty range applies to any experimental value. Some pieces of apparatus state the degree of uncertainty, in other cases you will have to make a judgement. Suppose you are asked to measure the volume of water in the measuring cylinder shown in Figure 11.1. The bottom of the meniscus of a liquid usually lies between two graduations and so the final figure of the reading has to be estimated. The smallest division in the measuring cylinder is 4 cm³ so we should report the volume as 62 (±) 2 cm³. The same considerations apply to other equipment such as burettes and alcohol thermometers that have analogue scales. The uncertainty of an analogue scale is half the smallest division.

## Uncertainty in digital instruments

A top pan balance has a digital scale. The mass of the sample of water shown here is 100.00 g but the last digit is uncertain. The degree of uncertainty is (±) 0.01 g: the smallest scale division. The uncertainty of a digital scale is (±) the smallest scale division.

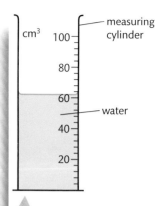

**Figure 11.1** The volume reading should be taken from the bottom of the meniscus. You could report the volume as 62 cm³ but this is not an exact value.

**The uncertainty of a digital scale is (±) the smallest scale division.**

## Other sources of uncertainty

Chemists are interested in measuring how properties change during a reaction and this can lead to additional sources of uncertainty. When time measurements are taken for example, the reaction time of the experimenter should be considered. Similarly there are uncertainties in judging, for example, the point that an indicator changes colour when measuring the equivalence point in a titration, or what is the temperature at a particular time during an exothermic reaction, or what is the voltage of an electrochemical cell. These extra uncertainties should be noted even if they are not actually quantified when data are collected in experimental work.

The mass of the water is recorded as 100.00 (+) 0.01 g.

An analytical balance is one of the most precise instruments in a school laboratory. This is a digital instrument. Analytical balances are more precise than top pan balances as they have a shield to remove any fluctuations due to air currents.

## Significant figures in measurements

The digits in the measurement up to and including the first uncertain digit are the **significant figures** of the measurement. There are two significant figures, for example, in 62 cm³ and five in 100.00 g. The zeros are significant here as they signify that the uncertainty range is (±) 0.01 g. The number of significant figures may not always be clear. If a time measurement is 1000 s, for example, are there one, two, three, or four significant figures? As this is ambiguous, scientific notation is used to remove any confusion as the number is written with one non-zero digit on the left of the decimal point.

| Measurement | Significant figures | Measurement | Significant figures |
|---|---|---|---|
| 1000 s | unspecified | 0.45 mol dm$^{-3}$ | 2 |
| 1 × 10$^3$ s | 1 | 4.5 × 10$^{-1}$ mol dm$^{-3}$ | 2 |
| 1.0 × 10$^3$ s | 2 | 4.50 × 10$^{-1}$ mol dm$^{-3}$ | 3 |
| 1.00 × 10$^3$ s | 3 | 4.500 × 10$^{-1}$ mol dm$^{-3}$ | 4 |
| 1.000 × 10$^3$ s | 4 | 4.5000 × 10$^{-1}$ mol dm$^{-3}$ | 5 |

## Exercises

1   What is the uncertainty range in the measuring cylinder in the close up photo here?

2   A reward is given for a missing diamond, which has a reported mass of 9.92 (±) 0.05 g. You find a diamond and measure its mass as 10.1 (±) 0.2 g. Could this be the missing diamond?

3   Express the following in standard notation:
   **(a)** 0.04 g      **(b)** 222 cm$^3$      **(c)** 0.030 g      **(d)** 30 °C

4   What is the number of significant figures in each of the following?
   **(a)** 15.50 cm$^3$      **(b)** 150 s      **(c)** 0.0123 g      **(d)** 150.0 g

## Experimental errors

The experimental error in a result is the difference between the recorded value and the generally accepted or literature value. Errors can be categorized as **random** or **systematic**.

You should compare your results to literature values where appropriate.

### Random errors

When an experimenter approximates a reading, there is an equal probability of being too high or too low. This is a random error.

Random errors are caused by:

• the readability of the measuring instrument
• the effects of changes in the surroundings such as temperature variations and air currents
• insufficient data
• the observer misinterpreting the reading.

As they are random, the errors can be reduced through repeated measurements; the readings that are randomly too high will be balanced by those that are too low if sufficient readings are taken.

This is why it is good practice to duplicate experiments when designing experiments. If the same person duplicates the experiment with the same result the results are **repeatable**; if several experimenters duplicate the results they are **reproducible**.

Suppose the mass of a piece of magnesium ribbon is measured several times and the following results obtained:

$$0.1234 \text{ g} \quad 0.1232 \text{ g} \quad 0.1233 \text{ g} \quad 0.1234 \text{ g} \quad 0.1235 \text{ g} \quad 0.1236 \text{ g}$$

$$\text{average mass} = \frac{0.1234 + 0.1232 + 0.1233 + 0.1234 + 0.1235 + 0.1236}{6} \text{ g}$$

$$= 0.1234 \text{ g}$$

The mass is reported as 0.1234 (±) 0.0002 g as it is in the range 0.1232 to 0.1236 g.

## Systematic errors

Systematic errors occur as a result of poor experimental design or procedure. They cannot be reduced by repeating the experiments. Suppose the top pan balance was incorrectly zeroed in the previous example and the following results were obtained:

$$0.1236 \text{ g} \quad 0.1234 \text{ g} \quad 0.1235 \text{ g} \quad 0.1236 \text{ g} \quad 0.1237 \text{ g} \quad 0.1238 \text{ g}$$

All the values are too high by 0.0002 g.

$$\text{average mass} = \frac{0.1236 + 0.1234 + 0.1235 + 0.1236 + 0.1237 + 0.1238}{6} \text{ g}$$

$$= 0.1236 \text{ g}$$

Examples of systematic errors include the following:

- measuring the volume of water from the top of the meniscus rather than the bottom will lead to volumes which are too high
- overshooting the volume of a liquid delivered in a titration will lead to volumes which are too high
- using an acid–base indicator whose end point does not correspond to the equivalence point of the titration
- heat losses in an exothermic reaction will lead to smaller temperature changes.

Systematic errors can be reduced by careful experimental design.

## Accuracy and precision

The smaller the systematic error, the greater is the **accuracy**. The smaller the random uncertainties, the greater the **precision**. The masses of magnesium in the earlier example are measured to the same precision but the first set of values is more accurate. Precise measurements have small random errors and are reproducible in repeated trials; accurate measurements have small systematic errors and give a result close to the accepted value (Figure 11.2).

**TOK** Systematic errors cannot be reduced by simply repeating the measurement in the same way. If you were inaccurate the first time you will be inaccurate the second.

So, how do you know that you have a systematic error? Why do you trust one set of results more than another?

 When evaluating investigations, distinguish between systematic and random errors.

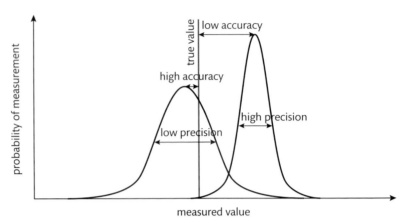

Figure 11.2 The set of readings on the left are of high accuracy and low precision. The readings on the right are of low accuracy and high precision.

## Exercises

5  Repeated measurements of a quantity can reduce the effects of:

 I   random errors
 II  systematic errors

 **A**  I only      **B**  II only      **C**  I and II      **D**  neither I or II

6  A student makes measurements from which she calculates the enthalpy of neutralization as 58.5357 kJ mol$^{-1}$. She estimates that her result is precise to ±2%.

 Which of the following gives her result expressed to the appropriate number of significant figures?

 **A**  59 kJ mol$^{-1}$      **B**  58.5 kJ mol$^{-1}$      **C**  58.54 kJ mol$^{-1}$      **D**  58.536 kJ mol$^{-1}$

7  Using a measuring cylinder, a student measures the volume of water incorrectly by reading the top instead of the bottom of meniscus. This error will affect:

 **A**  neither the precision nor the accuracy of the readings
 **B**  only the accuracy of the readings
 **C**  only the precision of the readings
 **D**  both the precision and the accuracy of the readings

8  A known volume of sodium hydroxide solution is added to a conical flask using a pipette. A burette is used to measure the volume of hydrochloric acid needed to neutralize the sodium hydroxide. Which of the following would lead to a systematic error in the results?

 I    the use of a wet burette
 II   the use of a wet pipette
 III  the use of a wet conical flask

 **A**  I and II only      **B**  I and III only      **C**  II and III only      **D**  I, II, and III

9  Which type of errors can cancel when differences in quantities are calculated?

 I   random errors
 II  systematic errors

 **A**  I only      **B**  II only      **C**  I and II      **D**  neither I or II

10  Measurements are subject to both random errors and to systematic errors. Identify the correct statements.

 I    Systematic errors can be reduced by modifying the experimental procedure.
 II   A random error results in a different reading each time the same measurement is taken.
 III  Random errors can be reduced by taking the average of several measurements.

 **A**  I and II only      **B**  I and III only      **C**  II and III only      **D**  I, II, and III

11  The volume of a water sample was repeatedly measured by a student and the following results were recorded.

| | I | II | III | IV | V |
|---|---|---|---|---|---|
| Volume (± 0.1) / cm³ | 38.2 | 38.1 | 38.2 | 38.3 | 38.2 |

The true volume of the sample is 38.5 cm³.

Which is the correct description of the measurements?

|   | Accuracy (± 0.1) / cm³ | Precision (± 0.1) / cm³ |
|---|---|---|
| **A** | yes | yes |
| **B** | yes | no |
| **C** | no | yes |
| **D** | no | no |

**12** The time for a 2.00 cm sample of magnesium ribbon to react completely with 20.0 cm³ of 1.00 mol dm⁻³ hydrochloric acid is measured five times. The readings are 48.8, 48.9, 49.0, 49.1, and 49.2 (±) 0.1 s.

State the value that should be quoted for the time measurement.

## Percentage uncertainties and errors

An uncertainty of 1 s is more significant for time measurements of 10 s than it is for 100 s. It is helpful to express the uncertainty using absolute, fractional or percentage values.

$$\text{fractional uncertainty} = \frac{\text{absolute uncertainty}}{\text{measured value}}$$

This can be expressed as a percentage:

$$\text{percentage uncertainty} = \frac{\text{absolute uncertainty}}{\text{measured value}} \times 100\%$$

The percentage uncertainty should not be confused with **percentage error**. Percentage error is a measure of how close the **experimental value** is to the literature or accepted value.

$$\text{percentage error} = \frac{\text{accepted value} - \text{experimental value}}{\text{accepted value}} \times 100\%$$

## Propagation of uncertainties in calculated results

Uncertainties in the raw data lead to uncertainties in processed data and it is important that these are propagated in a consistent way.

### Addition and subtraction

Consider two burette readings:

- initial reading (±) 0.05 / cm³ = 15.05
- final reading (±) 0.05 / cm³ = 37.20

What value should be reported for the volume delivered?

The initial reading is in the range 15.00 to 15.10 cm³.

The final reading is in the range: 37.15 to 37.25 cm³.

The maximum volume is formed by combining the maximum final reading with the minimum initial reading:

$$\text{vol}_{max} = 37.25 - 15.00 = 22.25 \text{ cm}^3$$

The minimum volume is formed by combining the minimum final volume with the maximum initial reading:

$$\text{vol}_{min} = 37.15 - 15.10 = 22.05 \text{ cm}^3$$

**Precise measurements have small random errors and are reproducible in repeated trials. Accurate measurements have small systematic errors and give a result close to the accepted value.**

percentage uncertainty
$$= \frac{\text{absolute uncertainty}}{\text{measured value}}$$
$$\times 100\%$$

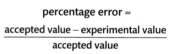

percentage error =
$$\frac{\text{accepted value} - \text{experimental value}}{\text{accepted value}}$$
$$\times 100\%$$

therefore the volume = 22.15 (±) 0.1 cm$^3$

The volume depends on two measurements and the uncertainty is the sum of the two absolute uncertainties.

## Multiplication and division

Working out the uncertainty in calculated values can be a time-consuming process. Consider the density calculation:

| | Value | Absolute uncertainty | % Uncertainty |
|---|---|---|---|
| mass / g | 24.0 | (±) 0.5 | $= \dfrac{0.5}{24.0} \times 100\% = 2\%$ |
| volume / cm$^3$ | 2.0 | (±) 0.1 | $= \dfrac{0.1}{2.0} \times 100\% = 5\%$ |

| | Value | Maximum value | Minimum value |
|---|---|---|---|
| density / g cm$^{-3}$ | $= \dfrac{24.0}{2.0} = 12.0$ | $= \dfrac{24.5}{1.9} = 12.89$ | $= \dfrac{23.5}{2.1} = 11.19$ |

| | Value | Absolute uncertainty | % Uncertainty |
|---|---|---|---|
| density / g cm$^{-3}$ | 12 | $= 12.89 - 12.00 = (\pm) 0.89$ | $= \dfrac{0.89}{12} \times 100\% = 7.4\%$ |

The density should only be given to two significant figures given the uncertainty in the mass and volume values, as discussed in the next section. The uncertainty in the calculated value of the density is 7% (given to one significant figure). This is equal to the sum of the uncertainties in the mass and volume values: (5% + 2% to the same level of accuracy). This approximate result provides us with a simple treatment of propagating uncertainties when multiplying and dividing measurements.

When multiplying or dividing measurements, the total percentage uncertainty is the sum of the individual percentage uncertainties. The absolute uncertainty can then be calculated from the percentage uncertainty.

## Significant figures in calculations

### Multiplication and division

Consider a sample of sodium chloride with a mass of 5.00 (±) 0.01 g and a volume of 2.3 (±) 0.1 cm$^3$. What is its density?

Using a calculator:

$$\text{density } (\rho) = \frac{\text{mass}}{\text{volume}} = \frac{5.00}{2.3} = 2.173\,913\,043 \text{ g cm}^{-3}$$

Can we claim to know the density to such precision when the value is based on less precise raw data?

The value is misleading as the mass lies in the range 4.99 to 5.01 g and the volume is between 2.2 and 2.4 cm$^3$. The best we can do is to give a range of values for the density.

The maximum value is obtained when the maximum value for the mass is combined with the minimum value of the volume:

$$\rho_{max} = \frac{\text{maximum mass}}{\text{minimum volume}} = \frac{5.01}{2.2} = 2.277\ 273\ \text{g cm}^{-3}$$

The minimum value is obtained by combining the minimum mass with a maximum value for the volume:

$$\rho_{min} = \frac{\text{minimum mass}}{\text{maximum volume}} = \frac{4.99}{2.4} = 2.079\ 167\ \text{g cm}^{-3}$$

The density falls in the range between the maximum and minimum value.

The second significant figure is uncertain and the reported value must be reported to this precision as $2.2\ \text{g cm}^{-3}$. The precision of the density is limited by the volume measurement as this is the least precise.

This leads to a simple rule. Whenever you multiply or divide data, the answer should be quoted to the same number of significant figures as the least precise data.

## Addition and subtraction

When values are added or subtracted, the number of decimal places determines the precision of the calculated value.

Suppose we need the total mass of two pieces of zinc of mass 1.21 g and 0.56 g.

$$\text{total mass} = 1.77\ (\pm)\ 0.02\ \text{g}$$

This can be given to two decimal places as the balance was precise to $(\pm)\ 0.01$ g in both cases.

Similarly, when calculating a temperature increase from 25.2 °C to 34.2 °C.

$$\text{temperature increase} = 34.2 - 25.2\ °\text{C} = 9.0\ (\pm)\ 0.2\ °\text{C}$$

### Worked example

Report the total mass of solution prepared by adding 50 g of water to 1.00 g of sugar. Would the use of a more precise balance for the mass of sugar result in a more precise total mass?

#### Solution

total mass = 50 + 1.00 g = 51 g

The precision of the total is limited by the precision of the mass of the water. Using a more precise balance for the mass of sugar would not have improved the precision.

### Worked example

The lengths of the sides of a wooden block are measured and the diagram on page 538 shows the measured values with their uncertainties.

> Whenever you multiply or divide data, the answer should be quoted to the same number of significant figures as the least precise data.

> Whenever you add or subtract data, the answer should be quoted to the same number of decimal places as the least precise value.

> When evaluating procedures you should discuss the precision and accuracy of the measurements. You should specifically look at the procedure and use of equipment.

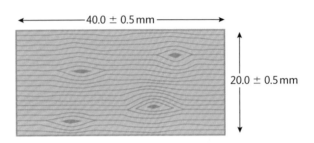

What is the percentage and absolute uncertainty in the calculated area of the block?

### Solution

area = 40.0 × 20.0 mm² = 800 mm² (area is given to three significant figures)

% uncertainty of area = % uncertainty of length + % uncertainty of breadth

$$\text{\% uncertainty of length} = \frac{0.5}{40.0} \times 100\% = 1.25\%$$

$$\text{\% uncertainty of breadth} = \frac{0.5}{20.0} \times 100\% = 2.5\%$$

% uncertainty of area = 1.25 + 2.5 = 3.75 ≈ 4%

$$\text{absolute uncertainty} = \frac{3.75}{100} \times 800 \text{ mm}^2 = 30 \text{ mm}^2$$

area = 800 (±) 30 mm²

## Discussing errors and uncertainties

An experimental conclusion must take into account any systematic errors and random uncertainties. You should recognize when the uncertainty of one of the measurements is much greater than the others as this will then have the major effect on the uncertainty of the final result. The approximate uncertainty can be taken as being due to that quantity alone. In thermometric experiments, for example, the thermometer often produces the most uncertain results, particularly for reactions which produce small temperature differences.

Can the difference between the experimental and literature value be explained in terms of the uncertainties of the measurements or were other systematic errors involved? This question needs to be answered when evaluating an experimental procedure. Heat loss to the surroundings, for example, accounts for experimental enthalpy changes for exothermic reactions being lower than literature values. Suggested modifications, such as improved insulation to reduce heat exchange between the system and the surroundings, should attempt to reduce these errors. This is discussed in more detail in Chapter 5 (page 222).

### NATURE OF SCIENCE

Lord Kelvin (1824–1907): 'When you can measure what you are speaking about and express it in numbers, you know something about it, but when you cannot measure it, when you cannot express it in numbers, your knowledge is of a meagre and unsatisfactory kind.'

Data are the lifeblood of scientists. This may be qualitative, obtained from observations, or quantitative, collected from measurements. Quantitative data are generally more reliable as they can be analysed mathematically but nonetheless will suffer from unavoidable uncertainties.

*contd …*

---

**To find the absolute uncertainty in a calculated value for *ab* or *a/b*:**

1 Find the percentage uncertainty in *a* and *b*.

2 Add the percentage uncertainties of *a* and *b* to find the percentage uncertainty in the calculated value.

3 Convert this percentage uncertainty to an absolute value.

---

The calculated uncertainty is generally quoted to not more than one significant figure if it is greater or equal to 2% of the answer and to not more than two significant figures if it is less than 2%.

Intermediate values in calculations should not be rounded off to avoid unnecessary imprecision.

*contd ...*

This analysis helps identify significant relationships and eliminate spurious outliers. Scientists look for relationships between the key factors in their investigations. The errors and uncertainties in the data must be considered when assessing the reliability of the data.

A key part of the training and skill of scientists is being able to decide which technique will produce the most precise and accurate results. Although many scientific results are very close to certainty, scientists can never claim 'absolute certainty' and the level of uncertainty should always be reported. With this in mind, scientists often speak of 'levels of confidence' when discussing experimental outcomes.

Science is a collaborative activity. Scientific papers are only published in journals after they have been anonymously peer reviewed by fellow scientists researching independently in the same field. The work must represent a new contribution to knowledge and be based on sound research methodologies.

## Exercises

**13** A block of ice was heated for 10 minutes. The diagram shows the scale of thermometer with the initial and final temperatures.

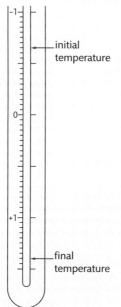

What is the temperature change expressed to the appropriate precision?

**A**  1.40 ± 0.01 K  **B**  2.05 ± 0.01 K  **C**  2.050 ± 0.005 K  **D**  2.1 ± 0.1 K

**14** A thermometer which can be read to a precision of ±0.5 °C is used to measure a temperature increase from 30.0 °C to 50.0 °C.

What is the percentage uncertainty in the measurement of the temperature increase?

**A**  1%  **B**  2.5%  **C**  3%  **D**  5%

**15** What is the main source of error in experiments carried out to determine enthalpy changes in a school laboratory?

**A**  uncertain volume measurements
**B**  heat exchange with the surroundings
**C**  uncertainties in the concentrations of the solutions
**D**  impurities in the reagents

**16** The mass of an object is measured as 1.652 g and its volume as 1.1 cm³. If the density (mass per unit volume) is calculated from these values, to how many significant figures should it be expressed?

**A**  1  **B**  2  **C**  3  **D**  4

**17** The number of significant figures that should be reported for the mass increase which is obtained by taking the difference between readings of 11.6235 g and 10.5805 g is:

**A**  3  **B**  4  **C**  5  **D**  6

**18** A 0.266 g sample of zinc is added to hydrochloric acid. 0.186 g of zinc is later recovered from the acid. What is the percentage mass loss of the zinc to the correct number of significant figures?

**A** 30% **B** 30.1% **C** 30.07% **D** 30.08%

**19** A $0.020 \pm 0.001$ g piece of magnesium ribbon takes $20 \pm 1$ s to react in an acid solution.

The average rate can be calculated from these data:

$$\text{average rate} = \frac{\text{mass of Mg}}{\text{time taken to dissolve}}$$

Identify the average rate that should be recorded.

**A** $0.001 \pm 0.0001$ g s$^{-1}$      **C** $0.0010 \pm 0.0001$ g s$^{-1}$
**B** $0.001 \pm 0.001$ g s$^{-1}$      **D** $0.0010 \pm 0.001$ g s$^{-1}$

**20** The concentration of a solution of hydrochloric acid = $1.00 (\pm) 0.05$ mol dm$^{-3}$ and the volume = $10.0 (\pm) 0.1$ cm$^3$. Calculate the number of moles and give the absolute uncertainty.

**21** The enthalpy change of the reaction:

$$CuSO_4(aq) + Zn(s) \rightarrow ZnSO_4(aq) + Cu(s)$$

was determined using the procedure outlined on page 222. Assume that:

- zinc is in excess
- all the heat of reaction passes into the water.

The molar enthalpy change can be calculated from the temperature change of the solution using the expression:

$$\Delta H = \frac{-c(H_2O) \times (T_{final} - T_{initial})}{[CuSO_4]}$$

where $c(H_2O)$ is the specific heat capacity of water, $T_{initial}$ is the temperature of the copper sulfate before zinc was added, and $T_{final}$ is the maximum temperature of the copper sulfate solution after the zinc was added.

The following results were recorded:

$T_{initial} (\pm) 0.1 / °C = 21.2$

$T_{final} (\pm) 0.1 / °C = 43.2$

$[CuSO_4] = 0.500$ mol dm$^{-3}$

**(a)** Calculate the temperature change during the reaction and give the absolute uncertainty.
**(b)** Calculate the percentage uncertainty of this temperature change.
**(c)** Calculate the molar enthalpy change of reaction.
**(d)** Assuming the uncertainties in any other measurements are negligible, determine the percentage uncertainty in the experimental value of the enthalpy change.
**(e)** Calculate the absolute uncertainty of the calculated enthalpy change.
**(f)** The literature value for the standard enthalpy change of reaction = $-217$ kJ mol$^{-1}$. Comment on any differences between the experimental and literature values.

> There should be no variation in the precision of raw data measured with the same instrument and the same number of decimal places should be used. For data derived from processing raw data (for example, averages), the level of precision should be consistent with that of the raw data.

# 11.2 Graphical techniques

## Understandings:

- Graphical techniques are an effective means of communicating the effect of an independent variable on a dependent variable, and can lead to determination of physical quantities.
- Sketched graphs have labelled but unscaled axes, and are used to show qualitative trends, such as variables that are proportional or inversely proportional.
- Drawn graphs have labelled and scaled axes, and are used in quantitative measurements.

## Applications and skills:

- Drawing graphs of experimental results, including the correct choice of axes and scale.
- Interpretation of graphs in terms of the relationships of dependent and independent variables.

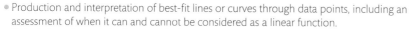

- Production and interpretation of best-fit lines or curves through data points, including an assessment of when it can and cannot be considered as a linear function.
- Calculation of quantities from graphs by measuring slope (gradient) and intercept, including appropriate units.

A graph is often the best method of presenting and analysing data. It shows the relationship between the **independent variable** plotted on the horizontal axis and the **dependent variable** on the vertical axis and gives an indication of the reliability of the measurements.

## Plotting graphs

When you draw a graph you should:

- Give the graph a title.
- Label the axes with both quantities and units.
- Use the available space as effectively as possible.
- Use sensible linear scales – there should be no uneven jumps.
- Plot all the points correctly.
- A line of best fit should be drawn smoothly and clearly. It does not have to go through all the points but should show the overall trend.
- Identify any points which do not agree with the general trend.
- Think carefully about the inclusion of the origin. The point (0, 0) can be the most accurate data point or it can be irrelevant.

## The 'best-fit' straight line

In many cases the best procedure is to find a way of plotting the data to produce a straight line. The 'best-fit' line passes as near to as many of the points as possible. For example, a straight line through the origin is the most appropriate way to join the set of points in Figure 11.3.

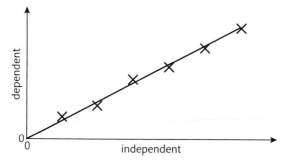

The best-fit line does not necessarily pass through any of the points plotted. Sometimes a line has to be extended beyond the range of measurements of the graph. This is called **extrapolation**. Absolute zero, for example, can be found by extrapolating the volume/temperature graph for an ideal gas (Figure 11.4).

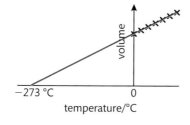

> The independent variable is the *cause* and is plotted on the horizontal axis. The dependent variable is the *effect* and is plotted on the vertical axis.

**Figure 11.3** A straight-line graph which passes through the origin shows that the dependent variable is proportional to the independent variable.

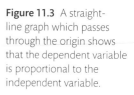

**Figure 11.4** The straight line can be extrapolated to lower temperatures to find a value for absolute zero.

The process of assuming that the trend line applies between two points is called **interpolation**.

Two properties of a straight line are particularly useful: the gradient and the intercept.

## Finding the gradient of a straight line or curve

The equation for a straight line is $y = mx + c$.

- $x$ is the independent variable
- $y$ is the dependent variable
- $m$ is the gradient
- $c$ is the intercept on the vertical axis.

The gradient of a straight line ($m$) is the increase in the dependent variable divided by the increase in the independent variable.

This can be expressed as

$$m = \frac{\Delta y}{\Delta x}$$

The triangle used to calculate the gradient should be as large as possible (Figure 11.5).

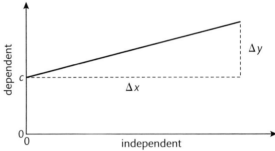

**Figure 11.5** The gradient ($m$) can be calculated from the graph. $m = \Delta y/\Delta x$.

The gradient of a straight line has units; the units of the vertical axis divided by the units of the horizontal axis.

The gradient of a curve at any point is the gradient of the tangent to the curve at that point (Figure 11.6).

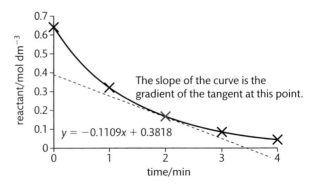

The slope of the curve is the gradient of the tangent at this point.

$y = -0.1109x + 0.3818$

**Figure 11.6** This graph shows how the concentration of a reactant decreases with time. The gradient of a slope is given by the gradient of the tangent at that point. The equation of the tangent was calculated by computer software. The rate at the point shown is $-0.11$ mol dm$^{-3}$ min$^{-1}$. The negative value shows that that reactant concentration is decreasing with increasing time.

## Errors and graphs

Systematic errors and random uncertainties can often be recognized from a graph (Figure 11.7). A graph combines the results of many measurements and so minimizes the effects of random uncertainties in the measurements.

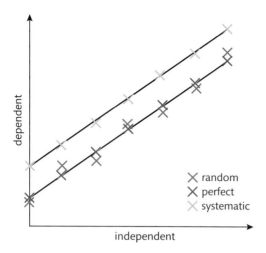

Figure 11.7 A systematic error produces a displaced straight line. Random uncertainties lead to points on both sides of the perfect straight line.

The presence of an outlier also suggests that some of the data are unreliable (Figure 11.8).

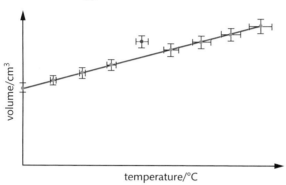

Figure 11.8 A graph showing an outlier which does not fit the line.

## Choosing what to plot to produce a straight line

Sometimes the data need to be processed in order to produce a straight line.

For example, when the relationship between the pressure and volume of a gas is investigated, the ideal gas equation $PV = nRT$ can be rearranged to give a straight line graph when $P$ is plotted against $1/V$:

$$P = nRT\frac{1}{V}$$

The pressure is **inversely proportional** to the volume. This relationship is clearly seen when a graph of $1/V$ against $P$ gives a straight line passing through the origin at constant temperature (Figure 11.9).

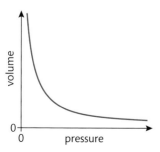

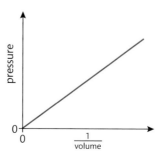

**TOK** We often dismiss results which don't fit the expected pattern because of experimental error. When are you justified in dismissing a data point which does not fit the general pattern?

**TOK** Data can be presented in a variety of graphical formats. How does the presentation of the data affect the way the data are interpreted?

Figure 11.9 The pressure of a gas is inversely proportional to the volume. A graph of $P$ against $1/V$ produces a straight line through the origin.

## The use of log scales

We saw in Chapter 8 (page 356) that the pH scale condenses a wide range of $H^+(aq)$ concentrations into a more manageable range. In a similar way, it is sometimes convenient to present data, for example successive ionization energies, on a logarithmic scale (page 88). Log scales also allow some relationships to be rearranged into the form of a straight line. Consider the following two examples.

1   Suppose, for example, a reaction is expected to follow the following rate law:

$$\text{rate} = k[A]^n$$

where $n$ is the order with respect to A (see Chapter 6, page 289), and $k$ is the rate constant.

Taking logarithms on both sides gives:

$$\ln \text{rate} = \ln k[A]^n = n \ln[A] + \ln k$$

Thus a plot of ln rate on the vertical axis and ln [A] on the horizontal axis would give a straight line with a gradient of $n$ and a vertical intercept of ln $k$ (Figure 11.10).

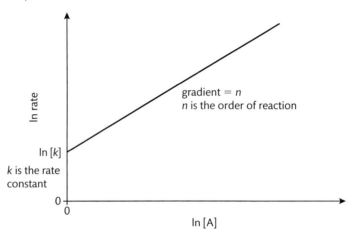

**Figure 11.10** The order of reaction can be found from the gradient of a ln rate against ln [A] graph.

2   The Arrhenius equation relates the rate constant of a reaction to temperature:

$$k(T) = Ae^{\frac{-E_a}{RT}}$$

where $E_a$ is the activation energy, $R$ is the universal gas constant, and $T$ is temperature measured in kelvin.

Taking natural logs on both sides:

$$\ln k(T) = \ln Ae^{\frac{-E_a}{RT}}$$

$$\ln k(T) = \ln A + \ln e^{\frac{-E_a}{RT}}$$

$$= \ln A - \frac{E_a}{RT}$$

Thus a plot of ln $k(T)$ against $(1/T)$ gives a straight line. The activation energy can be calculated from the gradient ($m = -E_a/R$) (Figure 11.11).

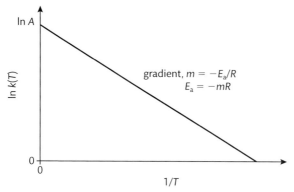

Figure 11.11 The activation energy of a reaction can be calculated from the gradient when ln $k(T)$ is plotted against $1/T$.

## Sketched graphs are used to show qualitative trends

Many of the graphs shown in this chapter, such as Figure 11.11, have labelled but unscaled axes. These are called sketched graphs, and are generally used to show qualitative trends, such as when variables are proportional or inversely proportional.

Drawn graphs used to present experimental data must have labelled and scaled axes if they are going to be used to display quantitative measurements.

## Using spreadsheets to plot graphs

There are many software packages which allow graphs to be plotted and analysed, the equation of the best fit line can be found, and other properties calculated. For example, the tangent to the curve in Figure 11.6 has the equation:

$$y = -0.1109x + 0.3818$$

so the gradient of the tangent at that point = $-0.11$ mol dm$^{-3}$ min$^{-1}$

The closeness of the generated line to the data points is indicated by the $R^2$ value. An $R^2$ of 1 represents a perfect fit between the data and the line drawn through them, and a value of 0 shows there is no correlation.

Care should, however, be taken when using these packages, as is shown by Figure 11.12.

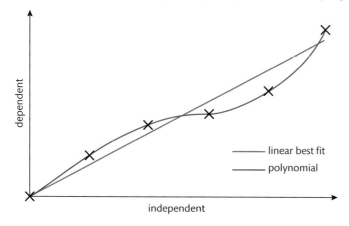

Figure 11.12 An equation which produces a 'perfect fit' is not necessarily the best description of the relationship between the variables.

The set of data points in Figure 11.12 can either be joined by a best-fit straight line which does not pass through any point except the origin:

$$y = 1.6255x \ (R^2 = 0.9527)$$

An infinite number of patterns can be found to fit the same experimental data . What criteria do we use in selecting the correct pattern?

**TOK**

or a polynomial which gives a perfect fit as indicated by the $R^2$ value of 1:

$$y = -0.0183x^5 + 0.2667x^4 - 1.2083x^3 + 1.7333x^2 + 1.4267x \ (R^2 = 1)$$

The polynomial equation is unlikely, however, to be physically significant. Any series of random points can fit a polynomial of sufficient length, just as any two points define a straight line.

## CHALLENGE YOURSELF

The closeness of the generated line to the data points is indicated by the $R^2$ value. $R$ is a correlation function computed from the formula:

$$R = \frac{\sum(Y_1 n - Y_1^{av})(Y_2 n_{calc} - Y_2^{av})}{\sqrt{\sum(Y_1 n - Y_1^{av})^2 \sum(Y_2 m_c - Y_2^{av})^2}}$$

with the sum over all the data points.

$Y_1 n$ is vertical coordinate of an individual data point value, and $Y_2 n$ the value calculated from the $x$ coordinate using the best-fit function. $Y^{av}$ is the average of $Y$ values.

$R$ can be used to measure the correlation between two sets of data points.

**1** Show that $R = 1$ for this set of data:

| $Y_1$ | 1 | 2 | 3 | 4 | 5 |
|-------|---|---|---|---|---|
| $Y_2$ | 1 | 2 | 3 | 4 | 5 |

**3** Calculate $R$ for this set of data:

| $Y_1$ | 1 | 2 | 3 | 4 | 5 |
|-------|---|---|---|---|---|
| $Y_2$ | 1 | 5 | 3 | 4 | 2 |

**2** Show that $R = -1$ for this set of data:

| $Y_1$ | 1 | 2 | 3 | 4 | 5 |
|-------|---|---|---|---|---|
| $Y_2$ | 5 | 4 | 3 | 2 | 1 |

### NATURE OF SCIENCE

The ideas of correlation and causation are very important in science. A correlation, often displayed graphically, is a statistical link or association between one variable and another. It can be positive or negative and a correlation coefficient can be calculated that will have a value between +1, 0 and −1. A strong correlation (positive or negative) between one factor and another is a necessary but not sufficient condition for a causal relationship. More evidence is usually required. There needs to be a mechanism to explain the link between the variables. There is, for example, a negative correlation between the concentration of chlorine monoxide and the concentration of ozone in the atmosphere over the Antarctic (Figure 11.13). Ozone levels are high at latitudes with low chlorine monoxide levels and low at latitudes with high chlorine monoxide levels, but the causal relationship can only be confirmed if a free radical mechanism, as discussed on page 195 is provided to explain the causal relationship.

One distinguishing factor between the 'harder' physical sciences and the 'softer' human sciences is that the former is concerned with simpler causal relationships. It is simpler to explain an increase in the rate of reaction than an increase in the annual rate of unemployment, as only a limited number of factors affect the former but many variables need to be considered when explaining the latter.

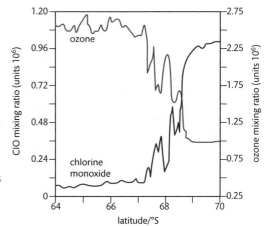

**Figure 11.13** A plot of chlorine monoxide and ozone concentrations over the Antarctic.

**22** The volume $V$, pressure $P$, temperature $T$, and number of moles of an ideal gas $n$ are related by the ideal gas equation: $PV = nRT$. If the relationship between pressure and volume at constant temperature of a fixed amount of gas is investigated experimentally, which one of the following plots would produce a linear graph?

**A** $P$ against $V$

**B** $P$ against $\dfrac{1}{V}$

**C** $\dfrac{1}{P}$ against $\dfrac{1}{V}$

**D** no plot can produce a straight line

**23** The volume and mass of different objects made from the same element, X, are measured independently. A graph of mass against volume, with error bars, is displayed.

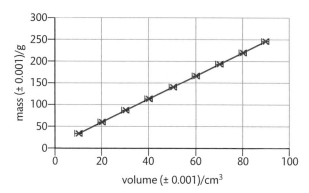

The literature values of the density of some elements are shown.

| Element | Density / g cm$^{-3}$ |
|---|---|
| aluminium | 2.70 |
| iron | 7.86 |
| copper | 8.92 |
| zinc | 7.14 |

These experimental results suggest:

| | Identity of X | Systematic errors | Random errors |
|---|---|---|---|
| **A** | aluminium | significant | not significant |
| **B** | aluminium | not significant | significant |
| **C** | inconclusive | not significant | not significant |
| **D** | inconclusive | significant | significant |

**24** In an experiment to measure the pH of distilled water at 25 °C the following results were obtained.

| Sample | pH |
|---|---|
| 1 | 6.69 |
| 2 | 6.70 |
| 3 | 6.69 |
| 4 | 6.68 |
| 5 | 6.70 |

The results are

**A** accurate and precise

**B** inaccurate but precise

**C** accurate but imprecise

**D** inaccurate and imprecise

**25** The amount of light absorbed by atoms at a characteristic wavelength can be used to measure the concentration of the element in a sample. A sample of sea water was analysed along with six standard solutions. Determine the concentration of chromium in the sea water by plotting a graph of the data.

| Chromium concentration/ µg dm$^{-3}$ | Absorbance at λ = 358 nm |
|---|---|
| 1.00 | 0.062 |
| 2.00 | 0.121 |
| 3.00 | 0.193 |
| 4.00 | 0.275 |
| 5.00 | 0.323 |
| 6.00 | 0.376 |
| sample | 0.215 |

**26** The activation energy for a reaction can be determined graphically using the Arrhenius equation:

$$k = Ae^{\frac{-E_a}{RT}}$$

Identify the plot which gives a straight line graph.

|   | Horizontal axis | Vertical axis |
|---|---|---|
| **A** | $T$ (where $T$ is in K) | ln $k$ |
| **B** | $1/T$ (where $T$ is in K) | ln $k$ |
| **C** | $1/T$ (where $T$ is in  C) | $k$ |
| **D** | $1/T$ (where $T$ is in K) | $k$ |

# 11.3 Spectroscopic identification of organic compounds

## Understandings:

- The degree of unsaturation or index of hydrogen deficiency (IHD) can be used to determine from a molecular formula the number of rings or multiple bonds in a molecule.
- Mass spectrometry (MS), proton nuclear magnetic resonance spectroscopy ($^1$H NMR), and infrared spectroscopy (IR) are techniques that can be used to help identify and to determine the structure of compounds.

### Guidance

- *The electromagnetic spectrum (EMS) is given in the data booklet in section 3. The regions employed for each technique should be understood.*
- *The operating principles are not required for any of these methods.*

## Applications and skills:

- Determination of the IHD from a molecular formula.
- Deduction of information about the structural features of a compound from percentage composition data, MS, $^1$H NMR, or IR.

### Guidance

- *The data booklet contains characteristic ranges for IR absorptions (section 26), $^1$H NMR data (section 27), specific MS fragments (section 28), and the formula to determine IHD. For $^1$H NMR, only the ability to deduce the number of different hydrogen (proton) environments and the relative numbers of hydrogen atoms in each environment is required. Integration traces should be covered but splitting patterns are not required.*

## Analytical techniques

Chemical analysts identify and characterize unknown substances, determine the composition of a mixture, and identify impurities. Their work can be divided into three types of analysis:

- **qualitative analysis**: the detection of the *presence* but not the quantity of a substance in a mixture; for example, forbidden substances in an athlete's blood
- **quantitative analysis**: the measurement of the *quantity* of a particular substance in a mixture; for example, the alcohol levels in a driver's breath
- **structural analysis**: a description of how the atoms are arranged in molecular structures; for example, the determination of the structure of a naturally occurring or artificial product.

Many instruments are available to provide structural analysis but they generally work by analysing the effect of different forms of energy on the substance analysed.

- **Infrared spectroscopy** is used to identify the bonds in a molecule.
- **Mass spectrometry** is used to determine relative atomic and molecular masses. The fragmentation pattern can be used as a fingerprint technique to identify unknown substances or for evidence for the arrangements of atoms in a molecule.
- **Nuclear magnetic resonance spectroscopy** is used to show the chemical environment of certain isotopes (hydrogen, carbon, phosphorus, and fluorine) in a molecule and so gives vital structural information.

No one method is definitive, but a combination of techniques can provide strong evidence for the structure.

## Mass spectrometry

### Determining the molecular mass of a compound

The mass spectrometer was introduced in Chapter 2 where we saw it was used to find the mass of individual atoms and the relative abundances of different isotopes. The instrument can be used in a similar way to find the relative molecular mass of a compound. If the empirical formula is also known from compositional analysis, the molecular formula can be determined. The technique also provides useful clues about the molecular structure.

### Fragmentation patterns

The ionization process in the mass spectrometer involves an electron from an electron gun hitting the incident species and removing an electron:

$$X(g) + e^- \rightarrow X^+(g) + 2e^-$$

The collision can be so energetic that it causes the molecule to break up into different fragments. The largest mass peak in the mass spectrum corresponds to a parent ion passing through the instrument unscathed, but other ions, produced as a result of this break up, are also detected.

**Using spectra to confirm the structure of a compound**
Full details of how to carry out this experiment with a worksheet are available online.

A mass spectrometer. The molecules are ionized and accelerated towards a detector. The sensor array can be seen through the round window (lower left).

The molecular ion or parent ion is formed when a molecule loses one electron but otherwise remains unchanged.

The **fragmentation pattern** can provide useful evidence for the structure of the compound. A chemist pieces together the fragments to form a picture of the complete molecule, in the same way that archaeologists find clues about the past from the pieces of artefacts discovered in the ground.

Consider Figure 11.14, which shows the mass spectrum of ethanol.

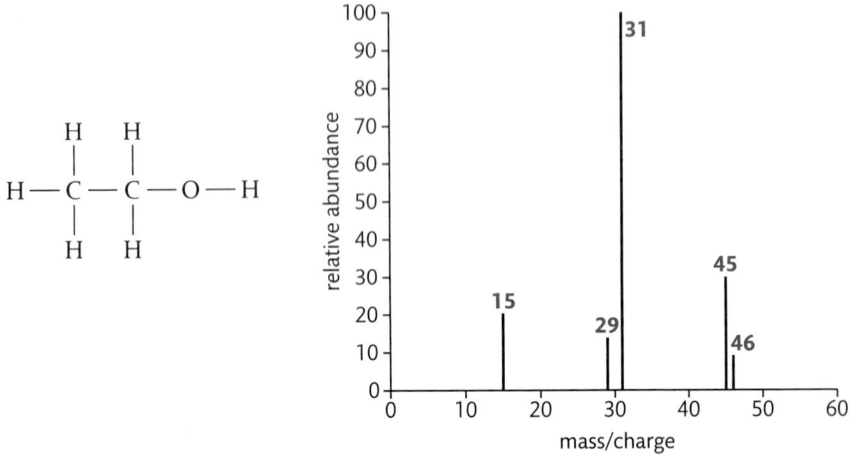

**Figure 11.14** The structure of ethanol and its mass spectrum.

The molecular ion corresponds to the peak at 46. The ion that appears at a relative mass of 45, one less than the parent ion, corresponds to the loss of a hydrogen atom.

Figure 11.15 shows fragmentation paths that explain the rest of the spectrum.

**Figure 11.15** Possible fragmentation pattern produced when ethanol is bombarded with high energy electrons.

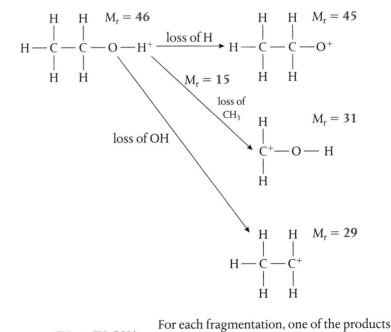

**The parent ion can break up into smaller ions in a mass spectrometer. A compound is characterized by this fragmentation pattern.**

**Figure 11.16** Two possible ways in which the C–C bond can break in ethanol. Only the charged species can be detected, as electric and magnetic fields have no effect on neutral fragments.

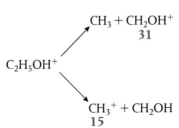

For each fragmentation, one of the products keeps the positive charge. So, for example, if the C–C bond breaks in an ethanol molecule, two outcomes are possible, as seen in Figure 11.16.

The fragmentation shown in Figure 11.16 explains the presence of peaks at both 15 and 31. Generally the fragment that gives the most stable ion is formed.

The cleavage of the C—O bond leads to the formation of the $C_2H_5^+$ ion in preference to the $OH^+$ ion in the example above, so there is an observed peak at 29 but not at 17.

Full analysis of a mass spectrum can be a complex process. We make use of the mass difference between the peaks to identify the pieces which have fallen off. You are expected to recognize the mass fragments shown below. You are not expected to memorise the details as the data are given in section 28 of the IB data booklet.

| Mass lost | Fragment lost |
|---|---|
| 15 | $CH_3\cdot$ |
| 17 | $OH\cdot$ |
| 18 | $H_2O$ |
| 28 | $CH_2{=}CH_2$, $C{=}O\cdot$ |
| 29 | $CH_3CH_2\cdot$, $CHO\cdot$ |
| 31 | $CH_3O\cdot$ |
| 45 | $COOH\cdot$ |

Don't forget to include the positive charge on the ions detected by the mass spectrometer when identifying different fragments.

## Worked example

A molecule with an empirical formula $CH_2O$ has the simplified mass spectrum below. Deduce the molecular formula and give a possible structure of the compound.

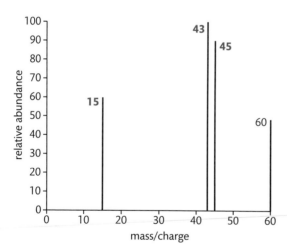

## Solution

empirical formula = $CH_2O$; molecular formula = $C_nH_{2n}O_n$

We can see that the parent ion has a relative mass of 60.

$M_r = n(12.01) + 2n(1.01) + n(16.00) = 30.03n$

$n = \dfrac{60}{30.03} = 2$

molecular formula = $C_2H_4O_2$

From the spectrum we can identify the following peaks:

| Peaks | Explanation |
|---|---|
| 15 (60 − 45) | presence of $CH_3^+$ loss of COOH from molecule |
| 43 (60 − 17) | presence of $C_2H_3O^+$ loss of OH from molecule |
| 45 (60 − 15) | presence of $COOH^+$ loss of $CH_3$ from molecule |

The structure consistent with this fragmentation pattern is:

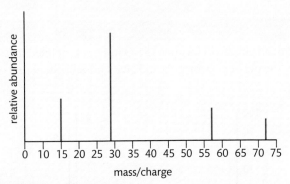

## Exercises

**27** The mass spectrum shown below was produced by a compound with the formula $C_nH_{2n}O$.

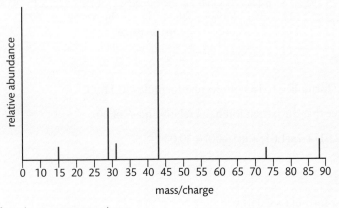

Which ions are detected in the mass spectrometer?

I    $C_2H_3O^+$
II   $C_3H_5O^+$
III   $C_4H_8O^+$

  **A**   I and II only       **B**   I and III only       **C**   II and III only       **D**   I, II, and III

**28** While working on an organic synthesis, a student isolated a compound X, which they then analysed with a mass spectrometer.

Identify X from the mass spectrum shown.

  **A**   $CH_3CH_2CH_3$       **B**   $C_3H_7CO_2H$       **C**   $C_2H_5CO_2CH_3$       **D**   $(CH_3)_2CHCO_2H$

**29** The mass spectra of two compounds are shown below. One is propanone ($CH_3COCH_3$) and the other is propanal ($CH_3CH_2CHO$). Identify the compound in each case and explain the similarities and differences between the two spectra.

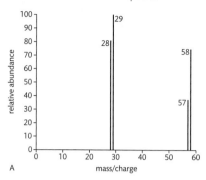

A

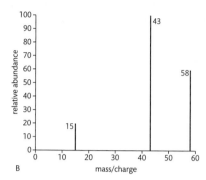

B

**30** The simplified mass spectrum of a compound with empirical formula $C_2H_5$ is shown below.

(a) Explain which ions give rise to the peaks shown.
(b) Deduce the molecular structure of the compound.

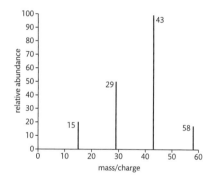

# The degree of unsaturation/IHD

The **degree of unsaturation** or **index of hydrogen deficiency (IHD)** provides a useful clue to the structure of a molecule once its formula is known. It is a measure of how many molecules of $H_2$ would be needed in theory to convert the molecule to the corresponding saturated, non-cyclic molecule. Cyclohexane and hex-1-ene, for example, have the same molecular formula ($C_6H_{12}$) and so have the same degree of unsaturation and IHD. One molecule of hydrogen is needed to convert them to the saturated alkane hexane ($C_6H_{14}$). Similarly ethene, with a double bond, has an IHD of 1 whereas the more unsaturated ethyne, with a triple bond, has an IHD of 2.

The IHD values of a selection of molecules are tabulated below.

| Molecule | Saturated non-cyclic target | Index of hydrogen deficiency (IHD) |
|---|---|---|
| $C_2H_4$ | $C_2H_6$ | 1 |
| $C_2H_2$ | $C_2H_6$ | 2 |
| cyclobutane and but-1-ene, $C_4H_8$ | $C_4H_{10}$ | 1 |
| $C_2H_5OH$ | $C_2H_5OH$ | 0 |
| $C_2H_4O$ | $C_2H_6O$ | 1 |
| $C_2H_5Cl$ | $C_2H_5Cl$ | 0 |

## CHALLENGE YOURSELF

**4** Show that the IHD of a molecule with the molecular formula $C_nH_pO_qN_rX_s$, is given by the general formula:

IHD = ½ × [2n + 2 − p − s + r]

Explain why $q$, the number of oxygen atoms, doesn't appear in the general formula?

## Exercises

**31** Deduce the IHD of the following by copying and completing the table below.

| Molecule | Corresponding saturated non-cyclic molecule | IHD |
|---|---|---|
| $C_6H_6$ | | |
| $CH_3COCH_3$ | | |
| $C_7H_6O_2$ | | |
| $C_2H_3Cl$ | | |
| $C_4H_9N$ | | |
| $C_6H_{12}O_6$ | | |

## Different regions of the electromagnetic spectrum give different information about the structure of organic molecules

**TOK**

The physical analytical techniques now available to us are due to advances in technology. How does technology extend and modify the capabilities of our senses? What are the knowledge implications of this?

Spectroscopy is the main method we have of probing into the atom and the molecule. There is a type of spectroscopy for each of the main regions of the electromagnetic spectrum. As discussed in Chapter 2 (page 69), electromagnetic radiation is a form of energy transferred by waves and characterized by its:

- **wavelength** ($\lambda$): the distance between successive crests or troughs
- **frequency** ($\nu$): the number of waves which pass a point every second.

The electromagnetic spectrum can be found in section 3 of the IB data booklet. Typical wavelengths and frequencies for each region of the spectrum are summarized in the table below.

- The distance between two successive crests (or troughs) is called the wavelength.
- The frequency of the wave is the number of waves which pass a point in one second.

For electromagnetic waves, the wavelength and frequency are related by the equation

$$c = \nu\lambda$$

where $c$ is the speed of light.

| Type of electromagnetic radiation | Typical frequency ($\nu$) / $s^{-1}$ | Typical wavelength ($\lambda$) / m |
|---|---|---|
| radio waves (low energy) | $3 \times 10^6$ | $10^2$ |
| microwaves | $3 \times 10^{10}$ | $10^{-2}$ |
| infrared | $3 \times 10^{12}$ | $10^{-4}$ |
| visible | $3 \times 10^{15}$ | $10^{-7}$ |
| ultraviolet | $3 \times 10^{16}$ | $10^{-8}$ |
| X rays | $3 \times 10^{18}$ | $10^{-10}$ |
| gamma rays | greater than $3 \times 10^{22}$ | less than $10^{-14}$ |

It should be noted from the table that $\nu \times \lambda = 3.0 \times 10^8$ m s$^{-1}$ = $c$, the speed of light. This gives $\nu = c/\lambda$.

In infrared spectroscopy, the frequency of radiation is often measured as number of waves per centimetre (cm$^{-1}$), also called the **wavenumber**.

Microwave cookers heat food very quickly as the radiation penetrates deep into the food. The frequency used corresponds to the energy needed to rotate water molecules, which are present in most food. The radiation absorbed by the water molecules makes them rotate faster. As they bump into other molecules the extra energy is spread throughout the food and the temperature rises.

As well as transferring energy, the electromagnetic radiation can also be viewed as a carrier of information. Different regions give different types of information, by interacting with substances in different ways.

- **Radio waves** can be absorbed by certain nuclei, causing them to reverse their spin. They are used in NMR and can give information about the environment of certain atoms.
- **Microwaves** cause molecules to increase their rotational energy. This can give information about bond lengths. It is not necessary to know the details at this level.
- **Infrared radiation** is absorbed by certain bonds causing them to stretch or bend. This gives information about the bonds in a molecule.
- **Visible light** and **ultraviolet light** can produce electronic transitions and give information about the electronic energy levels within the atom or molecule.
- **X rays** are produced when electrons make transitions between inner energy levels. They have wavelengths of the same order of magnitude as the inter-atomic distances in crystals and produce diffraction patterns which provide direct evidence of molecular and crystal structure.

## CHALLENGE YOURSELF

5 Calculate the energy of a photon of visible light with a frequency of $3.0 \times 10^{14} \text{ s}^{-1}$. Express your answer in kJ $\text{mol}^{-1}$.

## Infrared (IR) spectroscopy

### The natural frequency of a chemical bond

A chemical bond can be thought of as a spring. Each bond vibrates and bends at a natural frequency which depends on the bond strength and the masses of the atoms. Light atoms, for example, vibrate at higher frequencies than heavier atoms and multiple bonds vibrate at higher frequencies than single bonds.

Simple diatomic molecules such as HCl, HBr, and HI, can only vibrate when the bond stretches (Figure 11.17a). The HCl bond has the highest frequency of these three as it has the largest bond energy and the halogen atom with the smallest relative atomic mass.

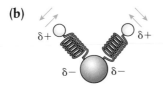

**Figure 11.17** IR radiation can cause a bond to stretch or bend.

In more complex molecules, different types of vibration can occur, such as bending, so that a complex range of frequencies is present (Figure 11.17b).

### Using infrared radiation to excite molecules

The energy needed to excite the bonds in a molecule and so make them vibrate with greater amplitude, occurs in the IR region (Figure 11.18). A bond will only interact with the electromagnetic infrared radiation, however, if it is polar. The presence of separate areas of partial positive and negative charge in a molecule allows the electric field component of the electromagnetic wave to excite the vibrational energy of the molecule. The change in the vibrational energy produces a corresponding change in the dipole moment of the molecule. The intensity of the absorption depends on the polarity of the bond. Symmetrical non-polar bonds in $N≡N$ and $O=O$ do not absorb radiation, as they cannot interact with an electric field.

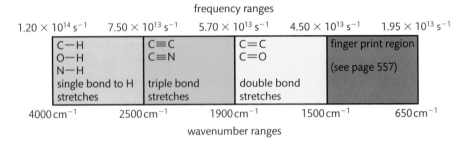

**Figure 11.18** The natural frequencies of some covalent bonds.

## Stretching and bending in a polyatomic molecule

In a polyatomic molecule such as water, it is more correct to consider the molecule stretching and bending as a whole, rather than considering the individual bonds. Water, for example, can vibrate at three fundamental frequencies as shown in Figure 11.19. As each of the three modes of vibration results in a change in dipole of the molecule, they can be detected with IR spectroscopy.

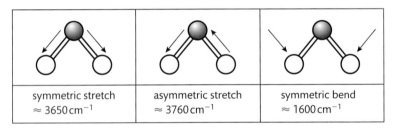

**Figure 11.19** The three vibrational modes of the water molecule are all IR active as they each produce a change in the dipole moment of the molecule.

For a symmetrical linear molecule such as carbon dioxide, there are four modes of vibration (Figure 11.20). However, the symmetric stretch is IR inactive as it produces no change in dipole moment. The dipoles of both $C=O$ bonds are equal and opposite throughout the vibration.

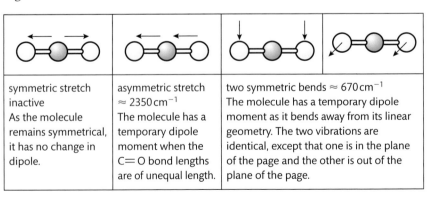

**Figure 11.20** Three of the vibrational modes of the carbon dioxide molecule are IR active. The symmetric stretch produces no change in dipole and so is IR inactive.

You are not expected to remember the characteristic wavenumbers. A more complete list is given in section 26 of the IB data booklet.

## Matching wavenumbers with bonds

The absorption of particular wavenumbers of IR radiation helps the chemist identify the bonds in a molecule. The precise position of the absorption depends on the environment of the bond, so a range of wavenumbers is used to identify different bonds. Characteristic infrared absorption bands are shown in the table on page 557.

| Bond | Wavenumber / cm$^{-1}$ | Intensity |
|---|---|---|
| C—O | 1050–1410 | strong |
| C=C | 1620–1680 | medium-weak; multiple bands |
| C=O | 1700–1750 | strong |
| C≡C | 2100–2260 | variable |
| O—H, hydrogen bonded in carboxylic acids | 2500–3000 | strong, very broad |
| C—H | 2850–3090 | strong |
| O—H, hydrogen bonded in alcohols and phenols | 3200–3600 | strong |
| N—H | 3300–3500 | strong |

Some bonds can also be identified by the distinctive shapes of their signals: for example, the O—H bond gives a broad signal and the C=O bond gives a sharp signal.

## Exercises

**32** Which of the following types of bond is expected to absorb IR radiation of the longest wavelength?

| | Bond order | Mass of atoms bonded together |
|---|---|---|
| **A** | 1 | small |
| **B** | 1 | large |
| **C** | 2 | small |
| **D** | 2 | large |

**33** The infrared spectrum was obtained from a compound and showed absorptions at 2100 cm$^{-1}$, 1700 cm$^{-1}$, and 1200 cm$^{-1}$. Identify the compound.

    **A** $CH_3COOCH_3$     **B** $C_6H_5COOH$     **C** $CH_2=CHCH_2OH$     **D** $CH≡CCH_2CO_2CH_3$

**34** A molecule absorbs IR at a wavenumber of 1720 cm$^{-1}$. Which functional group could account for this absorption?

    I    aldehydes
    II   esters
    III  ethers

    **A** I only     **B** I and II     **C** I, II, and III     **D** none of the above

**35** An unknown compound has the following mass composition: C, 40.0%; H, 6.7%; O, 53.3%. The largest mass recorded on the mass spectrum of the compound corresponds to a relative molecular mass of 60.

    **(a)** Determine the empirical and molecular formulas of the compound.
    **(b)** Deduce the IHD of the compound.
    **(c)** The IR spectrum shows an absorption band at 1700 cm$^{-1}$ and a very broad band between 2500 and 3300 cm$^{-1}$. Deduce the molecular structure of the compound.

**36** Draw the structure of a sulfur dioxide molecule and identify its possible modes of vibration. Predict which of these is likely to absorb IR radiation.

Hydrogen bonds can be detected by a broadening of the absorptions. For example, hydrogen bonding between hydroxyl groups changes the O—H vibration; it makes the absorption much broader and shifts it to a lower frequency.

Molecules with several bonds can vibrate in many different ways and with many different frequencies. The complex pattern can be used as a 'fingerprint' to be matched against the recorded spectra of known compounds in a database (Figure 11.21). A comparison of the spectrum of a sample with that of a pure compound can also be used as a test of purity.

**Figure 11.21** The IR spectrum of heroin (blue) compared with that of an unknown sample (black). The near-perfect match indicates that the sample contains a high percentage of heroin. Spectral analysis such as this can identify unknown compounds in mixtures or from samples taken from clothing or equipment. The technique is widely used in forensic science.

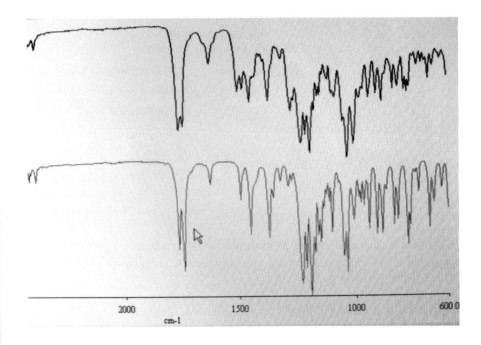

Consider the spectrum of propanone (Figure 11.22). The baseline at the top corresponds to 100% transmittance and the key features are the troughs which occur at the natural frequencies of the bonds present in the molecule.

**Figure 11.22** The molecular structure and spectrum of propanone.

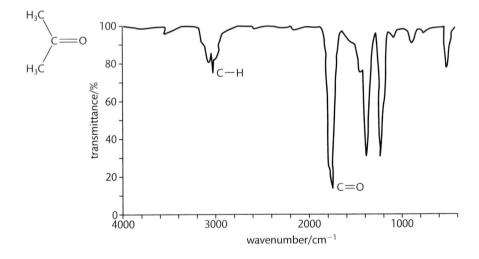

The absorption at just below 1800 cm$^{-1}$ shows the presence of the C=O bond and the absorption near 3000 cm$^{-1}$ is due to the presence of the C—H bond. The more polar C=O bond produces the more intense absorption.

The presence of the C–H bond can again been seen near 3000 cm$^{-1}$ in the spectrum of ethanol (Figure 11.23). The broad peak at just below 3400 cm$^{-1}$ shows the presence of hydrogen bonding which is due to the hydroxyl (OH) group.

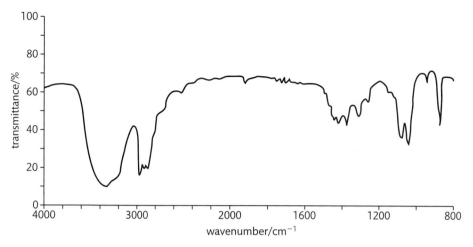

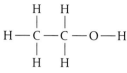

**Figure 11.23** The IR spectrum of ethanol. Note that the horizontal axis has a non-linear scale. This is common for many instruments, so you should always take care when reading off values for the wavenumbers of the absorptions.

## NATURE OF SCIENCE

Scientists use models to clarify certain features and relationships that are not directly observable. These models can become more and more sophisticated but they can never become the real thing. Models are just a representation of reality. The IR spectra of organic molecules for example are based on the bond vibration model, in which the covalent bond between two atoms is compared to a spring, with its natural frequency depending on the bond strength and the masses of an atom in the same way that the natural frequency of a spring depends on its stiffness and mass. We often use our everyday experiences to help us construct models to understand processes that are occurring on a scale beyond our experience. This is the strength of such models as it helps our understanding; the same mass/spring model can be used to explain a float bobbing up and in water for example. However, models also have limitations.

Scientists often take a complex problem and reduce it to a simpler, more manageable one that can be treated mathematically. We should not forget that the bond vibration model is a simplification – albeit an effective one. It is molecules, and not individual bonds, that are vibrating, as we saw in the examples of water and carbon dioxide (page 556).

## Exercises

**37** Identify the bonds which will produce strong absorptions in the IR region of the electromagnetic spectrum.

    I     C—O bond
    II    C=C bond
    III   C=O

   **A**   I and II only       **B**   I and III only       **C**   II and III only       **D**   I, II, and III

**38** State what occurs at the molecular level when IR radiation is absorbed.

**39** Cyclohexane and hex-1-ene are isomers. Suggest how you could use infrared spectroscopy to distinguish between the two compounds.

**40** The intoximeter, used by the police to test the alcohol levels in the breath of drivers, measures the absorbance at 2900 cm$^{-1}$. Identify the bond which causes ethanol to absorb at this wavenumber.

**41** A molecule has the molecular formula $C_2H_6O$. The infrared spectrum shows an absorption band at 1000–1300 cm$^{-1}$, but no absorption bands above 3000 cm$^{-1}$. Deduce its structure.

The Spectra Database for Organic Compounds was opened in 1997 and has given the public free access to the spectra of many organic compounds. The total accumulated number of visits reached 350 million at the end of February 2011, and the database has sent information from Japan to all over the world. The open exchange of information is a key element of scientific progress.

## CHALLENGE YOURSELF

**6** A bond has an IR absorption of 2100 cm$^{-1}$. Calculate the wavelength of the radiation and the natural frequency of the bond?

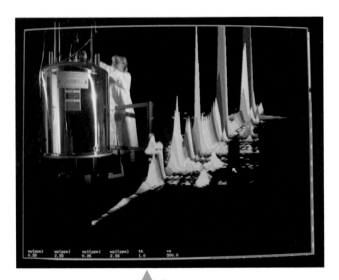

Screen display of a nuclear magnetic resonance spectrum. In the background, a scientist is seen loading a sample into the NMR spectrometer's magnet.

**Figure 11.24** A spinning nucleus can be thought of as a small bar magnet. The energy between the two states depends on the strength of the external magnetic field (applied by an electromagnet) and the chemical environment of the nucleus.

## Nuclear magnetic resonance (NMR) spectroscopy

### The principles of NMR

Nuclear magnetic resonance spectroscopy, a powerful technique for finding the structure and shape of molecules, depends on a combination of nuclear physics and chemistry. The nuclei of atoms with an odd number of protons such as $^1H$, $^{13}C$, $^{19}F$, and $^{31}P$, spin and behave like tiny bar magnets. If placed in an external magnetic field, some of these nuclei will line up with an applied field and, if they have sufficient energy, some will line up against it (Figure 11.24). This arrangement leads to two nuclear energy levels; the energy needed for the nuclei to reverse their spin and change their orientation in a magnetic field can be provided by radio waves.

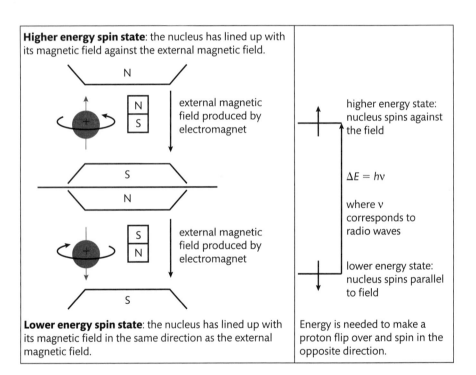

**Higher energy spin state**: the nucleus has lined up with its magnetic field against the external magnetic field.

N

external magnetic field produced by electromagnet

external magnetic field produced by electromagnet

**Lower energy spin state**: the nucleus has lined up with its magnetic field in the same direction as the external magnetic field.

higher energy state: nucleus spins against the field

$\Delta E = h\nu$

where $\nu$ corresponds to radio waves

lower energy state: nucleus spins parallel to field

Energy is needed to make a proton flip over and spin in the opposite direction.

In practice, a sample is placed in an electromagnet. The field strength is varied until the radio waves have the exact frequency needed to make the nuclei flip over and spin in the opposite direction. This is called **resonance** and can be detected electronically and recorded in the form of a spectrum (Figure 11.25).

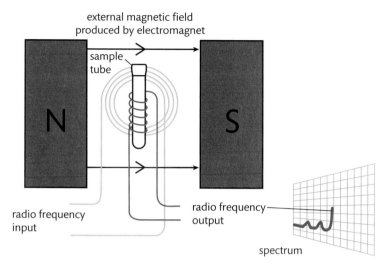

external magnetic field
produced by electromagnet

NMR spectroscopy is non-invasive as the small quantities of the sample are recovered unchanged after the experiment.

## Hydrogen nuclei in different chemical environments have different chemical shifts

As electrons shield the nucleus from the full effects of the external magnetic field, differences in electron distribution produce different energy separations between the two spin energy levels. The technique is a very useful analytical tool, as nuclei in different **chemical environments** produce different signals in the spectrum. Proton or $^1H$ NMR is particularly useful. The hydrogen nuclei, present in all organic molecules, effectively act as spies and give information about their position in a molecule.

The signals are measured against the standard signal produced by the 12 hydrogen nuclei in tetramethylsilane (TMS), the structure of which is shown in Figure 11.26.

$$CH_3 - Si - CH_3$$

with $CH_3$ above and $CH_3$ below the Si.

**Figure 11.26** Tetramethylsilane (TMS). Each of the 12 hydrogen atoms is bonded to a carbon atom, which in turn is bonded to two other hydrogen atoms. The silicon atom is bonded to four methyl groups. All the hydrogen atoms are in the same environment so only one signal is recorded.

The position of the NMR signal relative to this standard is called the **chemical shift** of the proton. Hydrogen nuclei in particular environments have characteristic chemical shifts. Some examples are given in the table below. A more complete list is given in section 27 of the IB data booklet.

| Type of proton | Chemical shift / ppm |
|---|---|
| TMS | 0 |
| —C**H**₃ | 0.9–1.0 |
| RO—C(=O)—C**H**₂— | 2.0–2.5 |

| Type of proton | Chemical shift / ppm |
|---|---|
| $R-\overset{\overset{\displaystyle O}{\|\|}}{C}-CH_2-$ | 2.2–2.7 |
| $-C\equiv C-H$ | 1.8–3.1 |
| $R-O-CH_2-$ | 3.3–3.7 |
| $R-\overset{\overset{\displaystyle O}{\|\|}}{C}-O-CH_2-$ | 3.7–4.8 |
| $R-\overset{\overset{\displaystyle O}{\|\|}}{C}-O-H$ | 9.0–13.0* |
| $R-O-H$ | 1.0–6.0* |
| $-HC=CH_2$ | 4.5–6.0 |
| ⬡—OH | 4.0–12.0* |
| ⬡—H | 6.9–9.0 |
| $R-\overset{\overset{\displaystyle O}{\|\|}}{C}-H$ | 9.4–10.0 |

\* Signals from the hydrogen atoms in the —OH groups are very variable owing to hydrogen bonding.

## Interpreting ¹H NMR spectra

The ¹H NMR spectrum of ethanal is shown in Figure 11.27.

**Figure 11.27** The ¹H NMR spectrum of ethanal shows two peaks because the hydrogen atoms are in two different environments. The **integrated trace** indicates the relative number of hydrogen atoms in the two environments.

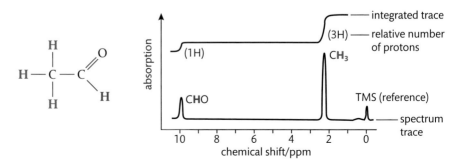

The spectrum trace has a peak at 9.7, which corresponds to the **CHO** proton and a peak at 2.1 which corresponds to the three protons in the **CH₃** group. The area under the $CH_3$ peak is three times larger than that under the CHO peak as it indicates the relative number of protons in each environment. The integrated trace gives this information more directly, as it goes up in steps which are proportional to the number of protons. This spectrum is analysed in more detail later in the chapter (page 567).

(page 567)

Avoid losing marks through carelessness. The number of peaks does not simply give the number of different chemical environments – it gives the number of different chemical environments in which hydrogen atoms are located.

## Worked example

The NMR spectrum of a compound which has the molecular formula $C_3H_8O$ is shown here.

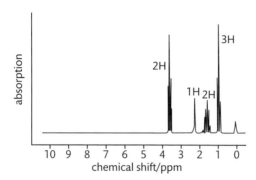

(a) Draw the full structural formulas and give the names of the three possible isomers of $C_3H_8O$.

(b) Identify the substance responsible for the peak at 0 ppm and state its purpose.

(c) Identify the unknown compound from the number of peaks in the spectrum.

(d) Identify the group responsible for the signal at 0.9 ppm.

### Solution

(a) The structures and names are:

propan-1-ol

propan-2-ol

methoxyethane

(b) Tetramethylsilane is used as a reference standard.

(c) For each structure, I–IV identifies the different environments of the H atoms in the molecule. 1–3 represents the number of atoms in each environment. There are four peaks in the spectrum. Propan-1-ol has four peaks with the correct areas.

(d) The peak at 0.9 ppm corresponds to the $CH_3$ group.

## Exercises

**42** The $^1$H NMR spectrum of a compound exhibits three major peaks and the splitting patterns below.

| Chemical shift / ppm | Peak area |
|:---:|:---:|
| 1.0 | 3 |
| 2.0 | 3 |
| 2.3 | 2 |

Identify the compound.

    **A** $CH_3CH_2CH_3$    **B** $CH_3CH_2CHO$    **C** $CH_3CH_2COCH_3$    **D** $CH_3CH_2CH_2CH_2CH_3$

**43** The low resolution $^1$H NMR spectrum of a fuel Y is shown.

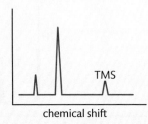

chemical shift

Identify Y.

    **A** $CH_3OH$    **B** $C_2H_6$    **C** $C_2H_5OH$    **D** $CH_3OCH_3$

**44** How many peaks will the following compounds show in their $^1$H NMR spectra?

(a) $CH_3{-}\overset{\overset{\displaystyle O}{\|}}{C}{-}O{-}CH_3$

(b) $CH_3{-}O{-}CH_3$

(c) $CH_3{-}\overset{\overset{\displaystyle CH_3}{|}}{\underset{\underset{\displaystyle CH_3}{|}}{C}}{-}CH_3$

(d) $CH_3{-}\overset{\overset{\displaystyle CH_3}{|}}{\underset{\underset{\displaystyle Cl}{|}}{C}}{-}H$

**45** Describe and explain the $^1$H NMR spectrum of $CH_3CH_2OH$.

### NATURE OF SCIENCE

The use of IR and radio wave technology has allowed us to gain information about individual molecules which was previously thought to be unattainable. Technology originally emerged before science, but new technologies drive developments in science. Evidence can now be obtained using instrumentation which gathers information beyond the normal range of human sense perception. Improvement in mass spectrometry, nuclear magnetic resonance, and infrared spectroscopy have made identification and structural determination of compounds routine. We now understand what happens when a molecule vibrates and rotates and the flipping of a proton's spin can give us crucial information about what is happening within a human cell (MRI is discussed on page 529). In recent decades, the growth in computing power and sensor technology has allowed scientists to collect increasingly larger amounts of data which can be interpreted to give objective scientific evidence.

## Analytical chemistry depends on combining information

The techniques discussed in this chapter provide the analytical chemist with different types of information. The skill of the analyst is to combine these methods to give a complete description of the structure of the substance being studied. For example, infrared spectroscopy gives some information about the bonds present in a molecule, but often this information needs to be supplemented with data from other sources to give a complete structure of the molecule.

## Worked example

(a) An unknown compound is found to have the following composition:

|   | % composition by mass |
|---|---|
| C | 85.6 |
| H | 14.4 |

Deduce the empirical formula of the compound.

(b) The mass spectrum of the compound is shown below. Deduce the molecular formula and the IHD of the compound.

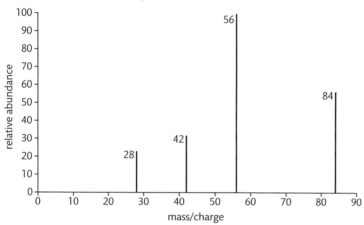

(c) Is the molecule likely to contain a $CH_3$ group? Explain your answer.

(d) The infrared spectrum shows one absorption close to 2900 cm$^{-1}$, but there is no absorption close to 1600 cm$^{-1}$. State what can be deduced from this information.

(e) Deduce the molecular structure from the $^1$H NMR spectrum shown.

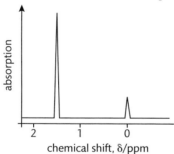

## Solution

(a) To find the empirical formula calculate the relative number of moles:

|  | C | H |
|---|---|---|
| mass / g | 85.6 | 14.4 |
| moles | $= \dfrac{85.6}{12.01}$ $= 7.13$ | $= \dfrac{14.4}{1.01}$ $= 14.3$ |
| simple ratio | $= \dfrac{7.13}{7.13}$ $= 1.00$ | $= \dfrac{14.4}{7.13}$ $= 2.02$ |

The empirical formula is $CH_2$.

(b) The mass spectrum shows a parent ion at 84. The molecular formula is $C_nH_{2n}$.

$$n(12.01) + 2n(1.01) = 84$$

$$14.03n = 84$$

$$n = \frac{84}{14.03} = 5.99$$

The molecular formula is $C_6H_{12}$.

The saturated non-cyclic compound with six carbons is $C_6H_{14}$, so the IHD = 1. The molecule contains a C=C or a ring.

(c) The absence of peaks at 15 or 69 (84 − 15) suggests that the molecule probably does not contain a methyl group.

(d) The absorption close to 2900 $cm^{-1}$ is due to the C—H bond.

The absence of an absorbance at 1600 $cm^{-1}$ suggests that the molecule does not contain a C=C bond. It must, therefore, have a ring structure.

(e) The NMR spectra shows only one peak, so all the hydrogen atoms are in the same chemical environment. This confirms that the molecule has a ring structure. It is cyclohexane.

## 21.1 Spectroscopic identification of organic compounds

## Understandings:

- Structural identification of compounds involves several different analytical techniques, including IR, $^1$H NMR, and MS.
- In a high-resolution $^1$H NMR spectrum, single peaks present in low resolution can split into further clusters of peaks.
- The structural technique of single crystal X-ray crystallography can be used to identify the bond lengths and bond angles of crystalline compounds.

### Guidance
- *The operating principles are not required for any of these methods.*
- *High resolution $^1$H NMR should be covered.*
- *The precise details of single crystal X-ray crystallography need not be known in detail, but students should be aware of the existence of this structural technique in the wider context of structural identification of both inorganic and organic compounds.*

## Applications and skills:

- Explanation of the use of tetramethylsilane (TMS) as the reference standard.
- Deduction of the structure of a compound given information from a range of analytical characterization techniques (X-ray crystallography, IR, $^1$H NMR, and MS).

### Guidance
*Students should be able to interpret the following from $^1$H NMR spectra: number of peaks, area under each peak, chemical shift, and splitting patterns. Treatment of spin–spin coupling constants will not be assessed but students should be familiar with singlets, doublets, triplets, and quartets.*

# Further NMR spectroscopy

## Tetramethylsilane (TMS) as the reference

As we discussed earlier, NMR signals are measured against a standard produced by the 12 hydrogen nuclei in tetramethylsilane (TMS). Because the hydrogen nuclei are all in the same environment, one signal is recorded. Also, because silicon has a lower electronegativity than carbon, TMS absorbs radio waves in a different region from that absorbed by hydrogen nuclei attached only to carbon. This ensures that the standard signal does not overlap with any signals under investigation.

The chemical shift (represented by δ) of a proton in a molecule is defined as:

$$\delta = \left(\frac{\nu - \nu_0}{\nu_0}\right) \times 10^6 \text{ ppm}$$

where $\nu$ and $\nu_0$ are the frequencies of the radio waves absorbed by the protons in the sample and TMS respectively. Although the absolute frequency of the signal depends on the strength of the magnetic field, the chemical shift – relative to the standard – stays the same. This allows a standard spectrum to be produced. TMS has the additional advantages that it is chemically inert and is soluble in most organic solvents. It can be easily removed from the sample as it has a low boiling point.

## High-resolution ¹H NMR spectroscopy

The NMR spectrum of an organic compound does not generally consist of a series of single peaks shown in the low-resolution spectra presented earlier. Instead, a sensitive, high-resolution NMR machine reveals a hidden structure, with the single peaks split or resolved into a group of smaller parts. For example, compare the low-resolution spectrum of ethanal (Figure 11.27) with Figure 11.28 below, which was obtained under more carefully controlled operating conditions.

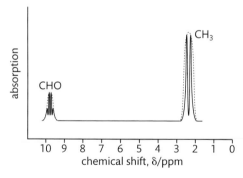

**Figure 11.28** The high-resolution ¹H NMR spectrum of ethanal. The dotted lines show the low resolution spectra.

The splitting of the peaks occurs as the effective magnetic field, experienced by particular nuclei, is modified by the magnetic field produced by neighbouring protons. This effect is known as **spin–spin coupling**. Here the magnetic field experienced by the protons in the methyl group, for example, depends on the spin of the proton attached to the carbon atom of the carbonyl group (CHO). The local magnetic field is increased when the magnetic field of the CHO proton is aligned with the external field and decreased when aligned against it. As the energy separation between the two spin states of a proton depends on the local magnetic field, this results in two possible values for the energy difference between the two nuclear energy levels for the $CH_3$ protons (Figure 11.29).

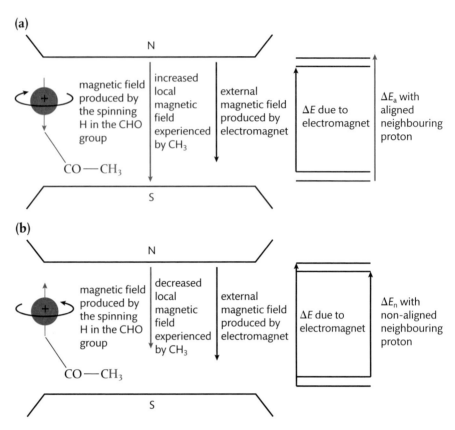

**Figure 11.29** (a) The alignment of the magnetic field due to the CHO proton with the external field increases the local magnetic field and the splitting ($\Delta E$) between the energy levels of the $CH_3$ protons. (b) The non-alignment of the magnetic field due to the CHO proton with the external field decreases the local magnetic field and the splitting ($\Delta E$) between the energy levels of the $CH_3$ protons.

Instead of one signal corresponding to one energy difference, $\Delta E$, two signals corresponding to $\Delta E_a$ and $\Delta E_n$ are produced. Each line corresponds to a different spin of the neighbouring proton. As they are both equally likely, the lines are of equal intensity (Figure 11.30).

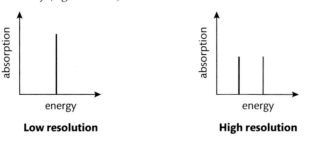

**Low resolution**

**High resolution**

**Figure 11.30** One signal in a low-resolution spectrum produces a doublet in a high-resolution spectrum when there is one proton on a neighbouring carbon atom.

In a similar way, the low-resolution peak corresponding to the CHO proton is split due to the different magnetic fields produced by the combinations of spin for the three protons of the neighbouring methyl group. As there are two possible orientations for each proton, a total of $2^3$ combinations are possible, resulting in four different local magnetic fields. This produces four signals with relative intensities 1, 3, 3, 1 – as shown in the table below.

| | | ↓↑↑ | ↓↓↑ | |
| | | ↑↓↑ | ↓↑↓ | |
| External magnetic field | ↑↑↑ | ↑↑↓ | ↑↓↓ | ↓↓↓ |
| | All protons aligned with external magnetic field. | Two protons with and one against external magnetic field. | One proton with and two against external magnetic field. | All protons against external magnetic field. |

## Worked example

Predict the splitting pattern produced by a neighbouring —$CH_2$— group.

### Solution

There are $2^2$ different combinations.

| ↑ ↑ | ↓ ↑ ↑ ↓ | ↓ ↓ |
|---|---|---|
| Both protons aligned with external magnetic field. | One proton aligned with and one against external magnetic field. | Both protons aligned against external magnetic field. |

Three lines are produced with relative intensities of 1, 2, 1.

The splitting patterns produced from different numbers of neighbouring protons can be deduced from Pascal's triangle and are summarized in the table below.

| Number of chemically equivalent protons causing splitting | Splitting patterns with relative intensities | | | | | | |
|---|---|---|---|---|---|---|---|
| 0 | | | | 1 | | | |
| 1 | | | 1 | | 1 | | |
| 2 | | | 1 | 2 | 1 | | |
| 3 | | 1 | | 3 | 3 | | 1 |
| 4 | 1 | | 4 | 6 | 4 | | 1 |

When analysing high-resolution NMR spectra, the following additional points should be noted:

- protons bonded to the same atom do not interact with one another as they are equivalent and behave as a group
- protons on non-adjacent carbon atoms do not generally interact with one another
- the O—H single peak in ethanol does not split unless the sample is pure as rapid exchange of the protons between ethanol molecules averages out the different possible spins.

## Worked example

The $^1H$ NMR spectrum of a compound with the empirical formula $C_2H_4O$ is shown.

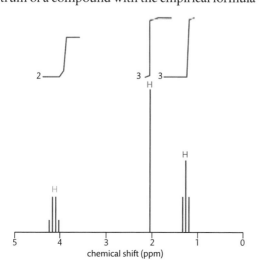

chemical shift (ppm)

If a proton has $n$ protons as nearest neighbours, its NMR peak is split into a group of $(n + 1)$ peaks. Thus, for $CH_3CH_2F$, we would expect the —$CH_2$— proton signal to be split into a quartet as it has three protons as nearest neighbours.

**TOK** Mathematics has been described as the science of patterns. Pascal's triangle has been known independently for over a thousand years by a number of different cultures. Why is mathematics such an effective tool in the natural sciences?

(a) Deduce the molecular formula of the compound.

(b) Draw possible structures of molecules with this molecular formula.

(c) Use section 27 of the IB data booklet to identify a structure which is consistent with the $^1$H NMR spectrum and account for the number of peaks and the splitting patterns in the spectrum.

**Solution**

(a) The $^1$H NMR spectrum shows the presence of eight hydrogens so the molecular formula is $C_4H_8O_2$. The hydrogens are in three different chemical environments, in a $2:3:3$ ratio.

From the formula, IHD $= 1$, so there is either a ring or one double bond.

(b) Possible structures: $CH_3CH_2CH_2COOH$, $CH_3CH(CH_3)COOH$, $CH_3CH_2COOCH_3$, $CH_3COOCH_2CH_3$, $HCOOCH_2CH_2CH_3$ and $HCOOCH(CH_3)_2$, although many of these do not fit the data about the $2:3:3$ ratio …

(c)

| Chemical shift / ppm | Integration | Type of proton | Splitting pattern | Structural information |
|---|---|---|---|---|
| 1.0–1.5 | 3H | $—CH_3$ | triplet | $CH_3$ next to $CH_2$ |
| 2.0–2.5 | 3H | (structure: $—CH_3$ attached to $C=O$ with RO and $CH_3$) 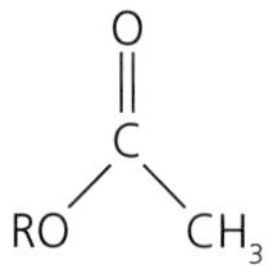 | singlet | $CH_3$ next to CO |
| 3.8–4.1 | 2H | 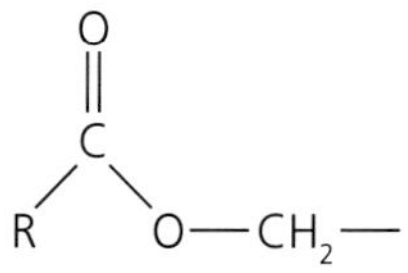 (structure: $C=O$ with R and $O—CH_2—$) | quartet | $OCH_2$ next to $CH_3$ |

The correct structure is $CH_3COOCH_2CH_3$

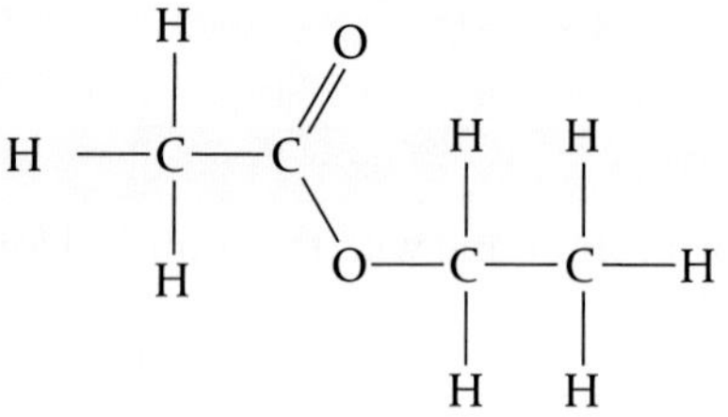

You need to be aware that the chemical shifts do not always exactly match the ones given in the IB data booklet.

The ethyl group pattern is easy to spot. The three-proton signal is split into a triplet and the two-proton signal is split into a quartet.

**Exercises**

46 **(a)** Draw the molecular structure of butanone.

**(b)** Use section 27 of the IB data booklet to predict the high resolution $^1$H NMR spectrum of butanone. Your answer should include the chemical shift, the number of hydrogen atoms, and the splitting pattern for the different environments of the hydrogen atoms.

47 Compare the $^1$H NMR spectra of ethanal and propanone. Your answer should refer to number of peaks, and the areas and splitting pattern of each peak.

**48** The key features of the $^1H$ NMR spectrum of a compound with the molecular formula $C_3H_6O_2$ are summarized below.

| Chemical shift / ppm | Number of H atoms | Splitting pattern |
|---|---|---|
| 1.3 | 3 | 3 |
| 4.3 | 2 | 4 |
| 8 | 1 | 1 |

What is the structure of this compound?

## X-ray diffraction

The most direct way to perceive an object is to shine light on it and then observe the light that is scattered from it. This is how we observe the world. The difficulty with examining individual atoms and molecules in this way is that the wavelength of visible light is too long for light to interact effectively with matter on this scale. Inter-atomic distances are of the order of $10^{-9}$ m which corresponds to the wavelength of X rays (see page 71).

When X rays pass through a crystalline solid they are scattered in an orderly way by their interaction with electrons in the substance. The scattered waves interact with each other to cause a **diffraction** pattern (Figure 11.31).

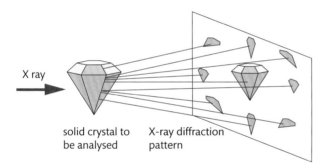

**Figure 11.31**  Electromagnetic waves, such as X rays, are diffracted when they interfere with each other due to the presence of objects in their path.

In places where the waves are in phase, with the peaks still aligned, the waves **interfere constructively** (Figure 11.32). This means that the waves reinforce each other, producing a resultant wave with a larger amplitude than the original waves.

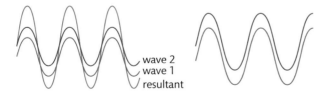

**Figure 11.32**  Constructive interference occurs when the waves are in phase: Waves reinforce each other to produce a region of high-intensity X rays on the screen.

**Destructive interference** occurs at places where the waves are out of phase by 180°, with the peak of one wave aligned with the trough of another (Figure 11.33). The waves cancel each other out completely if they have the same amplitude. This is called complete destructive interference.

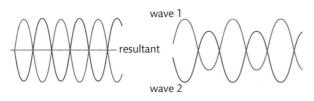

**Figure 11.33**  Destructive interference occurs when the waves are out of phase. Waves cancel each other out to produce a region of low-intensity X rays on the screen.

## CHALLENGE YOURSELF

7  Show that the path difference shown in green = $2d \sin \theta$ and deduce that for constructive interference to occur $n\lambda = 2d \sin \theta$.

Note that the details of the relationship between $\lambda$, $d$, and $\theta$ are only required in Option A.

**Figure 11.34**  The angle of diffraction at which constructive interference occurs ($\theta$) depends on the wavelength of the incident radiation ($\lambda$) and the inter atomic distance ($d$).

The cubic structure of sodium chloride was first determined by X-ray diffraction in 1913. There are approximately $10^{22}$ ions in a pinch of salt (0.001 g). The human brain has a capacity to store approximately $10^{16}$ bits of information. Can we know in detail a pinch of salt? How much can we know about the universe?

The answer is that NaCl has a regular structure that we can describe with just 10 pieces of information: all we need are the ionic radii and the geometry of the unit cell. An understanding of order and natural laws allows humans to gain significant knowledge of the universe despite its scale and complexity.

When X rays shine on a crystal, they are reflected in consecutive planes. The scattered waves interfere as they travel different distances as they pass through a crystal, and so are at different phases, dependent on their wavelength, when they hit the detector or screen. The diffraction pattern depends in a complex way on the relationship between the angle of incidence ($\theta$), the wavelength of the incident X rays ($\lambda$), and the distance between the atoms and their relative orientations ($d$) (Figure 11.34). Monochromatic X rays are used to ensure a simple correspondence between the diffraction pattern and the crystal structure. Similarly, the sample must be in the solid state as only orderly structures give ordered diffraction patterns that can be interpreted.

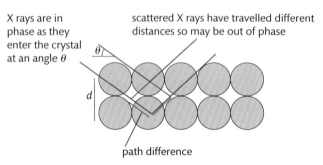

A map of the electron density in a solid can be determined directly from the X-ray diffraction pattern. One of the first applications of X-ray crystallography was to study inorganic ionic substances which have regular crystal structures, but it is now also applied to organic compounds. The electron density map of the organic molecule anthracene is shown in Figure 11.35. Contour lines connect points with the same electron density.

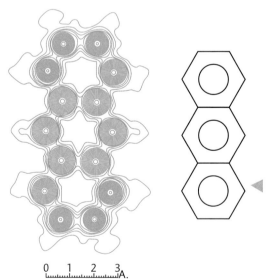

**Figure 11.35**  The electron density map of anthracene and its molecular structure. The carbon–carbon bond lengths and angles can be obtained directly from the map. The high electron density between the atoms shows the presence of covalent bonding.

The identity of the atoms can be determined from the electron density map as the pattern in electron densities are related to an element's electron configuration. It should be noted that hydrogen atoms, with only one electron, are not visible as their electrons densities are too low.

X-ray diffraction has been very successful in identifying the structure of important biochemical molecules despite the complex relationship between their structure and their X-ray diffraction pattern. The double helical structure of DNA can be mathematically determined from the 'X' in its diffraction pattern (see photograph on page 732) and the spacing of the large smudges at the top and bottom of the X-ray image is evidence for the repeating distance of 0.34 nm of the base pairs within the structure.

## NATURE OF SCIENCE

Science is highly collaborative and the scientific community is composed of people working in science, engineering, and technology. It is common to work in teams of people from many disciplines so that different areas of expertise and specializations can contribute to a common goal. There are a large number of national and international organizations for scientists working in the field. Teamwork of this sort takes place with the common understanding that science should be open minded but, of course, individual scientists are human and may have biases and prejudices. The story of the discovery of the structure of DNA is interwoven with tales of personal ambition and human conflict (see Chapter 13, page 732). The crucial importance of X-ray crystallography, and its cross disciplinary nature, is indicated by that fact that to date, 28 Nobel Prizes have been awarded to scientists working in the field. X-ray crystallography has played a vital role in diverse scientific disciplines – from physics and chemistry, to molecular biology and mineralogy.

Improvements in modern instrumentation and computing power have resulted in detailed knowledge of the structure of compounds. Dorothy Hodgkin took the first photograph of insulin in 1934 and published its refined structure in 1969. The determination of the three-dimensional structure of a protein molecule is a complex problem-solving exercise, which is now greatly aided by the use of computers. Whereas the diffraction pattern was originally collected on film, the data are now collected electronically and analysed using computer software, which is based on the work of a 19th century French mathematician, Jean-Baptiste Fourier. Fourier transforms allow complex signals to be analysed as a series of sine and cosine functions, which allows a mass of data which has been collected simultaneously, to be untangled and analysed separately. These Fourier transforms are used in other spectroscopic techniques. Dorothy Hodgkin won the Nobel Prize in Chemistry in 1964 for her work on the structures of vitamin $B_{12}$ and penicillin.

The Cambridge Crystallographic Database allows the chemical community to share structural information on the international stage. The International Union of Crystallography has members from a range of scientific disciplines and promotes international cooperation in the field.

## Exercises

**49** Which analytical technique would give bond length and bond angle data for a sample of a transition metal complex?

**50** When *monochromatic* X rays are directed towards a crystal, some undergo diffraction. What is meant by the term *monochromatic* and why is this important in X-ray crystallography?

**51** Why do hydrogen atoms not appear in an electron density map produced by X-ray diffraction?

**52** Explain why a sample must be in the solid state when X-ray diffraction is used to determine its structure.

**53** A simplified electron density map of a compound is shown.

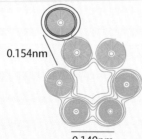

0.154nm

0.140nm

**(a)** Identify the compound from its bond length data.
**(b)** Explain why not all the atoms are shown in the electron density map.
**(c)** Deduce the degree of IHD of the compound.

## Practice questions

**1** A burette reading is recorded as 27.70 ± 0.05 cm³. Which of the following could be the actual value?

  I   27.68 cm³

  II  27.78 cm³

  III 27.74 cm³

  **A** I and II only    **B** I and III only    **C** II and III only    **D** I, II, and III

**2** A piece of metallic aluminium with a mass of 10.044 g was found to have a volume of 3.70 cm³. A student carried out the following calculation to determine the density.

Density (g cm⁻³) = $\dfrac{10.044}{3.70}$

What is the best value the student could report for the density of aluminium?

  **A** 2.715 g cm⁻³    **B** 2.7 g cm⁻³    **C** 2.71 g cm⁻³    **D** 2.7146 g cm⁻³

**3** Which experimental procedure is most likely to lead to a large systematic error?

  **A** Determining the concentration of an alkali by titration with a burette.

  **B** Measuring the volume of a solution using a volumetric pipette.

  **C** Determining the enthalpy change of neutralization in a beaker.

  **D** Measuring the volume of a gas produced with a gas syringe.

**4** Which would be the best method to decrease the random uncertainty of a measurement in an acid–base titration?

  **A** repeat the titration

  **B** ensure your eye is at the same height as the meniscus when reading from the burette

  **C** use a different burette

  **D** use a different indicator for the titration

**5** The ¹H NMR spectrum of X with molecular formula C₃H₆O is shown below.

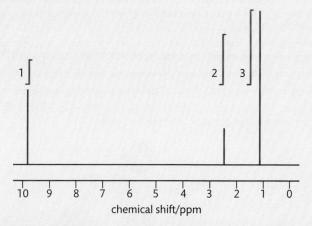

¹H NMR spectrum for question 5.

**(a)** Deduce which of the following compounds is X and explain your answer.

  **A** CH₃—CO—CH₃

  **B** CH₃—CH₂—CHO

  **C** CH₂=CH—CH₂OH    (2)

**(b)** Deduce which one of the peaks in the ¹H NMR spectrum of X would also occur in the spectrum of one of the other isomers, giving your reasoning.    (2)

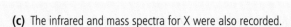

**(c)** The infrared and mass spectra for X were also recorded.

    **(i)** Apart from absorptions due to C—C and C—H bonds, suggest one absorption, in wavenumbers, that would be present in the infrared spectrum.   (1)

    **(ii)** Apart from absorptions due to C—C and C—H bonds, suggest one absorption, in wavenumbers, absent in this infrared spectrum but present in one of the other compounds shown in part (a).   (1)

**(d)** Suggest the formulas and *m/z* values of two species that would be detected in the mass spectrum.   (2)

*(Total 8 marks)*

**6** Infrared spectroscopy is commonly used as an analytical technique by inorganic, physical, and organic chemists.

**(a)** Explain why hydrogen bromide is IR active whereas bromine is IR inactive.   (1)

**(b)** The IR spectrum, mass spectrum, and $^1$H NMR spectrum of an unknown compound, X, of molecular formula $C_5H_{10}O_2$, are as follows.

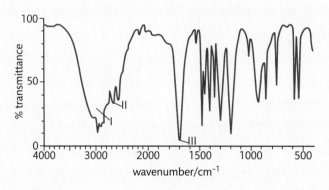

IR spectrum for question 6b.

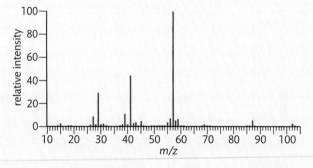

Mass spectrum for question 6b.

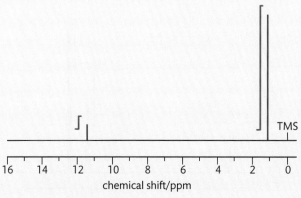

$^1$H NMR spectrum for question 6b.

**(i)** In the IR spectrum, identify the bond responsible for each of the absorptions labelled I, II, and III. (3)

**(ii)** In the mass spectrum, deduce which fragments the *m/z* values at 102, 57, and 45 correspond to. (3)

**(iii)** Identify the peak at 11.5 ppm in the $^1H$ NMR spectrum. (1)

**(iv)** State what information can be obtained from the integration traces in the $^1H$ NMR spectrum about the hydrogen atoms responsible for the peak at 1.2 ppm. (1)

**(v)** Deduce the structure of X. (1)

**(vi)** $CH_3COOCH_2CH_2CH_3$ is an isomer of X. Deduce two differences between the $^1H$ NMR spectrum of this isomer and that of X. (2)

*(Total 12 marks)*

**7** Infrared (IR) spectroscopy is widely used as a technique in analytical chemistry. Explain what happens at a molecular level during the absorption of IR radiation by carbon dioxide, $CO_2$.

*(Total 3 marks)*

**8** The IR spectrum, mass spectrum, and $^1H$ NMR spectrum of an unknown compound, X, of molecular formula $C_3H_6O_2$ are as follows.

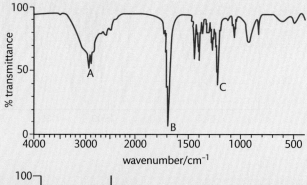

IR spectrum for question 8.

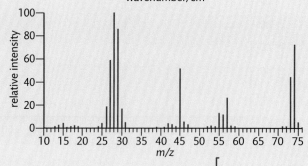

Mass spectrum for question 8.

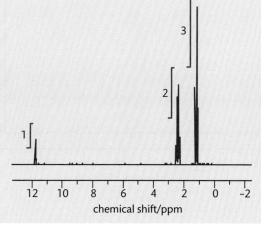

$^1H$ NMR spectrum for question 8.

**(a)** Identify the bonds responsible for the peaks A, B, and C in the IR spectrum of X. (2)

**(b)** In the mass spectrum of X, deduce which ions the $m/z$ values at 74, 45, and 29 correspond to. (3)

**(c)** Identify the peak at 11.73 ppm in the $^1$H NMR spectrum. (1)

**(d)** Deduce the structure of X. (1)

(*Total 7 marks*)

**9** The infrared spectrum of a substance, X, with empirical formula $C_3H_6O$ is given below.

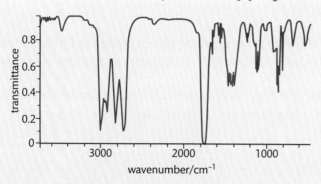

IR spectrum for question 9.

**(a)** Explain why the structural formula of X cannot be:

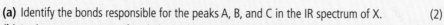

(2)

**(b)** The $^1$H NMR spectrum of X consists of three peaks. Deduce the structural formula of X and the relative areas under each peak. (2)

(*Total 4 marks*)

**10** Butan-1-ol, butan-2-ol, 2-methylpropan-1-ol, and 2-methylpropan-2-ol are four structural isomers with the molecular formula $C_4H_{10}O$.

**(a)** Details of the $^1$H NMR spectra of two of these alcohols are given below.

Spectrum 1

Two peaks: One at 1.3 ppm (relative to the TMS reference) with an integration trace of nine units, and the other at 2.0 ppm with an integration trace of one unit.

Spectrum 2

Four peaks: The first at 0.9 ppm with an integration trace of six units, the second at 1.7 ppm with an integration trace of one unit, the third at 2.1 ppm with an integration trace of one unit, and the fourth at 3.4 ppm with an integration trace of two units.

Consider the proton environments present in each of the alcohol molecules when answering the following questions.

**(i)** Identify which alcohol gives spectrum 1 and explain your answer by stating which hydrogen atoms in the molecule are responsible for each of the two peaks. (3)

**(ii)** Deduce which alcohol gives spectrum 2. Explain which particular hydrogen atoms in the molecule are responsible for the peaks at 0.9 ppm and 3.4 ppm. (3)

**(b)** The mass spectrum of one of the alcohols shows peaks at *m/z* values of 74, 59, and 45.

**(i)** Deduce which two of the alcohols could produce this spectrum and identify the species responsible for the three peaks. (4)

**(ii)** The spectrum also shows a significant peak at *m/z* = 31. Suggest which alcohol is responsible for this spectrum and deduce the species responsible for the peak at *m/z* = 31. (2)

**(c)** Explain why the infrared spectra of all four alcohols are very similar. (2)

*(Total 14 marks)*

**11** A feature of some $^1$H NMR spectra is the electron-withdrawing effect of electronegative atoms. These atoms cause nearby protons to produce peaks at higher chemical shift values, often in the range 2.5 to 4.5 ppm.

Consider the $^1$H NMR spectrum of an unknown compound, D, which has a molecular formula $C_4H_8O_2$ and is known to have an absorption in its IR spectrum corresponding to a C=O absorption.

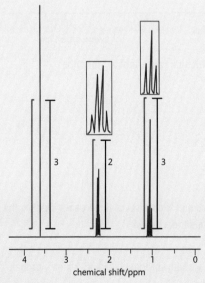

$^1$H NMR spectrum for question 11.

Use this information and the values in section 27 of the data booklet to deduce the structure of D.

*(Total 4 marks)*

**12 (a)** The mass spectrum of an unknown compound, X, of empirical formula $C_2H_4O$ is shown below.

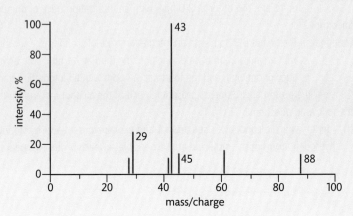

Mass spectrum for question 12a.

(i) Determine the relative molecular mass of X from the mass spectrum and deduce the formula of the molecular ion. (2)

(ii) Identify a fragment which gives rise to the peak at $m/z = 29$. (1)

(iii) Comment on the absence of a peak at $m/z = 59$. (1)

(b) The IR spectrum of X is shown below.

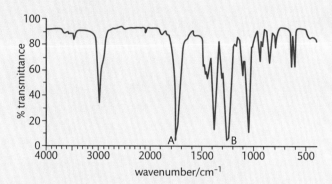

IR spectrum for question 12b.

(i) Use section 26 of the data booklet to identify the bonds which correspond to absorptions A and B. (1)

(ii) Deduce the name of the functional group present in X. (1)

(c) Typical proton chemical shift values are given in section 27 of the data booklet.

The $^1H$ NMR spectrum of X contains three peaks. Details of two of these are shown in the table below.

| Peak | Chemical shift / ppm | Relative peak area | Splitting pattern |
|---|---|---|---|
| first | 2.0 | 3 | singlet |
| second | 4.1 | 2 | quartet |
| third | | | |

(i) Deduce a possible structure for X that is consistent with the mass, IR, and $^1H$ NMR spectra. (1)

(ii) Complete the table above by suggesting the chemical shift of the third peak, and state its relative peak area and splitting pattern. (3)

(iii) Explain the splitting pattern of the peak at chemical shift 4.1 ppm. (2)

(Total 12 marks)

 To access weblinks on the topics covered in this chapter, please go to www. pearsonhotlinks.com and enter the ISBN or title of this book.

**12**

# Option A: Materials

| A.1 | Materials science involves understanding the properties of a material, and then applying those properties to desired structures. |
| A.2 | Metals can be extracted from their ores and alloyed for desired characteristics. ICP-MS/OES spectroscopy ionizes metals and uses mass and emission spectra for analysis. |
| A.3 | Catalysts work by providing an alternate reaction pathway for the reaction. Catalysts always increase the rate of the reaction and are left unchanged at the end of the reaction. |
| A.4 | Liquid crystals are fluids that have physical properties which are dependent on molecular orientation relative to some fixed axis in the material. |
| A.5 | Polymers are made up of repeating monomer units which can be manipulated in various ways to give structures with desired properties. |
| A.6 | Chemical techniques position atoms in molecules using chemical reactions whilst physical techniques allow atoms/molecules to be manipulated and positioned to specific requirements. |
| A.7 | Although materials science generates many useful new products, there are challenges associated with recycling and high levels of toxicity of some of these materials. |
| A.8 | Superconductivity is zero electrical resistance and expulsion of magnetic fields. X-ray crystallography can be used to analyse structures. |
| A.9 | Condensation polymers are formed by the loss of small molecules as functional groups from monomers join. |
| A.10 | Toxicity and carcinogenic properties of heavy metals are the result of their ability to form coordinated compounds, have various oxidation states, and act as catalysts in the human body. |

Light micrograph of high carbon steel. It contains 0.65% carbon by mass alloyed with iron. It is very strong but brittle and is used for cutting tools, high-strength wires and springs.

One of the key roles of the chemist is to transform natural resources which are readily available into more useful materials. Civilizations are sometimes characterized by the technology they have developed to accomplish this. The Bronze Age, for example, marks the time when the ancients were able to produce copper from smelted ores. The extraction of iron from its ores in the blast furnace is probably one of the most significant developments in the Industrial Revolution of the 18th century. These technological advances, however, often came without a full understanding of the underlying scientific principles. Today chemists are able to use their understanding of the bonding and structure of materials to develop new substances with properties to serve modern needs. This chapter discusses the materials we have used to make our life more comfortable, and our understanding more complete. We outline the extraction

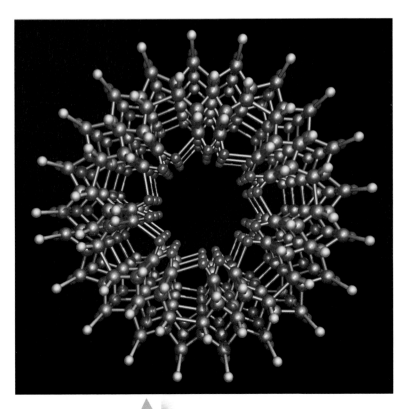

and analysis of metals, the properties of different addition plastics and their impact on their environment, the use of catalysts in improving the effectiveness of our chemistry to bring about important changes more effectively and more selectively, and liquid crystals, superconductors, and nanoparticles, which are modern materials with interesting properties.

Computer graphic of a molecular tube. Nanotechnology, which has grown rapidly since the 1990s, involves the construction of such devices. It has been described as 'the science of the very small with big potential' and could revolutionize computing, medicine, and manufacturing. Each of the coloured spheres represents a single atom: carbon (blue), oxygen (red) and hydrogen (yellow).

 **Materials science introduction**

## Understandings:

- Materials are classified based on their uses, properties, or bonding and structure.
- The properties of a material based on the degree of covalent, ionic, or metallic character in a compound can be deduced from its position on a bonding triangle.
- Composites are mixtures in which materials are composed of two distinct phases, a reinforcing phase that is embedded in a matrix phase.

### Guidance
- *Consider properties of metals, polymers, and ceramics in terms of metallic, covalent, and ionic bonding.*
- *See section 29 of the data booklet for a triangular bonding diagram.*

## Applications:

- Use of bond triangle diagrams for binary compounds from electronegativity data.
- Evaluation of various ways of classifying materials.
- Relating physical characteristics (melting point, permeability, conductivity, elasticity, brittleness) of a material to its bonding and structures (packing arrangements, electron mobility, ability of atoms to slide relative to one another).

### Guidance
*Permeability to moisture should be considered with respect to bonding and simple packing arrangements.*

## Materials are classified based on their uses, properties, or bonding and structure

Whereas most living things survive by adapting to their environment, human beings have been particularly effective at doing the opposite. We have adapted the material in our environment to meet our needs. Initially this was a trial and error process. We made buildings out of strong materials such as wood, stone, and iron, made windows and drinking implements from transparent glass, and attractive jewellery from shiny minerals or precious metals.

A more systematic scientific approach has led us to identify and measure the properties of different material more precisely and classify them into groups accordingly. Metals are strong and malleable, glasses are transparent and brittle, and ceramics are generally excellent insulators (superconductors are notable exceptions). In recent times our chemical understanding has allowed us to make great advances in the synthesis and uses of materials as we understand the link between their properties and their structure and composition. If the focus is on understanding the properties of a material, a classification based on its bonding and structure is helpful, whereas if we are interested in its properties and possible uses a classification based on the material type, metal, ceramic, composite, or polymer, is more appropriate.

## The properties of a material based on the degree of covalent, ionic, or metallic character can be deduced from its position on a bonding triangle

The structure and bonding of the different substances was discussed in Chapter 4. Although we generally classify solids as metallic, ionic, molecular, or giant covalent this is a simplification as many materials show intermediate properties. The bonding in a material is determined by the magnitude and difference of the electronegativities ($\chi$) of the constituent elements. This is illustrated by the triangle of bonding shown in Figure 12.1.

To understand the triangle, consider the position of the elements caesium and fluorine and the binary compound they react to form.

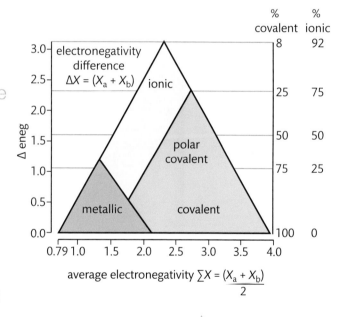

**Figure 12.1** Metals have low electronegativities and small electronegativity differences, which places them in the lower left corner. Ionic compounds are found at the top centre. Covalent structures are found in the lower right corner. They are made from non-metals that have high electronegativities.

| Substance | $\chi_{average}$ | $\Delta\chi$ | Position in triangle |
|---|---|---|---|
| CsF | $\frac{4.0 + 0.8}{2} = 2.4$ | $4.0 - 0.8 = 3.2$ | Top of the triangle as 100% ionic compound. Made up from the most electropositive metal and most electronegative non-metal. |
| Cs | 0.8 | $0.8 - 0.8 = 0$ | Bottom left as 100% metallic. Cs has the lowest absolute electronegativity. |
| $F_2$ | 4.0 | $4.0 - 4.0 = 0.0$ | Bottom right corner as 100% molecular covalent. |

The percentage ionic character of a compound can be approximated using the formula:

$$\% \text{ ionic characacter} = \frac{\Delta\chi}{3.2} \times 100\%$$

According to this equation, sodium chloride is 72% ionic and hydrogen chloride is 32% ionic. We describe the bonding in NaCl as ionic and HCl as polar covalent.

Locate the position of the following substances on the triangle of bonding:

(a) diamond

(b) silicon dioxide

(c) bronze (an alloy of copper and tin).

**Solution**

| | Substance | $\chi_{average}$ | $\Delta\chi$ |
|---|---|---|---|
| (a) | diamond | 2.6 | 0 |
| (b) | silicon dioxide | $\frac{1.9 + 3.4}{2} = 2.65$ | $3.4 - 1.9 = 1.5$ |
| (c) | Cu/Zn | $\frac{1.9 + 2.0}{2} = 1.95$ | $2.0 - 1.9 = 0.1$ |

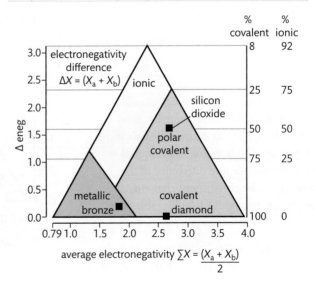

## There are four distinct classes of materials

Materials fall into four distinct classes: metals, polymers, ceramics, and composites. We have discussed the properties of metals in Chapter 4 and polymers in Chapter 10. Details of thermoplastic plastics, thermoset plastics, and elastomers are given later in this chapter.

## Ceramics are made by baking metal oxides and other minerals to high temperature

The term **ceramic** comes from the Greek word for pottery. This class of materials is so broad that it is often easier to define ceramics as all solid materials, except metals and their alloys, that are made by the high-temperature processing of inorganic raw materials. Their properties are generally the opposite of those found in the metals. Glasses and semiconductors can also be included in this class.

Ceramics can either form giant ionic or giant covalent structures, which explains why they are so hard. The presence of ions also explains their brittle properties. A shear force moves one layer of ions relative to another so that ions of the same charge are forced next to each other (Figure 12.2).

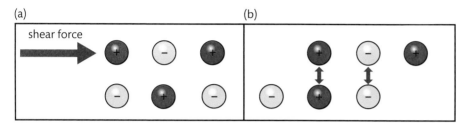

**Figure 12.2** Ionic materials and ceramics are brittle. (a) A strong force is applied to a layer of ions. (b) Ions of the same charge are now closer together and so the top layer repels the bottom layer and the structure falls apart.

Ceramics can be porous materials as there are gaps in their structure that allow water molecules to pass.

Glasses have many properties in common with ceramics as they are made from giant covalent structures such as silicon dioxide fused with some metal oxide with an ionic structure. The key difference is that glasses are transparent and waterproof. They are made by cooling the molten mixture of silicon dioxide and metal oxide quickly so the solid formed retains some of the disorder of the liquid. They are hard and brittle like the ceramics.

## Composites are mixtures composed of two distinct phases, a reinforcing phase that is embedded in a matrix phase

A **composite material** is a mixture of two materials. Generally a composite material is made up from fibres of a strong hard material embedded in a matrix of another material (Figure 12.3). The properties of the composite depend on the properties of its constituents.

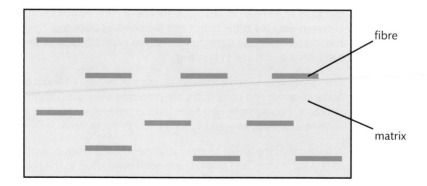

**Figure 12.3** A composite material has fibres of one material embedded in a matrix made from a different material.

If the composite is designed and fabricated correctly, it combines the strength of the fibre with the toughness of the matrix to achieve a combination of desirable properties not available in any single conventional material. Some composites also offer the advantage of being tailor-made so that properties, such as strength and stiffness, can easily be changed by changing the amount or orientation of the fibre.

The compositions of some common composites are shown on page 586.

| Composite | Fibre | Matrix |
|---|---|---|
| fibreglass | glass | plastic |
| carbon fibres | carbon | plastic |
| concrete | steel | cement |
| wood | cellulose | lignin |
| cermet | ceramic | metal |

Light micrograph of fibreglass. Fibreglass is a lightweight, extremely strong, and robust material. The plastic matrix may be a thermosetting plastic or thermoplastic.

**TOK** We can classify materials according to their composition, their bonding and structure, or their properties. No single classification is 'perfect'. How do we evaluate the different classification systems we use in the different areas of knowledge? How does our need to categorize the world help and hinder the pursuit of knowledge?

A technologist removing a sample of cermet from a furnace. Cermet is a composite material made from the ceramic boron carbide and the metal aluminium. The cermet is lighter than aluminium but stronger than steel.

## Some physical properties of materials

All solid materials have a number of physical properties. Here are some which affect how different materials are used.

| Property | Comments |
|---|---|
| Melting point | The temperature at which a solid begins to liquefy. Pure crystalline materials melt at constant temperature. Glasses have no defined melting point as they are generally mixtures. Thermosetting plastics do not melt when they are heated but burn. The carbon atoms combine with oxygen when the strong covalent bonds which hold the structure together are broken. Themoplastics have molecular covalent structures and so have intermediate melting points as only intermolecular forces are broken when the plastic melts. The melting points of metals generally increase across a period as more delocalized electrons are used in bonding and decrease down a group as an increase in ionic radius leads to reduced attraction between the ions in the lattice and the bonding electrons. The melting points of the transition metals are generally high as the d electrons are involved in bonding. |
| Permeability | The facility with which a material allows the passage of liquid or gas. Some ceramics and composites are porous as there are gaps in their structure. For example, pores can form in the matrix structure of cement which allows water to pass through the material. |
| Electrical conductivity | A measure of the ability to conduct a current at a given potential difference. Metals and graphite are good conductors in the solid state as they have delocalized electrons which are free to move throughout their structures. Ionic compounds can conduct electricity in the liquids state or in aqueous solution where their ions are free to move. Composites made from metal or graphite can conduct. |

| Property | Comments |
|---|---|
| Elasticity | The ability of a material to return to its origin shape once the stretching force has been removed. The physical reasons for elastic behaviour can be quite different for different materials. In metals, the atomic lattice changes size and shape when stretched. When the stretching force is removed, the lattice goes back to the original as the atoms are pulled back by the bonding electrons. Elastomers are elastic polymers, generally with double bonds in their structure. Their chains uncoil when a force is applied but return to a more stable coiled arrangement when the force is removed. More details are given later in the chapter (page 622). |
| Brittleness | A brittle material breaks into parts when it is stretched. Ionic and covalent bonds lead to brittle structures. Some ceramics and thermosetting are brittle. This property is the opposite of toughness. Metals and thermoplastics are tough. |
| Ductility / malleability | A ductile material can be stretched into long strands. Metals are ductile as their atoms can slide across each other without breaking their metallic bonds. The delocalized electrons adopt a new arrangement which ensures that the metallic bonding is maintained. A malleable material can be squeezed into any shape. Metals are malleable again because the delocalized electrons can accommodate any changes in structure without breaking the metallic bonding. |

Damaged concrete. Scanning electron microscope of cracks that have formed around a trapped air bubble in a sample of concrete that has been damaged through chemical reactions.

The properties of the different materials are summarized on page 588. These are only general rules and there are many exceptions.

| Property | Metal | Ceramic | Glass | Polymer | Composite |
|---|---|---|---|---|---|
| Melting point | Transition metals have the highest melting points as more electrons are involved in bonding. Group 1 metals have the lowest melting points. Pure metals have fixed melting points; alloys melt over a range of temperatures. | High: ionic and covalent bonds are strong. | High: covalent bonds are strong. | Thermoplastics have low melting points as intermolecular forces are weak. Thermosetting plastics don't melt but burn when heated to high temperature. | High: depends on the constituents. |
| Permeability | Low | Can be porous as there are gaps in the structure. | Low | No | Can be porous as there are gaps in the structure. |
| Electrical conductivity | High: there are delocalized electrons. | Low | Low, but some conductivity at very high temperature as ions are free to move. | Low, but some polymers with extended delocalized electrons have been synthesized which conduct electricity. | Generally low but can conduct if structure includes metal or graphite which have delocalized electrons. |
| Elasticity | Generally low: some metals show elastic properties; steel springs for example. The distance between the atoms increase when the metal is stretched but the atoms return to their original position due to the metallic bonding when the load is removed. | Low | Low | Low, but elastomers show elastic properties. Elastomers uncoil when a stretching force is applied but coil when force is removed. | Low, but carbon fibres show elastic properties. |
| Brittleness | Low | High: contain strong covalent or ionic bonds. When force is sufficiently strong to break these, the structure falls apart. | High: contain strong covalent or ionic bonds. When force is sufficiently strong to break these, the structure falls apart. | Some thermosetting plastics, which have a giant covalent structure, can be strong but brittle. Thermoplastics and elastomers are not brittle. | Generally low, but depends on composition. |
| Ductility | High: metal ions can be pulled apart without breaking the metallic bonds as the delocalized electrons can accommodate changes to the lattice structure. | Low | High | Low | Low |

The use of materials has characterized the development of different civilizations in history. In the stone age, humans used materials which could be modified for use by simple physical processing but the iron age involved chemistry in which the element was extracted from available minerals. Scientific knowledge during this period was limited and these were essentially technological developments which relied on empirical knowledge gained through trial and error. More modern times have been characterized by the use of materials such as aluminium and plastic. This has relied on the application of available technology; the extraction of reactive metals such as aluminium relied on the use of electricity, but more importantly on our understanding of the link between the properties of a material and its structure. The evolution of science has made our environment more accommodating through technological developments and more understandable in terms of the models and theories we have developed. Both these motivations continue to drive materials science forward. It is a cross-disciplinary area of science which attracts scientists of different skills with different objectives. We are now more aware of the impact on our environment of our use of natural resources. This has made us more aware of our ethical responsibilities as scientists and brought new challenges.

## Exercises

1   Identify which of the following statements refers to the composition of a composite material.

    **A**   It is a mixture in which one material acts as the matrix or glue.
    **B**   It contains at least three different materials, one of which is glue.
    **C**   It must contain a metallic element.
    **D**   It is a compound of two elements.

2   Use electronegativity values from section 8 of the data booklet to classify the bonding in the following materials: $Cl_2O$, $PbCl_2$, $Al_2O_3$, HBr, and NaBr.

3   Copper oxide can be added to give glass a blue or green colour. Deduce the position of copper oxide in the bonding triangle and describe the nature of its structure and bonding.

4   Explain why metals are ductile and ceramics are brittle.

5   Concrete is a composite of steel and cement. Outline its structure and suggest how the material could conduct electricity.

# A.2   Metals and inductively coupled plasma (ICP) spectroscopy

## Understandings:

- Reduction by coke (carbon), a more reactive metal, or electrolysis are means of obtaining some metals from their ores.
- The relationship between charge and the number of moles of electrons is given by Faraday's constant, $F$.
- Alloys are homogeneous mixtures of metals with other metals or non-metals.
- Diamagnetic and paramagnetic compounds differ in electron spin pairing and their behaviour in magnetic fields.
- Trace amounts of metals can be identified and quantified by ionizing them with argon gas plasma in inductively coupled plasma (ICP) spectroscopy using mass spectroscopy ICP-MS and optical emission spectroscopy ICP-OES.

### Guidance
- *Faraday's constant is given in the IB data booklet in section 2.*
- *Details of operating parts of ICP-MS and ICP-OES instruments will not be assessed.*

## Applications:

- Deduction of redox equations for the reduction of metals.
- Relating the method of extraction to the position of a metal on the activity series.
- Explanation of the production of aluminium by the electrolysis of alumina in molten cryolite.

- Explanation of how alloying alters properties of metals.
- Solving stoichiometric problems using Faraday's constant based on mass deposits in electrolysis.
- Discussion of paramagnetism and diamagnetism in relation to electron structure of metals.
- Explanation of the plasma state and its production in ICP-MS amd ICP-OES.
- Identify metals and abundances from simple data and calibration curves provided from ICP-MS and ICP-OES.
- Explanation of the separation and quantification of metallic ions by MS and OES.
- Uses of ICP-MS and ICP-OES.

**Guidance**
- *Only analysis of metals should be covered.*
- *The importance of calibration should be covered.*

## The method of extraction is related to its position in the activity series

The ability to extract metals was an important technological step in the development of our civilization. Some unreactive metals, such as gold and silver, occur in nature as the free element. More reactive metals are found in rocks or **ores** as compounds, combined with other elements present in the environment. These ores are usually oxides, sulfides, or carbonates of the metal mixed with impurities. The extraction of metals from these ores involves the reduction of the metal compounds (Chapter 9, page 416) and the removal of impurities.

The method of extraction is related to the position of the metal in the reactivity series.

| Metal | Method of extraction |
|---|---|
| potassium | electrolysis of molten compounds |
| sodium | |
| magnesium | |
| aluminium | |
| carbon | |
| zinc | reduction of oxides with carbon/carbon monoxide |
| chromium | |
| iron | |
| tin | |
| hydrogen | |
| copper | occur native in the ground or produced by heating the ore |
| silver | |
| mercury | |
| gold | |

*(arrow on left: decreasing reactivity, pointing downward)*

A more complete activity series is given in section 25 of the IB data booklet.

## Reduction of compounds using more reactive metals

The more reactive elements, at the top of the series, will reduce the oxides of the less reactive elements at the bottom of the series. The practical use of this route depends on the relative cost of the two metals involved.

Magnesium could in theory reduce iron(III) oxide but is generally not used as the magnesium is too expensive to be wasted in this way:

$$3Mg(s) + Fe_2O_3(s) \rightarrow 3MgO(s) + 2Fe(s)$$

However, aluminium is used to extract the more expensive chromium from its ores:

$$2Al(s) + Cr_2O_3(s) \rightarrow Al_2O_3(s) + 2Cr(s)$$

## Metals in the middle of the series are extracted from their oxides or sulfides with carbon

Coke, an impure form of carbon, formed by heating coal, is used as a relatively cheap reducing agent for metals in the middle of the activity series.

$$PbO(s) + C(s) \rightarrow Pb(s) + CO(g)$$

In the case of lead and zinc the sulfide is the most available ore. The sulfide is first roasted to produce the oxide, which is then reduced by carbon. Carbon monoxide is often the product of the reaction.

$$2ZnS(s) + 3O_2(g) \rightarrow 2ZnO(s) + 2SO_2(g)$$

$$ZnO(s) + C(s) \rightarrow CO(g) + Zn(s)$$

## Metal oxides can be reduced with carbon monoxide

Iron oxide is reduced with carbon monoxide in a blast furnace (Figure 12.4).

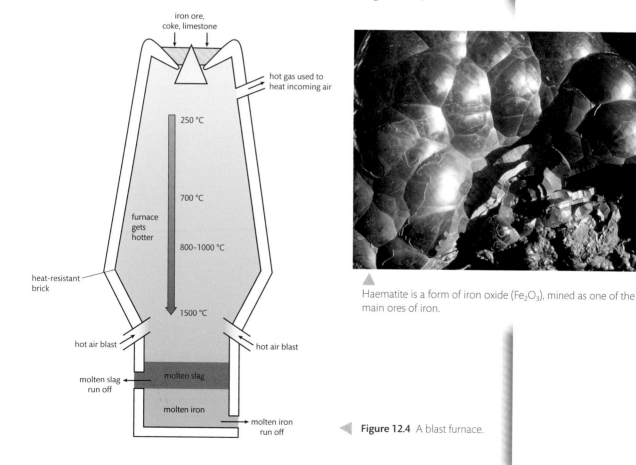

Haematite is a form of iron oxide ($Fe_2O_3$), mined as one of the main ores of iron.

**Figure 12.4** A blast furnace.

iron ore, coke, limestone

hot gas used to heat incoming air

250 °C

700 °C

furnace gets hotter

800–1000 °C

heat-resistant brick

1500 °C

hot air blast

hot air blast

molten slag run off

molten slag

molten iron

molten iron run off

Iron ore, coke, and limestone ($CaCO_3$) are added at the top of the blast furnace and a blast of hot air is blown in from near the bottom.

The coke burns in the preheated air to form carbon dioxide:

$$C(s) + O_2(g) \rightarrow CO_2(g) \qquad \Delta H = -298 \text{ kJ mol}^{-1}$$

The carbon monoxide acts as the **reducing agent** and reduces the iron(III) oxide:

$$Fe_2O_3(s) + 3CO(g) \rightarrow 2Fe(l) + 3CO_2(g)$$

## Less reactive metals can be produced by heating their ores

The less reactive metals at the bottom of the activity series can be extracted without carbon as the oxides are unstable at higher temperature. Mercury is produced when its sulfide ore, cinnabar, is heated in oxygen.

$$HgS(s) + O_2(g) \rightarrow Hg(l) + SO_2(g)$$

Cinnabar, an ore of mercury.

## More reactive metals are extracted from their molten compounds by electrolysis

As discussed in Chapter 9, reducing agents are suppliers of electrons. The most direct way to supply electrons is via an electric circuit. The more reactive metals at the top of the series, which cannot be reduced by carbon, are extracted using electrolysis. The electrolysis of aqueous compounds of these metals cannot be used, as the less reactive element hydrogen, present in the water, would be produced in preference to the metal at the cathode.

## The equations for the extraction can be deduced from changes in oxidation numbers

### Worked example

Copper is extracted from its sulfide ore by a combination of two reactions:

1  copper(I) sulfide is heated in air to produce copper(I) oxide and sulfur dioxide
2  the air supply is removed and copper(I) oxide is heated with excess copper(I) sulfide to produce sulfur dioxide and the metal.

Identify the element that is reduced in both redox reactions and deduce the equations.

1    Copper(I) sulfide has the formula $(Cu^+)_2 S^{2-} = Cu_2S$

We can write an unbalanced equation that has the oxidation numbers below each element:

$$Cu_2S + O_2 \rightarrow Cu_2O + SO_2 \qquad \text{unbalanced}$$
$$\phantom{Cu_2}{+1\ -2}\ \ \ \ 0\ \ \ \ \ \ \ {+1\ -2}\ \ \ \ {+4-2} \qquad \text{oxidation numbers (ON)}$$

- sulfur is oxidized: $(-2 \rightarrow +4)$: $\Delta(ON) = (+4) - (-2) = +6$
- oxygen is reduced: $(0 \rightarrow -2)$ : $\Delta(ON) = (-2) - (0) = -2$

To balance these changes: three Os must be reduced for each S. The copper is unchanged.

$$Cu_2S + 3/2O_2 \rightarrow Cu_2O + SO_2 \qquad \text{balanced}$$
$$\phantom{Cu_2}{+1\ -2}\ \ \ {3/2(0)}\ \ \ \ \ \ \ {+1\ -2}\ \ \ \ {+4\ 2(-2)}$$

multiplying by 2:

$$2Cu_2S + 3O_2 \rightarrow 2Cu_2O + 3SO_2 \qquad \text{balanced}$$

2    The unbalanced equation with oxidation numbers below each element:

$$Cu_2O + Cu_2S \rightarrow Cu + SO_2 \qquad \text{unbalanced}$$
$$\phantom{Cu_2}{+1\ -2}\ \ \ \ {+1\ \ 0}\ \ \ \ \ \ {+4}\ \ \ \ {-2} \qquad \text{oxidation numbers (ON)}$$

- sulfur is oxidized $(-2 \rightarrow +4)$: $\Delta(ON) = (+4) - (-2) = +6$
- copper is reduced $(+1 \rightarrow 0)$: $\Delta(ON) = (0) - (+1) = -1$

To balance these changes: six Cu must be reduced for each S oxidized. The oxygen is unchanged.

$$2Cu_2O + Cu_2S \rightarrow 6Cu + SO_2 \qquad \text{balanced}$$

## Aluminium is extracted from its ore (bauxite) by electrolysis

Aluminium is the most abundant metal in the Earth's crust and is found in the minerals **bauxite** and mica as well as in clay. It was, however, not discovered until 1825 by H.C. Oersted in Denmark. It is a reactive metal which means that its compounds are extremely difficult to break down by chemical reactions.

Nowadays, aluminium is a relatively cheap metal. The extraction of aluminium from the mineral bauxite involves three stages.

- **Purification**: the mineral is treated with aqueous sodium hydroxide. Bauxite is an impure form of hydrated aluminium oxide: $Al_2O_3.xH_2O$. The amphoteric nature of the oxide allows it to be separated from other metal oxides. Unlike most metal oxides, aluminium oxide dissolves in aqueous sodium hydroxide. The soluble aluminium oxide is separated by filtration from the insoluble metal oxides (iron(III) oxide) and sand.

$$Al_2O_3(s) + 2OH^-(aq) + 3H_2O(l) \rightarrow 2Al(OH)_4^-(aq)$$

The reaction can be reversed by passing carbon dioxide through the solution. Carbon dioxide forms the weak acid, carbonic acid, which neutralizes solution.

Bauxite is the primary ore from which aluminium is obtained.

**An amphoteric oxide is an oxide that can act either as an acid or a base.**

**In an electrolysis cell, the positive electrode is called the anode and the negative electrode is called the cathode.**

- **Solvation**: the purified aluminium oxide is dissolved in molten cryolite – a mineral form of $Na_3AlF_6$. This reduces the melting point of aluminium oxide and so reduces the energy requirements of the process. Pure aluminium oxide would not be a suitable electrolyte because it has a very high melting point and it is a poor electrical conductor even when molten. Its bonding is intermediate between ionic and polar covalent, as discussed earlier in the chapter.

- **Electrolysis**: the molten mixture is electrolysed (Figure 12.5). Graphite anodes are dipped into the molten electrolyte. The graphite-lined steel cell acts as the cathode.

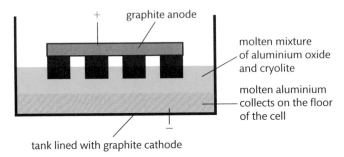

**Figure 12.5** The electrolysis of molten aluminium oxide.

The negatively charged $O^{2-}$ ions are attracted to the anode, where they lose electrons and are oxidized to oxygen gas:

$$2O^{2-}(l) \rightarrow O_2(g) + 4e^-$$

At the high temperature of the process, the oxygen reacts with the graphite anode to form carbon dioxide:

$$C(s) + O_2(g) \rightarrow CO_2(g)$$

As the graphite is burned away, the anode needs to be regularly replaced.

The positive aluminium ions, $Al^{3+}$, are attracted to the cathode, where they gain electrons and are reduced to molten aluminium:

$$Al^{3+}(l) + 3e^- \rightarrow Al(l)$$

The aluminium produced by this method is 99% pure with small amounts of silicon and iron impurities. As the electrolyte contains fluoride ions, fluorine gas is also produced in the process. This needs to be removed from the waste gases before they pass into the atmosphere as it would lead to environmental damage.

The need for high temperatures means that the process needs to be continuous to be economical. The cost of electricity is the most important factor to consider when

deciding the location of an aluminium plant and they are often sited near hydroelectric power stations. The high energy demand emphasizes the importance of recycling. The energy requirements of recycling aluminium are less than 5% of that needed to extract the metal directly.

## The amount of metal produced depends on the number of electrons supplied

The electric current ($I$) passing an point in an electric circuit is a measuring of the amount of charge ($Q$) passing each point in a given time, $t$.

$$\text{current } (I) = \frac{\text{charge } (Q)}{\text{time } (t)}$$

This allows the amount of charge delivered to an electrolysis cell to be calculated from the current and the time:

$$\text{charge } (Q) = \text{current } (I) \times \text{time } (t)$$

If the time is measured in seconds and the current in amperes, the charge is given in coulombs.

To calculate the number of electrons, $N(e)$, passing any point any second we need to divide the total charge by the charge of one electron ($e^- = 1.602189 \times 10^{-19}$ C). This value is given in section 5 of the IB data booklet.

$$N(e^-) = \frac{\text{charge } (Q)}{1.602189 \times 10^{-19} \text{ C}}$$

The amount of electrons, measured in moles, $n(e^-)$, can be obtained by dividing this number by Avogadro's constant ($L$).

$$n(e^-) = \frac{\text{charge } (Q)}{1.602189 \times 10^{-19} \text{ C} \times 6.02 \times 10^{23} \text{ mol}^{-1}}$$

This expression can be simplified by combining the constants to give a new constant:

$$\text{Faraday's constant } (F) = 1.602\,189 \times 10^{-19} \text{ C} \times 6.02 \times 10^{23} \text{ mol}^{-1} = 96\,500 \text{ C mol}^{-1}$$

**Faraday's constant** is the charge of 1 mol of electrons.

The amount of product formed by an electric current is chemically equivalent to the amount of electrons supplied; a statement of **Faraday's law of electrolysis**. These relationships allow the amount of metal produced during electrolysis to be calculated from the current and time using the stoichiometric strategies developed in Chapter 1.

### Worked example

Calculate the mass of aluminium that can be produced from an electrolytic cell in one year (365 days) operating with an average current of $1.20 \times 10^5$ A.

#### Solution

Equation at cathode:

$$Al^{3+}(l) + 3e^- \rightarrow Al(l)$$

$$\text{1 mol} \quad \text{3 mol} \quad \text{1 mol}$$

$$\frac{n(Al)}{n(e)} = \frac{1}{3}$$

$$n(Al) = \frac{1}{3} \times n(e)$$

charge ($Q$) = current ($I$) × time ($t$)

Faraday's constant is the charge of 1 mol of electrons.

Faraday's constant ($F$) = 96 500 C mol⁻¹

Faraday's law of electrolysis states that the amount of product formed by an electric current is chemically equivalent to the amount of electrons supplied.

The aluminium drink can is the world's most recycled container – more than 63% of all cans are recycled worldwide. You could watch three hours of television on the energy saved by recycling one aluminium can.

The number of moles of electrons can be calculated from the current:

$$n(e) = \frac{Q}{F} = \frac{I \times t}{F}$$

$$= \frac{1.20 \times 10^5 \text{ A} \times 365 \times 24 \times 60 \times 60 \text{ s}}{96\,500 \text{ C mol}^{-1}}$$

This gives

$$n(\text{Al}) = \frac{1}{3} \times \frac{1.20 \times 10^5 \times 365 \times 24 \times 60 \times 60}{96\,500} \text{ mol}$$

$$m(\text{Al}) = n(\text{Al}) \times M(\text{Al})$$

$$m(\text{Al}) = 26.96 \text{ g mol}^{-1} \times \frac{1.20 \times 10^5 \times 365 \times 24 \times 60 \times 60}{3 \times 96\,500} \text{ mol}$$

$$= 352\,680\,323 \text{ g}$$

$$= 352\,680.32 \text{ kg}$$

$$= 3.53 \times 10^5 \text{ kg}$$

### Exercises

6  **(a)** State the ore from which aluminium is extracted.
   **(b)** Explain why aluminium is not extracted from its oxide by carbon reduction in a blast furnace.
   **(c)** Describe and explain how aluminium atoms are formed during the extraction process.
   **(d)** Explain why aluminium cannot be obtained by electrolysis of an aqueous solution of an aluminium compound.
   **(e)** Explain the low conductivity of aluminium oxide.
   **(f)** Explain with chemical equations why the carbon anodes need to be replaced at regular intervals.

7  0.100 F of electric charge is passed through a saturated solution of copper(II) chloride. Calculate the mass of copper produced and the volume of chlorine gas produced, assuming the reaction is carried out under standard conditions of temperature and pressure.

8  A molten sample of titanium chloride was electrolysed using a current of 0.0965 A for 1000 s. 0.011 975 g of the metal was produced. Deduce the formula of the titanium chloride.

9  Methane is sometimes added to the preheated air in a blast furnace, instead of coke. Deduce the equation for the complete reaction between methane and haematite ($Fe_2O_3(s)$), in the presence of air.

10  The extraction of titanium involves the conversion of titanium(IV) oxide to titanium(IV) chloride. Carbon is oxidized to carbon monoxide in the process.

   **(a)** Deduce the chemical equation for the reaction.
   **(b)** Titanium(IV) chloride is reduced to the metal by magnesium. Deduce the equation for this reaction.

## Alloys are homogeneous mixtures of metals with other metals or non-metals

The iron produced by the blast furnace contains about 4% carbon. This high level of impurity makes the metal brittle and reduces its melting point. As this iron has limited uses, the majority is converted into an **alloy**: steel. An alloy is a homogeneous mixture containing at least one metal formed when liquid metals are added together and allowed to form a solid of *uniform* composition. Alloys are useful because they have a range of properties that are different from the pure metal. The presence of other elements in the metallic structure changes the regular arrangement of the metal atoms in the solid, making it more difficult for atoms to slip over each other, and so change the shape of the bulk material (Figure 12.6, page 597). Alloys are generally stronger than the pure metal. Alloying can also make metals more resistant to corrosion.

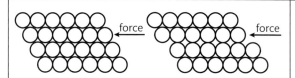

force → ← force ← force

**pure metal**
The shape of a pure metal can be changed as the atoms can easily slip over each other.

**alloy**
The presence of atoms of different sizes disrupts the regular structure and prevents the atoms from slipping across each other.

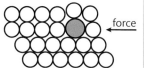

An alloy is a homogeneous mixture containing at least one metal formed when liquid metals are added together and allowed to form a solid of *uniform* composition.

**Figure 12.6** An alloy is a stronger, harder, and less malleable metal than the pure metal.

There is no single material called 'steel'. Instead, steel is the general name for a mixture of iron and carbon and other metals. Small differences in the composition of the steel can produce a range of different properties. This makes steel a versatile material with properties that can be adjusted to suit its use.

Changing the composition of an alloy is not the only way to adjust its properties. Different forms of heat treatment can change the structure of the alloy. The atoms in a piece of metal are not all arranged in a regular way. This is shown by the different orientation of the squares in Figure 12.7. Areas of regular structure are called 'crystal grains'. The properties of an alloy depend on the size and orientations of the grain boundaries.

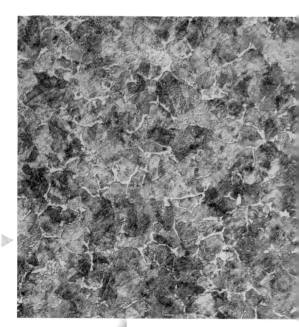

Light micrograph of high carbon steel. It contains 0.65% carbon by mass alloyed with iron. It is very strong but brittle and is used for cutting tools, high-strength wires, and springs.

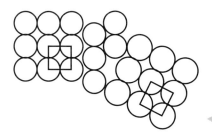

**Figure 12.7** The atoms in a metal are not all perfectly arranged in a regular way. Areas of regular structure are called 'crystal grains'.

The grain structure of brass, an alloy of copper and zinc..

**NATURE OF SCIENCE**

The history of the extraction of the metals can be used to measure the evolution of civilization. Most of the elements are metals and the history of their extraction illustrates many features about the development of science and technology. Fire was the crucial agency which brought about the extraction of metals and the mixing of alloys. Fire was originally considered to be an element, but later came to be recognized as a form of energy. It breaks down ores like malachite to the soft metal copper and facilitates the reduction of the ore haematite to the hard metal iron. As there was limited scientific understanding as to the basis of these changes, many experimental procedures were based on ritual or mysticism. The need to repeat experimental procedure was recognized but as the underlying theory was not understood it was couched in ritual language; to heat steel to the correct temperature to make a Japanese sword it has to glow 'to the colour of the morning sun'. The metal gold has always held a special place in different cultures and became a focus for alchemy; gold is precious because it is incorruptible and hence eternal. Gold resists decay and thus prolongs life. The alchemist saw a sympathy between the metals of the earth and health of the human body. We now see these false analogies as naïve, but should appreciate that many scientific theories are also analogies which have turned out to be false. The scientific theories of today solve the problems of today but they are only provisional.

## Paramagnetic and diamagnetic materials display different behaviour in magnetic fields because of their different electron spin pairings

Materials are classified as diamagnetic, paramagnetic, or ferromagnetic based on their behaviour when placed in an external magnetic field (Figure 12.8).

- **Diamagnetic materials** are repelled by an external magnetic field as the orbital motion of their electrons produces a very weak opposing magnetic field.
- **Paramagnetic materials** are attracted by an external magnetic field as they have unpaired electrons which behave like small magnetics which align with the external field. The level of magnetization is proportional and in the same direction as the applied field. All atoms have orbiting electrons and so show diamagnetic behaviour but paramagnetic behaviour dominates in cases of single atoms or ions with unpaired electrons.

Substances with paired electrons are diamagnetic, as electrons with opposite spins behave like minute bar magnets with opposing orientation and so cancel each other out.

**Figure 12.8** The electrons in an atom have two types of motion which both lead to magnetic effects, equivalent to that of the bar magnet shown. (a) Orbital motion leads to diamagnetic behaviour. (b) Electrons lead to paramagnetic behaviour.

Many individual atoms and ions have unpaired electrons and display paramagnetic effects. Chemical bonding often involves the pairing of electrons and so most materials with ionic and covalent structures are diamagnetic. Free radicals and some transition metal ion complexes have unpaired electrons and so display paramagnetic effects. The interaction of electrons is more complex in metallic structures and some metals are paramagnetic.

(a)

(b)

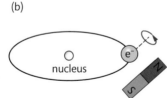

**Ferromagnetism** occurs when materials retain their magnetism after they have been removed from an external field. It occurs in materials containing iron, cobalt, and nickel where there is long-range ordering of the unpaired electrons, which remains in regions called **domains** after the external magnetic field is removed. Ferromagnetism is the largest effect, producing magnetizations sometimes orders of magnitude greater than the applied field.

Paramagnetic materials are attracted by an external magnetic field as they have unpaired electrons. Diamagnetic materials are weakly repelled by an external magnetic field. They have no unpaired electrons.

A free radical is a species with an unpaired electron.

### Worked example

Distinguish between the magnetic properties of $H_2O$ and $[Fe(H_2O)_6]^{3+}$.

#### Solution

All the electrons are paired in the water molecule and so it is diamagnetic.

The $Fe^{3+}$ in the complex ion has the electron configuration $[Ar]3d^5$ and so has 5 unpaired electrons. It is paramagnetic.

### Exercises

**11** Alloys of aluminium with nickel are used to make engine parts. Explain why this alloy is used rather than pure aluminium.

**12** Classify the period 3 atoms as paramagnetic or diamagnetic and explain your answer. Identify the element which is likely to show the strongest paramagnetic properties.

**13** Arrange the following atoms in order of increasing paramagnetism and explain your choice: K, Sc, V, Mn, Ga, As.

# Inductively coupled plasma (ICP) spectroscopy determines the identity and concentration of metals

## Inductively coupled plasma optical emission spectroscopy (ICP-OES)

Inductively coupled plasma (ICP) spectroscopy is one of the most powerful and popular analytical tools for the determination of metals and other elements in a variety of different samples. The technique is based upon an analysis of the element's emission spectra. We saw in Chapter 2 (page 71) that an emission spectrum is produced when the radiation from an excited sample is analysed. A line spectra is produced, with each line corresponding to an electron transition between different energy levels as electrons fall from a higher to lower energy levels. As each element has a unique set of energy levels it produces its own distinctive emission spectrum which can be used to identify the element (Figure 12.9).

The intensity of the lines depends on the concentration of the element in the sample. In ICP the sample is injected into a high-temperature **argon plasma** and the photons corresponding to the different frequencies are separated using a diffraction grating and counted using a photomultiplier which generates an electric signal.

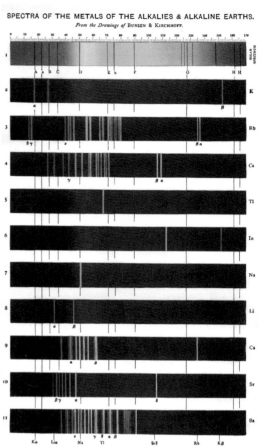

SPECTRA OF THE METALS OF THE ALKALIES & ALKALINE EARTHS.

*From the Drawings of* BUNSEN & KIRCHHOFF.

Flame emission spectra of Group 1 and Group 2 metals, as recorded by Robert Bunsen (1811–1899) and Gustav Kirchhoff (1824–1887). They were the first to observe that heated elements emitted a light of characteristic wavelength.

(a)

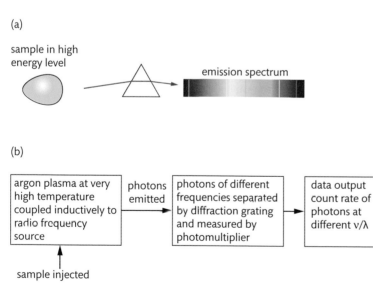

sample in high energy level

emission spectrum

(b)

| argon plasma at very high temperature coupled inductively to radio frequency source | photons emitted → | photons of different frequencies separated by diffraction grating and measured by photomultiplier | → | data output count rate of photons at different ν/λ |

sample injected

**Figure 12.9** (a) An emission spectrum is produced from an excited atom when an electron drops from a higher to a lower energy. The different lines correspond to different transitions. (b) In ICP the sample is excited by injecting it into an argon plasma. The emitted photons are analysed using a diffraction grating and photomultiplier. The high temperature of the argon plasma is generated by coupling the argon to a high-energy radio frequency coil.

## Plasma is a high energy state composed of isolated atoms, ions, and electrons.

The plasma state occurs at very high temperatures when some or all of the gaseous atoms have been ionized. The interactions in the plasma are dominated by charge interactions between positive ions and electrons. The atoms and ions in the plasma are excited and emit photons at characteristic frequencies.

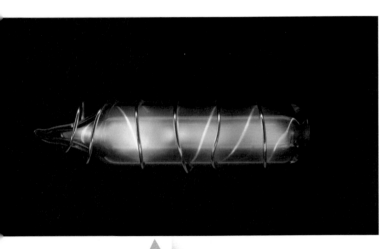

The high temperature of the argon plasma is generated by inductively coupling the gas to a high-energy radio frequency source.

The energy to form the argon plasma used in ICP is generated by a high-frequency radio frequency source, which is inductively coupled to the argon in a similar manner to the coils in an electric transformer. An electric discharge produces a 'seed' of ions and electrons in the argon which are then accelerated by the oscillating magnetic field of the radio waves, which results in further ionization as the excited electrons knock off electrons from other atoms. The processes continue until a high-temperature (10 000 K) plasma is formed. The induction coil controls the position of the plasma and keeps it away from the walls of the container, which would melt at such high temperatures.

An argon gas electric discharge plasma.

**The plasma is a high-energy state composed of isolated atoms, ions, and electrons.**

The plasma state is uncommon on earth, but is the most common state for the visible matter in the universe.

## Atoms from the sample are excited by colliding with the plasma particles and their emitted photons analysed.

Sufficient energy is available to convert the atoms of the injected sample to ions and promote the electrons to excited states, which then fall to the lower energy levels with the emission of photons at characteristic energies. The wavelength of the photons can be used to identify the element and the total number of photons is directly proportional to the concentration of the element in the sample.

## The concentration of an element can be determined from a calibration curve.

The number of photons emitted by sample atoms at a characteristic wavelength is proportional to the concentration of the element in a sample. Unknown concentrations can be determined by comparing its photo emission rate with those of some standard solutions over a range of concentrations on a **calibration curve** (Figure 12.10). A calibration curve is necessary as there are possible variations in the intensity of the signals due to the operating conditions of the plasma such as the flow rate of the argon and temperature of the plasma. The intensity of each line is compared to the intensities of the same line from samples with known concentrations of the elements. The concentrations are then computed by interpolation along the calibration lines. As each element produces a number of characteristic lines, different calibration curves can be produced for different wavelengths. Standard calibration curves for most elements are linear. The solutions used in the calibration are generally made by successive dilution of a standard solution. An acid solvent is often used in the analysis of metal samples. The concentration of the unknown solution should fall inside the calibrated region. Generally, the wavelengths of high intensity are selected for the analysis.

ppm = one part in a million $10^6$; ppb = one part in a billion $10^9$: they are units of concentration.

As the sample is vaporized and broken into atoms in the plasma, ICP determines the concentration of atoms irrespective of how they are combined together. It is an extremely sensitive method, allowing concentrations as low as 0.1 ppb (one part in $10^{10}$) to be measured.

## Worked example

The amount of lead in alloys used in electrical and electronic equipment needs to be carefully monitored as it can pose risks to human health.

A range of solutions were made up with different lead concentrations. The resulting calibration curve is shown, with the intensity measured in 1000 counts per second.

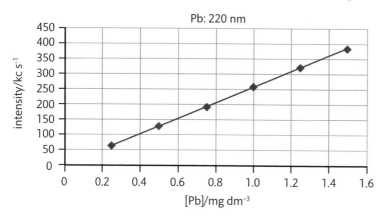

**Figure 12.10** A calibration curve for lead.

(a) Explain the number in the title of the graph.

(b) Suggest how the solutions used in the calibration curve were prepared, assuming the balance has a precision of (±) 0.0001 g and the concentrations need to be determined to three significant figures.

(c) Two alloy samples were tested using the same conditions.

| Alloy sample | Intensity / kc s$^{-1}$ |
|---|---|
| I | 120 |
| II | 20 |

Determine the concentration of lead in the two samples and comment on the reliability of the results.

### Solution

(a) 220 nm is the wavelength of the photons emitted.

(b) The smallest amount of Pb that can be accurately measured $\approx 0.0100$ g

To make the most concentrated solution (1.50 mg dm$^{-3}$) needs 0.0150 g in 10 dm$^3$ of solution, which is 0.00150 g in 1 dm$^3$ of solution.

Concentrated acid (solvent) is added to dissolve the Pb metal. (A mixture of concentrated nitric acid and hydrochloric acid is actually used.)

The other solutions were prepared by successive dilution of this most concentrated solution.

(c)

| Alloy sample | Intensity / kc s$^{-1}$ | [Pb] /mg dm$^{-3}$ |
|---|---|---|
| I | 120 | 0.469 |
| II | 20 | $\approx 0.078$ |

The concentration of II is less reliable as it is outside the range of the concentrations used in the calibration.

**NATURE OF SCIENCE**

The development of ICP spectroscopy illustrates the fuzzy boundary between pure and applied science. It is based on atomic processes and makes use of a state of matter not generally found on the Earth, but it is a very sensitive method of analysis which can show the presence of material which would be undetected by other methods, and has helped the production of improved materials. Improved instrumentation has allowed us to collect data beyond human sense perception.

### Inductively coupled plasma (ICP) mass spectroscopy (ICP-MS)

Inductively coupled plasma (ICP) mass spectroscopy is capable of detecting metals and non-metals at concentrations of one part in $10^{12}$. The sample is ionized with inductively coupled plasma and analysed using a mass spectrometer to separate and count the abundance of the ions. The technique is more effective with metals than non-metals. Metals have lower ionization energies and so form positive ions more readily. The ability to obtain isotopic information has made the method particularly effective in geochemistry.

**14 (a)** Describe the plasma state used in ICP spectroscopy.
  **(b)** Identify one element that cannot be identified by ICP spectroscopy.
  **(c)** Which method is more sensitive to measuring lower concentrations: ICP-OES or ICP-MS?
  **(d)** Identify the ICP method which is more effective in determining non-metal concentrations. Explain your answer.

**15** Levels of heavy metal ions in soil need to be carefully monitored as they can cause serious damage to the environment and human health.

A range of solutions were made up with different mercury concentrations. The resulting calibration curves are shown.

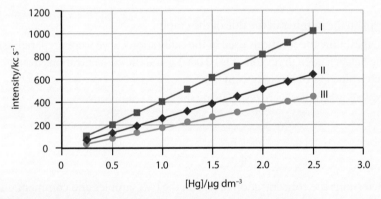

**(a)** Explain how three calibration curves could be produced for the same metal.
**(b)** One sample of soil was analysed in accordance with the methods for red line (II). It produced $3.00 \times 10^7$ counts in one minute. Deduce the mercury concentration of the sample.
**(c)** Deduce the intensity of photons produced by the sample when it is analysed in accordance with the blue line (I).
**(d)** Which line will produce the most precise concentration determination?

**16** The metallurgical properties of aluminium and its alloys are highly dependent on chemical composition. The presence of manganese increases the hardness of the alloy.

The manganese content in an alloy was determined by ICP-AES with alloys of known composition. The intensity signal = 120 kc s$^{-1}$. What is the manganese content in the alloy?

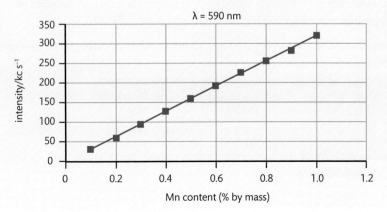

# A.3 Catalysts

## Understandings:

- Reactants adsorb onto heterogeneous catalysts at active sites and the products desorb.
- Homogeneous catalysts chemically combine with the reactants to form a temporary activated complex or a reaction intermediate.
- Transition metal catalytic properties depend on the adsorption/absorption properties of the metal and the variable oxidation states.
- Zeolites act as selective catalysts because of their cage structure.
- Catalytic particles are nearly always nanoparticles that have large surface areas per unit mass.

## Applications:

- Explanation of factors involved in choosing a catalyst for a process.
- Description of how metals work as heterogeneous catalysts.
- Description of the benefits of nanocatalysts in industry.

  ### Guidance
  - Consider catalytic properties such as selectivity for only the desired product, efficiency, ability to work in mild/severe conditions, environmental impact, and impurities.
  - The use of carbon nanocatalysts should be covered.

Catalysts play an essential role in the chemical industry. Without them many chemical processes would go too slowly to be economical. Catalysts work by providing reactions with alternative reaction mechanisms that have lower activation energies.

A catalyst can't make more of a product than would eventually be produced without it. It can however act *selectively* when two or more competing reactions are possible with the same starting materials, producing more of the desired product by catalysing only that reaction.

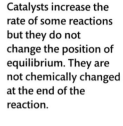

**Catalysts increase the rate of some reactions but they do not change the position of equilibrium. They are not chemically changed at the end of the reaction.**

The word *catalyst* derives from the Chinese word for marriage broker.

In the Haber process, chemists can produce ammonia at an economical rate at temperatures of 525 °C and a pressure of 20 atm ($2 \times 10^6$ Pa). To make one gram of ammonia at the same temperature and pressure but without a catalyst would require a reactor 10 times the size of the Solar System.

## Homogeneous and heterogeneous catalysis

Chemists divide catalysts into two types: **homogeneous** and **heterogeneous**. Homogeneous catalysts are in the same state of matter as the reactants, whereas in heterogeneous catalysis, the catalyst and the reactants are in different states. For example, the catalyst may be a solid and the reactants gases or liquids (Figure 12.11).

The area on the catalyst where the reaction takes place is called the **active site**. In heterogeneous catalysis the reactant molecules can only collide with the active sites on the *surface*. For the reactions to go significantly faster

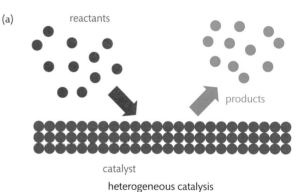

(a)

heterogeneous catalysis

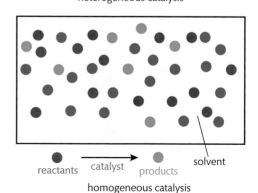

(b)

homogeneous catalysis

**Figure 12.11** Diagram representing (a) homogeneous catalysis and (b) heterogeneous catalysis.

there must be a significant drop in activation energy to compensate for this. There are more active sites available in homogeneous catalysed reactions and a small drop in activation energy can lead to a dramatic increase in rate.

Heterogeneous catalysis is generally preferred in industrial processes as the catalyst can be easily removed by filtration from the reaction mixture. The use of iron in the Haber process and vanadium(v) oxide in the Contact process is discussed in Chapter 7 (pages 327 and 328).

The use of homogeneous catalysis, which often requires expensive separation techniques, is generally reserved for the production of complex organic molecules. As they have greater activity, they work under milder conditions with greater selectivity. Enzyme-catalysed reactions in cells, which take place in aqueous solution, are examples of homogeneous catalysis.

## Examples of catalysts: transition metals

**A substance is adsorbed when it is weakly attached to a surface. It is absorbed when it enters pores in the material.**

| Industrial process | Catalyst |
|---|---|
| Haber process:<br>$N_2(g) + 3H_2(g) \rightleftharpoons 2NH_3(g)$ | finely divided iron |
| Contact process:<br>$2SO_2(g) + O_2(g) \rightleftharpoons 2SO_3(g)$ | vanadium(v) oxide, platinum |
| hydrogenation of unsaturated oils to make margarine | nickel |
| reaction of CO and $H_2$ to make methanol:<br>$CO(g) + 2H_2(g) \rightarrow CH_3OH(g)$ | copper |
| catalytic cracking, e.g.<br>$C_{10}H_{22}(g) \rightarrow C_4H_8(g) + C_6H_{14}(g)$ | $Al_2O_3/SiO_2$, zeolites |
| polymerization of ethene to poly(ethene) | Ziegler–Natta catalyst, $AlR_3 + TiCl_4$ |

Many catalysts are either transition metals or their compounds. Transition metals show two properties that make them particularly effective as catalysts.

- They have variable oxidation states. They are particularly effective catalysts in redox reactions.
- They adsorb small molecules onto their surface. Transition metals are often good heterogeneous catalysts as they provide a surface for the reactant molecules to come together with the correct orientation. The products desorb from the surface once the reaction is complete.

| Catalyst having variable oxidation state | Catalyst allowing adsorption onto surface |
|---|---|
| Vanadium(v) oxide as a catalyst:<br><br>$V_2O_5(s) + SO_2(g) \rightarrow V_2O_4(s) + SO_3(g)$<br>$V_2O_4(s) + \frac{1}{2}O_2(g) \rightarrow V_2O_5(s)$<br><br>Overall reaction<br>$SO_2(g) + \frac{1}{2}O_2(g) \rightarrow SO_3(g)$<br><br>Vanadium shows variable oxidation states. It is reduced from the +5 state to the +4 state and then oxidized back to the +5 state. | 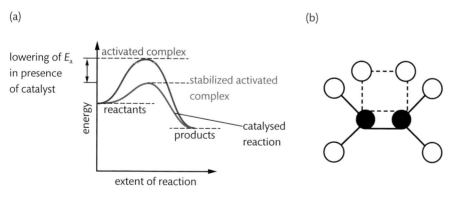 The reactants are both gases.<br><br>The reactants are both adsorbed on the Ni surface.<br><br>Bonds are broken and formed on the surface.<br><br>The product moves away from the surface. |
|  | Nickel, shown in blue, adsorbs both $C_2H_4$ and $H_2$ and provides a surface for reaction. It brings the reactants together with the correct orientation for a successful addition reaction. $C_2H_6$ is the product. |

## Activated complexes and intermediates

An **activated complex** is an unstable combination of reactant molecules that can go on to form products or fall apart to form reactants as it corresponds to a state with partial bonds of maximum energy in the reaction profile. A heterogeneous catalyst decreases the activation energy by stabilizing the activated complex (Figure 12.12).

An activated complex is an unstable combination of reactant molecules that can go on to form products or fall apart to form reactants.

(a)

(b)

Figure 12.12 Heterogeneous catalysis stabilizes the activated complex. (a) The activated complex has more energy than either the reactants or products. It is an unstable state with partial bonds as they are partially broken and partially formed. (b) Heterogeneous catalysis allows the formation of a stabilized activated complex.

The $V_2O_4$ formed with vanadium in the +4 oxidation state in the homogenous reaction above is a **reaction intermediate** (Figure 12.13). This is a species that occurs at a local minimum on the reaction profile that allows the reaction to follow a mechanism where all steps have lower activation energies then the uncatalysed reaction.

A reaction intermediate is a species that is produced and consumed during a reaction but does not occur in the overall equation.

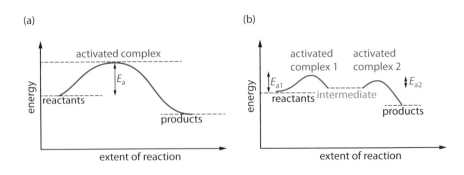

**Figure 12.13** Homogeneous catalysis can involve the formation of reaction intermediates. (a) A reaction of one step which involves no intermediate step. (b) A reaction of two steps in which an intermediate is formed. An intermediate is more stable than an activated complex as it corresponds to a local minimum on the reaction energy profile.

(a)

(b)

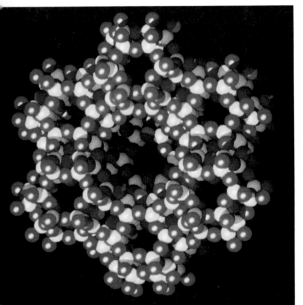

## Zeolites act as selective catalysts because of their cage structures

Zeolites are a family of naturally occurring minerals of aluminium silicates.

The open caged structure of zeolites gives them excellent catalytic properties.

- They offer a huge surface for reactants to be adsorbed. Almost every atom in the solid is at a surface and is therefore available as an active site.
- The shape and size of the channels makes them *shape-selective* catalysts. Only reactants with the appropriate geometry can interact effectively with the active sites, and only smaller molecules can escape so the products can be controlled.

Computer graphic representation of the structure of zeolite-Y, a mineral used in the catalytic cracking process in which large alkane molecules break down into smaller alkanes and alkenes. In this image, silicon and aluminium atoms are shown in yellow and oxygen atoms in red.

The word *zeolite* derives from the Greek words *zein* meaning to boil and *lithos* meaning stone. The first zeolite to be discovered released water when it was heated.

The open structure of zeolites is illustrated by the fact that a teaspoon of zeolite has a surface area of two tennis courts.

## Nanoparticles are effective heterogeneous catalysts as they have a large surface area per unit mass

**Nanoparticles** with very small particle size are particularly effective **heterogeneous catalysts** as they have a large number of active sites on the surface relative to their mass. The surface structure and electronic properties of the particles can also be modified to improve their

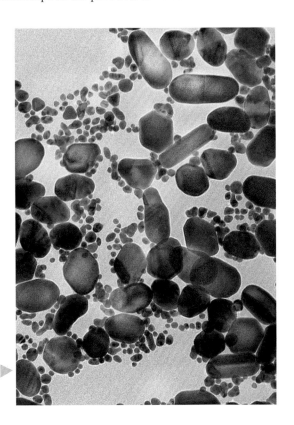

A coloured scanning electron micrograph (SEM) of gold nanoparticles.

catalytic performance. The benefits of nanoparticles are illustrated by the catalytic action of gold. Gold is relatively chemically inert, but in 1 nm clusters, which contain about 20 atoms, it becomes a very effective catalyst for a range of reactions which include the oxidation of carbon monoxide to form carbon dioxide in catalytic converters. The performance of a catalyst can be affected by local differences in composition, size, shape, and surface structure.

The hollow structures of carbon nanotubes discussed on page 629 also makes them very good candidates for shape-selective heterogeneous catalysis. They have large surface areas per unit mass, excellent electron conductivity, and are generally chemical stable. The catalytic properties can be varied by lining the tubes with different elements.

Supercomputer model of the structure of a gold nanoparticle (gold-coloured lattice) as it adsorbs carbon monoxide, CO (top). There are several hundred gold atoms in the lattice.

### NATURE OF SCIENCE

Think about how models are used in science. Catalysts were used to increase reaction rates before the development of an understanding of how they work. This led to models that are constantly being tested and improved.

## Catalytic activity can be modified with the use of promoters and inhibitors or inactivated by poisons

Catalytic activity can be deliberately modified with the use of **promoters** and **inhibitors**. The addition of promoters in small concentrations increases catalytic activity whereas inhibitors reduce the activity as they react with and remove the reaction intermediates.

Some catalysts have a limited working life as they can be **poisoned** or inactivated. Catalytic poisons block the active sites because they are adsorbed on the surface more strongly than reactant molecules. The iron catalysts in the Haber process work for between 5 and 10 years. Sulfur from traces of hydrogen sulfide in the natural gas used as the source of hydrogen presents the greatest problems. Similarly, the use of platinum as an effective catalyst for the Contact process is affected by even the smallest amounts of arsenic.

Other catalytic poisons include mercury(II) salts, carbon monoxide, and hydrogen cyanide.

## Catalyst choice depends on selectivity for only the desired product and environmental impact

The choice of catalyst will depend on a number of factors.

- Selectivity: does the catalyst give a high yield of the desired product?
- Efficiency: how much faster is the reaction with the catalyst?
- Life expectancy: for how long does it work before it is poisoned?

**TOK**

Some materials used as effective catalysts are toxic and harmful to the environment. Is environmental degradation justified in the pursuit of knowledge?

Palladium, platinum, and rhodium are used as catalysts in catalytic converters in cars. The value of these metals makes them an attractive target for thieves.

- Environmental impact.
- Ability to work under a range of conditions of temperature and pressure. A heterogeneous catalyst may melt and or become less effective if its operating temperatures are too high or its surface becomes coated with unwanted products.

Although some catalysts, such as the transition metals platinum and palladium, are very expensive, their use is economical. They reduce the energy costs of the process, increase yields, and can be reused as they are not chemically changed.

## NATURE OF SCIENCE

Catalysts are widely used in industry and it has been estimated that they contribute about one-sixth of the value of all manufactured goods in the industrialized world. Our understanding of the mechanisms of catalytic action has greatly improved recently because of the use of improved analytical spectroscopic and X-ray diffraction techniques. However, catalysis is a complex subject and there are still many areas where our understanding is incomplete. The growth in computing power has made modelling catalytic action much more powerful. These models can then be tested against the experimental results and modified accordingly.

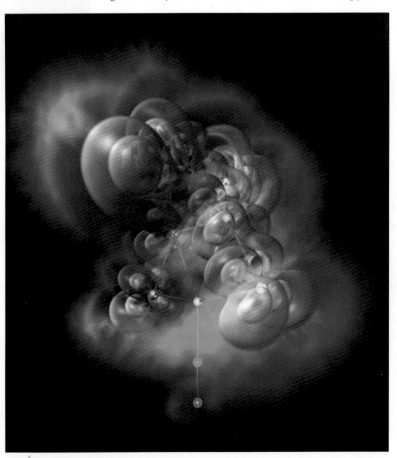

Platinum catalyst molecular modelling. Supercomputer model of the geometric and electronic structure of a platinum–carbon monoxide complex. A platinum cluster (seven yellow spheres) has adsorbed a carbon monoxide (CO) molecule (red and green spheres, bottom). The energetics of the bonding shown here is being studied because carbon monoxide can act to poison catalysts by adsorption on the surface of the metals used.

**17** Explain why transition elements and their compounds are effective heterogeneous and homogeneous catalysts.

**18 (a)** Although many catalysts are very expensive, their use does allow the chemical industry to operate economically. Outline the advantages of using catalysts in industrial processes.

**(b)** Sulfur in crude oil must be removed before the crude oil is refined as the sulfur can poison the catalysts. Explain how the sulfur impurities poison the catalyst.

**19 (a)** Distinguish between a reaction intermediate and an activated complex. Which species can, in theory, be isolated?

**(b)** Explain why heterogeneous catalysts are generally used in industrial processes.

**(c)** Suggest two reasons why gold nanotubes are effective catalysts.

**(d)** Suggest a reason why it is difficult to regulate for the toxicity of nanoparticles.

 # Liquid crystals

## Understandings:

- Liquid crystals are fluids that have physical properties (electrical, optical, and elasticity) that are dependent on molecular orientation to some fixed axis in the material.
- Thermotropic liquid crystal materials are pure substances that show liquid crystal behaviour over a temperature range.
- Lyotropic liquid crystals are solutions that show the liquid crystal state over a (certain) range of concentrations.
- Nematic liquid crystal phase is characterized by rod-shaped molecules which are randomly distributed but on average align in the same direction.

### Guidance

- *Soap and water is an example of lyotropic liquid crystals and the biphenyl nitriles are examples of thermotropic liquid crystals.*
- *Smectics and other liquid crystal types need not be discussed.*
- *Liquid crystal behaviour should be limited to the biphenyl nitrates.*

## Applications:

- Discussion of the properties needed for a substance to be used in liquid crystal displays (LCD).
- Explanation of liquid crystal behaviour on a molecular level.

### Guidance

*Properties needed for liquid crystals include: chemically stable, a phase which is stable over a suitable temperature range, polar so they can change orientation when an electric field is applied, and rapid switching speed.*

The solid and liquid states are discussed in Chapter 1 (page 11). When a solid crystal melts, the ordered arrangement of the particles breaks down, to be replaced by the disordered state of the liquid. Some crystals, however, melt to give a state which retains some of the order of the solid state. This intermediate state of matter with properties between the solid state and the liquid state is called the **liquid crystal** state. Liquid crystals have many of the physical properties of solid crystals; however, these properties can be easily modified. In digital watches, for example, a small electric field can alter optical properties by changing the orientation of some of the molecules. Some areas of the display go dark and others remain light, allowing the shape of different digits to be displayed. Over the past 40 years liquid crystals have gone from being an academic curiosity to the basis of big business.

Liquid crystals typically all contain long, thin, rigid, polar organic molecules. Imagine a large number of pencils put into a rectangular box and shaken. When you open

the box, the pencils will be facing in approximately the same direction, but will have no definite spatial organization. They are free to move, but generally line up almost parallel. This gives a simple model for the **nematic** type of a liquid phase liquid state. The molecules are randomly distributed as in a liquid, but the intermolecular forces are sufficiently strong to hold the molecule in one orientation in some regions or domains. These domains can be observed by viewing the liquid under a microscope with polarized light.

Although liquid crystals flow like a fluid, there is some order in their molecular arrangement. When viewed under a microscope using a polarized light, different regions, which have the molecules in different orientations, can be identified.

## Thermotropic liquid crystals show liquid crystal behaviour over a temperature range

The liquid crystal phase is only stable over a small range of temperatures. The directional order is lost and the liquid state is formed when the molecules have too much kinetic energy to be constrained in the same orientation by the intermolecular forces (Figure 12.14).

**Thermotropic** liquid crystal materials are pure substances that show liquid crystal behaviour over a temperature range.

**Figure 12.14** Thermotropic liquid crystals are formed in a temperature range between the solid and liquid state.

**Making a liquid crystal**
Full details of how to carry out this experiment with a worksheet are available online.

temperature increasing

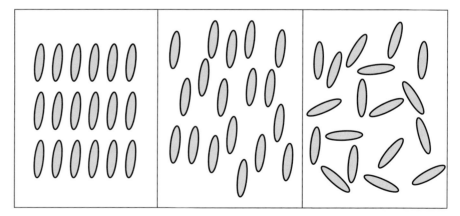

**Solid** The molecules have a regular arrangement and orientation.

**Liquid crystal** The molecules have an irregular arrangement and a regular orientation.

**Liquid** The molecules have an irregular arrangement and orientation.

## Lyotropic liquid crystals are solutions

Some substances can form a different type of liquid crystal state in solution. Consider a solution containing some rod-like molecules as the solute. At low concentrations, the molecules generally have a disordered orientation and an irregular arrangement. If the concentration is increased sufficiently the molecules will adopt an ordered structure and solid crystals will form. At intermediate concentrations a **lyotropic** liquid crystal state may be possible where the molecules have an irregular arrangement with a regular orientation (Figure 12.15).

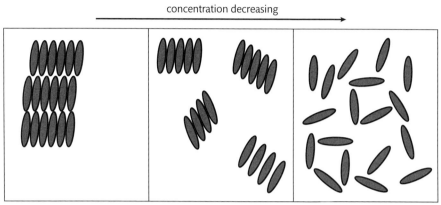

concentration decreasing

**Solid** The molecules have a regular arrangement and orientation.

**Liquid crystal** The molecules have an irregular arrangement and a regular orientation.

**Liquid** The molecules have an irregular arrangement and orientation.

The molecules that make up lyotropic liquid crystals generally consist of two distinct parts: a polar, often ionic, **head** and a non-polar, often hydrocarbon, **tail**. When dissolved in high enough concentrations in aqueous solutions, the molecules arrange themselves so that the polar heads are in contact with a polar solvent in an arrangement called a **micelle** (Figure 12.16).

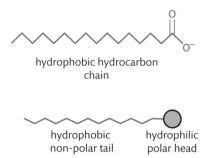

hydrophobic hydrocarbon chain

hydrophobic non-polar tail

hydrophilic polar head

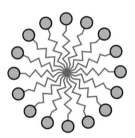

A micelle is formed when the molecules group together to form a spherical arrangement. The hydrophilic heads are exposed to water, shielding the non-polar tails.

Lyotropic liquid crystals are found in many everyday situations. Soaps and detergents, for example, form lyotropic liquid crystals when they combine with water. Many biological membranes also display lyotropic liquid crystalline behaviour.

Kevlar® can show lyotropic properties in solution as it is a rigid rod-shaped molecule due to its linked benzene rings. Although it is very resistant to most chemicals, Kevlar® is soluble in concentrated sulfuric acid as the hydrogen bonds between the chains are broken (Figure 12.17). At high concentrations a lyotropic liquid crystal state is formed. Some hydrogen bonding is present which forces the molecules into a parallel arrangement in localized regions like logs floating down a river.

**Figure 12.15** The phase transitions of lyotropic liquid crystals depend on both temperature and concentration.

**The phase transitions of thermotropic liquid crystals depend on temperature, while those of lyotropic liquid crystals depend on both temperature and concentration.**

Liquid crystal properties may play a central role in the processing of silk. The water-soluble silk molecules are stored in aqueous solution, but they can be assembled into rod-like units which form a lyotropic liquid crystal state.

**Figure 12.16** The formation of a micelle.

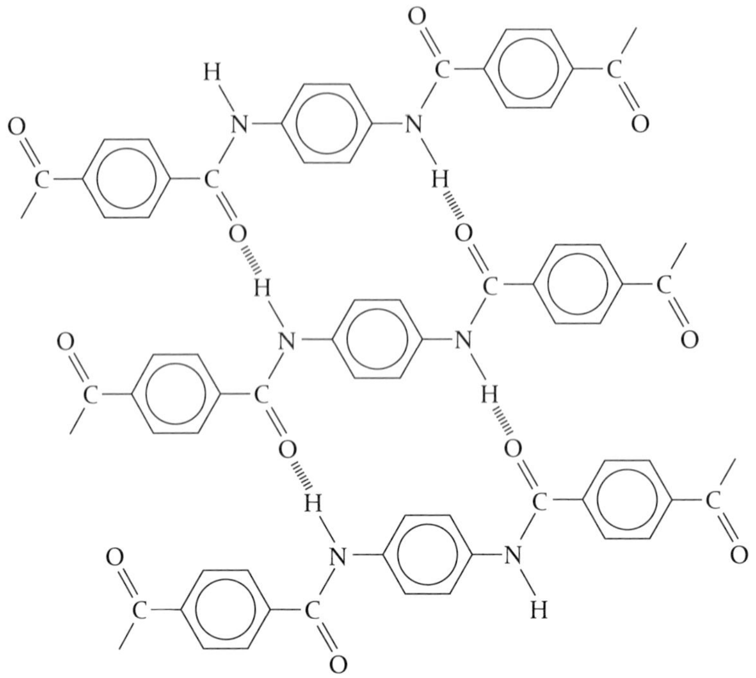

**Figure 12.17** The structure of Kevlar®. There are hydrogen bonds between the chains which can be broken when it is added to concentrated sulfuric acid.

The formation of Kevlar® is discussed on page 656.

## The elasticity and electrical and optical properties depend on the orientation of the molecule to some fixed axis in the material

The practical application of liquid crystals makes use of the dependence of their physical properties, such as their elasticity, and their electrical and optical behaviour on their molecular orientation to some fixed axis in the material.

To understand the optical properties of liquid crystals, we need to consider the behaviour of **polarized** light when it passes through a polarizing filter. We saw in Chapter 2 (page 70) that light is an electromagnetic wave. It is said to be polarized when the electric field vector vibrates in one plane only. A polarizing filter will only transmit light when it is aligned with the electric field. This is illustrated by the arrangement in Figure 12.18.

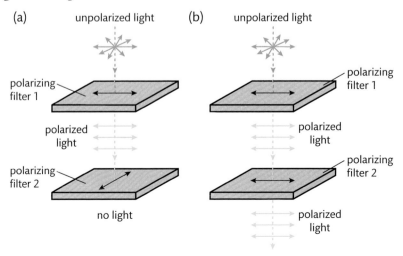

**Figure 12.18** (a) When the polarizing filters are crossed so that their planes of polarization are at right angles to one another, no light is transmitted. (b) When the polarizing filters are parallel, all of the light passing through the first filter also passes through the second.

The two polarizing filters used together transmit light differently depending on their relative orientations. The second polarizing filter is sometimes called the **analyser**.

The ability of liquid crystals to transmit light depends on their relative orientation to the plane of polarization.

TOK What attributes of the IB learner profile help scientists turn a lucky break into a scientific breakthrough?

## CHALLENGE YOURSELF

1   The molecular structure of cholesteryl benzoate is shown here.

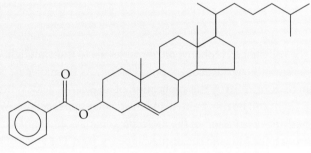

(a)   Identify a feature of its molecular structure that allows it to form a liquid crystal state.
(b)   Classify cholesteryl benzoate as a thermotropic or lyotropic liquid.

## Biphenyl nitriles show liquid crystal behaviour

The first liquid crystal molecules with suitable properties to be synthesized were the biphenyl nitriles (Figure 12.19).

$$C_5H_{11} — \bigcirc\bigcirc — \overset{\delta^+}{C}\equiv\overset{\delta^-}{N}$$

$$\delta^+ \qquad\qquad \delta^-$$

The molecule is polar as nitrogen has a greater electronegativity than carbon.

These molecules have three key features.

**Figure 12.19**  The biphenyl nitriles are liquid crystals. They are polar rigid rod-shaped molecules.

- Long alkyl chain: this limits the ability of the molecules to pack together and so lowers the melting point and helps maintain the liquid crystal state. The melting range can be varied by changing the size and shape of the hydrocarbon chain.
- Biphenyl groups: the two planar benzene rings make the molecule rigid and rod shaped.
- Nitrile group: the high electronegativity of nitrogen makes the functional group polar. This increases the intermolecular interactions between the molecules and allows the orientation of the molecule to be controlled by an electric field.

The presence of the unreactive alkyl groups and the two stable benzene rings increases the chemical stability of the molecule.

A number of rod-shaped molecules with thermotropic properties have been developed. Some examples are shown in Figure 12.20.

**Figure 12.20** Rod-shaped molecules that show thermotropic liquid crystal behaviour.

## The use of biphenyl nitriles in liquid crystal display devices

The ability of the rod-shaped biphenyl nitrile molecule to transmit light depends on its relative orientation to the plane of polarization. As the molecule is polar, this orientation can be controlled by the application of an electric field. When there is no applied voltage, light can be transmitted and the display appears light. When a small voltage is applied, the orientation of the molecules changes and light can no longer be transmitted through the film and the display appears dark. The areas of the display that are light and dark can thus be controlled, enabling different shapes to be displayed.

As discussed earlier, the nematic state for a thermotropic liquid crystal only exists within a small range of temperatures, which can limit the operating temperatures of LCDs.

Pentylcyanophenyl is suitable for liquid crystal displays (LCDs) as it has the following properties.

- It is chemically stable.
- It has a liquid crystal phase stable over a suitable range of temperatures.
- It is polar, making it able to change its orientation when an electric field is applied.
- It responds to changes of voltage quickly; i.e. it has a fast switching speed.

The dark areas of the display correspond to areas where a small voltage changes the orientation of the liquid crystal molecules, preventing light from passing through the film.

In general, no single compound can fulfil all the properties required for LCD applications, so complex mixtures are used. They contain 10–20 components, each one used to modify specific display properties, such as threshold voltage, switching speed, and temperature range.

## Twisted nematic LCDs

In a twisted nematic display, the liquid crystal material is located between two glass plates, all between two polarizing filters at right angles to each other. The surface of the glass plates is coated with a thin polymer layer with scratches in one direction. The molecules in contact with the glass line up with the scratches, like matches in the grooves of a piece of corrugated paper. Intermolecular bonds allow the molecules between the plates to form a twisted arrangement with the alignment varying smoothly across the cell (Figure 12.21).

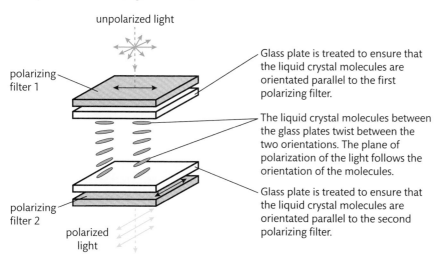

unpolarized light

polarizing filter 1

Glass plate is treated to ensure that the liquid crystal molecules are orientated parallel to the first polarizing filter.

The liquid crystal molecules between the glass plates twist between the two orientations. The plane of polarization of the light follows the orientation of the molecules.

Glass plate is treated to ensure that the liquid crystal molecules are orientated parallel to the second polarizing filter.

polarizing filter 2

polarized light

**Figure 12.21** Light passes through the LCD despite the orientation of the polarizing filters because the plane of polarization of light rotates with the orientation of the molecules.

In the 'off' state, the light passes through the second polarizing filter as the plane of polarization rotates with the molecular orientation as the light passes through the cell.

However, when a small threshold voltage is applied across the cell (the 'on' state), the situation changes. The polar liquid crystal molecules now align with the field and so the twisted structure is lost. The plane-polarized light is no longer rotated, and so no light is transmitted and the cell appears dark (Figure 12.22).

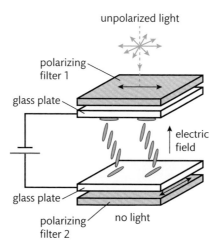

unpolarized light

polarizing filter 1

glass plate

electric field

glass plate

polarizing filter 2

no light

**Figure 12.22** The liquid crystal molecules align themselves parallel to the electric field when the threshold voltage is applied.

## CHALLENGE YOURSELF

**2** The diagram below is a representation of a liquid crystal display. A liquid crystal has the property of being able to rotate the plane of polarization of light.

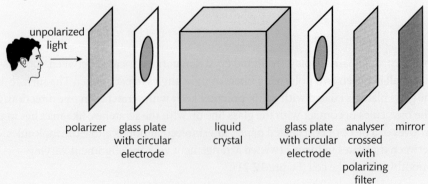

polarizer    glass plate        liquid     glass plate    analyser   mirror
             with circular      crystal    with circular  crossed
             electrode                     electrode      with
                                                          polarizing
                                                          filter

(a) State, and explain, what the observer would see if the liquid crystal were not present.
(b) State, and explain, what the observer would see if the liquid crystal were present.
(c) Outline how the application of a potential difference between the circular electrodes allows the observer to see the circle on the second glass plate.

### Exercises

**20 (a)** Distinguish between the liquid state and the liquid crystal state.
**(b)** Distinguish between a lyotropic liquid crystal and a thermotropic liquid crystal.
**(c)** Outline how a micelle forms in a soap solution.

**21** Distinguish between thermotropic liquid crystals and lyotropic liquid crystals and state the name of one example of each.

**22** The molecule below has liquid crystal properties.

$C_5H_{11}$ — ⬡⬡ — benzene ring with F, F

(a) Explain how the hydrocarbon chain adds to the chemical stability of the molecule.
(b) How does the presence of two fluorine atoms improve the liquid crystal properties?

**23** The structure of a terphenyl molecule is shown below:

$C_5H_{11}$ — ⬡⬡⬡ — $\overset{\delta^+}{C} \equiv \overset{\delta^-}{N}$

(a) State the molecular formula of the molecule.
(b) Suggest why the molecule can show liquid crystal behaviour at higher temperatures than the biphenyl molecules.

# A.5 Polymers

## Understandings:

- Thermoplastics soften when heated and harden when cooled.
- A thermosetting polymer is a prepolymer in a soft solid or viscous state that changes irreversibly into a hardened thermoset by curing.

- Elastomers are flexible and can be deformed under force but will return to nearly their original shape once the stress is released.
- High-density poly(ethene) (HDPE) has no branching, allowing chains to be packed together.
- Low-density poly(ethene) (LDPE) has some branching and is more flexible.
- Plasticizers added to a polymer increase the flexibility by weakening the intermolecular forces between the polymer chains.
- Atom economy is a measure of efficiency applied in Green Chemistry.
- Isotactic addition polymers have substituents on the same side.
- Atactic addition polymers have the substituents randomly placed.

### Guidance
*The equation for percent atom economy is provided in the IB data booklet in section 1.*

## Applications:

- Description of the use of plasticizers in poly(vinyl chloride) and volatile hydrocarbons in the formation of expanded polystyrene.
- Solving problems and evaluating atom economy in synthesis reactions.
- Description of how the properties of polymers depend on their structural features.
- Description of ways of modifying the properties of polymers including LDPE and HDPE.
- Deduction of structures of polymers formed from polymerizing 2-methylpropene.
- Consider only polystyrene foams as examples of polymer property manipulation.

**An addition polymer is formed when the double bonds of many monomer molecules open up to form a long continuous chain.**

In the 1930s some British scientists were investigating the reactions of ethene with other carbon compounds under high pressure. In some of the experiments, a hard waxy solid was produced, which was found to consist of only carbon and hydrogen atoms in the ratio 1 : 2. This accidental discovery has had a profound effect on all our lives. They had made poly(ethene). Plastics such as poly(ethene) are now the basis of many everyday materials. The **addition polymerization** reaction of ethene, in which many ethene molecules join together like a chain of paper clips, is outlined in Chapter 10 (page 488).

Computer graphic representation of the packed chains of the poly(ethene) molecule, a long-chain hydrocarbon with a high molecular mass. Poly(ethene) is made by the polymerization of $C_2H_4$, by heating under pressure in the presence of oxygen. It may be essentially considered to be a very long chain alkane.

$$
n \left( \begin{array}{c} H \\ \backslash \\ C = C \\ / \quad \backslash \\ H \quad\quad H \end{array} \right) \longrightarrow \left( \begin{array}{c} H \quad\quad H \\ | \quad\quad | \\ -C-C- \\ | \quad\quad | \\ H \quad\quad H \end{array} \right)_n
$$

monomer
ethene

polymer
poly(ethene)

The double bond in ethene breaks open and allows many molecules to link together to form a chain. The value of $n$ varies with the reaction conditions but it is generally in the thousands. The strength and melting points of the polymers increase with chain length, as the intermolecular forces increase with molecular size.

**Polymers** with different chemical compositions can be formed by changing the **monomer**: the formation of poly(ethene), poly(chloroethene), poly(propene), and polystyrene follow the same reaction scheme:

$$
n \left( \begin{array}{c} H \quad\quad H \\ \backslash \quad / \\ C = C \\ / \quad \backslash \\ H \quad\quad X \end{array} \right) \longrightarrow \left( \begin{array}{c} H \quad\quad H \\ | \quad\quad | \\ -C-C- \\ | \quad\quad | \\ H \quad\quad X \end{array} \right)_n
$$

monomer

polymer with a long straight chain of carbon atoms

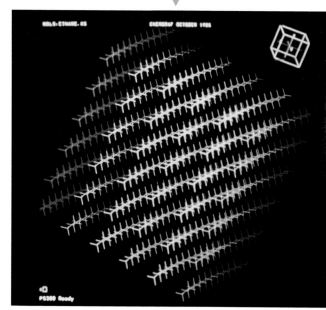

| Monomer | Polymer | Monomer | Polymer |
|---|---|---|---|
| ethene | polyethene | propene | polypropene |
|  | | | |
| chloroethene (vinyl chloride) | polychloroethene (PVC) | styrene | polystyrene |

### NATURE OF SCIENCE

Although plastics were one of the key materials of the last century the notion of very large molecules was not widely accepted by the scientific community until 1929. The story of the acceptance of the theory of large molecules is the story of Hermann Staudinger's determination to push forward an idea despite widespread resistance from his academic peers. The academic chemistry community at the beginning of the 20th century thought that the newly invented plastics and natural materials such as rubber, starch, and cellulose had structures in which bundles of small molecules were held together by unknown intermolecular forces. Staudinger's idea that there was a covalent bond between the units had little support. He was told by one of his colleagues to 'drop the idea of large molecules.' The eventual acceptance of Staudinger's theory was a key step in our scientific understanding that led to the practical development of polymer chemistry. Science is a human activity and disputes of this sort are common. They are constructive if they focus on the science and do not degenerate to personal squabbles.

### Worked example

Deduce the structure of the addition polymer formed from methylpropene. You should include three repeating units in the structure.

#### Solution

1   Draw three structures with the alkene double bond in the middle:

2   Open the double bond in each molecule so that single bonds extend in both directions:

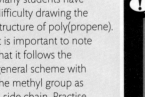

Changing the chemical composition of the monomer and the chain length is not the only strategy used to change the properties of a polymer. The description of a polymer as one straight chain is an oversimplification as branching can occur along the main chain. The relative orientation of all the groups along the chain can also affect the properties of the polymer.

## The density of poly(ethene) depends on the branching in the structure

The poly(ethene) used to make plastic bags has very different properties from the poly(ethene) used to make plastic buckets and toys. The carbon and hydrogen atoms are in the same ratio 1:2 but the molecules have different molecular structures. If poly(ethene) is polymerized at very high pressures, the reaction proceeds by a free radical mechanism and branched carbon chains are produced (Figure 12.23). This branching limits the interaction and alignment between neighbouring chains and the intermolecular forces are relatively weak. The resulting low-density polymer has a low melting point and quite flexible carbon chains.

Areas of regular arrangement between polymer molecules lead to a crystalline structure. Areas of irregular arrangement lead to amorphous forms.

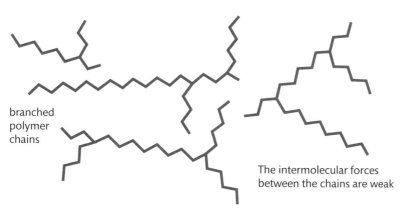

branched polymer chains

The intermolecular forces between the chains are weak

**Figure 12.23** Low-density poly(ethene) (LDPE). Branching limits the ability of the chains to pack closely. In this amorphous (non-crystalline) form, the intermolecular interactions between the chains are weak.

When ethene is polymerized at a lower temperature in the presence of a catalyst (a Ziegler catalyst with metal–carbon bonds) the reaction occurs by an ionic mechanism and a more crystalline structure is produced (Figure 12.24). In this high-density form the molecules have straight chains. It is more rigid, as the molecules are more closely packed with stronger intermolecular forces, and it has a higher melting point.

A range of poly(ethene)s with varying properties can be produced by modifying the extent and location of branching in the low-density form.

The plastic used to make this bag was LDPE, low-density poly(ethene).

intermolecular forces between the straight chains are relatively strong

**Figure 12.24** High-density poly(ethene) (HDPE). In this crystalline form the parallel chains are closely packed with relatively strong intermolecular bonds.

## Different orientations of side groups lead to isotactic and atactic forms

The presence of a methyl group in propene introduces a structural feature into the polymer chain not found in poly(ethene). Methyl groups can be arranged with different orientations relative to the carbon backbone. The **isotactic** form of the polymer, with methyl groups arranged on one side, is an example of a **stereoregular** polymer (Figure 12.25). It is crystalline and tough and can be moulded into different shapes. It is used to make car bumpers and plastic toys and can be drawn into fibres to make clothes and carpets.

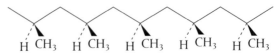

**Figure 12.25** Isotactic poly(propene) has a regular structure with the methyl groups pointing in the same direction, making it crystalline and tough.

The **atactic** form, produced when the methyl groups are randomly orientated, is softer and more flexible (Figure 12.26). It is useful as a sealant and in other waterproof coatings.

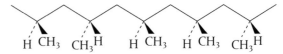

**Figure 12.26** Atactic poly(propene) has an irregular structure, which prevents the chains from packing together. It is soft and flexible.

Catalysts used to make stereoregular polymers are called Ziegler–Natta catalysts. The German chemist Karl Ziegler and Italian Guillio Natta shared the 1963 Nobel Prize for their work in this field.

The product of the polymerization reaction of propene can be controlled by using catalysts allowing chemists to tailor-make polymers with precise properties. A free-radical catalyst will produce the atactic polymer; a **Ziegler–Natta** catalyst, which leads to an ionic mechanism, will produce the more ordered isotactic form. The monomer binds to the catalyst surface with the correct orientation to produce the more ordered polymer. Other polymers with side chains, such as PVC, can also exist in isotactic and atactic forms.

## The properties of poly(vinyl chloride) are modified by using plasticizers

The non-systematic name for chloroethene is vinyl chloride and so the polymer of this monomer is more commonly known as poly(vinyl chloride) or PVC. The presence of the polar $C^{\delta+}$–$Cl^{\delta-}$ bond in PVC gives it very different properties from both poly(ethene) and poly(propene). The molecule has a permanent dipole, allowing a strong dipole–dipole intermolecular interaction to occur between neighbouring chains. The presence of the relatively large Cl atom also limits the ability of the chains to move across each other. The pure polymer is hard and brittle and has few uses. Its properties are radically improved, however, when **plasticizers**, such as di-(2-ethylhexyl)hexanedioate are added (Figures 12.27 and 12.28). The plasticizer molecules fit in between and separate the polymer chains. This allows the chains to slip across each other more easily. The most common plasticizers are di-esters such as the phthalates. The resulting plastic is softer and more flexible and is used, for example, to make credit cards. PVC with varying degrees of flexibility can be produced by varying the amount of plasticizer. The possible environmental impact of using plasticizers is discussed later (see page 633).

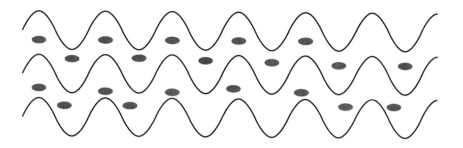

**Figure 12.27** The plasticizer molecules shown here in red separate the polymer chains. This allows them to move freely past each other.

(a)

(b)

**Figure 12.28** (a) Di-(2-ethylhexyl)hexanedioate and the (b) phthalates are common plasticizers. Note the presence of the two ester functional groups in both structures.

Light micrograph of fibres of PVC. PVC is a tough, white material, which softens with the application of a plasticizer.

Expanded polystyrene is widely used as a thermally insulating and protective packaging material.

## Expanded polystyrene is made by adding volatile hydrocarbons

Expanded polystyrene is made by **expansion moulding**. Polystyrene beads containing about 5% of a volatile hydrocarbon such as pentane are placed in a mould and heated. The heat causes the pentane to evaporate and bubbles of gas to form. The expansion of the gas causes the polymer to expand into the shape of the mould. The resulting plastic has a low density, is white, opaque, and an excellent thermal insulator. These properties should be contrasted with the polystyrene made without a foaming agent, which is colourless, transparent, and brittle.

## Polymers can be classified based on their response to heat and applied forces

### Thermoplastics soften when heated and harden when cooled

The plastics we have discussed are all examples of **thermosoftening** or **thermoplastic** polymers (Figure 12.29). They are made from polymer chains which interact only weakly via intermolecular forces. When they are heated one chain can slip across another making the polymer soften. They can be reheated and remoulded many times.

The intermolecular forces are strongest in crystalline regions, where the molecules are aligned. These areas increase the hardness of the bulk material. The molecules can slide across each other in amorphous regions which make the bulk material less brittle.

A **fibre** has a special crystalline structure in which all the molecules are aligned along the same direction. Isotactic poly(propene) can be made into such a strong fibre.

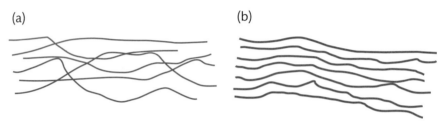

(a)  (b)

**Figure 12.29** Schematic of thermosoftening plastics. (a) They are made from polymer chains which interact only weakly via intermolecular forces. (b) If the chains are allowed to line up, the intermolecular forces increase and a strong fibre with a crystalline structure is produced.

More generally the crystalline regions are not aligned in the same direction. This can be increased if the polymer is stretched. This increases the strength of the polymer in the direction of the force, but may weaken it in other directions (Figure 12.30).

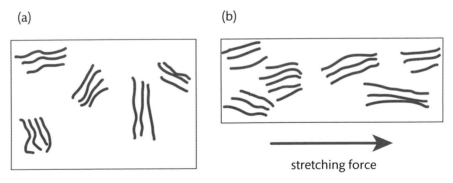

(a)  (b)

stretching force

**Figure 12.30** Stretching a thermoplastic increases the alignment between the crystalline regions of the polymer. The amorphous regions have been omitted for clarity. (a) Different crystalline regions of a thermoplastic where the molecules are aligned. (b) Stretching a thermoplastic increases the alignment between the different crystalline regions and increases the strength in this direction.

### Elastomer polymers show elastic properties when stretched

Elastomers are flexible and can be deformed under force but will return to nearly their original shape once the force is removed. Rubber, for example, is a natural hydrocarbon polymer which can be reversibly extended to over six times its natural length without losing its natural shape – which returns when the stretching force is removed. Although we have generally represented the polymer chains as relatively straight, this, as already discussed, is a simplification. Free rotation about the C—C bonds allows some polymer chains to be coiled into many different arrangements. These coils are straightened when the material is stretched but can return if the force applied to stretch the material is removed.

The elastic behaviour of a plastic can be modified with the addition of a small number of covalent bonds which allow some cross-links to form between the chains (Figure 12.31). This limited cross-linking restricts the overall movement of the molecules but allows some local movement.

**Figure 12.31** Two polymer chains ⌣— and ⌣— linked by a covalent bond ∫. The chains can be uncoiled when the polymer is stretched but return once the force is removed. The cross-link between the chains keeps the chains knotted together which increases the elasticity of the polymer.

The elastic properties of rubber can be linked to the presence of double bonds in the rubber structure ($-[CH_2-C(CH_3)=CH-CH_2]_n-$), which react with sulfur when the polymer is heated in the vulcanization process. The sulfur atoms form $-S-S-$ bridges between neighbouring chains which keeps the molecule knotted together. The molecules are free to unwind under stress but the cross-links restrict the relative movement between the chains

Poly(2-chlorobuta-1,3-diene) ($-[CH_2-CH=CCl-CH_2]_n-$), which also has an alkene double bond in the polymer chain, is an elastomer known as Neoprene.

## A thermosetting polymer is hardened by heating

There is more extensive cross-linking in the thermosetting polymers. A soft solid or viscous **prepolymer** state, made up from molecules of intermediate size, is first formed which then changes irreversibly into a hardened thermoset by curing. Covalent bonds are formed between adjacent chains of the polymers. These strong covalent cross-linkages give the material increased strength and rigidity. The extensive cross-links prevent the plastic from melting when it is reheated and so they cannot be softened or remoulded (Figure 12.32).

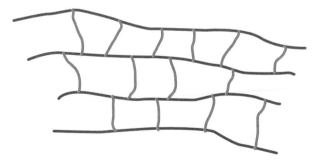

**Figure 12.32** Schematic of thermosetting plastics The polymer chains ⌣— are linked by a cross-links of covalent bonds ∫.

One of the first thermosetting plastics was Bakelite, formed from the co-monomers phenol and methanal (Figure 12.33). Bakelite has a hard rigid structure which does not melt once it has been heated and set. Modern resins are made in a similar way to Bakelite but melamine is used instead of phenol (see Exercise 27).

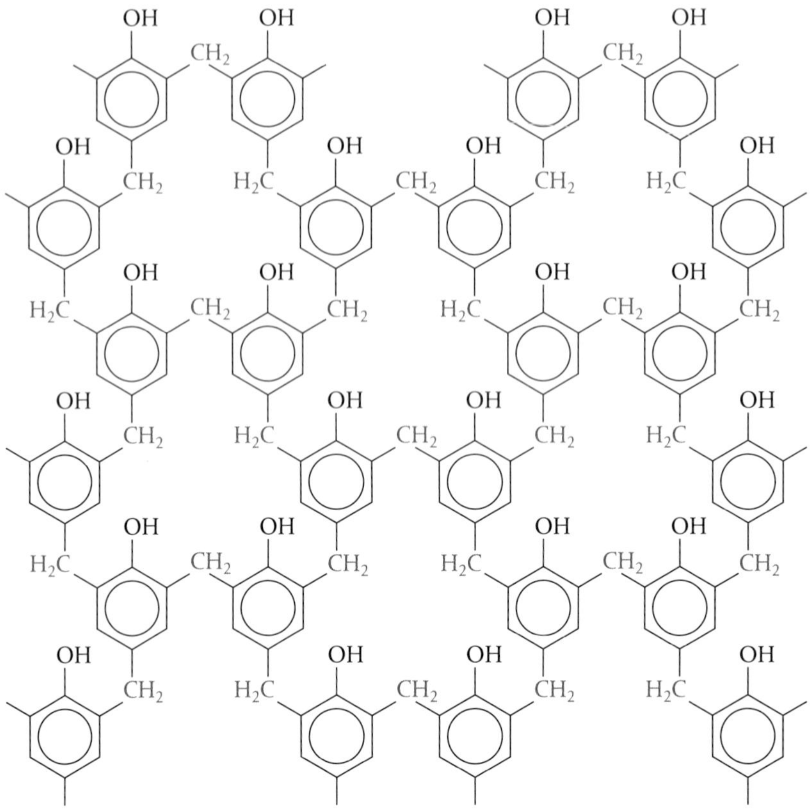

**Figure 12.33** The structure of Bakelite, a thermosetting plastic. Methanal ($CH_2O$) provides the $CH_2$ cross-links (shown in blue) between the benzene rings of phenol.

## Atom economy is a measure of efficiency applied in Green Chemistry

Green Chemistry is the sustainable design of chemical products and chemical processes. It aims to minimize the use and generation of chemical substances that are hazardous to human health and the environment. Traditionally, the efficiency of a reaction has been measured by calculating the percentage yield (the proportion of the desired product obtained compared to the theoretical maximum), but this is only a limited measure as it gives no indication of the quantity of waste produced. A synthetic route should maximize the atom economy by incorporating as many of the atoms of the reactants as possible into the desired product.

The **atom economy** of a reaction can be calculated from the equation provided in section 1 of the IB data booklet:

$$\% \text{ atom economy} = \frac{\text{molar mass of desired product}}{\text{molar mass of all reactants}} \times 100\%$$

Efficient processes have high atom economies, and are important for sustainable development, as they use fewer natural resources and create less waste. Addition polymerization reactions, for example, have an atom economy of 100% as all the reacting atoms end up in the polymer and there are no side products. Many real-world processes in drug synthesis, for example, use deliberate excess of reactants to increase the yield but have low atom economies.

Catalysts have a crucial role in improving atom economy.

% atom economy =
molar mass of desired product
molar mass of all reactants
× 100%

Chloroethene is the monomer used in the manufacture of PVC. It can be produced from 1,2-dichloroethane by the following reaction.

$$CH_2ClCH_2Cl \rightarrow CH_2{=}CHCl + HCl$$

Calculate the atom economy for the reaction.

**Solution**

molar mass of reactant $= (2 \times 12.01) + (4 \times 1.01) + (2 \times 35.45) = 98.96$

molar mass desired product $= (2 \times 12.01) + (3 \times 1.01) + (1 \times 35.45) = 62.50$

$$\% \text{ atom economy} = \frac{62.50}{98.96} \times 100\% = 63.2\%$$

## Exercises

**24** Identify which of the options below best describes a thermoplastic material.

| | Interaction within chains | Interaction between chains |
|---|---|---|
| A | Strong covalent | Strong van der Waals' forces |
| B | Strong covalent | Weak van der Waals' forces |
| C | Strong van der Waals' forces | Weak covalent |
| D | Weak covalent | Weak covalent |

Explain your answer.

**25 (a)** Draw a full structural formula showing the repeating unit in isotactic poly(propene).
**(b)** Poly(propene) can exist in isotactic and atactic forms. Sketch the structure and name the stereoregular polymer.
**(c)** Explain why the more crystalline form can be used to make strong fibres for carpets.
**(d)** Deduce how many monomer units of propene could be joined together to make a polymer with an average relative molecular mass of $2.1 \times 10^6$.
**(e)** Explain why only an *average* value can be given for the relative molecular mass.

**26** The properties of polystyrene and PVC can be modified during the manufacturing process.

**(a)** Distinguish between two forms of PVC and explain the difference in properties.
**(b)** Distinguish between two forms of polystyrene and explain the difference in properties.

**27** Melamine has the following structure:

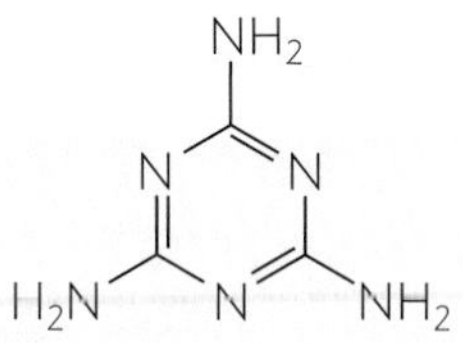

**(a)** It can be produced from urea in the following reaction.

$$6(NH_2)_2CO \rightarrow C_3H_6N_6 + 6NH_3 + 3CO_2$$

Calculate the atom economy for the reaction.
**(b)** Melamine combines with a co-monomer methanol to form a resin. Suggest a structure for this thermosetting plastic.
**(c)** Explain why thermoplastics such as poly(ethene) melt whereas thermosetting plastics such as the melamine resin do not.
**(d)** Discuss the role of cross-linking in the structures of thermosetting plastics and elastomers.

**28 (a)** Explain the use of expanded polystyrene as a packaging material.
**(b)** Describe how the expanded form is produced.

# A.6 Nanotechnology

## Understandings:

- Molecular self-assembly is the bottom-up assembly of nanoparticles and can occur by selectively attaching molecules to specific surfaces. Self-assembly can also occur spontaneously in solution.
- Possible methods of producing nanotubes are arc discharge, chemical vapour deposition (CVD), and high-pressure carbon monoxide (HIPCO).
- Arc discharge involves either vaporizing the surface of one of the carbon electrodes, or discharging an arc through metal electrodes submersed in a hydrocarbon solvent, which forms a small rod-shaped deposit on the anode.

## Applications:

- Distinguishing between physical and chemical techniques in manipulating atoms to form molecules.
- Description of the structure and properties of carbon nanotubes.
- Explanation of why an inert gas, and not oxygen, is necessary for CVD preparation of carbon nanotubes.
- Explanation of the production of carbon from hydrocarbon solvents in arc discharge by oxidation at the anode.
- Deduction of equations for the production of carbon atoms from HIPCO.
- Discussion of some implications and applications of nanotechnology.
- Explanation of why nanotubes are strong and good conductors of electricity.

### Guidance

- Possible implications of nanotechnology include uncertainty as to toxicity levels on a nanoscale, unknown health risks with new materials, concern that human defence systems are not effective against particles on the nanoscale, responsibilities of the industries and governments involved in this research.
- Conductivity of graphene and fullerenes can be explained in terms of delocalization of electrons. An explanation based on hybridization is not required.

In 1959 the Nobel Prize winning physicist Richard Feynman gave a ground breaking talk about the physical possibility of making, manipulating, and visualizing things on a small scale and arranging atoms 'the way we want'. Feynman challenged scientists to develop a new field where devices and machines could be built from tens or hundreds of atoms. This field is now called **nanotechnology**, which has been described as 'the science of the very small with big potential'.

Richard Feynman (1918–1988). His article 'There's plenty of room at the bottom' made predictions about nanotechnology before it was practically possible.

Individual silicon atoms (yellow) can be positioned to store data. This data can be written and read using a scanning tunnelling microscope.

Nanoscience research has rapidly grown internationally since the 1990s and it is now widely accepted that it will play an important role in the development of future technologies.

## Nanotechnology involves structures in the 1–100 nm range

Nanotechnology is defined as the research and technology development in the 1–100 nm range. Nanotechnology creates and uses structures that have novel properties because of their small size. It builds on the ability to control or manipulate matter on the atomic scale.

Nanotechnology is an interdisciplinary subject which covers chemistry, physics, biology, and material science. To the chemist, who is familiar with the world of molecules and atoms, 1 nm ($10^{-9}$ m) is relatively large, whereas 1 mm ($10^{-6}$ m) is considered small on an engineering scale. There are two general ways that are available to produce nanomaterials. The **top-down** approach starts with a bulk material and breaks it into smaller pieces. The **bottom-up** approach builds the material from atomic or molecular species. It is important to understand that, on the nanoscale, materials behave very differently to their bulk properties. The rules are very different from those that apply to our everyday world. The electron, for example, behaves more like a wave on the nanoscale scale and is less localized in space and can tunnel through what should be impenetrable barriers. Substances that are insulators in bulk form might become semiconductors when reduced to the nanoscale. Melting points can change due to an increase in surface area. These quantum effects and the large surface-area-to-volume ratios can lead to the same material having a range of size-dependent properties. The colour of a material, for example, can depend on its size.

It is theoretically possible to store the information in all the books of the world in a cube of material the size of the 'barest piece of dust that can be made out by the human eye'.

**TOK**

'Before you become too entranced with gorgeous gadgets ... let me remind you that information is not knowledge, knowledge is not wisdom ...' (Arthur C Clarke)

What is the difference between knowledge and information?

### NATURE OF SCIENCE

Science is an exciting and challenging adventure involving much creativity and imagination as well as exacting and detailed thinking and application. Richard Feynman was well known for flashes of intuition and the pleasure he took 'in finding things out'. He likened the scientific endeavour to understand the natural world to someone trying to understand the rules of chess by observation alone. 'You might discover after a bit, for example, that when there's only one bishop around on the board that the bishop maintains its colour. Later on you might discover the law for the bishop as it moves on the diagonal which would explain the law that you understood before – that it maintained its colour – and that would be analogous to discovering one law and then later finding a deeper understanding of it. Then things can happen, everything's going good, and then all of a sudden some strange phenomenon occurs in some corner, so you begin to investigate that – it's castling, something you didn't expect.' It is things we don't understand that are the most interesting. The direct influence of Feynman on nanotechnology is open to debate, but it is notable that Feynman's vision of atomically precise fabrication was cited by Bill Clinton during his presidential address when he proposed financial backing for scientific research in nanotechnology in January 2000. All science has to be funded, and political and economic factors are important factors in determining where the money goes. Science is a human activity and Nobel laureates have more political influence than their less experienced colleagues.

## Individual atoms can be visualized and manipulating using the scanning tunnelling and atomic force microscopes

One significant step in the bottom-up approach to the subject was the development of the scanning tunnelling microscope (STM) (see page 92) and the atomic force microscope (AFM), which can visualize and manipulate individual atoms in a physical way due to the interactions between the atoms of the probe and the atoms of the material under scrutiny.

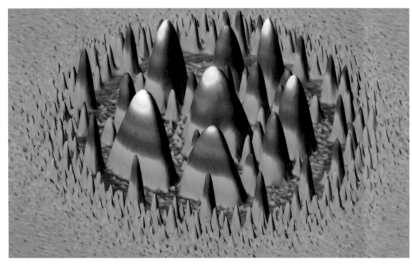

Coloured atomic force micrograph (AFM) of molecules of yttrium oxide ($Y_2O_3$) on a thin film of yttrium. A thin probe is moved across the surface and its movements as it follows the contours of the surface are translated into an image.

## Self-assembly can occur spontaneously in solution due to intermolecular interactions

Although ionic crystals naturally grow in solution as the opposite charged ions organize themselves into a lattice structure, the self-assembly of covalent structures is more complex.

Simple molecules such as water and glucose, for example, are just below 1 nm in size. The synthesis of nanoscale materials, which are 10–100 times larger, from such molecules is difficult using conventional chemical methods. It would involve large numbers of molecules spontaneously self-assembling. The process does, however, occur in nature where highly complex molecular structures such as proteins are built from the simple building blocks of 20 amino acids. This is possible as the amino molecules *recognize* and bind to each other by intermolecular interactions such as **hydrogen bonding** and **van der Waals'** forces. DNA-assisted assembly methods can be used in a similar way to make nanoscale materials. Strands of the molecule act as an 'intelligent sticky tape' allowing only certain base pairings to occur. Molecules can only bind to bases of the DNA when specific hydrogen bonding interactions occur. The field has developed in many directions, with chemists synthesizing ever more complex and finely tuned super-molecules.

### NATURE OF SCIENCE

The top-down perspective of Richard Feynman contrasts with the bottom-up approach first advocated by Eric Drexler, who envisaged molecular machines 'manoeuvring things atom by atom'. Drexler's views are controversial and have been criticized by Nobel Laureate Rick Smalley who has argued that fundamental physical principles would prevent them from ever being possible. Smalley believes that Drexler's speculations of molecular assemblers have threatened the public support for development of nanotechnology as some are concerned that these molecular assemblers could somehow get out of control. An understanding of science is vital when society needs to make decisions involving scientific issues but how does the public judge such issues? As experts in their particular fields, scientists have a role in answering such questions responsibly.

## Nanowires are used in electronic devices

Two examples of nanotechnology which are of interest are nanowires and nanotubes. Scientists hope to build tiny transistors from nanowires which can be as small as 1 nm in diameter, for use in computer chips and other electronic devices. These are generally constructed in a bottom-up approach in which atoms are organized on a surface by growing the nanowires on a donor substrate.

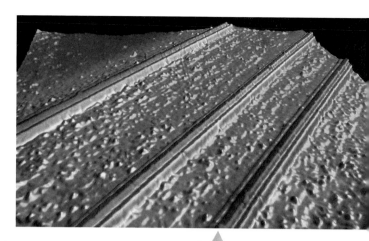

Coloured scanning tunnelling micrograph of nanowires. Just 10 atoms wide, these wires could be used in computers operating at the limits of miniaturization.

## Carbon nanotubes are made from pentagons and hexagons of carbon atoms

The structure of buckminsterfullerene, $C_{60}$, was discussed in Chapter 4. The inclusion of pentagons into the hexagonal structure of graphite allows the carbon atoms to form a closed spherical cage (Figure 12.34). The discovery of $C_{60}$ was one of the key developments in nanochemistry.

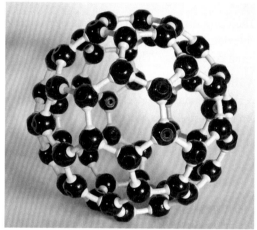

**Figure 12.34** $C_{60}$ has a structure consisting of interlinking hexagonal and pentagonal rings that form a hollow spherical shape similar to a soccer ball.

The discovery of $C_{60}$ led to the discovery of a whole family of structurally related carbon nanotubes. These resemble a rolled-up sheet of graphite, with the carbon molecules arranged in repeating hexagons. The tubes, which have a diameter of 1 nm, can be closed if pentagons are present in the structure (Figure 12.35).

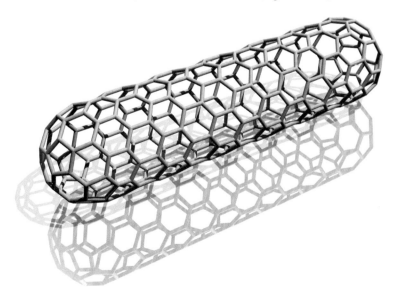

**Figure 12.35** The carbon nanotube is capped owing to the presence of pentagons at the ends of the structure.

## Single-walled carbon nanotubes (SWNTs) and multi-walled carbon nanotubes (MWNTs) can be made

A whole series of molecules, including structures with multiple walls of concentric tubes, have been produced. Carbon nanotubes have proved to have very useful properties.

Bundles of carbon nanotubes have tensile strengths between 50 and 100 times that of iron, as there is strong covalent bonding within the walls of the nanotube.

Different tubes have different electrical properties because, at the nanoscale, the behaviour of electrons is very sensitive to the dimensions of the tube. The electron behaves more like a wave than a particle at these dimensions, and its electrical properties are determined by the relationship between the wavelength of the electron and the tube length. Some tubes are conductors and some are semi-conductors.

Their properties can also be altered by trapping different atoms inside the tubes. Silver chloride, for example, can be inserted into a tube and then decomposed to form an inner coat of silver. The resulting tube is a thin metallic electrical conductor.

As tubes have large surface areas and specific dimensions, they have the potential to be very efficient and size-selective heterogeneous catalysts. Their mechanical (stiffness, strength, toughness), thermal, and electrical properties allow a wide variety of applications, from batteries and fuel cells, to fibres and cables, to pharmaceuticals and biomedical materials.

> In 1996 scientists at the IBM Research Laboratory in Zurich built the world's smallest abacus. Individual $C_{60}$ molecules could be pushed back and forth by the ultra-fine tip of a scanning tunnelling microscope.

> The world's smallest test tube has been made from a carbon nanotube. One end of the tube is closed by a fullerene cap that contains both pentagons and hexagons. The tube has a volume of $10^{-24}$ dm$^3$.

## Graphene is a single atomic plane of graphite

The 2010 Nobel Prize for Physics was awarded to Andre Geim and Konstantin Novoselov for their *'groundbreaking experiments regarding the two-dimensional material graphene'*.

Graphene is the thinnest material known and yet it is also one of the strongest. It conducts electricity as efficiently as copper as there is extensive delocalization of electrons throughout the structure and it out performs all other materials as a conductor of heat. Graphene is almost completely transparent, yet so dense that even the smallest atom, helium, cannot pass through it. All these properties are quantum effects related to the single atom thickness of its structure.

Graphene is composed of hexagonally arranged carbon atoms (spheres) linked by strong covalent bonds. It transports electrons highly efficiently and may one day replace silicon in computer chips and other technology applications.

## Carbon nanotubes are made by arc discharge, chemical vapour deposition (CVD), and high-pressure carbon monoxide (HIPCO)

Open carbon nanotubes are generally formed when gaseous carbon atoms aggregate to form hexagonal arrangements with the same chicken wire structure as graphite. Closed tubes are formed if the conditions allow for the additional formation of carbon pentagons. The techniques used differ in the source of the carbon atoms, the method used to vaporize the carbon atoms, and the type of tubes generated. The carbon atoms need to be produced in an oxygen-free atmosphere so as to prevent combustion to carbon dioxide.

MWNT are easier to produce in high volume quantities than SWNT.

| Method | Source of carbon | Details | Product |
|---|---|---|---|
| Arc discharge | Graphite | A large electric discharge is passed between two graphite electrodes in an inert atmosphere of low pressure helium or liquid nitrogen. The carbon atoms condense at the cathode and form carbon nanotubes. This was the method used to first make $C_{60}$. | A complex mixture is produced which requires further purification to separate the CNTs from the soot and the residual catalytic metals present in the crude product. |
| | Hydrocarbon solvent | An electric arc is discharged between metal electrodes submersed in a hydrocarbon solvent. A small rod-shaped deposit is formed on the anode. | |
| Laser ablation | Graphite | A high-powered laser atomizes a high-temperature graphite target in an inert atmosphere. | SWNT are produced. |
| Chemical vapour deposition (CVD) | Hydrocarbon gas | A hydrocarbon gas is passed over heterogeneous metal catalysts in a silica or zeolite support. Nanotubes form on the catalyst's surface as the carbon atoms condense from the atomized hydrocarbon. | Both MWNT and MZNT can be made, depending on the temperature. |
| High-pressure carbon monoxide (HIPCO) process | Carbon monoxide | An iron/carbon monoxide complex $Fe(CO)_5$ breaks up to produce iron nanoparticles, which act as a catalyst for the disproportionation of carbon monoxide: $$CO(g) + CO(g) \rightarrow C(s) + CO_2(g)$$ This allows the carbon nanotubes to form on the surface of the iron particles. | SWNT tubes are produced. |

## Implications of nanotechnology

Nanotechnology has the potential to provide significant advances over the next 50 years. Applications will be broad, including healthcare, medicine, security, electronics, communications, and computing.

| Area | Current and potential uses |
|---|---|
| agriculture | nanoporous zeolites for slow release of water and fertilizers |
| healthcare/medicine | biological nanosensors as diagnostic tools |
| energy | nanoscale catalyst-enhanced fuels for better efficiency nanomaterials for fuel cells/batteries/solar cells |
| electronics | carbon nanotube electronic components |
| ICT | flat panel flexible displays using nanotechnology high-density data storage using nanomagnetic effects faster processing using quantum computers |
| water treatment | nanomembranes for water treatment |

Quantum dot nanoparticle probes, used to target and image tumours through the incorporation of antibodies that bind to the target cancer cells.

Nanotechnology will have an impact on the ethical, legal, and political issues that face the international community in the near future. It is important that international bodies such as UNESCO promote a dialogue between the public and the scientific communities.

While scientists are very excited about the potential of nanotechnology, there are some concerns about the problems that the new technologies might cause. New technologies always carry new risks and concerns. There are unknown health effects

631

and concerns that the human immune system will be defenceless against nanoscale particles. As they have very different properties from their related bulk materials, they need to be handled differently. The toxicity of the materials, for example, depends on the size of particles. Many applications only require very small numbers of nanoparticles, so this reduces risks considerably. However some uses involve large quantities, for example sunscreens. Large-scale manufacture can lead to explosions. The small particle size and large surface area increase the rate of reactions to dangerous levels. Like any new chemical products, a full risk assessment is required, both for the production of new materials and for their subsequent uses. It is the responsibility of scientists to carry out these trials, assess the risks, and engage in debate with the public to ensure that concerns are addressed and the scientific facts of the technology are communicated.

## Exercises

**29** Carbon atoms can be constructed into various shapes, including balls, tubes, and pipes.

   **(a)** A carbon nanotube has a diameter of 1 nm and is 10 μm long. How many diameters does this length represent?

   **(b)** These tubes are believed to be stronger than steel. Explain the tensile strength of the tubes on a molecular level.

   **(c)** One problem in the synthesis of nanotubes is that a mixture of tubes with different lengths and orientations is produced. Suggest why this is a problem.

   **(d)** Suggest two reasons why carbon nanotubes could be effective catalysts.

   **(e)** Describe and explain the effect of the length of a carbon nanotube on its electrical conductivity.

**30** The wavelength of UV light is in the range 1–400 nm. Many modern sunscreens contain nano-sized particles of titanium dioxide which do not absorb ultraviolet radiation.

   **(a)** Suggest how these nanoparticles are able to protect the skin from ultraviolet radiation.

   **(b)** Suggest a reason why it is difficult to regulate for the toxicity of nanoparticles.

**31** *A Boy and His Atom* is the world's smallest movie. The boy in the picture is made up from about 130 atoms of carbon and oxygen.

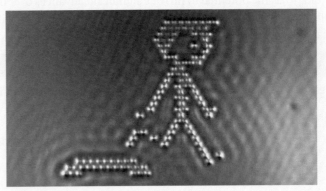

   **(a)** Estimate the height of the boy in the picture.

   **(b)** Suggest a method used to move the atoms to make the animation.

## A.7  Environmental impact: plastics

## Understandings:

- Plastics do not degrade easily because of their strong covalent bonds.
- Burning of poly(vinyl chloride) releases dioxins, HCl gas, and incomplete hydrocarbon combustion products.
- Dioxins contain unsaturated six-membered heterocyclic rings with two oxygen atoms, usually in positions 1 and 4.
- Chlorinated dioxins are hormone disrupting, leading to cellular and genetic damage.
- Plastics require more processing to be recycled than other materials.
- Plastics are recycled based on different resin types.

### Guidance

- *Dioxins do not decompose in the environment and can be passed on in the food chain.*
- *Consider polychlorinated dibenzodioxins (PCCD) and PCBs as examples of carcinogenic chlorinated dioxins or dioxin-like substances.*

## Applications:

- Deduction of the equation for any given combustion reaction.
- Discussion of why the recycling of polymers is an energy intensive process.
- Discussion of the environmental impact of the use of plastics.
- Comparison of the structures of polychlorinated biphenyls (PCBs) and dioxins.
- Discussion of the health concerns of using volatile plasticizer in polymer production.
- Distinguish possible resin identification code (RIC) of plastics from an IR spectrum.

### Guidance

- *House fires can release many toxins due to plastics (shower curtains, etc.). Low smoke zero halogen cabling is often used in wiring to prevent these hazards.*
- *Consider phthalate esters as examples of plasticizers.*
- *Resin identification codes (RIC) are in the IB data booklet in section 30.*
- *Structures of various materials molecules are in the IB data booklet in section 31.*

## Health concerns of using volatile plasticizer in polymer production

Plasticizer molecules have molecular covalent structures and so are generally volatile. Although they are trapped within the polymer structure, they are not chemically bonded to it and so can easily be released into the environment when a plastic ages and breaks down. There is some concern of the health effects of human exposure to the phthalate plasticizers. Many different phthalates exist with different properties, uses, and health effects. There is some evidence that phthalates effect the development of the male reproductive system in laboratory animals and phthalates are often classified as 'endocrine disruptors' or 'hormonally active agents' because of their ability to interfere with the endocrine system in the body. Experiments on laboratory animals have shown that they are potential carcinogens. The relatively high exposure of children to phthalates is of particular concern as PVC is present in many toys and childcare items. Levels are controlled in some countries to below 0.1% by mass. The evidence of adverse effects on human health is limited and more research is needed in this area.

Plastic waste is not biodegradable and persists for a long time, causing environmental problems.

## Plastics do not degrade easily because of their strong covalent bonds

As most plastic products have a short life cycle plastics account for about 10% by mass of our total waste and about 25% by volume. This leads to two problems:

• plastics are produced from crude oil which is non-renewable;
• most plastics are not biodegradable and waste placed in landfill does not degrade for hundreds of years.

Polymers are not broken down naturally as bacteria do not have the enzymes needed to breakdown the strong covalent C—C bond found in synthetic polymers.

Much of our plastic waste has been used to **landfill** disused quarries. However, suitable sites are becoming harder to find and reducing the amount of plastic dumped into landfills is a high priority.

Some poly(ethene) plastic bags, with added natural polymers such as starch, cellulose, or protein, however, can be made to biodegrade. The bacteria in the soil decompose the natural polymer and so the bag is broken down into smaller pieces. The synthetic polymer chains that remain have an increased surface area which speeds up the rate of decay further. One problem with biodegradability is that conditions in a landfill are often not suitable. The need to make sites watertight to prevent soluble products leaking into the environment also limits the supply of oxygen, preventing the bacteria from acting.

Landfill sites are used to dispose of about 90% of the world's domestic waste.

## Incineration of plastics reduces bulk, releases energy but produces air pollution

As the addition polymers are made up from mainly carbon and hydrogen, they are a concentrated energy source. Waste plastic can be burned and used as a fuel – but there are problems.

Biodegradable plastics are produced using plant-based starch. These bioplastics break down much faster than petroleum plastics and also produce little, if any, toxic by-products when burned.

634

- Carbon dioxide is a greenhouse gas.
- Carbon monoxide produced during incomplete combustion is poisonous.
- The combustion of PVC poses a particular problem as the hydrogen chloride produced causes acid rain. It must be removed from the fumes before they are released into the atmosphere.

Complete combustion of PVC produces water, carbon dioxide, and hydrogen chloride (HCl).

Deduce an equation for the reaction using $(CH_2CHCl)_n$ as the molecular formula of the polymer.

### Solution

The unbalanced equation:

$$(CH_2CHCl)_n + O_2 \rightarrow CO_2 + H_2O + HCl$$

1  Balancing carbon and chlorine: there are $2nC$ and $nCl$ on the left – use this information on the right:

$$(CH_2CHCl)_n + O_2 \rightarrow 2nCO_2 + H_2O + nHCl$$

2  Balancing the hydrogens: there are $3nH$ on the left – again, use this information on the right:

$$(CH_2CHCl)_n + O_2 \rightarrow 2nCO_2 + nH_2O + nHCl$$

3  Balancing the oxygens: there are $5nO$ on the right – use this information on the left:

$$(CH_2CHCl)_n + \frac{5n}{2}O_2 \rightarrow 2nCO_2 + nH_2O + nHCl$$

Chemical waste incinerator, where toxic chemicals are broken down by high temperatures into harmless or non-toxic products.

## Incomplete combustion of PVC produces dioxins

The complete combustion of plastics is rarely possible in reality, and dioxins can be unintentionally generated as by-products, depending on the incineration conditions. Dioxins contain unsaturated six-member heterocyclic rings with two oxygen atoms, usually in positions 1 and 4.

1.4-dioxin

polychlorinated dibenzo-*p*-dioxin

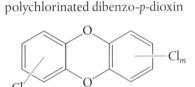

▲ Environmentalists investigating dioxin contamination of soil at Times Beach, Missouri.

Each benzene ring can have up to four chlorine atoms. They are 10 000 times more poisonous than the cyanide ion and they disrupt the action of hormones and can cause cellular and genetic damage. The molecules do not readily decompose in the environment and so can be passed on in the food chain. Dioxins persist in fat and liver cells. Symptoms of dioxin poisoning are cirrhosis of the liver, damage to heart and memory, concentration problems, and depression. The skin disease chloracne is a result of the body attempting to remove the poison through the skin. Dioxin can cause malfunctions in fetuses. It was one of the herbicides present in the defoliant called Agent Orange used during the Vietnam War.

## Polychlorinated biphenyls (PCBs) and polychlorinated dibenzofurans are dioxin-like substances and are also carcinogenic

The polychlorinated biphenyls have a high electrical resistance and are used in electrical transformers and capacitors. The structure is shown below. They contain a number of chlorine atoms attached to two connected benzene rings (biphenyl).

They are released into the environment from poorly maintained hazardous waste sites and the incomplete burning of waste from industrial incinerators. PCBs can accumulate in the leaves and above-ground parts of plants and food crops. They are also taken up into the bodies of small organisms and fish. As a result, people who ingest fish may be exposed to PCBs that have bioaccumulated in the fish they are ingesting. The polychlorinated dibenzofurans, shown below, are a group of toxic compounds associated with PCBs. They are produced in incinerators and are also carcinogenic.

## House fires can release many toxins when plastic objects burn

The combustion products of plastics are a serious concern in the event of a house fire. Although PVC is often used for its fire-retarding properties, we have seen that it produces a nasty cocktail of dangerous gases, including the dioxins and hydrogen chloride, when it does burn. The hydrogen chloride reacts with any water present to form hydrochloric acid.

One possible solution to this problem is to use low-smoke zero-halogen cabling made from plastics such as poly(propene). These give off only limited amounts of smoke and no hydrogen chloride. They are particularly used in underground areas where smoke levels can build up. These materials also have a reduced environment impact if they are incinerated after use.

### NATURE OF SCIENCE

There is some dispute over the carcinogenic properties of the phthalates. Testing the chemicals on animals raises many ethical issues and the only data available are based on tests on rats and mice. It may be true that what causes cancer in humans also causes cancer in rodents, but the reverse is not necessarily true. The IB has a strict animal experimentation policy.

**TOK** Do animals have the same rights as human beings? Is experimenting on rats more acceptable than experimenting with monkeys? What criteria have you used to justify your answer?

## Plastics require more processing to be recycled than other materials

Ideally materials should be reused so that no waste is produced. If this is not possible, the best alternative is recycling as it reduces:

• the use of raw materials
• energy costs
• the level of pollutants
• the need of land for waste disposal.

One challenge is the separation and purification of the materials. Although methods of mechanical separation have been developed, ideally the plastics should be collected separately to reduce costs. Plastics are recycled based on different resin types and the **resin identification codes** are listed in section 30 of the IB data booklet. Recycled materials tend to be of a lower grade quality than new materials due to the problems of purification.

The recycling symbol on the bottom of a bleach bottle indicates that the plastic is high-density poly(ethene). Different plastics can be identified by different numbers. This assists in sorting plastics before they are recycled.

As thermoplastics can be melted down and remoulded they can be recycled mechanically. This is the simplest and cheapest method: the used plastics are cut into small pieces, separated according to their relative density in a floating tank, and heated and extruded to form new shapes.

Chemical methods involve **depolymerization**. The used plastics are heated in the absence of air and split up into their monomers in a process known as **pyrolysis**. The products are separated by fractional distillation and used as chemical feedstock by the petrochemical industry to make other products including plastics. There are energy costs in both processes.

For recycling to be successful and self-sustainable, the costs of recycling must be less than those needed to produce new materials.

Brooms made from recycled plastic.

Unfortunately, plastics require more processing to be recycled than other materials. There are costs in collecting and sorting the different used plastics. There are often lots of additives in plastic products, such as reinforcements, fillers, and colorants and mixtures of plastics are much weaker than the individual plastics so the recycled product is often of lower quality than the original with only a limited range of uses.

## Plastics can be identified from their IR spectrum

As recycling companies don't usually know exactly what it is they are getting, it is important that they are able to identify plastics and process them appropriately. The plastics are first ground into little pellets and then passed on a conveyer belt where they are identified by a spectrometer which triggers the sorting process.

As discussed in Chapter 11, the positions of absorption bands in the IR spectrum gives information about the presence or absence of specific functional groups in a molecule. The whole spectrum constitutes a 'fingerprint' that can be used to identify the plastic. Although the IR spectra for poly(ethene) and poly(propene) are very similar (as they both made up from C—C and C—H bonds), they are not identical. As discussed in Chapter 11, the vibrations of the individual bonds are not independent as it is the whole molecule that vibrates. These differences are sufficient to distinguish between the two isomers.

The IR spectrum of PVC is shown in Figure 12.36. The absorption band between 600 and 700 cm$^{-1}$ due to the presence of the C—Cl bond is a key feature of the spectrum.

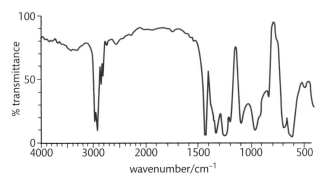

**Figure 12.36** The IR spectrum of PVC. Note the absorption band at 600–700 cm$^{-1}$.

IR spectroscopy can also be used to test the quality of the materials during all stages of the manufacturing process.

---

### Worked example

The infrared spectrum of a compound shows a strong absorption at 1000–1400 cm$^{-1}$ but no absorption between 2850 and 3090 cm$^{-1}$. Deduce the structure of the polymer using information in section 26 of the IB data booklet.

#### Solution

Absorption 1000–1400 cm$^{-1}$: C—F present

No absorption 2850–3050 cm$^{-1}$: no C—H present

It has the structure

$$\left[\begin{array}{c} \overset{\displaystyle F}{\underset{\displaystyle F}{C}} - \overset{\displaystyle F}{\underset{\displaystyle F}{C}} \end{array}\right]_n$$

The polymer is called poly(tetrafluoroethene) or Teflon®.

It is said that the American space programme would have floundered without Teflon because the material was used to make so many things, from space suits to the bags used to hold samples of moon rock. It is now used to make non-stick pans, Gore-Tex® fabric, and hip joint replacements. Science has been used to solve many problems and improve human life, but it can also inadvertently cause environmental problems. Risk benefit analyses, risk assessments, and the precautionary principle are all parts of the scientific way of addressing the common good.

The discovery of the addition polymers poly(ethene) and Teflon both included some elements of luck. The significance of serendipity in scientific discovery was discussed on page 617.

Different countries have different recycling policies. For recycling to be successful, economic and political factors need to be considered. If it is not economical to recycle plastic at the moment perhaps we should bury the plastics separately so that future generations could recover it later. Plastic disposal is a global problem with local solutions.

## CHALLENGE YOURSELF

**3** Explain why the absorption of C—X bonds for the halogens occurs at such wavenumbers compared to the C—H stretch.

**TOK**
One aspect of 'caring' in the IB Learner profile is to show a personal commitment to service and act to make a positive difference to the environment. What impact do your actions make on your local environment? Are there ethical obligations for humanity to treat the natural environment in a certain way?

## Exercises

**32 (a)** Plastics have replaced many traditional materials. Suggest two properties which make plastic more suitable than wood for making children's toys.
**(b)** Increased use of polymers has led to problems of waste disposal. State one method of waste disposal and discuss issues other than cost associated with its use.
**(c)** Explain why synthetic polyalkenes are not generally biodegradable.
**(d)** Explain how a poly(ethene) bag can be made more biodegradable.

**33** Discuss the advantages and disadvantages of incineration as a method of disposal compared with landfill sites.

**34** Discuss the advantages and challenges of recycling plastics.

**35** The general structure of the some pollutants is given in section 31 of the IB data booklet.

**(a)** State the range of permissible values for $n$ and $m$ for the polychlorinated biphenyls.
**(b)** State the range of permissible values for $n$ and $m$ for the polychlorinated dibenzofurans.

**36** Compare the IR spectra of ethene and its polymer.

## A.8 Superconducting metals and X-ray crystallography

## Understandings:

- Superconductors are materials that offer no resistance to electric currents below a critical temperature.
- The Meissner effect is the ability of a superconductor to create a mirror image magnetic field of an external field, thus expelling it.
- Resistance in metallic conductors is caused by collisions between electrons and positive ions of the lattice.
- The Bardeen–Cooper–Schrieffer (BCS) theory explains that below the critical temperature electrons in superconductors form Cooper pairs which move freely through the superconductor.
- Type 1 superconductors have sharp transitions to superconductivity whereas Type 2 superconductors have more gradual transitions.

- X-ray diffraction can be used to analyse structures of metallic and ionic compounds.
- Crystal lattices contain simple repeating unit cells.
- Atoms on faces and edges of unit cells are shared.
- The number of nearest neighbours of an atom/ion is its coordination number.

### Guidance

- *Only a simple explanation of BCS theory with Cooper pairs is required. At low temperatures the positive ions in the lattice are distorted slightly by a passing electron. A second electron is attracted to this slight positive deformation and a coupling of these two electrons occurs.*
- *Operating principles of X-ray crystallography are not required.*
- *Only pure metals with simple cubic cells, body centred cubic cells (BCC), and face centred cubic cells (FCC) should be covered.*

## Applications:

- Analysis of resistance versus temperature data for Type 1 and Type 2 superconductors.
- Explanation of superconductivity in terms of Cooper pairs moving through a positive ion lattice.
- Deduction or construction of unit cell structures from crystal structure information.
- Application of the Bragg equation, $n\lambda = 2d\sin\theta$, in metallic structures.
- Determination of the density of a pure metal from its atomic radii and crystal packing structure.

### Guidance

- *Perovskite crystalline structures of many superconductors can be analysed by X-ray crystallography but these will not be assessed.*
- *Bragg's equation will only be applied to simple cubic structures.*

## Resistance in metallic conductors is caused by collisions between electrons and the positive ions in the lattice

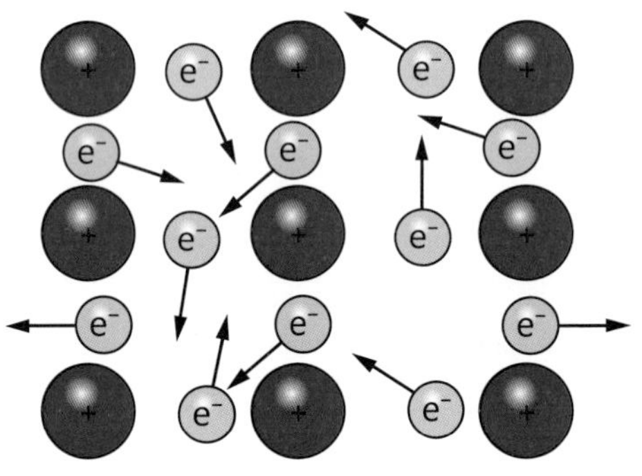

**Figure 12.37** A piece of metal which does not have current flowing through it. The arrows represent the random thermal motion of the electrons (their average speed at room temperature is hundreds of km s⁻¹).

As discussed in Chapter 4, a solid piece of metal, at room temperature, consists of a regular lattice of metal ions with the delocalized valence electrons moving in the spaces (Figure 12.37). The motion of the free electrons is random.

When a power source such as a battery is connected to the metal another motion is added to the random thermal motion of the electrons. This is more regular and results in a general 'drift' of electrons through the metal from the negative terminal of the power source to the positive terminal (Figure 12.38). A typical drift velocity for electrons in metals is 1 mm s⁻¹.

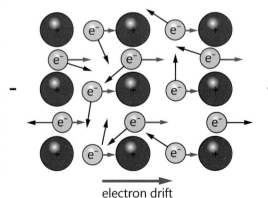

electron drift

**Figure 12.38** When a metal is connected to a battery there is a general drift of electrons from the negative terminal of the power source to the positive terminal.

The resistance of a piece of metal is due to collisions between the delocalized electrons and the positive ions which 'get in their way' and impede their movement through the metal. During a collision, some of the electron's kinetic energy is transferred to the ion, which increases the amplitude of their lattice vibrations. This increases the average kinetic energy of the ions and therefore the temperature of the metal.

The resistance of metals generally increases with temperature as the ions are vibrating with larger amplitude and so they get more in the way of the moving electrons. By contrast, the resistance of semi-conductors decreases with an increase in temperature as more electrons have sufficient energy to be free from individual atoms and available for conduction. Type 1 superconductors are exceptional in that their resistance falls to zero at low temperature (Figure 12.39).

(The temperature dependence of Type 2 superconductors will be discussed in more detail later.)

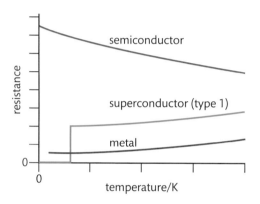

**Figure 12.39** The variation of resistance with temperature for different materials.

## Superconductors are materials that offer no resistance to electric currents below a critical temperature

 A superconductor is a material that conducts electricity without resistance.

The resistance of metals generally decreases with temperature. Superconductors show extreme properties in that the resistance falls to zero at a critical temperature. The effect was first observed by the Dutch physicist Heike Kamerlingh Onnes in 1811 and it was completely unexpected. The fact that a coil of wire made from a superconductor could carry an electric current round and round forever without needing a power source defied explanation.

### NATURE OF SCIENCE

Onnes' work in low temperature physics would not have been possible without his team of expert glassblowers and technicians needed to build and maintain the delicate equipment needed for such work. He had the best equipped and best organized laboratory in the world at the time. His original goal was to be the first to make liquid helium, which was the last gas to be liquefied, needing a temperature of 4 K. His success can be contrasted to the work of his British competitors, Dewar and Ramsey, which was hampered by the personal enmity between the pair. Ramsey, for example, had access to all the helium in Britain but would not share this precious resource with Dewar. Science is a human activity and scientists need to work in a team to be effective.

 What role do personal disagreements play in the pursuit of knowledge?

We now believe that the current in a Type 1 superconductor is carried by a **Cooper pair** of electrons. The formation of a Cooper pair is illustrated in Figure 12.40.

Superconductivity was first observed as a low temperature effect, when the positive ions have low vibrational energy. The presence of an electron, at such temperatures, distorts the lattice structure locally and attracts the oppositely charged positive ions. The positive ions become more closely packed and a region of high positive charge density is formed. A second electron is then attracted into the same region, and the two electrons form a Cooper pair.

**Figure 12.40** The formation of Cooper pairs.

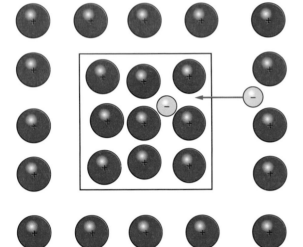

A second electron is attracted into the distorted region where the positive ions are more densely packed. It forms a Cooper pair with the electron that was responsible for the original distortion.

An electron attracts positive ions and so distorts the local structure of the lattice. The positive ions are more closely packed within this region.

Cooper pairing is a quantum effect. Electrons have a spin of ½ and are fermions which follow Pauli's exclusion principle. A Cooper pair has a spin of +1 or 0 and behaves as a boson. Bosons do not follow Pauli's exclusion principle.

The electron pair is more difficult to impede than a single electron, in the same way that a pair of people holding hands would be harder to stop than an individual, and the Cooper pair passes through the crystal lattice unimpeded and the material has no resistance.

Leon N. Cooper (born 1930), giving a lecture. He shared the 1972 Nobel Prize in Physics with Bardeen and Schrieffer for their work on superconductivity. The theory is known as the BCS superconductivity theory, after their initials. The theory involves electron pairs, which are named Cooper electron pairs in his honour.

The best conductors at room temperature are gold, silver, and copper. They do not show any superconducting properties as they have the smallest lattice vibrations and so cannot be distorted in a way that allows for the formation of a Cooper pair.

## The Meissner effect is the ability of a superconductor to create a mirror image magnetic field of an external field, thus expelling it

The German physicist, Walther Meissner, showed that superconductors were perfect diamagnets: they move away when placed in an external magnetic field. There is no magnetic field in the interior of the material as the external magnetic field induces eddy currents around the exterior which produces a magnetic field equal and opposite to the external field that originally induced them (Figure 12.41). The currents screen the interior of the material from the external magnetic field which is forced to pass around the superconductor.

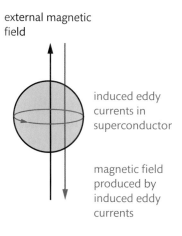

external magnetic field

induced eddy currents in superconductor

magnetic field produced by induced eddy currents

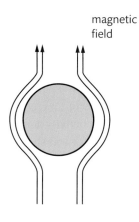

magnetic field

**Figure 12.41** There is no external field in the interior of a superconductor, as illustrated by the shaded circle.

## Type 1 superconductors have sharp transitions to superconductivity whereas Type 2 superconductors have more gradual transitions

Superconductors can be classified as Type 1 or Type 2 according to their behaviour in an external magnetic field. Type 1 materials lose their perfect diamagnetic properties once the magnetic field exceeds a critical value (Figure 12.42). They don't behave as superconductors at higher magnetic fields which eventually rip apart the Cooper pair needed for superconductivity.

opposing magnetic field produced by induced currents

opposing magnetic field = external magnetic field

external magnetic field          critical magnetic field

**Figure 12.42** The response of Type 1 superconductors to an external magnetic field.

Type 2 superconductors lose their magnetic properties more gradually (Figure 12.43).

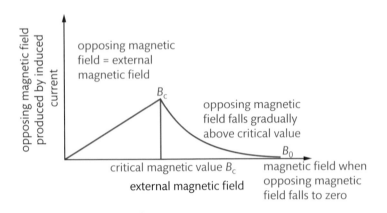

**Figure 12.43** The response of Type 2 superconductors to an external magnetic field.

A Type 2 superconductor is said to exist in a mixed state in regions between the critical value $B_c$ and $B_0$. Under these conditions, regions of the magnetic field thread through the bulk material which then loses its superconducting properties in these regions. The superconductivity of the bulk material is thus reduced and will eventually fall to zero at $B_0$ when the magnetic field passes through the whole material.

## Type 1 and Type 2 superconductors

### Type 1 superconductors are metals and metalloids

The 'Type 1' category of superconductors mainly consists of metals and metalloids that show *some* conductivity at room temperature. The variation of resistance for a Type 1 superconductor was shown in Figure 12.42 – it falls sharply to zero at a critical temperature.

The critical temperatures of some Type 1 superconductors are shown in the table.

| Material | Material type | $T_c$ / K |
|----------|---------------|-----------|
| Ti | metal | 0.40 |
| Zn | metal | 0.88 |
| Al | metal | 1.19 |
| Cr | metal | 3.00 |
| Sn | metal | 3.72 |
| Hg | metal | 4.15 |

Type 1 superconductors have been of limited practical use as the critical magnetic fields and temperatures are so low that they can only be maintained using expensive liquid helium.

Type 1 superconductors are sometimes called 'soft' superconductors.

### Type 2 superconductors are metallic compounds and alloys

Type 2 superconductors are generally made up from metallic compounds and alloys. Their resistance does not fall so sharply to zero as the temperature is lowered (Figure 12.44).

The recently discovered superconducting 'perovskites' (metal-oxide ceramics that normally have a ratio of 2 metal atoms to every

**Figure 12.44** The variation of resistance with temperature for the Type 2 superconductor $YBa_2Cu_3O_7$.

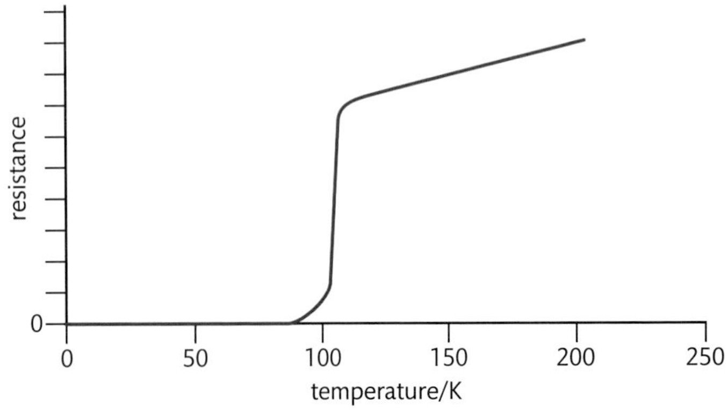

3 oxygen atoms) belong to this Type 2 superconductor group. They achieve higher critical temperatures than Type 1 superconductors by a mechanism that is still not completely understood, although it is thought to be linked to the planes of $CuO_4$ units within the structure.

Type 2 superconductors are also known as the 'hard' superconductors.

## All high-temperature superconductors are Type 2 semiconductors

One of the first high-temperature superconductors was lanthanum barium copper oxide, discovered in 1987, which has a critical temperature of 30 K. Other copper oxide superconductors were soon discovered. Superconductors with a critical temperature above 77 K are particularly useful as this is the boiling point of liquid nitrogen – which is a very inexpensive compared to the liquid helium needed for the low temperature superconductors. High-temperature superconductors are Type 2 conductors.

| Material | Material type | $T_c$ / K |
|----------|---------------|-----------|
| $YBa_2Cu_3O_7$ | ceramic | ≈ 90 |
| TlBaCaCuO | ceramic | ≈ 125 |

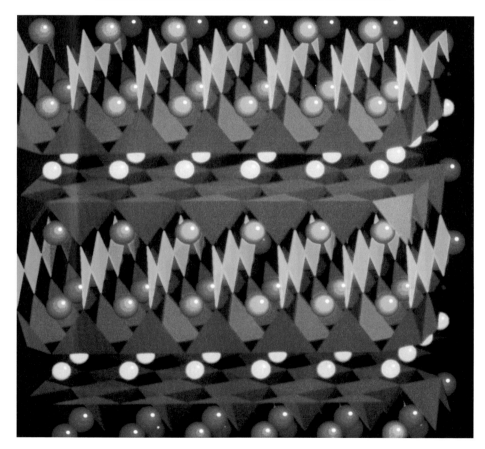

## CHALLENGE YOURSELF

4 The mineral perovskite has the formula $CaTiO_3$. Deduce the oxidation state of Ti in the mineral.

5 One copper oxide superconductor has the formula $YBa_2Cu_3O_7$. Assuming that Y is in the +3 state, deduce the oxidation number of Cu and comment on your answer.

Molecular computer graphic showing the crystal structure of one of the new generation of high-temperature superconductors; this is yttrium barium copper oxide ($YBa_2Cu_3O_7$). Discovered in 1987, the new superconducting ceramic materials are expected to lead to a technological revolution. The picture highlights the square-pyramidal (red) and square-planar (green) coordination of copper by oxygen ions in this orthorhombic structure. Yttrium ions are the yellow spheres, and barium ions the blue spheres.

Demonstration of magnetic levitation of one of the new high-temperature superconductors – yttrium barium copper oxide ($YBa_2Cu_3O_7$). The photograph shows a small, cylindrical magnet floating freely above a nitrogen-cooled, cylindrical specimen of a superconducting ceramic (made by IMI Ltd). The glowing vapour is from liquid nitrogen, which maintains the ceramic within its superconducting temperature range.

Superconducting magnets played a crucial role in the hunt for the Higg's boson at the Large Hadron Collider in CERN. A large magnetic field is needed to steer the elementary particles around the 27 km long circular tunnel under the French–Swiss border. Operations had to be halted at an earlier stage for a year as several tonnes of helium, needed to maintain the low temperatures for superconductivity, had leaked into the tunnel.

**NATURE OF SCIENCE**

The technical development of high-temperature superconductors poses a number of problems. It is a multi-disciplinary problem and the skills of the chemist are needed to synthesize ceramics of different composition. One problem is that ceramic materials are too brittle to be produced on a large scale. The skills of the physicist are needed to investigate and explain their unusual properties. There is still quite a lot of dispute about the mechanism of Type 2 conductivity and material scientists and engineers need to apply the unusual properties of superconductors to new technologies.

## The structure of solids

The structures of many solids can be understood using a simple model in which atoms are represented by spheres. In many pure metal structures these spheres are packed densely in a cubic structure.

### The cubic close-packed crystal structure has a coordination number of 12

In the cubic close-packed structure one layer of atoms (A) is arranged in a closely packed layer so that each sphere is surrounded by a hexagon of other spheres. A second layer (B) is then placed on top of the second layer by inserting the atoms in the holes between the atoms in the layer below it. A third layer of atoms (C) is then added with the atoms similarly placed in the holes of the second layer so that they do not overlap with the first layer. The ABC pattern is then repeated, which leads to a close-packed cubic structure (Figure 12.45). The atoms have a maximum coordination number of 12 (six atoms in the same plane, three above and three below), and are as tightly packed together as possible. The spheres fill 74% of the available space. This arrangement of atoms is favoured by several metals, including gold and silver.

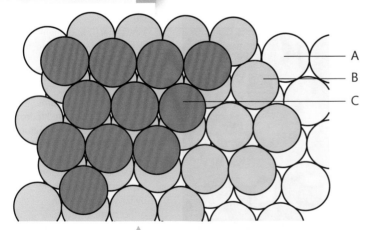
A
B
C

**Figure 12.45** A cubic close-packed crystal structure.

**The coordination number of an atom is the number of nearest neighbours it has.**

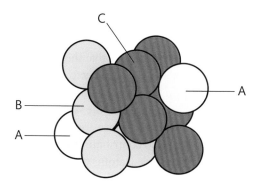

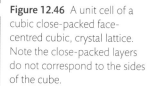

**Figure 12.46** A unit cell of a cubic close-packed face-centred cubic, crystal lattice. Note the close-packed layers do not correspond to the sides of the cube.

This structure is also described as a face-centred cubic cell (FCC), as the atoms can be thought of occupying the corners and centres of each face of the cube, as seen in the expanded structure shown in Figure 12.46. This represents a **unit cell**; the whole crystal structure can be built up by stacking these together in the same way that a wall is built from bricks.

> A close-packed structure is one in which atoms occupy the smallest total volume with the least empty space.

> A unit cell is the smallest unit that when stacked together repeatedly, reproduces the entire crystal.

## A body-centred cubic cell (BCC) crystal structure has a coordination number of 8

Some metals do not have a close packed structure. One common form is the body-centred cubic structure in which one atom is placed at the centre of a cube of eight nearest atoms.

Sodium, potassium, and iron have a body-centred cubic crystal structure.

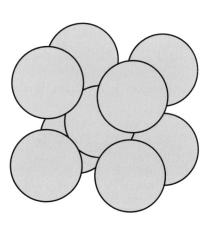

**Figure 12.47** A unit cell of a body-centred cubic crystal lattice.

## Counting the number of atoms in a unit cell

The coordination number of an atom in a body-centred structure is 8, as can be seen by focusing attention on the atom in the centre of the cube shown in Figure 12.48. All the atoms, however, have the same coordination number. Each atom on the corner is a member of eight other unit cells and so has eight nearest neighbours in the centre of each of these eight unit cells.

> Atoms on the corner of each cube are shared by eight unit cells. Each atom contributes an eighth of an atom to a unit cell.

Similarly, the coordination number of atoms in a face-centred cubic structure can be determined by focussing on one of the atoms in a corner. In Figure 12.48 this atom is shaded in yellow; it has three neighbouring atoms on the faces within the unit cell as closest neighbours, but twelve overall as it is part of eight unit cells.

The atoms at the centre of a face are shared by two unit cells and so can be thought of as equivalent to half an atom.

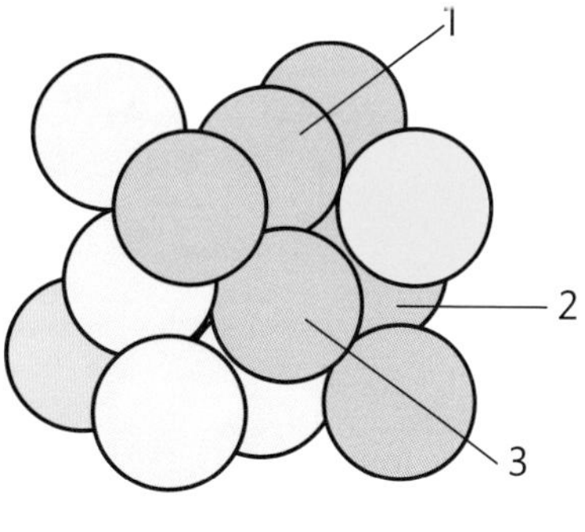

**Figure 12.48** The yellow sphere has three neighbouring spheres on the faces within the unit cell but twelve overall as it is a member of eight other unit cells. Each face atom can be thought of as being equivalent to a ½ sphere (3 × ½ × 8 = 12).

The same result is obtained by focussing attention on an atom in the centre of a face, shown in pink in Figure 12.49. This atom is bonded to four atoms in the corner of the

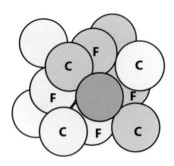

**Figure 12.49** The pink sphere has four neighbouring spheres on the corners and four on the faces above and below.

Atoms on the face of each cube are shared by two unit cells. Each atom contributes half of an atom to a unit cell.

same face, and four atoms on faces above and below, again giving a coordination number of 12.

We have seen that the atom in the centre of a cube belong exclusively to one unit cell, whereas atoms on the corner are shared by eight other unit cells and so contribute ⅛ of an atom to a unit cell, and atoms on a face are shared by two other unit cells and so contribute ½ an atom. These results can be extended: atoms on the edge of a cube are shared by four units cells and so contribute a ¼ of an atom.

| Position of an atom in cubic unit cell | Contribution to unit cell |
|:---:|:---:|
| centre | 1 |
| corner | ⅛ |
| face | ½ |
| edge | ¼ |

### Worked example

Calculate how many atoms there are in a body-centred cubic (BCC) unit cell.

**Solution**

| Location of atoms | Number of atoms | Contribution | Total atoms |
|:---:|:---:|:---:|:---:|
| centre | 1 | 1 × 1 | 1 |
| corner | 8 | 8 × ⅛ | 1 |

total = 1 + 1 = 2

There are two atoms.

### Worked example

Calculate how many atoms there are in a face-centred cubic (FCC) unit cell.

**Solution**

| Location of atoms | Number of atoms | Contribution | Total atoms |
|:---:|:---:|:---:|:---:|
| centre of face | 6 | 6 × ½ | 3 |
| corner | 8 | 8 × ⅛ | 1 |

total = 1 + 3 = 4

There are four atoms.

## Calculating the density of a metal

The density of a metal is an intensive property – it is independent of the size of the sample and can be determined by considering a unit cell of the material.

The atomic radius of copper is given in section 9 of the IB data booklet. Copper has a face-centred cubic structure.

(a) Calculate the length of a unit cell.

(b) Determine the density of the metal.

**Solution**

(a) The diagonal of a face has three atoms connected together.

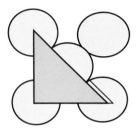

$\sqrt{2}$ (face diagonal)

1 (length of unit cell)

the diagonal of the cube $= r(M) + 2r(M) + r(M) = 4r(M)$

the length of a unit cell $= \dfrac{4r(M)}{\sqrt{2}}$

$$= 4 \times \dfrac{122}{\sqrt{2}} \times 10^{-12}\text{ m}$$

$$= 345 \times 10^{-12}\text{ m}$$

(b) the volume of a cube $= (3.45 \times 10^{-10})^3 \text{ m}^3$

number of atoms $= 4$

mass of individual atom $= \dfrac{63.55}{6.02 \times 10^{23}}\text{ g}$

mass of unit cell $= 4 \times \dfrac{63.55}{6.02 \times 10^{23}}\text{ g}$

density $= \dfrac{4 \times \dfrac{63.55}{6.02 \times 10^{23}}}{(3.45 \times 10^{-10})^3}\text{ g m}^{-3}$

$$= 10\,300\text{ g m}^{-3}$$

$$= 10.3\text{ kg m}^{-3}$$

The atomic radius of sodium is given in section 9 of the IB data booklet.

(a) Calculate the length of a unit cell.

(b) Determine the density of the metal.

## CHALLENGE YOURSELF

6 Calculate the percentage occupied by the atoms in a FCC unit cell.

**Solution**

(a) The diagonal of cube has three atoms connected together.

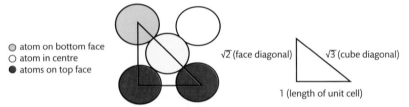

○ atom on bottom face
○ atom in centre
● atoms on top face

$\sqrt{2}$ (face diagonal)  $\sqrt{3}$ (cube diagonal)

1 (length of unit cell)

the diagonal of the cube = $r(M) + 2r(M) + r(M) = 4r(M)$

the length of a unit cell $= \dfrac{4r(M)}{\sqrt{3}}$

$$= \dfrac{4 \times 160 \times 10^{-12}}{\sqrt{3}} \text{ m}$$

$$= 370 \times 10^{-12} \text{ m}$$

(b) the volume of a cube = $(3.70 \times 10^{-10})^3 \text{ m}^3$

number of atoms = 2

mass of individual atom $= \dfrac{22.99}{6.02 \times 10^{23}} \text{ g}$

mass of unit cell $= 2 \times \dfrac{22.99}{6.02 \times 10^{23}} \text{ g}$

density $= \dfrac{2 \times \dfrac{22.99}{6.02 \times 10^{23}}}{(3.70 \times 10^{-10})^3} \text{ g m}^{-3}$

$$= 1500 \text{ kg m}^{-3}$$

## CHALLENGE YOURSELF

7 Calculate the percentage occupied by the atoms in a BCC unit cell.

8 A unit cell of the mineral perovskite is shown. Deduce the formula of the mineral.

○ Ca
○ Ti
● O

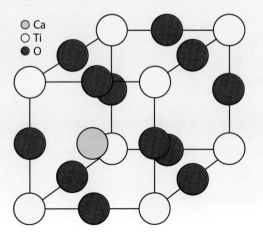

## The structure of solids is determined by X-ray diffraction

As discussed in Chapter 11, one of the best ways of determining the structure of a solid is X-ray diffraction. A crystal can produce a diffraction pattern with bright spots being produced by the constructive interference of X-rays at certain angles. Constructive interference occurs when the path difference between parallel rays is equal to an integer number of wavelengths (Figure 12.50).

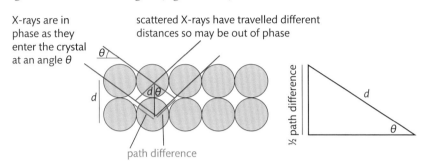

X-rays are in phase as they enter the crystal at an angle $\theta$

scattered X-rays have travelled different distances so may be out of phase

½ path difference

$d$

$d$

path difference

Figure 12.50 The scattered X-rays from different layers of a crystal travel different distances. Constructive interference occurs when the path difference is equal to an integer number of wavelengths.

The angle $\theta$ at which constructive interference occurs is related to the wavelength $\lambda$ and distance between the atoms. We see from the right-angled triangle in Figure 12.51 that:

$$\tfrac{1}{2} \times \text{path difference} = d \sin \theta$$

$$\text{path difference} = n\lambda = 2d \sin \theta$$

This is known as the **Bragg equation** and is given in section 2 of the IB data booklet.

Researcher using X-ray diffraction crystallography equipment to determine a crystal structure. A beam of monochromatic X-rays is generated and directed at the crystal (held in the apparatus at the back of the photograph). The repeated pattern of the crystal lattice acts as a diffraction grating, diffracting the beam in a way which depends on the lattice's arrangement and spacing. The scattered rays then strike a detector plate; the intensity at each point is recorded on X-ray sensitive photographic film, or else, as here, by electronic equipment which digitizes the data for analysis and presentation on a computer.

### Worked example

X-rays of wavelength $150 \times 10^{-12}$ m are scattered by a sodium crystal lattice. Bright spots occur at angles of 13.68° and 28.25°. Determine (a) the interatomic distance and (b) the atomic radius of sodium.

### Solution

(a) $n\lambda = 2d \sin \theta$

• with $n = 1$ and $\theta = 13.68°$

$$d = \frac{\lambda}{2\sin\theta}$$
$$= \frac{150 \times 10^{-12}}{2 \times \sin 13.68°} \text{ m}$$
$$= 317 \times 10^{-12} \text{ m}$$

• with $n = 2$ and $\theta = 28.25°$

$$d = \frac{2\lambda}{2\sin\theta}$$
$$= \frac{2 \times 150 \times 10^{-12}}{2 \times \sin 28.25°}$$
$$= 317 \times 10^{-12} \text{ m}$$

The interatomic distance is 317 pm.

(b) Assuming the atoms are touching:

$$r = \frac{d}{2} = 158.5 \times 10^{-12} \text{ m}$$

The atomic radius of sodium is 158.5 pm.

**TOK**

The scale at which we can investigate the world depends on the wavelength of the radiation we use to gather information. How reliable is our knowledge of the microscopic world compared to what we know at the macroscopic level? Can we ever get a complete picture of the world if we only use a selection of the wavelengths available?

## Exercises

**37** The resistance of two metals at low temperature is shown on the graph below.

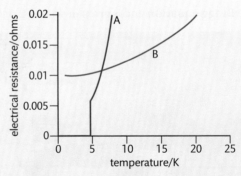

(a) Identify which of the graphs refers to a superconductor.
(b) Explain the different behaviour of the two materials with reference to their conduction mechanism.

**38** Explain why the temperature of a metal rises as an electric current is passed through it.

**39** Distinguish between Type 1 and Type 2 superconductors.

**40** The unit cell of a primitive cube is shown.

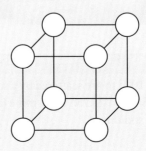

Calculate how many atoms there are in a unit cell of this structure.

**41** Potassium has a body-centred cubic close-packed structure. The atomic radius of potassium is 220 nm.

  **(a)** Calculate the length of a unit cell.
  **(b)** Determine the density of the metal.

**42** Gold has a face-centred cubic close-packed structure. The atomic radius of gold is 144 pm.

  **(a)** Calculate the length of a unit cell.
  **(b)** Determine the density of the metal.

**43** X-rays of wavelength $150 \times 10^{-12}$ m are scattered by a copper crystal lattice. A bright spot occurs at an angle of 17.9°. Determine the interatomic distance and the atomic radius of copper.

# A.9 Condensation polymers

## Understandings:

- Condensation polymers require two functional groups on each monomer.
- $NH_3$, HCl, and $H_2O$ are possible products of condensation reactions.
- Kevlar® is a polyamide with a strong and ordered structure. The hydrogen bonds between O and N can be broken with the use of concentrated sulfuric acid.

## Applications:

- Distinguish between addition and condensation polymers.
- Completion and descriptions of equations to show how condensation polymers are formed.
- Deduction of the structures of polyamides and polyesters from their respective monomers.
- Explanation of Kevlar's strength and its solubility in concentrated sulfuric acid.

  **Guidance**
  *Consider Green Chemistry polymers.*

## Condensation polymers can be formed from monomers with two functional groups

**Condensation** polymers can be formed when monomers, with *two functional groups*, undergo a condensation reaction with neighbouring monomers on both sides. A long chain is formed in the same way as a human chain can be formed when people link hands. Small molecules such as $H_2O$, $NH_3$, and HCl are released during the process.

## PET is a polyester

A **polyester** is formed when the acid monomer has two —COOH groups and the alcohol monomer has two —OH groups. The chain can extend in both directions, forming a polyester. When describing these reactions it is sometimes helpful to think about the functional groups sticking out in both directions as if from a box, with the box representing the rest of the molecule. For example:

$$\text{HOOC} \boxed{\quad} \text{COOH} + \text{HO} \boxed{\quad} \text{OH}$$

$$\downarrow$$

$$\text{HOOC} \boxed{\quad} \overset{\overset{\text{O}}{\|}}{\text{C}} - \text{O} \boxed{\quad} \text{OH} + H_2O$$

ester link

653

Focusing on the functional groups in this way enables us to deduce the repeating unit for any specified monomers.

Polyethylene terephthalate (PET) is formed when the two monomers ethane-1,2-diol and benzene-1,4-dicarboxylic acid (terephthalic acid) are heated to a temperature of 200 °C. The carboxylic acid and hydroxyl groups combine to form an ester in a condensation reaction:

$$HO-C(=O)-C_6H_4-C(=O)-OH + HO-CH_2-CH_2-OH \rightarrow H_2O + HO-C(=O)-C_6H_4-C(=O)-O-CH_2-CH_2-OH$$

As the ester produced has a —COOH group at one end and an —OH group at the other, it can react further and form a polymer chain with the release of one water molecule at each stage, as shown below.

$$HO-C(=O)-C_6H_4-C(=O)-O-CH_2-CH_2-OH + HO-C(=O)-C_6H_4-C(=O)-O-CH_2-CH_2-OH$$

$$\downarrow$$

$$\left(-O-CH_2-CH_2-O-C(=O)-C_6H_4-C(=O)-\right)_n + (2n-1)H_2O$$

The use of PET bottles instead of glass for containers of soft drinks increases the volume of drink transported by 60% as less packaging is needed.

A tube made of PET is about to be inserted within the weakened section of the blood vessel.

The resulting polymer is a polyester with many ester functional groups. Polyesters can be used as fibres to make clothing. They have high tensile strength due to their crystalline structure and the relatively strong intermolecular forces between the chains because of the polarity of the ester groups. Polyester fabrics were revolutionary when they first appeared in the 1950s because they do not crease.

As PET resembles glass in its crystalline clarity and its impermeability to gases, it is also used to make bottles for soft drinks. It has the additional advantages that is has low density, does not shatter when dropped, and is recyclable.

PET is unreactive and non-toxic, which makes it ideal as tubing used to repair damaged blood vessels in heart bypass operations. It is also used as a skin substitute for people who have suffered severe burns.

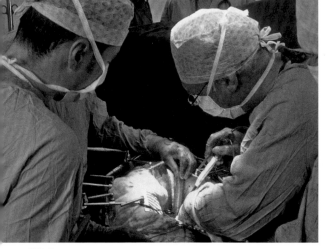

## Nylon is a polyamide

Most synthetic polyamides are formed when one monomer has two —COOH groups and the other monomer has two —NH$_2$ groups. Amide links form between the molecules and the chain can extend in both directions. We can describe these reactions in a similar way to the formation of polyesters, focusing on the functional groups as shown above.

$$\text{HOOC}—\blacksquare—\text{COOH} + \text{H}_2\text{N}—\blacksquare—\text{NH}_2$$

$$\downarrow$$

$$\text{HOOC}—\blacksquare—\overset{\displaystyle O}{\overset{\|}{C}}—\underset{\underset{H}{|}}{N}—\blacksquare—\text{NH}_2 + \text{H}_2\text{O}$$

amide link

The most common form of nylon is known as 6,6-nylon because both its monomers have six carbon atoms. They are 1,6-diaminohexane and hexanedioic acid:

$$\text{H}_2\text{N}—(\text{CH}_2)_6—\text{NH}_2 + \text{HOOC}—(\text{CH}_2)_4—\text{COOH}$$

$$\downarrow$$

$$\underset{\underset{H}{|}}{\overset{\overset{H}{|}}{N}}—(\text{CH}_2)_6—\underset{\underset{H}{|}}{N}—\overset{\overset{O}{\|}}{C}—(\text{CH}_2)_4—C\overset{O}{\underset{OH}{}} + \text{H}_2\text{O}$$

Thus, the repeating unit is:

$$\left(\underset{\underset{H}{|}}{N}—(\text{CH}_2)_6—\underset{\underset{H}{|}}{N}—\overset{\overset{O}{\|}}{C}—(\text{CH}_2)_4—\overset{\overset{O}{\|}}{C}\right)_n$$

The more reactive acid chloride, hexanedioyl chloride, is generally used instead of the di-acid. In this reaction, hydrogen chloride is the other condensation product.

$$\text{H}_2\text{N}—(\text{CH}_2)_6—\text{NH}_2 + \text{Cl}—\overset{\overset{O}{\|}}{C}—(\text{CH}_2)_4—\overset{\overset{O}{\|}}{C}—\text{Cl}$$

$$\downarrow$$

$$\left(\underset{\underset{H}{|}}{N}—(\text{CH}_2)_6—\underset{\underset{H}{|}}{N}—\overset{\overset{O}{\|}}{C}—(\text{CH}_2)_4—\overset{\overset{O}{\|}}{C}\right)_n + (2n-1)\text{HCl}$$

Nylon was discovered in 1935 by Wallace Carothers and his team working for the DuPont Company. He had earlier invented a synthetic rubber, neoprene, and was looking to make a synthetic fibre to replace silk. The supply of silk from Japan was vulnerable to the worsening trade relations with America. Commercial production of nylon began in 1939, just before the start of World War II but sadly, Carothers did not live to see the development of his invention. He took his own life by cyanide poisoning due to depression in 1937. Nylon was heralded as being 'as strong as steel, as fine as a spider's web'. One of the earliest major products was women's stockings – 64 million pairs were sold during the first year. Nylon was used in the war to make parachutes and tents as well as in surgical stitching. Seventy-five years later, nylon is still one of the most common polymers in use worldwide.

▲ Laboratory preparation of nylon. The polymer forms at the interface between the upper aqueous layer and the lower non-polar layer and can be wrapped around a glass rod and drawn out of the solution.

**Condensation polymers form between monomers which each have two functional groups to react. Addition polymers form between unsaturated monomers that break their double bond as they react.**

## Kevlar® is a polyamide

Kevlar® is a plastic that can stop a bullet. It is another condensation polymer and has a structure similar to nylon-6,6 with the carbon chain replaced by benzene rings, as shown below.

As the polymer consists of a long chain of benzene rings interconnected by hydrogen bonds it has a very regular structure. The chains line up parallel to one another allowing hydrogen bonds to form between the $NH_2$ groups from one chain and the $C=O$ groups from the next when they have the correct relative orientation (Figure 12.17).

## Phenol and methanal form a condensation polymer

A phenol–methanal polymer is made by adding acid or alkali to a mixture of the monomers. The phenol and methanal react together to form a condensation polymer. The reaction is more complex than the previous examples as the monomers do not have two functional groups at either ends. The initial reaction involves a substitution reaction in the 2 or 4 position of the benzene ring, as shown:

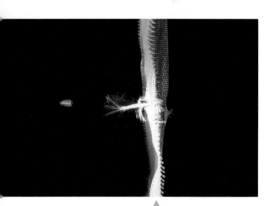

A 0.22 calibre bullet hitting Kevlar®. The bullet is travelling at 220 m s⁻¹.

The products now react with another benzene ring in a condensation reaction with the release of one molecule of water, as shown below:

As both benzene rings have reactive 2, 4 and 6 positions, a network structure can be built up through a series of similar reactions (Figure 12.33).

Bakelite has a hard rigid structure. It is a thermosetting plastic – it does not melt once it has been heated and set. It is a good electrical and thermal insulator and was previously used in a wide variety of applications such as telephone and radio casings before it was generally replaced by PVC. Phenol–methanal resins are still used in many machine and electrical components.

## Green Polymers

Green Chemistry aims to reduce the demand for resources and energy, decrease waste, and reduce environmental pollution.

Principles of green polymer production include:

- high resource effectiveness and high atom economy
- clean production processes, which prevent waste and reduce greenhouse gas emissions
- use of renewable resources and renewable energy
- low carbon footprint.

Although 'green polymers' are not exclusively biomaterials and many existing addition polymers and polymerization processes could be argued to meet the demands of Green Chemistry, many are biopolymers.

The crude oil that is the raw material for many addition polymers will run out, and the technology to produce plastics from crop plants is steadily improving. Carbohydrates, proteins, and polyesters are prominent condensation polymers that are chemically modified to meet the demands of polymer processing and applications. In 2011, the world's largest beverage company announced a plan to make PET bottles from only bio-based material.

### NATURE OF SCIENCE

An age is often defined by its key materials. We have had the Stone Age, Iron Age, and Bronze Age and perhaps today could be characterized as a time of plastics. The materials of the future will be based on future technological developments, but the need to manage our finite resources and reduce human impact on the environment are key factors in determining the direction of future research. These are political as well as scientific choices. Ideally we would like to use solar power to convert the greenhouse gases carbon dioxide and water into biomass by photosynthesis, which can then serve as a feedstock for biofuels and bioplastics. The reality is not that simple. Land is also needed for food production for example.

In the long term, the move to biomass as the raw material for plastics production is probably unavoidable. Oil reserves are finite. Any country can grow plants, while oil is distributed unevenly around the world. In the shorter term, the pace of the changeover will depend on the price of oil, and unpredictable political factors that affect oil production.

**TOK** Technology and new materials are developed to improve the quality of human life. How do we measure the quality of human life? What happens when technologies are developed which have an adverse effect on human life? Can the genie ever be put back in the bottle?

Biopolymer production. A microbiologist (left) and molecular biologist (right) monitoring bacterial growth and production of a biopolymer for use in plastics and other products. The bacteria are growing in a nutrient broth containing glycerol, a co-product of biodiesel production. A biopolymer is a polymer produced by a living organism.

### Worked example

Poly(ethylene furanoate) (PEF) is a green polymer made from bio-based monomers.

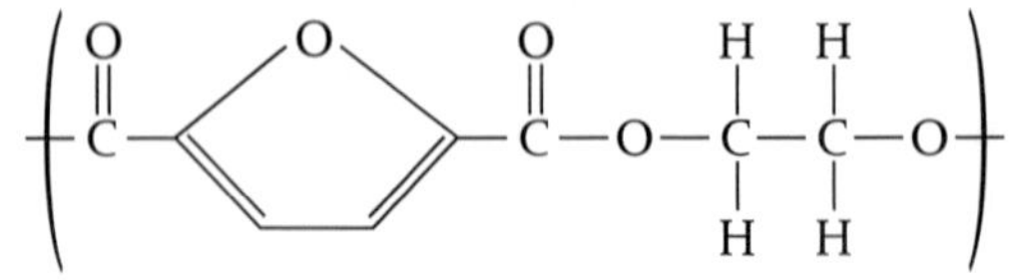

Deduce the structure of the two monomers from which it is made.

#### Solution

Find the ester link and break it to form an acid and an alcohol.

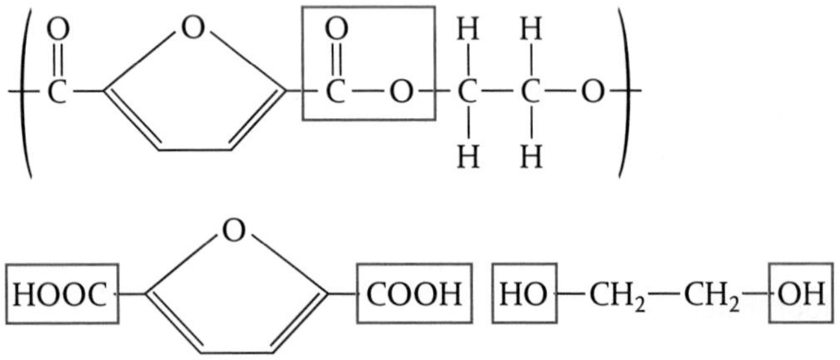

### Exercises

**44** Nylon-6,10 is made from the monomers 1,6-diaminohexane and decanedioic acid. Draw the repeating unit of this polymer.

**45** PLA has been called the first carbon neutral plastic. It has the structure below.

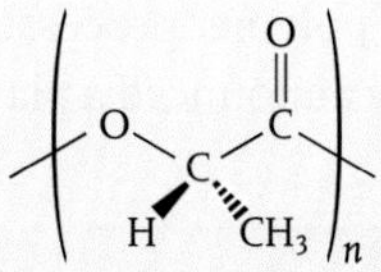

Deduce the structure of the monomer.

**46** Draw the structures of the polymers and any by-products formed from the following pairs of monomers.

(a) $HO-CH_2-CH_2-CH_2-OH + HO-CO-CH_2-CH_2-CO-OH$
(b) $H_2N-CH_2-(CH_2)_4-CH_2-NH_2 + Cl-CO-CH_2-CH_2-CO-Cl$

**47** This compound is a monomer for a condensation polymer.

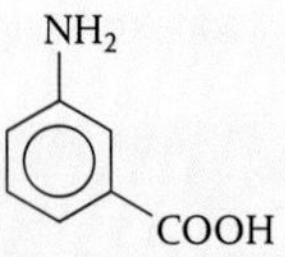

(a) Identify the functional groups in the monomer which allow it to act as a monomer.
(b) Deduce the by-product of the polymerization reaction.
(c) Deduce the structure of the resulting polymer. You should include at least three monomer units in your answer.
(d) Kevlar® is a polymer produced from monomers which have functional groups in the 1,4 positions of the benzene ring. Explain the strength of the polymer in terms of the orientation of the two functional groups.
(e) Explain why Kevlar® has a lower density than steel.

**48** The structures of three polymers are shown below. Deduce the structural formula of the monomers in each case.

**(a)**

$$-C-C-C-C-C-C-$$

with H, $CH_3$, H, $CH_3$, H, $CH_3$ on top and H, H, H, H, H, H on bottom.

**(b)**

$$-O-CH-C-O-CH-C-O-$$

with $CH_3$, O and $CH_3$, O substituents.

**(c)**

$$\left[\begin{array}{c} H \quad CH_3 \\ -C-C- \\ H \quad CO_2CH_3 \end{array}\right]_n$$

## Understandings:

- Toxic doses of transition metals can disturb the normal oxidation/reduction balance in cells through various mechanisms.
- Some methods of removing heavy metals are precipitation, adsorption, and chelation.
- Polydentate ligands form more stable complexes than similar monodentate ligands due to the chelate effect, which can be explained by considering entropy changes.

## Applications:

- Explanation of how chelating substances can be used to remove heavy metals.
- Deduction of the number of dative coordinate bonds a ligand can form with a central metal ion.
- Calculations involving $K_{sp}$ as an application of removing metals in solution.
- Compare and contrast the Fenton and Haber–Weiss reaction mechanisms.

### Guidance
- Ethane-1,2-diamine acts as a bidentate ligand and $EDTA^{4-}$ acts as hexadentate ligand.
- $K_{sp}$ values can be found in section 32 of the IB data booklet.
- The Haber–Weiss reaction generates free radicals naturally in biological processes. Transition metals can catalyse the reaction, with the iron catalysed (Fenton) reaction being the mechanism for generating reactive hydroxyl radicals.

## Heavy metals are toxic

Heavy metals are serious water pollutants because they are poisonous. Heavy metal ions have large densities and are thought to interfere with the normal functioning of key enzymes which normally bond to other necessary ions in the body such as $Ca^{2+}$, $Mg^{2+}$, or $Zn^{2+}$. Heavy metal ions disturb the normal oxidation/reduction balance in cells through various mechanisms. Even very small traces of heavy metals can have very significant harmful effects.

- Mercury ions have a particular attraction for sulfur atoms, and will bond to certain amino acids in enzymes and thus make them ineffective. The enzyme which acts as a sodium pump in the workings of the central nervous system is particularly sensitive to high mercury concentrations.

The phrase 'as mad as a hatter' originates from the fact that people who made hats were routinely exposed to high concentrations of mercury ions which were present in the salts used to treat felt.

- Lead is absorbed into the bloodstream where it deactivates the enzymes that make haemoglobin. This results in a build-up of aminolaevulinic acid (ALA) that causes the symptoms of lead poisoning.
- Cadmium mimics the action of zinc and replaces it in enzymes, which make them ineffective.

The sources of each of these pollutants and their possible health and environmental hazards are summarized in the following table.

| | Mercury | Lead | Cadmium |
|---|---|---|---|
| Source | • paints<br>• batteries<br>• agriculture | • lead pipes<br>• lead paint and glazes<br>• tetraethyl lead in petrol | • metal plating<br>• rechargeable batteries<br>• pigments<br>• by-product of zinc refining |
| Health hazard | • the most dangerous of the metal pollutants; causes serious damage to the nerves and the brain<br>• symptoms of mercury poisoning result from damage to the nervous system: depression, irritability, blindness and insanity<br>• Minamata disease | • burning pains in the mouth and digestive system followed by constipation or diarrhoea<br>• in severe cases there is a failure of the kidneys, liver, and heart which can lead to coma and death<br>• can cause brain damage, particularly in young children | • replaces zinc in enzymes making them ineffective<br>• itai-itai disease makes bones brittle and easily broken<br>• kidney and lung cancer in humans |
| Environmental hazard | • reproductive system failure in fish<br>• inhibits growth and kills fish<br>• biological magnification in the food chain | • toxic to plants and domestic animals<br>• biological magnification in the food chain | • toxic to fish<br>• produces birth defects in mice |

## CHALLENGE YOURSELF

**10** The names and structural formulas of the amino acids are given in section 33 of the IB data booklet. Identify the amino acid which is likely to bond to $Hg^{2+}$ ions.

## Ion exchange can be used to remove metal ions

Resins or zeolites can be used to exchange the metal ions in polluted water with hydrogen ions. 'Y' is used to show the resin or zeolite in the following equations:

$$H^+-Y-H^+(\text{ion exchange}) + M^{2+}(aq) \rightarrow Y-M^{2+}(\text{ion exchange}) + 2H^+(aq)$$

The $H^+$ ions can then combine with $OH^-$ ions released from the resin as it absorbs negative ions to form water:

$$H^+(aq) + OH^-(aq) \rightarrow H_2O(l)$$

## Metal ions can be removed by chemical precipitation

Heavy metal ions such as cadmium, lead, and mercury are easily removed by **precipitation** as sulfide salts, as their solubility in water is very low. Carefully controlled amounts of hydrogen sulfide gas are bubbled through a solution containing heavy metal ions, which are precipitated as sulfides and which can then be removed by filtration. For example, for cadmium ions:

$$Cd^{2+}(aq) + H_2S(g) \rightarrow CdS(s) + 2H^+(aq)$$

The excess hydrogen sulfide (being acidic) can then be easily removed.

The insoluble sulfides can also be formed when a soluble sulfide is added. For example, with lead ions:

$$Pb^{2+}(aq) + S^{2-}(aq) \rightarrow PbS(s)$$

Similarly, some metals can be removed as insoluble hydroxides on the addition of aqueous sodium hydroxide:

$$Cr^{3+}(aq) + 3OH^-(aq) \rightarrow Cr(OH)_3(s)$$

Some metals can be removed as insoluble phosphates:

$$Al^{3+}(aq) + PO_4^{3-}(aq) \rightarrow AlPO_4(s)$$

## Metal ions can be removed from solution by chelating agents

We saw in Chapter 3 (page 124) that transition metal ions can form complex ions with ligands. The ligand will donate a lone pair to form a dative covalent bond with a metal ion in a Lewis acid–base reaction (Figure 12.51).

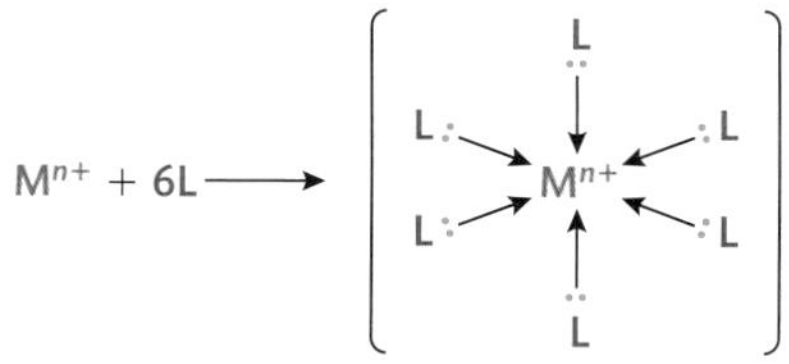

$$M^{n+} + 6L \longrightarrow$$

**Figure 12.51** $M^{n+}$ forms a complex ion with six monodentate (single-toothed) ligands.

EDTA$^{4-}$ (old name ethylenediaminetetraacetic acid) is a molecule which has six atoms (two nitrogen atoms and four oxygen atoms) with lone pairs available to form dative covalent bonds to a central transition ion (Figure 12.52).

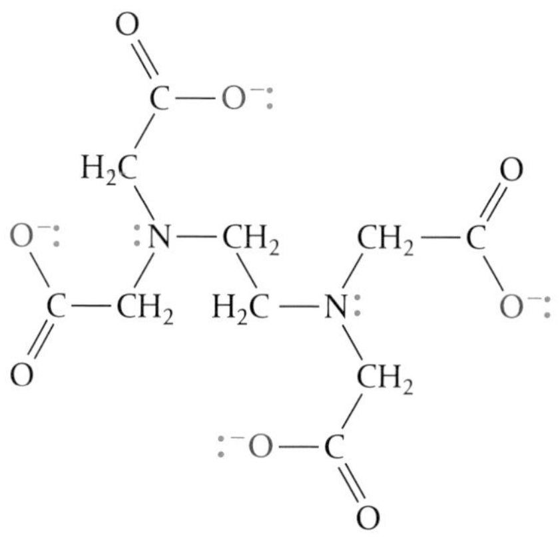

**Figure 12.52** The polydentate ligand EDTA$^{4-}$ can take the place of six monodentate ligands as it has six lone pairs available.

EDTA$^{4-}$ is thus equivalent to six monodentate ligands and is described as a **hexadentate** (six-toothed) ligand. It can occupy all the octahedral sites and grip the central ion in a six-pronged claw called a **chelate**.

A chelate is a complex containing at least one polydentate ligand. The name is derived from the Greek word for claw.

A molecular model of a molecule of EDTA$^{4-}$. The atoms of the molecule are colour-coded: carbon (black), nitrogen (blue), hydrogen (turquoise) and oxygen (red). As a chelating agent, EDTA$^{4-}$ can bind with positive metal ions (cations) using nitrogen and oxygen atoms to form up to six bonds.

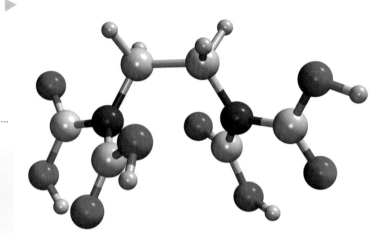

## CHALLENGE YOURSELF

**11** Assuming the transition metal ion, $M^{n+}$, is originally surrounded by water molecules, the ligand replacement reaction can be represented as:

$$[M(H_2O)_6]^{n+} + EDTA^{4-} \rightarrow [M(EDTA)]^{n-4} + 6H_2O$$

Predict the entropy change for this reaction and explain the stability of the chelate formed.

---

### Worked example

The structure of ethane-1,2-diamine is shown in section 16 of the IB data booklet. It is generally represented as en.

(a) Deduce the number of dative coordinate bonds the en ligand can form with a central metal ion.

(b) Deduce the coordination number and the oxidation state of the central metal ion in the complex $[Ni(en)_2Br_2]^+$

### Solution

(a) The ligand has two N atoms which can form dative coordinate bonds . It is a bidentate ligand.

(b) Each en ligand forms two bonds and each $Br^-$ ion forms one bond. The coordination number is 6.

There are two $Br^-$ ligands but en is neutral. Overall the complex has a 1+ charge. The charge on the central nickel ion is 3+. Check: $+3 + (2 \times -1) = +1$.

Oxidation no = +3.

## The solubility product is a measure of the solubility of an ionic compound

The above discussion is a simplification; no ionic substance is completely insoluble. A dynamic equilibrium is set up between insoluble solid and the aqueous ions. Consider, for example, mercury sulfide:

$$HgS(s) \rightleftharpoons Hg^{2+}(aq) + S^{2-}(aq)$$

The equilibrium constant for this reaction, $K_c$, can be deduced from the equilibrium law:

$$K_c = \frac{[Hg^{2+}(aq)] \, [S^{2-}(aq)]}{[HgS(s)]}$$

This differs from the examples discussed in Chapter 7 in that it is a *heterogeneous* equilibrium. As the molar concentration of a pure substance [HgS(s)] is constant, we can simplify this expression further to give a new equilibrium constant, known as the **solubility product, $K_{sp}$**:

$$K_{sp} = [Hg^{2+}(aq)]\,[S^{2-}(aq)]$$

As the $K_{sp}$ for a compound is an equilibrium constant, it changes only with temperature.

Solubility products give a measure of the solubility of an ionic compound.

The relationship between solubility as measured by the concentration of a saturated solution, and the solubility product is investigated in the following worked example.

$K_{sp}$ values are listed in section 32 of the IB data booklet.

## Worked example

State an expression for solubility product of $Cu(OH)_2$ and deduce an expression for $K_{sp}$ in terms of its solubility $s$.

### Solution

$$Cu(OH)_2(s) \rightleftharpoons Cu^{2+}(aq) + 2OH^-(aq)$$

If the solubility is $s$ then $[Cu^{2+}(aq)] = s$ and $[OH^-(aq)] = (2s)$

$$K_{sp} = [Cu^{2+}(aq)]\,[OH^-(aq)]^2$$
$$= s \times (2s)^2$$
$$= 4s^3$$

Solids with low solubility have small $K_{sp}$ values. The value of $K_{sp}$ can be used to predict the concentrations of solutions needed for chemical precipitation to occur. If the product of the ionic concentrations exceeds the solubility product, the solid will be precipitated.

## CHALLENGE YOURSELF

13 Use the equilibrium law discussed in Chapter 7 to deduce a more general expression for the solubility product, $K_{sp}$, of compound $M_pX_q(s)$ in terms of its solubility, $s$. Given the equilibrium formed by a metal M and a non metal X:
$$M_pX_q(s) \rightleftharpoons pM^{m+}(aq) + qX^{n-}(aq)$$

## Worked example

Zinc(II) ions ($Zn^{2+}$) can be removed by bubbling hydrogen sulfide through polluted water.

The solubility product of zinc sulfide is $1.60 \times 10^{-24}$ mol$^2$ dm$^{-6}$ at 25 °C.

(a) Calculate the concentration of $Zn^{2+}$ ions in a saturated solution of zinc sulfide.

(b) Suggest how the addition of hydrogen sulfide solution reduces the concentration of $Zn^{2+}$ ions in a saturated solution.

## CHALLENGE YOURSELF

12 Calculate the concentration of pure water and outline how the concentration of other pure substances can be calculated.

**Consider the equilibrium formed by a metal ion M⁺ and a non-metal X⁻:**

$$MX(s) \rightleftharpoons M^+(aq) + X^-(aq)$$

$K_{sp} = [M^+]\,[X^-]$ is called the solubility product constant. $K_{sp}$ depends only on temperature.

**Solution**

(a) In a saturated solution: $ZnS(s) \rightleftharpoons Zn^{2+}(aq) + S^{2-}(aq)$

$$K_{sp} = [Zn^{2+}(aq)] \, [S^{2-}(aq)] = 1.60 \times 10^{-24}$$

When no other ions are present: $[Zn^{2+}(aq)] = [S^{2-}(aq)]$

$$1.60 \times 10^{-24} = [Zn^{2+}(aq)]^2$$

$$[Zn^{2+}] = \sqrt{1.60 \times 10^{-24}}$$

$$= 1.26 \times 10^{-12} \text{ mol dm}^{-3}$$

(b) As the product of the ion concentrations is constant, an increase in $[S^{2-}]$ will lead to a decrease in $[Zn^{2+}]$ and the zinc will be precipitated out of solution.

## The common ion effect

In the worked example above, we saw that an increase in the concentration of sulfide ions led to a decrease in the solubility of the zinc ions in solutions. This is a general result known as the **common ion effect**.

Consider, for example, the solubility of calcium phosphate:

$$Ca_3(PO_4)_2(s) \rightleftharpoons 3Ca^{2+}(aq) + 2PO_4^{3-}(aq)$$

An increase in the concentration of either phosphate ions or calcium ions, that is ions *common* to the compound and the added solution, will – according to Le Chatelier's Principle – shift the equilibrium to the left and decrease the solubility of the compound.

## Harmful hydroxyl free radicals can be formed in the body from hydrogen peroxide

The way in which toxic doses of transition metals disturb the normal oxidation/reduction balance in cells is illustrated by the Fenton and Haber–Weiss reactions, which both involve the production of hydroxyl free radicals from the hydrogen peroxide produced enzymatically in the body. The mechanisms by which metals exert their toxicity in living organisms are complex but can be related to the formation of the hydroxyl free radical and other reactive oxygen species which have the potential to induce damage in biological systems. The hydroxyl radical is one of the most reactive oxidants that can be formed in a biological system.

Iron(II) and other transition metal ions such as cobalt and copper, for example, react with hydrogen peroxide and produce hydroxyl free radicals in a **Fenton reaction**:

$$Fe^{2+} + H_2O_2 \rightarrow Fe^{3+} + {}^{\bullet}OH + OH^-$$

The optimal pH for the reaction occurs between 3 and 6. If the pH is too high the iron(III) ions react with hydroxide ions to form a precipitate of iron(III) hydroxide and the hydrogen peroxide decomposes to give oxygen.

## The Haber–Weiss reaction generates free radicals naturally in biological processes

The Haber–Weiss reaction is another reaction route which explains how the highly reactive and toxic hydroxyl radical (HO•) can be generated from hydrogen peroxide, this time by its reaction with the superoxide ion ($O_2^-\bullet$), which is a normal cellular metabolite.

$$O_2^-\bullet + H_2O_2 \rightarrow O_2 + OH^- + OH\bullet$$

The reaction is very slow under normal conditions but can be catalysed by transition metal ions in what can be described as a superoxide-driven Fenton reaction.

Fe(III) ions are first reduced by superoxide ions to iron(II) ions:

$$O_2^-\bullet + Fe^{3+} \rightarrow O_2 + Fe^{2+}$$

The hydrogen peroxide is then oxidized by iron(II) in a Fenton reaction:

$$H_2O_2 + Fe^{2+} \rightarrow Fe^{3+} + OH^- + OH\bullet$$

## NATURE OF SCIENCE

The Fenton reaction generally occurs in chemical and biological systems as well as in the natural environment. Its importance has been long recognized, among other places, in food chemistry, in material ageing, and in environmental science. It is, however, the case that the simple reaction (of $Fe^{2+}$ ions with $H_2O_2$), observed by Fenton over a century ago, continues to be the subject of controversy. It is perhaps paradoxical that a reaction that is successfully applied in environment protection is thought to be a factor in the ageing process and the development of a variety of diseases, but chemistry is guided by thermodynamics not a moral compass. Our knowledge of the Fenton reaction is based on indirect evidence which is still developing as our technology develops.

 **TOK** Will we ever directly observe a reaction mechanism? What evidence would confirm to you that a reaction mechanism is correct? Which ways of knowing are you using here?

## Exercises

**49** Describe briefly how heavy metal ions function as poisons.

**50** The structure of the oxalate ion, $C_2O_4^{2-}$, is shown in section 16 of the IB data booklet. It is generally represented as ox.

    **(a)** Deduce the number of dative coordinate bonds the ligand can form with a central metal ion.

    **(b)** Deduce the coordination number and the oxidation state of the central metal ion in the complex $[Fe(ox)_3]^{3-}$.

**51** The solubility product of nickel sulfide is $2.0 \times 10^{-26}$ mol$^2$ dm$^{-6}$. Calculate the solubility of nickel sulfide.

**52** Deduce an expression for the solubility product of the following compounds:

    **(a)** PbS         **(b)** $Cu_2S$         **(c)** $AlPO_4$         **(d)** $Ni(OH)_2$

**53** Silver ions ($Ag^+$) can be removed by mixing sodium chloride solution with polluted water. The solubility product of silver chloride is $1.6 \times 10^{-10}$ mol$^2$ dm$^{-6}$ at 25 °C.

    **(a)** Calculate the concentration of $Ag^+$ ions in a saturated solution of silver chloride.

    **(b)** Calculate the concentration of the $Ag^+$ ion in a 0.100 mol dm$^{-3}$ solution of sodium chloride.

**54** Deduce an expression relating the solubility product constant $K_{sp}$ to the solubility $s$ for the following ionic compounds:

    **(a)** AgBr         **(b)** $Ni(OH)_2$         **(c)** $Hg_2S$

    **(d)** $Ca_3(PO_4)_2$         **(e)** $Cr(OH)_3$

**55** Lead(II) ions ($Pb^{2+}$) can be removed from polluted water by adding sodium sulfide and water. The solubility product of lead sulfide is $1.30 \times 10^{-28}$ at 25 °C.

    **(a)** Deduce an expression for the solubility product of lead(II) sulfide.

    **(b)** Calculate the concentration of $Pb^{2+}$ ions in a saturated solution of lead sulfide.

    **(c)** Suggest how the addition of sodium sulfide solution reduces the concentration of $Pb^{2+}$ ions in a saturated solution.

**56** When excess iron(II) is mixed with hydrogen peroxide, quantitative oxidation of $Fe^{2+}$ ions by $H_2O_2$ occurs. Explain this result with reference to the Fenton reaction.

**57** **(a)** State the equations for the two steps of the Haber–Weiss reaction when it is catalysed by $Fe^{3+}$ ions.

    **(b)** Identify the step which is a Fenton reaction.

    **(c)** Identify the oxidation state of oxygen in the superoxide ion and deduce the number of electrons transferred when the superoxide ion is oxidized in the Haber–Weiss reaction.

## Practice questions

1 Aluminium and its alloys are widely used in industry.

(a) Aluminium metal is obtained by the electrolysis of alumina dissolved in molten cryolite.
 (i) Explain the function of the molten cryolite. (1)
 (ii) State the half-equations for the reactions that take place at each electrode. (2)
(b) Outline two different ways that carbon dioxide may be produced during the production of aluminium. (2)

*(Total 5 marks)*

2 (a) Explain why iron is obtained from its ores using chemical reducing agents but aluminium is obtained from its ores using electrolysis. (2)
(b) Both carbon monoxide and hydrogen can be used to reduce iron ores. State the equations for the reduction of magnetite, $Fe_3O_4$, with
 (i) carbon monoxide (1)
 (ii) hydrogen. (1)

*(Total 4 marks)*

3 Alloys are important substances in industries that use metals.

(a) Describe an alloy. (1)
(b) Explain how alloying can modify the structure and properties of metals. (2)

*(Total 3 marks)*

4 Compare the modes of action of homogeneous and heterogeneous catalysts. State **one** example of each type of catalysis using a chemical equation **and** include state symbols.

*(Total 4 marks)*

5 (a) Name a thermotropic liquid crystal. (1)
(b) Explain the liquid crystal behaviour of the thermotropic liquid crystal named in part (a), on the molecular level. (4)

*(Total 5 marks)*

6 Poly(vinyl chloride) (PVC) and poly(ethene) are both polymers made from crude oil.

(a) Explain why PVC is less flexible than poly(ethene). (2)
(b) State how PVC can be made more flexible during its manufacture and explain the increase in flexibility on a molecular level. (2)
(c) PVC can exist in isotactic and atactic forms. Draw the structure of the isotactic form showing a chain of at least six carbon atoms. (1)

*(Total 5 marks)*

7 Landfill sites are used to dispose of about 90% of the world's domestic waste, but incineration is being increasingly used in some countries.

(a) State one advantage of each method. (2)
(b) Suggest why some biodegradable plastics do not decompose in landfill sites. (1)

*(Total 3 marks)*

8 (a) State the materials used for the positive and negative electrodes in the production of aluminium by electrolysis. (2)
(b) Aluminium is one of the most abundant elements found on Earth. Discuss why it is important to recycle aluminium. (2)

*(Total 4 marks)*

**9** Nano-sized 'test-tubes' with one open end, can be formed from carbon structures.

(a) Describe these 'test-tubes' with reference to the structures of carbon allotropes. (2)

(b) These tubes are believed to be stronger than steel. Explain the strength of these 'test-tubes' on a molecular level. (1)

(c) Carbon nanotubes can be used as catalysts.

　(i)　Suggest two reasons why they are effective heterogeneous catalysts. (2)

　(ii)　State **one** potential concern associated with the use of carbon nanotubes. (1)

*(Total 6 marks)*

**10** The structure of 4-pentyl-4-cyanobiphenyl, a commercially available nematic crystalline material used in electrical display devices, is shown below.

$$C_5H_{11} - \bigcirc - \bigcirc - CN$$

(a) Explain how the three different parts of the molecule contribute to the properties of the compound used in electrical display devices.

　(i)　CN

　(ii)　$C_5H_{11}$

　(iii)　$\bigcirc\!-\!\bigcirc$ (3)

(b) Describe and explain in molecular terms the workings of a twisted nematic liquid crystal. (4)

*(Total 7 marks)*

**11** Liquid crystal displays are used in digital watches, calculators, and laptops.
Describe the liquid crystal state, in terms of molecular arrangement, and explain what happens as temperature increases.

*(Total 3 marks)*

**12** Several monomers are produced by the oil industry and used in polymer manufacture. Examples include propene, styrene, and vinyl chloride.

(a) (i)　Draw the structural formula of propene. (1)

　(ii)　Isotactic poly(propene) has a regular structure, while atactic poly(propene) does not. Draw the structure of isotactic poly(propene), showing a chain of at least six carbon atoms. State and explain how its properties differ from those of atactic poly(propene). (3)

(b) Styrene can be polymerized to polystyrene, which is a colourless, transparent, brittle plastic. Another form of the polymer is expanded polystyrene. Outline how expanded polystyrene is produced from polystyrene, and state how its properties differ from those of polystyrene. (4)

(c) Many plastic materials are disposed of by combustion. State two disadvantages of disposing of poly(vinyl chloride) in this way. (2)

*(Total 10 marks)*

**13** Poly(ethene) is the most commonly used synthetic polymer. It is produced in low-density and high-density forms. Identify which form has the higher melting point. Explain by reference to its structure and bonding.

*(Total 4 marks)*

**14 (a)** The properties of poly(vinyl chloride), PVC, may be modified to suit a particular use. State the main method of modifying PVC and the effect this has on its properties. (2)

**(b)** Outline two disadvantages of using polymers such as poly(propene) and PVC, and give one disadvantage that is specific to PVC. (3)

*(Total 5 marks)*

**15** The diagram below represents a section of a polymer.

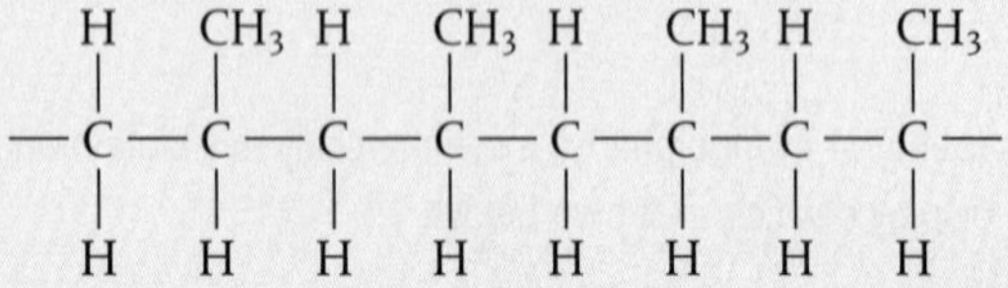

**(a)** Draw the structure of the monomer from which this polymer is manufactured. (1)

**(b)** Polymers A and B both have the structure shown above, but the average chain length is much greater in A than in B. Suggest two physical properties that would be different for A and B. (2)

**(c)** Polymers A and B both have isotactic structures. Polymer C is manufactured from the same monomer but is not isotactic. State the name used to describe this different structure and outline how the structure differs. (2)

*(Total 5 marks)*

**16** Identify **two** raw materials mixed with the iron ore in a blast furnace. In each case, outline its purpose and write an equation to show what happens to it in the blast furnace.

*(Total 5 marks)*

**17** Polymers have replaced more traditional materials such as metal and wood. Suggest **one** polymer property, different in each case, that makes polymers more suitable than traditional materials.

*(Total 2 marks)*

**18** Kevlar is a condensation polymer that is often used in liquid crystal displays. A section of the polymer is shown below.

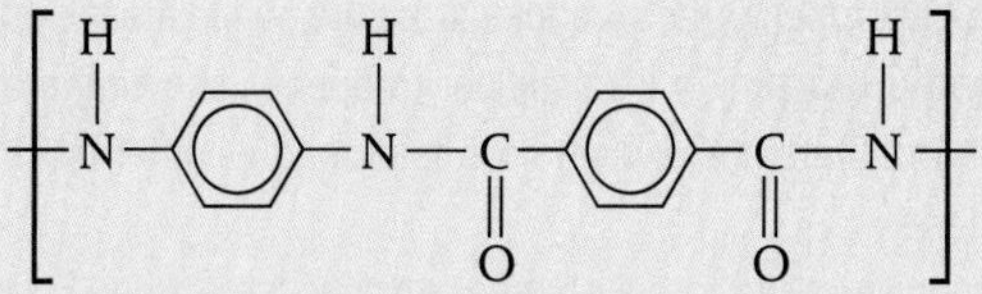

**(a)** Describe the liquid crystal properties of Kevlar. (3)

**(b)** Explain the strength of Kevlar in terms of its structure and bonding. (2)

**(c)** Explain why a bullet-proof vest made of Kevlar should be stored away from acids. (2)

*(Total 7 marks)*

**19** Industrial effluent is found to be highly contaminated with silver and lead ions. A sample of water contains $8.0 \times 10^{-3}$ mol dm$^{-3}$ Ag$^+$ and $1.9 \times 10^{-2}$ mol dm$^{-3}$ Pb$^{2+}$. On the addition of chloride ions both AgCl ($K_{sp} = 1.8 \times 10^{-10}$) and PbCl$_2$ ($K_{sp} = 1.7 \times 10^{-5}$) precipitate from the solution. Determine the concentration of Cl$^-$ needed to initiate the precipitation of each salt and deduce which salt precipitates first.

*(Total 5 marks)*

**20 (a)** Heavy metal ions can be removed from waste water by adding hydroxide ions. When hydroxide ions are added to a solution containing nickel ions, a precipitate of nickel(II) hydroxide, $Ni(OH)_2$, is formed. The solubility product of nickel(II) hydroxide is $6.50 \times 10^{-18}$ at 298 K. Determine the mass of nickel ions that remains in one litre (1.00 dm³) of water at 298 K with a pH of 7 after the precipitation reaction has occurred. (4)

**(b)** Suggest, with an explanation, a chemical method by which this amount of nickel dissolved in the water could be reduced even further. (2)

*(Total 6 marks)*

To access weblinks on the topics covered in this chapter, please go to www. pearsonhotlinks.com and enter the ISBN or title of this book.

**13**

Option B: Biochemistry

# Essential ideas

**B.1** Metabolic reactions involve a complex interplay between many different components in highly controlled environments.

**B.2 and B.7** Proteins are the most diverse of the biopolymers responsible for metabolism and structural integrity of living organisms. Analyses of protein activity and concentration are key areas of biochemical research.

**B.3** Lipids are a broad group of biomolecules that are largely non-polar and are therefore insoluble in water.

**B.4** Carbohydrates are oxygen-rich biomolecules that play a central role in metabolic reactions of energy transfer.

**B.5** Vitamins are organic micronutrients with diverse functions and which must be obtained from the diet.

**B.8** DNA is the genetic material that expresses itself by controlling the synthesis of proteins by the cell.

**B.9** Biological pigments include a variety of chemical structures with diverse functions and which absorb specific wavelengths of light.

**B.10** Most biochemical processes are stereospecific and involve only molecules with a certain configuration of chiral carbon atoms.

**B.6** Our increasing knowledge of biochemistry has led to several environmental problems, while also helping to solve others.

Calcium carbonate ($CaCO_3$) plates on the surface of a marine organism, shown in blue in this coloured scanning electron micrograph (SEM). These plates are shed and sink to the ocean floor, forming an important part of deep-sea sediments and rocks such as chalk and limestone. Metabolic processes, controlled by enzymes, synthesize the structural components of organisms, which are later returned to the environment.

Living things show unique properties. They extract and transform energy from their environment to build complex structures, and have the ability to self-regulate and self-replicate. Yet all living organisms are made of molecules that individually are no different from any other molecules found in non-living matter. Somehow the interactions between component molecules in living things must explain the complex processes that we associate with life. Biochemistry is the subject that seeks to find such molecular level explanations for biological phenomena.

Although biochemistry is a relatively young discipline, it is a rapidly advancing area of knowledge, and applications of research are found in the fields of health, diet, and medicine as well as in new technologies. In recent years many of the Nobel Prizes in chemistry – generally considered to be the most prestigious recognition of leading research in chemistry – have been given to scientists working in this field. Prizes have been awarded for major advances made in our understanding of proteins, of chemical interactions at receptors, and of the detailed action of DNA.

Biochemical molecules are an excellent example of the relationship between molecular structure and function, a theme that will be carried through this chapter. As biomolecules are all organic in nature, it is recommended that you are first familiar with the work in Chapter 10, Organic Chemistry. After studying the features of the major groups of biomolecules, this chapter ends with a consideration of some of the impacts and possible solutions to environmental problems related to biochemistry.

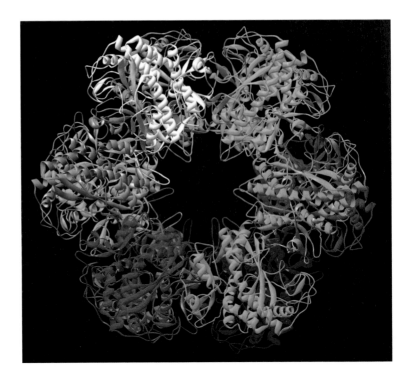

Computer model of the enzyme glutamine synthetase. Enzymes are proteins that catalyse all biochemical reactions. Their activity depends on their specific three-dimensional structure, which is determined by their chemical composition. In turn this is controlled by the exact molecular sequence in the nucleic acid DNA. Glutamine synthetase is a complex protein, having a quaternary structure made of six different polypeptide subunits – shown in different colours here. It catalyses the reaction for the synthesis of the amino acid glutamine.

## B.1  Introduction to biochemistry

### Understandings:
- The diverse functions of biological molecules depend on their structures and shapes.
- Metabolic reactions take place in highly controlled aqueous environments.
- Reactions of breakdown are called catabolism and reactions of synthesis are called anabolism.
- Biopolymers form by condensation reactions and are broken down by hydrolysis reactions.
- Photosynthesis is the synthesis of energy-rich molecules from carbon dioxide and water using light energy.
- Respiration is a complex set of metabolic processes providing energy for cells.

  **Guidance**
  *Intermediates of aerobic respiration and photosynthesis are not required.*

### Applications:
- Explanation of the difference between condensation and hydrolysis reactions.
- The use of summary equations of photosynthesis and respiration to explain the potential balancing of oxygen and carbon dioxide in the atmosphere.

### Biochemical reactions are organized in metabolic pathways

The scientific study of the origin of life has been described as one of the last frontiers of the life sciences, as so many questions remain unanswered. There is though general agreement that life began in an aqueous environment, and that a key event was the development of a membrane that enclosed and defined a volume of space, known as a **cell**. Within this membrane-bound environment, sequestered from the outside, specific conditions such as temperature, pH, and chemical concentrations can be generated and controlled. Cells are the basic unit of structure and function in all living things. Complex organisms contain vast numbers of cells, which together carry out all the life processes.

At any one time within the microscopic volume of a living cell, thousands of chemical reactions occur (Figure 13.1). The sum of all these reactions taking place in an organism is known as **metabolism**. This complex chemistry is dependent on a high level of order where every compound has a distinct function. Some features of metabolism are:

• Reactions are controlled in sequences and cycles known as **metabolic pathways**. The product of each step is the reactant for the next. Compounds taking part in metabolism are known as **metabolites**.

• Every reaction is controlled by a specific catalyst called an **enzyme**.

• Similar pathways and enzymes exist in a wide range of different organisms.

• Reactions can be coupled so that energy from one reaction is used to drive another.

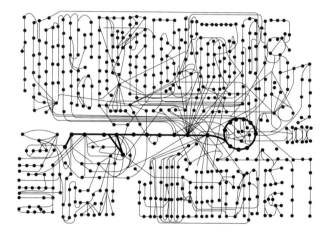

Given the complexity of metabolism, it is useful to classify pathways according to their broad purpose. Later in this chapter, specific examples of metabolic processes will be discussed in more detail.

## Anabolism: pathways of synthesis

The part of metabolism concerned with building up or synthesis is known as **anabolism**. The reactants are small molecules called **precursors**, and the products are larger, more complex molecules of higher energy. Anabolic pathways therefore require energy. Examples include the synthesis of proteins from amino acids, nucleic acids from nucleotides, and carbohydrates from the process of photosynthesis.

## Catabolism: pathways of breakdown

Metabolic reactions of breakdown or degradation are known as **catabolism**. Catabolic reactions release energy and produce energy-poor end-products, such as carbon dioxide and water. Examples include the breakdown of glucose in respiration or the oxidation of fatty acids.

The energy from catabolic reactions is used to drive anabolic reactions. This is known as **energy coupling** and involves an intermediary energy carrier called adenosine triphosphate, which is known as **ATP**.

The term **emergent properties** is used in biology to describe the properties that result from interactions between components in cells and between cells in multicellular organisms. It is a manifestation of 'the whole is greater than the sum of the parts'.

Metabolism is the sum of the chemical reactions occurring in a living organism.

Figure 13.1 A simplified diagram of some metabolic pathways. Each dot represents a metabolite and every line represents a chemical reaction. Pathways, cycles, end-products, and coupled reactions can be identified.

Metabolism is dependent on a regular supply of diverse nutrients in the diet. Many differences in human health across the world are the result of differences in the supply of nutritious food.

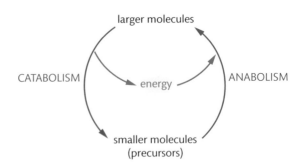

**Figure 13.2** The relationship between anabolic and catabolic pathways of metabolism.

Anabolism refers to metabolic pathways of synthesis; catabolism refers to metabolic pathways of breakdown.

Anabolic and catabolic processes take place simultaneously in a cell, but they are separately controlled. This is possible because the metabolic pathway for the biosynthesis of a molecule is usually different from the pathway for its breakdown, and involves different enzymes. Otherwise, metabolism would involve so-called **futile cycles** where stable complex structures would not exist in cells, but would be broken down as they form.

**NATURE OF SCIENCE**

The complexity of the chemical environment in biochemical systems makes it necessary to use advanced techniques for the isolation of different compounds. Elucidation of metabolic pathways has often been the result of analyses carried out *in vitro*, that is where components are isolated from their usual biological environment. As much as possible, biochemists need to check that data obtained in this indirect way are fully transferable to *in vivo* conditions, that is those within living cells. Similar considerations arise when data obtained from within one living system are used as a basis of knowledge for a different living system, such as carrying out drug trials on animals.

## Biomolecules are diverse organic molecules

Of the approximately 100 elements found on Earth, only 27 have been found to be essential components of living things, and the majority of these are present in very small amounts – known as **trace elements**. The molecules found in cells are mostly organic compounds containing about 96% by mass hydrogen, oxygen, carbon, and nitrogen. Sulfur, phosphorus, calcium, and iron are also present in significant amounts.

**Biomolecules**, the molecules present in living things, represent an immense diversity of structures. Many of them, such as proteins, nucleic acids, and polysaccharides, are **macromolecules**, having relative molecular masses of several thousand. Despite their size and complexity, macromolecules can be described relatively easily in terms of the small units from which they are made, commonly referred to as building blocks, which are linked together by covalent bonds. Most macromolecules are polymers and so the building blocks are monomers – molecules such as glucose and amino acids. Many of these monomers have functions in their own right, for example as energy carriers or molecular messengers. The reactions of build-up and breakdown of all these molecules follow a similar pattern, described below.

## Condensation and hydrolysis reactions

Biopolymers are **condensation polymers**, because their synthesis involves the loss of a molecule of water for each covalent bond that forms between two monomers. An example of this, esterification, was described in Chapter 10. But in order to form a polymer, the monomers must each have *two functional groups*, which can be considered as two active ends of the molecule, so they can link together in a similar way to people forming a chain by linking hands on both sides. The reaction is catalysed by enzymes, which are often known as **polymerases**.

Note that condensation polymerization differs from addition polymerization, also described in Chapter 10. Addition reactions lead to only one product, with no elimination of a small molecule.

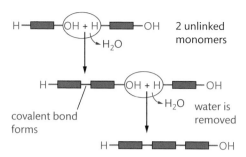

The breakdown of these molecules reverses the above reaction, adding a molecule of water for each covalent bond broken. The water is split with –H and –OH attaching separately to the product molecules. These are **hydrolysis** reactions and occur during chemical **digestion**. They are catalysed by enzymes, and can also be favoured by heat and acidic or alkaline conditions.

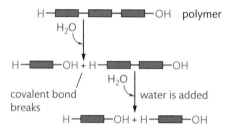

Examples of condensation and hydrolysis reactions include the synthesis and breakdown of proteins from amino acids and polysaccharides from sugars. Lipids, although they do not form polymers, also involve condensation and hydrolysis reactions between their sub-units. These are all discussed in more detail later in this chapter. These reactions are summarized below.

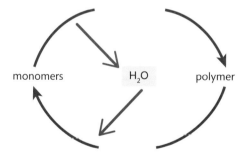

**Figure 13.3** Condensation reactions involve loss of a molecule of water for every covalent bond formed.

**Figure 13.4** Hydrolysis reactions involve addition of a molecule of water for every covalent bond broken.

## The activity of biological molecules is dependent on their structures and shapes

A recurring theme in biochemistry is the relationship between molecular structure and function. In other words, molecules seem to be 'chosen' for particular tasks in cells on the basis of their chemical nature and often their three-dimensional shape. Structural molecules like collagen and cellulose are tough and insoluble, whereas a chemical messenger such as the hormone insulin must interact specifically with receptor molecules. The catalytic action of enzymes depends entirely on their ability to form a temporary binding to their substrate, while nucleic acids are able to store and transmit genetic information using chemical sequences.

**NATURE OF SCIENCE**

As more and more data have been obtained on biochemical pathways, similar reaction patterns are seen in metabolic processes in species that may not be closely related. For this reason biochemistry is now a major part of the study of evolutionary biology. This is an example of how an interdisciplinary approach can contribute to deeper knowledge and understanding.

## Living cells transform energy

Living things absorb energy from their environment and use it to synthesize their own complex structures from simple starting molecules, and to carry out functions such as movement and reproduction. As energy is used in life processes, most of it is returned to the environment as heat.

### Photosynthesis converts light energy into chemical energy

The primary source of energy for life is the Sun. Green plants (and some other organisms) are able to capture solar energy and use it to synthesize energy-rich biomolecules. This process is known as **photosynthesis**, and all organisms, directly or indirectly, depend on it for their supply of food. Simply put, without photosynthesis there would be no life on Earth.

The key to photosynthesis is the absorption of light by **photosynthetic pigment** molecules. The primary pigment is **chlorophyll**, whose structure is described on page 740. The light energy trapped drives a series of redox reactions, in which – remarkably – water is split into hydrogen and oxygen. The oxygen is released as a waste product and the hydrogen ultimately reduces carbon dioxide to simple sugar molecules. This summary does not attempt to do justice to the complexity of the process, which involves many intermediates, electron carriers, and enzymes. But, in essence, photosynthesis transforms the energy-poor molecules carbon dioxide and water into energy-rich sugar with the release of oxygen. The overall reaction of photosynthesis can be summarized as follows.

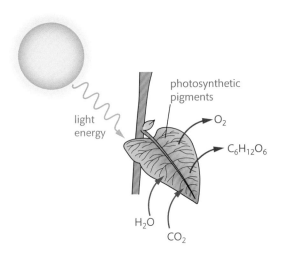

$$6CO_2 + 6H_2O \;\rightarrow\; \rightarrow \;\rightarrow\; C_6H_{12}O_6 + 6O_2$$

(The multiple arrows indicate that this is only a summary of the process, not a representation of a single reaction.)

### Respiration makes energy available for life processes

Living things obtain energy-rich molecules such as glucose either through their own process of photosynthesis, or by the intake of energy-rich molecules in food. Broadly speaking, green plants do the former and animals the latter. The release of this energy in a controlled way inside cells is known as **respiration**. It is essential to life, taking place in every living cell continuously.

Respiration is often likened to burning a fuel in oxygen, though in reality it is a much more complex and highly controlled process. But, like burning, it does involve reactions of oxidation where the amount of energy released depends on the extent of oxidation achieved. The details of respiration are complex, involving up to 50

Photosynthesis is the synthesis of energy-rich molecules from carbon dioxide and water using light energy.

**Figure 13.5** Summary of the reactants and products of photosynthesis.

Note that *respiration*, which is a biochemical process, is completely different from *breathing*, which is a physical process used to bring about gas exchange. Confusion between the two is generated by many sources, including the fact that the word for breathing is related to 'respire' in several languages, including French, Italian, and Spanish.

different chemical reactions, each controlled by a specific enzyme. Although different metabolites can be used as respiratory substrates, they are usually first converted into glucose, $C_6H_{12}O_6$.

The first stage of respiration, known as **glycolysis**, is common to all cells and does not use oxygen. Only a small proportion of the energy in glucose is released, as most is trapped in the products of this stage. In the absence of oxygen, known as **anaerobic conditions**, this is the only energy released, and it is enough to keep some cells alive, temporarily in the case of muscle cells and permanently in the case of some bacteria. Products of anaerobic respiration such as lactate and ethanol are therefore energy-rich molecules (as we know from the burning of ethanol described on page 491). In some ways this is like the incomplete combustion of fuels discussed in Chapter 10.

In the presence of oxygen, known as **aerobic conditions**, the oxidation of glucose is complete, and much more energy is released. This is why most cells are dependent on a continuous supply of oxygen. The end products of aerobic respiration are the energy-poor molecules carbon dioxide and water.

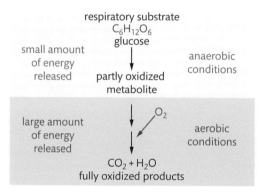

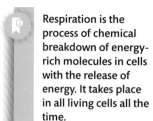
**Respiration is the process of chemical breakdown of energy-rich molecules in cells with the release of energy. It takes place in all living cells all the time.**

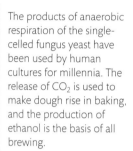
The products of anaerobic respiration of the single-celled fungus yeast have been used by human cultures for millennia. The release of $CO_2$ is used to make dough rise in baking, and the production of ethanol is the basis of all brewing.

**Figure 13.6** Summary of aerobic and anaerobic respiration.

Aerobic respiration involves a series of coupled redox reactions, where reactants known as **cytochromes** are successively reduced and then re-oxidized. Ultimately, oxygen acts as the **terminal electron acceptor** when it is reduced to water. The structures of cytochromes are described on page 744.

The overall equation for the aerobic respiration of glucose can be represented as follows:

$$C_6H_{12}O_6 + 6O_2 \;\rightarrow\;\rightarrow\;\rightarrow\; 6CO_2 + 6H_2O$$

Multiple arrows are again used to show that this is a multi-step reaction, and the representation is a summary only. Note that the reactants and products are the same as for the combustion of glucose.

Respiration releases heat. Here water vapour is rising from decaying organic matter on an active compost heap. Microorganisms living in the compost are releasing significant heat as a result of their high rate of respiration.

**Aerobic respiration uses $O_2$ and completely oxidizes glucose to $CO_2$ and $H_2O$. It releases much more energy than anaerobic respiration, which occurs in the absence of oxygen.**

## CHALLENGE YOURSELF

**2** Compare the oxidation states of carbon in $C_6H_{12}O_6$ and in $CO_2$ to examine the redox processes involved.

## Summary of photosynthesis and respiration

Photosynthesis and respiration are metabolic redox processes. Photosynthesis is an anabolic, energy-storing process which reduces carbon dioxide to sugar. Respiration is a catabolic, energy-yielding process which oxidizes sugar to carbon dioxide.

The overall chemical changes in photosynthesis and respiration are the reverse of each other – but in no way do these processes involve a reversal of their chemical steps. Yet together they provide a balance of chemicals, as the waste products of respiration are the raw materials for photosynthesis.

**Figure 13.7** Chemical cycling and energy flow through photosynthesis and respiration.

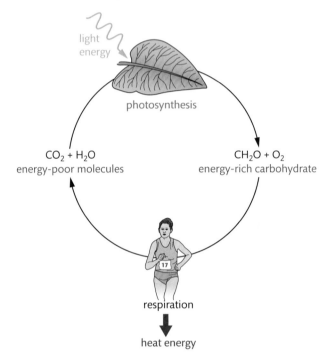

Photosynthesis acts as a **carbon sink**, as it removes carbon dioxide from the atmosphere, while respiration and combustion, which release carbon dioxide, are **carbon sources**. Human activities such as deforestation have decreased the carbon sink, and increased the carbon source by burning fossil fuels. Consequently, there is a change in the balance of gases in the atmosphere, and the increasing level of carbon dioxide linked to climate change is a source of widespread concern.

Note in Figure 13.7 that while chemicals are cycled and reused through living things, energy flows and is ultimately lost as heat. This means that life is dependent on a continuing supply of solar energy.

**Matter cycles and energy flows through biochemical processes.**

Data from the Mauna Loa research station in Hawaii provide a record of atmospheric carbon dioxide concentration since 1958. Taking into account seasonal fluctuations and variances, the overall trend has been an increase in carbon dioxide levels from about 315 ppm to about 390 ppm in the last 50 years. Carbon dioxide is a greenhouse gas that absorbs and re-radiates infrared radiation, and so this dramatic increase in its concentration is widely accepted as a major factor influencing climate change.

### Exercises

**1** Write an equation for the hydrolysis of the molecule $C_{18}H_{32}O_{16}$ (a trisaccharide) into its monomers, which are all isomeric with glucose.

**2** State the features of molecules that are able to form condensation polymers, and describe what happens during the polymerization reaction.

**3** State whether the following metabolic processes are anabolic or catabolic.

**(a)** protein synthesis      **(b)** oxidation of fatty acids
**(c)** anaerobic respiration      **(d)** DNA replication

**4** Outline the conditions required for photosynthesis to take place, and explain why it can be described as a redox process.

**5** State and explain the difference in energy yield between aerobic and anaerobic respiration.

# B.2 & B.7 Proteins and enzymes

## B.2 Proteins and enzymes

## Understandings:

- Proteins are polymers of 2-amino acids, joined by amide links (also known as peptide bonds).
- Amino acids are amphoteric and can exist as zwitterions, cations, and anions.
- Protein structures are diverse and are described at the primary, secondary, tertiary, and quaternary levels.
- A protein's three-dimensional shape determines its role in structural components or in metabolic processes.
- Most enzymes are proteins that act as catalysts by binding specifically to a substrate at the active site.
- As enzyme activity depends on the conformation, it is sensitive to changes in temperature, pH, and the presence of heavy metal ions.
- Chromatographic separation is based on different physical and chemical principles.

### Guidance

- The names and structural formulas of the amino acids are given in the IB data booklet in section 33.
- Reference should be made to alpha helix and beta pleated sheet, and to fibrous and globular proteins with examples of each.

## Applications and skills:

- Deduction of the structural formulas of reactants and products in condensation reactions of amino acids, and hydrolysis reactions of peptides.
- Explanation of the solubilities and melting points of amino acids in terms of zwitterions.
- Application of the relationships between charge, pH, and isoelectric point for amino acids and proteins.
- Description of the four levels of protein structure, including the origin and types of bonds and interactions involved.
- Deduction and interpretation of graphs of enzyme activity involving changes in substrate concentration, pH, and temperature.
- Explanation of the processes of paper chromatography and gel electrophoresis in amino acid and protein separation and identification.

### Guidance

In paper chromatography the use of $R_f$ values and locating agents should be covered.

## B.7 Proteins and enzymes

## Understandings:

- Inhibitors play an important role in regulating the activities of enzymes.
- Amino acids and proteins can act as buffers in solution.
- Protein assays commonly use UV-vis spectroscopy and a calibration curve based on known standards.

## Applications and skills:

- Determination of $V_{max}$ and the value of the Michaelis constant $K_m$ for an enzyme by graphical means, and explanation of their significance.
- Comparison of competitive and non-competitive inhibition of enzymes with reference to protein structure, the active site, and allosteric site.
- Explanation of the concept of product inhibition in metabolic pathways.

- Calculation of the pH of buffer solutions, such as those used in protein analysis and in reactions involving amino acids in solution.
- Determination of the concentration of a protein in solution from a calibration curve using the Beer–Lambert law.

**Guidance**
- *The effects of competitive and non-competitive inhibitors on $K_m$ and $V_{max}$ values should be covered.*
- *The Henderson–Hasselbalch equation is given in the IB data booklet in section 1.*
- *For UV-vis spectroscopy, knowledge of particular reagents and wavelengths is not required.*

## The functions of proteins

Proteins are in many ways the most remarkable of the biomolecules. It is estimated that as many as ten million different protein molecules may exist in nature, each with a unique structure and function. From this almost overwhelming diversity, we can classify two main types of proteins.

Coloured scanning electron micrograph (SEM) of hair shafts growing from the surface of human skin. Hair is made of the fibrous protein keratin, anchored in hair follicles. The outer layer of skin consists of dead keratinized cells that detach giving this flaky appearance.

**Fibrous proteins**

- structural components

- elongated molecules with dominant secondary structure

- insoluble in water

**Globular proteins**

- tools that operate at the molecular level – as enzymes, carriers, receptors

- compact spherical molecules with dominant tertiary structure

- soluble in water

Fibrous proteins are responsible for structure, support, and movement, whereas globular proteins drive the reactions of metabolism. Some specific examples of each type are given below.

| Role of protein | Named example | Type of protein | Specific function |
|---|---|---|---|
| structure | keratin | fibrous | protective covering in hair, wool, claws |
| structure | collagen | fibrous | connective tissue in skin and tendons |
| enzyme (catalyst) | polymerase | globular | catalyzes anabolic reactions such as DNA synthesis |
| communication | insulin | globular | controls and maintains the concentration of glucose in the blood |
| transport | hemoglobin | globular | carries oxygen |

How can it be that this same type of molecule, the protein, is used for both the walls of the reactor and the reactions within? The answer lies in the fact that proteins are as diverse and unique in their structures as they are in their functions, and that this variety is rooted in their molecular building blocks.

## The structure of proteins

### Amino acids are the building blocks of proteins

Proteins are polymers – long-chain molecules – of monomer units called **amino acids**. Each amino acid contains an amino group (—NH₂) and an acid group (—COOH) bonded to the same carbon atom.

amino group    carboxylic acid group

They are called 2-amino acids. Because the chain is numbered starting with the carboxylic acid group, the amino group is attached to carbon 2. This carbon atom is also bonded to a hydrogen atom and to a group usually known as 'R'. The R group differs from one amino acid to the next, and is therefore the feature that defines the amino acid. About 20 different amino acids are found in naturally occurring proteins. Each is given a standard three-letter abbreviation, for example the smallest amino acid glycine, where R = H, is known as Gly.

A complete list of all the amino acids used in proteins is given in section 33 of the IB data booklet. Amino acids can be classified according to the chemical nature of their R group, usually on the basis of their different polarities, as shown in the examples below.

In addition to the 20 common amino acids of proteins, over 150 other amino acids occur in biology in different forms other than in proteins. Fungi and higher plants have a particularly large variety of non-protein amino acids, some of which are toxic to other forms of life.

| Type of amino acid | R group contains | Named example | Structure |
|---|---|---|---|
| non-polar / hydrophobic | hydrocarbon | alanine, Ala | $H_2N—CH—COOH$ with $CH_3$ |
| polar but uncharged | hydroxyl, —OH, sulfhydryl, —SH, or amide, $—CONH_2$ | serine, Ser | $H_2N—CH—COOH$ with $CH_2—OH$ |
| basic (positively charged at pH 6.0–8.0) | amino, $—NH_2$ | lysine, Lys | $H_2N—CH—COOH$ with $CH_2—CH_2—CH_2—CH_2—NH_2$ |
| acidic (negatively charged at pH 6.0–8.0) | carboxylic acid, —COOH | aspartic acid, Asp | $H_2N—CH—COOH$ with $CH_2—COOH$ |

Amino acids are crystalline compounds with high melting points, usually above 200 °C, and they have much greater solubility in water than in non-polar solvents. In addition, amino acids usually move in an electric field. These properties are all typical of ionic compounds, and so suggest that amino acids contain charged groups. The charges are a result of acid–base behaviour, which is best explained in terms of Brønsted–Lowry theory.

In aqueous solution and in crystalline form, amino acids commonly exist with both positive and negative charges within the molecule, known as **zwitterions**. They are sometimes referred to as **internal salts**, as the charges result from an internal acid–base reaction, with the transfer of a proton ($H^+$) from the acid —COOH group to the basic $–NH_2$ group in the same amino acid.

**CHALLENGE YOURSELF**

3 All amino acids except glycine are chiral, and exist in the L form in nature. By reference to section 33 of the IB data booklet, determine which two amino acids found in proteins have *two* chiral carbon atoms.

undissociated form                    zwitterion

As amino acids contain both an acidic group and a basic group, they are **amphoteric**
or **amphiprotic**, as described in Chapter 8. In aqueous solution they will accept and
donate $H^+$ according to changes in the pH of the medium as shown below.

**1**   As an acid, donating $H^+$:

$$H_3N^+ - \overset{\overset{\displaystyle H}{|}}{\underset{\underset{\displaystyle R}{|}}{C}} - COO^- \rightleftharpoons H_2N - \overset{\overset{\displaystyle H}{|}}{\underset{\underset{\displaystyle R}{|}}{C}} - COO^- + H^+$$

**2**   As a base, accepting $H^+$:

$$H_3N^+ - \overset{\overset{\displaystyle H}{|}}{\underset{\underset{\displaystyle R}{|}}{C}} - COO^- + H^+ \rightleftharpoons H_3N^+ - \overset{\overset{\displaystyle H}{|}}{\underset{\underset{\displaystyle R}{|}}{C}} - COOH$$

Note that in the zwitterion it is the conjugates of the acid and the base that are
responsible for this property. As the pH of the medium affects the equilibrium
position of these reactions, it influences the charge of an amino acid as follows:

• at high pH (low $[H^+]$), reaction 1 above is favoured as the $-NH_3^+$ group loses its $H^+$ and
  forms an anion
• at low pH (high $[H^+]$), reaction 2 above is favoured as the $-COO^-$ group gains $H^+$ and
  forms a cation.

These effects of pH on charge are summarized below. This example assumes that the R
group is an uncharged group, for example the amino acid alanine.

$$H_3N^+ - \overset{\overset{\displaystyle H}{|}}{\underset{\underset{\displaystyle CH_3}{|}}{C}} - COOH \rightleftharpoons H_3N^+ - \overset{\overset{\displaystyle H}{|}}{\underset{\underset{\displaystyle CH_3}{|}}{C}} - COO^- \rightleftharpoons H_2N - \overset{\overset{\displaystyle H}{|}}{\underset{\underset{\displaystyle CH_3}{|}}{C}} - COO^-$$

cation                        neutral                        anion

ISOELECTRIC POINT

← decreasing pH                                   increasing pH →

So amino acids tend to be positively charged at low pH and negatively charged at high
pH. The intermediate pH at which the amino acid is electrically neutral is known as
its **isoelectric point**. With no net charge at this pH, amino acids will not move in an
electric field. Also at this point, the molecules will have minimum mutual repulsion
and so be the least soluble. Section 33 in the IB data booklet gives the pH of the
isoelectric point of each amino acid alongside its structure, and some examples are
shown in the table on page 683.

| Common name | Symbol | Structural formula | pH of isoelectric point |
|---|---|---|---|
| glycine | Gly | $H_2N—CH_2—COOH$ | 6.0 |
| alanine | Ala | $H_2N—CH—COOH$<br>$\quad\quad\mid$<br>$\quad\quad CH_3$ | 6.0 |
| lysine | Lys | $H_2N—CH—COOH$<br>$\quad\quad\mid$<br>$CH_2—CH_2—CH_2—CH_2—NH_2$ | 9.7 |
| aspartic acid | Asp | $H_2N—CH—COOH$<br>$\quad\quad\mid$<br>$\quad\quad CH_2—COOH$ | 2.8 |

This shows that amino acids such as alanine and glycine, which have uncharged R groups, have the same isoelectric point of pH 6.0. But where the R group contains an acidic or a basic group, then the $pK_a$ and $pK_b$ values of these groups will also influence the charge as pH changes. This is why aspartic acid and lysine, for example, have very different isoelectric points. This difference is exploited in techniques for separating amino acids, to be discussed later in this chapter.

The equations above also show that amino acids act as **pH buffers**. By reacting with both $H^+$ ions and $OH^-$ ions, amino acids cause the pH to be resistant to change on addition of small amounts of acid or alkali, as explained in Chapter 8. The buffering role of amino acids is important in helping to maintain a constant pH in cells, a crucial need for biological solutions. Many of the protein components, especially enzymes, are extremely sensitive to changes in pH and can be made inactive by significant fluctuations. For example, human blood has a pH of 7.4, and an increase or a decrease of more than 0.5 pH units can be fatal. Clearly, effective buffering is a must. There are several different buffer systems at work in the human body, including those that use amino acids and proteins.

Like amino acids, proteins also have isoelectric points. Fresh milk has a pH of about 6.7 and at this pH the protein casein carries a negative charge and is dispersed in solution. As it sours, bacteria growing in the milk produce acids that lower the pH and so reduce the charges on the molecules. When it reaches pH 4.6 this is the isoelectric point of casein, so now the protein becomes less soluble, precipitating from solution as the familiar 'curdled milk'. This is the first step in cheese making.

**Amino acids are amphoteric and can act as buffers in solution.**

A trough of curdled milk in a cheese-making factory. The curd is solidified milk formed by lowering the pH and so precipitating the protein at its isoelectric point.

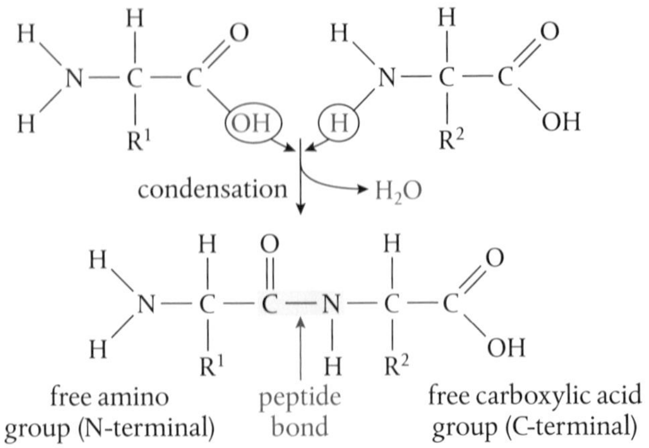

**Figure 13.8** Formation of a dipeptide by condensation of two amino acids.

## Amino acids link together through condensation reactions

Amino acids are able to react together in a condensation reaction in which a molecule of water is eliminated and a new bond is formed between the acid group of one amino acid and the amino group of the other. This bond is a substituted **amide link** known as a **peptide bond**, and two amino acids linked in this way are known as a **dipeptide**. By convention the free —$NH_2$ group (known as the N-terminal) is put on the left of the sequence and the free —COOH group (C-terminal) on the right.

We can see that the dipeptide still has a functional group at each end of the molecule, with —$NH_2$ at one end and —COOH at the other. So it can react again by another condensation reaction, forming a **tripeptide** and eventually a chain of linked amino acids known as a **polypeptide**.

### Worked example

Draw a tripeptide with the following sequence:

$$Cys — Val — Asn$$

### Solution

Look up the structures (the R groups) of the amino acids in section 33 of the IB data booklet and draw them out in the same order as given in the question.

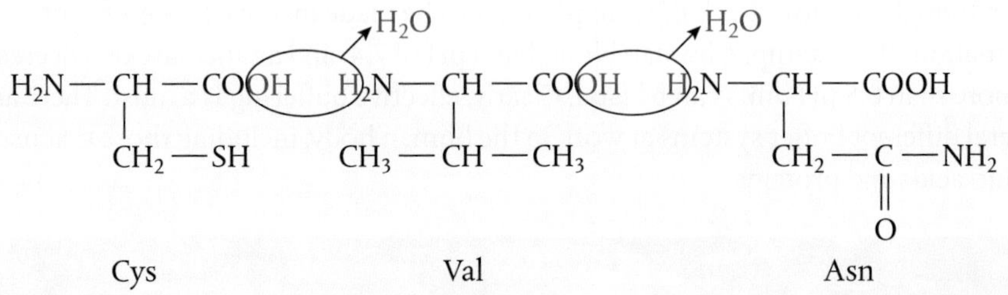

Now draw peptide bonds between the carbon of the —COOH group and the nitrogen of the —$NH_2$ group, ensuring that $H_2O$ is released, and that each atom has the correct number of bonds in the final structure.

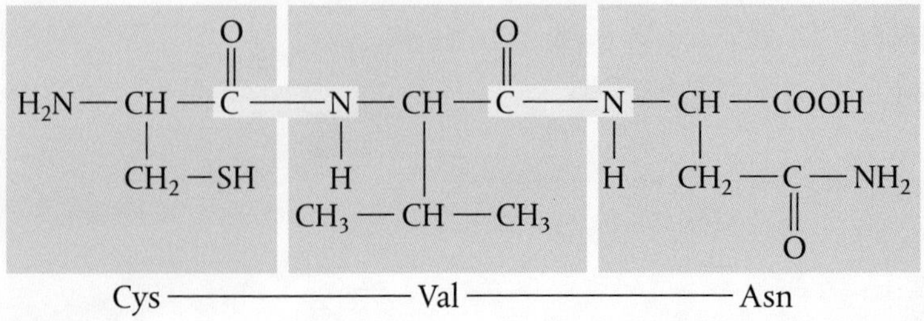

We can write a general equation for the synthesis of a polypeptide from its amino acids as follows

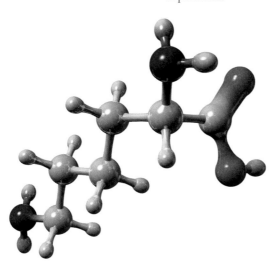

repeat unit

In just the same way as letters linked together in different orders make different words (e.g. eat, ate, tea), so amino acids linked together in different sequences make different peptides. The three amino acids above could have been linked for example as: Asn—Cys—Val or Cys—Asn—Val, all of which would be different tripeptides with different properties.

The sequence in which the amino acids are linked to form the chain is of great significance as it will determine the exact nature of the polypeptide. This is where the extraordinary variety of protein structures comes from.

Consider making a necklace by joining together 20 different colours of beads, with each colour being used as many times as you like. In every position you would have a choice of 20 different possibilities, so just imagine how many different combinations of beads you could have. Building polypeptides from amino acids presents a similar situation – at any point in the chain there are 20 different possibilities. Even for a tripeptide there are $20 \times 20 \times 20 = 8000$ different possible combinations. But proteins are typically made from polypeptide chains with 50 or more amino acids, so the number of possible structures becomes enormous. A polypeptide with 50 amino acids has $20^{50}$ different possible sequences: $1.1 \times 10^{65}$ variations.

We will now move on to look at how the sequence of amino acids in the polypeptide uniquely determines the structure and therefore the function of the protein. Understanding protein structure can seem quite complex, so for convenience it is divided into four levels of organization, known as primary through to quaternary.

Molecular model of the amino acid lysine $NH_2(CH_2)_4CH(NH_2)$ COOH. Lysine is known as an **essential amino acid** because it cannot be synthesized by the body and so must be obtained in the diet. Carbon atoms are shown in blue, hydrogen in gold, oxygen in red, and nitrogen in dark blue.

**Figure 13.9** Different coloured beads can be strung together in different combinations to make a wide variety of different necklaces. In a similar way, different sequences of amino acids link together to give rise to an almost infinite variety of proteins.

## CHALLENGE YOURSELF

4 By reference to section 33 of the IB data booklet, determine which amino acid contains a secondary amine group. How might this affect its properties in a peptide chain?

## The primary structure of proteins is the amino acid sequence

The **primary structure** of a protein refers to the number and sequence of amino acids in its polypeptide chain. Held together by peptide bonds, this forms the covalent backbone of the molecule. Interestingly, once the primary structure has been determined, all the other levels of protein structure follow – so it really does dictate the entire structure and function of the protein.

**Figure 13.10** Primary structure of a small polypeptide. Peptide bonds are highlighted in blue.

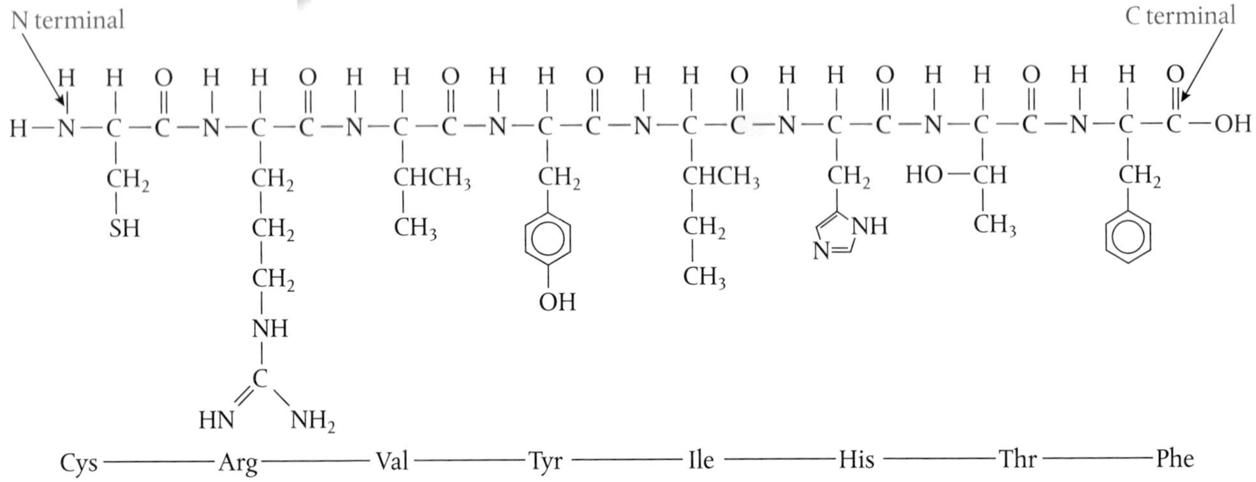

N terminal          C terminal

Cys ——— Arg ——— Val ——— Tyr ——— Ile ——— His ——— Thr ——— Phe

Sickle-cell anaemia is a condition that results from a single amino acid change in one chain of 146 amino acids in the protein haemoglobin. The resulting change in the conformation of haemoglobin means that it is not able to carry oxygen efficiently. It is a common condition in many African countries, as the altered red blood cells provide some immunity to malaria.

Often considered the father of modern molecular biology, Fred Sanger of Cambridge, England, is one of only four people to have been awarded two Nobel Prizes. In 1958 he was awarded the Chemistry Prize for establishing the sequence of the 51 amino acids in insulin chain B. This was the first protein to have its primary structure elucidated in this way and it was the culmination of 12 years of work. In 1980 Sanger shared the Nobel Prize in Chemistry for similar work on the base sequencing of nucleic acids.

So what determines the primary structure of a protein? The answer to this question when it came in the early 1960s was considered to be one of the most important discoveries of molecular biology. DNA (deoxyribose nucleic acid), which determines genetic information, acts by dictating to cells the primary structure of their proteins. In other words, the expression of genes is through the proteins that an organism synthesizes. So it is the primary structure of our proteins that gives each of us our unique genetic characteristics.

Protein sequencing is now a routine operation in biochemical research, with machines able to deduce the entire sequence of a large protein very quickly. This is a major part of **proteomics**, the study that explores the relationship between structure and function of proteins. The synthesis of new so-called **designer proteins** through protein engineering has many applications in pharmaceutical and environmental research. Protein sequences are also the aspect of protein structure used in studies of biochemical evolution to determine the relationships between organisms.

## The secondary structure of proteins is regular hydrogen bonding

The **secondary structure** refers to folding of the polypeptide chain as a result of hydrogen bonding between peptide bonds along its length. Hydrogen bonds can form between the —C=O group of one peptide bond and the —N—H group of another peptide bond further along the chain which will cause the chain to fold. The exact configuration of this will be influenced by the R groups along the chain and so differs in different proteins and even in different sections of the same protein.

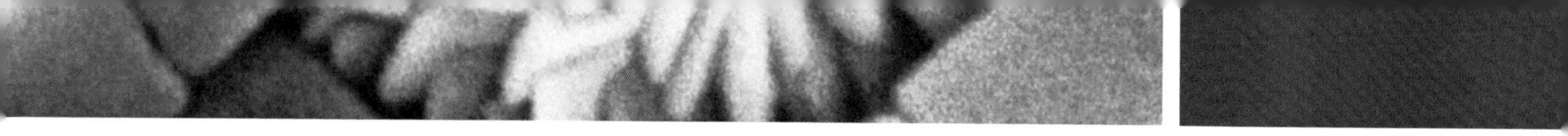

We can distinguish two main types of secondary structure, the α-**helix** and the β-**pleated sheet**.

The α-helix is a regular coiled configuration of the polypeptide chain resulting from hydrogen bonds forming between two peptide bonds four amino acid units apart. This twists the chain into a tightly coiled helix, much like a spiral staircase, with 3.6 amino acids per turn, as shown in Figure 13.11.

The α-helix is flexible and elastic as the intra-chain hydrogen bonds easily break and re-form as the molecule is stretched. A good example of the α-helix is found in keratins, structural proteins found in hair, skin, and claws.

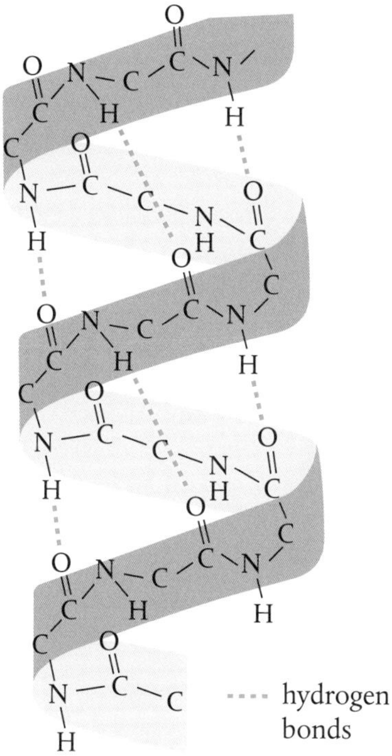

---- hydrogen bonds

**Figure 13.11** α-helical secondary structure of keratin. The amino acid backbone winds in a spiral, held by hydrogen bonds shown in blue.

Human hair (made of the protein keratin) grows approximately 15 cm in one year, which means that 9.5 turns of the α-helix must be produced every second.

Hair stretches to almost double its length when exposed to moist heat but contracts to its normal length on cooling, because the hydrogen bonds in the secondary structure easily break and re-form. This is why hair is often much curlier in humid conditions.

The β-pleated sheet is a structure composed of 'side by side' polypeptides which are in extended form, not tightly coiled as in the α-helix. They are arranged in pleated sheets that are cross-linked by inter-chain hydrogen bonds, as shown in Figure 13.12.

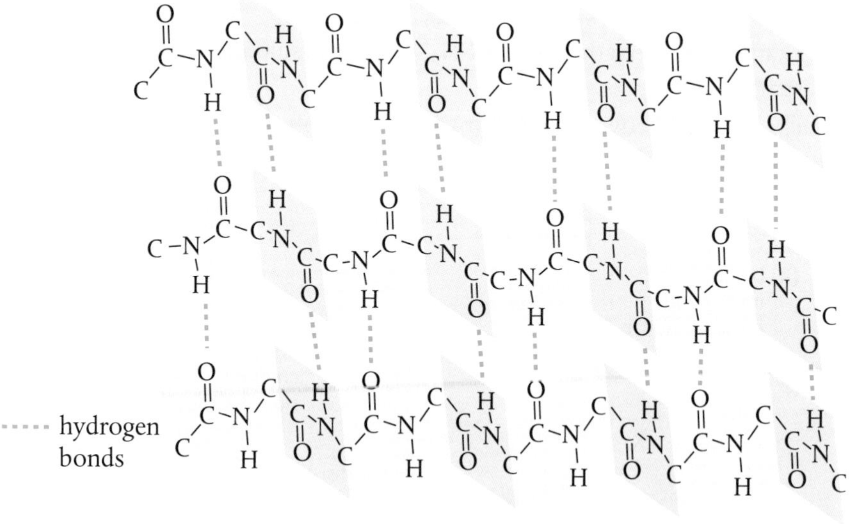

**Figure 13.12** β-pleated sheet secondary structure of silk fibroin. The polypeptides run parallel to each other, held by hydrogen bonds shown in blue.

---- hydrogen bonds

A spider's web outlined with drops of morning dew. The web's fibres are made of the protein fibroin containing a β-pleated sheet secondary structure and spun from special secreting glands. A typical web may contain 20 metres of fibroin.

The β-pleated sheet is flexible but inelastic. A good example is found in fibroin, the protein in the fibres spun by spiders and silkworms and also found in the beaks and claws of birds.

Keratin and fibroin with their well-defined secondary structure are fibrous proteins. Their toughness and insolubility in water make them ideal for their structural roles. They are simpler structures with more repetitive amino acid sequences than globular proteins, in much the same way as the bricks in a building are mostly alike.

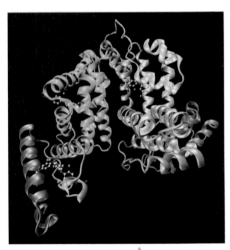

Computer artwork showing the structure of the protein albumin from human blood. The spiral regions of $\alpha$-helical structure can be clearly seen as well as the overall three-dimensional conformation.

Make sure you are clear on the difference between hydrogen bonds in the secondary structure, which form between groups in the peptide bonds, and hydrogen bonds in the tertiary structure, which form between the side chains.

## The tertiary structure of proteins is the result of interactions between the R groups

The **tertiary structure** refers to the further twisting, folding, and coiling of the polypeptide chain as a result of interactions between the R groups, known as **side chains**. The structure that results is a very specific compact three-dimensional structure, known as the protein's **conformation**. It is the most stable arrangement of the protein, taking into account all the possible interactions along the entire length of the polypeptide. Note that the interactions between the side chains are all *intra*-molecular forces, as they occur within the one polypeptide chain.

This conformation is particularly important in the globular proteins, which include all the enzymes and protein hormones. They are water soluble because their structure positions nearly all of the polar (or hydrophilic) side chains on the outer surface of the molecules where they can interact with water, and most of the non-polar (or hydrophobic) side chains in the interior out of contact with water. The interactions that stabilize this conformation are of the following types, summarized in Figure 13.13.

(a) *Hydrophobic interactions* – between non-polar side chains.
For example, between two alkyl side chains in valine; these weak interactions, based on London (dispersion) forces between induced dipoles, produce non-polar regions in the interior of the protein.

(b) *Hydrogen bonding* – between polar side chains.
For example, between the $-CH_2OH$ group in serine and the $-CH_2COOH$ group in aspartic acid.

(c) *Ionic bonding* – between side chains carrying a charge.
For example, between the $-(CH_2)_4NH_3^+$ group in lysine and the $-CH_2COO^-$ group in aspartic acid.

(d) *Disulfide bridges* – between the sulfur-containing amino acid cysteine.
These are covalent bonds, and hence the strongest of these interactions.

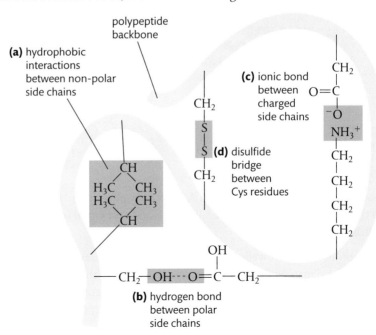

**Figure 13.13** Summary of the interactions that contribute to the tertiary structure of a protein.

These interactions can all be upset by changes in the medium such as to temperature, pH, or the presence of metal ions. When a protein loses its specific tertiary structure as a result of such disruptions, it is said to be **denatured**. The familiar sight of the white of an egg solidifying on heating is an example of this. Denaturation of enzymes renders them biologically inactive, which is one of the reasons why intracellular conditions must be tightly controlled. We will come back to this on page 695.

## Quaternary structure of a protein is the association between different polypeptides

Some proteins comprise more than one polypeptide chain, and in these cases the association between these chains is known as the **quaternary structure**. This association involves similar forces and bonds to those found in the tertiary structure – hydrophobic interactions, hydrogen bonds, ionic bonds, and disulfide bridges.

For example, the protein collagen, which is found in skin and tendons and is actually the most abundant protein in the human body, is a triple helix of three polypeptide chains, with inter-chain hydrogen bonds between them. This helps to give it a stable rope-like structure that is resistant to stretching.

Another example is the protein hemoglobin, responsible for carrying oxygen in the blood, which is made up of four polypeptide chains that fit together tightly in the protein assembly. The structure–function relationship of this pigment molecule is discussed further on page 741.

Many proteins consist of only one polypeptide chain, and so do not have a quaternary structure.

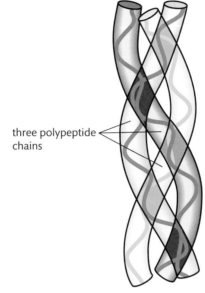

three polypeptide chains

**Figure 13.14** Triple-helical quaternary structure of collagen.

β₂   β₁

α₂   α₁

**Figure 13.15** Quaternary structure of hemoglobin, an assembly of four polypeptides.

The process of 'perming' that introduces more curls into hair involves first breaking the disulfide bridges between the cysteine residues in the keratin using a reducing agent. New disulfide bridges are formed when the hair is chemically re-oxidized while it is twisted around rollers. The size of the roller determines the position of the new disulfide bridges that form. As these are covalent bonds they do not break on normal treatments like washing and combing, and so are said to be 'permanent'. Similar processes are used in straightening curly hair.

## Summary of the bonds and forces involved in protein structure

| Protein structure | Nature of interactions |
|---|---|
| primary | covalent (amide / peptide) bonds between amino acids |
| secondary | hydrogen bonds within the polypeptide chain involving groups in the peptide bonds |
| tertiary | interactions between side chains including hydrophobic interactions, hydrogen bonds, ionic bonds, disulfide bridges |
| quaternary | interactions between polypeptide chains, including the same interactions as in the tertiary structure |

**NATURE OF SCIENCE**

Because of the almost infinite variety of protein structures, for a long time they were considered to be more likely than DNA to be the store of hereditary information. Biochemists were surprised to find from experimental results that in fact it is DNA and not protein which carries the genetic code. The evidence came from separate experiments on the ability of DNA to achieve transformation of bacteria, and on the use of radioactive isotopes to demonstrate that viruses inject DNA and not protein into their host cells. Data from both experiments were necessary for broad conclusions to be reached. Subsequent evidence proved that although proteins are not the carriers of hereditary information, they are the molecules through which it is expressed.

### Exercises

6 **(a)** Using the three-letter word symbols for amino acids, show all the possible tripeptides that can form from the three amino acids tyrosine, valine, and histidine.

   **(b)** Deduce the number of different peptides that could form from the four amino acids tyrosine, valine, histidine, and proline.

7 Consult section 33 of the IB data booklet to consider the following amino acids: leucine, glutamic acid, threonine, lysine, serine.

   Which of these amino acids:

   **(a)** is most likely to be found in the interior of a globular protein?
   **(b)** contains a secondary alcohol group?
   **(c)** will be negatively charged at pH 5.0?
   **(d)** will be positively charged at pH 7.0?

8 Explain the differences in the structure and properties of fibrous and globular proteins.

9 Hydrogen bonds occur in the secondary and the tertiary structures of proteins. Describe the different origins of these.

## Enzymes are globular proteins

The complexity of metabolism demands a highly sensitive control system which can respond to the changing needs of the cell. This is achieved through the action of **enzymes**, the biological catalysts that control every reaction in biochemistry. Because enzymes are specific for each reaction and can be individually controlled, they determine the cell's reactivity at the molecular level.

Enzymes are globular proteins, and exist in compact spherical shapes when in aqueous solution in cells. Their well-defined tertiary structure gives them a specific three-dimensional shape, which is essential for enzyme activity. Enzymes are typically relatively large molecules, containing several hundred amino acids, and some also have a quaternary structure. For example, many of the enzymes involved in the first stage of respiration are dimeric proteins, meaning they contain two polypeptide chains.

In addition, some enzymes require non-protein molecules to be bound for activity. These are known as **co-factors** and may be organic, when they are known as **coenzymes**, or inorganic, such as metal ions. Common examples include vitamins, many of which act as precursors for coenzymes.

Enzyme action is the basis of the brewing and cheese-making industries, possibly the oldest forms of biotechnology. Cheeses and fermented drinks are often associated with specific place names, according to the different flavours produced by enzymes in local microorganisms.

**Enzymes are biological catalysts that control all biochemical reactions. They are protein molecules.**

Many serious or fatal illnesses are the results of the failure of a single enzyme. For example, the condition phenylketonuria (PKU) that can lead to mental retardation is the consequence of a malfunction in the enzyme responsible for the breakdown of the amino acid phenylalanine in the liver. This condition is the reason why many food and drinks that contain aspartame are labelled 'contains a source of phenylalanine'.

## Enzymes form a complex with the substrate

Enzymes are catalysts and so increase the rate of a chemical reaction without themselves undergoing permanent chemical change. The reactant in the reaction catalysed by the enzyme is known as the **substrate**. The presence of the enzyme provides a reaction route of lower activation energy and so enables the reaction to occur more quickly at the same temperature.

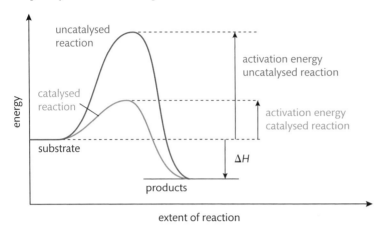

**Figure 13.16** Graph showing reaction route of lower activation energy in the presence of an enzyme. This means that at a specified temperature a higher proportion of particles will have sufficient energy to react and so the overall rate of reaction is increased.

The action of the enzyme is due to its ability to form a temporary binding to the substrate where it is held by relatively weak forces of attraction, forming an **enzyme–substrate complex**. This binding occurs at a small region of the enzyme known as the **active site**, which is typically a pocket or groove on the surface of the protein. The substrate is usually a much smaller molecule than the enzyme, and therefore fits within it. Formation of the complex depends on a 'chemical fit' or compatibility between the substrate and the side chains of the amino acids at the active site of the enzyme. This involves non-covalent interactions such as hydrophobic interactions, dipole–dipole attractions, hydrogen bonds, and ionic attractions. The binding in the complex puts a strain on the substrate molecule, and this facilitates the breaking and the forming of bonds. Once the substrate has reacted, the product formed no longer fits in the active site and so it detaches. The enzyme is then released unchanged and is able to catalyse further reactions.

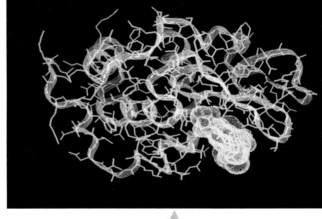

Computer graphics representation of the enzyme lysozyme, which breaks down polysaccharides. The protein is shown in blue with its backbone traced out as the magenta ribbon. The substrate is shown in yellow bound to the active site. Note that the substrate is much smaller than the enzyme.

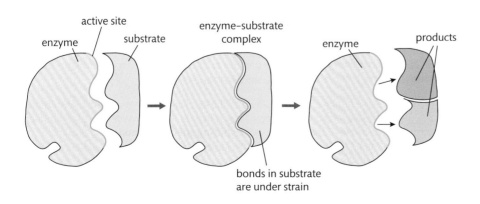

**Figure 13.17** Enzymes operate as catalysts by forming a complex with their substrate in which the reaction occurs.

Using **E** for enzyme, **S** for substrate, and **P** for product, we can summarize the action of enzymes as follows:

$$\mathbf{E} + \mathbf{S} \rightleftharpoons \mathbf{E\text{-}S} \rightleftharpoons \mathbf{E\text{-}P} \rightleftharpoons \mathbf{E} + \mathbf{P}$$

Note that all the reactions are shown as equilibrium reactions, and so are reversible depending on the conditions.

## Enzymes are specific for the reaction they catalyse

Many enzymes are known to be very specific for their substrate. For example, different proteases, enzymes that hydrolyse proteins, target only specific peptide bonds between certain amino acids. The specificity of an enzyme for its substrate results from its conformation, as this determines the arrangement of the side chains of the amino acids at its active site and therefore its ability to bind precisely with the substrate. The exact nature of the interactions leading to the enzyme–substrate complex is a subject of ongoing research.

### NATURE OF SCIENCE

Development of enzyme theory provides a case study of how a scientific model may change over time. In 1890 the German chemist Emil Fischer proposed a model known as the **lock and key** mechanism to describe the fit between an enzyme and its substrate, and to explain the specificity of enzymes. This is illustrated in Figure 13.18. But this model cannot readily explain all aspects of enzyme inhibition, and does little to explain the catalytic action, because a lock does not change a key the way an enzyme changes a substrate. Later work on proteomics recognized that enzymes are less rigid structures than the lock and key model suggests, and in 1958, Daniel Koshland of Rockefeller University, New York, proposed a modification known as the **induced-fit** mechanism of enzyme action. This suggests that in the presence of the substrate, the active site undergoes some conformational changes, shaping itself to allow a better fit. So instead of the substrate fitting into a rigid active site, this is a more dynamic relationship where the side chains at the active site change into the precise positions that allow the binding to occur. It has been compared to putting on a rubber glove that is shaped to the specific shape of the hand as it is pulled over the fingers. It is thought that the distortion that occurs as enzyme and substrate approach may be critical to catalysis.

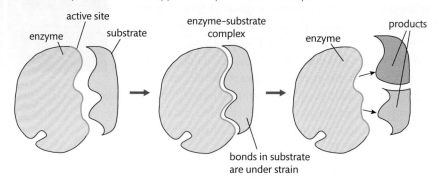

**Figure 13.18** Induced fit model of enzyme action. The approach of the substrate induces a conformational change at the active site. This enables the substrate to bind and undergo reaction. As the products are released, the enzyme reverts to its original state.

More recent research suggests that enzymes may be even more flexible structures in which the active site continually reshapes by its interactions with the substrate until the time the substrate is completely bound to it. This is known as the **shifting specificity model** and recognizes the involvement of the entire enzyme molecule rather than just the active site in the catalytic event. Evidence for these developments in enzyme theory has come largely from X-ray protein crystallography, and from advances in computer modelling that enable accurate three-dimensional predictions of enzyme structure to be made.

## Enzyme kinetics indicate that saturation occurs in the formation of the complex

The rate of enzyme-catalysed reactions can be followed using the same principles as those for other reactions discussed in Chapter 6. When graphs of substrate concentration against rate of reaction are plotted, the curves show the distinctive shape of **saturation**. Interpretation of these data lends support to the mechanism of enzyme action proceeding via an enzyme–substrate complex.

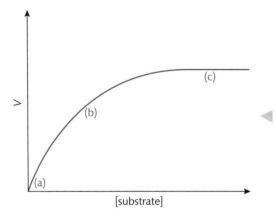

**Figure 13.19** The relationship between substrate concentration and rate for an enzyme-catalysed reaction. Note the symbol $V$ (velocity) is used to describe the rate of enzyme reactions.

The following points can be deduced from the graph.

**(a)** At low substrate concentration, the rate of the reaction is proportional to the substrate concentration. Enzyme is available to bind to the substrate.

**(b)** As the substrate concentration is increased the rate decreases and is no longer proportional to the substrate concentration. Some of the enzyme has its active sites occupied by substrate and is not available.

**(c)** At high substrate concentration the rate is constant and independent of substrate concentration. At this point the enzyme is saturated with substrate.

All enzymes show this saturation effect, but they vary widely with respect to the substrate concentration required to produce saturation. The mathematical expression describing the kinetics is known as the **Michaelis–Menten equation** after the German biochemist Leonor Michaelis and the Canadian medical scientist Maud Menten.

There are two features of Michaelis–Menten kinetics to note, which are shown in Figure 13.20 and explained below.

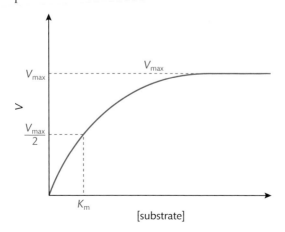

**Figure 13.20** The derivation of $V_{max}$ and $K_m$ from the rate–concentration graph.

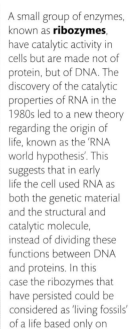

A small group of enzymes, known as **ribozymes**, have catalytic activity in cells but are made not of protein, but of DNA. The discovery of the catalytic properties of RNA in the 1980s led to a new theory regarding the origin of life, known as the 'RNA world hypothesis'. This suggests that in early life the cell used RNA as both the genetic material and the structural and catalytic molecule, instead of dividing these functions between DNA and proteins. In this case the ribozymes that have persisted could be considered as 'living fossils' of a life based only on nucleic acids.

## CHALLENGE YOURSELF

**5** What do you think is the order of the reaction with respect to the substrate in Figure 13.19 for each of the regions (a) to (c)?

693

## 1 The maximum velocity $V_{max}$

This is the maximum velocity of the enzyme under the conditions of the experiment. $V_{max}$ has the units of rate. It varies greatly from one enzyme to another, and with pH and temperature. The rate of enzyme reactions is sometimes expressed as the **turnover number**, defined as the number of molecules of substrate that can be processed into products per enzyme molecule per unit of time. For example, the enzyme catalase is a very fast enzyme with a turnover rate of up to 100 000 molecules of its substrate $H_2O_2$ per second.

## 2 The Michaelis constant $K_m$

This is the substrate concentration at which the reaction rate is equal to one half its maximum value. In other words, $[S] = K_m$ when the rate is $V_{max}/2$.

$K_m$ has the units of concentration and its value gives information about the affinity of the enzyme for its substrate. It is an inverse relationship – a low value of $K_m$ means that the reaction is going quickly even at low substrate concentrations. A higher value means that the enzyme has a lower affinity for its substrate. These relationships can be seen in Figure 13.21. The value of $K_m$ also varies with pH and with temperature.

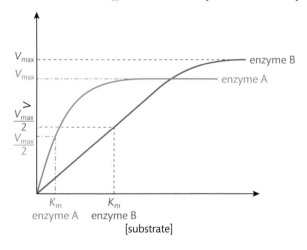

**Figure 13.21** The rate–concentration graphs for two different enzymes, A and B. It can be seen that the rate is higher at low substrate concentration for A, and so the value for its $K_m$ is lower.

The table below gives the $K_m$ values for some enzymes.

| Enzyme | Substrate | $K_m$ / mmol dm$^{-3}$ |
|---|---|---|
| catalase | hydrogen peroxide | 25.0 |
| hexokinase | glucose | 0.15 |
| carbonic anhydrase | hydrogencarbonate ion $HCO_3^-$ | 9.0 |

These differences also determine how responsive an enzyme will be to changes in substrate concentration. An enzyme with a low $K_m$, such as hexokinase, is saturated with substrate under most cell conditions and so will act at a more or less constant rate regardless of variations in substrate concentration. An enzyme with a high $K_m$, such as catalase, is not normally saturated with substrate so its activity will be more sensitive to changes in the concentration of substrate.

Enzyme names are often quite long and appear complex, but in most cases they are logically derived. The name of the substrate is followed by the type of reaction followed by the suffix –ase. So, for example, 'pyruvate dehydrogenase' acts on pyruvate to remove hydrogen; 'glucose isomerase' converts glucose into its isomer fructose.

## Enzyme activity is influenced by its physical and chemical environment

We have seen that the action of an enzyme depends on how its specific three-dimensional shape enables it to bind to the substrate. So any conditions that alter its conformation will affect its catalytic action. We will describe three of these factors here.

**TOK** To what extent do the use of metaphors and models, such as 'lock and key' and 'induced fit', enhance our knowledge of enzyme action?

### 1 Temperature

We know from Chapter 6 that the rate of a reaction is increased by a rise in temperature due to the increase in the average kinetic energy of the particles. For enzymic reactions, this means there is an increase in the frequency of collisions between molecules of enzyme and substrate that have greater than the activation energy, leading to a higher rate of reaction. But this is only true up to a certain temperature. Beyond this, the effect of the increase in kinetic energy is to change the conformation of the protein by disrupting the bonds and forces responsible for holding it in its tertiary structure. Consequently, the enzyme is no longer able to bind the substrate at the active site and its catalytic activity is diminished. This explains the shape of the curve shown in Figure 13.22.

The temperature corresponding to the maximum rate of reaction for a particular enzyme is known as its **optimum temperature**. Most enzymes in the human body have an optimum value close to 37 °C, which is body temperature. Organisms that are adapted to very different environments, such as bacteria in hot springs or algae on glaciers, produce enzymes with optimum values closer to their ambient temperatures.

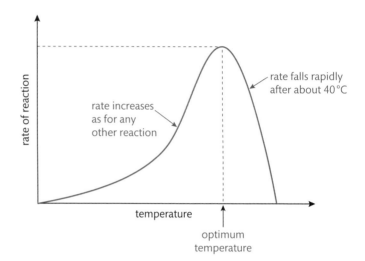

**Figure 13.22** The effect of temperature on the activity of an enzyme.

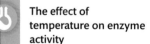

**The effect of temperature on enzyme activity**
Full details of how to carry out this experiment with a worksheet are available online.

Coloured scanning electron micrograph of granules of biological detergents showing the enzymes encapsulated in their structure. The enzymes help break down biomolecules such as those in blood, which may stain clothing. These enzymes are often the result of protein engineering with different optimum temperatures. Synthetic enzymes are also used in biodegradable plastics and in the textiles and food industries.

Note that loss of the tertiary structure, which is known as **denaturation**, does not mean loss of the covalent backbone of the protein molecules, which is known as **digestion**. Nonetheless, denaturation is usually an irreversible process, as you might know from the impossibility of uncooking an egg! Lowering the temperature usually causes what is called **deactivation** of an enzyme rather than denaturation. This prevents the enzyme from working but as it does not change the tertiary structure, it is usually reversible. This is why, for example, food that has been preserved by freezing soon spoils on thawing due to resumption of microbial activities as the temperature rises.

The effect of temperature on enzymes and other proteins is one of the main reasons why controlling the temperature is so important to many organisms, and why a change in the human core temperature of a couple of degrees Celsius is usually fatal.

## 2 pH

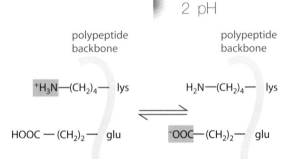

**Figure 13.23** The influence of pH on the state of ionization of acidic and basic groups in the side chains of a protein. For simplicity the diagram shows side chains of only two amino acids, lysine (lys) and glutamic acid (glu). In lysine R = $-(CH_2)_4-NH_2$ and in glutamic acid R = $-(CH_2)_2-COOH$.

The pH of a solution has several effects on the activity of an enzyme. It directly influences the state of ionization of acidic or basic groups in the side chains of the protein. From Le Chatelier's principle we can predict that at low pH (high [H$^+$]), acidic and basic groups become protonated, and at high pH (low [H$^+$]) they become deprotonated. The precise influence of pH depends on the p$K_a$ and p$K_b$ values of the acidic and basic groups, and so varies in different enzymes. These changes in ionization within the protein structure alter the attractive forces stabilizing the enzyme, and crucially affect its shape and its ability to recognize the substrate.

More specifically, changes in the ionization of side chains of amino acids at the active site will affect the ability of the enzyme to form a complex with the substrate. In most cases there is a clear optimum value for pH at which the enzyme has maximum activity. The optimum pH value for an enzyme gives a clue to the likely amino acids at its active site – typically, enzymes show maximum activity when the pH is close to the p$K_a$ value of the groups at its active site. Unlike for temperature, different enzymes in the same organism can have a wide variation in the optimum values of their pH, as shown in Figure 13.24.

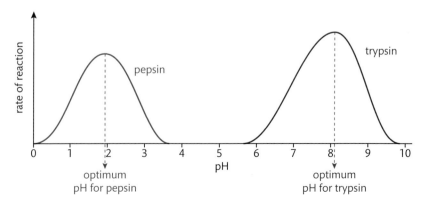

**Figure 13.24** The effect of pH on two different digestive enzymes in the human body.

These differences in the pH optima of different enzymes can be an important way of controlling enzyme activity. In the example shown in Figure 13.24, the enzyme pepsin is most active in the stomach, where the pH is very low. However, it becomes inactive once it is moved with the digested food into the more alkaline environment of the intestine, where trypsin is active. Their optimum values correspond to the pH in the different regions of the digestive tract where they are active. Extremes of pH denature an enzyme in much the same way as described for high temperature; an egg which has been dropped into strong acid looks 'cooked' in the same way as if it had been heated, due to changes in the tertiary structure of its protein.

## 3 Heavy metal ions

Heavy metals such as lead, copper, mercury, and silver are poisonous, primarily due to their effects on enzymes. When these metals are present as positive ions, they react with sulfhydryl groups, −SH, in the side chains of cysteine residues in the protein, forming a covalent bond with the sulfur atom and displacing a hydrogen ion. This disrupts the folding of the protein, and may change the shape of the active site and its ability to bind substrate. This is a form of inhibition, discussed below.

cysteine residue in protein

Ag bound to cysteine causing conformational change in the protein

**Figure 13.25**
Enzyme inhibition by $Ag^+$ ions. Binding of the metal to a sulfhydryl group in the amino acid cysteine may change the conformation of the enzyme at the active site.

## Chemical inhibitors modify enzyme activity

Inhibitors are chemicals that bind to enzymes and decrease their catalytic activity. Enzyme inhibition is an important aspect of the regulation of enzyme activity. Biochemical research using inhibitors has helped to provide a lot of information on details of enzyme action and metabolic pathways, and often plays a central role in drug design.

There are two main types of inhibitor, distinguished by where they bind to the enzyme:

- competitive inhibitors that bind at the active site
- non-competitive inhibitors that bind at a different location on the enzyme.

The optimum values of temperature and pH for an enzyme refer to the conditions where the enzyme and substrate are maximally able to bind and form a complex.

Inorganic dyes used to darken hair, such as 'Grecian Formula', contain a soluble lead salt which interacts with the sulfur atoms in the hair protein keratin to produce lead sulfide, PbS, which is black. The amount of darkening depends on the proportion of cysteine residues in the hair. Ancient Greeks used to line their waterways with lead and it was noticed that people who bathed often in this water had darker hair. Lead poisoning from the drinking water is believed to have contributed to the decline of both the Greek and the Roman empires. Concerns over the toxicity of lead salts have caused these hair dyes to be banned in many countries.

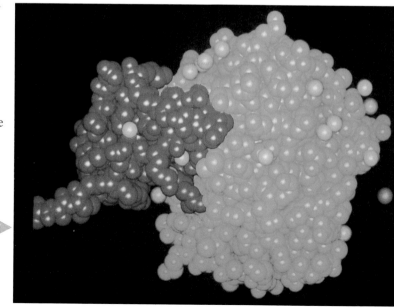

Computer graphics model of the digestive enzyme chymotrypsin, shown in green, with an inhibitor, shown in red. The small blue objects are water molecules. Chymotrypsin's action is to break down protein molecules, but the inhibitor prevents this from happening by binding at the active site.

## 1 Competitive inhibitors

Chemicals that bind at the active site of the enzyme are known as **competitive inhibitors** because they compete with the substrate for the binding position. They usually have a chemical structure similar to that of the substrate, so in a sense they mimic its ability to bind. But once they are bound they do not react to form products, instead blocking the active site and making it unavailable to the substrate.

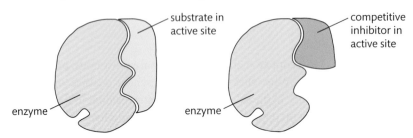

**Figure 13.26** Binding of a competitive inhibitor at the active site of an enzyme.

Increasing the concentration of substrate reduces the extent of inhibition as relatively fewer of the inhibitor molecules are able to bind. In this type of inhibition $V_{max}$ is not altered as there is still a substrate concentration where full activity of the enzyme can be achieved. But as it takes a higher substrate concentration to reach this rate, $K_m$ is increased. These relationships are shown in Figure 13.27.

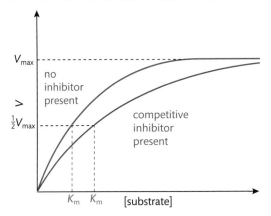

**Figure 13.27** Effect of a competitive inhibitor on the rate of an enzyme-catalysed reaction. $V_{max}$ is not altered by the inhibitor but $K_m$ is increased.

A good example of a competitive inhibitor is malonate inhibiting the enzyme succinate dehydrogenase. As its name suggests, the enzyme acts to remove hydrogen from succinate, which converts it into fumarate. This reaction occurs during aerobic respiration. The structures of the substrate succinate and the inhibitor malonate are sufficiently similar for them both to be able to bind at the same active site.

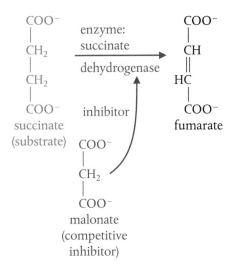

**Figure 13.28** The action of malonate as a competitive inhibitor for the enzyme succinate dehydrogenase. It possesses the correct chemical groups to be able to compete with succinate for binding at the active site.

## CHALLENGE YOURSELF

**6** What are the IUPAC names for succinate, fumarate and malonate?

## 2 Non-competitive inhibitors

Chemicals that bind to the enzyme at a position other than the active site are known as **non-competitive inhibitors**. Their binding causes a conformational change in the protein structure that alters the active site, inhibiting its ability to bind to the substrate. The term **allosteric site** refers to the binding site of the non-competitive inhibitor on the enzyme.

Increasing the concentration of substrate will not reduce the extent of this type of inhibition as the enzymes have effectively been decommissioned by the inhibitor and are unavailable. $V_{max}$ is decreased and cannot be restored no matter how high the substrate concentration. But, as is shown in Figure 13.30, the value of $K_m$ is unchanged because the uninhibited enzymes are perfectly functional.

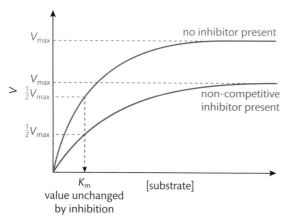

As non-competitive inhibitors do not bind at the active site, they do not necessarily possess similar chemical features to the substrate.

## Summary

The table below summarizes some of the main differences between competitive and non-competitive inhibitors.

|  | Competitive inhibition | Non-competitive inhibition |
|---|---|---|
| binding site on enzyme | binds at active site | binds at allosteric site |
| effect on $V_{max}$ | not affected | decreased |
| effect on $K_m$ | increased | not affected |

We have seen that metal ions such as $Ag^+$, $Hg^{2+}$, $Pb^{2+}$, and $Cu^{2+}$ can act as non-competitive inhibitors of enzyme activity, and many poisons such as DDT and cyanide behave similarly. Antibiotics, such as penicillin (described in Chapter 15), kill bacteria by inhibiting one of their key enzymes. Many anticancer drugs also work in this way, in order to block cell division in the tumour.

In healthy cells, enzyme inhibition is often an important means of controlling metabolic activity. One example is that the product of a reaction sometimes acts as an inhibitor of the enzyme for its synthesis, thereby setting up a feedback loop regulating its own concentration. This is known as **product inhibition**.

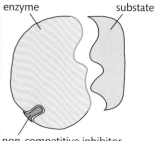

non-competitive inhibitor binds at allosteric site

**Figure 13.29** Binding of a non-competitive inhibitor to an enzyme changes the active site so that the substrate cannot bind.

**Figure 13.30** Effect of a non-competitive inhibitor on the rate of an enzyme-catalysed reaction. $V_{max}$ is reduced by the inhibitor but $K_m$ is unchanged.

*Allosteric inhibition* is not covered here. This is a broader term which can include both competitive and non-competitive inhibition, as well as negative and positive modulators. Here we refer to the allosteric site only in the context of the binding site of non-competitive inhibitors.

**Competitive inhibitors bind *at* the active site of the enzyme, non-competitive inhibitors bind *away* from the active site.**

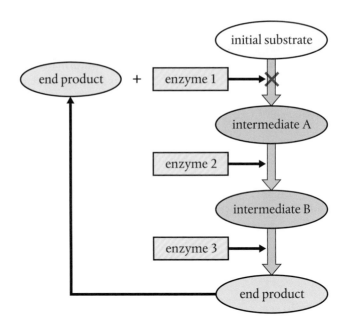

**Figure 13.31** Product inhibition in a biochemical pathway. The end product of the reaction acts as an inhibitor for the first enzyme leading to its production, so as its concentration builds up it effectively switches off its own synthesis. The synthesis of many amino acids is regulated in this way.

Inhibitors are described as **irreversible** when their binding to the enzyme is permanent, usually because it involves the formation of a covalent bond. Cyanide is an example of an irreversible inhibitor of the enzyme cytochrome oxidase, which catalyses the reduction of oxygen to water in the last step of aerobic respiration.

### Exercises

**10 (a)** State four characteristics of enzymes.
  **(b)** Sketch a graph of the rate of an enzyme reaction against temperature and explain its shape.

**11 (a)** Draw a graph of the rate of an enzyme reaction against substrate concentration.
  **(b)** On the same axes sketch how this graph would change in the presence of a competitive inhibitor.
  **(c)** State the effect of a competitive inhibitor on the values of:
    **(i)** $V_{max}$
    **(ii)** $K_m$

**12** Compare enzymes and inorganic catalysts, with reference to two similarities and three differences.

## Analysis of proteins

Analysis of protein content is a major aspect of research in biochemistry. For example, clinical analysis of protein levels in body fluids can be used to confirm pregnancy or can be used to help diagnose a variety of diseases. Food analysts are interested in knowing the total concentration and type of proteins in foods, and the pharmaceutical industry often uses altered protein levels to test the efficacy of a drug.

Many different approaches and techniques are used in protein analysis. We will consider here two main aspects of this work:

• analysis of the amino acid composition of an isolated protein
• analysis of the protein concentration of a sample.

### Analysis of the amino acid composition of a protein

The first step in the analysis is to break the peptide bonds between the amino acids in the protein structure through **hydrolysis** reactions, usually using acid. These reactions reverse the condensation reactions discussed on page 675, and occur commonly in cells during enzyme-catalysed protein digestion. (Note that determination of the amino acid composition of a protein is not the same as knowing its primary structure, as the *sequence* of the amino acids will not be known.)

Separation of the resulting amino acid mixture into its components can then be achieved in two ways.

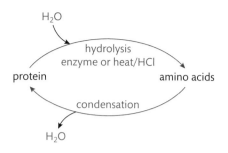

**Figure 13.32** Hydrolysis of protein produces amino acids; condensation of amino acids produces proteins.

## 1 Chromatography

Chromatography is a useful technique for separating and identifying the components of a mixture. The basic principle is that the components have different affinities for two phases, a **stationary phase** and a **mobile phase**, and so are separated as the mobile phase moves through the stationary phase. As amino acids are colourless in solution they are usually treated with a **locating reagent** at the end of the process which makes them take on colour to aid their identification.

**Paper chromatography** is an example of partition chromatography, in which the components are separated on the basis of their different solubilities in the two phases. It is used mainly for qualitative analysis. The paper contains about 10% water, and this is the stationary phase. Water is adsorbed by forming hydrogen bonds with the −OH groups in the cellulose of the paper. The solvent is the mobile phase as it rises up the paper by capillary action. As it does so it dissolves the components of the mixture to different extents, so carrying them at different rates.

The procedure is simple to run. A small sample of the amino acid mixture is spotted near the bottom of the chromatographic paper, and this position, known as the **origin**, needs to be clearly marked (in pencil so as not to interfere with the experiment). The paper is then suspended in a chromatographic tank containing a small volume of solvent, ensuring that the spot is above the level of the solvent.

> When measuring the distances to calculate $R_f$ values, be careful to measure from the origin and not from the bottom of the paper. Similarly, the solvent moves as far as the solvent front, not to the top of the paper.

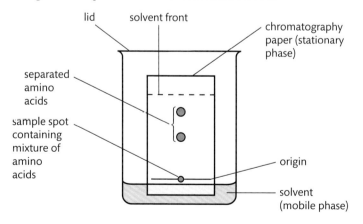

**Figure 13.33** Apparatus used to separate amino acids by paper chromatography.

As the solvent rises up the paper it will pass over the spot. Amino acids in the spot will distribute themselves between the two phases and so move up the paper at different speeds. As a result they become spread out according to their different solubilities. When the solvent reaches almost to the top of the paper, its final position is marked and is known as the **solvent front**. The paper is removed from the tank and developed by spraying it with the locating reagent **ninhydrin**. Most amino acids will now appear

**Separation of amino acids by chromatography**
Full details of how to carry out this experiment with a worksheet are available online.

701

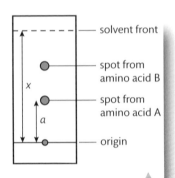

solvent front

spot from amino acid B

spot from amino acid A

origin

*x*

*a*

**Figure 13.34** Calculation of $R_f$ values in chromatography.

In chromatography, the $R_f$ value can be used to identify the components of a mixture.

$$R_f = \frac{\text{distance moved by amino acid}}{\text{distance moved by solvent}}$$

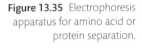

purple and can be distinguished as separate isolated spots up the length of the paper. The final result is known as a **chromatogram**.

The position of each amino acid on the chromatogram can be represented as an $R_f$ value (retention factor), which is calculated as shown below.

$$R_f = \frac{\text{distance moved by amino acid}}{\text{distance moved by solvent}}$$

So, for amino acid A, $R_f = \dfrac{a}{x}$

Specific amino acids have characteristic $R_f$ values when measured under the same conditions, so can be identified by comparing the values obtained with data tables. It is helpful to spot known amino acids alongside the mixture to act as markers for the experiment.

## 2 Electrophoresis

Electrophoresis is a technique for the analysis and separation of a mixture based on the movement of charged particles in an electric field. As we saw on page 682, amino acids carry different charges depending on the pH, and these differences can be exploited to separate them when placed in a buffered solution at a particular pH.

• When the pH is equal to their isoelectric point, amino acids will not move as they carry no net charge.
• When the pH > their isoelectric point, the amino acids exist as anions and move to the anode.
• When the pH < their isoelectric point, the amino acids exist as cations and move to the cathode.

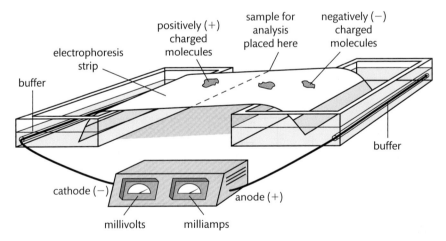

**Figure 13.35** Electrophoresis apparatus for amino acid or protein separation.

The rate of movement of the ions will depend on the number of charges on the ion and the molecular mass – smaller, more highly charged ions migrate faster. The voltage used and the temperature also affect the rate of movement.

In gel electrophoresis, the medium is a gel, typically made of polyacrylamide. The amino acid mixture is placed in wells in the centre of the gel and a voltage is applied. Depending on the pH of the buffer used, different amino acids will move at different rates and in different directions towards the oppositely charged electrodes. When separation is complete they can be detected with a stain such as ninhydrin or made to fluoresce under UV light, and identified by comparison with known samples or from data tables.

Electrophoresis can also be used to separate and identify intact proteins according to their different rates of migration towards the poles.

## Worked example

Gel electrophoresis was carried out using a buffer at pH 6.0 on a mixture of glycine, alanine, lysine, glutamic acid, and aspartic acid. Use section 33 of the IB data booklet to identify which amino acids

(a) will remain close to the origin

(b) will move fastest towards the anode

(c) will move fastest towards the cathode.

### Solution

From their isoelectric points, at pH 6.0 the amino acids will exist as follows:

glycine: neutral; alanine: neutral; lysine: cation; glutamic acid: anion; aspartic acid: anion

Therefore:

(a) glycine and alanine will not move

(b) glutamic acid and aspartic acid will move towards the anode, and aspartic acid will move more quickly as it is a smaller molecule

(c) lysine will move towards the cathode.

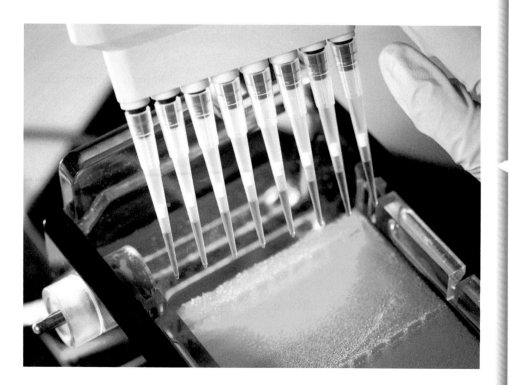

Multi-pipette used to place protein samples into agarose gel in a buffer solution for electrophoresis. The protein molecules will separate according to their different attractions to opposite electrical poles across the polyacrylamide gel (polyacrylamide gel electrophoresis or PAGE). This technique is used to detect whether proteins associated with particular diseases are found in the blood.

## Determination of the pH of buffer solutions

Electrophoresis and other aspects of experimental work used in protein studies and analysis require the use of buffer solutions. Buffers resist the change in the pH of a solution on the addition of small amounts of acid or base, and can be prepared to operate at a wide range of pH. The composition and mode of action of buffers was discussed in Chapter 8, and you might find it useful to review this first before going on to this section on the calculation of the pH of a buffer solution.

The pH of a buffer solution, that is its $H^+$ concentration, will depend on the interactions among its components. We will consider here an acidic buffer made of the generic weak acid HA and its salt MA.

The equilibria that exist in the buffer will be:

$$HA(aq) \rightleftharpoons H^+(aq) + A^-(aq)$$

$$MA(aq) \rightarrow M^+(aq) + A^-(aq)$$

We can make two approximations, based on some assumptions about these reactions, which will help to make the calculations easier.

1  The dissociation of the weak acid is so small that it can be considered to be negligible. So we can make the approximation

$$[HA]_{initial} \approx [HA]_{equilibrium}$$

2  The salt is considered to be fully dissociated into its ions. So we can approximate

$$[MA]_{initial} \approx [A^-]_{equilibrium}$$

The equilibrium expression for the acid is

$$K_a = \frac{[H^+][A^-]}{[HA]}$$

Therefore $[H^+] = K_a \dfrac{[HA]}{[A^-]}$

remembering that all values in this expression must be *equilibrium* concentrations. But from the approximations justified above, we know that $[HA]_{equilibrium} \approx [HA]_{initial}$ and $[A^-]_{equilibrium} \approx [MA]_{initial}$, so we can substitute these values as follows:

$$[H^+] = K_a \frac{[HA]_{initial}}{[MA]_{initial}}$$

which is usually given as

$$[H^+] = K_a \frac{[acid]}{[salt]}$$

By taking the negative logarithms of both sides of the equation, we can derive:

$$pH = pK_a + \log_{10} \frac{[salt]}{[acid]}$$

For basic buffer solutions the equivalent equations are:

$$[OH^-] = K_b \frac{[base]}{[salt]} \quad \text{and} \quad pOH = pK_b + \log_{10} \frac{[salt]}{[base]}$$

Joseph Henderson (1878–1942) was an American biochemist who developed equations showing that acid–base balance in the blood is regulated by buffers. Karl Hasselbalch (1874–1962), a Danish chemist and a pioneer in the use of pH measurement in medicine, converted the equations to logarithmic form in his work on studying acidosis in the blood. We now know that different buffers in the blood work together to keep the pH tightly controlled at 7.4. Any fluctuation in this value is so crucial that pH levels below 7.0 (acidosis) and above 7.8 (alkalosis) are, in the words of the medical profession, 'incompatible with life'.

These equations, known as the Henderson–Hasselbalch equations, are given in section 1 of the IB data booklet. The beauty of these expressions is that they enable us to know the pH of a buffer solution directly from:

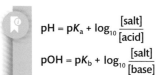

$$pH = pK_a + \log_{10}\frac{[salt]}{[acid]}$$

$$pOH = pK_b + \log_{10}\frac{[salt]}{[base]}$$

• the $K_a$ or $K_b$ values of its component acid or base and
• the ratio of initial concentrations of acid and salt used to prepare the buffer.

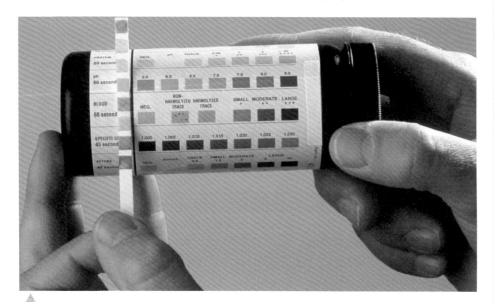

Urine analysis using a multiple test stick against a reference chart. The pads test for pH as well as for various components of the urine. Body fluids such as urine are effectively buffered for pH, so alterations in the urine pH can provide insights into medical conditions and disease.

## Worked example

Calculate the pH of a buffer solution at 298 K, prepared by mixing 25 cm³ of 0.10 mol dm⁻³ ethanoic acid, $CH_3COOH$, with 25 cm³ of 0.10 mol dm⁻³ sodium ethanoate, $Na^+CH_3COO^-$. $K_a$ of $CH_3COOH = 1.8 \times 10^{-5}$ at 298 K.

### Solution

$pK_a$ of $CH_3COOH = -\log_{10}(1.8 \times 10^{-5}) = 4.74$

As there are equal volumes and concentrations of $CH_3COOH$ and $NaCH_3COO$, then [acid] = [salt].

$$pH = pK_a + \log_{10}\frac{[salt]}{[acid]} = 4.74 + \log_{10}(1) = 4.74 + 0 = 4.74$$

Note that $\log_{10}(1) = 0$

This example shows that when a buffer solution contains equal amounts in moles of acid and salt (or base and salt), the last term in the Henderson–Hasselbalch expression becomes zero, so pH = $pK_a$ (or pOH = $pK_b$). This relationship is extremely useful when it comes to preparing buffers of a specified pH. All we have to do is choose an acid with a $pK_a$ value close to the required pH and then, if necessary, adjust the concentrations of acid and salt accordingly.

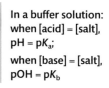

In a buffer solution:
when [acid] = [salt],
pH = $pK_a$;
when [base] = [salt],
pOH = $pK_b$

The buffer solution can be prepared by reacting the acid with enough strong alkali to convert one half of it into salt, as described on page 381.

### Worked example

How would you prepare a buffer solution of pH 3.75 starting with methanoic acid (HCOOH) and NaOH?

**Solution**

From the IB data booklet we have $pK_a$ (HCOOH) = 3.75, so a buffer with equal amounts in moles of this acid and its salt NaHCOO will have pH = 3.75.

This equimolar solution is prepared by reacting the acid with enough NaOH, so that one half of it is converted into salt and therefore [HCOOH] = [HCOO⁻].

Alternatively, the buffer can be prepared by mixing the acid directly with an appropriate amount of its salt.

### Worked example

How much $0.10 \text{ mol dm}^{-3}$ butanoic acid solution and solid potassium butanoate should be used to make $1.00 \text{ dm}^3$ of pH 5.00 buffer solution? State the assumptions made in the calculation.

**Solution**

From the IB data booklet butanoic acid has $pK_a = 4.83$.

$$pH = pK_a + \log_{10} \frac{[A^-]}{[HA]}$$

$$\therefore 5.00 - 4.83 = \log_{10} \frac{[\text{butanoate ion}]}{0.10 \text{ mol dm}^{-3}}$$

taking antilogs of both sides give

$$10^{0.17} = \frac{[\text{butanoate ion}]}{0.10 \text{ mol dm}^{-3}} = 1.5$$

$$\therefore [\text{butanoate ion}] = 0.15 \text{ mol dm}^{-3}$$

The molar mass of potassium butanoate is $126.12 \text{ g mol}^{-1}$

$$\therefore 1.00 \text{ dm}^3 \text{ of } 0.15 \text{ mol dm}^{-3} \text{ solution} = 0.15 \text{ mol} \times 126.12 \text{ g mol}^{-1} = 19 \text{ g}$$

So 19 g potassium butanoate should be added to $1.00 \text{ dm}^3$ of $0.10 \text{ mol dm}^{-3}$ butanoic acid.

The following assumptions were made:

- [butanoate ion]$_{\text{equilibrium}}$ = [potassium butanoate]$_{\text{initial}}$
- [butanoic acid]$_{\text{equilibrium}}$ = [butanoic acid]$_{\text{initial}}$
- no volume change occurs on mixing the solution.

## Analysis of the protein concentration of a sample

**Protein assays** refer to investigative procedures used to measure the concentration of protein in a sample. A technique commonly used in protein assays is **UV-visible spectroscopy**, often known as **UV-vis**.

As with other forms of spectroscopy, UV-vis depends on the fact that molecules interact with different parts of the electromagnetic spectrum according to their chemical composition. In this case we are interested in their interaction with visible and ultraviolet light. This radiation has the range approximately 180–750 nm, and has sufficient energy to excite the electrons in the occupied higher energy levels in complex molecules, such as proteins. When a full range of wavelengths of UV-vis radiation is passed through a sample, an **absorption spectrum** is obtained in which each characteristic absorption corresponds to an electronic transition. As seen in Figure 13.36, absorption spectra show wavelength ($\lambda$) on the horizontal axis and the intensity of absorption ($A$) on the vertical axis.

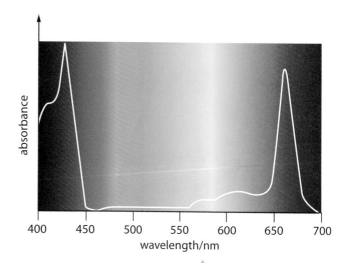

**Figure 13.36** Absorbance spectrum of chlorophyll, showing absorption peaks at approximately 430 nm and 660 nm, the red and blue parts of the spectrum. Green light is barely absorbed and so is transmitted, giving the colour that we see. Chlorophyll is a pigment molecule, associated with proteins in plant cells. It is discussed further on page 740.

Substances that appear coloured absorb certain wavelengths of light in the visible region and transmit the remaining wavelengths. This is why chlorophyll appears green, as we see in Figure 13.36. When the energy needed to excite an electron is in the ultraviolet region of the spectrum and all visible light is transmitted, the substance appears colourless.

Absorption spectra are obtained from a **spectrophotometer**, which is commonly used as a data-logging device. The main parts of a spectrophotometer are shown in Figure 13.37.

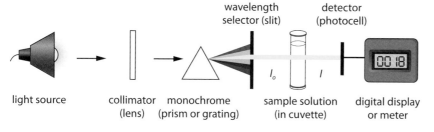

**Figure 13.37** Simplified diagram of a spectrophotometer. The desired range of wavelength of light is selected and passed through the solution of a sample in the cuvette. The photometer detects the light that is absorbed and sends a signal to a digital display.

UV-vis absorption spectra are useful for quantitative measurements, such as protein assays. Generally the wavelength of maximum absorbance is selected for the analysis. The amount of light absorbed at this wavelength (the absorbance, $A$) is given by the relationship $\log_{10}(I_0/I)$ where:

$I_0$ = the intensity of light before passing through the sample

$I$ = the intensity of light after passing through the sample

The absorbance depends on:

- the molar absorptivity, $\varepsilon$, defined as the absorbance of a 1.00 mol dm$^{-3}$ solution in a 1.00 cm cell at a specified wavelength
- the concentration of the solution, $c$
- the path length, $l$.

This can be expressed as:

$$\log_{10}(I_0/I) = \varepsilon\, l\, c$$

This is known as the Beer–Lambert law and is given in section 1 of the IB data booklet.

The Beer–Lambert law expresses the linear relationship between the absorbance and concentration of a compound at a fixed wavelength.

Biuret reagent showing the presence of protein in the right-hand flask. The biuret reagent causes peptide bonds in the protein to form a complex with copper(II) ions in alkaline solution, giving the solution a deep violet colour. The intensity of the colour increases with the concentration of protein present, and can be analysed by UV-vis spectroscopy.

It follows from this relationship that the absorbance of a compound at a fixed wavelength is directly proportional to its concentration. This can be used as the basis of determining the concentration of protein in a sample.

Protein analysis by UV-vis typically involves first reacting the sample with a reagent that generates a colour change which is dependent on the amount of protein present. This will promote absorption in the UV-vis range. Several different reagents can be used which react with different groups within the protein molecules, such as peptide bonds, aromatic side-groups, or basic groups. A common process uses the biuret reagent, which generates a purple colour by reaction with peptide bonds.

A relatively easy way to convert absorbance data into concentration is by use of a **calibration curve**. This is based on **standard solutions**, those with a known concentration of protein, which are prepared to cover a range of concentrations on either side of the value being investigated. Typically, at least five dilutions of a standard of known concentration are prepared. These are then each treated with the appropriate reagent to generate colour. Their absorbance is measured at the selected wavelength and plotted on a graph to obtain the calibration curve, as shown in Figure 13.38.

The absorbance of the solution to be analysed is then measured at the same wavelength as the standard solutions, and its protein concentration determined from the calibration curve, as shown in Figure 13.39. Where calibration curves have been generated by data-logging, appropriate software can often be used for this calculation. It is important that the sample and standard solutions are treated in the same way with respect to the type and amount of reagent added, buffer solutions used, and the temperature.

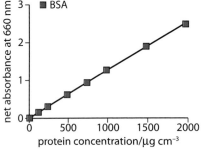
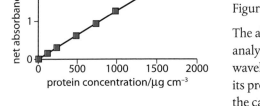

**Figure 13.38** Calibration curve using the protein standard BSA, bovine serum albumin.

Although we refer to calibration *curves*, the best results are obtained by interpolation on the *linear* part of the graph. Ideally, several calibration standards should be used and a regression function fitted to the data.

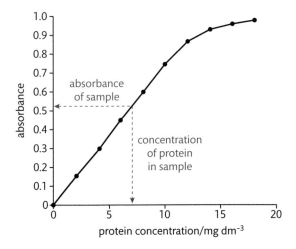

**Figure 13.39** A calibration curve used to find the concentration of a sample. The graph is linear at low concentrations, in accordance with the Beer–Lambert law.

## Worked example

The following tubes were set up using pipettes to measure volume. Tubes 1–6 contained dilutions of the protein standard solution bovine serum albumin (BSA) with an initial concentration of 5.00 mg protein $cm^{-3}$. The last row in the table refers to a tube of protein solution of unknown concentration. The absorbance of all tubes was measured at 540 nm.

| Tube number | Volume BSA / $cm^3$ | Volume distilled $H_2O$ / $cm^3$ | Volume reagent / $cm^3$ | Conc. protein / mg $cm^{-3}$ | Absorption at 540 nm |
|---|---|---|---|---|---|
| 1 | 0.00 | 2.00 | 2.00 | | 0.00 |
| 2 | 0.10 | 1.90 | 2.00 | | 0.34 |
| 3 | 0.30 | 1.70 | 2.00 | | 0.67 |
| 4 | 0.50 | 1.50 | 2.00 | | 1.02 |
| 5 | 0.70 | 1.30 | 2.00 | | 1.35 |
| 6 | 1.00 | 1.00 | 2.00 | | 1.65 |
| 2.00 $cm^3$ protein sample | | 0.00 | 2.00 | | 1.11 |

(a) Complete the column of conc. protein (mg $cm^{-3}$) for tubes 1–6 in the table.

(b) Plot a calibration curve of absorbance versus concentration for tubes 1–6.

(c) Use the curve to calculate the protein concentration in the unknown sample.

## Solution

..................................................................................................................

(a) conc. protein (mg protein $cm^{-3}$) = $\dfrac{\text{conc. BSA (mg protein cm}^{-3}) \times \text{vol BSA (cm}^{3})}{\text{total volume in tube (cm}^{3})}$

$$\therefore \text{conc. protein} = \frac{5.00 \text{ (mg protein cm}^{-3}) \times \text{vol BSA added (cm}^{3})}{4.00 \text{ (cm}^{3})}$$

| Tube number | Conc. protein / mg $cm^{-3}$ |
|---|---|
| 1 | 0.000 |
| 2 | 0.125 |
| 3 | 0.375 |
| 4 | 0.625 |
| 5 | 0.875 |
| 6 | 1.250 |

**(b)**

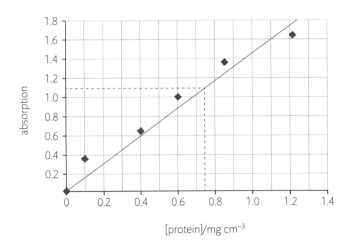

**(c)** Absorbance of 1.11 corresponds to protein concentration 0.750 mg cm$^{-3}$ in the sample tested.

### Exercises

**13 (a)** When carrying out paper chromatography on a sample of hydrolysed protein, explain why it is important to avoid handling the paper.
Make reference to section 33 in the IB data booklet to answer parts (b) and (c).

**(b)** Explain why in gel electrophoresis the amino acid isoleucine migrates towards the anode at high pH and towards the cathode at low pH.

**(c)** You are attempting to separate a mixture of glutamic acid and histidine by gel electrophoresis. Give a suggested pH for an appropriate buffer solution to use, and say in which direction each amino acid would migrate.

**14** Given 100 cm$^3$ of 0.05 mol dm$^{-3}$ methanoic acid, HCOOH, what volume of 0.05 mol dm$^{-3}$ NaOH would you need to add to prepare a buffer of pH 4.23? (Assume $K_a$ of HCOOH = $1.77 \times 10^{-4}$.)

**15** Explain the use of protein standards in preparing a calibration curve for the calculation of protein concentration.

## B.3 Lipids

## Understandings:
- Fats are more reduced than carbohydrates and so yield more energy when oxidized.
- Triglycerides are produced by condensation of glycerol with three fatty acids and contain ester links. Fatty acids can be saturated, monounsaturated, or polyunsaturated.
- Phospholipids are derivatives of triglycerides.
- Hydrolysis of triglycerides and phospholipids can occur using enzymes or in alkaline or acidic conditions.
- Steroids have a characteristic fused ring structure, known as a steroidal backbone.
- Lipids act as structural components of cell membranes, in energy storage, thermal and electrical insulation, transport of lipid soluble vitamins, and as hormones.

### *Guidance*
- *The structures of the fatty acids are given in the data booklet in section 34.*
- *Specific named examples of fats and oils do not have to be learned.*

## Applications and skills:

- Deduction of the structural formulas of reactants and products in condensation and hydrolysis reactions between glycerol and fatty acids and/or phosphate.
- Prediction of the relative melting points of fats and oils from their structures.
- Comparison of the processes of hydrolytic and oxidative rancidity in fats with respect to the site of reactivity in the molecules and the conditions that favour the reaction.
- Application of the concept of iodine number to determine the unsaturation of a fat.
- Comparison of carbohydrates and lipids as energy storage molecules with respect to their solubility and energy density.
- Discussion of the impact of lipids on health, including the roles of dietary high-density lipoprotein (HDL) and low-density lipoprotein (LDL), cholesterol, saturated, unsaturated, and *trans* fat and the use and abuse of steroids.

### Guidance
*The structural differences between cis and trans fats are not required.*

The term **lipid** is used as an umbrella term for a range of biomolecules such as fats and oils, steroids, and phospholipids. They are characterized by being hydrophobic or insoluble in water. They are, though, soluble in non-polar solvents, and this property is often used in extracting them from cells. Lipids contain the elements carbon, hydrogen, and oxygen, but the ratio of hydrogen to oxygen is greater than in carbohydrates – in other words they are more reduced molecules.

## Functions of lipids

### Lipids are essential molecules in a variety of roles in cells

Lipids contain stored energy that is released when they are broken down in the reactions of respiration in cells. Because lipids are more reduced than carbohydrates, they can effectively undergo *more* oxidation and so release *more* energy per unit mass when used as a respiratory substrate. The difference is significant: a gram of lipid releases almost twice as much energy as a gram of carbohydrate. However, partly due to their insolubility, the energy in lipids is not so readily available as it is in carbohydrates, as more reactions are involved in the breakdown. So the energy is released more slowly. The fat stores in animals, known as **adipose tissue** or **blubber**, serve as reservoirs of energy, swelling and shrinking as fat is deposited and withdrawn. Plants also sometimes store lipids for energy, for example as oils in seeds.

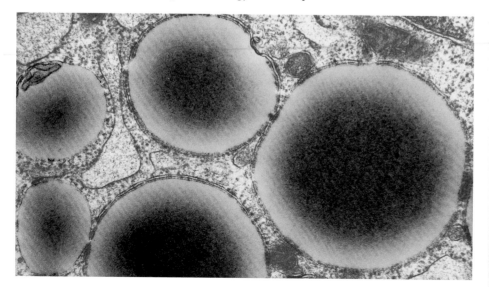

## CHALLENGE YOURSELF

7 Even though the concept of oxidation number is of limited use in organic chemistry, predict how you would expect the oxidation state of carbon to compare in a simple carbohydrate and in a simple lipid molecule. See if you can check this with some simple examples from each group.

You are more likely to take a glucose tablet than suck a lump of cheese, for example, when you are running a marathon. But if you were going on an expedition to the Arctic, you would take lots of lipids like cheese and butter, as they make ideal storage molecules. These differences are because the energy in carbohydrates is more readily available, but lipids are a denser energy store.

Electron micrograph of lipid droplets shown in green in a fat cell. These cells form adipose tissue, which stores energy as an insulating layer of fat.

711

Stored fat helps to protect some body organs, such as the kidneys, and a layer of fat under the skin acts as a thermal insulator. This is why animals that live in cold climates, such as seals and polar bears, have significant fat stores. Lipids also act as electrical insulators. In nerve cells a special layer of phospholipids called the myelin sheath gives electrical insulation to the nerves, and speeds up nervous transmission.

Some hormones, such as the sex hormones testosterone and estrogen, are made of lipids in the form of steroids. Bile acids, which aid digestion of fat in the intestine, are also steroid based. In addition, lipids help to absorb fat-soluble vitamins such as A, D, E, and K.

Lipids also play an important structural role. The phospholipids are a major component of membranes that enclose cells. Here they help to determine the selective transport of metabolites across cell boundaries. A different lipid molecule, cholesterol, is also important in plasma membrane structure, where it influences the fluidity and so the permeability of the membrane.

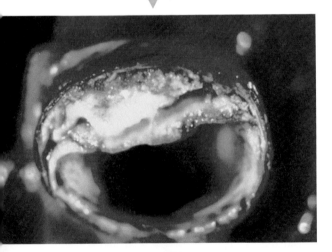

Magnified view of a slice through an artery showing a thick deposit caused by the disease atherosclerosis. The deposit is composed of a mixture of fats, cholesterol, and dead muscle cells. It disrupts blood flow and can break off in fragments blocking smaller blood vessels, leading to strokes and heart disease.

## Excess lipids in the diet can have negative effects on health

Excess lipids in the diet are increasingly linked to negative effects on health. These arise largely due to their low solubility that causes some lipids to be deposited in the walls of the main blood vessels. This can restrict blood flow, a condition known as **atherosclerosis**. It is usually associated with high blood pressure and can lead to heart disease.

In addition, because of the body's ability to convert excess fats into adipose tissue, a diet too rich in lipids can lead to the excess accumulation of body fat known as **obesity**. This is linked to many other health issues including diabetes and a variety of cancers. The molecule that is often the main culprit in circulatory diseases is **cholesterol**. It is present in the human diet, particularly from animal fat, and is also synthesized in the body. Because cholesterol is insoluble in blood, it is transported bound in different lipoproteins, the most well known of which are **LDL** (low-density lipoprotein) and **HDL** (high-density lipoprotein). These have gained the somewhat simplistic terms 'bad cholesterol' and 'good cholesterol' respectively. The names reflect the fact that high levels of LDL cholesterol are associated with increased deposition in the walls of the arteries, while high levels of HDL cholesterol seem to protect against heart attack. It is believed that HDL tends to carry cholesterol away from the arteries, so slowing its build-up. The main sources of LDL cholesterol are saturated fats and *trans* fats, the chemical nature of which is discussed in the next section.

**TOK**

Debate exists as to whether people who need two airline seats because they are obese should have to pay for this themselves or have the second seat paid for as part of a disability coverage. To what extent should health problems perceived as resulting from life-style choices be distinguished from other forms of disability?

Clearly the type of fat consumed is as important as the total amount. In general an intake of poly-unsaturated fats, such as those found in fish, many nuts, and corn oil, is considered beneficial in lowering levels of LDL cholesterol. Also, a type of fatty acid known as omega-3-poly-unsaturated fatty acid, found for example in fish oils and flax seeds, has been shown to be linked with reduced risk of cardiovascular disease as well as with optimum neurological development. These fatty acids cannot be manufactured by the body so are known as **essential fatty acids** and must be taken in the diet.

The essential fatty acids linoleic acid and linolenic acid are known as omega-6 and omega-3. The names refer to the position of the first double bond in the molecule relative to the terminal —$CH_3$ group. This is referred to as omega (the last letter in the Greek alphabet), to represent its distance from the —COOH group. These structures are given in section 34 of the IB data booklet.

## Uses and abuses of steroids

As noted above, lipids in the form of steroids are found in some hormones. Female steroid hormones are used in contraceptive pill formulations and in HRT (hormone replacement therapy) sometimes prescribed during menopause. Possible side-effects of these steroid treatments must be monitored and ongoing research is essential to provide data about long-term usage.

Male steroid hormones are collectively called androgens, of which **testosterone** is the most important. Medical uses of testosterone include treatment of disorders of the testes and breast cancer. These hormones are also known as **anabolic steroids** due to their role in promoting tissue growth, especially of muscles. Synthetic forms of them are used medically to help gain weight after debilitating diseases. They have also been used as **performance-enhancing drugs** by athletes in sports such as weight-lifting and cycling, as they can increase strength and endurance. Their use is banned by most sporting authorities for medical and ethical reasons.

The American Food and Drug Administration (FDA) recommends that pregnant women and nursing mothers should limit their intake of fish to two servings per week, due to concerns about mercury contamination. However, studies have also shown the importance of omega-3 fatty acids, which are found in fish, for fetal health and development of the brain. The obvious tension between these opposing recommendations leaves women with a difficult choice. One possible solution is to choose fish with low mercury levels, such as salmon and sardines; another is to use omega-3 fatty acid dietary supplements.

Scientist centrifuging urine samples sent for anti-doping testing at the laboratories of the Italian National Olympic Committee. The samples are analysed for performance-enhancing drugs such as anabolic steroids, using techniques such as liquid chromatography/mass spectrometry. Drug testing like this has become a focus of national and international sporting authorities and uses increasingly accurate technology. Anabolic steroids can cause changes in secondary sexual characteristics resulting from hormone imbalances, and can be associated with increased risk of liver cancer.

## Structures of different lipids

The structures of the three main types of lipids – triglycerides, phospholipids, and steroids – will be considered here in turn.

## Structure of triglycerides: fats and oils

**Triglycerides** are the major constituent of fats and oils. They are esters formed by condensation reactions between **glycerol** and **three fatty acids**.

Glycerol is a molecule with three carbon atoms, each of which has an alcohol group, as shown below.

$$\begin{array}{c}
H \\
| \\
H-C-O-H \\
| \\
H-C-O-H \\
| \\
H-C-O-H \\
| \\
H
\end{array}$$

glycerol

Following the guidelines in Chapter 10, see if you can give glycerol its IUPAC name? The answer is propane-1,2,3-triol; however, we will continue to refer to it as glycerol as this name is widely used.

Fatty acids are long-chain carboxylic acids R-COOH. For example, the fatty acid palmitic acid, $C_{15}H_{31}COOH$, has the following structure:

An esterification reaction takes place between an acid —COOH group and each —OH group in glycerol, eliminating water as each ester link forms.

**Figure 13.40** Esterification is a condensation reaction in which a molecule of water is released as each —OH group in glycerol condenses with the fatty acid —COOH group. The zig-zag lines represent the hydrocarbon chains of the fatty acid.

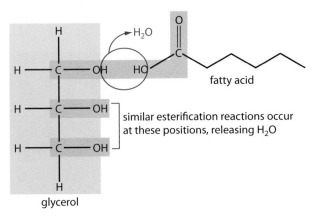

glycerol

similar esterification reactions occur at these positions, releasing $H_2O$

fatty acid

So one glycerol condenses with *three* fatty acids to form the *triglyceride*.

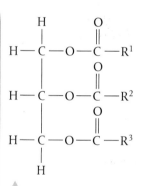

## Figure 13.41 and triglyceride structure

**ester linkage**

**glycerol**

a triglyceride

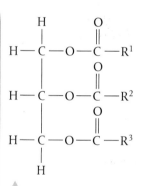
Figure 13.41 A triglyceride.

In most natural oils and fats the three fatty acids that form one triglyceride molecule are not all the same. They can be designated $R^1$, $R^2$, and $R^3$ as shown in Figure 13.42.

The fatty acids differ from each other in the following two ways, which give rise to the specific properties of different fats and oils.

1   The length of their hydrocarbon chain: the most abundant fatty acids have an even number of carbon atoms with chains between 14 and 22 carbon atoms long.

2   The number and position of carbon–carbon double bonds in the hydrocarbon chain:
    • fatty acids with no double bonds are said to be **saturated**
    • fatty acids with a single double bond are described as **mono-unsaturated**
    • fatty acids with several double bonds are described as **poly-unsaturated**.

Because fats and oils usually contain a variety of fatty acids, they are classified according to the predominant types of unsaturation present.

## Saturated fatty acids

Saturated fatty acids have the general formula $C_nH_{2n+1}COOH$. The carbon chain, made from only carbon–carbon single bonds, has tetrahedral bond angles (109.5°) which allow the molecules to pack relatively closely together. This leads to significant London (dispersion) forces between them. As a result they form saturated triglycerides with relatively high melting points that are solids at room temperature. They are known as **fats** and are derived mostly from animals. Common examples are butter and lard.

Figure 13.42 A triglyceride containing three different fatty acids.

*(i)* Fatty acids with an odd number of carbon atoms are rarely found in land-based animals, but are very common in marine organisms.

**Saturated fatty acids contain all single carbon–carbon bonds; unsaturated fatty acids contain one or more double carbon–carbon bonds in the hydrocarbon chain.**

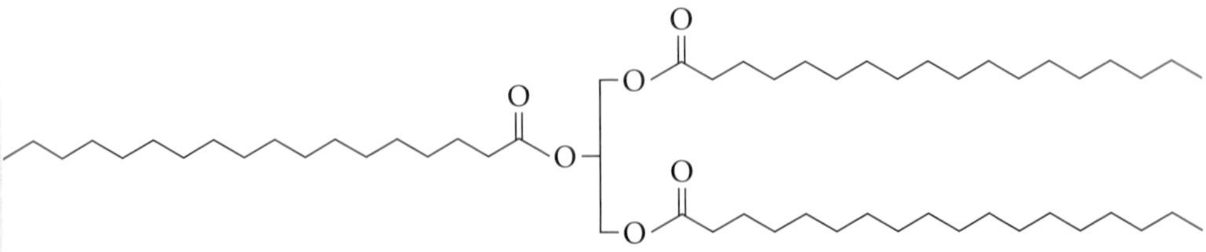

**Figure 13.43** A saturated triglyceride.

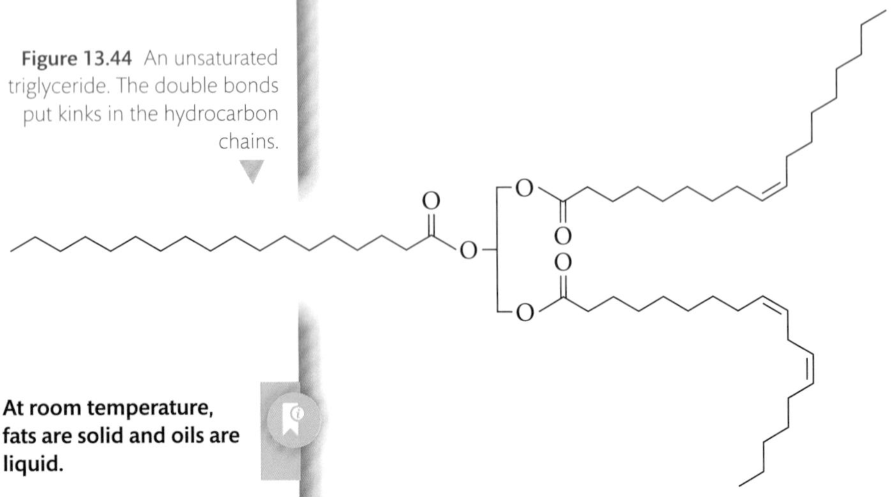

**Figure 13.44** An unsaturated triglyceride. The double bonds put kinks in the hydrocarbon chains.

At room temperature, fats are solid and oils are liquid.

The melting points of fatty acids increase with their molar mass and degree of saturation.

Assortment of dietary oils (liquids) and fats (solids). Oils have a lower melting point because they contain unsaturated fatty acids. These lower the level of cholesterol in the blood.

## Unsaturated fatty acids

By contrast, the unsaturated fatty acids, containing one or more carbon–carbon double bonds with 120° bond angles, have kinks in the chains that make it more difficult for the molecules to pack closely together. They form unsaturated triglycerides which have weaker intermolecular forces and lower melting points, so are liquids at room temperature. They are known as **oils**, and are found mostly in plants and fish. Common examples are corn oil and cod liver oil.

As commonly occurring fats and oils consist of a mixture of triglycerides, they usually do not have sharp melting points. Generally, the melting points increase with increasing molar mass (length of the hydrocarbon chains) and with increasing degree of saturation. The table below illustrates this by comparing the melting points of fatty acids with similar molar mass.

| Fatty acid | Formula | M / g mol$^{-1}$ | Number of double bonds | Melting point / °C | Common source | |
|---|---|---|---|---|---|---|
| linolenic | $C_{17}H_{29}COOH$ | 278 | 3 | −11 | soyabean oil | increasing saturation |
| linoleic | $C_{17}H_{31}COOH$ | 280 | 2 | −5 | corn oil | |
| oleic | $C_{17}H_{33}COOH$ | 282 | 1 | 16 | olive oil | |
| stearic | $C_{17}H_{35}COOH$ | 284 | 0 | 70 | beef fat | |

As noted earlier, a strong correlation has been shown between diets rich in saturated fats and elevated levels of LDL cholesterol, with associated increase in the incidence of heart disease.

### NATURE OF SCIENCE

Public knowledge concerning the health effects of excess lipids in the diet is the result of many published studies of long-term data. Scientists have shared their results through peer-reviewed publications and have helped to explain the links between diet and health. The widely accepted relationship between *trans* fats, excess saturated fat, and cholesterol with cardiovascular disease has helped to direct policies on food production and education.

## Determination of the degree of unsaturation in a fat uses iodine

Unsaturated fatty acids are able to undergo **addition reactions** by breaking the carbon–carbon double bond(s) and adding incoming groups to the new bonding positions created on the carbon atoms. This is a characteristic reaction of alkenes, described in Chapter 10. Iodine ($I_2$) is able to react with unsaturated fats in this way.

$$\underset{/}{\overset{\backslash}{C}} = \underset{\backslash}{\overset{/}{C}} \quad + \ I_2 \quad \longrightarrow \quad -\overset{\overset{I}{|}}{\underset{|}{C}} - \overset{\overset{I}{|}}{\underset{|}{C}} -$$

The equation shows that one mole of iodine will react with each mole of double bonds in the fat. Therefore the higher the number of double bonds per molecule, the larger the amount of iodine that can react. This is expressed as the **iodine number**, defined as the number of grams of iodine which reacts with 100 grams of fat. It is therefore a measure of the amount of unsaturation in the fat.

Determination of the iodine number of a fat usually involves reacting a known amount of the fat with a known amount of iodine, and waiting for the reaction to be completed. The amount of excess iodine remaining can then be calculated by titration with $Na_2S_2O_3$(aq), from which the amount of reacted iodine can be determined.

### Worked example

Linoleic acid has the formula $C_{18}H_{32}O_2$. Determine the iodine number of linoleic acid.

#### Solution

The formula for linoleic acid can be expressed as $C_{17}H_{31}COOH$, from which we can deduce that it has two carbon–carbon double bonds.

$\therefore$ 2 moles $I_2$ will react with 1 mole linoleic acid

$M$(linoleic acid) = 280 g mol$^{-1}$

$M(I_2)$ = 254 g mol$^{-1}$

$\therefore$ 280 g linoleic acid reacts with $(2 \times 254)$ = 508 g $I_2$

100 g linoleic acid reacts with $\dfrac{508 \ g \times 100 \ g}{280 \ g}$ = 181 g $I_2$

$\therefore$ iodine number = 181

The lower the iodine value, the higher the proportion of saturated fatty acids in the fat; the iodine number of saturated fatty acids will, of course, be zero. The table below gives some iodine values for some common fats and oils.

| Fat or oil | Iodine number |
|---|---|
| soyabean oil | 122–134 |
| olive oil | 80–90 |
| bacon fat | 47–67 |
| beef fat | 35–45 |

A similar reaction to the addition of iodine is addition of hydrogen, known as **hydrogenation**. This is sometimes carried out by the food industry to increase the saturation of oils. The process of partial hydrogenation produces *trans* fats, which are associated with some of the health problems discussed earlier. The structure of these fats is discussed in section 13.10, page 751.

### Rancidity of fats

When fats used in the food industry are stored for long periods of time, they can undergo chemical change which causes them to become **rancid**. This is characterized by disagreeable smells, taste, texture, or appearance. There are two main causes of this.

#### Hydrolytic rancidity

This occurs when the fat breaks down by hydrolysis reactions, using the water present in food. The site of reactivity is the ester linkages in the triglycerides.

$$
\begin{array}{ccc}
\begin{array}{l}
CH_2O - \overset{\displaystyle O}{\overset{\|}{C}} - R^1 \\[4pt]
CHO - \overset{\displaystyle O}{\overset{\|}{C}} - R^2 \quad + \ 3H_2O \\[4pt]
CH_2O - \overset{\displaystyle O}{\overset{\|}{C}} - R^3 \\[4pt]
\text{fat}
\end{array}
&
\rightarrow
&
\begin{array}{l}
CH_2OH \\[4pt]
CHOH \quad + \\[4pt]
CH_2OH \\[4pt]
\text{glycerol}
\end{array}
\quad
\begin{array}{l}
HO - \overset{\displaystyle O}{\overset{\|}{C}} - R^1 \\[4pt]
HO - \overset{\displaystyle O}{\overset{\|}{C}} - R^2 \\[4pt]
HO - \overset{\displaystyle O}{\overset{\|}{C}} - R^3 \\[4pt]
\text{fatty acid}
\end{array}
\end{array}
$$

This is the reverse of the condensation reaction described on page 714. The reaction occurs more readily in the presence of heat, such as during deep-fat frying. It is also catalysed by the enzyme **lipase**, and can be favoured in the presence of certain bacteria. The rancid smell and flavour is due to the release of free fatty acids, such as butanoic and octanoic acids which are released from rancid milk. As hydrolytic rancidity is favoured by higher temperatures, it can be substantially reduced by refrigeration.

#### Oxidative rancidity

This occurs when unsaturated fats react with oxygen from the air. The site of reactivity is the carbon–carbon double bonds in unsaturated triglycerides. The products responsible for the rancidity are volatile aldehydes and ketones. The process, known as auto-oxidation, is often accelerated by light and enzymes or metal ions. It proceeds via a free-radical mechanism and so yields a mixture of products. Oxidative rancidity is characteristic of fats and oils that have a high proportion of carbon–carbon double bonds, such as oily fish like herring. It can be controlled, but not eliminated, by the addition of **antioxidants**.

As they cannot undergo auto-oxidation, saturated fats are more stable than unsaturated fats.

Different cultures use varied sources of lipids and so different methods to extend their shelf-life. Examples of preservation include processing, packaging, and chemical additives.

## Structure of phospholipids

Phospholipids are similar to triglycerides in that they are also derived from fatty acids and glycerol, but have only two fatty acids condensed onto the glycerol molecule. The third –OH position of the glycerol has, instead, condensed with a phosphate group. Different phospholipids vary in their fatty acid chains and in the group attached to the phosphate. One of the most common phospholipids, **lecithin**, is shown in Figure 13.45.

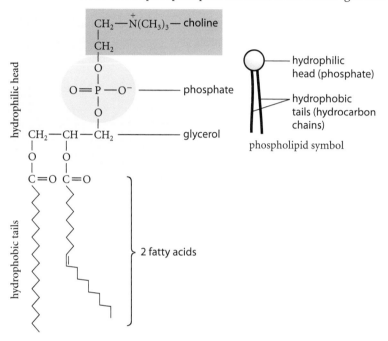

Whale oil was a traditional source of lipids for many countries, and was widely used as a food substance, a lubricant, and as a fuel for lighting. Over-harvesting of whales led to a depletion of stocks by the mid-1800s, and kerosene from crude oil became the major alternative fuel.

**Figure 13.45** Representations of the structure of phospholipids.

Phospholipids are characterized by having a polar, or hydrophilic, 'head' (the phosphate group) and two non-polar, or hydrophobic, 'tails' (the hydrocarbon chains of the fatty acids). As a result they will spontaneously form a **phospholipid bilayer** which maximizes the interactions between the polar groups and water, while creating a non-polar, hydrophobic interior.

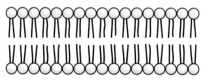

**Figure 13.46** Phospholipid bilayer.

This phospholipid bilayer provides the basis of membrane structure.

## Hydrolysis of fats and phospholipids

Triglycerides and phospholipids are broken down in hydrolysis reactions to yield their component molecules. The reactions use water and can occur in acidic or in alkaline conditions, or catalysed by enzymes known as **lipases**. This occurs during the digestion of lipids in the gut, where the activity of the enzymes is controlled largely by local changes in pH. Lipid digestion is generally a slow process and may take several hours before soluble products are released. Hydrolysis reactions are also responsible for hydrolytic rancidity.

Alkaline hydrolysis produces the salt of the fatty acid and is used in the manufacture of soap. For this reason, this reaction of reverse esterification is sometimes called **saponification**.

For example,

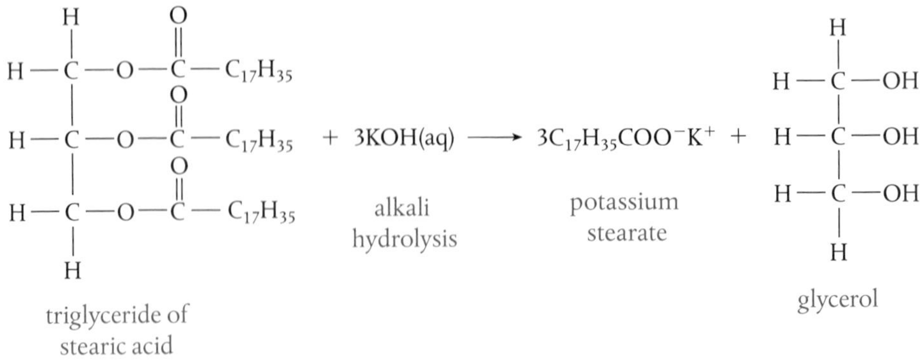

triglyceride of
stearic acid

$+ 3KOH(aq) \longrightarrow 3C_{17}H_{35}COO^-K^+ +$

alkali
hydrolysis

potassium
stearate

glycerol

## Structure of steroids

Steroids are lipids with a structure consisting of four fused rings, known as a **steroidal backbone**. One of the most important steroids is cholesterol, which has the following structure. It is given in the IB data booklet in section 34.

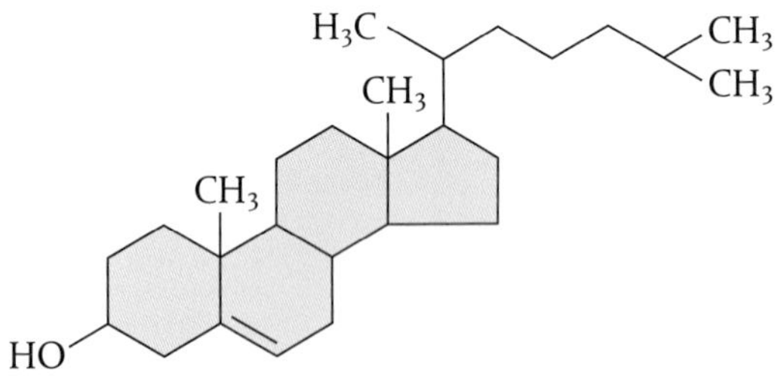

Cholesterol is used as a precursor in the synthesis of many biomolecules, including other steroids such as the sex hormones, bile acids, and Vitamin D. It is an essential component of cell membranes as it helps to provide fluidity and permeability to the structure. The hydroxyl group interacts with the polar head groups of phospholipids in the membrane, while the non-polar rings and hydrocarbon chain interact with the hydrophobic tails of the phospholipid bilayer. The uses, and problems, of cholesterol and other steroids were discussed earlier in this section.

### Exercises

**16** A sample of fat containing 0.02 moles of fatty acid was found to react with 10.16 g of iodine. Determine the number of carbon–carbon double bonds present in the fatty acid.

**17** The following table shows the melting point for a number of common fatty acids found in dietary fats and oils.

| Name of acid | Formula | Structural formula | Melting point / °C |
|---|---|---|---|
| lauric | $C_{11}H_{23}COOH$ | $CH_3(CH_2)_{10}COOH$ | 44 |
| myristic | $C_{13}H_{27}COOH$ | $CH_3(CH_2)_{12}COOH$ | 58 |
| palmitic | $C_{15}H_{31}COOH$ | $CH_3(CH_2)_{14}COOH$ | 63 |
| stearic | $C_{17}H_{35}COOH$ | $CH_3(CH_2)_{16}COOH$ | 70 |
| oleic | $C_{17}H_{33}COOH$ | $CH_3(CH_2)_7CH=CH(CH_2)_7COOH$ | 16 |
| linoleic | $C_{17}H_{31}COOH$ | $CH_3(CH_2)_4CH=CHCH_2CH=CH(CH_2)_7COOH$ | –5 |

**(a)** Which of the fatty acids are solids at a room temperature of 25 °C?
**(b)** Describe and explain the trend in the melting points in the first four fatty acids listed.
**(c)** Describe and explain the pattern in the melting points of the last three acids mentioned.

**18** Explain the different chemical basis of the two types of rancidity which can occur in lipids.

# B.4 Carbohydrates

## Understandings:

- Carbohydrates have the general formula $C_x(H_2O)_y$.
- Haworth projections represent the cyclic structures of monosaccharides.
- Monosaccharides contain either an aldehyde group (aldose) or a ketone group (ketose) and several –OH groups.
- Straight-chain forms of sugars cyclize in solution to form ring structures containing an ether linkage.
- Glycosidic bonds form between monosaccharides forming disaccharides and polysaccharides.
- Carbohydrates are used as energy sources and energy reserves.

  ### Guidance
  - *The component monosaccharides of specific disaccharides and the linkage details of polysaccharides are not required.*
  - *The distinction between α- and β-forms, and the structure of cellulose is not required.*

## Applications and skills:

- Deduction of the structural formulas of disaccharides and polysaccharides from given monosaccharides.
- Relationship of the properties and functions of monosaccharides and polysaccharides to their chemical structures.

  ### Guidance
  *The straight-chain and α-ring forms of glucose and fructose are given in the data booklet in section 34.*

Carbohydrates (literally *hydrated carbon*) are composed of the three elements carbon, hydrogen, and oxygen, with the hydrogen and oxygen always in the same ratio as in water i.e. 2 : 1. They therefore can be expressed by the general formula $C_x(H_2O)_y$. Note that this higher ratio of oxygen represents a more oxidized state for the carbon atoms than in lipids. There are two main types of carbohydrates – the simple sugars or **monosaccharides** and the condensation polymers of these known as **polysaccharides**.

## Functions of carbohydrates

The monosaccharides, for example **glucose** and **fructose**, are readily soluble in water and are mostly taken up by cells quite rapidly. They are used as the main substrate for respiration, releasing energy for all cell processes. They also act as precursors in a large number of metabolic reactions, leading to the synthesis of other molecules such as fats, nucleic acids, and amino acids.

Polysaccharides, being insoluble, are used as the storage form of carbohydrates. Animals mostly use **glycogen** for storage of carbohydrates in the liver and muscles, while plants store **starch** in their cells. These energy reserves can be broken down into monosaccharides, which are then oxidized in respiration to release energy for the cell's activities.

Animals generally make little use of carbohydrates for structural materials, but plant cells are very dependent on carbohydrates for their structure. The polysaccharide **cellulose**, which is found in the walls of all plant cells, is claimed to be the most abundant organic compound on Earth.

**TOK**

## Structure of carbohydrates

### Monosaccharides are simple sugars

The monosaccharides are the simplest form of carbohydrates and are usually classified according to the number of carbon atoms that they contain. Some of the most common are the **triose** sugars (C3), the **pentose** sugars (C5), and the **hexose** sugars (C6). All monosaccharides can be represented by the empirical formula $CH_2O$. Hexose sugars, for example, all have the molecular formula $C_6H_{12}O_6$.

These sugar molecules all have two or more hydroxyl groups (—OH) and a carbonyl group (—C=O). Their large number of polar hydroxyl groups is responsible for their ready solubility in water.

Many isomers of sugars exist, representing different structural arrangements of the same number and type of atoms in different molecules. For example, $C_6H_{12}O_6$ exists in many forms including glucose and fructose. The straight-chain forms of these sugars are shown below.

glucose: an aldose sugar     fructose: a ketose sugar

> **Monosaccharides contain a carbonyl group and at least two hydroxyl groups. They have the empirical formula $CH_2O$.**

In aqueous solution these sugars undergo an internal reaction resulting in the more familiar ring structures shown below.

glucose     fructose

These representations of the ring forms of sugars are known as **Haworth projection formulas**. The edge of the ring nearest the reader is represented by bold lines, and the letter C for the carbons in the ring are usually omitted from the structure.

The formation of the ring in glucose and fructose makes possible another type of isomer, so-called alpha and beta forms which are discussed further in section B.10.

The straight-chain and α-ring forms of glucose and fructose are given in section 34 of the IB data booklet so they do not have to be learned.

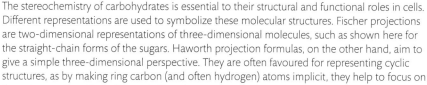

The stereochemistry of carbohydrates is essential to their structural and functional roles in cells. Different representations are used to symbolize these molecular structures. Fischer projections are two-dimensional representations of three-dimensional molecules, such as shown here for the straight-chain forms of the sugars. Haworth projection formulas, on the other hand, aim to give a simple three-dimensional perspective. They are often favoured for representing cyclic structures, as by making ring carbon (and often hydrogen) atoms implicit, they help to focus on the nature and position of the substituent groups.

Haworth formulas can, however, be misleading as they suggest that the five-membered ring of fructose and six-membered ring of glucose are planar, which is not the case. In reality these exist as puckered rings in different conformations which can interconvert by rotation around single bonds.

Scientists depend on models and visualizations to communicate knowledge, but it is often the case that a single representation is inadequate. Understanding can therefore be enhanced by the use of a variety of models, including computer simulations and mathematical models.

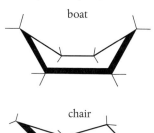

## Disaccharides are two simple sugars linked together

Disaccharides form by linking two monosaccharides together in a condensation reaction. A molecule of water is eliminated as an −OH group from each sugar molecule react together. The resulting bond between the monosaccharides is known as a **glycosidic link**. Disaccharides are all soluble molecules that can be hydrolysed into two monosaccharides by acid hydrolysis or by enzyme-catalysed reaction. Combining different monosaccharides will produce different disaccharides.

For example, two α-glucose molecules condense to form the disaccharide maltose, as shown here. The glycosidic link is known as 1–4 because $C_1$ in one molecule is bonded to $C_4$ in the other molecule. The molecular formula of maltose is $C_{12}H_{22}O_{11}$.

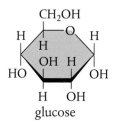

Sucrose is a disaccharide of glucose and fructose, whose structures are shown below. The condensation reaction involves the −OH group at $C_1$ of glucose. Deduce the structural formula of sucrose.

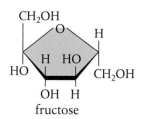

Sugar is an important trade product from many countries. Sugar cane is the world's largest crop, and is exported largely from tropical and sub-tropical regions of Brazil, India, China, and Thailand. Sugar beet grows only in the temperate zones of North America and Europe, though countries in these regions are usually net importers of sugar. Both crops yield sugar in the form of sucrose.

Lactose is a disaccharide found in milk. Many people suffer from 'lactose intolerance', which is usually a genetic condition, characterized by an inability to digest lactose owing to a lack of the enzyme lactase. The condition is more prevalent in many Asian and South African cultures where dairy products are less traditionally part of the adult diet. By contrast, people with ancestry in Europe, the Middle East, and parts of East Africa, where mammals are often milked for food, typically maintain lactase production throughout life.

The production of ethanol as a biofuel usually involves the fermentation of carbohydrates from crops such as corn and sugar cane. This is at the heart of the **food versus fuel** debate on land and resource use.

### Solution

The monosaccharides are joined by a glycosidic link as follows:

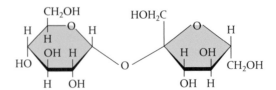

## Polysaccharides are the polymers of sugars

Polysaccharides form by repetitions of the reaction shown above, leading to a long chain of monosaccharide units held together by glycosidic bonds. Due to their large size, polysaccharides are all insoluble molecules, and so make an ideal storage form of the energy-rich carbohydrates. Cellulose forms a rigid structure which provides support to plant cells.

The most common polysaccharides are:

• starch – carbohydrate store in plants
• glycogen – carbohydrate store in animals
• cellulose – structural material in plants.

These are all polymers of glucose, but differ from each other in the isomer of glucose used and in the amount of cross-linking in the chain. For example, starch consists mostly of a straight-chain polymer of α-glucose with 1–4 linkages.

### Worked example

Glycogen is a branched polysaccharide which contains α-glucose molecules linked with both 1–4 and 1–6 glycosidic bonds. Use the structure of α-glucose in your IB data booklet to draw a section of the molecule showing both types of linkages.

### Solution

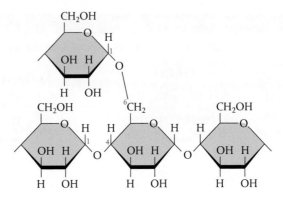

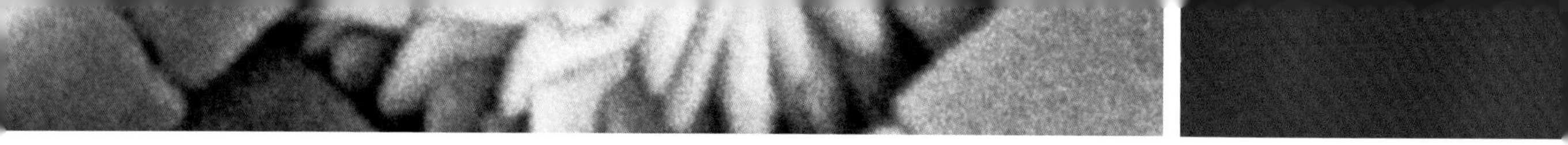

The structure of cellulose is described in section B.10.

## Exercises

**19 (a)** State the empirical formula of all monosaccharides.
   **(b)** State and explain the difference in solubility of monosaccharides and polysaccharides.

**20** The disaccharide lactose is made from the monomers shown below.

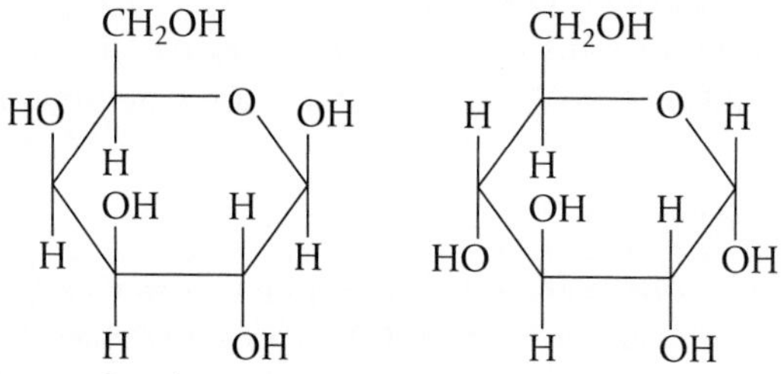

β-galactose          α-glucose

Deduce the structural and molecular formula of lactose, and name the bond between the sugars.

# B.5 Vitamins

## Understandings:

- Vitamins are organic micronutrients which (mostly) cannot be synthesized by the body but must be obtained from suitable food sources.
- The solubility (in water or fat) of a vitamin can be predicted from its structure.
- Most vitamins are sensitive to heat.
- Vitamin deficiencies in the diet cause particular diseases and affect millions of people worldwide.

## Applications and skills:

- Comparison of the structures of vitamins A, C, and D.
- Discussion of the causes and effects of vitamin deficiencies in different countries and suggestion of solutions.

### Guidance

- *The structures of vitamins A, C, and D are provided in the IB data booklet section 35.*
- *Specific food sources of vitamins or names of deficiency diseases do not have to be learned.*

Given the complexity of metabolic processes, it is not surprising that organisms need an equally complex array of molecules to maintain health, and these are known as **nutrients**. In terms of the human diet, **micronutrients** are those needed in extremely small amounts, generally less than 0.005% of body mass, quantities so small that they are usually measured in mg or µg per day. These substances are needed to enable the body to produce enzymes, hormones, and other biomolecules. As tiny as the amounts are, however, the consequences of their absence are severe and are known as **deficiency diseases**. Micronutrients include the **vitamins** and many so-called **trace minerals** such as Fe, Cu, Zn, I, Se, Mn, Mo, Cr, Co, and B.

## Vitamins are organic micronutrients

Vitamins are organic compounds, needed in small amounts for normal growth and metabolism, which (with the exception of vitamin D) are not synthesized in the body.

They are usually broken down by the reactions in which they are involved, so must be taken in from suitable food sources in the diet. They are often classified according to their relative solubility in water or in lipid.

## Water-soluble vitamins

Vitamins that are water soluble have polar bonds and the ability to form hydrogen bonds with water. They are transported directly in the blood, and excesses are filtered out by the kidneys and excreted. Vitamins B and C are water soluble.

The structures of some important vitamins are given in section 35 of the IB data booklet, so they do not have to be learned.

## Lipid-soluble vitamins

Vitamins that are lipid soluble are mostly non-polar molecules with long hydrocarbon chains or rings. They are slower to be absorbed and excesses tend to be stored in fat tissues where they can produce serious side-effects. Vitamins A, D, E, and K are fat soluble.

| Vitamin | Structure | Solubility and properties |
|---|---|---|
| A, retinol | | • fat soluble<br>• hydrocarbon chain and ring are non-polar and influence the solubility more than the one —OH group<br>• involved in the visual cycle in the eye, and particularly important for vision in low light intensity |
| C, ascorbic acid | | • water soluble<br>• several —OH groups enable hydrogen bonds to form with water<br>• acts as cofactor in some enzymic reactions, important in tissue regeneration following injury, and resistance to some diseases |
| D, calciferol | | • fat soluble<br>• predominantly a hydrocarbon molecule with four non-polar rings and only one —OH group<br>• chemically similar to cholesterol<br>• stimulates the uptake of calcium ions by cells and important in the health of bones and teeth |

Vitamin C contains several functional groups (—OH and —C=C—) that are relatively easily oxidized. This is why the vitamin is easily destroyed by most methods of food processing and storage, and is therefore best obtained from *fresh* fruits and vegetables. In general, the water-soluble vitamins are the most sensitive to heat, but other vitamins also lose some activity after being heated.

## NATURE OF SCIENCE

The discovery of vitamins (*vital amines*) is an example of scientists seeking a cause for specific observations. In the 1700s, many sailors on long voyages suffered from a disease known as scurvy, with symptoms of bleeding gums, poor resistance to infection, and dark spots on the skin. Although the concept of a disease resulting from the *lack* of a dietary component was not understood, it was discovered that these symptoms could be prevented by providing a nutrient that is present in citrus fruits. The vital ingredient was later identified as vitamin C. Similarly, in 1905, it was noted that the disease beriberi could be prevented by eating an ingredient in unpolished rice, later identified as vitamin B.

These and similar correlations led to the **hypothesis of deficiency diseases** – the concept that a *lack* of something in the diet could cause disease. This was formulated in 1912 and now forms the basis of much healthcare practice.

British people are sometimes known as 'limies' in America, because of the earlier practice of the British Navy to supplement the diet of sailors with limes to prevent scurvy.

## Vitamin deficiencies are a form of malnutrition

The absence of a regular, balanced supply of the diverse nutrients needed in the diet is known as **malnutrition**. This describes a broad spectrum of conditions, including vitamin deficiency diseases, which are always associated with compromised health. The main focus of malnutrition has traditionally been the large variety of nutrient-deficiency diseases, and in particular the incidence of these in under-developed countries. But increasingly the world is seeing a dramatic increase in diseases caused by high consumption of processed, energy-dense but micronutrient-poor foods.

The causes of malnutrition arising from vitamin deficiency are varied and widespread. They include:

• lack of distribution of global resources
• depletion of nutrients in the soil and water
• lack of education about, or understanding of, the importance of a balanced diet
• over-processing of food for transport and storage
• the use of chemical treatments such as herbicides in food production.

'Freedom from hunger and malnutrition is a basic human right and their alleviation is a fundamental prerequisite for human and national development.'

World Health Organization

Vitamin A is an antioxidant and is needed for healthy eyesight. It is related to carotene and found in orange and yellow fruit and vegetables. As it is fat soluble, it has been found that it can be effectively added to margarine in a process known as **vitamin fortification**. The potential of rice as a vehicle for vitamin A fortification is also being explored, given that rice is an important staple in many countries where the prevalence of vitamin A deficiency is high. Vitamin B is a term for a group of eight distinct water-soluble vitamins, which are most commonly found in unprocessed foods such as whole grains. Their deficiency causes a range of diseases including beriberi, forms of anaemia, and mental disorders. Cereals are commonly fortified with B vitamins. As vitamin $B_{12}$ contains cobalt, which is available only from animal sources, vegetarians and vegans may be at particular risk of deficiency. Vitamin C deficiency is characterized by lower resistance to infection and can develop into scurvy. It is best prevented by a diet rich in fresh fruits and vegetables. Vitamin D is made by the action of sunlight on the skin and is important for healthy bones.

Food label showing fortification of foods with vitamins.

727

The World Health Organization has identified vitamin A as the most important vitamin deficiency in global health terms. It is estimated that more than half of all countries, especially in Africa and South-East Asia, have a significant incidence of vitamin A deficiency, which is the leading cause of preventable blindness in children and increases the risk of disease and death from severe infections.

To what extent is mass medication through the food we eat an infringement of personal freedom? Are there ways of striking a balance between the claim of the scientists or government that they know what is best for health, and the right of an individual to choose what to eat?

Exposure to sunlight is an important source of vitamin D, but it is also the case that ultraviolet light has a damaging effect on the skin and can be the cause of skin cancers. Protection from this necessitates the use of sunscreens, and those with a protection factor of 8 or greater will block UV rays that produce vitamin D. This makes it even more important to include good sources of vitamin D in the diet when sun exposure is limited in this way. Mandatory vitamin D fortification is increasing, usually applied to milk and margarine, as the vitamin is fat soluble.

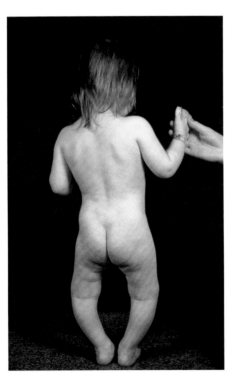

Child suffering from rickets. Rickets is a disease in growing children in which the bones do not harden and are malformed. It is due to a deficiency in vitamin D, which is necessary for the uptake of calcium.

In summary, there exist many possible solutions to the varying challenges of malnutrition. These include:

- the fortification of different staple foods with micronutrients
- the availability of vitamin supplements in many forms
- the possible improvements to nutrient content of food through genetic modification
- increased labelling of foods with content information
- education regarding the nature of a balanced diet and promotion of the importance of personal responsibility in dietary choices.

**NATURE OF SCIENCE**

The manufacture and sale of vitamin supplements is a major industry in many countries. Debate is widespread on the extent to which a balanced diet can provide sufficient quantities of vitamins, or whether supplementation is necessary for optimum health. Part of the controversy is a result of claims made by Linus Pauling in 1970 that 'megadoses' of vitamin C could be effective in preventing the common cold, and possibly certain cancers and heart disease as well. As the only person ever to have won two unshared Nobel Prizes, Pauling was a scientist and humanitarian of significant authority, and so his claims led to a surge in the sales of vitamin C. This happened despite the fact that his megavitamin claims lacked the evidence needed for acceptance by the scientific community. The existence of conflicting information and advice, and the pressure of advertising, can make it difficult for individuals to make an informed choice. Scientists have a duty to share their findings with the public in ways that help people to understand the issues and make valid judgments.

### Exercises

**21** Make reference to section 35 in the IB data booklet.

   **(a)** Identify two functional groups common to all three vitamins shown.

   **(b)** Identify one vitamin that is water soluble and one vitamin that is fat soluble. Explain the differences in solubility in terms of their structures and intermolecular forces.

**22** Suggest ways in which vitamin deficiency diseases can be alleviated.

# B.8 Nucleic acids

## Understandings:

- Nucleotides are the condensation products of a pentose sugar, phosphoric acid, and a nitrogenous base – adenine (A), guanine (G), cytosine (C), thymine (T), or uracil (U).
- Polynucleotides form by condensation reactions.
- DNA is a double helix of two polynucleotide strands held together by hydrogen bonds.
- RNA is usually a single polynucleotide chain that contains uracil in place of thymine, and a sugar ribose in place of deoxyribose.
- The sequence of bases in DNA determines the primary structure of proteins synthesized by the cell using a triplet code, known as the genetic code, which is universal.
- Genetically modified organisms have genetic material that has been altered by genetic engineering techniques, involving transferring DNA between species.

### Guidance
- *Structures of the nitrogenous bases and ribose and deoxyribose sugars are given in the data booklet in section 34.*
- *Knowledge of the different forms of RNA is not required.*

## Applications:

- Explanation of the stability of DNA in terms of the interactions between its hydrophilic and hydrophobic components.
- Explanation of the origin of the negative charge on DNA and its association with basic proteins (histones) in chromosomes.
- Deduction of the nucleotide sequence in a complementary strand of DNA or a molecule of RNA from a given polynucleotide sequence.
- Explanation of how the complementary pairing between bases enables DNA to replicate itself exactly.
- Discussion of the benefits and concerns of using genetically modified foods.

### Guidance
- *Limit expression of DNA to the concept of a four-unit base code determining a twenty-unit amino acid sequence. Details of transcription and translation are not required.*
- *Details of the process of DNA replication are not required.*

## The role of nucleic acids

**Deoxyribonucleic acid (DNA)** and **ribonucleic acid (RNA)** are collectively known as the nucleic acids. As is evident from their name they are acidic molecules found in the nucleus of cells (though RNA is also found elsewhere). DNA is responsible for storing the information that controls the genetic characteristics of an organism, and for passing it on to the next generation. RNA enables the information stored in DNA to be expressed by controlling the primary structures of proteins synthesized.

In order to carry out its functions, DNA needs to have the following features:

- it must be a very stable molecule, able to retain its precise chemical structure in cell conditions
- it must contain some 'code' that stores genetic information
- it must be able to replicate, in other words to produce an exact copy of itself.

The race to interpret all the known data about DNA and to come up with a model that could explain its structure and function was a major focus of biochemical research during the 1950s. When the double helical structure was suggested by Francis Crick and James Watson in their letter to *Nature* in 1953, it was immediately heralded as one of the most significant discoveries of the time. In a remarkably simple and elegant way, this model explained the unique ability of DNA to store and copy information exactly, as we will see in this section.

## The structure of nucleic acids

Like other biological macromolecules, DNA and RNA are polymers. They are built from monomers known as **nucleotides** and so are described as **polynucleotides**. Nucleic acids typically contain thousands of nucleotides, and are among the largest macromolecules found in cells.

### Nucleotides are the building blocks of nucleic acids

Nucleotides are made up from three components.

1  A pentose (C5) sugar: $C_5H_{10}O_5$ in DNA it is **deoxyribose**, in RNA it is **ribose**.

$^5CH_2OH$ ... $^5CH_2OH$

The difference between these sugars is in the groups attached to $C^2$ – *deoxy*ribose lacks an –OH.

2  A phosphate group $PO_4^{3-}$ (derived from phosphoric acid $H_3PO_4$) It is often denoted as (P)

$$O = P \begin{array}{c} O^- \\ | \\ \\ | \\ O^- \end{array} O^-$$

3  An organic nitrogenous base, of which there are two types. **Purines** are larger and contain two fused rings; **pyrimidines** are smaller and contain a single ring. There are two different purines and three different pyrimidines: each is described by the first letter of its name using a capital letter, as shown in the table below.

| Purine base | adenine, A 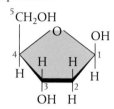 | guanine, G 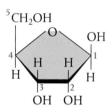 | |
|---|---|---|---|
| Pyrimidine base | cytosine, C | thymine, T | uracil, U |

The structures of the five bases are given in section 34 of the IB data booklet so they do not have to be learned. You should, however, be able to recognize which are purines, which are pyrimidines, and which pairs are able to link through hydrogen bonding.

Adenine, guanine, and cytosine are found in both DNA and RNA. Thymine is found exclusively in DNA and uracil is found exclusively in RNA.

The nucleotide forms as the pentose sugar, phosphate, and base join together by condensation reactions, releasing water. The base always condenses to $C_1$ of the sugar, and the phosphate to $C_5$. This is known as 'five prime' (5').

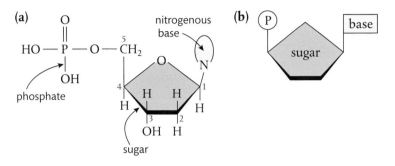

**Figure 13.47** (a) The structure of a deoxyribonucleotide. (b) A convenient short-hand form for drawing a nucleotide.

Ribonucleotides are found in RNA: they contain ribose sugar and either A, G, C, or U. Deoxyribonucleotides are found in DNA: they contain dexoyribose sugar and either A, G, C, or T.

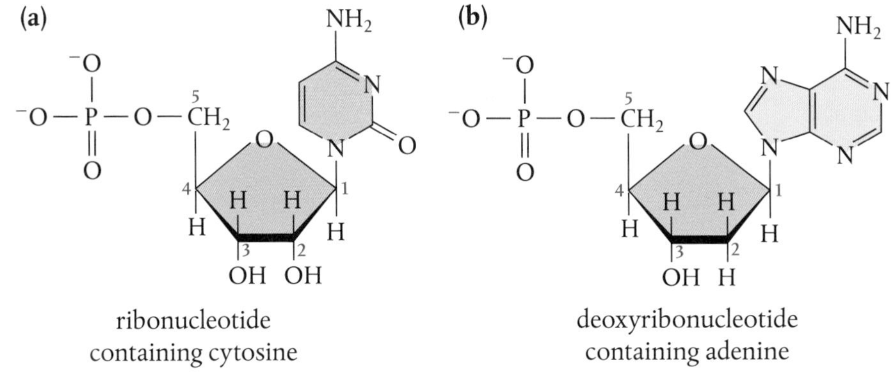

**(a)**

ribonucleotide
containing cytosine

**(b)**

deoxyribonucleotide
containing adenine

**Figure 13.48** (a) A ribonucleotide; (b) a deoxyribonucleotide.

## Nucleotides condense to form polynucleotides

Nucleotides link together in condensation reactions involving the phosphate at the 5' end of one nucleotide and the −OH group at the 3' (three prime) position of the other nucleotide. In this way they are able to build up a chain held together by covalent bonds between alternating sugar and phosphate residues. These bonds are phosphodiester links, as shown in Figure 13.49.

Note that the nitrogenous bases do not take part in the polymerization of the nucleotides but remain attached to the sugar at $C_1$.

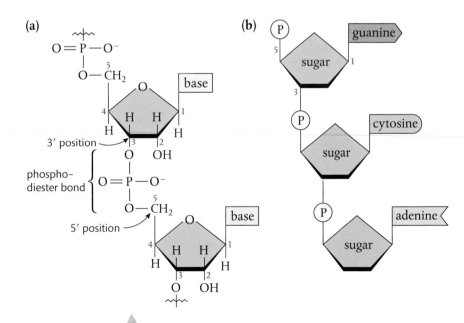

**Figure 13.49** (a) Part of a polynucleotide showing the phosphodiester bond. Note that the phosphate group carries a negative charge. (b) A short-hand form of a polynucleotide.

731

The story of the discovery of the structure of DNA shows how different approaches to solving the same problem can lead to a consistent conclusion. James Watson and Francis Crick, working in Cambridge, England, tackled the question largely by building molecular models, while Maurice Wilkins and Rosalind Franklin, working in London, approached it through X-ray crystallography. It is, however, also a story interwoven with tales of personal ambition and human conflict, that reflects some failure of the different teams of scientists to collaborate and communicate effectively. It is now widely recognized that, although Nobel Prizes for the discovery of DNA were awarded to Crick, Watson, and Wilkins in 1962, the crystallography work done by Franklin was crucial to the discovery. Franklin died in 1958, aged 37, and Nobel Prizes are not awarded posthumously.

Rosalind Franklin's famous X-ray photograph of DNA, which involved over 100 hours of exposure. It has been described as 'the most beautiful X-ray photograph of any substance ever taken.' The cross of bands indicates the helical nature of DNA.

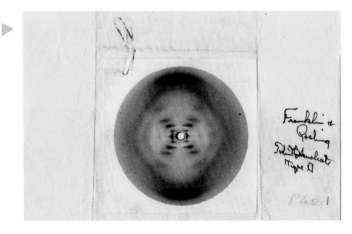

Computer artwork of the molecular structure of DNA. The two strands of the double helix, made of alternating sugar and phosphate groups, are shown in blue/green and pink/green. The diagonal lines show the stacked bases, which form complementary pairs held together with hydrogen bonds. The sequence of bases along the strand is the genetic code.

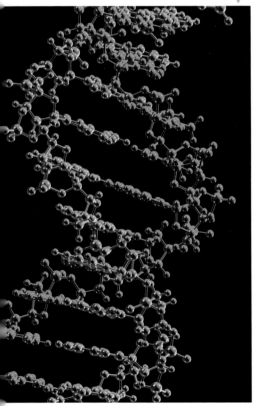

## DNA is a double helix of two polynucleotides

In DNA two polynucleotide strands are coiled around the same axis forming a **double helix** with the sugar–phosphate backbone on the outside and the nitrogenous bases on the inside. The two strands are held together by hydrogen bonds that form between bases on each strand. Due to the chemistry of the bases and the conformation of the helix, only certain **base pairings** involving one purine with one pyrimidine are possible: adenine forms a pair with thymine, and guanine always forms a pair with cytosine. These are known as **complementary pairs**.

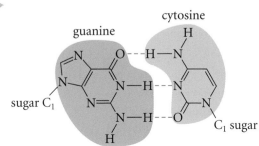

**Figure 13.50** Base pairs form only between adenine and thymine, and between guanine and cytosine. Note there are two hydrogen bonds between A and T and three hydrogen bonds between G and C.

The double helical structure with its paired bases is often described as a twisted ladder where the sides are the sugar–phosphate backbones and the rungs are the base pair (Figure 13.51).

Ten nucleotide residues make up one complete turn of the helix and this has the length of 3.4 nm. The two polynucleotide strands in the helix are said to be **anti-parallel**, meaning they run in opposite directions (3' → 5' and 5' → 3') and so are effectively upside down relative to each other, as shown in Figure 13.52.

This model fulfils all the expectations of DNA outlined earlier.

- Its stability is achieved by the fact that it maximizes hydrophobic interactions between the non-polar stacked bases in the sequestered environment in the middle of the molecule, while allowing polar and charged groups in the sugar–phosphate backbone to interact with the aqueous solution.
- The sequence of bases in the polynucleotide strand is effectively a digital code of information, with infinite variety possible.

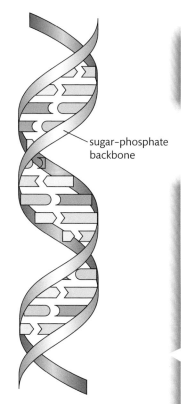

sugar–phosphate backbone

**Figure 13.51** The double helical structure of DNA.

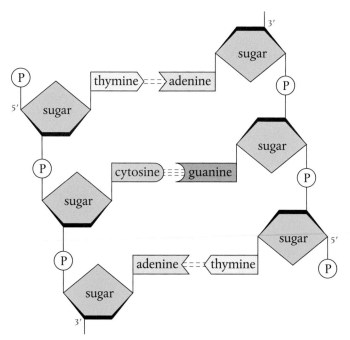

**Figure 13.52** Part of a DNA molecule. The two anti-parallel polynucleotide strands are held together by hydrogen bonds between the complementary bases.

- The base pairing between complementary strands provides a means for replication of the code. In a famous piece of understatement, Watson and Crick's 1953 paper concludes: '*It has not escaped our notice that the specific pairing we have postulated immediately suggests a possible copying mechanism for the genetic material.*' We will look at this mechanism in more detail later.

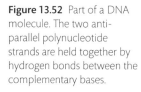

**In the structure of DNA, only the following base pairs exist:**
A=T, G≡C.

DNA fragments are observed to migrate towards the positive electrode in electrophoresis, indicating that they are negatively charged. The double helix structure of DNA shows that the origin of this charge is on the phosphate groups that link the sugars together in the backbone of the molecule. The negative charge causes DNA to associate with proteins known as **histones** that have a high proportion of basic amino acids, and so carry positive charges at cell pH. The combination of DNA and histones helps to stabilize the DNA within the **chromosomes** in the nucleus.

**DNA carries a negative charge due to its phosphate groups.**

**RNA differs from DNA in that it has**

- **ribose sugar instead of deoxyribose**
- **the base uracil instead of thymine**
- **a single-stranded structure.**


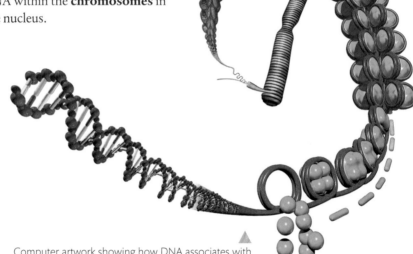

Computer artwork showing how DNA associates with histones. The DNA double helix is tightly coiled around histone proteins, shown as green spheres, which are tightly packaged together in groups of eight. These are then coiled together and further packaged into chromosomes, shown in the centre, which are the structures visible within the nucleus.

**TOK** Watson laughed when asked if he and Crick would patent their discovery of DNA, saying that 'there was no use for it'. 20 years later when the process for making recombinant DNA was developed at Stanford University, USA, by Boyer and Cohen, the technique was patented – leading to a revenue of $255 million in the biotech industry before the patent expired in 1997. This has opened many controversies, including the question of right of ownership of biological knowledge. What limits do you think should apply to patenting, which implies sole rights to use information?

## RNA is a single-stranded polynucleotide molecule

As we have noted, RNA differs from DNA in that it contains ribose sugar in place of deoxyribose and the base uracil in place of thymine. But in other ways its polynucleotide structure is constructed in the same manner as that of DNA, and it too carries information in its sequence of bases.

However, RNA exists as a single-stranded polynucleotide chain and does not generally form a double helix. It is a less stable molecule than DNA and is usually more short-lived in the cell. RNA is also able to cross the nuclear membrane and so can move between the nucleus and the cytoplasm.

## DNA is expressed through protein synthesis

DNA is the genetic material containing all the information for the development of the individual coded in the base sequences along its length. This code, which is essentially built from four 'letters', directs the synthesis of proteins by determining the sequence of their amino acids – their primary structure. Essentially, this means that the 4-unit code of bases in DNA must be translated into a 20-unit code to account for all the amino acids found in proteins. This occurs in two main steps, known as **transcription** and **translation**.

DNA is confined to the nucleus, but protein synthesis occurs on **ribosomes** in the cytoplasm of the cell. So DNA must allow a copy to be made of the relevant part of its information in the form of RNA, which then takes it to the ribosome. We can think of it as similar to the way in which we might copy a recipe from a book that stays in the library, and then take it to the place where we will use the information. The synthesis of RNA from DNA, known as **transcription**, occurs when the two strands of DNA separate by breaking the hydrogen bonds between the paired bases, a process often referred to as **unzipping**. Each strand of DNA can then act as a **template** for the assembly of a complementary strand of RNA from ribonucleotides. The specific base pairing ensures that ribonucleotides complementary to the bases in DNA are aligned in sequence, as shown in Figure 13.53. Note that the base uracil (U) which is used in RNA is complementary to adenine (A) in DNA. In this way the code in DNA is copied exactly. The entire process is controlled by enzymes.

Once formed, the RNA detaches from its DNA template and leaves the nucleus for the ribosome while the DNA re-forms the double helix.

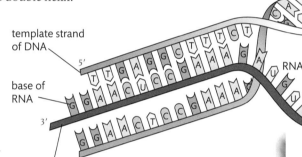

template strand of DNA

base of RNA

DNA

RNA

5′

3′

5′

**Figure 13.53** Production of RNA from DNA in transcription. Note that the base uracil which is present in RNA base pairs with adenine in DNA.

sugar–phosphate backbone of RNA

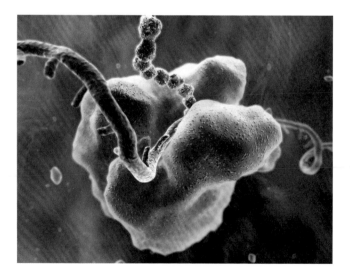

Computer artwork of a protein being synthesized at a ribosome. RNA, shown in purple, passes between the subunits of the ribosome and provides the instructions for the assembly of the protein. The sequence of bases in the RNA is a copy of the sequence in the DNA and determines the sequence of amino acids in the protein.

At the ribosome, the sequence of bases in RNA is used to determine the sequence of amino acids in a polypeptide. This is known as **translation** and involves the use of a different form of RNA that works like an adaptor. At one end this molecule recognizes a specific triplet of bases known as a **codon** in the transcribed RNA, and at the other end it recognizes a corresponding amino acid. As codons in the RNA are read sequentially, the adaptor molecule brings the appropriate amino acids into position, where they link together by peptide bonds to form a polypeptide.

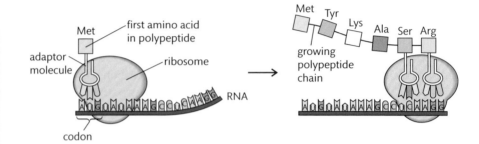

Therefore, the sequence of bases in the DNA, via RNA, determines the sequence of amino acids in the protein. The specific relationship between the bases and amino acids is known as the **genetic code**. As we saw above, it is a **triplet code** which means that each sequence of three bases in RNA specifies one amino acid to be inserted into the protein. For example, the sequence GGA specifies glycine while GCA specifies alanine. The universal nature of the code, the fact that the same codon specifies the same amino acid in all organisms, makes possible many of the developments in biotechnology and genetic engineering which have occurred over the last 50 years.

> **The genetic code is a triplet code. A sequence of three bases in RNA codes for one amino acid and is known as a codon.**

The Human Genome Project was the international, collaborative research programme whose goal was the complete mapping of the entire human DNA, three billion base pairs. The project began in 1990 and the complete sequence was published in 2003.

### NATURE OF SCIENCE

That the genetic code uses a triplet of bases was postulated initially from logic, but needed experimental data to be confirmed:

- a single base code would have 4 letters, and so could specify only 4 amino acids
- a double base code would have 4 × 4 combinations and so could specify 16 amino acids – still not enough
- the triplet code gives 4 × 4 × 4 = 64 different combinations - more than enough to code for the 20 amino acids that exist.

The hypothesis led to the development of experiments that confirmed the existence of the triplet code, and then determined the amino acid specification of each codon. Elucidation of the genetic code was the subject of the Nobel Prize awarded in Physiology or Medicine in 1968. The 64 variants of the triplet code means that most amino acids are coded for by more than one codon.

The term **central dogma**, which was coined by Crick, is sometimes used to summarize these ideas that genetic information flows in one direction in cells, from DNA to RNA to protein. As the primary structure of a protein determines its higher levels of structure and therefore its function, DNA is expressed through protein activity.

## DNA replication makes a copy of the genetic information

The process by which a molecule of DNA makes an exact copy of itself is known as **DNA replication**. It always occurs during cell division and ensures that every cell in an organism (with the exception of the sex cells used in reproduction) contains an identical set of genetic information. The process involves separation of the strands in the double helix by breaking the hydrogen bonds between the base pairs, and then using each strand as a template for the synthesis of a new strand. Again the specific base pairing ensures that only a base sequence complementary to that of the template strand will be produced. As DNA replication results in new molecules that contain one strand from the parent molecule and one newly synthesized strand, it is sometimes referred to as **semi-conservative replication**.

**Figure 13.55** The central dogma of molecular biology. The genetic code in DNA is copied to RNA and used to direct the synthesis of a polypeptide at the ribosome.

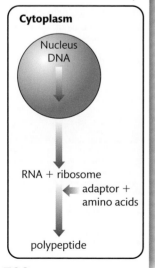

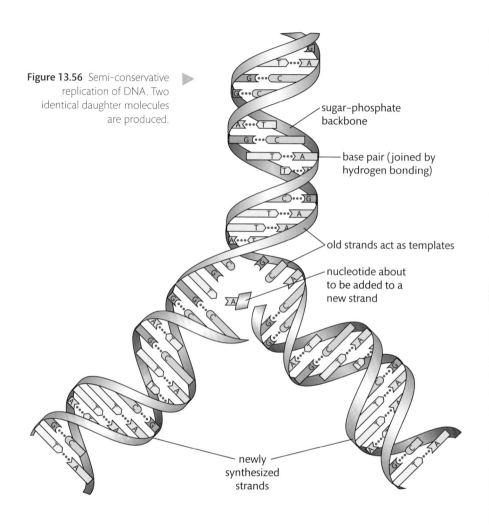

**Figure 13.56** Semi-conservative replication of DNA. Two identical daughter molecules are produced.

sugar–phosphate backbone

base pair (joined by hydrogen bonding)

old strands act as templates

nucleotide about to be added to a new strand

newly synthesized strands

## DNA can be transferred between species

The universal nature of the genetic code makes it possible for DNA from one organism to be expressed by directing protein synthesis when it is transferred into the DNA of a different species. This is the basis of **genetic engineering** which gives rise to **genetically modified organisms** (**GMOs**).

Techniques of inter-species DNA transfer are now advanced, and a wide range of genetically modified foods, known as **GM foods**, are marketed in many countries. The genetic modification may add a gene to yield a new product, inactivate a gene to remove undesired behaviour, or modify a gene for higher yields. Examples include corn which contains a bacterial gene that produces a natural pesticide, rice which produces higher concentrations of vitamin A, and tomatoes that remain fresh for longer. While genetically modified foods such as these promise certain benefits, their development also raises many issues and is the subject of on-going debate. Some aspects of both sides of this debate are summarized here.

Make sure you do not confuse DNA replication with transcription. Although they both involve the separation of DNA strands and the use of a single-stranded template, they are very different processes, controlled by different enzymes and making different products.

DNA profiling makes it possible to identify an individual from a small sample of their DNA. This has played an increasing role in forensics with applications in the criminal system, victim identification, immigration, and paternity cases. DNA sequencing is also used in studies of biochemical evolution and human migration.

**TOK**
Many countries have DNA databases, with information stored – particularly of individuals who have been convicted of crime. This raises questions of privacy and the right of governments to have access to personal information. Would it be more ethical to record the DNA of every citizen of a country, or would it magnify the concerns about 'big brother'?

Cans of genetically modified tomato puree. The photograph is from the UK where labelling of GM foods is mandatory.

## Benefits of GM foods

Some GM foods and GMOs have the following qualities:

- longer shelf-life
- improved flavour, texture, and nutritional value
- increased resistance to diseases and pests, reducing the use of pesticides
- produce a supply of substances such as vitamins and vaccines
- increased crop yields
- tolerance of a wider range of growing conditions, such as drought resistance.

## Concerns over GM foods

Many people, however, express the following concerns:

- lack of information about long-term effects
- changes to the natural ecosystem through cross-pollination
- possible links to increased allergies
- risk of altering natural composition of food
- concerns of breeding species that are resistant to control
- in some cases lack of information through food labelling.

Different countries have adopted very different approaches to the marketing of GM foods. In the European Union (EU), strict rules apply to the labelling of GM foods, while in the USA and Canada there is no mandatory labelling of GM content. It has been said that the EU is adopting the 'precautionary principle' in this regard, and this raises several concerns for international trade. At issue is the right for consumers to make informed choices about their food supply.

**A genetically modified organism is one whose DNA has been altered, often by the insertion of DNA from a different species.**

### Exercises

**23 (a)** Outline how nucleotides are linked together to form polynucleotides, explaining the nature of the bonds involved.
**(b)** Describe the forces that stabilize the DNA molecule.

**24** One strand of DNA contains the following base sequence

AATCGCATATAATTCGCTAGC

**(a)** What is the base sequence in the other strand in the double helix?
**(b)** What is the sequence of bases in the RNA synthesized using the first strand as a template?
**(c)** How many amino acids are coded for by this section of RNA?

**25** State three perceived benefits and three potential concerns of the use of genetically modified foods.

# B.9 Pigments

## Understandings:

- Biological pigments are coloured compounds produced by metabolism.
- The colour of pigments is due to highly conjugated systems with delocalized electrons, which have intense absorption bands in the visible region.
- Porphyrin compounds, such as hemoglobin, myoglobin, chlorophyll, and many cytochromes, are chelates of metals with large nitrogen-containing macrocyclic ligands.
- Hemoglobin and myoglobin contain heme groups with the porphyrin group bound to an iron(II) ion.
- Cytochromes contain heme groups in which the iron ion interconverts between iron(II) and iron(III) during redox reactions.
- Anthocyanins are aromatic, water-soluble pigments widely distributed in plants. Their specific colour depends on metal ions and pH.
- Carotenoids are lipid-soluble pigments, and are involved in harvesting light in photosynthesis. They are susceptible to oxidation, catalysed by light.

### Guidance

*The structures of chlorophyll, heme B, and specific examples of anthocyanins and carotenoids are given in the data booklet in section 35; details of other pigment names and structures are not required.*

## Applications and skills:

- Explanation of the sigmoidal shape of hemoglobin's oxygen dissociation curve in terms of the cooperative binding of hemoglobin to oxygen.
- Discussion of the factors that influence oxygen saturation of hemoglobin, including temperature, pH, and carbon dioxide.
- Description of the greater affinity of oxygen for fetal hemoglobin.
- Explanation of the action of carbon monoxide as competitive inhibition with oxygen binding.
- Outline of the factors that affect the stabilities of anthocyanins, carotenoids, and chlorophyll in relation to their structures.
- Explanation of the ability of anthocyanins to act as indicators based on their sensitivity to pH.
- Description of the function of photosynthetic pigments in trapping light energy during photosynthesis.
- Investigation of pigments through paper and thin-layer chromatography.

### Guidance

- *Explanation of cooperative binding in hemoglobin should be limited to conformational changes occurring in one polypeptide when it becomes oxygenated.*
- *Knowledge of specific colour changes with changing conditions is not required.*

The bright colours of the spectacular flower of *Zingiber spectabile* are the result of different pigment molecules. Photographed in Costa Rica.

Biological pigments are coloured compounds which are produced by metabolism. They include the bright colours in the wings of insects and the feathers of birds, the wide variety of colours of flowers and seaweeds, and the chemicals that give colour to human skin, hair, eyes, and blood. What does this diverse group of molecules have in common?

All pigment molecules have intense absorption bands in the visible region of the spectrum. The colour that we see is the light that is *not* absorbed, but instead is reflected. For example, we saw on page 707 that chlorophyll appears green because it absorbs red and blue light, but reflects the green. The colour seen is the complementary colour to that absorbed, which occupies an opposite position in the colour wheel, as seen in Figure 13.57.

Figure **13.57** Complementary colours are opposite each other in the colour wheel.

Differences in the colours of hair, eyes, and skin are due to differences in the concentration of the pigment melanin.

Pigment molecules absorb visible light because of the nature of their chemical bonds. In most cases they are **highly conjugated** structures, meaning that electrons in p orbitals are delocalized through alternating single and double bonds and through benzene ring structures. As these electrons are not held tightly in one position, they are able to become excited as they absorb certain wavelengths of light energy. The part of the molecule responsible for absorbing the radiation is called the **chromophore**. Important groups of pigments include the porphyrins, carotenoids, and anthocyanins.

**NATURE OF SCIENCE**

Observations of colour can be made qualitatively by the ability of an individual to detect changes in the environment. But these are subjective measures, which are imprecise and difficult to reproduce. Scientific studies of pigments are more reliably based on quantitative measurements of absorbance data. Improvements in technology involving digital probes have greatly enhanced the speed and accuracy of obtaining this absorbance data.

## Porphyrins

Figure 13.58 The structure of a porphyrin ring.

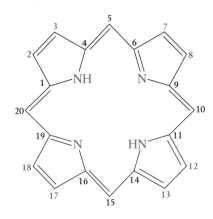

Porphyrin ring compounds, such as hemoglobin and chlorophyll, contain the planar ring structure shown in Figure 13.58. It is made up of four heterocyclic rings, containing carbon and nitrogen, linked by bridging carbon atoms. The ring acts as a ligand, forming a chelate with a metal involving coordinate bonds. Different porphyrin compounds contain different metals and also differ in the nature of the substituent groups which are attached to the carbon atoms labelled 2, 3, 7, 8, 12, 13, 17, and 18 in Figure 13.58.

## Chlorophyll: the primary photosynthetic pigment

Several different forms of chlorophyll exist, but the pigment always contains magnesium. This is why magnesium deficiency in the soil leads to loss of the green colour in leaves.

Yellow patches on leaves caused by chlorophyll deficiency due to lack of magnesium.

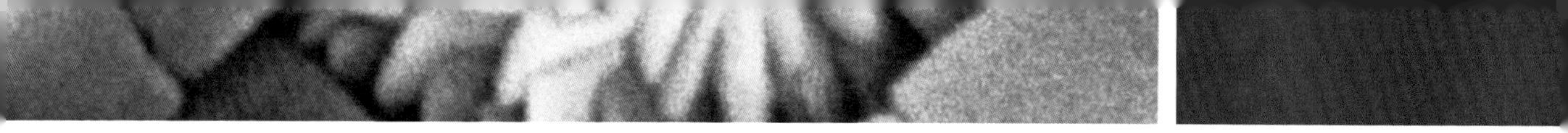

Chlorophyll is the primary pigment in photosynthesis, acting to absorb light energy. We saw on page 707 that chlorophyll absorbs light strongly in the blue part of the spectrum and to a lesser extent in the red. Other photosynthetic pigments, known as **accessory pigments**, harvest light in different parts of the spectrum and pass their energy to chlorophyll. As a result, chlorophyll undergoes a redox change, passing electrons to a series of **electron transport carriers**. Ultimately, chlorophyll is reduced back to its original state by gaining electrons from water. The process stores 'reducing power' which is able to reduce carbon dioxide to carbohydrate in reactions that do not depend on light energy.

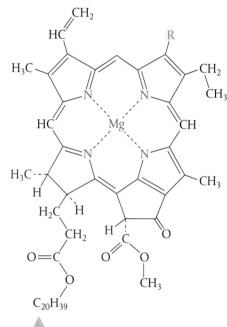

**Figure 13.59** The structure of chlorophyll:
R = –CH$_3$ in chlorophyll a
R = –CHO in chlorophyll b

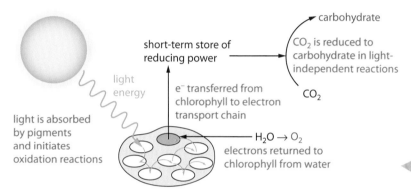

**Figure 13.60** The absorption of light by photosynthetic pigments initiates redox reactions that ultimately lead to the storage of chemical energy in carbohydrates.

The thermal stability of chlorophyll depends on the pH. In acidic solution Mg is lost from the porphyrin ring and replaced by two H$^+$ ions. This causes a colour change from green to olive-brown as the chromophore is altered. Cooking food often breaks cell membranes releasing acids which decrease the pH and bring about this change. Chlorophyll is more stable in alkaline conditions, which is why sodium hydrogencarbonate is sometimes added to water during cooking. The bright green colour of chlorophyll is often used as an indication of the freshness of food.

> The structures of chlorophyll and the heme group are given in section 35 of the IB data booklet.

## Hemoglobin and myoglobin: the oxygen-carrying team

The heme group, which is common to hemoglobin and myoglobin, contains iron – usually in the +2 oxidation state. Heme is a prosthetic group within protein molecules. Hemoglobin contains four heme groups, each bound within a polypeptide chain. In other words it is a protein with a quaternary structure. Myoglobin, on the other hand, contains one heme group and a single polypeptide chain.

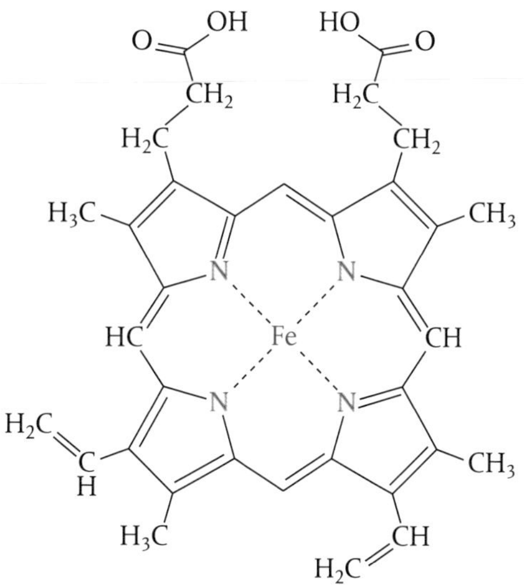

**Figure 13.61** The structure of heme.

Computer graphics model of the protein hemoglobin. The yellow balls represent $Fe^{2+}$ ions in the centre of the four porphyrin rings, shown in green. The protein environment of the iron, shown as the red strands, enables oxygen to be bound, carried, and released, without the iron being oxidized.

Iron deficiency is a prevalent micronutrient deficiency globally. Because of iron's role in hemoglobin, its deficiency leads to a serious condition known as anemia – with symptoms of fatigue, poor endurance, and lowered immunity. Iron is found in red meats, green leafy vegetables, nuts, and seeds. While its dietary deficiency is a cause of concern in many parts of the world, the question of how best to alleviate this is complicated by the fact that iron supplementation may increase susceptibility to malaria, which is also widespread.

When the iron atom in hemoglobin or myoglobin is oxidized to Fe(III), this form of the pigment appears brown rather than red and is unable to bind with oxygen. It is the form of myoglobin seen in cooked meat or meat that has 'gone off' through oxidation.

**Figure 13.62** The binding curve of hemoglobin and oxygen is sigmoidal, showing cooperative binding. Note that partial pressure is effectively a measure of oxygen concentration. These graphs are often referred to as oxygen dissociation curves.

Hemoglobin is designed to carry oxygen in the blood and myoglobin to store it, mostly in muscles. Both molecules do this by binding reversibly with molecular oxygen, $O_2$, which forms a weak bond with the iron atom. This binding does not change the oxidation of Fe, which remains in the +2 state, so the products are said to be **oxygenated** rather than oxidized, and are known as **oxyhemoglobin** and **oxymyoglobin** respectively. Due to the number of their heme groups, hemoglobin can bind four molecules of $O_2$, while myoglobin can bind one. The equation below summarizes these reactions, using Hb to represent hemoglobin and Mb to represent myoglobin.

$$Hb + 4O_2 \underset{\text{in respiring cells}}{\overset{\text{in lungs}}{\rightleftharpoons}} \underset{\text{oxyhemoglobin}}{Hb–(O_2)_4}$$

$$Mb + O_2 \rightleftharpoons \underset{\text{oxymyoglobin}}{Mb–O_2}$$

The reversible nature of these reactions is central to their role. Clearly, hemoglobin needs to associate with oxygen in the lungs, and dissociate to release the oxygen at respiring cells.

The binding of hemoglobin to oxygen is **cooperative** in nature. This means that the ability to bind oxygen is increased by the initial binding of oxygen to a heme group in the molecule. In simple terms this means that the uptake of oxygen by the second, third and fourth heme groups within a molecule gets easier as oxygen binds. This can be seen in the shape of the graph below, which is described as **sigmoidal** or S-shaped.

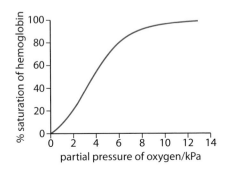

This cooperative effect is due to subtle changes that occur in the quaternary structure as oxygen binds. A conformational shift caused by the binding of oxygen at one heme group makes the other heme groups more receptive to oxygen. It is an allosteric effect. From the graph we can deduce the following about how this affects hemoglobin's ability to bind $O_2$.

- At low concentrations of $O_2$, hemoglobin has a low affinity for $O_2$.
- At high concentrations of $O_2$, hemoglobin has a high affinity for $O_2$.

In other words, the equilibrium

$$Hb + 4O_2 \rightleftharpoons Hb\text{--}(O_2)_4$$

shifts to the right in the lungs, causing oxygen uptake where oxygen concentration is high, and shifts to the left in respiring cells, releasing oxygen where oxygen concentration is low. This fits exactly with the metabolic requirements.

Other factors that influence the binding of oxygen to hemoglobin are temperature, pH, and carbon dioxide. The effects of these are shown in Figure 13.63.

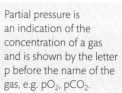

Partial pressure is an indication of the concentration of a gas and is shown by the letter p before the name of the gas, e.g. $pO_2$, $pCO_2$.

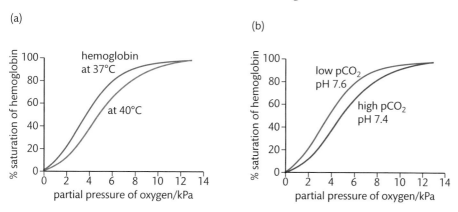

(a)      (b)

**Figure 13.63** Oxygen dissociation curves: (a) the influence of temperature; (b) the influence of pH/carbon dioxide.

Figure 13.63(a) shows that increasing temperature reduces the affinity of hemoglobin for $O_2$, as the dissociation curve has shifted to the right. This means that oxyhemoglobin more readily releases its oxygen in conditions of higher temperature, for example in cells during high metabolic activity such as exercise.

Figure 13.63(b) shows that decreasing pH reduces the affinity of hemoglobin for $O_2$, because the curve has shifted to the right as the acidity increases. Note that increases in the concentration of $CO_2$ have the same effect, as carbon dioxide dissolves to form carbonic acid and increases the acidity of the blood. During respiration, carbon dioxide is produced, decreasing the pH and so causing oxyhemoglobin to dissociate more and release oxygen where it is needed.

The response of oxygen dissociation curves to changes in pH or $CO_2$ is known as the Bohr effect. It was first described in 1904 by the Danish physiologist Christian Bohr, the father of Neils Bohr (see Chapter 2).

The equation below summarizes the factors that influence the equilibrium position in the oxygenation of hemoglobin.

$$Hb + 4O_2 \underset{\substack{\text{in respiring cells, low }pO_2 \\ \text{higher temperature} \\ \text{low pH / high }pCO_2}}{\overset{\substack{\text{in lungs, high }pO_2 \\ \text{lower temperature} \\ \text{high pH / low }pCO_2}}{\rightleftharpoons}} \quad \underset{\text{oxyhemoglobin}}{Hb\text{--}(O_2)_4}$$

The four polypeptide chains in adult hemoglobin are two α-chains and two β-chains. Before birth hemoglobin in the fetus has a different structure with two α-chains and

**Figure 13.64** Both fetal hemoglobin and myoglobin have a higher affinity for oxygen than adult blood.

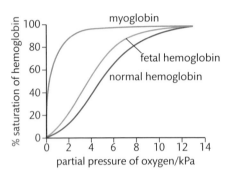

Animals that have evolved to live at high altitude where the oxygen concentration is low have developed hemoglobin with a higher affinity for oxygen.

**Factors that increase hemoglobin's affinity for $O_2$ displace the oxygen dissociation curve to the left; factors that decrease hemoglobin's affinity displace the oxygen dissociation curve to the right.**

two γ-chains. This form has a higher affinity for oxygen, as seen in Figure 13.64. The fact that its oxygen dissociation curve lies to the left of adult blood indicates that it is able to extract oxygen from the maternal blood. Following birth the fetal hemoglobin levels decline and after six months adult hemoglobin becomes the predominant form.

Myoglobin also has an oxygen dissociation curve to the left of that of hemoglobin, which means it has greater affinity for oxygen and can pick it up from hemoglobin for storage. Note that its dissociation curve is not sigmoidal in shape as there can be no cooperative binding within its one heme structure.

Carbon monoxide is a toxic gas, primarily because of its ability to bind to hemoglobin. Its affinity for hemoglobin is about 200 times that of oxygen, and so it effectively makes the hemoglobin unavailable to carry oxygen to respiring cells. Binding of carbon monoxide to hemoglobin forms carboxyhemoglobin, which does not readily dissociate.

$$Hb + CO \rightarrow Hb-CO$$
$$\text{carboxyhemoglobin}$$

Carbon monoxide poisoning can occur from the burning of fossil fuels with insufficient ventilation and from smoking tobacco.

## Cytochromes : electron-transport carriers

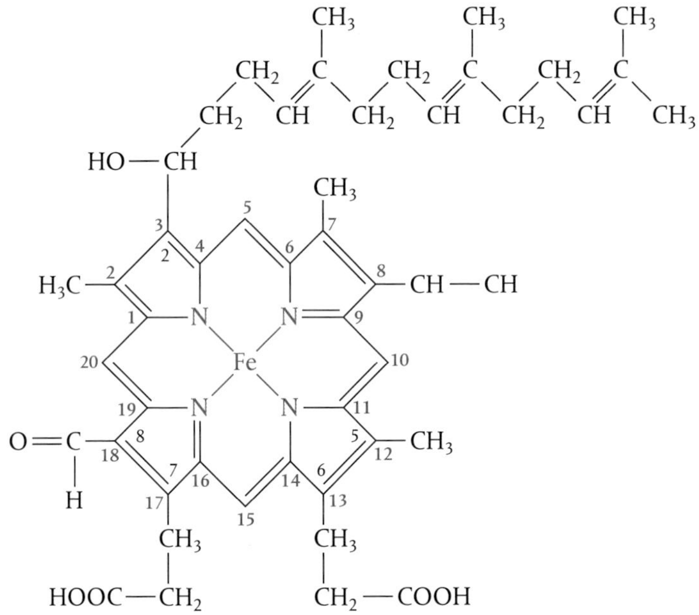

**Figure 13.65** Heme structure of cytochromes.

**In hemoglobin and myoglobin, the iron of the heme group remains in the Fe(II) state during $O_2$ transport. In cytochromes, the iron changes reversibly between Fe(II) and Fe(III) during electron transport.**

Cytochromes are a varied group of protein molecules that also contain the heme prosthetic group. They are found embedded in membranes and are responsible for electron transport during the redox reactions of aerobic respiration and photosynthesis. During the reactions they become successively reduced and then re-

Computer artwork of the molecular structure of the protein cytochrome c. The secondary structure of alpha helices is shown, along with the heme group surrounding the iron ion, shown in red. Cytochromes act as electron carriers in aerobic respiration, with the iron being successively reduced and re-oxidized in the process. They are found in the membranes of all cells..

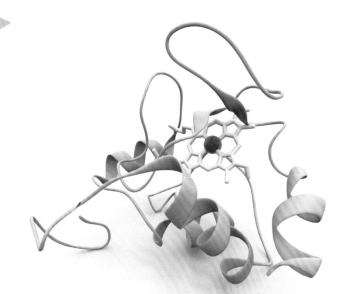

oxidized as they in turn accept and then pass on electrons. They are organized in sequence, corresponding to their electrode potentials, so that the electrons effectively flow down an electrochemical gradient.

Interestingly, despite the similarity of their structure with hemoglobin, their carrier mechanism is quite different. In cytochromes the iron of the heme group interconverts its oxidation state between +2 and +3 as the cytochrome undergoes redox change. The final cytochrome involved in aerobic respiration passes its electrons to the terminal acceptor oxygen with the formation of water. This is also the site of inhibition of the poison cyanide: by blocking the chain it prevents aerobic respiration from occurring, which is why it is such a potent poison.

## Carotenoids

Carotenoids are a group of pigments containing long hydrocarbon chains with many double bonds. They range in colour from yellow to red, and are fat soluble due to the long non-polar hydrocarbon chain. The structure of β-carotene, a carotenoid commonly found in fruit and vegetables, is shown in Figure 13.66.

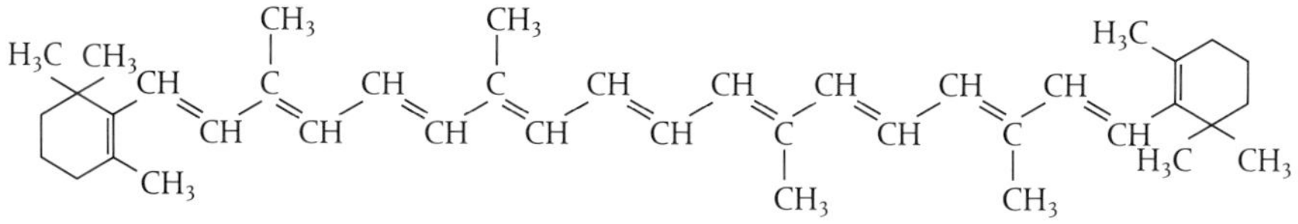

**Figure 13.66** The structure of β-carotene.

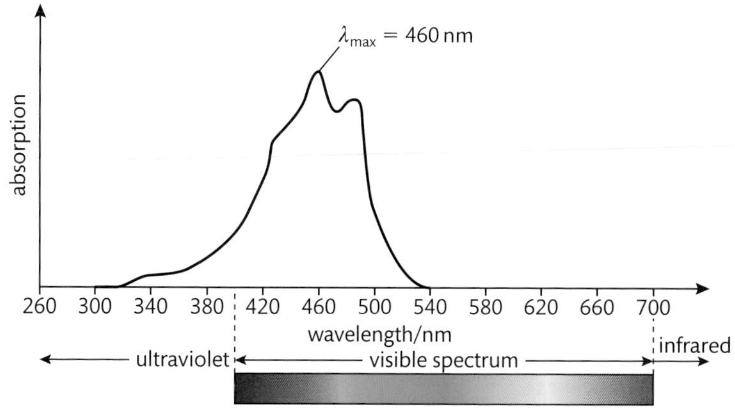

**Figure 13.67** The UV-visible spectrum of carotene. Blue/violet light is absorbed, due to conjugation in the long hydrocarbon chain, and so carotene appears orange.

α- and β-carotene are vitamin A precursors, and so play an important role in promoting healthy vision. Carotenoids are found in plant leaves, where they help in the harvesting of light for photosynthesis. They are accessory pigments, as described on page 741, which help to pass light energy to chlorophyll.

Plants use anthocyanins and carotenoids to attract pollinators and agents for seed dispersal. Some animals use the colours as warnings of poisons, and pigments also help to protect from UV damage.

The multiple conjugated carbon–carbon double bonds which give the carotenoids their colour also make them susceptible to oxidation, including that catalysed by light. This is why they are able to act as antioxidants. Oxidation can lead to a loss of vitamin A activity, as well as loss of colour and 'off' odours due to the release of volatile compounds. The chemical changes that occur during oxidation are not fully understood, but involve conversion of *trans*-carotenoids into *cis*-isomers. Oxidation of carotenoids can be reduced by preventing exposure to air and light, and by decreasing storage time.

Processed food commonly contains artificial colour additives. Countries differ in the compounds approved for this purpose and in the way in which the information is communicated to the consumer. In Europe the compounds are designated as 'E numbers', while in North America they are usually listed by chemical name.

Assortment of fruits that contain zeaxanthin, which is a carotene. Zeaxanthin is important in the physiology of the eye and is thought to play a role in reducing the risk of cataracts.

## Anthocyanins

Anthocyanins are a widely distributed group of pigments, responsible for many of the pink, red, and blue colours of plants. They absorb strongly in the blue and green parts of the spectrum. They are aromatic compounds with a three-ring $C_6C_3C_6$ structure and conjugated carbon–carbon double bonds.

**Figure 13.68** Flavylium cation, an anthocyanin.

The word 'anthocyanin' is derived from two Greek words: *anthos* meaning flower and *kyanos* meaning blue.

The polar hydroxyl groups allow the molecules to form hydrogen bonds, which increase their solubility in water. Consequently they are found dissolved in the aqueous cell sap rather than in the lipid-rich membranes.

Anthocyanins are formed by a reaction between sugars and proteins that requires light. This is why fruit often changes colour as it ripens and the sugar concentration increases. The colour of anthocyanins also changes as the pH of cell sap changes; they are generally pink in acidic solution, purple in neutral solution and turn greenish-yellow in alkaline solution.

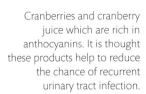

Cranberries and cranberry juice which are rich in anthocyanins. It is thought these products help to reduce the chance of recurrent urinary tract infection.

The sensitivity of anthocyanins to pH means that they can be used as pH indicators. The colour changes arise from transfer of $H^+$ from OH groups, which alters the conjugation and so the absorbance at the chromophore. For example, the red flavylium cation changes to the blue molecule quinonoid as pH increases.

(AH$^+$) flavylium     ⇌     (A) quinonoid
red                               blue

Adding acid will shift the equilibrium back to the left so the red colour reappears.

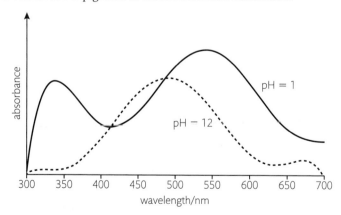

Red cabbage indicator in acid and alkaline solutions. The colour change is due to changes in ionization of anthocyanins.

## Worked example

The anthocyanins can be used as acid–base indicators. Identify the wavelength $\lambda_{max}$ which corresponds to maximum absorbance at the different pH values shown and suggest the colour of the pigment in acid and in basic conditions.

### Solution

| pH | $\lambda_{max}$ | Colour absorbed | Colour of pigment |
|---|---|---|---|
| 1 | 550 | green | red |
| 12 | 475 | blue | orange/yellow |

The changing colours of leaves with the seasons is due to changes in the relative amounts of chlorophylls, carotenoids, and anthocyanins present. Chlorophyll is often lost first as the temperature decreases, and the bright orange, yellow, and red colours seen in many leaves are due to the higher proportion of carotenes and anthocyanins.

The anthocyanins also form deeply coloured coordination complexes with $Fe^{3+}$ and $Al^{3+}$ ions that are present in metal cans. This sometimes causes a discolouration in canned fruit.

The bright colours of autumn leaves are mainly due to carotenoids and anthocyanins. Photographed in Washington State, USA.

## Analysis of pigments

Pigment extracts from plants typically contain a mixture of different pigment molecules. They are suitable for analysis by two different types of chromatography.

- Paper chromatography, which was described on page 701.
- Thin-layer chromatography, described below.

Thin-layer chromatography is an example of adsorption chromatography, which follows the same basic principles as paper chromatography. The stationary phase in this case is a thin layer of adsorbent particles of alumina or silica which may be only 0.2 mm thick. It is supported on glass or thin plastic plate. The mobile phase is the solvent, chosen according to the chemical nature of the pigments. Small spots of the pigment extract are placed on the origin, and capillary action causes the different compounds in the spot to separate, leading to identification from their $R_f$ values.

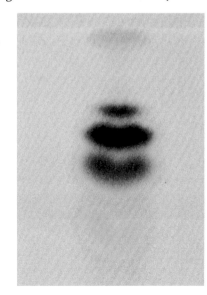

Thin-layer chromatogram (TLC) of an extract of pigments from chloroplasts. TLC plastic sheets are coated with a silica gel and a drop of the extract was placed at the bottom of the origin. The sheet was then placed in a beaker of solvent. The chromatogram shows the different solubilites of pigments in the extract in the solvent. The pigments can be identified as carotene, pheophytin, chlorophyll a, chlorophyll b, and carotenoids. The line across the top of the image is the solvent front.

Thin-layer chromatography is generally a quicker process than paper chromatography, and works efficiently on smaller samples. It is also a more sensitive technique with results which are more easily reproduced.

Exercises

**26** With respect to hemoglobin and cytochromes, explain the difference between being *oxidized* and being *oxygenated*.

**27** The absorbance spectra of anthocyanins are very sensitive to changes in pH. Identify the wavelength $\lambda_{max}$ which corresponds to maximum absorbance and suggest the colour of the pigment at the different pHs shown.

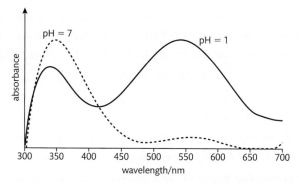

**28** Explain the following observations in terms of the molecular structure of the pigments involved.

    **(a)** When carrots are boiled, little colouration of the water occurs; when they are fried, the oil changes colour to orange.

    **(b)** When red cabbage is boiled, the water turns purple-red. When vinegar is added the colour changes to bright red.

**29** Three compounds were separated using thin-layer chromatography on a silica gel stationary phase.

| Compound | Distance travelled / cm |
|---|---|
| A | 2.5 |
| B | 7.5 |
| C | 10.0 |
| solvent | 15.0 |

Calculate the $R_f$ values and comment on the relative polarity of the components.

**30** Explain the difference in the shapes of the oxygen dissociation curves of hemoglobin and myoglobin in terms of their protein structures.

# B.10   Stereochemistry in biomolecules

## Understandings:

- With one exception, amino acids are chiral, and only the L-configuration is found in proteins.
- Naturally occurring unsaturated fat is mostly in the *cis* form, but food processing can convert it into the *trans* form.
- D- and L-stereoisomers of sugars refer to the configuration of the chiral carbon atom furthest from the aldehyde or ketone group, and D forms occur most frequently in nature.
- Ring forms of sugars have isomers, known as $\alpha$ and $\beta$, depending on whether the position of the hydroxyl group at carbon 1 (glucose) or carbon 2 (fructose) lies below the plane of the ring ($\alpha$) or above the plane of the ring ($\beta$).
- Vision chemistry involves the light activated inter-conversion of *cis* and *trans* isomers of retinal.

## Applications and skills:

- Description of the hydrogenation and partial hydrogenation of unsaturated fats, including the production of *trans* fats, and a discussion of the advantages and disadvantages of these processes.
- Explanation of the structure and properties of cellulose, and comparison with starch.
- Discussion of the importance of cellulose as a structural material and in the diet.
- Outline of the role of vitamin A in vision, including the roles of opsin, rhodopsin, and *cis-* and *trans*-retinal.

**Guidance**

- *Names of the enzymes involved in the visual cycle are not required.*
- *Relative melting points of saturated and cis/trans unsaturated fats should be covered.*

**NATURE OF SCIENCE**

The existence of stereospecific environments is universal in biological systems. This is in contrast to reactions that take place outside living cells, which more commonly involve racemic mixtures rather than one enantiomer. This difference has sometimes been used as a broad guiding distinction between living and non-living matter.

As we learned in Chapter 10, stereoisomers represent different spatial arrangements of the atoms in a molecule, and their study involves a three-dimensional approach. Many biopolymers can exist as stereoisomers, and metabolic reactions are usually stereospecific, meaning that only one form of the isomer has the required activity. In this section we will consider examples of stereochemistry in each of the main groups of biomolecules we have studied.

## Stereochemistry in proteins

In amino acids, the amino group, the carboxylic acid group, a hydrogen atom, and a variable group R are all attached to the same carbon atom, known as the α-carbon or carbon-2 in the numbering of the chain. So with four different groups attached, this carbon atom is chiral. This means that amino acids are optically active and can exist as two different stereoisomers, known as enantiomers. The stereochemistry of alanine is shown in Figure 13.69.

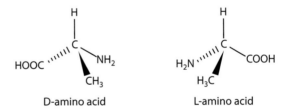

D-amino acid          L-amino acid

**Figure 13.69** L and D forms of the amino acid alanine where R = $CH_3$.

The only exception is glycine, in which R = H and so there is no chiral carbon atom.

The different stereoisomers of the amino acids are most commonly known as the L and D forms, applying a convention that compares their absolute configuration to that of glyceraldehyde. The L and D forms of amino acids have identical physical properties and chemical reactivities *apart from* the direction in which they rotate plane-polarized light and their reactions with reagents that are chiral. This last point is crucial in biochemistry. As enzymes, themselves made of proteins, are chiral molecules, they distinguish completely between the L and D forms of amino acids. Biological systems have evolved to use only the L forms of amino acids.

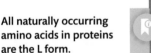 **All naturally occurring amino acids in proteins are the L form.**

## CHALLENGE YOURSELF

8 How many stereoisomers exist for threonine and isoleucine? Refer to section 33 of the IB data booklet.

 D-amino acids are scarce in nature but are widely used in the pharmaceutical industry, occurring in many drugs, including antibiotics such as penicillin and some anti-cancer agents. Preparation of D-amino acids industrially involves the use of enzymes to resolve racemic mixtures of amino acids. Recent research on preparing D-amino acids by direct synthesis is a promising development that could provide much cheaper synthetic routes for many drugs.

## Stereochemistry in lipids

Unsaturated fatty acids in fats and oils contain carbon–carbon double bonds. These exist in two forms, known as *cis–trans* isomers, which arise due to the restriction on rotation around the double bond. They were introduced in Chapter 10, page 516.

• The *cis* form occurs when the same group, for example hydrogen, has the same orientation relative to the double bond.

$$CH_3 \ CH_2 \ CH_2 \quad CH_2 \ CH_2 \ CH_2 \quad CH_2 \ CH_2 \ \overset{\overset{\displaystyle O}{\|}}{C} \quad C=C \quad CH_2 \ CH_2 \ OH$$

• The *trans* form occurs when the same group has opposite orientation across the double bond.

$$CH_3 \ CH_2 \ CH_2 \quad CH_2 \ CH_2 \ CH_2 \quad H \quad C=C \quad CH_2 \ CH_2 \ OH \quad CH_2 \ CH_2 \ \overset{\overset{\displaystyle C}{\|}}{O}$$

With the exception of some dairy products, most naturally occurring unsaturated fats are in the *cis* form. Molecules of the *cis* isomer cannot easily arrange themselves side by side to solidify, so they tend to have lower melting points than the corresponding *trans* isomer.

**Hydrogenation** of fats takes place in the food industry when hydrogen is added across the carbon–carbon double bonds using a finely divided metal catalyst such as nickel.

$$\overset{-CH_2 \qquad CH_2-}{\underset{H \qquad \qquad H}{C=C}} \ + \ H-H \ \overset{Ni}{\rightarrow} \ \overset{-CH_2 \qquad CH_2-}{\underset{H \qquad \quad H}{H-C-C-H}}$$

The product is a fat that, being more saturated, has a higher melting point, and therefore is a more convenient form for packing and storage as a solid or semi-solid. Fats made in this way also break down less easily under conditions of high temperature frying and usually have a longer shelf-life than liquid oils. Most margarines and shortening come into this category.

There is, however, a problem with the process. In **partial hydrogenation**, only some of the carbon–carbon double bonds in a fat are broken, and those that remain often get chemically modified from the *cis* position to

Foods containing *trans* fats produced by hydrogenation. The process is used to solidify fats and extend their shelf-life, but has been linked to increased risk of heart disease.

the *trans* position. The resulting fatty acids are therefore known as **trans fats** and are particularly prevalent in processed foods. Evidence shows that consuming *trans* fats raises the level of LDL cholesterol, which is a risk factor for heart disease. *Trans* fats also reduce the blood levels of HDL cholesterol, which protects against heart disease.

## Stereochemistry in carbohydrates

All simple sugars are chiral molecules as they contain at least one chiral carbon atom. The stereoisomers are described as D and L, again in reference to their configuration relative to glyceraldehyde. For sugars having two or more chiral carbon atoms, the prefixes D and L refer to the configuration of the chiral carbon atom furthest away from the carbonyl carbon.

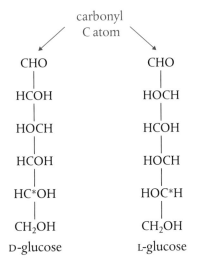

*this C atom determines notation D or L

D sugars are the most abundant form in nature.

The conversion of sugars in the straight-chain form to the ring form, described on page 722, creates an additional type of isomer, known as α and β forms. These are distinguished by the relative position of the groups attached to the carbon atoms that close the ring by forming an ether link with oxygen.

In glucose, α and β forms are determined by the positions of the −OH group at $C_1$.

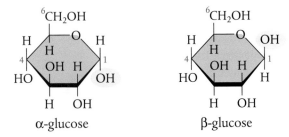

α-glucose          β-glucose

The alpha form has the −OH at $C_1$ on the opposite side of the ring to $C_6$. In the Haworth structure this is represented as a downwards projection. The beta form has the −OH on the same side of the ring as $C_6$, giving an upwards projection.

## CHALLENGE YOURSELF

9 Which form of glucose, α or β, would you expect to be the more stable and why?

In fructose, the designations are similar, but with the focus on $C_2$ instead of $C_1$.

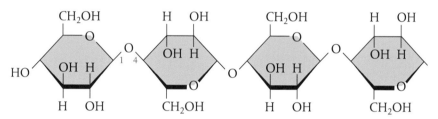

α-fructose   β-fructose

The structural differences between α and β glucose have a large effect on the properties of their polymers.

• Starch and glycogen are polymers of α-glucose. Starch forms a relatively compact spiral structure and is stored as starch grains in plant cells. The structure of starch shown on page 724.

• Cellulose is a polymer of β-glucose. It is a linear polymer with 1–4 links known as β-glycosidic links. These position the sugars at a different angle from the α-glycosidic links found in starch so the cellulose chain forms an uncoiled linear structure with alternate glucose monomers 'upside down' with respect to each other. This enables the hydroxyl groups to form hydrogen bonds with the hydroxyls of other cellulose molecules lying parallel.

cellulose: 1-4 linkage of β-glucose monomers

Consequently, cellulose forms cables, known as microfibrils, of parallel chains that give it a rigid structure. Cellulose is found in all plant cell walls and is one of the main sources of support in plant cells. This is why wood, which is rich in cellulose, is such a useful building material.

Starch and glycogen can be relatively easily hydrolysed into glucose by the action of digestive enzymes, but the human body does not produce an enzyme to hydrolyse the β-glycosidic links in cellulose. (The required enzyme, known as **cellulase**, is secreted by some bacteria, such as those living in the gut of ruminants.) Cellulose therefore passes through the gut largely chemically intact, contributing to the bulk of the faeces. Medical studies have indicated that this **dietary fibre** is of benefit to the health of the large intestine. The cellulose fibrils abrade the wall of the digestive tract and stimulate the lining to produce mucus which helps in the passage of undigested food through the gut. Fibre in the diet helps to reduce conditions such as constipation, haemorrhoids, and, possibly, colorectal cancer. In general, foods derived from plants with little or no processing are likely to be a good source of fibre.

The World Health Organization cites a low fruit and vegetable intake as a key risk factor in chronic diseases such as diabetes, obesity, and some cancers. Our growing understanding of the significance of fibre in the diet has led to an increase in the marketing of 'whole foods' such as grains and plant foods such as vegetables and salads. But fruit and vegetable intake varies considerably among countries, largely reflecting the prevailing economic, cultural, and agricultural environments. In developed countries fresh fruit and vegetable intake has decreased with increasing dependence on fast foods that are highly processed. It is estimated that globally 2.7 million deaths per year can be traced to low fruit and vegetable intake.

**Starch and glycogen are polymers of α-glucose, cellulose is a polymer of β-glucose.**

Coloured scanning electron micrograph of cellulose microfibrils in a plant cell wall. Microfibrils measure between 5 nm and 15 nm in diameter.

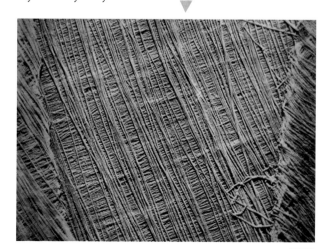

## Stereochemistry in vitamins

Vitamin A, also known as retinal, is involved in the so-called **visual cycle**, the photochemical changes associated with our ability to detect light.

**Figure 13.70** The isomerization of the 11-*cis* form of retinal to the all-*trans* form is induced by light energy. Note the change in stereochemistry at $C_{11}$ alters the shape of the molecule, and so its ability to bind to opsin.

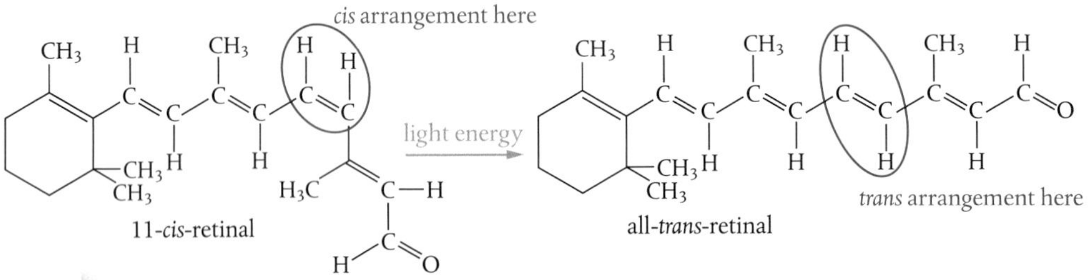

The retina of the eye contains two types of light-sensitive cells, known as **rods** and **cones**. The rods are stimulated by light of lower intensity and do not provide colour vision. The major photoreceptor pigment in rods is a large conjugated protein molecule called **rhodopsin**. This consists of a protein, **opsin**, tightly bound to **11-*cis*-retinal**, which is derived from vitamin A. When rhodopsin is exposed to light, a transformation of 11-*cis*-retinal occurs, changing it to **all-*trans* retinal**.

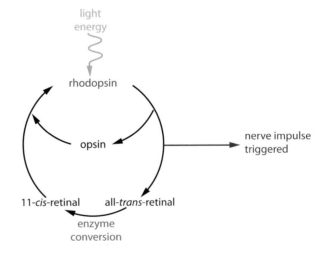

The structures of 11-*cis* and all-*trans* retinal are given in section 35 of the IB data booklet.

This causes the all-*trans* isomer to dissociate from the opsin, which triggers a nerve impulse. Rhodopsin is regenerated from opsin and 11-*cis*-retinal after the all-*trans* form isomerizes back to the 11-*cis* form in a series of steps catalysed by enzymes. A summary of the visual cycle is given in Figure 13.71.

**Figure 13.71** The visual cycle in rod cells.

Rods are responsible for our vision in low light intensity, and at the sides of the eye. This is why we see outlines of objects but not colours in the dark and at the peripheries of our vision. Most people find this hard to believe as our brain 'fills in' the information from other sources, but if you hold an object of unknown colour at the corner of your eye while looking straight ahead, you will not be able to distinguish its colour.

### Exercises

**31** Explain why partial hydrogenation of fats is associated with a problem that does not arise from the complete hydrogenation of fats.

**32** Cellulose and starch are both polymers of glucose but they have very different properties. Explain this by making reference to their structural units.

**33** What is meant by photochemical isomerization in the visual cycle?

# B.6 Biochemistry and the environment

## Understandings:

- Xenobiotics refer to chemicals that are found in an organism but which are not normally present there.
- Biodegradable/compostable plastics can be consumed or broken down by bacteria or other living organisms.
- Host–guest chemistry involves the creation of synthetic host molecules that mimic some of the actions performed by enzymes in cells, by selectively binding to specific guest species, such as toxic materials in the environment.
- Enzymes have been developed to help in the breakdown of oil spills and other industrial wastes.
- Enzymes in biological detergents can improve energy efficiency by enabling effective cleaning at lower temperatures.
- Biomagnification is the increase in concentration of a substance in a food chain.
- Green Chemistry, also called sustainable chemistry, is an approach to chemical research and engineering that seeks to minimize the production and release to the environment of hazardous substances.

## Applications and skills:

- Discussion of the increasing problem of xenobiotics such as antibiotics in sewage treatment plants.
- Description of the role of starch in biodegradable plastics.
- Application of host–guest chemistry to the removal of a specific pollutant in the environment.
- Description of an example of biomagnification, including the chemical source of the substance. Examples could include heavy metals or pesticides.
- Discussion of the challenges and criteria in assessing the 'greenness' of a substance used in biochemical research, including the atom economy.

### Guidance

- *Specific names of 'green chemicals' such as solvents are not expected.*
- *The emphasis in explanations of host–guest chemistry should be on non-covalent bonding within the supramolecule.*

## Xenobiotics: strangers to life

**Xenobiotics** are chemical compounds that are found in a living organism, but which are foreign to that organism. The term is also used to describe chemicals found in higher-than-normal concentrations, or compounds that are not produced naturally but only by synthetic processes – in other words chemicals that are foreign to the biosphere.

Examples of xenobiotics are:

- drugs, including antibiotics such as penicillin
- food additives
- pollutants, such as PCBs and dioxins
- insecticides, such as DDT
- heavy metals, such as mercury and lead ions
- hormones, such as estrogens
- plastics, such as PVC.

Within an organism, xenobiotics can have a wide variety of effects. Non-polar molecules pass relatively easily across the hydrophobic cell membranes. They enter cells where they may be modified by enzymes and then detoxified. This is how many drugs are broken down in the body. In agriculture, pesticides may be metabolized by similar processes, sometimes leading to resistance to the effect of the chemical.

However, if the xenobiotic cannot be modified in the organism it may build up in the cells. The increasing concentration of the substance in an organism is known as **bioaccumulation**. For example, mercury compounds in the form of methylmercury, which is non-polar, cross into the brain, where they build up causing mercury poisoning. Similarly, lead, in the form of tetraethyl lead from petroleum, can accumulate in fat tissues.

Scientist monitoring a water reservoir by sampling fish to analyse the mercury concentrations in their bodies. A nearby gold mine uses mercury to amalgamate the gold and this mercury is a xenobiotic, polluting the surrounding areas. Photographed in French Guiana.

Molecular model of a polychlorinated biphenyl (PCB) molecule. The carbon atoms in the phenyl rings are shown in blue, chlorine is shown in green, and hydrogen in white. PCBs are organic compounds that are highly stable, good insulators, and have low electrical conductivity. They were widely used in capacitors and transformers. The discovery in the 1960s that PCBs are toxic and carcinogenic and can act as **xenoestrogens** led to tight regulation of their use, but due to their stability they persist in the environment and in living tissue.

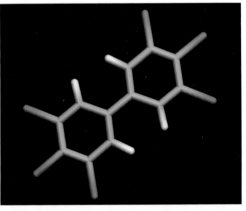

An increasing area of concern is the existence of **pharmaceutically active compounds** such as antibiotics, painkillers, and chemotherapy drugs in the environment. These may be discharged from industries or hospitals, or passed through the human body and released unmodified or partially metabolized in urine. Sewage treatment plants may break the xenobiotic down through bacterial action, but too often this process is incomplete. As a result, the compounds are released into the effluent, where they can be taken up by fish living downstream.

The waste water from sewage treatment may also contain sex hormones such as the female estrogens that have been released in human urine, particularly due to use of the synthetic contraceptive pill. There is some concern that male fish may absorb sufficient quantities of estrogens to be 'feminized' and unable to breed. Related concerns about disruptions to reproductive cycles arise from the widespread presence of so-called xenoestrogens, chemicals that imitate the effects of estrogen. Examples include polychlorinated biphenyls (PCBs) and bisphenol A.

Bisphenol A is an organic compound widely used in making polymers such as the polycarbonate plastics that are used in reusable water bottles, food containers, and water pipes. Bisphenol A has become controversial because it may mimic hormones, especially estrogens, and so give rise to a range of health problems. Studies have shown that risk of the chemical leaching from the plastic is increased when it is heated, and so particular concern has been expressed about its use in babies' bottles that are routinely heated during sterilization. While debate continues about safe levels, many industries have withdrawn these products and several governments have legislation pending to limit their use.

## Biomagnification

Although biological processes can produce many harmful substances, such as snake venom and irritants, natural toxins do not build up in the environment as they are broken down by enzymes. By contrast, some of the synthetic chemicals produced by humans are not broken down naturally as there are no enzymes to achieve this. Consequently, they build up in air, water, soil and living cells, and in some cases their concentration can increase in food webs to potentially harmful levels.

**Biomagnification** refers to the increase in concentration of a xenobiotic substance in a food web. It occurs when a xenobiotic cannot be metabolized, and so is taken up directly when one organism feeds on another, causing the greatest effect for animals that feed at the top of a food chain. A well-studied example of this is the insecticide DDT, dichlorodiphenyltrichloroethane.

Water bottle label showing that it does not contain bisphenol A, BPA. The chemical has been withdrawn from many applications due to concern over its xenoestrogenic properties.

DDT is a complex aromatic molecule, which was used to great effect starting during World War II to control the mosquitoes that are responsible for the spread of diseases such as malaria and typhus. The World Health Organization suggests that five million human lives were saved in the early years of its use. DDT is readily soluble in fat, and does not undergo metabolic breakdown. It therefore bioaccumulates in tissues and passes unchanged through food chains.

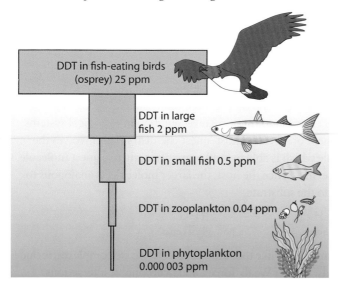

The bald eagle feeds high in the food chain and is therefore susceptible to the effects of biomagnification.

**Figure 13.72** Data on DDT concentrations taken from an estuary in Long Island Sound, USA. Ospreys at the top of the chain have 10 million times the concentration of DDT present in the phytoplankton.

757

Concerns over the environmental impact of DDT and other pesticides, particularly on bird life, were brought to the public attention through the publication of the book *Silent Spring* by American biologist Rachel Carson in 1962. This book is largely credited as launching the environmental movement that is now global in scope.

Who should determine the balance between the individual's right to freedom from disease and society's right to freedom from environmental degradation?

**Bioaccumulation refers to the build up of a substance within an organism; biomagnification refers to the build up of a substance in a food web.**

The Stockholm Convention on Persistent Organic Pollutants (POPs) identified twelve chemicals, known as 'the dirty dozen', whose use should be banned. Although legislation to this effect now exists in many countries, many of the chemicals are stable and persist in the environment. There is concern that climate change causing melting of the polar ice is re-mobilizing some of these banned chemicals into the Arctic atmosphere.

Figure 13.72 illustrates the biomagnification of DDT at each feeding level, known as a **trophic level**. As, for example, the small fish feed on a vast number of zooplankton, the concentrations of DDT are multiplied at each level. So the large fish and birds that feed high in the food chain accumulate elevated concentrations of DDT, as much as 10 million times the original concentration.

In the 1960s it was noticed that birds of prey, such as ospreys and peregrine falcons, suffered a serious decline in their numbers. The cause was traced to a thinning of their eggshells that made the eggs break under their parent's weight, and this was found to be due to the toxic effects of the high levels of DDT in their tissues. This and other negative environmental impacts eventually led to a ban on the use of indiscriminate spraying of DDT in many countries by the 1970s. Nonetheless, some continued use of DDT persists in vector control, particularly in countries where malaria is a serious health risk, and this remains controversial.

Other examples of bioaccumulation include organic molecules such as dioxins and PCBs, as well as heavy metals such as mercury and uranium. Data collected on these effects have been used to influence government policies and health advisories.

**NATURE OF SCIENCE**

It is the responsibility of scientists to consider the ways in which their research and findings impact the environment, and to find ways of amelioration. This involves risk assessment and long-term data collection. The issues presented raise ethical issues which cross national boundaries and demand international collaboration by scientists from different disciplines.

## Amelioration: responses to xenobiotics

Clearly, the widespread existence of xenobiotics in organisms and in the environment is a major cause of concern for human health and for biodiversity. *Amelioration* refers to approaches that seek to lessen the problems and improve the outlook. We will consider some examples here.

### Host–guest chemistry

We saw in section B.3 that enzymes and substrates form complexes as a result of molecular recognition and specific binding. The complexes are held together by forces other than covalent bonds which depend on the three-dimensional shape of the molecules. This and similar examples of molecular recognition in biological systems have inspired the development of so-called host–guest chemistry. This involves the synthesis of a **host** molecule which is able to bind non-covalently to a guest molecule, and form a **supermolecule**. In essence the host, the larger molecule, is analogous to the enzyme, and the guest to the substrate.

$$\text{H} + \text{G} \rightleftharpoons \text{H--G}$$
$$\text{host} \quad \text{guest} \qquad \text{host--guest complex}$$

The forces within the supermolecule, like those in enzyme–substrate complexes, include ionic bonds, hydrogen bonds, van der Waals' forces, and hydrophobic interactions.

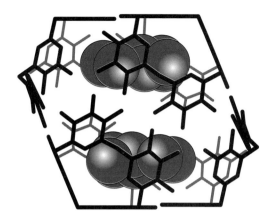

**Figure 13.73** Host–guest complex showing two guest molecules (pyrene butyric acid) in blue trapped within the structure of the host molecule which is a six-chain nanocapsule held together by hydrogen bonds.

Host–guest chemistry can be applied to the removal of some xenobiotics in the environment. The xenobiotic is the guest, and its chemical features determine the synthesis of the host, which is designed to bind to it. Many host molecules have a cage-like or tube-like structure which traps the guest molecule. The technique has been used in the removal of radioactive ions such as cesium-137 from nuclear waste.

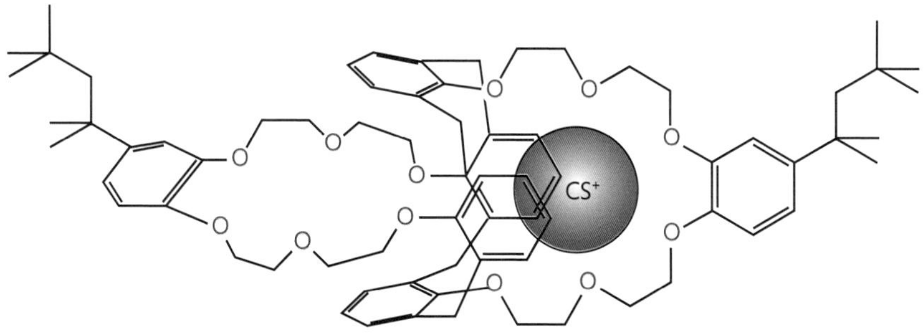

**Figure 13.74** Host molecule (known as BOBCalix6) shown with a positively charged cesium ion held inside one of its cavities. This host molecule was specifically developed to bind to the cesium-137 ion, by application of the thermodynamics of ion binding.

Another example is the removal of aromatic amines, which are derived from the cosmetics industry and are known to be carcinogenic. Drugs and drug metabolites are also targets of research for suitable host molecules for their removal.

**The associations between the host and guest molecules in a supermolecule are all non-covalent.**

## Biodegradable substances

Substances that cannot be broken down by natural processes, which mostly involve microbial action, are said to be **non-biodegradable**. Compounds in this category often contain carbon–halogen bonds or stable aromatic structures, which enzymes are not able to break. This is why many plastics, such as PVC and polystyrene, and compounds like DDT persist in the environment indefinitely.

On the other hand, a compound is **biodegradable** if it can undergo bacterial degradation into end products that are found in nature, and therefore are not harmful to the environment. Much research attention has been given to the development of biodegradable plastics, and two main types exist.

**1    Plant-based hydro-biodegradable plastic**

This plastic has a high starch content and is often obtained from corn. Genetic modification of grasses may help to produce similar plastics. The breakdown is initiated by hydrolysis and produces carbon dioxide and water. Swelling of starch grains can help to break up the plastic. At high temperatures it decomposes relatively quickly, but when buried in a landfill it may take much longer to decompose and may produce methane.

759

Biodegradable food packaging. Apples sealed in a wrapper made from starch-based plastic. The starch used to make this packaging was sourced from a non-genetically modified crop, as seen in the 'Non GM' label.

 Biodegradable substances are those that can be broken down in natural processes.

Coloured transmission electron micrograph (TEM) of an oil-degrading bacterium, shown in yellow, collected from a deep-sea oil plume in the Gulf of Mexico after the Deepwater Horizon oil spill in April 2010. This is a previously unknown species of bacteria that helped in the breakdown of oil from the spill around one kilometre below the ocean's surface.

**2    Petroleum-based oxo-biodegradable plastic**

This is derived from a by-product of the oil industry. Additives, often cobalt, are used to act as catalysts for the breakdown process, which can be programmed for different times depending on the use of the plastic. The plastic degrades into microfragments which are dispersed and eventually broken down by bacteria.

Plastics are sometimes described as **compostable**, which means they can be broken down in a compost pile, along with natural food products and garden waste.

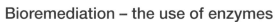

Waste plastic is a major international problem, and estimates suggest only 3% of plastic is recycled globally. Use of oxo-biodegradable plastics is becoming mandated in many rapidly-developing countries in the Middle East and Africa to help mitigate the problems of plastic disposal. This puts pressure on other countries to use this plastic in their export goods. Some critics though express concerns over the use of artificial additives in these plastics.

## Bioremediation – the use of enzymes

Although as a fossil fuel, crude oil is a natural product, it can be present in sufficient concentrations to be considered xenobiotic. This is the case, for example, when oil spills occur on land or at sea, depositing millions of litres into the adjacent environment. Organisms such as sea birds and marine mammals are then at risk from physical damage and from the toxic effects of the crude oil spill.

Ways to ameliorate the impact of oil spills include the use of microorganisms which are able to break the oil down by using it as a food source and oxidize it in respiration. This is known as **bioremediation**.

As crude oil contains a large number of different compounds, many different chemical reactions are involved in its breakdown. Microorganisms have evolved different enzymes that are specific for the degradation of different hydrocarbons in the oil so breakdown of the oil takes the combined action of a community of bacteria and fungi. Most of these are found naturally in the environment.

Over time, microbes are a dependable means of breaking down oil in the environment, although some of the larger and more highly branched molecules seem resistant to breakdown by enzymes. Environmental conditions such as temperature, supply of nutrients,

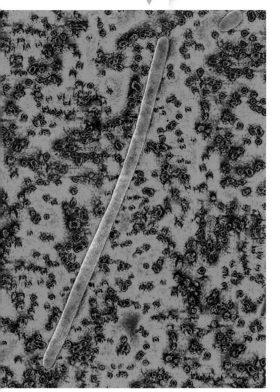

and availability of oxygen all influence the efficiency of the process, and in many cases the process may be too slow to prevent ecological damage. Research is ongoing to find ways to enhance the enzymic processes involved.

The use of enzymes in bioremediation also includes processes for the clean-up of industrial waste such as effluents from paper mills, textile industries, and the leather industry.

# Green Chemistry

Concerns over health and environmental impact have put the chemical industry under a lot of pressure for greater accountability. New regulations and rising oil prices have contributed to the need for significant changes to be made. This has become formalized to some extent with the establishment of **Green Chemistry**, also known as **sustainable chemistry**, as a field in its own right. The term 'Green Chemistry' was first coined in 1991, and is now a recognizable and rapidly growing area of study.

In essence, Green Chemistry is chemistry for the environment. Twelve principles have been developed which cover such concepts as mimimizing production of waste, the use of safe solvents, the design of energy-efficient processes, and increasing the atom economy of processes. In other words, it seeks to reduce the footprint of chemical manufacturing processes while improving product and environmental safety. In the context of biochemical research, Green Chemistry has contributed to some innovative processes. A few examples are discussed below.

## Food and drink

Carbon dioxide under pressure is known as supercritical carbon dioxide, and can penetrate into substances and act as a solvent. It is cheap and non-toxic. It is used in the extraction of caffeine in the preparation of decaffeinated coffee, replacing previously used toxic solvents. It is also used to remove fungicide contaminants from wine-bottle corks, and to pull pungent oil out of sesame seeds.

## Bioplastics

Plastics derived from corn starch which has been converted into a resin by bacteria can replace traditional oil-based plastics. Genetically engineered plants such as tobacco may be able to harvest useable plastics.

## Cosmetics

Production of esters for face creams has traditionally used sulfuric acid at high temperatures, but can be done using enzymes at room temperature.

## Clothing industry

Enzymes can replace polluting detergents and improve energy efficiency by enabling effective cleaning at lower temperatures.

Wool dyed with natural products. Green Chemistry seeks to limit the use of toxic dyes and solvents which are widely used in the textile industry.

Renewably sourced textile fibres such as bamboo and eucalyptus may replace synthetic materials from the petrochemical industry or fabrics such as cotton which rely on heavy use of fertilizers.

Many of the applications of Green Chemistry are still developing, and are the focus of active biochemical research. With better education, it is hoped that individuals will exert consumer choice in helping to promote some of these innovative practices. Green Chemistry provides an opportunity for the chemical industry to be both forward-looking and environmentally responsible.

### Exercises

**34** State three types of association found in host–guest supermolecules.

**35** Explain what is meant by biomagnification and why it is such a problem.

**36** State three examples of the use of enzymes in helping to ameliorate environmental problems.

### Practice questions

**1** The structures of the amino acids cysteine and serine are shown in section 33 of the IB data booklet. They can react with each other to form a dipeptide.
   **(a)** State the type of reaction occurring when amino acids react together and identify the other product of the reaction. (2)
   **(b)** Draw the structures of the two possible dipeptides formed in the reaction between one molecule each of cysteine and serine. (2)
   **(c)** Six tripeptides can be formed by reacting together one molecule of each of the amino acids arginine, histidine, and leucine. Predict the primary structures of these six tripeptides using the symbols shown in Section 33 of the IB data booklet to represent the amino acids. (3)
   **(d)** When many amino acid molecules react together a protein is formed. These proteins have primary, secondary, and tertiary structures.
       **(i)** State the type of intermolecular force responsible for maintaining the secondary structure. (1)
       **(ii)** State **two** other ways in which the tertiary structure of the protein is maintained. (2)

*(Total 10 marks)*

**2** **(a)** Maltose is a disaccharide of $\alpha$-glucose.
       **(i)** Use information from section 34 of the IB data booklet to draw the structure of maltose. (3)
       **(ii)** Use molecular formulas to show the reaction for the breakdown of maltose into its monomers. (2)
       **(iii)** State the name of this type of metabolic process. (1)
   **(b)** Cellulose is a polysaccharide of $\beta$-glucose.
       **(i)** Draw a monomer of cellulose. (1)
       **(ii)** Describe and explain the differences in the properties of cellulose and starch. (3)

*(Total 10 marks)*

**3** The graph below shows the effect of temperature on the rate of a reaction catalysed by an enzyme in the human body.

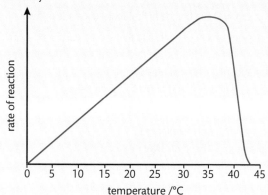

**(a)** With reference to the structure and function of enzymes, explain the shape of the graph. (5)

**(b)** Describe how the graph might be different if it showed the effect of temperature on the rate of a reaction catalysed by an enzyme in a plant adapted to a very cold climate. (2)

*(Total 7 marks)*

**4 (a)** The structures of some fatty acids are given in section 34 of the IB data booklet.

    **(i)** Determine the iodine number of linoleic acid. (3)

    **(ii)** A different fatty acid known as X is isolated, and it is found to have a similar molecular mass to that of linoleic acid, but a lower iodine number. What can you conclude about its structure? (1)

    **(iii)** State and explain which fatty acid, linoleic acid or X, would have the higher melting point. (2)

**(b)** Rancidity in fats can occur as a result of two separate processes. Name these processes, and describe how they differ in the site of reactivity and the conditions that favour the reaction. (6)

**(c)** Compare and contrast the use of lipids and carbohydrates as a source of energy. (3)

*(Total 15 marks)*

**5** Hemoglobin is a protein with a quaternary structure.

**(a)** Justify the statement that hemoglobin is a globular protein. (3)

**(b)** Sketch a graph that shows the cooperative nature of the binding of hemoglobin to oxygen. (4)

**(c)** Explain how the cooperative nature of the hemoglobin–oxygen binding is a consequence of the quaternary structure. (2)

**(d)** Annotate your graph in part (b) to show how hemoglobin's oxygen dissociation curve is changed by the presence of a higher concentration of carbon dioxide. Explain how this change affects the oxygen saturation of the blood when it is close to cells that are actively respiring. (3)

**(e)** Uncooked meat on display for sale is often wrapped in a plastic film which is permeable to air. Deduce why air is allowed to reach the meat. (2)

**(f)** State and explain two ways in which the oxygen dissociation curve for myoglobin differs from that of hemoglobin. (4)

*(Total 18 marks)*

**6** Foods derived from genetically modified organisms were introduced in the early 1990s. State **one** benefit and **one** concern of consuming genetically modified foods. (2)

**7** Deoxyribonucleic acid (DNA) is a double helical molecule made of two polynucleotide chains.

   **(a)** State the components of a nucleotide, and the type of reaction by which they join together. (2)

   **(b)** Explain in terms of the structure of the nucleotide, why DNA fragments move towards the positive electrode during electrophoresis. (2)

   **(c)** A sequence of bases in one strand of DNA is given below:

GCCTACTTAGCTA

   State the corresponding base sequence in:

     **(i)** the complementary strand of DNA;

     **(ii)** the RNA derived from this complementary strand of DNA. (2)

**8** **(a)** Explain why pigments such as anthocyanins are coloured. (2)

   **(b)** The wavelength of visible light lies between 400 and 750 nm. The absorption spectrum of a particular anthocyanin is shown below.

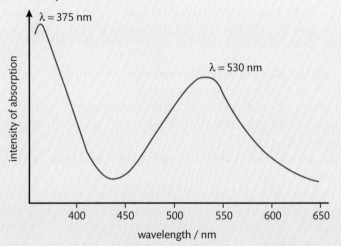

     **(i)** Explain what effect, if any, the absorption at 375 nm will have on the colour of the anthocyanin. (1)

     **(ii)** Explain what effect, if any, the absorption at 530 nm will have on the colour of the anthocyanin. (1)

   **(c)** List **two** factors which could alter the precise colour of a particular anthocyanin. (2)

(Total 6 marks)

**9** The structures of some anthocyanins and carotenoids are given in section 35 of the IB data booklet. Deduce and explain whether anthocyanins and carotenoids are water soluble or fat soluble. (4)

**10 (a)** Predict and explain the solubilities in water of vitamins A and C from their structures given in section 35 of the IB data booklet. (2)

**(b)** If excess amounts of vitamins A and C are consumed, predict with a reason which one is more likely to be stored in the body. (1)

**(c)** Suggest three reasons why vitamin deficiency diseases are prevalent in many parts of the world. (3)

*(Total 6 marks)*

**11 (a)** Outline the meaning of the term xenobiotic. (2)

**(b)** Describe the role of starch in biodegradable plastics. (2)

**(c)** Explain why a plastic such as PVC, poly(chloroethene), is non-biodegradable. (2)

*(Total 6 marks)*

To access weblinks on the topics covered in this chapter, please go to www.pearsonhotlinks.com and enter the ISBN or title of this book.

# 14

## Option C: Energy

# Essential ideas

An oil refinery. In the last 50 years oil has overtaken coal as the world's most important source of energy, however it is a limited resource, and eventually chemists will need to consider other sources of carbon.

We are completely dependent on our energy resources. Our ability to harness energy has allowed us to transform our world and give us control of what we do and when and where we do it. All this energy can be traced back to the formation of the Earth and the solar system. We are currently very dependent on the use of fossil fuels, which are a chemical store of solar energy from millions of years ago, and nuclear fuels, which are present in the earth. The energy of fossil fuels has its origins in the reorganization of electrons as they form new chemical bonds. The energy of nuclear fuels comes from mass changes in the centre of the atom as protons and neutrons adopt a more stable arrangement. Although the quantity of energy we have available to us will not change, the ability of this energy to do useful work does. Energy is constantly being degraded and so we will need to find and use alternative high-quality energy sources. The Sun again offers many options. Life itself is driven by the chemical changes of photosynthesis, which start with the electrons in a double bond being

excited to higher energy levels. This reaction has always been the ultimate source of our food but can also be harnessed to provide biomass fuels. We can use the solar energy indirectly by capturing the kinetic energy of the winds or the potential energy of raindrops. Perhaps the most attractive, but challenging, option is to try and replicate the solar fusion reactions here on Earth, as this could meet all of our energy needs. A less ambitious method uses organic dyes to duplicate the action of chlorophyll and catch the energy of a photon by excited electrons in conjugated organic molecules.

Whatever energy source we use in the future it will need to be more sustainable and environmentally friendly than those used in the last 300 years. The release of carbon atoms, which have been stored up naturally over millions of years, into the atmosphere as carbon dioxide in such a short time interval has had a significant effect on our climate. It is difficult to predict the future, but it is clear our use of energy will have to change.

View from the International Space Station (ISS) of the city lights of north-western Europe. This image highlights our ability to change our planet by harnessing energy supplies. North is to the left of the photo – London is at the bottom left and Paris at the centre.

# C.1 Energy sources

## Understandings:

- A useful energy source releases energy at a reasonable rate and produces minimal pollution.
- The quality of energy is degraded as heat is transferred to the surroundings. Energy and materials go from a concentrated into a dispersed form. The quantity of the energy available for doing work decreases.
- Renewable energy sources are naturally replenished. Non-renewable energy sources are finite.
- Energy density $= \dfrac{\text{energy released from fuel}}{\text{volume of fuel consumed}}$
- Specific energy $= \dfrac{\text{energy released from fuel}}{\text{mass of fuel consumed}}$
- The efficiency of an energy transfer $= \dfrac{\text{useful output energy}}{\text{total input energy}} \times 100\%$

## Applications and skills:

- Discussion of the use of different sources of renewable and non-renewable energy.
- Determination of the energy density and specific energy of a fuel from the enthalpies of combustion, densities, and the molar mass of fuel.
- Discussion of how the choice of fuel is influenced by its energy density or specific energy.
- Determination of the efficiency of an energy transfer process from appropriate data.
- Discussion of the advantages and disadvantages of the different energy sources in C.2 through to C.8.

People use a great range of energy sources. Some of these, such as wood fire burning, are ancient technologies while others, such as nuclear power and solar cells, are very recent. Most of our energy derives from the Sun, which drives the climate and photosynthesis. Humans can harness this energy directly using photovoltaic cells or indirectly by burning fossil fuels.

Oil is the fossil fuel that currently provides the world's economy with the most energy but this will change as our finite resources run out. Fossil fuels are **non-renewable** energy sources – they are used at a rate faster than they can be replaced. Another non-renewable energy source is uranium, which gives up energy as its nuclei splits to form smaller more stable nuclei.

In this section we are going to review some basic energy concepts and consider a variety of the most important energy technologies.

## A useful energy source releases energy at a reasonable rate and produces minimal pollution

Energy is defined as the ability to do work. Very little can happen without it – if we apply a force over a distance we do work – and to do this we need energy. Although our energy sources are being run down, this is not happening to the *quantity* of energy in the universe. The **conservation of energy** tells us that energy cannot be created or destroyed. It can only be converted from one form into another. The problem is that the *quality* of our energy is being degraded – if we lose energy to the environment it is no longer available to do useful work.

A room where everything is at the same temperature has low-quality energy, as there is no way that we can make the energy more spread out than it already is. Placing a piece of burning wood into the room, however, introduces some high-quality energy; the heat produced during the exothermic combustion reaction can be used to power an engine which can do useful work. During this process some of the energy will become spread out in the room where it can no longer be useful, so the quality of the energy has decreased.

Sources of energy are either hot bodies, like the Sun, or objects that store high-quality potential energy, like the water in a reservoir or the chemical energy of a fossil fuel.

An energy source needs to be cheap, plentiful, and readily accessible and provide high-quality energy at a suitable rate – not too fast or too slow. It should do this in a way that has minimal effect on the environment. Rain water, for example, is a generally a poor energy source; although it possesses gravitational potential energy it releases this energy at too slow a rate for it to be useful. The construction of a dam, however, allows this energy to be released at a more useful rate. A nuclear bomb, unlike a nuclear reactor, releases energy at too fast a rate for it to be used safely. Current high-quality energy sources which meet these criteria include fossil fuels, nuclear fission, electrochemical cells, solar energy, biomass, and alternative sources such as wind, waves, tidal, and hydroelectric.

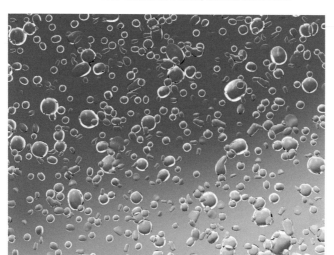

> The conservation of energy states that energy cannot be created or destroyed. It can only be converted from one form into another.

> In any cyclical process designed to convert heat to work, some energy is always degraded. Degraded energy is energy that is no longer available for the performance of useful work.

Water droplets on a window pane. The water droplets are a source of energy but they deliver the energy at too slow a rate to be useful.

A fuel is a substance that can release energy by changing its chemical or nuclear structure.

Water can give up its potential energy at a useful rate if it is stored up to be released later. This is a view of the Shasta dam, a hydroelectric power station located at Redding, California.

A **fuel** is a substance that can release energy by changing its chemical or nuclear structure. Fossil fuels release energy during a chemical reaction whereas uranium releases its energy during a fission reaction.

## Renewable energy sources are naturally replenished

Water will give up its energy when it is released from the dam to drive the turbines to generate hydroelectricity, but this source can be replenished by natural rainfall. It is a **renewable** source. A renewable source is one that is replenished at a rate faster than it is used. Wood for example is a renewable resource as trees can be grown to replace those chopped down to provide wood as fuel, but coal is non-renewable as it takes millions of years for fossil fuels to form.

## The energy density of a fuel is the energy produced per unit volume and the specific energy is the energy produced per unit mass

In Chapter 5 we discussed the enthalpy change of combustion. This is the enthalpy change that occurs when one mole of the substance is burnt completely in an excess of oxygen under standard conditions. This is a natural choice when comparing the energy changes of different reactions but is not necessarily the most relevant when factors such as storage and transport of a fuel need to be considered.

$$\text{Energy density} = \frac{\text{energy released from fuel}}{\text{volume of fuel consumed}}$$

$$\text{Specific energy} = \frac{\text{energy released from fuel}}{\text{mass of fuel consumed}}$$

The **energy density** of a fuel is the energy produced per unit volume whereas the **specific energy** of a fuel is the energy produced per unit mass.

The two terms are related via the density of the fuel, as the following worked example illustrates.

### Worked example

The enthalpies of combustion of a range of organic compounds are given in section 13 of the IB data booklet. Calculate the specific energy and energy density of hexane from its density, which is 0.6548 g cm$^{-3}$ under standard conditions.

**Solution**

Formula = $C_6H_{14}$

$M / \text{g mol}^{-1} = (6 \times 12.01) + (14 \times 1.01) = 86.2$

$$\Delta H_c \,/\, \text{kJ mol}^{-1} = -4163$$

$$\text{Specific energy} \,/\, \text{kJ g}^{-1} = \frac{-4163}{86.2} = 48.3$$

$$\text{Energy density} \,/\, \text{kJ cm}^{-3} = 48.3 \times 0.6548 = 31.6$$

The specific energies of some fuels are tabulated below.

| Fuel | Specific energy / MJ kg$^{-1}$ |
|------|-------------------------------|
| fusion fuel | $3 \times 10^9$ |
| $^{238}$U | $9 \times 10^8$ |
| gasoline (petrol) | 45.8 |
| natural gas | 55.5 |
| coal | 33.0 |
| wood | 17.0 |
| hydrogen(g) | 142 |

We can see that nuclear fuels have the highest specific energies and fossil fuels have higher specific energies than the related renewable sources.

## Energy conversions are never 100% efficient

A **primary source** of energy is often not used directly but converted to a **secondary source** such as electricity and some energy is inevitably lost during the conversion.

The **efficiency** of an energy transfer is defined as:

$$\text{efficiency} = \frac{\text{useful output energy}}{\text{total input energy}} \times 100$$

No matter how well a power plant is designed it can never convert energy from one form into another with 100% efficiency. Energy is always dissipated during energy transformations. This is a consequence of the **second law of thermodynamics**. The efficiency of different power stations depends on the design but typical values for fossil fuel power stations are tabulated below.

| Fossil fuel | Typical efficiency values |
|-------------|---------------------------|
| gas | 40–50% |
| oil | 35–45% |
| coal | 35–40% |

The efficiency is generally less than 50% as the random motion of the heated gas particles needs to be converted into the coordinated motion of the particles in the solid turbine and some energy is inevitably lost in the process. It has been estimated that the complete conversion of 10 J of heat energy into 10 J work has about the same likelihood as a group of monkeys typing Shakespeare's complete works.

The specific energy of a fuel is the energy produced per unit mass.

Nuclear fuels have a higher energy density and specific energy than fossil fuels.

The International Energy Agency is an autonomous organization which works to ensure reliable, affordable, and clean energy for its 28 member countries and beyond. The International Renewable Energy Agency (IRENA) was founded in 2009 to promote increased adoption and sustainable use of renewable energy sources (bioenergy, geothermal energy, hydropower, ocean, solar, and wind energy).

$$\text{efficiency} = \frac{\text{useful output energy}}{\text{total input energy}} \times 100$$

The maximum efficiency with which heat can be converted to work depends on the temperature of the heat source and the surroundings to which the heat is dissipated. A jet engine is more efficient than a car engine because it runs at a higher temperature. If an engine was operating in an environment at 0 K then all the random motion of the gases would be lost and the process would be 100% efficient, but it is impossible to achieve absolute zero.

Cooling towers of the Ferrybridge coal-fired power station in England. A lot of low-quality energy is released into the environment in the hot steam.

## Worked example

A coal-burning power station generates electrical power at a rate of $550 \times 10^6 \, J \, s^{-1}$. The power station has an overall efficiency of 36% for the conversion of heat into electricity.

(a) Calculate the total quantity of electrical energy generated in one year of operation.

(b) Calculate the total quantity of heat energy used in the generation of this amount of electricity.

(c) Calculate the mass of coal that will be burned in one year of operation, assuming that coal has the enthalpy of combustion of graphite.

### Solution

(a) Total electrical energy in one year = $550 \times 10^6 \times 60 \times 60 \times 24 \times 365$
$$= 1.73 \times 10^{16} \, J$$

(b) $\dfrac{\text{useful output energy}}{\text{total input energy}} = \dfrac{\text{useful electrical energy}}{\text{total input heat energy}} = 0.36$

$$\text{heat energy in} = \dfrac{\text{electrical energy generated}}{0.36}$$
$$= 4.82 \times 10^{16} \, J$$

(c) heat energy = $4.82 \times 10^{16} \, J$
$$= 4.82 \times 10^{13} \, kJ$$

$$\text{moles of coal (or graphite)} = \dfrac{4.82 \times 10^{13}}{394}$$
$$= 1.22 \times 10^{11} \, mol$$

$$\text{mass} = 1.22 \times 10^{11} \, mol \times 12.01 \, g \, mol^{-1}$$
$$= 1.47 \times 10^{12} \, g$$
$$= 1.47 \times 10^9 \, kg$$

## CHALLENGE YOURSELF

1 1000 kJ of electrical energy are supplied every hour to a television set. 300 kJ are given out as light and 20 kJ are given out as sound. Identify an additional energy transfer process that occurs during the working of a television and calculate the energy efficiency of the television.

**NATURE OF SCIENCE**

Albert Szent-Györgyi said 'Discovery consists of seeing what everybody has seen and thinking what nobody has thought.' The scientific ideas behind the concepts of energy, both its quantity and its quality, arose from simple observations of the world around us. Everyone is familiar with the fact that heat is observed to go from hot to cold objects, but only a few scientists understood the significance of this. The theories relating heat and work are very broad in their application. They were originally developed in the 19th century to increase the efficiency of the steam engine – an issue of crucial economic importance at the time, as a country's power was intimately linked with its use of steam power. They can now be applied to explain many aspects of the physical world. The broad application of the theories is linked to the precise mathematical language in which they are expressed. We are able to assign numbers to the quantity and quality of energy.

**TOK**

The theoretical advances in understanding the relationship between heat and movement were often stimulated by political and economic considerations. Sadi Carnot's *Reflections on the Motive Power of Fire*, which was one of the most important pieces of writing on the efficiency of steam engines, was written while he was a semi-retired military officer after Napoleon's final defeat in 1815.

In what ways might social, political, cultural, and religious factors affect the types of research that are financed and undertaken, or rejected?

1 Consider the following energy sources:

- biomass
- fossil fuels
- geothermal
- hydroelectricity
- nuclear fission
- nuclear fusion
- solar electricity
- solar heating
- tidal
- wind power

(a) Identify the sources which are derived from recent solar radiation.

(b) Identify the sources which are derived from ancient solar radiation.

(c) Identify the sources which are derived from the formation of Earth.

(d) Identify the sources which are renewable and explain your answer with reference to your answers to part (a)–(c).

2 $4.00 \times 10^7$ kJ are required to heat a home in a typical winter month.

(a) The house can be heated directly with a gas boiler burning methane gas (efficiency 85%). Calculate the mass of methane required in one month using this method of heating.

(b) The home can also be heated using electricity from a natural gas-burning power plant (efficiency 50%). Determine the mass of methane needed to generate the electricity needed to heat the house.

3 The enthalpies of combustion of methane and hydrogen are given in section 13 of the IB data booklet.

(a) Calculate the specific energies of $CH_4$ and $H_2$.

(b) Use the ideal gas equation to calculate the density of the two gases at s.t.p. and hence calculate the energy density of the two gases.

(c) Identify the best fuel based on this information and discuss the practical difficulties involved in its widespread use.

## CHALLENGE YOURSELF

2 Factual learning in chemistry is a non-spontaneous 'unnatural' process in which the entropy of your brain decreases. Why doesn't this contradict the second law of thermodynamics?

# C.2 Fossil fuels

## Understandings:

- Fossil fuels were formed by the reduction of biological compounds that contain carbon, hydrogen, nitrogen, sulfur, and oxygen.
- Petroleum is a complex mixture of hydrocarbons that can be split by a physical process into different component parts, called fractions by fractional distillation.
- The tendency of a fuel to auto-ignite, which leads to 'knocking' in a car engine, is related to molecular structure and measured by the octane number.
- The performance of hydrocarbons as fuels is improved by the cracking and catalytic reforming reactions.
- Coal gasification and liquefaction are chemical processes that convert coal to gaseous and liquid hydrocarbons.
- A carbon footprint is the total amount of greenhouse gases produced during human activities. It is generally expressed in equivalent tons of carbon dioxide.

## Applications and skills:

- Discussion of the effect of chain length and chain branching on the octane number.
- Discussion of the reforming and cracking reactions of hydrocarbons; and explanation of how these processes improve the octane number.
- Deduction of equations for cracking and reforming reactions, coal gasification, and liquefaction.
- Discussion of the advantages and disadvantages of the different fossil fuels.

### Guidance
*The cost of production and availability (reserves) of the fossil fuels and impact on the environment should be considered.*

- Identification of the various fractions of petroleum, their relative volatility, and their uses.
- Calculations of the carbon dioxide added to the atmosphere when different fuels burn and determination of carbon footprints for different activities.

## Fossil fuels were formed by the reduction of biological compounds

The fossil fuels have been described as 'sunshine in the solid, liquid, and gaseous form', as their energy comes from sunlight which was trapped by green plants millions of years ago. Fossil fuels are produced by the slow and partial decomposition of plant and animal matter that is trapped in the absence of air. Oxygen is lost from the biological molecules containing carbon, hydrogen, nitrogen, sulfur, and oxygen at a faster rate than other elements, which results in reduced biological compounds which are often hydrocarbons.

## Coal is the most abundant fossil fuel

Coal is a combustible sedimentary rock formed from the remains of plant life which have been subject to geological heat and pressure. Most coal was formed during the carboniferous period (286–360 millions of years ago). The action of pressure and heat changed plant material in stages from peat to lignite to bituminous soft coal and finally to anthracite. At each stage the percentage of carbon increases. Anthracite is formed under conditions of very high heat and pressure and is almost pure carbon, but coal generally contains between 80% and 90% carbon by mass. Coal occurs in many areas, though the majority of the world's supplies are in the northern hemisphere. It is by far the most plentiful of the Earth's fossil fuels.

### CHALLENGE YOURSELF

**3** Suggest a source of the sulfur in coal and crude oil and explain why this is a problem.

### Worked example

A number of carbon fuels are used domestically to provide heating during the winter months.

| | Percentage composition | | | | Specific energy / kJ g$^{-1}$ |
|---|---|---|---|---|---|
| | C | H | O | N | |
| wood | 50 | 6 | 43 | 1 | 10–13 |
| peat | 59 | 6 | 33 | 2 | 13 |
| bituminous coal | 88 | 5 | 5–15 | 1 | 30 |
| anthracite | 95 | 2–3 | 2–3 | trace | 31 |

**(a)** Describe the relationship between the oxygen content of a fuel and its specific energy.

**(b)** Describe how the composition of the fuels changes as they are exposed to high pressure.

**(c)** State two advantages of coal use over wood.

**(d)** State one advantage of the use of wood.

**(e)** Discuss some of the disadvantages of the use of coal.

### Solution

**(a)** The less oxygen a compound contains the greater its specific energy.

**(b)** Oxygen (and water vapour) are lost.

**(c)** Coal is the most abundant fossil fuel and has high specific energy and energy density.

**(d)** It is a renewable.

**(e)** Difficult and expensive to mine and transport; produces sulfur oxides, which lead to acid deposition, particulates (soot), which lead to global dimming, and carbon dioxide, a greenhouse gas which leads to global warming; mining has an environmental impact.

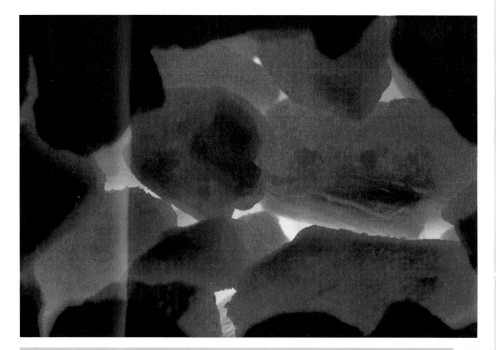

Burning anthracite. Anthracite has a fixed carbon content of 92–98%. It burns with a short blue flame and no noticeable smoke.

Coal fuelled much of the Industrial Revolution, which led to important advances in both science and technology. The development of steam power was crucial to a country's economy, but to understand the link between heat and work scientists had to unravel the nature of energy – its quality and its quantity and the underlying molecular basis for the laws governing the transfer of heat into work. Whatever the field, whether it is pure science or engineering technology, there is boundless scope for creative and imaginative thinking.

Exercises

**4**   An analytical chemist determines the percentage composition by mass of a sample of coal.

| C | H | O | N | S |
|---|---|---|---|---|
| 84.96 | 5.08 | 7.55 | 0.73 | 1.68 |

   **(a)** Determine the empirical formula of the coal.
   **(b)** Explain how the combustion of the coal could produce acid rain. Give equations to illustrate how the elements in the coal can produce acidic gases.

**5**   The coal burned in a 500 MW ($500 \times 10^3$ kJ s$^{-1}$) power station has a specific energy of 33.0 kJ g$^{-1}$.

   **(a)** Determine the mass of the coal burned each second when the power station is operating at full capacity, assuming an efficiency of 38%.
   **(b)** The empirical formula of the coal can be approximated as CH. Calculate the mass of carbon dioxide produced each second.

# Crude oil is a valuable fuel and chemical feedstock

Crude oil is one of the most important raw materials in the world today. It is a complex mixture of straight-chain and branched-chain saturated alkanes, cycloalkanes, and

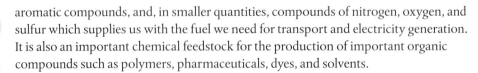

aromatic compounds, and, in smaller quantities, compounds of nitrogen, oxygen, and sulfur which supplies us with the fuel we need for transport and electricity generation. It is also an important chemical feedstock for the production of important organic compounds such as polymers, pharmaceuticals, dyes, and solvents.

Crude oil was formed over millions of years from the remains of marine animals and plants, which were trapped under layers of rock. Under these conditions of high temperature and high pressure, organic matter decays in the presence of bacteria and the absence of oxygen. Crude oil is a limited resource and eventually reservoirs will be so depleted that chemists will need to consider other sources of carbon, both as a fuel and as a chemical feedstock.

In the last 50 years oil has overtaken coal as the world's most important source of energy. Oil and gas are easier to extract than coal since they are fluids and can be pumped up from underground reserves. It is now possible to extract oil from beneath the sea. There are risks and benefits in using oil as a source of energy or as a source of carbon to make new products.

Petrol or gasoline is a highly concentrated and convenient energy source for use in transport. It could be argued, however, that burning hydrocarbons, with their resulting environmental side-effects such as smog and global warming, is a misuse of this valuable resource. When the great Russian chemist Dmitri Mendeleyev (Chapter 3, page 97) visited the oilfields of Azerbaijan at the end of the 19th century, he is said to have likened the burning of oil as a fuel to 'firing up a kitchen stove with banknotes'.

We still use about 90% of the refined product as a fuel. However, as supplies decrease, this proportion may fall. Crude oil will last longer if we conserve energy and recycle materials, such as plastics. Burning fuels derived from crude oil is the most convenient and economical option at the moment, but alternative energy sources and feedstocks may be developed.

Polymers, for example, could also be made from coal, of which there are still large reserves, and from renewable biological materials such as wood, starch, or cotton.

The words used to describe the different liquid fuels can cause confusion. Petroleum is a broad category that includes both crude oil and petroleum products. The terms "oil" and "petroleum" are sometimes used interchangeably. In this text we have used crude oil. The liquid fuel used in cars is either called gasoline or petrol. We have used the word gasoline.

The Organization of the Petroleum Exporting Countries (OPEC) is an intergovernmental organization set up to stabilize oil markets in order to secure an efficient, economic, and regular supply of petroleum. There are political implications in being dependent on imported oil and gas. Price fluctuations have a significant effect on national economies; supplies and energy resources are therefore an important bartering tool in political disputes.

A gasoline pump supplies energy to a car at a rate of about 34 MW (34 MJ s$^{-1}$).

Petrochemical plants take crude oil, separate it into fractions, and process it to make useful organic compounds.

## Crude oil needs to be refined before it is used as a fuel

Crude oil is of no use before it is **refined**. Sulfur impurities, mainly in the form of hydrogen sulfide, must first be removed as they would block the active sites of the catalysts used in later chemical processing. The acidic hydrogen sulfide is removed by dissolving it in basic potassium carbonate solution:

$$H_2S(g) + CO_3^{2-}(aq) \rightleftharpoons HS^-(aq) + HCO_3^-(aq)$$

The hydrogen sulfide can be recovered from solution by later reversing the reaction. It is burned in air to form sulfur dioxide:

$$2H_2S(g) + 3O_2(g) \rightarrow 2SO_2(g) + H_2O(l)$$

The sulfur dioxide produced can then react with more hydrogen sulfide to produce elemental sulfur:

$$2H_2S(g) + SO_2(g) \rightarrow 3S(s) + 2H_2O(l)$$

This desulfurization step also reduces acid rain pollution which would otherwise result if the sulfur was burned with the oil.

The crude oil is then separated into different **fractions** on the basis of their boiling points (Figure 14.1). In this **fractional distillation** process the crude oil is heated to a temperature of about 400 °C.

At this temperature all the different components of the mixture are vaporized and allowed to pass up a **distillation column**. The level at which the molecules condense depends on their size. The smaller molecules containing between one and four carbon atoms collect at the top as the **refinery gas** fraction. Molecules of successively larger molecular mass condense at lower levels corresponding to their higher boiling points. The different fractions and their uses are tabulated below.

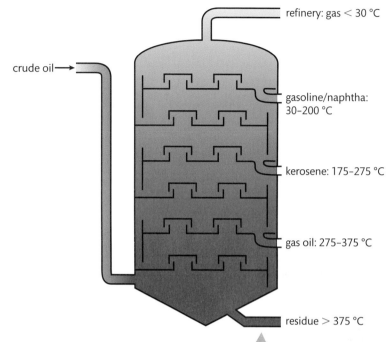

**Figure 14.1** The fractional distillation of crude oil.

| Fraction | Number of carbon atoms | Use |
|---|---|---|
| refinery gas | 1–4 | fuel and as a feedstock for petrochemicals |
| gasoline/naphtha | 5–10 | gasoline (petrol): fuel for cars<br>naphtha: chemical feedstock |
| kerosene | 10–16 | fuel for jets, paraffin for heating |
| gas oil | 13–25 | fuel for diesel engines, power plants, and heating |
| residue | >25 | oil-fired power stations, polishing waxes, lubricating oils, bitumen used to surface roads |

The residue from a fractionating column consists of hydrocarbons with high boiling points under normal atmospheric conditions. **Vacuum distillation** can be used to vaporize these compounds and separate them at relatively low temperatures. Higher temperatures would lead to the molecules breaking up before separation takes place. The fraction with between 5 and 10 carbon atoms is the most in demand as it is used in cars. As a liquid it is convenient to handle and deliver and has a relatively low boiling point so it is easy to vaporize, which assists combustion.

## Cracking breaks down large alkanes to smaller alkanes and alkenes

Fractional distillation is a physical process and although some of the compounds distilled can be used directly, further treatment is generally needed. The demand for the different fractions does not necessarily match the amounts present in the crude oil supplied and so the hydrocarbon molecules from the crude oil need to be chemically changed. Hydrocarbons with up to 12 carbon atoms are in the most demand as they are more easily vaporized and therefore make the best fuels. The supply of these molecules can be increased by breaking down or **cracking** larger molecules. For example, the cracking of heptane:

Molecular graphics representation of the structure of the synthetic zeolite catalyst ZSM-5, showing its microchannel architecture. Zeolite minerals containing a silica-alumina crystalline structure are used as catalysts in the cracking process by which crude oil is refined.

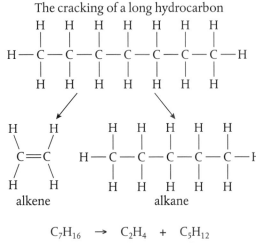

The cracking of a long hydrocarbon

alkene    alkane

$$C_7H_{16} \rightarrow C_2H_4 + C_5H_{12}$$
alkene    alkane

Other examples:

$$C_{16}H_{34} \rightarrow C_8H_{18} + C_8H_{16}$$
alkane    alkene

$$C_{10}H_{22} \rightarrow C_8H_{18} + C_2H_4$$
alkane    alkene

As we can see, the reaction also produces useful alkenes (e.g. $C_8H_{16}$ and $C_2H_4$), which can be used to make addition polymers and other important products.

When the process is achieved by heating the starting materials it is called **thermal cracking**. In **catalytic cracking** the use of a catalyst allows the reaction to occur at a lower temperature of 500 °C and helps to give the required product by controlling the mechanism. The reactions that occur are complicated but generally involve the formation of **carbocations** (page 518), which are produced and then rearranged on the catalyst surface. Large and intermediate-sized alkanes are passed over an alumina ($Al_2O_3$) and silica ($SiO_2$) catalyst, which is in powdered form to increase its surface area. The lower temperature requires less energy and so reduces the cost of the process. Zeolites, which are naturally occurring minerals of aluminium, silicon, and oxygen, are also good catalysts for this process as their crystal structures contain an extensive network which offers the hydrocarbons a large surface area for reaction. Some carbon is, however, formed during the process and this can coat the catalyst and stop it working. The catalyst

Catalytic cracking uses high temperature and a catalyst to break down (crack) heavy oil fractions into lighter, more useful oils. The oil is heated to 500 °C and passed over a catalyst such as zeolite crystals. The vessel where the cracking takes places is the barrel-shaped grey one on the right.

is cleaned or regenerated by separating it from the reaction mixture using steam jets. The carbon coat is then removed by heating. The heat produced from the combustion of this carbon can be used to sustain the cracking reaction.

Catalytic cracking tends to produce branched-chain alkanes and compounds which contain the benzene ring (aromatics) – which burn more evenly in a car engine than their straight-chain isomers and are used in high-quality gasoline. This is discussed in more detail later in the chapter.

**Hydrocracking** can also produce compounds which can be used in high-quality gasoline. In this process a heavy hydrocarbon fractions is mixed with hydrogen at a pressure of about 80 atm ($80 \times 1.0 \times 10^5$ Pa) and cracked over palladium on a zeolite surface. A high yield of branched-chain alkanes and cycloalkanes and some aromatic compounds is produced.

## The tendency of a fuel to auto-ignite is measured by the octane number

The four strokes of a typical gasoline engine are:

| Piston position | Action |
|---|---|
| moves to increase volume of chamber | air and fuel intake |
| moves to decrease volume of chamber | compression stroke and spark ignition near end of compression |
| moves to increase volume of chamber | expansion of gases caused by production of gases and increase temperature |
| moves to decrease volume of chamber | exhaust gases expelled |

In the compression stroke of an internal combustion engine, a cylinder-full of fuel and air is squashed into a smaller volume and ignited with a spark plug. Some fuels auto-ignite without the need of a spark plug as the fuel–air mixture is compressed by the piston. This premature ignition is known as '**knocking**' as it gives rise to a knocking sound in the engine. Knocking reduces the efficiency of the engine as the energy of the exploding and expanding gas is not applied fully to the piston at the optimum time and can damage an engine. Straight-chain molecules have a greater tendency to knock. The branched-chain isomer of octane, 2,2,4-trimethylpentane (isooctane) does not suffer from premature ignition and is considered to be the standard by which other fuels are judged. Hence the performance of a fuel is given by its **octane number**, which is based on a scale on which the 2,2,4-trimethylpentane has a value of 100 and the straight-chain molecule heptane, which auto-ignites relatively easily, has an octane number of 0. A fuel with an octane rating of 96 burns as efficiently as a mixture of 96% 2,2,4-trimethylpentane and 4% heptane. Fuels with high octane numbers can be more highly compressed, which results in more power per piston stroke.

**The octane number indicates the resistance of a motor fuel to knock. Octane numbers are based on a scale on which 2,2,4-trimethylpentane (isooctane) is 100 (minimal knock) and heptane is 0 (maximum knock).**

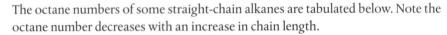

## CHALLENGE YOURSELF

4  **(a)** Suggest a value for the octane number of octane.

**(b)** Since the octane number system was developed, a number of compounds have been found with an octane number greater than 100. Predict which straight-chain alkanes have an octane number of above 100.

The octane numbers of some straight-chain alkanes are tabulated below. Note the octane number decreases with an increase in chain length.

|         | RON  | MON  | Average octane number |
|---------|------|------|-----------------------|
| butane  | 94   | 89.6 | 92                    |
| pentane | 62   | 62.6 | 62                    |
| hexane  | 24.8 | 26   | 25                    |
| heptane | 0    | 0    | 0                     |

The octane number of some isomers of hexane and other molecules with six carbon atoms are given in this table.

| Compound          | Average octane number |
|-------------------|-----------------------|
| hexane            | 25                    |
| (*trans*) hex-2-ene | 93                  |
| cyclohexane       | 83                    |
| benzene           | 106                   |

From these results we can see the following patterns:

• cyclic compounds have higher octane numbers than linear structures
• alkenes have a higher octane number than the isomeric cycloalkane
• aromatic compounds with the benzene ring have even higher octane numbers.

## CHALLENGE YOURSELF

5  Use the data in the table to investigate the relationship between octane number and bond enthalpies.

| Compound             | Average octane number |
|----------------------|-----------------------|
| octane               | −19                   |
| 2,4-dimethylhexane   | 65                    |
| 2,2,4-trimethylpentane | 100                 |

**TOK**

In 1922 Thomas Midgley found that the octane number of a fuel could be increased with the addition of tetraethyl lead ($Pb(C_2H_5)_4$) and this led to the widespread use of leaded gasoline. Its use has, however, now been phased out in most countries as it both inhibits the action of catalytic convertors and is a source of lead air pollution. Lead is a heavy metal poison with cumulative neurological effects that are particularly damaging to young children. Methanol (octane number 107) and ethanol (octane number 108) are now, for example, both added to gasoline instead of tetraethyl lead.

## Catalytic reforming increases the octane number of a fuel

In **catalytic reforming** the atoms in a molecule can rearrange to form a more branched chain or a cyclic or aromatic compound. The process is often referred to as plat forming if Pt is used as the catalyst, but other rare and expensive metals, such as Pd, Ir, or Rh, can also be used.

Hexane, for example, can be converted to benzene and hydrogen in a **dehydrogenation** reaction:

$$C_6H_{14} \rightarrow C_6H_6 + 4H_2$$

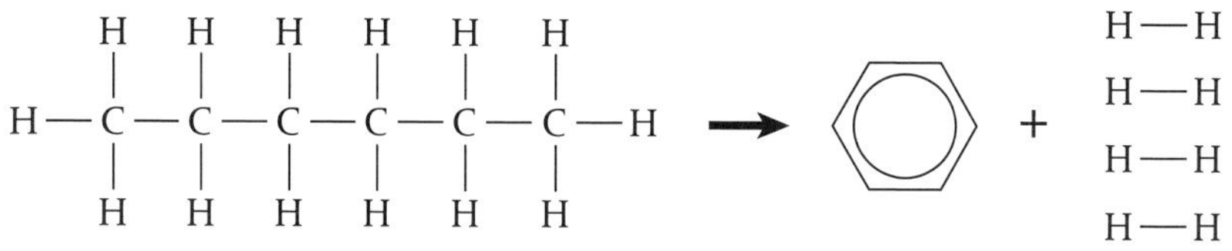

and heptane can be converted into methylbenzene and hydrogen:

$$C_7H_{16} \rightarrow C_6H_5CH_3 + 4H_2$$

The branching in a molecule can also be increased in a process called **isomerization** by heating the molecules in the presence of a catalyst such as $AlCl_3$.

Octane, for example, can be converted into 2,2,4-trimethylpentane:

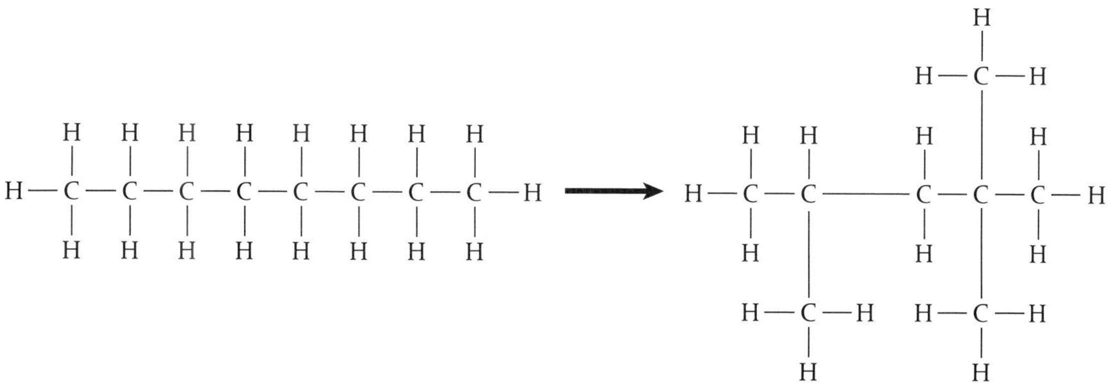

## Alkylation involves the octane number by reacting lower mass alkenes with alkanes to form higher mass alkanes

The alkenes produced in the cracking process can further increase the quality of the crude oil by **alkylation**. This can be thought of as a little like the reverse of a cracking reaction in that an alkene and an alkane with short carbon chains combine together to form a high mass alkane with a branched chain. The alkane is effectively adding across the double bond in the alkene – with a hydrogen atom bonding to one of the carbons in the double bond (shown in red) and the rest of the molecule (R shown in blue) adding to the other carbon of the double bond.

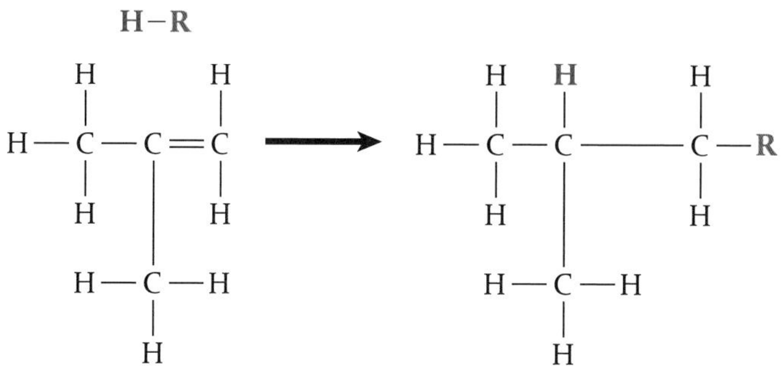

The hydrogen atom (in red) bonds to the carbon atom in the double bond which has the least number of hydrogens. So 2,2,4-trimethylpentane can be produced from the reaction between methylpropane and methylpropene with an acidic catalyst.

## Supplies of liquid fuels can be increased by coal liquefaction

Liquid hydrocarbon fuels can also be produced by reacting coal with hydrogen under high pressure in the presence of a catalyst. The resulting mixture of hydrocarbons can then be separated by fractional distillation. As the cost of crude oil increases as a resource this will be an increasingly economic option.

The direct conversion of coal to liquids by hydrogenation process can be summarized by:

$$nC + (n+1)H_2 \rightarrow C_nH_{2n+2}$$

where $n > 4$

The **Fischer–Tropsch** process involves using a mixture of carbon monoxide and hydrogen as the feedstock and produces a variety of alkanes along with water:

$$(2n+1)H_2 + nCO \rightarrow C_nH_{2n+2} + nH_2O$$

The growing demand for crude oil, accompanied by the declining crude oil reserves and the concerns over energy security, has intensified the interest in direct coal liquefaction. This occurs particularly in countries which are rich in coal resources, but short of crude oil.

### Exercises

6   Draw the molecular structure of 2,2,4-trimethylpentane (isooctane).

7   **(a)** Deduce an equation for the cracking of $C_{11}H_{24}$ in which an alkene and an alkane are formed in the ratio 3:1.
   **(b)** Explain why cracking is a useful process.
   **(c)** Although alkanes can be cracked with heat alone, it is more common for oil companies to use catalysts. Suggest two reasons for this.

8   **(a)** State the name and formula of two compounds present in gasoline.
   **(b)** Explain how the compounds are isolated from crude oil.
   **(c)** Explain why these components are used in gasoline.
   **(d)** Discuss two different methods that can be used to increase the yield of gasoline from a given quantity of crude oil.
   **(e)** State equations to represent each of these reactions.

9   Consider the following organic compounds.

   - pentane
   - pentene
   - benzene
   - cyclopentane

   State the order of increasing octane number and explain your choice.

10   Consider the following organic compounds.

   - pentane
   - hexane
   - heptane
   - ethanol

   State the order of increasing octane number and explain your choice.

**11** Crude oil currently provides a greater percentage of the world's energy than any other energy source.

(a) State three reasons for its wide use as an energy source.

(b) Describe briefly how crude oil is formed in nature.

(c) Describe the processes by which the crude material is made ready for use.

## Natural gas is mainly methane

Methane is the primary constituent of natural gas, which also contains nitrogen and sulfur compounds (hydrogen sulfide) as impurities. Natural gas was formed millions of years ago by the action of heat, pressure, and perhaps bacteria on buried organic matter. The gas is trapped in geological formations capped by impermeable rock. It is also formed from the decomposition of crude oil and coal deposits. It can occur almost entirely on its own, dissolved under pressure in oil; or in a layer above the oil in a reservoir. Natural gas can also be found associated with coal, when it is a major hazard as it forms an explosive mixture with air.

Oil spills from oil pipelines are issues that demand international cooperation and agreement.

Natural gas is the cleanest of the fossil fuels to burn, due to its high H : C ratio. Impurities can easily be removed, so the combustion of natural gas produces minimal amounts of carbon monoxide, hydrocarbons, and particulates. Where it is available as mains gas it flows through pipes to wherever it is needed, so little energy is used to get the gas from the ground to the consumer. Setting up such a distribution network, however, involves a massive capital investment and in some countries liquefied gas (butane or propane) is an option for domestic heating and cooking.

Aerial view of production rigs in the Vakhitovskoye natural gas field, Orenberg, Russia.

### Worked example

Consider the following specific energies of different fuels.

The financial costs and the political risks involved in constructing international pipelines are the main reasons why the international trade in natural gas has been relatively slow. At present most natural gas is consumed in the countries in which it is found.

| Fuel | Specific energy / kJ g$^{-1}$ | Carbon content by mass / % |
|------|------|------|
| coal | 32 | 94 |
| oil | 42 | 83 |
| natural gas | 55 | 75 |
| wood | 15 | 70 |
| hydrogen | 142 | 0 |

(a) Suggest an explanation for the trend in specific energies between coal, oil, natural gas, and hydrogen.

(b) The choice of fuel also depends on other factors besides specific energies. One of these is the amount of carbon dioxide produced. Explain why this is an important factor to consider.

(c) Calculate the carbon dioxide production for each 1000 kJ of energy from each source and identify the best and worst fuel on this basis.

## Solution

(a) Hydrogen has a higher enthalpy of combustion than carbon as it forms stronger bonds with oxygen. As the percentage carbon content decreases and the hydrogen content increases the specific energy increases.

(b) Carbon dioxide is a greenhouse gas and causes global warming.

(c)

| Fuel | Specific energy / kJ g$^{-1}$ | Mass needed to produce 1000 kJ / g | Carbon content by mass / % | Carbon burnt / g | Carbon dioxide produced / g |
|---|---|---|---|---|---|
| coal | 32 | $= \dfrac{1000}{32}$ $= 31.3$ | 94 | $= \dfrac{1000}{32} \times 0.94$ | $= \dfrac{1000}{32} \times 0.94 \times \dfrac{44.01}{12.01}$ $= 108$ |
| oil | 42 | $= \dfrac{1000}{42}$ $= 23.8$ | 83 | $= \dfrac{1000}{42} \times 0.83$ | $= \dfrac{1000}{42} \times 0.83 \times \dfrac{44.01}{12.01}$ $= 72$ |
| natural gas | 55 | $= \dfrac{1000}{55}$ $= 18.2$ | 75 | $= \dfrac{1000}{55} \times 0.75$ | $= \dfrac{1000}{55} \times 0.75 \times \dfrac{44.01}{12.01}$ $= 50$ |
| wood | 15 | $= \dfrac{1000}{15}$ $= 66.7$ | 70 | $= \dfrac{1000}{15} \times 0.70$ | $= \dfrac{1000}{15} \times 0.70 \times \dfrac{44.01}{12.01}$ $= 171$ |
| hydrogen | 142 | $= \dfrac{1000}{142}$ $= 7.0$ | 0 | 0 | 0 |

Hydrogen is the best and coal is the worst fuel on this basis.

## Supplies of methane can be increased by cracking larger hydrocarbons or from coal gasification

Coal can be converted to the more environmentally clean methane by the process of **coal gasification**. The crushed coal is mixed with superheated steam, and a mixture of carbon monoxide and hydrogen known as **synthesis gas** is produced.

$$C(s) + H_2O(l) \rightarrow CO(g) + H_2(g)$$

Synthesis gas can be used directly as a fuel. It can be processed further to make methane; it is mixed with additional hydrogen in the presence of a heated catalyst:

$$CO(g) + 3H_2(g) \rightarrow CH_4(g) + H_2O(g)$$

Synthetic natural gas can also be made by heating crushed coal in the presence of steam with a potassium hydroxide catalyst to produce methane and carbon dioxide:

$$2C(s) + 2H_2O(g) \rightarrow CH_4(g) + CO_2(g)$$

### Exercises

**12** Describe a process that can be used to convert a more available fossil fuel to the less available hydrocarbon-based source of energy. State equations to show how methane and pentane are formed during these processes.

**13** State three reasons for not relying on carbon-containing fuels in the future.

**14** Synthesis gas can be considered as carbon monoxide and hydrogen mixed in equal amounts.

**(a)** Use section 13 in the IB data booklet to predict the enthalpy of combustion of a mixture which contains one mole each of the two components.

**(b)** Deduce how much energy could be available if the same carbon monoxide was first converted to methane, and the methane was used as a fuel.

**(c)** A student wishes to compare the energy available from equal volumes of methane and synthesis gas. Predict which sample will produce the most energy and explain your choice.

**15 (a)** Identify the major constituent of natural gas and write a balanced chemical equation for its combustion.

**(b)** Compare natural gas with other fossil fuels as a source of air pollution for a given amount of energy and account for any differences.

**(c)** Compare the relative supplies of natural gas and other fossil fuels.

**(d)** Suggest a process by which the natural supplies of the major component in natural gas can be increased and state the equations which describe the chemical reactions involved in the process.

## The past and future of fossil fuels

As civilization has advanced, the carbon content of fuel has decreased. Coal was the fossil fuel used first. It is the most abundant and easiest to obtain of all the fossil fuels and most similar in properties to charcoal, which was generally used as a fuel by primitive cultures. Coal has generally been replaced today by gasoline and natural gas as the fuel of choice as they have higher specific energies and energy densities and are easier to transport. The two fluids, gas and oil, are also cleaner burning and produce less carbon dioxide per unit energy.

The advantages and disadvantages of the three fossil fuels are summarized below.

The choice of fossil fuel used by different countries depends on historical, geological, and technological factors. Different societies have different priorities in their energy choices.

**All fossil fuels are non-renewable and produce the greenhouse gas carbon dioxide.**

|  | Coal | Crude oil | Natural gas |
|---|---|---|---|
| Advantages | • Cheap and plentiful throughout the world. <br> • Can be converted into synthetic liquid fuels and gases. <br> • Safer than nuclear power. <br> • Ash produced can be used in making roads. | • Easily transported in pipelines or by tankers. <br> • Convenient fuel for use in cars as volatile and burns easily. <br> • Sulfur impurities can be easily removed. | • Produces fewer pollutants per unit energy. <br> • Easily transported in pipelines and pressurized containers. <br> • Does not contribute to acid rain. <br> • Higher specific energy. |
| Disadvantages | • Produces many pollutants. <br> • Produces $CO_2$, $SO_2$, particulates (electrostatic preceptors can remove most of these). <br> • Difficult to transport. <br> • Waste can lead to visual and chemical pollution. <br> • Mining is dangerous. | • Limited lifespan and uneven world distribution. <br> • Contributes to acid rain and global warming. <br> • Transport can lead to pollution. <br> • Carbon monoxide is a local pollutant produced by incomplete combustion of gasoline in internal combustion engines. <br> • Photochemical smog produced as secondary pollutant due to reactions of the primary pollutants (nitrogen oxides and hydrocarbons) released from internal combustion engines. | • Limited supplies. <br> • Contributes to global warming. <br> • Risk of explosion due to leaks. |

**The carbon footprint is a measure of the total amount of carbon dioxide emissions that is directly and indirectly caused by an activity or a product.**

## Carbon footprint

One measure of the impact our activities have on the environment is given by our **carbon footprint**. The carbon footprint is a measurement of all the greenhouse gases we individually produce. It has units of mass of carbon dioxide equivalent and depends on the amount of greenhouse gases we produce in our day-to-day activities through the use of fossil fuels – such as heating, transport, and electricity.

### NATURE OF SCIENCE

'Carbon footprint' has become a widely used term in the public debate on our responsibilities in the fight against global climate change. There is, however, limited consensus on how to quantify a carbon footprint. Some issues are:

- should the carbon footprint include just carbon dioxide ($CO_2$) emissions or include other greenhouse gas emissions such as methane as well?
- should it be restricted to carbon-based gases or can it include substances that don't have carbon in their molecules such as dinitrogen monoxide, which is another greenhouse gas?
- should it include other gases such as carbon monoxide (CO), which is a toxic primary pollutant that can be oxidized to carbon dioxide in the atmosphere?

Words that scientists agree on which have an impact on the public must be clearly understood. Scientific discourse with the public needs to take account of this.

### Worked example

On a typical winter's day $1.33 \times 10^6$ kJ of energy is needed in a home.

The specific energy densities and approximate empirical formulae of wood and coal and the efficiency of the heating systems are tabulated below.

| Fuel | Formula of fuel | Specific energy / kJ g$^{-1}$ | Efficiency of heating / % |
|------|-----------------|-------------------------------|---------------------------|
| coal | CH | 31 | 65 |
| wood | $C_5H_9O_4$ | 22 | 70 |

**(a)** Calculate the percentage mass of carbon in the two fuels.

**(b)** Determine the carbon footprint from using the two forms of heating in terms of the mass of carbon dioxide produced by the two fuels.

**(c)** Suggest a reason why the carbon footprint calculation for wood does not give a full account of its impact on the environment.

### Solution

**(a)**

| Fuel | Formula of fuel | Percentage mass of C |
|------|-----------------|----------------------|
| coal | CH | $= \dfrac{12.01}{12.01 + 1.01} \times 100$ <br> $= 92.2\%$ |
| wood | $C_5H_9O_4$ | $= \dfrac{5 \times 12.01}{(5 \times 12.01) + (9 \times 1.01) + (4 \times 16.00)} \times 100$ <br> $= 45.1\%$ |

**(b)**

| Fuel | Calorific content of fuel needed / kJ | Mass of fuel needed / g | Mass of carbon burned / g | Mass of $CO_2$ produced / kg |
|---|---|---|---|---|
| coal | $= \dfrac{1.33 \times 10^6}{0.65}$ $= 2.05 \times 10^6$ | $= \dfrac{1.33 \times 10^6}{0.65 \times 31}$ $= 66\,000$ | $= 0.922 \times \dfrac{1.33 \times 10^6}{0.65 \times 31}$ $= 60\,800\ (= 60.8\ \text{kg})$ | $= 60.8 \times \dfrac{44.01}{12.01}$ $= 223\ (\text{kg})$ |
| wood | $= \dfrac{1.33 \times 10^6}{0.70}$ $= 1.9 \times 10^6$ | $= \dfrac{1.33 \times 10^6}{0.70 \times 22}$ $= 86\,400$ | $= 0.451 \times \dfrac{1.33 \times 10^6}{0.70 \times 22}$ $= 38\,900\ (= 38.9\ \text{kg})$ | $= 38.9 \times \dfrac{44.01}{12.01}$ $= 142\ (\text{kg})$ |

**(c)** Growing the trees to produce the wood absorbs carbon dioxide due to photosynthesis.

## Exercises

**16 (a)** State three reasons why most of the world's energy consumption is provided by fossil fuels.
  **(b)** Identify the energy source that currently provides the greatest proportion of the world's total energy demand and explain your answer.

**17** State three reasons why, worldwide, gas is preferred to oil as a fuel in power stations.

**18** Oxygenates are oxygen-containing organic compounds that are added to gasoline because they have high octane numbers. Methylbenzene is an aromatic molecule with a benzene ring which is added to gasoline because it too has a high octane number. The enthalpies of combustion of the two compounds are given in section 13 of the IB data booklet.

  **(a)** Calculate the mass of each fuel needed to produce 10 000 kJ of energy.
  **(b)** Determine the carbon footprint in terms of the mass of carbon dioxide added to the atmosphere in producing this amount of energy from the two fuels.
  **(c)** Suggest a second reason why oxygenates are added to gasoline.

# C.3 & C.7

# Nuclear fusion and fission

## C.3  Nuclear fusion and fission

# Understandings:

**Nuclear fusion**
- Light nuclei can undergo fusion reactions as this increases the binding energy per nucleon.
- Fusion reactions are a promising energy source as the fuel is inexpensive and abundant, and no radioactive waste is produced.
- Absorption spectra are used to analyse the composition of stars.

**Nuclear fission**
- Heavy nuclei can undergo fission reactions as this increases the binding energy per nucleon.
- $^{235}$U undergoes a fission chain reaction:

$$^{235}_{92}\text{U} + {}^{1}_{0}\text{n} \rightarrow {}^{236}_{92}\text{U} \rightarrow \text{X} + \text{Y} + \text{neutrons}$$

*Guidance*
*The workings of a nuclear power plant are not required.*

- The critical mass is the mass of fuel needed for the reaction to be self-sustaining.
- $^{239}$Pu, used as a fuel in 'breeder reactors', is produced from $^{238}$U by neutron capture.
- Radioactive waste may contain isotopes with long and short half-lives.

### Guidance
*Safety and risk issues include: health, problems associated with nuclear waste and core meltdown, and the possibility that nuclear fuels may be used in nuclear weapons.*

- Half-life is the time it takes for half the number of atoms to decay.

## Applications and skills:

### Nuclear fusion
- Construction of nuclear equations for fusion reactions.
- Explanation of fusion reactions in terms of binding energy per nucleon.
- Explanation of the atomic absorption spectra of hydrogen and helium, including the relationships between the lines and electron transitions.

### Nuclear fission
- Deduction of nuclear equations for fission reactions.

### Guidance
*Students are not expected to recall specific fission reactions.*

- Explanation of fission reactions in terms of binding energy per nucleon.
- Discussion of the storage and disposal of nuclear waste.
- Solution of radioactive decay problems involving integral numbers of half-lives.

### Guidance
*The equations, $N = N_0 e^{-\lambda t}$ and $T_{\frac{1}{2}} = \dfrac{ln2}{\lambda}$ are given in section 1 of the IB data booklet.*

## C.7   Nuclear fusion and nuclear fission

## Understandings:

### Nuclear fusion
- A binding energy curve is given in the IB data booklet in section 36. The mass defect ($\Delta m$) is the difference between the mass of the nucleus and the sum of the masses of its individual nucleons.
- The nuclear binding energy ($\Delta E$) is the energy required to separate a nucleus into protons and neutrons.
- The mass defect (4m) is the difference between the mass of the nucleus and the sum of the masses of its individual nucleons.

### Nuclear fission
- The energy produced in a fission reaction can be calculated from the mass difference between the products and reactants using Einstein's mass–energy equivalence relationship $E = mc^2$.
- The different isotopes of uranium in uranium hexafluoride can be separated, using diffusion or centrifugation, causing fuel enrichment.

### Guidance
*The workings of a nuclear power plant are not required.*

- The effusion rate of a gas is inversely proportional to the square root of the molar mass (Graham's law).

### Guidance
*Graham's law of effusion is given in the IB data booklet in section 1.*

- Radioactive decay is kinetically a first-order process with the half-life related to the decay constant by the equation $\lambda = \dfrac{ln2}{t_{\frac{1}{2}}}$.

### Guidance
*Decay relationships are given in the IB data booklet in section 1.*

- The dangers of nuclear energy are due to the ionizing nature of the radiation it produces, which leads to the production of oxygen free radicals such as superoxide ($O_2^-$), and hydroxyl (HO•). These free radicals can initiate chain reactions that can damage DNA and enzymes in living cells.

### Guidance
*Safety and risk issues include: health, problems associated with nuclear waste, and the possibility that nuclear fuels may be used in nuclear weapons.*

## Applications and skills:

### Nuclear fusion
- Calculation of the mass defect and binding energy of a nucleus.

### Guidance
*A binding energy curve is given in the IB data booklet in section 36.*

- Application of the Einstein mass–energy equivalence relationship, $E = mc^2$, to determine the energy produced in a fusion reaction.

**Nuclear fission**

- Application of the Einstein mass–energy equivalence relationship to determine the energy produced in a fission reaction.
- Discussion of the different properties of $UO_2$ and $UF_6$ in terms of bonding and structure.
- Solution of problems involving radioactive half-life.
- Explanation of the relationship between Graham's law of effusion and the kinetic theory.
- Solution of problems on the relative rate of effusion using Graham's law.

Many people fear radioactivity: they associate it with the fall-out of atomic bombs or disasters such as the explosion at the Fukushima nuclear power station. It is, however, a natural process, constantly occurring all around us. It is the result of naturally unstable atomic nuclei changing into more stable ones. Nuclear reactions can also occur artificially when atoms are bombarded with protons, neutrons, or other high-energy particles. Nuclear reactions should be contrasted to chemical reactions which only involve the outer electrons of an atom. Atoms change their identity in nuclear reactions but not in chemical reactions.

As discussed in Chapter 2, atoms with different numbers of neutrons are known as isotopes. The neutrons help provide a strong nuclear force, of short range, which binds the nucleus together despite the electrical repulsion between the positively charged protons. This force is about 100 times more powerful than the electric force at such short distances and is also 'blind' to electric charge and acts equally on protons and neutrons, binding them together. In relatively light nuclei, the strong force counteracts the electric force, provided the number of neutrons and protons is about equal. In heavy nuclei, however, there have to be more neutrons than protons to combat the repulsion between protons. The extra neutrons are there because the strong force acts mainly between neighbouring protons. The electric force, on the other hand, can act over longer distances. A proton at one side of the nucleus will feel some electric repulsion from a proton at the other side, but not a strong force attraction from protons or neutrons. This means that the repulsive electric force begins to overcome the attraction of the strong force. The presence of extra neutrons dilutes the electric force and prevents the nucleus from blowing apart. The balance between the forces determines whether a particular nucleus will be stable or unstable.

When the stable nuclei of the elements are plotted on the graph of number of protons against number of neutrons they all fall in an area enclosed by two curved lines known as the **band of stability** (Figure 14.2).

Nuclear reactions involve the protons and neutrons in the nucleus, and the atoms may be converted to other elements. In chemical reactions only valence electrons are involved and atoms do not change their identity.

**Figure 14.2** The stable nuclei of the elements all fall in an area known as the band of stability. A nucleus emits alpha radiation if it has too few neutrons (too many protons), and beta particles if it has too many neutrons.

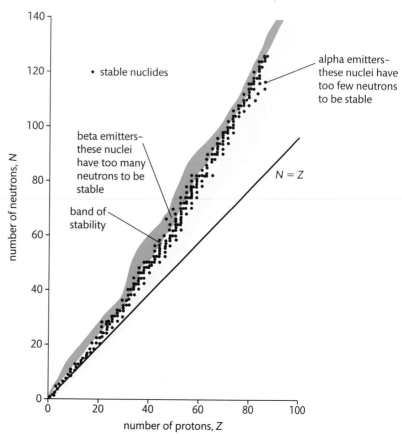

When a nucleus contains either too many or too few neutrons, it is radioactive and changes to a more stable nucleus by giving out radiation. This may be of several different forms which differ in ionization and penetration abilities.

**Alpha particles**, emitted by nuclei with too many protons to be stable, are composed of two protons and two neutrons.

**Beta particles**, emitted by nuclei with too many neutrons, are electrons which have been ejected from the nucleus owing to neutron decay.

**Gamma rays** are a form of electromagnetic radiation which are given out as a result of the **nucleons** reorganizing themselves.

A nucleon is a proton or a neutron.

## Some particles in the particles zoo

Nuclear reactions can involve a wide range of particles and types of radiation. The positron, for example, is the antiparticle of the electron. It has the same mass as an electron but the opposite charge. When a positron collides with an electron both particles are destroyed and their mass converted to the equivalent amount of energy.

A small selection of these subatomic particles is tabulated below.

| Particle/ radiation | Relative charge | Relative mass | Symbol | Description |
|---|---|---|---|---|
| proton | +1 | 1 | $_1^1H$ | hydrogen nucleus |
| alpha | +2 | 4 | $_2^4He$ | helium nucleus |
| beta | −1 | 0 | $_{-1}^0e$ | electron |
| positron | +1 | 0 | $_{+1}^0e$ | antiparticle of the electron |
| gamma (photon) | 0 | 0 | $\gamma$ | electromagnetic wave |

Note the charge does not need to be given as a (right) superscript as it is implied in the left subscript. The alpha particle has a charge of +2 as the atomic number of helium is +2. The beta particle has a charge of −1 as it has subscript of −1.

## The mass defect is the difference between the mass of the nucleus and the sum of the masses of its individual nucleons

The absolute mass of the elementary particles is given in section 4 of the IB data booklet and reproduced below.

| Elementary particle | Mass / amu | Mass / kg |
|---|---|---|
| proton | 1.008 665 | $1.672622 \times 10^{-27}$ |
| neutron | 1.007 265 | $1.674927 \times 10^{-27}$ |
| electron | 0.000 549 | $9.109383 \times 10^{-31}$ |

One atom of carbon-12 has a mass of 12 amu.

1 amu is defined as 1/12 of the mass of an atom of the isotope $_6^{12}C$.

1 amu = $1.66 \times 10^{-27}$ kg

A helium atom is made from two protons, two neutrons and two electrons. Adding the masses of its constituent particles we have:

predicted mass of helium atom = 2 (1.008665 + 1.007265 + 0.000549 ) amu
$$= 4.032958 \text{ amu}$$

This value should be contrasted with the actual mass of a helium atom, which is 4.002603 amu. The total mass of the atom is less than the sum of the masses of the separate elementary particles. This mass difference is called the **mass defect**.

mass defect for helium = 4.032958 − 4.002603 = 0.030355 amu

The mass of the electrons was included for convenience; the mass defect is due to the protons and neutrons binding together in the nucleus. The mass defect ($\Delta m$) is the difference between the mass of the nucleus and the sum of the masses of its individual nucleons.

To understand the reason for this mass defect we need to bring in one of the most significant results from Einstein's Special Theory of Relativity. Einstein showed that mass and energy are equivalent and related by the famous equation $E = mc^2$. In forming a nucleus, mass appears to have been lost because it has been converted to energy which is given out as the protons and neutrons fuse together. This energy is called the **binding energy**.

The mass defect ($\Delta m$) is the difference between the mass of the nucleus and the sum of the masses of its individual nucleons.

The binding energy is the energy released when a nucleus is made from protons and neutrons or the energy required to separate a nucleus into separate nucleons.

## Worked example

Calculate the binding energy of the helium nucleus in kJ mol$^{-1}$.

### Solution

When calculating the binding energy we need to use consistent units of mass and energy.

The conversion factor is given in section 2 of the IB data booklet.

$1 \text{ amu} = 1.66 \times 10^{-27} \text{ kg}$

$\Delta m = 0.030355 \times 1.66 \times 10^{-27} \text{ kg}$

$\Delta E = \Delta mc^2$

$\Delta E = 0.030355 \times 1.66 \times 10^{-27} \times (3.0 \times 10^8)^2 \text{ J}$

$\quad = 4.535 \times 10^{-12} \text{ J}$

$\quad = 2.73 \times 10^9 \text{ kJ mol}^{-1}$

The nuclear binding energy is a quantitative measure of nuclear stability.

## Exercises

**19** **(a)** Calculate the binding energy and mass defect for deuterium ($^2_1$H) whose measured mass is 2.01355 amu.
   **(b)** Calculate the binding energy per nucleon for $^4_2$He and $^2_1$H.
   **(c)** Calculate the energy change for the proposed nuclear reaction: $2\,^2_1$H → $^4_2$He.
   **(d)** Identify the nuclide which is more stable.

Atomic energies can also be given in MeV, which is often more convenient than the SI unit of the joule. The electron volt is the energy given to an electron when it is accelerated through a potential difference of 1 V. One mole of electrons, with an energy of 1 eV of energy have $6.02 \times 10^{23} \times 1.6 \times 10^{-19} \text{ J} = 96 \text{ kJ mol}^{-1}$ of energy. This is the order of magnitude of enthalpy changes in chemical reactions.

$$\text{potential difference} = \frac{\text{energy gained}}{\text{charge}}$$

$$\text{energy gained} = \text{potential difference} \times \text{charge}$$

$1\ \text{eV} = 1\ \text{V} \times 1.60 \times 10^{-19}\ \text{C} = 1.60 \times 10^{-19}\ \text{J}$

The binding energy of an individual atom of helium, for example, is

$\dfrac{4.538 \times 10^{-12}}{1.60 \times 10^{-19} \times 4} = 7.09$ eV and the binding energy of a deuterium is 1.1 eV.

## Binding energy graphs can be used to understand nuclear stability

$^{4}_{2}\text{He}$ is more stable than $^{2}_{1}\text{H}$ because it has a higher binding energy per nucleon. A graph of binding energy per nucleon versus mass number indicates the relative stability of the atomic nuclei.

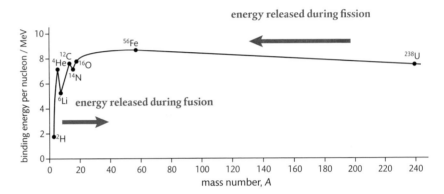

**Figure 14.3** Graph of atomic nuclei binding energies; y axis plotted against mass number, x axis. Nuclear stability is due to the strong nuclear force overcoming the electromagnetic repulsion between the protons. Isotopes on the left of this graph undergo nuclear fusion while isotopes on the right undergo nuclear fission.

The curve in the binding energy graph indicates that the binding energy per nucleon tends to increase sharply to a peak at $^{56}_{26}\text{Fe}$, which corresponds to the most stable isotope, and then gradually diminishes. As binding energy is the energy released when the nuclei are formed it is important to understand that $^{56}_{26}\text{Fe}$ is the most stable nuclei because it has the *least* energy.

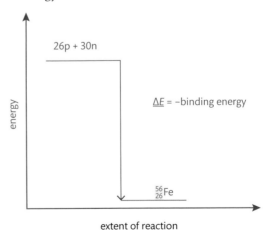

**Figure 14.4** The binding energy is the energy released when the nucleus is formed from its constituent protons and neutrons. $^{56}_{26}\text{Fe}$ is the most stable nucleus as it has the lowest energy.

Energy will be given out in any process that leads to an increase in the binding energy per nucleon.

**Nuclear fusion**, which is the joining of very light nuclei, can occur for isotopes such as deuterium, which are found to the left of the $^{56}_{26}\text{Fe}$ maximum on the graph.

**Nuclear fission**, which is the splitting of a heavy nucleus, can occur for isotopes to the right of the $^{56}_{26}\text{Fe}$ maximum, such as $^{238}_{92}\text{U}$.

## Light nuclei can undergo fusion reactions as this increases the binding energy per nucleon

Nuclear fusion brings together nuclei of small or lighter elements to form heavier elements, with the release of energy. We have already considered the fusion of $^{2}_{1}\text{H}$ nuclei to form $^{4}_{2}\text{He}$:

$$2\,^{2}_{1}\text{H} \rightarrow\,^{4}_{2}\text{He}$$

Note that as the number of protons has not changed, the charge, as represented by the subscripts in the formula of the different isotopes, is balanced $(2 \times 1 = 2)$. Similarly the superscripts, which refer to the number of protons and neutrons are also balanced $(2 \times 2 = 4)$.

### Worked example

The energy of the Sun is produced from fusion reactions. The primary reaction that fuels the fires of the Sun is believed to be the fusion of four hydrogen atoms to yield one helium nucleus.

(a) Complete the reaction below by identifying $a$, $p$, and $r$.

$$4^{1}_{1}\text{H} \rightarrow\,^{4}_{2}\text{He} + a^{r}_{p}\text{X}$$

(b) Explain why energy is given out in the reaction.

**Solution**

(a) Equating the charges on both sides gives $4 = 2 + ap$

Equating the mass on both sides gives $4 = 4 + ar$

This suggests $r = 0$, $p = +1$, $a = 2$: two positrons are produced.

$$4^{1}_{1}\text{H} \rightarrow\,^{4}_{2}\text{He} + 2^{0}_{1}\text{e}$$

(b) Energy is given out in the fusion reaction because the total mass of the products is slightly less than the total mass of the reactants. Mass is converted to the equivalent amount of energy.

## The elements in the stars can be identified by their absorption spectra

All objects that have a temperature above 0 K give out a range of electromagnetic radiation of different wavelengths. The amount and peak wavelength of the radiation depends on the temperature of the body. The higher the temperature, the more radiation is emitted and the shorter the wavelength of the bulk of the radiation. At the temperatures we experience on Earth most objects radiate in the infrared part of the electromagnetic spectrum, but the Sun has a sufficiently high temperature (the surface temperature is 5700 K) to give out all the colours of the spectrum. It is a source of white light with a maximum intensity occurring in the yellow region of the spectrum.

This is not the complete story, however, as the Sun is surrounded by an 'atmosphere' which is at a lower temperature than the Sun itself. The gases in this region can absorb some wavelengths of the Sun's emitted radiation, producing dark absorption lines in

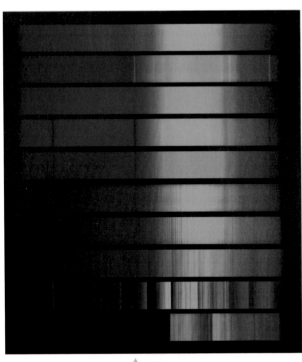

the spectrum. These dark bands can be used to identify elements present in the gases surrounding the Sun. The Sun's spectrum shows dark lines that represent absorbed radiation from the elements hydrogen and helium.

## The absorption lines correspond to the electrons being excited from lower to higher energy levels

Hydrogen and helium atoms and helium ions are present in the outer layers of the sun. At very high temperatures the atoms are stripped of their electrons and the intensely hot mixture of positive nuclei and free electrons is called **plasma**. Hydrogen atoms and helium ions ($He^+$ ions) are both one-electron systems and have similar patterns in their energy levels. As we saw in Chapter 2, the energy levels converge with increasing energy. The absorption lines in the visible region of the spectrum of hydrogen are due to the electron being excited from the $n = 2$ energy level.

The energy levels of the hydrogen atom and helium ion ($He^+$ ion) are compared below.

Diagram of the spectra of stars, showing a set of dark absorption lines which indicate the presence of certain elements, such as hydrogen and helium, in the outer atmosphere of the star. The stars from top to bottom are : Lambda Cephei, P Cygni, Beta Orionis, Alpha Canis Majoris , Alpha Canis Minoris, Alpha Aurigae, Alpha Hydrae , Alpha Orionis, Omicron Ceti, and Y Canum Venaticorum.

| Energy level | Energy H atom / kJ mol⁻¹ | Energy He⁺ ion / kJ mol⁻¹ |
|:---:|:---:|:---:|
| 1 | −1312.0 | −5250 |
| 2 | −327.5 | −1310.0 |
| 3 | −145.4 | −581.8 |
| 4 | −81.9 | −327.5 |
| 5 | −52.0 | −209.6 |
| ∞ | 0 | 0 |

Note that all the energy levels have negative values as the fully ionized state with $n = \infty$ corresponds to zero energy.

The energy levels for helium have lower energy than the corresponding states for hydrogen due to increased nuclear charge which attracts the electron more closely to the nucleus.

**Plasma is a high-energy state composed of isolated atoms, ions, and electrons.**

## CHALLENGE YOURSELF

**6** Compare the energy levels of the hydrogen atom and the helium ion. Explain the values of the corresponding energy levels.

### Worked example

**(a)** Determine the wavelength absorbed when an electron in a helium ion is excited from the $n = 3$ to the $n = 4$ level.

**(b)** Identify the region of the spectrum in which this transition occurs.

### Solution

**(a)** $\Delta E = -327.5 - -581.8$ kJ mol⁻¹ = +254.3 kJ mol⁻¹

[convert kJ per mol to J per ion]

$$\frac{254.3 \times 10^3}{6.02 \times 10^{23}} = 4.22 \times 10^{-19} \text{ J}$$

Use the equation $E = h\nu$

$$\nu = \frac{4.22 \times 10^{-19}}{6.63 \times 10^{-34}}$$
$$= 6.37 \times 10^{14} \text{ s}^{-1}$$

Use the equation $c = \nu\lambda$

$$\lambda = \frac{3.0 \times 10^{8}}{6.37 \times 10^{14}}$$
$$= 4.70 \times 10^{-7} \text{ m}$$

**(b)** The electromagnetic spectrum is shown in section 3 of the IB data booklet. This line occurs in the visible region of the spectrum.

The energy levels of the helium atom are more complicated. Assuming one electron remains in the 1s orbital, the second electron can have either paired or unpaired spin and the energy levels split into sub-levels, so, for example, there are two energy states with the $1s^{1}2s^{1}$ configuration.

There are selection rules which limit the range of possible transitions; the spin of the electron does not change during a transition so parallel states can only be excited to parallel states and s electrons can only be excited to p levels, for example.

| 'Excited' electron | Relative spins | Energy / kJ mol$^{-1}$ | Relative spin | Energy / kJ mol$^{-1}$ |
|---|---|---|---|---|
| 1s | | | opposite | −2371 |
| 2s | parallel | −460 | opposite | −383 |
| 2p | parallel | −349 | opposite | −325 |
| 3s | parallel | −180 | opposite | −161 |
| 3p | parallel | −152 | opposite | |
| 3d | parallel | −146 | opposite | −146 |
| 4p | | | opposite | −82 |
| ∞ | | 0 | | 0 |

### Worked example

Determine the energy and wavelength produced by the transition from 2p to 3d with the electrons having opposite spins and deduce whether the electron transition occurs in the visible region.

**Solution**

$$\Delta E = h\nu = \frac{hc}{\lambda}$$

To fall in the visible region

For red light ($\lambda = 700 \times 10^{9}$m)

$$\Delta E_{min} = h\nu_{min} = \frac{hc}{\lambda_{max}}$$
$$= \frac{6.63 \times 10^{-34} \text{ J s} \times 3.00 \times 10^{8} \text{ m s}^{-1}}{700 \times 10^{-9} \text{ m}}$$
$$= 2.84 \times 10^{-19} \text{ J}$$
$$= 171 \text{ kJ mol}^{-1}$$

For blue light ($\lambda = 400 \times 10^9$ m)

$$\Delta E_{max} = h\nu_{max} = \frac{hc}{\lambda_{min}}$$

$$= \frac{6.63 \times 10^{-34} \text{ J s} \times 3.00 \times 10^8 \text{ m s}^{-1}}{400 \times 10^{-9} \text{ m}}$$

$$= 4.97 \times 10^{-19} \text{ J}$$

$$= 299 \text{ kJ mol}^{-1}$$

For the 2p to 3d transition:

$$\Delta E = -146 - -325 = 179 \text{ kJ mol}^{-1}$$

This line falls in the visible region of the spectrum.

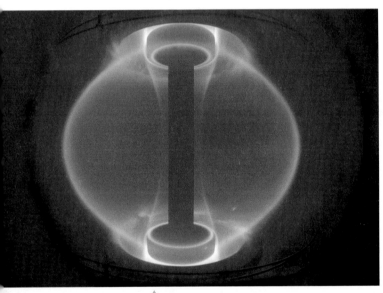

Spherical ball of plasma (pink) inside the START device at Culham, England. The START (Small Tight Aspect Ratio Tokamak) device changes the shape of the plasma from a torus (ring) to a sphere.

## Nuclear fusion as a possible source of energy

The fusion of 1 g of hydrogen will release as much energy as the combustion of $10^3$ kg of coal but unfortunately there are practical difficulties in carrying out such fusion reactions on Earth. Very high temperatures are needed for the protons to have sufficient kinetic energy to overcome the mutual electrostatic repulsion and fuse together. The energy needed to initiate the uncontrolled fusion reaction in a hydrogen bomb, for example, is produced by the fission of U-235 or Pu-239. Controlled fusion reactions are more difficult as there are some technical problems:

- the production of plasma state which must be held together long enough to fuse the nuclei
- enough energy must be produced to make the process profitable.

The hot plasma can be confined by **magnetic confinement**. Atoms of the appropriate hydrogen isotope are injected into a donut-shaped container called a **tokamak** where they are subjected to strong magnetic and electric fields. The electric field accelerates the positive ions and so increases the kinetic energy of the nuclei until the nuclei fuse. The hot matter is prevented from touching the walls of the container by the magnetic field. A metal such as sodium or lithium is then used to absorb and transfer the heat produced to a generator. The tokamak at Princeton University has achieved high enough temperatures for fusion to occur but the energy output has not yet equalled the energy input. A super-cooled magnet is used to generate the magnetic field but there are technical difficulties associated with maintaining such low temperatures near the high temperatures needed to produce the plasma state.

As no single nation can solve the world's energy problems on their own, scientists from all over the world work together on the ITER project. ITER is an acronym of International Thermonuclear Experimental Reactor and Latin for 'the way' or 'the road'. This aims to harness the energy produced by the fusion of atoms to help meet mankind's energy needs.

In the **inertial confinement** method, tiny glass spheres are filled with deuterium or a deuterium/tritium mixture at a pressure of several hundred atmospheres. The fuel pellets are then subjected to UV radiation generated by high-energy lasers. Under this photon bombardment the atoms are squeezed together to cause them to fuse. Molten lithium is then used to absorb the energy from fusion and transfer it to a steam generator to produce electricity. This method has not yet been found to be successful.

## The advantages of nuclear fusion

There are advantages to nuclear fusion.

- The fuel is abundant: there are about $10^{23}$ deuterium atoms in one litre of sea water.
- Fusion is considered to be less dangerous than fission with regard to radioactive materials: most radioactive isotopes produced by fusion have short half-lives and are therefore only a threat for a short time
- Massive transport of radioactive materials is not required and no waste has to be stored.

In 1989 two respected chemists, Stanley Pons and Martin Fleishmann, claimed to have achieved a fusion reaction during a simple electrolysis experiment. The claims were dismissed by other scientific groups as the results of the experiment were not reproducible. Is it always possible to obtain replicable results in the natural sciences? Are reproducible results possible in other areas of knowledge?

**TOK**

### Exercises

**20** The hydrogen bomb is an example of uncontrolled nuclear fusion which involves two isotopes of hydrogen. Deduce the missing coefficients and species in the following equations.

    **(a)** $^2_1H + ^3_1H \rightarrow ^4_2He + \ldots$

    **(b)** $^4_2He + ^{14}_7N \rightarrow ^1_1H + \ldots$

**21** Diagram 1 shows some of the energy levels of the hydrogen atom. Diagram 2 is a representation of part of the absorption spectrum of atomic hydrogen, with the black lines showing the absorption lines.

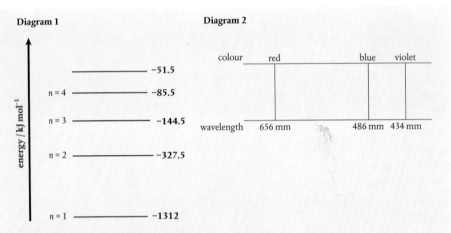

Diagram 1

Diagram 2

(a) Calculate the energy change that corresponds to each of the three lines.

(b) Identify the three transitions that give rise to these transitions.

(c) Explain why the lines in the absorption bands of atomic hydrogen, shown in diagram 2, converge as the wavelength of the lines decreases.

22 When 1.0 g of hydrogen undergoes fusion $6.72 \times 10^{-3}$ g of matter is converted into energy. Burning coal releases 30 kJ g$^{-1}$.

(a) Determine the specific energy of hydrogen in nuclear fusion.

(b) Compare the two methods of energy production and check the claim that the fusion of 1 g of hydrogen releases as much energy as the combustion of $20 \times 10^3$ kg of coal.

23 The first fusion reactors on the Earth are likely to use a reaction between deuterium ($^2$H) and tritium ($^3$H) to produce energy, as it produces large amounts of energy at relatively low temperatures.

$$^2_1H + {}^3_1H \rightarrow {}^4_2He + {}^1_0n$$

Calculate the energy produced, given the following data:

|  | Mass/amu |
|---|---|
| $^1n$ | 1.008 665 |
| $^2_1H$ | 2.014 102 u |
| $^3_1H$ | 3.016 049 u |
| $^4_2He$ | 4.002 602 |

# Heavy nuclei can undergo fission reactions as this increases the binding energy per nucleon

In the same way that small atoms would be expected to form larger nuclei by fusion due to their relatively low binding energy per nucleon, we expect large nuclei to break down into smaller nuclei. Nuclear fission can occur naturally, or it can be induced by bombardment with a particle such as a neutron. **Artificially induced fission** is the operating basis behind nuclear reactions, which were first observed in 1938 when two German scientists, Otto Hahn and Fritz Strassmann, discovered barium among the products formed when uranium was bombarded with neutrons. The results were explained by Lise Meitner and Otto Frisch based on Bohr's 'droplet' model of the nucleus, in which neutrons and protons are compared to the molecules in a drop of liquid. In the same way that the spherical shape of a drop distorts into a dumbbell shape and then splits into fragments when water is added, a nucleus will split when the number of neutrons is increased.

| Target nucleus shown as the large circle absorbs a neutron (small circle). | Nucleus has too many neutrons and excess vibrational energy. | Vibrations produce dumb bell shape. | Repulsive forces between protons stretch the nucleus. | Fission occurs. Fragments separate and give out extra neutrons. |
|---|---|---|---|---|

**Figure 14.5** The water droplet model of nuclear fission.

The additional neutron causes the uranium nuclei to divide like a biological cell undergoing **fission**, with the production of energy. A wide variety of possible products can be formed when the nucleus of an atom of $^{235}_{92}U$ is struck with a neutron. For example:

$$^{235}_{92}U + ^{1}_{0}n \rightarrow ^{141}_{56}Ba + ^{92}_{36}Kr + 3\,^{1}_{0}n$$

A large amount of energy is produced as the total mass of the products is slightly less than the total mass of the reactants. The mass is converted into an equivalent amount of energy, which is given out. The neutrons released in the fission of one nucleus can trigger the fission of other uranium atoms in a **chain reaction**.

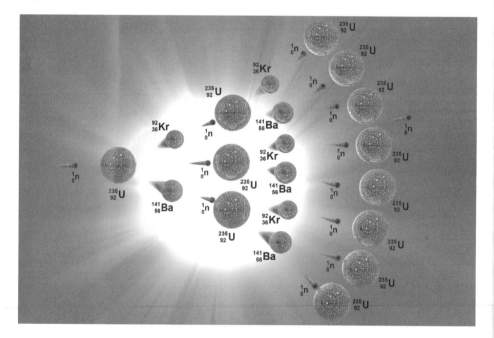

In a nuclear chain reaction, a neutron strikes a $^{235}_{92}U$ atom, splitting it into atoms of krypton and barium and releasing energy along with three neutrons, which go on to strike three more $^{235}_{92}U$ atoms. Uncontrolled chain reactions can be used in weapons. Chain reactions can be controlled using neutron-absorbing materials such as boron.

Nuclear reactors are designed to ensure that, on average, only one neutron from each reaction goes on to initiate a further reaction. If more reactions took place the chain reaction could run out of control. With less than one neutron available the number of reactions would decrease and the fission process would soon stop.

The chance that a given neutron goes on to cause a fission reaction depends on:

• the number of potential nuclei in the neutron's path
• the speed of the neutrons.

The neutrons produced by the fission process are generally moving too quickly to initiate further reactions and need to be slowed down by **moderators** in the reactor. The moderators slow down the neutrons sufficiently so that they are absorbed more easily by the nuclei. **Control rods** absorb neutrons. They are introduced or removed from the reactor to control the chain reaction. They are made of materials which can absorb neutrons, such as graphite and cadmium.

### The critical mass is the minimum mass of fissionable material needed to sustain a chain reaction

For a fissile material to sustain a chain reaction there must be enough fissionable material to allow the neutron released in one fission process to have a good chance of finding another fissile nuclei before escaping from the bulk material. The **critical mass** is the minimum mass of a fissionable material needed to sustain a chain reaction. The exact value of the critical mass depends on the exact nature of the fuel being used and the shape of the assembly. Naturally occurring uranium contains less than 1% of $^{235}_{92}U$ so enriched uranium fuel is needed to sustain the reaction. **Enrichment** is the process by which the percentage composition of $^{235}_{92}U$ is increased to make nuclear fission more likely.

The critical mass is the minimum mass of a fissionable material needed to sustain a chain reaction.

$^{235}_{92}U$ accounts for about 0.72% of all naturally occurring uranium.

View of the top of the reactor at a nuclear power station in Kent, England, showing a technician standing on top of the reactor charge transfer plate into which the uranium fuel rods fit.

### Exercises

**24** Incomplete equations for nuclear reactions of a number of different isotopes of uranium are given below.

| I | $^{233}_{92}U \rightarrow {}^4_2He + W$ |
|---|---|
| II | $^{235}_{92}U + {}^1_0n \rightarrow {}^{141}_{56}Ba + {}^{92}_{36}Kr + X$ |
| III | $^{239}_{92}U \rightarrow Y + {}^0_{-1}e$ |
| IV | $^{233}_{92}U + {}^1_0n \rightarrow {}^{140}_{58}Ce + Z + 2\,{}^1n$ |

**(a)** Identify the missing species W, X, Y, and Z.
**(b)** State which of the nuclear reactions above is/are used to produce electricity in nuclear power plants. Explain your choice.
**(c)** Explain the origin of the energy produced in the reaction identified in part (b).

**25** Explain why natural uranium cannot be used directly as a nuclear fuel.

## Fuel enrichment involves the separation of different isotopes of uranium

Isotopes have the same chemical properties but have different physical properties. Heavier atoms will move on average more slowly than lighter atoms. This is the principle behind one method of fuel enrichment. Gaseous uranium hexafluoride ($UF_6$) is forced through a semipermeable membrane. Molecules containing the different isotopes of uranium will, on average, move at different average speeds. This produces a slight separation between the molecules containing $^{235}_{92}U$ and $^{238}_{92}U$. If the process is repeated many times better separations can be achieved.

(a)

(b)

This side has been enriched in the molecules with a larger mass

This side has been enriched with the molecules of smaller mass

**Figure 14.6** (a) A mixture of the two gases is allowed to effuse into another container. (b) The blue molecules have a smaller mass and so move with a higher average speeds so a partial separation occurs. The relative concentration of the lighter blue molecules is higher on the right and the concentration of the red molecules is higher on the left.

## $UF_6$ is the only compound of uranium sufficiently volatile to be used in the gaseous diffusion process

The oxidizing nature of fluorine allows the uranium to form the +6 oxidation state. $UF_6$ has a molecular covalent structure with the U atom surrounded by an octahedron of six fluorine atoms. The covalent bonds in the molecule are polar due to the different electronegativities of the uranium and fluorine but the molecule is non-polar as the bond polarities cancel each other out due to symmetry. Although $UF_6$ is a solid at room temperature and atmospheric pressure, it sublimes if heated to 56.5 °C. The intermolecular bonds between the molecules are relatively weak for a molecule with so many electrons. The fluorine atoms have a partial negative charge, which repels other F atoms from neighbouring molecules.

**Figure 14.7** The structure of $UF_6$.

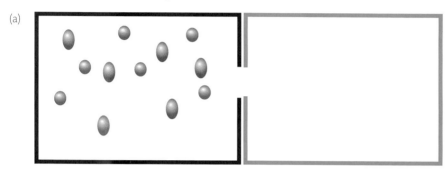

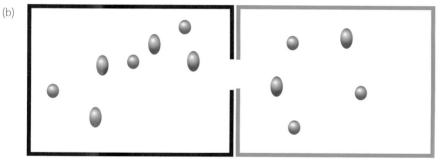

The F atoms in neighbouring molecules repel each other

801

### CHALLENGE YOURSELF

7 Explain why it is fortunate for the enrichment process that fluorine consists of only a single isotope.

The properties of uranium hexafluoride should be contrasted with those of uranium dioxide, which is an ionic solid with a melting point of 2865 °C. The difference can be explained by the higher oxidation state of uranium in the hexafluoride. The hypothetical $U^{6+}$ ion doesn't exist in compounds because it would have such a high charge density that the outer electrons of the $F^-$ ion would be distorted to the extent that it would not remain an isolated ion. The negative ion would be so polarized that two of the electrons from the 'fluoride ion' would be shared with the 'positive ion'.

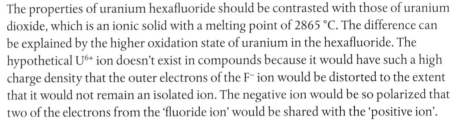

**Figure 14.8** The high charge density of the hypothetical $U^{6+}$ ion is too high for it to exist. Instead the +6 state forms covalent bonds. The electrons on the fluorine are pulled toward the uranium ion.

### All molecules have same average kinetic energy at the same temperature so heavier molecules move more slowly

We saw in Chapter 1 that the absolute temperature of gas is a measure of its average kinetic energy.

Consider a mixture of two gases, A and B, at the same temperature.

$$KE_A^{ave} = KE_B^{ave}$$

$$\tfrac{1}{2}m_A v_A^{ave\,2} = \tfrac{1}{2}m_B v_B^{ave\,2}$$

$$\frac{m_A}{m_B} = \frac{v_B^{ave\,2}}{v_A^{ave\,2}}$$

$$\sqrt{\frac{m_A}{m_B}} = \frac{v_B^{ave}}{v_A^{ave}}$$

As the rate of effusion is proportional to the average speed we arrive at a result known as **Graham's law**.

As the time it takes for the two gases to effuse is inversely proportional to the average speeds we also have:

$$\frac{v_B^{ave}}{v_A^{ave}} = \frac{t_A}{t_B} = \sqrt{\frac{m_A}{m_B}}$$

Graham's law states that the rate of effusion of a gas is inversely proportional to the square root of the molecular or molar masses.

### Worked example

Determine the relative times for the same amount of the hexafluorides of the two isotopes of uranium to diffuse.

#### Solution

mass of $^{235}UF_6 = 235 + (6 \times 19) = 349$

mass of $^{238}UF_6 = 238 + (6 \times 19) = 352$

$$\frac{t_{238}}{t_{235}} = \sqrt{\frac{m_A}{m_B}} = 1.004$$

Graham's law explains the difficulty of the isotope separation process. The ratio of the time it takes for the same amount of $^{235}UF_6$ and $^{238}UF_6$ to diffuse is only 1.004. As very little separation occurs in any one stage the process needs to be repeated up to 4000 times to achieve the necessary enrichment.

The dioxide is often used as a fuel for nuclear reactors as it has a higher melting point than the element and as it is already oxidized does not burn at the high temperatures of the reactor.

## The different isotopes of uranium in uranium hexafluoride can be separated, using centrifugation

The other method of fuel enrichment uses centrifugation as the method of the separation. The UF$_6$ containing a mixture of both isotopes is placed into a centrifuge and spun at a very high speeds. Molecules with the smaller mass are easier to accelerate and so follow a sharper circular path with a smaller radius. The heavier $^{238}$UF$_6$ molecules tend to move out toward the walls of the centrifuge and the lighter $^{235}$UF$_6$ molecules stay more in the centre where they can be pumped out. The same process is repeated many times to produce a gas mixture that is sufficiently enriched in $^{235}$U. At a uranium enrichment plant, thousands of centrifuges are linked together in long cascades.

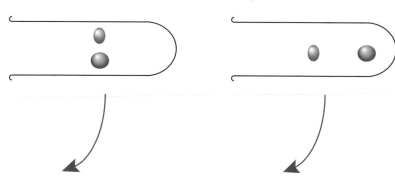

As the test tube rotates the molecule with the heavier mass moves to the bottom. A mixture richer in the light isotope can then be removed from the middle of the tube and centrifuged repeatedly for better separation.

**Figure 14.9** The isotopes are separated as the mixture is spun in a centrifuge at high speeds.

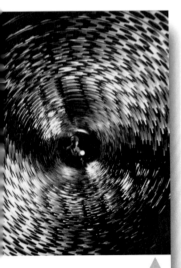

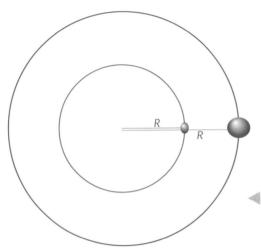

◀ **Figure 14.10** The blue particle with a small mass is more readily rotated around a sharper circular path with a smaller radius.

To produce a fuel richer in U-235, the mined uranium is converted into uranium hexafluoride gas. This is spun in a centrifuge. The molecules containing heavier U-238 tend to collect at the outside and are led off. The gas richer in U-235 is passed to further stages of purification before conversion into usable fuel.

### NATURE OF SCIENCE

There is no such thing as a centrifugal force. Both molecules experience a centripetal force as they move in a circle towards the centre of the circle. The confusion arises as the rotating particles behave as if they are being pushed outwards, but the wide use of the term in everyday language such as the piece of lab equipment called a 'centrifuge' and in science fiction has led to much confusion. In science we often explain the familiar in terms of the unfamiliar. Why are tables hard? Because the chemical bonds between the atoms are strong. What is the natural state of motion? To continue with the same speed in a straight line, although we rarely see this in our experience because of the invisible force friction.

Science is not just refined common sense.

The centrifuges must spin very quickly – in the range of 100 000 revolutions per minute. The technology to achieve this is out of the reach of most countries, although recent development of inexpensive, high-precision computer-controlled machining equipment has made things somewhat easier.

Only a very small number of countries have the necessary enrichment technology to develop nuclear weapons. The International Atomic Energy Authority aims to limit the spread of this technology. There are disputes about whether some countries are developing nuclear energy as an energy source or for use in weapons.

### Exercises

**26 (a)** Compare the bonding and structure in $UF_6$ and $UO_2$ and explain any differences.
  **(b)** Comment on the relative radioactivity of two samples of the compounds which have not been enriched.
  **(c)** The fuel typically used in fission reactors is based on the metal oxide. Suggest why the oxide is used rather than the pure metal.

**27** The boiling points of some covalent substances are tabulated below.

| Substance | Boiling point / °C |
| --- | --- |
| $UF_6$ | 56.6 |
| $Br_2$ | 58.8 |
| $I_2$ | 184 |
| $S_8$ | 444.6 |

  **(a)** Discuss the trend in boiling points of the elements.
  **(b)** Comment on the boiling point of $UF_6$ with reference to your answer in part (a).
  **(c)** Discuss why $UF_6$ is a suitable compound to use in the enrichment of uranium.
  **(d)** Explain why the nuclear enrichment process involve many separation stages.

**28 (a)** Explain the advantage of enriching the uranium used in a nuclear reactor.
  **(b)** Suggest a possible international risk of a fuel-enrichment programme.

The intermolecular forces in $UF_6$ are anomalous and do not follow the normal trends. It is unusual in that it has a relatively low boiling point for such a large molecule. This can be explained by the polar nature of the bonds, as outlined above. When results do not fit a general pattern we have first to check that the discrepancy is not due to experimental error. If the discrepancy is real we are challenged into modifying our theories. There are more factors to consider than just the number of electrons in determining the interaction between non-polar molecules. Ideally our theories should be able to make accurate predictions. You can now *explain* the low boiling point but would you have been able to *predict* it?

## Uncontrolled nuclear reactions are used in nuclear weapons

When the number of neutrons is not controlled, a fission reaction can release an enormous amount of energy in a very short time. This happened when the fission bombs were dropped on Hiroshima and Nagasaki in Japan during World War II. Weapons have been designed using both $^{235}_{92}U$ and $^{239}_{94}Pu$, which is a by-product of the peaceful use of $^{235}_{92}U$ for energy.

Einstein's equation $E = mc^2$ is the equation of life, as it explains how the Sun produces the energy that supports life on Earth. But it is an also an equation of death, as is demonstrated by the terrible destruction of Hiroshima and Nagasaki. Laura Fermi (wife of Enrico who won the Nobel Prize in 1938 for his work on neutron bombardment) said 'To moral questions there are no universal answers. Some men said the atom bomb should not have been built but Enrico did not think this would be a solution. It is no good trying to stop knowledge from going forward. Whatever Nature has in store for mankind, unpleasant as it may be, men must accept, as ignorance is never better then knowledge.' Should scientists be held morally responsible for the applications of their discoveries? Is there any area of scientific knowledge the pursuit of which is morally unacceptable?

Is knowledge always better than ignorance?

Some argue against the use of nuclear power. For them, the risk of an uncontrolled nuclear reaction happening in a power station is not worth taking as it would lead to a thermal meltdown of the core and the release of dangerous radioactive material into the environment. It is also claimed that nuclear power stations could be targets for terrorist attack.

 The French philosopher Auguste Compte said that to know is to predict. Is this always true in the sciences? Can the statement be applied to other areas of knowledge?

Hiroshima, after it had been destroyed by a US atomic bomb dropped on the morning of the 6th August 1945. It was the first atomic bomb to be used in warfare, the second being used over Nagasaki three days later. Over 220 000 people died in the attacks, and thousands were injured.

Since World War II, when the destructive nature of nuclear bombs was witnessed for the first time, the threat of their use has acted as a deterrent to countries planning to act aggressively against the nuclear powers. Non-proliferation treaties have been formulated which attempt to limit nuclear technology to a small number of nations.

## $^{239}_{94}$Pu used as a fuel in 'breeder reactors' is produced from $^{238}_{92}$U by neutron capture

Fast breeder reactors were developed because the supply of fissionable $^{235}_{92}$U is limited. Breeder reactors convert the more abundant uranium isotope $^{238}_{92}$U into fissionable $^{239}_{94}$Pu.

$^{238}_{92}$U can capture fast moving neutrons to form the heavier uranium isotope:

$$^{238}_{92}U + ^{1}_{0}n \rightarrow ^{239}_{92}U$$

which then decays to $^{239}_{93}$Np with the emission of a beta particle:

$$^{239}_{92}U \rightarrow ^{239}_{93}Np + ^{0}_{-1}e$$

and the $^{239}_{93}$Np further decays to $^{239}_{94}$Pu with the emission of another beta particle:

$$^{239}_{93}Np \rightarrow ^{239}_{94}Pu + ^{0}_{-1}e$$

In the fast breeder reaction the $^{239}_{94}$Pu is bombarded with a neutron and undergoes a fission reaction. For example:

$$^{239}_{94}Pu + ^{1}_{0}n \rightarrow ^{145}_{56}Ba + ^{93}_{38}Sr + 2\,^{1}_{0}n$$

No moderators are needed in a plutonium reactor because plutonium requires faster neutrons for fission than $^{235}_{92}$U.

There are major concerns associated with the use of breeder reactors.

- Plutonium is toxic.
- Plutonium can be concentrated from reactor grade to weapons grade easily. It can be easily separated from the uranium isotopes as they are atoms of different elements with different chemical properties.
- Breeder reactors are less efficient than those fuelled by uranium and require liquid metals as coolants. The escape of liquid sodium from a breeder reactor and its subsequent contact with water would be disastrous.
- They could be more susceptible to accidents.
- All nuclear reactors produce radioactive by-products that are difficult to store and dispose of.

The use of nuclear energy is monitored internationally by the International Atomic Energy Agency. It was set up in 1957 as the world's 'Atoms for Peace' organization within the United Nations family. The IAEA is the world's centre of cooperation in the nuclear field.

The use of nuclear energy carries risks as well as benefits. Who should ultimately be responsible for assessing these? How do we know what is best for society and the individual?

**TOK**

### NATURE OF SCIENCE

Science is highly collaborative and the scientific community is composed of people working in science, engineering, and technology. As well as collaborating on the exchange of results, scientists work on a daily basis in collaborative groups on a small and large scale within and between disciplines and countries, facilitated even more by virtual communication. IAEA and the ITER project are examples of such large-scale collaboration.

### Exercises

**29** When the nucleus of $^{235}_{92}$U is split under neutron bombardment about 1/1000 of the mass is converted to the equivalent amount of energy.

    **(a)** Calculate how much energy would be produced by the fission of 1.0 kg of $^{235}_{92}$U?

    **(b)** The specific energy of coal is 30 kJ $g^{-1}$. Calculate the mass of coal that would need to be burned to produce the same mass of energy.

**30** $^{226}_{88}$Ra decays naturally with the emission of an alpha particle to form an isotope of radon (Rn). The masses of the particles involved in the reaction are tabulated.

| Rn | 226.0254 amu |
|---|---|
| Ra | 222.0176 amu |
| $\alpha$ | 4.0026 amu |

Determine the energy released in the decay process.

**31** Consider the following fission reaction in which a neutron collides with a nucleus of uranium-235 and the following reaction takes place.

$$^{235}_{92}U + ^1_0n \rightarrow ^{96}_{37}Rb + ^{138}_{55}Cs + 2\,^1_0n$$

The masses of the relevant particles are tabulated

| | |
|---|---|
| $^{235}_{92}U$ | 235.0439 amu |
| $^1_0n$ | 1.0087 amu |
| $^{96}_{37}Rb$ | 95.9342 amu |
| $^{138}_{55}Cs$ | 137.9112 amu |

(a) Explain why the equation is not simplified by cancelling a neutron from both sides.

(b) Determine the energy produced by the nuclear reaction in kJ mol$^{-1}$.

**32** $^{228}_{90}Th$ is a radioactive isotope that emits alpha particles.

(a) Deduce the equation for the alpha emission.

(b) The masses of the nuclides in the decay process are shown below:

| Nuclide | Mass / amu |
|---|---|
| $^{228}_{90}Th$ | 228.028 726 |
| decay product | 224.020 196 |
| alpha particle | 4.002 604 |

Calculate the mass difference between the $^{228}_{90}Th$ isotope and the products.

(c) Determine the energy released in kJ mol$^{-1}$ during the reaction.

(d) Assuming that coal releases 28 kJ g$^{-1}$, calculate the mass of coal that would need to be burned to produce the same amount of energy.

**A radioactive decay simulation**

Full details of how to carry out this experiment with a worksheet are available online.

# Nuclear waste is still radioactive

One of the potential hazards associated with the use of nuclear energy is that the products of fission reactions are still dangerously radioactive. The neutron:proton ratio of the isotopes produced does not fall in the stability belt shown in Figure 14.3.

Some radioactive isotopes are long-lived. $^{238}_{92}U$, for example, has a half-life of $4.47 \times 10^9$ years, which is approximately the age of the Earth, so only half the $^{238}_{92}U$ that existed when the Earth formed has since decayed away. Other isotopes, such as $^{214}_{84}Po$, have half-lives of a fraction of a second. The long half-lives of certain artificially produced isotopes are of particular concern when handling radioactive waste. One by-product of nuclear reactors, $^{237}_{93}Np$ has a half-life of 2.2 million years. Any site for storing waste contaminated with such isotopes must be one that is unlikely to be disturbed in the future. Otherwise radioactive material may escape into the environment.

# The half-life of radioactive isotopes

Although we cannot predict at which instant a particular nucleus will decay, the overall rate at which a collection of nuclei decays is regular and can be quantified by its **half-life**. This is the time taken for:

• half the mass of an isotope to decay

• the concentration of an aqueous isotope to fall to half its initial value

• the number of atoms of the isotope to fall to half their original number

• the activity of an isotope to fall to half its initial value.

### Worked example

Bismuth-212 has a half-life of 1 hour. Deduce how long it would take for 16.00 g of the isotope to decay so that only 1.00 g remained.

### Solution

The half-life is the time taken for the mass to fall to half its value. Construct a table:

| Time / hours | Mass of isotope remaining / g |
|:---:|:---:|
| 0 | 16.00 |
| 1 | 8.00 |
| 2 | 4.00 |
| 3 | 2.00 |
| 4 | 1.00 |

The decay will take 4 hours.

A decay curve for the isotope in the worked example is shown in Figure 14.11. It is an exponential curve and in theory never falls to zero.

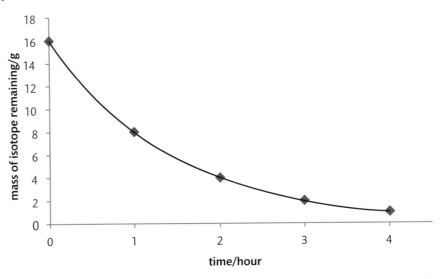

**Figure 14.11** A decay curve for an isotope which has a half-life of 1 hour.

The half-life of an isotope depends intimately on the balance of forces within a nucleus.

What is the role of evidence in justifying religious belief?

## NATURE OF SCIENCE

### Carbon-14 dating

$^{14}_{6}C$ has too many neutrons to be stable. It can reduce the neutron : proton ratio when a neutron changes to a proton and an electron. The proton stays in the nucleus and changes the identity of the atom to nitrogen and the electron is ejected from the atom as a beta particle:

$$^{14}_{6}C \rightarrow \, ^{14}_{7}N + \, ^{0}_{-1}e$$

The relative abundance of $^{14}_{6}C$ present in living things, however, remains quite constant as the decayed atoms are continually replenished from $^{14}_{6}C$ present in carbon dioxide from the atmosphere during photosynthesis. When organisms die no more carbon is exchanged and the levels of $^{14}_{6}C$ fall due to beta decay.

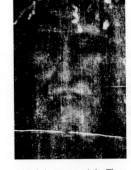

This process occurs at a regular rate and can be used to date carbon-containing materials. The half-life is 5730 years, so the carbon-14 to carbon-12 ratio falls by 50% every 5730 years after the death of a living organism. This creates a timescale which allows it to be used in the dating of archaeological objects. *continued*

*continued*

For many centuries people have believed the Turin Shroud was used to wrap the body of Jesus Christ after his death. Carbon-14 measurements have dated the shroud to have been made no earlier than 1260 ACE. The linen was found to have come from flax grown sometime between 1260 and 1390.

Scientists adopt a sceptical attitude to knowledge claims. This does not mean that they disbelieve everything, but rather that they suspend judgement until they have a good reason to believe a claim to be true or false. Such reasons are based on evidence and argument.

## Radioactive decay is a first-order process

As radioactive decay is a first-order process, the rate of decay of a nucleus A can be expressed in the following form:

$$\text{rate of decay} = \lambda[A]$$

where $\lambda$ is called the **decay constant**. It is essentially a first-order rate constant, but is exceptional in that it does not change with temperature.

This expression can be integrated to give:

$$\ln([A]_t) = -\lambda t + \ln([A]_0)$$

where $[A]_0$ is the initial concentration

$$\ln\frac{[A]_t}{[A]_0} = -\lambda t$$

Note the decay equations are given in section 1 of the IB data booklet.

Expressing this equation in exponential form gives:

$$\frac{[A]_t}{[A]_0} = e^{-\lambda t}$$

We can look at the relationship between the decay constant $\lambda$ and the half life $t_{1/2}$.

when $t = t_{1/2}$ the $[A]_t = \frac{1}{2}([A]_0)$

$$\ln(\tfrac{1}{2}) = -\lambda t_{1/2}$$

$$\ln 2 = \lambda t_{1/2}$$

This means that the half-life is independent of the starting concentrations, which is a key characteristic of radioactive decay.

> rate of decay $= \dfrac{d[A]_t}{dt} = \lambda[A]_t$
> where $[A]_t$ is the concentration of A at time $t$.

### Worked example

A radioactive sample contains a solution with an initial concentration of $1.400 \times 10^{-6}$ mol dm$^{-3}$. The concentration of $^{240}\text{AmCl}_3$ decreases to $1.365 \times 10^{-6}$ mol dm$^{-3}$ after 2 hours. Determine the half-life of $^{240}\text{Am}$.

**Solution**

$$\ln\frac{[A]_t}{[A]_0} = -\lambda t$$

$$\ln\frac{1.365 \times 10^{-6}}{1.400 \times 10^{-6}} = -\lambda \times 2 \text{ hr}$$

$$\lambda = \frac{1}{2} \times \ln\frac{1.400 \times 10^{-6}}{1.365 \times 10^{-6}} \text{ hr}^{-1}$$

$$= 0.012\,659 \text{ hr}^{-1}$$

$$t_{1/2} = \frac{\ln 2}{\lambda} = \frac{\ln 2}{0.012659} \text{ hr}$$

$$= 55 \text{ hr}$$

### Worked example

$^{226}_{88}$Ra has a half-life of 1620 years. Determine the decay constant, $\lambda$, and deduce the proportion of the sample that remains after 100 years.

**Solution**

$$t_{\frac{1}{2}} = \frac{\ln 2}{\lambda}$$

$$\lambda = \frac{\ln 2}{t_{\frac{1}{2}}}$$

$$= \frac{\ln 2}{1620}$$

$$= 0.000428 \text{ yr}^{-1}$$

$$\ln\frac{[A]_t}{[A]_0} = -\lambda t$$

$$= -0.000428 \text{ yr}^{-1} \times 100 \text{ yr}$$

$$= -0.0428$$

$$\frac{[A]_t}{[A]_0} = e^{-0.0428}$$

$$= 0.958$$

$$= 95.8\%$$

## Nuclear waste can be high level or low level

An important aspect of the nuclear industry is the disposal of radioactive waste. The spent fuel rods from nuclear power stations are **high-level waste** whereas the containers which hold the fuel are classified as **low-level waste**. The method of disposal depends on the level of the waste and the length of time it remains active. Low-level wastes have low levels of activity and short half-lives. High-level wastes have high activity and long half-lives.

Sources and characteristics of low- and high-level waste

| Nature of waste | Source | Characteristics |
|---|---|---|
| low level | • hospitals: items such as clothing, paper towels which are used where radioactive materials are handled<br>• fuel containers | • activity is low<br>• short half-life<br>• high volume |
| high level | • nuclear industry: spent fuel rods<br>• military | • activity is high<br>• long half-life<br>• low volume |

### Disposal of low-level waste

As the decay process produces heat energy, low-level waste is stored in cooling ponds of water until the activity has fallen to safe levels. The water is then passed through an ion-exchange resin, which removes the isotopes responsible for the activity, and diluted before being released into the sea. Other methods of disposal include keeping the waste in steel containers inside concrete-lined vaults.

## Disposal of high-level waste

As we have seen, the products formed from nuclear reactors with long half-lives can maintain dangerously high levels of radioactivity for thousands of years. Unfortunately, there is no way to speed up the rate of the decay process. Waste disposal presents a formidable problem because products from the decay process may themselves undergo further nuclear reactions. Remotely controlled machinery removes the spent rods from the reactor and transfers them to deep pools where they are cooled by water containing a neutron absorber. The fuel rods are often cased in ceramic or glass and then packed in metal containers before being buried deep in the Earth, either in impervious granite rock or in deep unused mines. The site selected for the disposal must safely contain the material for a very long period of time and prevent it from entering the underground water supply. Because there is always the problem that land masses may move (for example, in an earthquake) and the radioactive material escape, the waste is buried in remote places that are geologically stable.

Drilling machinery being used to excavate underground boreholes into which nuclear waste may be placed. Before long-term nuclear waste is stored underground, the area must be examined for geological activity.

Used fuel cooling and storage pond. Fuel rods are placed in the storage ponds awaiting reprocessing. The spent fuel is still highly radioactive and continues to generate heat. The water absorbs the heat and shields the operators from the radiation emitted by the fuel.

## Comparison between fossil fuel and nuclear power stations

| Fossil fuel | Nuclear fission |
| --- | --- |
| ordinary chemical combustion reaction to produce heat | nuclear fission to produce heat from mass defect: $$\Delta E = \Delta mc^2$$ |
| products are $CO_2$ (greenhouse gas) + $SO_2$ (acid rain) + particulates (global dimming) | products can be highly radioactive; no $CO_2$ is produced; accidents can release radioactive materials |
| fuel does not have to be enriched | U-235 fuel has to be enriched |
| fuels burnt in a furnace; requires air | fuel rods in an airtight building require neutrons |
| all fuel can be used up | spent fuel is highly radioactive |
| fly ash can be used to make roads | nuclear waste has to be stored and safely disposed of |
| no meltdown possible | failure of control system can lead to meltdown |

# The dangers of nuclear energy are due to the ionizing nature of the radiation

Every radioactive decay involves the emission of ionizing radiation. As alpha, beta, and gamma radiation pass through a substance, collisions occur which result in electrons being removed. When biologically important molecules such as DNA are ionized mutations can occur.

**NATURE OF SCIENCE**

We live in a sea of radiation. In recent years, some have expressed a fear for the effects of radiation. People don't want to live near nuclear reactors and are frightened by reports of links between excess exposure to sunlight and skin cancer. Several factors combine to heighten the public's anxiety about both the short-range and long-range effects of radiation. Perhaps the most important source of fear is the fact that radiation can't be generally detected by individuals. Furthermore, the effects of exposure to radiation might not appear for months or years or even decades. Scientists have a responsibility to society to report evidence accurately to enable the public to be fully aware of the relative risks of radiation.

Ionization occurs when the radiation carries enough energy to remove an electron from an atom or molecule. The ability to ionize water is the threshold that marks the difference between ionizing and non-ionizing radiation as water makes up, by mass, 70–90% of all living tissue. The ionization energy of water is 1216 kJ mol$^{-1}$.

When ionizing radiation passes through living tissue, electrons are removed from water molecules to produce $H_2O^+$ ions.

$$H_2O \rightarrow H_2O^+ + e^-$$

The $H_2O^+$ ion contains an unpaired electron and is an extremely reactive **free radical**. It is one of the strongest oxidizing agents that can exist in aqueous solution. It destroys biologically active molecules by either removing electrons or removing hydrogen atoms. $H_2O^+$ can, for example, dissociate to produce a hydroxyl radical and a hydrogen ion:

$$H_2O^+ \rightarrow HO\bullet + H^+$$

This often leads to damage to the membrane, nucleus, chromosomes, or mitochondria of the cell that can inhibit cell division, result in cell death, or produce a malignant cell.

A variety of other reactions are possible in the track of the charged particle. Hydrogen peroxide can be formed by the combination of two hydroxyl radicals:

$$2HO\bullet \rightarrow H_2O_2$$

One of most important electron acceptors is molecular oxygen, which readily accepts electrons to give rise to a series of partially reduced species which include the superoxide ion ($O_2^-$):

$$O_2 + e^- \rightarrow O_2^-$$

Hydrogen peroxide ($H_2O_2$), the hydroxyl radical (HO•) and peroxyl (ROO•) and alkoxyl (RO•) radicals are other reactive oxygen species which may be involved in the initiation and propagation of free radical chain reactions and which are potentially highly damaging to cells.

Harmful effects of reactive oxygen species on the cell include:

• damage to DNA

• oxidation of polyunsaturated fatty acids in lipids

• oxidation of amino acids in proteins.

Nuclear incidents have a global effect; the accidents at Three Mile Island, Chernobyl, and the problems at Fukushima caused by a tsunami could be discussed to illustrate the potential dangers.

An aerial view of the abandoned city of Pripyat, Ukraine, showing how nature is beginning to recapture the area. Pripyat is a ghost town near the Chernobyl Nuclear Power Plant. On 26th April 1986, reactor number 4 of the Chernobyl Nuclear Power Plant went out of control, leading to meltdown and an explosion. Around 1000 square kilometres of land were directly contaminated by radioactive fall-out and a 30 km exclusion zone was created. A concrete sarcophagus, the Object Shelter, was built to contain the radioactive materials, but within the restricted area the radiation is still lethal to humans.

## Exercises

**33** **(a)** It has been suggested that the fission products from nuclear reactions should be isolated for 10 half-lives. Calculate the fraction of a radioactive species that remains after this length of time.
   **(b)** Deduce the percentage of the material that has decayed in this time.

**34** Consider a sample of a radioactive isotope with a half-life of 19.2 s. What would its count rate be after 96 s if it started with an initial count rate of 1200 disintegrations per second?

**35** One fission reaction of $^{235}_{92}U$ that can take place in a nuclear reactor can lead to the production of an atom of strontium-90 and two neutrons. Deduce the identity of the other nuclide produced.

**36** Radioactive waste from nuclear power stations is often divided into high-level and low-level wastes. Describe the materials present in these wastes and the methods used for their storage and disposal.

**37** It has been estimated that the $^{14}_{6}C$ in the atmosphere is responsible for producing 60 atoms of $^{14}_{7}N$ and 60 electrons every hour for each gram of carbon. This gives a disintegration rate of 60 counts $hr^{-1} g^{-1}$. A sample of a sea shell found near the sea shore was found to have a count rate of 4 counts $hr^{-1} g^{-1}$. Estimate the age of the shell.

**38** $^{238}_{94}Pu$ decays by emission of an $\alpha$-particle to form an isotope of uranium (U).

   **(a)** State the nuclear equation for this decay.
   **(b)** The half-life of $^{238}_{94}Pu$ is 88 years. Explain why the activity of a sample may be considered to be constant over a period of one year.
   **(c)** Determine the percentage of the plutonium remaining after 20 years.

**39** A sample of waste produced by the reaction of $^{235}_{92}U$ contains 10.0 kg of $^{90}_{38}Sr$. The activity of the sample is $5.1 \times 10^{16} s^{-1}$ and the half-life of the isotopes is 28.4 yr.

   **(a)** Determine the activity after a period of 80 years.
   **(b)** Comment on the implications of your answer in part (a) on the problems associated with using uranium as an energy source.

**40** Radiation is characterized as ionizing when it removes an electron from a water molecule. The energy needed to do this is 1216 kJ $mol^{-1}$. Deduce that the dividing line between ionizing and non-ionizing radiation falls in the ultraviolet region of the electromagnetic spectrum.

## C.4 Solar energy

### Understandings:

- Light can be absorbed by chlorophyll and other pigments with a conjugated electronic structure.
- Photosynthesis converts light energy into chemical energy:

$$6CO_2 + 6H_2O \rightarrow C_6H_{12}O_6 + 6O_2$$

- Fermentation of glucose produces ethanol which can be used as a biofuel:

$$C_6H_{12}O_6 \rightarrow 2C_2H_5OH + 2CO_2$$

- Energy content of vegetable oils is similar to that of diesel fuel, but vegetable oils are not used in internal combustion engines as they are too viscous.
- Transesterification between an ester and an alcohol with a strong acid or base catalyst produces a different ester:

$$RCOOR^1 + R^2OH \rightarrow RCOOR^2 + R^1OH$$

- In the transesterification process, involving a reaction with an alcohol in the presence of a strong acid or base, the triglyceride vegetable oils are converted to a mixture mainly comprising alkyl esters and glycerol, but with some fatty acids.
- Transesterification with ethanol or methanol produces oils with lower viscosity that can be used in diesel engines.

### Applications and skills:

- Identification of features of the molecules that allow them to absorb visible light.

**Guidance**

*Only a conjugated system with alternating double bonds needs to be covered.*

- Explanation of the reduced viscosity of esters produced with methanol and ethanol.
- Evaluation of the advantages and disadvantages of the use of biofuels.
- Deduction of equations for transesterification reactions.

Solar energy has been described as the ultimate energy source and we have seen that a lot of the energy we have on the Earth originates from the Sun. All our fossil fuel supplies were derived from the Sun through photosynthesis. We have seen that solar energy is produced by a series of fusion reactions which convert hydrogen to helium. About 98% of the Sun's energy is emitted in the form of heat and light and the remaining given out as X-rays and gamma rays.

There are many advantages to solar energy.

- It will be readily available as long as we need it, is free, and requires no purification.
- It is a clean and safe form of energy. The environmental impact is relatively small, although large areas of land are needed.
- It is often available where it is needed, so no transportation is needed.
- Political problems are reduced as the Sun is available to 'all'.

The use of solar energy has, however, been limited because of some disadvantages with its use.

- Other energy sources have been relatively inexpensive.
- Solar energy is widely dispersed and so must be concentrated before it is used.
- Solar energy is not available at night when the demand for energy is at its highest.
- As the supply varies with weather conditions and time of day, an effective method of storing solar energy is needed.

Solar energy can be collected in a number of ways:

- Thermal (passive collection): the Sun's heat is used to heat water or other objects, which are then used for other purposes.
- Thermal (active collection): the Sun's heat is used to bring about an endothermic change. The energy is then given out when the process is later reversed.
- The solar energy can be converted to chemical energy (biomass) using photosynthesis and then given out when the chemical products are used as fuels.
- The solar energy can be converted to electricity by means of photovoltaic and dye-sensitized solar (DSSC) cells.
- The solar energy can be captured indirectly in its derived forms of wind and hydroelectricity.

# Light can be absorbed by chlorophyll and other pigments with a conjugated electronic structure

Photosynthesis converts about 1% of incident solar radiation into chemical energy. Some of the solar energy is reflected or used to heat the surface of the Earth. Plants do not cover the Earth's surface completely or absorb all wavelengths of light. Although an inefficient process, photosynthesis does provide a crucial route for harnessing vast amounts of the solar energy that the Earth receives.

The process begins in the chloroplasts of plant cells, which contain chlorophyll and carotenoid molecules that can absorb incoming photons and capture their energy. This energy can then be used to drive a complex sequence of redox reactions which converts carbon dioxide and water to the energy-rich glucose molecule. Leaves appear green because chlorophyll absorbs blue and red light. Carotenoid molecules absorb violet and blue light but are not as abundant as chlorophyll molecules in leaves. They only make themselves known to us in the orange/yellow leaves of autumn, when the chlorophyll molecules are decaying.

 Photosynthesis recycles all the atmospheric carbon dioxide every 300 years and all the oxygen every 2000 years.

## The chromophores in the molecule absorb light

Visible light produces electronic transitions in organic molecules. The amount of light absorbed at different wavelengths depends on the molecular structure. The colour of a substance is determined by which colour(s) it transmits or reflects. This is the **complementary** colour(s) to the ones absorbed.

### Worked example

The absorbance of an artificial dye is shown. Identify the wavelength which corresponds to maximum absorbance ($\lambda_{max}$) and use the colour wheel in section 17 of the IB data booklet to deduce the colour of the dye.

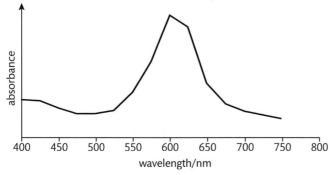

### Solution

- The wavelength that corresponds to the maximum absorbance is 600 nm.
- Orange light is absorbed.
- The dye is blue (the complementary colour of orange).

The part of the molecule responsible for absorbing the photon of radiation is called the **chromophore**. Unsaturated groups such as C=C, C=O, —N=N—, and the benzene ring are examples of chromophores. The wavelengths that correspond to the maximum absorbance for some chromophores are shown in the table.

| Chromophore | $\lambda_{max}$ / nm |
|---|---|
| C=C | 175 |
| C=O | 190 and 280 |
| C=C—C=C | 210 |
| —NO$_2$ | 270 |
|  | 190 and 260 |

A compound is more likely to absorb visible light and appear coloured when it contains a **conjugated system** of alternate double and single bonds. The more extensive the conjugation the longer the wavelength of the light absorbed. Benzene is a conjugated system and so absorbs at longer wavelengths than the alkenes with a single double bond.

The relationship between the wavelength of the radiation absorbed and the length of the conjugated system can be explained using the wave model of the electron discussed in Chapter 2 (page 74). The wavelength of the light absorbed by a conjugated system increases with length in the same way, and for essentially the same reason, that a guitar string produces a lower note as its length increases.

## Chlorophyll absorbs red and blue light

Chlorophyll contains a planar heterocyclic unit called a porphyrin whose structure consists of four pyrrole rings linked by a single bridging carbon atom (Figure 14.12). Each pyrrole ring contains four carbon atoms and one nitrogen atom.

There are two closely related forms of chlorophyll that have different R groups – chlorophyll *a* has a methyl (CH$_3$) group and chlorophyll *b* has an aldehyde (CHO) group. Chlorophyll acts a polydentate ligand with four nitrogen atoms forming four dative covalent bond with a central metal ion to form a chelate complex (see page 125).

The extensive conjugation in chlorophyll, which stretches beyond the porphyrin ring, allows it to absorb visible light. The two different forms of chlorophyll, which differ only in one group that is attached to the ring, absorb light at different wavelengths; chlorophyll a absorbs red light and chlorophyll b absorbs blue light. As the two molecules span a large region of the visible spectrum they harvest more solar energy than either would individually. Only green light is not absorbed and this is the colour that we see.

A conjugated system contains alternate double and single bonds. The benzene ring is a conjugated system. The wavelength of the light absorbed by an organic molecule increases with the length of the conjugated system.

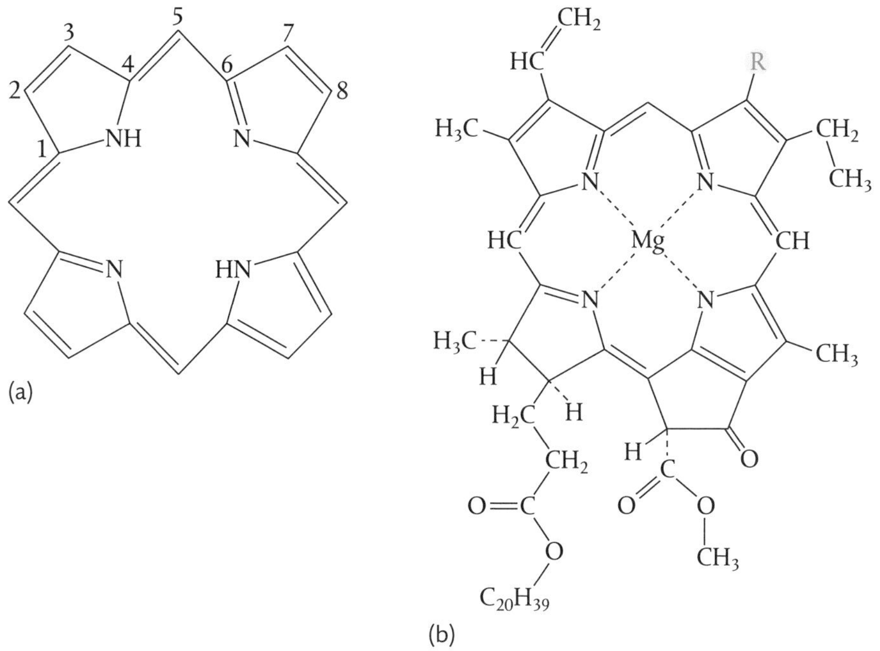

**Figure 14.12** (a) The structure of a porphyrin ring. (b) The structure of chlorophyll. $R = CH_3$ (chlorophyll a) or $R = CHO$ (chlorophyll b).

(a)

(b)

Carotenoids are the most widespread pigments in nature. A large majority are produced by algae.

## Carotenoids

Carotenoids are the most common pigments in nature. They absorb light in the violet and green range and so range in colour from yellow to red. There are only low levels of carotenoids in grass but a large majority are produced by algae.

The majority of the carotenoids are derived from a 40-carbon polyene chain. The hydrocarbon carotenoids are known as **carotenes**. In $\alpha$- and $\beta$-carotene, the chain is terminated by cyclic end-groups (Figure 14.13).

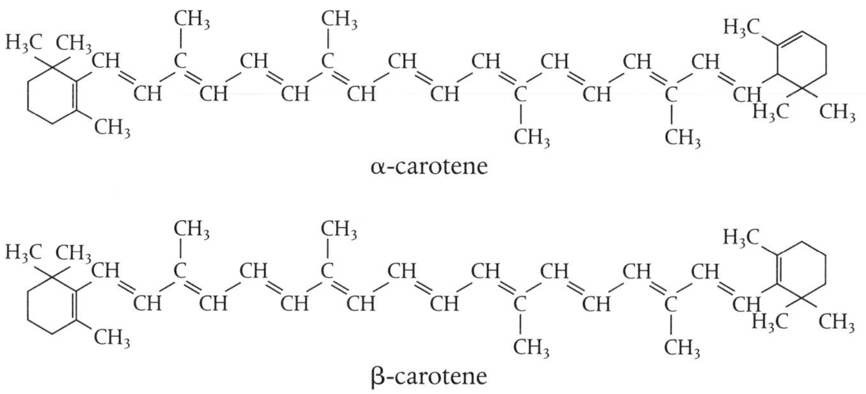

α-carotene

β-carotene

**Figure 14.13** The structures of $\alpha$- and $\beta$-carotene.

## CHALLENGE YOURSELF

**10** Study the structure of the two forms of carotene. Deduce the molecular formula of the two molecules and distinguish between them.

Carotenoids are structurally related to vitamin A. Vitamin A is a primary alcohol and can be oxidized to the aldehyde, retinal.

**vitamin A**

The conjugated system of retinal absorbs visible light. The energy gained allows retinal to change its geometry, which results in an electrical signal being sent along the optic nerve to the brain.

## Exercises

**41 (a)** Explain why $CH_2$=CH—CH=$CH_2$ shows an absorption band at a longer wavelength than $CH_3$—CH=CH—$CH_3$.
   **(b)** Explain why the absorption bands disappear when bromine is added.
   **(c)** Explain why benzene is colourless and nitrobenzene is yellow.

**42** A simplified colour wheel is given in section 17 of the IB data booklet. The effect of conjugation is illustrated by the spectra of the diphenylpolyenes, as shown in the table below.

| Diphenylpolyenes | | $n$ | $\lambda_{max}$ / nm |
|---|---|---|---|
| | | 2 | 328 |
| | | 3 | 358 |
| $C_6H_5$—[CH=CH]$_n$—$C_6H_5$ | | 4 | 394 |
| | | 5 | 403 |
| | | 6 | 420 |

**(a)** Describe the relationship between $n$ and $\lambda_{max}$.
**(b)** Suggest which members of series absorb in the visible region.
**(c)** Suggest the colour of $C_6H_5$—(CH=CH)$_5$—$C_6H_5$ and $C_6H_5$—(CH=CH)$_6$—$C_6H_5$.
**(d)** Explain the limitations to your answer in parts (b) and (c).

**43** The spectrum of β-carotene is shown in Figure 14.14 and the structure in Figure 14.13. Explain why the molecule absorbs in the visible region of the spectra and suggest the colour of the pigment.

**Figure 14.14** The spectrum of β-carotene.

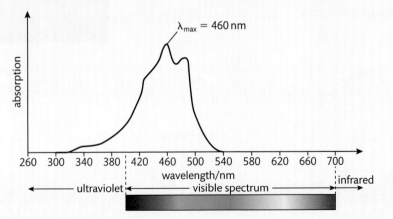

**Figure 14.15** The conjugated system of 4-aminobenzoic acid enables it to act as a sunscreen.

Moderate exposure to UV light results in the production of the natural pigment melanin, and darkens the skin. Repeated over-exposure to the sun, however, can cause premature ageing and increases the risk of skin cancer. Conjugated compounds can be used as sunscreens as they absorb dangerous ultraviolet radiation. For example, 4-aminobenzoic acid absorbs UV radiation at 265 nm and is a component of many sunscreens (Figure 14.15). It is also known as para-aminobenzoic acid (PABA).

## Photosynthesis converts light energy into chemical energy

The energy of the excited chlorophyll molecule drives the sequence of redox reactions that is photosynthesis.

This reaction can be divided into two half-reactions. One half-reaction involves the reduction of carbon dioxide to glucose:

$$6CO_2 + 24H^+ + 24e^- \rightarrow C_6H_{12}O_6 + 6H_2O$$

Twenty-four electrons are needed to reduce six molecules of carbon dioxide to one molecule of glucose as the oxidation number of each carbon decreases from +4 to 0.

The electrons are generated from the oxidation of twelve molecules of water to form oxygen. The oxidation number of twelve oxygen atoms increases from −2 to 0.

The equation for the oxidation half-reaction is:

$$12H_2O \rightarrow 6O_2 + 24H^+ + 24e^-$$

Adding the two half-reactions:

$$6CO_2 + 24H^+ + 24e^- \rightarrow C_6H_{12}O_6 + 6H_2O$$

$$12H_2O \rightarrow 6O_2 + 24H^+ + 24e^-$$

gives

$$6CO_2 + 12H_2O \rightarrow C_6H_{12}O_6 + 6H_2O + 6O_2$$

which can be simplified to:

$$6CO_2 + 6H_2O \rightarrow C_6H_{12}O_6 + 6O_2$$

The products of photosynthesis can be used for food, as a primary fuel or converted to other fuels such as ethanol. These biofuels are a renewable energy source. Wood is a form of biomass and a primary fuel but has a lower specific energy than fossil fuels due to its relatively high oxygen content.

## Ethanol can be used as a biofuel

The most useful biofuels are liquids which can be used in internal combustion engines.

Ethanol can be made from biomass by fermenting plants high in starches and sugars.

$$C_6H_{12}O_6 \rightarrow 2C_2H_5OH + 2CO_2$$

This process can be carried out at approximately 37 °C in the absence of oxygen by yeast which provide an enzyme which catalyses the reaction.

### Worked example

(a) State the equation for the complete combustion of ethanol.
(b) The enthalpy of combustion of ethanol is −1367 kJ mol$^{-1}$. Calculate the specific energy of by ethanol in kJ g$^{-1}$.
(c) Compare this value with the corresponding value for octane and explain the difference.

### Solution

(a) $C_2H_5OH(l) + 3O_2(g) \rightarrow 3H_2O(l) + 2CO_2(g)$

(b) heat produced by one mole (46.08) = −1367 kJ

$$\text{heat produced by } 1.00\text{ g} = \frac{1367}{46.08}\text{ kJ g}^{-1}$$
$$= 29.67\text{ kJ g}^{-1}$$

(c) heat produced by one mole (114.26) = −5470 kJ g$^{-1}$

$$\text{heat produced by } 1.00\text{ g} = \frac{5470}{114.26}\text{ kJ g}^{-1}$$
$$= 47.87\text{ kJ g}^{-1}$$

Less heat is produced per unit mass with ethanol because it is already partially oxidized.

Gasohol is a mixture of 10% ethanol and 90% unleaded gasoline. The ethanol can be produced from several types of plant material and in most cases gasohol can be substituted for gasoline with only minor changes in fuel consumption and performance. The advantages of using ethanol include:

• it is renewable
• it has a higher octane rating than normal gasoline
• it produces lower emissions of carbon monoxide (by up to 30%) and nitrogen oxides
• it decreases a country's dependence on oil.

One disadvantage is that the ethanol absorbs water as it can form hydrogen bonds with the water molecules in the atmosphere. This leads to the ethanol separating from the hydrocarbon components in the fuel as well as causing corrosion.

Methanol can also be used; it is produced by heating wood in the presence of steam and limited amounts of oxygen. A mixture of hydrogen, carbon monoxide, and carbon dioxide is initially produced. The hydrogen and carbon monoxide can then react further to form the liquid fuel methanol.

Particulates in the form of soot and unburned hydrocarbons are hazardous by-products of the process and carbon monoxide is a toxic gas.

## CHALLENGE YOURSELF

**11** A possible incomplete equation for the conversion of wood into hydrogen, carbon monoxide, and carbon dioxide is:

$$2C_{16}H_{23}O_{11} + 19H_2O + O_2 \rightarrow xH_2 + yCO + zCO_2$$

(a) Identify the oxidation number of all the elements in the equation.
(b) Identify the elements which are oxidized and reduced in the reaction.
(c) Deduce the value of $x$ by balancing the hydrogen atoms.
(d) Determine the value of $y$ and $z$ by balancing the changes of oxidation numbers and the number of carbon atoms.
(e) Deduce how many methanol molecules can be produced from one wood molecule.

Methane can be made from the bacterial breakdown of plant material in the absence of oxygen. The process can be controlled to produce a clean burning biogas like natural gas.

Carbohydrates, for example, produce a mixture which is about 50% methane:

$$C_6H_{12}O_6 \rightarrow 3CO_2 + 3CH_4$$

Fats, however, produce 72% methane:

$$2C_{15}H_{31}COOH + 14H_2O \rightarrow 9CO_2 + 23CH_4$$

## The advantages and disadvantages of using biofuels

### Advantages

- Cheap and readily available
- if crops/trees are replanted can be a renewable and sustainable source.

### Disadvantages

- The production of biomass involves the use of land which could be used for other purposes, such as growing food
- high cost of harvesting and transportation in large volumes
- most of the land considered for biomass production would need the massive application of fertilizers
- lower specific energy than fossil fuels
- greenhouse gases still produced
- biomass is not renewable if crops/trees are not replanted.

## The energy content of vegetable oils

The idea of using vegetable oil as an engine fuel dates back to Rudolf Diesel (1858–1913), who used peanut oil to run his first engine at the World Exhibition in Paris in 1900. In 1911, he said, 'The diesel engine can be fed with vegetable oils and would help considerably in the development of agriculture of the countries which use it.'

Vegetable oil was, however, forgotten as a renewable source of power when the crude oil industry produced a hydrocarbon 'diesel fraction' that would power a modified 'diesel engine'. The vegetable oils are not ideal fuels. They are about 11 to 17 times more viscous than diesel fuel and have low volatility, which means they do not burn completely and form deposits in the fuel injector of diesel engines.

Vegetable oils are **esters** of **propane-1,2,3-triol (glycerol)** and long-chain carboxylic acids, called **fatty acids**.

**glycerol**      **fatty acids**      **triglyceride**

The triglyceride oil molecules can be thought of as having 'tuning fork' structures, with the three long limbs being the fatty acid chains. The oils are viscous as there are relatively strong van der Waals' forces between the long fatty acid limbs of each molecule.

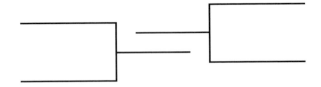

**Figure 14.16** The fatty acid chains align themselves so as to allow close packing between the oil molecules, which makes the liquid viscous.

## Transesterification with ethanol or methanol produces oils with lower viscosity that can be used in diesel engines

The process used to convert these oils to biodiesel is called **transesterification**, in which the triglyceride oil is reacted with methanol or ethanol to form glycerol and a methyl or ethyl ester with reduced viscosity due to the smaller size of the molecules.

The triglyceride is reacted with the alcohol in the presence of a catalyst, usually a strong base like sodium hydroxide or a strong acid. The ethanol or methanol replaces the glycerol in the oil and forms an ester with the fatty acids, and free glycerol is regenerated.

$$
\begin{array}{llll}
\underset{\textbf{triglyceride}}{
\begin{array}{c}
\quad\;\; O \\
\quad\;\; \| \\
CH_2O\!-\!C\!-\!R_1 \\
| \quad\quad\quad O \\
R_2\!-\!C\!-\!O\!-\!CH \quad\; \| \\
| \quad\quad\quad\; \\
CH_2O\!-\!C\!-\!R_3
\end{array}}
&
+\; 3\,C_2H_5OH
\xrightarrow[\text{Catalyst}]{OH^-}
&
\underset{\textbf{glycerol}}{
\begin{array}{c}
CH_2OH \\
| \\
CHOH \\
| \\
CH_2OH
\end{array}}
&
\underset{\textbf{ethyl esters}}{
\begin{array}{c}
O \\
\| \\
C_2H_5\!-\!O\!-\!C\!-\!R_1 \\
O \\
\| \\
C_2H_5\!-\!O\!-\!C\!-\!R_2 \\
O \\
\| \\
C_2H_5\!-\!O\!-\!C\!-\!R_3
\end{array}}
\end{array}
$$

**triglyceride**      **ethanol**      **glycerol**      **ethyl esters**

The reaction is reversible, so the alcohol must be added in excess to drive the reaction towards the right, according to Le Chatelier's principle, to ensure complete conversion. The heavier and more viscous glycerol settles out and may be purified for use in the pharmaceutical, cosmetic, or detergent industries.

The biodiesel produced is less viscous than the original oil as it is made up from smaller molecules which do not pack together so effectively, reducing the van der Waals' intermolecular forces. It is biodegradable, nontoxic, and has significantly fewer emissions when burned than crude oil-based diesel.

The oils used can either be grown specifically for the purpose, or waste oil from other sources which has been treated to remove impurities, such as free fatty acids, can be used. Blends of 20% biodiesel with 80% crude oil diesel can be used in unmodified diesel engines. Biodiesel can be used in its pure form but may require certain engine modifications to avoid maintenance and performance problems.

**44 (a)** Solar energy has been described as the ultimate energy source. Identify energy sources which derive from photosynthesis and other indirect sources.

  **(b)** Discuss the advantages and disadvantages of the use of biomass as a fuel.

**45 (a)** State the chemical equation for the photosynthesis of glucose.

  **(b)** Identify the molecule needed by plants to photosynthesize.

  **(c)** Identify the structural feature which allows this molecule to carry out this function.

  **(d)** Glucose can be converted to ethanol, which can be used as a fuel. State the name and equation of the process and describe the conditions needed.

**46 (a)** When biomass decomposes in the absence of oxygen, biogas is formed. Name the main gas present in biogas.

  **(b)** When wood and crop residues are burnt in a limited amount of oxygen, a mixture of gases known as producer gas is formed. Identify the two combustible gases present in producer gas.

  **(c)** When wood is burnt in an enclosed space the combustion produces harmful pollutants. Identify the pollutants.

  **(d)** Suggest why biomass is likely to become more important in the future as a fuel.

**47** One part of the Earth's surface receives $1.25 \times 10^6$ J of solar energy. Green plants such as algae absorb $1.25 \times 10^4$ J of this energy.

  **(a)** Determine the percentage of the sun's energy absorbed by green plants.

  **(b)** Suggest two reasons why the remainder of the Sun's energy is not absorbed by green plants.

  **(c)** Identify the process by which green plants use the Sun's energy to convert water and carbon dioxide into glucose and state the equation for the reaction.

  **(d)** State two forms of biomass which can be converted into energy.

**48** State some of the advantages of using biodiesel.

# C.5 Environmental impact: global warming

## Understandings:

- Greenhouse gases allow the passage of incoming solar short-wavelength radiation but absorb the longer-wavelength radiation from the Earth. Some of the absorbed radiation is re-radiated back to Earth.

### Guidance

*Greenhouse gases to be considered are $CH_4$, $H_2O$, and $CO_2$.*

- There is a heterogeneous equilibrium between the concentration of atmospheric carbon dioxide and aqueous carbon dioxide in the oceans.
- Greenhouse gases absorb IR radiation because there is a change in dipole moment as the bonds in the molecule stretch and bend.
- Particulates such as smoke and dust cause global dimming as they reflect sunlight, as do clouds.

## Applications and skills:

- Explanation of the molecular mechanisms by which greenhouse gases absorb IR radiation.
- Discussion of the evidence for the relationship between the increased concentration of gases and global warming.
- Discussion of the sources, relative abundance, and effects of different greenhouse gases.
- Discussion of the different approaches to the control of carbon dioxide emissions.
- Discussion of pH changes in the ocean due to increased concentration of carbon dioxide in the atmosphere.

## Greenhouse gases absorb long-wavelength IR radiation from the Earth

**Figure 14.17** The greenhouse effect is a process by which the Earth warms up. The surface of the Earth absorbs some solar radiation and re-radiates some at a longer (infrared, IR) wavelength which can be absorbed and re-radiated by gases such as carbon dioxide in the atmosphere.

The temperature of the Earth is maintained by a steady-state balance between the energy received from the Sun and the energy leaving the Earth and going back into space. Incoming solar radiation is in the visible and ultraviolet region. Some of this radiation is reflected back into space and some is absorbed by gases in the atmosphere. Most of the solar radiation passes through the atmosphere, however, and warms the surface of the Earth. The warm Earth surface then **radiates** some of this energy as **longer wavelength infrared** radiation which is **absorbed** by **greenhouse molecules** such as carbon dioxide and water vapour in the lower atmosphere. A covalent bond is like a spring in that it vibrates at a natural frequency. When infrared radiation has the same frequency as a covalent bond, the molecule absorbs the radiation and the bonds increase their vibrational energy. This makes the air warmer, causing it to radiate heat in turn. Some of this radiation is **re-radiated** back to the Earth's surface and some is re-radiated back into space (Figure 14.17). This natural process is called the **greenhouse effect** because the Sun's energy is absorbed in a way that is similar to the way light energy is trapped by the glass in a greenhouse. The glass lets light energy in but does not let heat energy out.

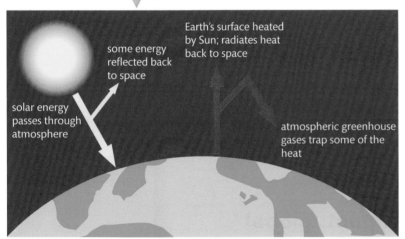

some energy reflected back to space

Earth's surface heated by Sun; radiates heat back to space

solar energy passes through atmosphere

atmospheric greenhouse gases trap some of the heat

## Greenhouse gases and their sources

Avoid using journalistic terms such as 'bounce off', 'trapped', or 'reflected' when talking about the greenhouse effect.

The greenhouse effect occurs naturally but there are concerns that human activities may be increasing its effect, leading to **global warming**. Water is the main greenhouse gas owing to its great abundance, but as it is produced from natural processes, its contribution to global warming is generally not considered. The level of carbon dioxide produced from burning fossil fuels has been increasing steadily over the last 150 years. Levels of carbon dioxide have been measured at Mauna Loa in Hawaii since the International Geophysical Year in 1957 (Figure 14.18).

The Mauna Loa Observatory monitors all atmospheric constituents that may contribute to climatic change, such as greenhouse gases and aerosols, and those which cause depletion of the ozone layer.

The increase in levels of carbon dioxide can be compared to changes in average global temperatures during the same period (Figure 14.19). It is estimated that carbon dioxide contributes about 50% to global warming.

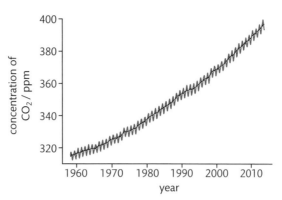

**Figure 14.18** Graph showing the rising concentration of atmospheric $CO_2$ between 1958 and 2012 measured 4170 m up on Mauna Loa, Hawaii. The graph reveals the steady rise of $CO_2$ levels in the atmosphere each year due to increasing fossil fuel consumption. The regular wobbles reflect seasonal plant growth in the spring and decay in the autumn in the northern hemisphere each year.

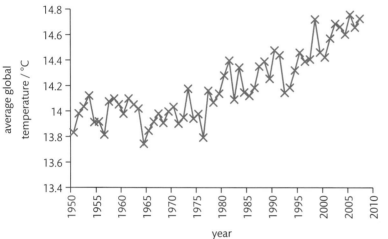

**Figure 14.19** Global average temperatures from 1950 to 2007.

Not all gases are equally effective at absorbing infrared radiation. The ability to absorb infrared radiation depends on the change in dipole moment that occurs as a molecule vibrates. Symmetric non-polar diatomic molecules such as $N_2$ and $O_2$ are not greenhouse gases as they do not absorb infrared radiation. The ability of a gas to absorb infrared is quantified by what is known as the **greenhouse factor**, which compares the ability of a substance to absorb infrared to carbon dioxide's ability to do so. Ten molecules of water, for example, have the same global warming effect as one molecule of carbon dioxide, while one molecule of methane has the same effect as 30 molecules of carbon dioxide.

| Gas | Main source | Greenhouse factor | Relative abundance / % | Overall contribution to increased global warming / % |
|---|---|---|---|---|
| water ($H_2O$) | evaporation of oceans and lakes | 0.1 | 0.10 | – |
| carbon dioxide ($CO_2$) | increased levels owing to combustion of fossil fuels and biomass | 1 | 0.036 | 50 |
| methane ($CH_4$) | anaerobic decay of organic matter; increased levels caused by intensive farming | 30 | 0.0017 | 18 |
| dinitrogen oxide ($N_2O$) | increased levels due to use of artificial fertilizers, needed for example in increased production of biomass | 160 | 0.0003 | 6 |

**NATURE OF SCIENCE**

The graph below demonstrates the correlation between carbon dioxide levels and temperature through the last glacial cycle. The upper curve shows $CO_2$ concentration in parts per million while the lower curve is a reconstruction of atmospheric temperature from measurements of the isotope deuterium. Both are plotted against age, measured in thousands of years before the present (BP), with the present at the far left.

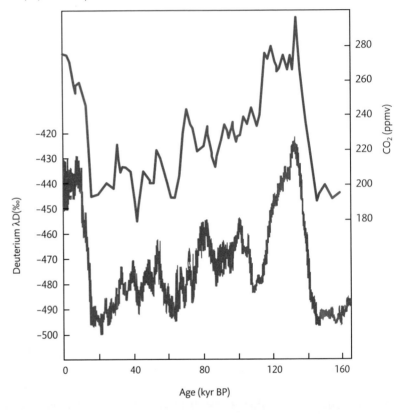

**Figure 14.20** The graph showing the correlation between carbon dioxide levels and temperature through the last glacial cycle.

The data are not enough to prove the causal link between $CO_2$ concentration and temperature. Both changes could be due to changes in a third variable.

The ideas of correlation and cause are very important in science. A correlation is a statistical link or association between one variable and another. A strong correlation (positive or negative) between one factor and another suggests some sort of causal relationship between the two factors but more evidence is usually required before scientists accept the idea of a causal relationship. To establish a causal relationship, scientists need to have a plausible scientific mechanism linking the factors. This has been proposed in the case of the greenhouse effect. Ideally, however, the relationship between the variables needs to be experimentally investigated with all other possible key variables being controlled. This is often impossible; levels of carbon dioxide cannot be added to the environment in such a controlled way and so we need to rely on computer models.

## Influence of increasing amounts of greenhouse gases on the atmosphere

There is now little doubt that since the 19th century the amount of carbon dioxide and other anthropogenic greenhouse gases in the atmosphere have increased dramatically and that the average temperature of the Earth has also increased, even if rather erratically. It has been suggested that levels of carbon dioxide will double in about 100 years. Allowing for the effect of all the gases, the temperature of the Earth could rise by 2 °C within 50 years. There are three likely effects resulting from this:

- changes in agriculture such as crop yields
- changes in biodistribution due to desertification and loss of cold water fish habitats
- rising sea levels because of thermal expansion and the melting of polar ice caps and glaciers.

## There is a heterogeneous equilibrium between atmospheric carbon dioxide and aqueous carbon dioxide in the oceans

About 50% of the carbon dioxide produced by the combustion of fossil fuels is absorbed by plants during photosynthesis or dissolved by the oceans. There is a heterogeneous equilibrium between concentrations of atmospheric carbon dioxide and aqueous carbon dioxide in the oceans.

$$CO_2(g) \rightleftharpoons CO_2(aq)$$

The carbon dioxide reacts with the water to form carbonic acid:

$$CO_2(aq) + H_2O(l) \rightleftharpoons H_2CO_3(aq)$$

The carbonic acid then reacts to form hydogencarbonates or carbonates:

$$H_2CO_3(aq) \rightleftharpoons H^+(aq) + HCO_3^-(aq)$$

$$HCO_3^-(aq) \rightleftharpoons H^+(aq) + CO_3^{2-}(aq)$$

This leads to higher ocean acidity, mainly near the surface, where the carbon dioxide is absorbed. This higher acidity inhibits shell growth in marine animals and is suspected to be a cause of reproductive disorders in some fish.

## Ocean acidification affects shell-forming animals

Over the past 300 million years, oceans have been slightly basic, with pH levels averaging about 8.2. Today, the pH has decreased to around 8.1. This drop of 0.1 represents a 25% increase in acidity. If the levels of carbon dioxide continue to increase, the pH of the oceans could fall further affecting shell-forming animals such as corals, oysters, shrimp, and lobster.

Since 1850, glaciers have been in retreat worldwide. It is thought that global warming has accelerated this trend in recent years.

## CHALLENGE YOURSELF

**12** Shell formation occurs mainly near the ocean's surface as the water at lower depths is colder and under more pressure. Explain this statement with reference to the relative solubility of calcium carbonate and calcium hydrogencarbonate.

### Exercises

**49 (a)** Suggest why the first measurements of $CO_2$ levels were taken at Mauna Loa in Hawaii and at the South Pole.
   **(b)** In 1959 the concentration of carbon dioxide was 316 ppm. In 2007 the reading was 384 ppm. Calculate the percentage increase in $CO_2$ levels between 1959 and 2007.
   **(c)** Identify the major source of the increased $CO_2$ during this period.
   **(d)** Explain the annual fluctuations in carbon dioxide levels.
   **(e)** Identify two different means by which $CO_2$ can be removed from the atmosphere naturally and give balanced equations for both of these.
   **(f)** Suggest how the depletion of tropical forests can lead to an increase in carbon dioxide levels.
   **(g)** Describe how $CO_2$ interacts with infrared radiation on the molecular level.

**50** Carbon dioxide is about 50 times more soluble in water than oxygen and about 100 times more soluble than nitrogen.

**(a)** Explain the relatively high solubility of carbon dioxide.

**(b)** Predict the sign of the enthalpy change of solution of carbon dioxide and deduce how its solubility changes with an increase in temperature.

**(c)** It has been suggested that the high levels of carbon dioxide could lead to a positive feedback process whereby increases in global temperatures are amplified and rise out of control. Suggest a possible mechanism for this positive feedback process.

**(d)** Suggest how the photosynthesis of phytoplankton could lead to a negative feedback process in which increases in temperature are reduced.

**51** The formation of sea shells can be described by the following reaction.

$$Ca^{2+}(aq) + CO_3^{2-}(aq) \rightarrow CaCO_3(s)$$

Explain how the formation of sea shells reduces atmospheric levels of carbon dioxide.

**52** Explain how a fall in pH from 8.2 to 8.1 represents a 25% increase in acidity.

## Global dimming

As we can see, the pattern in global temperatures is complicated. The fall in temperatures during the 1960s, for example, has been linked to the increase in particulates produced by volcanic activity during this period. Particulates can lower the temperature by scattering light so that less radiation reaches the Earth. This effect is called **global dimming** and first came to scientists' attention when pan evaporation rates were measured in the 1950s: less water than expected was evaporating from a full pan of water, suggesting the amount of solar radiation reaching the Earth was decreasing.

The incomplete combustion of coal, oil, and wood produces tiny airborne particles of soot, ash, sulfur compounds, and other pollutants which reflect sunlight back into space, preventing it reaching the earth's surface. The particles also act as nucleating agents for the formation of water droplets. Polluted clouds are more reflective than unpolluted clouds as they contain more water droplets. It is suggested that global dimming has limited the full effects of the global warming. A reduction in particulate pollution could lead to even larger global temperature increases than initially predicted.

**NATURE OF SCIENCE**

The factors affecting the temperature of the planet are very complex and interrelated. Scientists make mathematical models to predict the outcome of possible futures. The energy flow for the Earth and atmosphere is complicated, however. Computer simulations that model the climate of the Earth must take all factors into consideration. One concerned group, 'Climate prediction', have been doing calculations on thousands of computers in homes and schools all around the world to gain the power needed to run their computer model.

## Three strategies for reducing carbon dioxide levels

There are essentially three strategies for reducing carbon dioxide levels in the atmosphere.

| Strategy | Action |
|---|---|
| increased energy efficiency and conservation | • use of insulation and more efficient appliances<br>• reducing personal energy use by turning off lights and electronics when not in use<br>• reducing distance travelled in vehicles or using more efficient modes of transport such as hybrid cars or public transport |

| Strategy | Action |
|---|---|
| reduced dependence on carbon-based energy resources | • use alternative sources such as solar, wind, geothermal, hydropower, wave, tidal, or nuclear power <br> • use reduced-carbon fuels such as natural gas <br> • the potential use of biomass depends on the processes by which it is converted to energy |
| capture and storage of carbon from fossil fuels or from the atmosphere | • carbon dioxide can be removed from the atmosphere and stored within plants and soil, supporting the plants <br> • alternatively, carbon dioxide can be captured either before or after fossil fuel is burned and then be stored (sequestered) within the Earth <br> • reduce deforestation and plant more trees |

## NATURE OF SCIENCE

The study of global warming encompasses a broad range of concepts and ideas and is transdisciplinary. As well as collaborating on the exchange of results, scientists work on a daily basis in collaborative groups on a small and large scale within and between disciplines, laboratories, organizations, and countries, facilitated even more by virtual communication. The IPCC is officially composed of about 2500 scientists. They produce reports summarizing the work of many more scientists from all around the world. Some of their work has been controversial and aroused strong emotions amongst scientists and the public.

Some people question the reality of climate change and question the motives of scientists who have 'exaggerated' the problem. How do we assess the evidence collected and the models used to predict the impact of human activities? What effect does a highly sensitive political context have on objectivity? Can politicians exploit the ambiguity of conclusions coming from the scientific community for their own ends?

**TOK**

The first world climate conference in 1979 recognized the need for action against climate change. The Intergovernmental Panel on Climate Change (IPCC) was set up by the United Nations in 1988. Since then there have been a number of agreements and commitments for action. The 2007 Nobel Peace Prize was awarded to the IPCC and Al Gore (former Vice President of the United States, 1993–2001).

## Exercises

**53 (a)** Carbon dioxide contributes to the greenhouse effect. Identify one natural source of this gas.
  **(b)** Identify a second carbon-containing greenhouse gas and state its source.
  **(c)** Identify an air pollutant that counteracts the greenhouse effect and describe how it achieves this.
  **(d)** Using carbon dioxide as an example, explain how greenhouse gases contribute to global warming.
  **(e)** Describe the effects of global warming.

**54 (a)** Describe the greenhouse effect in terms of radiations of different wavelengths.
  **(b)** Water vapour acts as a greenhouse gas. State the main natural and artificial sources of water vapour in the atmosphere.
  **(c)** Discuss the relative contributions of carbon dioxide and methane to the greenhouse effect.

**55** Particulates are a type of primary air pollutant produced in several industries by the burning of fuels.

  **(a)** State one type of fuel that is very likely to produce particulates when burned.
  **(b)** Deduce the equation for a combustion reaction of methane in which particulates are formed.

When describing the greenhouse effect, do not base the whole of your answer only on rising sea levels and their causes. The effects on climate, agriculture, and biodiversity and so on should also be included.

# C.6 Electrochemistry, rechargeable batteries, and fuel cells

## Understandings:

• An electrochemical cell has internal resistance due to the finite time it takes for ions to diffuse. The maximum current of a cell is limited by its internal resistance.

### Guidance
*A battery should be considered as a portable electrochemical source made up of one or more voltaic (Galvanic) cells connected in series.*

- The voltage of a battery depends primarily on the nature of the materials used, while the total work that can be obtained from it depends on the quantity of the materials.
- In a primary cell the electrochemical reaction is not reversible. Rechargeable cells involve redox reactions that can be reversed using electricity.
- A fuel cell can be used to convert chemical energy, contained in a fuel that is consumed, directly to electrical energy.

**Guidance**

*Hydrogen and methanol should be considered as fuels for fuel cells. The operation of the cells under acidic and alkaline conditions should be considered. Students should be familiar with proton-exchange membranes (PEM) fuel cells.*

- Microbial fuel cells (MFCs) are a possible sustainable energy source using different carbohydrates or substrates present in wastewaters as the fuel.

**Guidance**

*The Geobacter species of bacteria, for example, can be used in some cells to oxidize ethanoate ions ($CH_3COO^-$) under anaerobic conditions.*

- The Nernst equation, $E = E^0 - \left(\dfrac{RT}{nF}\right) \ln Q$, can be used to calculate the potential of a half-cell in an electrochemical cell under non-standard conditions.

**Guidance**

*The Nernst equation is given in the data booklet in section 1.*

- The electrodes in a concentration cell are the same but the concentration of the electrolyte solutions at the cathode and anode are different.

## Applications and skills:

- Distinction between fuel cells and primary cells.
- Deduction of half-equations for the electrode reactions in a fuel cell.
- Comparison between fuel cells and rechargeable batteries.

**Guidance**

*The lead–acid storage battery, the nickel–cadmium (NiCad) battery, and the lithium-ion battery should be considered.*

- Discussion of the advantages of different types of cells in terms of size, mass, and voltage.
- Solution of problems using the Nernst equation.
- Calculation of the thermodynamic efficiency ($\Delta G/\Delta H$) of a fuel cell.
- Explanation of the workings of rechargeable and fuel cells including diagrams and relevant half-equations.

**Guidance**

*Students should be familiar with the anode and cathode half-equations and uses of the different cells.*

Some of the problems of burning our limited supplies of oil were discussed in sections C2 and C5. Crude oil is a valuable feedstock for the chemical industry while the combustion of hydrocarbons releases large quantities of the greenhouse gas carbon dioxide into the atmosphere. It is clear that one of the most important challenges for the chemist is to develop other, more environmentally friendly, sources of energy. Electrochemistry is an important field of technological development in this area as it could offer a cleaner way of producing energy. **Primary electrochemical cells**, in which the electrons transferred in a spontaneous redox reaction produce electricity, are discussed in Chapter 9 (page 432). They are a useful way to store and transport relatively small amounts of energy, but as they cannot be recharged their disposal can pose environmental problems.

## There is resistance in both the external circuit and the battery

As discussed in Chapter 4, a solid piece of metal, at room temperature, consists of a regular lattice of metal ions with the delocalized valence electrons moving in the spaces between them. The motion of the free electrons is random. When a battery is connected to the metal another motion is added to the random thermal motion of the electrons. This is more regular and results in a general 'drift' of electrons through the metal from the negative terminal of the power source to the positive terminal.

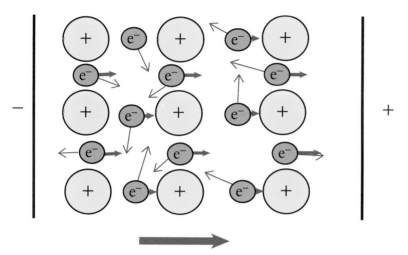

Figure 14.21 When a metal conducts electricity there is a general drift of electrons from the negative terminal of the power source to the positive terminal.

The resistance of a piece of metal is due to collisions between the delocalized electrons and the positive ions which 'get in the way' of the electrons and impede their movement through the metal.

Similarly, within a battery the current is carried by ions which experience some **internal resistance** as they pass between the terminals as it takes a finite time for them to diffuse in the electrolyte.

## Electric circuits

Consider the following circuit in which a cell is placed in a circuit with an external resistor $R$.

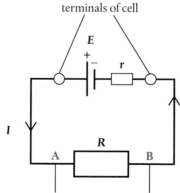

$V_{AB}$ = potential difference between A and B
= energy given out as each unit of charge passes between the two points A and B in the circuit

Figure 14.22 A cell of EMF $E$ is placed in a circuit with a external resistor $R$. The internal resistance of the cell is $r$.

The **potential difference** (V) or voltage between two points in a circuit is a measure of the energy given out as each unit of charge passes between the two points.

$$\text{potential difference } (V) = \frac{\text{energy } (E)}{\text{charge } (Q)}$$

831

**Current** is the rate of flow of electric charge.

$$\text{current } (I) = \frac{\text{charge } (Q)}{\text{time } (t)}$$

The **resistance** of a component in a circuit is the ratio of the potential difference across the component and the current passing through it.

$$\text{resistance } (R) = \frac{\text{potential difference } (V)}{\text{current } (I)}$$

The **electromotive force** (E) of a cell is a measure of the total energy made available by the chemical reactions in the cell per unit charge transferred. Not all this energy is available to the charge as it passes through the outside circuit because some energy is wasted due to **internal resistance** as the ions pass through the cell.

The terminal potential, $V$, is generally less than the electromotive force, $E$.

The voltage drop $(E - V)$ depends on the internal resistance, $r$.

• For the external circuit:

$$V = IR$$

• For the complete circuit, including the internal resistance of the cell:

$$E = I \times (R + r)$$

$$E = V + Ir$$

$$E - V = Ir$$

The maximum current will be delivered when the external resistance $R \approx 0$.

$$\frac{E}{R + r} = I$$

$$\frac{E}{r} \approx I_{max}$$

The maximum current of a cell is limited by its internal resistance.

A battery is made up of one or more voltaic cells, connected in series.

The maximum current of a cell is limited by its internal resistance.

The flow of electric current is often compared metaphorically to the flow of water and explained using a similar vocabulary. Are the terms 'current' and 'internal resistance' accurate descriptions of reality?

## The voltage of a battery depends primarily on the nature of the electrodes and the electrolytes

We have seen that a voltaic cell generates an **electromotive force (E)** as electrons flow from the half-cell with the more negative potential to the half-cell with the more positive potential. The magnitude of this voltage depends on the *difference* in the tendencies of these two half-cells to undergo reduction. Standard cell potentials can be calculated from the reduction potentials in section 24 of the IB data booklet.

The reaction quotient (Q) is a measure of the relative concentrations of products and reactants present during a reaction at a particular point in time. Q is the equilibrium expression with non-equilibrium concentrations.

## The Nernst equation can be used to calculate the potential of a half-cell under non-standard conditions

To understand how the voltage depends on the composition of the electrolyte it is useful to consider how the Gibbs free energy changes with the **reaction quotient**. The reaction quotient (Q) is a measure of the relative concentrations of products and reactants present during a reaction at a particular point in time. Q is the equilibrium expression with non-equilibrium concentrations.

In Chapter 6 (page 341) we saw that the Gibbs free energy change of a reaction and the equilibrium constant are related by the equation:

$$\Delta G = -RT \ln K$$

where $R$ is the molar gas constant, $T$ is the temperature in K, and $\Delta G^{\ominus}$ is the difference in free energy change assuming that *all* the reactants are converted into products in their standard states.

To form an expression for $\Delta G$ at other compositions consider the following graph which shows how the Gibbs free energy changes with composition. As the reaction proceeds from reactant to products the Gibbs free energy falls to a minimum. This is the position of equilibrium. The same position is reached if the reaction proceeds in the opposite direction, starting from the products.

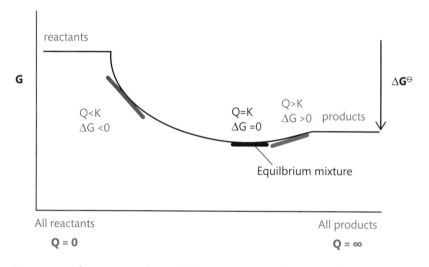

- $Q = 0$ corresponds to no reaction and $Q = \infty$ corresponds to complete reaction.
- When $Q$ is smaller than the equilibrium constant further reaction is possible and $\Delta G < 0$. The reaction can continue with a decrease in free energy. The slope of the red line is negative.
- When $Q$ is larger than the equilibrium constant further reaction is not possible and $\Delta G > 0$. The slope of the blue line is positive.
- At equilibrium $Q = K$. The slope of the black line is zero and $\Delta G = 0$.

The equation which describes this behaviour more precisely is:

$$\Delta G = -RT \ln K + RT \ln Q = -RT \ln \frac{K}{Q}$$

$\Delta G = \Delta G^{\ominus} + RT \ln Q$

We saw in Chapter 9 (page 445) that the electrode potential $E$ is related to Gibbs free energy by the relation:

$\Delta G^{\ominus} = -nFE^{\ominus}$

where $n$ is the number of electrons involved in the reaction and $F$ is the charge of one mole of electrons.

More generally we can include non-standard conditions:

**Figure 14.23** The Gibbs free energy is at a minimum at equilibrium.

You would not be expected to derive the equations used in this section.

$\Delta G = -nFE$

$-nFE = -nFE^{\ominus} + RT \ln Q$

$E = E^{\ominus} - RT/nF \ln Q$

Under standard conditions the concentrations of all the ions = $1.00 \text{ mol dm}^{-3}$, $Q = 1$, and $E = E^{\ominus}$ as we would expect.

This is called the **Nernst equation** and is given in section 1 of the IB data booklet.

We can see from this equation that the voltage of a cell depends on:

• the nature of the half cells, $E^{\ominus}$

• the temperature $T$ of the solutions

• the concentration of the ions in solution, $Q$.

### Worked example

Consider the copper/zinc voltaic cell, $Zn\|Zn^{2+} \frown Cu^{2+}(aq)\|Cu(s)$, discussed on page 432. The cathode reaction is:

$$Cu^{2+}(aq) + 2e^- \rightleftharpoons Cu(s)$$

and the anode reaction is:

$$Zn(s) \rightleftharpoons Zn^{2+}(aq) + 2e^-$$

Calculate the cell potential when $[Zn^{2+}(aq)]$ is $0.0100 \text{ mol dm}^{-3}$ and $[Cu^{2+}(aq)] = 0.100 \text{ mol dm}^{-3}$ with a temperature of 25 °C.

**Solution**

The cell reaction is:

$$Zn(s) + Cu^{2+}(aq) \rightleftharpoons Zn^{2+}(aq) + Cu(s)$$

$$Q = \frac{[Zn^{2+}(aq)]}{[Cu^{2+}(aq)]} = \frac{0.0100}{0.100} = 0.100$$

We do not need to consider the concentration of the solids from the equation as they remain constant during the reaction. The amount and volume of the electrodes change proportionally.

$$E^{\ominus} = +0.34 - -0.76 = 1.10 \text{ V}$$

$E = E^{\ominus} - RT/nF \ln Q$

$$= 1.10 - \frac{8.31 \times 298}{2 \times 9.65 \times 10^4} \times \ln 0.100$$

$$= 1.13 \text{ V}$$

## The electrodes in a concentration cell are the same

The electrodes in a concentration cell are the same but the concentration of the electrolyte solutions at the electrodes are different. A **concentration cell** is a voltaic cell where the two half-cells are made of the same materials but differ in the concentration of the electrolyte.

Consider the voltaic cell made up from two $Cu^{2+}(aq)/Cu$ half-cells made from two copper sulfate solutions of different concentrations.

Calculate the cell potential when $[Cu^{2+}(aq)]$ is $0.00100$ mol dm$^{-3}$ and $[Cu^{2+}(aq)] = 0.100$ mol dm$^{-3}$ at a temperature of $25\,°C$.

**Solution**

According to Le Chatelier's principle, the reduction is more likely to occur at higher $[Cu^{2+}(aq)]$ and oxidation at lower $[Cu^{2+}(aq)]$:

• cathode reaction:

$$Cu^{2+}(aq) + 2e^- \rightleftharpoons Cu(s)$$

$[Cu^{2+}(aq)]_{cathode} = 0.100$ mol dm$^{-3}$

• anode reaction:

$$Cu(s) \rightleftharpoons Cu^{2+}(aq) + 2e^-$$

$[Cu^{2+}(aq)]_{anode} = 0.00100$ mol dm$^{-3}$

• cell reaction:

$$Cu(s) + Cu^{2+}(aq) \rightleftharpoons Cu^{2+}(aq) + Cu(s)$$
$$\phantom{Cu(s) + Cu^{2+}}0.100 \phantom{(aq) \rightleftharpoons } 0.00100$$

$$Q = \frac{[Cu^{2+}(aq)]_{anode}}{[Cu^{2+}(aq)]_{cathode}} = \frac{0.00100}{0.100} = 0.0100$$

$$E^{\ominus} = 0\ V$$

$$E = E^{\ominus} - RT/nF\ lnQ$$
$$= 0 - \frac{8.31 \times 298}{2 \times 9.65 \times 10^4} \times \ln 0.0100$$
$$= +0.0285\ V$$

The worked example can be generalized to give the following equation:

$$E = -(RT/nF)\ lnQ = E = -(RT/nF)\ ln\left(\frac{[M^{n+}]_{anode}}{[M^{n+}]_{cathode}}\right)$$
$$E = RT/nF\ ln\left(\frac{[M^{n+}]_{cathode}}{[M^{n+}]_{anode}}\right)$$

A positive potential will be produced if the concentration of the ions is higher in the cathode half-cell. According to Le Chatelier's principle the reduction half-cell is more likely to move to the right at higher $[M^{n+}]_{cathode}$.

# The total work that can be obtained from a cell depends on the quantity of materials used

An exothermic reaction produces heat $(-\Delta H_{sys})$. Some of this heat can be used for useful work, but some $(q)$ is needed, however, to ensure that the total entropy of the universe increases despite any local decrease $(-\Delta S_{sys})$ in the entropy of the system.

$$\frac{q}{T} = -\Delta S_{sys}$$
$$q = -T\Delta S_{sys}$$

total energy available as heat = $(-\Delta H_{sys})$

heat wasted to ensure that $\Delta S_{total} > 0$ is $q = -T\Delta S_{sys}$

free energy available to do useful work = $-\Delta H_{sys} - q$

$$= -\Delta H_{sys} + T\Delta S_{sys}$$

$$= -\Delta G_{sys}$$

The Gibbs free energy of a reaction is a measure of the energy available to do useful work.

This is the origin of the term *free* energy – it is the energy free to do useful work.

For one mole of reaction:

$$\Delta G = -nFE$$

where $n$ is the amount of electrons that is transferred during one mole of reaction.

The amount of energy available increases with the number of electron transferred. The total work that can be obtained from a cell depends on the quantity of the materials used.

We also know that power $= \dfrac{\text{work}}{\text{time}} = \dfrac{\text{voltage} \times \text{charge}}{\text{time}} = VI$

Larger batteries deliver more power as they deliver more charge per unit time. Increasing the size of the electrodes, for example, decreases the internal resistance. This increases the power delivered as the current is increased.

### Exercises

**56** Determine the potential of the following cells at 25 °C.

**(a)** $Zn|Zn^{2+}(aq, 0.100 \text{ mol dm}^{-3})\|Ni^{2+}(aq, 0.00100 \text{ mol dm}^{-3})|Ni(s)$
**(b)** $Mn|Mn^{2+}(aq, 0.100 \text{ mol dm}^{-3})\|Pb^{2+}(aq, 0.000100 \text{ mol dm}^{-3})|Pb(s)$
**(c)** $Zn|Zn^{2+}(aq, 1.50 \text{ mol dm}^{-3})\|Fe^{2+}(aq, 0.100 \text{ mol dm}^{-3})|Fe(s)$

**57** Consider the cell $Zn|Zn^{2+}(aq)\|Pb^{2+}(aq)|Pb(s)$

The cell has a potential of 0.60 V when the $[Pb^{2+}(aq)] = 0.100 \text{ mol dm}^{-3}$

**(a)** Determine the concentration of the $Zn^{2+}$ ions.
**(b)** Suggest how the concentrations could be altered to increase the voltage to 0.65 V.
**(c)** Suggest how the potential of the cell in part (a) could be decreased without changing the concentrations.

**58** A concentration cell is made from two $Zn|Zn^{2+}(aq)$ electrodes.

Solution A has a $Zn^{2+}$ concentration of 0.110 mol dm$^{-3}$

Solution B has a $Zn^{2+}$ concentration of 0.220 mol dm$^{-3}$

**(a)** Identify which solution should be used at the cathode (positive electrode) to produce a positive voltage.
**(b)** Calculate the voltage of the cell.

## Secondary cells can be recharged and so have longer life times than primary cells

We have so far discussed **primary cells** where the electrochemical reaction is irreversible. The cell reactions involve the production of aqueous ions or gas molecules which become dispersed during the reaction. In this section we will discuss **secondary cells**. These can be recharged and so have a longer life than primary cells. Rechargeable batteries are expensive to buy at first but they become more economical with use.

A primary cell/battery is one that cannot be recharged. A secondary cell/battery is one that can be recharged.

## Lead–acid battery is used for heavy power applications

The lead–acid battery is used for heavy power applications as, due to the quantity of materials used, it can deliver a high current for short periods of time. This is just what is needed to start an internal combustion engine. The lead–acid battery relies on the ability of lead to exist in two oxidation states, +2 and +4, and the insolubility of lead(II) sulfate, $PbSO_4$. Both the electrodes are made from lead, but the negative electrodes are additionally filled with a paste of lead(IV) oxide. The electrolyte is sulfuric acid. As each cell produces a voltage of 2 V, a battery of six cells is needed to produce the 12 V needed in a car engine. The high density of lead limits the uses of the battery.

### Discharging a lead–acid battery

• Half-reaction at the negative electrode – lead is oxidized to lead(II) sulfate:
$$Pb(s) + SO_4^{2-}(aq) \rightarrow PbSO_4(s) + 2e^-$$

• Half-reaction at the positive electrode – lead(IV) oxide is reduced to lead(II) sulfate
$$PbO_2(s) + 4H^+(aq) + SO_4^{2-}(aq) + 2e^- \rightarrow PbSO_4(s) + 2H_2O(l)$$

Adding the two half-reactions gives the complete reaction for the discharge of the cell:
$$Pb(s) + 2H_2SO_4(aq) + PbO_2(s) \rightarrow 2PbSO_4(s) + 2H_2O(l)$$

Note the sulfuric acid is used up during the discharge process.

### Charging a lead–acid battery

As the lead(II) sulfate produced in the discharging process is insoluble, it is not dispersed into the electrolyte and the process can be reversed. When the lead(II) sulfate on the two electrodes is connected to a d.c. supply, electrolysis occurs and one electrode is oxidized back to lead(IV) oxide while the other is reduced to lead.

• Reduction half-reaction:
$$PbSO_4(s) + 2e^- \rightarrow Pb(s) + SO_4^{2-}(aq)$$

• Oxidation half-reaction:
$$PbSO_4(s) + 2H_2O(l) \rightarrow PbO_2(s) + 4H^+(aq) + SO_4^{2-}(aq) + 2e^-$$

During the charging process, especially of older batteries, some water may be lost. The lead–acid battery needs to be topped up with water at intervals to make up for this loss. This provides a convenient method for testing the state of a battery, as the density decreases as the acid is used up.

## Nickel–cadmium batteries

Rechargeable nickel–cadmium batteries are used in electronics and toys. When the battery is discharged, the positive electrode is nickel hydroxide and the negative electrode is cadmium hydroxide. The electrolyte is aqueous potassium hydroxide.

During the charging process the cadmium(II) hydroxide is reduced to the element and nickel(II) hydroxide is oxidized to $Ni^{3+}$ in the form of $NiO(OH)$.

### Charging a nickel–cadmium battery

• Reduction half-reaction:
$$Cd(OH)_2(s) + 2e^- \rightarrow Cd(s) + 2OH^-(aq)$$

Electricity is used in motor vehicles to provide the initial power to start the engine. Once the engine is running, the power from the engine is used to recharge the battery.

• Oxidation half-reaction:

$$Ni(OH)_2(s) + OH^-(aq) \rightarrow NiO(OH)(s) + H_2O(l) + e^-$$

## Discharging a nickel–cadmium battery

The reverse reactions occur when it is discharged. The discharge process can be summarized by the equation:

$$2NiO(OH)(s) + Cd(s) + 2H_2O(l) \rightarrow 2Ni(OH)_2(s) + Cd(OH)_2(s)$$

This reaction can be reversed as both metal hydroxides are insoluble.

These batteries have a **discharge memory**. If their normal cycle of use involves short periods of discharge followed by periods of recharge, they can be discharged for longer periods.

Nickel cadmium batteries must be disposed of responsibly as cadmium is a toxic metal.

Different countries have different recycling programmes but heavy metal pollution is an international problem. Batteries that are not recycled and end up in landfills can leak toxic materials into the environment.

**NATURE OF SCIENCE**

The use of heavy metals such as lead and cadmium pose an environmental problem as the metals are poisonous. High cadmium levels can lead, for example, to depressed growth, kidney damage, fetal deformity, and cancer. The power of scientific knowledge and technology to transform societies is unparalleled. It has the potential to produce great universal benefits but can cause harm to people and the environment. Risk assessment and the precautionary principle are all parts of the scientific way of addressing the common good.

## The lithium-ion battery

One of the most promising new reusable batteries is the lithium-ion battery, which benefits from lithium's low density and high reactivity (Figure 14.24). It can store a lot of electrical energy per unit mass. As lithium metal is reactive steps must be taken to prevent it from forming an oxide layer which would decrease contact with the electrolyte. At the cathode it is placed in the lattice of a metal oxide ($MnO_2$), and at the anode it is mixed with graphite. A non-aqueous polymer-based electrolyte is used.

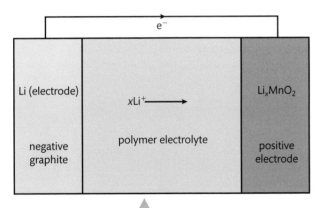

**Figure 14.24** The lithium-ion battery.

## Discharging a lithium-ion battery

• Negative electrode – lithium is oxidized:

$$Li \rightarrow Li^+(polymer) + e^-$$

• Positive electrode – assuming Li is present as $Li^+$, it is the Mn which is reduced:

$$Li^+(polymer) + MnO_2(s) + e^- \rightarrow LiMnO_2(s)$$

The two half-reactions are reversed when the battery is recharged.

Lithium-ion batteries are used in cell (mobile) phones, lap-top computers, and cameras.

### Worked example

Assuming Li has an oxidation number of +1, deduce the oxidation number of Mn in the mixed oxide $LiMnO_2$ and hence show that the Mn has been reduced in the half-reaction:

$$Li^+(polymer) + MnO_2(s) + e^- \rightarrow LiMnO_2(s)$$

## Solution

The oxidation number of Li = +1 and of O = –2.

For the mixed oxide $LiMnO_2$: $+1 + Ox\ (Mn) + 2(-2) = O$

therefore oxidation state of Mn = +3

The oxidation number of Mn has been decreased from +4 in $MnO_2$ to +3. A decrease in oxidation number is reduction.

## The hydrogen fuel cell

Hydrogen is a possible alternative fuel to hydrocarbons. It could reduce our dependence on fossil fuels and reduce the amount of carbon dioxide released into the atmosphere. One mole of hydrogen can release 286 kJ of heat energy when it combines directly with oxygen:

$$H_2(g) + \tfrac{1}{2}O_2(g) \rightarrow H_2O(l) \qquad \Delta H^\ominus = -286 \text{ kJ mol}^{-1}$$

As this is a redox reaction that involves the transfer of electrons from hydrogen to oxygen, it can be used to produce an electric current if the reactants are physically separated. This is the basis of a **fuel cell**, where the reactants are continuously supplied to the electrodes. The hydrogen–oxygen fuel cell operates with either an acidic or alkaline electrolyte.

> **TOK** Are oxidation numbers 'real' or are they artificial constructs invented by the chemist?

### The hydrogen–oxygen fuel cell with an alkaline electrolyte

The hydrogen–oxygen fuel cell most commonly has an alkaline electrolyte (Figure 14.25).

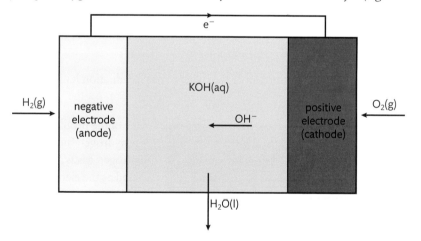

**Figure 14.25** The hydrogen–oxygen fuel cell with an alkaline electrolyte.

- Half-reaction at the negative electrode (anode) – $H_2(g)$ is oxidized at the anode:

$$2H_2(g) + 4OH^-(aq) \rightarrow 4H_2O(l) + 4e^-$$

- Half-reaction at the positive electrode (cathode) – $O_2(g)$ is reduced at the cathode:

$$2H_2O(l) + O_2(g) + 4e^- \rightarrow 4OH^-(aq)$$

The overall reaction is the sum of the oxidation and reduction half-reactions:

$$2H_2(g) + \cancel{4OH^-(aq)} + 2H_2O(l) + O_2(g) + \cancel{4e^-} \rightarrow 4H_2O(l) + \cancel{4e^-} + \cancel{4OH^-(aq)}$$

$$2H_2(g) + O_2(g) \rightarrow 2H_2O(l)$$

The fuel cell will function as long as hydrogen and oxygen are supplied. The electrodes are often made of porous carbon with added transition metals such as nickel. The potassium hydroxide provides the hydroxide ions that are transferred across the cell.

## The hydrogen–oxygen fuel cell with an acidic electrolyte

The hydrogen–oxygen fuel cell can also function in acidic solution (Figure 14.26). The **proton exchange membrane** fuel cell has a membrane usually made from the strong and durable plastic (Teflon) which allows $H^+$ ions to move from the anode to the cathode. Both electrodes are coated with tiny particles of platinum to catalyse the reaction.

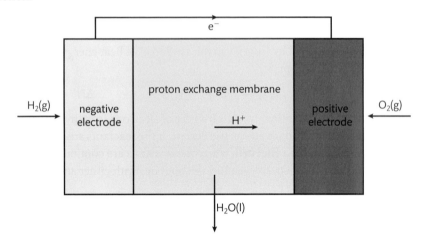

**Figure 14.26** The hydrogen–oxygen fuel cell with an acidic electrolyte.

• Half-reaction at the negative electrode (anode) – $H_2(g)$ is oxidized at the anode:
$$2H_2(g) \rightarrow 4H^+(aq) + 4e^-$$
• Half-reaction at the positive electrode (cathode) – $O_2(g)$ is reduced at the cathode:
$$4H^+(aq) + O_2(g) + 4e^- \rightarrow 4H_2O(l)$$

Again the overall reaction is the sum of the oxidation and reduction half-reactions:
$$2H_2(g) + O_2(g) \rightarrow 2H_2O(l)$$

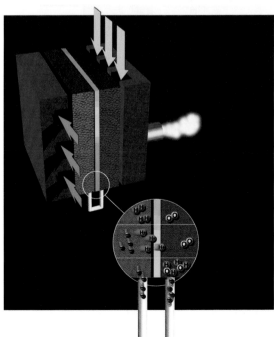

The hydrogen fuel cell is a clean and efficient power source. Hydrogen is pumped into the cell (blue arrows), where the hydrogen nuclei (blue, inset) are separated from their electrons (yellow, inset). The electrons flow around a conducting loop (beige) as an electric current which can be harnessed. The hydrogen nuclei pass through a membrane (yellow, inset) and combine with the electrons and oxygen from the air (pale blue arrows) to form steam (white).

One of the problems with the hydrogen fuel cell is that hydrogen gas is almost never found as the element in nature and has to be extracted from other sources. Hydrocarbons, including fossil fuels and biomass (waste organic matter) for example, can be processed to break down into hydrogen and carbon dioxide. The alternative is to electrolyse water. For the whole process to be environmentally clean, the hydrogen should be generated using renewable resources such as wind power.

## Methanol is oxidized using catalysts in the methanol fuel cell

Methanol is an alternative fuel used in a fuel cell. Methanol is a stable liquid at normal environmental conditions, has a high energy density, and is easy to transport. As the efficiency of methanol fuel cells is quite low they are used in cases where energy and power density are more important factors.

In the direct methanol fuel cell (DMFC), the fuel is oxidized under acidic conditions on a catalyst layer to form carbon dioxide. The $H^+$ ions formed are transported across a proton exchange membrane from the anode to the cathode where they react with oxygen to produce water and electrons are transported through an external circuit from anode to cathode. Water is consumed at the anode and is produced at the cathode.

- Half-reaction at the negative electrode (anode) – methanol reacts with $H_2O(l)$, the carbon is oxidized from −2 to +4, and six electrons are produced:
$$CH_3OH(g) + H_2O(l) \rightarrow CO_2(g) + 6H^+(aq) + 6e^-$$
- Half-reaction at the positive electrode (cathode) – $O_2(g)$ is reduced at the cathode, the six electrons available will reduce three Os reduced from 0 to −2:
$$6H^+(aq) + \tfrac{3}{2}O_2(g) + 6e^- \rightarrow 3H_2O(l)$$

Adding the equations for the two half-reactions we obtain the overall equation:

$$CH_3OH(g) + H_2O(l) \rightarrow CO_2(g) + 6H^+(aq) + 6e^-$$
$$6H^+(aq) + \tfrac{3}{2}O_2(g) + 6e^- \rightarrow 3H_2O(l)$$
$$CH_3OH(g) + \tfrac{3}{2}O_2(g) \rightarrow CO_2(g) + 2H_2O(l)$$

## Biomass is oxidized by bacteria in the microbial fuel cell (MFC)

**Microbial fuel cells** (MFC) may one day offer a cheap and renewable source of energy. They can be used to harness the energy produced from the microbial oxidation of a huge range of organic substances. Bacteria are very small organisms which oxidize many organic compounds into $CO_2$ and $H_2O$ with the production of energy. Some of this energy is needed by the organisms to grow and maintain their metabolism, but the rest can be harvested and used to generate electricity.

The bacteria live in the anode and convert the organic biomass under anaerobic conditions into carbon dioxide with the production of $H^+$ ions and electrons. The bacteria transfer the released electrons to an insoluble electron acceptor which acts as the anode and the electrons then flow through an electrical circuit to the cathode where they reduce oxygen. The protons flow through the proton exchange membrane to the cathode.

- Half-reaction at the negative electrode (anode) – glucose is oxidized by the bacteria, six Cs are oxidized from 0 to +4, so twenty-four electrons are released:
$$C_6H_{12}O_6(aq) + 6H_2O(l) \rightarrow 6CO_2(g) + 24H^+(aq) + 24e^-$$
- Half-reaction at the positive electrode (cathode) – $O_2(g)$ is reduced at the cathode, the 24 electrons available will reduce 12 Os from 0 to −2:
$$24H^+(aq) + 6O_2(g) + 24e^- \rightarrow 12H_2O(l)$$

The overall equation is that of aerobic respiration:

$$C_6H_{12}O_6 + 6H_2O \rightarrow 6CO_2(g) + 24H^+(aq) + 24e^-$$
$$24H^+(aq) + 6O_2(g) + 24e^- \rightarrow 12H_2O(l)$$
$$C_6H_{12}O_6 + 6O_2(g) \rightarrow 6CO_2(g) + 6H_2O(l)$$

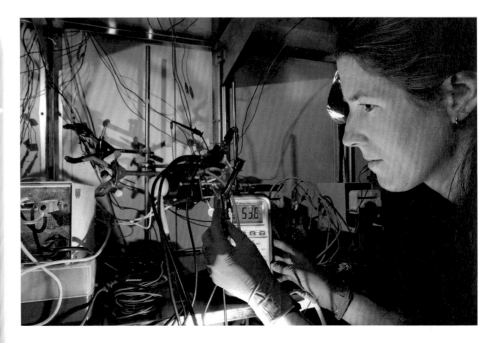

Researcher testing the electrical output of a microbial fuel cell. This fuel cell (centre) comprises a chamber filled with an organic solution and Geobacter bacteria. Within the fuel cell are small electrodes. The bacteria colonize the anode electrode and oxidize the organic compounds. The reaction allows the bacteria to transfer electrons directly to the anode – the electrons then flow to the cathode electrode, generating electricity.

The substrates used in MFCs range from carbohydrates, volatile fatty acids, and alcohols to amino acids and proteins. One issue with these compounds, however, is that they can undergo alternative microbial reactions. The ethanoate ion is commonly used, however, as it does not undergo these side reactions and is only oxidized by the Geobacter species of bacteria under anaerobic conditions.

The Geobacter bacteria produce current densities in microbial fuel cells that are higher than any known organism.

The half-cell reactions with ethanoic acid are as follows.

• Half-reaction at the negative electrode (anode) – ethanoic acid is oxidized by the bacteria, two Cs are oxidized from 0 to + 4 so eight electrons are produced:
$$CH_3COOH(aq) + 2H_2O(l) \rightarrow 2CO_2(g) + 8H^+(aq) + 8e^-$$
• Half-reaction at the positive electrode (cathode) – $O_2(g)$ is reduced at the cathode, the eight electrons available will reduce four Os from 0 to −2:
$$8H^+(aq) + 2O_2(g) + 8e^- \rightarrow 4H_2O(l)$$

The overall equation is:
$$CH_3COOH(aq) + 2O_2(g) \rightarrow 2CO_2(g) + 2H_2O(l)$$

It is not feasible at the moment to power full scale MFCs with pure substrates from an economic point of view. The use of second generation biofuels or organic waste streams is highly promising because it combines the treatment of the waste with the generation of energy.

Microbial fuel cells offer many potential advantages over hydrogen fuel cells. For example, hydrogen fuel cells require a very pure source of a highly explosive gas that is difficult to store and distribute. Furthermore, hydrogen is generally derived mainly from fossil fuel rather than renewable sources. In contrast, the energy sources for microbial fuel cells are renewable organics, including some that are, literally, 'dirt cheap'.

## Thermodynamic efficiency of a cell

$$\text{efficiency} = \frac{\text{useful output energy}}{\text{total input energy}} \times 100$$

$$\text{maximum efficiency} = \frac{-\Delta G_{sys}}{-\Delta H_{sys}} \times 100\%$$

$$\text{maximum efficiency} = \frac{-\Delta G_{sys}}{-\Delta H_{sys}} \times 100\%$$

The maximum efficiency is also called the **thermodynamic efficiency** of a cell.

For the hydrogen–oxygen fuel cell, when water is produced as a liquid the net reaction is:

$$H_2(g) + \tfrac{1}{2}O_2(g) \rightarrow H_2O(l)$$

$\Delta H_f^{\ominus}$ (kJ mol$^{-1}$) = $-285.8$ kJ mol$^{-1}$
$\Delta G_f^{\ominus}$ (kJ mol$^{-1}$) = $-237.1$ kJ mol$^{-1}$

$$\text{efficiency} = \frac{237.1}{285.8} \times 100\% = 82.96\%$$

When water is produced as gas the reaction is:

$$H_2(g) + \tfrac{1}{2}O_2(g) \rightarrow H_2O(g)$$

$\Delta H_f^{\ominus}$ (kJ mol$^{-1}$) = $-241.8$ kJ mol$^{-1}$
$\Delta G_f^{\ominus}$ (kJ mol$^{-1}$) = $-228.6$ kJ mol$^{-1}$

$$\text{efficiency} = \frac{228.6}{241.8} \times 100\% = 94.54\%$$

.........................................
## CHALLENGE YOURSELF

**13** Explain the increased efficiency of a hydrogen–oxygen fuel cell which produces steam compared to water.
.........................................

## Similarities and differences between fuel cells and rechargeable batteries

In a fuel cell, the fuel is supplied continuously whereas in rechargeable batteries the energy is stored inside the batteries. Some advantages and disadvantages of the different systems are summarized below.

| Fuel cell/battery | Advantages | Disadvantages |
|---|---|---|
| fuel cell | • more efficient than direct combustion as more chemical energy is converted to useful energy <br> • no pollution <br> • low density | • hydrogen is a potentially explosive gas <br> • hydrogen must be stored and transported in large/ heavy containers <br> • very expensive; technical problems due to catalytic failures, leaks, and corrosion |
| lead–acid | • can deliver large amounts of energy over short periods | • heavy mass <br> • lead and sulfuric acid could cause pollution |
| cadmium nickel | • longer life than lead–acid batteries | • cadmium is very toxic <br> • produces a low voltage <br> • very expensive |
| lithium ion | • low density <br> • high voltage <br> • does not contain a toxic heavy metal | • expensive <br> • limited life span |

## Exercises

**59** **(a)** Determine $\Delta G_{reaction}$ for the complete combustion of methanol, using data in section 12 of the IB data booklet.

**(b)** Calculate the thermodynamic efficiency of a methanol fuel cell.

**60** The reaction taking place when a lead–acid storage battery discharges is:

$$Pb(s) + PbO_2(s) + 2H_2SO_4(aq) \rightarrow 2PbSO_4(s) + 2H_2O(l)$$

**(a)** Use oxidation numbers to explain what happens to the Pb(s) in terms of oxidation and reduction during this reaction.

**(b)** Write a balanced half-equation for the reactions taking place at the negative terminal during this discharge process.

**(c)** Identify the property of $PbSO_4$ which allows this process to be reversed.

**(d)** State one advantage and one disadvantage of using a lead–acid battery.

**61** Sucrose, $C_{12}H_{22}O_{11}$, has been used as substrate for a microbial fuel cell.

**(a)** Identify the electrode where the bacteria live and explain your choice.

**(b)** Use the changes of oxidation number of carbon atoms to deduce the half-reaction at the negative electrode.

**(c)** Use the changes of oxidation number of oxygen atoms to deduce the half-reaction at the positive electrode.

**(d)** Deduce the overall reaction that occurs with sucrose as a substrate.

**62** One type of fuel cell uses hydrogen as the fuel with hot aqueous potassium hydroxide as the electrolyte. The overall equation for the process is:

$$2H_2 + O_2 \rightarrow 2H_2O$$

**(a)** State the two half-equations for the reactions involving each reactant.

**(b)** Hydrogen is a more expensive source of chemical energy than gasoline. Explain why fuel cells are considered to be more economical than gasoline engines.

# C.8 Photovoltaic and dye-sensitized solar cells (DSSC)

## Understandings:

- Molecules with longer conjugated systems absorb light of longer wavelength.
- The electrical conductivity of a semiconductor increases with an increase in temperature whereas the conductivity of metals decreases.

### Guidance
*The relative conductivity of metals and semiconductors should be related to ionization energies.*

- The conductivity of silicon can be increased by doping to produce n-type and p-type semiconductors.

### Guidance
*Only a simple treatment of the operation of the cells is needed. In p-type semiconductors, electron holes in the crystal are created by introducing a small percentage of a Group 13 element. In n-type semiconductors inclusion of a Group 15 element provides extra electrons.*

- Solar energy can be converted to electricity in a photovoltaic cell.

### Guidance
*In a photovoltaic cell the light is absorbed and the charges separated in the silicon semiconductor.*

- DSSCs imitate the way in which plants harness solar energy. Electrons are 'injected' from an excited molecule directly into the $TiO_2$ semiconductor.

### Guidance
- *The processes of absorption and charge separation are separated in a dye-sensitized solar cell.*
- *Specific redox and electrode reactions in the Gratzel DSSC should be covered. An example is the reduction of $I_2/I_3^-$ ions to $I^-$.*

- The use of nanoparticles coated with light-absorbing dye increases the effective surface area and allows more light over a wider range of the visible spectrum to be absorbed.

## Applications and skills:

- Relation between the degree of conjugation in the molecular structure to the wavelength of the light absorbed.
- Explanation of the operation of the photovoltaic and dye-sensitized solar cell.
- Explanation of how nanoparticles increase the efficiency of DSSCs.
- Discussion of the advantages of the DSSC compared to the silicon-based photovoltaic cell.

We saw in Chapter 3 that silicon has some properties intermediate between the metals and non-metals. This is perhaps most significantly illustrated by its electrical conductivity. Silicon is a **semiconductor** and the main element in the electronics industry.

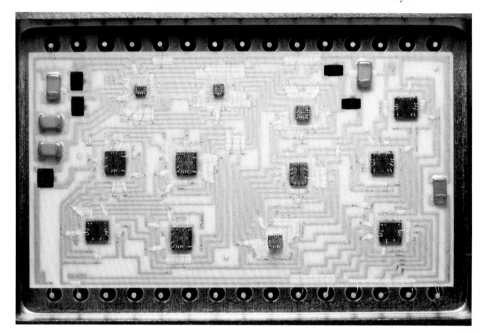

Macrophotograph of an integrated circuit or silicon chip.

## Silicon is a semiconductor

Metals are good electrical conductors because they have delocalized electrons that can move freely between the positive ions in a metal lattice. The conductivity of metals can be related to their low ionization energies, and the small number of electrons they have in their outer energy levels. The outer electrons are relatively free to leave the atom and move to the vacant orbitals of neighbouring atoms. We saw in Chapter 3 (page 105) that ionization energies generally increase across a period. This accounts for the lower electrical conductivity of silicon. However, silicon does have a higher electrical conductivity than other non-metals on the right of the Periodic Table and is said to be a semiconductor.

Extra electrons can also be released by giving them more energy, either by increasing the voltage or by exposing them to light. This allows the silicon to act as a gate for electron flow in electric circuits, and this property is used in photovoltaic cells.

## Comparing conductors and semiconductors

A semiconductor is a material that increases its electrical conductivity with temperature. The increase in thermal energy allows more electrons to be released from

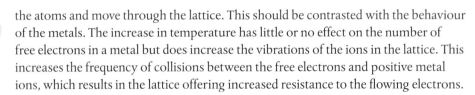

A semiconductor is a material that increases its electrical conductivity with temperature.

the atoms and move through the lattice. This should be contrasted with the behaviour of the metals. The increase in temperature has little or no effect on the number of free electrons in a metal but does increase the vibrations of the ions in the lattice. This increases the frequency of collisions between the free electrons and positive metal ions, which results in the lattice offering increased resistance to the flowing electrons.

## The structure and properties of silicon

Silicon is not a very good conductor of electricity under normal conditions. The outer electrons occupy sp³ hybrid orbitals and are needed to form four covalent bonds to neighbouring atoms. At absolute zero, it has no conductivity as the bonding electrons are fixed in place and unable to move about the crystal (Figure 14.27).

As the temperature increases, however, the thermal energy provides the necessary energy to free some electrons from the covalent bonds between the silicon atoms and the conductivity increases dramatically. This leaves an atom with a vacant site or **hole** and a net positive charge. Another atom in the lattice has more than its normal allocation of four electrons (Figure 14.28).

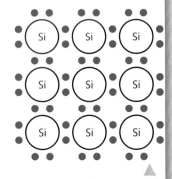

Figure 14.27  The structure of silicon.

Figure 14.28  An increase in thermal energy can allow an electron to migrate to another atom in the crystal.

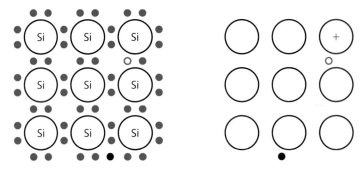

Silicon is said to be an **intrinsic** semiconductor as the origin of the electrical conductivity is from *within* the lattice. The number of positive holes is the same as the number of electrons.

Electrons move through the lattice to occupy these holes and leave holes behind. This can be represented as the migration of positively charged holes in the opposite direction to the movement of electrons (Figure 14.29).

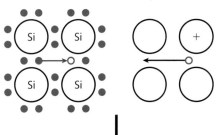

## Silicon can be doped by adding small amounts of Group 13 and 15 elements

The conductivity of silicon can also be significantly increased if small concentrations of similarly sized atoms of other elements are added to the lattice. The added substances are called **dopants**. The silicon crystals are exposed to the vapour of the substance to be added in a furnace. This process needs to be carefully controlled to concentrations of a few parts in a billion. The low concentrations ensure that the dopant atoms are well separated, allowing them to fit into the silicon lattice without disrupting it.

Figure 14.29  The migration of an electron from left to right to fill a vacant site can be represented as the migration of a positively charged hole in the opposite direction. The current can now be carried by the liberated electron or the migration of the positive hole.

### Doping with Group 15 elements makes n-type semiconductors

The doping of silicon with a Group 15 element such as arsenic results in the crystal having extra free electrons. The arsenic only needs four of its five outer electrons to form covalent bonds to its neighbouring silicon atoms. This leaves one electron free to

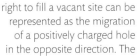

migrate through the crystal (Figure 14.30). The added atoms are called **donor** atoms because they donate electrons to the material.

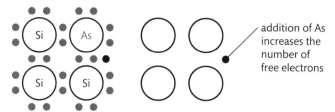

**Figure 14.30** The addition of an arsenic atom adds a free electron to the lattice.

Silicon doped with arsenic is classed as an **n-type semiconductor** because its electrical conductivity is due to *negative* carriers (i.e. electrons). It is important to note that the addition of donor atoms leaves the lattice uncharged as the extra electrons are balanced by extra protons in the nucleus of the Group 15 element.

## Doping with Group 13 elements makes p-type semiconductors

The doping of silicon with a Group 13 element such as gallium similarly results in an extra hole in the structure. The gallium can provide only three of the four electrons needed to form the four covalent bonds, which leaves a hole in the structure (Figure 14.31). These holes can migrate as electrons move from other sites to fill the holes. The added atoms are called **acceptor** atoms because they accept electrons to fill the holes in the bonds.

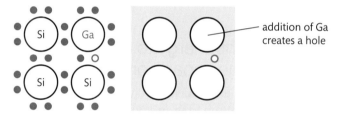

**Figure 14.31** The addition of a gallium atom creates a hole in the lattice.

Silicon doped with gallium is a **p-type semiconductor** because its electrical conductivity is due to *positive* carriers (i.e. the holes). Doping increases the conductivity of the silicon because less energy is needed to get the extra electrons or holes moving.

## An n–p junction can be used to make a diode

A diode is the simplest possible semiconductor device. A diode allows current to flow in one direction but not the other. For example, if an **n–p junction** is connected to an external battery as shown in Figure 14.32, neither the free electrons of the n-type semiconductor nor the holes of the p-type semiconductor will pass the junction and the diode has high resistance.

**Figure 14.32** The many free electrons of the n-type semiconductor do not pass the junction as they are attracted to the positive terminal of the battery. The many free holes of the p-type semiconductor do not pass the junction as they are attracted to the negative terminal of the battery.

However, if the poles of the external battery are reversed, the conductivity dramatically increases as both the holes and the electrons can now pass the junction (Figure 14.33).

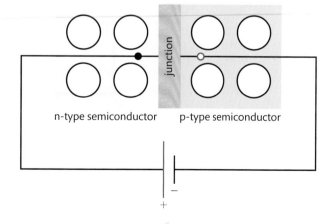

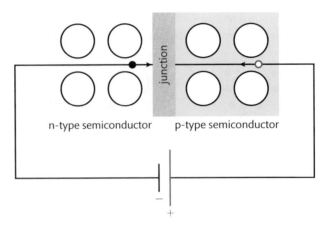

n-type semiconductor      p-type semiconductor

This allows the n–p junction to be used a rectifier as it converts alternating current into direct current.

### Exercises

**63** Compare the properties of semiconductors with metals and insulators and relate the properties to ionization energies.

**64 (a)** Suggest why germanium is a semiconductor, while diamond, an allotrope of carbon, is an insulator.
   **(b)** Describe and explain the changes in electrical properties that occur in germanium when small amounts of boron are added.

**65** Suggest which element is commonly added to germanium to make an n-type semiconductor and explain your choice.

## The conversion of light energy to electricity involves light absorption and charge separation

The methods of converting light to electricity involve the absorption of a photon of light and the separation of an electron from an atom or molecule to form an ion–electron pair. This is illustrated in the idealized situation below. If the ion and electron are allowed to recombine directly then the cell is effectively short-circuited and the absorbed light is lost in the form of heat.

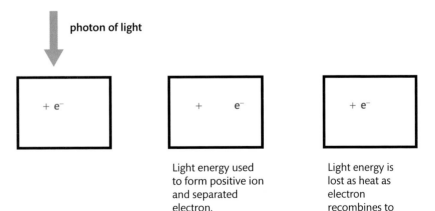

photon of light

+ e⁻          +      e⁻          + e⁻

Light energy used to form positive ion and separated electron.

Light energy is lost as heat as electron recombines to form neutral atom

**Figure 14.34** Light is absorbed but no electricity is generated as the opposite charges are allowed to recombine.

Alternatively, if the positive ion and electron are forced to separate, due to the electric field in a p–n junction in a photovoltaic cell or at a surface between the dye, electrolyte, and semiconductor in a dye sensitized cell, an electric current is produced as the electron passes around the external circuit before recombining.

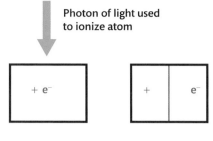

**Photon of light used to ionize atom**

Ions and electrons separated (for example by p–n junction)

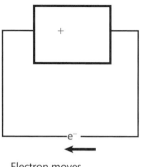

Ions and electrons separated.
In photovoltaic cells by p–n junction.
In DSSC at surfaces between the dye, semiconductor, and electrolyte.

Electron moves around external circuit. Light energy used to generate an electric current

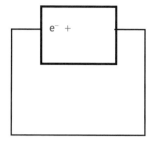

Electron returns from neutral atom

**Figure 14.35** Light is absorbed and electricity generated as the electron is forced to take an external path to recombine with its ion.

As we will see in a photovoltaic cell a semiconductor assumes both tasks of light absorption and charge separation whereas the tasks are separated in a dye-sensitized solar cell.

## Solar energy can be converted to electricity in a photovoltaic cell

Photovoltaic cells provide a means of converting sunlight directly into electricity. Applications range from calculators and watches, to space flight. The cells can also be used as a domestic energy source, providing electricity for the home. They offer an alternative energy source which is non-polluting and does not contribute to global warming.

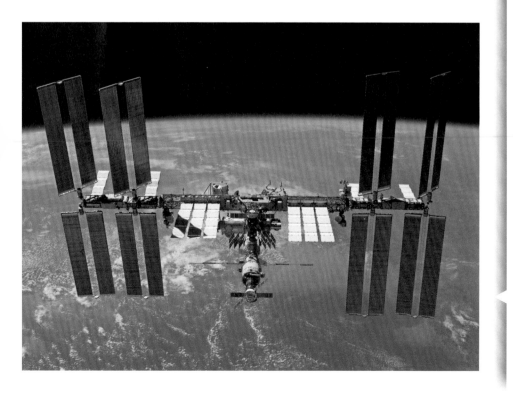

This solar array on the international space station consists of many solar panels designed to convert the energy in sunlight into electrical energy.

## A photovoltaic cell includes sheets of n-type and p-type silicon

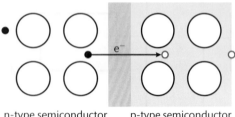

n-type semiconductor    p-type semiconductor

**Figure 14.36** Electrons pass from the n-type semiconductor to fill the holes on the p-type semiconductor.

A photovoltaic cell includes sheets of n-type and p-type silicon, typically in close contact. As discussed earlier, both n-type and p-type semiconductors have no overall charge as the number of electrons is balanced by the number of protons. However, when n-type and p-type semiconductors are placed together, electrons in the narrow area near the junction flow from the n-type to the p-type semiconductor and fill the positive holes (Figure 14.36). The region is known as the **depletion layer** as the charge carriers are effectively removed from this region.

This process cannot continue indefinitely because the electron exchange results in both sides of the junction becoming charged. The n-type semiconductor has lost electrons and becomes positively charged and the p-type semiconductor has gained electrons and becomes negatively charged. The resulting electric field opposes further exchanges of electrons and positive holes.

If the two layers are connected by an external circuit and light of the correct energy strikes the surface of the cell and is absorbed, more electrons and positive holes are created. The electrons and positive holes are prevented from recombining directly by the electric field in the p–n junction. Instead, electrons from the n-type conductor have sufficient energy to leave and pass through the external circuit to fill the holes in the p-type conductor. This further increases the positive charge of the n-type semiconductor so positive holes are repelled internally across the junction.

Simultaneously, the negative charge of the p-type semiconductor is increased so electrons are repelled across towards the junction (Figure 14.37).

**Figure 14.37** The workings of a photovoltaic cell.

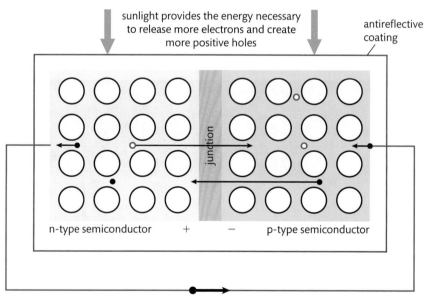

The process can continue as long as the cell is exposed to sunlight. As silicon is a very shiny material, an **antireflective coating** is applied to the top of the cell to reduce light losses due to reflection.

## Advantages and disadvantages of photovoltaic cells

### Advantages of photovoltaic cells

Photovoltaic cells have the potential to be a very important energy source for the future because:

- the Sun is an unlimited energy source
- use of photovoltaic cells would reduce our dependency on fossil fuels
- they do not incur the environmental problems associated with fossil fuels or nuclear fission
- they are easy to maintain as they have no moving parts.

### Disadvantages of photovoltaic cells

- There are some technological difficulties to be overcome before photovoltaic cells can be widely used:
- they only generate electricity when in sunlight so their use must be linked to an electrical storage system
- their efficiency is only 10–20%; only photons with sufficient energy to create an electron–hole pair are absorbed, the rest of the light simply passes through the cell
- large areas need to be covered with cells to produce electricity at the required levels
- the necessary purification and treatment of silicon to an appropriate standard is expensive.

Rows of panels containing photovoltaic cells capable of transforming the Sun's radiation into electrical energy.

 The first use of solar cells was to provide NASA spacecraft with electricity. The low efficiency of the energy transfer was of little concern as the intensity of the radiation was so high.

**NATURE OF SCIENCE**

All science has to be funded and the source of the funding is crucial in decisions regarding the type of research to be conducted. Pure research with no obvious direct benefit to anyone can be funded by governments, whereas applied research aims to produce a particular technological product. The first voltaic cells were produced by NASA for space probes and were only later used on Earth.

## Dye-sensitized solar cells (DSSC)

In a **dye-sensitized solar cell** (**DSSC**), the anode is composed of a porous layer of titanium dioxide nanoparticles, covered with a molecular dye that absorbs sunlight, much like the chlorophyll in green leaves. The cathode is a transition metal wire. In the photovoltaic cell the silicon acts as both the source of the electrons, as well as providing the electric field to separate the charges and create a current. In the DSSCs, the titanium(IV) oxide, $TiO_2$, semiconductor is only used to help remove the electrons from positive ions formed when they are ejected from a molecule. The electrons are provided by a separate photosensitive dye.

### DSSCs use a dye with a conjugated structure

The dye has a conjugated structure made up from $sp^2$ hybridized carbon atoms which each have p orbitals which overlap to form an extended system of π electrons.

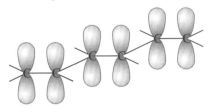

**Figure 14.38** A conjugated system of $sp^2$ hybridized carbon atoms. The p orbitals can overlap to form an extended delocalized π system of electrons.

The structure of one dye used in some cells is shown below. The molecule acts as a bidentate ligand and forms two dative covalent bonds with the transition metal ion ruthenium. It is the complex ion which absorbs the photon of light. The π system extends over the twelve carbon atoms, two nitrogen atoms and the four oxygen atoms in the molecule.

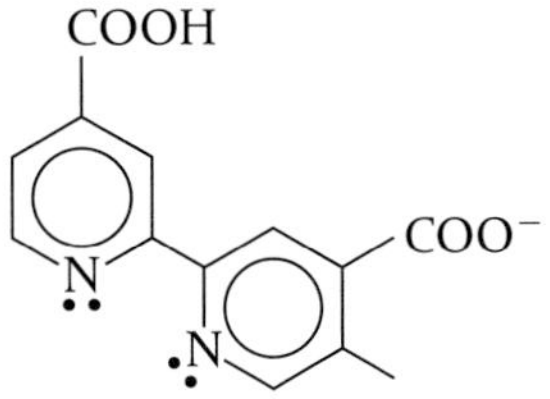

COOH

COO⁻

N

N

**Figure 14.39** A dye molecule with an extended π system of electrons.

Benzene rings and other double bonds can make up a conjugate system.

**TOK**

A conjugated system can be compared to a violin string. The longer the violin string the longer the wavelength of the sound produced and the longer the conjugate system the longer the wavelength of the light absorbed. The similarities arise as an electron can be considered as a wave which extends over the π system. What role do models and metaphors play in the acquisition of knowledge?

### The dye absorbs a photon and injects an electron into a $TiO_2$ layer at the anode

The initial charge separation occurs at the surface between the dye, semiconductor, and electrolyte.

The dye absorbs a photon of light: and becomes excited, shown as Dye*:

$$Dye \xrightarrow{h\nu} Dye^*$$

The excited electron then moves to the $TiO_2$ semiconductor and the dye becomes ionized:

$$Dye^* \rightarrow Dye^+ + e^-(TiO_2)$$

The electron is prevented from recombining with the positively charge dye molecule because the dye takes an electron from the electrolyte ion X⁻ instead.

$$Dye^+ + X^-(electrolyte) \rightarrow Dye + X(electrolyte)$$

The large surface area of the $TiO_2$ nanoparticles allows it to play a secondary role in scattering photons back into the transparent film where they can be absorbed by the dye.

## The electron passes through the external circuit to the platinum electrode where it reduces the electrolyte

The electron flows from the semiconductor through the external circuit to the positive platinum electrode where it reduces the electrolyte X back to $X^-$:

$$X(electrolyte) + e^- \rightarrow X^-(electrolyte)$$

The flow of charge is completed in the electrolyte by $X^-$ ions diffusing to the anode where they replace the $X^-$ ions originally oxidized by the dye.

### Worked example

In a Gratzel dye-sensitized solar cell the anode is made from a $TiO_2$ semiconductor covered with an organic dye molecule (S). The electrolyte is made from an $I_3^-/I_2$ mixture. The tri-iodide is formed when iodide ions and iodine molecules are present in solution:

$$I_2(aq) + I^-(aq) \rightarrow I_3^-(aq)$$

(a) Describe how light is absorbed by the molecule S.
(b) Describe how the positive and negative charges are separated at the anode.
(c) Describe the redox reactions that occur at the cathode and anode.

### Solution

(a) S has an extended conjugated $\pi$ system of electrons which allows it to absorb light in the visible region of the spectrum.
(b) The excited dye molecule injects an electron into the semiconductor:
$$S^* \rightarrow S^+ + e^-(TiO_2)$$
The ionized dye immediately loses its positive charge as it accepts an electron from the $I_3^-$ ion:
$$2I_3^- + 2S^+ \rightarrow 2S + 3I_2$$
(c) Cathode:
$$3I_2 + 2e^- \rightarrow 2I_3^-$$
Anode:
$$2S^+ + 2I_3^- \rightarrow 2S + 3I_2$$

## Advantages and disadvantages of DSSCs

### Advantages of DSSCs

• DSSCs are energy efficient as the dyes are very effective at converting photons to excited electrons. The large surface area of the nanoscale titanium dioxide anode scatters the light so that there is a high chance that a photon is absorbed.
• They use low-cost materials and are simple to manufacture.
• They can replace existing technologies such as rooftop solar collectors, where mechanical reliability and low density are important factors.
• Can work even in low-light conditions, allowing them to work under cloudy skies and non-direct sunlight where other cells would 'cutout'.

## Disadvantages of DSSCs

- The current efficiency, which is the current produced per unit area, is still relatively low.
- Dyes will degrade when exposed to ultraviolet radiation.
- At low temperatures, liquid electrolytes can freeze, stopping power production and potentially leading to physical damage. Higher temperatures cause the liquid to expand, making sealing the panels a serious problem. More recent cells replace the liquid $I_3^-/I_2$ electrolyte with a thin-film of $CsSnI_3$. They are more efficient, more stable, and last longer.
- Typically, dye molecules have poorer absorption in the red part of the spectrum compared to silicon, which means that fewer of the photons in sunlight can be used for electrical current generation.

**NATURE OF SCIENCE**

The operation of a dye-sensitized solar cell mimics photosynthesis and uses $TiO_2$ nanoparticles which scatter light as they are of the same scale as the wavelength of visible light. They are products which apply our scientific understanding of chemistry, physics, and biology.

### Exercises

**66** Explain how a photovoltaic cell works.

**67** Discuss three advantages and three disadvantages of using photovoltaic cells to power a car.

**68** Pure silicon is a semiconductor. Explain how the addition of small amounts of gallium or arsenic changes the conductivity of silicon.

**69 (a)** Compare the workings of a photovoltaic cell and a DSSC by describing the processes by which the light is absorbed and the resulting charges separated.
  **(b)** Explain what happens if the charges are not separated and directly recombine.

### Practice questions

**1** It is now widely accepted that the increased production of carbon dioxide is leading to global warming.

  **(a)** Describe how carbon dioxide acts as a greenhouse gas. (2)
  **(b)** Discuss the influence of increasing amounts of greenhouse gases on the environment. (3)

  *(Total 5 marks)*

**2** High-level and low-level wastes are two types of radioactive waste. Compare the half-lives and the methods of disposal of the two types of waste. (3)

**3** The initial products of the fractional distillation of oil often undergo cracking. State the major reason for catalytic cracking. (2)

**4** Compare the processes of nuclear fission and nuclear fusion. (2)

**5** The half-life of $^{234}_{92}Ra$ is 1600 years. Determine the length of time taken for 93.75% of the radium to disintegrate. (2)

**6 (a)** Explain what is meant by 'degraded energy'. (2)
  **(b)** A nuclear power station uses $^{235}_{92}U$ as fuel. Outline how the fuel produces energy. (4)
  **(c)** Explain what is meant by the critical mass of a fissile material. (1)

  *(Total 7 marks)*

**7 (a)** Most of the world's energy comes from fossil fuels. State two reasons for this. (2)

**(b)** Define the term 'specific energy'. (1)

**(c)** Identify a fuel which has a higher specific energy than fossil fuels. (1)

**(d)** A natural gas power station has an output power of $600 \times 10^6$ J s$^{-1}$ and an overall efficiency of 30%. The specific energy density of the fuel is $60 \times 10^3$ J g$^{-1}$. Determine the rate of consumption of natural gas in the power station. (3)

*(Total 7 marks)*

**8 (a)** Determine the percentage of carbon by mass in the fuels coal (CH), gasoline ($C_8H_{18}$), and natural gas ($CH_4$). (1)

**(b)** Suggest two reasons why coal has been replaced by gasoline and natural gas today as the fuel of choice. (2)

**(c)** One fuel that has been proposed as a replacement for carbon-containing substances is hydrogen. State two advantages of using hydrogen as a fuel. (2)

*(Total 5 marks)*

**9** The enthalpies of combustion of propane and butane are given in section 13 of the IB data booklet.

**(a)** Calculate the specific energies of $C_3H_8$ and $C_4H_{10}$. (2)

**(b)** Use the ideal gas equation to calculate the density of the two gases at s.t.p. and hence calculate the energy density of the two gases. (3)

**(c)** One danger of using gas for domestic purposes is the possibility of faulty gas tubing. Which gas would escape at the faster rate if the gas tubing connected to the bottle of the different gases had a leak? (1)

*(Total 6 marks)*

**10 (a)** State the name of the process by which green plants capture the Sun's energy and convert carbon dioxide and water into glucose. (1)

**(b)** Identify a molecule in plants which absorbs sunlight and explain how it is able to carry out this function with reference to its molecular structure. (2)

**(c)** State the half-equation in which oxygen is oxidized from carbon dioxide to glucose. (1)

**(d)** State the overall equation for the full redox reaction. (1)

**(e)** Glucose can be converted into ethanol, which can be used in fuel cells.

    **(i)** Identify this process by name and write the equation for the chemical reaction. (2)

    **(ii)** Determine the thermodynamic efficiency of a fuel cell fuelled by ethanol. (3)

**(f)** Glucose may be used as a fuel in a microbial cell. Describe the function of the bacteria in this process. (3)

*(Total 13 marks)*

**11** Consider the following organic compounds.

- ethanol
- pentane
- hexane
- benzene

**(a)** Explain the term octane number. (2)

**(b)** State the order of increasing octane number and explain your choice. (4)

*(Total 6 marks)*

**12** $^{235}_{92}U$ decays by alpha decay emitting a helium nucleus.

**(a)** Deduce the identity of the decay product. (2)

**(b)** Deduce the time it takes for 75% of the sample to decay. (2)

*(Total 4 marks)*

**13 (a)** Discuss the effects of fossil fuel use on the environment. (3)
   **(b)** Suggest steps that could be taken to reduce these effects. (6)
   **(c)** The average cost of gasoline varies dramatically from country to country. Discuss the implications of this for the average carbon footprint. (3)

*(Total 12 marks)*

**14 (a)** State the name and formula of two compounds present in gasoline. (2)
   **(b)** Describe and explain the process by which these compounds are obtained from crude oil. (4)
   **(c)** Describe a method that can be used to increase the yield of gasoline from a given quantity of crude oil that contains $C_{14}H_{30}$. (2)

*(Total 8 marks)*

**15 (a)** Use section 13 of the IB data booklet to calculate the specific energy of methane and methanol. (2)
   **(b)** Deduce the average oxidation number of carbon in the two compounds. (1)
   **(c)** Suggest a possible relationship between the oxidation number and specific energy. (1)
   **(d)** Calculate the specific energy of glucose and discuss the validity of your hypothesis. (3)

*(Total 7 marks)*

**16** Vegetable oils have a similar energy content to diesel fuel.

   **(a)** Explain why vegetable oils are not used in internal combustion engines. (2)
   **(b)** Describe the process by which vegetable oils are converted to more useful fuels. (2)

*(Total 4 marks)*

**17** Fuel cells may be twice as efficient as the internal combustion engine. Although fuel cells are not yet in widespread use, NASA has used a basic hydrogen–oxygen fuel cell as the energy source for space vehicles.

   **(a)** State the half-equations occurring at each electrode in the hydrogen–oxygen fuel cell in an alkaline medium. (2)
   **(b)** Describe the composition of the electrodes and state the overall cell equation of the nickel–cadmium battery. (3)

*(Total 5 marks)*

**18** The high activity of lithium metal leads to the formation of an oxide layer on the metal which decreases the contact with the electrolyte in a battery.

   **(a)** Describe how this is overcome in the lithium-ion battery. (2)
   **(b)** Describe the migration of ions taking place at the two electrodes in the lithium-ion battery when it produces electricity. (2)
   **(c)** Discuss one similarity and one difference between fuel cells and rechargeable batteries. (2)

*(Total 6 marks)*

**19** Describe the use of silicon in photovoltaic cells. Include the following in your description:

   • why pure silicon is a better conductor than non-metals such as sulfur and phosphorus
   • how a p-type semiconductor made from silicon is different from pure silicon
   • how sunlight interacts with semiconductors.

*(Total 5 marks)*

**20** Nuclear fission and nuclear fusion occur to increase the binding per nucleon.

    **(a)** Identify the nuclide which has the highest binding energy per nucleon. (1)

    **(b)** Define the *binding energy* of a nucleus. (1)

    **(c)** In a nuclear reactor, a nucleus of $^{235}_{92}$U absorbs a neutron and fissions into $^{141}_{56}$Ba and $^{92}_{36}$Kr. State the equation for this fission process and explain how it can lead to a chain reaction. (3)

    **(d)** The mass defect in the reaction in part (c) is $3.1 \times 10^{-28}$ kg. Calculate the energy released (in kJ mol$^{-1}$). (3)

    **(e)** The nuclear fuel has typically 3% of $^{235}_{92}$U. Calculate the specific energy of the fuel. (3)

    **(f)** Describe how the amount of $^{235}_{92}$U is increased from its natural levels of abundance. (3)

*(Total 14 marks)*

**21** Consider the nuclear reaction between two isotopes of hydrogen to produce an isotope of helium.

$$^{2}_{1}H + ^{1}_{1}H \rightarrow ^{3}_{2}He$$

The masses of the relevant particles are:

| | Mass / amu |
|---|---|
| $^{2}_{1}H$ | 2.014102 |
| $^{1}_{1}H$ | 1.00728 |
| $^{3}_{2}He$ | 3.01603 |

    **(a)** State the name of this type of reaction. (1)

    **(b)** Calculate the energy produced during the process (in kJ mol$^{-1}$). (4)

    **(c)** Identify which of the nuclei has the largest binding energy per nucleon and explain your choice. (2)

    **(d)** Identify the main practical problem that has to be overcome if the energy from this reaction is to be harnessed to produce useful energy commercially. (1)

*(Total 8 marks)*

**22** Discuss two direct methods by which solar energy can be converted to electricity. (8)

**23 (a)** A nuclear power plant that uses $^{235}_{92}$U as fuel produces $2.00 \times 10^{4}$ kJ of useful energy every second. The efficiency of the power station is 42% and each fission reaction of $^{235}_{92}$U gives out $2.8 \times 10^{-11}$ J of energy. Determine the mass of $^{235}_{92}$U fuel used each hour. (3)

    **(b)** Describe how and explain why some reactors are used to produce plutonium-239. (3)

    **(c)** $^{239}_{94}$Pu has a half-life of $2.40 \times 10^{4}$ years. Determine its decay constant. (1)

    **(d)** Calculate the time taken for the activity of $^{239}_{94}$Pu to fall to 1.00% of its initial value. (2)

*(Total 9 marks)*

To access weblinks on the topics covered in this chapter, please go to www.pearsonhotlinks.com and enter the ISBN or title of this book.

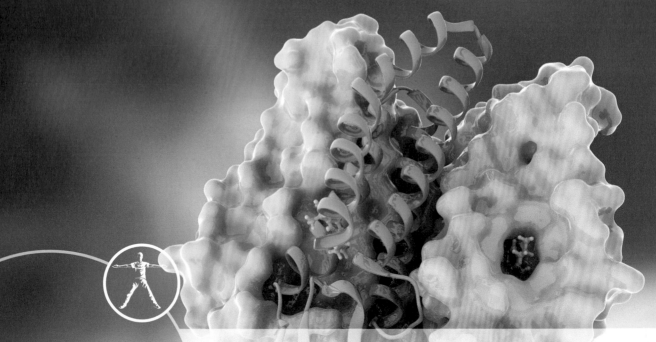

# 15 Option D: Medicinal chemistry

# Essential ideas

**D.1** Medicines and drugs have a variety of different effects on the functioning of the body.

**D.2** Natural products with useful medicinal properties can be chemically altered to produce more potent and safe medicines.

**D.3** Potent medical drugs prepared by chemical modification of natural products can be addictive and become substances of abuse.

**D.4** Excess stomach acid is a common problem that can be alleviated by compounds that increase the stomach pH by neutralizing or reducing its secretion.

**D.5** Antiviral medications have recently been developed for some viral infections while others are still being researched.

**D.7** Chiral auxiliaries allow the production of individual enantiomers of chiral molecules.

**D.8** Nuclear radiation, whilst dangerous owing to its ability to damage cells and cause mutations, can also be used to both diagnose and cure diseases.

**D.9** A variety of analytical techniques is used for detection, identification, isolation, and analysis of medicines and drugs.

**D.6** The synthesis, isolation, and administration of medications can have an effect on the environment.

Computer model showing the structure of anaesthetic drug molecules on the lower left and right, bound to a protein molecule shown in grey. The protein has five sub-units and acts as an ion channel. The binding of the drug to the surface of the protein inhibits its action, and this helps to induce and maintain general anaesthesia during surgery. Research and development in drug design often focuses on the chemical interactions between drugs and specific receptor target molecules in the body.

For thousands of years it has been known that chemicals with medical properties are found in extracts of animal organs, plant tissue, and minerals found in the local environment. In many cultures this knowledge has been passed from generation to generation within communities, and continues to be an important aspect of health management for many people today.

The 20th century saw a major new development in healthcare with the production of synthetic molecules specifically for the treatment of illnesses. Without question, this has been one of the most significant achievements of the last 100 years. The development of targeted drugs and vaccines has meant that smallpox has been eradicated, millions of people have survived infections such as malaria and tuberculosis, and other diseases such as polio are on their way to extinction. Untold numbers of people owe their lives to the action of medicines.

But at the same time – and as with many other great innovations – the pharmaceutical industry has brought new challenges.

- Abuses, excesses, and the problem of antibiotic resistance have to be faced.
- Nuclear medicine contributes greatly to diagnosis and therapy especially of cancer, but raises new issues of radiation hazard and disposal.
- The appearance of new diseases such as avian flu highlights the need for the industry to be proactive in developing new drugs – the AIDS pandemic is a reminder of what happens when the spread of an infectious disease is not checked.

859

In addition, there are huge discrepancies in the availability of drugs in different parts of the world, leading to continued suffering and death from diseases for which effective treatments exist.

In this chapter we study applications of chemistry in drug design, development, and administration by some case-study examples. Note that a knowledge of organic chemistry from Chapter 10 is important to help you interpret this information fully.

Digital composite image showing a biochemist using a virtual reality system to investigate molecular interactions. The large purple ribbon-like molecule is an enzyme of HIV and the blue helical object is half of a section of DNA. This system allows researchers to manipulate computer-generated stereo images of molecules to study their interactions. This is one approach used in structure-based drug design.

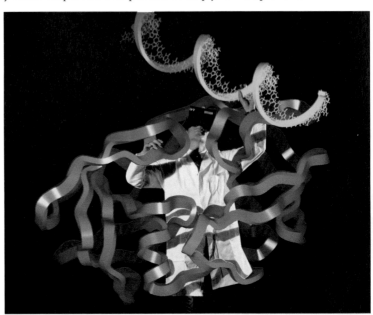

# D.1 Pharmaceutical products and drug action

## Understandings:

- In animal studies, the therapeutic index is the lethal dose of a drug for 50% of the population ($LD_{50}$) divided by the minimum effective dose for 50% of the population ($ED_{50}$).
- In humans, the therapeutic index is the toxic dose of a drug for 50% of the population ($TD_{50}$) divided by the minimum effective dose for 50% of the population ($ED_{50}$).
- For ethical and economic reasons, animal and human tests of drugs (for $LD_{50}/ED_{50}$ and $TD_{50}/ED_{50}$ respectively) should be kept to a minimum.
- The therapeutic window is the range of dosages between the minimum amount of the drug that produce the desired effect and a medically unacceptable adverse effect.
- Dosage, tolerance, addiction, and side-effects are considerations of drug administration.
- Bioavailability is the fraction of the administered dosage that reaches the target part of the human body.
- The main steps in the development of synthetic drugs include identifying the need and structure, synthesis, yield, and extraction.
- Drug–receptor interactions are based on the structure of the drug and the site of activity.

## Applications and skills:

- Discussion of experimental foundations for therapeutic index and therapeutic window through both animal and human studies.
- Discussion of drug administration methods.
- Comparison of how functional groups, polarity, and medicinal administration can affect bioavailability.

## The human body has many natural systems of defence

The functioning of the human body involves an incredibly intricate balance of thousands of different reactions occurring simultaneously. The sum of all these processes is known as **metabolism**. Inevitably, this complex system can suffer from many types of defect and breakdown, through injury, through genetically or environmentally caused abnormalities, and through accumulated changes with age. In addition, we are constantly under attack from microorganisms which can enter the body, alter its functioning, and so cause disease.

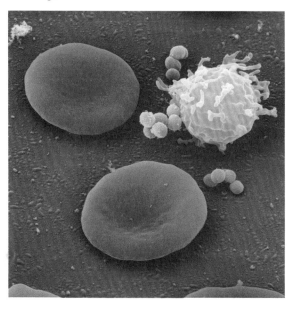

Coloured scanning electron micrograph of bacteria, shown in yellow, in the blood alongside red blood cells and a white blood cell. The white blood cell will destroy the bacteria, protecting the body from disease.

Happily, the human body is well equipped with equally complex systems of defence and healing processes. Rather like in a battle of war, we describe attacking microorganisms as **invaders** and the body's responses as different **lines of defence**, activated as the invaders penetrate more deeply. Often the responses of the body manifest themselves as symptoms of disease. For example, we may experience fever as the body raises its temperature to fight a bacterial infection. Although these symptoms generally need to be monitored, they are not usually themselves cause for concern.

When considering how best to fight disease, it is essential that we keep the focus on maximizing the effectiveness of the body's natural defence systems. At best, medicines work by supplementing our natural healing processes.

Computer artwork of the inflammatory response. Bacteria, shown in gold, are seen entering the body through a cut in the skin, and the blood capillary beneath the site of entry is releasing white blood cells, shown in purple and green, into the tissue. These cells will destroy the bacteria and activate the immune response.

## Medicines and drugs: some terminology

The terms 'medicines' and 'drugs' are sometimes used interchangeably, and sometimes have slightly different meanings in different parts of the world. They are most clearly defined as follows.

The therapeutic effect is the beneficial effect of a medical treatment.

- **Drug**: a chemical that affects how the body works. This includes changes for the better *and* for the worse. The term is sometimes associated with substances which are illegal in many countries, such as cocaine, ecstasy, and heroin, but it has a broader meaning.
- **Medicine**: a substance that improves health. Medicines, which may be natural or synthetic, therefore contain beneficial drugs. Synthetic medicines also contain other ingredients, which are non-active but help in the presentation and administration of the drug. The beneficial effect of a medicine is known as its **therapeutic** effect.

The word *placebo* is Latin for 'I will please'. The term *nocebo*, Latin for 'I will harm', is sometimes used to describe a condition worsened by a belief that a drug used is harmful. One example is a person dying of fright after being bitten by a non-venomous snake.

### NATURE OF SCIENCE

The placebo effect – the power of suggestion – is a well-documented phenomenon. It occurs when patients gain therapeutic effect from their belief that they have been given a useful drug, even when they have not. Although there is no rigorous explanation for this effect, it is generally accepted that about one-third of a control group taking a placebo show some improvements. This fact is used in double-blind tests in all major clinical trials as discussed on page 868.

To establish a causal link between the placebo and therapeutic effect, scientists need to establish a mechanism. This needs experimental evidence and data which are objective and reproducible. But studies on the placebo effect are fraught with subjectivity and difficulties of interpretation. Other factors could have contributed to the claimed therapeutic effects, such as spontaneous improvement, fluctuation of symptoms, answers of politeness, and patient misjudgement, and these all need to be accounted for by control experiments. Without a scientific explanation, the placebo effect continues to be somewhat controversial.

## Drugs can be administered in different ways

The way a drug is delivered to the patient's body depends on many factors. These include the chemical nature of the drug, the condition of the patient, and the most effective way of getting the drug to the target organ. For example, some chemicals, including proteins such as insulin, are decomposed by the action of the digestive enzymes in the gut, so they cannot be administered as pills, but must instead be injected directly into the blood. Likewise, a patient in a coma might be unable to swallow an ingested pill so the drug must be delivered in another way.

The following methods are all used to administer drugs.

| Method of administering drug | Description | Example |
|---|---|---|
| oral | taken by mouth | tablets, capsules, pills, liquids |
| inhalation | vapour breathed in; smoking | medications for respiratory conditions such as asthma; some drugs of abuse such as nicotine and cocaine |
| skin patches | absorbed directly from the skin into the blood | some hormone treatments, e.g. estrogen, nicotine patches |
| suppositories | inserted into the rectum | treatment of digestive illnesses and haemorrhoids |
| eye or ear drops | liquids delivered directly to the opening | treatments of infections of the eye or ear |
| parenteral: by injection (see Figure 15.1) | intramuscular (into muscle) | many vaccines |
| | intravenous (into the blood, the fastest method of injection) | local anaesthetics |
| | subcutaneous (under the skin) | dental injections |

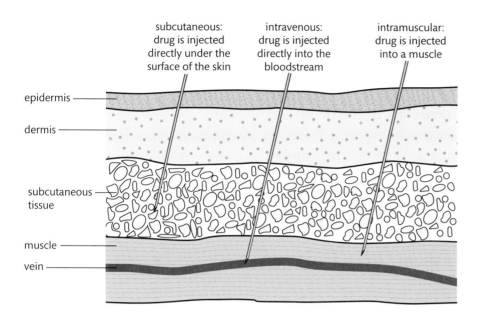

subcutaneous: drug is injected directly under the surface of the skin

intravenous: drug is injected directly into the bloodstream

intramuscular: drug is injected into a muscle

epidermis

dermis

subcutaneous tissue

muscle

vein

**Figure 15.1** Different parenteral methods for the administration of drugs.

## Bioavailability of drugs: the amount that reaches the target

Not all of an administered drug reaches its target in the body. This is because the drug may be broken down in metabolic processes or may be incompletely absorbed into the blood. The fraction of an administered drug that reaches the blood supply is known as its **bioavailability**. By this definition, drugs that are administered by intravenous methods have a bioavailability of 100%, so this is used as the basis of comparison.

Bioavailability is an important consideration when calculating how much of a drug to administer, known as the **dosage**.

Figure 15.2 shows a typical result of the bioavailability of a drug taken orally, compared with the same amount of the same drug taken intravenously.

Factors that influence bioavailability are discussed below.

> **Bioavailability is the fraction of the administered dosage that reaches the bloodstream.**

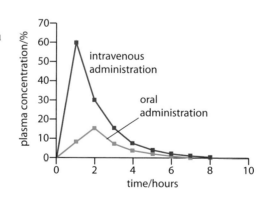

**Figure 15.2** Bioavailability of a drug when administered orally and intravenously. The absolute bioavailability is calculated from the ratio of the areas under the two curves.

## Administration of the drug

The relatively low bioavailability of a drug taken orally, shown in Figure 15.2, is known as the **first-pass effect**, and means that as little as 20–40% of an orally ingested drug may reach the bloodstream. This is because after swallowing, these drugs pass into the digestive system where biological catalysts known as **enzymes** may alter them chemically. Once absorbed from the digestive system, they are passed in the blood to the liver where further metabolic breakdown reactions occur.

Other methods of drug administration avoid the first-pass effect as they provide more direct routes into the bloodstream. So in general an oral dose of a drug needs

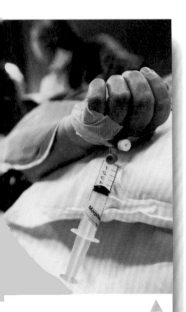

to be about four times higher than the dosage of the same drug administered intravenously. The strong analgesic morphine has a bioavailability of only about 30% when taken orally as the remainder is metabolized by the liver. For more effective pain management, morphine is therefore administered intravenously.

### The solubility of the drug

Water solubility is important for circulation in the aqueous solution in the blood, but lipid solubility helps in the passage of the drug through membranes during absorption. Codeine is more lipid soluble than morphine as it is a less polar molecule (as can be seen on page 881), and has a bioavailability of about 90%.

### Functional groups in the drug

Functional groups in the drug can also influence bioavailability, particularly acid–base groups. The $pK_a$ and $pK_b$ values of these groups in the molecule will determine the charges carried on the drug at different pH values, and therefore its reactivity and solubility in different parts of the body.

## Physiological effects of drugs are complex

Because of the complexity of metabolism, a drug will interact in many different ways and produce more than one physiological effect. The situation is made more complicated by the fact that different individuals respond in different ways to administered drugs. Healthcare providers therefore need to keep several considerations in mind when prescribing drugs and evaluating an individual's response to the medication.

### Side-effects

The overall effects of a drug in the body can be classified as follows:

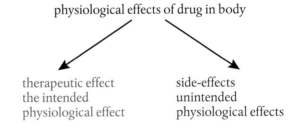

physiological effects of drug in body

therapeutic effect
the intended
physiological effect

side-effects
unintended
physiological effects

**Side-effects** are defined as physiological effects which are not intended, and they vary greatly from one drug to another, and with the same drug in different people. Sometimes side-effects may be beneficial, such as the fact that aspirin, taken for pain relief, helps protect against heart disease. Other times the side-effects may be relatively benign, such as causing drowsiness, nausea, or constipation. But of greater concern are side-effects which are much more adverse, such as causing damage to organs. The impact of these side-effects must be evaluated throughout the drug treatment. Patients must also be made aware of the possible side-effects of a drug to help in monitoring the treatment and to make possible adjustments in lifestyle. For example, in some cases this will mean not driving or operating machinery. One of the most dramatic – and tragic – examples of adverse side-effects was the deformities produced in unborn children resulting from the thalidomide drug. This is discussed on pages 869 and 901.

Syringe attached to a cannula in a patient's hand to administer the painkilling drug morphine intravenously during surgery.

## Tolerance and addiction

When a person is given repeated doses of a drug, **tolerance** can develop, which means a reduced response to the drug for the same dose. So higher doses are needed to produce the same effect, and this increases the chances of toxic side-effects. The mechanism by which tolerance to a drug develops is not always understood – it could be that the body has become able to metabolize and break down the drug more efficiently, or that the drug receptors in cells become less effective. For some drugs, tolerance develops to one effect of the drug and not to other effects.

A related but different condition is **dependence** or **addiction**. This occurs when a patient becomes dependent on the drug in order to feel normal, and suffers from **withdrawal symptoms** if the drug is not taken. Symptoms can be mild, such as headaches suffered on withdrawal from dependence on caffeine, or serious if the drug is toxic or shows tolerance, such as opiates, alcohol, and barbiturates.

## Dosage

The **dosing regime** for a drug refers to the specific quantity of drug to be taken at one time, and the frequency of administration. Calculations of dosage must take bioavailability into account, as well as possible side-effects and potential problems of tolerance and addiction. Determining appropriate dosage is usually quite difficult as there are so many variables involved – for example the age, sex, and weight of the patient, as well as factors such as diet and environment. Interactions with other drugs must also be considered. Ideally the dosage should result in constant levels of the drug in the blood, but this is almost impossible to achieve other than by a continuous, intravenous drip. Other methods of administration will inevitably lead to fluctuations in the blood drug level between doses. The important thing is that the concentration in the bloodstream must remain within a certain range: above this range, unacceptable side-effects may occur, below it there may not be effective therapeutic outcomes. This target range is known as the **therapeutic window**.

The range of concentrations that defines the therapeutic window varies greatly from one drug to the next. For drugs that have a small therapeutic window, drug levels in the blood must be monitored closely to maintain effective dosing without giving a toxic dose.

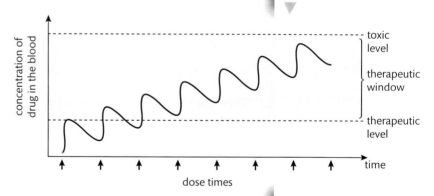

The therapeutic window can be quantified as the **therapeutic index** (**TI**). This is the ratio of the dose that produces toxicity to the dose that produces a clinically effective response in a population. The relevant terms in the equation are:

- The minimum effective dose, $ED_{50}$, is the dose that produces the therapeutic effect in 50% of the population.
- The lethal dose, $LD_{50}$, is the dose that is lethal to 50% of the population. This is used in animal trials.
- The toxic dose, $TD_{50}$, is the dose that is toxic to 50% of the population. This is used in human studies.

Tolerance occurs when repeated doses of a drug result in smaller physiological effects.

Addiction occurs when the dependency on a drug leads to withdrawal symptoms if it is withheld.

It is possible to experience addiction even to one's own hormones and neurotransmitters (chemicals used for communication). For example, some people are addicted to exercise as this leads to the release of chemicals that can produce a 'high'. Susceptible people are driven to exercise increasingly, and they suffer withdrawal symptoms such as depression if they cannot fulfil this need.

**Figure 15.3** The therapeutic window.

The therapeutic window is the range of a drug's concentration in the blood between the minimum amount that produces its therapeutic effect and a medically unacceptable adverse effect.

In animal studies lethal doses are determined; however, in human trials the upper limit is the toxic dose. This means that the therapeutic index is defined differently in the two groups:

- in animals TI = $\dfrac{LD_{50}}{ED_{50}}$

- in humans TI = $\dfrac{TD_{50}}{ED_{50}}$

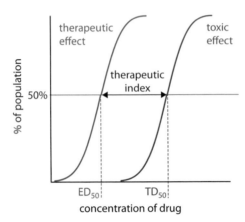

**Figure 15.4** The therapeutic index is determined from data on the responses of the population to different dosages of the drug.

The therapeutic index is a measure of a drug's safety because a higher value indicates a wide margin between doses that are effective and doses that are toxic. A low therapeutic index means a low margin of safety, where a slight change in the dose may produce an undesirable adverse side-effect.

Some examples of the relative values of the therapeutic index of some common drugs are compared in the table below.

| Drug | Therapeutic effect | Therapeutic index (TI) |
|---|---|---|
| penicillin | antibiotic | increasing value of therapeutic index |
| morphine | analgesic | |
| cocaine | stimulant | |
| ethanol | depressant | |
| warfarin | anticoagulant in blood | |

Penicillin has a high therapeutic index, and is therefore quite forgiving in terms of the dose administered. This means it is safe if taken in higher doses than that required for therapeutic effect. On the other hand, warfarin, with a very low therapeutic index, has a low margin of safety and the correct dosage is crucial. The difference in the therapeutic window of these two drugs is shown in Figure 15.5. In general, drugs with a low therapeutic index are those where bioavailability critically alters the therapeutic effects.

**Figure 15.5** Therapeutic index of (a) penicillin and (b) warfarin.

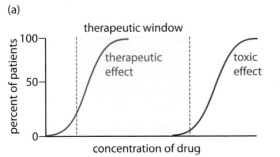

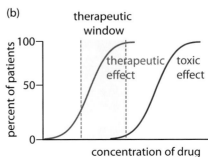

## Drug action depends on interactions with receptors

The activity of most drugs is determined by their ability to bind to a specific receptor in the body. Receptors are usually proteins, which includes enzymes, chemical structures on cell membranes, or DNA. The binding of the drug prevents or inhibits the normal biological activity, and so interrupts the development of disease. Drug–receptor interactions depend on a 'chemical fit' between the drug and receptor – in general the better the fit, the greater the activity of the drug. The binding of drug and receptor usually involves different types of non-covalent bonding, such as ionic bonds, hydrogen bonds, van der Waals' forces, and hydrophobic interactions.

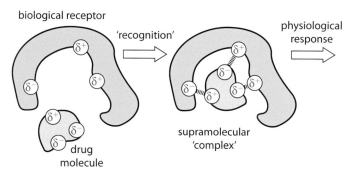

**Figure 15.6** A drug often combines with a receptor through hydrogen bonding to form a supramolecular complex.

Understanding drug–receptor interactions has made an important contribution to advances in approaches to drug design.

## The development of new synthetic drugs is a long and costly process

Pharmaceutical companies and research groups are constantly developing new drugs, seeking those that are more effective and have fewer toxic side-effects than pre-existing drugs for the same condition. In addition, there is demand for drugs for new conditions such as new viral strains of flu. Every new drug developed represents a major investment of cost, and so the industry is very selective in its focus. Consequently, a large amount of research goes into drugs for conditions such as obesity, depression, cancer, cardiovascular disease, and ulcers, which are prevalent in the developed world where the market can support the cost. Much less attention and fewer resources are given to researching drugs for conditions such as tropical diseases prevalent in the developing world.

Most countries have stringent controls over the development and licensing of drugs. For every new drug that reaches the market, thousands of candidate molecules fail to meet the criteria and are rejected. The average time for development of a drug from its first identification to the market is about 10–12 years.

Knowledge of drug–receptor interactions has revolutionized the process by which new drugs are developed. Most research now focuses on identifying a suitable molecular target in the body and designing a drug to interact with it. This approach, known as **rational drug design**, is very different from the time when pharmaceutical companies worked mostly on a 'trial and error' basis, starting with a natural remedy and trying to improve on nature with no real insight into the mechanism of the action of the drug at the molecular level.

Supramolecular chemistry refers to the properties of assemblies of two or more molecules held together by intermolecular forces, most importantly hydrogen bonding. It involves molecular recognition by the different components, known as **host–guest** interactions. In addition to its applications in drug design, it is the subject of research for developing chemical sensors to act as a 'chemical nose' and extract specific substances from mixtures such as caffeine from coffee, urea from the blood in kidney machines, and heavy metals from industrial waste.

Malaria is a disease that is both curable and preventable. But a child dies of malaria every 10 seconds; more than one million people die of malaria every year. Why do you think this is?

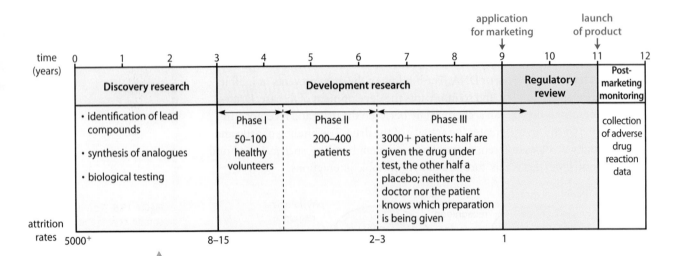

**Figure 15.7** Stages in the discovery and development of a new medicine.

John le Carré's novel *The Constant Gardener* is a fictional tale of drug trials administered by a large pharmaceutical company on AIDS patients in Kenya. It touches on issues such as drug side-effects and synergies, client selection for trials, the drive for profit by the pharmaceutical industry, and the role of government and NGO pharmaceutical watchdogs. Although it is not based on facts of a specific case, it raises some relevant questions and is a good read. It is also available as a movie.

All drugs carry risks as well as benefits. Who should ultimately be responsible for assessing the risk-to-benefit ratio of a drug in an individual – the pharmaceutical company, a government watchdog body, the doctor, or the patient?

**TOK**

Once a target molecule has been identified, the next step is to find a lead compound – one that shows the desired pharmaceutical activity which will be used as a start for the drug design and development process. (Note: 'lead' here is pronounced to rhyme with 'need', not the element Pb!) Lead compounds are often derived from plants, for example, an anti-cancer agent extracted from yew trees led to the development of Taxol, and digitalis extracted from the foxglove flower led to heart medications. Microorganisms too have provided rich sources of lead compounds, particularly in the development of antibiotics.

The effectiveness of the lead compound is optimized by synthesizing and testing many chemically related compounds known as **analogues**. A process called **combinatorial chemistry** enables the production and testing of vast numbers of candidate medicines in a very short time. Following extensive laboratory tests, a potential medicine is then tested on animals, under strict legislative control. For ethical and economical reasons, animal and human testing of drugs should be kept to a minimum. Data on the safety and effectiveness of a drug enable researchers to predict the clinical therapeutic index of a drug candidate at an early stage. From this, the value of the therapeutic index for humans and the dose to be administered in human trials are determined.

Figure 15.7 shows that there are usually three phases to the subsequent human trials, involving an increasing number of patients. The effectiveness of the drug is judged by the relative improvement in the patients who had received the real medication as compared with those on placebo in Phase III.

Today many countries maintain post-marketing safety surveillance programmes for all approved drugs, and databases are available detailing adverse drug reactions. This has sometimes led to the withdrawal of a drug from the market after years of usage.

During the early 1960s the drug thalidomide was marketed, initially in Germany, and prescribed to pregnant women in many countries to help with 'morning sickness' in their early months of pregnancy. Tragically, the drug had devastating effects on the development of the fetus, and up to 12 000 children were born with severe birth defects, most notably missing or malformed limbs, and many more did not survive infancy. By the time the deformities in the newborns were linked with the thalidomide drug, it had been widely marketed in at least 46 countries. This tragedy has led to the addition of further regulatory steps in drug licensing.

The thalidomide drug was never marketed in the USA because of the intervention of Frances Kelsey, a pharmacologist working at the Food and Drug Administration (FDA). Despite pressure from thalidomide's manufacturer and the fact that it was already approved in over 20 countries, she registered concerns about the drug's ability to cross the placenta into the fetal blood. Her insistence that further tests be carried out was dramatically vindicated when the effects of thalidomide became known. For her insightful work in averting a similar tragedy in the USA she was given a Distinguished Federal Service Award by President Kennedy.

## Exercises

1  List the three different ways in which drugs can be injected into the body. Predict, giving a reason, which of the three methods will result in the drug having the most rapid effect.

2  State what is meant by *tolerance* towards a drug and explain why it is potentially dangerous.

3  **(a)** Explain why the therapeutic index is defined differently in animal studies and in humans.
   **(b)** Outline the factors that must be considered when determining the dosage of a drug.
   **(c)** Why can it be challenging to determine the dosage of a drug that has a low therapeutic index?

4  Describe three factors that influence the bioavailability of a drug.

## Quick reference for functional group identities

In the following sections on different classes of drugs, reference will be made to the functional groups of the molecules which are generally associated with their activity. It is important that you can recognize and identify these groups in different molecules. Some, but not all, of them were introduced in Chapter 10, so a brief summary of the important ones found in drugs is given here. (Note that R and R′ refer to carbon containing or alkyl groups.)

| Structure of functional group | Name of functional group | Structure of functional group | Name of functional group |
|---|---|---|---|
| $\underset{/}{\overset{\backslash}{C}}=\underset{\backslash}{\overset{/}{C}}$ | alkenyl | $R-N\underset{H}{\overset{H}{<}}$ | primary amino |
| $-\overset{\mid}{\underset{\mid}{C}}-OH$ | hydroxyl | $R-N\underset{R'}{\overset{H}{<}}$ | secondary amino |
| $\underset{R'}{\overset{R}{>}}C=O$ | ketone | $R-N\underset{R'}{\overset{R''}{<}}$ | tertiary amino |
| arene | arene | $-C\underset{N-H}{\overset{O}{<}}\;H$ | carboxyamide |
| $-C\underset{OH}{\overset{O}{<}}$ | carboxylic acid | $-C\underset{O-R}{\overset{O}{<}}$ | ester |
| $R-O-R'$ | ether | (heterocyclic ring with N) | a heterocyclic ring, containing atoms other than C, usually N |

▲ Close-up of the deformed hand and forearm of a 'thalidomide baby'. Thalidomide is a sedative drug that was administered to many pregnant women in the 1960s. It was withdrawn from the market after it was found to cause serious fetal abnormalities. This tragedy led to major changes in drug testing protocols.

It is easy to confuse *amine* and *amide*. Amines are organic derivatives of ammonia, $NH_3$. In amides, the N is attached to a carbonyl carbon ($-C=O$), so these are derivatives of carboxylic acids. There is no $-C=O$ group in an amine.

## D.2 Aspirin and penicillin

## Understandings:

### Aspirin
- Mild analgesics function by intercepting the pain stimulus at the source, often by interfering with the production of substances that cause pain, swelling, or fever.
- Aspirin is prepared from salicylic acid.
- Aspirin can be used as an anticoagulant, in prevention of the recurrence of heart attacks and strokes, and as a prophylactic.

### Penicillin
- Penicillins are antibiotics produced by fungi.
- A beta-lactam ring is a part of the core structure of penicillins.
- Some antibiotics work by preventing cross-linking of the bacterial cell walls.
- Modifying the side-chain results in penicillins that are more resistant to the penicillinase enzyme.

## Applications and skills:

### Aspirin
- Description of the use of salicylic acid and its derivatives as mild analgesics.
- Explanation of the synthesis of aspirin from salicylic acid, including yield, purity by recrystallization, and characterization using IR and melting point.
- Discussion of the synergistic effects of aspirin with alcohol.
- Discussion of how aspirin can be chemically modified into a salt to increase its aqueous solubility and how this facilitates its bioavailability.

### Penicillin
- Discussion of the effects of chemically modifying the side-chain of penicillins.
- Discussion of the importance of patient compliance and the effects of the over-prescription of penicillin.
- Explanation of the importance of the beta-lactam ring on the action of penicillin.

#### Guidance
- *Students should be aware of the ability of acidic (carboxylic) and basic (amino) groups to form ionic salts, for example soluble aspirin.*
- *Structures of aspirin and penicillin are available in the data booklet in section 37.*

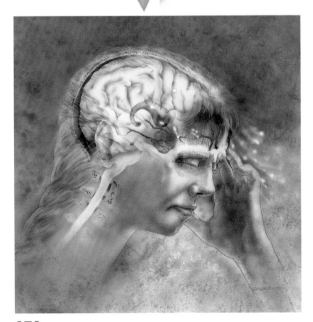

Conceptual artwork of a person suffering from a headache showing inflamed blood vessels and nerves around the brain. Analgesics work in different ways to block the pathway between the source of pain and perception by the brain.

## Aspirin: a mild analgesic

Our body's ability to perceive pain is one of our very best defence mechanisms. We act immediately to try to eliminate the source of pain – and so act to reduce further damage to ourselves. Removing our hand from a hot plate, being aware that a sharp object has pierced our skin, or being virtually incapable of moving a broken limb are all examples of our innate abilities to protect ourselves.

But we all know that the sensation of pain is unpleasant – at best. At worst, it can dominate the senses and cause a debilitating effect, especially as many people have medical conditions that result in chronic pain. And so the need exists for painkillers, a class of drugs known as **analgesics**. Note though that pain is a symptom of a bigger problem – an injury or a disease – and therefore long-term relief is dependent on treating the underlying cause.

Pain is detected as a sensation by the brain when nerve messages are sent from various **pain receptors** located around the body. These receptors are themselves stimulated by chemicals known as **prostaglandins**, which are released from cells damaged by thermal, mechanical, or chemical energy. Once released, prostaglandins also mediate the **inflammatory response** by causing the dilation (widening) of blood vessels near the site of injury. In turn this can lead to swelling and increased pain. In addition, prostaglandins have an effect on the temperature regulation of the body that may result in increased temperature known as **fever**.

To be effective, a painkiller must intercept or block this pathway somewhere between the source of pain and the receptors in the brain.

Aspirin and non-steroidal anti-inflammatory drugs (NSAIDs) such as ibuprofen are **mild analgesics**. They act by preventing stimulation of the nerve endings at the site of pain and inhibit the release of prostaglandins from the site of injury. This gives relief to inflammation and fever as well as to pain. Because these analgesics do not interfere with the functioning of the brain, they are also known as **non-narcotics**.

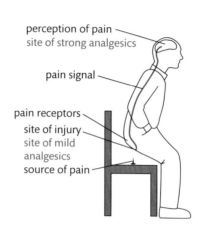

**Figure 15.8** Pathways of pain in the body. Different types of analgesic have different sites of action.

perception of pain
site of strong analgesics

pain signal

pain receptors
site of injury
site of mild analgesics
source of pain

Mild analgesics block sensation of pain at the source.

The name 'Aspirin' was originally a trademark belonging to the pharmaceutical company Bayer. After Germany lost World War I, Bayer was forced to surrender this trademark (and also the one for 'Heroin') to the UK, France, Russia, and the USA as part of the reparations of the Treaty of Versailles in 1919.

## Development of aspirin

From the time of Hippocrates in about 400 BCE it was known that chewing willow bark could give relief to pain and fever. But it was not until the early 1800s that it was demonstrated that the active ingredient in the bark is salicin, which is converted to **salicylic acid** in the body (*salix* is the Latin name for willow). Although salicylic acid proved to be effective in treating pain, it tasted awful and caused the patient to vomit.

carboxylic acid
COOH
OH hydroxyl

**Figure 15.9** The structure of salicylic acid (2-hydroxybenzoic acid).

In 1890 the Bayer Company in Germany made an ester derivative of salicylic acid, which was more palatable and less irritable to the body, while still being effective as an analgesic. It was named **aspirin**, in recognition of the plant spirea which produces a similar compound. Aspirin manufacture began that year, and it became one of the first drugs to enter into common usage. Today it continues to hold its place as the most widely used drug in the world, with an estimated production of over 100 billion standard tablets every year. It is widely used in the treatment of headache, toothache, and sore throat. Also, because it is effective in reducing fever, known as an **antipyretic**, and inflammation, it is used to provide relief from rheumatic pain and arthritis.

**TOK**
It could be argued that whereas mild analgesics seek to eliminate pain at source, strong analgesics only alter our ability to perceive pain. Do these two approaches depend only on sense perception or also on other ways of knowing?

carboxylic acid
COOH    O
        ||
   O—C—CH₃    ester

**Figure 15.10** The structure of aspirin (2-ethanoyloxybenzenecarboxylic acid or acetylsalicylic acid, ASA).

## The synthesis of aspirin

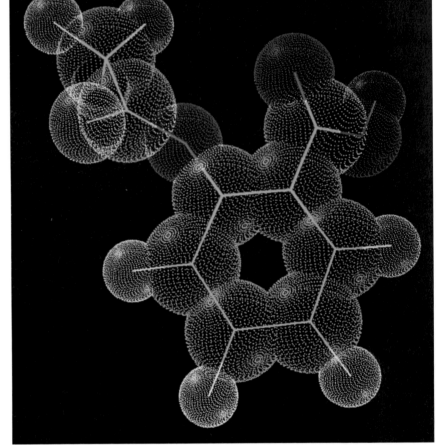

Computer graphic of a molecule of aspirin, 2-ethanoyloxybenzenecarboxylic acid. The carboxylic acid group, −COOH, is shown top right and the ester group −COOCH₃, top left. The ester group is introduced by reaction of salicylic acid, 2-hydroxybenzoic acid, with ethanoic anhydride in an esterification reaction.

**Synthesis of aspirin**
Full details of how to carry out this experiment with a worksheet are available online.

Salicylic acid, 2-hydroxybenzoic acid, is converted into aspirin through esterification, which is a condensation reaction. The process usually uses ethanoic anhydride, $(CH_3CO)_2O$, and can be represented as follows.

salicylic acid    ethanoic anhydride    aspirin    ethanoic acid

Concentrated sulfuric acid or phosphoric acid is added to the reactants and the mixture is warmed gently. The aspirin product must then be isolated and purified from the mixture.

The product is first cooled to cause crystals to form, and then suction filtered and washed with chilled water. Aspirin has a very low solubility in water at low temperature, so this process removes the soluble acids while not leading to the loss of the aspirin product.

Purification involves a technique known as **recrystallization**. This involves dissolving the impure crystals in a minimum volume of hot ethanol, which is a better solvent for

**Recrystallization** purifies a substance by causing it to crystallize from a hot saturated solution during cooling. Impurities stay in the solution.

the impurities than for the aspirin product. A saturated solution of aspirin is formed. As this solution is then cooled *slowly*, the solubility of the aspirin decreases and it crystallizes out of solution first. It can be separated by filtration, as the impurities and unreacted salicylic acid remain in solution.

The purity of the product can be confirmed by **melting point determination**. Pure substances have well-defined melting points which are altered by the presence of impurities. Special apparatus is usually used to carry out this determination and the results are compared with data. Pure aspirin has a melting point of 138–140 °C, and salicylic acid has a melting point of 159 °C. A mixture would have a lower and less well-defined melting point.

The yield can be calculated from the stoichiometry of the reaction, using the mass of salicylic acid used and the mass of product obtained. See Exercise 5 on page 875.

Infrared (IR) spectroscopy can be used in the characterization of aspirin and related molecules. As described in Chapter 11, page 555, the absorption of particular wavenumbers of IR radiation helps to identify the presence of certain functional groups in a molecule. Characteristic IR absorption bands are given in section 26 of the IB data booklet.

The infrared spectra of salicylic acid and aspirin are shown in Figure 15.11.

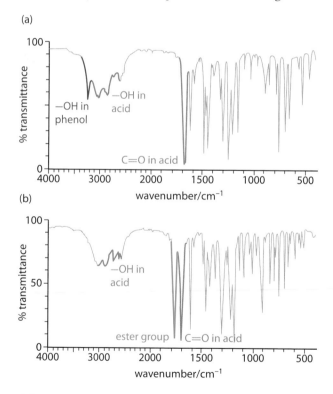

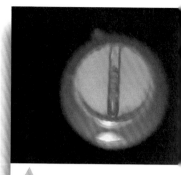

Magnified view through a lens of a melting point determination in a melting point apparatus. The crystals of the sample in the tube are slowly heated electrically until they melt, and the temperature is obtained from a thermometer. Several readings will be averaged and compared with standard literature values to determine the purity of the sample.

**Figure 15.11** IR spectra of (a) salicylic acid and (b) aspirin.

Comparisons of the spectra reveal similarities and differences between the two molecules. The major similarities in the spectra are:

- strong peaks from 1050 to 1410 cm$^{-1}$ due to C—O in alcohol/ester
- strong peaks from 1700 to 1750 cm$^{-1}$ due to C=O in carboxylic acid
- both have broad peaks from 2500 to 3000 cm$^{-1}$ due to OH in carboxylic acid
- both have peaks from 2850 to 3090 cm$^{-1}$ due to C—H (overlapping the broad —OH peak).

The major differences in the spectra are:

- a second peak from 1700 to 1750 $cm^{-1}$ due to presence of ester group in aspirin
- a peak from 3200 to 3600 $cm^{-1}$ in salicylic acid due to the presence of its –OH group; this peak is not present in the aspirin spectrum.

## Physiological effects of aspirin

In 1982 the British chemist John Vane won the Nobel Prize in Medicine for his discovery that aspirin works by blocking the synthesis of prostaglandins. This finding explains the analgesic effects of aspirin, as well as its effectiveness in reducing fever and inflammation, and some of its significant side-effects. The latter can be both positive and negative, as discussed below.

Aspirin is an **anticoagulant**, meaning it reduces the ability of the blood to clot. This makes it useful in the treatment of patients at risk from heart attacks and strokes. Many people use a low daily dose of aspirin as a prophylactic for this purpose. But this same side-effect means that aspirin is not suitable (and could be potentially dangerous) if taken by a person whose blood does not clot easily, or for use following surgery when blood clotting must be allowed to occur. Recent research has also shown that regular intake of a low dose of aspirin may reduce the risk of colon cancer, although additional data are needed before aspirin is routinely recommended for this use.

Negative side-effects of aspirin include irritation and even ulceration of the stomach and duodenum, possibly leading to bleeding. A large number of people, especially those prone to asthma, are also allergic to aspirin, so it must be used with caution. It is not recommended for children under 12 because its use has been linked to Reye's syndrome, a rare and potentially fatal liver and brain disorder.

The physiological effects of aspirin are more acute when it is taken with ethanol in alcoholic drinks. This effect is known as **synergy**, and means that care must be taken when consuming alcoholic drinks alongside medication. The synergistic effects of ethanol and aspirin can cause increased bleeding of the stomach lining and increased risk of ulcers.

## Modification of aspirin for absorption and distribution

Aspirin is available in many formulations, which include various coatings and buffering components. These can delay the activity of the aspirin until it is in the small intestine to help alleviate some of its side-effects.

Aspirin is taken orally and transported in the plasma of the blood in aqueous solution. It has a low solubility in water as it is a largely non-polar molecule. Its bioavailability can be increased by increasing its solubility in water through chemical modification. This involves reacting aspirin with an alkali such as NaOH or $NaHCO_3$, so that it forms an ionic salt.

aspirin is not very soluble

sodium salt of aspirin is more soluble

sodium 2-ethanoyloxybenzenecarboxylate

---

A **prophylactic** refers to a medical treatment that is taken to prevent disease. This is in contrast to drugs which are administered in response to the symptoms of disease.

---

Drugs which contain an acidic or a basic group can be chemically modified to form an ionic salt which increases their aqueous solubility.

Formulations that contain the salt of the acid are known as **soluble aspirin** or **dispersible aspirin**.

Soluble aspirin is dissolved in water and taken into the body by drinking. The increased aqueous solubility of the drug is the result of converting the carboxylic acid group into an ionic salt.

**NATURE OF SCIENCE**

The aspirin story started with anecdotal evidence that extracts from willow tree bark gave relief from pain. From this, scientists progressed to isolate the active ingredient, and later to modify its structure and demonstrate a mechanism for its action. The discovery, synthesis, and development of aspirin at all stages shows the importance of observations and the replication of data.

## Exercises

**5** **(a)** Aspirin is prepared by reacting salicylic acid with excess ethanoic anhydride. In an experiment, 50.05 g of salicylic acid was converted into 55.45 g of aspirin. What was the percentage yield?
  **(b)** How could you check the purity of your product?

**6** Describe how chemical modification of aspirin can increase its bioavailability.

**7** **(a)** Aspirin is described as a *mild analgesic* and as an *anticoagulant*. Explain the meaning of these two terms.
  **(b)** Why can it be dangerous to consume alcoholic drinks when taking aspirin medication?

# Penicillin: an early antibiotic

## The discovery of antibiotics

The first example of a chemical used to kill pathogens came from the observation that certain dyes used in the dyestuffs industry were able to kill some microorganisms. It led in 1891 to the treatment of malaria using methylene blue. Paul Ehrlich of Berlin (page 880) introduced the concept of a 'magic bullet', a chemical designed to target a specific disease but not touch the host cells, and successfully treated syphilis patients with an arsenical drug. Systematic screening for other potential antimicrobials led to the discovery of the sulfonamide drugs, such as Prontosil® in 1933, with their seemingly miraculous ability to cure septicaemia. By 1940, the use of sulfonamides had dramatically reduced the number of deaths of mothers in childbirth.

However, it was the discovery of the chemicals known as **penicillins** that truly revolutionized modern medicine, as this gave birth to drugs now known as **antibiotics**. These are chemicals, usually produced by microorganisms, which have action against other microorganisms. Their discovery is generally credited to Alexander Fleming, who was a Scottish microbiologist, working in 1928 on bacteria cultures. He noticed that a fungus (or mould) known as *Penicillium notatum* had contaminated some of his cultures, and was therefore about to discard them as spoiled. However, his eye was drawn to the fact that the mould had generated a clear region around it where no bacterial colonies were growing. He concluded that something produced by the mould was specifically inhibiting the bacterial growth. Fleming published his findings, but as he and his collaborators were not chemists, they did not pursue the work of isolating and identifying the active ingredient.

Fleming's original culture plate of the fungus *Penicillium notatum*, photographed 25 years after the discovery in 1928. The clear region around the fungus where bacterial growth is inhibited can be clearly seen.

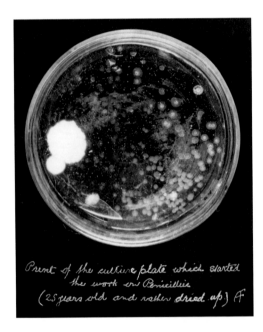

*Print of the culture plate which started the work on Penicillin (25 years old and rather dried up) AF*

During World War II, when penicillin supply could not meet demand, it was a common practice to collect the urine from patients being treated to isolate and reuse the penicillin it contained. It was estimated that as much as 80% of early penicillin formulations was lost from the body in the urine.

### NATURE OF SCIENCE

The story of Fleming's discovery of penicillin is often described as serendipitous – a fortunate discovery made by chance or by accident. But it was more than that. Would not the majority of people who noticed the plates were contaminated simply have thrown them away, likely disappointed at the 'failed experiment'? The difference was that Fleming had the insight to observe the plates carefully and ask the right questions about why a clear ring appeared around the fungal growth. Scientists are trained to be observant and to seek explanations for what they see, and this must include the unexpected. As Louis Pasteur once famously said, 'Chance favours only the prepared mind'. Consider to what extent scientific discoveries are only possible to scientists who are trained in the principles of observation and interpretation.

In the early 1940s, the Australian bacteriologist Howard Florey and German-born biochemist Ernst Chain, working in Oxford, England, picked up the research and successfully isolated penicillin as the antibacterial agent produced by the penicillium mould. It was used for the first time in human trials in 1941. This was in the midst of World War II when there was an unprecedented demand for such a treatment for bacterial infections resulting from war wounds. Its rapid development and distribution is known to have saved thousands of lives in the later years of the war. For their work in discovering penicillin, Fleming, Florey, and Chain shared the Nobel Prize in Medicine in 1945.

The main research and production of penicillin was moved to the USA in 1941 to protect it from the bombs attacking Britain during the war. Large-scale production methods were developed using deep fermentation tanks containing corn steep liquor with sterile air being forced through.

## The action of penicillin

The isolation and development of penicillin occurred, however, before there was any understanding of its chemical structure or its mode of action. It was the work of British biochemist Dorothy Hodgkin in 1945 using X-ray crystallography that determined the structure of **penicillin G**, the major constituent of the mould extract.

The structure of penicillin can be considered as a dipeptide formed from two amino acids, cysteine and valine. The molecule contains a nucleus of a five-membered ring

Dorothy Hodgkin (1910–1994), the British X-ray crystallographer who discovered the structures of penicillin, vitamin B12, and insulin. She was awarded the Nobel Prize in Chemistry in 1964.

containing a sulfur atom known as thiazolidine, attached to a four-membered ring containing a cyclic amide group, known as **beta-lactam**. This ring consists of one nitrogen and three carbon atoms, and is the part of the molecule responsible for its antibacterial properties.

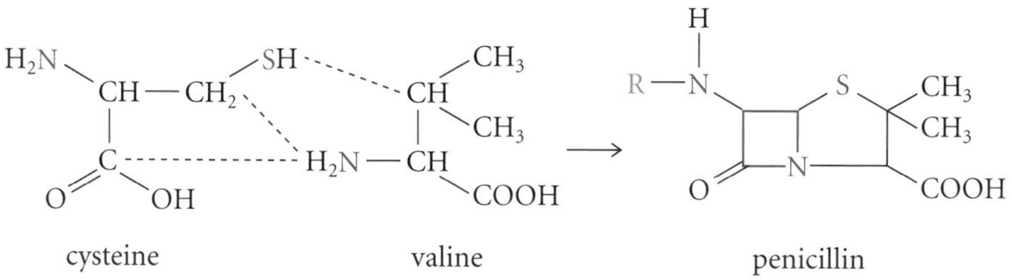

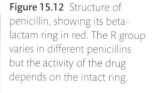

**Figure 15.12** Structure of penicillin, showing its beta-lactam ring in red. The R group varies in different penicillins but the activity of the drug depends on the intact ring.

This structure is highly unusual as beta-lactam rings were unknown before the discovery of penicillin. The bond angles in this ring are reduced to about 90°, despite the fact that because they have sp² and sp³ hybridized atomic orbitals the atoms in the ring seek to form bonds with angles of 120° and 109.5° respectively. This puts a strain on the bonds, effectively weakening them. Consequently the ring breaks relatively easily, and this is the key to the molecule's biological activity.

The action of these beta-lactam antibiotics is to disrupt the formation of cell walls of bacteria by inhibiting a key bacterial enzyme, **transpeptidase**. As the drug approaches the enzyme, the high reactivity of the amide group in the ring causes it to bind irreversibly near the active site of the enzyme as the ring breaks. Inactivation of the enzyme in this way blocks the process of cell wall construction within the bacterium because it prevents polypeptide cross-links from forming between the mucopeptide chains. Without these strengthening links, the cell wall is unable to support the bacterium, and so it bursts and dies.

Penicillin's action is effective against a wide range of bacteria, many of which are responsible for infections of the ear, nose, throat, and mouth as well as sites of infection from wounds.

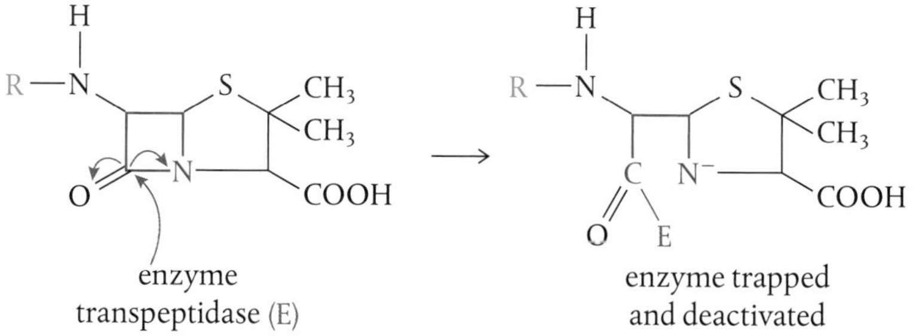

enzyme
transpeptidase (E)

enzyme trapped
and deactivated

## CHALLENGE YOURSELF

1   Work out the hybridization of each of the carbon atoms in the structure of penicillin given here.

**Figure 15.13** The action of penicillin. By means of its highly reactive beta-lactam ring, the antibiotic binds and deactivates the transpeptidase enzyme. This leads to a halting of bacterial cell wall construction causing bacterial death.

Bacterial cell walls are chemically quite distinct from cell walls in plants and cell membranes in plants and animals. The polypeptide chains used to build the cross-links to strengthen the bacterial cell wall contain the amino acid d-alanine. Only its optical isomer, l-alanine, is found in humans. So penicillin selectively targets bacteria and is generally not toxic to animals.

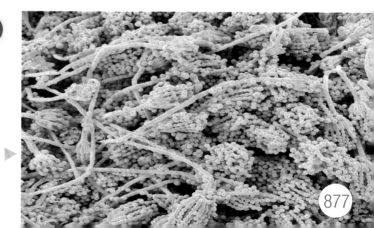

Coloured scanning electron micrograph of *Penicillium* sp. growing on bread. This is the mould that is used to produce the antibiotic penicillin.

**Ring strain in the beta-lactam ring is responsible for the activity of penicillins.**

A disadvantage of penicillin G is that it is broken down by stomach acid, and so has to be injected directly into the blood. Different forms of penicillin have been developed by modifying the side chain (the part denoted as 'R' in Figures 15.12 and 15.13), and these enable the drug to retain its activity even when ingested in pill form. The use of penicillin is limited by the significant number of people who suffer from allergic responses to it.

## Antibiotic resistance: bacteria fight back

Confirmation that the beta-lactam ring is crucial to penicillin's antibacterial action comes from studies that show the drug loses all activity when this ring is broken. This is what happens in the presence of some bacteria which show **antibacterial resistance**.

Bacterial resistance to penicillin – and also to other antibiotics – has become a major problem in modern medicine. This was observed as early as the 1940s when penicillin proved to be ineffective against some populations of bacteria. It is now known that these resistant bacteria produce an enzyme, **penicillinase** or **beta-lactamase**, which can open penicillin's four-membered ring and render it inactive. The spread of these resistant bacteria in a population is increased by exposure to the antibiotic, as this wipes out the non-resistant strains and so gives the resistant strains a competitive advantage.

Responses to the challenge of antibiotic resistance to penicillin include the following.

**Figure 15.14** A graph showing the rapid increase in the number of different β-lactamase enzymes identified since 1970.

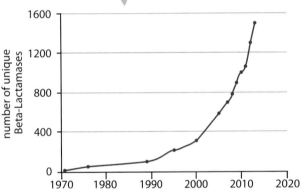

• The synthesis of different forms of penicillin which are able to withstand the action of penicillinase. These include methicillin, which has now largely been replaced by oxacillin, due to the spread of methicillin-resistant bacteria.

**Figure 15.15** The structures of (a) methicillin and (b) oxacillin. Both drugs are made by modifying the side chains in penicillin (denoted by R in Figures 15.12 and 15.13, and shown in green here) make the drug resistant to the penicillinase enzyme.

These two penicillin derivatives still have the beta-lactam ring, but have modified side-chains which prevent the binding of the penicillinase enzyme, and so protect the ring from cleavage before it finds its target.

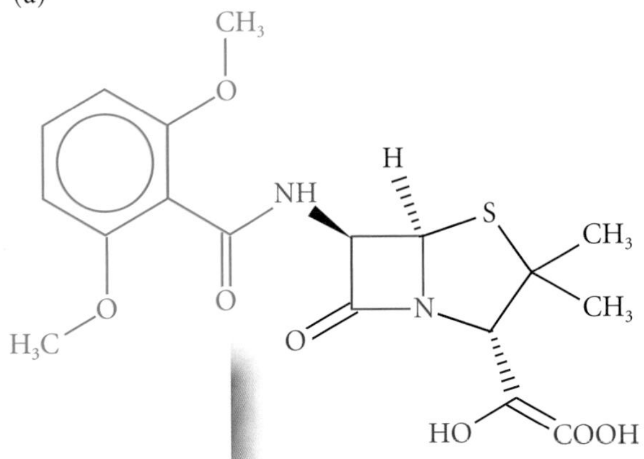

• The control and restriction of the use of antibiotics by legislation to make them prescription-only drugs. In addition, doctors are encouraged not to over-prescribe antibiotics when other treatments can be effective.

(a)

CH₃

H₃C

(b)

H₃C

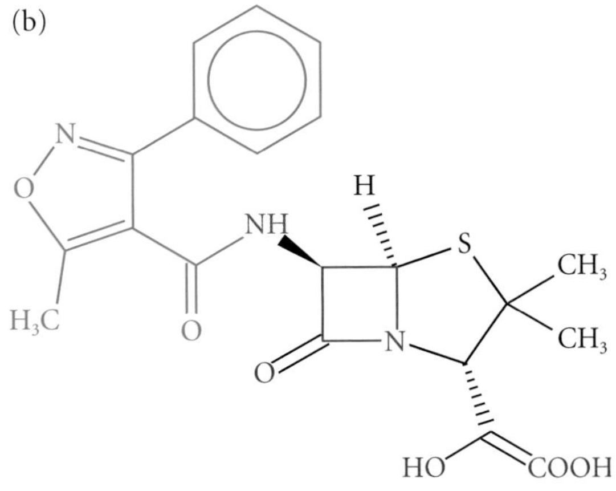

- The education of patients in the importance of completing the full course of treatment with an antibiotic, referred to as 'patient compliance'. This is essential to prevent resistant bacteria prolonging the disease or spreading into the community.

The problems of antibiotic-resistant bacteria are discussed further on page 933.

The problems of antibiotic-resistant bacteria are discussed further on page 933.

### Exercises

8  **(a)** With reference to the structure given in section 37 of the IB data booklet, determine the molecular formula of penicillin.
   **(b)** Mark on the molecule where the side chain can be modified and explain why this is done.
   **(c)** Refer to the part of the molecule responsible for its antibiotic properties, and explain the basis of its mode of action.

9  Discuss three ways in which human activities have caused an increase in the resistance to penicillin in bacterial populations.

## D.3   Opiates

## Understandings:

- The ability of a drug to cross the blood–brain barrier depends on its chemical structure and solubility in water and lipids.
- Opiates are natural narcotic analgesics that are derived from the opium poppy.
- Morphine and codeine are used as strong analgesics. Strong analgesics work by temporarily bonding to receptor sites in the brain, preventing the transmission of pain impulses without depressing the central nervous system.
- Medical use and addictive properties of opiate compounds are related to the presence of opioid receptors in the brain.

## Applications and skills:

- Explanation of the synthesis of codeine and diamorphine from morphine.
- Description and explanation of the use of strong analgesics.
- Comparison of the structures of morphine, codeine, and diamorphine (heroin).
- Discussion of the advantages and disadvantages of using morphine and its derivatives as strong analgesics.
- Discussion of side-effects and addiction to opiate compounds.
- Explanation of the increased potency of diamorphine compared to morphine based on their chemical structure and solubility.

### Guidance
*Structures of morphine, codeine, and diamorphine can be found in the data booklet in section 37.*

## The opiates bind to receptor sites in the brain

We have seen that aspirin acts as a mild analgesic. A completely different group of compounds, the **opiates** (also known as **opioids**), act as **strong analgesics**. This means that they kill pain by preventing the transmission of pain impulses in the brain, rather than at the source (see Figure 15.8 on page 871).

Opiates are natural analgesics that are derived from **opium**, which is found in poppy seeds. The first records of cultivation of the opium poppy go back to Mesopotamia more than 5000 years ago. This crop has had a very long, complex, and bloody history. It seems likely that no chemical product ever has been responsible for more wars, economic fortunes, and legislative changes, and this is still the case today.

Flower and seed head of *Papaver somniferum*, the opium poppy.

The analgesic properties of the opiates arise because we possess so-called **opioid receptors** in the brain to which they bind temporarily. This binding blocks the transmission of impulses between brain cells that would signal pain. In other words, strong analgesics interfere with the *perception* of pain without depressing the central nervous system.

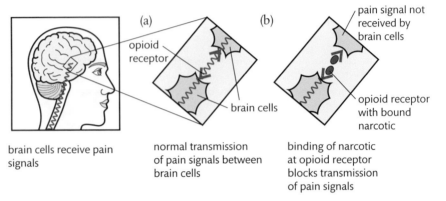

(a)

opioid receptor

brain cells

brain cells receive pain signals

normal transmission of pain signals between brain cells

(b)

pain signal not received by brain cells

opioid receptor with bound narcotic

binding of narcotic at opioid receptor blocks transmission of pain signals

**Figure 15.16** The action of strong analgesics is to bind at opioid receptors in the brain cells and so block the transmission of pain signals.

Because these analgesics act on the brain, they may cause possible changes in behaviour and mood, so they are also known as **narcotics**. Opioids are the most effective painkillers for severe pain, but due to their side-effects and potential problems with dependence, their usage must be monitored through medical supervision.

## Strong analgesics must enter the brain

The target for the opiates is the brain. This presents a challenge as the brain is surrounded by a membrane-bound structure, known as the **blood–brain barrier**, which protects it by restricting the chemicals that can enter from the blood. Like all membranes, this structure is made largely of lipids which are non-polar molecules. The blood–brain barrier is therefore a hydrophobic, non-polar environment, not easily crossed by polar molecules. For a drug to penetrate this barrier and enter the brain, it will be more effective when it itself is non-polar and lipid soluble.

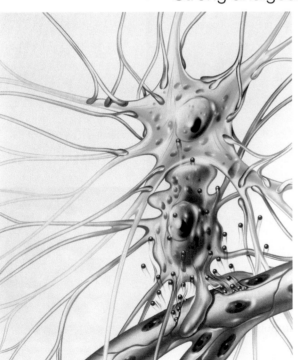

 The blood–brain barrier was first discovered by the German scientist Paul Ehrlich in the late 19th century, when he observed that a blue dye introduced into the blood of an animal coloured all its organs blue except the brain. Later experiments involved injecting the dye into the spinal fluid, when it was found that the brain became dyed but the rest of the body did not. This tight control over the movement of substances between fluids in the brain and blood vessels helps to protect the brain. But one of the challenges in treating brain diseases such as tumours involves outwitting this natural defence of the brain so that it will allow therapeutic chemicals to enter.

Illustration of the transmission of a drug from a blood capillary into a nerve cell of the brain. Small molecules which leave the blood, shown as blue spheres, have to pass through the cell shown in orange which supports and selectively screens molecules from the nerve cell of the brain, shown in green. This blood–brain barrier stops harmful molecules from reaching the brain. Molecules which are more non-polar such as heroin are able to cross this barrier more easily.

The analgesic properties of the opiates depend largely on their ability to move from the blood, where aqueous solubility is important, into the brain where lipid solubility is important to cross the barrier. The solubilities of the drugs are determined by their chemical structure.

## The structures and synthesis of opioids

The narcotic drugs derived from opium are primarily morphine and its derivatives.

We will consider three of these here: **codeine**, **morphine**, and **diamorphine** (known as **heroin**).

The structure and effects of these drugs are compared in the table below.

| | Codeine | Morphine | Diamorphine (heroin) |
|---|---|---|---|
| structure | | | |
| functional groups | • arene<br>• ether (2)<br>• alkenyl<br>• hydroxyl (1)<br>• tertiary amino | • arene<br>• ether<br>• alkenyl<br>• hydroxyl (2)<br>• tertiary amino | • arene<br>• ether<br>• alkenyl<br>• ester (ethanoate) (2)<br>• tertiary amino |
| obtained from | raw opium (0.5%)<br>usually prepared from morphine | raw opium (10%) | found in opium, but usually obtained by reaction of morphine |
| therapeutic uses | • sometimes used in a preparation with a non-narcotic drug such as aspirin or paracetamol in the second stage of the pain management ladder<br>• also used in cough medications and in the short-term treatment of diarrhoea | • used in the management of severe pain, such as in advanced cancer<br>• can be habit forming and can lead to dependence, so use must be regulated by a medical professional | • used medically only in a few countries legally for the relief of severe pain<br>• the most rapidly acting and the most abused narcotic<br>• initially produces euphoric effects, but very high potential for causing addiction and increasing tolerance<br>• dependence leads to withdrawal symptoms and many associated problems |

Notice that these three drugs have a common basic structure that accounts for their similar properties, as well as some different functional groups. Morphine is the principle drug derived from opium. When administered through intravenous injection it has about six times the bioavailability as when taken orally. The two –OH groups in morphine give it some polarity which limits its ability to cross the blood–brain barrier.

Codeine is found at low levels in opium but is more commonly prepared from morphine. It is therefore known as a **semi-synthetic** drug. The reaction converts one

## CHALLENGE YOURSELF

2 Suggest why ethanoic anhydride may be more effective than ethanoic acid for carrying out the esterification of morphine.

The process used in the methylation of morphine to form codeine has evolved over time. The reaction was first carried out in 1881 by reacting morphine with methyl iodide, $CH_3I$, in alkaline solution.

morphine + $CH_3I$ + KOH → codeine + KI + $H_2O$

But the reaction is inhibited by the water released. Later methods involve the use of methylbenzene, $C_6H_5CH_3$, which acts to remove water from the reaction mixture by distillation.

of the −OH groups into the methyl ether, so is known as methylation. This change makes codeine a less polar molecule than morphine and so it can cross the blood–brain barrier more easily. However, the conversion also causes a significant drop in the binding at the opioid receptors, which makes codeine a weaker analgesic than morphine.

Diamorphine (heroin) is produced from morphine by an esterification reaction in which both −OH groups are converted into ethanoate (ester) groups by reaction with ethanoic acid ($CH_3COOH$) or ethanoic anhydride (($CH_3CO)_2O$). This reduces the polarity significantly, making diamorphine much more lipid soluble than morphine and so more able to cross the blood–brain barrier. This is why it is faster acting than the other opioid drugs.

The synthesis of codeine and diamorphine from morphine is summarized below.

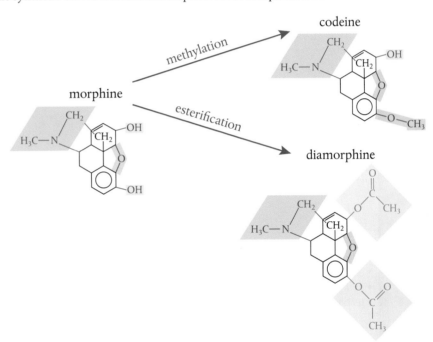

As a result of their structures and solubilities, these three drugs differ in their effectiveness as follows:

- codeine:
- morphine:
- diamorphine:

increasing strength as analgesics
increasing narcotic effects
increasing side-effects

So diamorphine has a much greater potency than morphine, reaching the brain cells faster and in higher concentration. It is more active by a factor of two. Note that this also applies to its greater side-effects as well as to its characteristics of tolerance and dependence. Inside the brain diamorphine must undergo metabolic change before it can act at the opioid receptors. The ester links are broken by enzymes called **esterases**. For this reason diamorphine is described as a **pro-drug**, meaning that its metabolic products, mostly morphine, actually bring about its effects. The molecular structure of diamorphine can be thought of as a way of 'packaging' the morphine so that it can reach its target more efficiently.

Another derivative of morphine known as 6-acetylmorphine, which contains the ester link at only one of the positions, is even more potent than heroin as it does not need to undergo this hydrolysis reaction before interacting with the brain cells. It is produced as a metabolite from heroin in the body, but due to its high activity it is an extremely dangerous drug when taken in pure form.

The so-called opium wars involving China, Britain, France, and India in the late 19th century erupted from trade disputes involving opium. They ended in the imposition of several treaties by western countries on China, including the yielding of Hong Kong to Britain, which ended in 1997. Opium production continues to be a major, if illegal, crop, particularly in South West Asia. Afghanistan produces most of the world's opiates, and increasingly is processing more of the crop into heroin within the country. According to a United Nations (UN) report in 2013, the cultivation of opium has been steadily increasing in Afghanistan, despite eradication attempts and UN-backed incentive programmes to reduce production.

## NATURE OF SCIENCE

The analgesic action of opium derivatives has been known for hundreds of years, well in advance of an understanding of their effects. Morphine was first isolated in 1803, and was administered during the American Civil War in the 1860s. As there was little useful information available on dosage, side-effects, and dependence, its use caused the deaths and addiction of many soldiers. Diamorphine went on the market in 1898, marketed as 'heroin' because it was believed to be the 'heroic' drug that would banish pain forever. It had to be withdrawn from general distribution 5 years later when its addictive properties became evident. Over time, this 'hit and miss' approach to pain management has evolved into official protocols with clear guidelines. This has been possible because data on the action of opiates has been widely collected and shared, so that their uses and potential problems have more fully evaluated. Data collection and analysis of trends and causal links is an ongoing aspect of medical science.

# Advantages and disadvantages of using strong analgesics

## Pain management

The World Health Organization (WHO) has developed a three-step 'analgesic ladder' to be a simple guideline to encourage better global standards of pain management.

1  use mild analgesics
2  add a weak opioid such as codeine or tramadol
3  in severe intractable pain, use strong opioids such as morphine, methadone, or possibly diamorphine.

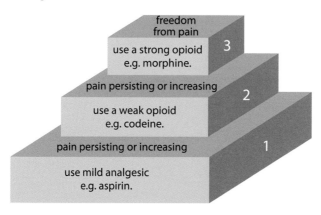

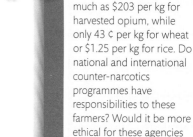

Morphine is a chiral molecule and exists naturally as a single stereoisomer (−). When it was first synthesized it was made as a racemic mixture of the naturally occurring stereoisomer with its (+) enantiomer. When these were separated and tested, it was found that the (+) form, which does not occur in nature, has no analgesic activity.

**TOK** A UN source states that farmers can earn as much as $203 per kg for harvested opium, while only 43 ¢ per kg for wheat or $1.25 per kg for rice. Do national and international counter-narcotics programmes have responsibilities to these farmers? Would it be more ethical for these agencies to buy rather than burn the opium crops?

Despite the fact that cost-effective methods of pain control exist, they are not widely used everywhere. There are cultural, societal, political, and economic factors that influence the availability of painkillers globally. Recognizing this as a deep problem, coalitions of doctors in many countries are pushing towards the goal of making access to pain management a universal human right.

**Figure 15.17** The WHO three-step analgesic ladder.

In step 3, cases of severe pain, intravenous morphine is the most widely used analgesic. In some places, notably the UK and a few European countries, diamorphine (heroin) is available as a legally prescribed, controlled drug.

## Side-effects

Strong analgesics have several other effects that can sometimes be used for therapeutic purposes, but sometimes are considered adverse side-effects. They include:

• constipation
• suppression of the cough reflex
• constriction of the pupil in the eye
• narcotic effects, which are discussed below.

The constipating effects of mild opioids are sometimes used in medication. A mixture of kaolin and morphine is used to treat cases of diarrhoea, as the morphine reduces the muscle contractions in the lower gut and so slows down the passage of faecal matter. It is not used as a painkiller in this context.

## Narcotic effects and addiction

The word 'narcotic' is derived from a Greek word meaning numbness or stupor. Narcotics depress brain function, induce sleep, and are potentially addictive. Diamorphine is the most potent narcotic, causing the problem of heroin addiction.

In the short-term, heroin induces a feeling of well-being and contentment, as it causes a dulling of pain and a lessening of fear and tension. There is often a feeling of euphoria in the initial stages after intake. But relatively quickly, heroin users start to show dependence, so they cannot function properly without the drug and suffer from withdrawal symptoms such as cold sweats and anxiety when it is withheld. This is compounded by an increasing tolerance to the drug, so higher doses are needed to bring about relief. In most countries access to the drug usually involves dealing in an illegal market, and the cost of the supply is often beyond the individual's means. This in turn may lead to crime and other social problems. As the drug is taken by injection, the user commonly picks up infections such as HIV and hepatitis from unclean needles. In short, the life of the heroin addict is usually profoundly altered by the drug.

Helping heroin addicts to break their dependence is a slow and difficult process. Sometimes an alternate analgesic, **methadone**, is administered. Methadone is taken orally and has a longer duration of action. This can reduce drug craving and prevent symptoms of withdrawal. Although its use is controversial in some countries, research has shown that methadone maintenance is an effective treatment for opioid dependence and has substantially reduced the death rates of addicts receiving it.

**TOK**

Laws often exist to protect people from things that can do them harm – such as making it compulsory to wear a seat belt in a car or banning certain chemical substances. Some argue that these laws impinge on personal rights and freedoms; others argue that they validate the rights to safety of society at large. To what extent do you think these points of view are in opposition with each other?

Heroin user slumped after injecting himself with diamorphine. The tourniquet around his arm is used to make the veins stand out to ease injection. Heroin, a strong analgesic, is a highly addictive drug with powerful narcotic effects.

### Exercises

**10** Codeine, morphine, and heroin are described as strong analgesics.

(a) State two functional groups common to codeine, morphine, and heroin.
(b) A patient has been prescribed morphine following surgery. State the main effect and a major side-effect she will experience.

**11** By reference to its chemical structure, explain why diamorphine is more potent in its action as a strong analgesic than morphine.

**12** The medical use of diamorphine is allowed only in some countries. Give arguments in favour and against its legal controlled use.

# D.4 pH regulation of the stomach

## Understandings:
- Non-specific reactions, such as the use of antacids, are those that work to reduce the excess stomach acid.
- Active metabolites are the active forms of a drug after it has been processed by the body.

## Applications and skills:
- Explanation of how excess acidity in the stomach can be reduced by the use of different bases.
- Construction and balancing of equations for neutralization reactions and the stoichiometric application of these equations.
- Solving buffer problems using the Henderson–Hasselbalch equation.
- Explanation of how compounds such as ranitidine (Zantac) can be used to inhibit stomach acid production.
- Explanation of how compounds like omeprazole (Prilosec) and esomeprazole (Nexium) can be used to suppress acid secretion in the stomach.

### Guidance
- *Antacid compounds should include calcium hydroxide, magnesium hydroxide, aluminium hydroxide, sodium carbonate, and sodium bicarbonate (sodium hydrogencarbonate).*
- *Structures for ranitidine, omeprazole, and esomeprazole can be found in the data booklet in section 37.*

## Excess acidity in the stomach is potentially harmful

The body keeps a tight control over the pH in cells and extra-cellular fluids, as changes in the H⁺ concentration have significant effects on the activity of many molecules, especially enzymes. The gastro-intestinal tract, or **gut**, generates and maintains different pH environments along its length, which play an important role in controlling the activity of digestive enzymes.

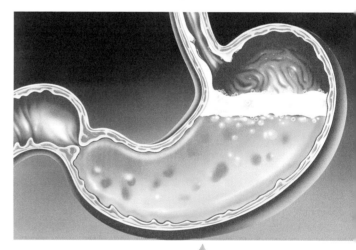

Illustration of a raft of foaming antacid on top of the contents of a human stomach. Heartburn is caused by a rising of the stomach's acidic contents into the oesophagus, shown in the upper centre, causing inflammation and a sense of pain. Antacids neutralize the acid to bring relief.

The stomach is unusual in that it generates a pH as low as 1–2 by the production of hydrochloric acid, HCl. The acid is released from specialized cells called **parietal cells** in gastric glands in the lining of the stomach wall. The acid environment not only kills bacteria that may have been ingested with food, but also provides the optimum environment for the action of its digestive enzymes. However, some factors, such as excess alcohol, smoking, caffeine, stress, and some anti-inflammatory drugs, can cause excess production of this acidic secretion, known as **gastric juice**. This can lead to the following problems:

- acid indigestion – feeling of discomfort from too much acid in the stomach
- heartburn – acid from the stomach rising into the oesophagus (often called acid reflux)
- ulceration – damage to the lining of the gut wall, resulting in loss of tissue and inflammation.

The term **dyspepsia** is used to refer to feelings of pain and discomfort in the upper abdomen, which include indigestion and heartburn.

Ulcers can occur in different regions of the gut, and there are distinct differences in the relative frequency of occurrence of the different types of ulcer. For example, in the British population duodenal ulcers are more common, whereas in Japan gastric ulcers predominate. The reasons for the different occurrences are probably based on diet, but there are other possible causes, including genetics.

## NATURE OF SCIENCE

The study of dyspepsia provides a good example of what scientists call *cause and effect*. Excess stomach acid (cause) brings about the symptoms of indigestion and heartburn (effect). The relationship is known as a causal relationship because a mechanism exists to explain the link between the variables. (This is different from a correlation, which is a mutual relationship between two variables that lacks a linking mechanism. For example, in the last 50 years there has been an increase in both atmospheric $CO_2$ and in obesity - but there is no mechanism to suggest that obesity is the *cause* of this atmospheric change. Correlation does not always imply causation.)

Understanding the cause and effect relationship of excess stomach acid and dyspepsia leads to two different approaches to the treatment:

1 reduce or remove the cause

2 ameliorate the effects.

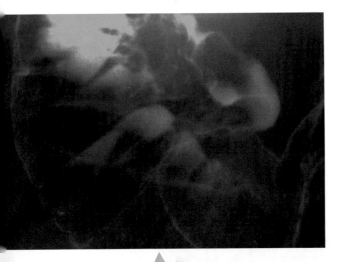

False-colour double contrast X-ray showing a duodenal ulcer as the oval pink feature in the upper centre-right. Ulcers can cause severe pain. Healing is promoted by antibiotics and by drugs that block the secretion of acid.

## Some drugs work to prevent the production of excess acid

In the early 1980s, a surprising discovery was made. Researchers in Australia identified a bacterium, known as *Helicobacter pylori*, that was shown to be a cause of stomach ulcers and linked to the risk of developing stomach cancer. The *Helicobacter* burrows into the mucus lining of the stomach, causing inflammation. This leads to loss of mechanisms that protect the stomach wall from its hostile acidic contents, and so tissue breakdown occurs. Conditions such as chronic inflammation and ulcers were not previously thought to be related to microorganisms, and so the discovery of *Helicobacter* led to significant changes in treatment regimens. Antibiotics are now frequently prescribed for these conditions, and used in combination with the drugs that reduce acid secretion (described below).

The presence of *Helicobacter* in the stomach can be tested using a breathalyser. The patient is given a drink containing urea that has been labelled with non-radioactive carbon-13. If present, the bacteria will break down the urea, causing the release of carbon-13 labelled $CO_2$ in the breath.

## H$_2$-receptor antagonists

The body is equipped with complex mechanisms to protect it from the self-harm that could result from uncontrolled release of stomach acid. Together these mechanisms ensure that gastric juice is released only when required – stimulated by the presence of food and distension (stretching) of the stomach walls. Several transmitters and chemical messengers called hormones are involved, and of these **histamine** is of specific interest.

Histamine has the structure shown in Figure 15.18.

**Figure 15.18** The structure of histamine, a chemical transmitter in the body that stimulates stomach acid production by binding at H$_2$ receptors.

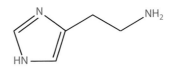

Histamine has different functions in the body and several different receptor sites. In the stomach it stimulates secretion of stomach acid by interacting at receptors known as $H_2$ (not to be confused with hydrogen gas!) in the parietal cells in the gastric glands. This histamine interaction initiates a sequence of events, leading to the release of acid into the stomach lumen. This suggests that a possible target for a drug which will reduce stomach acid secretion would be to block the histamine–$H_2$ interaction. Drugs which do this and which compete with histamine for binding at the $H_2$ receptors are known as **$H_2$-receptor antagonists**.

Ranitidine (Zantac) is an example of an $H_2$-receptor antagonist drug. It was developed from analogues of histamine using knowledge of the $H_2$-receptor structure, and refined from earlier drugs to increase its potency. In many countries it is now available as an over-the-counter drug, but higher dosages need prescription.

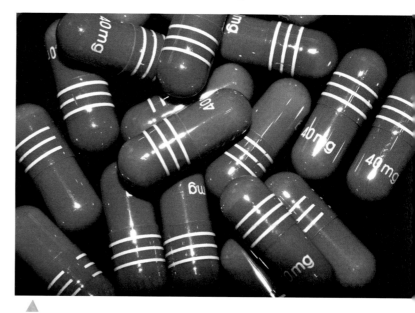

**Figure 15.19** The structure of ranitidine (Zantac), an $H_2$-antagonist that inhibits stomach acid production.

Zantac is quite widely used, but in many cases has been superseded by the proton pump inhibitors described below.

## Proton pump inhibitors

In the last step of gastric acid secretion, the parietal cells in the gastric glands pump protons ($H^+$) across their membranes and into the lumen of the stomach. For each $H^+$ ion pumped into the lumen, one $K^+$ ion is pumped in the opposite direction so there is no charge build-up. Movement of the ions occurs against their concentration gradients and so requires energy. This is provided by the hydrolysis of an energy carrier known as ATP, using the enzyme ATPase which is embedded in the cell membrane. The enzyme is therefore known as the **$H^+/K^+$ ATPase** or simply as a **gastric proton pump**.

Drugs which inhibit the proton pump will directly prevent the release of acid into the stomach lumen. The first proton pump inhibitor was omeprazole, marketed as Prilosec, which was followed by the release of esomeprazole or Nexium when the patent for Prilosec expired in 2001. These drugs, shown in Figure 15.20, are amongst the world's most largely used medications.

Nexium pills, showing their distinctive purple colour with racing stripes. Prilosec was the original purple pill marketed by AstraZeneca, and this design was modified with the launch of Nexium to suggest its increased potency. Prilosec and Nexium are both proton pump inhibitors that reduce the secretion of stomach acid, but scientists are divided on their relative effectiveness.

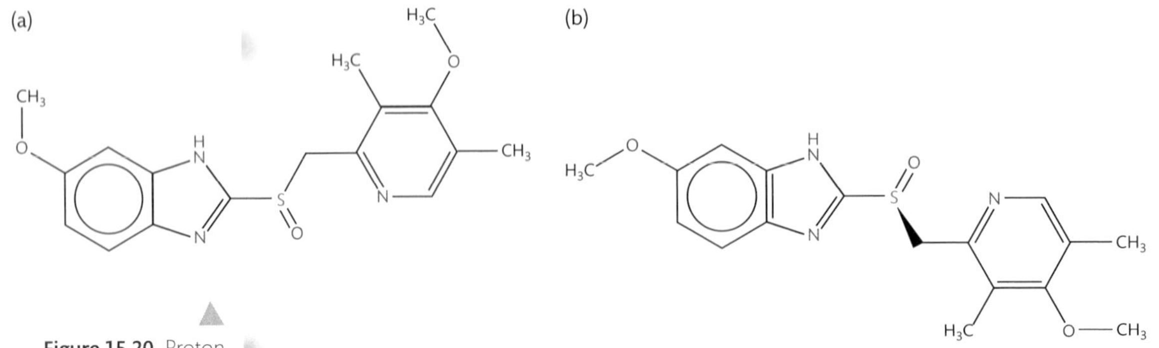

(a)

(b)

**Figure 15.20** Proton pump inhibitor drugs (a) omeprazole (Prilosec) and (b) esomeprazole (Nexiom).

If you study the formulas of omeprazole and esomeprazole, which can also be found in section 37 of the IB data booklet, you could be forgiven for thinking they look the same. They are in fact the same structure. Like many drugs, they exist as stereoisomers: omeprazole is a racemic mixture of the *R* and *S* forms, whereas esomeprazole is only the *S* enantiomer (*es*-omeprazole). There is evidence that the *S* form has greater potency as a proton pump inhibitor, leading to claims that this molecule alone, marketed as Nexium, is more effective than equivalent amounts of Prilosec. This is reflected in the higher price of Nexium. There are, however, counter claims that this is simply a marketing strategy, as in fact the two enantiomers interconvert in the body and so the drugs are equally effective. Medical doctors often face a choice when prescribing medicines, and conflicting information such as this makes it difficult. The situation demands data, the lifeblood of science, and this needs to be as objective and free from bias as possible.

## Summary of the action of $H_2$-receptor antagonists and proton pump inhibitors in reducing stomach acid secretion

**Figure 15.21** Summary of the targets of drugs that reduce the production of stomach acid.

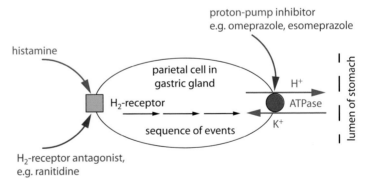

**Investigation of the effectiveness of antacids**
Full details of how to carry out this experiment with a worksheet are available online.

## Antacids are weak bases which neutralize excess acid

Drugs to help combat excess stomach acid are known as **antacids**. They work by neutralizing the hydrochloric acid, so relieving the symptoms. Antacids are usually *weakly* basic compounds, often metal oxides, hydroxides, carbonates, or hydrogencarbonates. Strong bases cannot be used because they are caustic and would cause direct harm to the stomach. The antacids used do not directly coat the ulcer or induce healing, but according to the dictum 'no acid, no ulcer', they do allow the stomach lining time to mend. Antacids are used for a wide variety of non-specific digestive disorders.

Antacids which contain metal hydroxides include calcium hydroxide, magnesium hydroxide, and aluminium hydroxide. These neutralize hydrochloric acid with the formation of a salt and water, as shown below:

- calcium hydroxide, $Ca(OH)_2$

$$Ca(OH)_2(aq) + 2HCl(aq) \rightarrow CaCl_2(aq) + 2H_2O(l)$$

- magnesium hydroxide, $Mg(OH)_2$

$$Mg(OH)_2(aq) + 2HCl(aq) \rightarrow MgCl_2(aq) + 2H_2O(l)$$

- aluminium hydroxide, $Al(OH)_3$

$$Al(OH)_3(aq) + 3HCl(aq) \rightarrow AlCl_3(aq) + 3H_2O(l)$$

Several antacid formulations contain both aluminium and magnesium compounds, as they complement each other well. Magnesium salts tend to be faster acting, but aluminium compounds, because they dissolve more slowly, tend to provide longer-lasting relief. In addition, magnesium salts tend to act as a laxative, whereas aluminium salts cause constipation. Aluminium has been linked with the development of Alzheimer's disease, and although this is by no means proven, many people carefully limit its intake.

Antacids which contain metal carbonates and hydrogencarbonates include sodium carbonate and sodium hydrogencarbonate. These neutralize hydrochloric acid with the formation of a salt, water, and carbon dioxide, as shown below:

- sodium hydrogencarbonate, $NaHCO_3$

$$NaHCO_3(aq) + HCl(aq) \rightarrow NaCl(aq) + H_2O(l) + CO_2(g)$$

- sodium carbonate, $Na_2CO_3$

$$Na_2CO_3(aq) + 2HCl(aq) \rightarrow 2NaCl(aq) + H_2O(l) + CO_2(g)$$

The gas released can cause bloating of the stomach and flatulence. To reduce this side-effect, antifoaming agents are often added to the formulation. Some antacids also contain alginates which float to the top of the stomach, forming a 'raft' which acts as a barrier preventing reflux into the oesophagus.

Note that because antacids change the pH of the stomach, they can alter other chemical reactions, including the absorption of other drugs. Although they are over-the-counter drugs, they should not be taken for an extended period without medical supervision.

## pH and buffering

As we noted, biological systems are very sensitive to changes in pH. This is why complex buffering systems exist in cells that help to prevent major fluctuations in the pH. Buffers resist the change in the pH of a solution on the addition of small amounts of acid or base, and can be prepared to operate at a wide range of pH. The composition and mode of action of buffers was discussed in Chapter 8, and you might find it useful to review this first before going on to this section on the calculation of the pH of a buffer solution.

The pH of a buffer solution, that is its $H^+$ concentration, will depend on the interactions among its components. We will consider here an acidic buffer made of the generic weak acid HA and its salt MA.

The equilibria that exist in the buffer will be as follows.

1  weak acid:  $\quad\quad\quad\quad\quad HA(aq) \rightleftharpoons H^+(aq) + A^-(aq)$

2  salt:  $\quad\quad\quad\quad\quad\quad\quad MA(aq) \rightarrow M^+(aq) + A^-(aq)$

We can make two approximations, based on some assumptions about these reactions, which will help to make the calculations easier.

An antacid tablet dissolving in a glass of water. The fizzing is due to the release of carbon dioxide as the sodium carbonate reacts with water. Antacids neutralize stomach acid and so relieve the symptoms of indigestion, heartburn, or stomach ulcer.

## CHALLENGE YOURSELF

3  Why do sodium carbonate and sodium hydrogencarbonate react as weak bases? Consider possible hydrolysis reactions of their conjugate ions.

Remember from Chapter 8:

acid + base → salt + $H_2O$

acid + carbonate/hydrogencarbonate → salt + $H_2O$ + $CO_2$

In stoichiometry questions concerning antacids, remember that the molar ratio of antacid to acid will vary with different antacids. So make sure you are basing your answer on the correct balanced equation.

1  The dissociation of the weak acid is so small that it can be considered to be negligible. The equilibrium lies so far to the left that we can make the approximation:

$$[HA]_{initial} \approx [HA]_{equilibrium}$$

2  The salt is considered to be fully dissociated into its ions. The equilibrium lies so far to the right that we can make the approximation:

$$[MA]_{initial} \approx [A^-]_{equilibrium}$$

The equilibrium expression for the acid is $K_a = \dfrac{[H^+][A^-]}{[HA]}$

Therefore $[H^+] = K_a \dfrac{[HA]}{[A^-]}$

Remember that all values in this expression must be *equilibrium* concentrations.

From the approximations justified above, we know that

$$[HA]_{equilibrium} \approx [HA]_{initial} \quad \text{and} \quad [A^-]_{equilibrium} \approx [MA]_{initial}$$

so we can substitute these values as follows.

$[H^+] = K_a \dfrac{[HA]_{initial}}{[MA]_{initial}}$ , which is usually given as $[H^+] = K_a \dfrac{[acid]}{[salt]}$

By taking the negative logarithms of both sides of the equation, we can derive:

$$pH = pK_a + \log_{10} \frac{[salt]}{[acid]}$$

For basic buffer solutions the equivalent equations are:

$[OH^-] = K_b \dfrac{[base]}{[salt]}$ and $pOH = pK_b + \log_{10} \dfrac{[salt]}{[base]}$

These equations, known as the Henderson–Hasselbalch equations, are given in section 1 of the IB data booklet. The beauty of these expressions is that they enable us to know the pH of a buffer solution directly from the following:

- the $K_a$ or $K_b$ values of its component acid or base and
- the ratio of initial concentrations of acid and salt used to prepare the buffer.

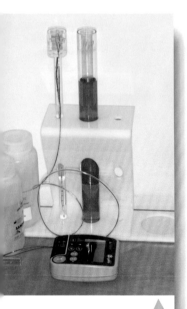

pH testing equipment used to diagnose oesophageal reflux disease. The tubes contain water and buffer solution used to calibrate the sensors and recorder shown at the bottom.

$pH = pK_a + \log_{10} \dfrac{[salt]}{[acid]}$

$pOH = pK_b + \log_{10} \dfrac{[salt]}{[base]}$

Joseph Henderson (1878–1942) was an American biochemist, who developed equations showing that acid–base balance in the blood is regulated by buffers. Karl Hasselbalch (1874–1962), a Danish chemist and a pioneer in the use of pH measurement in medicine, converted the equations to logarithmic form in his work on studying acidosis in the blood. We now know that different buffers in the blood work together to keep the pH tightly controlled at 7.4. Fluctuation in this value is so crucial that pH levels below 7.0 (acidosis) and above 7.8 (alkalosis) are, in the words of the medical profession, 'incompatible with life'.

## Worked example

Calculate the pH of a buffer solution at 298 K, prepared by mixing 25 cm³ of 0.10 mol dm⁻³ ethanoic acid ($CH_3COOH$) with 25 cm³ of 0.10 cm³ sodium ethanoate ($Na^+CH_3COO^-$). $K_a$ of $CH_3COOH = 1.8 \times 10^{-5}$ at 298 K.

## Solution

$pK_a$ of $CH_3COOH = -\log_{10} (1.8 \times 10^{-5}) = 4.74$

As there are equal volumes and concentrations of $CH_3COOH$ and $NaCH_3COO$, then [acid] = [salt].

$$pH = pK_a + \log_{10} \frac{[salt]}{[acid]} = 4.74 + \log_{10} (1) = 4.74 + 0 = 4.74$$

(Note that $\log_{10} (1) = 0$)

This example shows that when a buffer solution contains equal amounts in moles of acid and salt (or base and salt), the last term in the Henderson–Hasselbalch expression becomes zero, so $pH = pK_a$ (or $pOH = pK_b$). This relationship is extremely useful when it comes to preparing buffers of a specified pH. All we have to do is choose an acid with a $pK_a$ value close to the required pH and then, if necessary, adjust the concentrations of acid and salt accordingly.

The buffer solution can be prepared by reacting the acid with enough strong alkali to convert one half of the acid into salt, as described on page 381.

> **In a buffer solution when [acid] = [salt], $pH = pK_a$**
>
> **When [base] = [salt], $pOH = pK_b$.**

### Worked example

How would you prepare a buffer solution of pH 3.75 starting with methanoic acid (HCOOH) and NaOH?

### Solution

From the IB data booklet, $pK_a$ (HCOOH) = 3.75, so a buffer with equal amounts in moles of this acid and its salt ($Na^+HCOO^-$) will have pH = 3.75.

This equimolar solution is prepared by reacting the acid with enough NaOH so that one half of the acid is converted into salt and therefore $[HCOOH] = [HCOO^-]$.

Alternatively, the buffer can be prepared by mixing the acid directly with an appropriate amount of its salt.

### Worked example

How much 0.10 mol $dm^{-3}$ butanoic acid solution and solid potassium butanoate should be used to make 1.00 $dm^3$ of pH 5.00 buffer solution? State the assumptions made in the calculation.

### Solution

From the IB data booklet, butanoic acid $pK_a = 4.83$.

$$pH = pK_a + \log_{10} \frac{[A^-]}{[HA]}$$

$$5.00 - 4.83 = \log_{10} \frac{[\text{butanoate ion}]}{0.10 \text{ mol dm}^{-3}}$$

Take anti-logs of both sides:

$$10^{0.17} = \frac{[\text{butanoate ion}]}{0.10 \text{ mol dm}^{-3}} = 1.5$$

[butanoate ion] = 0.15 mol dm$^{-3}$

The molar mass of potassium butanoate is 126.12 g mol$^{-1}$

1.00 dm$^3$ of 0.15 mol dm$^{-3}$ solution = 0.15 mol × 126.12 g mol$^{-1}$ = 19 g

So 19 g potassium butanoate should be added to 1.00 dm$^3$ of 0.10 mol dm$^{-3}$ butanoic acid.

The following assumptions were made:

• [butanoate ion]$_{equilibrium}$ = [potassium butanoate]$_{initial}$
• [butanoic acid]$_{equilibrium}$ = [butanoic acid]$_{initial}$
• no volume change occurs on mixing the solution

### Exercises

**13** Suggest why the action of drugs in lowering the production of stomach acid is considered to be indirect in the case of $H_2$-receptor antagonists, but direct in the case of gastric proton pump inhibitors.

**14** Magnesium hydroxide and aluminium hydroxide can act as antacids.

  **(a)** Write an equation for the reaction of hydrochloric acid with each of these antacids.
  **(b)** Identify which antacid neutralizes the greater amount of acid if 0.1 mol of each antacid is used.
  **(c)** Explain why potassium hydroxide is not used as an antacid.

**15 (a)** 100 cm$^3$ of a buffer is prepared which contains 0.100 mol dm$^{-3}$ butanoic acid and 0.200 mol dm$^{-3}$ sodium butanoate. What is the change in pH when 2.00 cm$^3$ of 0.100 mol dm$^{-3}$ HCl is added to this buffer? The p$K_a$ of butanoic acid is 4.82.
  **(b)** How would the pH of the buffer alter if 20 cm$^3$ of distilled water was added to the original solution?

## D.5 Antiviral medications

## Understandings:

• Viruses lack a cell structure and so are more difficult to target with drugs than bacteria.
• Antiviral drugs may work by altering the cell's genetic material so that the virus cannot use it to multiply. Alternatively, they may prevent the viruses from multiplying by blocking enzyme activity within the host cell.

## Applications and skills:

• Explanation of the different ways in which antiviral medications work.
• Description of how viruses differ from bacteria.
• Explanation of how oseltamivir (Tamiflu) and zanamivir (Relenza) work as preventative agents against flu viruses.
• Comparison of the structures of oseltamivir and zanamivir.
• Discussion of the difficulties associated with solving the AIDS problem.

  ***Guidance***
  *Structures for oseltamivir and zanamivir can be found in the IB data booklet in section 37.*

## Viruses: nature's most successful parasites

Figure 15.22 shows that viruses come in different shapes and sizes and are all extremely small. Their diameters range from 20 to 300 nm, which means that they are **sub-microscopic**. In other words they cannot be studied with a light microscope, but only with an electron microscope.

Viruses are such small and simple structures that there is debate about whether they can be classified as living organisms in their own right. They contain only two main components, protein and nucleic acid (either RNA or DNA), have no cellular structure, and are only capable of reproducing inside another living cell. In all these ways they are different from bacteria, which have a complex cellular structure and the ability to survive and reproduce independently from other living cells.

Viruses are in fact the original hijackers – they literally take over the functioning of another cell, the so-called **host cell**, and use it to carry out their own reproduction. The host cell's components are used in the assembly of new viral particles and in the process the cell eventually dies, releasing thousands of viral particles into the organism. Viruses are usually somewhat specific for their host, and different strains exist that infect bacteria, plants, and animals.

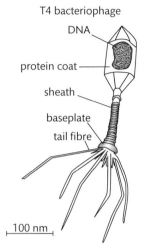

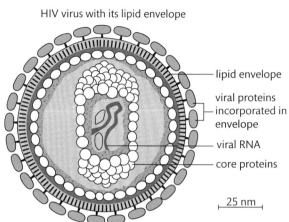

**Figure 15.22** Examples of viruses.

T4 bacteriophage
- DNA
- protein coat
- sheath
- baseplate
- tail fibre

100 nm

HIV virus with its lipid envelope
- lipid envelope
- viral proteins incorporated in envelope
- viral RNA
- core proteins

25 nm

## The war against viruses

The body's defence system usually responds to viral infections by producing specific **antibodies**, which act against a virus in the **immune response**. This often leads to protection, known as **immunity**, against repeated infections with the same virus. But sometimes the virus is not completely eradicated from the body and remains dormant in cells. This can cause a flare-up on another occasion, such as some herpes infections which cause cold sores. Another example is the chicken pox virus that can cause the different disease shingles years after the original infection.

Despite the body's defences, viral infections claim the lives of millions of people each year and are responsible for an even greater number of illnesses, many of them serious. Diseases such as measles, meningitis, and polio are caused by viruses, as are more recent diseases

**TOK** The words *virus* and *infection* have been adopted in technological jargon to describe a type of malicious software that inserts itself into computer files and replicates, usually causing harm to the system. Does the use of these terms depend on a knowledge of their biological origin? To what extent is knowledge implicit in language?

Artwork of a SARS virus particle inside a cell. SARS (severe acute respiratory syndrome) is an often fatal lung disease that first appeared in China in late 2002 and spread rapidly through the world via air travel. The virus is related to the type that causes the common cold. Like all viruses it cannot replicate by itself but instead uses the machinery of the host cell to produce more copies of itself.

**Antibiotics are effective against bacteria but not against viruses.**

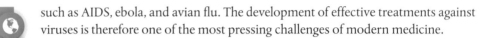

such as AIDS, ebola, and avian flu. The development of effective treatments against viruses is therefore one of the most pressing challenges of modern medicine.

Treating viral infections is particularly difficult because the viruses live within host cells and so cannot be easily targeted. Antibiotics such as penicillin are effective against bacteria, because they can target a structure such as a cell wall, but there are no equivalent structures to target in viruses. This is why antibiotics are not effective against viruses. In a sense viruses are so stripped-down structurally that there is little for a drug to target.

Another problem is the speed at which viruses can multiply, so that they are often spread through the organism by the time that symptoms appear. In addition, virus particles have a tendency to **mutate** rapidly, which means that they make small changes in their genetic material, and this changes their susceptibility to drugs.

There have, though, been successes in the treatment of viral infections. Vaccines were first introduced in the 18th century, and today are a major aspect of preventative healthcare, known as **prophylactic** treatment. Vaccines work by stimulating the body to prepare specific antibodies which can give immunity. Successful vaccination programmes have reduced the incidence of diseases such as cholera, polio, and measles. In 1980 the World Health Organization declared that smallpox has been eradicated from all parts of the world.

### NATURE OF SCIENCE

Edward Jenner (1749–1823) pioneered the work that eventually led to the global eradication of the devastating disease smallpox. Yet his methods would not stand the test of today's ethical standards for scientific experimentation. Jenner observed that people who suffered from the relatively mild disease of cowpox did not seem to contract smallpox (a more serious disease). He tested his theory on an eight-year-old boy by first injecting him with pus from a cowpox pustule, and when the boy had recovered from cowpox, injected him with pus from a smallpox pustule. The boy did not develop smallpox. When he was told he needed more proof, Jenner repeated the practice on more children, including his own baby son. Despite the evidence, Jenner's work was slow to be accepted as many people found the idea of inoculating the body with disease to be repulsive. But eventually the results spoke for themselves, and the use of vaccination became widespread.

Jenner used intuition and careful observation to design a process that he believed would be beneficial to others. Consider other cases where scientists may have had to balance the courage of their convictions with contrary public perception.

Mutations in a virus can, however, limit the effectiveness of some vaccines. For example, flu vaccines are useful only against the known strains, and as these change through mutation, different vaccines usually have to be prepared and administered every year.

The main strategy to treat viral infections is the administration of specific medicines known as **antivirals**. These all interfere in some way with the viral life cycle and so prevent the release of new viral particles from the cell. Some antivirals work by altering the cell's DNA, its genetic material, so that the virus cannot use it to multiply. Others block enzyme activity within the host cell which prevents the virus from reproducing. One reasonably effective antiviral drug is Amantadine, which has a cage-like structure and causes changes in the cell membrane that prevent the entry of a virus into the host cell. It is therefore best used as a prophylactic treatment or given before the infection has spread widely – a difficult task given the speed at which infections can strike.

Some recent advances in the development of antivirals for the flu virus are discussed below.

Polio is a highly infectious disease caused by a virus which invades the nervous system. It most commonly affects children under five years old, leaving many who survived crippled and paralysed. There is no cure, but there are effective vaccines, which have been available since the 1950s. Immunization programmes have eradicated polio from most of the world, but the disease is still endemic in Afghanistan, Nigeria, and Pakistan. The Global Polio Eradication Initiative was launched in 1988 and tracks all new cases on a weekly basis. Its goal is to eradicate polio worldwide by immunizing every child until transmission stops.

The word 'vaccine' is derived from the Latin word *vacca* for cow. It was first used by Edward Jenner in 1798 in the context of his work on cowpox and smallpox.

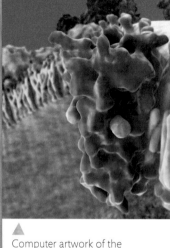

# Flu viruses: a case study in antivirals

Influenza, commonly known as the flu, is such a common disease that most of us can expect to experience it during our lives. Its symptoms include chills, headache, sore throat, and weakness, but it can develop into much more serious illnesses such as pneumonia. Flu infections can be particularly serious in the elderly and those with compromised immune systems. It is estimated that about half a million people die of flu every year, and there are constant fears of a global outbreak, known as a **pandemic**.

In November 1918, the same month in which World War I ended, a flu pandemic started in which 20 million people died in less than 2 years. It is believed that the outbreak started with a relatively harmless strain of flu that slowly evolved into a very virulent strain. Its effects were global, with large numbers of casualties in the Pacific region, Africa, and North America. It is considered to be the worst pandemic of all time, often referred to as the 'Spanish flu'.

Flu is caused by two main types of virus known as influenza A and B. They are spherical viruses and have RNA as their genetic material. Flu viruses have specific proteins on their surface, of which two play a key role in their life cycle.

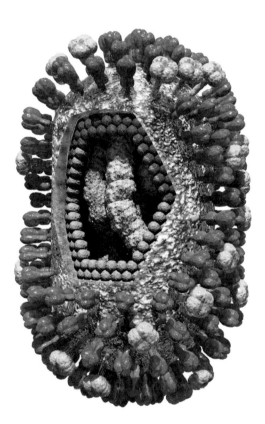

1 **Hemagglutinin (H)** is a glycoprotein that enables the viral particle to 'dock' with the host cell before it enters.

2 **Neuraminidase (N)** is an enzyme that catalyses a cleavage reaction which allows the new viral particles to escape from the host cell and spread infection. The enzyme snips off a type of sugar molecule, sialic acid, from glycoproteins on the surface of the host cell membrane.

▲ Computer artwork of the action of an antiviral drug, shown in blue, blocking an ion channel in the viral surface. This prevents the release of the viral genetic material into the host cell, and so interrupts the viral replication and infection cycle. Viral surface proteins are shown in red and yellow in the background.

Cut-away computer artwork of an influenza virus particle. The surface shows two types of protein spike, hemagglutinin (shown in red) and neuraminidase (shown in yellow). These determine the strain of virus and are essential to its life cycle. Other viral proteins are shown in purple, and the genetic material, RNA, is shown in yellow in the core.

These two molecules come in a variety of subunits which control the infectivity of the virus. The naming system of viruses, such as H1N1 and H5N1, refers to the different forms of these molecules that are present.

In 2009 a new strain of the influenza A virus, known as H1N1, was identified as causing flu infections. As people had little natural immunity to this strain, the infection spread globally causing serious illness and death, and the World Health Organization (WHO) declared it a pandemic. The alert was lifted in 2010 when the number of infections had declined steeply. Debate continues on whether the pandemic designation was an exaggerated response, possibly triggered by economic interests in increased sales of vaccines and antivirals. It is believed that more than 250 000 people died of the disease, mostly in Africa and South-East Asia.

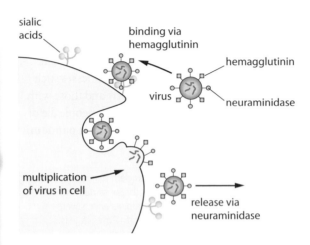

**Figure 15.23** Summary of the life cycle of the flu virus showing the roles of hemagglutinin and neuraminidase.

It may be of help to you to learn a little bit more about enzymes and inhibitors – read pages 697–699 in the Biochemistry option chapter.

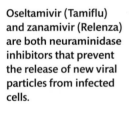

The action of hemagglutinin and neuraminidase is shown in Figure 15.23.

If the action of either of these viral proteins was affected, it would evidently interrupt the viral life cycle. Of the two, neuraminidase seems to be a better target for drug design and so it has become a focus for research.

As an enzyme, neuraminidase binds to its reactant sialic acid, the **substrate**, at a specific region known as the **active site**. It is this binding between enzyme and substrate that gives the catalytic action, as it provides a reaction pathway of lower activation energy. Chemicals that interfere with this binding are called **inhibitors** and usually have a specific fit with the enzyme.

The three-dimensional structure of neuraminidase became known through X-ray crystallography in 1993, including details on its active site. This enabled researchers to design a molecule which could bind at the active site and so block the binding of substrate and act as an inhibitor.

**Oseltamivir (Tamiflu) and zanamivir (Relenza) are both neuraminidase inhibitors that prevent the release of new viral particles from infected cells.**

The first neuraminidase inhibitors were designed by a team in Australia, and led to the production of zanamivir (Relenza), which was approved for use in 2000. It was closely followed by the production of oseltamivir (Tamiflu). As can be seen in Figure 15.24 and the table on page 41, both drugs have a chemical structure similar to sialic acid and so are able to bind at the active site in neuraminidase. This class of drug is active against both influenza A and B viruses. Tamiflu and Relenza are claimed to reduce the symptoms of flu and shorten the time of its effects, but must be taken within 48 hours of the appearance of symptoms.

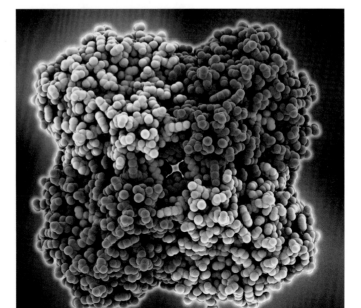

Molecular model of the neuraminidase enzyme found on the surface of the influenza virus, in a complex with the drug oseltamivir. Binding of the drug at the enzyme's active site inhibits its action, and so prevents the release of new viral particles from the host cell.

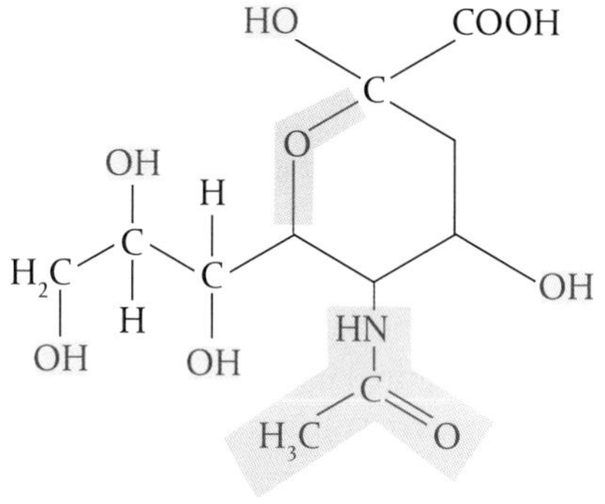

The structure of the neuraminidase substrate sialic acid, showing the similarity of its structure to that of the inhibitors oseltamivir and zanamivir.

**Figure 15.24** The structure of the neuraminidase substrate sialic acid, showing the similarity of its structure to that of the inhibitors oseltamivir and zanamivir.

## CHALLENGE YOURSELF

**4** Suggest why neuraminidase inhibitors can be described as *competitive* inhibitors.

The table below compares and contrasts the two drugs Tamiflu and Relenza.

| | Oseltamivir (Tamiflu) | Zanamivir (Relenza) |
|---|---|---|
| structure | 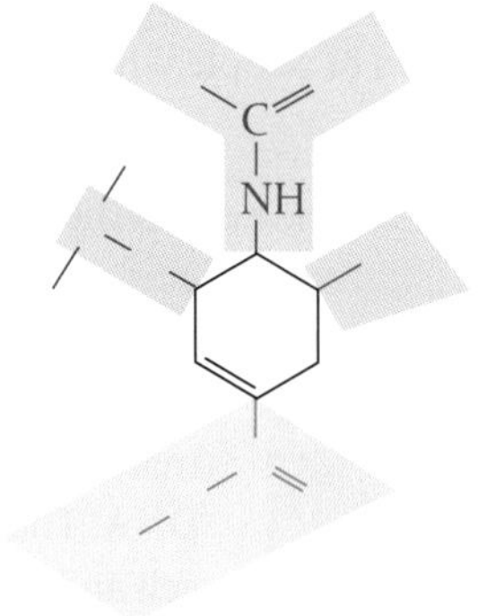 | 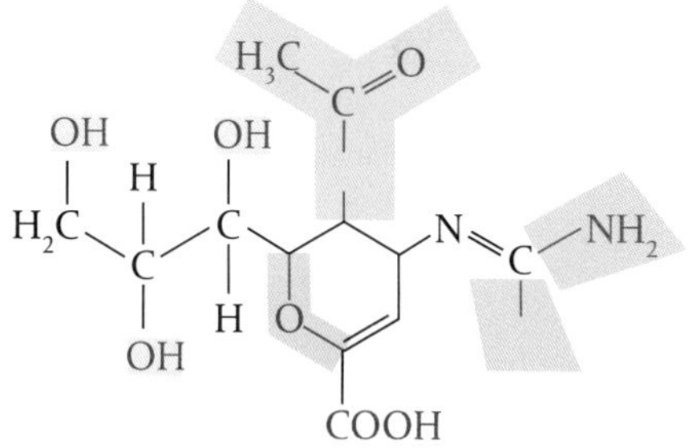 |
| functional groups | alkenyl<br>ether<br>primary amino<br>carboxyamide<br>ester | alkenyl<br>ether<br>primary amino<br>carboxyamide<br>carboxylic acid<br>hydroxyl (3) |
| drug action | neuraminidase inhibitor | neuraminidase inhibitor |
| administration | orally | inhalation |
| resistance to drug | some rare strains of flu virus have shown resistance | no resistance reported |
| counter-effects | nausea, vomiting | possible asthma |

Antiretroviral drugs are expensive and so have been very poorly distributed in the countries where they are generally needed the most. The Clinton Health Access Initiative Foundation (CHAI) began as a campaign to address the HIV/AIDS crisis in the developing world and strengthen health systems there. A major achievement is that nearly six million people now have access to HIV medications at costs reduced to about $200 per person per year. This includes a large number of HIV-positive children who were previously left untreated. It is estimated that one child dies every two minutes from mother to child transmission of HIV, and global efforts are focused on preventing this, especially in Cambodia, Ethiopia, Lesotho, Malawi, Tanzania, and Vietnam.

The structures of oseltamivir and zanamivir are given in section 37 of the IB data booklet.

Computer artwork of HIV replication. The viral particles, shown in green, surround the white blood cell, shown in blue, and attach to its surface using specific proteins for recognition. Viral RNA, shown in pink, is then injected into the cell and using reverse transcriptase synthesizes DNA which integrates into the host's chromosome. This can be seen in the white cell nucleus in the centre. New viral particles are assembled within the cell and are shown at the bottom budding from the cell, taking part of the membrane as an envelope.

# AIDS : a viral pandemic

The condition known as **AIDS**, acquired immune deficiency syndrome, caused by the human immunodeficiency virus (HIV), was first diagnosed in humans in 1981. The infection is transmitted from person to person through sexual or parenteral exposure to fluids such as blood, semen, and mucus that contain HIV. The disease AIDS is characterized by a failure of the immune system, so that the body falls prey to life-threatening opportunistic infections such as pneumonia and forms of cancer. The infection has spread at an alarming rate through the global population and it is estimated that approximately 33 million people are currently **HIV positive**, with a likelihood of developing AIDS. Although cases have been reported in all regions of the world, a very high proportion of people who are HIV positive live in sub-Saharan Africa.

HIV primarily infects vital white blood cells in the immune system. These cells are called **CD4+ T cells**. The virus binds to specific receptor proteins on the cell surface and then penetrates the cell. HIV is a **retrovirus**, which means that its genetic material is in the form of RNA rather than DNA. The virus releases its RNA into the cell and the enzyme **reverse transcriptase** controls the synthesis of viral DNA from this RNA. The viral DNA integrates into the cell's own DNA and replicates with it when the cell divides. Viral particles are produced within the host cell, and are released in large numbers when the cell dies.

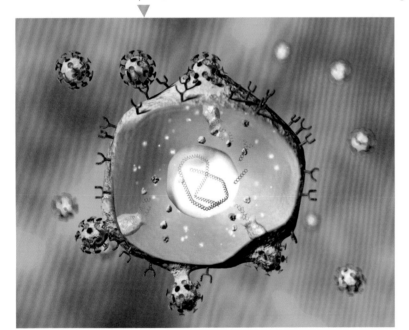

## The fight against HIV infection

There are three main reasons why HIV is proving even more challenging than other viruses to defeat.

**1** The virus destroys helper T cells, the very cells in the immune system that should be defending the body against the virus.

**2** The virus tends to mutate very rapidly, even within a patient. It is thought that there is more variation in HIV in a single patient than in the influenza virus worldwide in a year. These variations mean that the virus 'escapes' the immune response, so the patient has to make a response to the new virus.

**3** The virus often lies dormant within host cells, so the immune system has nothing to respond to.

Despite the challenges, great progress has been made in the development of specific antivirals for HIV infection. The drugs are known as **antiretroviral drugs**, **ARVs**, and about 20 of these are now commonly available. Although these drugs do not cure the patient, they can give lasting suppression of the HIV infection. This means that with appropriate treatments, HIV infection can be considered as a potentially chronic disease rather than as a fatal disease. Antiretroviral treatment during pregnancy can also effectively prevent transmission of the disease from mother to child.

Antiretroviral drugs target and interrupt the following different stages in the HIV life cycle:

• binding and fusion of the virus to the receptor on the CD4 cell membrane
• reverse transcription of viral RNA to DNA in the host cell
• integration of viral DNA into the host chromosome
• release of new viral particles by budding from the host cell surface.

Of these targets, inhibitors of the viral enzyme reverse transcriptase are the most widespread. They include drugs such as AZT, also known as zidovudine, which was the first antiretroviral drug to be approved. It has been found that the best results occur when a combination of different ARVs is used. Combination treatments typically include two different reverse transcriptase inhibitors plus a third drug, all of which can be taken as a single pill once daily. The cost for most combination treatments is approximately $12 000 per patient per year.

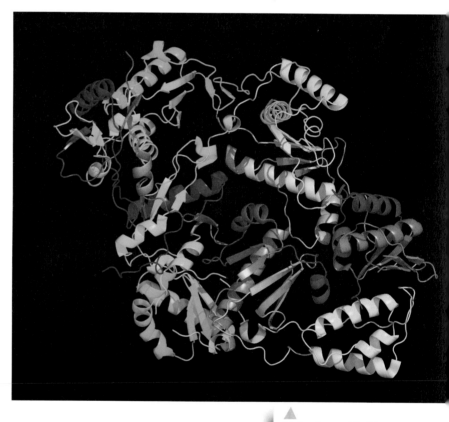

The development of ARVs is a field which is advancing rapidly as more drugs become available. Medical doctors must consider how to tailor a prescription to individual patients, who may benefit from different regimens of different drugs. Considerations of side-effects, potency, expense, convenience, and prevention of transmission must all be weighed. ARV treatments generally need to be sustained throughout life.

Intense research on developing a vaccine for HIV/AIDS is ongoing. There are some hopes that a therapeutic vaccine may be possible to help control the infection in people who are HIV-positive. But the development of a preventative vaccine that would give immunity to people who are HIV-negative has so far not been possible. This is mainly because of the problem of the variable nature of the virus within cells, and the fact that the immune response seems to act too slowly in the case of HIV infection.

Molecular model of the HIV enzyme reverse transcriptase complexed with the inhibitor efavirenz. Binding of the inhibitor to the enzyme prevents HIV reproducing in the host cell. Efavirenz is therefore an effective antiretroviral drug that reduces the spread of HIV infection.

**NATURE OF SCIENCE**

The development of effective antivirals is a good example of the inter-disciplinary nature of many scientific endeavours. Technological advances in the areas of electron microscopy and X-ray crystallography have provided insights into structures that could not otherwise be known. Advances in molecular biology have helped explain the role of viral proteins and genetic material in the viral life cycle. This cumulative knowledge has helped to drive research in the pharmaceutical industry, resulting in the availability of effective new drugs for many diseases. At best, science is a collaborative process in which findings from different disciplines contribute to the achievement of a common goal.

## Exercises

**16** Why are viral infections not able to be treated with antibiotics?

**17** With reference to the structure of the influenza virus, explain why it is possible to suffer from flu several times during a lifetime.

**18** Explain why the antivirals Tamiflu and Relenza must be taken within a very short time after the appearance of the symptoms of flu.

**19** Discuss some of the challenges and successes in the global response to the AIDS pandemic.

# D.7 Taxol: a chiral auxiliary case study

## Understandings:
- Taxol is a drug that is commonly used to treat several different forms of cancer.
- Taxol naturally occurs in yew trees but is now commonly synthetically produced.
- A chiral auxiliary is an optically active substance that is temporarily incorporated into an organic synthesis so that it can be carried out asymmetrically with the selective formation of a single enantiomer

## Applications and skills:
- Explanation of how Taxol (Paclitaxel) is obtained and used as a chemotherapeutic agent.
- Description of the use of chiral auxiliaries to form the desired enantiomer.
- Explanation of the use of a polarimeter to identify enantiomers.

### Guidance
*The structure of Taxol is provided in the IB data booklet in section 37.*

## Optical isomerism: chiral drugs exist in two forms with different activities

As we learned in Chapter 10, chiral molecules have two mirror image forms, known as enantiomers, and arise wherever a carbon atom in a molecule is bonded to four different groups.

**Figure 15.25** A chiral molecule gives rise to a pair of enantiomers.

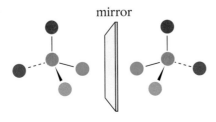

mirror

Although the two enantiomers of a molecule usually have identical chemical properties, they can react differently in the presence of a chiral environment, such as with the enzymes and receptors in the body. Figure 15.26 shows a hypothetical interaction between a chiral drug and its chiral binding site, and illustrates why only one of its enantiomers is biologically active. Given that about two-thirds of the drugs on the market are chiral, this difference in the physiological properties of their two enantiomers is very significant.

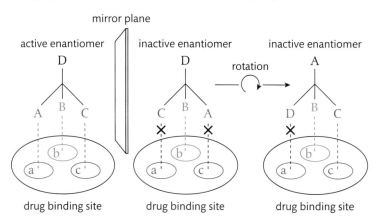

Biological synthesis reactions within cells (*in vivo*) produce only one enantiomeric form. So when a drug is harvested from a natural source, such as morphine from opium seed, only a single enantiomer is obtained. But when drugs are produced by synthetic processes outside the body (*in vitro*) they yield a mixture of enantiomers, known as a **racemate**. Pharmaceutical companies then face the challenge of finding out the physiological effects of each isomer, before determining whether the drug can be marketed as the racemic mixture or whether a single enantiomer must be produced.

The major impetus for this research activity in stereochemistry came from the thalidomide tragedy, described earlier in this chapter (page 869). The drug was manufactured and sold as a racemic mixture, as shown in Figure 15.27. It was discovered later that only the (*R*) isomer had the desired effect on inducing sleep in pregnant women. Its enantiomer, the (*S*) form, was **teratogenic**, meaning that it caused serious deformities in the fetus.

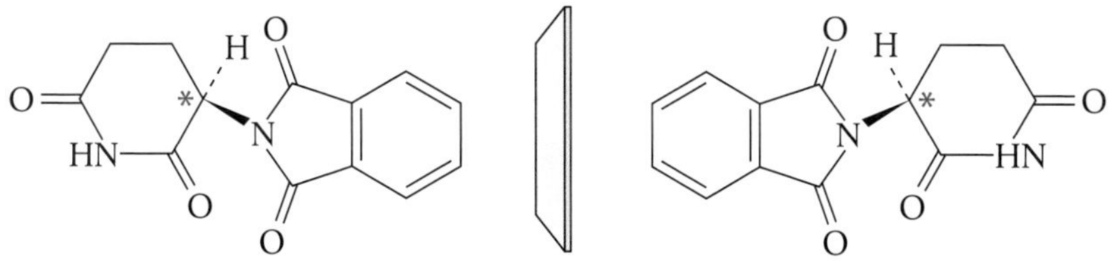

(*R*)-thalidomide
(sleep-inducing)

(*S*)-thalidomide
(teratogenic)

It is known that the two forms of the thalidomide drug interconvert under physiological conditions, so administering a pure isomer would not protect against the teratogenic effects. Nonetheless, the drug is still of some interest to researchers. It is thought that the action of the (*S*) form is to prevent the development of new blood vessels and this makes it an interesting agent for suppressing tumour growth in cancer and in treatment of HIV/AIDS and leprosy. Thalidomide is administered in some places for these purposes, but its marketing remains highly controversial.

Drugs that are marketed as racemates include fluoxetine (Prozac) and the anti-inflammatory drug Ibuprofen, which, like thalidomide, undergoes enantiomer inter-conversion *in vivo*. Although there is currently no regulatory mandate to develop new drugs exclusively as single enantiomers, it is becoming increasingly common to do

**Figure 15.26** The different behaviour of a pair of enantiomers in a chiral environment. The active enantiomer has a three-dimensional structure that allows the drug to interact with its binding site at positions a, b, and c. The inactive enantiomer cannot be aligned to interact at all three positions simultaneously.

Many drugs are chiral and so exist as two forms – these forms should be considered as two separate drugs, with different properties, during research and development. Often only one form has the intended therapeutic effect.

**Figure 15.27** The two enantiomers of the drug thalidomide. The chiral carbon atom is marked with a red asterisk *.

TOK To what extent do you think consumers can be free from prejudice regarding the use of the thalidomide drug, given its dark history? Is opposition likely to be based on emotion or on rational distrust of the scientific research? Are reactions based on emotion less valid than those that question the science?

> **Chemotherapy means the treatment or control of disease by chemical agents. It is generally used in the context of cancer treatment.**

this. It is estimated that of the chiral drugs on the market, approximately 50% are single enantiomers. The development of a single enantiomer drug is described below with respect to the **chemotherapeutic** drug Taxol.

## Taxol is a powerful anti-cancer drug

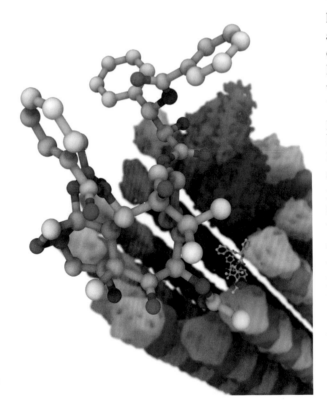

Taxol, shown as a ball and stick model, bound to microtubules that are shown in yellow and blue. The drug acts by stabilizing the microtubules that are involved in cell division. Binding of the drug makes the microtubules unable to disassemble and so they cannot move chromosomes around the cell. Atoms are represented as colour-coded spheres: carbon in grey, oxygen in red, and nitrogen in blue, with hydrogen atoms omitted.

Taxol is sometimes known as Paclitaxel, and is one of a group of related compounds known as **taxoids**. Taxol was first identified in 1971 from a screening programme carried out by the US National Cancer Institute, testing for new anti-cancer agents. It has potent effects against solid tumours, and was approved for use as a chemotherapeutic agent in 1992. It is used primarily in the treatment of breast and ovarian cancers.

Taxol's anti-cancer properties are a result of its ability to bind to a protein called **tubulin** in cells. Tubulin is the main component of **microtubules**, which form structures called **spindles** during cell division. When Taxol binds at the microtubules, it prevents the spindle fibres from breaking down, and this halts the cell division cycle. In this way Taxol prevents growth of the tumour.

Taxol was first isolated from the bark of Pacific yew trees (*Taxus sp.*) in the 1970s. This practice soon led to controversy about the environmental impact of harvesting from this natural source. Yew bark contains only about 0.0004% Taxol, so vast amounts of bark were needed. The process of stripping the bark kills the trees, which take 200 years to mature and are part of a sensitive ecosystem. This concern spearheaded many research groups to find methods of synthesizing the drug and its analogues.

Branch of the Pacific yew tree, *Taxus brevifolia*, a source of the anti-cancer drug Taxol. It is extracted from the bark of the tree (shown here peeled back). Demand for the drug exceeds the supply from the trees – which grow very slowly and are found only in old-growth forests on the northwest coast of North America.

# Asymmetric synthesis: the production of a single enantiomer of Taxol

A major challenge in the design of synthesis routes is that Taxol is a 'very chiral' molecule with 11 chiral carbon centres. This means it can exist as a large number of enantiomers, which may have different effects in the body, including the possibility of harmful physiological effects. Only one enantiomer has the desired therapeutic activity. Isolating this desired enantiomer from its racemic mixture is possible, but it is a wasteful process as much of the product is not used. It is therefore of more interest to pharmaceutical companies to find ways of directly synthesizing a single enantiomer, a process known as **asymmetric synthesis** or **enantioselective synthesis**.

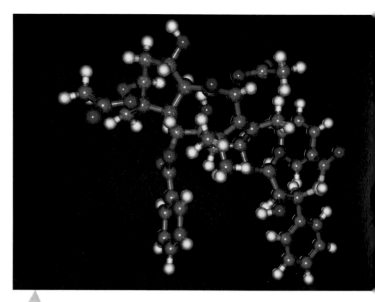

Computer graphic of a molecule of Taxol. The structure of Taxol, shown as a computer graphic above, and as a structural formula to the left. The atoms and their bonds are colour coded in the photograph: carbon in dark blue, hydrogen in white, oxygen in red, and nitrogen in light blue. Taxol has the chemical formula $C_{47}H_{51}NO_{14}$. Its complex structure and stereochemistry makes it difficult to synthesize commercially.

**The synthesis of Taxol needs to be stereospecific.**

In 2001, the Nobel Prize in Chemistry was awarded to three pioneers in the field of enantioselective synthesis. William Knowles of the USA, Ryoji Noyori of Japan, and K. Barry Sharpless of USA developed different techniques using chiral catalysts for the large-scale production of a desired isomer. Their work has many applications, including an industrial process for the production of the drug l-DOPA, used in the treatment of Parkinson's disease.

One strategy to achieve this uses a **chiral auxiliary**. This is a chiral molecule which binds to the reactant, physically blocking one reaction site through steric hindrance, so ensuring that the next step in the reaction can only take place from one side. This effectively forces the reaction to proceed with a specified stereochemistry. Once the specific enantiomer of the new product has been set, the auxiliary can be taken off and recycled. This is illustrated in Figure 15.28, using the relatively simple example of converting propanoic acid (which is non-chiral) into 2-aminopropanoic acid (which is chiral). The use of a chiral auxiliary has been employed successfully in the synthesis of Taxol.

Because Taxol is such a complex molecule, its commercial synthesis from simple molecules involves about 30 steps, and has such a poor yield it is impractical.

A more efficient process now uses the extraction of a compound which is related to Taxol from the needles and leaves of yew trees from Europe and the Himalayas. Harvesting the leaves does not damage the trees in the way that removal of bark does, and so this is a more sustainable approach. The related compound, known as 10-DAB, is then chemically modified to form Taxol. The process is known as **semi-synthetic synthesis** as it starts with a precursor obtained from nature.

Although the semi-synthetic route addresses some of the environmental concerns associated with harvesting from tree bark, it also creates some new challenges for the pharmaceutical industry. The overall conversion of 10-DAB to Taxol requires 13

## CHALLENGE YOURSELF

**5** The structure of Taxol is shown here. See if you can identify all 11 chiral carbon atoms.

both enantiomers are produced

without a chiral auxiliary →

and

2-aminopropanoic acid

propanoic acid

with a chiral auxiliary →

→ auxiliary removed →

only one enantiomer produced

**Figure 15.28** The production of a single enantiomer using a chiral auxiliary.

Needles of yew trees, which are a source of 10-DAB, a precursor in the semi-synthetic synthesis of Taxol. Harvesting naturally occurring compounds from needles does not harm the trees.

solvents and a range of other organic reagents. The large number of steps is associated with a low yield of product.

A promising development is the discovery that some fungi produce Taxol in fermentation reactions. In addition, plant cell fermentation technology is being developed in which Taxol is extracted directly from plant cell cultures and purified by chromatography. These processes have the potential to eliminate the use of many hazardous solvents and are part of innovations in Green Chemistry.

**NATURE OF SCIENCE**

Advances in technology have led to developments of chemical processes which can now synthesize complex drugs previously obtainable only from natural sources. This allows for much more sustainable production of some pharmaceuticals. As the demand for chemotherapeutic agents continues to increase worldwide, there is pressure on the industry to match this with a sustainable supply.

Enantiomers can be identified using a polarimeter, as described in Chapter 10 (page 522). The instrument measures the rotation of plane-polarized light by the optically active compound using an analyser.

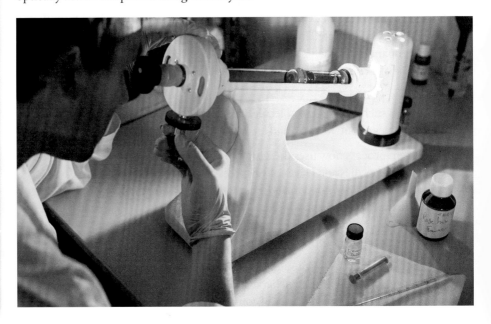

Technician using a polarimeter to determine the optical rotation of a solution. This is used as a measure of the quality of an extract or synthetic preparation.

20 **(a)** Describe the original source of Taxol and the environmental impact of obtaining the drug from this source.

**(b)** Taxol has been described as a 'very chiral molecule'. Explain the meaning of this statement and why processes to synthesize Taxol® chemically are complex and must be carefully controlled.

21 Describe how chiral auxiliaries can be used to synthesize only the desired enantiomeric form of a drug from a non-chiral starting compound. Explain why it is important to use only the desired enantiomeric form of a drug and give an example of what can happen if a racemic mixture is used.

# D.8 Nuclear medicine

## Understandings:
- Alpha, beta, gamma, proton, neutron, and positron emissions are all used for medical treatment.
- Magnetic resonance imaging (MRI) is an application of NMR technology.
- Radiotherapy can be internal and/or external.
- Targeted alpha therapy (TAT) and boron neutron capture therapy (BNCT) are two methods which are used in cancer treatment.

### Guidance
*Isotopes used in nuclear medicine include Tc-99m, Lu-177, Y-90, I-131, and Pb-212.*

## Applications and skills:
- Discussion of common side-effects from radiotherapy.
- Explanation of why technetium-99m is the most common radio isotope used in nuclear medicine based on its half-life, emission type, and chemistry.
- Explanation of why lutetium-177 and yttrium-90 are common isotopes used for radiotherapy based on the type of radiation emitted.
- Balancing nuclear equations involving alpha and beta particles.
- Calculation of the percentage and amount of radioactive material decayed and remaining after a certain period of time using the nuclear half-life equation.
- Explanation of TAT and how it might be used to treat diseases that have spread throughout the body.

### Guidance
*Common side-effects discussed should include hair loss, nausea, fatigue, and sterility. Discussion should include the damage to DNA and growing or regenerating tissue.*

## Unstable atomic nuclei emit radiation

The chemical reactivity that we have studied so far has been based on changes in the distribution of *electrons* in atoms. In all these cases we have assumed the nucleus to be a stable and inert part of the atom. But in reactions considered in *nuclear* chemistry, the atomic nucleus is itself a reactive part of an atom because it is actually unstable.

The stability of an atom's nucleus depends on the number and type of nuclear particles present, the so-called **nucleons**, which vary in different isotopes of the same element.

- Stable nuclei have balanced forces among the nucleons and so are not reactive.
- Unstable nuclei have unbalanced forces and an excess of internal energy, and so they spontaneously decay to form more stable nuclei, in a process known as **radioactivity**. These unstable nuclei are known as **radionuclides**.

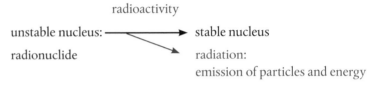

Radioactivity involves the emission of energy and particles from the nucleus as an atom decays into a more stable form. The emissions are known as radiation.

The 'trifoil' is the international symbol for dangerous radiation. The symbol can be magenta or black on a yellow background. It is posted where radioactive materials are stored or used, and acts as a warning for people to protect themselves from exposure to radioactivity.

radioactivity

unstable nucleus: ⟶ stable nucleus

radionuclide

radiation: emission of particles and energy

**Natural radionuclides** occur in the environment in air, water, and soil. They include $^{235}U$, $^{3}H$, $^{40}K$, and $^{14}C$. All elements with $Z = 84$ (Po, polonium) and higher are naturally radioactive, which means they have no stable naturally occurring isotope.

**Induced** or **artificial radionuclides** are nuclei that are made to be unstable through procedures that usually involve bombardment reactions with neutrons or helium nuclei at great speed. Many radionuclides used in nuclear medicine are produced in this way.

### NATURE OF SCIENCE

The discovery of radioactivity is another famous example of how scientists have sometimes stumbled across the unexpected, shown the intuition to probe into the cause, and opened the doors for further inquiry. Henri Becquerel was a French physicist who studied phosphorescence in the late 1800s. By chance he noticed that photographic plates became fogged when close to uranium salts, even in the absence of sunlight. He traced the cause to radiation from the uranium and showed that the emission caused gases to ionize. This discovery of radioactivity in 1896 inspired the work of Pierre and Marie Curie, who went on to discover other sources of natural radioactivity and for the first time isolated the elements polonium and radium. The Nobel Prize in Physics in 1903 was awarded jointly to Henri Becquerel and the Curies.

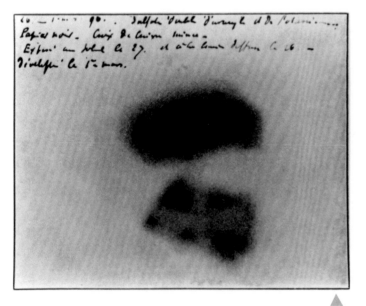

The photograph that led to the discovery of radioactivity by Henri Becquerel in 1896. Dark patches show where he put crystals of uranium salt on a photographic plate. His comments are above. He expected that when exposed to sunlight the plate would be fogged by X-rays from the salt, but found that it became fogged by uranium salt alone when left in a drawer. Becquerel realized that he had found a new form of radiation.

Atomic nuclei have a highly complex structure, and knowledge of this field is advancing rapidly, largely through the discoveries of particle physics involving particle accelerator data. New particles have been discovered and more is being learned of the forces responsible for giving atoms mass and for enabling them to exist together in the nucleus. We now know that neutrons and protons are not fundamental particles in the nucleus, but are themselves made up of more fundamental particles called **quarks**. Quarks are arranged in sets of three, and changes in their type gives rise to some forms of radiation. It is also the case that most particles have **antiparticles**, which have equivalent mass but opposite charge. For example, the **positron** is the antiparticle of an electron with the same mass but with a positive charge. When particles and antiparticles collide, mutual destruction occurs and energy is released as a form of radiation called **gamma rays**.

The complexities of this field rapidly become beyond the purposes of our needs here to explore nuclear medicine. For this study we will focus on the atomic particles introduced in Chapter 2 and given in section 4 of the IB data booklet.

| Particle | Position | Charge | Relative mass |
|----------|----------|--------|---------------|
| proton | nucleus | + | 1 |
| neutron | nucleus | 0 | 1 |
| electron | outside nucleus | – | 0.0005 |

When radionuclides decay into a more stable form, one or more of the following events occurs in the nucleus:

- the ejection of a neutron
- the ejection of a proton
- the conversion of a neutron to a proton with the ejection of an electron, known as a **beta particle**
- the conversion of a proton to a neutron with the ejection of a **positron**
- the release of additional energy by the emission of photons, known as **gamma rays**.

These changes give rise to the different types of radiation, and result in the formation of a new nuclide, which may itself be radioactive and continue to decay. Sometimes a change in the number of protons occurs, so the product is a different element from the parent radionuclide. We will see this in the examples that follow, using **nuclear equations** to show the changes in the number of nuclear particles. Remember the convention used to show mass number and atomic number introduced in Chapter 2:

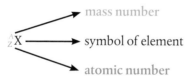

$$^A_Z X$$

mass number
symbol of element
atomic number

## The main types of radiation are alpha, beta, and gamma

### Alpha radiation

Alpha radiation is the ejection of particles from the nucleus that carry a charge of 2+ and have a mass of 4 atomic mass units. Alpha particles are equivalent to a nucleus of helium and can be denoted as $^4_2\text{He}$ or $^4_2\alpha$.

Emission of an alpha particle causes the mass number of a radionuclide to decrease by 4 units and the atomic number to decrease by 2 units.

For example, uranium is converted into thorium by alpha decay:

$$^{238}_{92}\text{U} \rightarrow {}^4_2\alpha + {}^{234}_{90}\text{Th}$$

### Beta radiation

Beta radiation is the ejection of electrons from the nucleus. They are formed during the conversion of neutrons to protons, so the mass number stays the same and the atomic number increases by 1 unit. Beta particles are electrons and so have negligible mass and a negative charge. They are denoted as $^0_{-1}\beta$.

For example, thorium is converted into proactinium by beta decay:

$$^{234}_{90}\text{Th} \rightarrow {}^0_{-1}\beta + {}^{234}_{91}\text{Pa}$$

One of the goals of the ancient alchemists was to convert base metals such as lead into noble metals such as gold. This possibility was debunked with the development of atomic theory in the 18th century, which explained the separate identity of each element. Yet through radioactivity, one element can be converted into another. This was at first a startling realization, described by Rutherford as 'a manifestation of sub-atomic chemical change'. Bombardment techniques have since enabled very small amounts of gold to be produced from other elements, but the process is of no real interest due to its high energy demand.

**Nuclear medicine uses alpha, beta, gamma, neutron, and positron emissions.**

When you have written a nuclear equation, check that it is balanced for the total numbers of particles in the mass number (*A*) and atomic number (*Z*) on both sides of the equation. Even though the identity of the atoms changes, the total number of particles must be accounted for during the reaction.

## Gamma radiation

Gamma radiation is the emission of energy as electromagnetic waves (or photons). The photons have very short wavelength, in the range 0.0005 to 0.1 nm, and have frequencies above $10^{19}$ Hz. They are denoted as $\gamma$. Gamma radiation results from energy changes in the nucleus and does not alter the atomic number or the mass number. It often accompanies alpha or beta radiation as the energy of the radionuclide is lowered during radioactive decay.

### Worked example

Write nuclear equations for the following reactions, making reference to section 5 of the IB data booklet:

**(a)** the alpha decay of an isotope of radon that has mass number 219

**(b)** the beta decay of carbon-14.

### Solution

**(a)** Radon is Rn with Z = 86 so the radionuclide is $^{219}_{86}\text{Rn}$.

Alpha decay will result in a decrease in Z of 2 units and a decrease in A of 4 units. So the new element has Z = 84, which is polonium, Po.

$$^{219}_{86}\text{Rn} \rightarrow {}^{215}_{84}\text{Po} + {}^{4}_{2}\alpha$$

**(b)** The radionuclide carbon-14 is $^{14}_{6}\text{C}$.

Beta decay will result in an increase in Z of 1 unit and no change in A. So the new element has Z = 7, which is nitrogen, N.

$$^{14}_{6}\text{C} \rightarrow {}^{14}_{7}\text{N} + {}^{0}_{-1}\beta$$

## Radioactive emissions have an ionizing effect

Radioactivity is known as **ionizing radiation** because it has enough energy to interact with an atom and cause the removal of electrons, so the atom becomes ionized. Radiation can cause the release of electrons other than those in the outer shell, and form highly unstable radicals. Some radicals are so reactive that they exist for only a fraction of a second, immediately reacting with nearby molecules causing chemical changes such as oxidation.

The ionizing effects of radiation are the reason why radioactivity is dangerous to living cells. Exposure to emissions causes ionization of the biological molecules in cells or in water, which may form radicals such as hydrogen, H•, and hydroxyl, OH•. The major effect is on the genetic material (DNA), which has a double-helical structure and can break when ionized. This can lead to cell death or to mutations that can be linked to cancer.

All forms of radioactive emission discussed here are ionizing, though they differ in what is known as their **ionization density**. This refers to the average energy released along a unit length of their track. Alpha particles with their +2 charge and relatively large mass, have a high ionization density. X-rays and $\gamma$-rays have a lower ionization density, which means that at the same dose they produce radicals more sparsely within a cell.

The higher ionizing density of alpha particles causes them to release most of their energy to a small region in the cell. They are therefore more destructive to biological

(a)

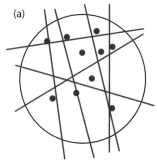

(b)

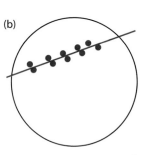

**Figure 15.29** Representation of different ionization densities. Each red dot represents an ionization, and the two examples represent the same dose with the same total number of ionizations: (a) low ionizing density radiation such as gamma rays; (b) high ionizing density such as alpha particles.

material than the same dose of lower ionizing density particles. This is the basis of a form of radiotherapy known as TAT, discussed on page 914.

The ionizing effects of radiation in cells mean that exposure to radioactive sources should generally be avoided where possible. Yet it is this same property of radioactivity that makes it such a useful and successful tool in the diagnosis and treatment of many medical conditions and diseases.

## Half-life of an isotope determines the rate of radioactive decay

Radioactive substances spontaneously decay at a rate that depends only on the nature of the substance. The reaction is not affected by changes in temperature, pressure, or the presence of other substances. Radioactive decay follows first-order reaction kinetics, as explained in Chapter 6.

In a first-order reaction for a reactant N, the rate expression is:

$$\text{rate} = k\,[N]$$

Although we do not need to explain the mathematics involved here, this equation can be expressed in the integrated form as follows:

$$\ln\frac{N_t}{N_0} = -kt$$

where $N_0$ = concentration of reactant at $t = 0$, $N_t$ = concentration of reactant at time $t$, and 'ln' refers to natural logarithms (log to base e).

The **half-life**, $t_{1/2}$, is the time taken for the concentration of a reactant to decrease to one half its original value, so at this time $N_t = N_0/2$. Substituting into the equation:

$$\frac{\ln(N_0/2)}{\ln N_0} = -k\,t_{1/2} \text{ so } \ln 2 = k\,t_{1/2}$$

$$\therefore t_{1/2} = \frac{\ln 2}{k} = \frac{0.693}{k}$$

$$k = \frac{0.693}{t_{1/2}}$$

This shows that the half-life of a specific radioactive decay process is constant. It depends only on the rate constant of the reaction, usually known as a **decay constant**, $\lambda$, in this context. So the rate of radioactive decay does not depend on the starting amount of radionuclide.

For a particular isotope, it will take exactly the same time for any amount to be reduced to one half its initial value: 1000 g decaying to 500 g will take the same time as 1.0 mg decaying to 0.5 mg.

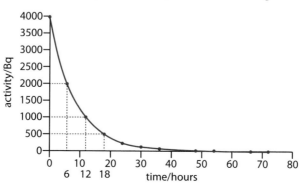

The half-life of a reaction is the time taken for an initial quantity of substance to fall to one half of its value.

The expression $t_{1/2} = \frac{\ln 2}{k}$ is given in the IB data booklet.

All radioactive decay reactions are first-order reactions. First-order reactions have a constant half-life.

**Figure 15.30** Radioactive decay of Tc-99m, showing its half-life of 6 hours.

The value of the half-life of an isotope has an inverse relationship with the rate of the radioactive decay. Short half-lives indicate high rates of decay and vice versa. The rate of radioactive emission is referred to as the isotope's **activity**, and is a measure of the number of occurrences of nuclear disintegration per unit time. The SI unit of activity is the becquerel (Bq), in which one unit equals the decay of one nucleus per second.

### Worked example

An isotope of radium, $^{226}_{88}Ra$, has a half-life of 1620 years. Calculate the rate constant for the decay of radium-226.

### Solution

Substitute the given value for $t_{1/2}$ into the equation $k = 0.693/t_{1/2}$

$$k = \frac{0.693}{1620 \text{ years}} = 4.28 \times 10^{-4} \text{ year}^{-1}$$

Note that the units of the rate constant of a first-order reaction are time$^{-1}$, and the units of time in this solution must be consistent with those for the half-life.

If we consider the graph of technetium-99m (see Figure 15.30), from the fact that $t_{1/2} = 6$ hours, we can deduce that:

• after one half life, 6 hours, ½ sample remains
• after two half-lives, 12 hours, $(½)^2 = ¼$ sample remains
• after three half-lives, 18 hours, $(½)^3 = ⅛$ sample remains, etc.

It follows that if $n$ intervals of 6 hours are allowed to pass, the amount remaining will be $(0.5)^n$ of the original amount. This means that

$$\frac{N_t}{N_0} = (0.5)^n \quad \text{where}$$

$\frac{N_t}{N_0}$ = proportion of isotope remaining

$n$ = number of half lives = $\frac{t}{t_{1/2}}$

The equation
$$\frac{N_t}{N_0} = (0.5)^{t/t_{1/2}}$$
is given in section 1 of the IB data booklet.

We can use this equation to calculate the amount of isotope decayed and remaining at any interval of time, from knowledge of either the half-life or the decay constant.

### Worked example

What amount of $^{128}_{53}I$ will be left when 3.65 mol of this isotope is allowed to decay for 15.0 min? The half-life of $^{128}_{53}I$ is 25.0 min.

### Solution

number of half-lives = $\frac{15.0 \text{ min}}{25.0 \text{ min}} = 0.6$

$$\frac{N_t}{N_0} = (0.5)^{t/t_{1/2}}$$

proportion remaining = $(0.5)^{0.6} = 0.6597$

∴ amount remaining = $3.65 \text{ mol} \times 0.6597 = 2.41 \text{ mol}$

Note that the measure of initial and final concentrations can be in any unit – mass, moles, activity, etc. – but they must be consistent within the calculation and the solution.

As a quick check, it is obvious that the time interval is less than a half-life, so it makes sense that the amount remaining is more than half the original amount.

# Nuclear radiation in medical treatment

'Nuclear medicine' refers to the use of radiation in healthcare practice, which is now a major part of medical care in two main areas:

in the *diagnosis* of disease, by helping to provide detailed information about an individual's internal organs – the techniques used are known as **nuclear imaging**

in the *treatment* of disease, particularly cancer, through the destruction of targeted cells – this is known as **radiotherapy**.

## Diagnostic techniques in nuclear medicine

Diagnostic techniques usually involve first attaching a radionuclide, known as a **tracer**, to a biologically active molecule, making a drug called a **radiopharmaceutical**. This is then taken orally or by injection. The tracer allows the progress of the drug to be traced as it emits gamma rays from inside the body, which can then be detected by a **gamma camera**. Nuclear imaging has the clear advantage over X-ray techniques in that it can be applied to soft tissue as well as to bones, and enables the internal functioning of an organ to be observed from outside the body.

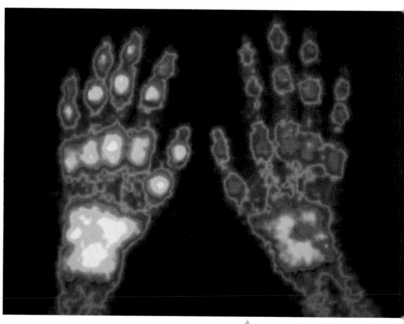

False colour gamma camera scan of the hands of a person with extensive rheumatoid arthritis affecting the wrists and fingers. The radioisotope has accumulated in the inflamed tissue around the arthritic joints and shows as brighter areas. The hand on the left is particularly severely affected. The gamma rays generate small flashes of light, which are amplified and processed by the camera.

Radiopharmaceuticals are designed to target a certain part of the body where there may be abnormality or disease. For example, iodine is taken up by the thyroid gland and glucose is particularly taken up by the brain, so the tracer is attached to these molecules. The medical practitioner can view organs from different angles and so observe indications of abnormality. For example, so-called cold spots develop where isotopes are only partially taken up and hot-spots develop where isotopes are taken up in excess, and either can indicate a malfunction in the organ. It is easier to interpret these if images are taken over a period of time.

The tracers used in radiopharmaceuticals must emit gamma rays with enough energy to escape from the body and must have a half-life just long enough for the scan to be complete before its decay. The radiopharmaceutical most widely used in diagnosis is technetium-99m, $^{99}_{43}\text{Tc}$. This isotope is used in about 80% of all nuclear imaging procedures as it has the following advantages.

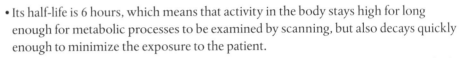

- Its half-life is 6 hours, which means that activity in the body stays high for long enough for metabolic processes to be examined by scanning, but also decays quickly enough to minimize the exposure to the patient.
- Its decay involves the release of gamma rays and low-energy electrons. Without high-energy beta emission, the radiation dose is low. Low-energy gamma rays escape the body and are accurately detected by the gamma camera.
- Technetium is chemically versatile, so acts as a tracer by bonding to a range of biologically active substances. These are chosen according to the organ to be studied.

Technetium is an artificial element that is generated in nuclear reactors from molybdenum-99 which decays to technetium-99.

## Positron emission tomography (PET)

This is a type of scanner that gives three-dimensional images of tracer concentration in the body. The radionuclide contains a positron-emitting tracer and is injected into the patient's body where it accumulates in the target tissue. Positrons are emitted from the tracer and these combine immediately with electrons, releasing energy as gamma rays. Detection of the gamma rays by a camera enables their origin to be precisely determined. A common tracer used with PET scanners is fluorine-18, which is bonded to glucose in the radiopharmaceutical. The uptake and use of glucose is different in cancer cells from in healthy cells and these differences will be visible on the scan.

A relatively new procedure combines PET with CT (computerized tomography) scans that use X-rays to obtain images. The combined technique, PETCT, gives better diagnosis of a wide variety of diseases.

## Magnetic resonance imaging (MRI)

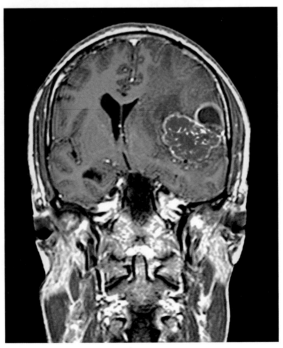

Since 1977, when MRI was first used to produce images of internal body organs and soft tissue, it has developed into one of the most widely used diagnostic techniques in modern medicine. MRI is an application of nuclear magnetic resonance (NMR) spectroscopy, described in Chapter 11, and so uses the fact that hydrogen atoms, $^1H$, have a magnetic moment due to their odd number of protons. In the presence of a powerful magnet, radio waves are used to generate an electronic signal that can be decoded by a computer to produce two- or three-dimensional images.

Coloured MRI scan through the head of a male patient. A cancerous tumour is shown in bright red compressing the left side of the brain. Information from scans such as this can help doctors to determine the best treatments for disease.

MRI is particularly useful in the diagnosis of living tissue because hydrogen atoms are present in water, which makes up about 70% of the body by mass.

MRI does not use ionizing radiation, in contrast to other imaging techniques, so is considered relatively non-invasive. Radio waves are low-energy waves and there are no known hazards of the exposure of the body to the strength of magnetic fields applied. MRI scans give detailed images of almost any part of the body and are widely used in cancer detection, the diagnosis of soft tissue injuries, and in monitoring degenerative diseases.

The term *MRI* is used for the application of NMR technology in medicine, purposefully avoiding reference to nuclear energy. This is thought to lessen the public concerns about technologies connected with nuclear energy.

## Radionuclide therapy

Cancer is one of the largest causes of death globally, and remains one of the most difficult diseases to treat. Cancer cells arise when normal cells lose their regulatory mechanisms for the control of growth and division, and are characterized as rapidly growing abnormal cells, often known as a **tumour**. One of the challenges in treating cancer is to target the cancerous cells and prevent their division, while minimizing damage to the normal cells.

The fact that they are rapidly dividing can make cancerous cells particularly sensitive to damage by radiation. This is because its ionizing effect primarily affects DNA that controls cell division. Although radiation kills healthy cells too, and this is a major consideration in the administration of radiotherapy, they are often damaged to a lesser extent due to their different rates of cell division. Radiotherapy treatments involve irradiating the area containing the growth, with the aim of controlling or eliminating the cancer. Alongside surgery and chemotherapy, radiotherapy is a widely-used aspect of cancer treatment.

Radionuclides used in therapy are ideally strong beta-emitters that also emit gamma radiation to enable imaging. Lutetium-177 and yttrium-90 are widely used on the basis of their emissions. Yttrium-90 is increasingly also being used in arthritis treatment.

There are several words related to cancer that are useful to know. *Oncology* is the study of cancer; a *carcinogen* is a chemical that causes cancer; *metastasis* refers to the spread of cancer cells through other organs in the body.

### 1 External radiotherapy or teletherapy

In teletherapy, an external source of radiation is directed at the site of cancer in the body from a radioactive source, usually cobalt-60. This undergoes beta decay producing the stable product nickel-60.

$$^{60}_{27}Co \rightarrow {}^{60}_{28}Ni + {}^{0}_{-1}\beta + \gamma\text{-rays}$$

This reaction also emits gamma radiation, which is penetrating and damaging to cells, especially cancer cells.

Other more recent developments in external radiotherapy procedures include:

- linear accelerator: a type of particle accelerator in which microwave technology is used to accelerate electrons, which are then aimed at a heavy metal target to produce high-energy X-rays which are precisely directed at the tumour.

Sometimes therapeutic procedures are given to patients as *palliative* measures, that is used to relieve pain when attempts to cure the disease are not possible. Do patients always have a right to access all information about their treatment? Is it ever ethically acceptable to deceive people?

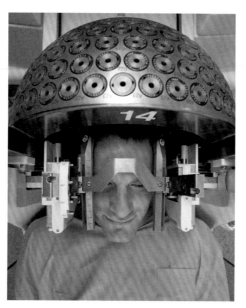

Patient set-up for gamma knife radiosurgery. The collimator helmet allows a single dose of gamma radiation to be directed through the ports of the helmet and targeted at a specific region of the patient's brain. Each beam of radiation provides a low dose and has a minimal effect on the tissue it passes through to reach its target, a brain tumour.

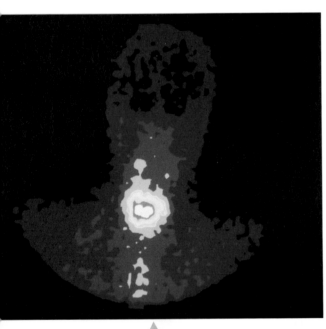

Coloured SPECT (single photon emission computed tomography) scan showing thyroid cancer. The cancerous cells are seen as white and yellow areas in the neck of the patient. SPECT scans of the thyroid gland are made by injecting the patient with the radioactive tracer iodine-131, which concentrates in the thyroid and can be detected by gamma camera.

- gamma knife radiosurgery: tiny beams of gamma radiation are focused on a tumour from approximately two hundred cobalt-60 sources, causing a strong dose to be delivered at the site where the beams converge.

Both of these techniques promise greater precision in the targeting of the ionizing radiation at the tumour with minimum damage to the surrounding healthy tissue. This is particularly important in the case of brain cancer treatment where avoiding damage to the rest of the brain is so important.

## 2 Internal radionuclide therapy

In internal radionuclide therapy, a radioactive material is taken into the body, either in solid form as an implant or as a liquid. An implant is introduced near the site of the tumour and left there for a period of time. It is usually a radioactive metal in the form of a wire, seed, or tube and is a gamma or beta emitter. Sometimes, this treatment involves the patient needing to be isolated while the implant is in place due to their emission of radiation – which could be dangerous to others.

Radioactive liquids are introduced either orally or by injection. Examples include:

- phosphorus-32 is used for blood disorders
- strontium-89 is used for secondary bone cancers, especially for pain control
- iodine-131 is used for thyroid cancer.

The incidence of thyroid cancer has increased sharply all over the world in the last few decades. This may be due in part to more sensitive diagnostic procedures, but it is thought that increasing exposure to radiation and possibly environmental carcinogens may have also had an effect. Studies of people who lived close to the nuclear accident in Chernobyl, Ukraine, in 1986 have shown a clear dose–response relationship in which higher absorption of radiation from iodine-131 led to an increased risk of developing thyroid cancer.

**Figure 15.31** Targeted alpha therapy uses an alpha-emitting radionuclide to bind to an antibody on the target cancer cell and then destroy it by ionizing radiation.

A promising development in this field is **targeted alpha therapy**, TAT, which is also known as radioimmunotherapy. This has the potential to be effective in the treatment of dispersed cancers, that is those that have spread beyond the original tumour, a process known as **metastasis**. TAT uses alpha-emitting radionuclides specifically directed at the biological target by attaching them to carriers such as antibodies. These carry the radionuclide to exactly the right place. Alpha particles are effective in this role because:

- they have very high ionizing density and so a high probability of killing cells at the target
- alpha particle radiation is short range and so minimizes unwanted irradiation of normal tissue surrounding the targeted cancer cells.

TAT using lead-212 is showing promise for the treatment of pancreatic, ovarian, and melanoma cancers.

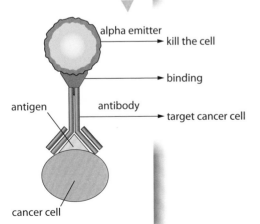

An experimental development of this is **boron neutron capture therapy** (BNCT), which is used particularly in the treatment of brain and neck tumours. Effectively, this technique generates the alpha particles at the target. First the patient is given a high dose of the non-radioactive isotope boron-10, which concentrates in malignant brain tumours. This is followed by irradiation with neutrons of sufficient energy to be absorbed by the boron – this is the *boron neutron capture*. The reaction is accompanied by the emission of high-energy alpha particles, which are in position to kill the cancer cells in the tumour. The reaction of neutron capture is as follows:

$$^{10}_{5}B + ^{1}_{0}n \rightarrow ^{11}_{5}B \rightarrow ^{4}_{2}\alpha + ^{7}_{3}Li$$

The targeted nature of this treatment depends on the extent to which boron-10 is selectively absorbed by the tumour and not taken up significantly by healthy cells. Other non-radioactive isotopes are being explored for possible application in this role for tumours at other sites in the body. Radionuclide therapy continues to advance as new treatments become available. The goal in all these approaches is to limit the exposure of all healthy cells to radiation and to use treatments with the minimum toxic side-effects.

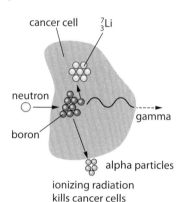

**Figure 15.32** Boron neutron capture therapy releases alpha radiation at the target in the body.

## Side-effects of radiotherapy

External radiotherapy tends to cause more general side-effects than internal therapy. Improvements in radiotherapy processes have in many cases reduced the range and severity of the side-effects of many of the treatments. Nonetheless, side-effects of radiotherapy do occur, mainly as a result of the effects of radiation on the surrounding tissue. The ionizing effects of radiation cause changes in the DNA of healthy as well as cancerous cells, particularly in those that divide rapidly, such as hair follicle cells.

As with all forms of medical treatment, individuals vary greatly in their responses to radiotherapy, but some of the most common side-effects are:

- fatigue – rest and regular hydration are important during treatment
- nausea – more common when the treatment is in the area of the digestive system
- hair-loss – this occurs within the treatment area and is usually temporary
- sterility – more likely if treatment is close to ovaries or testes
- skin reaction – skin may become red, sore, or itchy in local area of irradiation.

**NATURE OF SCIENCE**

The ionizing effects of radiation can both cause cancer and be used in its diagnosis and treatment. This apparent dichotomy evidently presents a challenge, and scientists have to balance the risk of exposure against potential benefits. In this they carry a heavy responsibility. Access to data can help to quantify the risk, and it is therefore important for medical personnel, industry, and governments to maintain data banks and records of the relationship between exposure and the incidence of disease.

Patch of bare skin on a man's cheek showing facial hair loss following radiotherapy for leukaemia. Radiotherapy is used to kill cancerous cells, but can affect other rapidly growing cells, such as those in hair follicles.

**22 (a)** Formulate the nuclear equation for the decay of $^{90}Y$, which is a beta emitter.

**(b)** The $^{90}Y$ isotope has a half-life of 64 hours. Calculate how much of a 65.0 g sample would remain after 4 days.

**23** $^{228}Ac$ is radioactive. After one day it is found that 0.33 mg of a 5.0 mg sample remains. What is its half-life?

**24 (a)** Outline the characteristics of Tc-99m that make it so suitable for use in diagnostic procedures.

**(b)** State the characteristics of Lu-177 and Y-90 that make them useful in radiotherapy.

**25 (a)** Describe what is meant by targeted alpha therapy.

**(b)** Explain two characteristics of alpha particles that enable them to be particularly effective in cancer treatments.

# D.9 Drug detection and analysis

## Understandings:

- Organic structures can be analysed and identified through the use of infrared spectroscopy, mass spectroscopy, and proton NMR.
- The presence of alcohol in a sample of breath can be detected through the use of either a redox reaction or a fuel cell type of breathalyser.

## Applications and skills:

- Interpretation of a variety of analytical spectra to determine an organic structure including infrared spectroscopy, mass spectroscopy, and proton NMR.
- Description of the process of extraction and purification of an organic product. Consider the use of fractional distillation, Raoult's law, the properties on which extractions are based and explaining the relationship between organic structure and solubility.
- Description of the process of steroid detection in sport utilizing chromatography and mass spectroscopy.
- Explanation of how alcohol can be detected with the use of a breathalyser.

### Guidance

- Students should be able to identify common organic functional groups in a given compound by recognition of common drug structures and from IR (section 26 of the data booklet), $^1H$ NMR (section 27 of the data booklet), and mass spectral fragment (section 28 of the data booklet) data.
- A common steroid structure is provided in the data booklet (section 34).

Today's multi-billion dollar drug industry is a far cry from early efforts to isolate medicines from natural products. Whereas then there was little knowledge of chemical structure or quantitative analysis, now the pharmaceutical industry has at its disposal advanced chemical knowledge and an array of technological instruments that make analysis ever more precise. In this section, we look at how some chemical techniques of purification and analysis are used in the drug industry and in the related field of drug detection.

## Drug isolation and purification

In the synthesis of drugs, it is common for the product to contain a mixture of compounds formed, as well as unreacted components, including reactants, solvents, and catalysts. Isolation of the required product in pure form is therefore an essential, and often a lengthy, part of the synthesis process. In essence, the techniques used in achieving this exploit differences between the physical properties of the required product and the other components of the mixture. We will consider applications of two main properties used in this process.

- differences in solubilities in different solvents
- differences in volatility.

## Organic structure and solubility

The solubility of a compound depends on its ability to interact and form stable bonds with the solvent, as discussed in Chapter 4 (page 179).

Organic molecules that dissolve well in organic solvents such as hexane or benzene are generally non-polar molecules which interact through London (dispersion) forces. These solutes typically have a high hydrocarbon content, such as long carbon chains and aromatic rings, and a smaller proportion of functional groups that are polar. On the other hand, organic compounds that dissolve well in water have a higher proportion of functional groups that are polar, as they interact by forming hydrogen bonds. These solutes include hydroxyl (–OH), carboxyl (–COOH), and amino (–NH₂) groups. Functional groups in aldehydes and ketones, amides, and esters also provide some polarity in the molecule. Aqueous solubility is enhanced by the presence of ionic groups such as salts.

As we saw earlier in the chapter, solubility is an important factor in determining the ability of drugs to reach their target in the body, which is why drugs like aspirin are sometimes modified to increase their aqueous solubility. Another example is the drug fluoxetine, which is converted to its more soluble ionic salt by reaction with hydrochloric acid.

> Molecules which are largely non-polar dissolve better in non-polar solvents; molecules with a higher proportion of polar or ionic groups dissolve better in water.

fluoxetine is not
very soluble

$+$ HCl $\longrightarrow$

fluoxetine hydrochloride (Prozac®)
is more soluble

This reaction produces the antidepressant drug Prozac.

During isolation processes, solubility differences can be used to separate the components of a mixture. Choosing a solvent which selectively dissolves a particular component is known as **extraction**. This is what happens, for example, when coffee beans are decaffeinated by extracting caffeine with liquid carbon dioxide.

**Solvent extraction** exploits the fact that a solute may show the greatest difference in solubility between two solvents that are immiscible. When given the chance to dissolve in both, the solute becomes unequally distributed between the two, known as **partition**.

Compounds with a higher solubility in non-polar solvents can be separated from aqueous solutions using a separating funnel because they form a separate layer, and the lower layer can be drained away. Here the lower aqueous layer has been coloured purple to make the separation more visible.

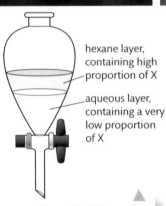

hexane layer, containing high proportion of X

aqueous layer, containing a very low proportion of X

**Figure 15.33** Separating funnel. The ground glass top makes a tight seal which is important during shaking. The two solvents are immiscible and so form two distinct phases. The tap at the bottom allows all of the lower aqueous layer to be drained away.

**Solvent extraction uses two immiscible solvents in which the required solute has very different solubilities.**

Salting out is used to separate proteins from solution, and uses the principle that large covalent molecules are less soluble in strong electrolytes than in water. Addition of an ionic compound such as common salt, NaCl, is made to an aqueous solution of proteins. The aqueous solubility of proteins decreases and so they precipitate from the solution, and can then be separated by filtration.

## CHALLENGE YOURSELF

**6** Water and ethanol are soluble in all proportions, but when potassium carbonate, $K_2CO_3$, is added they can be made immiscible and form two separate layers. This is known as **salting out**. Refer to the intermolecular forces involved to suggest why this might happen.

Solvent extraction can be illustrated by the following example.

- A product mixture is an aqueous solution that contains the required product X. It is known that X has a higher solubility in hexane than in water.
- The aqueous mixture is added to a **separating funnel** and a volume of hexane is added. The funnel is shaken vigorously and then placed in a stand to allow the contents to settle. Hexane is less dense than water and so forms the upper layer.
- Product X has dissolved more in the hexane than the water. The lower aqueous layer can be drained away, leaving the hexane layer containing X in solution.
- X can then be recovered by evaporation of the hexane.

Solvent extraction is used in the preparation of penicillin. The drug is extracted from aqueous solution using trichloromethane as the solvent.

Note that **recrystallization**, described on page 872, is another important technique that can be used in the purification of drug products from mixtures. This process also exploits differences in solubility between the required product and impurities.

## Organic structure and volatility

The boiling point of an organic compound is determined by the strength of the forces between its molecules, as these must be broken in order to separate the molecules and form the gas phase. So the stronger the intermolecular forces, the higher the boiling point and the less volatile the substance. The factors that influence the strength of intermolecular forces in organic compounds were discussed in Chapter 4 and Chapter 10, and are summarized here.

- Molecular size: volatility lowers with increasing molecular size due to increases in the London (dispersion) forces.
- Polarity: more polar functional groups cause lower volatility due to their ability to form hydrogen bonds or dipole–dipole interactions. The influence of functional groups on lowering volatility is in the order:

amide > carboxyl > hydroxyl > ketone > aldehyde > amino > ester > ether

**Fractional distillation** is a separation technique which exploits differences in volatility. It is based on the same principle of evaporation and condensation as the simple distillation process illustrated on page 492, but achieves better separation through the use of a fractionating column. The process results in **fractions**, each of which contains a mixture of liquids which boil within a narrow temperature range. Fractional distillation is used in the isolation of drug products from liquid mixtures, and as part of the process used to separate **chemical feed-stock**, such as phenols and toluene, used in the synthesis of many drugs.

 Fractional distillation is a major part of the oil industry. The process is responsible for separating crude oil, which contains thousands of different compounds, into more useful fractions such as fuel oil, kerosene, naphtha, gasoline, and gases.

The theory of fractional distillation is based on a relationship known as Raoult's law. To explain this, we first need to introduce the concepts of mole fraction and vapour pressure.

The **mole fraction** of a substance, shown with the symbol $\chi$ (the Greek letter 'chi'), refers to the fraction of the moles of the substance in a mixture. For example, in a mixture of A and B, the mole fraction of A is the number of moles of A divided by the total number of moles:

$$\chi_A = \frac{n(A)}{n(A)+n(B)} \quad \text{and} \quad \chi_B = \frac{n(B)}{n(A)+n(B)}$$

The sum of the mole fractions is:

$$\chi_A + \chi_B = \frac{n(A)}{n(A)+n(B)} + \frac{n(B)}{n(A)+n(B)} = 1$$

Note that mole fraction has no units.

The mole fraction of a substance is the fraction of the moles of the substance in a mixture. The sum of the mole fractions of all the components of a mixture is equal to 1.

## Worked example

What are the mole fractions of the components of a solution made by mixing 500 g of ethanol with 500 g of water?

### Solution

As data are given without decimal places, we will use integer values for relative atomic mass here. First calculate the number of moles of each component.

$$M(C_2H_5OH) = (12 \times 2) + 16 + (1 \times 6) = 46 \text{ g mol}^{-1}$$

$$\therefore n(C_2H_5OH) = \frac{\text{mass}}{M} = \frac{500 \text{ g}}{46 \text{ g mol}^{-1}} = 10.87 \text{ mol}$$

$$M(H_2O) = (1 \times 2) + 16 = 18 \text{ g mol}^{-1}$$

$$\therefore n(H_2O) = \frac{\text{mass}}{M} = \frac{500 \text{ g}}{18 \text{ g mol}^{-1}} = 27.78 \text{ mol}$$

Total number of moles = 10.87 + 27.78 = 38.65 mol

$$\chi(C_2H_5OH) = \frac{10.87}{38.65} = 0.28 \text{ and } \chi(H_2O) = \frac{27.78}{38.65} = 0.72$$

The mole fraction of water could also be calculated by subtracting the value for ethanol from 1 (1 − 0.28 = 0.72).

The **vapour pressure** is the pressure exerted by a vapour in equilibrium with its liquid at a given temperature in a closed system.

$$\text{liquid} \xrightleftharpoons[\text{condense}]{\text{boil / evaporate}} \text{vapour}$$

The further this equilibrium lies to the right, the higher the vapour pressure, as more molecules exist in the gas state to exert pressure on the liquid surface. Compounds that are more volatile, that is those that have weaker intermolecular forces and lower boiling points, therefore exert a higher vapour pressure than less volatile compounds at the same temperature.

Consider a solution made of two liquid components, A and B. The vapour above the solution will contain molecules of A and of B, and therefore each of these components contributes to the total vapour pressure. But their relative contribution will depend on their relative volatilities.

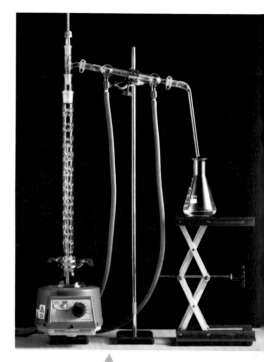

Fractional distillation apparatus using an electric heater. The vapour that is released from the top of the column has been through several cycles of boiling and condensation. This vapour is cooled by water in the condenser and forms a liquid that is enriched in the more volatile component.

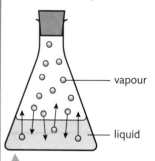

**Figure 15.34** In a closed system at equilibrium, the rate of evaporation equals the rate of condensation. The vapour pressure is the pressure exerted on a liquid by its vapour under these conditions.

Equilibrium vapour pressure is the pressure exerted by a vapour on its liquid when the rate of evaporation equals the rate of condensation.

Substances that are more volatile have weaker intermolecular forces and lower boiling points than less volatile substances.

The total vapour pressure of a solution is equal to the sum of the vapour pressures of each component in the mixture. The vapour pressure of each component is proportional to its mole fraction in the solution.

Using $P$ for vapour pressure:

$$P_{total} = P_A + P_B$$

The vapour pressures of each component, $P_A$ and $P_B$, are calculated by **Raoult's law**. This states that the vapour pressure of a volatile substance in a solution is equal to the vapour pressure of the pure substance multiplied by its mole fraction in the solution.

Using $P°$ to represent the vapour pressure of a pure substance:

$$P_A = P°_A \times \chi_A \text{ and } P_B = P°_B \times \chi_B$$

$$P_{total} = P_A + P_B = P°_A \times \chi_A + P°_B \times \chi_B$$

In other words, the vapour pressure of a solution of two liquids depends on the vapour pressures and proportion of each liquid present. The relationship applies only to so-called **ideal solutions**, those which contain fully miscible liquids. In these cases the liquid components behave in the same way when mixed in the solution as they do when pure. Chemically alike compounds in which the intermolecular forces are similar form ideal solutions.

Raoult's law is summarized in Figure 15.35.

**Figure 15.35** Vapour pressure of a solution of two liquids, A and B, of varying composition. Note that at any point on the $x$-axis, the sum of the mole fractions of A + B = 1. The total vapour pressure, $P_{total}$ shown in red is equal to the sum of the vapour pressures of each component.

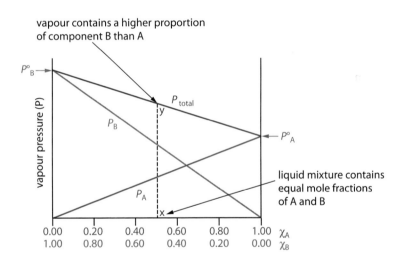

Note that a more volatile component refers to one that exerts a higher vapour pressure. The two terms are often used interchangeably.

Figure 15.35 shows that the total vapour pressure of a solution is equal to the sum of the component vapour pressures for any composition of the mixture. In simple terms, from any point on the horizontal axis, add up the corresponding values for the blue line and the green line, and you will get the value for the red line.

We can see that, in this example, component B has a higher vapour pressure than component A, as shown by comparing the vapour pressures of the pure substances marked on the graph, $P°_A$ and $P°_B$. To understand the significance of this, let us compare the compositions of the solution and its vapour at the points marked as x and y.

- x represents the solution when it contains equal amounts of each component A and B – the mole fraction of each is 0.5.
- y represents the total vapour pressure of that equimolar mixture. This shows that B makes a larger contribution to the total vapour pressure than A, so the vapour must contain a higher proportion of molecules of B.

The vapour above a solution of two liquids is always enriched in the more volatile component, relative to their mole fractions in the solution.

Fractional distillation is an application of Raoult's law. When a solution boils, it produces a vapour which is enriched in its more volatile component. When that vapour is collected, it condenses to form a solution which is also enriched in the more volatile component. By repeating the cycle of boiling and condensation, more and more separation of the components can be achieved.

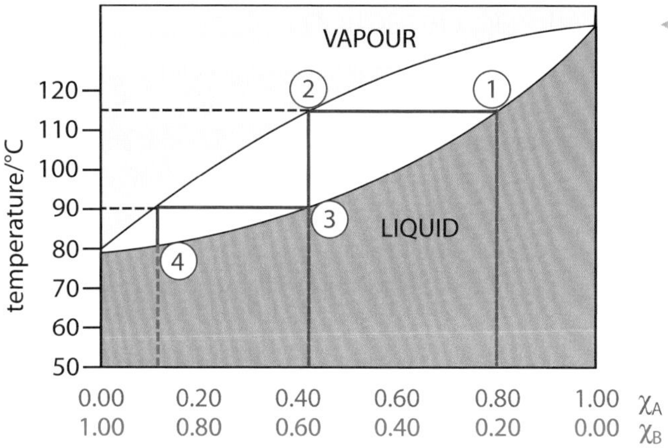

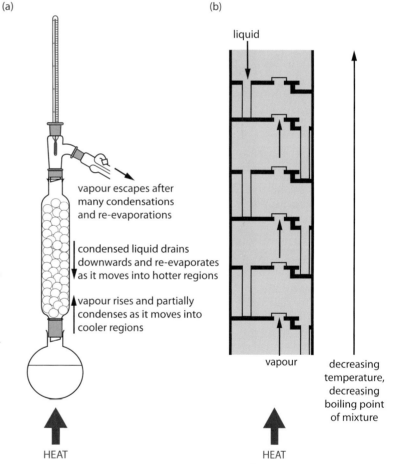

▲ **Figure 15.36** Temperature–composition graph for a mixture of two solutions, A and B.

A solution boils when its total vapour pressure reaches the external pressure. So the vapour pressure–composition graph in Figure 15.35 can be converted into a boiling point–composition graph, such as shown in Figure 15.36. The lower curve represents the liquid composition, and the upper curve represents the vapour composition. The two curves are joined by horizontal **tie lines**, shown in red, which indicate the same temperature at each point.

Figure 15.36 can be used to illustrate the process of fractional distillation as follows.

- Point 1: a starting solution that contains mole fraction 0.80 of A and 0.20 of B boils at 115°C.
- Point 2: the vapour at 115°C has a different composition from the starting solution.
- Point 3: condensation of this vapour forms a solution with a composition of approximately mole fraction 0.40 of A and 0.60 of B.
- Point 4: the solution in point 3 boils at 90°C and condenses to form a liquid which has mole fraction 0.10 of A and mole fraction 0.90 of B.

So overall the ratio of A:B in the solution has changed from 80:20 to 10:90 in three cycles. The proportion of the more volatile component B has increased significantly.

Fractional distillation uses a column such as that shown in Figure 15.37. The surface area inside the column is increased by the presence of glass beads or glass projections. As the solution boils, vapour rises up the column until it condenses and falls back down. This vapour is then reboiled by ascending vapour, and the process repeats. The temperature decreases as the vapour rises up the column, allowing for a succession of boil–condense cycles. Eventually, the vapour exiting the flask is collected and condensed to form a liquid enriched in the more volatile component.

**Figure 15.37** Columns for fractional distillation: (a) as used in laboratories and (b) as typically used in industry. Both columns have a large internal surface area to maximize the surface for condensation. At each boil–condense cycle, the liquid falls down to the higher temperature and the vapour rises to the lower temperature.

## Drug detection

The abuse of drugs in sporting competitions and concerns over drink driving are familiar items in the news. The ethical, health, and safety issues arising from the use of some drugs has led to specific guidelines surrounding their use in most countries. Laws govern which substances are banned and what are acceptable limits for certain activities. As part of this legislative control, governments have instigated surveillance methods for checking on the presence and concentration of drugs in individuals in the population. These methods use modern techniques of chemical analysis, as described below.

### Steroid detection

Steroids are lipids with a structure consisting of four fused rings, known as a **steroidal backbone**. An example of a steroid is cholesterol, which has the following structure.

This is given in section 34 of the IB data booklet.

Steroids are found in some hormones, especially the sex hormones. Male steroid hormones are collectively called androgens, of which **testosterone** is the most important. These hormones are known as **anabolic steroids**, due to their role in promoting tissue growth, especially of muscles. They have been used as **performance-enhancing drugs** by athletes in sports such as weight-lifting and cycling, as they can increase strength and endurance. Anabolic steroids are usually synthesized from testosterone, and include drugs such as nandrolone, stanozolol, and furazabol.

The use of anabolic steroids is banned by most sporting authorities for medical and ethical reasons. These compounds are toxic to the liver and can be associated with an increased risk of cancer and heart problems. They also disturb the hormone balance in the body, causing changes in secondary sexual characteristics such as hair distribution and risks to fertility. Most sporting authorities have introduced procedures for the collection of body fluid samples taken from athletes at the time of competition, which are analysed for the presence of banned substances.

The most common method used for detection of steroids in blood and urine samples is known as **gas chromatography–mass spectrometry**, GC-MS. This uses the two techniques of chromatography and mass spectrometry combined in sequence:

- gas chromatography separates the chemical mixture into pure chemicals
- mass spectroscopy identifies and quantifies the components.

### Gas chromatography

Chromatography is a useful technique for separating and identifying the components of a mixture. The basic principle is that the components have different affinities for two

---

Cholesterol is a steroid which is found widely in living things as it is a component of cell membranes. When taken in excess in the diet, cholesterol is associated with certain circulatory diseases such as atherosclerosis and coronary heart disease, described further on page 712.

The World Anti-Doping Agency was formed in 1999 in response to the rapidly increasing widespread use of anabolic steroids in sports. The agency's mission is to harmonize anti-doping policies and regulations within sports organizations and among governments. A major achievement has been the development and implementation of a World Anti-Doping Code, which was been broadly accepted by most governments and sporting bodies. The code specifies that anti-doping laboratories need to be accredited by meeting international standards.

The term *doping* is believed to be derived from the Dutch word *dop*, which was an alcoholic drink used by Zulu warriors to enhance their skills in battle. The word was first adopted for the use of illegal drugging of racehorses, and passed into more general usage as the use of enhancing performance through chemicals became more common.

phases, a **stationary phase** and a **mobile phase**, and so are separated as the mobile phase moves through the stationary phase. In gas chromatography, the phases are:

- stationary phase – a microscopic layer of a non-volatile *liquid*, usually a polymer, which is coated on the walls of an inert solid support
- mobile phase – an inert carrier *gas*, such as helium.

Separation of the components of a mixture is determined by the different rates at which they move through the instrument. These rates differ according to the boiling points and solubilities of each component, as these determine the relative associations of the molecules with the liquid (stationary) and gas (mobile) phases. The components therefore partition themselves between the two phases. Molecules which spend more time in the gas phase move more quickly, while those with higher boiling points and greater solubility in the liquid move more slowly.

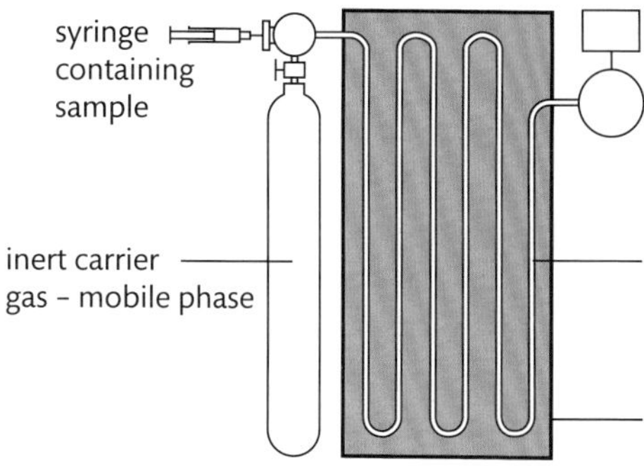

As shown in Figure 15.38, the sample is introduced into the instrument by injection and then heated so that it boils. The gas is mixed with the inert carrier gas and passed into the column. The temperature in the column is controlled, and is typically lower than the initial temperature, so that some components of the mixture condense and may dissolve in the liquid phase on the walls of the column. Depending on how they partition themselves between the liquid and gas phases, each component of the mixture will be **eluted** at a specific interval of time, known as its **retention time**. Changing the temperature of the column controls the retention times, and therefore the amount of separation of the components achieved. A detector is used to record the passage of each compound as a peak, and the area under the peak is a measure of its concentration relative to a known standard.

An example of a simple gas chromatogram is shown in Figure 15.39. The retention time for component X, $t_R$, is measured from the time of the injection of the sample.

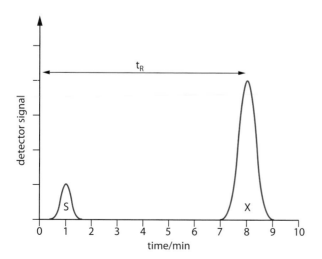

In gas chromatography–mass spectrometry, some of the eluted sample is passed directly to a mass spectrometer for identification. This avoids the need to identify compounds from their retention times.

Gas chromatography (GC) is sometimes known as gas-liquid chromatography (GLC) or gas-liquid partition chromatography (GLPC) to clarify the phases involved. Any of these terms can be used as they describe the same process.

**Figure 15.38** Gas-liquid chromatography apparatus.

- syringe containing sample
- recorder
- detector
- outlet tube
- inert carrier gas – mobile phase
- column – coated with stationary phase
- thermostatically controlled oven

**Figure 15.39** Gas chromatogram showing the retention time for compound X in a sample. The retention time for the peak marked S is the so-called void time, the minimum time for a compound that does not react with the stationary phase to be eluted.

**Components of a mixture are separated in gas chromatography on the basis of their boiling points and relative solubilities in the gas and liquid phases. More volatile components are eluted more quickly and so have shorter retention times.**

**Figure 15.40** Summary of gas chromatogram–mass spectrometer.

## Mass spectrometry

The principles of mass spectrometry were described in Chapter 11 (page 549). The instrument vaporizes the sample and then generates positive ions from the components. These ions are then accelerated and deflected in a magnetic field, and separated according to their different deflections. In the mass spectrometer, molecules often fragment into structures which can be identified from their charge to mass ratio ($m/z$). Molecules tend to break in predictable places so fragmentation patterns give clues to their structure. The use of computer databases of known fragmentation patterns allows a wide range of compounds to be identified. Specific mass spectrometer fragments with their masses are given in section 28 of the IB data booklet.

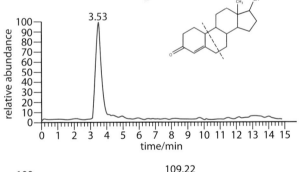

Figure 15.41 shows the combined results from gas chromatography–mass spectrometry used to analyse a sample and detect the presence of the steroid drug nandrolone.

## Techniques used for the detection of ethanol

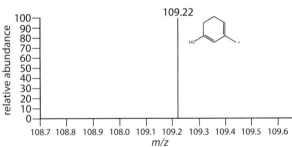

Ethanol, $C_2H_5OH$, is the alcohol present in beer, wine, and hard liquor drinks – which are widely used in many diets and cultures.

**Figure 15.41** GC-MS spectra of nandrolone. The upper diagram shows the gas chromatogram, and the lower diagram the mass spectrum in which a molecular fragment is clearly identified.

The polar —OH group enables ethanol to form hydrogen bonds with water, making it readily soluble in aqueous solution. So ethanol is able to pass quickly from the gut to the blood and circulate to all parts of the body. This is why the effects of ethanol are noticeable a very short time after intake. Ethanol acts as a **depressant**, which means it decreases the activity of the central nervous system, which causes short-term changes in behaviour and long-term dependency.

A person whose judgement is changed by the presence of ethanol in the blood is said to be **impaired**, which is a potentially dangerous condition. As a result, most countries have set legal limits for allowable levels of ethanol concentration for activities such as driving, and have instigated procedures to test body fluid samples from individuals. These tests usually measure the **blood alcohol concentration** as mass per volume, that is milligrams of ethanol per $cm^3$ of blood ($mg\ cm^{-3}$).

The maximum legal blood alcohol concentration (BAC) for motor vehicle use varies by country. Values typically range from 0.2 to 0.8 $mg\ cm^{-3}$, though Brazil, Hungary, Russia, and Nepal have a zero value for the allowable limit. Legislation has changed in many countries to lower the limit in response to widespread concerns over alcohol-related road traffic accidents. Publically available breathalyser tests are being used increasingly, and in France vehicle drivers are required by law to carry such a device. Vehicles can be fitted with breathalyser immobilizers, or alcolocks, that prevent the use of the vehicle by an impaired driver.

Ethanol is a volatile compound and so establishes equilibrium in the lungs between the solution in the blood and gas, which is released in exhaled breath.

$$C_2H_5OH(aq) \rightleftharpoons C_2H_5OH(g)$$

in blood      in exhaled breath

The equilibrium constant $K_c$ for this reaction has a fixed value at a particular temperature so measurement of ethanol in the breath can be used to assess the blood alcohol concentration. Instruments that measure ethanol concentration in a sample of breath and convert it into blood alcohol concentration are known as **breathalysers**.

Roadside breathalysers use redox chemistry to measure ethanol concentration. As described in Chapter 10 (page 493), ethanol is oxidized to ethanal and ethanoic acid by the oxidizing agent potassium dichromate(VI), $K_2Cr_2O_7$. During the reaction, chromate(VI) is reduced to chromate(III), which causes a colour change from orange to green.

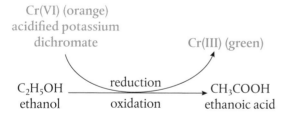

Cr(VI) (orange)
acidified potassium
dichromate

Cr(III) (green)

$C_2H_5OH$   reduction   $CH_3COOH$
ethanol    oxidation    ethanoic acid

The extent of the colour change can be measured using a photocell and so be used to determine the ethanol concentration. The test is often used as preliminary test which may lead to further, more accurate, tests using **intoximeters**.

An instrument known as an **alcosensor** uses the electrochemical processes in a **fuel cell** to measure ethanol concentration. The fuel cell consists of two platinum electrodes with a porous acid electrolyte between. Exhaled air is passed over the cell and any ethanol present is oxidized to ethanoic acid at the anode.

$$C_2H_5OH(g) + H_2O(l) \rightarrow CH_3COOH(l) + 4H^+(aq) + 4e^-$$

Protons and electrons released from this reaction pass to the cathode where they reduce oxygen to water.

$$O_2(g) + 4H^+(aq) + 4e^- \rightarrow 2H_2O(l)$$

Alcohol is a depressant, and long-term use of large quantities can radically impact a person's health and lifestyle.

Alcohol breath test. The roadside breathalyser gives an immediate reading of whether the level of alcohol in the motorist's blood is over the legal limit

The concentration of the alcohol in exhaled air is directly related to the concentration of the alcohol in the blood.

The overall reaction is the oxidation of ethanol to ethanoic acid and water.

$$C_2H_5OH(g) + O_2(g) \rightarrow CH_3COOH(l) + H_2O(l)$$

The electric current produced by the reaction is measured by a computer and used to calculate the blood alcohol concentration. Fuel cell intoximeters are accurate and portable, and widely used.

### NATURE OF SCIENCE

Advances in technology have led to increasingly precise means of detecting the presence of drug derivatives in body fluids and in the environment. This means that concentrations which were previously too low to be measured can now be reported accurately. This has made tighter regulation of drug use possible, in some cases leading to changes in regulations and laws. Authorities and governments often depend on scientific data such as spectral evidence in making judgements and enforcing the law. It is therefore essential that the data collected are reliable and include clearly stated uncertainties.

## Organic structure analysis and identification

A major part of the preparation of drugs in the pharmaceutical industry is the characterization of products. This uses modern techniques of analysis and identification, including mass spectroscopy, infrared spectroscopy, and proton NMR. These techniques were all introduced and explained in Chapter 11, and the principles of their usage are exactly the same when applied to the analysis of drugs. Therefore there is no new information on the processes here, but we will see how their applications can be used in the drug industry. We will take as an example the characterization of aspirin following its preparation from salicylic acid, which was described on page 872. You may find it useful to review this section first.

### Mass spectroscopy

This is used to confirm the presence of a compound through the peak of the parent molecular ion. The presence or absence of fragment peaks in the spectrum helps confirm the structure. Impurities can often be determined through the presence of their characteristic molecular ion and/or fragment peaks.

Notice that several peak on the mass spectra have 'shadow peaks' at (M + 1). For example, in Figure 15.42(b), aspirin has a small peak at 139 as well as 138, and at 121 as well as 120. These smaller peaks are most likely due to the presence of $^{13}C$ in the molecular fragments.

| Salicylic acid $C_7H_6O_3$ | Aspirin $C_9H_8O_4$ |
|---|---|
| COOH OH (benzene ring structure) | COOH O—C=O CH₃ (benzene ring structure) |
| molecular ion $C_7H_6O_3^+$ <br> $m/z = 138$ | molecular ion $C_9H_8O_4^+$ <br> $m/z = 180$ |

The presence of the molecular ions can be seen in the two spectra, as identified in Figure 15.42. This helps to confirm the identity of the compounds tested. Notice that the size of the molecular ion peak in aspirin is relatively small – this is not an unusual situation and indicates that fragmentation of the majority of the molecular ions has occurred before they pass through the deflector and hit the detector.

The mass spectra of salicylic acid and of aspirin are shown in Figure 15.42.

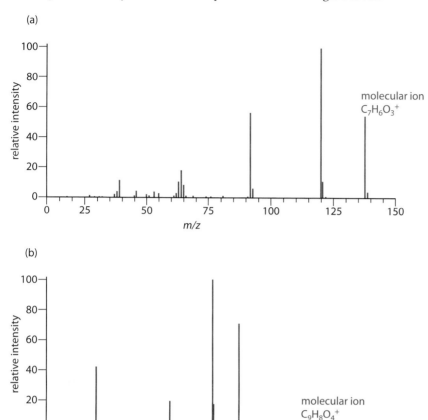

Figure 15.42 Mass spectra of (a) salicylic acid and (b) aspirin.

Other peaks in the spectra generally indicate the presence of molecular fragments. For example, the peak at 121 in Figure 15.42(a) could be due to the molecular ion $C_7H_5O_2^+$, formed by loss of OH•.

m/z = 138     loss of OH•     m/z = 121

Can you think of a possible identity for the peak at 138 in Figure 15.42(b) that is not a molecular fragment? The answer is that it could be the molecular ion of unreacted salicylic acid, the starting material in the synthesis of aspirin. This tells us that mass spectrometry alone cannot always provide evidence for the purity of a sample.

## Infrared spectroscopy (IR)

Functional groups in compounds show as characteristic absorption peaks in infrared spectroscopy. The groups are influenced to some extent by the environment of the bond, so every organic compound has its own specific infrared spectrum. This can therefore act as a molecular fingerprint as the identify of an unknown compound can

**Figure 15.43** HNMR spectrum of aspirin, 2-acetoxybenzoic acid

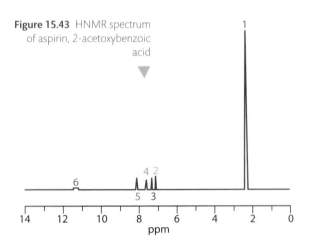

be determined by comparison of the IR spectrum with those of pure compounds stored in a database of IR spectra. The infrared spectra of aspirin and salicylic acid are discussed on page 873.

## Proton NMR

Proton NMR ($^1$H NMR) is a very sensitive technique which enables chemists to check the identity of the sample from the chemical shifts, the number of peaks, and integrated area as well as the splitting patterns. The presence of impurities will show as additional peaks with their own characteristics.

Figure 15.43 shows the $^1$H NMR spectrum of aspirin.

This can be interpreted with colour coding as follows:

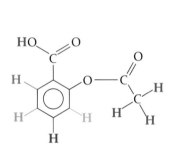

| Peak | Chemical shift / ppm | Type of proton | Splitting pattern |
|------|---------------------|----------------|-------------------|
| 1 | 2.3 | 3 equivalent protons on the –CH$_3$ group in the ester group | singlet |
| 2 | | | doublet |
| 3 | range 7–8 | 4 protons attached within the aromatic ring, each in slightly different chemical environments | triplet |
| 4 | | | triplet |
| 5 | | | doublet |
| 6 | 11 | –OH of carboxylic acid; but the peak is so broad that it is almost not visible | singlet |

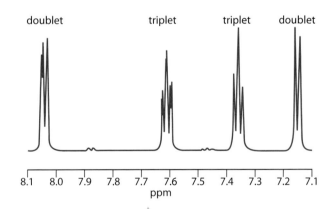

doublet    triplet    triplet    doublet

**Figure 15.44** The protons of the benzene ring show splitting into doublets and triplets according to their coupling with adjacent protons.

The splitting pattern of peaks 2–5 can be shown in more detail in a higher resolution spectrum.

The ratio of the peaks, based on the integrated area rather than the height of the peaks and taking into account the splitting pattern, is as follows:

Peak:  **1 : 2 : 3 : 4 : 5 : 6**
Integrated area ratio:   3 : 1 : 1 : 1 : 1 : 1

An $^1$H NMR spectrum of salicylic acid would similarly show four aromatic peaks due to the protons attached to the benzene ring, but would lack the singlet observed at 2.3 as it has no ester group containing a methyl group.

## Exercises

**26** Which one of the following pairs of liquids might be used in carrying out solvent extractions? Explain your choice.

    **A**   benzene and hexane         **C**   water and ethanol
    **B**   methylbenzene and water     **D**   benzene and methylbenzene

**27 (a)** State what is meant by an ideal solution.
    **(b)** Explain what happens to the boiling point of a mixture present at increasing height in a fractionating column.

**28** Infrared spectroscopy can be used to detect ethanol in breath samples.

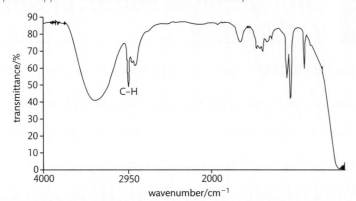

**Figure 15.45** Infrared absorption spectrum of ethanol in the gas phase.

**(a)** Use the structure of ethanol to identify peaks on this spectrum (Figure 15.45).
**(b)** State which of these peaks can be used to distinguish ethanol from water vapour in the breath.
**(c)** People who suffer from diabetes often exhale propanone vapour in their breath. Suggest why they may therefore give a false positive result in the infrared spectroscopy test for ethanol.

**29** Caffeine has the following structure:

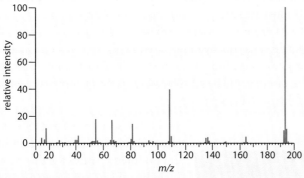

**(a)** In the mass spectrum given in Figure 15.46, what peak supplies the strongest evidence for the presence of caffeine?

**Figure 15.46** Mass spectrum for question 29.

**(b)** Identify two characteristic absorptions in the infrared spectrum (Figure 15.47) that are consistent with the structure of caffeine.

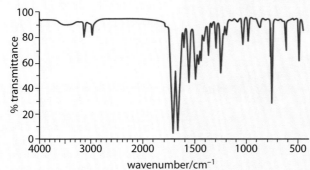

**Figure 15.47** Infrared spectrum for question 29.

**(c)** How many peaks would you expect in the $^1$H NMR spectrum of caffeine? What would be their relative areas and splitting patterns?
**(d)** Name three functional groups present in caffeine.

## D.6 Environmental impact of some medications

### Understandings:
- High-level waste (HLW) is waste that gives off large amounts of ionizing radiation for a long time.
- Low-level waste (LLW) is waste that gives off small amounts of ionizing radiation for a short time.
- Antibiotic resistance occurs when microorganisms become resistant to antibacterials.

### Applications and skills:
- Description of the environmental impact of medical nuclear waste disposal.
- Discussion of environmental issues related to left-over solvents.
- Explanation of the dangers of antibiotic waste, from improper drug disposal and animal waste, and the development of antibiotic resistance.
- Discussion of the basics of Green Chemistry (sustainable chemistry) processes.
- Explanation of how Green Chemistry was used to develop the precursor for Tamiflu (oseltamivir).

  ### Guidance
  *The structure of oseltamivir is provided in the IB data booklet in section 37.*

In this chapter we have explored many of the ways in which modern medicine has made significant contributions to advances in human health. Better diagnosis and treatments of many conditions have led to improvements in the quality of life, and increases in longevity in many parts of the world.

A recurring theme has been an awareness of how side-effects of medications may directly impact health. Consequently, side-effects to the patient are monitored and negative effects avoided wherever possible. In a parallel way, the activities of the pharmaceutical industry in drug preparation, administration, and disposal produce side-effects in the environment. Many of these are negative and potentially damaging to human health. It is thus equally important that these environmental side-effects are monitored, with policies and procedures put in place to minimize their negative impact. Failure to do so would be self-defeating, as the quality of the environment is critical to the health of all living things.

> The 12 principles of Green Chemistry are given on pages 940–941. You do not need to learn these, but you may find it useful to refer to them in this study.

In this last section, we will look at some of the challenges and possible solutions to the environmental impact of the medical industry, including the role of Green Chemistry. This branch of chemistry, also known as Sustainable Chemistry, has developed since 1991, and focuses on 12 principles. These principles cover concepts such as avoiding waste, maximizing

Water pollution monitoring in Gujarat, India. A scientist collects a sample of polluted water as it pours from a pipe into a shallow ditch. The water has been stained dark yellow by the presence of poisonous organochloride chemicals, especially 2,6-dichlorobenzenamine and 2,4,5-trichlorobenzene which are used in the pharmaceutical industry. In this major industrial area, wastes are often disposed of by dumping them in any convenient open space or watercourse.

the amount of raw material that ends up in the product, and the use of safe solvents. In essence, Green Chemistry seeks to reduce the footprint of chemical manufacturing processes while improving product and environmental safety. As we will see, it has many applications in the pharmaceutical industry.

## Solvent waste: the major emission of the drug industry

Most drugs are complex molecules, so their synthesis and extraction involves multiple steps. In many parts of this process, organic solvents are used. These may be toxic and are often left over at the end of the synthesis, leading to problems of disposal. It is estimated that up to 80% of the mass of reactants that does not end up in the pharmaceutical product is due to solvents, including water. Disposal of solvents often involves incineration, which can release toxins into the environment. Overall, solvents are by far the biggest contributor to the emissions of the pharmaceutical industry.

Solvent use is therefore a serious concern in the pharmaceutical industry. The suitability of solvents can be assessed by three factors:

1 toxicity to workers – whether the solvent is carcinogenic (cancer causing) or associated with other health issues

2 safety of the process – whether the solvent is highly flammable, explosive, or can cause toxic by-products

3 harm to the environment – whether the solvent will contaminate soil and ground water, cause ozone depletion, or contribute to greenhouse gas formation when released or burned.

On the basis of these criteria, examples of some common solvents can be classified as preferred or undesirable as shown below.

| Preferred solvents | Undesirable solvents |
|---|---|
| water, $H_2O$ | dichloromethane, $CH_2Cl_2$ |
| ethanol, $C_2H_5OH$ | methanal, $HCHO$ |
| 2-propanol, $CH_3CH(OH)CH_3$ | tetrachloromethane, $CCl_4$ |
| propanone, $CH_3COCH_3$ | diethyl ether, $C_2H_5OC_2H_5$ |
| ethyl ethanoate, $CH_3COOC_2H_5$ | benzene, $C_6H_6$ |

It can be seen that chlorinated compounds, ethers, and many aromatic compounds are considered problematic, and should wherever possible be replaced by water, alcohols, or possibly esters.

One of the principles of Green Chemistry is the use of *safer solvents and to avoid the use of auxiliaries where possible.* Water is clearly the safest solvent for the environment, and supercritical carbon dioxide ($CO_2$ under pressure) can also be used in some processes. Another principle of Green Chemistry is to *prevent waste.* Pharmaceutical companies are finding ways to reduce and reuse solvents in the synthesis process, so that there is less waste released into the environment. Detailed analysis of the entire energy costs has shown that solvent

Apparatus for supercritical extraction of compounds from plants. The extraction occurs at high pressure and temperature using carbon dioxide as a solvent, known as supercritical carbon dioxide, and avoids the use of environmentally harmful solvents. Photographed in the Green Chemistry research group laboratory in the University of York, UK.

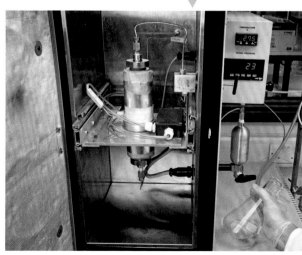

Left-over organic solvents are the major emission of the pharmaceutical industry. Solvent recycling can substantially cut emissions to air, water, and soil.

recycling programmes can run at significantly lower costs than the total cost of the production of new solvent and burning of waste. Case-studied examples include the production of the arthritis drug Celebrex by Pfizer, where scenarios with and without solvent recycling were rigorously compared.

## Nuclear waste: an increasing problem in the drug industry

The use of nuclear chemistry in the diagnosis and treatment of disease is a rapidly expanding area of medicine, as was discussed in section D.8 (page 905). Many of the techniques used are associated with some radioactive waste, which can potentially be hazardous to living things and the environment. Disposal of medical nuclear waste is therefore a growing problem that must be faced by the medical industry.

The method of disposal used depends on the level of waste and the length of time it remains radioactive, which is determined by its half-life.

- **High-level waste** gives off large amounts of ionizing radiation for a long time. The isotopes have long half-lives.

Yellow barrels containing solid low-level radioactive waste such as contaminated glass, metal, rags, and equipment. The equipment shown compresses the barrels to one-fifth of their original size, before they are stored in concrete vaults. Photographed in Oak Ridge National Laboratory, Tennessee, USA.

- **Low-level waste** gives off small amounts of ionizing radiation for a short time. The isotopes have short half-lives.

Most of the waste generated by nuclear medicines is low-level waste. It includes items such as clothing, protective shoe covers, paper towels, and implements that have become contaminated with radioactive material. Disposal of this low-level waste usually involves first interim storage in sealed containers that are safe, secure, and environmentally sound. The radioactivity typically decays in hours or days, and the waste can then be disposed of by conventional means – compaction, landfill, or sewers for liquids.

The International Atomic Energy Agency (IAEA) provides recommendations for the classification of nuclear waste, but the actual definition of low-level waste is set by individual countries. As the level of activity for this waste is usually quite variable, there may be some radioactive components in the mixture that have relatively high activity.

Spent isotopes from medical diagnosis techniques may generate some high-level waste, although this amount is quite small relative to the amount of high-level waste from spent fuel rods generated by the nuclear energy industry. The medical waste is often toxic as well as radioactive, and can have damaging effects in the environment.

Disposal of high-level waste is a complex problem because products of the decay process may themselves be radioactive and continue to emit ionizing radiation. The decay processes also often emit significant amounts of heat. High-level waste is usually stored first under water in reinforced cooling ponds for 5 to 10 years, and then transferred to dry storage in heavily shielded structures, often buried deep in the Earth. It is essential to prevent the radioactive waste from entering the underground water supply.

Innovations in Green Chemistry may help to reduce nuclear waste, for example by extracting enriched uranium from incinerator ash using supercritical carbon dioxide.

An alternative innovative approach is to reduce the use of radioactive isotopes in diagnosis, by replacing them with fluorescent dyes. This has given promising results in some early trials and has substantially reduced the radioactive waste.

Aerial view of construction work at the Hanford liquefied high-level atomic waste storage facility at Richland, Washington State, USA. Each tank has a capacity of four million litres of liquefied high-level waste and has a double-shell construction. The tanks are surrounded by reinforced concrete and covered with ten feet of earth. Long-term storage such as this is sited in regions that are believed to be geologically stable.

## Antibiotic waste: are we killing the cures?

The problem of antibiotic-resistant bacteria, which we discussed with respect to penicillin on page 879, applies to most other antibiotics as well. This presents a major challenge to modern medicine, as many antibiotics are simply no longer effective as therapeutic agents against bacterial infections.

### NATURE OF SCIENCE

Scientific innovations sometimes bring unintended burdens as well as benefits to society. This is certainly the case with some of the environmental impacts of the pharmaceutical industry. The responsibility to ameliorate the effects then falls to the scientists, who often must work in cooperation with governments and regulatory authorities. While scientific advances are clearly the source of some of these issues, it is also scientific developments that will most appropriately address the concerns.

Antibiotic resistance has become a major problem with some strains of tuberculosis (TB), and treatment now requiring the use of several different antibiotics together. It is estimated that today 1 in 7 new TB cases is resistant to the drugs most commonly used to treat it. Antibiotic-resistant TB bacteria have been identified in many countries and are a particular concern in Russia, India, South Africa, and Peru. Antibiotic resistance must be faced on a global scale, as no country can protect itself from the importation of resistant pathogens through travel and trade.

Hospitals often face a particular problem in dealing with antibiotic-resistant bacteria. So-called **superbugs** are bacteria such as methicillin-resistant *Staphylococcus aureus* (MRSA) that carry several resistant genes, and cause infections that are extremely difficult to treat. Extensive use of **broad-spectrum antibiotics**, that is those that are used against a wide range of bacteria, has also enabled infections such as *Clostridium difficile* to thrive.

Coloured scanning electron micrograph (SEM) of methicillin-resistant *Staphylococcus aureus*, known as MRSA. The bacteria are shown here in yellow on the microscopic fibres of a wound dressing. These bacteria are a major problem in hospitals because they are resistant to many commonly prescribed antibiotics. They can cause wound infections, pneumonia, and blood poisoning in vulnerable people, such as those who have recently had surgery.

Antibiotic resistance arises by genetic mutation in bacteria and would normally account for a very small proportion of the bacterial population. But increased exposure to the antibiotic dramatically increases the number of resistant organisms, as it effectively kills off the competition. The spread of antibiotic resistance can be traced to the beginning of the large scale commercial production and distribution of antibiotics. It is estimated that over the last 50 years, millions of tonnes of antibiotic compounds have been released into the biosphere. Perhaps surprisingly, less than half of these antibiotics produced are used for treatment of disease in humans. Other uses include:

• therapeutic use in aquaculture and household pets
• growth promotion and prophylactic use in animal livestock
• pest control in agriculture
• sanitizers in toiletries and household cleaning products
• sterilization and culture selection in research and industry.

The use of antibiotics in animal feeds is worth particular note. The drugs are given to lower the incidence of disease in the stock as a precautionary measure, in other words administered to healthy animals. The antibiotics pass through animal waste into the soil and water and so enter the human food chain, where they increase exposure of bacteria to the antibiotic.

Another source of antibiotics in the environment is through improper drug disposal. Expired, unused antibiotics are frequently discarded by households and by the medical profession, and this can result in contamination of surface, ground, and drinking water supplies. Studies have also shown that in some countries, effluent from pharmaceutical production plants can be contaminated with antibiotics.

There are no simple solutions to the problem of antibiotic-resistant bacteria. Strict measures of infection control and antibiotic use are a global priority. These must be backed up by efforts to minimize release of antibiotics into the environment, including the destruction of their activity before disposal. Individuals can contribute to the solution by avoiding overuse, and complying with instructions to complete a prescribed dose.

## Obtaining the Tamiflu precursor: a Green Chemistry case study

Oseltamivir (Tamiflu), described on page 897, is an antiviral that may lessen the spread of the flu virus within the body by preventing the release of new viral particles from their host cells. The drug has attracted particular attention as it is the only orally administered antiviral that may be effective in cases of H5N1 (avian flu) infection.

The key precursor for the synthesis of Tamiflu is **shikimic acid**, or its salt shikimate, with the following structure:

This compound is found in low concentrations in many plants, but the Chinese star anise, *Illicium verum*, which grows in Vietnam and South-West China, has been a favoured source. Shikimate is found in the star-shaped fruit of the tree, and can be extracted in a lengthy chemical process. But the low yields from this process are blamed for the worldwide shortage of Tamiflu in 2005, and again during the flu pandemic of 2009 when many governments stock-piled the drug.

There are therefore active efforts worldwide to prospect for alternate sources of the shikimate precursor. Some of the promising developments in this field, which are all applications of Green Chemistry, include the following.

- The production of shikimate from fermentation reactions of genetically engineered bacteria. This process has been developed by the pharmaceutical company Roche.
- The harvesting of shikimate from the needles of several varieties of pine trees. Even though yields are quite low, the needles represent a plentiful resource.
- The extraction of shikimate from suspension cultures of the Indian sweetgum tree. This is an inexpensive natural source and does not involve genetic manipulation.

## Green Chemistry success stories in the pharmaceutical industry

At first glance, the principles of Green Chemistry seem to be rather obvious common sense statements rather than innovative ideas. Maybe this is their very strength. By putting the focus on prevention rather than amelioration and on reduction rather than excess, Green Chemistry principles have challenged the status quo of many chemical processes.

The following are some examples of Green Chemistry success stories in the pharmaceutical industry, which illustrate some of the principles.

• The production of the drug Viagra by Pfizer uses a modified reaction route that produces just a quarter of the waste of the original process. It reduces the amount of solvent and avoids the use of toxic and hazardous reagents.

• The synthesis of the anti-inflammatory drug ibuprofen has been altered from a six-step to a three-step reaction route. This has increased the atom economy of the process from 40% to 77% and reduced the energy demand.

• Synthesis of the analgesic drug Lyrica was modified to use a natural reagent of an enzyme with water as a solvent to reduce the use of non-renewable organic materials. This has eliminated the emissions of more than 3 million tonnes of $CO_2$ compared with the original process.

The challenge to scientists is to consider the environmental footprint of an *entire* chemical process from cradle to grave. The use of safer chemicals and solvents, shorter synthesis pathways and renewable resources in production, and the recycling and treatment of waste are all part of this.

## Exercises

**30** Describe some of the problems caused by left-over solvents in the pharmaceutical industry.

**31** State some of the sources of low-level radioactive waste arising from nuclear medicine, and explain how this must be treated.

**32** 'The very success of antibiotics in fighting disease has led to the widespread emergence of resistant strains, which today threatens their very usefulness'. Discuss this statement.

**33** What is meant by 'patient compliance' in the context of antibiotic prescriptions?

**34** Outline the general processes that should be followed to promote Green Chemistry in the manufacture of drugs.

## Practice questions

**1** Antibiotics treat infections by stopping the growth of bacteria or destroying them.

    **(a)** Identify the side-chain by drawing a circle around the side-chain in the structure of benzylpenicillin given below. (The structure of penicillin is given in section 37 of the IB data booklet.)   (1)

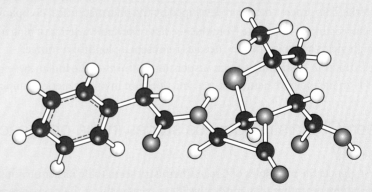

    **(b)** Discuss **two** problems associated with the over-prescription of penicillin and explain how these are overcome.   (3)

        *(Total 4 marks)*

**2** Chiral auxiliaries are used in drug design. Describe how a chiral auxiliary works.   (2)

**3** Two substances commonly used in antacid tablets are magnesium hydroxide and aluminium hydroxide.

**(a)** State an equation to represent a neutralization reaction with one of the above antacids. (1)

**(b)** State and explain whether 0.1 mol of magnesium hydroxide is more effective or less effective than 0.1 mol of aluminium hydroxide. (1)

*(Total 2 marks)*

**4** **(a)** State **two** differences in structure between viruses and bacteria. (2)

**(b)** Describe **two** ways in which antiviral drugs work. (2)

**(c)** Discuss **two** difficulties associated with the development of drugs for the effective treatment of AIDS. (2)

*(Total 6 marks)*

**5** Morphine is a strong analgesic which is administered parenterally.

**(a)** Explain why morphine is normally injected intravenously. (1)

**(b)** Diamorphine (heroin) is a more effective painkiller than morphine. The structures of morphine and diamorphine are shown in section 37 of the IB data booklet. Explain at the molecular level why diamorphine is absorbed into fatty tissue more rapidly than morphine. (2)

*(Total 3 marks)*

**6** During drug development, trials are conducted to determine the therapeutic window. Explain the meaning of the term 'therapeutic window' and discuss its importance in drug administration. (4)

**7** Examples of strong analgesics are morphine, codeine, and diamorphine (heroin). Their structures are shown in section 37 of the IB data booklet.

**(a)** Identify **two** functional groups present in all three of these analgesics. (2)

**(b)** Identify **one** functional group present in morphine, but not in diamorphine. (1)

**(c)** State the name of the type of chemical reaction which is used to convert morphine into diamorphine. (1)

*(Total 4 marks)*

**8** The first penicillin to be used was benzylpenicillin (Penicillin G), and its structure is shown below.

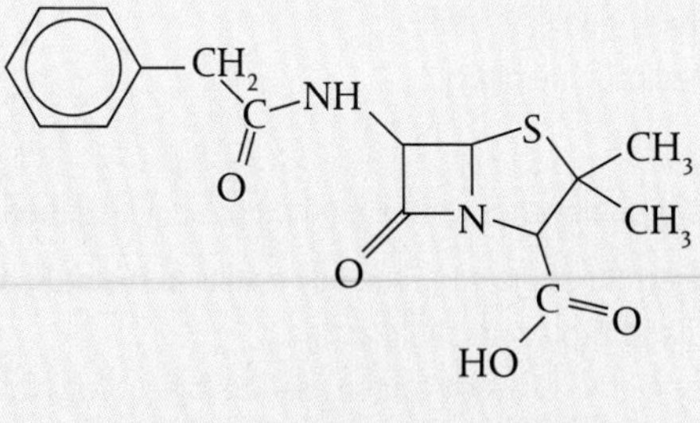

**(a)** Explain how penicillins are able to act as antibacterials. (2)

**(b)** Modern penicillins have a similar structure to Penicillin G but a different side-chain. State **two** advantages of modifying the side-chain. (2)

**(c)** The active part of penicillins is the beta-lactam ring. Determine the functional group present in the beta-lactam ring and explain why the ring is important in the functioning of penicillin as an antibacterial. (3)

*(Total 7 marks)*

**9** Paroxetine, whose structure is shown below, is a drug prescribed to people suffering from mental depression.

**(a)** Identify the **two** chiral carbon atoms in the structure above with an asterisk (*).        (2)

**(b)** Explain, with an example, the importance of chirality in drug action.        (2)

**(c)** Describe the use of chiral auxiliaries to synthesize the desired enantiomer of a drug.        (2)

**(d)** Paroxetine is usually prescribed in the form of its hydrochloride salt.

    **(i)**   Explain why it is used in this form.        (2)

    **(ii)**  State the structural feature of a molecule of paroxetine that enables it to form a salt. (1)

*(Total 9 marks)*

**10** Drugs can be prescribed for treating various diseases and assisting in healing the human body; however, any drug presents potential risks. The properties of three drugs are summarized below.

| Drug | Physiological effect | Side-effects | Therapeutic window |
|------|----------------------|--------------|--------------------|
| **A** | high | severe | medium |
| **B** | moderate | moderate | narrow |
| **C** | low | minimal | wide |

Suggest which drug (**A**, **B**, or **C**) could be

**(a)** considered safe enough to be taken by patients without supervision.        (1)

**(b)** administered **only** by qualified staff.        (1)

**(c)** used **only** in a medical emergency.        (1)

*(Total 3 marks)*

**11** The effectiveness of a drug depends on the method of administration.

**(a)** One method of injecting drugs into the body results in the drug having a very rapid effect. State the method and explain its rapid action.        (2)

**(b)** List the **two** other methods which can be used to inject drugs into the body.        (1)

**(c)** Identify the method of administration used to treat respiratory diseases such as asthma.        (1)

*(Total 4 marks)*

**12** Ethanol, a depressant, is sufficiently volatile to pass into the lungs from the bloodstream. The roadside breathalyser test uses acidified potassium dichromate(VI) which reacts with any ethanol present in the breath and converts it to ethanoic acid.

**(a) (i)**  State the oxidation and reduction half-equations that occur in the breathalyser when ethanol is present in the breath.        (2)

    **(ii)**  Describe the colour change that occurs to the acidified dichromate(VI) if ethanol is present in the breath.        (1)

**(b)** Police use the intoximeter, an infrared spectrophotometer, to confirm a roadside breathalyser test. Explain how the amount of ethanol is determined from the infrared spectrum. (2)

*(Total 5 marks)*

**13** Iodine-123 is better than iodine-131 for diagnostic work in assessing thyroid function. It has a half-life of 13.3 hours and decays by electron capture. Iodine-131 has a half-life of 8 days and decays by beta emission.

**(a)** With reference to its half-life, suggest why the use of iodine-123 may be favoured. (1)

**(b)** Write the equation for the decay of iodine-131. (1)

*(Total 2 marks)*

**14** A mixture of two miscible liquids, A and B, may be separated by fractional distillation.

**(a)** Sketch the general form of the boiling point/composition diagram for the mixture. (3)

**(b)** State and explain the change in the boiling point of the mixture at increasing height in the fractionating column. (3)

*(Total 6 marks)*

**15** Outline a current Green Chemistry approach for isolating Taxol®. Explain why this approach is less harmful to the environment than traditional approaches. (2)

 To access weblinks on the topics covered in this chapter, please go to www.pearsonhotlinks.com and enter the ISBN or title of this book.

# Green chemistry

The twelve principles of green chemistry:

## 1 Prevention

It is better to prevent waste than to treat or clean up waste after it has been created.

## 2 Atom economy

Synthetic methods should be designed to maximize the incorporation of all materials used in the process into the final product.

## 3 Less hazardous chemical synthesis

Whenever practicable, synthetic methods should be designed to use and generate substances that possess little or no toxicity to people or the environment.

## 4 Designing safer chemicals

Chemical products should be designed to effect their desired function while minimizing their toxicity.

## 5 Safer solvents and auxiliaries

The use of auxiliary substances (e.g. solvents or separation agents) should be made unnecessary whenever possible and innocuous when used.

## 6 Design for energy efficiency

Energy requirements of chemical processes should be recognized for their environmental and economic impacts and should be minimized. If possible, synthetic methods should be conducted at ambient temperature and pressure.

## 7 Use of renewable feedstocks

A raw material or feedstock should be renewable rather than depleting whenever technically and economically practicable.

## 8 Reduce derivatives

Unnecessary derivatization (use of blocking groups, protection/de-protection, and temporary modification of physical/chemical processes) should be minimized or avoided if possible, because such steps require additional reagents and can generate waste.

## 9 Catalysis

Catalytic reagents (as selective as possible) are superior to stoichiometric reagents.

## 10 Design for degradation

Chemical products should be designed so that at the end of their function they break down into innocuous degradation products and do not persist in the environment.

## 11 Real-time analysis for pollution prevention

Analytical methods need to be further developed to allow for real-time, in-process monitoring and control prior to the formation of hazardous substances.

## 12 Inherently safer chemistry for accident prevention

Substances and the form of a substance used in a chemical process should be chosen to minimize the potential for chemical accidents, including releases, explosions, and fires.

## Experimental work is an integral part of chemistry

Chemistry is an experimental science. During your IB chemistry course your learning will involve a significant amount of laboratory work. This will help you to understand some of the concepts, teach you important skills, and give you opportunities to extend your knowledge through investigations. And it is often the best part about studying chemistry!

Laboratory work usually involves 'hands-on' experimental work, which leads to the collection of **primary data**. These are data obtained directly, such as by measuring changes in a variable during an experiment or by collecting information through surveys or observations. **Secondary data** refers to data obtained from another source, such as via reference material or third-party results. The source of secondary data must always be cited in a report. Analysis of secondary data can also form an important part of experimental work.

Much of your laboratory work is likely to involve communication technology, through the use of data-logging devices and software such as spreadsheets, databases, and graph-plotting programs. The use of simulations and the development and analysis of models are also important skills.

### NATURE OF SCIENCE

Advances and progress in chemistry are based on the scientific method. This consists of systematic observation, measurement, and experiment and the formulation, testing, and modification of hypotheses. Central to this process is the gathering of empirical and measurable evidence based on sound, reproducible experimental work.

## Health, safety, and the environment

Considerations of health and safety are a crucial aspect of experimental work. The best sources of information for carrying out risk assessments are **MSDS, material safety datasheets**, which should be available whenever you are handling chemicals. The Laboratory Safety Institute (LSI) has developed useful guidelines on laboratory practice, which are summarized in the IB chemistry guide. It is also important that you consider the environmental effects of your work in the laboratory and learn safe procedures for the storage, use, and disposal of chemicals. Micro-scale chemistry and Green Chemistry both present opportunities to limit the waste and environmental impact of your work.

International hazard symbols used in laboratories ensure that safety information is conveyed irrespective of the working language.

*continued*

*continued ....*

From top left to bottom right, the symbols represent:

- dangerous to the environment
- toxic
- gas under pressure
- corrosive
- explosive
- flammable
- caution – used for less serious health hazards like skin irritation
- oxidizing
- biohazard.

# Practical skills

The choice of apparatus for carrying out reactions and for accurate measurement involves considerations of safety, efficiency, precision, and availability. The list below summarizes some of the most important skills for practical chemistry; it is hoped you will become familiar with these either through direct experimentation, through demonstration, or through simulation/virtual experimentation.

- choice of glassware for different tasks/measurements
- collection of gases by displacement of water
- accurate measurement of mass using a balance, including heating to constant mass
- precipitation and gravimetric analysis
- use of filtration apparatus, possibly including suction
- use of pipette with filler, and burette
- titration techniques including acid–base and redox
- preparation of standardized solutions and serial dilutions
- safe choice and practices for heating chemicals
- calorimetry
- use of pH meter and indicators
- use of probes for data-logging
- construction of voltaic and electrolytic cells
- use of colorimeter/spectrophotometer
- use of molecular models
- use of separating funnel and decantation
- simple distillation and reflux techniques
- recrystallization and melting point determination
- use of a centrifuge
- paper chromatography and TLC plates with $R_f$ calculations
- preparation and use of standard curves for calibration and determination of concentration.

**TOK** It is now possible to observe and carry out many virtual experiments electronically. Are there ways of knowing that cannot be used in this medium? Do you think the quality of the learning that takes place is different in a virtual versus a real environment?

## Assessment of experimental work

In addition to supporting your learning throughout the course, experimental work also forms part of the assessment of the IB programme. In Section A of Paper 3, questions will test your understanding of laboratory procedures and applications. The table below shows the experiments that are specified as part of the course, so be sure that you are familiar with these.

| Sub-topic | | Page number | Experiment |
|---|---|---|---|
| 1.2 | The mole concept | 22 | The obtaining and use of experimental data for deriving empirical formulas from reactions involving mass changes |
| 1.3 | Reacting masses and volumes | 49 | Use of the experimental method of titration to calculate the concentration of a solution by reference to a standard solution |
| 1.3 | Reacting masses and volumes | 43 | Obtaining and use of experimental values to calculate the molar mass of a gas from the ideal gas equation |
| 5.1 | Measuring energy changes | 219 | A calorimetry experiment for an enthalpy of reaction should be covered and the results evaluated |
| 8.2 | Properties of acids and bases | 354 | Students should have experience of acid–base titrations with different indicators |
| 8.3 | The pH scale | 358 | Students should be familiar with the use of a pH meter and universal indicator |
| 9.2 | Electrochemical cells | 426 | Performance of laboratory experiments involving a typical voltaic cell using two metal/metal ion half-cells |
| 10.1 | Fundamentals of organic chemistry | 473 | Construction of 3D models (real or virtual) of organic molecules |
| 15.1 | Energy cycles | 246 | Performance of lab experiments which could include single replacement reactions in aqueous solutions |
| 19.1 | Electrochemical cells | 416 | |

Experimental work is also the focus of the Internal Assessment component, discussed in the next chapter.

# Internal assessment

## The investigation

During your two-year IB Chemistry course, you are expected to carry out an individual scientific investigation, sometimes known as an **exploration**. This must be written up as a full report, and contributes to your final assessment on the course.

The investigation will be based on a topic of your own interest, and have a purposeful research question and scientific rationale. Your approach and methodology may rely on the collection of primary data through experimental work, or it may involve analysis of secondary data. Possibilities include the use of spreadsheets for analysis and modelling, extraction and analysis of data from a database, or the use of open-ended simulations. The investigation may also use a mix of approaches and data sources. In all cases, the investigation is marked according to the same five criteria, which are summarized below. Note the following general points:

- The written investigation is marked by your teacher (internally).
- The reports of a sample of students from your class will be re-marked by the IB, a process known as moderation, which ensures that the same standards are applied across all candidates.
- The mark awarded for your investigation contributes 20% towards your final IB result.
- The investigation is expected to take approximately 10 hours to complete.
- The investigation should be about 6 to 12 pages in length in regular font size.
- The investigation can be based on a topic within the course content, or it can be on extension material beyond the topic specifications in the IB Chemistry guide.

The investigation should provide clear evidence of the knowledge and skills that you have acquired with respect to the Nature of Science, and an awareness of the aims of the course. You also have the opportunity here to demonstrate the attributes of the IB learner profile.

## The assessment criteria

The investigation will be marked using a best-fit approach to match the level of work with the descriptors given as mark bands. Each criterion is marked separately, and makes a specific contribution to the final mark out of 24 (later scaled to 20% of the overall IB assessment), as shown below.

|  | Personal engagement | Exploration | Analysis | Evaluation | Communication |
|---|---|---|---|---|---|
| mark out of 24 | 2 | 6 | 6 | 6 | 4 |
| % of IA mark | 8% | 25% | 25% | 25% | 17% |

The marking descriptors for each criterion are shown below, with some additional notes for guidance. You are strongly recommended to focus only on the descriptor of the highest level in each case, shown in red here – there is no point in aiming for less!

## Personal engagement

| Mark | Descriptor |
| --- | --- |
| 0 | The student's report does not reach a standard described by the descriptors below. |
| 1 | **The evidence of personal engagement with the exploration is limited with little independent thinking, initiative, or creativity.**<br>The justification given for choosing the research question and/or the topic under investigation does not demonstrate **personal significance, interest, or curiosity**.<br>There is little evidence of **personal input and initiative** in the designing, implementation, or presentation of the investigation. |
| 2 | **The evidence of personal engagement with the exploration is clear with significant independent thinking, initiative, or creativity.**<br>The justification given for choosing the research question and/or the topic under investigation demonstrates **personal significance, interest, or curiosity**.<br>There is evidence of **personal input and initiative** in the designing, implementation, or presentation of the investigation. |

Your report should include some background to the choice of your investigation and what inspired you in the planning. Maybe it was something you thought about in class, or during an experiment, or something you read? You will be credited for an investigation that is innovative and somewhat unique, that shows evidence of independent thinking and creativity in any or all stages. Try to demonstrate personal interest and genuine enthusiasm in your report.

## Exploration

| Mark | Descriptor |
| --- | --- |
| 0 | The student's report does not reach a standard described by the descriptors below. |
| 1–2 | The topic of the investigation is identified and a research question of some relevance is **stated but it is not focused**.<br>The background information provided for the investigation is **superficial** or of limited relevance and does not aid the understanding of the context of the investigation.<br>The methodology of the investigation is only appropriate to address the research question to a very limited extent since it takes into consideration few of the significant factors that may influence the relevance, reliability, and sufficiency of the collected data.<br>The report shows evidence of limited awareness of the significant safety, ethical, or environmental issues that are **relevant to the methodology of the investigation\***. |
| 3–4 | The topic of the investigation is identified and a relevant but not fully focused research question is described.<br>The background information provided for the investigation is mainly appropriate and relevant and aids the understanding of the context of the investigation.<br>The methodology of the investigation is mainly appropriate to address the research question but has limitations since it takes into consideration only some of the significant factors that may influence the relevance, reliability, and sufficiency of the collected data.<br>The report shows evidence of some awareness of the significant safety, ethical, or environmental issues that are **relevant to the methodology of the investigation\***. |
| 5–6 | The topic of the investigation is identified and a relevant and fully focused research question is clearly described.<br>The background information provided for the investigation is entirely appropriate and relevant and enhances the understanding of the context of the investigation.<br>The methodology of the investigation is highly appropriate to address the research question because it takes into consideration all, or nearly all, of the significant factors that may influence the relevance, reliability, and sufficiency of the collected data.<br>The report shows evidence of full awareness of the significant safety, ethical, or environmental issues that are **relevant to the methodology of the investigation.\*** |

\* This indicator should only be applied when appropriate to the investigation.

Your report must have a clearly stated and focused research question, and give the scientific context of the work. This means relating it to your knowledge of the topic studied. The methodology used must show how relevant data are collected, taking into account factors that influence reliability of results. Consider control variables, choice of apparatus, and how many data will be sufficient for useful analysis. Note that five data points are usually considered necessary to establish a trend line. Where appropriate, make sure you have demonstrated awareness of related health, safety, and environmental issues. References to sources must, of course, be properly quoted.

## Analysis

| Mark | Descriptor |
|------|------------|
| 0 | The student's report does not reach a standard described by the descriptors below. |
| 1–2 | The report includes **insufficient relevant** raw data to support a valid conclusion to the research question. Some **basic** data processing is carried out but is either too **inaccurate or too insufficient to lead to a valid** conclusion. The report shows evidence of little consideration of the impact of measurement uncertainty on the analysis. The processed data are incorrectly or insufficiently interpreted so that the conclusion is invalid or very incomplete. |
| 3–4 | The report includes relevant but incomplete quantitative and qualitative raw data that could support a simple or partially valid conclusion to the research question. Appropriate and sufficient data processing is carried out that could lead to a broadly valid conclusion but there are significant inaccuracies and inconsistencies in the processing. The report shows evidence of some consideration of the impact of measurement uncertainty on the analysis. The processed data are interpreted so that a broadly valid but incomplete or limited conclusion to the research question can be deduced. |
| 5–6 | The report includes sufficient relevant quantitative and qualitative raw data that could support a detailed and valid conclusion to the research question. Appropriate and sufficient data processing is carried out with **the accuracy** required to enable a conclusion to the research question to be drawn that is fully **consistent** with the experimental data. The report shows evidence of full and appropriate consideration of the impact of measurement uncertainty on the analysis. The processed data are correctly interpreted so that a completely valid and detailed conclusion to the research question can be deduced. |

In this part of the report you must record data, both qualitative and quantitative, and demonstrate how the data are processed. This includes showing accuracy in calculations, the correct use of units, and consideration of the impact of error propagation. Data should be tabulated where possible. Graphs must be clearly titled, have appropriate scales and labelled axes with units, and show accurately plotted data points. Suitable best-fit lines or curves need to be marked distinctly. Your processed data need to be interpreted carefully in the context of the research question to develop a valid conclusion.

## Evaluation

| Mark | Descriptor |
|------|------------|
| 0 | The student's report does not reach a standard described by the descriptors below. |
| 1–2 | A conclusion is **outlined** which is not relevant to the research question or is not supported by the data presented. The conclusion makes superficial comparison to the accepted scientific context.<br>Strengths and weaknesses of the investigation, such as limitations of the data and sources of error, are **outlined** but are restricted to an **account of the practical or procedural issues** faced.<br>The student has **outlined** very few realistic and relevant suggestions for the improvement and extension of the investigation. |
| 3–4 | A conclusion is **described** which is relevant to the research question and supported by the data presented.<br>A conclusion is described which makes some relevant comparison to the accepted scientific context.<br>Strengths and weaknesses of the investigation, such as limitations of the data and sources of error, are **described** and provide evidence of some awareness of the **methodological issues\*** involved in establishing the conclusion.<br>The student has **described** some realistic and relevant suggestions for the improvement and extension of the investigation. |
| 5–6 | A detailed conclusion is **described and justified** which is entirely relevant to the research question and fully supported by the data presented.<br>A conclusion is correctly **described and justified** through relevant comparison to the accepted scientific context.<br>Strengths and weaknesses of the investigation, such as limitations of the data and sources of error, are **discussed** and provide evidence of a clear understanding of the **methodological issues** involved in establishing the conclusion.<br>The student has **discussed** realistic and relevant suggestions for the improvement and extension of the investigation. |

\* The report shows evidence of full awareness of the significant safety, ethical or environmental issues that are **relevant to the methodology of the investigation**.

You must give a conclusion that is both justified by the results presented, and puts the findings in a broader context. This involves comparison with literature values and accepted data sources. This is a good place to show off your relevant scientific knowledge, and you should aim to include molecular level explanations for your findings where possible. Full consideration of errors is essential, and should lead you to evaluate the methodology chosen and suggest relevant modifications. Make sure the modifications are specific to the weaknesses identified. A table with three columns can help you to keep this part of the report focussed, as shown in the example below:

| Error/design limitation | Impact on results | Suggested modification |
|-------------------------|-------------------|------------------------|
| some of the $CO_2$ collected by displacement of water may have dissolved in the water | volume of $CO_2$ measured is less than the volume released by the reaction | collect gas over warm water to reduce it solubility |

## Communication

| Mark | Descriptor |
|------|------------|
| 0 | The student's report does not reach a standard described by the descriptors below. |
| 1–2 | **The presentation of the investigation is unclear, making it difficult to understand the focus, process, and outcomes.**<br>The report is not well structured and is unclear: the necessary information on focus, process, and outcomes is missing or is presented in an incoherent or disorganized way.<br>The understanding of the focus, process, and outcomes of the investigation is obscured by the presence of inappropriate or irrelevant information.<br>There are many errors in the use of subject-specific terminology and conventions\*. |

| Mark | Descriptor |
|------|------------|
| 3–4 | **The presentation of the investigation is clear. Any errors do not hamper understanding of the focus, process, and outcomes.** <br><br> The report is well structured and clear: the necessary information on focus, process, and outcomes is present and presented in a coherent way. <br><br> The report is relevant and concise thereby facilitating a ready understanding of the focus, process, and outcomes of the investigation. <br><br> The use of subject-specific terminology and conventions is appropriate and correct. Any errors do not hamper understanding. |

\* For example, incorrect/missing labelling of graphs, tables, images; use of units, decimal places.

A good scientific report communicates in clear and concise language with no superfluous comments. There is no fixed narrative style or outline of sub-headings expected, but your report should follow a logical sequence and make correct use of the subject-specific terms. Scientific journal articles provide a good source of ideas for how to structure your report. This criterion will be judged holistically on the overall report.

# Making the most of your Internal Assessment opportunity

## 1 Start early

Your school will give guidance on when you are expected to work on your investigation and will probably issue internal deadlines. But you can start thinking about possible topics from the beginning of the course, and research ideas and approaches. Keep a record of your resources and outlines, and allow your ideas to develop as your knowledge grows in the course.

## 2 Be aware of the criteria

As you choose your research question and design your investigation, keep a close eye on the assessment criteria as given here. Remember the marks you are given are determined by how well your work matches these specific descriptors, so keep checking.

## 3 Seek and follow feedback

Your teacher may give you some guidance on your early ideas and suggest modifications. Don't be afraid to ask for help as you develop your plan, as this may well make your work more efficient and will not affect your assessment.

## 4 Be enthusiastic!

This is your chance to put the Nature of Science into action. You are in charge of your choice of topic, and have the flexibility here to be creative, so enjoy it fully.

# Theory of knowledge

## Introduction

In TOK you are encouraged to think critically about the process of knowing. Which ways of knowing do you use to justify your chemical knowledge? Does chemistry give you a 'true' picture of reality? How does the knowledge you gain in your chemistry class differ from that gained in other subjects? What are the ethical implications of technological developments in the subject? Chemistry has been hugely successful in giving us explanations of the material world and has also made a significant contribution to improving our quality of life, but does it offer certainty?

## Ways of knowing: perception

What does the figure on the right represent?

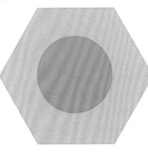

To many people this is simply a circle and a hexagon, but to an IB chemistry student it should have more significance. It can be interpreted as a benzene ring for example. How you choose to interpret the picture will depend on the context in which it is presented and your prior knowledge. This illustrates an important point: perception is an active process, which includes an element of personal interpretation.

## Chemistry and technology

Chemistry deals with **empirical knowledge**. This is knowledge acquired by the senses, enhanced, if necessary, by technology. We are now able to see things which are beyond the direct limits of our senses. Look at the photograph below. Is this what a metal surface really looks like?

## The scientific method

Should the natural sciences be regarded more as a method or more as a system of knowledge?

Richard Feynman (1918–1988), one of the great physicists of the 20th century, gave the following description of the scientific method:

> " In general we look for a new law by the following process. First we guess it. Then we compute the consequences of the guesses to see what would be implied if the law was right. If it disagrees with experiment, it is wrong. In that simple statement is the key to science … It does not make any difference how smart you are, or what is your name – if it disagrees with experiment it is wrong … It is true that one has to check a little to check that one is wrong. "

During your IB chemistry course, you are continually challenged to think about the Nature of Science. To what extent is Feynman's view of the scientific method still a valid description today? Does a single method adequately describe scientific studies in all disciplines from astronomy to geology? Could you

◀ This picture is obtained by firing a beam of polarized $^3$He atoms towards a metal surface. The metal can be seen as a lattice of positive metal ions (blue) in a sea of electrons (red).

use your experience in the chemistry laboratory or on the group 4 project to write your own definition of the scientific method?

## Ways of knowing: induction (reason)

How do individual observations lead to theories and scientific laws of nature? Imagine an experiment in which you test the pH of some aqueous solutions of different oxides.

| Oxide | Acid/alkali |
|---|---|
| $Na_2O(s)$ | alkali |
| $MgO(s)$ | alkali |
| $CO_2(g)$ | acid |
| $SO_2(g)$ | acid |
| $CaO(s)$ | alkali |
| $N_2O_5(g)$ | acid |

Two possible explanations which fit the pattern are:

- All solid oxides are alkalis. All gaseous oxides are acidic.
- All metal oxides are alkalis. All non-metal oxides are acidic.

We have used **induction** to draw the two general conclusions. Inductive logic allows us to move from specific instances to a general conclusion. Although it appeals to common sense, it is logically flawed. Both conclusions are equally valid, based on the evidence, but both conclusions could be wrong. Just because something has happened many times in the past does not prove that it will happen in the future. This is the **problem of induction**. The philosopher Bertrand Russell illustrated the danger of generalization by considering the case of the philosophical turkey. The bird reasoned that since he had been fed by the farmer every morning, he always would be. Sadly, this turkey discovered the problem with induction on Thanksgiving Day! Are you acting in the same way as the turkey when you draw conclusions in your experimental work?

How do we justify the use of induction? Consider the following form of reasoning.

- On Monday I used induction and it worked.
- On Tuesday I used induction and it worked.
- On Wednesday I used induction and it worked.
- On Thursday I used induction and it worked.
- On Friday I used induction and it worked.
- Therefore I know that induction works.

## What form of reasoning is used here to justify induction?

Karl Popper (1902–1994) realized that scientific verification doesn't actually prove anything and decided that science finds theories, not by verifying statements, but by **falsifying** them. Popper believed that even when a scientific theory had been successfully and repeatedly tested, it was not necessarily true. Instead, it had simply not yet been proved false. Observing a million white swans does not prove that all swans are white, but the first time we see a black swan, we can firmly disprove the theory.

No matter how many times we record in our notebooks the observation of a white swan, we get no closer to proving the universal statement that all swans are white. Black swans inhabit lakes, rivers, and coastal areas in Australia.

## Ways of knowing: deduction (reason)

Deductive logic allows us to move from general statements to specific examples.

The conclusion of deductive logic must be true if the general statements on which it is based are correct. Deductive reasoning is the foundation of mathematics. We can use this reasoning to test our scientific hypotheses. Consider again the pH of the oxides tabulated earlier. The two competing hypotheses could be distinguished by considering the pH of a non-metal oxide such as phosphorus oxide, which is a solid at room temperature. If we use the two hypotheses as starting points (**premises**), they lead to two different conclusions using deductive reasoning.

• All solid oxides are alkalis.
• Phosphorus oxide is solid.

Therefore: phosphorus oxide is an alkali.

OR

• All non-metal oxides are acidic.
• Phosphorus oxide is a non-metal oxide.

Therefore: phosphorus oxide is an acid.

When the pH of phosphorus oxide solution is tested and shown to be an acid we can be certain that the first hypothesis is false, but we cannot be sure that the second is definitely true.

If it survives repeated tests, it may, however, become accepted as scientific truth, but this is not certain. No matter how many tests a hypothesis survives, we will never prove that it is true in the same way as mathematical proof is true. All scientific knowledge is provisional.

There are still problems, however, with this view of science. When your results don't match up with the expected values in a chemistry investigation, do you abandon the accepted theories or do you explain the differences as being due to experimental error, faulty instruments, or contaminated chemicals?

How have scientists and philosophers made use of Karl Popper's ideas? Are we any closer to proving scientific principles are 'true'?

When are you justified in dismissing a data point which does not fit the general pattern?

## Same data, different hypothesis

It is always possible to think of other hypotheses that are consistent with the given set of data. The hypothesis: 'Oxides with one oxygen in the formula are alkalis, oxides with more than one oxygen are acids' also fits the data presented. For the same reason, an infinite number of patterns can be found to fit the same experimental data.

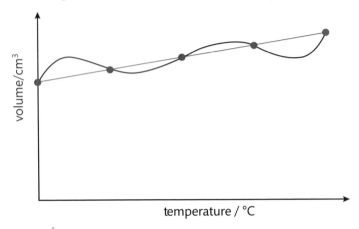

The curve and straight line in the graph both fit the experimental data.

You may argue that the straight line in the graph above is more suitable as it is simpler, but on what grounds do we base the assumption that simplicity is a criterion for truth? The idea that the simplest explanations are the best is inspired by the principle – named after the medieval philosopher William of Occam – known as Occam's razor.

## Rejecting anomalous results: confirmation bias

We often dismiss results which don't fit the expected pattern because of experimental error. In the example below, is it reasonable to reject the point not on the line?

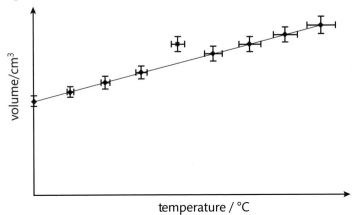

# Are the models and theories that scientists use merely pragmatic instruments or do they actually describe the natural world?

Scientists use models to clarify certain features and relationships. They can become more and more sophisticated but they can never become the real thing. Models are just a representation of reality. The methane molecule, for example, can be represented in a number of forms. All these models of methane are based on the Bohr model of the atom discussed in Chapter 2. Although this is one of the most successful scientific models, it is not complete as it fails to explain the electron arrangement of atoms after calcium in the Periodic Table. To explain the chemistry of all the elements, a more sophisticated model that involves considering an electron as a wave is needed.

need imagination to form a mental representation of something when it is beyond sense experience. Imagination is also associated with creativity, problem-solving, and originality; all key skills of the scientists.

The wave–particle duality of the electron illustrates a general knowledge issue. Two sources of knowledge can often give conflicting results and it is for us to see if the conflict is real or a limitation of our ways of knowing.

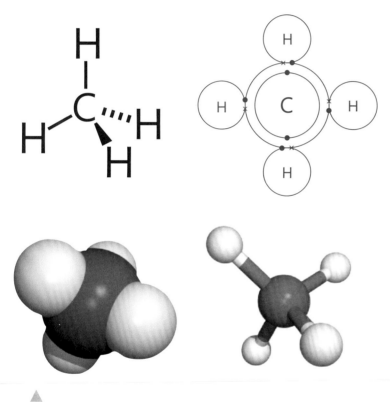

▲ Different models of the methane molecule

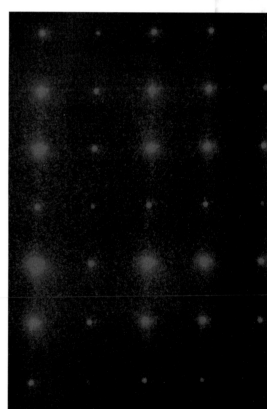

▲ This is a diffraction grating pattern formed by laser light (red), which has passed through an array of crossed gratings. Light is generally considered as a wave.

The evidence for the wave nature of electrons comes from the diffraction pattern observed when a beam of electrons is passed through a metal structure, which is similar to that observed when light is passed through a diffraction grating (see right). We now recognize that the 'true' nature of the electron, or indeed anything, cannot be completely described by a single model. Both the wave model and the particle model are needed. This should not surprise us as models are often based on our everyday experience which does not apply to the small scale of the atom. To understand nature at this level, scientists must go beyond their experience and use their imagination. Scientists

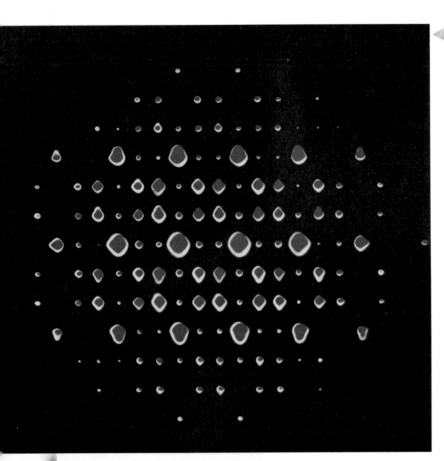

This is an electron diffraction pattern of a binary alloy of 90% titanium and 10% nickel. The pattern can be explained by considering an electron as a wave.

J. J. Thomson won the 1906 Nobel Prize in Physics for measuring the mass of an electron, that is for showing it to be a 'particle'. His son G. P. Thomson won the 1937 Nobel Prize in Physics for showing the electron to be a 'wave'. This is not necessarily a contradiction. It is a question of particles sometimes behaving as waves. Our everyday classification of phenomena into wave' and 'particle' breaks down at the subatomic scale. This limitation of our experience should not, however, shackle our understanding of the sub-atomic world.

# Science and pseudoscience: alchemy and homeopathy

If you have ever dropped sugar into a glass of a carbonated water you will have noticed that it fizzes. Can you offer an explanation for this?

If someone suggested that it was because there was an 'evil demon' present in the drink who was responding angrily to being assaulted by sugar granules you would probably reject this as a non-scientific explanation, but what makes this non-scientific? A scientific theory must be testable. It is difficult to imagine an experiment which could be designed to prove the 'evil demon' theory *false*. A theory that can be used to explain everything explains nothing.

It is worth reflecting, however, that many of the experimental techniques of chemistry have their origins in the pseudoscience of alchemy.

The alchemist's hunt for the Philosopher's Stone, which was believed to give eternal life and could turn base metals into gold, seems very naïve to us now, but how do you think our chemical knowledge will be viewed 500 years on?

Add sugar to any of these drinks and awake an evil demon! ▶

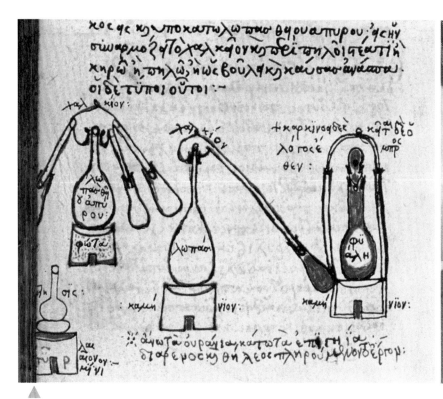

A page from a treatise on alchemy written by Zosimus of Panapolitus (4th century). Some of the equipment drawn is found in a modern chemistry laboratory.

In 1661, with the publication of *The Sceptical Chemist*, Robert Boyle established chemistry as a separate science. He is famous for *Boyle's law*, which states the relationship between pressure and volume for a fixed mass of gas.

There are a number of activities that are claimed by those who practise them to be scientific, such as astrology, homeopathy, and crystology. The label 'science' can add authority to the claims, but how do we distinguish a genuine science from a fake or **pseudoscience**?

Ernest Rutherford, the father of nuclear physics, described himself as an alchemist as he was able to change one element into another by nuclear reactions.

## A web and hierarchy of disciplines

The IB Diploma programme refers to group 4 as 'Sciences', while the Theory of Knowledge programme refers to two separate areas of knowledge, the human sciences and the natural sciences, which broadly represent groups 3 and 4 respectively. What is the distinction between these two areas of knowledge? Can you think of subjects that might be classified in either group? The IB course 'computer science' has at different times been classified as a group 3 subject (individuals and societies), a group 5 subject (mathematics) but now is part of group 4. What arguments can be made for placing it in these different categories?

Is it possible to place the different scientific disciplines in a hierarchy and which criteria would you use for your choice? Chemical theories can help our understanding of biology: for example, hydrogen bonding explains the double helix structure of DNA. But much of chemistry relies on physics: for example, hydrogen bonding is explained in terms of electrostatic attraction.

Is this direction of explanation ever reversed? The view that one subject can be explained in terms of the components of another is called **reductionism**. Is physics in some way 'better' than the other sciences? Where would you place mathematics, which has been described as both the queen and servant of the sciences in this hierarchy? Our knowledge of the Periodic Table and atomic structure suggests that there are limits to the number of elements in nature. Is chemistry in some way the most complete science? Which of the natural sciences is most clearly based on direct observation?

Homeopathy is an alternative therapy that aims to treat diseases by giving extremely dilute doses of compounds that cause the same symptoms as the disease. The more dilute the dosage, the more powerful the remedy. Some of the most powerful doses are so dilute that it is likely they do not contain a single molecule of the active substance. Practitioners attribute this to the 'memory' of the water in which they have been diluted. Conventional science has subjected these claims to intense scrutiny, but firm evidence of anything other than the placebo effect has not yet been found.

## How does chemical knowledge change with time?

We have seen that the inductive and falsification theories of science give an incomplete description of how science progresses. An alternative view was offered by Thomas Kuhn (1922–1996). Kuhn suggested that science does not develop by the orderly accumulation of facts and theories, but by dramatic revolutions which he called **paradigm shifts**. In this context, a paradigm can be thought of as a model or world view accepted by the scientific community. Kuhn distinguished between periods of **normal science** in which new discoveries are placed within the current paradigm and **extraordinary science** which produces results which do not fit the current paradigm. Isaac Newton, John Dalton, Charles Darwin, and Albert Einstein are all revolutionary scientists who changed the way we look at the world by proposing new paradigms.

The idea of a paradigm shift can be illustrated by considering the picture below.

As Kuhn says 'What were ducks in the scientists' world before the revolution, are rabbits afterwards ...'

Atomic theory is one of the most important paradigms of chemistry. Dalton's model of the atom as being indivisible collapsed with the discovery of the proton, neutron, and electron.

▲
In one paradigm, the picture can be interpreted as a duck; in another paradigm, it can be interpreted as a rabbit. Turn the page through 90° and experience a paradigm shift.

## Paradigm shifts: phlogiston theory and the discovery of oxygen

When a solid such as magnesium burns, it crumbles into an ash. It seems quite natural to assume that the metal is giving something off as it burns. It was originally believed that all flammable materials contain phlogiston (a word derived from the Greek for flame), which was absorbed by the air as substances burn. In this theory, substances stop burning when all the phlogiston has been released or when the air is saturated with the phlogiston released. The crisis for the paradigm occurred when careful

According to the phlogiston paradigm, a substance is released into the air when a candle burns. We now know that the carbon and hydrogen in the candle combine with oxygen in the air to form carbon dioxide and water.

measurements showed that a mass increase occurred during combustion. Some explained this result within the phlogiston paradigm by suggesting that phlogiston could have a negative mass but that explanation was rejected in favour of the modern oxygen theory of combustion.

As substances burn more brightly in oxygen, the gas was originally called 'dephlogisticated air' by Joseph Priestley, one of the scientists credited with its discovery. However, the discovery of oxygen made the term 'phlogiston' meaningless.

A widely held stereotype of scientific progress is that of an idealistic young innovator challenging the ideas of the establishment. This is rationalized in Kuhn's model of science because individual scientists are often reluctant to make such leaps. So what is the role of creative thinking in scientific progress? The need to be a risk taker and think out of the box is emphasized by Richard Feynman: 'One of the ways of stopping science would be to only experiment in the region where you know the law'.

Max Planck said 'A new scientific theory does not triumph by convincing its opponents and making them see the light, but rather because its opponents eventually die out and a new generation grows up that is familiar with it'.

## Shared and personal knowledge

The subject of chemistry has a body of highly structured and systematic shared knowledge. It is the work of many individuals and is in a sense anonymous – although there would have been no Hamlet without Shakespeare, atomic theory would have been developed without Dalton. While individuals can and do contribute to this body of knowledge, their work is subject to peer review and their experimental results need to be replicated by others if they are going to be accepted by the scientific community.

We all, however, have difference experiences of chemistry, and this gives us personal knowledge of the subject. This includes procedural knowledge of how to do something such as a titration. Personal knowledge can be formed from a number of ways of knowing such as our memories, our experimental observations, and the significance we associate with different ideas. Like public knowledge, personal knowledge also evolves with time. What you now know about the atom is quite different to what you knew five years ago. Personal knowledge, unlike public knowledge, can be forgotten!

## Ways of knowing: language

The language of alchemy was cryptic and secretive as the knowledge it communicated was thought to be too powerful to share with the general public. The names of many chemicals were derived from their natural origin and were not related to their composition.

The language of modern chemistry, by contrast, is precise, and is an effective tool for thought. When asked to draw the different isomers of $C_7H_{16}$ it is very easy to draw the same structure twice. The IUPAC nomenclature, however, allows you to distinguish the different isomers.

| heptane | 2-methylhexane | 3-methylhexane |
| --- | --- | --- |
| 2,2-dimethylpentane | 2,3-dimethylpentane | 2,4-dimethylpentane |
| 3,3-dimethylpentane | 3-ethylpentane | 2,2,3-trimethylbutane |

The nine isomers of $C_7H_{16}$. The names help you to distinguish the different structures.

The use of oxidation numbers has also allowed us to develop a systematic nomenclature for naming inorganic substances.

Chemistry, of course, also has its own universal language. Balanced equations allow us to use mathematics to solve chemical problems. The ability to attach numbers to substances allows the chemist to use mathematics as a precise tool to investigate the material world. Language should be a tool and not an obstacle to knowledge.

## Measurement: the observer effect

Measurement has allowed the chemist to attach numbers to the properties of materials, but the act of measurement can change the property being measured. Adding a thermometer to a hot beaker of water, for example, will cause the temperature to decrease slightly and adding an acid–base indicator, which is itself a weak acid, will slightly change the pH of the solution.

Generally, such effects can be ignored, as measures are taken to minimize them. Only a few drops of indicator are used, for example, and thermometers are designed to have a low heat capacity. The **observer effect** can cause significant problems at the atomic scale, however, which led the physicist Werner Heisenberg (1901–1976) to comment: 'What we observe is not nature itself but nature exposed to our mode of questioning'. The observer effect is also significant in the human sciences. Can your school director observe a 'normal' chemistry class?

## Knowledge and belief

It should be clear from the previous discussion that science does not offer complete certainty and absolute truth. Do you *know* that sodium chloride is made up from $Na^+$ and $Cl^-$ ions or do you simply *believe* this to be the case? What is needed to change a belief into knowledge?

## Chemistry and ethics

Progress in science and technology affects our lives. Often these effects are positive – drugs and medicines have made our lives safer, and the development of new materials has made our lives more comfortable – but technological developments can also bring suffering and injustice. Industry and technology have had a negative impact on the environment. How do we decide what is the right and wrong use of science? These are ethical questions. There is often disagreement about what is 'right' and ideas of what is considered to be acceptable often change over time. Ethical issues raise difficult questions about risk versus benefits. In many cases, the science is so new that judging long-term benefits and risks is difficult. Developments in chemistry can create new ethical issues. There are also more direct concerns about how scientists should conduct their work. Scientists generally work in communities, not in isolation, and are expected to report their results honestly and openly in an atmosphere of trust. Science is, however, a human endeavour and scientists, like the rest of humanity, can be motivated by envy, vanity, and ambition.

▲
Methyl orange is a weak acid. The addition of the indicator will change the pH of the solution it is measuring.

▲
The dangers of dioxin pollution were discussed in Chapter 12. Dioxin toxicity research has involved tests on rats. Are such tests ethically justified?

Is science, or ought it to be, value-free? Some would argue that it is the aim of science to describe the world as it is and not as it should be. The natural sciences and ethics are different areas of knowledge which use different ways of knowing to answer different questions. It is for society to decide what to do with scientific issues – that is the moral question.

Some people do, however, fear the consequence of scientists 'interfering with nature'. The arguments for and against the use of genetically modified foods, for example, were discussed in Chapter 13. Who decides what is and what is not a legitimate area of scientific research? The scientific community or society at large? The fear of scientific discoveries is, of course, understandable. As discussed in Chapter 15, scientists believed that thalidomide was so safe that it was prescribed to pregnant women to control morning sickness, with tragic consequences. Who is responsible when things go wrong?

## Ways of knowing: imagination

E. J. Corey, whose Nobel prize winning work on organic syntheses is described in Chapter 10, wrote:

> " The synthetic chemist is more than a logician and strategist; he is an explorer strongly influenced to speculate, to imagine and even to create. "

Our imagination can help us to solve problems and develop original ideas. We may use imagination to make connections between separate ideas, to build models or create theories. But to what extent should we trust our imagination, given that is derived in the mind rather than through sense perception? Can imagination reveal truths that reality hides? What other examples of the discoveries of chemists described in this book illustrate the importance of imagination?

## The knowledge framework in chemistry

An area of knowledge can be characterized by a knowledge framework which provides a tool for comparing different areas of knowledge.

| Scope/applications | Concepts/language |
|---|---|
| Chemistry is about understanding the nature of matter and its interactions.  It helps us understand and control the material world and can be used to improve human life.<br><br>Chemistry is a central science which has applications in the biological, material, and environmental sciences. There are ethical considerations that limit its scope of inquiry. Chemicals can damage our environment and be used as weapons. | Chemical knowledge is shared using natural languages in books, journals, and meetings. Chemical equations and mathematics are used to formulate and solve quantitative problems.  Key chemical concepts include mass, charge, bonding and structure, and energy. Everyday metaphors are used to understand the microscopic world; atoms can be thought of as billiard balls and electrons as waves. Units and chemical nomenclature are required to communicate shared knowledge precisely. |

### Methodology

Chemists follow a scientific methodology with an emphasis on experimental work. Results are explained using theories and models and evaluated by peer review. Many ways of knowing are involved in the sciences. Intuition and creativity are needed to produce hypotheses and reason to provide coherent explanations. Knowledge is shared using natural language and problems formulated and solved using chemical symbols and mathematical language. Observations and measurements are made using sense perception, and emotion can provide the personal motivation for a scientist to focus on a particular area of research. The scientific approach assumes that the material world behaves in a coherent way and is rationally comprehensible. Experimental results and well-established theories count as facts and explanations which reduce chemical change and structure to simple, well-understood concepts such as mass, charge, and attractive and repulsive forces. Models can be used to simplify a problem to simple cause and effect relationships. The scope of the subject is limited by the dangerous nature of some substances to the individual and the environment.

## Historical development

Many of the techniques of chemistry originate from alchemy. Lavoisier attached numbers to substances and helped chemistry develop as a physical science. Mendeleyev's Periodic Table systematized a mass of chemical information, and Atomic Theory explained the structure of the Periodic Table and the nature of chemical interactions. It was originally believed that a 'vital force' was needed to explain organic chemistry but we now realize that it fits in with the rest of our chemical understanding.

## Links to personal knowledge

Our shared chemical knowledge has grown from the personal knowledge of individuals such as Boyle, Avogadro, Mendeleyev, Dalton, Bohr, Lewis, Gibbs, Brønsted, Lowry, and Kebulé. Their contributions have made the subject more systematic and coherent. Individual chemists have to take some responsibility for the consequences of their work. They must use their knowledge responsibly and consider the full implications of their work.

## Chemistry and TOK assessment

In your TOK essays, you are expected to make connections between the knowledge issues raised and your own experiences as a learner. It is helpful to support your argument with examples drawn from your IB diploma courses as well as from other sources. In your TOK presentations, you are asked to apply your TOK thinking skills to a contemporary issue. This can be an opportunity, for example, to reflect on the moral and ethical implications of scientific developments. Your chemistry course offers a wide range of experiences for reflection.

## Some examples of prescribed essay titles for you to consider

- What similarities and differences are there between historical and scientific explanations?                     (May 2010)

- A model is a simplified representation of some aspect of the world. In what ways may models help or hinder the search for knowledge?                    (May 2011)
- What is it about theories in the human and natural sciences that makes them convincing?                     (May 2012)
- In what ways may disagreement aid the pursuit of knowledge in the natural and human sciences?                    (May 2013)
- 'Knowledge is nothing more than the systematic organization of facts.' Discuss this statement in relation to two areas of knowledge.                    (May 2014)
- 'That which is accepted as knowledge today is sometimes discarded tomorrow.' Consider knowledge issues raised by this statement in two areas of knowledge.                    (May 2014)

# Advice on the extended essay

The Extended Essay is a compulsory part of the IB Diploma. It is an independent 40-hour research project in an IB subject of your choice. The final essay is up to 4000 words of formally presented, structured writing. The marks awarded for the Extended Essay and TOK are combined to give a maximum of three bonus points.

An Extended Essay in chemistry must have a clear chemical emphasis and not be more closely related to another subject. For example, a chemistry Extended Essay in an area such as biochemistry will be assessed on its chemical and not its biological content. It should include chemical principles and theory.

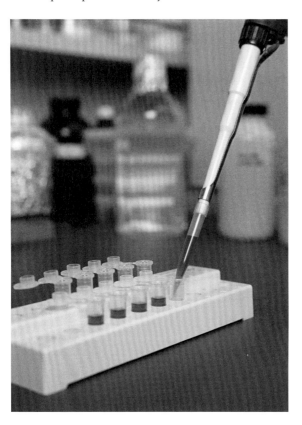

The best chemistry Extended Essays are often based on experiments carried out in a school laboratory.

## Some advice

### Before you start

Read a copy of the subject-specific details of an Extended Essay in chemistry, including the assessment criteria. Read some previous essays and try to identify their strengths and weaknesses. Draw up a list of possible research questions including the techniques you would use to address these questions. Many of the best essays are written by students investigating relatively simple phenomena using apparatus and materials that can be found in most school laboratories.

You may find it useful to consider some of the following techniques when planning your research; it is often appropriate to use a combination of two or more of these approaches:

- titration: acid–base or redox
- chromatography: paper, partition, thin-layer, column
- electrophoresis
- spectrophotometry
- measuring mass or volume changes
- calorimetry
- qualitative and quantitative analysis
- separation and purification techniques in organic chemistry
- use of data-logging probes for some of the above.

Think carefully about which technique(s) you will be using when planning your research. Acid–base and redox titrations, for example, can be used to analyse a range of problems.

## The research question

The research question is the key to a successful Extended Essay. You should choose a topic that interests you as you will be spending 40 hours on this. Your question must be sharply focused. For example, *'What is the ratio of oxygen and chlorine produced at the anode during the electrolysis of different concentrated solutions of aqueous sodium chloride solution?'* is better than *'What happens during the electrolysis of salt?'*

## The research process

- Safety is a priority. Don't do anything in the laboratory without checking with your supervisor.

- Use a range of resources to find out what others have done in the area. Textbooks or the internet should never be the only source of information.
- Keep written records of everything that you do and make a note of all references, including the date when internet sites were accessed so that you can build up your footnotes and bibliography as you go along.
- Record all experimental data, including the dates when the experiments were performed and any uncertainties in your measurements. In your preliminary investigations, write down any problems and challenges you encountered and record any modifications. Use your imagination to design new equipment if necessary.

## While writing the essay

Make sure that you address your stated research question and the Extended Essay assessment criteria.

- Include explanations of any theory not covered in the IB subject guide, including the chemistry of any specialized techniques you have used.
- Use the appropriate chemical language and make sure that all chemical equations are balanced.
- Include sufficient details of any experimental procedure to allow others to repeat the work.
- Check any calculations and make sure that all experimental data are presented correctly.
- Discuss the limitations of the experimental method and any systematic errors.
- Consider any questions which are unresolved at the end of your research and suggest new questions and areas for possible further investigation.
- Let your enthusiasm and interest for the topic show and emphasize clearly your own personal contribution.
- Ensure that your word count is close to 4000. You will often find you can cut quite a number of words as you polish your essay at the end.

## After completing the essay

- Check and proofread the final version carefully.
- Use the assessment criteria to grade your essay. Are you satisfied with the grade you award yourself?

## The assessment criteria

All Extended Essays are assessed according to five criteria, labelled A–E. Each criterion has several descriptors corresponding to different achievement levels. By judging which of these levels most closely matches the work in the essay, the appropriate mark is assigned for each criterion. The final grade awarded for the essay is determined by totalling these five marks. The maximum number of marks available is 34.

The table below gives the descriptor for the highest achievement level for each criterion together with the maximum number of marks available. The Extended Essay criteria and advice to achieve high marks for each criterion

| Criterion and Marks | Assessment focus | Advice/questions to ask yourself |
|---|---|---|
| **A: Focus and method – 6 marks**<br>• Topic<br>• Research question<br>• Methodology | Assesses the explanation of the focus of the research (this includes the topic and the research question), how the research will be undertaken, and how this focus is maintained throughout the essay. | Your research question must be formulated as a question, and given context by researching the existing literature. The methodology could include practical work in the laboratory or be based on secondary sources. The rationale for choosing an experimental procedure should be clearly explained. |
| **B: Knowledge and understanding – 6 marks**<br>• Context<br>• Subject-specific terminology and concepts | Assesses the extent to which the research relates to chemistry, and additionally the way in which this knowledge and understanding is demonstrated through the use of appropriate terminology and concepts. | Does the essay focus on the chemistry aspect of the investigation? You are expected to apply your chemical knowledge appropriately and explain the underlying principles behind your research question and methodology. You should use acknowledged scientific sources and they should be relevant and effectively referenced. You must try to maintain a consistent linguistic style and use chemical nomenclature and terminology, including chemical and structural formulas, balanced equations with state symbols, significant figures and SI units. |
| **C: Critical thinking – 12 marks**<br>• Research<br>• Analysis<br>• Discussion and evaluation | Assesses the extent to which critical thinking skills has been used to analyse and evaluate the research undertaken. | Does your data support and clarify your argument? Your analysis could include data tables, graphs, mathematical transformations, and statistical analysis. The rationale behind any statistical test should be explained and the significance of the results discussed. You should avoid investigations with a large number of variables as they can be unfocused and incoherent. Any limitations of your investigation including poor experimental design, systematic errors and any unresolved issues should be discussed. You must comment on the quality, balance and quantity of your sources and the validity and reliability of your data, including the uncertainties of any measurements. You should suggest ways in which the investigation could be extended. |

| Criterion and Marks | Assessment focus | Advice/questions to ask yourself |
|---|---|---|
| **D: Presentation – 4 marks**<br><br>• Structure<br>• Layout | Assesses the extent to which the presentation follows the standard format expected from academic writing and the extent to which this aids communication. | Does your presentation conform to accepted academic standards? The use of numbered and headed paragraphs helps you clearly present your argument. Only use charts, images or tables if they contribute towards your argument. Large tables of primary raw data collected should be labelled and put in an appendix. Graphs or charts showing processed data should highlight only the most pertinent aspects and you should avoid the use of excessive graphs, charts and tables as they hinder communication. When your experimental procedure is long or complex it can be placed in the appendix and summarized in the body of the essay. This summary should however include all the key elements that contribute to the quality of the investigation. Similarly include sample calculations in the text to illustrate how your data was processed. A bibliography is essential and any unoriginal material must be carefully acknowledged otherwise it will be considered as a case of possible academic misconduct. |
| **E: Engagement – 6 marks**<br><br>• Process<br>• Research focus | This assesses your engagement with your research focus and the research process. | You are expected to reflect on the decision-making and planning process during your investigation. You must explain why you chose your question and the methodology used. You must complete a 'Reflections on Planning and Progress Form' (RPPF) which should refer to:<br><br>• the approach and strategies you chose, and their relative success<br><br>• the 'Approaches to Learning' skills you have developed, and their effectiveness<br><br>• how the research process has changed your conceptual understandings<br><br>• how you responded to unexpected challenges |

| Criterion and Marks | Assessment focus | Advice/questions to ask yourself |
|---|---|---|
| | | • how additional questions emerged during the research process |
| | | • what you would do differently if you were given the opportunity to repeat the process. |
| | | Your reflections should be personal and demonstrate that you have learned from the experience. You should show evidence of your thinking, creativity and originality. |

## Bibliography and references

It is required that you acknowledge all sources of information and ideas in an approved academic manner. Essays that omit a bibliography or that do not give references are unacceptable. Your supervisor or school librarian will be able to give you advice on which format to follow. One acceptable format is:

Author(s), Year, *Title*, Place of Publication, Publisher.

C. Brown and M. Ford, 2014, *Higher Level Chemistry 2nd edition*, UK, Pearson Baccalaureate.

Internet references should include the title of the extract used as well as the website address, the date it was accessed, and, if possible, the author. You should always exercise caution when using information from websites that do not give references or that cannot be cross-checked against other sources. The more important a particular point is to the essay, the more the quality of its source needs to be evaluated. There are websites available online which can assist you in these tasks.

## Viva voce

Remember to use a range of resources including the internet and any libraries available.

After you have handed in the final version you will be given a short interview or *viva voce* by your supervisor, who is required to write a report on your project. This is an opportunity to discuss the successes and challenges of the project and for you to reflect on what you have learned from the experience.

# World Studies Extended Essay

As you think about topics for an Extended Essay in chemistry, it may be that you find an area of current global interest, which overlaps with another subject. In this case, it may be appropriate to submit the essay as World Studies, which is a separate IB Extended Essay subject. An essay in World Studies must have the following characteristics:

- it must focus on an *issue of contemporary global significance*
- it must involve an in-depth *interdisciplinary study*, making reference to at least two IB subjects.

The approach to a World Studies Extended Essay is to identify a global issue and find a local example that lends itself to research and analysis, using the methodologies of two different subjects. This gives a grounded appreciation and understanding of the issue under study. As part of the research, you are encouraged to keep records of your thoughts and ideas in the 'researchers reflection space'. This helps to show development in your global perspective and some of the challenges in the research.

Areas of study which could have chemical content include:

- environmental and/or economic sustainability
- health and development
- science, technology and society.

The Extended Essay process is one on the most distinctive features of the Diploma programme and is a great preparation for your further studies. Enjoy it!

## During the course

Take responsibility for your own learning. When you finish your study of a particular topic in class, that is a good time to check that you have covered and understood everything detailed by the IB that can be assessed. This information is shown at the start of each sub-section in the book in two pale-yellow boxes, *Understanding* and *Applications and Skills*, as shown in the examples below. The notes on *Guidance* direct you to the IB data booklet or help explain the detail required.

## Understanding:

- Qualitative data include all non-numerical information obtained from observations not from measurement.
- Quantitative data are obtained from measurements, and are always associated with random errors/ uncertainties, determined by the apparatus, and by human limitations such as reaction times.

**Guidance:**
*SI units should be used throughout the programme.*

## Applications and skills:

- Distinction between random errors and systematic errors.
- Record uncertainties in all measurements as a range (±) to an appropriate precision.
- Discussion of ways to reduce uncertainties in an experiment.
- Propagation of uncertainties in processed data, including the use of percentage uncertainties.
- Discussion of systematic errors in all experimental work, their impact on the results, and how they can be reduced.
- Estimation of whether a particular source of error is likely to have a major or minor effect on the final result.
- Calculation of percentage error when the experimental result can be compared with a theoretical or accepted result.

**Guidance**
- *Note that the data value must be recorded to the same precision as the random error.*
- *The number of significant figures in a result is based on the figures given in the data. When adding or subtracting, the answer should be given to the least number of decimal places. When multiplying or dividing the final answer is given to the least number of significant figures.*

Check that you have completed all the *Exercises* at the end of each sub-topic, and checked your answers with those given on the eText.

### Exercises

**36** Identify the bonds which will produce strong absorptions in the IR region of the electromagnetic spectrum.

   I    $C-O$ bond
   II   $C=C$ bond
   III  $C=O$

  **A**  I and II only    **B**  I and III only    **C**  II and III only    **D**  I, II, and III

**37** State what occurs at the molecular level when IR radiation is absorbed.

Spend extra time on parts of the course where you are less confident of your knowledge and understanding. Use additional sources of information such as other books, journals, movies, and the web links in this book to help to spark your curiosity, deepen your understanding, and grasp the wider contexts of the topic. The more you do, the more you will enjoy the course and the more successful you will be.

The *Practice questions* at the end of each chapter are mostly IB questions from recent IB examination papers, so they are a very good way of testing yourself at the end of each topic. The answers used by examiners in marking the papers are also given on the eText.

1   What is the electron configuration of the $Cr^{2+}$ ion?

   **A**  [Ar] $3d^54s^1$       **B**  [Ar] $3d^34s^1$       **C**  [Ar] $3d^64s^1$       **D**  [Ar] $3d^44s^0$

2   What is the relative atomic mass of an element with the following mass spectrum?

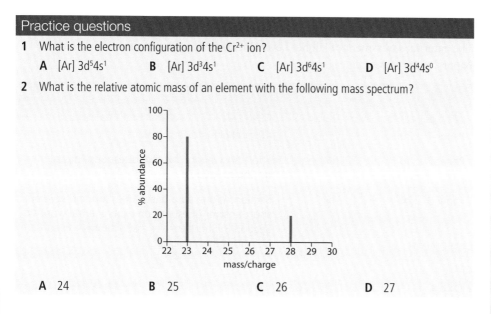

   **A**  24             **B**  25            **C**  26          **D**  27

You will also be assessed on experimental work through the Internal Assessment, and by some short questions on experimental work in Paper 3. The best way to prepare for this is to take a lively interest in the laboratory work throughout the course and always relate it to the theory.

# Preparing for the examination

Organize your time for review well ahead of the examination date, planning on a topic by topic basis. While you are studying make sure that you test yourself as you go – being able to recognize the content on the page is very different from being able to produce it yourself on blank paper. Effective revision generally involves using lots of scrap paper for testing your knowledge and understanding. Practise writing balanced equations, drawing diagrams, structural formulas, and so on.

Try to make your studying cumulative; this means building up a connected picture of knowledge and understanding by seeing how the topics are inter-related and reinforcing the same concepts. It can feel a bit like doing a jigsaw, where the more you have done the easier it gets to add in the new pieces.

There is no choice of questions in the examination, so make sure that you do not miss anything out. When you have finished your review of a particular topic, it is a good idea to test yourself with IB questions and time yourself according to how much time you are given for each type of question.

## In the examination

The external assessment of Higher Level Chemistry consists of three examination papers, as follows.

| | % of total mark | Duration / hours | Description of examination |
| --- | --- | --- | --- |
| Paper 1 | 20 | 1 | 40 multiple-choice questions |
| Paper 2 | 36 | 2¼ | Short-answer and extended-response questions on Topics 1–21 |
| Paper 3 | 24 | 1¼ | Section A: one data-based question and several short-answer questions on experimental work<br>Section B: Short-answer and extended-response questions from one option |

### Paper 1: Multiple-choice questions on Topics 1–21 (Chapters 1–11)

You are not allowed to use your calculator or the IB data booklet in this paper, but you are given a copy of the Periodic Table. The questions will give you any other data that you need, and any calculations will be straightforward.

There is no penalty for wrong answers so make sure that you do not leave any blanks. Read *all* the given answers A–D for each question. It is likely that more than one answer is close to being correct but you must choose the best answer available.

### Paper 2: Written answers on Topics 1–21 (Chapters 1–11)

### Paper 3: Written answers on laboratory work and the options (Chapters 12–15)

You are given 5 minutes reading time for Paper 2 and Paper 3. There is no choice of question in either paper; you are expected to answer *all questions*. You are allowed to use a calculator and will be provided with a copy of the IB data booklet.

- Note the number of marks given in brackets for each part of a question and use this to guide you in the detail required. In general, one mark represents one specific fact or answer.
- Take note of the **command terms** used in the questions as these also give an important clue about exactly what is required. It is a good idea to underline the command terms on the question paper to help you focus your answer.
- Sometimes questions include several different instructions, and it can be easy to miss a part of the question; avoid this by crossing off the parts of the question on the paper as you go, much as you cross items off a shopping list so you can see what you might have missed.

Remember these questions are testing your knowledge and understanding of *chemistry*, so be sure to give as much relevant detail as you can, with equations and specific examples wherever possible. The examiner can only give you credit for what you write down so do not assume anything. Show off!

It is essential that you show all your workings in calculations very clearly. Also pay attention to significant figures and include units in your answers. When a question has several parts which all follow on from each other, you will not be penalized more than once for the same mistake. So, for example, if you make a mistake in part (a) of a question, but then use that wrong answer in a correct method in part (b), you will still get full marks for part b) – *provided that your method was clear*. So never give up! (This is known as 'error carried forward' in examiner-speak, and is shown as ECF in the mark schemes.)

In Paper 3 make sure that you follow the guidelines on the front of the paper. After section A turn to the option you have studied in section B, and do not be distracted by the other questions on the paper.

# Index

# Index

# Index

# Index